134.00

Contemporary Authors ®

Explore your options!

Gale databases are offered in a variety of formats

GALE

The information in this Gale publication is also available in some or all of the formats described here. Your Gale Representative will be happy to fill you in. Call toll-free 1-800-877-GALE.

GaleNet SM
your information community

GaleNet

A number of Gale databases are now available on GaleNet, our new online information resource accessible through the Internet. GaleNet features an easy-to-use end-user interface, the powerful search capabilities of BRS/SEARCH retrieval software and ease of access through the World Wide Web.

Diskette/Magnetic Tape

Many Gale databases are available on diskette or magnetic tape, allowing systemwide access to your most-used information sources through existing computer systems. Data can be delivered on a variety of mediums (DOS-formatted diskettes, 9-track tape, 8mm data tape) and in industry-standard formats (comma-delimited, tagged, fixed-field).

CD-ROM

A variety of Gale titles are available on CD-ROM, offering maximum flexibility and powerful search software.

Online

For your convenience, many Gale databases are available through popular online services, including DIALOG, NEXIS, DataStar, ORBIT, OCLC, Thomson Financial Network's I/Plus Direct, HRIN, Prodigy, Sandpoint's HOOVER, the Library Corporation's NLightN and Telebase Systems.

ISSN 0010-7468

Contemporary Authors®

**A Bio-Bibliographical Guide to
Current Writers in Fiction, General Nonfiction,
Poetry, Journalism, Drama, Motion Pictures,
Television, and Other Fields**

TERRIE M. ROONEY,
JENNIFER GARIEPY,
Editors

volume 153

GALE

DETROIT · NEW YORK · TORONTO · LONDON

STAFF

Jennifer Gariepy and Terrie M. Rooney, *Editors, Original Volumes*

Joann Cerrito and Kathleen J. Edgar, *Contributing Senior Editors*

David M. Galens, Margaret Mazurkiewicz, Mary Ruby
Lynn M. Spampinato, and Brandon Trenz, *Contributing Editors*

Christine M. Bichler and Stacy A. McConnell, *Associate Editors*

Carol A. Brennan, Jay Daniel, Laurie DiMauro, Nancy Edgar, Mary Gillis, Nancy Godinez,
Marian Gonsoir, Jeanne M. Lesinski, Michelle M. Motowski, Susan Reicha, Joe Reiner, Paula Pyzik Scott,
Pamela Shelton, Ken Shepherd, Les Stone, Deborah Straub, Michaela A. Swart, Linda Tidrick,
Arlene True, and Elizabeth Wenning, *Sketchwriters*

Pamela Willwerth Aue, *Managing Editor*

Victoria B. Cariappa, *Research Manager*

Barbara McNeil, *Research Specialist*

Julia C. Daniel, Michele P. LaMeau, Tracie A. Richardson,
Norma Sawaya, and Cheryl L. Warnock, *Research Associates*

Alfred A. Gardner I, *Research Assistant*

∞™ This book is printed on acid-free paper that meets the minimum requirements
of American National Standard for Information Sciences-
Permanence Paper for Printed Library Materials, ANSI Z39.48-1984.

Library of Congress Catalog Card Number 62-52046
ISBN 0-7876-0130-6
ISSN 0010-7468

Printed in the United States of America

10 9 8 7 6 5 4 3 2 1

Contents

Indexing note: All *Contemporary Authors* entries are indexed in the *Contemporary Authors* cumulative index, which is published separately and distributed with even-numbered *Contemporary Authors* original volumes and odd-numbered *Contemporary Authors New Revision Series* volumes.

As always, the most recent *Contemporary Authors* cumulative index continues to be the user's guide to the location of an individual author's listing.

Contemporary Authors
was named an
**"Outstanding
Reference Source,"**
*by the
American Library
Association Reference
and Adult Services
Division after its
1962 inception.
In 1985 it was listed by
the same organization
as one of the
twenty-five most
distinguished reference
titles published in the
past twenty-five years.*

Preface

Contemporary Authors (*CA*) provides information on approximately 100,000 writers in a wide range of media, including:

- Current writers of fiction, nonfiction, poetry, and drama whose works have been issued by commercial publishers, risk publishers, or university presses (authors whose books have been published only by known vanity or author-subsidized firms are ordinarily not included)

- Prominent print and broadcast journalists, editors, photojournalists, syndicated cartoonists, graphic novelists, screenwriters, television scriptwriters, and other media people

- Authors who write in languages other than English, provided their works have been published in the United States or translated into English

- Literary greats of the early twentieth century whose works are popular in today's high school and college curriculums and continue to elicit critical attention

A *CA* listing entails no charge or obligation. Authors are included on the basis of the above criteria and their interest to *CA* users. Sources of potential listees include trade periodicals, publisher's catalogs, librarians, and other users.

How to Get the Most out of *CA:* Use the Index

The key to locating an author's most recent entry is the *CA* cumulative index, which is published separately and distributed with even-numbered original volumes and odd-numbered revision volumes. It provides access to *all* entries in *CA* and *Contemporary Authors New Revision Series* (*CANR*). Always consult the latest index to find an author's most recent entry.

For the convenience of users, the *CA* cumulative index also includes references to all entries in these Gale literary series: *Authors and Artists for Young Adults, Authors in the News, Bestsellers, Black Literature Criticism, Black Writers, Children's Literature Review, Concise Dictionary of American Literary Biography, Concise Dictionary of British Literary Biography, Contemporary Authors Autobiography Series, Contemporary Authors Bibliographical Series, Contemporary Literary Criticism, Dictionary of Literary Biography, Dictionary of Literary Biography Documentary Series, Dictionary of Literary Biography Yearbook, DISCovering Authors, DISCovering Authors: British, DISCovering Authors: Canadian, DISCovering Authors: Modules* (including modules for Dramatists, Most-Studied Authors, Multicultural Authors, Novelists, Poets, and Popular/Genre Authors), *Drama Criticism, Hispanic Literature Criticism, Hispanic Writers, Junior DISCovering Authors, Major Authors and Illustrators for Children and Young Adults, Major 20th-Century Writers, Native North American Literature, Poetry Criticism, Short Story Criticism, Something about the Author, Something about the Author Autobiography Series, Twentieth-Century Literary Criticism, World Literature Criticism,* and *Yesterday's Authors of Books for Children.*

A Sample Index Entry:

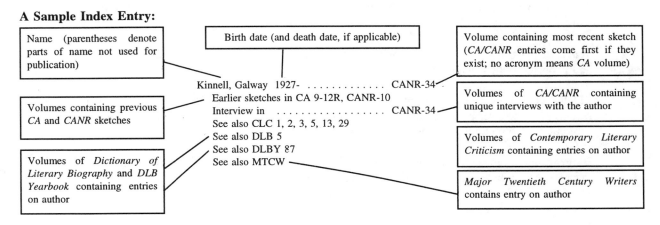

How Are Entries Compiled?

The editors make every effort to secure new information directly from the authors; listees' responses to our questionnaires and query letters provide most of the information featured in *CA*. For deceased writers, or those who fail to reply to requests for data, we consult other reliable biographical sources, such as those indexed in Gale's *Biography and Genealogy Master Index*, and bibliographical sources, including *National Union Catalog, LC MARC*, and *British National Bibliography*. Further details come from published interviews, feature stories, and book reviews, as well as information supplied by the authors' publishers and agents.

An asterisk (∗) at the end of a sketch indicates that the listing has been compiled from secondary sources believed to be reliable but has not been personally verified for this edition by the author sketched.

What Kinds of Information Does an Entry Provide?

Sketches in *CA* contain the following biographical and bibliographical information:

- **Entry heading:** the most complete form of author's name, plus any pseudonyms or name variations used for writing

- **Personal information:** author's date and place of birth, family data, ethnicity, educational background, political and religious affiliations, and hobbies and leisure interests

- **Addresses:** author's home, office, or agent's addresses, plus e-mail and fax numbers, as available

- **Career summary:** name of employer, position, and dates held for each career post; resume of other vocational achievements; military service

- **Membership information:** professional, civic, and other association memberships and any official posts held

- **Awards and honors:** military and civic citations, major prizes and nominations, fellowships, grants, and honorary degrees

- **Writings:** a comprehensive, chronological list of titles, publishers, dates of original publication and revised editions, and production information for plays, television scripts, and screenplays

- **Adaptations:** a list of films, plays, and other media which have been adapted from the author's work

- **Work in progress:** current or planned projects, with dates of completion and/or publication, and expected publisher, when known

- **Sidelights:** a biographical portrait of the author's development; information about the critical reception of the author's works; revealing comments, often by the author, on personal interests, aspirations, motivations, and thoughts on writing

- **Biographical and critical sources:** a list of books and periodicals in which additional information on an author's life and/or writings appears

Obituary Notices in *CA* provide date and place of birth as well as death information about authors whose full-length sketches appeared in the series before their deaths. These entries also summarize the authors' careers and writings and list other sources of biographical and death information.

Related Titles in the *CA* Series

Contemporary Authors Autobiography Series complements *CA* original and revised volumes with specially commissioned autobiographical essays by important current authors, illustrated with personal photographs they provide. Common topics include their motivations for writing, the people and experiences that shaped their careers, the rewards they derive from their work, and their impressions of the current literary scene.

Contemporary Authors Bibliographical Series surveys writings by and about important American authors since World War II. Each volume concentrates on a specific genre and features approximately ten writers; entries list works written by and about the author and contain a bibliographical essay discussing the merits and deficiencies of major critical and scholarly studies in detail.

Available in Electronic Formats

CD-ROM. Full-text bio-bibliographic entries from the entire *CA* series, covering approximately 100,000 writers, are available on CD-ROM through lease and purchase plans. The disc combines entries from the *CA, CANR,* and *Contemporary Authors Permanent Series* (*CAP*) print series to provide the most recent author listing. It can be searched by name, title, subject/genre, nationality/ethnicity, personal data, and as well as advanced searching using boolean logic. The disc is updated every six months. For more information, call 1-800-877-GALE.

Online. The *Contemporary Authors* database is made available online to libraries and their patrons through online public access catalog (OPAC) vendors. Currently, *CA* is offered through Ameritech Library Services' Vista Online (formerly Dynix), and is expected to become available through CARL Systems and The Library Corporation. More OPAC vendor offerings will soon follow.

GaleNet. *CA* is available on a subscription basis through GaleNet, a new online information resource that features an easy-to-use end-user interface, the powerful search capabilities of the BRS/Search retrieval software, and ease of access through the World Wide Web. For more information, call 1-800-877-GALE.

Magnetic Tape. *CA* is available for licensing on magnetic tape in a fielded format. Either the complete database or a custom selection of entries may be ordered. The database is available for internal data processing and nonpublishing purposes only. For more information, call 1-800-877-GALE.

Suggestions Are Welcome

The editors welcome comments and suggestions from users on any aspects of the *CA* series. If readers would like to recommend authors for inclusion in future volumes of the series, they are cordially invited to write: The Editors, *Contemporary Authors,* 835 Penobscot Bldg., 645 Griswold St., Detroit, MI 48226-4094; call toll-free at 1-800-347-GALE; or fax at 1-313-961-6599.

CA Numbering System and Volume Update Chart

Occasionally questions arise about the *CA* numbering system and which volumes, if any, can be discarded. Despite numbers like "29-32R," "97-100" and "153," the entire *CA* print series consists of only 133 physical volumes with the publication of *CA* Volume 153. The following charts note changes in the numbering system and cover design, and indicate which volumes are essential for the most complete, up-to-date coverage.

CA First Revision
- 1-4R through 41-44R (11 books)
 Cover: Brown with black and gold trim.
 There will be no further First Revision volumes because revised entries are now being handled exclusively through the more efficient *New Revision Series* mentioned below.

CA Original Volumes
- 45-48 through 97-100 (14 books)
 Cover: Brown with black and gold trim.
- 101 through 153 (52 books)
 Cover: Blue and black with orange bands.
 The same as previous *CA* original volumes but with a new, simplified numbering system and new cover design.

CA Permanent Series
- *CAP*-1 and *CAP*-2 (2 books)
 Cover: Brown with red and gold trim.
 There will be no further *Permanent Series* volumes because revised entries are now being handled exclusively through the more efficient *New Revision Series* mentioned below.

CA New Revision Series
- *CANR*-1 through *CANR*-54 (54 books)
 Cover: Blue and black with green bands.
 Includes only sketches requiring significant changes; **sketches are taken from any previously published *CA*, *CAP*, or *CANR* volume**.

If You Have: You May Discard:

If You Have:	You May Discard:
CA First Revision Volumes 1-4R through 41-44R **and** *CA Permanent Series* Volumes 1 and 2	*CA* Original Volumes 1, 2, 3, 4 Volumes 5-6 through 41-44
CA Original Volumes 45-48 through 97-100 **and** 101 through 153	**NONE:** These volumes will not be superseded by corresponding revised volumes. Individual entries from these and all other volumes appearing in the left column of this chart may be revised and included in the various volumes of the *New Revision Series*.
CA New Revision Series Volumes *CANR*-1 through *CANR*-54	**NONE:** The *New Revision Series* does not replace any single volume of *CA*. Instead, volumes of *CANR* include entries from many previous *CA* series volumes. All *New Revision Series* volumes must be retained for full coverage.

A Sampling of Authors and Media People
Featured in This Volume

Colin Bateman
Bateman's career as a journalist earned him numerous awards. He was able to translate this success to fiction writing with the publication of his first novel, the comedic, political thriller *Divorcing Jack.*

Robert Benchley
A noted humorist and actor, Benchley was a member of the fabled Algonquin Round Table as well as the star of a series of humorous short films. His writings include *Love Conquers All* and *My Ten Years in a Quandary and How They Grew.*

Bonnie Bremser
As the wife of Beat poet and convicted armed robber Ray Bremser, Bonnie Bremser's life was a bizarre combination of literary and criminal activity. She recounts her story in her autobiography, *Troia: Mexican Memories.*

Po Bronson
Often compared to Joseph Heller's bitingly comic novel *Catch-22,* Bronson's first novel, *Bombardiers,* is a satiric look at American decadence as portrayed by a group of work-obsessed, corrupt bond traders.

Deepak Chopra
One of the most successful purveyors of self-help merchandising, Chopra is a medical doctor who has parlayed his dedication to mind/body health into a million-selling industry that includes books such as *Ageless Body, Timeless Mind.*

Hillary Rodham Clinton
First Lady Clinton has added author to her growing list of achievements with the 1996 publication of *It Takes a Village: And Other Lessons Children Teach Us,* a book that draws upon her considerable work on behalf of children.

Charles D'Ambrosio
A short story writer with a number of honors to his credit, including the Aga Khan Fiction Prize and inclusion in the 1991 edition of *Best American Short Stories,* D'Ambrosio is the author of the acclaimed collection *The Point.*

Susan J. Douglas
Douglas is the author of *Where the Girls Are: Growing up Female with the Mass Media,* a book that focuses on feminine culture as it was portrayed in the films, television programs, and music of the 1950s and 1960s.

Neal Gabler
Respected film historian Gabler is the author of *An Empire of Their Own: How the Jews Invented Hollywood,* as well as a lauded biography of 1930s gossip reporter Walter Winchell, *Winchell: Gossip, Power, and the Culture of Celebrity.*

James Finn Garner
Garner is the author of the popular *Politically Correct Bedtime Stories,* a work that, via its humorous reworkings of classic children's stories, skewers the politically correct movement.

Anita Faye Hill
Hill's *Race, Gender, and Power in America: The Legacy of the Hill-Thomas Hearings* collects essays examining the legal and media frenzy following her harassment allegations against U.S. Supreme Court nominee Clarence Thomas.

Howard Korder
Often compared to David Mamet, Korder is the author of numerous plays, including *Search and Destroy, Night Maneuver,* and *The Lights,* which won the 1994 Obie Award for best playwriting.

Joacquim Maria Machado de Assis
A prolific author of plays, poems, novels, and short stories, Machado de Assis is one of the most lauded men of letters in Brazilian history. Among his more popular works are the novels *Epitaph of a Small Winner* and *Dom Casmurro.*

Alison Moore
Moore won a Notable Book of the Year honor from the American Library Association for her 1993 short story collection, *Small Spaces between Emergencies.* She is also the author of the acclaimed novel *Synonym for Love.*

Luigi Pirandello
The recipient for the Nobel Prize in Literature in 1934, Pirandello is considered one of the most influential dramatists of the twentieth century, especially for his thematic use of philosophy and his progressive approach to play structure.

Whit Stillman
Stillman is a highly regarded screenwriter/director who has defined himself as a stylist of quirky comedies of manners; his films include *Metropolitan,* which dissects New York's upper classes, and the popular *Barcelona.*

A

ABEL, Emily K. 1942-

PERSONAL: Born in 1942.

ADDRESSES: Office—University of California, Los Angeles, School of Public Health, Los Angeles, CA 90095-1772.

CAREER: Writer, historian, educator. Professor of Health Services at the University of California, Los Angeles.

WRITINGS:

(Editor, with Elizabeth Abel) *The Signs Reader: Women, Gender, and Scholarship,* University of Chicago Press (Chicago, IL), 1983.

Terminal Degrees: The Job Crisis in Higher Education, Praeger Publishers (New York), 1984.

Love Is Not Enough: Family Care of the Frail Elderly, American Public Health Association (Washington, DC), 1987.

(Editor, with Marjorie L. Pearson) *Across Cultures: The Spectrum of Women's Lives,* Gordon and Breach (New York), 1989.

(Editor, with sister, Margaret K. Nelson) *Circles of Care: Work and Identity in Women's Lives,* State University of New York (Albany, NY), 1990.

Who Cares for the Elderly? Public Policy and the Experience of Adult Daughters, Temple University Press (Philadelphia), 1991.

SIDELIGHTS: Emily K. Abel is a feminist and historian whose writings are noted for their insightful blend of qualitative research and personal anecdotes gleaned from interviews, a method which critics have maintained offers readers a broad perspective on is-

sues such as caregiving, work in the home, underemployment of the highly educated, and the impact of public policy on private lives. As both an editor of anthologies of critical essays and an author of sociological studies, Abel has garnered praise for the clarity with which she examines issues that some critics regard as underrepresented in feminist scholarship. While she has at times been faulted for failing to pursue radical alternatives to the situations she examines, her work has also been lauded for bringing critical attention to issues that have long affected the lives of American women.

At the center of *Terminal Degrees: The Job Crisis in Higher Education,* Abel's 1984 portrayal of the decline in opportunities for people with doctorate degrees in American universities and colleges, is a critique of the traditional merit system in determining job security and availability, and of the growing reliance on part-time and adjunct teaching faculty in institutions of higher education. "She speaks with skill and sympathy about both the relative privileges of highly educated middle-class people and the many ways in which they are like any other workers in the United States of the 1980s," observed Magali Sarfatti Larson in *Contemporary Sociology.* Critics highlighted Abel's inclusion of the personal stories of numerous would-be academics; "Abel presents a picture of despondency and self-blame that haunts its victims," remarked Joan Smith in the *Women's Review of Books.* Although some critics faulted the author for failing to examine in greater depth how displaced academics could join forces with tenured members of their profession in order to change the structure of higher education for the betterment of all, *Terminal Degrees* "is the right step in that direction," Smith declared.

In *Circles of Care: Work and Identity in Women's Lives,* a collection of essays published in 1990 that Abel edited with her sister, Margaret K. Nelson, contributors "explore the social, historical, and economic conditions that define caregiving as women's work and shape the rewards, stresses, and overall experience of this form of socially necessary labor," according to Sandra Lynn Morgen in *American Anthropologist.* The essays in this volume compare levels of stress and job satisfaction across the spectrum of caregiving, from family members caring for sick relatives in the home, to nurses in institutions for the sick, elderly, or disabled, to less formal situations such as adult daycare facilities. Vicki Smith remarked in a review of *Circles of Care* in *Signs,* "The contributions to this volume quite successfully show how care and connectedness simultaneously can be a source of strength and subordination for women, both in paid and unpaid work." "This book broadened my perspective on the scope of women's involvement in caregiving and provided new insights into its meanings and consequences for them," declared Linda S. Noelker in *Contemporary Sociology.*

Abel collected statistical data to prove that, contrary to common belief, most of the elderly in the United States are cared for by their families, and in most of those homes, the burden of care falls on the adult female in the household. In her 1991 volume *Who Cares for the Elderly? Public Policy and the Experience of Adult Daughters* Abel examines this situation in light of the lack of public policy support for such informal caregiving and the emotional and financial costs to the caregiver-daughter, relying on interviews with fifty women who care for their elderly mothers in their homes. The author's reliance on interview data gives the reader of *Who Cares for the Elderly?* "a sense of the everyday issues caregiving women face as they seek to reconcile their own sense of the importance of what they do with its invisibility and the devaluation by the larger society," according to Deanne Bonnar in the *Women's Review of Books.* "The book is well-written," declared Shelley I. White-Means in the *Journal of Consumer Affairs,* "and allows the reader to share, in a very personal way, the joys, dilemmas, and frustrations of women who provide care for their frail elderly mothers."

BIOGRAPHICAL/CRITICAL SOURCES:

PERIODICALS

American Anthropology, September, 1991, pp. 748-749.

Bloomsbury Review, March, 1992, p. 23.
Change, May-June, 1985, p. 61.
Contemporary Sociology, November, 1985, pp. 732-733; July, 1991, pp. 622-623.
Journal of Consumer Affairs, summer, 1993, pp. 187-189.
Journal of Higher Education, March-April, 1986, pp. 226-227.
Journal of Marriage and Family, May, 1992, pp. 475-476.
Los Angeles Times Book Review, January 6, 1985, p. 8.
New York Review of Books, February 13, 1986, pp. 35-42.
Publishers Weekly, April 26, 1991, pp. 51-52.
Signs, summer, 1992, pp. 837-38; autumn, 1992, p. 205.
Women's Review of Books, March, 1985, pp. 4-5; January, 1989, p. 24.

* * *

ACKERMAN, James D. 1950-

PERSONAL: Born August 14, 1950, in Orangeburg, SC; son of James D. (in U.S. Navy) and Marjorie R. (a homemaker; maiden name, Carter) Ackerman; married Arlee M. Montalvo, 1976 (divorced, 1987); married Elvia J. Melendez, September 19, 1994. *Ethnicity:* "Caucasian." *Education:* Humboldt State University, B.A., 1973, M.A., 1976; Florida State University, Ph.D., 1981.

ADDRESSES: Home—7 Brisas del Yunque, Canovanas, PR. *Office*—University of Puerto Rico, P.O. Box 23360, San Juan, PR 00931-3360; fax 787-764-3875. *E-mail*—ackerman@upracd.upr.clu.edu.

CAREER: University of Puerto Rico, San Juan, professor, 1981—.

MEMBER: International Association for Plant Taxonomy, Botanical Society of America, American Society of Plant Taxonomists, Ecological Society of America, Association for Tropical Biology, American Orchid Society, CBS, IVCN.

WRITINGS:

The Orchids of Puerto Rico and the Virgin Islands, University of Puerto Rico Press (San Juan, PR), 1992.

An Orchid Flora of Puerto Rico and the Virgin Islands, New York Botanical Garden, 1995.

Contributor of more than fifty articles to scientific journals.

WORK IN PROGRESS: Flora of the Greater Antilles: Orchidaceae, publication by New York Botanical Garden expected in 1999; research on the pollination of orchidaceae.

SIDELIGHTS: James D. Ackerman told *CA:* "My primary motivation for writing is a desire to communicate the results of scientific studies. I try to communicate in the simplest possible terms, with the basic concepts and goals clearly defined. As a young scientist, I found these were often implied or obscure in the work of others, and I strive to avoid the same pitfalls. I write on botany, ecology, and evolutionary biology, for these are the subjects that have fascinated me almost since I was a child."

* * *

ADAMSON, Robert 1943-

PERSONAL: Born May 17, 1943, in Sydney, New South Wales; married Cheryl Adamson, 1973 (marriage ended); married Juno Gemes, 1988.

ADDRESSES: 47 Cheero Point Rd., Cheero Point, New South Wales 2254, Australia.

CAREER: Worked as a pastry cook, fisherman, and journalist in the 1960s; *New Poetry* magazine, Sydney, associate editor, 1968-70, editor, 1970-75, assistant editor, 1975-77; Prism Books, Sydney, editor and director, 1970-77. Big Smoke Books, Sydney, founding editor and director (with Dorothy Hewett), 1979—; Paper Bark Press, founder (with Michael Wilding), 1988—. Prism Books and *New Poetry* magazine, designer, 1970—; Big Smoke Books, designer, 1979—.

AWARDS, HONORS: Australia Council fellowship, 1976, 1977; Grace Leven prize, 1977.

WRITINGS:

POETRY

Canticles on the Skin, Illumination Press, 1970.

The Rumour, New Poetry (Sydney), 1971.
Swamp Riddles, Island Press (Sydney), 1974.
Theatre I-XIX, Pluralist Press (Sydney), 1976.
Cross the Border, New Poetry, 1977.
Selected Poems, Angus and Robertson, 1977.
Where I Come From, Big Smoke (Sydney), 1979.
The Law at Heart's Desire, Prism (Sydney), 1982.
The Clean Dark, Paper Bark Press (Cheero Point, New South Wales), 1989.
Robert Adamson Selected Poems, 1970-1989, University of Queensland Press (Queensland), 1990.
Waving to Hart Crane, Adamson, 1994.

NOVELS

(With Bruce Hanford) *Zimmer's Essay,* Wild and Woolley (Sydney), 1974.
Wards of the State: An Autobiographical Novella, Angus and Robertson (Pymble, New South Wales), 1992.

OTHER

(Editor, with Manfred Jurgensen) *Australian Writing Now,* Outrider/Penguin (Indooroopilly, Queensland), 1988.

Manuscript Collection: Australian National Library, Canberra.

* * *

ADATTO, Kiku 1947-

PERSONAL: Born in 1947. *Education:* Has earned a Ph.D.

ADDRESSES: Agent—c/o Basic Books, 10 East 53rd St., New York, NY 10022.

CAREER: Freelance journalist and lecturer in American culture at Harvard University, Cambridge, MA.

WRITINGS:

Picture Perfect: The Art and Artifice of Public Image Making, Basic Books (New York), 1993.

SIDELIGHTS: In 1990, Kiku Adatto published the findings of a study she conducted that compared network news coverage of the 1968 and 1988 American presidential campaigns. Her article, published in the

New Republic, revealed that in 1968 the average presidential "sound bite" was just over forty seconds, while its counterpart in 1988 averaged less than ten seconds in length. Adatto concluded that substantive news stories augmented by clips from candidates' speeches sometimes lasting as long as a minute had been replaced twenty years later with stories that often critiqued candidates' appearance rather than what they had to say. These findings form the basis for Adatto's 1993 book, *Picture Perfect,* in which the author examines the power of the image over the American public in the realms of popular cinema, advertising, and art photography, as well as in television news coverage.

"Where television's political reporting has gone wrong," remarked Bob Schieffer in a *Washington Monthly* review of *Picture Perfect,* "is in failing to examine the candidates' ideas and assessing the substance of what they are trying to illustrate with their manufactured images." Adatto's analysis suggested to critics that television journalists have replaced longer, more substantively critical reporting with "theater criticism," that is, commentary on the images candidates generate. The result, according to Adatto, is a sometimes naive, sometimes cynical reproduction of these images which, the author contends, often fails to undermine the images' power. "Even as we tell ourselves knowingly that the camera can and does lie, part of us remains doggedly devoted to its images as keepsakes of reality," observed Carl Sessions Stepp in the *American Journalism Review.*

In three central chapters of *Picture Perfect,* Adatto traces the origin of the power of the images generated by candidates and their handlers. She contends that no matter how aware the American public may be of the artificiality of the "photo opportunities" in which candidates pose as heroic and strong public figures, these images tap into popular myths that are so attractive that their spells bewitch the public nonetheless. Adatto examines the appearance of these myths in popular film and art photography, but this aspect of her thesis failed to impress reviewers as much as her discussion of political reporting. Several critics faulted this turn away from what they perceived as the book's original concern: the causes and effects of the shrinking sound bite. Others criticized Adatto's failure to explore possible solutions to a problem that has come to seem endemic to television—a media once believed to offer direct access to reality.

Many critics expressed the opinion that the most persuasive part of *Picture Perfect* is the author's cri-

tique of the increasing focus of television journalism on the artificiality of the images generated by presidential candidates and their handlers, and the consequent shift away from coverage of the important social and political issues that ought to be at the forefront in a presidential campaign. "Adatto's lesson for the television reporters is fairly simple," Schieffer remarked: "Do not underestimate the power of imagery—real or otherwise, but ignore it when it cannot be backed by content."

Overall, critical response to *Picture Perfect* was mixed. While some commentators stressed the significance of Adatto's cautionary tale of the shrinking sound bite as a sign of what is being lost in political reporting, the lack of possible solutions to this dilemma, and the book's shift away from the world of politics toward the world of art and popular culture disappointed others. "The book is classic cultural criticism," wrote Joshua Gamson in *Contemporary Sociology:* "provocative, concerned, covering a broad territory . . . often wildly speculative, deeply ambivalent about the past and the future, and sloppy in its claims about effect." Nonetheless, critics found much to recommend in *Picture Perfect,* specifically the author's trenchant analysis of an important issue in contemporary American society.

BIOGRAPHICAL/CRITICAL SOURCES:

PERIODICALS

American Journalism Review, July/August, 1993, pp. 45, 47.
Boston Globe, May 25, 1993, p. 66.
Contemporary Sociology, January, 1994, pp. 132-33.
New Republic, June 21, 1993, pp. 30-33, 36.
Washington Monthly, April, 1993, pp. 54-57.*

* * *

A. E.
 See RUSSELL, George William

* * *

AGNEW, Spiro T(heodore) 1918-1996

OBITUARY NOTICE—See index for *CA* sketch: Born November 9, 1918, in Baltimore, MD; died of acute

leukemia, September 17, 1996, in Berlin, MD. Politician, lawyer, and author. Considered one of the most infamous Vice Presidents in United States history, Agnew enjoyed a meteoric rise in politics when he went from Baltimore, Maryland, County Executive to the vice presidency in just three years. Born in Baltimore to Greek immigrants, Agnew was a World War II veteran and earned his law degree from the University of Baltimore. He moved to the suburbs, built a private law practice, and had his first taste of politics serving on the Parent-Teacher Association at his children's schools. He joined the Republican Party and was appointed to the Baltimore County Board of Zoning Appeals in 1957. He was elected Baltimore County Executive in 1962 as a progressive-minded candidate, the first Republican to hold the post since 1895. Agnew ran for governor in 1966 and won, looking more progressive than his Democratic opponent. But he soon championed arch-conservative causes and often berated anti-war and civil rights demonstrators. He was asked to join presidential candidate Richard Nixon in the 1968 election and, when he and Nixon won, became "hatchet man" for the president, according to a contributor in the *Washington Post.* But Agnew's political career came to a scandalous end when he resigned from office in 1973 after pleading no contest to tax evasion charges that were brought after an investigation of alleged bribes. Agnew resigned October 10 of that year, but maintained throughout his life that he never took bribes. He returned to his private law practice and wrote his memoirs, *Go Quietly . . . or Else,* in 1980. Agnew also penned the novel *The Canfield Decision,* in 1976.

OBITUARIES AND OTHER SOURCES:

PERIODICALS

Chicago Tribune, September 22, 1996, sec. 4, p. 8.
Los Angeles Times, September 18, 1996, p. A1.
New York Times, September 19, 1996, pp. A1, B15.
Washington Post, September 19, 1996, pp. B1, B7.

* * *

AKAR, John J(oseph) 1927-1975

PERSONAL: Born May 20, 1927, in Rotifunk, Sierra Leone; died of heart disease, June 23, 1975; son of Joseph Philip and Tikidankay (Mansaray) Akar; married Constance Eleanor Wright, November 24, 1956; children: Jacqueline Jasmin, Pamela Juli, Melissa Dankay, Michelle Mayilla, Cynthia Collette, Emily Yama. *Education:* Attended Otterbein College, 1946-49; University of California at Berkeley, B.A., 1950; attended Lincoln's Inn, London, 1950-53; attended London School of Economics, 1950-52.

CAREER: Free-lance broadcaster, 1950-55; affiliated with the Voice of America, 1955-56; Sierra Leone Broadcasting System, director, 1957-67; Sierra Leone Hotels and Tourist Board, secretary, 1960-67; Commonwealth Broadcasting Secretariat, London, England, secretary, 1967-69; Ambassador to the United States from Sierra Leone, 1969-75; High Commissioner to Canada, 1970-75. Danforth visiting lecturer to the United States, 1964-66; member of Sierra Leone Museum Committee; chair of Sierra Leone National Museums, Monuments, and Relics Commission; founder of National Dance Troupe of Sierra Leone. Chiefdom counsellor, Bumpeh Chiefdom, Rotifunk, Sierra Leone; actor on stage and in films.

MEMBER: American Federation of Television and Radio Artists, Rotary Club.

AWARDS, HONORS: Honorary Trustee, Baker University, Baldwin, KS; named to the Order of the British Empire; chevalier Cedars of Lebanon, 1959; received Sierra Leone Independence Medal, 1961; Independence Competition Prize, Congress for Cultural Freedom, 1961, for *Cry Tamba;* honorary doctorates, Albright College, Reading, PA, and Otterbein College, Westerville, OH; Neuffield Scholar, University of Edinburgh, Scotland.

WRITINGS:

Cry Tamba (play), West African Review, 1954.

Also author of additional plays, including *Valley without Echo* (1949), produced by the British Council in 1954, and *The Second Chance,* 1954. Contributor to periodicals in Jamaica. Also composer of the Sierra Leone national anthem.

SIDELIGHTS: John J. Akar was a diplomat, broadcaster, actor, and author of the play *Valley without Echo,* one of the first African plays to be produced in Europe. For his second play, *Cry Tamba,* Akar won the Independence Competition Prize, awarded by the Congress for Cultural Freedom in 1961.

After completing his education at colleges in the United States and England, Akar worked as a broadcaster with the Voice of America and with the Sierra

Leone Broadcasting System. In 1969, Akar joined the diplomatic service as ambassador to the United States and High Commissioner to Canada. During his career, he appeared on stage as an actor in London and on Broadway, and was the composer of the music for the Sierra Leone national anthem.

BIOGRAPHICAL/CRITICAL SOURCES:

BOOKS

African Authors: A Companion to Black African Writing, Volume 1: 1300-1973, Black Orpheus Press, 1973.

PERIODICALS

West African Review, July, 1954.

OBITUARIES:

PERIODICALS

New York Times, July 1, 1975, p. 32.

* * *

ALI, Agha Shahid 1949-

PERSONAL: Born February 4, 1949, in New Delhi, India. *Education:* University of Kashmir, Srinagar, B.A. 1968; University of Delhi, M.A. (English literature), 1970; Pennsylvania State University, M.A. (English), 1981, Ph.D., 1984; University of Arizona, Tucson, M.F.A., 1985.

ADDRESSES: Office—Department of English, Bartlett Hall, University of Massachusetts, Amherst, MA 01003.

CAREER: University of Delhi, lecturer in English, 1970-75; Pennsylvania State University, instructor, 1976-83; University of Arizona, Tucson, graduate assistant, 1983-85; JNC Companies, Tucson, communications editor, 1985-87; Hamilton College, Clinton, NY, assistant professor of English and creative writing, 1987-93; University of Massachusetts, Amherst, associate professor of English, 1993—. Visiting professor of creative writing, State University of New York, Binghamton, spring, 1989.

AWARDS, HONORS: Breadloaf Writers' Conference scholarship, 1982, 1983; Academy of American Poets

prize, 1983: Pennsylvania Council on the Arts fellowship, 1983; Ingram Merrill Foundation fellowship, 1987; New York Foundation for the Arts fellowship, 1993.

WRITINGS:

POETRY

Bone-Sculpture, Writers Workshop (Calcutta), 1972.
In Memory of Begum Akhtar and Other Poems, Writers Workshop, 1979.
The Half-Inch Himalayas, Wesleyan University Press (Middletown, CT), 1987.
A Walk through the Yellow Pages, Sun/Gemini Press (Tucson, AZ), 1987.
A Nostalgist's Map of America, Norton (New York), 1991.
The Beloved Witness: Selected Poems, Viking Penguin (New Delhi), 1992.

OTHER

T.S. Eliot as Editor, University of Michigan Research Press (Ann Arbor), 1986.
(Translator) *The Rebel's Silhouette: Selected Poems,* by Faiz Ahmed Faiz, Peregrine Smith (Salt Lake City), 1992.*

* * *

ALLAHAR, Anton L. 1949-

PERSONAL: Born January 19, 1949, in Trinidad. *Education:* Attended Ryerson Polytechnic University, 1970-73; University of Toronto, B.A. (with honors), 1975, M.A., 1976, Ph.D., 1981.

ADDRESSES: Office—Department of Sociology, Social Science Center, University of Western Ontario, London, Ontario N6A 5C2, Canada; fax 519-661-3200. *E-mail*—allahar@sscl.uwo.ca.

CAREER: University of Toronto, Ontario, assistant professor, 1981-84; University of Western Ontario, London, assistant professor of sociology, 1994-89, associate professor of sociology, 1989-95, professor of sociology, 1996—, member of Centre for Interdisciplinary Historical Studies and Political Economy Research Group. Has lectured and given conference papers at colleges and universities, including Carleton University, Ottawa, Ontario, St., Stephens College, Oxford, Fanshawe College, London, England, Uni-

versity of Windsor, University of the West Indies, University of Toronto, Dalhousie University, St. Mary's University, Halifax, Nova Scotia, Universidad de la Havana, York University, and Trent University.

MEMBER: Canadian Association of Latin American and Caribbean Studies, Canadian Institute of Caribbean and Latin American Studies, Canadian Sociology and Anthropology Association, Association of Caribbean Studies (United States), Caribbean Studies Association (Puerto Rico), Instituto del Caribe (Cuba), Society for Caribbean Studies (England), Centre for Research on Latin America and the Caribbean, Ontario Cooperative Programme in Latin American and Caribbean Studies.

WRITINGS:

The Sugar Planters of Colonial Cuba, Two-Thirds Editions (Toronto, Ontario), 1982.
Sociology and the Periphery: Theories and Issues, Garamond Press (Toronto), 1989, revised edition, 1995.
Class, Politics, and Sugar in Colonial Cuba, Edwin Mellen (Lewiston, NY), 1990.
(Editor with R. G. Cecil) *Is There Life after Debt?,* Inter-American Organization for Higher Education (Montreal, Quebec), 1993.
(With James E. Cote) *Generation on Hold: Coming of Age in Advanced Industrial Society,* Stoddart Publishing (Toronto), 1994.

Contributor to books, including *The Social World,* edited by Lorne Tepperman and R. J. Richardson, McGraw-Hill Ryerson (Toronto), 1986, 3rd edition, edited by Tepperman and James Curtis, 1994; *Conflicts of Interest: Canada and the Third World,* edited by Jamie Swift and Brian Tomlinson, Between-the-Lines (Toronto), 1991; and *The Racist Imagination: The Sociology of Racism in Canada,* edited by Vic Satzewich, University of Toronto Press (Toronto), 1996. Contributor to scholarly journals, including *New Community, Transition, Canadian Ethnic Studies, Colonial Latin American Historical Review, Indo Caribbean Review,* and *Canadian Journal of Latin American and Caribbean Studies.* Editor in chief, *International Journal of Comparative Race and Ethnic Studies,* 1994—.

WORK IN PROGRESS: Social Inequality: Canadian Dimensions, with James Cote, for James Lorimer (Toronto); *Political Identities: Ethnicity versus Nationalism.*

ALVI, Moniza 1954-

PERSONAL: Born February 2, 1954, in Lahore, Pakistan; married Robert Coe, 1995. *Education:* University of York, 1973-76, B.A. (honors), 1976; Whitelands College, London, postgraduate certificate in education, 1977; London University Institute of Education, M.A. (education), 1985.

ADDRESSES: Office—c/o Oxford University Press, Walton St., Oxford OX2 6DP, England.

CAREER: Scott Lidgett School, London, teacher, 1978-80; Aylwin School, London, teacher, 1980—, English department head, 1989—.

AWARDS, HONORS: The Poetry Business prize (co-winner with Peter Daniels), 1992.

WRITINGS:

POETRY

(With Peter Daniels) *Peacock Luggage,* Smith Doorstop Books (London), 1992.
The Country at My Shoulder, Oxford University Press (Oxford), 1993.

*　　*　　*

AMARAL, Jose Vazquez
　　See VAZQUEZ AMARAL, Jose

*　　*　　*

ANTON, Ted 1957-

PERSONAL: Born January 30, 1957, in Bronx, NY; son of Gus (a graphic artist) and Bertha (a bookkeeper) Anton; married Maja C. Eaton (an attorney), May 24, 1986; children: Cam, Marja Anton Eleni. *Ethnicity:* "Greek-American." *Education:* Attended London School of Economics and Political Science, London, 1977-78; Columbia University, B.A., 1979; University of Iowa, M.A. and M.F.A., both 1984. *Politics:* Conservative Democrat. *Religion:* Greek Orthodox. *Avocational interests:* Jazz.

ADDRESSES: Office—Department of English, DePaul University, 802 West Belden Ave., Chicago, IL

60614-3214; fax 708-771-5864. *E-mail*—tanton @condor.depaul.edu. *Agent*—Ellen Levine, Ellen Levine Literary Agency, Inc., 15 East 26th St., New York, NY 10020.

CAREER: DePaul University, Chicago, IL, associate professor of English, 1989—. Mary Kuntz Press, member of board of directors; Center for Latino Research, member of board of directors. A.Y.S.O. soccer coach, 1995—; volunteer for Junior Great Books, 1994—.

MEMBER: National Association of Science Writers, American Association for the Advancement of Science, Association of Educators in Journalism and Mass Communications, National Writers Union.

AWARDS, HONORS: National Teachers as Writers Award, 1989; nominated for National Magazine Award in Reporting, 1993; grant from Fund for Investigative Journalism, 1993; senior Fulbright fellow, 1994.

WRITINGS:

(Editor with Rick Mc Cart) *The New Science Journalists,* Ballantine (New York), 1995.
Eros, Magic, and the Murder of Professor Culianu (nonfiction), Northwestern University Press (Evanston, IL), 1996.

Contributor of articles to periodicals, including *Chicago, Chicago Tribune, The Sciences,* and *Lingua Franca.* Contributor to anthologies, including *Best American Essays,* 1990, 1991, 1992.

WORK IN PROGRESS: Dream Street, a novel.

* * *

ARMANTROUT, (Mary) Rae 1947-

PERSONAL: Born April 13, 1947, in Vallejo, CA; married Charles Korkegian, 1971; children: one son. *Education:* California State University, San Diego, 1965-68; University of California, Berkeley, B.A., 1970; California State University, San Francisco, M.A., 1975.

ADDRESSES: Home and office—4774 East Mountain View Dr., San Diego, CA 92116.

CAREER: California State University, San Francisco, teaching assistant, 1972-74; California State University, San Diego, lecturer, 1980-82; University of California, San Diego, La Jolla, lecturer, 1980—.

AWARDS, HONORS: California Arts Council fellowship, 1989; Fund for Poetry award, 1993.

WRITINGS:

POETRY

Extremities, The Figures (Great Barrington, MA), 1978.
The Invention of Hunger, Tuumba (Berkeley, CA), 1979.
Precedence, Burning Deck (Providence, RI), 1985.
Necromance, Sun and Moon Press (Los Angeles, CA), 1991.
Made to Seem, Sun and Moon Press, 1995.

* * *

ARONSON, Steven M. L.

PERSONAL: Education: Attended Yale University.

CAREER: Holt, Rinehart & Winston, New York City, senior editor; Harcourt Brace Jovanovich, New York City, co-publisher; Pierpont Morgan Library, New York City, fellow.

AWARDS, HONORS: Edgar Allan Poe Award (with co-author Natalie Robins) for best fact crime book, Mystery Writers of America, 1986, for *Savage Grace.*

WRITINGS:

Hype (nonfiction), Morrow, 1983.
(With Natalie Robins) *Savage Grace* (nonfiction), Morrow, 1985.

Also author of articles for *House and Garden* and *Architectural Digest.*

SIDELIGHTS: In two books, Steven M. L. Aronson probes Americans' fascination with those who have achieved celebrity status. The first is entitled *Hype,* which the author defines as "much more ado about something than that something is ever worth." In the bulk of the book Aronson skewers noteworthy ex-

amples of the process of hype—how people become "products" and gain notoriety through clever packaging and relentless public relations. His targets include model Cheryl Tiegs, romance writer Barbara Cartland (the "empress of hype"), gossip columnist "Suzy," and an assortment of self-promoters and trendsetters in entertainment, fashion, and even plastic surgery. In the magazine section of the *Chicago Tribune,* Aronson lamented that hype in his view has become the "currency of the land."

With his second book, *Savage Grace,* Aronson teamed up with poet Natalie Robins to explore a darker underside to Americans' curiosity about the lives of the rich and famous. In 1972, twenty-six-year-old Tony Baekeland, intelligent, handsome, and heir to an immense plastics fortune, stabbed his mother to death in London. Diagnosed as a schizophrenic, Tony spent seven years in a British mental institution. When he was released, he returned to New York, where he tried, unsuccessfully, to kill his grandmother by repeatedly stabbing her. He was arrested and imprisoned on New York City's Riker's Island, where he committed suicide by asphyxiating himself with a plastic bag.

Savage Grace is an oral history of this macabre story. To assemble the story, the authors interviewed scores of prominent people who knew the Baekelands intimately: authors such as James Jones, William Styron, and Francine du Plessix Gray, as well as fashion designers, millionaires, French countesses, Italian princes—the jet-set of two continents. The private story that emerges from their testimony is even more lurid than the public one. Readers meet Tony's eccentric father, Brooks Baekeland, who tries to help his son overcome an adolescent stuttering problem by forcing him to read aloud at dinner parties—from the eighteenth-century erotic writer, the Marquis de Sade. One source alleges that to "cure" Tony of his homosexuality, his mother repeatedly committed incest with him. What emerges is a series of events that has often been likened to a Greek tragedy, with its recurrent theme of wealthy dynasties collapsing into murder, incest, and insanity.

The critical reaction to *Savage Grace* was mixed. Some reviewers criticized the book for a lack of narrative coherence. In the *New York Times Book Review,* for example, Jennifer Allen wrote that the authors "seem set on making up in length what they have left out in narration. Scores of people have been tracked down and quoted, if only to bloat the book with yet another fuzzy recollection." Other commen-

tators praised the work, with Christopher Schemering of *Washington Post Book World* citing the book's "brutal clarity." *Time* reviewer William A. Henry commended it for its "arresting detail." Daniel Goleman of the *New York Times* concluded: "*Savage Grace* is a fascinating . . . exploration of the decadence of wealthy people without purpose." *Savage Grace* was voted "best fact crime" book by the Mystery Writers of America in 1986.

BIOGRAPHICAL/CRITICAL SOURCES:

PERIODICALS

Chicago Tribune (magazine section), June 26, 1983.
Globe and Mail (Toronto), August 31, 1985.
Los Angeles Times Book Review, June 12, 1983, p. 4; December 8, 1985, p. 14.
Newsweek, August 5, 1985, p. 66.
New York Review of Books, June 16, 1983, pp. 30-31.
New York Times, July 10, 1985, p. 19.
New York Times Book Review, July 28, 1985, p. 10.
Spectator, January 4, 1986, pp. 26-27.
Time, August 12, 1985, p. 58.
Times Literary Supplement, December 27, 1985, p. 1474.
Village Voice, May 31, 1983, pp. 54-55.
Washington Post Book World, September 15, 1985, p. 8.*

* * *

ASH, Stephen V. 1948-

PERSONAL: Born November 22, 1948, in El Centro, CA; son of Omar L. and Juanita (Vaughan) Ash; married Jean Cumming, June 20, 1970. *Ethnicity:* "White." *Education:* Gettysburg College, B.A., 1970; University of Tennessee, M.A., 1974, Ph.D., 1983.

ADDRESSES: Home—1802 Pinoak Ct., Knoxville, TN 37923. *Office*—Department of History, 1101 McClung Tower, University of Tennessee, Knoxville, TN 37996; fax 423-974-3915.

CAREER: Independent historian in Knoxville, TN, 1983-90; University of Tennessee, Knoxville, instructor, 1989-95, assistant professor of American history, 1995—. University of Tennessee, Chattanooga, adjunct instructor, 1994. *Journal of East Tennessee History,* managing editor, 1993—.

MEMBER: Organization of American Historians, Society of Civil War Historians, Conference of Historical Journals, Southern Historical Association, Tennessee Historical Society, Virginia Historical Society, East Tennessee Historical Society, Phi Kappa Phi.

AWARDS, HONORS: John T. Moore Memorial Award, Tennessee Historical Society, 1977, for a journal article; Tennessee History Book Award, Tennessee Historical Commission and Tennessee Library Association, and Outstanding Academic Book Citation, *Choice,* both 1988, for *Middle Tennessee Society Transformed;* fellow of American Council of Learned Societies, 1988; fellow of Virginia Historical Society and Andrew W. Mellon Foundation, both 1989; History in the Media Award, East Tennessee Historical Society, 1991, for the newspaper series "Past Times."

WRITINGS:

Meet Me at the Fair! A Pictorial History of the Tennessee Valley Agricultural and Industrial Fair, Tennessee Valley Fair (Knoxville, TN), 1985.

Tennessee's Iron Industry Revisited: The Stewart County Story, Land Between the Lakes Association (Golden Pond, KY), 1986.

The Knoxville News-Sentinel: A Century of Front Pages, Knoxville News-Sentinel Co. (Knoxville), 1986.

Beyond Their Dreams (video documentary), produced by University of Tennessee (Knoxville), 1986.

Middle Tennessee Society Transformed, 1860-1870: War and Peace in the Upper South, Louisiana State University Press (Baton Rouge, LA), 1988.

Messages of the Governors of Tennessee, Volume IX: *1907-1921,* Volume X: *1921-1933,* Tennessee Historical Commission (Nashville, TN), 1990.

Past Times: A Daybook of Knoxville History, Knoxville News-Sentinel Co., 1991.

When the Yankees Came: Conflict and Chaos in the Occupied South, 1861-1865, University of North Carolina Press (Chapel Hill, NC), 1995.

Contributor of articles and reviews to books, including *Houston and Crockett, Heroes of Tennessee and Texas: An Anthology,* edited by Herbert L. Harper, Tennessee Historical Commission, 1986. Contributor to periodicals, including *Virginia Magazine of History and Biography, Historian, Tennessee Historical Quarterly, Maryland Historian,* and *Journal of Southern History.*

WORK IN PROGRESS: Tennesseans and Their History, a college-level textbook; research on the South in the early Reconstruction period.

* * *

ASSIS, Joaquim Maria Machado de
 See MACHADO de ASSIS, Joaquim Maria

B

BAILEY, Jackson Holbrook 1925-1996

OBITUARY NOTICE—See index for *CA* sketch: Born September 22, 1925, in Portland, ME; died of cancer, August 2, 1996, in Brattleboro, VT. Educator, producer, and author. Bailey gained prominence in the area of Asian studies. He began his teaching career in 1959 at Earlham College in Richmond, Indiana, after having served in the Far East with the American Friends Service Committee as a program director. During his forty-five-year career at Earlham, Bailey produced many documentaries on Japan; along with former Ambassador to Japan, Edwin O. Reischauer, he produced thirty-two programs on Japanese history for public television. Bailey also went on to direct the Great Lakes College Association's Center for East Asian Studies. Among his credits are awards from the Lilly Endowment, the National Endowment for the Humanities, and honors from the Emperor of Japan (1988). He was the author of many articles for such publications as the *Journal of Asian Studies*. Bailey was a contributor to several editions of *Studies on Asia* and edited several publications himself, including *Listening to Japan: An Anthology* and *Japan: The Changing Tradition*. Bailey was also the author of *Ordinary Lives, Extraordinary People: A Study of Political and Economic Change in a Tohoku Village*.

OBITUARIES AND OTHER SOURCES:

PERIODICALS

New York Times, August 8, 1996, p. D22.

BALTZELL, E(dward) Digby 1915-1996

OBITUARY NOTICE—See index for *CA* sketch: Born November 14, 1915, in Philadelphia, PA; died of a heart attack, August 17, 1996, in Boston, MA. Sociologist, educator, and author. Baltzell gained a reputation in the field of sociology for his studies about white Anglo-Saxon Protestants. Although his second wife disputes the claim, Baltzell is credited with coining the acronym WASP, to refer to the ethnic group. Baltzell graduated from the University of Pennsylvania in 1939, before serving with the U.S. Naval Reserve during World War II. In 1947, he joined the faculty of his Alma Mater as an instructor. He remained at the University until his retirement nearly forty years later. Named a fellow of the American Academy of Arts and Sciences, Baltzell also was the Danforth fellow in the Society for Religion in Higher Education at the Princeton Theological Seminary from 1967 until 1968. Among his books are *Philadelphia Gentleman: The Making of a National Upper Class*, *Protestant Establishment: Aristocracy and Caste in America* (in which he used the term WASP), *Puritan Boston and Quaker Philadelphia: Two Protestant Ethics and the Spirit of Class Authority and Leadership*, *The Protestant Establishment Revisited*, and *Judgment and Sensibility: Religion and Stratification*.

OBITUARIES AND OTHER SOURCES:

BOOKS

Who's Who in America, 50th edition, Marquis, 1995.

PERIODICALS

Chicago Tribune, August 20, 1996, section 3, p. 11.
New York Times, August 20, 1996, p. B6.

* * *

BARUCHELLO, Gianfranco 1924-

PERSONAL: Born August 29, 1924, in Livorno, Italy; son of Mario and Maria (Mezzera) Baruchello; married Agnese Naldoni, 1974; children: Paolina. *Education:* Studied in Rome; Doctor Juris, 1945.

ADDRESSES: Home—Via di Santa Cornelia, m. 695 (Prima Porta), Rome, Italy; 8 Rue Linne, Paris 75005, France. *Agent*—Gallerie Milano, Via Manin 3, Milan 20121, Italy; Gallerie Krief, 50 Rue Mazarine, Paris 75006, France.

CAREER: Painter. Also writer, performance artist, and filmmaker. Has created and appeared in numerous films and videos, including *Costretto a scomparire, Perforce,* and *Complemento di colpa,* all 1968; *Norme per gli olocausti, Per una giornata di malumore nazionale, Non accaduto,* and *I giorni di Lua,* all 1969; *Lap* and *Peep Sea Show,* both 1971; *A partire dal dolce,* 1980; *Dietro l'iride,* 1985; *Quando il giallo si dissolve, Un lieve rossore nel tempo,* and *Quell'episodio dell'immaginazione che chiamano la realta,* all 1990; *68/91* and *Punto di fuga,* both 1991; *Cinque esercizi di mesia difficolta, Lavoro personale di G.B. al Paintbox,* and *Immagini per il satellite RAISAT,* all 1992.

AWARDS, HONORS: Chevalier des arts et des lettres.

WRITINGS:

Mi viene in mente, Schwarz (Italy), 1966.
Multipurpose Object, Marcatre/Lerici (Italy), 1966.
La quindicesima riga, Lerici (Italy), 1967.
Avventure nell'armadio di plexigass, Feltrinelli (Italy), 1968.
Una settantina di idee, Bianco e Nero 7/8 (Italy), 1968.
Come ho dipinto certi miei quadri, Geiger (Italy), 1976.
(With Gilbert Lascault) *Alphabers d'Eros,* Galilee (Italy), 1976.

(With Henry Martin) *Fragments of a Possible Apocalypse,* Multhipla (Italy), 1978.
Sentito vivere, Exit (Italy), 1978.
La stazione del Conte Goluchowsky, Exit, 1978.
L'Altra Casa, Galilee, 1981.
Marcel Duchamp in 20 Photos, Gregory, 1981.
Agricola Cornelia Soc. per Azioni, Exit, 1981.
La scomparsa di Amanda Silvers, Exit, 1982.
(With Martin) *How to Imagine: A Narrative on Art and Agriculture,* Documentext/McPherson Publishing (New Paltz, NY), 1983.
(With Martin) *Why Duchamp: An Essay on Aesthetic Impact,* Documentext/McPherson Publishing, 1985.
Uomini di Pane, Geiger, 1986.
Mille Titoli, Exit/Essegi, 1987.
Bellissimo il Giardino, Exit, 1989.
Se tanto mi da canto, Roma Studio, 1990.
Dall'archivio dei Cinque Cuori, Essegi, 1991.
Miss Omissis, Exit, 1991.
Al Polo Nord, rotolando, Exit, 1992.

SIDELIGHTS: Gianfranco Baruchello, best known for his work as an artist, has also been heralded as a charming and unconventional author. Baruchello is the creator of works of abstract expressionism, assemblages and drawings of found objects, films and videos, and aluminum sheets covered with tiny drawings and objects. In *Contemporary Artists,* Henry Martin (Baruchello's occasional co-author) listed the painter's other work as "a vast series of aesthetic activities that include objects, films, theater pieces, books, video tapes, stage sets, postal happenings, sound tracks, sculptures, narrative series of drawings, assemblages of odds and ends and cardboard cut-outs in plexiglass cases and wooden boxes." In 1972, Baruchello set about running a farm as a work of art. This decade-long endeavor followed the example of artist Marcel Duchamp, who promoted the idea that, in the hands of an artist, anything can become art.

From this experience came *How to Imagine: A Narrative on Art and Agriculture* (1983), a book created with the help of Martin. The pair tape-recorded (and Martin later translated) Baruchello's musings on a variety of subjects that were inspired by his farm, Agricola Cornelia. *New York Times* reviewer Donald Hall marveled at the artist's verbal talents, and identified him as being one of the few individuals who are "natural wonders, geysers of idea, charm, and nonsense." The book's unconventional style makes for unusual, somewhat difficult reading; according to Hall, the "spirited monologue starts from earth and extends into politics, Duchamp, the soul, Christo,

bees, feminism, lettuce and death. . . . At first it is difficult to read, it moves so swiftly; we exhaust ourselves trying to keep up with Mr. Baruchello's leaps and zags. . . . But the text teaches the reader to read itself. It is worth the effort; Mr. Baruchello is not only an original and intuitive thinker but funny and charming."

In 1985, Baruchello and Martin produced *Why Duchamp: An Essay on Aesthetic Impact.* Using the same conversational technique used to produce *How to Imagine,* the team turned again to the subject Marcel Duchamp, who died in 1968. Duchamp introduced the concept of "ready-made" art, as in his work called "In Advance of the Broken Arm," which was nothing more than a snow shovel suspended from the ceiling. In a *New York Times Book Review* article about *Why Duchamp,* Calvin Tomkins suggested that Baruchello's "real gift may be for conversation." Also, the reviewer noted the sympathy and understanding that he showed for his subject: "Mr. Baruchello knew Duchamp, and it is easy to see why they became friends. The mind that emerges from these pages is playful, allusive, witty, surprising, unpretentious and iconoclastic." The book has a simple agenda: to find inspiration in the artist's life and work, and to cast Duchamp as a liberator whose theories and example allowed artists to express themselves in any way they chose. Baruchello has clearly applied this permission to his own life, in painting, in farming, and in his individual way of "writing" books.

BIOGRAPHICAL/CRITICAL SOURCES:

BOOKS

Contemporary Artists, 4th edition, edited by Joann Cerrito, St. James Press, 1996, p. 85-87.

PERIODICALS

New York Times Book Review, April 15, 1984, p. 20; July, 21, 1985, p. 28; September 8, 1985, p. 15.

* * *

BATEMAN, Colin 1962-

PERSONAL: Born in 1962. *Education:* Attended Oxford University.

ADDRESSES: Home—Ireland. *Agent*—c/o Arcade Publishing, 141 Fifth Ave., New York, NY 10010.

CAREER: Journalist and writer.

AWARDS, HONORS: Received journalism fellowship for Oxford; Betty Trask Award, 1995; Northern Ireland Press Award.

WRITINGS:

Divorcing Jack, Arcade Publishing (New York), 1995.

SIDELIGHTS: Colin Bateman's first novel, *Divorcing Jack,* is a comic, political thriller. The hero of *Divorcing Jack,* Dan Starkey, like his creator, is an Irish newspaper columnist. Facing the end of his marriage due to a drunken indiscretion, Starkey takes up with his new lover only to find her murdered soon after. The remaining three quarters of the novel is a game of hunter and hunted. Starkey tries to solve the mystery of his lover's death while hiding from those who believe him responsible: the police, an IRA-connected thug named Cow Pat Coogan and a Loyalist skinhead gang.

Set in an Ireland plagued by terrorism, the political groups add tension and intrigue to the tale. John Ferguson, writing in the *Boston Globe,* noted that Bateman's "wicked sense of fun make[s] this a thrill ride worth tagging along for." To relieve some of this tension, Bateman injects humor into the story. In his *New York Times Book Review* piece, critic D. Keith Mano cited several amusing lines from *Divorcing Jack.* Included was the hero's observation: "The pouches beneath my eyes sagged like fridge-black bananas." *Spectator* critic Michael Bywater praised the novel's "good action" and predicted that the success of *Divorcing Jack* will allow Bateman to "live well on his royalties."

BIOGRAPHICAL/CRITICAL SOURCES:

PERIODICALS

Booklist, September 1, 1995, p. 39.
Boston Globe, August 24, 1995, p. 67.
New York Times Book Review, August 27, 1995.
Publishers Weekly, July 24, 1995, p. 48.
Spectator, March 11, 1995.*

BAUER, Tricia

PERSONAL: Born in Baltimore, MD; married Bill Bozzone.

ADDRESSES: Home—P.O. Box 34, West Redding, CT 06896-0034. *Office*—Millbrook Press, 2 Old New Milford Rd., Brookfield, CT 06804.

CAREER: Writer. Millbrook Press, Brookfield, CT, director of special markets and rights for children's books.

MEMBER: Poets and Writers.

WRITINGS:

Working Women and Other Stories (short stories), Bridge Works (Bridgehampton, NY), 1995.

Also author of *Boondocking* (novel), 1997. Contributor of fiction and poetry to anthologies, including *The Next Parish Over,* edited by Patricia Monaghan, New Rivers Press, 1993, and *Eating Our Hearts Out,* edited by Leslea Newman, Crossing Press, 1993. Contributor of fiction and poetry to periodicals, including *Western Humanities Review, Calyx, American Literary Review, Carolina Quarterly, American Voice, Black Warrior Review,* and *Massachusetts Review.* Contributor of travel features to the *New York Times* and the *International Herald Tribune* (Paris).

* * *

BEHRENS, Ellen 1957-

PERSONAL: Born July 25, 1957, in Fremont, OH; daughter of William (an oil painter and potter) and Dorothy (an artist) Cox; married David Behrens, June 8, 1979 (divorced, April, 1988). *Ethnicity:* "White." *Education:* Denison University, B.A., 1979; Bowling Green State University, M.F.A., 1990. *Politics:* Democrat. *Religion:* Protestant. *Avocational interests:* Sports, music, the arts.

ADDRESSES: Home—Sandusky, OH. *Office*—Delphi Chassis Systems, 2509 Hayes Ave., Sandusky, OH 44870. *E-mail*—ebehrens@umich.edu.

CAREER: Adjunct instructor at colleges and universities, 1990-94; Delphi Chassis Systems, Sandusky, OH, educational development counselor, 1994—.

Ohio Arts Council, artist in residence, 1991—; Firelands College, member of Technologies Advisory Board; Sandusky City Schools, community advisor.

MEMBER: Associated Writing Programs, Teachers and Writers Collaborative, Ohioana Library Association, Bowling Green State University Creative Writing Alumni Association (member of board of directors).

AWARDS, HONORS: Grant, Ohio Arts Council, 1992.

WRITINGS:

None but the Dead and the Dying (novel), Baskerville Publishers (Dallas, TX), 1996.

Work represented in anthologies, including *What's a Nice Girl Like You. . . ,* Crossing Press (Freedom, CA), 1992; and *Ohio Fiction Writers,* edited by Jan Saari, 1995. Contributor to periodicals, including *Descant, Fiction,* and *Echoes.* Advisory editor, *Mid-American Review,* 1994—.

WORK IN PROGRESS: For All Seasons, a literary novel; research on amusement parks, state parks, and the Great Lakes trade.

SIDELIGHTS: Ellen Behrens told *CA:* "I have been writing fiction since about the age of six, when I discovered that all those words I was learning to spell were mine to arrange into sentences and little stories. I grew up in the small town of Clyde, Ohio, which was Sherwood Anderson's setting for *Winesburg, Ohio,* and I was the daughter of artists. I remember summers the four of us kids spent at outdoor art shows, watching the people and listening to the other artists talk. I learned about language there, that some people said words that we weren't ever supposed to utter, and that no doubt impressed me.

"Mostly I wrote about characters who weren't anything like me, because the last person I wanted to be was myself (thank goodness I've made peace with myself since). They lived in places where I had never been and did things I could only imagine doing. They were Nancy Drew imitations and fans who got to meet their favorite television stars. Those manuscripts have met their appropriate demise, but they were necessary practice along the way.

"At Denison University, encouraged by the first published authors I had ever met, I started my first novel

which, though not deceased, has been comatose for many years in a box somewhere. I read Toni Morrison's work for the first time, and it was a case of love at first sight that has endured. I read the works of contemporary poets and fiction writers, met established writers as they made their way around the country, stopping at Granville.

"Later, after a marriage and divorce and a few years in the business world, I returned to Ohio and to the Master of Fine Arts program at Bowling Green State University, where I started reading and writing again. I went back to the small town nuances of a place like Clyde for my first novel. Despite living in four states in 1987, my travels made me appreciate the subtleties of cornfields and one-lane township roads, quick thickets of woods in the middle of wheat, the rhythmic click of a single traffic signal in the dark of night, and the brush of factory grease in the air.

"I write to share what I see and feel in places nobody else thinks twice about. I write to prove them wrong who say, 'Who would want to read about that?' I write, now, to celebrate the very places I thought I needed to leave, to share what I have discovered in coming home."

* * *

BELAND, Pierre 1947-

PERSONAL: Born October 4, 1947, in Quebec City, Quebec, Canada; son of Rene (a geologist) and Andree (Boulanger) Beland; children: Martine, Eliane. *Education:* Dalhousie University, Ph.D.

ADDRESSES: Home and office—460 Champ-de-Mars, No. 504, Montreal, Quebec H2Y 1B4, Canada.

CAREER: St. Lawrence National Institute of Ecotoxicology, Montreal, Quebec, senior research scientist, 1987—. International Joint Commission, member, 1995—. *Military service:* Canadian Navy, served in Student Reserve.

WRITINGS:

Beluga: A Farewell to Whales, Lyons & Burford (New York City), 1996.

Author of a suspense novel, McClellend & Stewart (Toronto, Ontario), in press.

BELLOS, David 1945-

PERSONAL: Born in 1945, in England; son of Nathaniel and Katherine (Schapiro) Bellos. *Education:* University of Oxford, B.A., 1967, M.A., 1970, D.Phil., 1971. *Religion:* Jewish. *Politics:* "None." *Avocational interests:* Cycling.

ADDRESSES: Office—Department of Romance Languages and Literatures, Princeton University, Princeton, NJ 08544.

CAREER: University of Edinburgh, Edinburgh, Scotland, lecturer in French, 1972-82; University of Southampton, Southampton, England, professor of French, 1982-85; University of Manchester, Manchester, Lancashire, England, professor of French, 1986-96; Princeton University, Princeton, NJ, professor of French and comparative literature, 1997—.

AWARDS, HONORS: IBM France translation prize, French-American Foundation, 1988, for translation of *Life: A User's Manual;* Chevalier dans l'ordre des palmes academiques, 1988; Prix Goncourt de la Biographie, 1994, for *Georges Perec: A Life in Words.*

WRITINGS:

TRANSLATOR

(And editor) Leo Spitzer, *Essays on Seventeenth-Century French Literature,* Cambridge University Press, 1983.
Georges Perec, *Life: A User's Manual,* Godine, 1987.
Perec, *W: Or the Memory of Childhood,* Godine, 1988.
Perec, *Things: A Story of the Sixties,* Collins Harvill, 1990.
Perec, *"53 Days,"* Harvill, 1992.
Kadare, *The Pyramid,* Harvill, 1996.
Kadare, *The File on H,* Harvill, 1996.

Also translator of Perec's *Winter Journey,* 1985.

MONOGRAPHS

Honore de Balzac, *La Cousine Bette,* Grant & Cutler, 1980.
Balzac, *Old Goriot,* Cambridge University Press, 1987.

OTHER

Balzac Criticism in France, Clarendon Press, 1976.
Georges Perec: A Life in Words (biography), Godine, 1993.

WORK IN PROGRESS: A critical biography of French filmmaker Jacques Tati.

SIDELIGHTS: David Bellos, who has written or translated more than one hundred books and articles in English and French on nineteenth- and twentieth-century French literature, is well known for his English translations of works by French novelist and short story writer Georges Perec. Bellos is credited with introducing Perec's works to English-speaking audiences, beginning with his translation of Perec's *Winter Journey* in 1985 and *Life: A User's Manual* in 1987. *Life* presents Perec's views on modern society through physical and psychological descriptions of several tenants in a Parisian apartment building. The characters' experiences encompass both the mundane details of everyday life and more intriguing events including mystery and murder. In a review of this work for the *New York Times Book Review,* Paul Auster asserted that it "could not have been an easy assignment for a translator, but apart from a number of small lapses here and there, David Bellos seems to have done an admirable job."

Critics generally praise Bellos's translations as musical, persuasive, and highly accurate. However, Gabriel Josipovici, in a review of *Life: A User's Manual* in the *Times Literary Supplement,* argued that Bellos rendered some book titles and quotations inconsistently, claiming that "this might seem a trivial objection, but hundreds of such details combine to give the impression of something slightly clumsy and unfocused, which is the precise opposite of the effect of the book in French." The ensuing debate in the *TLS,* Bellos told *CA,* did much to raise the profile of literary translation in the United Kingdom.

Many critics have found, as Dan Gunn observed in a review of *Things: A Story of the Sixties* in the *Times Literary Supplement,* that while "those with French may find themselves turning back to Perec's original; those without French should be assured that what is found there is never a disappointment." Bellos published a biography of Perec in 1993 (reissued with corrections in the United Kingdom in 1996), entitled *Georges Perec: A Life in Words,* which was praised by *Publishers Weekly* as an "exhaustive biography" that represented "remarkable" investigative work by

Bellos. The review also stated that Bellos's biography should renew interest in Perec's writing. In French translation, it won the Prix Goncourt for biography in 1994.

BIOGRAPHICAL/CRITICAL SOURCES:

PERIODICALS

Le Monde, March 25, 1994.
Los Angeles Times, December 12, 1993.
New York Review of Books, November 3, 1994.
New York Times Book Review, November 15, 1987, p. 7; January 8, 1989, p. 16.
Publishers Weekly, October 11, 1993, p. 75.
Times Literary Supplement, May 13, 1983, p. 496; October 30-November 5, 1987, p. 1191-92; February 10-16, 1989, p. 148; August 10, 1990, p. 841; December 3, 1993.

* * *

BENCHLEY, Robert (Charles) 1889-1945

PERSONAL: Born September 15, 1889, in Worchester, MA; died of a brain hemorrhage, November 21, 1945; married Gertrude Darling, 1914; children: Nathaniel. *Education:* Attended Harvard University, 1908-12.

CAREER: Wrote advertising copy for the Curtis Publishing Company early in his career; freelance humorist, c. 1915-45; *Vanity Fair* (magazine), journalist, 1919-20, managing editor, 1920-29; journalist for *Tribune Magazine,* 1919-20; drama editor for *Life,* beginning 1923; Paramount Studios, Los Angeles, CA, writer of film subtitles, beginning 1928.

Acted in stage productions, including *Music Box Review,* 1926; acted in short and full-length films, including: (And writer) *The Sex Life of the Polyp,* 1928; (and writer) *The Treasurer's Report,* 1928; (and writer) *The Spellbinder,* 1929; (and writer) *Stewed, Fried, and Boiled,* 1929; (and writer) *Furnace Trouble,* 1929; (and writer) *Lesson Number One,* 1929.

Appeared in films during the 1930s, including *The Sport Parade,* 1932; *Dancing Lady,* 1933; *Headline Shooter,* 1933; (and writer) *Your Technocracy and*

Mine, 1933; *Rafter Romance*, 1934; *Social Register*, 1934; *China Seas*, 1935; (and writer) *How to Sleep*, 1935; (and writer) *How to Break 90 at Croquet*, 1935; *Piccadilly Jim*, 1936; (and writer) *How to Be a Detective*, 1936; (and writer) *How to Behave*, 1936; (and writer) *How to Train a Dog*, 1936; (and writer) *How to Vote*, 1936; (and writer) *The Romance of Digestion*, 1936; *How to Start the Day*, 1937; *A Night at the Movies*, 1937; *Live, Love, and Learn*, 1937; *The Broadway Melody of 1938*, 1938; (and writer) *The Courtship of the Newt*, 1938; (and writer) *An Evening Alone*, 1938; (and writer) *How to Figure Income Tax*, 1938; (and writer) *How to Read*, 1938; (and writer) *How to Sub-let*, 1938; (and writer) *How to Watch Football*, 1938; (and writer) *Music Made Simple*, 1938; (and writer) *Opening Day*, 1938; (and writer) *An Hour for Lunch*, 1938; (and writer) *How to Raise a Baby*, 1938; (and writer) *Mental Poise*, 1938; (and writer) *Dark Magic*, 1939; (and writer) *Day of Rest*, 1939; (and writer) *Home Early*, 1939; (and writer) *Home Movies*, 1939; (and writer) *How to Eat*, 1939; (and writer) *That Inferior Feeling*, 1939; (and writer) *See Your Doctor*, 1939.

Appeared in films during the 1940s, including *Hired Wife*, 1940; (and writer) *The Trouble with Husbands*, 1940; *Nice Girl?* 1941; (and writer, with others) *The Reluctant Dragon*, 1941; *Three Girls about Town*, 1941; *You'll Never Get Rich*, 1941; *Bedtime Story*, 1941; (and writer) *The Forgotten Man*, 1941; (and writer) *How to Take a Vacation*, 1941; (and writer) *Nothing but Nerves*, 1941; (and writer) *Crime Control*, 1941; (and writer) *Waiting for Baby*, 1941; *I Married a Witch*, 1942; *The Major and the Minor*, 1942; *Take a Letter, Darling*, 1942; (and writer) *Keeping in Shape*, 1942; (and writer) *The Man's Angle*, 1942; (and writer) *The Witness*, 1942; *My Tomato*, 1943; *Flesh and Fantasy*, 1943; *The Sky's the Limit*, 1943; *The Song of Russia*, 1943; *Young and Willing*, 1943; (and writer) *No News is Good News*, 1943; *Her Primitive Man*, 1944; *Janie*, 1944; *National Barn Dance*, 1944; *Practically Yours*, 1944; *See Here, Private Hargrove*, 1944; (and writer) *Important Business*, 1944; (and writer) *Why Daddy?* 1944; *Duffy's Tavern*, 1945; *It's in the Bag*, 1945; *Kiss and Tell*, 1945; *Pan-Americana*, 1945; *The Road to Utopia*, 1945; *The Stork Club*, 1945; *Snafu*, 1945; *Weekend at the Waldorf*, 1945; (and writer) *I'm a Civilian Here Myself*, 1945; *The Bride Wore Boots*, 1946; *Janie Gets Married*, 1946.

AWARDS, HONORS: Academy Award, 1935, for best short film, for *How to Sleep*.

WRITINGS:

BOOKS; HUMOR

Of All Things, [New York, NY], 1921.
Love Conquers All, [New York, NY], 1922.
Pluck and Luck, [New York, NY], 1925.
The Early Worm, [New York, NY], 1927.
20,000 Leagues under the Sea, or, David Copperfield, [New York, NY], 1930.
The Treasurer's Report and Other Aspects of Community Singing, [New York, NY], 1930.
No Poems, or, Around the World Backwards and Sideways, [New York, NY], 1932.
From Bed to Worse, or, Comforting Thoughts about the Bison, [New York, NY], 1934.
My Ten Years in a Quandary and How They Grew, [New York, NY], 1936, Blue Ribbon Books, 1939; Aeonian Press (Leyden, MA), 1976.
After 1903—What?, [New York, NY], 1938.
(With Charles Bennett, Joan Harrison, and James Hilton) *Foreign Correspondent*, Warner Bros., 1940.
Inside Benchley, [New York, NY], 1942.
Benchley beside Himself, [New York, NY], 1943.
Benchley—Or Else!, [New York, NY], 1947.
Chips Off the Old Benchley, illustrated by Gluyas Williams, Harper (New York, NY), 1949; introduction by Frank Sullivan, Aeonian Press, 1976.
The Benchley Roundup, selected by Nathaniel Benchley, illustrated by Williams, Harper, 1954; Chicago University Press, 1983.
Benchley Lost and Found: 39 Prodigal Pieces, illustrated by Peter Arno and others, Dover, 1970.
A Good Old-Fashioned Christmas, illustrated by Williams, Ipswich Press (Ipswich, MA), c. 1981.
The Best of Robert Benchley, illustrated by Arno, Herbert F. Roese, Adam Johm Barth, and others, Avenel Books (New York, NY), 1983.
Benchley at the Theatre, Ipswich, 1986.

Contributor of humor and reviews to periodicals, including *Harvard Lampoon*, *Vanity Fair*, *Life*, *Tribune Magazine*, *New York World*, *The Bookman*, and *New Yorker*.

Also author or co-author of film scripts, including *You'd Be Surprised*, 1926; (and actor) *The Sex Life of the Polyp*, 1928; (and actor) *The Treasurer's Report*, 1928; (and actor) *The Spellbinder*, 1929; (and actor) *Stewed, Fried, and Boiled*, 1929; (and actor) *Furnace Trouble*, 1929; (and actor) *Lesson Number One*, 1929; *Sky Devils*, 1932; *The Sport Parade*, 1932;

(and actor) *Your Technocracy and Mine,* 1933; *Dancing Lady,* 1933; *The Gay Bride,* 1934; *The Gay Divorcee,* 1934; (and actor) *How to Sleep,* 1935; (and actor) *How to Break 90 at Croquet,* 1935; *Murder on a Honeymoon,* 1935; (and actor) *How to Be a Detective,* 1936; (and actor) *How to Behave,* 1936; (and actor) *How to Train a Dog,* 1936; (and actor) *How to Vote,* 1936; (and actor) *The Romance of Digestion,* 1936; *Dancing Pirate,* 1936; (and actor) *The Courtship of the Newt,* 1938; (and actor) *An Evening Alone,* 1938; (and actor) *How to Figure Income Tax,* 1938; (and actor) *How to Read,* 1938; (and actor) *How to Sub-let,* 1938; (and actor) *How to Watch Football,* 1938; (and actor) *Music Made Simple,* 1938; (and actor) *Opening Day,* 1938; (and actor) *An Hour for Lunch,* 1938; (and actor) *How to Raise a Baby,* 1938; (and actor) *Mental Poise,* 1938; (and actor) *Dark Magic,* 1939; (and actor) *Day of Rest,* 1939; (and actor) *Home Early,* 1939; (and actor) *Home Movies,* 1939; (and actor) *How to Eat,* 1939; (and actor) *That Inferior Feeling,* 1939; (and actor) *See Your Doctor,* 1939; *Foreign Correspondent,* 1940; (and actor) *The Trouble with Husbands,* 1940; (and actor) *The Forgotten Man,* 1941; (and actor) *How to Take a Vacation,* 1941; (and actor) *Nothing but Nerves,* 1941; (and actor) *Crime Control,* 1941; (and actor) *Waiting for Baby,* 1941; (and actor) *Keeping in Shape,* 1942; (and actor) *The Man's Angle,* 1942; (and actor) *The Witness,* 1942; (and actor) *No News Is Good News,* 1943; (and actor) *Important Business,* 1944; (and actor) *Why Daddy?* 1944; (and actor) *I'm a Civilian Here Myself,* 1945.

SIDELIGHTS: American humorist and actor Robert Benchley has made a large and varied contribution to our culture. He was known for both his acting and writing talents as well as his integral participation with the Algonquin Round Table, a group of well-regarded writers, including Robert Sherwood and Dorothy Parker, who gathered at the Algonquin Hotel. His short humorous pieces saw print first in magazines, then were collected in books such as *Love Conquers All, The Early Worm,* and *My Ten Years in a Quandary and How They Grew.* He not only acted in films during the late 1920s, 1930s, and 1940s, but wrote many comic short films that were shown with features in movie theaters during those decades. One such, *How to Sleep,* which Benchley both wrote and starred in, garnered an Academy Award in 1935.

As a screenwriter, Benchley is perhaps best remembered for his series of short subject films in which he also performed, especially those with the words "How to" in the titles. Besides the aforementioned

award-winner, noteworthy examples include *How to Train a Dog, How to Figure Income Tax,* and *How to Watch Football.* As Greg S. Faller reported in the *International Dictionary of Films and Filmmakers,* in this series "he usually played a bumbling 'expert' or 'authority' trying to explain something complicated . . . about modern living." Benchley also worked, however, on the scripts of feature films, including one effort by the famed British director Alfred Hitchcock, *Foreign Correspondent* (1940). He acted in more feature films during the 1930s and 1940s, including *China Seas, I Married a Witch,* and *Janie.* Faller observed that in these films, Benchley was "always playing a *bon vivant* or a befuddled, amiable interloper. Either character allowed him to demonstrate upper-class wit, ironic double-talk, hesitant confusion, and a certain clumsiness." Benchley continued to write for and act in films until his death from a brain hemorrhage in 1945.

The popularity of Benchley's humorous books has continued long after his death. His son, Nathaniel, made selections of his own favorites from his father's opus, and published it in 1954 as *The Benchley Roundup.* This has been reprinted in later years; one such edition was lauded in the *Saturday Review* in 1965 as "wry and ceaselessly clever," and another hailed by the *Washington Post Book World* in 1983 as "a delightful book." In 1970, Dover Publications came out with a volume of several previously uncollected Benchley essays, called *Benchley Lost and Found: 39 Prodigal Pieces.* *Publishers Weekly* heralded its printing by calling it "a miniature lode for Benchley-lovers."

There is some disagreement among critics about whether Benchley's humor has held up over time. Reviewing *Benchley at the Theatre,* a 1986 collection of pieces from Benchley's stint as a drama critic, Julius Novick in the *New York Times Book Review* charged that the author's "bland, chatty facetiousness . . . in the aggregate begins to weigh rather heavily." An *Atlantic* reviewer discussing the same volume, however, praised Benchley's "insouciant lightness of touch," and acclaimed his "very funny—still funny—writing." *Time* concluded *Benchley at the Theatre* to be a "rare and delightful scrapbook."

BIOGRAPHICAL/CRITICAL SOURCES:

BOOKS

Altman, Billy, *Laughter's Gentle Soul: The Life of Robert Benchley,* W. W. Norton, 1996.

Benchley, Nathaniel, *Robert Benchley,* (New York, NY), 1956.

Cook, Samantha, editor, *International Dictionary of Films and Filmmakers,* second edition, *Volume 4: Writers and Production Artists,* St. James Press (Detroit, MI), 1993.

Gehring, Wes D., *Mr. B, or, Comforting Thoughts about the Bison: A Critical Biography of Robert Benchley,* Greenwood Press (Westport, CT), 1992.

Redding, Robert, *Starring Robert Benchley: Those Magnificent Movie Shorts,* University of New Mexico Press (Albuquerque, NM), 1973.

Rosmond, Babette, *Robert Benchley: His Life and Good Times,* Doubleday (Garden City, NY), 1970.

PERIODICALS

Atlantic, January, 1986, pp. 95-96.

New York Times Book Review, January 19, 1986, p. 21.

Publishers Weekly, June 22, 1970, p. 65.

Saturday Review, July 31, 1965, p. 26.

Time, January 6, 1986, p. 92.

Washington Post Book World, November 27, 1983, pp. 12-13.*

* * *

BENN, Gottfried 1886-1956

PERSONAL: Born May 2, 1886, in Mansfeld, Westprignitz, Germany; died July 7, 1956, in Berlin, Germany; son of a clergyman; married first wife (deceased); married second wife (deceased). *Education:* Studied medicine.

CAREER: Private physician in Berlin, Germany, beginning c. 1917. *Military service*—Served as a doctor for the German Army in both World Wars.

AWARDS, HONORS: Accepted into the Prussian Academy of the Arts, 1932; Georg Bucher Preis from the German Academy of Language and Poetry, 1951.

WRITINGS:

Morgue (poetry), [Germany], 1912.

Fleisch (poetry; title means, "Flesh"), [Germany], 1917.

Statische Gedichte (poetry; title means, "Static Poems"), 1949; Arche (Zurich, Switzerland), [Germany], c. 1983.

Doppelleben (autobiography; title means, "Double Life"), [Germany], 1950.

Fruhe Prosa und Reden, Limes-Verlag (Wiesbaden, Germany), 1950.

Primal Vision (collected poetry and prose), 1961; Boyars (London), c.1976.

Gesammelte Werke (eight volumes; collected poetry and prose), edited by Dieter Wellershoff, Limes-Verlag, c. 1970.

Selected Poems, edited by Friedrich Wilhelm Wodtke, Oxford University Press (London, England), 1970.

Lyrik: Auswahl letzter Hand, with essay by Max Rychner, Limes-Verlag, c. 1977.

Das Gottfried-Benn-Brevier: Aphorismen, Reflexionen, Maximen aus Werken u. Briefen, Limes-Verlag, 1979.

Gottfried Benn: Das Nichts und der Herr am Nebentisch (collected poetry), with biographical essay by Joachim Dyck, K. Wagenbach (Berlin, Germany), c. 1986.

Prose, Essays, Poems, edited by Volkmar Sander, with foreword by E. B. Ashton, and introduction by Reinhard Paul Becker, Continuum (New York, NY), 1987.

Samtliche Werke (four volumes; title means "Works"), Klett-Cotta (Stuttgart, Germany), 1986-1991.

Der Ptolemaer (selections), Klett-Cotta, c. 1988.

The Voice behind the Screen, translated by Simona Draghici, Plutarch Press (Washington, DC), 1996.

Also the author of a libretto for a musical with composer Paul Hindemith.

CORRESPONDENCE

Briefe an F. W. Oelze: 1932-1945, Limes-Verlag, 1977.

Briefwechsel mit Paul Hindemith, Limes-Verlag, c. 1978.

Briefe an F. W. Oelze: 1945-1949, Limes-Verlag, c. 1979.

Briefe an F. W. Oelze: 1950-1956, Limes-Verlag, c. 1980.

Gottfried Benn, Max Rychner: Briefwechsel, 1930-1956, Klett-Cotta, 1986.

Briefe an Elinor Buller, Klett-Cotta, 1992.

Gottfried Benn, Egmont Seyerlen: Briefwechsel, 1914-1956, Klett-Cotta, 1993.

SIDELIGHTS: German poet, essayist, and novelist Gottfried Benn had a few poems published beforehand, but it was in 1912 that he captured critical attention with his poetic cycle, *Morgue.* As Michael Hofmann reported in the *Times Literary Supplement,* the poems of this collection were "written in an hour, published in a week, and notorious ever since for their bleak aestheticism, their macabre juxtapositions, their reduction of human life to a bizarre and pitiful spectacle of no content or significance." Benn continued writing poetry, for which he is best known, but also wrote novels and essays. Though perhaps not as severely as in *Morgue,* his literary efforts continued in something of a nihilistic vein. As Michael Hamburger in another *Times Literary Supplement* piece translated Jurgen Schroeder's words about the writer in his biography of him, "Benn was predestined to cast the basic socio-political experience of the 20th century, that is, the still largely unfathomed experience of alienation, powerlessness and isolation of the individual, into its most communicable and enjoyable form."

Benn became a controversial figure when he first embraced Adolf Hitler's National Socialist (Nazi) Party in 1933, then repudiated it a short time later. Nazi literary critics subsequently denounced his creative work. In more recent years, a great deal of critical attention has been directed toward his correspondence in an effort to understand his ideological shifts and contradictions. Volumes of Benn's letters to such friends as businessman F. W. Oelze and composer Paul Hindemith have been collected and published in Germany since the 1970s. English-language translations of Benn's poems and prose are available; some of these titles include *Primal Vision, Prose, Essays, Poems,* and *Selected Poems.* Benn himself claimed to hold a somewhat disparaging view of his own creative talents; Hofmann quoted an English translation of the author's comments from a 1922 collection of his works: "Two hundred pages, how paltry, one would have to be ashamed of it if one were still alive. Not a document worth mentioning; I would be amazed if anyone were to read it." Benn went on to say that he felt "quite remote from them [i.e. the selections]. . . . whatever happens, I don't care for them." Nevertheless, he received honors for his creations, including induction into the Prussian Academy of Arts in 1932, and the Georg Buchner Preis in literature in 1951.

Benn was born the son of a clergyman in Mansfeld, Germany, in 1886. He pursued an education in medicine, a profession he continued to practice during his literary career. It was presumably during his years of medical study that he first attained the cynical view of human life that was a conspicuous feature of the poems in *Morgue.* After his schooling, Benn served as a German Army physician in World War I, then, after the war, he set up a private practice in Berlin, specializing in skin and venereal diseases. Like many other Germans, he developed a contempt for the Weimar Government that allowed Germany to fall into economic decline during the 1920s and 1930s. Because of this, Benn initially applauded the Nazis' rise to power, believing it would empower and restore order to the beleaguered German people.

After Hitler arrested fellow Nazi leader Ernst Roehm and had him shot in 1934, however, Benn—according to the *Encyclopedia of the Third Reich*—labeled Nazism and its offshoots as "popular organs of excretion." Though, as the *Encyclopedia* subsequently reported, Benn "came under party fire, was expelled from the Reich Writing Chamber, and was forbidden to publish," Hitler's army employed his services as a physician during World War II. Benn did not seem to object to serving the Third Reich in this capacity; Hofmann quoted one of Benn's translated prose pieces about his accommodations during the war: "Nothing dreamier than barracks! Room 66 faces the drill ground; before it grow three small rowan trees A battalion band rehearses in a corner It is the fifth year of war, and here is a completely secluded world." Yet Benn was not a loyal servant of the Nazi regime. Hamburger reported that the writer's correspondence with Oelze contains letters "only thinly veiling his wish for the defeat of the army whose uniform he continued to wear."

After the defeat of the Nazis, Benn regained his literary reputation, both in his native Germany and in the rest of the world, but in the words of the *Encyclopedia of the Third Reich,* "he could never quite silence" criticism of his initial support for Hitler's regime. Benn created several distinguished works during the late 1940s and early 1950s, including *Statische Gedichte.* Discussing the poems of Benn's later years, Hofmann asserted that "these . . . are his most moving; they have a Chinese asceticism and sorrow; they use the music of simple words, in basic quatrains; they arise from the daily conditions of Benn's life, a walk, an evening in a bar, a gift of flowers, a book he has been reading." Benn died in 1956.

Latter-day critical opinion of Benn's work includes that of Peter Washington, who reviewed an English-

language collection, *Primal Vision,* in the *Spectator.* He found in the volume a "mixture of egoism and ecstacy, personal disgust and *weltschmerz.*" He also noted that "Benn's verse" is "always vivid." Hamburger, in another *Times Literary Supplement* issue, also critiqued Benn's *Lyrik: Auswahl letzer Hand.* He complained that in it, the poet and essayist "is presented as a 'classic', not as the 'enfant terrible' he delighted in being." Of *Das Nichts und der Herr am Nebentisch,* a collection of Benn's efforts in several genres edited by Joachim Dyck in 1986, J. Glenn concluded in *World Literature Today* that it "will undoubtably prove to be one of the more useful" editions of the German writer's work.

Volumes of Benn's correspondence have also been received with critical interest. Of *Briefwechsel mit Paul Hindemith,* Benn's letters to a composer with whom he collaborated on a libretto, Richard Exner observed in *World Literature Today* that "we learn a lot about Benn if we read these letters carefully." Of *Briefe an F. W. Oelze: 1932-1945* Exner noted in the same periodical that "undoubtedly" the letters therein "are among the most significant intellectual documents we have of Benn outside of what we would more strictly call his oeuvre." Exner also reviewed the two volumes containing Benn's correspondence during the years between 1945 and 1956 in *World Literature Today.* He claimed that "in these letters Benn comes to life as nowhere else in his work or other epistolary activity." Exner went on to explain: "Oelze managed, to sum it up, to penetrate Benn's isolation, which was largely self-imposed. . . . In many of his letters to Oelze, Benn also showed a sociable side which he otherwise seemingly lacked altogether."

BIOGRAPHICAL/CRITICAL SOURCES:

BOOKS

Dierick, Augustinus Petrus, *Gottfried Benn and His Critics: Major Interpretations, 1912-1992,* Camden House (Columbia, SC), c. 1992.

Holthusen, Hans Egon, *Gottfried Benn: Leben, Werk, Widerspruch, 1886-1992,* Klett-Cotta (Stuttgart, Germany), c. 1986.

Manyoni, Angelika, *Consistency of Phenotype: A Study of Gottfried Benn's Views on Lyric Poetry,* Lang (New York, NY), c. 1983.

Ritchie, James McPherson, *Gottfried Benn: The Unreconstructed Expressionist,* Wolff (London, England), 1972.

Schroder, Jurgen, *Gottfried Benn: Poesie u. Sozialisation,* Kohlhammer (Stuttgart, Germany), 1978.

Zentner, Christian, Friedemann Bedurftig, and Amy Hackett, editors, *Encyclopedia of the Third Reich,* Macmillan (New York, NY), 1991.

PERIODICALS

Spectator, March 6, 1976, p. 25.

Times Literary Supplement, October 28, 1977, p. 1257; October 3, 1980, pp. 1095-1096; September 26, 1986, pp. 1055-1056.

World Literature Today, autumn, 1978, pp. 624-625; winter, 1980, p. 101; spring, 1981, pp. 311-312; winter, 1987, p. 98.*

—*Sketch by Elizabeth Wenning*

* * *

BENNETT, William (John) 1943-

PERSONAL: Born July 31, 1943, in Brooklyn, NY; son of F. Robert (a banker) and Nancy (a medical secretary) Bennett; married Mary Elaine Glover (a child-development specialist) in 1982; children: John, Joseph. *Education:* Williams College, B.A., 1965; University of Texas, Ph.D., 1970; Harvard University Law School, J.D., 1971. *Politics:* Republican. *Religion:* Roman Catholic.

ADDRESSES: Office—862 Venable Pl. N.W., 1766 I St. N.W., Suite 890, Washington, DC 20012; and Republican National Committee, 1414 Sadlers Wells Dr., Herndon, VA 22070-2837.

CAREER: Boston University, Boston, MA, assistant to president, 1972-76; National Humanities Center, Triangle Park, NC, executive director, 1976-79, president and director, 1979-81; National Endowment for the Humanities, Washington, DC, chairman, 1981-85; U.S. Department of Education, Washington, DC, secretary of education, 1985-88; Dunnels, Duvall, Bennett and Porter, Washington, DC, partner, 1988—; Executive Office of the President, Washington, DC, director of national drug policy, 1989-90; Empower America, Washington, DC, co-director, 1993—. Instructor, Government School, 1966, and Boston Police Academy, 1975; assistant professor, University of Southern Mississippi, 1967-68, University of Texas, 1970, Boston University, 1971-76, and University of Wisconsin, 1973; resident

advisor and tutor, Harvard University, 1969-71. Adjunct associate professor, University of North Carolina and North Carolina State University, 1979-81. Government representative to UNESCO, 1983.

MEMBER: National Academy of Education, American Society for Political and Legal Philosophy, Society for Values in Higher Education, National Humanities Faculty, Southern Education Communications Association.

AWARDS, HONORS: Has received numerous honorary degrees from various universities and colleges, including Williams College, Gonzaga University, George Washington University, Manhattan College, Central State University, and University of Notre Dame.

WRITINGS:

(With Terry Eastland) *Counting by Race: Equality from the Founding Fathers to Bakke and Weber,* Basic Books (New York, NY), 1979.

Our Children and Our Country: Improving America's Schools and Affirming the Common Culture, Simon & Schuster (New York, NY), 1988.

(Contributor) *What Your Need to Know about AIDS,* edited by Jo Ann Gasper, Servant Books (Ann Arbor, MI), 1989.

The De-Valuing of America: The Fight for Our Culture and Our Children, Summit Books (New York, NY), 1992.

(Editor and author of commentary) *The Book of Virtues: A Treasury of Great Moral Stories,* Simon & Schuster, 1993, published as *The Book of Virtues for Young People: A Treasury of Great Moral Stories,* Silver Burdett (Parsippany, NJ), 1996.

The Index of Leading Cultural Indicators: Facts and Figures on the State of American Society, Simon & Schuster, 1994.

(Editor and author of commentary) *The Moral Compass: Stories for a Life's Journey,* Simon & Schuster, 1995.

Also author of booklets and reports, *Why Judge?: A Conversation about Jurisprudence with William J. Bennett; To Reclaim a Legacy: A Report on the Humanities in Higher Education,* 1984; *Completing the Reagan Revolution,* 1986; *First Lessons: A Report on Elementary Education in America,* 1986; *American Education: Making It Work,* 1988.

SIDELIGHTS: In 1985 William Bennett was appointed Secretary of Education by President Ronald Reagan. Four years later President George Bush asked Bennett to direct the national drug policy. Well-known in political circles as what Jane Sims Podesta described in *People* as "an outspoken critic of the academic establishment," Bennett spent his years in Washington, DC as an advocate for improving America's educational system and a warrior in the war against drugs.

Jonathan Yardley described Bennett in the *Washington Post Book World:* "Bennett conveyed the impression of having more depth than glitz; to be sure he insisted on fobbing himself off as a partisan of rock 'n' roll, but he openly confessed to reading books and in public utterances he quoted from philosophers of higher standing than Robert Fulghum and Kahlil Gibran. Of greater significance, he displayed a willingness—no, a pugnacious eagerness—to take on difficult issues of the sort customarily skirted." Yardley continued: "He wasn't always polite, he wasn't always judicious and he wasn't always right, but he browbeat his constituency into thinking about important questions."

As U.S. Secretary of Education, Bennett focused a great part of his energies and career studying and exploring the current state of education in America. In addition to his work at the Department of Education, Bennett was an assistant to the president of Boston University and a respected instructor at various colleges and universities.

Bennett's book, *Our Children and Our Country: Improving America's skills and Affirming the Common Culture,* is a collection of 24 speeches the U.S. Education Secretary gave concerning the nation's education system. Patrick Reardon writes of *Our Children and Our Country:* "Bennett says the three R's of reading, writing and arithmetic need to be supplemented by the three cs—content, character and choice. That means, essentially, that schools should teach the classics and build 'moral quality' and that parents should have a choice of where to send their children." Cynthia Parsons notes in the *Los Angeles Times Book Review* that in his speeches Bennett "says several times—and of course he is correct—that the family is an important basic unit and should be strengthened. But something like one-half of all U.S. schoolchildren today come to school from unstable family units. These children need the bread of comprehensive care (housing, health, job skills) and

imaginative schooling; not the cake of a classics curriculum."

Bennett's two books, *The Book of Virtues: A Treasury of Great Moral Stories* and *The Moral Compass: Stories for a Life's Journey,* are collections of age-old stories, poetry, and essays that highlight the necessity and importance of morality and virtue in our everyday life. According to John Allen Paulos in the *New York Times Book Review* Bennett's books are "well stocked with inspirational writings taken from the Greeks (Aesop, Plato), the Bible (David and Goliath, Ecclesiastes), American folklore (Washington and the cherry tree), allegorical stories (Tolstoy's *How Much Land Does a Man Need?*), Shakespeare, Grimms' fairy tales, and writings by Goethe, Longfellow, Robert Frost, Oscar Wilde (oddly) and numerous others." Jean Porter points out in *Christian Century* that through the publication of these tales Bennett offers readers "a substantial contribution to a longstanding tradition of moral discourse."

Martha C. Nussbaum writes in her review of *The Book of Virtues* that Bennett "believes that the project of forming good character can and should be undertaken in a democracy independently of political debate about the issues that divide us. Despite the many vexing issues that separate us, he argues, we can agree in a general way about the traits of character that distinguish a good person and a good citizen."

And Katherine Paterson notes in the *New York Times Book Review* that Bennett book, *The Book of Virtues for Young People,* is a "huge compilation of vintage poems, stories and essays. [Bennett] may be the loudest voice, but it is only one of many urging harassed parents to return to 'family values.'"

BIOGRAPHICAL/CRITICAL SOURCES:

PERIODICALS

Christian Century, October 5, 1994, pp. 896-897.
Los Angeles Times Book Review, December 25, 1988, p. 6; March 6, 1994, p. 8.
Nation, March 21, 1987, pp. 368-371.
National Review, October 9, 1995, pp. 60-61.
New Republic, December 12, 1988, pp. 32-38; January 10 & 17, 1994, pp. 38-42; November 27, 1995, pp. 36-38.
New York Times Book Review, November 14, 1993, p. 14; October 15, 1995, p. 32.
Observer, December 3, 1995, p. 14.
People, June 11, 1990, pp. 97-100.

Tribune Books, September 18, 1988, p. 6.
Washington Post Book World, January 26, 1992, p. 3; January 2, 1994, p. 2.*

* * *

BERLE, Gustav 1920-1996

OBITUARY NOTICE—See index for *CA* sketch: Born March 4, 1920, in Germany; died of cardiopulmonary arrest, September 22, 1996, in Hollywood, FL. Publisher, author, business professional and professor. A highly educated advertising and public relations professional, Berle wrote 14 books after his retirement between 1986 and 1993. Most of the subjects were business (especially how-to books for small business people), the environment and retirement. Berle graduated from the City College of New York and earned a doctorate in business administration from the University of Hawaii. He started his career as a public relations consultant in Baltimore and later founded the *Northern Star,* a suburban weekly. Berle started writing immediately after retiring in 1986 and one of his most well-known titles is *The Green Entrepreneur: Business Opportunities That Can Save the Earth and Make You Money,* published in 1991. His other works include *Retiring to Your Own Business* (1993), *Do-It-Yourself Business Book* (1988), and *Instant Business Plans* (1993). A member of Mensa, Berle was a business professor at the University of Baltimore and Florida International University.

OBITUARIES AND OTHER SOURCES:

PERIODICALS

Washington Post, September 24, 1996, p. B7.

* * *

BERLINER, Michael S. 1938-

PERSONAL: Born July 4, 1938, in Columbus, OH; son of Abe (an accountant) and Helen (Kolitz) Berliner; married Judith Block (a research biologist), June 17, 1961; children: Dana. *Education:* University of Michigan, B.A., 1960, M.A., 1964; Boston University, Ph.D., 1970. *Politics:* "Laissez-faire capitalism."

ADDRESSES: Home—2334 Kelton Ave., West Los Angeles, CA 90064. *Office*—Ayn Rand Institute, 4640 Admiralty Way, No. 715, Marina del Rey, CA 90292. *E-mail*—mail@aynrand.org. *Agent*—Perry Knowlton, Curtis Brown Ltd., 10 Astor Place, New York, NY 10003.

CAREER: California State University, Northridge, professor and chairperson of department of social and philosophical foundations of education, 1970-84; Ayn Rand Institute, Marina del Rey, CA, executive director, 1985—. Trustee, Foundation for the New Intellectual. *Military service:* U.S. Army, 1960.

MEMBER: American Philosophical Association.

WRITINGS:

(Editor) *Letters of Ayn Rand,* Dutton, 1995.
(Author of introduction) *The Morality of Individualism* (Russian translation of Ayn Rand essays), Maket (St. Petersburg), 1995.

Also contributor to periodicals, including *Educational Forum, Objectivist Forum,* and *Los Angeles Times.*

SIDELIGHTS: Michael S. Berliner told *CA:* "As the archivist of Ayn Rand's papers and as a former philosophy professor, my purpose in compiling *Letters of Ayn Rand* was to provide Ayn Rand's admirers and potential new readers with insight into the life, career, and intellectual development of this influential novelist and philosopher."

Letters of Ayn Rand chronicles the voluminous correspondence of the Russian-born philosopher and novelist. The book contains letters to luminaries, including architect Frank Lloyd Wright, film mogul Cecil B. DeMille, actress Barbara Stanwyck, politician Barry Goldwater, and noted author H. L. Mencken, as well as responses to fan mail from the reading public. Christopher Cox noted in the *New York Times Book Review* that "the frequent citations . . . make *Letters of Ayn Rand,* edited by Michael S. Berliner, the authoritative companion to her work." In the *National Review,* Florence King described the collection as a "labor of love," while Suzanne Parker remarked in the *Detroit Free Press,* "With our culture drifting, groping, grasping for guidance, *Letters of Ayn Rand* is a breath of fresh air." Cox concluded that "the brutal honesty of her letters provides not only a wealth of serious thought but also some of the most entertaining passages in a remarkable volume that easily rises to the level of literature."

BIOGRAPHICAL/CRITICAL SOURCES:

PERIODICALS

Detroit Free Press, July 5, 1995, p. 6D.
National Review, October 9, 1995, pp. 61-62.
New York Times Book Review, August 6, 1995, p. 9.
Washington Post Book World, July 9, 1995, p. 4.

* * *

BETTS, Clive 1943-

PERSONAL: Born August 6, 1943, in Southampton, England; son of William Gordon (an electrician) and Olive (Greeves) Betts; married Eleri Davies (a university lecturer), 1966; children: Aced, Catrin. *Ethnicity:* "Welsh." *Education:* University of Wales, University College of Wales, Aberystwyth, B.A. (with honors), 1964. *Religion:* Anglican.

ADDRESSES: Home—12 Pentwyn Isaf, Caerphilly, Glamorgan CF83 2NR, Wales. *Office—Western Mail,* Cardiff CF1 1WR, Wales.

CAREER: Western Mail, Cardiff, Wales, Welsh affairs correspondent and author of the weekly column "Clive Betts on Wednesday."

MEMBER: Caerphilly Civic Society.

WRITINGS:

Culture in Crisis, Ffynnon (Wirral, Merseyside, England), 1976.
A Oedd Heddwch?, Gwasg ap Dafydd (Cardiff, Wales), 1978.
Cardiff and the Eisteddfod, Gwasg ap Dafydd, 1978.
The Political Conundrum, Gomer Press (Llandysul, Wales), 1993.

WORK IN PROGRESS: Research on Welsh history.

* * *

BEVIS, William W. 1941-

PERSONAL: Born June 25, 1941, in New York, NY; son of Herman W. Bevis and Jennie Lyde; married Juliette Crump; children: three. *Education:* University of California—Berkeley, Ph.D., 1968.

ADDRESSES: Home—2500 Raymond, Missoula, MT 59802. *Office*—University of Montana, Missoula, MT 59812.

CAREER: Author. University of Montana, Missoula, associate professor of English, 1974-78, professor of English, 1978—.

MEMBER: Western Literature Association, Association for Study of Literature and the Environment (ASLE).

AWARDS, HONORS: Western States Book Award for Creative Nonfiction, 1995, for *Borneo Log: The Struggle for Sarawak's Forests.*

WRITINGS:

Mind of Winter: Wallace Stevens, Meditation, and Literature, University of Pittsburgh Press, 1988.
Ten Tough Trips: Montana Writers and the West, University of Washington Press (Washington), 1990.
Borneo Log: The Struggle for Sarawak's Forests, University of Washington Press (Washington), 1995.

WORK IN PROGRESS: The Hmong in Missoula and Laos; Environment and Chaos in the Russian Far East.

SIDELIGHTS: William Bevis, a professor of English at the University of Montana, began his book writing career with a typically professorial topic: a 1988 study of the American poet, Wallace Stevens, entitled *Mind of Winter: Wallace Stevens, Meditation, and Literature.* In 1990, Bevis's second work was published. The book, *Ten Tough Trips: Montana Writers and the West,* analyzes the work of authors dealing with the American West and specifically Bevis's adopted home of Montana (the author grew up in New York) and contains autobiographical material. Bevis's 1995 work, *Borneo Log: The Struggle for Sarawak's Forests,* details the devastating effects of tropical logging Bevis witnessed while living in Borneo and Japan on sabbatical.

Bevis's first book, *Mind of Winter,* received attention in various academic quarterlies. Reviewers noted the ranging nature of the narrative, which includes extensive discussions of Buddhist and Hindu philosophy, as well as western views of consciousness to the point of including brain function diagrams. As Tim Armstrong wrote of *Mind of Winter* in *The New England Quar-*

terly: "In some ways it is less an academic work than that delightfully American genre the encyclopedia-quest: it has the scope (if few of the delights) of *Moby Dick* or *Zen and the Art of Motorcycle Maintenance.*" Other critics responded more favorably to the volume, including *ANQ*'s Jacqueline Vaught Brogan, who asserted: "Despite the critical acumen of this book, and despite the proliferation of asides, tangents, and extensions providing the larger context of his argument, Bevis has managed to write something on the order of a *meditation* itself . . . , one which successfully evokes the *meditative nothingness, suchness,* or *detachment* characteristic of much of Steven's best verse." Roger R. Labbe, in a review in the *Wallace Stevens Journal,* also responded favorably to *Mind of Winter,* declaring that "Bevis does an excellent job of discussing a difficult subject, an aconceptual state of consciousness for which the West lacks a decent vocabulary."

Robert Gish, reviewing Bevis's *Ten Tough Trips* in *Western Historical Quarterly,* compared this second book of Bevis's to Robert Persig's *Zen and the Art of Motorcycle Maintenance.* Gish provided a positive assessment of the volume, contending that Bevis's writing went "right to the heart of why novels, autobiographies, poetry, and prose matter—or can matter in our lives." *Ten Tough Trips* explores past and present writers whose subject was the American West, though Bevis occasionally includes autobiographical information. The book begins with earlier writers who saw in the West a vision of paradise that Bevis suggests was somewhat naive and, ultimately, destructive. Later sections of the book deal with more realistic views of the land by current authors such as Ivan Doig and Norman Maclean. Bevis also discusses the writings of Native Americans—both earlier authors such as D'Arcy McNickle and newer voices including James Welch.

Bevis's move from writing about English literature to considering visions of the wilderness and their effect on the land became complete in the author's next work, *Borneo Log.* Bevis narrated the sad plight of tropical forests using information he gathered during the nearly two years that he spent in Sarawak, a Malaysian state, and also in Japan, a country responsible for much of the Sarawak logging.

Liz Caile, reviewing *Borneo Log* for the *Bloomsbury Review,* applauded Bevis's ability to make vivid points. For example, she quoted his characterization of the rain forests of Southeast Asia as "a going concern for over a hundred million years, with about

10 years left." Caile characterized the book as "beautifully and comprehensively written," an assessment with which others agreed. In 1995, *Borneo Log* won the Western States Book Award for creative nonfiction.

BIOGRAPHICAL/CRITICAL SOURCES:

PERIODICALS

ANQ, January, 1991, p. 44.
Bloomsbury Review, July/August, 1991, p.10; spring, 1995.
Christian Science Monitor, January 8, 1991, p.13.
Journal of Religion, January 1992, pp. 164-65.
Library Journal, September 15, 1995, p. 90.
New England Quarterly, June 1990, pp.319-22.
Virginia Quarterly Review, autumn, 1989, pp. 120, 122.
Wallace Stevens Journal, 1989, pp. 229-231.
Western Historical Quarterly, February, 1992, pp. 119-20.

* * *

BHATT, Sujata 1956-

PERSONAL: Born May 6, 1956, in Ahmedabad, India; married Michael Augustin, 1988; children: one daughter. *Education:* Goucher College, B.A. (philosophy and English), 1980; University of Iowa Writers' Workshop, M.F.A., 1986.

ADDRESSES: Agent—c/o Carcanet Press, 208 Corn Exchange Bldgs., Manchester M4 3BQ, England.

CAREER: Freelance writer and translator. University of Victoria, British Columbia, Lansdowne Visiting writer/professor, spring, 1992.

AWARDS, HONORS: Alice Hunt Bartlett award, 1988; Dillons Commonwealth Poetry prize, 1989; Poetry Society Book Recommendation, 1991, for *Monkey Shadows;* Cholmondeley award, 1991.

WRITINGS:

POETRY

Brunizem, Penguin (Manchester, Carcanet, and New Delhi), 1988.
Monkey Shadows, Penguin, 1991.

Freak Waves (chapbook), Reference West (Victoria, British Columbia), 1992.
The Stinking Rose, Penguin, 1995.

* * *

BIERMANN, Pieke 1950-

PERSONAL: Born March 22, 1950, in Stolzenau, Lower Saxony, Germany; daughter of Theodor (a clerk) and Anneliese (Zinke) Biermann; married Thomas Woertche (a publicist and critic), October 15, 1993. *Education:* Attended universities in Germany and Italy; University of Hannover, M.A., 1976.

ADDRESSES: Home—Olivaer Platz 15, 10707 Berlin, Germany. *Office*—P.O. Box 15 14 10, 10676 Berlin, Germany; fax 49-30-881-6207. *Agent*—Michael Meller Literary Agency, Osterwaldstrasse 9-10, 80805 Munich, Germany; fax 49-89-36-63-72.

CAREER: Professional translator from Italian and English into German. Radio writer and novelist.

MEMBER: German Translators and Writers Union, IG Medien.

AWARDS, HONORS: Award from Ingeborg Bachmann Wettbewerb, 1990; two German Crime Fiction Awards, 1991, for *Violetta,* and 1994, for *Herzrasen.*

WRITINGS:

Potsdamer Ableben (novel), Rotbuch Verlag (Berlin, Germany), 1987.
Violetta (novel), Rotbuch Verlag, 1990, translation by Ines Rieder and Jill Hannum, Serpent's Tail (New York), 1996.
Herzrasen (novel), Rotbuch Verlag, 1993.
Vier, Fuenf, Sechs (novel), A. Knaus Verlag (Munich, Germany), in press.

Work represented in anthologies, including *Women on the Case,* edited by Sarah Paretsky, Delacorte (New York), 1996. Contributor of stories and articles to magazines.

WORK IN PROGRESS: Research on Berlin's security networks for a "literary reportage," to be published by A. Knaus under the title *Der Asphalt unter Berlin.*

SIDELIGHTS: Pieke Biermann told *CA:* "I have been writing since childhood, but I did not try to do it professionally until the early 1980s. I began with documentary features for radio and television and reviews for periodicals. I have been a translator since the 1970s, but I only translate one book per year.

"I started writing fiction in 1986, thanks to a fury about what journalism and the culture business were about to become. Since then I have written novels and short stories. All of them are set in Berlin and deal with the city's people, transformations, and historical, topographical, human, and anti-human realities.

"My novels are, somehow, historiography of the present. My stories all have a female narrator, though not the same one for each story, and her 'I's are a strange kind of memorial for women who could and did exist only in a place like Berlin.

"What influences my work most is reality, the reality as it reflects this city. I am very curious about Berlin, and the longer I live here (about twenty years now) the more curious I become. Nobody has 'written this city' since 1933. I do, because I think that Berlin is a kind of universal metropolis, much like New York, Chicago, Los Angeles, London, Paris, Barcelona, or Mexico City.

"My novels and stories are realistic narratives, so they have to be crime fiction. Both series will have seven parts in the end. The novels seem to need about three years each, the stories less. The stories will become a single collection, as soon as they are completed, and I intend to publish them under the title *Berlin, Kabbala.*"

* * *

BIGGERS, Earl Derr 1884-1933

PERSONAL: Born August 26, 1884, in Warren, OH; died of a heart attack, April 5, 1933, in Pasadena, CA; son of Robert J. and Emma Derr Biggers; married Eleanor Ladd, 1912; children: Robert Ladd. *Education:* Harvard University, B.A., 1907.

CAREER: Traveler (newspaper), Boston, MA, staff, columnist and drama critic, 1908-12; playwright and novelist, 1912-33.

WRITINGS:

PLAYS

If You're Only Human, produced, 1912.
Inside the Lines, (produced in Baltimore, MD, and New York, NY, 1915; produced in London, 1917), Bobbs Merrill (Indianapolis, IN), 1915.
(With Lawrence Whitman) *A Cure for Curables* (adaptation of a story by Cora Harris), produced in New York, NY, 1918.
See-Saw, produced in New York, NY, 1919.
(With Christopher Morley) *Three's a Crowd,* produced in New York, NY, 1919; produced in London, 1923.
The Ruling Passion, published in *Reference Scenarios,* Palmer Institute of Authorship, 1924.

NOVELS; EXCEPT AS NOTED

Seven Keys to Baldpate, Bobbs Merrill, 1913.
Love Insurance, Bobbs Merrill, 1914.
(With Robert Welles Ritchie) *Inside the Lines,* Bobbs Merrill, 1915.
The Agony Column, Bobbs Merrill, 1916; published as *Second Floor Mystery,* Grosset and Dunlap (New York), 1930.
Fifty Candles, Bobbs Merrill, 1926.
Earl Derr Biggers Tells Ten Stories (short stories), Bobbs Merrill, 1933.

"CHARLIE CHAN" NOVEL SERIES; FIRST PUBLISHED IN SATURDAY EVENING POST

The House without a Key, Bobbs Merrill, 1925.
The Chinese Parrot, Bobbs Merrill, 1926.
Behind That Curtain, Bobbs Merrill, 1928.
The Black Camel, Bobbs Merrill, 1929.
Charlie Chan Carries On, Bobbs Merrill, 1930.
Keeper of the Keys, Bobbs Merrill, 1932.

ADAPTATIONS: Many films and television films featuring Charlie Chan have been made, including an animated series; also a comic book about Chan has been published.

SIDELIGHTS: Earl Derr Biggers wrote several other novels, and had plays produced in New York City and London, England, but his best-known legacy to readers is his creation of the fictional detective, Charlie Chan. Biggers penned the first Chan novel, *The House without a Key,* in 1925. He followed it with five more books featuring the portly Chinese sleuth. Many of Biggers' Charlie Chan novels were

adapted for the screen and as a result, Biggers reaches a larger audience. As Henry Kratz explained in the *Critical Survey of Mystery and Detective Fiction,* "[i]t must be admitted that Charlie Chan's status as a folk hero depends more on the cinema image" than on the novels themselves. Kratz also declared Biggers' most famous character "to rank with Tom Sawyer and Tarzan of the Apes," and noted that Chan "has inspired the creation of numerous other 'cross-cultural' detectives."

Biggers served as a columnist and a drama critic for *Traveler,* a Boston newspaper. Apparently he was zealous in the latter capacity, because Kratz reported that "he was discharged for writing overly critical reviews." Biggers left the paper in 1912 and later that year he saw the production of his first play, *If You're Only Human;* the year following, his first novel, *Seven Keys to Baldpate,* was published. Margaret J. King in *Twentieth-Century Crime and Mystery Writers* described *Seven Keys* as one of several "mystery-romances cast in the melodramatic mold," while Kratz observed that it "was exceedingly popular."

Over a decade later, Biggers introduced readers to Chan. The first volume—as well as subsequent books—appeared first in serialized form in *The Saturday Evening Post.* As Kratz put it, Biggers "had already been practicing his craft for a number of years. He had developed a smooth and readable colloquial style in the four novels and numerous short stories he had already published." Further, "[i]n the several plays he had written or collaborated on he had developed a knack for writing dialogue. Thus, he was at the peak of his literary powers in 1925, when Charlie Chan first burst into print." Chan, an investigator for the Honolulu Police Department, begins his fictive career as a detective sergeant, but through the course of the novels rises to the level of inspector. He is overweight, yet agile, and brings an Eastern sensitivity to his cases. King explained that "as a Chinese on the side of law and order, Chan was in part designed to counteract the image of the sinister or deviously clever Oriental which had dominated foreign adventure novels from the 19th century." Yet racial stereotypes are not the only ones flouted in the Chan adventures. The detective most often becomes involved in plots concerning romantic pairings; the heroines of these, according to Kratz, "are usually proud and independent liberated women, concerned about their careers."

The earlier novels are set in Hawaii, but in the later ones, including *Behind That Curtain,* Chan travels to locales such as San Francisco and Lake Tahoe. In the earlier books, the viewpoint is not Chan's; in later works, the reader becomes much better acquainted with the detective's personal life and thought processes. Biggers' last Chan novel, *Keeper of the Keys,* was published in 1932, one year before the author died of a heart attack.

BIOGRAPHICAL/CRITICAL SOURCES:

BOOKS

Henderson, Lesley, *Twentieth-Century Crime and Mystery Writers,* third edition, St. James Press (Chicago, IL), 1991.

Magill, Frank N., editor, *Critical Survey of Mystery and Detective Fiction* (four volumes), Salem Press (Pasadena, CA), 1988.*

* * *

BIRCHMORE, Fred (Agnew) 1911-

PERSONAL: Born November 29, 1911, in Athens, GA; son of Fred Gillam (a dairy supplier) and Nela (a homemaker; maiden name, Agnew) Birchmore; married Willa Deane Stuckey, December 21, 1939; children: Rebecca Birchmore Campen, Fred C., Melinda Birchmore Musick, Daniel A. *Ethnicity:* "Caucasian." *Education:* University of Georgia, A.B., 1932, M.A., J.D., 1934; University of Cologne, exchange scholar. *Politics:* Independent. *Religion:* Methodist.

ADDRESSES: Home—613 Milledge Terr., Athens, GA 20606-4945. *E-mail*—103264,1476@compuserve.

CAREER: Athens Realty Co., Athens, GA, owner, 1946-75, retiring in 1975. Also worked as a lawyer and college professor. *Military service:* U.S. Navy, 1944-46; became lieutenant junior grade.

MEMBER: Kiwanis Club (president, 1974; district lieutenant governor, 1978).

AWARDS, HONORS: Hixson Award from Kiwanis Club; community awards.

WRITINGS:

Around the World on a Bicycle, University of Georgia Press (Athens, GA), 1939, reprinted, Cucumber Island Storytellers, 1996.

Miracles in My Life, Cucumber Island Storytellers, in press.

SIDELIGHTS: Fred Birchmore told *CA:* "An exchange scholar to the University of Cologne in Germany, I purchased a German bicycle and traveled through the Scandinavian countries before classes began. My companion was a member of the Hitler Youth Movement, and we saw the German Army on maneuvers, preparing for the blitzkriegs of World War II. I met Hitler, and Sonja Henie taught me to ice skate. The copious notes I wrote while riding my bicycle became articles that appeared in the *Atlanta Journal* Sunday magazine.

"During the school year, I took advantage of the holidays by visiting the British Isles, running into the bicycle Tour de France, swimming around the Isle of Capri, living the good life. For spring holidays I was in Egypt, and calamity struck: my passport and all my money were stolen as I lay sleeping on the beach! Unable to leave the country, school slipped away from me and, when I finally received money and passport, it was too late to return. So I set out alone across Asia, traveling through countries that had not been visited by a foreigner since Alexander the Great, following camel trails through the Himalayas, and being pursued by tigers in the jungles.

"*Around the World on a Bicycle* is the true story of my adventures and misadventures."

* * *

BLACKSTOCK, Terri 1957-
(Terri Herrington; Tracy Hughes)

PERSONAL: Born December 7, 1957, in Belleville, IL; daughter of O. L. Ward (a retired Air Force Colonel and airline pilot) and Jo Ann Weathersby (a secretary; maiden name, Rogers); married, November 27, 1992; children: three. *Education:* Attended Hinds Junior College, 1975-1976; Northeast Louisiana University, B.A., 1981. *Religion:* Baptist. *Avocational interests:* Attending children's extracurricular activities and volunteering in church ministries.

ADDRESSES: Home—Clinton, MS. *Agent*—Greg Johnson, Alive Communications, 1465 Kelly Johnson Blvd., Suite 320, Colorado Springs, CO 80920. *E-mail*—TBlackstck@aol.com.

CAREER: Writer. Published romance and suspense novels under the names Terri Blackstock, Terri Herrington, and Tracy Hughes.

AWARDS, HONORS: Reviewers' Choice nomination for Best New Author, *Romantic Times,* 1986; Reviewers' Choice nomination for Best Dell Candlelight Ecstasy, *Romantic Times,* 1986, for *A Secret Stirring;* Golden Medallion Finalist for Best Traditional Romance, Romance Writers of America, 1987, for *Lovers' Reunion;* Golden Medallion for Best Short Contemporary Novel, Romance Writers of America, 1988, for *Stolen Moments;* Climbing Rose Award, North Louisiana Romance Writers, 1988; Lifetime Achievement Award for Best Continuing Series, *Romantic Times,* 1990, for the Calloway Corners Series; Special Achievement Award, *Romantic Times,* 1991, for *White Lies & Alibis;* Climbing Rose Award, North Louisiana Romance Writers, 1992; W.I.S.H. Award, *Romantic Times,* 1992, for Johnny Malone, a character in *Honorbound;* Reviewers' Choice nomination for Best Harlequin American, *Romantic Times,* 1992, for *Honorbound.*

WRITINGS:

"SUNCOAST CHRONICLES" SERIES

Evidence of Mercy, Zondervan, 1995.
Justifiable Means, Zondervan, 1996.
Ulterior Motives, Zondervan, 1996.
Presumption of Guilt, Zondervan, in press.

"SECOND CHANCES" SERIES

Never Again Goodbye, Zondervan, 1996.
When Dreams Cross, Zondervan, in press.

UNDER PSEUDONYM TERRI HERRINGTON

Blue Fire, Silhouette (New York), 1984.
Head over Heels, Dell (New York), 1986.
Lovers' Reunion, Silhouette, 1986.
Tender Betrayer, Dell, 1986.
A Secret Stirring, Dell, 1986.
Stolen Moments, Dell, 1987.
Tangled Triumphs, Silhouette, 1987.
Ticket to a Fantasy, Dell, 1987.
Wife Wanted, Silhouette, 1988.
Her Father's Daughter, HarperCollins, 1991.
Flashback, Silhouette, 1993.
One Good Man, HarperCollins, 1993.
Silena, HarperCollins, 1993.
Winner Take All, HarperCollins, 1995.

UNDER PSEUDONYM TRACY HUGHES

Impressions, Harlequin (New York, NY), 1986.
Quiet Lightning, Harlequin, 1986.
Above the Clouds, Harlequin, 1988.
Emerald Windows, Harlequin, 1989.
White Lies & Alibis, Harlequin, 1990.
Honorbound, Harlequin, 1991.
Second Chances, Harlequin, 1991.
Father Knows Best, Harlequin, 1992.
Sand Man, Harlequin, 1992.
Delta Dust, Harlequin, 1993.
Jo—Calloway Corner Series, Harlequin, 1993.
Catch a Falling Star, Harlequin, 1994.
Heaven Knows, Harlequin, 1994.
The Princess and the Pauper, Harlequin, 1994.
To Heaven and Back, Harlequin, 1995.
Daniel—Return to Calloway Corners, Harlequin, 1996.

SIDELIGHTS: Terri Blackstock began her writing career in 1983 when she sold the rights to her first romance novel. Since that time, she has released more than 30 additional titles and, in 1994, she began work in a new genre, the suspense novel. A renewed spirituality is also making its mark on her subsequent work; her "SunCoast Chronicles" series of suspense novels carry a Christian message. "I wanted to be able to tell the truth in my stories . . . and not just be politically correct. It doesn't matter how many readers I have if I can't tell them what I know about the roots of their problems and the solutions that have literally saved my life," she told *CA.* The author asserts that writing is her most important ministry, but she also is active in her church's ministries in Jackson, Mississippi.

However, Blackstock has not abandoned the romance format that has proved such a success for her; she is also working on a new romance series called "Second Chances." The first book in this series is *Never Again Goodbye,* the story of a woman who gives up her child for adoption. After learning that the adoptive mother has died, she reenters her daughter's life. *Never Again Goodbye* is the first romance novel that author has published as Terri Blackstock. Previously her work was published under the name Terri Herrington and the pseudonym Tracy Hughes. Blackstock has published romance novels with Silhouette, Harlequin, and Dell, and published mainstream novels with HarperCollins. Under all of these names, she has more than three and a half million books in print.

BLAIR, E(lizabeth) Anne 1946-

PERSONAL: Born September 7, 1946, in Melbourne, Australia; daughter of Ronald Raymond (a surveyor) and Jean (a homemaker; maiden name, Tredinnick) Johnston; married James Anderson Blair, September 7, 1980. *Ethnicity:* "Caucasian." *Education:* Monash University, B.A., 1968, Diploma of Education, 1969, Ph.D., 1993. *Politics:* "Australian Democrat." *Avocational interests:* Reading contemporary literature and biography, contemporary film and drama.

ADDRESSES: Home and office—41 Swallow St., Port Melbourne, Victoria 3207, Australia. *E-mail*—eablair@silas.cc.monash.edu.au.

CAREER: Teacher for Victorian State Education Department, 1970-73, and Presbyterian Ladies College, 1974-80; secondary schoolteacher in Melbourne, Australia, 1981-86; Monash University, Clayton, Australia, tutor, 1990, lecturer in history, 1993; Victorian University of Technology, Melbourne, lecturer in the history of Southeast Asia, 1994; Monash University, research fellow at National Centre for Australian Studies, 1995-96. Royal Melbourne Institute of Technology, lecturer, 1996.

WRITINGS:

(With Donald Horne) *How to Be Australia,* National Centre for Australian Studies, Monash University (Melbourne, Australia), 1994.
Lodge in Vietnam: A Patriot Abroad, Yale University Press (New Haven, CT), 1995.

WORK IN PROGRESS: A book on the experiences of Australian Brigadier F. P. "Ted" Serong in Vietnam, 1962-1975, presenting the western involvement in the second Indochina war from the perspective of this non-American military adviser.

SIDELIGHTS: E. Anne Blair told *CA:* "I am involved in the local politics of the Port Melbourne bayside region, where I live with my husband. I was the secretary of the Swallow Street residents' association from 1986 to 1992, during a cleanup of the chemically contaminated area surrounding Swallow Street, and during the following major development of the Melbourne bayside area. The Swallow Street group was ultimately successful in achieving all of the objectives for which it had been formed."

BLAND, Peter 1934-

PERSONAL: Born May 12, 1934, in Scarborough, Yorkshire; married Beryl Matilda Connolly, 1956; children: two daughters and one son. *Education:* Attended Victoria University, 1955-59.

ADDRESSES: Home and office—125 Kenilworth Ct., Lower Richmond Road, Putney, London SW15, England.

CAREER: New Zealand Broadcasting Corporation, "Poetry" program, Editor, 1960-64; Downstage Theatre Company, Wellington, co-founder and artistic director, 1964-68; freelance writer and actor in London. Regular contributor, *London Magazine,* 1964-1990. *Military service:* Royal Army Education Corps, 1952-54.

AWARDS, HONORS: University of New Zealand McMillan-Brown prize, 1958; Melbourne Arts Festival Literary award, 1960; New Zealand Arts Council fellowship, 1968; Cholmondeley award, 1977; Arvon Foundation award, 1980, 1990.

WRITINGS:

POETRY

(With John Boyd and Victor O'Leary) *Three Poets,* Capricorn Press (Wellington), 1958.
My Side of the Story; Poems 1960-64, Mate (Auckland), 1964.
Domestic Interiors, Wai-Te-Ata Press (Wellington), 1964.
The Man with the Carpet-Bag, Caxton Press (Christchurch), 1972.
Mr. Maui, London Magazine Editions (London), 1976.
Primitives, Wai-Te-Ata Press, 1979.
Stone Tents, London Magazine Editions, 1981.
The Crusoe Factor, London Magazine Editions, 1985.
Selected Poems, McIndoe (Dunedin), 1987.
Paper Boats, McIndoe, 1990.

PLAYS

Father's Day, produced in Wellington, 1967.
George the Mad Ad Man, produced in Wellington, 1967; produced in Coventry, 1969.

Manuscript Collection: Turnbull Library, Wellington.

BORNHOLDT, Jennifer Mary 1960-
 (Jenny Bornholdt)

PERSONAL: Born November 1, 1960, Lower Hutt, New Zealand; married Gregory O'Brien, 1994. *Education:* Victoria University, B.A. (English literature), 1984.

ADDRESSES: Agent—c/o Victoria University Press, P.O. Box 600, Wellington, New Zealand.

CAREER: Unity Books, Wellington, bookseller, 1989-92. Haines Recruitment Advertising, Wellington, copywriter, 1992—.

WRITINGS:

POETRY, AS JENNY BORNHOLDT

This Big Face, Victoria University Press (Wellington, New Zealand), 1988.
Moving House, Victoria University Press, 1989.
Waiting Shelter, Victoria University Press, 1991.
How We Met, Victoria University Press, 1995.

* * *

BORNHOLDT, Jenny
 See BORNHOLDT, Jennifer Mary

* * *

BOUVIER, Nicolas 1929-

PERSONAL: Born March 6, 1929, in Geneva, Switzerland; son of Auguste (a librarian) and Antoinette (Maurice) Bouvier; married Eliane Petitpierre, January 13, 1968; children: Thomas, Manuel. *Education:* Attended University of Geneva. *Religion:* Protestant.

ADDRESSES: Home—41 vie de Vandoervrer, CH 1223 Cologny, Geneva, Switzerland. *Office*—9 ou. Vibert, CH 1227 Carouge, Geneva, Switzerland.

CAREER: Freelance writer.

AWARDS, HONORS: Prix des critiques, Paris, France, 1982; Grand prix de la Ville de Geneve, 1987; Prix Scott-Moncrief, London, England, 1988.

WRITINGS:

L'Usage du Monde (travel), Droz (Geneva, Switzerland), 1963; translated by Robyn Marsack as *The Way of the World,* Marlboro Press (Marlboro, VT), 1992.

Japon (title means "Japan"), Rencontre (Lausanne, Switzerland), 1967.

Chronique Japonnaise (travel), L'Age d'homme (Lausanne, Switzerland); translated by Anne Dickerson as *The Japanese Chronicles,* Mercury House (San Francisco, CA), 1992.

Le Poisson-scorpion (novel), Burtil Galland (Vevey, Switzerland); translated by Marsack as *The Scorpion-Fish,* Carcanet (New York, NY), 1987.

Journal d'Aran et d'autres lieux: Feuilles de route (travel), Payot (Paris, France), c. 1990.

La Vie immediate: Ella Maillart: Photographies/textes (travel), Editions Payot (Lausanne, Switzerland), c. 1991.

Has also written for Swiss television.

SIDELIGHTS: Nicolas Bouvier is a native of Switzerland who writes in the French language. His works include travel pieces, television shows, and a novel. Many of his books have seen publication in other European countries besides the land of his birth; those that have appeared in English translation in the United States are *The Scorpion-Fish, The Way of the World,* and *The Japanese Chronicles.* Bouvier has been awarded the Grand prix de la Ville de Geneve, Paris's Prix des critiques, and London's Prix Scott-Moncrief for his creative efforts.

L'Usage du Monde was Bouvier's first book, published in 1963, though it was not translated into English as *The Way of the World* until 1992, years after American readers had discovered his 1987 novel *Le Poisson-scorpion (The Scorpion-Fish). The Way of the World* tells the story of how Bouvier and his friend Thierry traveled through several Balkan and Middle Eastern countries in an old Fiat automobile during the 1950s. When they ran low on cash and their car needed to be repaired, they stopped for varying stretches of time, living and working among the natives of such cities as Teheran, Iran, Istanbul, Turkey, and Belgrade, Yugoslavia. "Thus *The Way of the World* interweaves adventure with an abundance of shrewd insights gained by sharing in local peoples' lives for weeks or months on end," explained Dervla Murphy, reviewing the book in the *Times Literary Supplement.* Murphy also praised Bouvier's insight into the people of Bosnia, a region since fraught with ethnic fighting, and noted that "in his response to the ancient complexities of Iran, Bouvier is at his most perceptive, enabling us to see the last Shah and the Ayatollah Khomeini in perspective." Chris Goodrich in the *Los Angeles Times Book Review* lauded *The Way of the World* as well, calling its tone "thoughtful, mysterious, a bit poetic."

Chronique Japonnaise, under the translated title *The Japanese Chronicles,* hit bookstores in the United States in the same year as *The Way of the World,* but like that volume was also written prior to *The Scorpion-Fish. The Japanese Chronicles* is unusual among travel books about Japan in that it examines the lives of the Japanese poor and relates to readers the various ways in which these citizens economize. Bouvier also discusses within its pages the irony of a culture which guards against outsiders yet borrows much from both the Chinese and the Americans. Charles Solomon in the *Los Angeles Times Book Review* hailed it as "engaging," while a *Washington Post Book World* critic called it "a reverential and delicately nuanced portrait" of the eastern nation.

While *The Scorpion-Fish* is a novel, it employs a structure much like Bouvier's travel writing, chronicling the thoughts and feelings of a European traveling in an unnamed island that most reviewers have identified as Sri Lanka. The narrator reacts from everything to the large insects of the island and the poisonous fish of the title which is symbolic of the land itself, to the local monks who are sanctioned by the rest of the people in the acts of terrorism they commit. The narrator also suffers from tropical fevers and accompanying hallucinations, including the levitating ghost of a Catholic priest who died six years before. Critics had good things to say about *The Scorpion-Fish;* Victoria Scott in the *Los Angeles Times Book Review* asserted that "to read 'The Scorpion-Fish' . . . is to be drawn off the tourist track and into the life of Asia, where the distinction between fact and fiction has long been blurred—and hence, for those who can see, clarified." Sara Vogan in the *New York Times Book Review* concluded that "Bouvier has given us an insightful meditation on how we perceive the world we live in, the natural and the mystical."

BIOGRAPHICAL/CRITICAL SOURCES:

PERIODICALS

Los Angeles Times Book Review, December 6, 1987, p. 13; April 25, 1993, p. 6; August 22, 1993.

New York Times Book Review, September 27, 1987, p. 18.
Publishers Weekly, August 21, 1987, p. 52.
Times Literary Supplement, October 13, 1993, p. 28.
Washington Post Book World, May 24, 1992, p. 13.

* * *

BREMSER, Bonnie 1939-

PERSONAL: Born Bonnie Frazer, July 23, 1939, in Washington, DC; married Ray Bremser, 1959 (separated, 1973); children: Rachel (given up for adoption). *Education:* Attended Sweet Briar College.

ADDRESSES: Home—Cherry Valley, NY.

WRITINGS:

Troia: Mexican Memoirs, Croton Press (New York), 1969; republished as *For Love of Ray,* London Magazine Editions (London), 1971.

SIDELIGHTS: Bonnie Bremser portrayed herself and her experiences in Mexico during the 1960s in *Troia: Mexican Memoirs,* an autobiography which was published in 1971 as *For Love of Ray.* Bonnie Bremser is a largely self-taught writer who used the works of her husband and other Beat poets and writers as models to create *Troia.* This work is both a romantic love story and a picaresque tale told in an improvisational style. Bremser became part of the Beat literary movement that was known for its anti-establishment stance promoted by such influential figures as poet Allen Ginsberg and novelist Jack Kerouac.

In 1959, Bonnie Frazer married Beat poet Ray Bremser, who had been released from prison the previous year after serving a sentence for armed robbery. The couple, with their infant daughter Rachel, fled to Mexico City when Ray was again charged with armed robbery. In Mexico the family lived with the specter of Ray's arrest hanging over them. Bonnie turned to prostitution to earn a living and as a result of the great amount of stress in their lives, the couple separated and put their daughter up for adoption. Ray and Bonnie eventually reconciled and made a meager living in Hoboken, New Jersey.

While Ray served a second stint in prison for armed robbery, Bonnie passed the time by writing about their adventures in Mexico. Part of this journal was published in 1967 in the literary magazine *Down Here,* but it did not appear in its entirety until it was published as *Troia: Mexican Memoirs* in 1969. "*Troia* is rough-hewn and defiantly unconventional and true to the experience of the author," asserted Michael Perkins in the *Dictionary of Literary Biography.*

BIOGRAPHICAL/CRITICAL SOURCES:

BOOKS

Dictionary of Literary Biography, Volume 16: *The Beats: Literary Bohemians in Postwar America,* edited by Ann Charters, Gale (Detroit), 1983, pp. 33-35.

PERIODICALS

Times Literary Supplement, May 21, 1971, p. 586.*

* * *

BRIERLEY, Barry 1937-

PERSONAL: Born December 21, 1937, in Menomonie, WI; married Barbara Webster, September 1, 1984; children: Scott, Jodi; stepchildren: Matthew Druzkowski, Daniel Druzkowski, Luke Druzkowski. *Ethnicity:* "White."

ADDRESSES: Home—1852 South Saguaro Circle, Mesa, AZ 85202.

CAREER: Joston's, Owatonna, MN, staff artist, 1970-79; Wincraft, Winona, MN, manager of special graphics, 1983-87; writer, 1993—. *Military service:* U.S. Marine Corps, 1957-60; became sergeant.

MEMBER: Western Writers of America.

WRITINGS:

HISTORICAL NOVELS

Wasichu, Lagare, 1993.
Timeless Interlude at Wounded Knee, Blue Bird Publishing (Tempe, AZ), 1995.
White Horse, Red Rider, Bear Books, 1996.
Wasichu's Return, Bear Books, 1996.

Also author of the screenplay *Chesty's Traveling Road Show.*

WORK IN PROGRESS: Spirit Riders, a novel and screenplay; research on Butch Cassidy and on the Apache Indians.

* * *

BROCK-BROIDO, Lucie 1956-

PERSONAL: Born May 22, 1956, in Pittsburgh, PA. *Education:* Johns Hopkins University, B.A., 1979; Columbia University, M.F.A., 1982.

ADDRESSES: Home and office—c/o Dodge Hall, Writing Division, School of the Arts, Columbia University, New York, NY 10027.

CAREER: Harvard University, Cambridge, MA, Briggs-Copeland Assistant Professor in Poetry, 1988-93, and director, creative writing program, 1992-93; Bennington Writing Seminars, associate professor in poetry, 1993-95; Columbia University, NY, associate professor and director of poetry, 1993—. Princeton University, Princeton, NJ, visiting professor of poetry, 1995.

AWARDS, HONORS: Grolier Poetry prize, Blacksmith Series, Cambridge, 1983; poetry fellowship, Fine Arts Work Center, Provincetown, 1983; Hoyns fellowship in poetry, University of Virginia, 1984; National Endowment for the Arts poetry fellowship, 1985; *New Letters* Literary award, 1987; *New England Review* Narrative Poetry award, 1987; Massachusetts Artist fellowship in poetry, 1988; Harvard-Danforth award for distinction in teaching, 1989, 1990; *American Poetry Review* Jerome Shestack prize for poetry, 1991; Harvard University Phi Beta Kappa Teaching award, 1991.

WRITINGS:

POETRY

A Hunger, Knopf (New York), 1988.
The Master Letters, Knopf, 1995.

* * *

BRODSKY, Vera
 See LAWRENCE, Vera Brodsky

BRONSON, Po 1964-

PERSONAL: Born in 1964, in Seattle, WA; son of Duncan and Louise Bronson. *Ethnicity:* "Euro-American." *Education:* Stanford University, B.A., 1986; San Francisco State University, M.F.A., 1995. *Politics:* "Every four years." *Religion:* "Sex." *Avocational interests:* "Laughing, women with skunk stripes in their hair, soccer."

ADDRESSES: Office—2148 Market St., San Francisco, CA 94114. *Agent*—Peter Ginsberg, Curtis Brown Ltd., 10 Astor Place, New York, NY 10003.

CAREER: First Boston Corporation, San Francisco, CA, bond salesman, 1986-88; Citi Respect ("San Francisco Politics"), 1988-89; Mercury House (nonprofit publishing company), San Francisco, CA, associate publisher, 1989-95. Co-founder of the Writer's Grotto, San Francisco.

WRITINGS:

Bombardiers (novel), Random House (New York), 1995.
The First $20 Million is Always the Hardest (novel), Random House, 1997.

Contributor to *Wired* magazine and the *New York Times Magazine.*

SIDELIGHTS: Publishing executive and former bond salesman Po Bronson is the author of the critically-acclaimed *Bombardiers,* a satirical story of societal corruption and obsession with work routines as seen within the office of bond traders. Set in San Francisco, the novel revolves around Sid Geeder, a bond trader in his mid-thirties who hates his job with the Atlantic Pacific investment bank. Geeder is seeking a way out of Atlantic Pacific by cashing in his 100,000 shares of his company's stock, which is worth $4 million. Unfortunately, his superiors at the bank threaten to fire him if he tries to retire, which would cause Geeder to lose his take of the wealth. Geeder and several of his co-workers become increasingly sickened by the corrupt nature of bond-trading at the bank, especially when they learn that the company is plotting a buyout of the Dominican Republic. The title of Bronson's novel refers to bond traders who sell bonds that are sure to explode—that is, fail—thus triggering government bailouts, which create more bonds to sell and greater profits to be made by traders.

Many literary critics have likened Bronson's novel to Joseph Heller's *Catch-22,* among them Judith Wynn, who observed in her *Chicago Tribune* review: "What gallows humorist Joseph Heller did for Army bombardiers 34 years ago in 'Catch-22,' Bronson does for high finance in the '90s." Wynn also opined: "Po Bronson . . . has written a hilarious, distinctly terrifying first novel that might make you consider switching your cash into a nice, boring money market account. Or a mattress." *Hungry Mind Review* contributor Dwight Garner also recognized similarities between *Bombardiers* and *Catch-22.* "[T]he books do indeed share a similarly piquant sense of the absurd. The traders soon learn that, in order to be rewarded, it is 'better to talk in circles than to talk straight, just as it was better to sound sensible than to be sensible.'" Garner, however, found far more for which to praise Bronson than just his Helleresque writing style. "Bronson's an accomplished stylist who bowls you over with the sheer, onrushing audacity of his prose," Garner proclaimed, adding: "Bronson has written a subversive business novel that teems with manic energy and sour wit. He's a cultural bombardier, and happily, his aim feels unerringly true."

Other critics, although delighted with Bronson's novel, expressed concern that the corrupt world depicted in the story is not far from the truth. Reviewer John Rebschook, for example, wrote in *Bloomsbury Review:* "*Bombardiers* . . . is a wonderful romp through the world of money. . . . The book rings so true that you might be tempted to unload any bond funds you own. On the other hand, I have a feeling if Bronson ever decides to take aim at the world of equities, you probably won't feel any better about investing in stocks." *Los Angeles Times Book Review* contributor David Ignatius further explained the success of Bronson's novel: "What drives this book . . . is Bronson's vision of the modern U.S. economy as an absurd scam. He explains in one of the Swiftian rants that begin each chapter: 'They disguised it all with numbers. They bought and sold money, and every year the Fed pumped more money into the money they had sold. . . . The money was in sales, and the real money was in selling money.' A powerful insight in a book full of promise."

Bronson spent seven years working on his M.F.A. in creative writing at San Francisco State University. According to *Business Week*'s Jeffrey M. Laderman, Bronson's work has paid off. *Bombardiers,* Laderman wrote, "starts out fast and never lets up. Bronson's book [is] perhaps the most entertaining depiction of greed and dishonesty on Wall Street ever to see print. . . . Bronson is a major talent, able to craft the kind of passages you reread just to revel in prose with a compelling cadence all its own."

BIOGRAPHICAL/CRITICAL SOURCES:

BOOKS

Bronson, Po, *Bombardiers,* Random House (New York), 1995.

PERIODICALS

Bloomsbury Review, November/December, 1995, pp. 24, 26.
Business Week, February 27, 1995, pp. 21, 25.
Chicago Tribune, March 28, 1995, Tempo section, p. 3.
Hungry Mind Review, spring, 1995, pp. 43, 47.
Kirkus Reviews, October 15, 1994, p. 1363.
Los Angeles Times Book Review, March 12, 1995, pp. 1, 8.
New Statesman, March 17, 1995, p. 39.
New York Times Book Review, August 13, 1995, pp. 3, 24.
Observer Review, April 16, 1995, p. 18.
San Francisco Review of Books, March/April, 1995, pp. 12-13.
Time, April 3, 1995, p. 78.
Times Literary Supplement, April 7, 1995, p. 25.
Washington Post, February 12, 1995.

* * *

BROOKS, Richard A. 1931-

PERSONAL: Born August 5, 1931, in Brooklyn, NY. *Education:* Columbia College, A.B., 1953; Harvard University, A.M., 1954; Columbia University, Ph.D., 1959.

ADDRESSES: Office—Department of English, Speech and World Literature, College of Staten Island, City University of New York, Staten Island, NY 10301.

CAREER: New York University, began as assistant professor, became associate professor, 1964-67, director of Maison Francaise, 1964-67; Richmond College and Graduate Center, began as associate professor, became professor of humanities, 1967-77, chairman of department, 1967-77; College of Staten Is-

land, City University of New York, Staten Island, NY, professor of humanities, 1977—.

MEMBER: Modern Language Association, American Society of Eighteenth Century Studies, American Comparative Literature Association.

AWARDS, HONORS: New York University Arts and Sciences Research Fund grant, 1966-67; City University of New York travel grant, 1967; City University of New York Research Foundation research grants, 1971-77; National Endowment for the Humanities grant, 1972.

WRITINGS:

Voltaire and Leibniz, Librarie Droz (Geneva), 1964.
(Editor) *A Critical Bibliography of French Literature: The Eighteenth Century,* Syracuse University Press, 1968.
(Editor) *The Selected Letters of Voltaire,* New York University Press, 1973.
(Editor with Douglas W. Alden) *A Critical Bibliography of French Literature: The Twentieth Century,* Syracuse University Press, 1979.
(Editor with H. Gaston Hall) *A Critical Bibliography of French Literature: The Seventeenth Century,* Syracuse University Press, 1983.
(Editor with Raymond C. LaCharite) *A Critical Bibliography of French Literature: The Sixteenth Century,* Volume 2, revised edition, Syracuse University Press, 1985.*

* * *

BROWN, Tony
 See BROWN, William Anthony

* * *

BROWN, William Anthony 1933-
 (Tony Brown)

PERSONAL: Born April 11, 1933, in Charleston, WV; son of Royal and Catherine (Davis) Brown; married (divorced); children: Byron Anthony. *Education:* Wayne State University, B.A., 1959, M.S.W., 1961. *Politics:* Republican.

ADDRESSES: Office—Tony Brown Productions, 1501 Broadway, Suite 412, New York, NY 10036.

CAREER: Television journalist and writer. Worked briefly as a social worker, c. 1961; *Detroit Courier,* Detroit, MI, began as drama critic, became city editor; WTVS-TV, Detroit, writer, producer, and/or host of various programs, including *C.P.T. (Colored People's Time)* and *Free Play;* host of *Black Journal,* WNET-TV, 1970-77, *Tony Brown's Journal,* 1977 to c. 1980, 1982—, and *Tony Brown at Daybreak,* c. 1980-82. Founding dean of Howard University's School of Communications, 1971-74. Commentator for *All Things Considered,* National Public Radio. President of Tony Brown Productions, 1977—. *Military service:* U.S. Army, 1953-55.

MEMBER: National Association of Black Media Producers, National Association of Black Television and Film Producers, National Communications Council, Council for the Economic Development of Black Americans (founding member).

AWARDS, HONORS: Communicator for Freedom Award from Operation Push, 1973; Frederick Douglass Liberation Award, 1974; Public Service Award from National Urban League, 1977; Solomon Fuller Award from American Psychiatric Association, 1989; Image Award from National Association for the Advancement of Colored People, 1991; Emmy Award nomination from the Academy of Television Arts and Sciences, Peabody Award, and Russwurm Award, all for *Black Journal;* Black Emmy Award; Economic Empowerment Award from Southern Christian Leadership Conference.

WRITINGS:

(As Tony Brown) *Black Lies, White Lies: The Truth According to Tony Brown* (nonfiction), Morrow, 1995.

As Tony Brown, screenwriter, producer, and director of film *The White Girl,* 1988.

SIDELIGHTS: Tony Brown is a prominent, and controversial, television journalist and writer. He was born in 1933 in an impoverished area of Charleston, West Virginia. Raised by friends, Brown distinguished himself during his days as a high school student and, after serving in the army, he proved similarly successful with his collegiate studies. In the early 1960s, after earning a master's degree from Wayne State University, Brown began a career in

social work. But he soon left that career for work as a drama critic at the *Detroit Courier,* and eventually became city editor of that newspaper. It was during his time on staff at the *Courier* that Brown became increasingly active in local civil rights issues. Brown eventually left the *Courier* to serve as producer of *C.P.T.* (Colored People's Time), a program dedicated to African American topics and interests and broadcast by WTVS-TV, Detroit's public television station. After leaving *C.P.T.,* Brown continued to work in television as a producer of *Free Play.*

In 1970 Brown left Detroit for New York City to host *Black Journal,* another black-oriented show broadcast monthly on public television. This wide-ranging show incorporated editorials, interviews, and discussions treating various aspects and issues of the black community. With Brown as its host, *Black Journal* gained popularity and was eventually broadcast weekly, rather than monthly. On *Black Journal,* Brown established himself as a forthright personality unafraid of confrontation. He clashed with black leaders when he took a position in apparent support of Ethiopia's repressive government, and he clashed with other figures in broadcasting when he exposed what he considered to be racist aspects of the television industry.

In the mid-1970s Brown's candor ran him afoul of corporate sponsors who were, apparently, displeased with his controversial nature. Despite its popular success, *Black Journal* was faced with cancellation when the Corporation for Public Broadcasting revealed that it would withdraw sponsorship of Brown's program. Various black organizations pressured the corporation to renew sponsorship of Brown's program, and the corporation eventually yielded. *Black Journal* was then broadcast until 1977, when Brown grew dissatisfied with the restraints imposed on the show by various special interest groups, and left *Black Journal* for commercial syndication.

Brown's new show, *Tony Brown's Journal,* proved as successful as *Black Journal,* and by the early 1980s it was being broadcast in more than eighty American cities. Another show, *Tony Brown at Daybreak,* was also well received. Brown, however, felt that his show could be broadcast on even more stations and at more convenient hours for viewers. Consequently, he returned to public television in 1982. *Tony Brown's Journal* has been shown on PBS-TV affiliates since that time.

Throughout his career, Brown has regularly courted controversy. In addition to his public observations on racism within the broadcasting industry, he has continuously aligned himself with potentially unpopular and inflammatory issues and individuals, such as African-American Supreme Court nominee Clarence Thomas. During hearings ostensibly designed to evaluate his capacity to serve as a U.S. Supreme Court justice, then-judge Thomas was questioned by a Senate panel on a variety of issues, most notably on allegations of sexual harassment made by law professor Anita Hill, with whom Thomas had once worked. Brown has also denounced liberal African Americans for championing federal assistance as a corrective to racial inequality in the United States, declaring himself a member of the Republican Party, and contending that the Republican emphasis on capitalism itself is the means by which problems are most effectively resolved in free-market America.

Brown's iconoclasm is reflected in his 1995 volume *Black Lies, White Lies: The Truth According to Tony Brown.* In this tome Brown argues against integration as an effective means of resolving racial differences and calls instead for measures of separatism. In addition, he claims that medical factions have conspired against effective AIDS research and that, furthermore, racial genocide is a tangible threat to black Americans.

Critical reaction to *Black Lies, White Lies* was mixed. A *Publishers Weekly* contributor, while characterizing "Brown's basic theme on race relations"—that black Americans should not rely on government or white society to promote their best interests, and that white Americans should realize that all Americans are affected by societal influences—as "sound," concluded that the author "undermines" his argument by overgeneralizing about the leaders and members of the American black community. In his *Washington Post Book World* assessment, Richard D. Kahlenberg summarized Brown's various arguments and theories in *Black Lies, White Lies,* including his support of black separatism and his contention that the medical establishment is willfully sabotaging AIDS research and treatment in an attempt to wipe out the black population. Kahlenberg asserted: "From this murky brew of black separatism and conspiracy theory, flashes of insight manage to shine through. Brown launches a devastating critique of affirmative action policies." Nevertheless, Kahlenberg faulted Brown's prose style, arguing that "even his legitimate criticisms are often undercut by a sensationalist style that works better on television than in print." *Booklist*'s Ray Olson offered a highly favorable review of *Black Lies, White Lies,* calling Brown's explanations of his

belief in various conspiracy theories "very enlightening," and concluding that "Maybe [Brown] *should* be president."

In addition to writing *Black Lies, White Lies* and his various broadcasting endeavors, Brown has expressed himself in the film medium. In 1988 he wrote, directed, and produced *The White Girl,* a drama about a black college student who becomes a drug addict.

BIOGRAPHICAL/CRITICAL SOURCES:

BOOKS

Contemporary Black Biography, Volume 3, Gale (Detroit), 1993.

PERIODICALS

Booklist, October 15, 1995, p. 369.
Christian Science Monitor, August 23, 1988, pp. 1, 6.
Detroit Free Press, September 24, 1971.
Essence, October, 1980.
Jet, August 12, 1991.
Los Angeles Times, February 18, 1996.
New York Times, February 11, 1990.
Publishers Weekly, September 11, 1995, p. 70.
Wall Street Journal, August 5, 1991.
Washington Post, February 10, 1990.
Washington Post Book World, February 4, 1996.*

* * *

BROX, Jane (Martha) 1956-

PERSONAL: Born September 4, 1956, in Dracut, MA; daughter of John (a farmer) and Antoinette (a homemaker; maiden name, Rossi) Brox. *Ethnicity:* "Italian/Lebanese." *Education:* Colby College, B.A. (magna cum laude), 1978; special student, Harvard University, 1984; Warren Wilson College, M.F.A., 1988.

ADDRESSES: Home—1334 Broadway, Dracut, MA 01826.

CAREER: Has worked as a baker, a cook, and a bookstore clerk; has worked on her family farm; Harvard Extension School, Cambridge, MA, instructor and tutor in writing, workshop leader, 1994—;

freelance writer and poet, 1985—. Has also taught writing classes and workshops for the Brockport Writers' Forum and Harvard Summer School. Nonfiction writer-in-residence at the Loft, Minneapolis, MN, May, 1996. Has written commentary for National Public Radio's *Living on Earth* program.

MEMBER: PEN New England; Massachusetts Audubon Society; Trustees of the Reservations.

AWARDS, HONORS: Grants and fellowships from Yaddo, 1989 and 1992; the MacDowell Colony, 1989, 1991, 1993, 1994, 1995, 1996; the Virginia Center for the Arts and the Millay Colony, 1990; Ucross Foundation, 1991; Banff Centre, 1993; Massachusetts Cultural Council, 1994; National Endowment for the Arts, 1994; William Sloane Fellow award from the Breadloaf Writers' Conference, 1995; L. L. Winship/PEN New England Award for *Here and Nowhere Else,* 1996.

WRITINGS:

(Editor with Kathleen Aponick and Paul Marion, and contributor) *Merrimack: A Poetry Anthology,* Loom Press (Lowell, MA), 1992.
Here and Nowhere Else: Late Seasons of a Farm and Its Family (nonfiction), Beacon Press (Boston, MA), 1995.

Contributor to books, including *The Ucross Foundation Poetry Anthology,* Ucross Poetry Foundation, 1992; *The Great Blue Heron and Other Poems,* Adrienne Lee, 1996; *The Party Train: An Anthology of North American Prose Poetry,* New Rivers Press (Minneapolis, MN), 1996; *In Short* (essays), W. W. Norton (New York, NY), 1996; *Best American Essays, 1996,* Houghton Mifflin (Boston, MA), 1996. Also contributor of poetry, reviews, prose and essays to periodicals, including *Orion, A View from the Loft, Georgia Review, Gettysburg Review, Ohio Review, Boston Literary Review (BLR), Salamander, New England Review, Taos Review, Zone 3, Fiction, Virginia Quarterly Review, Hudson Review,* and the *Cumberland Poetry Review.*

WORK IN PROGRESS: Another book about the history of Massachusetts farms, focusing on the early twentieth century, when many original owners sold their farms to recent immigrants.

SIDELIGHTS: Poet and essayist Jane Brox began her life on a farm in Dracut, Massachusetts, in 1956. Her

father had inherited the farm from her grandfather, an immigrant who arrived from Lebanon in the late 19th century, and purchased the farm in 1901. Brox worked on the farm during her childhood, but left to study literature and pursue a writing career. Later, she returned to the family farm to help her aging father, and it was from this experience that she drew inspiration for *Here and Nowhere Else: Late Seasons of a Farm and Its Family,* an account of the joys found and dilemmas faced on the Broxes' longtime homestead.

Patti Doten, reviewing *Here and Nowhere Else* in the *Boston Globe,* hailed Brox's "keen and sensuous observations of the land she grew up on," but also noted that "throughout seeps an eerie, David Lynchian undercurrent that slashes through the bucolic to the pain and anguish beneath." Doten is referring to the fact that Brox's father, who has run the farm all his life, is in his eighties, and the only son who remains and who might conceivably carry on the Brox farming tradition struggles with drug abuse. Brox lets her readers know that there is a good chance the farm may die with her father.

The life and community centrality of the Brox family's farm is another major theme of *Here and Nowhere Else.* As Michael Kenney of the *Boston Globe* reported, "particularly on weekends there is a lively patronage from Lawrence's newer immigrants, Cambodians and Vietnamese families, many of whom, Brox says, tell her that they come out to enjoy sitting under the trees while their children run in the fields." The farm stand sells corn, tomatoes, beans, squash, blueberries, apples, and other fruits and vegetables during the harvest season.

Critics have responded positively to *Here and Nowhere Else.* Speaking of the problems facing the Brox farm, Maxine Kumin in the *New York Times Book Review* asserted that "Brox describes [them] crisply yet with great feeling," and judged the book to be "a poignant account." *Kirkus Reviews* declared that the volume's "surprising strength accrues line by line in Brox's keen observation and spare, poetic prose." Franklin Burroughs in the *Southern Review* affirmed that "the language of the book is concrete, with a stringency that balances the tendency of the pastoral toward elegy and reverie," and went on to conclude that the author's "most lyrical and affirmative passages are persuasive because they are ballasted by a thorough knowledge of costs and benefits, of the considerations and anxious calculations that are daily realities of farming."

Brox told *CA:* "A sense of place and the natural world have always played an important part in my work. I came to writing relatively late—I started writing poetry in my mid-twenties while I was living on Nantucket Island off the coast of Massachusetts.

"Even as I turned to writing prose, my work was informed by my attention to poetry. I began with prose poems: short meditations on the farm of my childhood, which dwelled on the things that marked the natural life of the place—white pines, peaches, apple trees. Sometimes I think I wrote myself back home. In writing those pieces, my attention turned more and more to the farm even as its place in the world became more tenuous: my father was aging, my brother wasn't capable of carrying on by himself.

"In my early thirties, I returned to Dracut in the Merrimack Valley of Massachusetts to help run my family's farm. I tended the greenhouse, some of the small crops, and ran the farm stand. As I worked and lived there, my wish to capture the spirit of the place and what it meant to my family became stronger. The prose poems I had written at a distance became connected with the narrative of the family. The result was my first book: *Here and Nowhere Else: Late Seasons of a Farm and Its Family.*

"In it I try not only to look at our own farm, but the legacy of the small New England farm in general. My father's story has been a strong influence on my work. His life had spanned much of the century in a place that had changed dramatically. He had remembered when the road was unpaved, when the first airplane had flown overhead, and now the farm is cut through by a busy state road, and small industries and housing tracts have grown up around it. It seemed essential to me to set down the story of the place and the older people of the place before it disappeared entirely.

"I began, also, to read about the history of the area, particularly of farming in New England, and such history began to inform the pieces I wrote. I came to see our farm as one of many similar stories of long association with the land. And the literary figures of this area had their influence on me as well. Henry David Thoreau, and of course, Robert Frost.

"My new work also involves the farm and this region. I am currently researching work for a new book that will chronicle the early years of this century when the farms were being abandoned by their original owners and taken up by immigrants who had

come to work in the textile mills in Lawrence and Lowell. I plan it to be a larger examination of place, a study of the evolution of agriculture in this valley, and a study, too, in the contrasts between urban and rural life. But there'll be some poetry in it too, I hope."

BIOGRAPHICAL/CRITICAL SOURCES:

BOOKS

Brox, Jane, *Here and Nowhere Else: Late Seasons of a Farm and Its Family,* Beacon Press (Boston, MA), 1995.

PERIODICALS

Boston Globe, June 15, 1995, pp. 69-70; September 13, 1995, pp. 61, 64.
Kirkus Reviews, April 1, 1995.
New York Times Book Review, August 6, 1995, p. 13.
Southern Review, fall, 1995, pp. 948-50.

* * *

BRUCE, Evangeline

PERSONAL: Daughter of Edward Bell (an American diplomat); married David Bruce (an ambassador), 1946; children: Alexandra (deceased), David, Nicholas. *Education:* Radcliffe College.

ADDRESSES: Office-c/o Sasha Bruce Youthwork Inc., 741 Eighth St. SE, Washington, DC 20003-2802.

AWARDS, HONORS: Legion d'Honneur, from the French government; the "Evangeline Bruce" rose was named in her honor and displayed in England at the Chelsea Flower Show, 1971.

WRITINGS:

Napoleon and Josephine: The Improbable Marriage, Scribner (New York), 1995.

SIDELIGHTS: As the daughter of an American diplomat to China and Japan, stepdaughter of a British diplomat, and widow of David Bruce, the distinguished American ambassador, Evangeline Bruce has lived in virtually every corner of the world, but was formally educated in France. Fascinated by French history, Bruce began writing a book some twenty years ago that was set in 1795, during the French Revolution. That material, coupled with the author's study of the relationship of Napoleon Bonaparte and Marie Josephine Rose Tascher de La Pagerie, is presented in Bruce's 1995 book, *Napoleon and Josephine: The Improbable Marriage.* Detailing the couple's passionate courtship, childless marriage, and subsequent divorce, *Napoleon and Josephine* puts particular emphasis on Napoleon's military leadership and Josephine's use of sex to advance her societal status.

Reviewer William Doyle, in his *New York Times Book Review* critique of Bruce's book, expressed appreciation for the author's firsthand knowledge of Paris, and remarked that Bruce writes of her subjects "with style and sympathy." While noting that "the story is a familiar one and, retold, adds little to the sum of our knowledge of two characters intensively written about almost from the moment they met," Doyle nevertheless deemed *Napoleon and Josephine* "an extremely readable account of their lives together, and an easy and attractive introduction to Napoleon and his private life."

Bruce's own life has all the makings of a best-seller. The daughter of an ambassador, she lived in China and Japan as a young child. When her father died, her mother married a British ambassador, and the family lived in various countries, including Italy, Sweden, France, Holland, Great Britain, and Switzerland. In the 1940s she took a job in the Office of Strategic Services, located in London, where she married her boss, David Bruce, who would later serve as ambassador to France during the Truman administration, ambassador to Germany under President Eisenhower, and ambassador to England during the Kennedy years. During their eight years in London, Evangeline and David Bruce were known for their hospitality and warmth as they entertained a vast array of people, from politicians and world leaders to artists and writers. David Bruce died in 1977, but Evangeline Bruce continues to spend some of each year at their home in London. Her primary residence, however, is Washington, DC, where she still plays the quintessential hostess and is famous for her gatherings of influential people of all walks of life. "If Washington were the Sistine Chapel," writer Sally Quinn told *Vanity Fair,* "Evangeline would be *up* there on the ceiling."

Evangeline Bruce's life has not been without its trials, and one of the most challenging she faced was the 1975 death of her daughter Alexandra, nicknamed Sasha by her family. Sasha, married to Greek national Marios Michaelides, was found at the family estate with a gunshot wound to her head. Initially her death was ruled a suicide, but her mentally and physically abusive husband was charged with her murder after an investigation three years later. However, Michaelides is protected by a treaty between the United States and his homeland and will not be extradited for trial. To honor her daughter, Bruce has founded the Sasha Bruce House, a shelter for runaway and homeless teenagers in Washington, DC, and Sasha Bruce Youthwork, a program employing dozens of social workers to counsel troubled teens.

BIOGRAPHICAL/CRITICAL SOURCES:

PERIODICALS

Architectural Digest, March, 1991, pp. 164-69, 202.
Vanity Fair, February, 1995, pp. 102-108, 141-142.*

* * *

BUCKNER, Rheuben
 See McCOY, Max

* * *

BULGER, William M. 1934-

PERSONAL: Born February 2, 1934, in Boston, MA; son of James and Jean (McCarthy) Bulger; married Mary Foley, July 2, 1960; children: William, James, Sarah, Patrick, Mary Bulger Hurley, Daniel, Kathleen Bulger Webb, Christopher, Brendan. *Ethnicity:* "Irish-American." *Education:* Attended Boston College. *Religion:* Roman Catholic.

ADDRESSES: Office—18 Tremont St., Boston, MA.

CAREER: Massachusetts House of Representatives, representative, 1961-70; Massachusetts Senate, member, 1971-96, president, 1978-96; University of Massachusetts at Amherst, president, 1996—. Boston Public Library, member of board of trustees. *Military service:* U.S. Army, 1953-55.

WRITINGS:

While the Music Lasts: My Life in Politics, Houghton (Boston, MA), 1996.

SIDELIGHTS: William M. Bulger told *CA:* "I believed that my memoir might serve to set the record straight and convey the truth. Others seemed determined to write my biography. I was sure that I could do better."

* * *

BUMILLER, Elisabeth 1956-

PERSONAL: Born May 15, 1956, in Aalborg, Denmark; daughter of Theodore R. (a travel and film lecturer) and Gunhild Eiken Moeller Rose Bumiller; married Steven R. Weisman (a newspaper editorial writer), October 23, 1983; children: Madeleine Elisabeth, Theodore Joseph. *Education:* Northwestern University, B.S.J., 1977; Columbia University, M.S.J., 1979. *Religion:* Episcopalian. *Avocational interests:* Gardening, cooking, running, reading.

ADDRESSES: Office—New York Times, 229 West 43rd St., New York, NY 10036. *E-mail*—bumiller@nytimes.com. *Agent*—Amanda Urban, International Creative Management, 40 West 57th St., New York, NY 10019.

CAREER: Washington Post, Washington, DC, reporter for "Style" section, 1979-87, reporter from Washington, New Delhi, Tokyo, and New York City, 1990-91, 1995; *New York Times,* New York City, reporter on metropolitan staff, 1995—.

WRITINGS:

May You Be the Mother of a Hundred Sons: A Journey among the Women of India, Random House (New York), 1990.
The Secrets of Mariko: A Year in the Life of a Japanese Woman and Her Family, Times Books (New York), 1995.

* * *

BURCHELL, Mary
 See COOK, Ida

BURNSIDE, John 1955-

PERSONAL: Born March 19, 1955, in Dunfermline, Fife, Scotland.

ADDRESSES: Agent—c/o Jonathan Cape, Random House, 20 Vauxhall Bridge Rd., London SW1V 2SA, England.

CAREER: Enterprise Systems, Thames Ditton, software engineer, 1988-90; Syntelligence, Redhill, Surrey, knowledge engineer, 1990-94. Self-employed, 1994—.

AWARDS, HONORS: Scottish Arts Council Book awards, 1988, 1991; Geoffrey Faber Memorial prize, 1994, for *Feast Days,*

WRITINGS:

POETRY

The Hoop, Carcanet (Manchester), 1988.
Common Knowledge, Secker and Warburg (London), 1991.
Feast Days, Secker and Warburg, 1992.
The Myth of the Twin, Jonathan Cape (London), 1994.
Swimming in the Flood, Jonathan Cape, 1995.

* * *

BUSCH, Hans (Peter) 1914-1996

OBITUARY NOTICE—See index for *CA* sketch: Born April 4, 1914, in Aachen, Germany; died September 17, 1996, in Bloomington, IN. Stage director, musician and author. The son of a conductor, Busch studied music his entire life and became a noted stage director of operas. Busch studied music in Geneva and Vienna and came to the United States in 1942. After serving in the U.S. Army during World War II, he was one of the first directors of National Broadcasting Corp. (NBC)'s television opera theater. He then joined the faculty of Indiana University and directed operas that earned national attention. He also wrote considerably about the composer Verdi's letters, most notably the book *Verdi's "Aida": The History of an Opera in Letters and Documents,* published in 1978. Busch also penned a book in his native tongue, *Giuseppe Verdi Briefe,* in 1979. During the 1970s, Busch stage directed operas for national com-

panies, including New York's Metropolitan Opera. Busch retired from the University of Indiana in 1980.

OBITUARIES AND OTHER SOURCES:

BOOKS

International Who's Who in Music and Musicians' Directory, Melrose, 1984.

PERIODICALS

New York Times, September 29, 1996, sec. 1, p. 45.

* * *

BUSH, Duncan 1946-

PERSONAL: Born April 6, 1946, in Cardiff, Wales; married Annette Jane Weaver, 1981; children: two sons. *Education:* University of Warwick, (first class honors in English and European literature), 1978; attended Wadham College, Oxford, 1978-81.

ADDRESSES: Home and office—Godre Waun Oleu, Brecon Rd., Ynyswen, Penycae, Powys SA9 1YY, Wales.

CAREER: Writer. Gwent College, Wales, director of writing program, 1984—.

MEMBER: Welsh Academy, 1982.

AWARDS, HONORS: Arts Council of Wales Poetry prize, 1984, for *Aquarium,* and 1986 for *Salt;* Arts Council of Wales Book of the Year award, 1995, for *Masks.*

WRITINGS:

POETRY

Aquarium, Poetry Wales Press (Bridgend), 1983.
Salt, Poetry Wales Press, 1985.
Black Faces, Red Mouths, Bedrock Press (Ynyswen), 1986.
Masks, Seren (Bridgend), 1994.

PLAYS

Cocktails for Three, produced in Oxford, 1979.
Ends, produced in Cardiff, 1980.
Sailing to America, produced in Cardiff, 1982.

Author of radio plays, including *In the Pine Forest* (adapted from *The Genre of Silence*), 1991; and *Are There Still Wolves in Pennsylvania?* (adapted from *Masks*), 1991. Also author of the television play *Sailing to America*, 1992.

NOVELS

The Genre of Silence, Seren, 1988.
Glass Shot, Secker and Warburg (London), 1991.

* * *

BUTLER, (Frederick) Guy 1918-

PERSONAL: Born January 21, 1918, in Cradock, Cape Province, South Africa; married Jean Murray Satchwell, 1940; children: three sons, one daughter. *Education:* Rhodes University, M.A., 1939; Brasenose College, Oxford, M.A., 1947.

ADDRESSES: Office—"High Corner," 122 High St., Grahamstown 6140, South Africa.

CAREER: University of the Witwatersrand, Johannesburg, lecturer in English, 1948-50; Rhodes University, Grahamstown, professor of English, 1952-86, honorary research fellow, 1987—. *Standpunte,* English editor, 1952-54; *Contrast,* advisory editor, 1960—; *New Coin,* editor, 1964-74. First president, Shakespeare Society of South Africa, 1985. *Military service:* South African Army in the Middle East, Italy, and the United Kingdom, 1940-45.

AWARDS, HONORS: CNA award, 1976; English Academy of Southern Africa Gold Medal, 1989; Lady Usher prize for literature, 1992. D.Litt.: University of Natal, 1970; University of the Witwatersrand, 1984; University of South Africa, 1989; Rhodes University, 1994. Honorary Life President, English Academy of South Africa, 1983, Shakespeare Society of South Africa, 1991; Honorary Life Vice-Chairman of National Arts Festival Committee, 1993.

WRITINGS:

POETRY

Stranger to Europe: Poems 1939-1949, Balkema (Cape Town), 1952; augmented edition, 1960.

South of the Zambezi: Poems from South Africa, Abelard Schuman (London), 1966.
On First Seeing Florence, New Coin-Rhodes University (Grahamstown, South Africa), 1968.
Selected Poems, Donker (Johannesburg), 1975; revised edition, 1989.
Songs and Ballads, David Philip (Cape Town), 1978.
Pilgrimage to Dias Cross, David Philip, 1987.

PLAYS

The Dam (produced in Cape Town, 1953), Balkema, 1953.
The Dove Returns (produced in Glencoe, Natal, 1955), Balkema, and Fortune Press (London), 1956.
Take root or Die (produced in Grahamstown, 1966), Balkema, 1970.
Cape Charade (produced in Grahamstown, 1967), Balkema, 1968.
Richard Gush of Salem (produced in Grahamstown, 1970), Maskew Miller (Cape Town), 1982.
Demea (produced in Grahamstown, 1990), David Philip, 1990.

OTHER

An Aspect of Tragedy, Rhodes University (Grahamstown), 1953.
The Republic of the Arts, Witwatersrand University Press (Johannesburg), 1964.
Karoo Morning: An Autobiography 1918-35, David Philip, 1977.
Bursting World: an Autobiography 1936-45, David Philip, 1983.
A Rackety Colt, or The Adventures of Thomas Stubbs (novel), Tafelberg (Cape Town), 1989.
Tales of the Old Karoo (short stories), Donker (Johannesburg), 1989.
A Local Habitation: An Autobiography (1945-90), David Philip, 1991.
Guy Butler: Essays and Lectures (1949-1991), David Philip, 1994.
(Editor) *A Book of South African Verse,* Oxford University Press (London), 1959.
(Editor) *When Boys Were Men,* Oxford University Press (Cape Town), 1969.
(Editor with Tim Peacock) *Plays from Near and Far: Twelve One-Act Plays,* Maskew Miller (Cape Town), c. 1973.
(Editor) *The 1820 Settlers: An Illustrated Commentary,* Human and Rousseau (Cape Town), 1974.

(Editor with Christopher Mann) *A New Book of South African Verse in English,* Oxford University Press (Cape Town), 1979; Oxford University Press (Oxford), 1980.

(Editor with N. Visser) *The Re-Interment on Buffelskop: My Diary, 7-15 June 1921 and 8-29 August 1921,* by S.C. Cronwright-Schreiner, Rhodes University (Grahamstown), 1983.

(Editor with David Butler) *Out of the African Ark,* Donker (Johannesburg), 1988.

(Editor with Jeff Opland) *The Magic Tree,* Longman (Cape Town), 1989.

C

CADDY, Caroline 1944-

PERSONAL: Born January 20, 1944, in Caroline Mavis Rumple, Perth, Western Australia; married Daniel C. Caddy, 1965 (died, 1972); children: one son, one daughter. *Education:* Received high school diploma of dental nursing.

ADDRESSES: Office—R.M.B. 9367 Tania Rd., Torbay 6330, Western Australia, Australia.

CAREER: Dental nurse, Perth, 1960-65. Self-employed in farming, teaching writing workshops, and working at clerical jobs, 1965—.

AWARDS, HONORS: Western Australian Literary Week award, 1991, for *Beach Plastic;* National Book Council Banjo Patterson award, and Phillips Fox Turnbull award, 1992, for *Conquistadors.*

WRITINGS:

POETRY

Singing at Night, Fremantle Arts Centre Press, 1981.
Letters from the North, Fremantle Arts Centre Press, 1984.
Beach Plastic, Fremantle Arts Centre Press, 1990.
Conquistadors, Penguin Australia (Perth), 1991.

* * *

CADUTO, Michael J. 1955-

PERSONAL: Born December 20, 1955, in Providence, RI; son of Ralph (a medical research techni-

cian) and Esther (a registered nurse; maiden name, Martone) Caduto; married Marie Levesque, September 15, 1990. *Ethnicity:* "Italian-American." *Education:* University of Rhode Island, B.S. (with highest distinction), 1978; University of Michigan, M.S. (summa cum laude), 1981. *Politics:* Independent. *Avocational interests:* Hiking, writing poetry and songs, reading, photography, human spirituality, guitar playing and singing, contra dancing, bicycling, swimming, travel, puns.

ADDRESSES: Office—Programs for Environmental Awareness and Cultural Exchange, P.O. Box 1052, Norwich, VT 05055.

CAREER: Audubon Society of Rhode Island, land management planner, 1975-78, teacher, 1976-78; W. Alton Jones Environmental Education Center, Greenwich, RI, teacher and naturalist, 1979; Pocono Lake Preserve, curator of exhibits and program director, 1979; VINS, worked in land management, 1982-85, and environmental education, 1982-83; Programs for Environmental Awareness and Cultural Exchange (PEACE), Norwich, VT, founder, 1984, director, 1984—. Vermont Council on the Arts, touring artist; teacher at colleges, including University of New Hampshire, Vermont State College, and Leslie College; presents workshops on ecological education, native cultures, and storytelling. Atlantic Center for the Environment, senior education fellow, also senior instructor at Living Rivers Environmental Education Program, 1980; Vermont Museum and Gallery Alliance, member.

MEMBER: World Wildlife Fund, Amnesty International, North American Association for Environmental Education, Wildlife Society (past president), Na-

tive American Rights Fund, Native American Heritage Association, Tree of Peace Society, Maryknoll Missionary Society, American Friends Service Committee, League for the Advancement of New England Storytelling, Southern Poverty Law Center, Phi Kappa Phi.

AWARDS, HONORS: Keepers of the Animals was chosen by *American Bookseller* as a "Pick of the List," 1991, and awarded the Choice Award, collections category, Association of Children's Booksellers, 1992; New England Regional Environmental Educator Award, 1992; Popular Award from American Society of Composers, Authors, and Publishers, 1995, for *All One Earth;* Art and Literary Award from New York State Outdoor Education Association; scholar of Vermont Council on the Humanities.

WRITINGS:

Ann Arbor Alive: The Ecology of a City, Ecology Center of Ann Arbor (Ann Arbor, MI), 1981.
A Guide on Environmental Values Education (in English and Spanish), UNESCO (Paris, France), 1985.
Pond and Brook: A Guide to Nature in Freshwater Environments, University Press of New England (Hanover, NH), 1990.
(With Joseph Bruchac) *Keepers of the Earth: Native American Stories and Environmental Activities for Children,* with teacher's guide, Fulcrum Publishing (Golden, CO), 1988.
(With Bruchac) *Keepers of the Animals: Native American Stories and Wildlife Activities for Children,* with teacher's guide, Fulcrum Publishing, 1991.
(With Bruchac) *Keepers of the Night: Native American Stories and Nocturnal Activities for Children,* Fulcrum Publishing, 1994.
(With Bruchac) *Keepers of the Life: Discovering Plants through Native American Stories and Earth Activities for Children,* with teacher's guide, Fulcrum Publishing, 1994.
All One Earth: Songs for the Generations, LUNABLU (Norwich, VT), 1994.
(With Bruchac) *Native American Gardening: Stories, Projects, and Recipes for Families,* Fulcrum Publishing, 1996.
Italian Tales of Wisdom, Fulcrum Publishing, in press.

Contributor to books, including *How Nature Works: Regenerating Kinship with Planet Earth,* edited by Michael J. Cohen, Stillpoint Publishing (Walpole, NH), 1988; *The Green Umbrella: Stories, Songs, Poems, and Starting Points for Environmental Assemblies,* edited by Jill Brand and others, A. and C. Black (London, England), 1991; and *Teacher's Read-Aloud Anthology,* edited by Margaret H. Lippert, Macmillan/McGraw (New York City), 1993. Contributor of more than a hundred articles and poems to magazines, including *Organic Gardening, Ranger Rick's NatureScope, Northeast Indian Quarterly, Vermont Life, New Alchemy Quarterly,* and *Journal of Environmental Education.*

WORK IN PROGRESS: A thematic collection of original tellings of world stories for children, for Fulcrum Publishing; continuing research on environmental ethics and spirituality.

SIDELIGHTS: Michael J. Caduto told *CA:* "God's purest creation is found in nature. Each day, as I am writing, I look out over the hills of trees, pastures, and wildflowers. I see the sun arching across the open sky or the clouds swirling overhead, and my creativity draws from the well. As I listen to birds call and watch them flit among the branches, my thoughts take wing. In the city, my vision is occluded by the walls of nearby buildings. In nature, however, my creative spirit begins anew each day as I rise with the sun in the east, grows in strength as the sun climbs to the south, and ebbs as the sun finds rest in the western sky.

"Body, mind, and spirit are one: all must be fed to maintain the strength of each. Twice during each writing day, I break for a vigorous walk. Whether the wildflowers are sprouting or in bloom, whether they are golden with fall color or have hardened into brown stalks protruding above the snowline, I am out among them. During these walks, I renew my connection to creation. At some point during my principal, midday walk, I stop to pray, to give thanks and ask for a true, open heart, through which a voice will flow with words that the creator has given me to speak in this world.

"I work on my own simply because there is no organization, university, or other institution that would pay me to pursue the creative projects and priorities that are most important to me. Each organization is a living organism, and its workers carry out the appointed tasks of the tissues and organs, the sinew and bones. It is a challenge for me to follow my muse while hewing to the strictured regimen required of one serving in a support role for an organization.

Although I earned an advanced degree and taught at colleges and universities, I have also worked as a dishwasher, factory worker, forester, land manager, carpenter, maker of fine furniture, and so on. Any time I find myself confined to doing the same thing repeatedly, especially when my creative self cannot find expression through my work, I become anxious and listless.

"I started out studying agriculture and working on a small farm, with the intention of having my own farm some day. Eventually I hope to cut back somewhat on the extensive traveling I must presently do to teach and perform stories and music. Instead, I will focus more on creative writing and songwriting. I also want to own a small farm where I can establish a large-scale garden and both study and manage the fields and forests. The balancing act and dynamic tension I face as a creative artist, ecologist, and student of the world focuses on how to give wings to my creative self while putting bread on the table, supporting my family, and meeting the mundane obligations that arise from sustaining my corporeal self in the material world."

* * *

CARLUT, Charles E. 1911-

PERSONAL: Born March 8, 1911, in Lyons, France; married in 1953; children: one. *Education:* Ecole de Science et Politique, Paris, diploma, 1932; Faculte Droit, Paris and Lyons, diploma, 1936; Ecole Prep Prof Fr a L'Etranger, Paris, diploma, 1938; Ohio State University, Ph.D., 1948.

ADDRESSES: Office—Department of Romance Languages, Ohio State University, Columbus, OH 43210.

CAREER: Department of Romance Languages, Ohio State University, Columbus, OH, instructor in French, 1938-40, 1946-48, began as assistant professor and became associate professor of French, 1948-65, professor of French, 1965-81.

MEMBER: Modern Language Association, American Association of Teachers of French, Society of French Professors of America.

AWARDS, HONORS: French Order of Merit, 1972; Palmes Academiques (France), 1973 and 1978.

WRITINGS:

(Editor with Germaine Bree) *France de Nos Jours,* Macmillan, 1957, 4th edition, 1975.
(Editor with Elaine Marks) *Recits de Nos Jours,* Macmillan, 1964.
(Author of introduction and notes) *Nineteenth Century French Short Stories,* Dell, 1966.
(With Walter Meiden) *French for Oral and Written Review,* Holt, Rinehart & Winston, 1968, 5th edition, 1993.
La Correspondence de Flaubert: Etude et Repertoire Critique, Ohio State University Press, 1969.
(With Alain Dubuisson) *Initiation au deriveur,* Editions Amphora (Paris), 1973.
(With Pierre H. Dube and J. Raymond Dugan) *A Concordance to Flaubert's L'education Sentimentale,* two volumes, Garland Publishing, 1978.
(With Pierre H. Dube and J. Raymond Dugan) *A Concordance to Flaubert's Madame Bovary,* two volumes, Garland, 1978.
(Editor) *Essais sur Flaubert en l'honneur du professeur Don Louis Demorest,* Nizet (Paris), 1979.
(With Pierre H. Dube and J. Raymond Dugan) *A Concordance to Flaubert's Salammbo,* two volumes, Garland Publishing, 1979.
(With Pierre H. Dube and J. Raymond Dugan) *A Concordance to Flaubert's La Tentation de Saint Antoine,* Garland Publishing, 1979.
(With Pierre H. Dube and J. Raymond Dugan) *A Concordance to Flaubert's Trois Contes,* Garland Publishing, 1979.
(With Pierre H. Dube and J. Raymond Dugan) *A Concordance to Flaubert's Bouvard et Pecuchet,* Garland, 1980.

Member of editorial staff of *French Review.*

BIOGRAPHICAL/CRITICAL SOURCES:

PERIODICALS

Modern Language Journal, March, 1965, p. 188; December, 1970, p. 616; autumn, 1984, p. 286; winter, 1988, p. 473; autumn, 1993, p. 382.*

* * *

CARSON, Ciaran 1948-

PERSONAL: Born October 9, 1948, in Belfast, Ireland; married Deirdre Shannon, 1982; children: two

sons, one daughter. *Education:* Queens University, Belfast, B.A.

*ADDRESSES: Office—*Arts Council of Northern Ireland, 181 A Stranmills Rd., Belfast BT9 5DU, Northern Ireland.

CAREER: Writer. Traditional arts officer, Arts Council of Northern Ireland, 1975—.

AWARDS, HONORS: Eric Gregory award; Alice Hunt Bartlett award; *Irish Time/*Aer Lingus award.

WRITINGS:

POETRY

The New Estate, Wake Forest University Press (Winston-Salem, NC), 1976.
The Irish for No, Gallery Press (Dublin), 1987.
The New Estate, and Other Poems, Gallery Press (Oldcastle, Meath), 1988.
Belfast Confetti, Silver Buckle Press (Madison, WI), 1993.
First Language: Poems, Wake Forest University Press, 1994.
Letters from the Alphabet, Gallery Press (Oldcastle, Meath), 1995.

OTHER

Irish Traditional Music, Appletree Press (Belfast), 1986.

* * *

CASART, Jonathan
 See ST. MARTIN, Hardie

* * *

CASART, Julian
 See ST. MARTIN, Hardie

* * *

CASSIDY, David (Bruce) 1950-

PERSONAL: Born April 12, 1950, in New Jersey; son of Jack Cassidy (an actor) and Evelyn Ward (an

actor and singer); stepson of Shirley Jones (an actor and singer); half brother of Shaun, Patrick, and Ryan; married Kay Lenz (an actor), April 3, 1977 (divorced); married Meryl Tanz (a horsebreeder), 1984 (divorced); married Sue Shifrin (a model, singer, and songwriter); children: (third marriage) Beau. *Education:* Studied psychology at Los Angeles City College; trained for the stage with David Craig· and Milton Katselas.

*ADDRESSES: Agent—*Melanie Greene Management, 152 South Roxbury Dr., Suite 5, Beverly Hills, CA 90212.

CAREER: Actor, singer, songwriter, and author. Before beginning his career in entertainment, worked in the mailroom of a textile company. Has also performed in regional theater. Tours and performs concerts featuring music of the Partridge Family and his own. Breeds and races thoroughbred horses.

Appeared in stage productions, including *The Fig Leaves Are Falling,* 1969; *Little Johnny Jones,* 1981; *Parade of Stars Playing the Palace,* 1983; *Joseph and the Amazing Technicolor Dreamcoat,* 1983; *And So to Bed; Time; Tribute;* and *Blood Brothers,* 1993. Appeared in films including *Instant Karma,* 1990, and *The Spirit of '76,* 1991. Television series appearances include *The Partridge Family,* 1970-74; and *David Cassidy—Man Undercover,* 1978-79; as well as episodes of *The Survivors, Adam-12, Bonanza, Police Story, Mod Squad, Ironside, Marcus Welby, M.D., The F.B.I.,* and *Alfred Hitchcock Presents.* Also appeared in the television movie *The Night the City Screamed,* and on specials, including *The Bob Hope Show, Thanksgiving Reunion with the Partridge Family, My Three Sons, Celebrity Challenge of the Sexes,* and *Parade of Stars.* Albums include *David Cassidy,* 1990, and *Nomads, Indians, Saints,* 1991.

MEMBER: Screen Actors Guild, American Federation of Television and Radio Artists, Actors' Equity Association, American Society of Composers, Authors and Publishers.

AWARDS, HONORS: Golden Apple Award (Discovery of the Year) from the Hollywood Women's Press Club, 1971; Emmy Award nomination, Best Actor in a Dramatic Role, 1978, for *Police Story;* received eighteen Gold Record Awards from the Recording Industry Association of America; two Grammy Award nominations.

WRITINGS:

(With Chip Deffaa) *C'mon Get Happy . . . Fear and Loathing on the Partridge Family Bus,* Warner Books, 1994.

SIDELIGHTS: David Cassidy's autobiography, *C'mon Get Happy . . . Fear and Loathing on the Partridge Family Bus,* written with Chip Deffaa, is a recollection of Cassidy's rise to stardom as a member of the hit 1970s television show *The Partridge Family;* it also discusses Cassidy's life after leaving the role of Keith Partridge. Named after the Partridge family's theme song *C'mon Get Happy,* the book describes the series that chronicled the lives of a middle-class widow and her five children, who supplement the family income by touring as a group of musicians and singers known as The Partridge Family. The clan tour in a painted, psychedelic, multicolored bus, driven by the kids' mother, portrayed by Cassidy's real-life stepmother Shirley Jones, renowned star of musicals such as *Oklahoma* and *Carousel.*

The Partridge Family gave Cassidy the opportunity to sing and perform to audiences worldwide, a factor which contributed to the sale of fifteen million copies of the single "I Think I Love You." Cassidy's popularity grew throughout the mid-1970s, resulting in guest appearances on popular television shows and interviews in trendy teen magazines. His image also appeared on lunchboxes and posters across America. Other Partridge Family hits include "Point Me in the Direction of Albuquerque" and "Doesn't Somebody Want to Be Wanted."

In *C'mon Get Happy,* Cassidy discusses his experiences as a 'teen idol' and remarks on his subsequent withdrawal from the limelight. He reports that his frustrations with his teen idol image stem from his role as the fun-loving, carefree Keith Partridge, someone who was never taken seriously by his audiences. According to Cassidy in *Interview,* Keith was "a cheerful dimwit, a shallow airhead [who was] supposed to be funny. . . . I didn't ever think that people would assume I was that guy but they did." Many of Keith's comedic moments involved his brother Danny, played by Danny Bonaduce, who later gained popularity as a radio disc jockey.

In Cassidy's opinion, Keith was a sharp contrast to the real David Cassidy. One thing Cassidy is serious about is his talent for music. The song "I Think I Love You" was a number one single in 1970 but Cassidy and his band members outside *The Partridge Family* held the song in contempt. As reported in the book, one band member's laughter had to be edited out of the final version. In 1975 Cassidy went into seclusion. He told *Interview* contributor Dimitri Ehrlich: "I went back to acting class. I got rid of my agent and started at the bottom again. In the early '80s I started working in regional theater, trying almost to demystify myself."

In his book, Cassidy describes his often turbulent relationship with his father, character actor Jack Cassidy; the inability of Hollywood to look beyond his Keith Partridge persona; several references to his romanic relations with women; and how two failed marriages led the ex-Partridge to seek therapy in 1987. According to *Entertainment Weekly* contributor Tim Appelo, Cassidy discusses his relationships with Meredith Baxter (star of *Family Ties*) and Susan Dey (who starred in *The Partridge Family* as Keith's sister Laurie, and later appeared in television shows such as *LA Law* and *Love and War*).

In addition to writing *C'mon Get Happy,* Cassidy performed the lead roles in productions of *Joseph and the Amazing Technicolor Dreamcoat* and *Blood Brothers.* He appeared in the latter work with his half brother Shaun Cassidy, who became a teen idol himself with a role on television's *The Hardy Boys Mysteries* and a singing career of his own (he scored a hit with a remake of the Ronnette's "Da Doo Ron Ron"). David Cassidy's work as Keith Partridge received renewed interest in the early 1990s when reruns of the show began airing on the Nickelodeon cable network. He also scored another hit record in 1990 with "Lying to Myself."

BIOGRAPHICAL/CRITICAL SOURCES:

PERIODICALS

Entertainment Weekly, July 9, 1994, p. 52.
Interview, May 1991, p. 106.
People, November 1, 1993, p.66-70.*

* * *

CESSAC, Catherine 1952-

PERSONAL: Born August 19, 1952, in Bordeaux, France; daughter of Rene and Raymonde (Deltour) Cessac. *Ethnicity:* "European." *Education:* Attended University of Bordeaux; University of Paris, Ph.D., 1994.

ADDRESSES: Home—115 ave. de la division Leclerc, F-92290 Chatenay, Malabry, France; fax 33-14-350-7149.

CAREER: Musicologist. Researcher, Centre de Musique Baroque, Versailles, France, 1993—.

AWARDS, HONORS: Bronze Medal from CNRS, 1995.

WRITINGS:

Marc-Antoine Charpentier, Fayard (Paris), 1988, Amadeus Press (Portland, OR), 1995.
Elisabeth Jacquet de la Guerre: Une femme compositeur sous le regne de Louis XIV, Actes Sud (Arles, France), 1995.

WORK IN PROGRESS: Nicolas Clerambault, for Fayard.

* * *

CHANG, Chen-Chi 1920-
(Ch'eng-chi Chang, Garma C. C. Chang)

PERSONAL: Born August 28 (one source says September 28), 1920, in Canton, China; married Yu Nien-Tze; children: one son, one daughter. *Education:* Educated at Kong Ka Monastery, Kan-Po, Tibet, 1944.

CAREER: Lecturer in Buddhism at University of Nanking, 1945-46; instructor in Chinese, Army Language School, 1952-53; New School of Social Research, New York City, lecturer in Buddhism, 1954-55; research fellow in Buddhism at Bollingen Foundation, 1954-62; College of Chinese Culture, Taipei, China, professor of Buddhism, 1964-65; assistant professor of oriental philosophy at University of Nebraska, 1965-66; Pennsylvania State University, University Park, associate professor of Asian religions, 1966-71, professor of Buddhism, 1971—. Consultant in advanced studies, Chung Hwa Institute, 1967.

WRITINGS:

Four Essays on Buddhism, Buddhist Association (United Kingdom), 1954.

(Author of preface) *Tibetan Yoga and Secret Doctrine,* Oxford University, 1958.
The Practice of Zen, Harper & Row (New York), 1959.
(Contributor) *Buddhism* (includes "Life in a Tibetan Vajrayana Monastery"), Braziller (New York), 1961.
(As Garma C. C. Chang; translator and author of annotations) *The Hundred Thousand Songs of Milarepa: The Life Story and Teaching of the Greatest Poet-Saint to Appear in the History of Buddhism,* University Books, 1962, abridged edition, Harper & Row, 1970.
The Essential Teachings of Tibetan Tantra, University Books, 1963.
(As Garma C. C. Chang; editor, translator, and author of annotations) *Teachings of Tibetan Yoga,* University Books, 1963, published as *Six Yogas of Naropa and Teachings on Mahamudra,* Snow Lion Publications, 1986.
(As Garma C. C. Chang) *The Buddhist Teaching of Totality: The Philosophy of Hwa Yen Buddhism,* Pennsylvania State University Press, 1971.
A Modern Interpretation of Buddhist Doctrines (in Chinese), Wisdom Torch (Taipei), 1973.
(General editor) *A Treasury of Mahayana Sutras: Selections from the Maharatnakuta Sutra,* Pennsylvania State University Press, 1983.

Also contributor to journals, including *Philosophy East and West, China Culture,* and *Tomorrow.*

BIOGRAPHICAL/CRITICAL SOURCES:

PERIODICALS

Choice, November, 1972, p. 1140.
Times Literary Supplement, May 18, 1973, p. 559.*

* * *

CHANG, Ch'eng-chi
See CHANG, Chen-Chi

* * *

CHANG, Garma C. C.
See CHANG, Chen-Chi

CHEYNEY-COKER, Syl 1945-

PERSONAL: Born June 28, 1945, in Freetown, West Africa. *Education:* Attended University of Oregon, 1967-70; attended University of California, 1970; Attended University of Wisconsin, 1971-72.

ADDRESSES: Office—Department of English, University of Maiduguri, P.M.B. 1069, Maiduguri, Nigeria.

CAREER: Writer. Has worked as a drummer, and as a factory and dock worker. Eugene *Register Guard,* OR, journalist, 1968-69; University of Wisconsin, Madison, teaching assistant, 1971; Radio Sierra Leone, head of cultural affairs, 1972-73; freelance writer, 1973-75; University of the Philippines, Quezon City, visiting professor of English, 1975-77. University of Maiduguri, Nigeria, lecturer, 1977-79, senior lecturer, 1979—.

AWARDS, HONORS: Food Foundation grant, 1970.

WRITINGS:

POETRY

Concerto for an Exile, Africana (New York), 1972, Heinemann (London), 1973.
The Graveyard Also Has Teeth, New Beacon (London), 1974.
The Blood in the Desert's Eyes: Poems, Heinemann (Portsmouth, NH), 1990.

OTHER

The Last Harmattan of Alusine Dunbar (novel), Heinemann (Oxford and Portsmouth), 1990.

* * *

CHILDERS, (Robert) Erskine 1870-1922

PERSONAL: Born June 25, 1870, in London, England; executed by firing squad on November 24, 1922, in Dublin, Ireland; son of Robert Caesar (an Orientalist) and Anna Mary Henrietta (Barton) Childers; married Mary Alden Osgood, January 5, 1904; children: Robert, Erskine. *Education:* Attended Haileybury College; Trinity College, Cambridge, B.A., 1893.

CAREER: Served as a clerk in the British House of Commons, 1895-1910; after settling in Ireland, smuggled weapons and fought for Irish home rule; elected to the Dail Eireann for County Wicklow, 1921; joined Irish Republican Army after Irish Free State established. *Military service:* Served in Britain's City Imperial Volunteer Battery of the Honourable Artillery Company during the Boer War; served in the British Royal Naval Air Service during World War I, attained the rank of Lieutenant-Commander, was mentioned in despatches and awarded the Distinguished Service Cross.

WRITINGS:

NONFICTION

In the Ranks of the C.I.V.: A Narrative and Diary of Personal Experiences with the C.I.V. Battery (Honourable Artillery Company) in South Africa, Smith, Elder (London, England), 1900.
(With Basil Williams) *The H.A.C. in South Africa: A Record of the Services Rendered in the South African War by Members of the Honourable Artillery Company,* Smith, Elder, 1903.
(Editor) *The Times History of the War in South Africa,* volume 5, Low, Marston, 1907.
War and the Arme Blanche, Arnold, 1910.
The Framework of Home Rule, Arnold, 1911.
German Influence on British Cavalry, Arnold, 1911.
The Form and Purpose of Home Rule: A Lecture, Ponsonby (Dublin, Ireland), 1912.
Military Rule in Ireland, Talbot Press (Dublin, Ireland), 1920.
Is Ireland a Danger to England?, Woodgrange Press (Dublin, Ireland), 1921.
(Editor with Alfred O'Rahilly) *Who Burnt Cork City: A Tale of Arson, Loot, and Murder,* Irish Labour Party and Trade Union Congress (Dublin, Ireland), 1921.
What the Treaty Means, Republic of Ireland (Dublin, Ireland), 1922.
Clause by Clause: A Comparison between the "Treaty" and Document No. 2, Republic of Ireland, 1922.
A Thirst for the Sea: The Sailing Adventures of Erskine Childers, edited by Hugh and Robin Popham, Stanford Maritime (London, England), 1979.

OTHER

The Riddle of the Sands, A Record of Secret Service Recently Achieved (novel), Smith, Elder, 1903;

Dodd, Mead (New York, NY), 1915; Hart-Davis (London, England), 1968; with line drawings by Charles Mozley, Dent (London, England), 1970; with introduction by E. F. Parker and illustrated by John O'Connor, Imprint Society (Barre, MA), 1971; with introduction by Norman Donaldson, Dover (New York, NY), 1976; with introduction and notes by Eric J. Grove, Naval Institute Press (Annapolis, MD), 1991; with introduction by David Trotter, Oxford University Press (Oxford, England), 1995.

ADAPTATIONS: The Riddle of the Sands was made into a British film in 1979.

SIDELIGHTS: Erskine Childers was a writer belonging both to his native England and his adopted Ireland. Though he wrote several works of nonfiction on the subjects of the British military and the struggle for Irish independence, he is attributed the status of father to the British spy novel. The tradition of this genre, according to Gareth W. Dunleavy in the *Dictionary of Literary Biography,* "runs from Childers to John Le Carre." The novel which earned Childers this place in literary history, *The Riddle of the Sands, A Record of Secret Service Recently Achieved,* was published in Great Britain in 1903, and in the United States in 1915. Though its premise of Germany invading Britain from the sea is now outdated, the book still enjoys popularity through late twentieth-century reprints, and was made into a British film in 1979.

The author was born Robert Erskine Childers in London, England, in 1870. His father was Robert Caesar Childers, a renowned expert on the Orient. Childers' father died, however, when he was six years old, and he went to live with Anglo-Irish relatives in County Wicklow, Ireland. He returned to England for his college education, receiving his bachelor's degree from Trinity College, Cambridge, in 1893. Shortly afterwards, he became a clerk in the British Parliament's House of Commons, but it was what Childers did on the weekends away from his job that became a greater influence on his career. He spent much of his leisure time sailing alone, and eventually he made trips into the North Sea, along the coasts of the Netherlands, Denmark, and Germany. The familiarity he gained with the Frisian Islands in particular would help him make *The Riddle of the Sands* extremely realistic.

The first book that Childers penned, however, was 1900's *In the Ranks of the C.I.V.: A Narrative and*

Diary of Personal Experiences with the C.I.V. Battery (Honourable Artillery Company) in South Africa. C.I.V. stands for City Imperial Volunteers, and, as the subtitle implies, *In the Ranks* is Childers' personal account of his service during the Boer War. He also collaborated with Basil Williams on the official version of the Honourable Artillery Company's history, 1903's *The H.A.C. in South Africa,* and later Childers edited the fifth volume of *The Times History of the War in South Africa.* In the same year that *The H.A.C. in South Africa* and *The Riddle of the Sands* were published, Childers visited Massachusetts, where he met the woman he would marry the following January, Mary Alden Osgood. Mary was better known as Molly.

The Riddle of the Sands brought Childers much success. He couched the novel in the form of a factual story, reported to the British military authorities but ignored. The narrator, Carruthers, is an upper-class member of the British Foreign Office, who, out of boredom, accepts an invitation from Davies—a more steady, practical type—to sail on the latter's small and frill-free yacht, the *Dulcibella.* Carruthers thinks they are going duck hunting, but actually Davies has enlisted his aide in solving a mystery. He has previously had a chance encounter with a German yacht piloted by an English captain named Dollmann, who tried to cause him to be stranded and shipwrecked. Davies wonders what Dollmann didn't want him to see and report. Together, Carruthers and Davies uncover a German plot to invade England by landing in Lincolnshire. Dollmann proves to be a disgruntled and disgraced former British naval officer, and throws himself into the ocean rather than be brought back to face trial. There is also a love interest in *The Riddle of the Sands* between Davies and Dollmann's daughter, inserted by Childers at his publisher's request.

As Dunleavy reported, *The Riddle of the Sands* "met with immediate public and critical approval." It fueled a movement in England to improve its military preparedness, and Childers continued to fan the fire with his next factual books, including 1910's *War and the Arme Blanche* and 1911's *German Influence on British Cavalry.* The author's goal in this pair of titles, according to Dunleavy, was to "argu(e) for modern weapons and training."

Dunleavy also noted in his *Dictionary of Literary Biography* essay that "Childers came back from the Boer War with inclinations toward home rule for Ireland." Before entering the Royal Naval Air Ser-

vice in order to fight for England in World War I, he published his first two books in favor of the Irish cause, *The Framework of Home Rule* and *The Form and Purpose of Home Rule: A Lecture.* Childers and his wife had also begun smuggling guns to Ireland before World War I; some of these weapons were used in the failed Easter Rising of 1916.

After the World War I, Childers increased his activities and writings on behalf of a free Ireland. The early 1920s saw him produce volumes such as *Military Rule in Ireland, Is Ireland a Danger to England?,* and *What the Treaty Means.* Childers learned about the "treaty" of the last title first-hand, because he was elected to the Dail Eireann for County Wicklow in 1921, and was part of the treaty delegation to London that year. The treaty established the Irish Free State, but divided Ireland into northern and southern portions, with only the south granted semi-independent status. Childers argued against this compromise, and when the Irish Free State was established, he joined the Irish Republican Army in opposition to it. In 1922, he was secretly tried by the Irish Free State for illegal possession of an automatic pistol, and executed by a firing squad. According to Dunleavy, Childers shook hands with the squad members and asked them to step closer to carry out their orders.

The Riddle of the Sands has been reprinted several times since Childers' death. Latter-day reviewers of the novel have been generally positive. D. H. Enright in the *Times Literary Supplement* compared Childers to Polish-English author Joseph Conrad, and asserted that "even if one isn't given to messing about in boats, the wanderings of the Dulcibella hold the attention by sheer gusto and authority." A 1971 *Time* magazine critique affirmed that the novel "is still the world's greatest sailing suspense tale." Benny Green in the *Spectator* judged it to be "perhaps the best, of those Edwardian call-to-arms thrillers," and concluded that *The Riddle of the Sands* "retains much of its old magnetism today."

The film adaptation of *The Riddle of the Sands* hit British movie theaters in 1979; the same year saw the publication of an edited version of Childers' sailing journals, *A Thirst for the Sea: The Sailing Adventures of Erskine Childers.* Childers, however, left another legacy besides his books, this one especially to his beloved Ireland. His second son, Erskine, became president of the Republic of Ireland in 1973.

BIOGRAPHICAL/CRITICAL SOURCES:

BOOKS

Boyle, Andrew, *The Riddle of Erskine Childers,* Hutchinson, 1977.
Dictionary of Literary Biography, Volume 70: *British Mystery Writers, 1860-1919,* Gale, 1988.
Twentieth-Century Crime and Mystery Writers, St. James Press, 1991.
Wilkinson, Burke, *The Zeal of the Convert,* Luce, 1976.
Williams, Basil, *Erskine Childers, 1870-1922,* Women's Printing Society, 1926.

PERIODICALS

Spectator, September 23, 1972, pp. 472-473.
Time, December 20, 1971, p. 91.
Times Literary Supplement, July 14, 1995, p. 9.*

—*Sketch by Elizabeth Wenning*

* * *

CHOPRA, Deepak (K.) 1946-

PERSONAL: Born in 1946, in New Delhi, India; immigrated to United States, 1970; naturalized U.S. citizen; son of Krishan Chopra (a physician); married; wife's name, Rita; children: Mallika (daughter), Gautam (son). *Education:* All India Institute of Medical Science, M.D.

ADDRESSES: Home—La Jolla, CA. *Office*—The Chopra Center for Well Being, 7630 Fay Ave., La Jolla, CA 92037. *Agent*—Muriel Nellis, Literary and Creative Artists, 3543 Albemarle St. NW, Washington, DC 20008; c/o Crown/Harmony, 201 East 50th St., 22nd Floor, New York, NY 10022; c/o The Ford Group, 872 La Jolla Rancho Rd., La Jolla, CA 92037.

CAREER: Physician, lecturer, and writer. Muhlenbert Hospital, Plainfield, NJ, intern, c. 1970-71; established private endocrinology practice in Boston, MA, 1971; affiliated with Tufts University, Medford, MA, Harvard University, Cambridge, MA, and Boston University, Boston, MA, 1971-c. 1985; New England Memorial Hospital (now Boston Regional Medical Center), Stoneham, MA, chief of staff, 1981-1985; Maharishi Ayur-Veda Products International, Inc.,

cofounder, 1985, sole stockholder, 1985-87, president, treasurer and clerk, 1985-88; Maharishi Ayur-Veda Health Center for Behavioral Medicine and Stress Management, Lancaster, MA, director, 1985-93; Sharp Institute for Human Potential and Mind/Body Medicine, La Jolla, CA, executive director, 1993—; Center for Mind/Body Medicine at L'Auberge, Del Mar, CA, director, 1993-95; associated with The Chopra Center for Well Being, La Jolla. Member of alternative medicine board of National Institute of Health. Coproducer of video *Growing Younger,* 1994.

MEMBER: American Association of Ayurvedic Medicine (founder).

AWARDS, HONORS: Christened Dhanvantari of Heaven on Earth by Maharishi Mahesh Yogi, 1989.

WRITINGS:

Creating Health: The Psychophysiological Connection, Houghton (Boston), 1985, published as *Creating Health: Beyond Prevention, Toward Perfection,* 1987, new edition with new introduction published as *Creating Health: How to Wake Up the Body's Intelligence,* 1991.

Return of the Rishi: A Doctor's Search for the Ultimate Healer (autobiography), Houghton, 1988, new edition with new introduction published as *Return of the Rishi: A Doctor's Story of Spiritual Transformation and Ayurvedic Healing,* 1991.

Quantum Healing: Exploring the Frontiers of Mind/Body Medicine, Bantam (New York), 1989.

(With Richard Averbach and Stuart Rothenberg) *Perfect Health: Maharishi Ayurveda, the Mind/Body Program for Total Well-Being,* Crown/Harmony (New York), 1990.

Perfect Health: The Complete Mind/Body Guide, illustrations by Stephen Van Damme, Crown/Harmony, 1991.

Unconditional Life: Mastering the Forces That Shape Personal Reality, Bantam, 1991, published as *Unconditional Life: Discovering the Power to Fulfill Your Dreams,* Bantam, 1992.

Creating Affluence: Wealth Consciousness in the Field of All Possibilities, New World Library, 1993.

Ageless Body, Timeless Mind: The Quantum Alternative to Growing Old, Crown/Harmony, 1993.

Restful Sleep: The Complete Mind/Body Program for Overcoming Insomnia, Crown/Harmony, 1994.

The Seven Spiritual Laws of Success: A Practical Guide to the Fulfillment of Your Dreams, Amber-Allen, 1994, New World Press, 1995.

Perfect Weight: The Complete Mind/Body Program for Achieving and Maintaining Your Ideal Weight, Crown/Harmony, 1994.

Journey into Healing: Awakening the Wisdom within You, Harmony, 1994, published as *Journey into Healing: A Step-by-Step Personal Guide Compiled from the Timeless Wisdom of Deepak Chopra, M.D.,* Crown/Harmony, 1994.

Perfect Digestion: The Key to Balanced Living, Crown/Harmony, 1995.

The Return of Merlin (novel), Crown/Harmony, 1995.

Living without Limits, American Medical Association Library, 1995.

Boundless Energy: The Complete Mind/Body Program for Overcoming Chronic Fatigue, Crown/Harmony, 1995.

The Way of the Wizard: Twenty Spiritual Lessons for Creating the Life You Want, Crown/Harmony, 1996.

Contributor to periodicals, including *Journal of the American Medical Association.* Member of scientific advisory board of *Longevity.*

WORK IN PROGRESS: Two novels, a fantasy and a thriller; a textbook.

SIDELIGHTS: Deepak Chopra is a prominent physician—sometimes categorized as a New Age guru—promoting alternative approaches to mental and physical well-being. Chopra began his career as a physician. After studying in India, he came to the United States in 1970 and completed his education, served a residency, and then opened a private practice. In addition, he taught at various institutions, including both Tufts University and Boston University, and served the New England Memorial Hospital as chief of staff.

By 1980 Chopra had become increasingly concerned with Western medicine's, and thus his own practice's, reliance on pharmaceuticals as a major means of restoring, or merely maintaining, healthy individuals. Chopra's search for alternatives to standard Western approaches eventually led him to the Maharishi Mahesh Yogi, an Indian spiritualist who teaches transcendental meditation. Through the Maharishi (who had gained celebrity in the 1960s with his counseling of several notable celebrities, including the Beatles musical group), Chopra became profoundly involved in transcendental meditation. In addition, he learned about Ayurvedic medicine, a holistic approach in which a patient's surroundings

and general attitude are considered in addition to more conventional mental and physical conditions.

In 1985 Chopra established the Maharishi Ayur-Veda Health Center for Behavioral Medicine and Stress Management. Here Chopra began applying his understanding of both Ayurvedic and Western practices. Two years later, he published *Creating Health: The Psychophysiological Connection,* the first of many works in which Chopra imposed his holistic perspective on various health-related subjects. This initial work, which was twice reprinted, first as *Creating Health: Beyond Prevention, Toward Perfection,* and then as *Creating Health: How to Wake Up the Body's Intelligence,* launched Chopra as a leading figure in alternative medicine, and his ensuing writings have established him as one of the most successful, and charismatic, figures in the counter-culture health movement sometimes termed New Age.

Creating Health proved immensely successful with book-buyers eager to discover an alternative to Western medicine and its reliance on drug medications. An ensuing volume, the autobiographical *Return of the Rishi: A Doctor's Search for the Ultimate Healer* (reprinted as *Return of the Rishi: A Doctor's Story of Spiritual Transformation and Ayurvedic Healing*) realized similar success and furthered Chopra's reputation as an accessible, credible physician with insights somewhat unique in Western medicine. The book chronicles Chopra's path to enlightenment, from his early days as an intern at a New Jersey hospital, to his discovery of Ayurveda methods, to his current success. Judith Hooper wrote in the *New York Times Book Review:* "Chopra's talent as a storyteller and his eye for the exemplary detail make this a rich and compelling book."

In ensuing volumes Chopra continued to elaborate on various aspects of holistic health. In 1991's *Perfect Health: The Complete Mind/Body Guide,* he emphasizes the health benefits gained by considering all aspects—as opposed to merely the ailing aspects—of given patients. And in *Unconditional Life: Mastering the Forces That Shape Personal Reality* (reprinted as *Unconditional Life: Discovering the Power to Fulfill Your Dreams*), he relates the manner in which individuals can realize greater health and stability by adjusting personal perspectives.

Among Chopra's most popular, and most controversial, publications is *Ageless Body, Timeless Mind: The Quantum Alternative to Growing Old,* a 1993 volume in which he contends that the aging process can be significantly effected and modified through such means as meditation, nutrition, and even personal expression. Aging, Chopra argues, is not necessarily a process of degeneration. It is, rather, a culmination of experiences and perceptions. As such, the elderly, for Chopra, constitute the storehouse for humankind's most profound knowledge and understanding. A contributor to *Kirkus Reviews* called the book "thoughtful" and "sometimes inspiring," while a reviewer for *Publishers Weekly* stated that despite Chopra's "inspirational conviction" in his material, the book was periodically "thin on substance."

Chopra's relatively radical insights into aging and the elderly powerfully appealed to a substantial segment of the American book-buying public, and the book eventually topped numerous bestseller lists. Chopra has enjoyed further success with such volumes as *The Seven Spiritual Laws of Success: A Practical Guide to the Fulfillment of Your Dreams* and *Journey into Healing: Awakening the Wisdom within You.* In addition, he has addressed specific health issues in such works as *Perfect Digestion: The Key to Balanced Living, Perfect Weight: The Complete Mind/Body Program for Achieving and Maintaining Your Ideal Weight,* and *Restful Sleep: The Complete Mind/Body Program for Overcoming Insomnia.*

Among Chopra's less likely publications is *The Return of Merlin,* a novel in which an apprentice to the Arthurian wizard Merlin travels through time and lands in the twentieth century, where he helps a police officer solve a crime. "This is a bold, occasionally brilliant retelling of Arthurian lore," judged a critic in *Publishers Weekly.* Pam Lambert, writing in *People Weekly,* declared: "Chopra weaves an intriguing story that also offers plenty to ponder." Chopra explained to a *Publishers Weekly* interviewer that he felt fiction was truthful in that "it reveals your innermost feelings and fantasies about situations, circumstances, people and events." He added, "If you write fiction and you do it with intensity and passion, you reveal yourself—and you write the truth."

Chopra benefits from widespread celebrity as a prolific writer whose new works regularly rank among national bestsellers. He is, moreover, a prominent figure on television, whether appearing as a guest on interview programs such as *The Oprah Winfrey Show* or as principal lecturer on public television broadcasts. Although he followed *The Return of Merlin* with the more characteristic *The Way of the Wizard: Twenty Spiritual Lessons for Creating the Life You Want,* he disclosed in 1995 that he is increasing inclined toward writing fiction.

BIOGRAPHICAL/CRITICAL SOURCES:

BOOKS

Chopra, Deepak, *Return of the Rishi: A Doctor's Story of Spiritual Transformation and Ayurvedic Healing,* Houghton, 1991.
Notable Asian Americans, Gale, 1995, pp. 59-60.

PERIODICALS

Booklist, January 15, 1987, p. 783; May 15, 1993, p. 1650; December 1, 1995, p. 586.
Chicago Tribune, September 13, 1995.
Entertainment Weekly, May 24, 1996, pp. 12-13.
Kirkus Reviews, April 15, 1990, p. 571; July 1, 1991, p. 833; May 15, 1993, p.636.
Library Journal, June 1, 1990, pp. 160, 162; October 1, 1991, p. 125; January, 1992, p. 200; June 15, 1993, p. 90; July, 1995, p. 118; January, 1996, p. 106.
New York Times Book Review, March 27, 1988, p. 39.
People Weekly, November 15, 1993, pp. 169-70; August 14, 1995, pp. 27-28.
Psychology Today, November/December, 1993, pp. 36-37.
Publishers Weekly, December 18, 1987, p. 48; April 20, 1990, p. 73; December 6, 1991, p. 45; June 28, 1993, p. 74; September 26, 1994, p. 67; May 8, 1995, p. 283; July 24, 1995, pp. 43-44.
Time, June 24, 1996, p. 64.
USA Today, January 4, 1990.

* * *

CLINTON, Hillary Rodham 1947-

PERSONAL: Born October 26, 1947, in Chicago, IL; daughter of Hugh Ellsworth (in business) and Dorothy (a homemaker; maiden name, Howell) Rodham; married William Jefferson Clinton (a politician), October 11, 1975; children: Chelsea Victoria. *Education:* Wellesley College, B.A. (with high honors), 1969; Yale University, J.D., 1973. *Politics:* Democrat. *Religion:* Methodist.

ADDRESSES: Home and office—White House, 1600 Pennsylvania Ave. NW, Washington, DC 20500-0002.

CAREER: Admitted to the bars of the State of Arkansas, U.S. District Court (east and west districts) of

Arkansas, U.S. Court of Appeals (8th circuit), 1973, admitted to the bar of the U.S. Supreme Court, 1975; Children's Defense Fund, Cambridge, MA, and Washington, DC, attorney, 1973-74; Carnegie Council on Children, New Haven, CT, legal consultant, 1973-74; Judiciary Committee of the U.S. House of Representatives, Washington, DC, counsel for the impeachment inquiry staff, 1974; University of Arkansas, Fayetteville, assistant professor of law, 1974-77, Little Rock, lecturer at law school, 1979-80; U.S. District Court (east district) of Arkansas, reporter for federal court speedy trial planning group, 1975-79; Rose Law Firm, Little Rock, AR, partner, 1977-92; First Lady of the United States, Washington, DC, 1993—; Committee on Health Care, committee head, Washington, 1993—.

Served on the board of directors of Legal Services Corporation, Washington, 1978-81 (chair, 1978-80); of Wal-Mart Stores, Inc., 1986-92; of TCBY Enterprises, Inc., 1989-92; of Lafarge Corp., 1990-92; also served on boards of Children's Defense Fund; Child Care Action Campaign; National Center on Education and the Economy; Children's Television Workshop; Public/Private Ventures; Arkansas Children's Hospital; and Franklin and Eleanor Roosevelt Institute. Served as a committee member for the Southern Regional Education Board's committee on quality education; Arkansas Educational Standards Committee, 1983-84.

MEMBER: American Bar Association (chair of commission of women in the profession, 1987-91); Arkansas Bar Association, National Democratic Party.

AWARDS, HONORS: Named Outstanding Layman of the Year by Phi Delta Kappa, 1984; named one of One Hundred Most Influential Lawyers in America by the National Law Journal, 1988, 1991; Lewis Hine Award, National Child Labor Law Committee, 1993; Albert Schweitzer Leadership Award, Hugh O'Brian Youth Foundation, 1993; Iris Cantor Humanitarian Award, University of California at Los Angeles Medical Center, 1993; Friend of Family Award, the American Home Economics Association, 1993; Charles Wilson Lee Citizen Service Award, Committee for Education Funding, 1993; Claude D. Pepper Award, National Association for Home Care, 1993; Commitment to Life Award, AIDS Project Los Angeles, 1994; Distinguished Service, Health Education and Prevention Award, National Center for Health Education, 1994; Cerviel Corporation Achievement Award, *Vista* magazine, 1994; Social Justice Award, United Auto Workers Union, 1994; Ernie Banks Posi-

tivism Trophy, Emil Verban Memorial Society, 1994; Ellen Browning Scripps Medal, Scripps College, 1994; Distinguished Pro Bono Service Award, San Diego Volunteer Lawyer Program, 1994; Special Achievement Award, Hispanic Public Corporation, 1994; Hippy U.S.A. Award, 1994; Distinguished Citizen Award, Coalition of Citizens With Disabilities in Illinois, 1994; AIDS Awareness Award, 1994; Ellington Shield against Helplessness, Duke Ellington School for the Performing Arts, 1994.

WRITINGS:

NONFICTION

It Takes a Village: And Other Lessons Children Teach Us, Simon & Schuster (New York), 1996.

Also author of *Handbook on Legal Rights for Arkansas Women.*

SIDELIGHTS: Liberals have heralded Hillary Rodham Clinton as a champion of women's and children's rights, an attorney of great capabilities and energy, and an active political partner of her husband, United States President William Jefferson Clinton. In her book, *It Takes a Village: And Other Lessons Children Teach Us,* Clinton focuses on the problems facing children and families in modern American society.

In addition to raising her own daughter, Clinton's authority in writing *It Takes a Village* stems from her involvement with children's issues and causes since her early law school days and her position as an attorney with the Children's Defense Fund. She has also served on the board of directors of that organization, and has been a legal consultant for the Carnegie Council on Children. Clinton continued her involvement with children's issues throughout her husband's tenure as Governor of Arkansas, and into his term as President. As she put it in her book, "I have spent much of the past 25 years working to improve the lives of children. My work has taught me that they need more of our time, energy, and resources." *It Takes a Village* is not the First Lady's first book, however. She wrote the *Handbook on Legal Rights for Arkansas Women* while her husband was governor of that state.

Clinton draws not only on her own experiences with her daughter Chelsea for *It Takes a Village,* but on her own childhood growing up with traditional middle-class parents in the Chicago area. She com-

pares the era in which she grew up with the modern one, admitting to longing for the more simpler time herself, but reminding readers that going backwards is not an option: "Those who urge a return to the values of the 1950s are yearning for the kind of family and neighborhood I grew up in and for the feelings of togetherness they engendered. I understand that nostalgia. I feel it myself when the world seems too much to take." Nevertheless, she maintains that "our past was not so picture-perfect. Ask African-American children who grew up in a segregated society, or immigrants who struggled to survive in sweatshops and tenements, or women whose life choices were circumscribed and whose work was underpaid." She further noted that "[t]he longing for 'the way things used to be' also obscures the larger settings in which the family finds itself today, as it struggles with broken homes, discrimination, economic downturns, urbanization, consumerism, and technology."

Yet Clinton's conservative critics may be surprised by some of the advice she offers in *It Takes a Village.* As Martha Brant and Evan Thomas reported in *Newsweek,* the First Lady "thinks everyone should wait until the age of 21 before having sex. She believes divorce has been made too easy and that couples should stay together for the sake of the kids." She does, however, advocate sexual education in the schools and openness about sexual subjects between parents and children. "No matter how great an effort adults make to convince young people to abstain," Clinton declares in *It Takes a Village,* "there will be some who are determined to embark on sexual experience. They need straight talk about contraception and sexually transmitted diseases to help them deal responsibly with the consequences of their actions." Another of her educational recommendations is to beef up discipline in the schools. "[D]iscipline and order are necessary for learning," the First Lady states. "I agree with those who advocate dress codes and even uniforms in some districts because they appear to diminish the frictions caused by brand-name consumerism and gang identification." According to Brant and Thomas, Clinton is also "sensitive that conservatives will translate the word 'Village' in her title"—the title comes from an African proverb advocating that the whole community take responsibility for child-rearing—"to mean 'Big Government.' She talks instead of a 'partnership' between government, churches, and charities."

Descriptions of government-aided programs that Clinton believes in, however, make up a significant portion of *It Takes a Village.* She discusses the

Abecedarian program in North Carolina, which gave a group of low-income African American households extra in-home educational help for infants, and managed to significantly raise the intelligence test scores of these children once they entered school. Clinton also praises a program which enlists the help of businesses in providing coupons for child care products to poor women who go for prenatal examinations. According to Katherine Paterson, reviewing *It Takes a Village* in *New York Times Book Review,* the book "is filled with such creative programs, which not only meet the needs of children and their parents but, in the long run, save our communities and our nation lives and money." Overall, Clinton reiterates her strong belief in universal health care for all children and expectant mothers. The First Lady also offers parents practical, everyday advice in *It Takes a Village.* She writes about what to look for in a day care center, and recommends books to read to preschoolers.

Book reviewers have had mixed reactions to *It Takes a Village.* Judith Shulevitz, in *New York* magazine felt that "the book seems to misread the current electoral mood, which is more concerned with getting rid of government than it is with enforcing particular values." Yet she conceded that "there are . . . a lot of wise ideas in this book." Douglas J. Besharov, opining in the *Washington Post Book World* had his reservations about *It Takes a Village,* but noted: "I came away from this book liking Hillary Rodham Clinton. Even as I was frustrated by her failure to subject her policy beliefs to critical examination, I was taken by her earnestly expressed concern for children and commitment to her own family." Richard Bernstein in the *New York Times* praised the First Lady's effort, labeling her tone "levelheaded, moderate, warmly common-sensical." Paterson hailed the work as "a gathering together of problems and real solutions, framed by stories that are fun to hear and laced with the occasional folksy observation." Phyllis Burke in the *Los Angeles Times Book Review* strongly lauded *It Takes a Village,* asserting that it "demonstrates intellectual vitality and openness to new ideas. This is a woman who is helping to shape the national dialogue." Burke went on to conclude that "[t]hroughout this book, there is the sound of tempered frustration and unshakable determination, a missionary's zeal and a mother's vulnerability. . . . It is not a book for cynics, but it will be welcomed by those who want to understand just who Hillary Rodham Clinton is and what we can do to help the children in our village."

BIOGRAPHICAL/CRITICAL SOURCES:

BOOKS

Boyd, Aaron, *First Lady: The Story of Hillary Rodham Clinton,* Morgan Reynolds (Greensboro, NC), 1994.

Clinton, Hillary Rodham, *It Takes a Village: And Other Lessons Children Teach Us,* Simon & Schuster (New York), 1996.

Dumas, Ernest, editor, *The Clintons of Arkansas: An Introduction by Those Who Know Them Best,* University of Arkansas Press (Fayetteville, AR), 1993.

Radcliffe, Donnie, *Hillary Rodham Clinton: A First Lady for Our Time,* Warner Books (New York), 1993.

PERIODICALS

Los Angeles Times Book Review, January 28, 1996, pp. 1, 12.

Newsweek, January 15, 1996, pp. 20-24, 26, 30-33.

New York, January 29, 1996, pp. 46-47.

New York Times, February 5, 1996, pp. C9, C13.

New York Times Book Review, February 11, 1996, p. 24.

Washington Post Book World, January 28, 1996, pp. 1, 10.*

—*Sketch by Elizabeth Wenning*

* * *

CODY, Paul 1953-

PERSONAL: Born December 23, 1953, in Newton, MA; son of John E. (a clerk) and Margaret (a clerk; maiden name, Christie) Cody; married Elizabeth Holmes (an editor and poet), September 26, 1987; children: Liam Scott, Austin James. *Education:* University of Massachusetts, Boston, B.A. (magna cum laude), 1982; Cornell University, M.F.A., 1987. *Politics:* "Mostly Democrat." *Religion:* "Interested in Catholicism and Buddhism; practice neither." *Avocational interests:* Journalism, sports, editing, history, crime, and mental illness.

ADDRESSES: Home and office—901 North Tioga St., Ithaca, NY 14850. *Agent*—Sloan Harris, International Creative Management, 40 West 50th St., New York, NY 10019. *E-mail*—dec5@cornell.edu.

CAREER: Free-lance writer, 1976—. Perkins School for the Blind, Watertown, MA, child-care worker, 1983-85; Cornell University, Ithaca, NY, lecturer in English, 1987-89; *Cornell* magazine, Ithaca, NY, associate editor and staff writer, 1991-96. Visiting professor of writing, Cornell University, 1997—.

AWARDS, HONORS: Arthur Lynn prize in fiction, Cornell University, 1987; grant in fiction writing, New York Foundation for the Arts, 1989; Stegner Fellowship, Stanford University, 1990 (declined).

WRITINGS:

The Stolen Child (novel), Baskerville (Dallas, TX), 1995.
Eyes like Mine (novel), Baskerville, 1996.

Contributor to numerous periodicals, including the *Boston Globe Harper's, The Quarterly,* and *Wind.*

WORK IN PROGRESS: A novel, *The Thing He Did;* research on Willard Asylum, a mental institution in upstate New York.

SIDELIGHTS: Paul Cody's first novel *The Stolen Child* is "horrifying and beautiful, sorrowful, measured, and truthful," wrote Bethany Clement in the *San Francisco Review of Books.* The story follows both the destinies of the title character—a youth who is kidnapped, later recovered, and institutionalized in his adult years as a result of the experience and the abuse that followed—and several other characters whose lives connected with and were changed by his ordeal. Cody explores the ways in which the child's mother and brother are troubled by the incident. The policeman who tried to trace the child's abductor and the waitress who unwittingly served the child and his kidnapper are also haunted by their memories. Clement concluded by calling Cody's book "impossibly and unexpectedly lovely."

Cody's second novel, *Eyes like Mine,* is also a portrait of a young life damaged by traumatic incidence. Protagonist Will Ross, a Boston-born working-class writer, begins at age 37 to reevaluate his life. Will was placed in a mental institution in his immediate post-teen years because of an obsession with serial killers. During his twenties he was a vagrant, wandering the countryside trying to sort out his identity. By the time the story begins, Will—like Cody himself—has graduated from the writing program at Cornell University, has married, and is expecting his first child. He tries to understand the means by which he got to his current place in life, and he tries to predict what will happen to him in the future. A *Kirkus Reviews* contributor called Cody a "rare" writer who is concerned with the large questions— love, life, death—that loom over life. The reviewer affirmed that Cody "has the talent to give those questions a rightful, elegant due."

Paul Cody told *CA:* "I've been writing since I was a child, I guess because I've always loved to read, and writing words on paper gave me the feeling that I could think about, shape, and in some sense influence my experience of the world by writing it down. And then in 1971-72, when I was 18 years old, I became an alcoholic and drug addict and spent seven years in and out of mental hospitals and detoxes, until I was finally taken by the police to Medfield State Hospital, southwest of Boston, in the summer of 1978. I was committed by a judge to 30 days in a locked ward and then spent a short time in a residential drug treatment program, where all the residents except me were there on pre-release status from state and federal prisons. I've been straight and sober, and writing steadily, since then.

"This has always been the single biggest influence on my work, and I'm probably drawn to my subjects— abducted and lost children, religious and drug-induced ecstasy, crime, marginality, insanity—because I'm trying on different levels to figure out why my life went so wrong and then so right. In a way, writing about darkness gives me the chance to visit the demons, and then find what I hope is light and redemption again and again. It's a way to participate in the mystery of life without going to church."

BIOGRAPHICAL/CRITICAL SOURCES:

PERIODICALS

Kirkus Reviews, January 15, 1996, p. 84.
San Francisco Review of Books, July/August, 1995, p. 4.

* * *

CODY, Robin 1943-

PERSONAL: Born March 1, 1943, in St. Helens, OR; son of Bob and Betty Cody. *Education:* Yale, B.A., 1965. *Avocational interests:* Rivers, outdoors.

ADDRESSES: Home—5003 S.E. Thirty-Fourth Ave., Portland, OR 97202.

CAREER: Writer.

AWARDS, HONORS: Oregon Book Award, 1995, and Pacific Northwest Booksellers Award, 1996, both for *Voyage of a Summer Sun: Canoeing the Columbia River.*

WRITINGS:

Umbrella Guide to Bicycling the Oregon Coast (travel guide), Epicenter Press (Seattle, WA), 1990.
Ricochet River (fiction), Knopf (New York), 1992.
Voyage of a Summer Sun: Canoeing the Columbia River (travelogue), Knopf, 1995.

SIDELIGHTS: Robin Cody is a writer whose fiction and nonfiction works share a foundation in the author's intimate knowledge of the Pacific Northwest. His first book-length publication, *The Umbrella Guide to Bicycling the Oregon Coast,* was dubbed "top-notch and useful," by Thomas K. Fry in the *Library Journal.* This was followed by a novel, *Ricochet River,* a coming-of-age story set in 1960 in a small logging town in Oregon. The book was warmly received. Constance Decker Thompson remarked in the *New York Times Book Review* that "much of the book's rich imagery springs from [its] very particular terrain." Cody is also the author of *Voyage of a Summer Sun: Canoeing the Columbia River,* a travelogue which chronicles the author's eighty-two-day voyage down the Columbia River in a canoe. Several reviewers found Cody's account of a river voyage superior to the average travelogue due to the author's extensive knowledge of the history and natural surroundings of the river.

In *Ricochet River,* Cody depicts the end of an era through the arrival of Jesse Howl, a teenage Native American boy, in a nearly all-white logging town in 1960 Oregon. A skillful athlete, Jesse wins guarded acceptance from the townspeople for his feats on the football field. But only Wade Curren, the novel's narrator, his girlfriend Lorna, and his family, with whom Jesse lives during his last year in high school, fully accept the young Klamath Indian. In *Ricochet River* critics found an apt representation of Eisenhower America as seen through the eyes of its three young protagonists, influenced by Elvis Presley and *American Bandstand* and struggling against the conservative small-town mores of their upbringing as they approach adulthood. "The author . . . has a naturalist's feel for the Pacific Northwest evident in his majestic descriptions of its clear blue and green rivers, its wildlife, salmon fishing and log-rolling," remarked a reviewer for *Publishers Weekly.* Barbara Quick, who reviewed the book for the *Los Angeles Times Book Review,* faulted the author for occasional sentimentality. However, she observed that the strength of *Ricochet River* is in the author's success "in creating a sense of place and a truly wonderful character in the person of Jesse Howl."

"The travel-narrative-cum-voyage-of-self-discovery is by now such a cliche that it should be outlawed," wrote Ted Conover in a *New York Times Book Review* assessment of Cody's third book, *Voyage of a Summer Sun.* "Trips need to carry their own weight, and this one does," he continued. The solo trip documented in *Voyage of a Summer Sun* takes Cody from the headwaters of the Columbia River in Canada out to the Pacific Ocean on the Washington-Oregon coast, some 1200 miles. "Cody . . . gives a sparkling account of his adventure, interweaving historical detail and natural history with childhood memories of the river," remarked a *Publishers Weekly* contributor. Not all critics were equally enthusiastic about the author's ruminations on the mostly catastrophic changes wrought on the environment of the river by human hands in the twentieth-century. However, many found the book a successful account of a daring voyage taken by an ordinary, if well-informed, individual. Brenda Grazis concluded in *Booklist:* "Cody's peppery wit and engaging interest in the river townsfolk and in the wildlife he encounters keep the narrative buoyant."

Cody is a writer whose works are set in the Pacific Northwest, drawing on the author's familiarity with the history, flora, and fauna of that area of the United States. His travelogue, *Voyage of a Summer Sun,* offers a portrait of the modern-day Columbia River, drawn through interviews with the people who continue to make their living from it. The work reveals the history of the area, combined with the author's naturalist observations on how the river has changed since he was a child. While Cody has at times been faulted for occasional lapses into sentimentality in his fiction or into moralizing in his nonfiction, he has garnered frequent praise for the wit and warmth with which he evokes life in the Pacific Northwest.

BIOGRAPHICAL/CRITICAL SOURCES:

PERIODICALS

Booklist, April 1, 1995, p. 1374.

Kirkus Reviews, February 1, 1995, pp. 119-20.
Library Journal, June 1, 1990, p. 158.
Los Angeles Times Book Review, May 10, 1992, p. 15.
New York Times Book Review, August 23, 1992, p. 16; June 11, 1995, p. 9.
Publishers Weekly, January 20, 1992, p. 44; February 20, 1995, p. 191.

* * *

COHEN, Marcel 1937-

PERSONAL: Born October 9, 1937, in Asnieres, France; son of Jacques and Marie (Salem) Cohen. *Ethnicity:* "White." *Education:* Attended Ecole Superieure de Journalisme and Ecole du Louvre, both Paris, France. *Religion:* Jewish.

ADDRESSES: Home—197 rue de Grenelle, 75007 Paris, France.

CAREER: Journalist, 1958—. Worked as a military correspondent, 1960-61.

AWARDS, HONORS: Grant for Macalester College from World Press Institute, 1970-71.

WRITINGS:

Du desert au livre: Entretiens avec Edmond Jabes, Pierre Belfond, 1981, translation by Pierre Joris published as *From the Desert to the Book,* Station Hill (Barrytown, NY), 1990.
Miroirs, Editions Gallimard, 1981, translation by Jason Weiss, Sun and Moon (College Park, MD), in press.
Le grand paon-de-nuit, Editions Gallimard, 1990, translation by Cid Corman published as *The Peacock Emperor Moth,* Burning Deck Press (Providence, RI), 1995.

UNTRANSLATED WORKS

Galpa (novel), Editions Le Seuil, 1969.
Malestroit: Chroniques du silence, EFR, 1973.
Voyage a Waizata, EFR, 1976.
Murs, EFR, 1979.
Je ne sais pas le nom, Editions Gallimard, 1986.

SIDELIGHTS: Marcel Cohen told *CA:* "After a difficult childhood, marked by the death of most of my family in the Nazis' camps, I started to hitchhike extensively all over Europe during high school vacations. At the age of twenty, I traveled from Paris to the Himalayas through Italy, Greece, Turkey, Iran, Afghanistan, Pakistan, and India, sleeping on truck platforms or sidewalks and spending several months in a Tibetan monastery. As a journalist, I have covered almost all kinds of events (except sports). In 1970 and 1971 I studied and traveled in the United States. Soon afterward I began to write about contemporary art for museums and art galleries.

"Although my main interest since childhood has been literature, I have always seen in journalism a privileged way of discovering the real race of this world. My first writings were poems. Accepted by the two Paris publishers to whom they were sent in 1968, they were never printed. My first novel *Galpa,* dealing with my experience of India, was considered by many critics to be a prose-poem. This ambiguity, to be considered a poet by novelists and a novelist by poets, still persists.

"In fact, belonging to a generation that can neither testify as a witness of the Shoah nor remain silent, I do not recognize myself in the linear form, the unity, the psychology, or the symbolism of the novel, and I do not recognize the habitual boundaries between prose and poetry. Scattered in dozens of small and unrelated chapters, my books have no real beginning or end. In many ways, they can be seen as an echo of the task that Samuel Beckett assigned to today's writers: 'to find a form to express the chaos.'

"The texts of *The Peacock Emperor Moth* are so short that, with some humor and irony, the writer Stacey Levine could call me the world's shortest writer."

* * *

COLE, Toby 1916-

PERSONAL: Born Marion Cholodenko, January 27, 1916, in Newark, NJ; changed her name for her professional career; daughter of Jacob (a builder) and Bessie Cholodenko; married Ben Irwin (Organizational Secretary of the New Theatre League), 1940 (divorced, 1945); married Aron Krich (a poet, publisher, and psychologist), August 3, 1946; children: John Kalen Krich. *Education:* Attended New Jersey

Junior College, 1935, New Theater School of the New Theatre League, 1936-38, and Cornell University, 1942.

ADDRESSES: Home—2951 Derby St., Berkeley, CA 94705.

CAREER: Federal Theater, WPA, actor, 1938-39; New Theatre League, New York City, organizational secretary, 1939-41; assistant to a Broadway producer Lee Sabinson (*Finian's Rainbow*), 1942; American-Russian Institute, New York City, librarian, 1943-46; Tamara Daykarhanova School for the Stage, registrar, 1946-47; playreader for Broadway producers, 1955-56; Actors and Authors Agency, New York City, founder, 1958, owner, 1958—.

WRITINGS:

(Editor) *Acting: A Handbook of the Stanislavski Method,* Lear, 1947, Crown, 1955.
(Editor and coauthor of introduction and biographical notes with Helen Krich Chinoy) *Actors on Acting: The Theories, Techniques, and Practices of the Great Actors of All Times as Told in Their Own Words,* Crown, 1949, revised edition, 1970.
(Editor with Helen Krich Chinoy) *Directing the Play,* Bobbs-Merrill, 1953, revised edition, 1963, published as *Directors on Directing: A Sourcebook of the Modern Theatre,* Prentice-Hall, 1963.
(Editor) *Playwrights on Playwriting: The Meaning and Making of Modern Drama,* Hill & Wang, 1960.
(Editor) *Venice: A Portable Reader,* Lawrence Hill, 1979.
(Editor) *Florence: A Traveler's Anthology,* Lawrence Hill, 1981.

Also author of unpublished work, *The World's First Ghetto: Venice 1516-1779.* A Toby Cole archive was established in 1983 by the Shields Library of the University of California, Davis.

BIOGRAPHICAL/CRITICAL SOURCES:

PERIODICALS

Library Journal, April 1, 1979; December 1, 1981, p. 2313.
Los Angeles Times Book Review, June 13, 1982, p. 10.
New York Times Book Review, June 3, 1979, p. 3.

COLEMAN, David (Firth) 1945-

PERSONAL: Born March 15, 1945, in Bedford, England; son of Ivor Firth and Beatrice (Jenkins) Coleman; married Julia Elizabeth Gould. *Education:* Attended Bedford Modern School and Sussex University; studied for the theater at the Guildhall School of Music and Dramatic Art.

ADDRESSES: Home—One Newry Rd., St. Margaret's Twickenham, Middlesex TW1 1PJ, England.

CAREER: Actor, singer, director, and author.

MEMBER: British Actors' Equity Association.

AWARDS, HONORS: Most Promising Actor award, *Plays and Players,* 1970, for *1776.*

WRITINGS:

(And author of lyrics) *Canary Blunt* (play), first performed at Latchmere Theatre, London, 1985.

Also author of television plays *Card Trick* and *I'm a Stranger Here Myself.**

* * *

COLEMAN, Ray 1937-1996

OBITUARY NOTICE—See index for *CA* sketch: Born June 15, 1937, in Leicester, England; died of cancer, September 10, 1996, in Shepperton, England. Biographer and journalist. Coleman gained fame for his biographies of John Lennon and Paul McCartney but in the early 1960s he was credited with bringing respectability to the music journalism scene, which at the time was dominated by sensationalist fan magazines. His most recent works were two collaborative autobiographies with Bill Wyman of the Rolling Stones and Gerry Marsden of Gerry and the Pacemakers, *Stone Alone* and *I'll Never Walk Alone,* respectively. Coleman began his journalism career in his hometown of Leicester, then moved on to papers in Brighton and Manchester before going to London in 1960 work on *Melody Maker.* He became editor of the magazine in 1963 and stayed until 1967 when he went to edit *Disc* magazine. But Coleman returned to *Melody Maker* in 1970 and stayed until 1979. Using his background of news reporting, Coleman published investigative and news articles in *Melody Maker* in

addition to the usual personality features and gave rock journalism more mainstream respectability. Coleman covered the rise of The Beatles, Elton John, David Bowie and the Rolling Stones and became trusted by many of them. His two-volume biography *Lennon,* published in 1984 (four years after Lennon's assassination by Mark David Chapman), was approved by the former Beatle's widow, Yoko Ono Lennon. Allan Kozinn, writing in the *New York Times,* noted Coleman was frank about his subjects' shortcomings yet didn't concentrate on "lurid backstage gossip." Coleman went on to publish autobiographies on Eric Clapton (*Clapton!,* 1986), Paul McCartney (*McCartney: Yesterday and Today*), Frank Sinatra (*Frank Sinatra: A Celebration*), and Rod Stewart.

OBITUARIES AND OTHER SOURCES:

PERIODICALS

Los Angeles Times, September 23, 1996, p. A16.
New York Times, September 22, 1996, p. 48.

* * *

COLEMAN, Victor (Art) 1944-

PERSONAL: Born September 11, 1944, in Lvov, Poland; Canadian citizen; married Elizabeth Toon, 1963 (divorced, 1967); married Sarah Miller, 1968 (divorced, 1972); married Jan-Marie Cooke, 1970; children: (first marriage) two daughters and one son; (second marriage) one daughter; (third marriage) one daughter. *Education:* Attended State University of New York, 1963-65; attended University of California, Berkeley Poetry Conference, summer, 1965.

CAREER: Writer. Copy clerk, *Toronto Star,* Toronto, 1962-64; Oxford University Press, Toronto, assistant production manager, 1965-66; The Coach House Press, Toronto, senior editor/production manager, 1967-74; A Space, Toronto, artistic director, 1975-78; National Film Theatre, Kingston, Ontario, programmer/administrator, 1980-82; The Music Gallery, Toronto, programmer/publicist, 1983-86; Coach House Talking Books, Toronto, producer, 1989-90; Toronto Small Press Group, Toronto, executive director, 1992—.

AWARDS, HONORS: Canada Council Arts award, 1974, 1977; Ontario Arts Council Writer's Project grant, 1990; Ontario Arts Council Works in Progress grant, 1991.

WRITINGS:

POETRY

From Erik Satie's Notes to the Music: "Nine Poems." Island Press (Toronto), 1965.
one/ eye/ love, Coach House Press (Toronto), 1967.
Light Verse, Coach House Press, 1969.
Back East, Bowering (Montreal), 1970.
Old Friends' Ghosts: Poems 1963-68, Weed/Flower Press (Toronto), 1970.
Some Plays: On Words, Intrepid Press (Buffalo, NY), 1971.
Strange Love, Coach House Press, 1972.
Parking Lots, Talonbooks (Vancouver), 1972.
America, Coach House Press, 1972.
Stranger, Coach House Press, 1974.
Speech Sucks, Talonbooks, 1974.
Terrific at Both Ends, Coach House Press, 1978.
Captions for the Deaf, Rumour (Toronto), 1979.
From the Dark Wood: Poems 1977-83, Underwhich Editions (Toronto), 1985.
Corrections: Rewriting Six of My First Nine Books, Coach House Press, 1985.
(With David Bolduc) *Honeymoon Suite,* Underwhich Editions, 1990.
Waiting for Alice, Eternal Network (Toronto), 1993.
Lapsed W.A.S.P.: Poems 1978-89, ECW Press (Toronto), 1994.

OTHER

Nothing Heavy or Fragile, Coach House/Music Gallery Talking Books, 1990.

Author of *The Party,* a play produced in 1981; also author of the screenplay *125 Rooms of Comfort,* 1974, and the radio play *Audiothon,* 1975.

* * *

COLLINS, Paul 1936-

PERSONAL: Born December 11, 1936, in Muskegon, MI; married Candace Brown; children: Michael, Michelle, Scott, Eric, Chauvon.

ADDRESSES: Office—Collins Fine Art, 615 Kent Hills Rd. NE, Grand Rapids, MI 49505.

CAREER: Artist for Collins Fine Art; has also worked for Gerald R. Ford Museum, Grand Rapids, MI; Martin Luther King Jr. Center for Nonviolent Social Change, Atlanta, GA; Joseph P. Kennedy Foundation, Washington, DC; Pushkin Museum, Moscow, Russia; and Palace de la Presidence du Senegal, Dakar, Senegal. Member of board of trustees, Robeson Players, 1972-80; member, American Indian Movement, 1972-84; advisory board member, John F. Kennedy Center for the Performing Arts, 1976-80; co-chair for Western Michigan-United Negro College Fund, 1989-90. Designed Martin Luther King Jr. Non-Violent Peace Prize Medal, 1979-80. *Exhibitions:* American Artist, Butler Institute of Art, Youngstown, OH, 1971; American Heritage Exhibition, Corcoran Gallery, Washington, DC, 1973; John F. Kennedy Center for Performing Arts, Washington, DC; Parthenon Museum, Nashville, TN; Museum of Science and Industry, Los Angeles, CA; Children's Museum, Indianapolis, IN; Avery Fisher Hall, Lincoln Center, New York City; and many others.

AWARDS, HONORS: Mead Book Award, Mead Paper Company, 1972; African Culture Award, Senegalese Government, 1973; Special Art Award, Stax Record Company, 1974; Paul Collins Humanist American Artist award, 1976; People's Choice Award, American Painters in Paris, 1976; Government of Senegal named a street after Collins, 1977; Official Naming Ceremony, Pine Ridge, South Dakota, "Bright Eagle," 1977; named among Twenty Outstanding Figure Painters and How They Work, 1979; Arts Council Award, Grand Rapids Arts Council, 1979; Black Achievement Award, 1979; Accademia della Arti e dell Lavoro, Italy, 1980; American Woman Commemorative Plaque, 1983; Fortieth Anniversary Symbol for Israel, 1988-89.

WRITINGS:

Twenty Figure Paintings and How They Work, Watson-Guptil, 1979.

Also illustrator of *Africa for the Africans,* 1972, and *Black Self Determination,* 1972; contributor to *Black Portrait of an African Journey,* 1973. Contributor to *Ebony* magazine.

BIOGRAPHICAL/CRITICAL SOURCES:

PERIODICALS

American Artist, April, 1976.
Booklist, February 15, 1872, p. 486.
Ebony, October, 1971.*

CONN, Stewart 1936-

PERSONAL: Born November 5, 1936, in Glasgow, Scotland; married Judith Clarke, 1963; children: two sons. *Education:* Attended Kilmarnock Academy and Glasgow University.

ADDRESSES: Agent—Lemons Unna and Durbridge Ltd., 24-32 Pottery Lane, London W11 4LZ, England.

CAREER: Writer. BBC, Edinburgh, Radio drama producer, Glasgow, then head of Drama (Radio), 1962-92; Edinburgh Royal Lyceum Theatre, literary adviser, 1973-75. Has served on literature and drama panels of the Scottish Arts Council. *Military service:* Royal Air Force.

AWARDS, HONORS: Eric Gregory award, 1963; Scottish Arts Council poetry prize and publication award, 1968, award, 1978; Edinburgh Festival Fringe award, for drama, 1981, 1988. Fellow, Royal Scottish Academy of Music and Drama, 1990.

WRITINGS:

POETRY

The Chinese Tower, M. Macdonald, 1967.
Stoats in the Sunlight, Hutchinson (London), 1968, published as *Ambush and Others Poems,* Macmillan (New York), 1970.
(With others) *Corgi Modern Poets in Focus 3,* edited by Dannie Abse, Corgi (London), 1971.
An Ear to the Ground, Hutchinson, 1972.
Thunder in the Air, Akros (Preston, Lancashire), 1976.
Under the Ice, Hutchinson, 1978.
In the Kibble Palace: New and Selected Poems, Bloodaxe (Newcastle upon Tyne), 1987.
The Luncheon of the Boating Party, Bloodaxe, 1991.
At the Aviary, Bloodaxe, 1995.
In the Blood, Bloodaxe, 1995.

PLAYS

Break-Down, produced in Glasgow, 1961.
Birds in a Wilderness, produced in Edinburgh, 1964.
I Didn't Always Live Here (produced in Glasgow, 1967), included in *The Aquarium, The Man in the Green Muffler, I Didn't Always Live Here,* 1976.
The King (produced in Edinburgh, 1967; produced in London, 1972), published in *New English Dramatists 14,* Penguin (London), 1970.

Broche, produced in Exeter, 1968.

Fancy Seeing You, Then (produced in London, 1974), published in *Playbill Two,* edited by Alan Durband, Hutchinson (London), 1969.

Victims (includes *The Sword, In Transit,* and *The Man in the Green Muffler*), (produced in Edinburgh, 1970), *In Transit,* New York, Breakthrough Press, 1972; *The Man in the Green Muffler,* included in *The Aquarium, The Man in the Green Muffler, I Didn't Always Live Here,* 1976.

The Burning (produced in Edinburgh, 1971), Calder and Boyars (London), 1973.

A Slight Touch of the Sun, produced in Edinburgh, 1972.

The Aquarium (produced in Edinburgh, 1973), included in *The Aquarium, The Man in the Green Muffler, I Didn't Always Live Here,* 1976.

Count Your Blessings, produced in Pitlochry, Pertshire, 1975.

Thistlewood (produced in Edinburgh, 1975), Woodhouse (Todmorden, Lancashire), 1979.

The Aquarium, The Man in the Green Muffler, I Didn't Always Live Here, Calder (London), 1976.

Play Donkey (produced in Edinburgh, 1977), Woodhouse, 1980.

(With Stephen Macdonald) *Billy Budd,* adaptation of the novel by Herman Melville, produced in Edinburgh, 1978.

Hecuba, produced in Edinburgh, 1979; revised version produced in Glasgow, 1989.

Herman, produced in Edinburgh, 1981; produced in London, 1986.

By the Pool, produced in Edinburgh, 1988; produced in London, 1989.

Hugh Miller, produced in Edinburgh, 1988.

Author of radio plays, including *Any Following Spring,* 1962; *Cadenza for Real,* 1963; *Song of the Clyde,* 1964; *The Canary Cage,* 1967; *Too Late the Phalarope,* from the novel by Alan Paton, 1984. Also author of television plays, including *Wally Dugs Go in Pairs,* 1973; *The Kite,* 1979; and *Blood Hunt,* 1986.

OTHER

Twelve More Modern Scottish Poets, edited by Charles King and Ian Crichton Smith, Hodder & Stoughton (London), 1986.

(Editor) *New Poems 1973-74,* Hutchinson (London), 1974.

(Editor) *Faber Book of Twentieth-Century Scottish Poetry,* Faber (London), 1992.

COOK, Ida (?)-1987
(Mary Burchell)

PERSONAL: Born in Sunderland, England; died in 1987, in England. *Education:* Attended Duchess' School, Northumberland. *Avocational interests:* Opera.

CAREER: Writer. Appeared as one of the first guests on television show *This Is Your Life,* 1956.

MEMBER: Romantic Novelists Association (former president).

WRITINGS:

NOVELS; AS MARY BURCHELL

Wife to Christopher, Mills & Boon (London), 1936.

Nobody Asked Me, Mills & Boon, 1937, Harlequin (Toronto), 1976.

Except My Love, Mills & Boon, 1937, Harlequin, 1973.

Call—And I'll Come, Mills & Boon, 1937, Harlequin, 1973.

But Not for Me, Mills & Boon, 1938, Harlequin, 1971.

Other Lips Have Loved You, Mills & Boon, 1938, as *Two Loves Have I,* Harlequin, 1976.

With All My Worldly Goods, Mills & Boon, 1938, Harlequin, 1961.

Yet Love Remains, Mills & Boon, 1938, Harlequin, 1975.

After Office Hours, Mills & Boon, 1939.

Little Sister, Mills & Boon, 1939, Arcadia House (New York), 1947.

One of the Family, Mills & Boon, 1939.

Such Is Love, Mills & Boon, 1939, Harlequin, 1975.

Yours with Love, Mills & Boon, 1940.

Pay Me Tomorrow, Mills & Boon, 1940, Harlequin, 1974.

One Man's Heart, Mills & Boon, 1940, Harlequin, 1972.

I'll Go with You, Mills & Boon, 1940.

Accompanied by His Wife, Mills & Boon, 1941, Harlequin, 1974.

Always Yours, Mills & Boon, 1941.

Just a Nice Girl, Mills & Boon, 1941, Harlequin, 1975.

Strangers May Marry, Mills & Boon, 1941, Harlequin, 1974.

Where Shall I Wander?, Mills & Boon, 1942.

Thine Is My Heart, Mills & Boon, 1942.

Love Made the Choice, Mills & Boon, 1942, Harlequin, 1975.

Dare I Be Happy?, Mills & Boon, 1943, Harlequin, 1975.

My Old Love Came, Mills & Boon, 1943.

Thanks to Elizabeth, Mills & Boon, 1944.

Take Me with You, Mills & Boon, 1944, Harlequin, 1965.

Dearly Beloved, Mills & Boon, 1944, Harlequin, 1967.

Away Went Love, Mills & Boon, 1945, Harlequin, 1964.

Cinderella after Midnight, Mills & Boon, 1945, Harlequin, 1964.

Meant for Each Other, Mills & Boon, 1945, Harlequin, 1966.

Wife by Arrangement, Mills & Boon, 1946, Harlequin, 1960.

It's Rumoured in the Village, Mills & Boon, 1946, Harlequin, 1973.

First Love—Last Love, Mills & Boon, 1946.

Find Out the Way, Mills & Boon, 1946.

Not without You, Mills & Boon, 1947.

Under Joint Management, Mills & Boon, 1947.

Ward of Lucifer, Mills & Boon, 1947, Harlequin, 1967.

The Brave in Heart, Mills & Boon, 1948, Harlequin, 1975.

If You Care, Mills & Boon, 1948.

Then Come Kiss Me, Mills & Boon, 1948, Harlequin, 1958.

Wish on the Moon, Mills & Boon, 1949.

If This Were All, Mills & Boon, 1949.

I Will Love You Still, Mills & Boon, 1949.

Choose Which You Will, Mills & Boon, 1949, Harlequin, 1966.

At First Sight, Mills & Boon, 1950.

A Letter for Don, Mills & Boon, 1950.

Love Him or Leave Him, Mills & Boon, 1950, Harlequin, 1961.

Tell Me My Fortune, Mills & Boon, 1951, Harlequin, 1975.

Mine for a Day, Mills & Boon, 1951.

Here I Belong, Mills & Boon, 1951.

Over the Blue Mountains, Mills & Boon, 1952, Harlequin, 1960.

Stolen Heart, Mills & Boon, 1952, Harlequin, 1962.

Sweet Adventure, Mills & Boon, 1952, Harlequin, 1968.

A Ring on Her Finger, Mills & Boon, 1953.

No Real Relation, Mills & Boon, 1953.

The Heart Must Choose, Mills & Boon, 1953.

The Heart Cannot Forget, Mills & Boon, 1953, Harlequin, 1966.

Meet Me Again, Mills & Boon, 1954, as *Nurse Alison's Trust,* Harlequin, 1964.

When Love's Beginning, Mills & Boon, 1954, Harlequin, 1969.

Under the Stars of Paris, Mills & Boon, 1954, Harlequin, 1976.

Yours to Command, Mills & Boon, 1955, Harlequin, 1964.

The Prettiest Girl, Mills & Boon, 1955.

Hospital Corridors, Mills & Boon, 1955, Harlequin, 1958.

For Ever and Ever, Mills & Boon, 1956, Harlequin, 1959.

Loving Is Giving, Mills & Boon, 1956, Harlequin, 1967.

On the Air, Mills & Boon, 1956, Harlequin, 1960.

To Journey Together, Mills & Boon, 1956, Harlequin, 1970.

Loyal in All, Mills & Boon, 1957, as *Nurse Marika, Loyal in All,* Harlequin, 1963.

Love Is My Reason, Mills & Boon, 1957, Harlequin, 1959.

Joanna at the Grange, Mills & Boon, 1957.

And Falsely Pledge My Love, Mills & Boon, 1957, Harlequin, 1965.

Dear Sir, Mills & Boon, 1958, Harlequin, 1961.

Dear Trustee, Mills & Boon, 1958, Harlequin, 1959.

The Girl in the Blue Dress, Mills & Boon, 1958, Harlequin, 1976.

Star Quality, Mills & Boon, 1959, as *Surgeon of Distinction,* Harlequin, 1959.

Honey, Mills & Boon, 1959, Harlequin, 1977.

Corner House, Mills & Boon, 1959.

Across the Counter, Mills & Boon, 1960, Harlequin, 1961.

Choose the One You'll Marry, Harlequin, 1960.

Paris—and My Love, Mills & Boon, 1960, Harlequin, 1961.

My Sister Celia, Mills & Boon, 1961, Harlequin, 1971.

Reluctant Relation, Mills & Boon, 1961, Harlequin, 1962.

The Wedding Dress, Mills & Boon, 1962, Harlequin, 1964.

House of Conflict, Mills & Boon, 1962, Harlequin, 1963.

Inherit My Heart, Mills & Boon, 1962, Harlequin, 1963.

Dangerous Loving, Mills & Boon, 1963.

Sweet Meadows, Mills & Boon, 1963.

Do Not Go, My Love, Mills & Boon, 1964, Harlequin, 1972.

The Strange Quest of Anne Weston, Mills & Boon, 1964, as *The Strange Quest of Nurse Anne,* Harlequin, 1965.

Girl with a Challenge, Mills & Boon, 1965, Harlequin, 1970.

Her Sister's Children, Mills & Boon, 1965.

A Song Begins, Mills & Boon, 1965, Harlequin, 1966.

The Other Linding Girl, Mills & Boon, 1966, Harlequin, 1970.

The Broken Wing, Mills & Boon, 1966, Harlequin, 1967, as *Damaged Angel,* Mill & Boon, 1967.

When Love Is Blind, Mills & Boon, 1967, Harlequin, 1968.

Though Worlds Apart, Mills & Boon, 1967, Harlequin, 1969.

The Marshall Family, Mills & Boon, 1967, Harlequin, 1968.

A Home for Joy, Mills & Boon, 1968, Harlequin, 1969.

Missing from Home, Mills & Boon, 1968, Harlequin, 1969.

The Curtain Rises, Mills & Boon, 1969, Harlequin, 1970.

The Rosewood Box, Mills & Boon, 1970.

Child of Music, Mills & Boon, 1970, Harlequin, 1971.

Second Marriage, Mills & Boon, 1971.

Music of the Heart, Harlequin, 1972.

Design for Loving, Mills & Boon, 1972.

Unbidden Melody, Mills & Boon, 1973, Harlequin, 1974.

Song Cycle, Harlequin, 1974.

Remembered Serenade, Harlequin, 1975.

Elusive Harmony, Mills & Boon, 1976, Harlequin, 1977.

Nightingales, Harlequin, 1980.

OTHER

We Followed Our Stars (autobiography), Morrow (New York), 1950.

(With Tito Gobbi) *My Life,* Macdonald & Jane's (London), 1979.

SIDELIGHTS: Under the pseudonym Mary Burchell, Ida Cook wrote over one hundred twenty novels during a career that spanned half a century. Penning romantic fictions that featured the worlds of opera and nursing, Cook successfully sold the first of her many novels to Mill & Boon, a major British publishing house, in 1936. Her goal was initially to earn enough money to fund the repeated trips she her sister Louise were making to Germany in order to aid Jews fleeing the country on the eve of World War II. Cook and her sister brought almost thirty people to safety, using their London flat as a temporary refuge; she recounts these adventures in her 1950 autobiography, *We Followed Our Stars,* which C. B. Burnett calls in the *Christian Science Monitor* "a moving picture of the heroism of two unassuming British subjects in perilous times."

Cook's romantic fiction is characterized by a low-key approach that emphasizes character development rather than scenes of untamed lust and wild passion; a happy ending is also found in each of her novels. In real life, the author and her sister had became ardent opera fans in the 1920s, following the purchase of their first gramophone recordings, and this interest filtered into many of Cook's works, especially *A Song Begins,* which features the character Sir Oscar Warrender, a conductor who is featured in several of Cook's later novels. The majority of Cook's books became well known to North American audiences after they were reprinted by Toronto's Harlequin publisher during the 1960s and 1970s. Throughout her life, Cook developed strong friendships with some of the major talents of twentieth-century opera, including Maria Callas, Clems Krauss, and Tito Gobbi, whom she helped write *My Life,* his 1979 autobiography.

BIOGRAPHICAL/CRITICAL SOURCES:

BOOKS

Cook, Ida, *We Followed Our Stars,* Morrow (New York), 1950.

Twentieth-Century Romance and Gothic Writers, Gale (Detroit), 1982, pp. 109-112.

PERIODICALS

Christian Science Monitor, April 28, 1950, p. 18.
New York Times Book Review, April 23, 1950, p. 24.
Times (London), February 5, 1987.*

* * *

COREN, Michael 1959-

PERSONAL: Born January 15, 1959, in London, England; son of Philip (a taxi driver) and Sheila (a homemaker; maiden name, Schneider) Coren; married Bernadette Barber (a teacher), July 4, 1987; children: Daniel, Lucy, Oliver. *Education:*

Nottingham University, B.A.; attended City University of London. *Politics:* Conservative. *Religion:* Christian.

ADDRESSES: Agent—Lucinda Vardey Agency, 297 Seaton St., Toronto Ontario M5A 2T6, Canada.

CAREER: Journalist and writer. *New Statesman,* London, England, reporter and home news editor; *GAT* (arts magazine), London, theatre editor; *The Tablet,* television editor. Writer and broadcaster, "Arts Comment," CJRT radio, and "Comment," Channel 4 television; interviewer, *Imprint,* TV-Ontario; has made numerous appearances on BBC television and radio. Host of "Lives and Times" series at Toronto's Harbourfront, 1990-94. Instructor, Humber School of Creative Writing, Toronto, 1992-93; researcher for screenwriter Colin Welland.

MEMBER: Royal Canadian Military Institute.

AWARDS, HONORS: Young Journalist of the Year nomination (United Kingdom), 1983.

WRITINGS:

Theatre Royal: One Hundred Years of Stratford East, Quartet (London), 1984.
The Outsiders, Quartet, 1985.
Gilbert: The Man Who Was G. K. Chesterton (biography), J. Cape (London), 1989, Paragon House (New York City), 1990.
The Invisible Man: The Life and Liberties of H. G. Wells (biography), Atheneum (New York City), 1993.
Aesthete: The Frank Diaries of Michael Coren, Random House (New York City), 1993.
The Man Who Created Narnia (juvenile biography), Lester, 1994.
Conan Doyle (biography), Bloomsbury, 1996.

Author of column, "Coren at Large," for *Books in Canada;* columnist for *Globe and Mail, Law Times,* and *Saturday Night.* Contributor of book reviews and articles to periodicals, including *Sunday Times, New Republic, Toronto Star, Maclean's, Toronto Life, Globe and Mail, Literary Review,* and *Reader's Digest.* Associate editor, *Canadian Catholic Review;* contributing editor, *Crisis.* Contributor to reference books, including *One Thousand Makers of the Twentieth Century, Dictionary of National Biography,* and *The Oxford Companion to Crime and Mystery Writing.*

Contributing writer for television productions, including *Man Alive,* for the Canadian Broadcasting Corporation, 1988-89, and *The Outsiders* (with Salman Rushdie) and *Comment,* both for British television; co-author, *Millennium* (televised Christmas special).

SIDELIGHTS: A native of England, journalist Michael Coren lives in Canada, where he is a prolific writer of articles, columns, and reviews on the arts for both British and Canadian publications. In addition, Coren has written several books, including biographies of such literary figures as British poet, novelist, and essayist G. K. Chesterton, whom Coren profiles in his 1989 work, *Gilbert: The Man Who Was G. K. Chesterton.* Opening with an account of Chesterton's death in 1936, Coren looks back at the colorful life of the English writer who was known as much for his books—*The Everlasting Man, Orthodoxy,* and *The Man Who Was Thursday*—as for his slovenly ways, anti-Semitism, and for such memorable sayings as "If a thing's worth doing, it is worth doing badly."

Coren's biography of Chesterton received mixed reviews, although several critics approved the biographer's method of handling charges that Chesterton—the converted-Catholic—was anti-Semitic. "One of the few virtues of Mr. Coren's biography is that he tackles this charge head-on," stated *Observer* reviewer Michael Davie. "He reprints some horrifying examples of Chesterton's attacks on Jews. But he also assembles telling points in Chesterton's defence."

Coren's biography of British novelist and essayist Herbert George Wells, *The Invisible Man: The Life and Liberties of H. G. Wells,* also discusses the professed anti-Semitism of Coren's subject. However, the book gives equal time to Wells's reputation as a philanderer and socialist. While Wells died in 1946, his novels, including *The Time Machine, The War of the Worlds,* and *The Island of Doctor Moreau,* have continued to find new and appreciative readers. Although Coren acknowledges Wells's success as a writer, the biographer sheds unflattering light on Wells's character. Commenting on Coren's portrayal of Wells, Andrew Motion writes in the *Washington Post Book World:* "The final part of [Wells's] long life is a grim story of failing powers and falling sales—and also of history proving that the worst things he had imagined were not bad enough to match reality. Coren softens his tone as he moves through these dark days, but at the close it's his irritation and disapprobation we remember most clearly, not his

sympathy." In another assessment of *Invisible Man,* *National Review* contributor Hadley Arkes reflects on the height of Wells's popularity: a time when the author gained audiences with various world leaders and was considered somewhat of a prophet. "It is Michael Coren's achievement to extract from this stunning record the puzzle that truly needs to be explained," Arkes declares: "How was this exalted reputation achieved by a man whose academic preparation was, to put it gently, thin; whose learning was meager; and whose philosophic understanding—as Mr. Coren makes clear—was indescribably shallow? . . . His friends thought him rollicking good company, and a genius besides. But as Michael Coren makes clear, he was a thoroughly bad man, and altogether a nasty piece of work."

Among Coren's other publications are *The Man Who Created Narnia,* a portrait of the late English author C. S. Lewis, and a biography of Arthur Conan Doyle, creator of the fictional detective Sherlock Holmes. In 1996's *Conan Doyle,* Coren provides a biographical study and no-frills record of the noted British author as both a man and a writer. Although Sherlock Holmes became one of world's most popular fictional characters, his creator, Coren relates, began to resent his creation's popularity. While audience response compelled him to turn out more and more Holmes stories, Conan Doyle desired to explore other subjects, especially historical fiction. Despite the money and popularity he gained from his detective stories, he finally killed Holmes off in one novel, only to infuriate his faithful following of readers. With his readers upset and his popularity on the wane, Conan Doyle grudgingly resurrected Holmes, explaining away his "death" as a hoax plotted by the sleuth. In *Conan Doyle* Coren describes the author's struggles and triumphs as a writer, while also exploring Conan Doyle's staunch devotion to spiritualism.

Conan Doyle was well-received by Patricia Craig in *New Statesman and Society.* "What [Coren] aims to do is set out the facts of Conan Doyle's life with as little fuss or eccentricity as possible," the critic states. "This is a plain and manly study (as befits its subject): short, sturdy and straightforward." Another reviewer, John Bemrose, commented in *Maclean's* that although Conan Doyle is remembered almost exclusively for his Holmes stories, Coren's portrayal of the author's life is "far more than a one-song affair: *Conan Doyle* is a moving portrait of a man who refused to rest on his laurels. The phlegmatic Holmes may have given his author wealth and social position, but Conan Doyle used them to wage tireless

campaigns for social justice, and to further his lifelong investigation of spiritualism, with its attempts to contact the dead." Bemrose also found Coren's biographical study "informative and admiring."

In addition to his biographical studies, Coren has written *Aesthete: The Frank Diaries of Michael Coren,* a collection of his writings as they appeared in *Frank* magazine. These humorous selections satirize various Canadian personalities, including Prime Minister Brian Mulroney, and many aspects of Canadian life, even targeting the Canadian Roman Catholic Church. "Coren's saving grace," writes George Kaufman in *Books in Canada,* "is that he spreads his malice indiscriminately across all classes, races, beliefs, and genders. In spite of the frequent cheap shots, *Aesthete* is a valuable mirror to Canadian society and deserves to be read by more than the small circle of *Frank* readers."

BIOGRAPHICAL/CRITICAL SOURCES:

PERIODICALS

Books in Canada, September 1993, pp. 40-41.
Globe and Mail (Toronto), March 11, 1989.
Horn Book, May/June, 1995, p. 370.
London Review of Books, April 8, 1993, pp. 17-18.
Maclean's, February 5, 1996, p. 60.
National Review, January 24, 1994, pp. 62, 64-65.
New Statesman and Society, January 12, 1996, p. 40.
Observer, January 29, 1989, p. 48.
Publishers Weekly, January 5, 1990, p. 58.
Times Literary Supplement, March 31, 1989, p. 330; January 15, 1993, p. 5.
Washington Post Book World, August 22, 1993, pp. 8-9.

* * *

COSSOLOTTO, Matthew 1953-

PERSONAL: Born November 27, 1953, in Detroit, MI; son of Lou and Virginia (maiden name, Ludascher) Cossolotto; married Lora Lackey, 1984; children: Katherine Hope. *Ethnicity:* "Italian American." *Education:* University of California, Berkeley, B.A., 1977; attended Lund University, 1975-76. *Politics:* Independent. *Avocational interests:* Languages, travel, cultural and international studies, politics and voting systems, tennis.

ADDRESSES: Home and office—3481 Wildwood St., Yorktown Heights, NY 10598; fax (914)245-9713.

CAREER: U.S. House of Representatives, Washington, D.C., legislative assistant to Congressman Leon E. Panetta, 1977-81, special assistant to Speaker James C. Wright, Jr., 1983-88; served in the Peace Corps, Sierra Leone, West Africa, 1981-82; MCI Communications Corp., Washington, D.C., senior manager of the Corporate Communications Department and speechwriter for William G. McGowan, 1988-92; PepsiCo Foods & Beverages International, Somers, NY, director of communications, 1992-95; GTE Corp., Stamford, CT, director of communications, 1995-96; Ovations International, Inc., Yorktown Heights, NY, founder and president, 1996—. President and board chair of the Center for Voting and Democracy, 1992-96. Has appeared on television and radio news programs.

MEMBER: Phi Beta Kappa.

WRITINGS:

NONFICTION

Almanac of Transatlantic Politics, Brassey's, 1991.
Almanac of European Politics: 1995, Congressional Quarterly (Washington, D.C.), 1995.

Contributor to *Vital Speeches of the Day,* 1996; also contributor to periodicals, including *Wall Street Journal, Washington Post, Christian Science Monitor, Los Angeles Times,* and *Newsday.*

WORK IN PROGRESS: Updates of the almanac; *The Reforming of America: A History of Voting and Democracy in the U.S.*

SIDELIGHTS: Matthew Cossolotto has had a distinguished career in the communications field. Born in Detroit, Michigan, in 1953, he began his career in the area of politics, serving as a legislative assistant to then-Congressman Leon Panetta in 1977. He took time off from working in Washington, D.C., to go to Sierra Leone, West Africa, as a Peace Corps volunteer. When he returned, Cossolotto became special assistant to Speaker of the House James Wright; he stayed in this capacity until 1988. He then left the political arena to become senior manager of MCI's Corporate Communications Department and serve as speechwriter to MCI's founder and chair, William G. McGowan. He fulfilled similar functions at PepsiCo Foods & Beverages International and GTE Corpora-

tion before starting his own communications and public affairs company, Ovations International, in 1996. With Ovations, Cossolotto plans to sponsor seminars on effective public speaking and other topics.

During his years of government service, Cossolotto made many trips to Europe. He visited Germany as part of a staff exchange program between the U.S. Congress and Germany's parliamentary body, the Bundestag. He also studied in Sweden during the course of his college education. He put some of the expertise gained from these experiences into his books, *Almanac of Transatlantic Politics* and *Almanac of European Politics: 1995. Almanac of European Politics: 1995* "is a compendium of information about the politics and government of all the countries in Europe," explained Valeria DeBenedetta in the Westchester, New York *Reporter Dispatch.* The Almanac contains up-to-date information about election results, political parties, and government leaders throughout Western Europe. The volume also contains facts about the European Union, the organization of European countries which has its own governmental agencies, including a popularly elected parliament.

In addition to his career in communications, Cossolotto has continued his involvement in politics. He has served during much of the 1990s as the founding president and board chair of the Center for Voting and Democracy, a nonpartisan organization concerned with reforming the voting system and raising voting levels in the United States. One of Cossolotto's causes within this organization, informed by his study of European politics, is to transform the voting system in the United States from a winner-take-all plurality system to one of proportional representation—the system followed by most European nations. The author explained the concept in *Speechwriter's Newsletter:* "Proportional systems come in all shapes and sizes, but the fundamental feature is that the parties or candidates win legislative seats in rough proportion to the votes received in an election. . . . John Stuart Mill and some of the other thinkers that are revered in political thought were real big proponents of proportional voting." He commented to DeBenedetta: "A large percentage of the population [in the United States] has never voted for a winner. That begins to gnaw at you and wear you down." A speech Cossolotto made on this issue, "What the U.S. Can Learn From European Politics," was included in *Vital Speeches of the Day* in 1996. An article in the *Speechwriter's Newsletter* confirmed that "Cossolotto is one of those rare speechwriters whose work has

appeared in *Vital Speeches* under his own name."
Cossolotto told *Speechwriter's Newsletter* he was
grateful for the inclusion of his speech in that publi-
cation because "it gets the idea of proportional voting
out to a different audience."

BIOGRAPHICAL/CRITICAL SOURCES:

PERIODICALS

Reporter Dispatch, August 7, 1995.
Speechwriter's Newsletter, March 1, 1996, pp. 1-2.

* * *

COX, Maxwell E(varts) 1922-1996

OBITUARY NOTICE—See index for *CA* sketch: Born
September 26, 1922, in Plainfield, NJ; died Septem-
ber 5, 1996, in Brooklyn, NY. Lawyer, civic leader,
and author. Cox was a prominent attorney in New
York and worked for the law firm that represented
billionaire Howard Hughes. He published a novel,
The Point of the Game, in 1969. Cox attended
Harvard University and Harvard Law School and was
hired by the Manhattan law firm of Simpson, Thacher
and Bartlett upon graduation. He then went on to
Davis and Cox, the firm that represented industrialist
Howard Hughes. Cox also worked with Jacobs,
Persinger and Parker for the past 15 years. Outside
the world of law, Cox was chair of the board of
governors for St. Ann's Episcopal School in Brooklyn
Heights and was senior warden of the school's parish,
St. Ann and the Holy Trinity. Cox was the brother of
Archibald Cox, the special prosecutor in the
Watergate case who was fired by President Nixon.

OBITUARIES AND OTHER SOURCES:

PERIODICALS

New York Times, September 8, 1996, p. 47

* * *

CROWE, Cameron 1957-

PERSONAL: Born July 13, 1957, in Palm Springs,
CA; married Nancy Wilson (a musician), c. 1990.
Education: Attended California State University.

ADDRESSES: Home—Seattle, WA. *Office*—Los An-
geles, CA. *Agent*—c/o Creative Artists Agency, 9830
Wilshire Blvd., Beverly Hills, CA 90212.

CAREER: Associated with *Rolling Stone,* San Fran-
cisco (now New York City), 1973-82; writer, 1981—;
screenwriter, 1982—; director of films, including *Say
Anything,* 1989; *Singles,* 1991; and *Jerry Maguire*
(and producer), 1997. Appeared in film *American Hot
Wax,* 1978. Creative consultant, *Fast Times at
Ridgemont High* (television series), 1986.

AWARDS, HONORS: Grammy Award nomination,
best album notes, Association of Recording Arts and
Sciences, 1986, for Bob Dylan's *Biograph.*

WRITINGS:

BOOKS

Fast Times at Ridgemont High: A True Story, Simon
 & Schuster, 1981.

SCREENPLAYS

Fast Times at Ridgemont High (adapted from Crowe's
 book), Universal, 1982.
The Wild Life, Universal, 1984.
Say Anything, Twentieth Century-Fox, 1989.
Singles, Warner Bros., 1991.
Jerry Maguire, TriStar, 1997.

OTHER

Contributor to periodicals, including *Circus, Creem,*
and *Rolling Stone.* Author of the album notes for Bob
Dylan's *Biograph* and Led Zeppelin's boxed set,
1990.

SIDELIGHTS: Cameron Crowe is a former *Rolling
Stone* writer who has distinguished himself as a film-
maker. Crowe came to *Rolling Stone* when he was
still in his teens after graduating from high school at
the age of fifteen. In 1978, while writing for *Rolling
Stone,* Crowe concocted a notion for a book project:
He would go undercover and re-enter high school for
one year, to record his experiences there. Crowe
soon found a cooperative school principal, who thus
enabled Crowe to regain first-hand experience of
high-school life. Once back in school, Crowe decided
to emphasize the lives of his more typical classmates.
"They're anonymous Joes who are *not* unwed moth-
ers or angel dust cases," he told Richard Harrington

in the *Washington Post,* "they're just average kids slugging through life."

The result of Crowe's endeavor was *Fast Times at Ridgemont High: A True Story,* in which he recounts a full range of events and incidences occurring throughout the 1978-79 school year at Ridgemont High School in Redondo Beach, California. Crowe's volume details the usual school occasions such as homecoming, the prom, and graduation. In addition, he relates several more personal details of fellow students. Notable here is one student's reflection on getting an abortion.

Some reviewers decried *Fast Times at Ridgemont High* as unconvincing while others found it plausible and, moreover, entertaining. *Washington Post* reviewer Jonathan Yardley was among the volume's detractors, arguing that Crowe's emphasis on life outside the classroom rendered his account "too predictable and too melodramatic to ring true." Charles Kaiser, however, wrote in the *New York Times Book Review* that *Fast Times at Ridgemont High* "is always pleasantly amusing" and he contended that "you'll probably laugh out loud at Cameron Crowe's often hilarious account of one of our least changed rituals."

In 1982 Crowe adapted *Fast Times at Ridgemont High* as a screenplay. Among the film's enthusiasts was Janet Maslin, who wrote in *New York Times* that Crowe and director Amy Heckerling had created an "appealing teen-age comedy with something of a fresh perspective on the subject." *Fast Times at Ridgemont High* was sufficiently successful to warrant Crowe further opportunity to work in Hollywood. He responded by writing the screenplay for *The Wild Life,* a teen-age sex comedy that ostensibly concerns a young man's trials and tribulations during the summer between high school and college. But Gene Siskel commented in his *Chicago Tribune* review that the film "is totally preoccupied with sex" and disliked the "depiction of males exploiting females." Janet Maslin, in her *New York Times* appraisal of *The Wild Life,* noted that Crowe "has come up with some promising new possibilities."

After *The Wild Life,* Crowe decided to direct his own work. In 1989 he completed *Say Anything,* a teen-oriented comedy about the unlikely high-school romance between an earnest youth and the school's most beautiful, most intelligent female student. Sheila Benson charged in her *Los Angeles Times* review that Crowe manages to succeed in his endeavor "to dig among the slag heaps of an almost mined-out genre—

the teen-age movie—and come up with one of the nicest of the species, a film of warmth, insight, humor and surprising originality." Likewise, *Chicago Tribune* reviewer Dave Kehr called *Say Anything* "a beautiful film, full of wit, freshness and surprise and graced with a vivid, convincing sense of character and place." Jay Carr, writing in *Boston Globe,* simply proclaimed *Say Anything* "a pleasure."

Crowe followed *Say Anything* by writing and directing *Singles,* a comedy about young adults living in Seattle. Among the characters in this film are Janet, an aspiring architect working as a waitress; Janet's lover, Cliff, a woefully dim and untalented rock singer; Janet and Cliff's neighbor Linda, an environmentalist; and Linda's new romantic interest, fellow environmentalist Steve. *Singles* charts the interactions of these and other characters as they wrestle with the problems of their lives. Desson Howe, writing in *Washington Post,* noted that *Singles* is "not art, but it's always diverting." Janet Maslin, writing in *New York Times* noted that the film "speaks so wryly to all the fun and trouble of being newly independent in one's early 20's."

Singles served as further indication that Crowe is content writing about life's more mundane aspects and individuals. "I really am happy writing about the people who don't get written about," Crowe told *New York Times* critic Michael Walker. He seemed unbothered by the seemingly uncommercial nature of such people as compelling film characters. He described his characters as "people who aren't tremendously glamorous, just living their lives."

BIOGRAPHICAL/CRITICAL SOURCES:

PERIODICALS

Boston Globe, April 14, 1989, p. 21.
Chicago Tribune, September 9, 1981; August 13, 1982; October 2, 1984; April 14, 1989.
Los Angeles Times, September 28, 1984; April 14, 1989; September 27, 1992, pp. 6, 80-81.
Nation, November 21, 1981, pp. 547-51.
New Statesman and Society, January 15, 1993, p. 34.
New Yorker, May 15, 1989, pp. 122-23.
New York Times, September 3, 1982; September 28, 1984; April 14, 1989, p. C11; September 6, 1992, p. B7-8; September 18, 1992, p. C3.
New York Times Book Review, September 13, 1981, p. 16.
Rolling Stone, October 1, 1992, pp. 57-60.

Washington Post, September 9, 1981, p. C9; August 13, 1982; October 1, 1984; April 14, 1989, p. C1; September 18, 1992, p. WW48.*

* * *

CROZIER, Andrew 1943-

PERSONAL: Born in 1943. *Education:* Cambridge University, M.A.; University of Essex, Wivenhoe, Ph.D.

ADDRESSES: Office—University of Sussex, Falmer, Brighton, Sussex BN1 9RH, U.K.

CAREER: University of Sussex, Brighton, senior lecturer in English.

WRITINGS:

POETRY

Loved Litter of Time Spent, Sumbooks (Buffalo), 1967.
Train Rides: Poems from '63 and '64, R. (Pampisford, Cambridgeshire), 1968.
Walking on Grass, Ferry Press (London), 1969.
In One Side and Out the Other, with John James and Tom Phillips, Ferry Press, 1970.
Neglected Information, Blacksuede Boot Press (Sidcup, Kent), 1973.
The Veil Poem, Burning Deck (Providence, RI), 1974.
Printed Circuit, Street (Cambridge), 1974.
Seven Contemporary Sun Dials, with Ian Potts, Ian Potts (Brighton), 1975.
Pleats, Great Works (Bishops Stortford, Hertfordshire), 1975.
Duets, Circle Press (Guildford, Surrey), 1976.
Residing, Aggie Weston's (Belper, Derbyshire), 1976.
High Zero, Street (Cambridge), 1978.
Were There, Many Press (London), 1978.
Utamaro Variations, Tetrad (London), 1982.
All Where Each Is, Agneau 2 (Edinburgh), 1985.

(With Donald Davie and C.H. Sisson) *Ghosts in the Corridor,* Paladin (London), 1992.

OTHER

(Editor with Tim Longville) *A Various Art,* Carcanet (Manchester), 1987.

* * *

CULLINAN, Patrick 1932-

PERSONAL: Born May 21, 1932, in Pretoria, South Africa. *Education:* Magdalen College, Oxford, B.A., M.A. (Italian and Russian), 1953.

CAREER: Freelance writer, 1963—. Farmer and sawmiller, eastern Transvaal, 1953-79; Co-founder of Bateleur Press; *The Bloody Horse,* editor, 1980-81; University of the Western Cape, lecturer in English, 1982-92.

AWARDS, HONORS: Olive Schreiner award, 1980; Pringle prize, 1983, 1984, 1990; Sanlam Literary award, 1989.

WRITINGS:

POETRY

The Horizon Forty Miles Away, Polygraph (Johannesburg), 1973.
The White Hall in the Orchard, David Philip (Cape Town), 1984.
Selected Poems 1961-1991, Artists' Press (Johannesburg), 1992.

Author of *Today Is Not Different,* 1978.

OTHER

Robert Jacob Gordon 1743-1795: The Man and His Travels at the Cape. Winchester-Struik (Cape Town), 1992.

D

DALE, Ernest 1917-1996

OBITUARY NOTICE—See index for *CA* sketch: Born February 4, 1917, in Hamburg, Germany; died of a cerebral aneurysm, August 16, 1996, in Manhattan, New York. Educator, business consultant, and writer. Dale gained recognition as a management consultant to firms such as International Business Machines (IBM) and DuPont. While pursuing post-graduate work, Dale began his teaching career in 1944 at Yale University. From there he moved on to Cornell University and the University of Virginia, among others. During the 1950s and 1960s, he served as the president of Ernest Dale Associates, a management consulting firm. He contributed articles to periodicals such as *New Republic* and *Atlantic Monthly*. His major works include *Management: Theory and Practice, Organization, The Decision-Making Process in the Commercial Use of High-Speed Computers, The Great Organizers,* and *Back to Basic: The Memoirs of Ernest Dale.*

OBITUARIES AND OTHER SOURCES:

BOOKS

Who's Who in Finance and Industry, 27th edition, Marquis, 1991.

PERIODICALS

New York Times, September 8, 1996, p. 47.

D'AMBROSIO, Charles

PERSONAL: Education: graduated from the Iowa Writer's Workshop.

ADDRESSES: Agent—c/o Little, Brown, and Company Inc., 34 Beacon St., Boston, MA 02108.

CAREER: Freelance writer.

AWARDS, HONORS: "The Point" included in *Best American Short Stories,* 1991; Aga Khan Fiction Prize, 1993, from the *Paris Review;* finalist in the first fiction category, 1995, *Los Angeles Times* Book Prizes, for *The Point.*

WRITINGS:

The Point (short stories; contains "The Point," "Her Real Name," "American Bullfrog," "Jacinta," "All Aboard," "Lyricism," and "Open House"), Little, Brown (Boston, MA), 1995.

Also contributor of stories to anthologies and periodicals, including *Best American Short Stories,* 1991; *New Yorker* and *Paris Review.*

SIDELIGHTS: Fiction writer and graduate of the Iowa Writer's Workshop Charles D'Ambrosio had one of his tales published in 1991's *Best American Short Stories.* Another garnered him the 1993 Aga Khan Fiction Prize from the *Paris Review* before his first collection of stories, *The Point,* was published in

1995. *The Point* has been widely acclaimed and has itself won another honor for D'Ambrosio—the book was a finalist in the first fiction category of 1995's *Los Angeles Times* Book Prizes.

The title tale of *The Point* was first published in the *New Yorker,* and later reprinted in *Best American Short Stories.* Its protagonist, Kurt Pittman, has lost his father to suicide. His mother, though still living, has become a hopeless alcoholic since her husband took his own life. She throws huge parties for other men and women who like to escape their relationship problems by getting drunk, and Kurt's function at these soirees is to escort overindulgent guests safely home. He listens to their troubles, and they often reward him with a few dollars. "I suppose it was better than a paper route," he says, during the course of his narration. Kurt's work for the particular evening of the story is shepherding home Mrs. Gurney, whose husband is cheating on her. The "point" of the story's title, which he has learned from listening to his mother's needy circle, in Kurt's words, is that "at a certain age, a black hole emerged in the middle of your life, and everything got sucked into it, and you knew, forever afterward, that it was there . . . and you pretended it wasn't there and never looked directly at it, if you could manage the trick." Later in the story, Kurt reveals that he was the one who discovered his father's body after he'd shot himself.

"Like 'The Point,'" asserted James McManus in the *New York Times Book Review,* "the six other stories in Mr. D'Ambrosio's collection are shapely and satisfying. The emotional territory he covers is familiar—a world of lapsed Catholics, of estranged married couples, of too-early death—but he consistently manages to isolate moments of understated splendor, to take unexpected angles on his characters' grief and desire." "Her Real Name" concerns a terminally-ill girl who flees her religiously strict father with a soldier; "Jacinta" covers the disintegration of a marriage after the death of a child; and "All Aboard" uses a galley ship rowed by slaves as a metaphor for a Catholic funeral. Erin McGraw, critiquing the fiction collection in the *Georgia Review,* offered these words of praise: "D'Ambrosio isn't afraid of letting humor seep into his stories about grief, meanness mix with innocence, farce play out in one ring while tragedy occurs in the next." She went on to remark that "D'Ambrosio fills his stories with shifting currents and angles of light, and the tragedies that sit at their centers are partially obscured by ordinary, daily, fussy life—cleaning up houses and buying newspa-

pers. The tragedies are no less real and no less acknowledged, but the newly clean houses are real too, and the newspapers, and everything modifies everything else." Leigh Allison Wilson, reviewing *The Point* in the *Washington Post Book World,* concluded: "Whether he's writing about a marriage gone off the tracks because of the death of a friend, the death of a child, or about a family blown apart by madness and suicide, at the heart of Charles D'Ambrosio's stories is the lolling, seductive possibility of hope, of clarity, of a perfect moment."

BIOGRAPHICAL/CRITICAL SOURCES:

BOOKS

D'Ambrosio, Charles, *The Point,* Little, Brown (Boston, MA), 1995.

PERIODICALS

Georgia Review, winter, 1995, pp. 950-959.
New York Times Book Review, February 26, 1995, p. 8.
Washington Post Book World, April 16, 1995, p. 11.*

* * *

DARUWALLA, Keki N(asserwanji) 1937-

PERSONAL: Born January 24, 1937, in Lahore, Pakistan; married; children: one child. *Education:* Attended Government College, Ludhiana; University of the Punjab, Lahore, M.A. (English).

ADDRESSES: Office—c/o Oxford University Press, Post Box 43, YMCA Library Bldg., 1st Floor, Jai Singh Rd., New Delhi 110 001, India.

CAREER: Writer. Member of the Indian Police Service, 1958—; superintendent of police, 1962—.

WRITINGS:

POETRY

Under Orion, Writers Workshop (Calcutta), 1970.
Apparition in April, Writers Workshop, 1971.
Crossing the Rivers, Oxford University Press (New Delhi), 1976.
Winter Poems, Allied (New Delhi), 1980.

The Keeper of the Dead, Oxford University Press, 1982.
Landscapes, Oxford University Press, 1987.

SHORT STORIES

Sword and Abyss, Vikas (Sahibabad), 1979.

OTHER

(Editor) *Two Decades of Indian Poetry 1960-1980,* Vikas, 1980.

* * *

DAVIDOW, Michael
 See DAVIDOW, Mike

* * *

DAVIDOW, Mike 1913-1996

OBITUARY NOTICE—See index for *CA* sketch: Born Michael Davidow, February 15, 1913, in Russia; died September 4, 1996, in Moscow, Russia. Journalist and author. Davidow was a naturalized U.S. citizen and served in the U.S. Army during World War II, but spent the last 13 years of his life in Moscow as a correspondent for the American Communist Party newspaper *People's Weekly World.* Educated at Brooklyn College, Davidow had a series of odd jobs before starting his writing career with the *Daily World,* formerly the *Daily Worker.* Davidow also authored several books and plays with a socialist outlook. In 1973 he wrote *Life without Landlords.* He also wrote the plays *The Long Life* (1964), *Eagle-Doves* (1966) and *The Closest Battlefield* (1969). Davidow remained a Communist even after the fall of the Soviet Union and sided with the hard-line parliamentarians during the 1993 showdown with Russian President Boris Yeltsin, remaining in the parliament building as it was shelled by tanks. Davidow also authored a pamphlet series from 1974 to 1976 titled *The Soviet Union through the Eyes of an American.*

OBITUARIES AND OTHER SOURCES:

PERIODICALS

Chicago Tribune, September 9, 1996, sec. 4, p. 7.

DAVIS, Bart 1950-

PERSONAL: Born December 13, 1950, in New York, NY; son of Byron and Beverly Davis; married; wife's name, Sharon (an attorney); children: Jordan, Ali. *Education:* State University of New York at Stony Brook, B.A., 1971, M.S.W., 1976. *Avocational interests:* Tennis, skeet shooting, coaching soccer.

ADDRESSES: Home—Port Washington, NY. *Agent*—Robert Gottlieb, William Morris Agency, 1325 Avenue of the Americas, New York, NY 10019. *E-mail*—author@li.net.

CAREER: Novelist and screenwriter. Science Museum of Long Island, member of board of directors; writing teacher at public schools; lecturer at educational institutions, including Herbert H. Lehman College of the City University of New York and State University of New York at Stony Brook. Associate producer of motion picture *Love or Money,* 1990.

MEMBER: Authors Guild, Association of Former Intelligence Officers, Writers Guild of America East.

WRITINGS:

NOVELS

Blind Prophet, Doubleday (New York City), 1983.
A Conspiracy of Eagles, Bantam (New York City), 1984.
Takeover, Bantam, 1986.
Full Fathom Five, Bantam, 1987.
The Doomsday Exercise, Bantam, 1989.
Raise the Red Dawn, Pocket Books (New York City), 1990.
Destroy the Kentucky, Pocket Books, 1991.
Atlantic Run, Pocket Books, 1993.
Voyage of the Storm, Pocket Books, 1995.
The Midnight Partner, Bantam, 1995.

OTHER

(Co-author) *Love or Money* (screenplay), Hemdale Releasing, 1990.
Full Fathom Five (screenplay), Concorde, 1991.
(With George Kalinsky) *Shooting Stars: The Collected Images of George Kalinsky* (nonfiction), Simon & Schuster (New York City), 1992.

Author of the videotape *Baby Alive.* Contributor to magazines.

WORK IN PROGRESS: A novel; a one-hour television series about fighter pilots.

SIDELIGHTS: Bart Davis told *CA:* "I am principally a novelist and screenwriter. My novels have been released internationally and translated into several other language, such as Japanese, Italian, Norwegian, and Bulgarian. I have also done *Shooting Stars,* a nonfiction book, in collaboration with the official photographer for Madison Square Garden, and a videotape on accident prevention for children. Most of my articles are on writing, education, and parenting.

"I have been fortunate to find two careers to love. The first one, years ago, in teaching, led to articles on a program that my partner and I had created for disruptive and troubled students in the Three Village School District. That led to a first novel and nine more.

"I think I am best as a structuralist, knowing how to plot and theme my work. I often have to remind myself to pay equal attention to the characters. As one editor put it: if *they* are interesting, everything they do is interesting. I write every day, for at least six hours, more if I am in a section that simply cannot be put down.

"*The Midnight Partner,* my latest novel, enabled me to explore several themes not possible in previous books: the stresses and strains of long marriage, the difficulty of raising children, the emotions triggered by infidelity, and the pressures of our North Shore lifestyle."

BIOGRAPHICAL/CRITICAL SOURCES:

PERIODICALS

Chicago Tribune, July 2, 1995.

* * *

DAVIS, Marilyn (Illaine) 1930-

PERSONAL: Born July 5, 1930, in Chatham, Ontario, Canada; daughter of Norman Huxley (a pharmacist) and Myrtle May (a homemaker; maiden name, McCreight) Davis. *Education:* University of Western Ontario, B.A., 1954, M.A., 1964; Ontario College of Education, University of Toronto, summer, 1955 and 1956; King's College, University of London, London, England, Ph.D., 1980. *Politics:* "Liberal and/or So-cialist (New Democratic Party)." *Religion:* Protestant. *Avocational interests:* Reading, swimming, bicycling, cats.

*ADDRESSES: Office—*The Writers Union of Canada, 24 Ryerson Ave., Toronto, Ontario M5T 2P3, Canada.

CAREER: University of Western Ontario, London, Ontario, Canada, began as teaching fellow, became instructor of English, 1960-64; University of Saskatchewan, Saskatoon, Canada, began as lecturer, became assistant professor of English, 1966-72; independent researcher. Research associate and lecturer on the subject of Nellie McClung.

MEMBER: Association of Canadian and Quebec Literatures, The Melville Society, Writer's Union of Canada.

AWARDS, HONORS: Philosophy Award, Brescia College, 1954; Canada Council fellow, 1959-60, 1965-66, 1967-68, 1970-71; Ontario Graduate fellow, 1963-64; Honor of Commonwealth scholarship, 1967-68; Study Leave grant, University of Saskatchewan, 1967-68; Canada Council summer grant, 1969; Canada Council research associate's grant, 1973-74; Social Sciences and Humanities Research Council of Canada allowance, 1980; Harbourfront International Festival of Authors (Toronto, Canada), invited to deliver an address on the subject of Nellie L. McClung, 1993; regional history award (Canadian Prairie and Northwest Territory), Canadian Historical Association of the Learned Societies of Canada, 1994, for *Firing the Heather: The Life and Times of Nellie McClung.*

WRITINGS:

(With Mary Hallett) *Firing the Heather: The Life and Times of Nellie McClung,* Fifth House Press (Saskatoon), 1993.
(Editor) *Stories Subversive: Through the Field with Gloves Off, Short Stories by Nellie L. McClung,* University of Ottawa Press (Ottawa, Ontario, Canada), 1996.

Contributor to journals, including *Tamarack Review, Canadian Literature, Journal of Canadian Fiction,* and *Canadian Children's Literature.* Reviewer for various publications, including *London Free Press, Alphabet, Canadian Forum,* and *Toronto Star.*

WORK IN PROGRESS: Two articles about Nellie L. McClung for periodical publication; edit and write

introduction for *Belinda; or, The Rivals,* by Abraham Holmes; a book on Herman Melville's *The Confidence Man.*

SIDELIGHTS: Marilyn Davis told *CA:* "My writing career, to date, is largely academic, and grows out of research projects and the adaptation of dissertations for book publication, though there is a variety of material in my mind to be turned into fiction—or, at this stage, *attempts* at fiction writing. My academic research tends more towards the explication of texts, and my particular interest is in those kinds of fictions which are 'difficult' and enigmatic because of their rich and complex texture of myth and symbol. It is satisfying detective work, and my hope is that this kind of analysis exposes the essential meaning and significance of the work in such a way as to make it more accessible and enriching to the interested reader or, at the very least, provocative in such a way as to stimulate further discussion, even controversy.

"A very different kind of work lay in my cooperation, with history colleague Mary Hallett, in the co-authoring of a biography, *Firing the Heather: The Life and Times of Nellie McClung.* At first I resisted involvement in a project whose framework was largely historical, as I am a specialist in nineteenth century North American Literature, Canadian and American. I finally agreed, however, and learned to enjoy working with varied kinds of manuscript material in Canadian provincial and federal archives.

"I knew little about McClung, Canadian first wave feminist, suffragist, social reformer, popular novelist, and short story writer. Her work had been passed off by orthodox literary critics as sentimental romanticism, and I was dubious about what more I could say. My study revealed the opposite: that McClung's literary stance was essentially anti-romantic, largely satiric, and realistic in its approach to women's issues. She dealt with many hush-hush topics of her time, such as: wife and child abuse, the maddening loneliness of pioneer farm women in their isolated prairie environment, the legalization of contraceptives to enable a woman to have control over her own body in place of constant debilitating pregnancies, and the need to change those laws which deprived women of their social and legal rights.

"That male critics in a pre-feminist period or with an anti-feminist bias should determine a woman author's place in Canadian literary history with no sensitivity to women's consciousness (I even wondered if they and I were reading the same texts!), seemed deplor-

able and in need of correction. Examining McClung's fiction from a feminist perspective I discovered strong-willed heroines who battle for self-determination by refusing the feminine limitations society would impose on them. They defy the patriarchal system and question the secondary nature of being female. Such stories are subversive for they attack stereotypical, sex-prejudiced views of women. Their heroines are rebels and necessary counter ideals to the passive, self-sacrificing Victorian heroines. Such work warrants special attention, in part, because many of these women's concerns are still with us, and also because we seek, in women's studies, to recover and understand the experiences of women, to reconstruct their past, and challenge the largely male critic's opinion of a woman writer's place in literary history. Taking a feminist literary perspective enriched and confirmed my own feminism.

"On the political side it is interesting to note that McClung was not only sought out as a speaker in Canada for her humorous and common sense attitude to the women suffrage issue, and for her witty retorts to male hecklers that had her audiences rolling in the aisles and coming back for more. Carrie Chapman Catt, president of the National American Women's Suffrage Association (NAWSA) in the United States, had heard McClung speak in Minneapolis, was impressed, and asked McClung to carry out a speaking tour in the U.S. in the fall of 1916. McClung proved as great a hit in the States as she was in Canada. As one American reporter noted: 'somebody seemed not to have opened the door but to have taken the side off the house and a west Canadian breeze blew in. . . . Everyone knew instinctively that here was a suffrage advocate of a type different from any ever seen here before. . . .' NAWSA workers were so impressed with the impact she made that they invited her back for tours in 1917 and 1918. In Minnesota workers pressed her to come to Duluth: 'the women in the northern part of the state are very much in need of rousing and we feel that you are just the person to do it.' The Canadian, Nellie McClung, took an active part in the American suffrage campaigns, as she did in Canada where she was known as the unofficial leading feminist and suffragist, and one of the most popular novelists of her day. The importance of a feminist biography like *Firing the Heather* is that it tells Canadian women today how they got where they are, and that many of the women's issues of McClung's day are still relevant to today's feminist activists. Much of McClung's fiction reflects her feminist concerns, but has not been studied by Canadian literary critics."

DEARMER, Geoffrey 1893-1996

OBITUARY NOTICE—See index for *CA* sketch: Born March 21, 1893, in London, England; died August 18, 1996, in Birchington-on-Sea, Kent, England. Author. Dearmer, who devoted his career to literary occupations, is remembered as one of the esteemed poets of the World War I era. After enlisting in the British Army in 1914 at the onset of war in Europe, Dearmer penned verse about his experiences in battle in Gallipoli, Turkey, and The Somme, France. From 1936 until 1958, Dearmer worked as an examiner and censor of plays to Lord Chamberlain. He served in that role until the job was eliminated. During most of those years, and continuing on to 1960, he also was on staff of the *Children's Hour* as an editor and contributor. Throughout his career, Dearmer published his work. Reviewers often commended his war poetry saying that Dearmer, a religious man, presented his haunting tales with optimism, unlike some of his contemporaries. Among his books of verse are *Poems, The Day's Delight,* and *Aught for Your Comfort?* His plays were published as *St. Paul* and *Referee.* His novels included *Saint on Holiday* and *They Chose to be Birds.* He compiled *Told on the Air: Broadcast Stories of Children,* issued in 1948, and many of his poems were republished in *A Pilgrim's Song: Selected Poems,* released during the year of his one-hundredth birthday.

OBITUARIES AND OTHER SOURCES:

BOOKS

International Authors and Writers Who's Who, International Biographical Centre, 1982.

PERIODICALS

Los Angeles Times, August 21, 1996, p. A12.
New York Times, August 21, 1996, p. B8.
Washington Post, August 21, 1996, p. C4.

* * *

DEFFAA, Chip 1951-

PERSONAL: Born May 18, 1951, in New Rochelle, New York; son of Louis P. and Alberta (Saby) Deffaa. *Education:* Princeton University, A.B., 1973.

ADDRESSES: Home—15 1/2 Van Houten St., Apt. #107, Paterson, NJ 07505-1037. *Agent*—c/o Kevin McShane, Fifi Oscard Agency, 24 West 40th St., New York, NY 10018.

CAREER: New York Post, New York City, jazz critic, 1986—.

AWARDS, HONORS: ASCAP-Deems Taylor Award, American Society of Composers, Authors, and Publishers, 1993.

WRITINGS:

Swing Legacy, Scarecrow Press (Metuchen, NJ), 1989.
Voices of the Jazz Age: Profiles of Eight Vintage Jazz Men, University of Illinois Press, 1990.
In the Mainstream: Eighteen Portraits in Jazz, Scarecrow Press, 1992.
Traditionalists and Revivalists in Jazz, Scarecrow Press, 1993.
(With David Cassidy) *C'Mon Get Happy . . . Fear and Loathing on the Partridge Family Bus,* Warner Books (New York, NY), 1994.
Blue Rhythms: Six Lives in Rhythm and Blues, University of Illinois Press, 1996.
Jazz Veterans: A Portrait Gallery, Cypress House Press (Mill Valley, CA), 1996.
(Editor) *F. Scott Fitzgerald: The Princeton Years,* Cypress House Press, 1996.

Contributor to *Entertainment Weekly, down beat, Video Review,* and *Jazz Times.*

WORK IN PROGRESS: Blue Rhythms, for University of Illinois Press.

SIDELIGHTS: Chip Deffaa, a critic for the *New York Post,* has penned several books on the musicians whose works inspired listeners to label the 1920s as "The Jazz Age." In the volumes *Voices of the Jazz Age: Profiles of Eight Vintage Jazz Men, Traditionalists and Revivalists in Jazz, Swing Legacy,* and *In the Mainstream: Eighteen Portraits in Jazz,* Deffaa presents vital interviews and memories of the Jazz Age. *Choice* contributor A. D. Franklin praises *Voices of the Jazz Age* because "the author presents an excellent synthesis of the interview material in a highly readable form."

Deffaa told *CA:* "As a jazz critic/historian, I have specialized in preserving the oral histories of veteran jazz musicians whose stories might otherwise be lost. I've traveled extensively to document the careers of older jazz men. My first 'role model' was neither a jazz musician nor a jazz critic/historian, but rather

the late travel and adventure writer, Richard Halliburton."

The interviews in *Voices of the Jazz Age* represent a variety of performers who played important roles in the Jazz Age. One chapter that drew critical attention was the section on Bix Beiderbecke, a trumpeter who succumbed to alcoholism at the age of twenty-nine. Roberta Lisker of *School Library Journal* lauded Deffaa for writing "clearly and lucidly" and remarked that the book "more than adequately narrates the careers of its subjects."

The critically acclaimed *Traditionalists and Revivalists in Jazz* contains profiles of fourteen obscure jazz artists. R. L. Greenhaw of *Choice* praised the "satisfying blend of anecdotal, factual, and entertaining material" and recommended the book's appendix for its discussion of "vintage recording restoration techniques." *Swing Legacy* offers another look at the jazz age with more interviews and historical commentary from Deffaa. K. R. Dietrich's comments in *Choice* reflected an appreciation for Deffaa's efforts. "Deffaa is clearly a fan of this music," noted Dietrich, adding that the pieces on the musicians are "candid and heartfelt."

Deffaa served as interviewer and coauthor on *C'Mon Get Happy . . . Fear and Loathing on the Partridge Family Bus*. Along with ex-Partridge David Cassidy, Deffaa chronicles the career of Cassidy from his days as a teen idol to the present. Tim Appelo of *Entertainment Weekly* praised Deffaa for his work on *C'Mon Get Happy* and credited him for his "able job of buffing [Cassidy's] prose."

Deffaa's 1996 work, *Blue Rhythms: Six Lives in Rhythm and Blues,* centers on the rise of Rhythm and Blues in the late 1940s. He documents this history through his interviews with six Rhythm and Blues singers from that period: La Vern Baker, Charles Brown, Ruth Brown, Floyd Dixon, Little Jimmy Scott, and Jimmy Witherspoon. According to *San Francisco Examiner* critic Philip Elwood, "Deffaa is a careful writer and indefatigable researcher. His initial questions spark the memory and revelations and observations spill out."

BIOGRAPHICAL/CRITICAL SOURCES:

PERIODICALS

Choice, December 1990, p. 639; January 1991, p. 789; February 1994, p. 944.

Entertainment Weekly, July 29, 1994, p. 52.
Examiner (San Francisco), August 30, 1996, p. C10.
School Library Journal, December 1990, p. 136.

* * *

DEKKERS, Midas 1946-

PERSONAL: Born in 1946, in the Netherlands.

ADDRESSES: Agent—c/o Macmillan Children's Book Group, 866 3rd Ave., New York, NY 10022.

CAREER: Writer. Biologist on television in the Netherlands.

WRITINGS:

NONFICTION; EXCEPT AS NOTED

(With others) *Natuurlijke historie,* Erven Thomas Rap (Amsterdam, Netherlands), 1976.
Bestiarium, Bakker (Amsterdam, Netherlands), 1977.
Het edelgedierte; over het vreemde verbond tussen mens en dier, Bakker, 1978.
(With Jan den Hengst) *Waterrijk; flora en fauna van ons zoete water,* Spectrum (Utrecht, Netherlands), 1981.
Het walvismeer; op de bres met Greenpeace (fiction), Stichting Greenpeace Nederland (Amsterdam), 1982, translated as *Arctic Adventure,* Orchard Books (New York), 1987.
(With others) *De Grote stad, Amsterdam,* Meulenhoff Informatief (Amsterdam), 1984.
Mummies, Contact (Amsterdam), 1986.
The Nature Book: Discovering, Exploring, Observing, Experimenting with Plants and Animals at Home and Outdoors (juvenile), translated by Jan Michael, illustrated by Angela de Vrede, Macmillan (New York), 1988.
Dearest Pet: On Bestiality, translated by Paul Vincent, Verso (London, England), 1994.
Birthday: Baby Animals Come into the World, Scientific Books for Young Readers (New York), 1995.

SIDELIGHTS: Midas Dekkers, who enjoys a successful career as a television biologist in the Netherlands, has penned many books on science and nature. Some of these works have been translated into English, notably a well-received 1988 science exploration book for children entitled *The Nature Book: Discovering,*

Exploring, Observing, Experimenting with Plants and Animals at Home and Outdoors. Tim Wynne-Jones in the Toronto *Globe and Mail* declared *The Nature Book* to be "excellently designed . . . for reading and using." Mary Cowen in the *Christian Science Monitor* praised the volume as well, calling it "an intriguing catalog of great ideas."

Dekkers's 1994 volume available in English aims at a more adult audience. The title, *Dearest Pet: On Bestiality,* sums up the subject of the book—incidences of and discussion about human sexual experiences involving animals. Dekkers asserts that actual cases are rare, but estimates that bestiality per capita is much higher in isolated rural communities with restrictive mores concerning sexual activity between humans. Nicola Shulman, reviewing *Dearest Pet* in the *Times Literary Supplement,* reported, however, that "Dekkers . . . thinks the bestiality statistics would be very much higher if animals could talk." Dekkers also discusses examples of bestiality throughout history, bringing to light a 1908 Austrian project to study matings between apes and humans, as well as the case of an army quartermaster fired from his job because of his sexual affinity for ducks. Dekkers also devotes pages to common human activities that he maintains are closely tied to bestiality; in Shulman's words, "the ordinary cherishing of pets, the ingestion of cows' milk, the consumption and use in surgery of other animals' organs, and even . . . the exchange of sweat between horse and rider." Shulman concluded her review by characterizing *Dearest Pet* as "engaging and eccentric and amusing."

BIOGRAPHICAL/CRITICAL SOURCES:

PERIODICALS

Christian Science Monitor, May 9, 1988, p. 25.
Globe and Mail [Toronto], October 30, 1987.
Times Literary Supplement, July 22, 1994, p. 12.*

* * *

De-la-NOY, Michael 1934-

PERSONAL: Born April 3, 1934, in Hessle, England. *Education:* Attended Bedford School, 1942-51. *Avocational interests:* "Drinking wine and going for very short walks."

ADDRESSES: Agent—c/o Scott Ferris Associates, Box 317, 15 Gledhow Gardens, London SW5 0AY, England.

CAREER: Press officer to the Archbishop of Canterbury, 1961-74; writer.

MEMBER: The Wig and Pen Club (London).

WRITINGS:

Before the Storm (poems), Outposts (Dulwich), 1958.
A Child's Life of Christ, Epworth (London), 1964.
Young Once Only: A Study of Boys on Probation, Epworth, 1965.
(Editor) *The Fields of Praise* (poems), Religious Education Press (Oxford), 1968.
A Day in the Life of God, Citadel Press (Derby), 1971.
Elgar: The Man, Viking (New York), 1983.
Denton Welch: The Making of a Writer, Viking, 1984.
(Editor) *The Journals of Denton Welch,* E. P. Dutton (New York), 1984.
The Honours System, Allison and Busby (London), 1985.
(Editor) *Fragments of a Life Story: The Collected Short Writings of Denton Welch,* Penguin (New York), 1987.
Acting as Friends: The Story of the Samaritans, Constable (London), 1987.
Eddy: The Life of Edward Sackville-West, Bodley Head (London), 1988.
Michael Ramsey: A Portrait, Collins (London), 1990.
Windsor Castle: Past and Present, Headline (London), 1990.
Exploring Oxford, Headline (London), 1991.
The Church of England: A Portrait, Simon and Schuster (London), 1993.
The Queen behind the Throne, Hutchinson (London), 1994.
The King Who Never Was: The Story of Frederick, Prince of Wales, Peter Owen (London), 1996.
Mervyn Stockwood: A Lonely Life, Mowbray (London), 1996.

Contributor to books, including the 1993 Missing Persons volume of the *Dictionary of National Biography.* Contributor to periodicals, including *Sunday Times, Observer, Times* (London), *Guardian, Independent, Times Educational Supplement, New Society, Illustrated London News, Musical Times, Field, New Humanist,* and *Commonwealth.* Also contributor of reviews to *Spectator* and *Literary Review.*

SIDELIGHTS: Michael De-la-Noy, former press officer to the Archbishop of Canterbury, has written several historical and biographical works ranging from 1965's study of troubled youth in *Young Once Only: A Study of Boys on Probation,* to an examination of the life of music composer Edward Elgar. Among De-la-Noy's subjects are Denton Welch, a writer who died in 1948 after suffering for thirteen years with injuries resulting from a bicycling accident, and Michael Ramsey, Primate of All England, in *Michael Ramsey: A Portrait,* published in 1990.

In *Denton Welch: The Making of a Writer, Fragments of a Life Story: The Collected Short Writings of Denton Welch,* and his edition of *The Journals of Denton Welch,* De-la-Noy sheds new light on the life and works of the British writer and painter Denton Welch. Heretofore, Welch's autobiographical journals had not been published in their entirety. In the 1950s, one author appraised Welch's content as controversial, and therefore felt "restricted by both the danger of libel and the fear of boring or shocking" early-1950s readers, according to Alan Hollinghurst in the *Times Literary Supplement.* De-la-Noy's *Journals,* however, are comprehensive and "contain little that can readily be dispensed with," Hollinghurst concluded, "and Michael De-la-Noy's new complete edition, along with his biography of Welsh, goes far to restitute the whole man."

In De-la-Noy's 1990 publication, *Michael Ramsey: A Portrait,* the author writes from his special vantage point as former press officer to Michael Ramsey, Archbishop of Canterbury from 1961 to 1974. De-la-Noy's biography of the late archbishop looks at Ramsey's life from childhood through his years at Cambridge, and then focuses on his career during the turbulent era of the 1960s. According to Eric James in the London *Times,* De-la-Noy writes from a close personal and professional relationship with Ramsey, observing that "De-la-Noy was treated more as a son than as a [press officer], until the abrupt end of his time in the archbishop's employ." Comparing De-la-Noy's biography to another volume on Ramsey written by Owen Chadwick, James declared both books "a fascinating study in judgement: not just the archbishop's but that of each author."

De-la-Noy again focuses on the modern Anglican Church in *The Church of England: A Portrait.* The author studies trends in the Church since Ramsey's time which he finds disturbing, including, according to Karen Armstrong in the *New Statesman and Society,* an "unconscious racism" that keeps black clergy-men from rising in the Church hierarchy, and "the rise of fundamentalism within the Anglican communion, which is no longer the broad, comprehensive Church it used to be." Despite these concerns, Armstrong decided that "De-la-Noy's conclusion that the Church has been hamstrung in its mission of compassion is harsh, since he has also presented us with a moving array of people who are trying creatively to make Christianity work." *Times Literary Supplement* reviewer Richard Harries, the Bishop of Oxford, declared that "De-la-Noy is critical, even bitter, about many aspects of the Church of England, but [*The Church of England: A Portrait*] is at heart an affectionate account by someone for whom the Church has meant and continues to mean much."

De-la-Noy told *CA:* "I have been fortunate to write biographies of people like Elgar, Denton Welch, Edward Sackville-West, Frederick, Prince of Wales (father of George III) and the Queen Mother who lived at a time when people still kept diaries and wrote letters—and more to the point, their correspondence was preserved. The invention of the telephone and the fax have spelt disaster for biographers. In any event, almost everyone worth writing about has now been written about, or already chewed over by the press. The future, I fear is bleak; but as everyone has always said that I may be proved wrong!"

BIOGRAPHICAL/CRITICAL SOURCES:

PERIODICALS

Los Angeles Times Book Review, June 9, 1985, p. 6.
New Statesman and Society, October 1, 1993, p. 38.
Observer, October 17, 1993, p. 17.
Times (London), December 6, 1984; March 3, 1990.
Times Literary Supplement, July 15, 1983, p. 751; December 21, 1984, pp. 1479-80; August 9, 1985, p. 886; January 7, 1994, p. 24.

* * *

de LESTRES, Alonie
 See GROULX, Lionel (Adolphe)

* * *

DENT, Richard J. 1951-

PERSONAL: Born May 13, 1951, in Indiana. *Education:* American University, Ph.D.

ADDRESSES: *Home*—3915 Oneida Pl., Hyattsville, MD 20782. *Office*—Department of Anthropology, American University, Washington, DC 20016; fax 202-885-1837. *E-mail*—rdent@american.edu.

CAREER: American University, Washington, DC, associate professor of anthropology and head of department, 1988—.

WRITINGS:

Chesapeake Prehistory, Plenum (New York City), 1995.

WORK IN PROGRESS: A book on Philadelphia archaeology.

* * *

DERKSEN, Jeff 1958-

PERSONAL: Born in 1958, in Murrayville, British Columbia. *Education:* David Thompson University Centre, B.A., 1984; University of Calgary, M.A., 1995.

ADDRESSES: *Office*—P.O. Box 61102 Kensington Postal Outlet, Calgary, Alberta T2N 456, Canada.

CAREER: Artspeak Gallery, Vancouver, British Columbia, founding board member, 1986-95; The New Gallery, Calgary, Alberta, board member, 1994-95; *Writing* magazine, Vancouver, British Columbia, editor, 1989-93; Kootenay School of Writing, Vancouver, British Columbia, founding board member, 1984—.

AWARDS, HONORS: Dorothy Livesay Poetry award, 1991; British Columbia Book prize, 1991, for *Down Time;* Alberta Writers' Guild Poetry prize, 1994, for *Dwell.*

WRITINGS:

POETRY

Memory Is the Only Thing Holding Me Back, DTUC Press (Nelson, British Columbia), 1984.
Until (chapbook), Tsunami Editions (Vancouver), 1987.
Down Time, Talonbooks (Vancouver), 1990.
Selfish (chapbook), Pomeflit (Vancouver), 1993.
Dwell, Talonbooks, 1994.

DERY, Mark 1959-

PERSONAL: Born December 24, 1959, in Boston, MA; son of Leslie (an artist) and Leslie (an artist; maiden name, Killam; present surname, Dery) Morrill; married Margot Mifflin (a writer), June 20, 1992; children: Thea Nicola. *Ethnicity:* "Caucasian." *Education:* Occidental College, B.A., 1982. *Politics:* "Unrepentantly leftist." *Religion:* "Church of the Subgenius." *Avocational interests:* "Xenologophilia—I collect strange words."

ADDRESSES: *Agent*—Linda Chester, Linda Chester Literary Agency, 630 5th Ave., New York, NY 10111. *E-mail*—markdery@well.com; http://www.well.com/user/markdery.

CAREER: Full-time cultural critic and freelance journalist.

MEMBER: National Writers Union.

WRITINGS:

Culture Jamming: Hacking, Slashing, and Sniping in the Empire of Signs (political monograph), Open Media (Westfield, NJ), 1993.
(Editor) *Flame Wars: The Discourse of Cyberculture* (nonfiction anthology), Duke University Press (Durham, NC), 1995.
Escape Velocity: Cyberculture at the End of the Century (nonfiction), Grove Press (New York, NY), 1996.

Contributor to books, including *Radiotext(e),* Autonomedia (Brooklyn, NY), 1992; *State of the Art: Issues in Contemporary Communications,* St. Martin's (New York, NY), 1992; *Present Tense: Rock and Roll and Culture,* Duke University Press, 1992; *Mondo 2000: A User's Guide to the New Edge,* Harper Perennial (New York, NY), 1992; *Memesis: The Future of Evolution/Ars Electronica Festival '96,* Springer Wien (New York), 1996; and *The Virtual Dimension: Architecture, Representation, and Crash Culture,* Princeton Architectural Press (Princeton, NJ), 1997. Also contributor to *Beyond Cyberpunk,* a hypercard database of essays and esoterica; contributor of articles to periodicals, including *21.C, World Art, Virtual City, Village Voice, New York Times, Wave, Wired, Adbusters Quarterly, New Media, Rolling Stone, ArtNews, Elle, South Atlantic Quarterly, Oz, Architecture New York, Andere Sinema,* and *Discovery Channel Online.*

WORK IN PROGRESS: A series of essays on millennial America, on topics from survivalism to sadomasochism, to be titled *The Pyrotechnic Insanitarium.*

SIDELIGHTS: Mark Dery has made a career for himself as a critic of popular culture and cyberculture. He has written extensively about the Internet, as well as "off-line" cyberculture, and is especially knowledgeable about fringe groups who utilize the Internet as an essential part of their existence. His 1995 book, *Flame Wars: The Discourse of Cyberculture,* contains essays about the impact of cyberculture by academics, science fiction writers, and information technology experts. Edwin Diamond and Stephen Bates, writing in *Nation,* called *Flame Wars* "a lively, lit-crit look at the prevailing weirdness of the new electronic culture." Caius van Nouhuys in the *Whole Earth Review* discussed the reader's need to "start thinking about how our society relates" to electronic media, and observed that "*Flame Wars* is a great place to start." John Noto in the *American Book Review* noted that the "overlap in subject matter among all these essays . . . serves to elucidate and highlight different perspectives."

In *Escape Velocity: Cyberculture at the End of the Century,* Dery explicates for readers what Peter Jukes in the *New Statesman and Society* described as "a parade of cyberpunk novelists, cybersex enthusiasts, technopagans, cyber rockers and underground roboticists." Jukes found the author's emphasis on the more bizarre cyberculture groups to be unwarranted, protesting that "since every manifestation is potentially important, nothing can be left out. From nanotechnology to neural networks, safe sex to smart drugs, Dery connects the most diverse and spurious developments." According to a *Kirkus Reviews* critic, however, Dery "presents a convincing overview of a coherent pancultural phenomenon."

Beth Rosenberg in the *Christian Science Monitor* declared that "Dery demonstrates an encyclopedic knowledge of cultural theory" in his analysis of cybercultural phenomenon. Yet, Dery's extensive knowledge of various cybercultures does not complicate *Escape Velocity* for the reader. According to *New York Times* reviewer Michiko Kakutani, Dery "manages to give the lay reader a lively and informative tour through the darker recesses of cyberculture, navigating its jargon-filled byways with an observant eye."

Dery told *CA:* "My aim in writing *Escape Velocity* was to pry loose the white-knuckled grip that millennial cyberhype—corporate futurology and New Age eschatology—has on our public discourse about culture and technology. I wanted to take back the future from the technocratic elite lionized by *Wired* magazine, relocating our cultural conversation about technology from the 'there and then' to the 'here and now,' wiring it into the power relations and social currents of our historical moment.

"But, at the same time that I wanted to deliver lethal firepower to the New Age credulity and free-market flackery that afflicts so much of the writing on cyberculture, I also wanted to spotlight the ragtag and bobtail swept along by futurist Alvin Toffler's Third Wave. *Escape Velocity* is equally about the rogue roboticists, cyberpunks, and other members of high-tech subcultures who have taken as their slogan cyberpunk novelist William Gibson's maxim, 'the street finds its own uses for things,' turning technology to perverse, sometimes subversive ends, using it in ways never intended or even imagined by its manufacturers.

"My larger goal, as a writer, is to write a cultural criticism that combines the lapidary craftsmanship of J. G. Ballard, the mordant social satire of William S. Burroughs, the historiography of Mike Davis, and the deadeye aim of Noam Chomsky. Following in the footsteps of Georges Bataille, I'm interested in the unspeakable and the unthinkable—the unlit, unfrequented corners of society, the nethermost regions of the self: freaks, forensic pathology, psychopharmacology, the occult, true crime, conspiracy theory, cannibalism, madness, medical museums, Art Brut, weird science, sexual deviance, soft tissue modification (by tribal peoples and postmodern primitives), creature features, alien abductions, Situationism, surrealism, science fiction, Satanic ritual abuse, the grotesque, the carnivalesque—in short, extremes and excess of every sort. I want to induce, in my reader, the vertigo that comes from leaning too far over the edge of the cultural abyss."

BIOGRAPHICAL/CRITICAL SOURCES:

PERIODICALS

American Book Review, December, 1994-February, 1995, p. 5.
Bay Guardian, March, 1996, p. 9.
Christian Science Monitor, May 14, 1996, p. 12.
Kirkus Reviews, December 15, 1995.
Library Journal, February 15, 1996, p. 168.

Nation, February 5, 1996, pp. 28-31; June 3, 1996, pp. 36-38.
New Statesman and Society, April 14, 1995, pp. 37-38; April 12, 1996, pp. 36-37.
New York Times, February 20, 1996.
New York Times Book Review, May 5, 1996, p. 23.
Whole Earth Review, spring, 1994, p. 99; spring, 1996, pp. 20-21.

* * *

de SOUZA, Eunice 1940-

PERSONAL: Born August 1, 1940, in Poona, India. *Education:* University of Bombay, B.A. (honors), 1960, Ph.D. 1988; Marquette University, Milwaukee, Wisconsin, M.A. 1963.

ADDRESSES: Office—St. Xavier's College, Bombay 400 001, India.

CAREER: St. Xavier's College, Bombay, lecturer in English, 1969—, head of the Department of English, 1990—; *Economic Times,* Bombay, arts columnist, 1973-84; *Indian Post,* Bombay, literary editor, 1987.

WRITINGS:

POETRY

Fix, Newground (Bombay), 1979.
Women in Dutch Painting, Praxis (Bombay), 1988.
Ways of Belonging: Selected Poems, Polygon (Edinburgh), 1990.
Selected and New Poems, St. Xavier's College (Bombay), 1994.

FOR CHILDREN

All About Birbal, India Book House (Bombay), 1969.
Himalayan Tales, India Book House, 1973.

Also author of *More About Birbal* and *Tales of Birbal,* both India Book House.

OTHER

(Editor, with Adil Jussawalla) *Statements: An Anthology of Indian Prose in English,* Orient Longman (Bombay), 1976.

D'ESTE, Carlo 1936-

PERSONAL: Born in 1936.

ADDRESSES: Office—c/o HarperCollins, 1000 Keystone Industrial Park, Scranton, PA 18512.

CAREER: Military historian and biographer, 1978—. Formerly, lieutenant colonel with the United States Army.

WRITINGS:

Decision in Normandy: The Unwritten Story of Montgomery and the Allied Campaign, Dutton (New York City), 1983.
Bitter Victory: The Battle for Sicily, 1943, Dutton, 1988.
World War II in the Mediterranean, 1942-1945, Algonquin (Chapel Hill, NC), 1990.
Fatal Decision: Anzio and the Battle for Rome, HarperCollins (New York City), 1991.
Patton: A Genius for War, HarperCollins, 1995.

SIDELIGHTS: A retired U.S. Army colonel, Carlo D'Este is considered one of the leading historians of Allied operations in the European theater during World War II. Beginning with 1983's *Decision in Normandy: The Unwritten Story of Montgomery and the Allied Campaign,* he has written several considerations of strategy, tactics, and command in such pivotal battles as the Normandy invasion and the amphibious assault on Anzio in southern Italy.

Decision in Normandy critiques the performance of British commander Bernard L. "Monty" Montgomery in the planning and execution of Operation Overlord, the invasion of Normandy that took place in June of 1944. D'Este maintains that Montgomery falsified accounts of the battle and revised his strategy for the campaign when Allied troops were unable to wrest the key city of Caen from German control. A *Publishers Weekly* reviewer deemed the book "controversial" due to its sharp criticism of British troops involved in the assault, and highlighted D'Este's "dramatic account of the development of ill feeling between Montgomery and the American generals Eisenhower, Bradley, and Patton." According to David Fraser in the *London Review of Books,* D'Este's examination of the invasion and the ensuing two-and-a-half month battle is "carefully researched, militarily perceptive and lucidly written." Military correspondent Drew Middleton agreed, hailing the book as "the best-researched, best-reasoned, best-

written account of [the Normandy] campaign that I have read," in his review for the *New York Times Book Review.*

Bitter Victory: The Battle for Sicily, 1943 "fills an important gap in the history of the Second World War," according to Michael Carver, who reviewed the 1988 volume for the *Times Literary Supplement.* In this work D'Este focuses on Operation Husky, the little-studied battle that gave rise to rivalries between such Allied commanders as Alexander, Bradley, Patton, Montgomery, and Eisenhower and which established a foothold for Allied forces in retaking Occupied Europe. A *Publishers Weekly* contributor noted the author's criticism of "the committee system of coalition warfare during this formative stage of the Allied partnership," and *New York Times Book Review* critic Walter Lord proclaimed *Bitter Victory* "a splendid campaign history."

In 1990 D'Este's *World War II in the Mediterranean, 1942-1945,* was published as the second volume in a series entitled "Major Battles and Campaigns." His analysis of strategy in the North African and Italian campaigns received critical praise; P. L. De Rosa declared in *Choice* that "Although [the] book covers all levels of the conflict, D'Este is at his best analyzing the Allied and Axis leadership."

In *Fatal Decision: Anzio and the Battle for Rome* D'Este examines Operation Shingle, code name for the invasion of Anzio, Italy. A reviewer for *Publishers Weekly* called the study "well researched and vividly told" in its account of the strategic and tactical errors that ultimately resulted in a bloody five-month-long deadlock. The assault occurred in January 1944; it would be May before Allied forces could finally break out from the beach. In the *American Historical Review,* historian Alan F. Wilt praised the book's "fast-paced narrative that features descriptive and interpretive passages as well as telling anecdotes," and Michael Howard in the *Times Literary Supplement* proclaimed *Fatal Decision* "a definitive account of this tragedy." He continued, "The comprehensiveness of [D'Este's] research, the clarity and compassion of his writing, and above all the scrupulous fairness of his judgments have already marked him out as a superb military historian, and here he has found a subject that gives full scope to his talents."

In D'Este's next military study, *Patton: A Genius for War,* published in 1995, the historian attempts to revise the boorish image of General George S. Patton

Jr. that was promoted by the popular 1970 film biography, *Patton.* D'Este offers readers a complex portrayal of the general who served in North Africa, Sicily, and the Battle of the Bulge. He depicts Patton—who was killed in an automobile accident in December 1945—as an ambitious soldier obsessed with heroism and haunted by a family legacy of military valor. According to D'Este, Patton suffered dyslexia and depression, wrote poetry for solace, believed himself a reincarnated Viking and Roman soldier, and abhorred cowardice above all else. British biographer Alistair Horne, who reviewed *Patton: A Genius for War* in the *New York Times Book Review,* remarked that "in sharp contrast to the imprint made by the George C. Scott film, from Carlo D'Este's excellent research emerges a deeply religious and well-read romantic, passionately caring of his soldiers." *Wall Street Journal* reviewer Mark Yost called the work "thoughtful" and noted that *Patton* "gives us a new understanding of this great and troubled man."

BIOGRAPHICAL/CRITICAL SOURCES:

PERIODICALS

American Historical Review, October 1992, pp. 1304-1305.
Choice, December 1990, p. 683.
London Review of Books, December 22, 1983, pp. 7-8; May 26, 1994, p. 3.
New York Times, September 8, 1988, p. C21.
New York Times Book Review, January 22, 1984, p. 10; November 27, 1988, p. 18; July 21, 1991, p. 27; December 10, 1995, pp. 9, 11.
Publishers Weekly, October 14, 1983, p. 51; July 1, 1988, pp. 61-62; April 12, 1991, p. 51.
Times Literary Supplement, September 16, 1988, p. 1022; September 6, 1991, pp. 11-12; June 10, 1994, p. 33.
Wall Street Journal, December 8, 1995, p. A10.*

* * *

De VOS, Susan 1953-

PERSONAL: Born December 30, 1953, in Nagoya, Japan; married Thomas L. McFarland, February 15, 1985; children: Diana. *Ethnicity:* "American." *Education:* University of California, Berkeley, A.B., M.P.P.; University of Michigan, Ph.D.

ADDRESSES: Office—Center for Demography and Ecology, 4412 Social Science Bldg., University of Wisconsin—Madison, Madison, WI 53706; fax 608-262-8400. *E-mail*—devos@ssc.wisc.edu.

CAREER: University of Wisconsin—Madison, associate scientist. University of Zimbabwe, visiting lecturer.

AWARDS, HONORS: Fulbright fellow, 1989.

WRITINGS:

Household Composition in Latin America, Plenum (New York), 1995.

Contributor to academic journals.

* * *

DEWITT, Katherine, Jr. 1943-

PERSONAL: Born March 21, 1943, in Oxford, NC; daughter of Wallace (an electrolytic platemaker) and Katherine (a bureaucrat; maiden name, Moore) DeWitt; children: Lucas Dewitt Sawyer. *Education:* University of the State of New York, B.A.

ADDRESSES: Agent—Dan Wright, Ann Wright Representatives, 136 East 56th St., New York, NY 10022.

CAREER: Advertising copywriter, 1965-89; writer.

MEMBER: Mensa, Washington Independent Writers.

WRITINGS:

(With James E. T. Lange) *Chappaquiddick: The Real Story,* St. Martin's (New York), 1993.

WORK IN PROGRESS: (With James E. T. Lange) *The Ripper Syndrome,* a multi-disciplinary study of serial killers; (with James E. T. Lange) an untitled exploration of the assassination of President Abraham Lincoln in 1865.

SIDELIGHTS: In *Chappaquiddick: The Real Story* Katherine DeWitt, Jr., writing with James E. T. Lange, recounts in detail the events leading up to the drowning death of Mary Jo Kopechne, a passenger in Senator Edward Kennedy's car on a July night in 1969. The authors explain that Kennedy, after driving off a bridge, neglected to inform police of the incident until a day later. Kopechne drowned in the accident, and the senator plead guilty to leaving the scene. Although such facts have led to much controversy surrounding the incident, the authors contend that Kennedy is "the living victim of Chappaquiddick."

In presenting their case, DeWitt and Lange offer brief biographies of Kennedy and Kopechne as well as a chronology of events. They delve into the controversy, debunking conspiracy theories such as the notion that Kopechne was driving the car, that she was dead before the accident, and that the Central Intelligence Agency orchestrated the event. In conclusion, the authors deem that Kennedy's explanation—that he was injured in the mishap and delayed reporting the event because he had "some kind of mental breakdown, whether caused by stress or injury"—is true. The volume is, in the words of Jeffrey Toobin in *Washington Post Book World,* a "pro-Kennedy" Chappaquiddick study.

BIOGRAPHICAL/CRITICAL SOURCES:

BOOKS

DeWitt, Katherine, and James E. T. Lange, *Chappaquiddick: The Real Story,* St. Martin's (New York), 1993.

PERIODICALS

Publishers Weekly, May 10, 1993, p. 65.
Washington Post Book World, July 11, 1993, p. 2.

* * *

DIAMOND, Sara 1958-

PERSONAL: Born in 1958; married Richard Hatch (a scientist). *Education:* University of California, Irvine, B.A., 1979; University of California, Berkeley, M.A., 1988, Ph.D., 1993.

ADDRESSES: Home—P.O. Box 2439, Berkeley, CA 94702. *E-mail*—102147.420@compuserve.com.

CAREER: Writer.

WRITINGS:

Spiritual Warfare: The Politics of the Christian Right, South End Press (Boston, MA), 1989.

Roads to Dominion: Right-Wing Movements and Political Power in the United States, Guilford (New York City), 1995.

Facing the Wrath: Confronting the Right in Dangerous Times, Common Courage Press (Monroe, ME), 1996.

WORK IN PROGRESS: A book on the Christian right, publication by Guilford expected in 1998; research on political sociology and cultural studies.

* * *

DOUGLAS, Susan J(eanne) 1950-

PERSONAL: Born in 1950.

ADDRESSES: Office—University of Michigan Department of Communications, 2020 Friezer, 105 South State St., Ann Arbor, MI 48109-1285.

CAREER: Hampshire College, Amherst, MA, professor of media and American studies; affiliated with the University of Michigan, Ann Arbor, MI. Media critic for *The Progressive.*

WRITINGS:

Inventing American Broadcasting, 1899-1922, Johns Hopkins University Press (Baltimore, MD), 1987.

Where the Girls Are: Growing up Female with the Mass Media, Times Books (New York, NY), 1994.

Contributor to periodicals, including the *Village Voice, Nation, TV Guide, Journal of American History, ARTnews,* and *In These Times.*

SIDELIGHTS: Media and American culture expert Susan J. Douglas, who is well known for her work as a media critic for the *Progressive* periodical, published her first book, *Inventing American Broadcasting, 1899-1922,* in 1987. Its focus is the development of radio and its role in shaping the United States' culture in the modern era, particularly during the earliest part of the 1920s. The volume was generally well received; Donald J. Marion in the *Library Jour-*

nal hailed it as "a solid work of scholarship," and C. H. Sterling in *Choice* lauded it as "a tour-de-force of insight."

Douglas garnered more critical and public attention, however, with her 1994 effort, *Where the Girls Are: Growing up Female with the Mass Media.* The volume is a study that juxtaposes principles of the feminist movement against the images of women prevalent in television, films, and the music industry during the movement's formative years. Douglas examines Disney film heroines of the 1940s and 1950s, and popular television shows that featured girls or women—from 1960s staples such as *Gidget* and *The Patty Duke Show* to the sexual objectification and stereotyping evident in such 1970s fare as *Charlie's Angels, Dynasty,* and *Dallas.* For instance, "for anyone who has ever sensed, yet found herself unable to articulate, the precise difference between *Bewitched* and *I Dream of Jeannie,*" declared Walter Kirn in *New York* magazine, "this . . . is essential reading." He went on to quote Douglas's book on the subject: "'The question of whether Samantha [protagonist of *Bewitched*] could use her powers, and under what circumstances, defined the entire series. . . . She often made mistakes, but because she had the traditional female traits of empathy, tact, flattery . . . all coupled with her magic, she was able repeatedly to rescue her husband, herself, and her marriage.'" By contrast, *I Dream of Jeannie*'s title character "was 'amorous and sexualized' 'not the ideal 1960s wife who happened to have magic powers.' Thus 'Captain Nelson tried in vain to contain Jeannie both physically and sexually, and in those episodes where Jeannie's bottle was lost, there was considerable tension until it was found.'"

Douglas also analyzes female vocal groups of the 1960s such as the Supremes, the Shirelles, and the Ronettes. As Carolyn See, reviewing *Where the Girls Are* in the *Washington Post,* reported, "women were still being given ambivalent messages from the culture, but—in song—they could get together and talk about them and, because all life is change, you could hate a boy (and all boy-girl games) one day and be totally taken up by a bad boy who treats you mean the next." According to Michiko Kakutani of the *New York Times,* Douglas "contends . . . that girl singing groups of the early 60's . . . were a 'pop culture harbinger' of the women's consciousness-raising groups of the late 60's and early 70's."

As the above quotations from Douglas's book indicate, she is unlike at least one of the current images

of feminist critics—the one that dismisses all of American popular culture as a conscious or unconscious influence that serves to enslave women and place them completely in a passive role. As Kirn put it, "Douglas is no mere ideological scold but an ambivalent champion of dreck." Though in *Where the Girls Are* Douglas does find negative messages in the media about such things as unattainable standards of female beauty, she also found much that was positive in, for instance, the female characters presented on television shows. Gidget's perkiness, quoted Kirn, was "'assertiveness masquerading as cuteness,' and was an 'absolutely critical mask for girls who wanted to take an active role in the world yet still be thought of as appealing.'" And, while in some ways *Charlie's Angels* played to men's sexual fantasies, it also presented strong, intelligent women working together to fight crime. Douglas has concluded, according to Kirn, that "'American women today are a bundle of contradictions because much of the media imagery we grew up with was itself filled with mixed messages about what women should and should not do.'"

Critics were for the most part at least somewhat approving of *Where the Girls Are.* Though Kirn protested that such detailed analysis "brought to bear" on the "slight materials" of pop culture was like "watching envelopes being opened by lasers or hot dogs set in their buns using cranes," Douglas had anticipated such attitudes in her book. Pop culture aficionado and author Pagan Kennedy quoted her humorous self-deprecation in a review for the *Women's Review of Books:* "I am a professor of media studies. You know what that means. I probably teach entire courses on the films of [1960s pop singer] Connie Francis. . . . All I do now, of course, is study [pop singer] Madonna." Even critics who praised Douglas's book, however, faulted her baby-boomer love for the 1960s. Kennedy, for instance, related: "Since I'm more than ten years younger than Douglas, I gritted my teeth as she elegized Beatlemania and the magic of growing up with hippiedom—at certain moments I could have sworn I heard the *Big Chill* soundtrack playing in the background." But she went on to note that "once Douglas begins talking about the years of her adulthood she becomes a hard-headed historian. Particularly impressive is her analysis of the media's simultaneous promotion and containment of the women's movement in the early seventies." See summed up her feelings about Douglas's volume by hailing it thus: "*Where the Girls Are* may be the funniest, most original, most brilliant piece of academic writing I've ever read."

BIOGRAPHICAL/CRITICAL SOURCES:

BOOKS

Douglas, Susan J., *Where the Girls Are: Growing up Female with the Mass Media,* Times Books, 1994.

PERIODICALS

Choice, April, 1988, p. 1235.
Library Journal, November 1, 1987, pp. 109-110.
New York, May 2, 1994, pp. 74-75.
New York Times, June 14, 1994, sec. C, p. 19.
Washington Post, June 3, 1994, sec. C, p. 2.
Women's Review of Books, June, 1994, p. 10.*

—*Sketch by Elizabeth Wenning*

* * *

DUGGAN, Laurence James 1949-
(Laurie Duggan)

PERSONAL: Born May 30, 1949, Melbourne. *Education:* Attended Sydney University, 1973-74; Monash University, Melbourne, B.A., 1976; attending Melbourne University, 1991—.

CAREER: Swinburne College, lecturer in media studies, 1976; Canberra College of Advanced Education, lecturer in media studies, 1983; freelance scriptwriter, 1978-83; *The Times on Sunday,* Melbourne, art critic, 1986-87; Victoria University of Technology, Melbourne, poetry teacher, 1994.

AWARDS, HONORS: Anne Elder award for a first book of poems, 1978; ANZ New Writing award, 1988; Wesley Michel Wright award, 1988.

WRITINGS:

POETRY, AS LAURIE DUGGAN

East: Poems 1970-1974, Rigmarole (Melbourne), 1976.
Under the Weather, Wild and Woolley (Sydney), 1978.
Adventures in Paradise, Experimental Art Foundation (Adelaide), 1982.
The Great Divide: Poems 1973-83, Hale and Iremonger (Sydney), 1985.

The Ash Range, Picador (Sydney), 1987.
All Blues, Northern Lights (London), 1989.
The Epigrams of Martial, Scripsi (Melbourne), 1989.
Blue Notes, Picador, 1990.
Memorials, Little Esther (Adelaide), 1995.

* * *

DUGGAN, Laurie
 See DUGGAN, Laurence James

* * *

DUNMORE, Helen 1952-

PERSONAL: Born in 1952, in Yorkshire, England; married; children: one son and one stepson. *Education:* York University, B.A. (English), 1973.

ADDRESSES: Agent—c/o Bloodaxe Books Ltd., P.O. Box 1SN, Newcastle-upon-Tyne NE99 1SN, England.

CAREER: Writer. Works as a nursery teacher.

AWARDS, HONORS: Poetry Book Society Choice; Poetry Book Society Recommendation, 1991, for *Short Days, Long Nights;* Alice Hunt Bartlett award.

WRITINGS:

POETRY

The Apple Fall, Bloodaxe (Newcastle-upon-Tyne), 1983.
The Sea Skater, Bloodaxe, 1986.
The Raw Garden, Bloodaxe, 1988.
Short Days, Long Nights: New & Selected Poems, Bloodaxe, 1991.
Secrets (for children), Bodley Head (London), 1994.
Recovering A Body, Bloodaxe, 1994.

NOVELS

Going to Egypt, MacRae (London), 1992.
Zennor in Darkness, Penguin (London), 1993.
In the Money (for children), Red Fox (London), 1993.
Burning Bright, Penguin, 1994.
A Spell of Winter, Viking (London), 1995.

DuPREE, Sherry Sherrod 1946-

PERSONAL: Born November 25, 1946, in Raleigh, NC; daughter of Matthew Needham (a railroad porter-supervisor) and Elouise (an elementary school teacher; maiden name, Heartley) Sherrod; married Herbert Clarence DuPree (an elementary school principal), January 11, 1975; children: Amil, Andre, Andrew. *Ethnicity:* "African American." *Education:* North Carolina Central University, B.S., 1968, M.A., 1969; University of Michigan, A.M.L.S., 1974, Ed.S., 1978; graduate study at the University of Florida, 1980-81. *Politics:* Democrat. *Religion:* Holiness Pentecostal. *Avocational interests:* Reading, making cloth flowers, playing piano.

ADDRESSES: Home—1825 N.W. 22nd Terrace, Gainesville, FL 32605. *Office*—Santa Fe Community College Library, Building P-208, P.O. Box 1530, 3000 N.W. 83rd St., Gainesville, FL 32606.

CAREER: Ann Arbor Public Schools, Tappan Junior High School Media Center, Ann Arbor, MI, instructional media specialist and department chair, 1970-76; University of Michigan Hospital, Ann Arbor, summer dietetic supervisor, 1970-73; University of Florida Libraries, Gainesville, FL, associate Afro-American and religion specialist for main branch, 1977-83; University of Florida, Institute of Black Culture, Gainesville, project director, 1982-93; Santa Fe Community College, Gainesville, reference librarian, 1983—; Bethume Cookman College, Daytona Beach, FL, extension professor of teacher education, 1986-89. Visiting professor in educational media at Eastern Michigan University, Ypsilanti, MI, 1975.

Founder and organizer of the DuPree African-American Pentecostal and Holiness Collection (materials on African American Pentecostal churches, etc.) at the New York Public Library's Schomburg Center for Research in Black Culture. Has also organized museum exhibit on African American gospel music for the University of Florida; exhibit traveled to the Billy Graham Center in Wheaton, IL. Member of board of directors for the Middle Atlantic Regional Press, Washington, DC; Institute for Black Family Development, Detroit, MI; Ocala Marine Institute Canopy; and Florida Ancestor's Project. Consultant; has made presentations on educational and religious issues in several locations, including Toronto, Ontario, Fort Lauderdale, FL, Los Angeles, CA, Atlanta, GA, Seattle, WA, Gainesville, FL, Washington, DC, Dallas, TX, Chicago, IL, New Orleans, LA, and Virginia Beach, VA.

MEMBER: American Library Association, Society of American Archivists, Zeta Phi Beta, Society for Pentecostal Studies, African American Religious Group, Writers Platform Association, Resources to Religions Caucus, National Association for Female Executives, Florida Library Association, Rosewood Massacre Forum, Alachua Library League, Billy Graham Archives Minority Council, Florida Community College Association, University of Florida Libraries Association (past president).

AWARDS, HONORS: Travel and pilot study grant from the Division of Sponsored Research, University of Florida, 1983; travel to collections grant from the National Endowment for the Humanities, 1983; educational research grants from International Business Machine, Inc. (IBM) and the National Council of Churches, Inc., both 1983; research matching grant from Santa Fe Community College, 1983; Governor's Achievement Award, from the governor of Florida, 1986; research grant from Howard University Divinity School, 1987; grant for the Holiness Pentecostal Project from the Gatorade Foundation, University of Florida, 1987; visiting fellowship from the Smithsonian Institution, African American History and Culture, 1987; research grants from the Black Seminarians of Princeton Theology Seminary and Nationwide Insurance Co., both 1988; travel grants from the Southern Regional Education Board, 1987-92; Santa Fe Community College Black Faculty Award, 1990; received one of the 7th Annual Ebony Appreciation Awards, 1990; grants for the Gospel Music Traveling Display from the Friends of the Library (Gainesville) and the City of Gainesville Commissioners, both 1994; grant from Santa Fe Community College to publish educational pamphlets on two Florida Folk Heritage Award winners, 1994 and 1995; Sojourner Truth Award from the Education Committee of the Gainesville Commission on the Status of Women, 1995.

WRITINGS:

NONFICTION

Biographical Dictionary of African-American, Holiness-Pentecostals: 1880-1990, Middle Atlantic Regional Press (Washington, DC), c. 1990.

(With husband, Herbert C. DuPree) *African-American (Good News) Music,* Middle Atlantic Regional Press, 1993.

(Contributor, with H. C. DuPree) *1993 Yearbook of American and Canadian Churches,* Abingdon Press (Nashville, TN), 1993.

African-American Pentecostals Movement: An Annotated Bibliography, Garland Publishing (New York), 1996.

Associate editor of *Pneuma: The Journal of the Society for Pentecostal Studies.* Also author or co-author of several booklets, including *Displays for Schools, Bible Lessons for Youth, What You Always Wanted to Know About the Card Catalog But Were Afraid to Ask, Busy Bookworm: Good Conduct Book, Library Skills, Exposed! Federal Bureau of Investigation (FBI) Unclassified Reports on Churches and Church Leaders,* and *The Silent Spokesman: Bishop Robert Clarence Lawson.*

Contributor to reference books, including *Biographical Dictionary of American Cult and Sect Leaders,* Garland, 1986; *Pentecostal Handbook: A Reference Guide to the Origins, Personalities, and Doctrines of the Pentecostal People in the United States of America,* Richard Crayne (Morristown, TN), 1986; *Black Holiness: A Guide to the Study of Black Participation in Wesley and Perfectionist and Glossolalia Pentecostal Movements,* Scarecrow, 1987; *Researching Modern Evangelicalism: A Guide to the Holdings of the Billy Graham Center, with Information on Other Collections,* Greenwood, 1990; *Religious Leaders of America: A Biographical Guide to Founders and Leaders of Religious Bodies, Churches, and Spiritual Groups in North America,* Gale (Detroit, MI), 1991; *Directory of African American Religious Bodies,* Howard University Press (Washington, DC), 1991 and 1995; *Encyclopedia of African American Religions,* Garland, 1993; *Called to Lead: Wisdom for the Next Generation of African American Leaders,* Moody Bible Press (Chicago, IL), 1995; *Encyclopedia of African American Culture and History,* Macmillan (New York), 1995.

Contributor to books, including *The Life and Times of Gospel Music,* Michael Friedman Publishing Group (New York), 1994; *True Love,* University of Florida Gospel Choir (Gainesville), 1994; *African American Steel Guitar Players,* Florida Department of State, 1995; *This Is My Song: A Collection of Gospel Music for the Family,* Crown (New York), 1995.

Contributor of articles to periodicals, including *Collection Building, Media Spectrum: Michigan Association for Media in Education, Florida Folklore Society Newsletter, Washington Post, New York Times, Gainesville Sun, Sun-Sentinel* (Ft. Lauderdale), *Detroit News,* and the *Miami Herald.*

WORK IN PROGRESS: "I am preparing references on the Rosewood Massacre featuring pictures of descendants, newspaper clippings, oral interviews, and legislative sources. Next, I will update *The Biographical Dictionary of African American Holiness Pentecostals.* I am writing on the roles of women and youth in Pentecostal churches. Also, I write on how Federal Bureau of Investigation (FBI) files were used to monitor black churches. I will continue to promote the Golden Era of Gospel Music with more publications and traveling exhibits."

SIDELIGHTS: Educator, librarian, archivist, and author Sherry Sherrod DuPree has dedicated much of her multi-faceted career towards preserving and explaining the history of the African American Pentecostal religious movement. She has penned books on the subject by herself, and with her husband, Herbert C. DuPree. Her titles include the *Biographical Dictionary of African-American, Holiness-Pentecostals: 1880-1990, The African American Pentecostal Movement: An Annotated Bibliography,* and a collaboration with Mr. DuPree, *African-American (Good News) Music.* She has also authored several booklets, some with educational or library purposes, others concerning the Pentecostal movement or civil rights. One noteworthy example, again written with her husband, was 1993's *Exposed! Federal Bureau of Investigation (FBI) Unclassified Reports on Churches and Church Leaders.* In addition to her published work, DuPree also created the DuPree African-American Pentecostal and Holiness Collection at the Schomburg Center for Research in Black Culture of the New York Public Library. She served as curator for a museum exhibit on the history of African American gospel music performers which originated at Santa Fe Community College but traveled to the Billy Graham Archives in Wheaton, Illinois.

As its title indicates, *Exposed!* is a documentation of the ways in which the Federal Bureau of Investigation (FBI) infiltrated and reported on the activities of many African American organizations, including churches. DuPree quotes from FBI memos that have become unclassified. In one dating from 1943, according to an article by Esmeralda Barnes in *Black Issues in Higher Education,* former FBI chief Herbert Hoover "requests coverage of all persons associated with Twentieth Century School of Bible Research." In another from the same year, an agent reports that "Bishop Joseph Croom's church, also known as the Triumph Church of the New Age, cannot be located in New York City." A memo from 1969 notes that "The Church of Lebanon, Tennessee, is located within the Negro community and has been attempting

to integrate the church with white citizens." DuPree explained the FBI's interest in such organizations to Barnes: "Many churches said their members should not fight in wars [because of unequal treatment of African Americans in the United States, especially in the South], and the FBI became very concerned. Black colleges also were of great concern to the FBI because they were seen as sources of agitation." The author added that "most Black colleges were religion-based. Church leaders influenced social change during the times of World War I, World War II and the Red scare." DuPree concluded of her work in *Exposed!:* "I don't pass judgment. I just give facts."

In *African-American Holiness Pentecostal Movement,* readers will become acquainted with many interesting figures, including that of Mother Laura Adorka Kofi. Mother Adorka founded a branch of Pentecostalism which featured a kosher diet, accentuated economic independence from whites, and held a belief that black people must return to Africa in order to find self-fulfillment. She was active during the 1920s, and her story has many parallels to Black Muslim leader Malcolm X. She, too, was assassinated, and, as noted in the *Pace of Santa Fe Community College,* "there is controversy about whether the murder was planned by a rival black organization or by suspicious white authorities." DuPree told the *Pace* that Mother Adorka "was a mover and shaker, and whites were frightened of her. She was not one to hide her heritage." G. Holloway, reviewing *African-American Holiness Pentecostal Movement* in *Choice,* predicted that "this volume will be indispensable to faculty and graduate students."

DuPree told *CA:* "I have filled many requests over the years from people needing information on various subjects. That is what I love to do. When a student minister requested information on a black Pentecostal church, I discovered how very little information had been published. I have conducted research in many libraries and archives. I have done computer searches and conducted oral interviews. My interest has turned into an unending research project. Young and older people (especially young people) are interested in this information and I feel strongly that it should be available. It is important to black history, religion, civil rights, and other disciplines to be able to read documented histories of the Pentecostal movement.

"In 1994, Barbara Kramer and I attracted a following to the Rosewood cause. Together we formed a group called the Rosewood Forum to research this massacre. Rosewood was located approximately 10 miles northwest of Cedar Key, Florida. The trouble erupted

on New Year's Day 1923 when white men were searching for a black man accused of assaulting a white woman. These white men rampaged through the Rosewood community, burning houses and buildings and driving every black resident away. In 1994, the Florida Legislature paid the Rosewood surviving descendants because the State of Florida did not protect its black citizens in 1923. This was the first attempt in U. S. history to pay reparations for racial violence.

"From 1993 to 1995, I was a consultant for the Bureau of Florida Folklife Programs, a unit of the Division of Historical Resources, Florida Department of State. The Florida Folklife Programs produced, in 1995, an audio cassette recording of African-American gospel steel guitar music in Florida. The recording features Willie Eason (known as the Father of African American steel guitar players), Aubrey Ghent, Henry Nelson, and others. Articles on this style of folk music were featured in *Newsweek* magazine, July 16, 1996, and *Guitar Magazine*, August, 1996. This music has been found mainly in Holiness Pentecostal churches. I also contributed along with Bob Stone to 'Folk Masters 1994,' a concert program book and radio listener's guide for the Smithsonian Folk Masters program at Wolf Trap, Virginia, where our Florida players performed.

"After I use the gathered resources for publications, I house them at the Schomburg Center, New York Public Library. The collection is the DuPree African American Pentecostal and Holiness Collection, accession number MG-325. Information concerning my publications and collections are available on the OCLC and RLIN library databases. Some special collections are in the *Library of Congress National Union Catalog of Manuscript Collections*. Gospel music materials are housed in three locations: the Black Music Research Collection, Columbus College, Chicago, IL; the Gospel Music Hall of Fame, Detroit, MI; and the Schomburg Center collection, New York."

BIOGRAPHICAL/CRITICAL SOURCES:

PERIODICALS

American Libraries, February, 1978, p. 99.
Black Issues in Higher Education, April 22, 1993, pp. 14-16.
Chicago Tribune, August 6, 1993, pp. 2, 7.
Choice, April, 1990, p. 1297; June, 1996, p. 1613.
Christian Century, August 11-18, 1993, p. 770.
Detroit News, October 21, 1989, p. A15.

Ebony, August, 1996.
Journal of American History, June, 1990, p. 183-99.
Miami Herald, July 25, 1994, p. 1.
Miami Times, September 14, 1989, p. C2.
Orlando Sentinel, February 27, 1993, p. B5.
Pace of Santa Fe Community College, April/May/June, 1996, pp. 1-2.
Sacramento Bee, September 26, 1993, p. B1.
Sun-Sentinel (Ft. Lauderdale, FL), October 21, 1989, pp. D1-D7.
Tampa Tribune, October 21, 1989; April 25, 1994.
Washington Post, August 7, 1993; July 24, 1995.
Western Journal of Black Studies, fall, 1995, p. 231.

* * *

DYGARD, Thomas J. 1931-1996

OBITUARY NOTICE—See index for *CA* sketch: Born August 10, 1931, in Little Rock, AK; died of heart failure, September 30, 1996, in Hazelton, PA. Children's author and journalist. A reporter and bureau chief for the Associated Press, Dygard is best known for his sports and adventure novels for children. His most recent book, *Running Wild,* featured a teenager who found happiness after joining a football team. Dygard began his career writing sports for the *Arkansas Gazette* after earning his degree from the University of Arkansas at Fayetteville. In 1954 he was offered a job with the Associated Press and went on to work in several of their bureaus, including Little Rock, Arkansas, Birmingham, Alabama, and New Orleans, Louisiana. He was also bureau chief in Tokyo, Japan, Chicago, Illinois, Indianapolis, Indiana, and Little Rock, Arkansas. Dygard started writing sports novels for young adults as a hobby and had his first one, *Running Scared,* published in 1977. He went on to publish a book every year until 1986 and some of the best-known are *Outside Shooter, Point Spread* and *Soccer Duel.* He retired from the Associated Press in 1993 and moved to Evansville, Indiana, but continued writing children's novels.

OBITUARIES AND OTHER SOURCES:

BOOKS

Something about the Author Autobiography Series, Volume 15, Gale, 1993.

PERIODICALS

New York Times, October 5, 1996, p. 52.

E

EARL, Donald (Charles) 1931-1996

OBITUARY NOTICE—See index for *CA* sketch: Born February 11, 1931, in Cambridge, England; died of liver cancer, August 20, 1996, in England. Professor and author. A prominent scholar on the Classics, Earl continued to teach and write about ancient Roman and Greek society even as interest in the field waned. His four books in the 1960s—*The Political Thought of Sallust, Tiberius Gracchus, a Study in Politics, The Moral and Political Tradition of Rome,* and *The Age of Augustus*—constitute an exhaustive study of Roman politics from the age of the Gracchi to Octavius Caesar. His most recent writings were contributions to periodicals, including *Athenaeum (Pavia), Historia, Journal of Roman Studies,* and *Latomus.* Earl was educated in Latin and Roman history at St. Catharine's College at Cambridge University in England and began his research on Sallust while studying for his doctorate, which led to his first book. Throughout his academic career, Earl lectured at Leeds University in England, Northwestern University in Illinois and was chair of the Classics Department at the University of Hull in England. He held the latter post until 1988, when the University disbanded the department. Earl stuck with the discipline, however, and became Dean of Arts at Hull in 1984. After retiring in 1988, he still taught Roman history at Hull part-time.

OBITUARIES AND OTHER SOURCES:

PERIODICALS

Times (London), September 25, 1996, p. 19.

EASTAWAY, Edward
See THOMAS, (Philip) Edward

* * *

EDELSON, Marshall 1928-

PERSONAL: Born May 31, 1928, in Chicago, IL; son of George I. and Ida (Bernstein) Edelson; married Zelda Sarah Toll (former head of publications, Peabody Museum, Yale University), December 27, 1952; children: Jonathan Toll, Rebecca Jo, David Jan Edelson Tolchinsky. *Education:* University of Chicago, Ph.B., 1946; Stanford University, A.B., 1949; University of Chicago, Ph.D., 1954, M.D., 1955; Western New England Institute for Psychoanalysis, 1966-71; American Psychoanalytic Association, certification in adult psychoanalysis, 1975. *Avocational interests:* Movies.

ADDRESSES: Office—Department of Psychiatry, Yale University School of Medicine, 25 Park St., Grace Education Building, 6th Floor, New Haven, CT 06519-1189.

CAREER: Psychoanalyst and educator. Presbyterian Hospital, Chicago, IL, intern, 1955-56; Sheppard and Enoch Pratt Hospital, Towson, MD, resident in psychiatry, 1956-59; University of Oklahoma, Oklahoma City, assistant professor of psychiatry, 1961-63; Austen Riggs Center, Stockbridge, MA, staff psychiatrist, 1964-68; Yale University, New Haven, CT, associate professor, 1968-76, professor of psychiatry, 1976—. Western New England Institute for Psychoanalysis, educational consultant, 1973—. *Military ser-*

vice: Psychiatrist, U.S. Army Medical Corps, 1959-61; became captain.

MEMBER: International Psychoanalytic Association, American Psychiatric Association (life fellow), American Medical Association, American Psychoanalytic Association, Western New England Institute for Psychoanalysis and Psychoanalytic Society.

AWARDS, HONORS: National Institute for Mental Health Career Teacher fellowship, 1962; Heinz Hartmann award, New York Psychoanalytic Institute, 1973; honorary M.A., Yale University, 1976; Psychiatric Residents Association Teaching Awards, Department of Psychiatry, Yale University, 1987 (first recipient), 1992, 1993, 1995; Stephen Fleck Faculty Award, exemplary physician and clinical teacher, Department of Psychiatry, Yale University, 1992; special award from psychiatric residents, Department of Psychiatry, Yale University, for "unsurpassed commitment to teaching excellence," 1994.

WRITINGS:

The Termination of Intensive Psychotherapy, Charles Thomas (Springfield, IL), 1963.

Ego Psychology, Group Dynamics, and the Therapeutic Community, Grune and Stratton (New York), 1964.

Sociotherapy and Psychotherapy, University of Chicago Press (Chicago, IL), 1970.

The Practice of Sociotherapy: A Case Study, Yale University Press (New Haven, CT), 1970.

(Editor with Theodore Lidz) Training Tomorrow's Psychiatrist, Yale University Press, 1970.

The Idea of a Mental Illness, Yale University Press, 1971.

Language and Interpretation in Psychoanalysis, Yale University Press, 1975.

Hypothesis and Evidence in Psychoanalysis, University of Chicago Press, 1984.

Psychoanalysis: A Theory in Crisis, University of Chicago Press, 1988.

Contributor to Explorations in General Theory in Social Science, Free Press, 1976; Psychiatry and the Humanities, Yale University Press, 1978, 1980; Applied Psycholinguistics and Mental Health, Plenum, 1980; Exploring Clinical Methods for Social Research, Sage Publications, 1985; Repression or Dissociation: Implications for Personality Theory, Psychopathology, and Health, University of Chicago Press, 1990; Interface between Psychoanalysis and Psychology, American Psychological Association

Press, 1992; and Psychotherapy Research and Practice: Bridging the Gap, BasicBooks, 1994. Also contributor to professional journals, including Psychoanalytic Study of the Child.

WORK IN PROGRESS: (With David N. Berg) Nothing to Do with Me: A Psychoanalyst's Journey Beyond Individual Psychology ("A memoir about experiences in groups and organizations"); "currently interested in group and organizational dynamics, and also in narrative paradigms for encoding knowledge; investigating the implications for theory and practice of focusing on the telling and enacting of stories in psychoanalysis and psychotherapy."

SIDELIGHTS: A practicing psychoanalyst and professor of psychiatry at Yale University Medical School, Marshall Edelson has worked at the interface of psychiatry and psychoanalysis, on the one side, and the social sciences (notably, sociology, linguistics, and cognitive psychology) and the humanities, on the other. His 1975 work Language and Interpretation in Psychoanalysis includes a detailed analysis of a poem by Wallace Stevens and a prelude by Johann Sebastian Bach, and employs Noam Chomsky's linguistics to demystify the intuitions of the psychoanalyst by proposing that they are unwitting responses to linguistic features in speech. 1971's The Idea of Mental Illness is also about language and semiotics. Edelson received the New York Psychoanalytic Institute's Heinz Hartmann Award in 1972 for his work on language and dreams.

In 1984's Hypothesis and Evidence in Psychoanalysis, Edelson continues to adhere to the main tenets of psychoanalytic theory, while taking note that others are debunking them, but at the same time he cautions that their claims will be held suspect so long as they "still feel free to indulge in their delusions that their heaps of clinical observations, case reports, vignettes, and anecdotes do meet scientific requirements for empirical evidence." In the 1984 book and 1988's Psychoanalysis: A Theory in Crisis, he defends psychoanalysis as a legitimate scientific discipline, and applies ideas from the philosophy of science to show how the task of formulating and testing psychoanalytic theory might be better carried out. The former work suggests that psychoanalysts should make use of probability theory and single-subject research to validate its hypotheses, and the later work argues strongly for the value of case studies, much more rigorously formulated, as a means for testing and not simply generating psychoanalytic hypotheses. "Edelson presents a cogent but highly abstract line of

reasoning," *Library Journal* reviewer Paul Hymowitz commented in a review of *Hypothesis and Evidence,* noting that the psychiatrist's work is a valuable first step toward reevaluating and refining the techniques whereby psychoanalysis' clinical successes are verified. Robert Wallerstein, writing in the *New York Times Book Review,* declared: "Dr. Edelson has committed himself with gusto, persistence, and intelligence . . . [to] a spirited defense of psychoanalysis as science—not necessarily as it is, but as it can be in the best of hands and as it should be."

Edelson was a leader in developing "the therapeutic community" in psychiatric inpatient settings. In 1964's *Ego Psychology, Group Dynamics, and the Therapeutic Community,* and 1970's *Sociotherapy and Psychotherapy* and *The Practice of Sociotherapy: A Case Study,* making use of knowledge of group dynamics and sociology, he showed that attending to the characteristic of the treatment milieu, and engaging patients in solving social problems that arise in the setting in which they are treated, are necessary for success. He argued for the value of a sociotherapy whose interventions, concerned with group dynamics and the relation of groups to each other, seek to change a social system, and showed how it complements a psychotherapy whose interventions, concerned with personality dynamics, seek to change an individual. In a critique for *Library Journal,* Morton Bard labeled *Sociotherapy and Psychotherapy* "tightly reasoned" and "intellectually controlled theory."

Edelson told *CA:* "My writing grows out of my work as a teacher and psychoanalyst. It is my way of struggling with the problems and questions that confront me as I do that work."

BIOGRAPHICAL/CRITICAL SOURCES:

BOOKS

Edelson, Marshall, *Hypothesis and Evidence in Psychoanalysis,* University of Chicago Press, 1984.

PERIODICALS

Ethics, July, 1985, p. 973.
Library Journal, March 1, 1970, p. 905; March 1, 1984, p. 109.
New Republic, January 21, 1985, p. 28.
New York Times Book Review, February 26, 1989, p. 36.
Times Literary Supplement, September 15, 1989, p. 1009.

EDGERTON, Leslie H. 1943-

PERSONAL: Born February 13, 1943, in Odessa, TX; son of Leslie H. and Dorothy Ella (a retailer; maiden name, Vincent) Edgerton; married Sheila K. Smith (a supervisor), October 11, 1968 (divorced, 1979); married Mary F. Goff (a hairstylist), May 4, 1986; children: Britney, Sienna, Michael. *Ethnicity:* "Caucasian." *Education:* Indiana University at Ft. Wayne, B.A. (with honors), 1994; graduate study at Vermont College. *Politics:* "Laissez-faire." *Religion:* Agnostic. *Avocational interests:* Reading and sports.

ADDRESSES: Home—4941 Maple Ridge Dr., Ft. Wayne, IN 46835-3930. *Office*—Bold Strokes Hair Design, Inc., 6772 State Blvd., Ft. Wayne, IN 46815. *Agent*—Maureen Lasher, P.O. Box 888, Pacific Palisades, CA 90272. *E-mail*—LEdger7633 @aol.com.

CAREER: Snobs Hair Designers, New Orleans, LA, artistic director, 1982-84; Busta at the Fairmont, New Orleans, stylist, 1984-85; Kenneth's, New Orleans, stylist, 1985-86; Bold Strokes Hair Design, Ft. Wayne, IN, owner, 1986—. Has served on the Milady Editorial Committee, and the National Book Review Committee for forthcoming books; media member of the Indiana University Publications Board, 1993-94. *Military service*—U.S. Navy, 1961-65, became radioman third class.

MEMBER: Writers Center of Indianapolis.

AWARDS, HONORS: Indiana University at South Bend Literary Award for short fiction, 1972; named one of "Indiana's Best Writers," 1993, by Arts Indiana; associate fellowship grant in literature from the Indiana Arts Commission, 1994; numerous hairdressing awards.

WRITINGS:

NONFICTION

You and Your Clients: Human Relations for Cosmetology, Delmar Publishing (Albany, NY), 1992.
Managing Your Business: Milady's Guide to the Salon, Milady Publishing (Bronx, NY), 1993.
SalonOvations's Guide to Becoming a Financially Solvent Salon, Milady Publishing, 1996.

Author of column published in *Nails Magazine.* Also contributor of articles to periodicals, including *Bride's, Kiwanis Magazine, Dental Economics,*

Bridal Trends, Circle K Magazine, Business Digest, Business People, Nails Magazine, Groom and Board, National Beauty School Journal, Your Home, Hair and Beauty News, SalonOvations, South Bend Tribune, American Salon, and *Cosmetology Today.*

FICTION

The Death of Tarpons (novel), University of North Texas Press (Denton, TX), 1996.
Monday's Meal (short stories), University of North Texas Press, 1997.

Also contributor of stories to periodicals, including *South Carolina Review, Kansas Quarterly, Arkansas Review, Chiron Review, Hopewell Review, Aethlon, Innisfree, The Analecta, Whiskey Island Magazine, Samsura, North Atlantic Review, My Legacy, Confluence,* and *New Press;* also contributor to the *Imaginary Friends* anthology.

WORK IN PROGRESS: Working on memoirs for University of North Texas Press, and on *SalonOvations Guide to Writing Nonfiction Book Proposals* for Milady Publishing; research on prisons in the United States; a young adult novel entitled *Mirror, Mirror;* a crime novel entitled *Just Like That.*

SIDELIGHTS: Leslie H. Edgerton has built a successful career in the hairstyling field, winning styling awards in three different states. Born in Odessa, Texas, in 1943, he worked during the 1980s as an artistic director and as a stylist at popular salons in New Orleans, Louisiana. When he moved to Fort Wayne, Indiana, however, he became the owner of his own salon, Bold Strokes Hair Design. Along the way, Edgerton has parlayed his expertise in styling and design into several nonfiction books on the subject, including 1992's *You and Your Clients: Human Relations for Cosmetology,* 1993's *Managing Your Business: Milady's Guide to the Salon,* and 1996's *SalonOvations's Guide to Becoming a Financially Solvent Salon.* Yet even before he became the author of nonfiction books, he was writing short stories, and garnered the 1972 Indiana University at South Bend Literary Award for short fiction. While still meeting the demands of owning a successful salon, Edgerton took classes to earn a bachelor's degree at Indiana University at Fort Wayne, then continued working towards a master of fine arts from Vermont College. He has contributed both short fiction and articles to periodicals, and a story to the *Imaginary Friends* anthology. His first novel, *The Death of Tarpons,* was published in 1996.

The Death of Tarpons is the story of Corey John, a Texan who, as an adult facing a battle with cancer, returns to his home state's Gulf Coast. He there recalls the summer he spent as a fourteen-year-old, fishing for tarpons with his grandfather—himself dying of cancer at that time. Edgerton's narrative focuses primarily on this recollection, and it is with immediacy that the reader shares the teenage Corey's discoveries about his parents. His father, Robert, is an abusive man immersed in his work and incapable of loving his son. His mother, Mary, sees mental illness as a means to avoid her husband. Corey's grandmother will never follow up on her promise to Robert to make him a partner in his restaurant business. It is only through his grandfather's love and attention during this harrowing season of realization that Corey learns not to repeat his father's mistakes in life.

Critics responded favorably to Edgerton's art in *The Death of Tarpons.* Robert Jordan, holding forth on the book's worth in the *Library Journal,* hailed it as an "exceptional first novel," and went on to recommend it highly for purchase by both public and academic libraries. A *Publishers Weekly* critic called *The Death of Tarpons* "inspirational," and declared that Edgerton's work "shines with wisdom."

Edgerton followed *The Death of Tarpons* with a collection of short stories entitled *Monday's Meal,* published by University of North Texas Press, which also brought out the novel. The University of North Texas Press may also be the vehicle which brings readers Edgerton's memoirs. The author continues to write nonfiction as well; he is working on another book for Milady Publishing, the house involved with some of his previous cosmetology related volumes, *SalonOvations Guide to Writing Nonfiction Book Proposals.* He also writes a regular column for *Nails Magazine.*

Edgerton told *CA* of his start in the writing field: "My writing career began shortly after my 'reading career' was launched somewhere around the enlightened age of six. Almost all of my literary output up until perhaps twenty years ago is only available 'in my room,' having passed—thankfully!—into oblivion. I cannot recall exactly when I decided to be a writer; I just know there wasn't a time in my life when that wasn't my goal. To achieve my aim of appearing in print, I determined early on in childhood that the accumulation of experience would serve as the focus of all my efforts, and indeed, that has remained my driving force throughout my entire life. The accumu-

lation of material goods or wealth has always seemed somewhat distasteful and never a desired objective, much to the chagrin I'm sure, of several of my ex-wives, who probably deserved that I paid more attention to that part of what is considered a normal American existence. I have not held up my part in accumulating things and am quite happy so long as I own a pair of jeans, t-shirt or sweater (in season), and at least one nourishing meal per day. And time to write. That is paramount and crucial to maintaining the life processes within my earthly unit.

"Who have been my influences? There are so many, changing virtually each week as I pick up a new author, but primarily have been Albert Camus (in particular, *The Stranger*), William Faulkner (although I can't read him when I'm writing—I end up with four rapes, two suicides, an arson attempt, an incest incident, and a lynching, and I'm still in the first paragraph—that's not what Bill does, but it *seems* that's what he does), early Raymond Carver, Lou Mathews (not a household word, but a terrific writer all the same), Louis-Ferdinand Celine, Jorge Luis Borges, William Shakespeare, John Donne, Jean Genet, Jean-Paul Sartre, Diane Lefer, Francois Camoin, Phyllis Barber, Doug Glover, Bret Lott, J. D. Salinger, Richard Brautigan, Kevin Cantry, William Goyen, Norman Mailer . . . the list would run in the hundreds if not thousands, and space gently urges that I desist. My first *real* teacher, Elaine Hemley-Gottlieb. I wish Pete Dexter would write more. Kurt Vonnegut. Enough!

"My writing process is that I write every blessed moment I am not earning my daily bread or involved in slumber (four hours per night). I keep about thirty-five pieces in motion at all times, including novels, short stories, magazine articles, queries, essays, and grocery lists. I've never experienced writer's block, probably because when I get stuck on one thing, I just open another file on the ol' Gateway 2000 computer and hack away at that one. I'm inspired by my wife Mary and my children. When I'm gone, I want them each to be able to say that 'Dad/Hubby sure could crank it out! And some of it is good. Some of it is even better than that. I'm sure proud of him.' As always, it turns out to be an ego thing.

"Each subject I've chosen has been for a unique reason. Rather than go into each book, let me talk about *The Death of Tarpons*. I began this with the word 'spatterdashers' (original title) which I'd seen used in an interview with a French writer in the *Paris Review*. I wish I could remember who it was. As a lover of words, I feel in love with this kinda ugly one. It was one of those utilitarian Anglo-Saxon numbers that meant exactly what it said. Spatterdashers was a literal term denoting an item of clothing men wore in pre-dry cleaner days that prevented spatter from dashing them. The more familiar version nowadays is 'spats.' Around this word, I added about sixty thousand words and then my publisher said we had to deep-six the title because nobody would know what it meant. I lost the argument that ensued, and deep down, I knew she was right. Although, I just picked up Gore Vidal's latest work, *Palimpsest,* and I wonder what kinds of conversations he had with his editor. . . . Put Vidal on my list of influences, too, if for nothing else, great titles.

"In search of experience, I went a little too far and ended up in prison for two years. That sort of cooled my ardor for collecting adventures . . . well, for a little while, anyway. At least, after my sojourn inside the walls, I limited things to those that were at least semi-legit, and, as they say, 'my hands have been clean for three decades.' I don't recommend prison for learning to write, although it does help with material. The problem is, paper is too hard to come by for the average inmate engaged in the writing trade.

"Indeed, I've just begun to pen my memoirs and in them I'll talk about my days at the Pendleton Reformatory. It only took thirty years to be able to do so, so if an aspiring author thinks the Jack London school of writing something to aspire to, perhaps he or she might want to start early enough to allow for a cooling down period of a quarter century or so.

"If I had to describe my philosophy of literature it would be this: Tell the truth and get out of the way. Figure on the reader having a functioning brain. Respect those who've earned respect and don't think much about those who don't; it'll give you a headache. Look in on your wife and kids once in a while and say something nice to them—they'll appreciate it and you'll feel good about it, even if it takes valuable time away from your writing. Don't own a dog who resists housebreaking. Teach your kids to never date anyone named after a day of the week and never play poker with someone named after a city. These are not only the rules of writing (for me) but for life, as well. Oh—and when you put little squiggly lines down on paper, try and make it interesting above all. There's way too much seriousness in the world and it's getting worse. Check the paper if you don't believe me."

BIOGRAPHICAL/CRITICAL SOURCES:

PERIODICALS

Library Journal, March 15, 1996, p. 94.
Publishers Weekly, February 12, 1996, p. 60.

* * *

EDMOND, Lauris (Dorothy) 1924-

PERSONAL: Born April 2, 1924; married Trevor Edmond, 1945; children: five daughters, one son. *Education:* University of Waikato, B.A., 1968; Victoria University, M.A., 1972.

ADDRESSES: Home and office—22 Grass St., Oriental Bay, Wellington, New Zealand.

CAREER: Writer. Huntly College, teacher, 1968-69; Heretaunga College, Wellington, teacher, 1970-72; Post-Primary Teachers Association, Wellington, editor, 1973-80; Massey University, Palmerston North, off-campus tutor and lecturer, 1980—. Writer-in-residence, Deakin University, Melbourne, 1985.

AWARDS, HONORS: New Zealand P.E.N. award, 1975; Katherine Mansfield-Menton fellowship, 1981; Commonwealth poetry prize, 1985; Lilian Ida Smith award, 1987. D.Litt.: Massey University, 1988. O.B.E. (Officer, Order of the British Empire), 1986.

WRITINGS:

POETRY

In Middle Air, Pegasus Press (Christchurch), 1975.
The Pear Tree and Other Poems, Pegasus Press, 1977.
Salt from the North, Oxford University Press (Wellington), 1980.
Seven, Wayzgoose Press (Wellington), 1980.
Wellington Letter, Mallinson Rendel (Wellington), 1980.
Catching It, Oxford University Press (Auckland), 1983.
Selected Poems, Oxford University Press, 1984.
Seasons and Creatures, Oxford University Press, and Bloodaxe (Newcastle upon Tyne), 1986.
Summer near the Arctic Circle, Oxford University Press 1988.

New and Selected Poems, Oxford University Press and Bloodaxe, 1991.
Scenes from a Small City, Daphne Brasell Association, 1994.
Selected Poems 1975-1994, Bridget Williams Books, 1994.

PLAYS

Between Night and Morning, produced in Wellington, 1980.

Also author of *The Mountain* (cycle of four radio plays), 1980-81.

OTHER

(Editor) *Dancing to My Tune: Verse and Prose,* by Denis Glover, Catspaw Press (Wellington), 1974.
(Editor) *Young Writing,* P.E.N. New Zealand Centre (Wellington), 1979.
(Editor) *A Remedial Persiflage,* by Chris Ward, Post Primary Teachers Association (Wellington), 1980.
(Editor) *The Letters of A.R.D. Fairburn,* Oxford University Press (Wellington), 1981.
High Country Weather (novel), Sydney, Allen and Unwin, and Wellington, Port Nicholson Press, 1984.
(Editor, with Carolyn Milward) *Women in Wartime: New Zealand Women Tell Their Story,* Government Printing Office (Wellington), 1986.
Hot October: An Autobiographical Story, Allen and Unwin (Sydney), 1989.
Bonfires in the Rain, Bridget Williams Books, 1991.
The Quick World, Bridget Williams Books, 1992.

* * *

EDMOND, Murray (Donald) 1949-

PERSONAL: Born in 1949.

ADDRESSES: Office—English Department, University of Auckland, Private Bag 92019, Auckland, New Zealand.

CAREER: Writer, actor, and director, Town and Country Players, Wellington. University of Auckland, lecturer in drama, 1991—. Editor, *Freed,* 1970-71.

WRITINGS:

POETRY

Entering the Eye, Caveman Press (Dunedin), 1973.
Patchwork, Hawk Press (Days Bay), 1978.
End Wall, Oxford University Press (Auckland), 1981.
Selected Poems, Oxford University Press, 1984.
Letters and Paragraphs, Caxton Press (Christchurch), 1987.
From the Word Go: Poems, Auckland University Press (Auckland), 1992.
The Switch: A Long Poem, Auckland University Press, 1994.

OTHER

(Editor, with Mary Paul) *The New Poets of the 80's: Initiatives in New Zealand Poetry,* Allen and Unwin (Wellington), 1987.

*　　*　　*

EDWARDS, I(orwerth) E(iddon) S(tephen)　1909-1996

OBITUARY NOTICE—See index for *CA* sketch: Born July 21, 1909, in London, England; died September 24, 1996, in London, England. Archeologist and author. Recognized as the leading authority on Egypt's Tomb of King Tutankhamun, Edwards wrote the popular and critically acclaimed book *Tutankhamun: His Tomb and Its Treasures* in 1976. He was Keeper of the Egyptian Antiquities in the British Museum from 1955 to 1974 and helped make "King Tut," the 14th Century B.C. Egyptian monarch, a household word in the United States and Britain. Edwards was the main force behind the Tutankhamun exhibit at the British Museum and his expertise was widely sought by the public when the exhibit toured the United States in 1977. After studying at England's Cambridge University, Edwards worked in the British Museum's department of Egyptian and Assyrian antiquities in 1934 and became an expert on ancient Egypt. Serving in Britain's Foreign Office in Cairo during World War II, Edwards studied the pyramids and published *The Pyramids of Egypt* a few years after the war. His other works include *Treasures of Tutankhamun,* published in 1972, and *Tutankhamun's Jewelry,* published in 1976. Edwards was a visiting professor at Brown University in Providence, Rhode Island, and a Glanville Memorial Lecturer at Cambridge University, England. He also contributed to and edited other archeology journals.

OBITUARIES AND OTHER SOURCES:

BOOKS

Who's Who, 146th edition, St. Martin's, 1994.

PERIODICALS

New York Times, October 7, 1996, p. B13.

*　　*　　*

ELLIS, Jerry　1947-

PERSONAL: Born November 28, 1947, in Fort Payne, AL; son of J. P. (a carpenter) and Viva (Buckles) Ellis; companion of Debi Holmes-Binney (a writer and publicist). *Ethnicity:* "Native American." *Education:* University of Alabama, B.A., 1970.

ADDRESSES: Home and office—1714 Smith Gap Rd. NW, Fort Payne, AL 35967. *Agent*—Charlotte Sheedy, Sterling Lord Literistic, Inc., 65 Bleecker St., New York, NY 10019.

CAREER: Writer, lecturer and Native American folk artist.

MEMBER: The Authors Guild, Inc.

AWARDS, HONORS: Pulitzer Prize nomination, 1991, for *Walking the Trail: One Man's Journey along the Cherokee Trail of Tears*.

WRITINGS:

Walking the Trail: One Man's Journey along the Cherokee Trail of Tears, Delacorte (New York City), 1991.
Bareback! One Man's Journey along the Pony Express Trail, Delacorte, 1993.
Marching through Georgia: My Walk with Sherman, Delacorte, 1995.
(Compiler) *In Short: A Collection of Brief Creative Non-Fiction,* Norton (New York City), 1996.

WORK IN PROGRESS: Power Spots: A Native American Adventure, on Native American sacred sites; and *Dove Story,* a children's book.

SIDELIGHTS: Jerry Ellis told *CA:* "I never dreamed of being a writer when I was a child growing up in the mountains of Fort Payne, Alabama—the site of an old Cherokee town. I wasn't even big on reading; I preferred to roam the woods and creeks where my Indian ancestors had once lived.

"I got the first hint that I would become a writer when I was twenty years old. I fell for a woman living in Oklahoma and began to write love letters to her.

"By the age of twenty-six, I had thumbed enough miles in the United States to circle the earth five times. I had heard so many stories and felt so much along the way that I was overtaken by a need to tell others about these experiences. I began to write stories and plays.

"In 1985 I moved to Hollywood to try to sell my screenplay. It was about the Cherokee Trail of Tears, where five thousand of my ancestors died in 1838, when seven thousand armed U.S. soldiers forced them to march barefooted nine hundred miles from their homes in the Deep South to Oklahoma in the heart of winter. I couldn't sell the script, but I felt compelled to tell the story, so, in 1989 I became the first person in modern history to walk those nine hundred miles. It was an extraordinary journey, and I wrote a book about it.

"During the journey, I gained insight into how my roots, American history, and my great fascination with travel and people was shaping my writing. I had, I felt, a kind of calling to write such books. I am currently working on my fourth book. In the past year I have visited thirty-five states to investigate Native American sacred sites, so I can write about the history and mythology of these places, as well as the adventure of the trek. It has been an extraordinary journey, filled with rare events and people. My partner, Debi Holmes-Binney, has been making a video documentary about the trip, and we've painted our car Betsy with murals of the most striking sites we have explored. This has drawn much excitement from onlookers, and they have become part of our journey to probe the spirit of America in the 1990s. As you might gather, I am a strong believer that life is too short and amazing not to try to make the most of it. The spiritual life can be fun and exciting."

ELTON, Hugh 1964-

PERSONAL: Born November 17, 1964, in Erith, Kent, England; married, wife's name Krista, December 12, 1992. *Ethnicity:* "White." *Education:* University of Sheffield, B.A. (with honors), 1986; Queen's College, Oxford, D.Phil., 1990.

ADDRESSES: Office—Department of History, Trinity College, Hartford, CT 06106; fax 860-297-5111. *E-mail*—Hugh.Elton@mail.trincoll.edu; http://shakti .trincoll.edu/~helton/index.html.

CAREER: Oxford University, Oxford, England, tutor in classics at Lincoln College, 1988; participated in archaeological field studies in Italy, Turkey, and France, 1991; Cambridge University, Cambridge, England, site assistant with Cambridge Archaeological Unit, 1991-92; Rice University, Houston, TX, visiting assistant professor of history, 1993-94; Trinity College, Hartford, CT, visiting assistant professor of history, 1994—. Conducted field studies in England, Greece, and Israel. Speaker at colleges and universities, including Emory University, 1994.

WRITINGS:

(Editor with J. F. Drinkwater, and contributor) *Fifth-Century Gaul: A Crisis of Identity?* Cambridge University Press (Cambridge, England), 1992.
Warfare in Roman Europe, A.D. 350-425, Clarendon Press (New York City), 1996.
Frontiers of the Roman Empire, Indiana University Press (Bloomington, IN), 1996.

Contributor to books, including *A Dictionary of Ancient History,* edited by G. Speake, Basil Blackwell (Oxford, England), 1994, published as *The Penguin Dictionary of Ancient History,* Penguin; and *Barbarians in the West,* edited by N. Christie, Oxford University Press (Oxford), in press. Contributor of articles and reviews to classical studies journals, including *Medieval Prosopography, Papers of the British School at Rome,* and *Britannia.*

SIDELIGHTS: Hugh Elton told *CA:* "In my book *Warfare in Roman Europe,* I discussed the military events involved in the decline of the late Roman Empire and the rise of the Barbarian West during the period A.D. 350-500, examining the military systems of Rome and her enemies, showing how they developed and interacted. The study produced a number of important conclusions. The discussion of the barbarian threat suggests that it had little coherence and

that, when compared with Roman forces, barbarian military capacities were low and did not improve during this period.

"This theme of relationships between Romans and non-Romans is also the subject of my second book *The Frontiers of the Roman Empire.* Here, I examine the Roman frontier as a series of overlapping zones—civil, economic, and military—with attention paid to processes on both sides of the border.

"My current research focuses on Cilicia in eastern Asia Minor in the Roman period. My next book will be a general study of Cilicia as a region in the Roman Empire. However, this research is at an early stage, and the precise form is not yet set. One question still to be resolved is whether to attempt archaeological field work in the region. I am working on several related papers: a study on bandits and social structures in the region, a paper on the political and military role of the Isaurians in the early Byzantine period, and an analysis of the political changes in the region between the second century B.C. and the first century A.D."

* * *

ELWARD, James (Joseph) 1928-1996
(Rebecca James)

OBITUARY NOTICE—See index for *CA* sketch: Surname is pronounced "*el*-word"; born November 22, 1928, in Chicago, IL; died of a heart attack, August 30, 1996, in Manhattan, New York. Actor and writer. Elward was an author of plays, television scripts, and novels, who received high praise when he completed the autobiographical novel of fashion executive Helen Van Slyke after her death. Credited as coauthor of the work, entitled *Public Smiles, Private Tears,* Elward contributed text that was consistent in style to that of Van Slyke. During his career, Elward was a writer of television programs for NBC, CBS, and ABC, beginning in 1956. He also acted in various theatrical productions. In addition he wrote plays, such as *Upbeat, Friday Night,* and *Best of Friends.* He authored the libretto of *The Man on the Bearskin Rug.* Among his television scripts were *The Remittance Man, Hide Me in the Mountains,* and *Music Power,* as well as work on serials such as *The Secret Storm, Love Is a Many Splendored Thing, The Guiding Light,* and *The Doctors.* He also penned novels as

Rebecca James, including *The House Is Dark, Tomorrow Is Mine,* and *Storms End.* In 1956, he received the Writers' Guild Award for best comedy script.

OBITUARIES AND OTHER SOURCES:

PERIODICALS

Chicago Tribune, September 3, 1996, section 3, p. 5.
New York Times, September 2, 1996, p. 22.

* * *

EMANUEL, James A(ndrew, Sr.) 1921-

PERSONAL: Born June 15, 1921, in Alliance, NE; married Mattie Johnson, 1950 (divorced 1974); children: one son (died 1983). *Education:* Howard University, B.A. (summa cum laude), 1950; Northwestern University, M.A., 1953; Columbia University, Ph.D., 1962.

ADDRESSES: Home and office—B.P. 339, 75266 Paris Cedex 06, France.

CAREER: Writer. Civilian Conservation Corps, Wellington, KS, canteen steward, 1939-40; elevator operator, Des Moines, IA, 1940-41; weighmaster, Rock Island, IL, 1941-42; United States War Department, Office of the Inspector General, Washington, D.C., confidential secretary, 1942-44; Pre-Induction Section, Army and Air Force Induction Station, Chicago, IL, civilian chief, 1950-53; Harlem YWCA Business School, New York, instructor, 1954-56; City College of New York, instructor, 1957-62, assistant professor, 1962-70, associate professor, 1970-72, professor of English, 1973-84; University of Grenoble, Fulbright Professor of American Literature, 1968-69; University of Warsaw, Fulbright Professor of American Literature, 1975-76; University of Toulouse, visiting professor of American Literature, 1971-73, 1979-81. Broadside Critics Series, Detroit, MI, general editor, 1969-75. *Military service:* 93rd Infantry Division, United States Army, 1944-46: Sergeant; Army Commendation Ribbon.

AWARDS, HONORS: John Hay Whitney fellowship, 1952, 1953; Saxton memorial fellowship, 1964; *Black American Literature Forum* Special Distinction award (for poetry), 1978.

WRITINGS:

POETRY

The Treehouse and Other Poems, Broadside Press (Detroit, MI), 1968.

At Bay, Broadside Press, 1969.

Panther Man, Broadside Press, 1970.

Black Man Abroad: The Toulouse Poems, Lotus Press (Detroit), 1978.

A Chisel in the Dark: Poems, Selected and New, Lotus Press, 1980.

A Poet's Mind, Regents (New York), 1983.

The Broken Bowl. New and Uncollected Poems, Lotus Press, 1983.

Deadly James and Other Poems, Lotus Press, 1987.

The Quagmire Effect, American College (Paris), 1988.

Whole Grain: Collected Poems, 1958-1989, Lotus Press, 1990.

De la rage au coeur, bilingual with French translations by Jean Migrenne, Amiot Lenganey (Thaon, France), 1992.

(With Godelieve Simons) *Blues in Black and White,* privately printed (Brussels, Belgium), 1992.

OTHER

Langston Hughes, Twayne (New York), 1967.

(Editor, with Theodore L. Gross) *Dark Symphony: Negro Literature in America,* Free Press (New York), 1968.

(With MacKinlay Kantor and Lawrence Osgood) *How I Write 2,* Harcourt Brace, (New York), 1972.

* * *

ENDO, Shusako 1923-1996

OBITUARY NOTICE—See index for *CA* sketch: Born March 27, 1923, in Tokyo, Japan; died from complications of hepatitis, September 29, 1996, in Tokyo. Author and playwright. Endo was a prolific writer and his favorite subject was the clash of cultures between the East and West. A Roman Catholic, he also wrote about religious faith, both Eastern and Western. His most recent novel was 1995's *Deep River,* a story about modern Japanese travelers who discover spirituality on a trip to India. Endo was baptized Roman Catholic when he was 12 at the urging of his aunt. Sickness kept him from combat in World War II and he attended Keio University after the war and went to Lyons, France, to study French Catholic writing. His first book, *Shiroihito,* was published in 1955. In addition to novels, Endo also wrote plays and was a humorist. John Updike once wrote of Endo in the *New Yorker:* "One can only marvel at the unobtrusive, persuasive effort of imagination that enables a modern Japanese to take up a viewpoint from which Japan is at the outer limit of the world." Because of his Catholicism, Endo's work was more understood by Western readers. In 1994, he was a contender for the Nobel Prize in Literature; throughout his career, Endo won several Japanese literary awards.

OBITUARIES AND OTHER SOURCES:

BOOKS

Dictionary of the Arts, Facts on File, 1994.

PERIODICALS

Los Angeles Times, September 30, 1996, p. A22.
New Yorker, January 14, 1980.
New York Times, September 30, 1996, p. B8.

* * *

ESPOSITO, Mary Ann 1942-

PERSONAL: Born August 3, 1942, in Buffalo, NY; daughter of Roy J. (a chemist) and Louise (a dietician; maiden name, Galasso) Saporito; married Guy M. Esposito (a physician), 1968; children: Elizabeth, Christopher. *Education:* Daeman College, B.A., 1964; University of New Hampshire, M.A. 1991; graduate of Cucina della Campania in Sorrento, Italy and of Italianissimo in Perugia, Italy. *Politics:* Independent. *Religion:* Catholic. *Avocational interests:* Travel, foreign language study.

ADDRESSES: *Home*—New Hampshire. *Office*—P.O. Box 1426, Portsmouth, NH 03802. *Agent*—Michael Jones, P.O. Box 397, Pelham, NH 03807.

CAREER: Public Broadcasting Service (PBS), host and creator of "Ciao Italia," a cooking show, Durham, NH, 1989—; Mary Ann Esposito, Inc. (a production company), president, 1996—; author of cookbooks. University of New Hampshire, Portsmouth, instructor in Italian cooking, 1985-90; European Heritage Institute, Richmond, VA, lecturer and

cook, 1990-91; Visiting and guest chef to numerous culinary institutes, including Boston University; has been a guest cook at Tre Vaselle in Torgiano, Italy, and La Cucina d'Edgardo in Montalcino, Tuscany; Strawberry Banke, Portsmouth, NH, president of board of trustees, 1980-84.

MEMBER: International Association of Cooking Professionals.

AWARDS, HONORS: Columbus Foundation Literary Award, Barnes and Noble, 1993, for *Ciao Italia;* Pirandello Lyceum Award, Barnes and Noble, 1995, for educational and entertainment contributions made by an Italian-American.

WRITINGS:

COOKBOOKS

Ciao Italia, Hearst Books/William Morrow (New York), 1991.
Nella Cucina, Hearst Books/William Morrow, 1993.
Celebrations Italian Style, illustrated by Tomie de Paola, Hearst Books/William Morrow, 1995.
Easy Book of Yeast Dough, William Morrow, 1997.

WORK IN PROGRESS: Research on the foods of northern Italy; a bread cookbook, to be published in 1997.

SIDELIGHTS: Since 1989, Mary Ann Esposito has hosted a weekly PBS cooking show called "Ciao Italia," on which she instructs her viewers in preparing a variety of authentic Italian dishes, and educates them about Italian history and folklore. According to a 1996 press release, "Ciao Italia" has aired on more than 250 public television stations, and "is one of the most-watched PBS cooking programs, with about one million viewers per episode per week." Esposito, whose cookbooks *Ciao Italia* and *Nella Cucina* are best-sellers, learned a great deal about Italian cooking from her Sicilian and Neapolitan-born grandmothers, but also attended cooking schools in Italy and earned a master's degree in Italian Renaissance history from the University of New Hampshire. The popular cook has appeared as a guest on a number of television shows, including NBC's "Today Show," ABC's "Home Show," and the Discovery Channel's "Low Cholesterol Gourmet," and has been profiled in such periodicals as *TV Guide, Quarterly Review of Wines, Family Circle, Ambassador,* and *Workbasket.* Esposito commented: "When it comes to holidays and special occasions, I am a hopeless sentimentalist. I regard these occasions as unique links in our lives that reaffirm our feelings for those we care about. For me, the preparing and sharing of food is one of the best expressions of those feelings."

BIOGRAPHICAL/CRITICAL SOURCES:

OTHER

Author quotes and other information obtained from press release from Fenneman Productions, Inc., and Mary Ann Esposito, Inc., 1996.

F

FIEDLER, Johanna 1946-

PERSONAL: Born in 1946, in Boston, MA; daughter of Arthur (a violist and symphony conductor) and Ellen (Bottomley) Fiedler. *Education:* Attended Sarah Lawrence College, 1963-67.

ADDRESSES: Office—c/o Doubleday, 1540 Broadway, New York, NY 10036. *Agent*—Gloria Loomis, Watkins Loomis Agency Inc., 133 East 35th St., Suite 1, New York, NY 10016.

CAREER: Metropolitan Opera, New York City, general press representative, 1975-89; writer, 1990—. Also publicist for National Symphony and program editor for New York Philharmonic.

WRITINGS:

Arthur Fiedler: Papa, the Pops and Me, Doubleday (New York City), 1994.

WORK IN PROGRESS: History of the Metropolitan Opera, 1966 to the Present, to be published by Doubleday as a Nan A. Talese imprint, in c. 1999.

SIDELIGHTS: Johanna Fiedler is the author of *Arthur Fiedler: Papa, the Pops and Me,* in which she recalls the life of her famous father, the former conductor of the Boston Pops orchestra. "Arthur Fiedler did more to popularize classical music—and, some think, to water it down—than any other American-born musician," wrote *Wall Street Journal* contributor Terry Teachout. In his fifty-year career with the Boston Pops, Fiedler undertook popular recordings and concerts, providing the funding that kept the Boston Symphony Orchestra or BSO, solvent. "Fiedler, who

in his old age looked like a cross between Santa Claus and Captain Kangaroo," Teachout explained, "was a natural media idol." According to the biography written by his eldest daughter, however, "despite his dashing, twinkly appearance and bluff, avuncular persona, [Fiedler] was a very difficult man," observed a *Publishers Weekly* contributor. "He and his wife both drank heavily, she eventually to her death, and family occasions among the Fiedlers . . . were the very model of dysfunctionalism."

Fiedler traces much of her father's unhappiness to the minimal respect he received as a musician from the Boston artistic community. "She thinks Serge Koussevitzky, the longtime BSO conductor, began to view him as a dangerous rival as Fiedler's popularity grew," declared Patti Doten in the *Boston Globe.* "And she feels her father never came to terms with the fact that he was not appreciated as a great musician and revered like Koussevitzky and Seiji Ozawa. She quotes Michael Steinberg, former artistic administrator and program annotator with the BSO, as saying that the musicians regarded Fiedler as "'a sort of lowlife who has to be taken seriously because the Pops season provides the money to keep the BSO going.'" "Throughout his life," wrote Lawson Taitte in the *New York Times Book Review,* "he behaved obsequiously to them, even though they paid him only $12,500 for the entire Pops season in 1961-62, exactly what he had been making 20 years earlier."

Most reviewers agree that Johanna Fiedler's depiction of her father is, in Taitte's words, "as unflinching as a Holbein or Whistler portrait." "We are persuaded," he added, "we see the renowned just as he was, every wrinkle and scowl line intact." The book reflects the author's own feelings of pain and abandonment. "Her

complaints against Fiedler *pere* seem valid," commented a *Kirkus Reviews* contributor, "but the dysfunctional Fiedler family nevertheless strikes the reader as having been more typical of the mid-century upper middle class than traumatic." Nonetheless, Taitte stated, "Ms. Fiedler convinces the reader that despite his failings she had genuine affection for her father." "This is a genuinely moving book," Teachout declared, "remarkable both for the fascinating story it tells and the spare, unsentimental prose in which it is written."

BIOGRAPHICAL/CRITICAL SOURCES:

PERIODICALS

Boston Globe, September 27, 1994, p. 33.
Kirkus Reviews, August 15, 1994, p. 1099.
New York Times Book Review, November 13, 1994, p. 73.
Publishers Weekly, August 15, 1994, pp. 79-80.
USA Today, November 11, 1994, p. D9.
Wall Street Journal, September 27, 1994, p. A14.

* * *

FINE, Doris Landau 1949-

PERSONAL: Born March 22, 1949, in Heidenheim, Germany; daughter of Jonas (an engineer) and Wanda (a nurse; maiden name, Krakowska) Landau; married Norman J. Fine, January 21, 1973; children: one son, one daughter. *Ethnicity:* "Jewish." *Education:* Boston University, B.S., 1971, M.S., 1976; Brandeis University, doctoral study, 1989—.

ADDRESSES: Home—Newton Highlands, MA. *Office*—Education Development Center, Inc., Newton, MA.

CAREER: Columbia Point Health Center, Dorchester, MA, physical therapist, 1971-73; Kinderschool of United Cerebral Palsy, South Natick, MA, staff member, 1973-75; Eunice Kennedy Shriver Center, Waltham, MA, assistant director of physical therapy, 1975-77; University of Massachusetts, adjunct faculty member, 1979-80; Waltham Public Schools, Waltham, physical therapist, 1980-82; Northeastern University, Boston, MA, lecturer in physical therapy, 1985-88; Youville Hospital, Cambridge, MA, member of pediatric evaluation team, 1988-90; Education

Development Center, Inc., Newton, MA, training specialist, 1992-93; Boston University, Boston, lecturer at Sargent College of Allied Health Professionals, 1993-96; Education Development Center, Inc., consultant, 1995—. Kids Are People Elementary School, physical therapist and staff trainer; Wheelock College, instructor, 1984.

MEMBER: Society for Disability Studies.

WRITINGS:

(With K. Blenk) *Making School Inclusion Work: A Guide to Everyday Practices,* Brookline Books (Cambridge, MA), 1995.

Contributor of articles and reviews to journals, including *Topics in Acute Care and Trauma Rehabilitation, Disability Studies Quarterly,* and *Journal of Educational Measures.*

WORK IN PROGRESS: An exploratory study of the experiences of secondary school students with spina bifida, and the experiences of their parents and teachers.

* * *

FLINT, Roland (Henry) 1934-

PERSONAL: Born February 27, 1934, in Park River, ND; married Janet Altic, 1962 (divorced 1973); married Rosalind Cowie, 1979; children: (first marriage) two daughters, one son. *Education:* University of North Dakota, B.A., 1958; Marquette University, M.A., 1960; University of Minnesota, Ph.D., 1968.

ADDRESSES: Home and office—8605 Milford Ave., Silver Spring, MD 20910.

CAREER: Marquette University, Milwaukee, WI, teaching assistant, 1959-60; University of Minnesota, Minneapolis, teaching assistant and instructor, 1960-68; Georgetown University, Washington, DC, assistant professor, 1968-75, associate professor, 1975-81, professor of English, 1981—. *Military service:* United States Marine Corps, 1954-56: became corporal; National Service medal.

MEMBER: Poetry Society of America (board of directors, 1984-86).

AWARDS, HONORS: National Endowment for the Arts Discovery grant, 1970, fellowship, 1981; Corcoran Gallery award in poetry, 1976; Stanley Young fellow in poetry, Bread Loaf Writer's Conference, 1981; Silver Medalist, Council for Advancement and Support of Education's National Professor of the Year award, 1987; Maryland State Arts Council grant, 1989, 1993; National Poetry Series selection, 1989, for *Stubborn;* Maxwell Anderson Award, University of North Dakota, 1993; Poet Laureate of Maryland Designate, 1995. Honorary Doctorate: North Carolina Wesleyan College, Rocky Mount, 1986.

WRITINGS:

POETRY

And Morning, Dryad Press (Washington, DC), 1975.
The Honey and Other Poems for Rosalind (chapbook), Unicorn (Huntington, WV), 1976.
Say It, Dryad Press, 1979.
Resuming Green: Selected Poems, 1965-1982, Dial Press (New York), 1983.
Sicily (chapbook), North Carolina Wesleyan College Press (Rocky Mount, NC), 1987.
Stubborn, University of Illinois Press (Urbana), 1990.
(With William Stafford) *Hearing Voices,* Willamette University Press (Salem, OR), 1991.
Pigeon, North Carolina Wesleyan College Press, 1991.
Pigeon in the Night (in Bulgarian and English), Fakel Press (Sofia), 1994.

OTHER

(Translator, with Betty Grinburg) *Words and Graphite,* by Boris Christov, Andina Publishing House (Varna), 1991.
(Translator, with Betty Grinburg and Lyubomir Nicolov) *Wings of the Messenger,* by Boris Christov, Petrikoff Publications (Sofia), 1991.
(Translator, with Vyara Tcholakova) *Pagan,* by Lyubomir Nicolov, Carnegie-Mellon Press (Pittsburgh, PA), 1992.

* * *

FOULKES, Paul 1923-

PERSONAL: Born March 19, 1923, in Mannheim, Australia; married, 1964; children: one son. *Educa-*

tion: University of Sydney, B.Sc., 1945, B.A., 1949; University of London, Ph.D., 1957.

ADDRESSES: Home—24 Granville Park, London SE13 7EA, England.

CAREER: University of Sydney, lecturer in physics, 1949-53; free-lance editor, translator, and writer since 1964.

WRITINGS:

(With Bertrand Russell) *Wisdom of the West: A Historical Survey of Western Philosophy in Its Social and Political Setting,* Doubleday, 1959, reprinted, Fawcett, 1966.

Subeditor on *Encyclopedia Britannica,* 1959-1964. Contributor of articles on philosophical logic to various learned journals.

* * *

FREEMAN, Castle (William), Jr. 1944-

PERSONAL: Born November 26, 1944, in San Antonio, TX; son of Castle William (a business executive) and Janet (a homemaker; maiden name, Cunningham) Freeman; married Alice Chaffee (an artist and designer), July 12, 1969; children: Alexander C., Sarah S. *Ethnicity:* "White." *Education:* Columbia University, B.S. (cum laude), 1968. *Avocational interests:* American and European history, natural history (especially botany and entomology).

ADDRESSES: Home—Newfane, VT. *Agent*—Christina Ward, Christina Ward Literary Agency, P.O. Box 505, North Scituate, MA 02060.

CAREER: Franklin Institute, Philadelphia, PA, technical writer, 1970-72; Stephen Greene Press, Brattleboro, VT, editor, 1976-80; *Old Farmer's Almanac,* Dublin, NH, author of the column "Farmer's Calendar," 1981—. *Country Journal,* copy editor, 1981-87.

MEMBER: Phi Beta Kappa.

AWARDS, HONORS: Award for New England Writers, St. Botolph's Club Foundation (Boston, MA), 1993.

WRITINGS:

The Bride of Ambrose (stories), Soho Press (New York City), 1987.
Spring Snow (essays), Houghton (Boston, MA), 1996.

Contributor of articles and stories to periodicals, including *Yankee, Harrowsmith, Atlantic Monthly, Harvard, Massachusetts Review,* and *Shenandoah.*

WORK IN PROGRESS: A collection of short stories "unified by common characters, setting, and themes."

SIDELIGHTS: Castle Freeman, Jr., told *CA:* "*Spring Snow* collects one-hundred-fifty-six of the brief essays I have written over the past sixteen years for *The Old Farmer's Almanac.* The essays examine with (I hope) charm, wit, and a little science, the creatures, tasks, events, history, weather, and other phenomena (chiefly, but not exclusively outdoor phenomena) of the New England hill country through the seasons of the year. The content of the essays varies, but they stick to the small, simple, and familiar: common animals and birds of the countryside, rather than exotics; family life and everyday jobs around a country place, rather than high adventure; snow, dirt roads, vegetable gardens, and so on, rather than glamour. If they are successful, the essays are reflective, amusing, informative, intelligent without being pretentious, and stylish without being affected. *Spring Snow* is solidly in the long line of rural writing that goes back before the ancient Greeks to the Old Testament, and proceeds up through E. B. White to the present."

* * *

FRENCH, Anne 1956-

PERSONAL: Born March 5, 1956, in Wellington, New Zealand; married Gary Alfred James Boire; children: one son. *Education:* Victoria University of Wellington, B.A. (honors), 1976, M.A., 1980; Auckland Secondary Teachers' College, Diploma in Teaching, 1977.

ADDRESSES: Home and office—P.O. Box 1799, Wellington, New Zealand.

CAREER: Victoria University of Wellington, teaching assistant, 1979; Oxford University Press, Wellington,

editor, 1980-82, Oxford University Press, Auckland managing editor, 1982-89, publisher, 1990-93; Museums of New Zealand, Wellington, managing editor, 1995—. *New Zealand Strategic Management,* Auckland, managing editor, 1994—. Writer-in-residence, Massey University, 1993.

AWARDS, HONORS: New Zealand Book award for poetry, 1988; PEN Best First Book of Poetry, 1988.

WRITINGS:

POETRY

All Cretans Are Liars, Auckland University Press (Auckland), 1987.
The Male as Evader, Auckland University Press, 1988.
Cabin Fever, Auckland University Press, 1990.
Seven Days on Mykonos, Auckland University Press, 1993.

OTHER

(Editor) *Elsdon Best-Maori Religion and Mythology, Part II,* Government Printing Office (Wellington), 1980.

* * *

FREUDENTHAL, Gad 1944-

PERSONAL: Born October 27, 1944, in Jerusalem, Palestine (now Israel); son of Heinz and Renate (Engel) Freudenthal; married M. C. Glangeaud (a psychologist); children: Emmanuel, Michael. *Education:* Attended Hebrew University of Jerusalem and Sorbonne, University of Paris I. *Religion:* Jewish.

ADDRESSES: Home—156 rue d'Aulney, 92290 Chatenay-Malabry, France. *Office*—Institut d'histoire des sciences, Centre National de la Recherche Scientifique, 13 rue du Four, 75006 Paris, France.

CAREER: Centre National de la Recherche Scientifique, Paris, France, director of research at Institute for the History of Science, 1982—.

WRITINGS:

(Editor) *Etudes sur Helene Metzger/Studies on Helene Metzger,* E. J. Brill (Leiden, Netherlands), 1990.

(Editor) *Studies on Gersonides: A Fourteenth-Century Jewish Philosopher-Scientist,* E. J. Brill, 1992.

Aristotle's Theory of Material Substance: Heat and Pneuma, Form and Soul, Oxford University Press (Oxford, England), 1995.

* * *

FRIEDLANDER, Henry (Egon) 1930-

PERSONAL: Born September 24, 1930, in Berlin, Germany; immigrated to the United States, naturalized citizen; married in 1953. *Education:* Temple University, B.A., 1953; University of Pennsylvania, M.A., 1954, Ph.D. (history), 1968.

ADDRESSES: Office—Department of Judaic Studies, 3111 James Hall, Brooklyn College, City University of New York, 2900 Bedford Ave., Brooklyn, NY 11210.

CAREER: American History Association, staff member of war document project, 1957-58; Louisiana State University, New Orleans, instructor in history, 1958-64; McMaster University, assistant professor, 1964-67; University of Missouri, St. Louis, assistant professor, 1967-70; City College, New York City, assistant professor of history, 1970-72, assistant professor of Jewish studies, beginning 1972; Brooklyn College, City University of New York, professor of history in Judaic Studies Program.

AWARDS, HONORS: Harrison fellow, 1955-56; Social Science Research Council fellow, 1956-57.

WRITINGS:

(Editor, with George Schwab) *Detente in Historical Perspective: The First CUNY Conference on History and Politics,* Cyrco Press (New York), c. 1975.

(Editor, with Sybil Milton) *The Holocaust: Ideology, Bureaucracy, and Genocide—The San Jose Papers,* Kraus International (Millwood, NY), 1980.

(Editor, with Sybil Milton) *Archives of the Holocaust: An International Collection of Selected Documents,* Garland (New York), 1989.

The German Revolution of 1918, Garland, 1992.

The Origins of Nazi Genocide: From Euthanasia to the Final Solution, University of North Carolina Press (Chapel Hill), 1995.

Contributor of articles and reviews to periodicals, including the *Journal of the American Medical Association.*

SIDELIGHTS: A professor of history specializing in Judaic studies, Henry Friedlander has written and edited several books designed to shed light on the crimes committed against individuals in Europe during World War II by Adolf Hitler and his Nazi soldiers. Friedlander's books depict not only the horror of the Holocaust, but the events and beliefs that contributed to it.

Among Friedlander's publications are several volumes of papers and letters written by Holocaust survivors and experts. These books include *The Holocaust: Ideology, Bureaucracy, and Genocide—The San Jose Papers* and *Archives of the Holocaust: An International Collection of Selected Documents,* both of which Friedlander edited with Sybil Milton. The first of these was published in 1980 and includes twenty-five papers that were originally presented at the San Jose, California, meetings of the National Conference of Christians and Jews in 1977 and 1978. Contained in the book are essays on the political, social, and moral issues surrounding the Holocaust, including writings on the corruption of thought and education in Nazi Germany, and the American response to the Holocaust. In his assessment of *The Holocaust, Religious Studies Review*'s Todd M. Endelman asserted that the book offers "conceptually sophisticated generalizations about key topics in the history of the Holocaust," while a *Choice* reviewer called it "an important and valuable contribution to Holocaust scholarship."

The concept of "racial cleansing" is the basis of another of Friedlander's books, *The Origins of Nazi Genocide: From Euthanasia to the Final Solution.* In this volume Friedlander describes how the Nazi program of euthanasia that resulted in the deaths of some 5,000 handicapped children was a precursor to the concentration camps that offered the Nazis their "final solution" for purging the German nation of Jews and others whom the Nazis believed were inferior and unclean. Although Hitler began the euthanasia program on the day World War II began in 1939, the practice of "race hygiene" had been in the works since the early 1930s, when a law was passed in Germany ordering the sterilization of individuals afflicted with any of a wide range of disorders, including mental illness, blindness, deafness, epilepsy, and alcoholism. *The Origins of Nazi Genocide* describes Hitler's "domestic purification" program that later

targeted the Jews, and the book offers a history of the events and thoughts that most likely led to the murders of thousands of innocents. Writing in the *New York Review of Books,* reviewer Gordon A. Craig lauded Friedlander's "admirably researched study," adding: "One of the distinguishing features of this study is the meticulous description of the administration of the euthanasia program . . . and the [Nazi] chain of command."

BIOGRAPHICAL/CRITICAL SOURCES:

PERIODICALS

Choice, October, 1981, p. 296; July/August, 1992, p. 1641.
Library Journal, September 15, 1981, p. 1730.
New York Review of Books, October 5, 1995, pp. 24-27.
Publishers Weekly, August 14, 1995, p. 67.
Religious Studies Review, July, 1982, p. 296.*

* * *

FRIEDMAN, Francine 1948-

PERSONAL: Born July 8, 1948, in Lima, OH; daughter of Ralph and Muriel Edelman; married Richard N. Friedman (a neurophysiologist), 1977; children: David, Danielle, Jonathan. *Education:* Syracuse University, A.B. (cum laude), 1970; McMaster University, M.A., 1971; Claremont Graduate School, M.I.S., 1972, Ph.D., 1978.

CAREER: Temple University, Philadelphia, PA, instructor, 1978; Jerusalem Institute for Federal Studies, Jerusalem, Israel, research fellow, 1978-79; Vanderbilt University, Nashville, TN, research associate at Center for European Studies, 1986-87, assistant professor of political science, 1988-89; Ball State University, Muncie, IN, associate professor of political science and director of Office of European Studies, 1990—. Hebrew University of Jerusalem, research fellow at Soviet and East European Research Center, 1978-79; Stanford University, researcher at Hoover Institution on War, Revolution, and Peace, 1980-81; St. Mary's University, instructor, 1981-82; University of Illinois at Urbana-Champaign, summer research associate, 1983, 1987, 1994.

MEMBER: American Political Science Association, American Association for the Advancement of Slavic Studies, Council on Foreign Relations, Indiana Academy of the Social Sciences, Indiana Political Science Association.

AWARDS, HONORS: Grants from American Philosophical Society, 1981-82, and U.S. Department of Education, 1992-93, 1993-94.

WRITINGS:

Yugoslavia: A Comprehensive English-Language Bibliography, Scholarly Resources (Wilmington, DE), 1993.
The Bosnian Muslims: Denial of a Nation, Westview (Boulder, CO), 1996.

Contributor to books, including *Governing Peoples and Territories,* edited by Daniel J. Elazar, Institute for the Study of Human Issues (Philadelphia, PA), 1982; *Crises in the Balkans: Views from the Participants,* edited by Constantine P. Danopoulos and Kostas G. Messas, Westview, in press; *The Role of Religion in the War in Bosnia,* edited by Paul Mojzes, in press; and *State-Society Relations in Yugoslavia, 1945-1992,* edited by Jill Irvine, Melissa Bokovoy, and Carol Tilly, in press. Contributor of articles and reviews to political science, social science, and Slavic studies journals, including *Canadian Review of Studies in Nationalism (Bibliography), International Interactions, Slavic Review, Canadian-American Slavic Studies, Southeastern Political Review* and *International Perspectives.*

* * *

FRYE, Charles A(nthony) 1946-1994

PERSONAL: Born March 18, 1946, in Washington, DC; died of lymphoma, October 8, 1994, in New Orleans, LA; divorced; children: Odeyo J., Sekou C., Anthony F., Lia M. *Education:* Howard University, B.A., 1968, M.A., 1970; University of Pittsburgh, Ph.D., 1976.

CAREER: Washington, DC, Public Library, librarian, 1968-69; Washington, DC, Public Schools, teacher, 1969-70; Howard University, Washington, DC, assistant professor, 1970-77; Fayetteville State University, director of interdisciplinary studies, 1977-78; Hampshire College, associate dean of students and associate professor of education, beginning c. 1978; Five College Black Studies Executive Committee, chair

and journal editor, 1983-85; taught at University of Massachusetts at Amherst; Southern University, New Orleans, professor of African philosophy and humanities, director of Center for African and African-American studies, until 1994.

MEMBER: National Council for Black Studies (chair and editor of council journal, 1980-82; member of board of directors), Association for Supervision and Curriculum Development.

AWARDS, HONORS: Advanced Study Fellowship, Ford Foundation, 1972-73.

WRITINGS:

The Impact of Black Studies on the Curricula of Three Universities, University Press of America, 1976.

Towards a Philosophy of Black Studies, R & E Research Associates, 1978.

(Editor) *Level Three: A Black Philosophy Reader,* University Press of America, 1980.

(Editor) *Values in Conflict: Blacks and the American Ambivalence toward Violence,* University Press of America, 1980.

From Egypt to Don Juan: The Anatomy of Black Philosophy, preface by August Coppola, University Press of America, 1988.

The Peter Pan Chronicles (novella), University Press of Virginia, 1989.

Contributor of reviews to *Journal of Negro History.*

SIDELIGHTS: A glance at Charles A. Frye's publications reveals his varied interests and areas of expertise. His first three books—*The Impact of Black Studies on the Curricula of Three Universities, Towards a Philosophy of Black Studies,* and *Level Three: A Black Philosophy Reader*—reflect his graduate training in both philosophy and higher education. Another of Frye's concerns is evident in his fourth text, *Values in Conflict: Blacks and the American Ambivalence toward Violence,* which not only addresses the contemporary phenomenon of violence but also examines social values as they relate to African Americans. His fifth text, *From Egypt to Don Juan: The Anatomy of Black Philosophy,* treats similar themes of blacks, race identity, and philosophy.

Though his mode of presentation for his sixth book, *The Peter Pan Chronicles,* shifts from analytic to creative writing, his thematic concern with contemporary black issues remains constant. The story is told through the unreliable eyes of a black patient, Raynard Parker, in an insane asylum. Parker was once assigned to sabotage the efforts of black civil rights activists in the 1960s, especially those of his friend Tommy Rollins, who Parker betrayed to government authorities. Unable to deal with the guilt of his actions, Parker suffers from severe time and space disorientation. Throughout the book he transforms figures in the asylum into people from his past, yielding a disjointed recreation of his activities in the 1960s.

Some reviewers of *The Peter Pan Chronicles* complained that they found it difficult to derive meaning from the novel's unorthodox narration. Others, however, found it a refreshing deviance from traditional fictional conventions. Charles C. Nash, writing in *Library Journal,* felt that Frye's technique resulted in a "brilliant collage of images" and that the book presented a terrifying yet convincing portrait of blacks in the United States.

BIOGRAPHICAL/CRITICAL SOURCES:

PERIODICALS

Library Journal, June 15, 1989.
Publishers Weekly, June 2, 1989, p. 78.*

G

GAARDER, Jostein 1952-

PERSONAL: Born in 1952, in Oslo, Norway; married; children: two sons.

ADDRESSES: Home—Oslo, Norway.

CAREER: Writer. Worked as a high school teacher of philosophy in Norway for eleven years.

AWARDS, HONORS: Norwegian Literary Critics' Award, and Norwegian Ministry of Cultural and Scientific Affairs' Literary Prize, both 1990, both for *The Solitaire Mystery; Sophie's World: A Novel about the History of Philosophy* was ranked number one in the world by Publishing Trends 1995 in their International Fiction Bestseller List.

WRITINGS:

NOVELS IN ENGLISH TRANSLATION

Sofies verden: Roman om filosofiens historie, Aschenhoug, 1991, translation by Paulette Moller published as *Sophie's World: A Novel about the History of Philosophy,* Farrar, Straus (New York), 1994.
The Solitaire Mystery, translation by Sarah Jane Hails, illustrations by Hilde Kramer, Farrar, Straus, 1996.
The Christmas Mystery, translation by Elizabeth Rokkan, illustrations by Rosemary Wells, Farrar, Straus, 1996.

OTHER

Froskeslottet, illustrations by Torill Maro Henrichsen, Aschenhoug, 1988.

Kabalmysteriet, Aschenhoug, 1990.
Julemysteriet, Aschehoug, 1992.
Bibi Bokkens magiske bibliotek, Universitetsforlaget, 1993.

SIDELIGHTS: Jostein Gaarder is a Norwegian writer who is probably best known to English-language readers for *Sophie's World: A Novel about the History of Philosophy,* a 1994 translation of his 1991 novel, *Sofies verden: Roman om filosofiens historie,* for readers in their mid-teens or older. In this work, a teenage Norwegian schoolgirl, Sophie, receives a series of inquisitive letters, posing such questions as "Who are you?" and "What does it take to live a good life?" Intrigued, Sophie begins corresponding with the sender of the mysterious letters. The ongoing correspondence quickly becomes a course in the history of philosophy from pre-Socratic to modern times.

Sophie eventually meets her instructor, Albert Knox, and as they continue their study of philosophy both characters come to suspect that they are actually characters in a novel. The suspicions of Sophie and Albert lead, in turn, to an investigation of metaphysics and the discovery that the duo are, indeed, characters in a novel, one being written by Albert Knag, a Norwegian military officer stationed in Lebanon. Knag is writing his novel for his daughter, Hilde. Knag's impending return to Norway provides a fair measure of suspense as *Sophie's World* builds to an appropriately quirky climax.

Upon publication in Scandinavia in 1991, *Sofies verden* developed into an exceptionally popular work. It achieved bestseller status in various European nations and was eventually acquired for American

publication. *Sophie's World* appeared in English translation in 1994 and proceeded to draw praise from reviewers. Among its supporters was Andrea Ashworth, who wrote in the *Times Literary Supplement* that the novel is "seductive and original." She concluded that "*Sophie's World* is, as it dares to congratulate itself, 'a strange and wonderful book.'"

Although some critics expressed reservations about Gaarder's book, they acknowledged the work's merits. John Vernon declared in the *New York Times Book Review* that "the history of philosophy becomes inserted into the tale of a Norwegian Nancy Drew like an aspirin into a piece of cheese," but conceded that "Mr. Gaarder's tour through the past of Western thought will perhaps have the good effect of encouraging some readers to seek out the real thing." And *Village Voice* reviewer Richard Gehr, while noting the book's "one-size-fits-all coziness," acknowledged that *Sophie's World* "is a concise, clearly written corrective to philosophic obscurantism."

BIOGRAPHICAL/CRITICAL SOURCES:

PERIODICALS

New York Times Book Review, September 25, 1994.
Sunday Times (London), January 29, 1995, p. 3.
Times Literary Supplement, January 13, 1995, p. 20.
Village Voice, November 15, 1994, p. 87.*

* * *

GAB
 See RUSSELL, George William

* * *

GABLER, Neal 1950(?)-

PERSONAL: Born c. 1950. *Education:* Attended the University of Michigan.

ADDRESSES: Office—c/o Alfred A. Knopf, Inc., 201 East 50th St., New York, NY 10022.

CAREER: Writer. Co-host of *Sneak Previews,* PBS-TV.

AWARDS, HONORS: Prize from *Los Angeles Times Book Review,* 1989, for *An Empire of Their Own: How the Jews Invented Hollywood.*

WRITINGS:

An Empire of Their Own: How the Jews Invented Hollywood, Crown (New York), 1988.
Winchell: Gossip, Power, and the Culture of Celebrity, Knopf (New York), 1994.

Contributor to periodicals, including *American Film, New York Times Book Review,* and *Video Review.*

SIDELIGHTS: Neal Gabler is a historian specializing in film and American culture. His first book, *An Empire of Their Own: How the Jews Invented Hollywood,* relates the achievements of such film moguls as Samuel Goldwyn, Louis B. Mayer, Jack Warner, and Harry Cohn, and it traces the development of Hollywood from its origins to the McCarthy era. In *An Empire of Their Own* Gabler maintains that these pioneering Jewish producers, most of whom hailed from Eastern Europe, managed to re-create themselves as American businessmen in an industry, motion pictures, that itself fosters such pursuits. Many films produced under these moguls perpetuated the image of America as what Ron Grossman, writing in the *Chicago Tribune,* described as "a land of miracles and a place where hard work and talent make dreams come true." Men like Goldwyn and Cohn, because of their Jewishness, might find themselves ordinarily cast as outsiders in America, Gabler contends, but in their films they sought to fashion an endearing image of America—one particularly evident in Frank Capra's films and the equally popular Andy Hardy series—as a nearly magical land of seemingly limitless riches and fairness.

An Empire of Their Own was well received upon publication in 1988. Molly Haskell, a noted author of film criticism, wrote in the *New York Times Book Review* that Gabler had produced an "enthralling book of social history," while another distinguished film authority, the *Los Angeles Times Book Review*'s Charles Champlin, hailed *An Empire of Their Own* as a "lively and scholarly history." Lindsay Anderson, noted as both a filmmaker and critic, wrote in the *Times Literary Supplement* that *An Empire of Their Own,* along with A. Scott Berg's *Goldwyn,* provides a "comprehensive and graphic account of Hollywood's dream factories."

Gabler followed *An Empire of Their Own* with *Winchell: Gossip, Power, and the Culture of Celebrity,* a biography of the influential newspaper and radio journalist Walter Winchell, who enjoyed particular popularity in the 1930s. Winchell became famous for his syndicated gossip column, originating in the *New York Graphic* during the 1920s, in which he emphasized the hardships, both personal and professional, of famous contemporaries. A nationwide radio show increased Winchell's fame in the 1930s and 1940s, when he served as a staunch advocate of America's war effort. Winchell's fortunes declined in the 1950s, when he supported Senator Joseph McCarthy's anticommunist investigations, and by the 1960s he was futilely attempting to find a distributor for his column.

For Gabler, Winchell is a key figure in the shift in emphasis in America from high culture to mass-market entertainment. Winchell, according to Gabler, fostered interest in celebrities and elevated celebrity behavior to the level of actual news. Gabler's rendering of Winchell's life, in turn, results in a history of these developments in American culture. "Writing that Winchell was 'arguably one of the principal architects' of modern American culture, Mr. Gabler turns the columnist's life into the springboard for a fascinating social history," observed Michiko Kakutani in her *New York Times* review of *Winchell.* She added that Gabler's "novelistic approach [gives] the reader a vivid, psychologically acute portrait of Winchell himself."

Likewise impressed with Gabler's achievement in *Winchell* was Frank Rich, who wrote in the *New York Times Book Review* that "Gabler captures the magnetism of Winchell's demonic energy." Rich described *Winchell* as "imaginatively written and authoritatively reported." And Murray Kempton, writing in the *Los Angeles Times Book Review,* noted: "Gabler is not to be envied the labors of his exhumations; but he has worked at them wonderfully and surprised us with the revelation that [Winchell's] bones do indeed live and are almost as vividly deplorable as when they were flesh."

BIOGRAPHICAL/CRITICAL SOURCES:

PERIODICALS

Chicago Tribune, December 26, 1988.
Los Angeles Times Book Review, September 25, 1988, pp. 2, 11-12; November 13, 1994, pp. 1, 10-11.

New York, October 24, 1994, pp. 73-4.
New York Review of Books, May 18, 1989, pp. 28-33.
New York Times, October 20, 1988, p. C24; November 7, 1989, pp. C17, C24; October 18, 1994, p. B3.
New York Times Book Review, October 23, 1988, pp. 1, 57-9; October 23, 1994, pp. 1, 31-3.
Times Literary Supplement, December 15, 1989, p. 1387.*

*　　*　　*

GALDOS, Benito Perez
See PEREZ GALDOS, Benito

*　　*　　*

GALE, Zona 1874-1938

PERSONAL: Born August 26, 1874, in Portage, WI; died of pneumonia, December 27, 1938, in Chicago, IL; buried at Silver Lake Cemetery in Portage, WI; daughter of Charles Franklin (a railroad engineer) and Eliza Beers (a teacher) Gale; married William Llewellyn Breese (a banker), 1928; children: (adopted daughter) Leslyn. *Education:* University of Wisconsin, Madison, B.L., 1895, M.A., 1899.

CAREER: Worked as a reporter for the Milwaukee *Evening Wisconsin,* 1895-96, the *Milwaukee Journal,* 1896-1901, and the *New York Evening World,* 1901-03; worked as a full-time writer in Portage, WI, after 1904. Served on the Wisconsin Library Commission, 1920-1932; as a member of the Wisconsin Board of Regents, 1923-29; on the Board of Visitors at the University of Wisconsin, 1936-38; as Wisconsin Delegate at the International Congress for Women, Chicago, 1933.

AWARDS, HONORS: Butterick Prize, 1911; Pulitzer Prize, 1921, for a dramatization of her novel, *Miss Lulu Bett;* D.Litt., Ripon College, 1922; D.Litt., University of Wisconsin, 1929; D.Litt., Rollins College, 1930.

WRITINGS:

Romance Island (novel), Bobbs-Merrill, 1906.
The Loves of Pelleas and Etarre (short stories), Macmillan, 1907.

Friendship Village (short stories), Macmillan, 1908.

Friendship Village Love Stories (short stories), Macmillan, 1909.

Mothers to Men (short stories), Macmillan, 1911.

Christmas (novel), Macmillan, 1912.

When I Was a Little Girl (short stories), Macmillan, 1913.

Neighborhood Stories (short stories), Macmillan, 1914.

Heart's Kindred, Macmillan, 1915.

A Daughter of the Morning (novel), Bobbs-Merrill, 1917.

Birth (novel), Macmillan, 1918.

Peace in Friendship Village (short stories), Macmillan, 1919.

Miss Lulu Bett (novel), Appleton, 1920.

The Neighbors (short stories), Huebsch, 1920.

Miss Lulu Bett (dramatization of the novel), Appleton, 1920.

Faint Perfume (novel), Appleton, 1923.

Preface to a Life (novel), Appleton, 1926.

Yellow Gentians and Blue (short stories), Appleton, 1927

Portage, Wisconsin and Other Essays (essays), Appleton, 1928.

Borgia (novel), Knopf, 1929.

Bridal Pond (novel), Knopf, 1930.

Papa La Fleur (novel), Appleton, 1933.

Old Fashioned Tales (short stories), Appleton-Century, 1933.

Light Woman (novel), Appleton-Century, 1937.

Frank Miller of Mission Inn (biography), Appleton-Century, 1938.

Magna (novel), Appleton-Century, 1939.

SIDELIGHTS: Now largely forgotten, Zora Gale was recognized during the 1920s as a leader in the American "revolt from the village," a movement fueled by the popularity of her *Miss Lulu Bett.* Originally a novel chronicling a woman's escape from small-town dullness and drudgery, *Miss Lulu Bett* was dramatized by Gale, who subsequently won the 1921 Pulitzer Prize in drama.

Raised in Portage, Wisconsin, Gale was an only child whose parents deeply influenced her life and work. Her father introduced her to the writings of Plato, Emerson, Darwin, and Swedenborg, impressing upon her a belief in philosophic idealism. Her mother, a possessive, highly devout woman, shaped Gale's perception of divinity as an all-pervading feminine life-force. Gale's mysticism, which grew stronger with the passing of years, was a blend of theosophy and transcendental pantheism, summed up and simplified in her motto: "Life is something more than that which we believe it to be." This was a recurring motif in her work.

Gale began her writing career working as a reporter in Milwaukee and then in New York City. She published her first novel, the flowery *Romance Island,* in 1906. Pressure from her mother to come home from New York to the idyllic life of Portage inspired Gale to write the first stories of Friendship Village—a town modelled on her home town—before she returned to Wisconsin in 1911. *Friendship Village, Friendship Village Love Stories,* and several other volumes present Gale's philosophy of love and community in stories filled with the sentiment, wholesomeness, and folksiness that marked her as a defender of the nineteenth-century village mythos. The success of her books provided her with the money and influence to actively support the various causes that drew her loyalty. Gale spoke and wrote on behalf of women's suffrage, trade unions, world peace, and the liberal Progressive Party of Wisconsin. During World War I, her pacifist activities led her Portage neighbors to suspect her of German sympathies, and they expressed pleasure when she was placed under federal surveillance. Hurt by this betrayal, Gale slowly came to see the Midwestern village as a mixture of good and bad elements—although not entirely as the suffocating, spiritual hell insisted upon by her literary contemporaries. Her disillusionment was voiced in *Birth, Peace in Friendship Village, Miss Lulu Bett,* and *Faint Perfume,* novels stripped of Gale's former romanticism and excess verbiage, and imbued with impressionistic realism. For several years in the early 1920s she was considered comparable to Sinclair Lewis in exposing middle-class dullness and provincialism. Receiving the Pulitzer Prize for *Miss Lulu Bett* in 1921 was the high point of Gale's career.

Gale's mother greatly influenced her daughter's spiritual life, maintaining a hold that was intensified by her death in 1923, when Gale turned away from realism to explore her growing mysticism. Beginning with *Preface to a Life,* her books became increasingly burdened with spiritual matters which outweighed her story lines, causing her decline in popular and critical favor. Gale spent her last years writing and speaking for her favorite causes.

Today Gale's stature is measured by the influence she exerted in promoting human rights and by *Miss Lulu Bett,* which a critic in the *Nation* hailed as belonging "among the very earliest of plays which broke away

from theatrical convention to establish upon the stage a new American literature."

BIOGRAPHICAL/CRITICAL SOURCES:

BOOKS

Derleth, August, *Still Small Voice: The Biography of Zona Gale,* D. Appleton-Century Company, 1940.
Dictionary of Literary Biography, Volume 9: *American Novelists, 1910-1945,* Gale, 1981.
Goist, Park Dixon, *From Main Street to State Street: Town, City, and Community in America,* Kennikat Press, 1977, pp. 13-20.
Herron, Ima Honaker, *The Small Town in American Literature,* Duke University Press, 1939, pp. 334-428.
Hilfer, Anthony Channell, *The Revolt from the Village: 1915-1930,* University of North Carolina Press, 1969, pp. 111-36.
Overton, Grant, *The Women Who Make Our Novels,* Dodd, Mead, & Co., 1928, pp. 143-56.
Phelps, William Lyon, *As I Like It,* Charles Scribner's Sons, 1923.
Reference Guide to American Literature, third edition, St. James, 1994.

PERIODICALS

Bookman (New York), January, 1909, p. 476; April, 1923, pp. 168-72.
Nation, December 28, 1918, pp. 809-10; February 2, 1921, p. 189; December 11, 1929, p. 725.
New Republic, August 11, 1920, pp. 315-16.
New York Times, December 28, 1920, p. 9.
Yale Review, winter, 1987, p. 221.

* * *

GARB, Tamar 1956-

PERSONAL: Born Tama Hammerschlag in 1956, in Jerusalem, Israel; daughter of Werner (an architect) and Cynthia (in business) Hammerschlag; took her stepfather's name when her mother married Ivor Garb; married Rasaad Jamie (a journalist), July, 1982; children: Gabriel Jamie. *Education:* University of London, Ph.D., 1990. *Religion:* Jewish. *Avocational interests:* Cooking, theater, movies, dining out, friendships.

ADDRESSES: Home—68 Lancaster Rd., London N4 UPT, England. *Office*—Department of Art, University College, Gower St., London WC1E 6BT, England.

CAREER: University College, London, England, lecturer and reader in art history.

MEMBER: Association of Art Historians, Association International des Critiques d'Art.

WRITINGS:

Women Impressionists, Rizzoli (New York), 1986.
Berthe Morisot (monograph), Cornell University Press (Ithaca, NY), 1987.
Sisters of the Brush: Women's Artistic Culture in Late Nineteenth-Century Paris, Yale University Press (New Haven, CT), 1994.
The Jew in the Text: Modernity and the Construction of Identity, edited with Linda Nochlin, Thames & Hudson (London), 1995.

SIDELIGHTS: Tamar Garb, a reader in art history at London's University College, has published several volumes profiling female Impressionist artists and the obstacles these women overcame in achieving recognition for their artistic talent.

Garb's first book, *Women Impressionists,* highlights the lives and accomplishments of Berthe Morisot and Mary Cassatt, the most widely recognized women Impressionists, as well as the lesser-known Eva Gonzales and Marie Braquemond, all of whom painted in Paris at the end of the nineteenth century and were influenced by some of the period's greatest male artists. Introduced to Impressionism by artist Edouard Manet, Morisot is considered one of France's greatest woman painters, while American-born Cassatt, who was advised by painter Edgar Degas, is lauded for her paintings with a mother-and-child theme. Manet also inspired and instructed Gonzales, but Gonzales died young, perhaps before she fully realized her potential. The fourth artist Garb profiles, Marie Braquemond, was the wife of Felix Braquemond, who recognized his wife's amazing talent with jealousy and tried to suppress her art. The stories of Gonzales and Braquemond, according to critics, make Garb's book most valuable, as Morisot and Cassatt have been widely represented elsewhere. For example, reviewer Belinda Thomson, writing in *Burlington* magazine, noted: "It was the less familiar figures, Eva Gonzales (often unfairly dismissed as a Manet clone) and Marie Braquemond (previously

overshadowed by the reputation of her husband), who stood most to gain from the present study." Although Thomson expressed a desire for more information about the artists Garb presents, the critic applauded Garb's work, judging *Women Impressionists* a "brief, judicious yet challenging account of a fascinating and relatively untapped subject leaves the reader eager for more, and that is as it should be."

Garb's third book, *Sisters of the Brush: Women's Artistic Culture in Late Nineteenth-Century Paris,* involves some of the same artists the author discusses in her first book, as well as far lesser-known talents, but Garb examines them as part of the Union of Women Painters and Sculptors, rather than individually. Organized in 1881, the Union sought to increase opportunities for women artists in Paris. At that time the art world in Paris was a man's domain; women were denied admission into Ecole des Beaux-Arts, the city's elite art academy, and little attention was paid by the press to the talents of women. In addition, art competitions were judged solely by men, and, though many women entered, few won prizes in those competitions. As the Union worked for equality in the arts, however, the male-dominated art world began to recognize the potential contribution of women artists. The Union gradually made headway, with its major triumph coming in 1896 when the prestigious Ecole opened its doors to women. Ironically, Garb indicates, the women who comprised the Union were actually quite conservative. Although militant about their equality in the arts, they were characteristically devoted wives and mothers who opposed the influence of women in other professions.

Sisters of the Brush was well-received by critics, among them Jill Lloyd, who remarked in the *Times Literary Supplement,* "Given that there are no personalities to bring it to life, [Garb's] text would make dry reading if it were not for the lively evocation of historical context. In the course of her account, Tamar Garb uncovers some fascinating paradoxes, characteristic of an age in transition." *Art Journal* contributor Mary Tompkins Lewis also applauded Garb's book, writing: "In its wide-ranging examination of contemporary perceptions of art and femininity and, moreover, in its articulation of their intersection on the painted and critical canvas, *Sisters of the Brush* reaches far beyond the conventional aesthetic judgments and heroic narratives of modernism to restructure our view of the Paris art world in the late nineteenth century from its margins." Art historian Julie Springer also praised *Sisters of the Brush* in her

review for *Belles Lettres:* "For art historians, *Sisters of the Brush* breaks new ground with its focus on women of the artistic minor league—women who may well represent the visual arts in Paris at the turn of the century more fully than a Morisot or Cassatt. . . . For the general reader, *Sisters of the Brush* provides a fascinating weave of art and gender politics, embellished with biographical vignettes of some pretty remarkable women."

BIOGRAPHICAL/CRITICAL SOURCES:

PERIODICALS

Art Journal, fall, 1994, pp. 90-92.
Belles Lettres, spring, 1995, p. 15.
Burlington, April, 1987, pp. 254-255.
Times Literary Supplement, October 7, 1994, p. 23.

* * *

GARCIA ROCHA, Rina 1954-

PERSONAL: Born March 20, 1954, in Chicago, IL; married Thomas Rocha. *Education:* Attended Columbia College, Santa Rosa Jr. College, and Northeastern Illinois University.

ADDRESSES: Home—5840 West Roosevelt Rd., Chicago, IL 60650.

CAREER: Poet. Has given numerous poetry readings in the Chicago area, including "Latina Art Expo '77."

MEMBER: Popular Culture Association, Movimiento Artistico Chicano (MARCH).

AWARDS, HONORS: One of Garcia Rocha's poems won publication in a national contest in 1967; Olga-Bush Journal Award; cash prize for two poems published in *Eluder.*

WRITINGS:

(Contributor) *Raza Art and Media Collective* (anthology), University of Michigan, 1977.
Eluder (poems), Alexander Books, 1980.

Contributor of poems to *Abrazo, Garland Court Review, Revista Chicano-Riquena,* and *Hojas Poeticas.*

GARNER, James Finn 1960(?)-

PERSONAL: Born c. 1960; married; wife's name, Lies; children: Liam. *Education:* University of Michigan, B.A. *Politics:* Democrat.

ADDRESSES: Home—Chicago, IL. *Office*—c/o Simon and Schuster, 1230 Avenue of the Americas, New York, NY 10020.

CAREER: Author and improvisational theater artist. Has appeared on Chicago Public Radio.

WRITINGS:

Politically Correct Bedtime Stories, Macmillan (New York), 1994.
Once Upon a More Enlightened Time, Macmillan, 1995.
Politically Correct Holiday Stories, Macmillan, 1995.

Also the author of an improvisational theater collection titled *Kafka for Kinder.* Contributor to periodicals, including *Chicago Tribune Magazine.*

ADAPTATIONS: Politically Correct Bedtime Stories was adapted for CD-ROM.

WORK IN PROGRESS: An animated *film noir* about one of his improvisational characters, Rex Koko, a private-eye clown.

SIDELIGHTS: When James Finn Garner heard that classic children's fairy tales were being revised to avoid material that might be considered offensive by various groups, "he was appalled," according to Jon Elsen, an interviewer for the *New York Times Book Review.* Garner decided to make fun of this trend, and the result is his 1994 effort, *Politically Correct Bedtime Stories.* In this volume Garner has rewritten thirteen popular stories, inserting politically correct terminology wherever he could. For instance, Rumpelstiltskin is not a dwarf but variously "vertically challenged" or a "man of nonstandard height," who is scolded for attempting to "interfere" with Esmeralda's "reproductive rights" by demanding her first-born child as payment for teaching her how to spin straw into gold. In Garner's version of "Little Red Riding Hood," the wolf manages to don Grandma's nightgown after eating her because he is "unhampered by rigid, traditionalist notions of what was masculine or feminine," and after Jack trades his mother's cow for three magic beans, Garner writes of Jack's mother: "She used to think her son was merely

a conceptual rather than a linear thinker, but now she was sure that he was downright differently abled."

Critics have applauded Garner's satire; Patricia T. O'Conner in the *New York Times Book Review* asserted that "somebody had to do it. And James Finn Garner has met the challenge manfully—or, rather, like a fully realized individual, secure in his personhood and in touch with his inner child." Jonathan Yardley in the *Washington Post Book World* was even more lavish in his praise of *Politically Correct Bedtime Stories;* he declared that "Garner isn't a mere writer, he's a virtuoso, a necromancer, a master of the tour de force—a Hans Nonsectarian Andersen for our very own time." Yardley further judged that Garner, in satirizing the extremes of political correctness, has committed "a public service of truly epic dimensions." Garner himself defended stories like the ones he altered to Elsen: "There's magic to storytelling, and fear and wonder, and when you tie obvious little agendas to it, kids see that. I don't think a kid was ever made sexist because he or she read 'Snow White.' I think they were made sexist because of how they were raised and what they see in society around them."

BIOGRAPHICAL/CRITICAL SOURCES:

BOOKS

Garner, James Finn, *Politically Correct Bedtime Stories,* Macmillan, 1994.

PERIODICALS

New York Times Book Review, May 15, 1994, p. 3.
Washington Post Book World, April 27, 1994, p. B2.*

* * *

GEIOGAMAH, Hanay 1945-

PERSONAL: Born in 1945, in Oklahoma, United States. *Education:* University of Indiana, B.A., 1980.

CAREER: Native American Theater Ensemble (NATE), artistic director, 1972-76; Native Americans in Arts, New York City, artistic director, 1980-82; University of California, Los Angeles, taught in theater department, 1982-92; Colorado College, Colorado Springs, visiting professor of theater, 1983;

American Indian Registry for the Performing Arts, Los Angeles, executive director, 1984-88; American Indian Dance Theater, conducted tours in U.S. and Europe, 1988-89; technical consultant advisor for the Wildwood Production feature film *Dark Wind,* 1989; American Indian Dance Theater, codirected the Theater's special on "Dance in America," *Great Performances,* PBS, 1989.

AWARDS, HONORS: Charles MacMahon Foundation Scholarship in Journalism, 1963; William Randolph Hearst National Writing Award, 1966-67; guest speaker, American Theater Association's 46th National Convention, 1982.

WRITINGS:

Body Indian (play), produced by American Indian Theater Ensemble, La Mama Theatre, New York City, 1972.
Foghorn (play), produced by Native American Theater Ensemble, West Berlin, West Germany, 1973.
New Native American Drama: Three Plays (includes *Body Indian, Foghorn,* and *49*), introduction by Jeffrey Huntsman, University of Oklahoma Press (Norman), 1980.

Also author of the play *49*. Editor of *American Indian Culture and Research Journal.*

SIDELIGHTS: Hanay Geiogamah is known for plays in which he employs humor, realism, and idiomatic language to subvert negative stereotypes about Native Americans and to address the alienation felt by Indians in contemporary American society. Critics have consistently praised Geiogamah for his compelling characterizations, his emphasis on survival and self-knowledge, and his realistic portrayal of the social and political conditions under which Native Americans live today. Jeffrey Huntsman has stated: "[Geiogamah's] purpose is, first, to present and thereby preserve *living* Indian traditions and, next, to demonstrate the facts of Indian life in America today, unvarnished by either Indian or non-Indian romanticizers."

Geiogamah's best-known plays, *Body Indian, Foghorn,* and *49,* are collected in *New Native American Drama: Three Plays.* Although these works often address such problems as alcoholism, poverty, and racism, they are considered optimistic in outlook because of their focus on the importance of developing pride, unity, and self-respect among Native Americans. For example, in *Foghorn,* Geiogamah satirizes the relationship between Natives and whites in America from colonial times to the present. While he attacks the long history of white exploitation of Indians, he does so in a way, as stated by Kenneth Lincoln, that "purges the anguish and celebrates what it means to be alive today in Indian America." Geiogamah himself has written: "Almost all the characters in [*Foghorn*] are stereotypes pushed to the point of absurdity. The satire proceeds by playful mockery rather than bitter denunciation." In addition to writing plays, Geiogamah has served as artistic director of several art and theater organizations, including the Native American Theater Ensemble (NATE), Native Americans in Arts, and the American Indian Dance Theater.

BIOGRAPHICAL/CRITICAL SOURCES:

BOOKS

Native North American Literature, Gale, 1994.

PERIODICALS

Booklist, July 1, 1980, pp. 1584-85.
Choice, December, 1980, p. 528.
Comparative Drama, summer, 1981, pp. 187-90.
Dance Magazine, January, 1990, p. 74.
Library Journal, July, 1980, p. 1535.
Los Angeles Times, February 10, 1989, p. 15.
MELUS, fall, 1989-90, pp. 69-81, 91-8.
World Literature Today, summer, 1981, p. 515.*

* * *

GILDEN, Mel 1947-

PERSONAL: Born in 1947.

ADDRESSES: Agent—c/o Pocket Books, Simon & Schuster Bldg., 1230 Ave. of the Americas, New York, NY 10020.

CAREER: Writer.

WRITINGS:

The Return of Captain Conquer, Houghton (Boston, MA), 1986.
Pokey to the Rescue, Wanderer Books (New York City), 1987.

RV and the Haunted Garage, Wanderer Books, 1987.

Harry Newberry and the Raiders of the Red Drink, Holt (New York City), 1989.

Outer Space and All That Junk, Lippincott (New York City), 1989.

Star Trek: The Next Generation: Boogeymen, Pocket Books (New York City), 1991.

The Planetoid of Amazement, HarperCollins (New York City), 1991.

Star Trek: The Starship Trap, Pocket Books, 1993.

The Pumpkins of Time (sequel to *Outer Space and All That Junk*), Harcourt (New York City), 1994.

The Jungle Book: A Novelization (based on script by Stephen Sommers and the novel by Rudyard Kipling), HarperPaperbacks, 1994.

My Brother Blubb, Pocket Books, 1994.

"FIFTH GRADE MONSTERS" SERIES; JUVENILE FICTION

M Is for Monster, Avon (New York City), 1987.

Born to Howl, Avon, 1987.

The Pet of Frankenstein, Avon, 1988.

Z Is for Zombie, Avon, 1988.

Monster Mashers, Avon, 1989.

Things That Go Bark in the Park, Avon, 1989.

Yuckers!, Avon, 1989.

The Monster in Creeps Head Bay, Avon, 1990.

How to Be a Vampire in One Easy Lesson, Avon, 1990.

Island of the Weird, Avon, 1990.

Werewolf, Come Home, Avon, 1990.

Monster Boy, Avon, 1991.

Troll Patrol, Avon, 1991.

The Secret of Dinosaur Bog, Avon, 1991.

"ZOOT MARLOWE" SERIES

Surfing Samurai Robots, Lynx Press (New York City), 1988.

Hawaiian U.F.O. Aliens, Roc (New York City), 1991.

Tubular Android Superheroes, Roc, 1991.

"BEVERLY HILLS 90210" SERIES; NOVELIZATIONS OF TELE-PLAYS

Beverly Hills 90210, HarperPaperbacks, 1991.

More Than Worlds, HarperPaperbacks, 1993.

Graduation Day, HarperPaperbacks, 1994.

"CYBERSURFERS" SERIES; WITH TED PEDERSEN

Pirates on the Internet, Price Stern Sloan (Los Angeles, CA), 1995.

Cyberspace Cowboy, Price Stern Sloan, 1995.

Ghost on the Net, Price Stern Sloan, 1996.

Cybercops and Flame Wars, Price Stern Sloan, 1996.

SIDELIGHTS: Mel Gilden's fiction spans a variety of genres. He has written novelizations of scripts from the television program *Beverly Hills 90210* and from the film *The Jungle Book,* adapted from Rudyard Kipling's classic children's book. He is best known, however, for the many science fiction and fantasy parodies he has published. In books such as *The Return of Captain Conquer, Outer Space and All That Junk, M Is for Monster, Surfing Samurai Robots,* and *Pirates on the Internet,* Gilden has carved a niche for himself as an adult, children's and young adult author. Critics compare his work to that of Daniel Pinkwater, Douglas Adams, and the Monty Python troupe of actors and praise it for its bizarre sense of fun. "Just check your sense of reality at the door," writes *School Library Journal* contributor Lyle Blake Smythers.

Gilden began his career as a novelist for young adults with *The Return of Captain Conquer,* "a wonderfully funny science fiction serial parody," declares Annette Curtis Klause in *School Library Journal,* "that stays true to its inner logic throughout." It tells of how Watson Congruent launches a search for his father, Sherlock, who has disappeared along with the memorabilia of the famous TV show that he sells to discriminating fans. The author explores a similar theme in *Harry Newberry and the Raiders of the Red Drink,* in which young Harry tries to find the reason why his mother (possibly the assistant of the comic book superheroine Tuatara) has been kidnapped by the evil Bonnie Android. "Gilden reels out a series of madcap adventures, one more wacky than the rest," states *Booklist* contributor Barbara Elleman.

Gilden's "Fifth Grade Monsters" series is intended for younger readers and tells about an entire classroom consisting of not-quite-usual children "straight out of Universal Studios," writes Elaine E. Knight in *School Library Journal,* including C. D. Bitesky, a junior vampire; the Steins, brother Frankie and sister Elisa; and Howie Wolfner, a young man with a definite hair problem once a month. The class's adventures cover more than fifteen volumes and emphasize how the word "monster" can be simply a descriptive rather than a judgmental term. "Allusions to classic monster films are everywhere," Knight concludes.

Outer Space and All That Junk tells of how thirteen-year-old Myron Duberville discovers that his eccen-

tric uncle Hugo, chairman of the board of Astronetics Corporation, is not in fact hallucinating when he claims that he has discovered aliens in the old junk heaped on city streets. He has collected and modified an old 1960 Chevrolet Belvedere in order to speed them on their way home. Opposed to Hugo are Pinch and Grinley, who want to remove him from the board of the company. Myron finds himself unwillingly roped into cooperating with his uncle's scheme in order to save both their lives. "Pinkwater fans," declares a *Kirkus Reviews* contributor, "will revel in this madcap adventure." In *The Pumpkins of Time,* Myron, Hugo, and Myron's cohort Princess return to combat time-travelling aliens who use giant pumpkins in their temporal journeys, "Gilden," Klause concludes in *School Library Journal,* "is becoming a force in his own right."

BIOGRAPHICAL/CRITICAL SOURCES:

PERIODICALS

Booklist, June 15, 1989, p. 1821; December 1, 1989, p. 742; October 15, 1994, p. 426.
Book Report, March/April, 1992, p. 59.
Kirkus Reviews, October 15, 1989, pp. 1529-1530.
Kliatt, September, 1991, p. 23; July, 1993, p. 16.
Locus, November, 1989, p. 55; March, 1990, p. 64; August, 1990, p. 48; April, 1991, p. 42; May, 1991, p. 33; August, 1991, p. 50; September, 1991, p. 59; November, 1991, p. 54.
Publishers Weekly, December 11, 1987, p. 65; July 4, 1994, p. 64.
School Library Journal, September, 1986, pp. 134-35; December, 1989, p. 100; January, 1991, p. 90; November, 1991, p. 117; October, 1994, p. 122.
Voice of Youth Advocates, August, 1994, p. 145.
Washington Post Book World, August 28, 1988, p. 9.
Wilson Library Bulletin, September, 1989, pp. 7-8.*

* * *

GIL-MONTERO, Martha 1940-

PERSONAL: Born September 27, 1940, in Cordoba, Argentina; immigrated to U.S., 1976, naturalized U.S. citizen, 1989; daughter of Rosendo (a civil engineer) and Beatriz Eugenia (Premoli) Gil-Montero; married Joseph A. Page (a law professor and writer), May 18, 1984. *Education:* Escuela Normal de Professores Alejandro Carbo, Cordobo, maestra nor-

mal, 1958; Cambridge University, lower certificate in English, 1959, certificate of proficiency in English, 1964; Goethe Institut, Radolfzell, West Germany, zeugnis, 1963; Alliance Francaise, Cordoba, diploma de capacidad in French, 1965; attended Universidad Autonoma de Mexico, 1966, and Georgetown University, 1985. *Politics:* Democrat. *Religion:* Roman Catholic.

ADDRESSES: Home—1001 26th St. N.W., No. 808, Washington, DC 20037. *Agent*—Carl D. Brandt, 1501 Broadway, New York, NY 10036.

CAREER: Author, editor, researcher, and lecturer, 1960—; Embassy of Argentina, Mexico City, Mexico, translator and interpreter, 1966; Embassy of Argentina, Washington, DC, assistant to the cultural attache, 1967-69, affiliated with Press and Cultural Office, 1979-80; head of Department of International Relations of the National Council of Science and Technology of Argentina, 1969-78. Translator and interpreter for Universidad Nacional de Cordoba, 1960-63, Industrias Kayser Argentina, 1961-63, and Editorial de la Universidad de Buenos Aires, 1969-70.

WRITINGS:

Mundomujer (poetry), Fulgor (Buenos Aires), 1970.
(Translator) Herbert Matthews, *Fidel Castro,* Cuarto Poder, 1971.
(Translator) Joseph A. Page, *Peron,* Vergara, 1984.
(Translator) James A. Whelan, *Out of the Ashes,* [Chile], 1989.
Brazilian Bombshell: The Biography of Carmen Miranda, Donald I. Fine, 1989.

Also author of several monographs on international science policy for National Council of Science and Technology of Argentina, 1969-78.

WORK IN PROGRESS: "An erotic-feminist-historical biography."

SIDELIGHTS: Argentine-born American Martha Gil-Montero is a former Argentine government official who wrote about Latin American show business legend Carmen Miranda in *Brazilian Bombshell: The Biography of Carmen Miranda.* A singer of Brazilian samba music, Miranda was famous for her provocative dancing style and exotic costumes, which featured large, elaborately decorated hats. Gil-Montero's book records Miranda's ascent to stardom in Brazil before she moved to the United States in 1939 to

appear in such Hollywood films as *That Night in Rio* and *The Gang's All Here.* Though the move boosted Miranda's career and brought her tremendous financial success, she often suffered from depression and became dependent on pills. Miranda's career waned during the late 1940s, and she died of a heart attack in 1955 at age forty-six. Gil-Montero's *Brazilian Bombshell,* however, emphasizes the positive aspects of the singer's life: "The most important part of the book is my real admiration for her music, mainly the Brazilian songs. I think that has to come back and that Americans should know about them," Gil-Montero told Rod Granger of *Inside Books.* Reviewers generally praised the biography as an important, well-researched book. Alan Ryan's comments in the *Washington Post* were typical: "Martha Gil-Montero's *Brazilian Bombshell* is just the sort of biography Carmen Miranda deserves: affectionate and generous, yet honest and realistic."

BIOGRAPHICAL/CRITICAL SOURCES:

PERIODICALS

Chicago Tribune, June 20, 1989.
City Paper, August 4, 1989.
Inside Books, July-August, 1989.
Voice Literary Supplement, August, 1989.
Washington Post, May 29, 1989.

* * *

GLASCO, Michael 1945-

PERSONAL: Born March 12, 1945, in Dallas, TX; son of Lowell and Pauline (Suddath) Glasco; married, December 27, 1969; wife's name, Elizabeth (director of computer records storage). *Ethnicity:* "Anglo." *Education:* Southern Methodist University, B.F.A., 1969, M.F.A., 1970. *Religion:* Roman Catholic. *Avocational interests:* Foreign travel, cooking, "golfing with my wife, Elizabeth."

ADDRESSES: Home—3244 Amherst, Dallas, TX 75225.

CAREER: Southern Methodist University, Dallas, TX, photography instructor, 1969-71; owner and operator of a commercial photography studio which did photography for national advertising campaigns and corporate annual reports, 1971-94; freelance writer,

1995—. Active in church outreach programs for the homeless and for poor neighborhoods in Dallas.

WRITINGS:

Angels in Tesuque (novel), Sunstone Press (Santa Fe, NM), 1995.

WORK IN PROGRESS: Another novel set on the Texas coast.

SIDELIGHTS: Texas author Michael Glasco spent twenty years as the owner and operator of his own successful commercial photography business before pursuing a career as a novelist. The first published result of this dramatic career shift is 1995's *Angels in Tesuque.* Set in a small pueblo in New Mexico, *Angels in Tesuque* is the story of Ben Touchstone, a half-white, half-Native American boy who is visited by an angel and counseled by other guardian spirits during his childhood. With the help of this spiritual guidance he overcomes poverty, racist taunts, and the difficulties he encounters with his alcoholic father and brother—the latter of whom is jealous and vows to ruin his life. Ben rises to become the first Native American U.S. Senator from his state, but faces blackmail as well as the temptation to betray his own people for political and financial gain. He is also, throughout his life, prone to a certain optimistic misinterpretation of the words and actions of others who are less honest than himself. As a *Publishers Weekly* reviewer pointed out, however, "Glasco keeps his sensitive hero on the right track through costly lessons." The critic praised *Angels in Tesuque* as an "earnest first novel."

Glasco told *CA:* "*Angels in Tesuque* is my first novel to be published, but the second novel I've written. The first remains unpublished, and has a modern-day international terrorist storyline set in Europe, the Middle East, and America.

"The idea for *Angels in Tesuque* came to me at dawn in Santa Fe, on Christmas morning, 1993. It was snowing and I was sipping coffee on my sister's porch, where the view stretches out to the hills surrounding Tesuque Pueblo. The idea for the novel came to me as quickly and as suddenly as that unexpected snowfall. Since I was very young, I've spent quite a lot of time in Santa Fe and the surrounding countryside. There is something magical and unique about the area, and the visual images are very powerful, as is the Native American culture.

"As far as undertaking writing novels, I think, after twenty years of commercial photography, that I had become 'burnt out.' I've always thought very visually, and after all those years behind the camera, writing seemed a quite natural thing for me to do. I had taken several creative writing courses taught by novelist Marshall Terry while an undergraduate at Southern Methodist University, but that was twenty-five years ago.

"The creative ideas come very quickly while I'm writing, and characters just appear in my imagination in a very visual way, usually accompanied at the same time by names, mannerisms, backgrounds, appearance, etc. Dialogue just seems to happen. I average about four to six pages a day on the computer.

"I've just concluded, along with my wife Elizabeth, a fifteen-city book signing tour in Texas, Arizona, Washington, and California. I really enjoyed meeting total strangers who had read all or part of my novel, and visiting with them about my book on a one-to-one basis.

BIOGRAPHICAL/CRITICAL SOURCES:

PERIODICALS

Publishers Weekly, September 18, 1995, p. 115.

* * *

GLISSANT, Edouard 1928-

PERSONAL: Born September 21, 1928, in Sainte-Marie, Martinique; came to United States, 1988; son of Edouard (a plantation manager) and Adrienne (Godard) Glissant; children: Pascal, Jerome, Olivier, Barbara, Mathieu. *Education:* Paris University, Sorbonne, D.Phil., 1953, state doctorate, 1977.

ADDRESSES: Home—213 Prescott, Baton Rouge, LA 70803-5309. *Office*—Louisiana State University, French Department, Baton Rouge, LA 70810.

CAREER: Lycee des Jeunes Filles, Fort-de-France, Martinique, instructor in philosophy, 1965; Institut Martiniquais d'Etudes (IME), Fort-de-France, founder, 1967, director, 1967-78; United Nations Educational, Scientific, and Cultural Organization (UNESCO), Paris, France, editor, 1981-88; Louisiana State University, Baton Rouge, LA, distinguished

professor and director of Center for French and Francophone Studies, 1988—. Cofounder of *ACOMA Review,* 1970.

AWARDS, HONORS: Received Ordre des Francophones D'Amerique, Quebec; Prix Renaudot, 1958, for *La Lezarde;* Prix Charles Veillon, 1965, for *Le quatrieme siecle;* award from Twelfth Putterbaugh Conference, Norman, OK, 1989; honorary Litt.D., York University, 1989; honorary doctorate degree, Glendon College, York University, 1989; Roger Callois International Prize, 1991.

WRITINGS:

POETRY

Un champ d'iles, [Paris], 1953.
La terre inquiete, Editions de Seuil (Paris), 1954.
Les Indes: Poemes de l'une et l'autre terre, Editions de Seuil, 1955.
Le sel noir, Editions de Seuil, 1959.
Le sang rive, Presence Africaine (Paris), 1960.
Poemes (contains *Un champ d'iles, La terre inquiete,* and *Les Indes*), Editions de Seuil, 1965.
Boises, [Martinique], 1977.
Pays reve, pays reel, Editions de Seuil, 1985.

ESSAY COLLECTIONS

Soleil de la conscience, Editions de Seuil, 1956.
L'intention poetique, Editions de Seuil, 1969.
Le discours antillais, Editions de Seuil, 1981, published in English as *Caribbean Discourse: Selected Essays,* 1989.

NOVELS

La Lezarde, Editions de Seuil, 1958, published in English as *The Ripening,* 1959.
Le quatrieme siecle, Editions de Seuil, 1964.
Malemort, Editions de Seuil, 1975.
La case du commandeur, Editions de Seuil, 1981.
Mahagony, Editions de Seuil, 1987.

OTHER

Monsieur Toussaint (play), Editions de Seuil, 1961, abridged version published as *Monsieur Toussaint: Version scenique,* [Martinique], 1978, published in English translation, 1982.

SIDELIGHTS: An important figure in Caribbean literature, Edouard Glissant writes of Martinique's ge-

ography, history, and diverse ancestry. In his work, Glissant rejects the common assumption that a Martinican identity must be based on either white supremacist values or on *negritude,* which Kenneth Ramchand defines as a "celebration of Africa as a cultural matrix; a favourable interpretation of the African past; a pride in Blackness: a contrast between a harmonious way of life and decadent White civilization lost in materialism." Instead, Glissant stresses that Martinicans can distinguish themselves by recognizing the "prophetic vision of the past" in terms of their present situation. Glissant's fiction is set in the Antilles, a group of islands in the West Indies, and often features nonchronological narration marked by occasional absences of capitalization and punctuation. Although such narrative strategies may confuse readers, they produce, according to Juris Silenieks, "evocations, referring to what might be images from Africa, the Middle Passage, *marronnage* [the state of runaway slaves], slavery, etc. . . .like brief flashes surging up from the collective unconscious, as it were, fading quickly into other images whose referential frame seems to be the present or myth and legend." In addition to praising Glissant for occasionally writing in *creole,* a combination of French and the rarely written local dialect, critics have recognized that his combination of varying narrative strategies and voices appropriately reflects a nation's evolving identity.

Glissant grew up in Sainte-Marie, Martinique, where his father was a plantation manager. After completing his studies at the Lycee Schoelcher in Fort-de-France and campaigning for the poet and political activist Aime Cesaire in 1945, Glissant went to France to study philosophy and ethnology at the Sorbonne and the Musee de l'Homme. There, he published several volumes of poetry, his first essay collection, *Soleil de la conscience,* the novels *La Lezarde* (*The Ripening*) and *Le quatrieme siecle,* and the play *Monsieur Toussaint.* Because of Glissant's involvement in the Societe Africaine de Culture, the Front Antillo-Guyanais pour l'Independance, and other West Indian political groups, the French government forbade him to travel outside of France. In 1965, however, Glissant was allowed to return to Martinique to teach philosophy courses at the Lycee des Jeunes Filles in Fort-de-France. He continued to write, publishing poetry with *Un champ d'iles, La terre inquiete, Les Indes: Poemes de l'une et l'autre terre,* the essay collection *L'intention poetique,* and the novel *Malemort.* In 1967, he established the Institut Martiniquais d'Etudes (IME), a school that stressed Antillean history, sponsored many cultural activities,

and was heralded as an alternative to the French government's public schools. Glissant returned to France in 1980, worked as an editor at the United Nations Educational, Scientific, and Cultural Organization (UNESCO), and completed the poetry collection *Pays reve, pays reel,* the volume of essays *Le discours antillais* (*Caribbean Discourse: Selected Essays*), and the novels *La case du commandeur* and *Mahagony.*

Glissant's interest in historical events that have influenced Martinique is developed in the poems "Les Indes" and "La terre inquiete" and in his second novel, *Le quatrieme siecle.* "Les Indes" and "La terre inquiete" relate how Columbus "found" the West Indies and how Africans were forcibly brought there as slaves. These poems focus on the sociocultural distance between Martinique, Africa, and Europe as well as the distinctions made between Martinicans of European descent, those whose African ancestors accepted their slave status, and those who were descended from *maroons,* nonassimilated fugitive slaves who lived in the jungle. Critics recognize that these poems end with hope for social growth. *Le quatrieme siecle* continues the theme of historical influence by focusing upon the young Mathieu Beluse and Papa Longoue, whose predecessors came from Africa as slaves. While Mathieu's progenitor accepts his position, Papa Longoue's becomes Martinique's first *maroon.* Mathieu seeks out the aging Papa, the *quimboiseur,* or healer, who explains important events in Martinican history to him. Scholars have noted that Mathieu's attempt to know and transcend his past parallels Glissant's own objectives as a Martinican writer.

Glissant's first novel, *The Ripening,* is set after the events described in *Le quatrieme siecle.* In the story, Mathieu explains how he and his compatriots, a group of young, idealistic political activists, planned the assassination of Thael, a minor government official, to ensure themselves a victory in the election of 1945. The narrative, which is told from both an adolescent and an adult perspective by Mathieu, proved confusing for some readers. The novel, however, drew praise for its descriptive passages and the characters' existential musings. The sagas of the Beluse and Longoue families continue in *La case du commandeur,* but the focus shifts to Marie Celat, known as Mycea in *The Ripening. La case du commandeur* traces Marie's birth and childhood, her marriage to Mathieu, his departure to Europe, the death of her sons, and her ensuing insanity. As the descendant of both slaves and *maroons,* Marie is

unable to fully accept either heritage; this ambivalence compromises her identity, results in her mental breakdown, and hints at the possible collapse of Martinican society. Juris Silenieks observed that despite *La case du commandeur*'s negativity, "attentive reading is likely to yield the novel's richness of meaning and poetic beauty and to extend its relevance beyond the regional context."

Glissant's third novel, *Malemort,* concerns three characters who search for escape from poverty and unemployment. *Malemort* spans almost 140 years of island history by juxtaposing and interweaving the fates of these modern Martinicans, who are often treated and referred to as one individual, with those of their predecessors. Hedi Bouraoui notes that Glissant's later work, *Mahagony,* takes a similar approach to history so that a "date, though specific, is simply a trigger for spontaneous memories transcending past, present, and future, and creating an effect of simultaneity that intentionally blurs events and relationships." Like *Malemort, Mahagony* is a polyphonic work, for the histories of the *maroons* are linked to that of the mahogany tree and the entire island. The events that enfold around the tree, which proves a source of comfort and protection for many *maroons*—including Gani in 1831, Maho in 1943, and Mani in 1978—involve characters from Glissant's earlier works. Marie Celat and other prominent female characters reappear, and Maho is recognizable as Beautemps, one of Mathieu's allies in *The Ripening.* Because the principal narrator, Mathieu, continually speaks to and about Glissant, his biographer, *Mahagony* also examines the relationship between story and storyteller.

Glissant's most famous essay collections, *L'intention poetique* and *Caribbean Discourse,* provide additional insight into his works. Daniel Racine described *L'intention poetique* as a "248-page 'meditation on the essence of language and its relationship with poetry' in which [Glissant] tries to define a poetics of the Antillean people derived from his culture and identity and different from Western poetics." *Caribbean Discourse* was published concurrently with *La case du commandeur* and includes essays on Antillean literature, economics, sociology, history, anthropology, linguistics, and discourse patterns. Wilbert J. Roget has found both collections representative of Glissant's desire "to develop in the Antillais complete rootedness in his land and his history so that he may be equipped to interact on equal footing with peoples of different cultural provenances."

BIOGRAPHICAL/CRITICAL SOURCES:

BOOKS

Dash, J. Michael, *Edouard Glissant,* Cambridge University Press, 1995.

PERIODICALS

French Review, December, 1979, pp. 224-31.
South Atlantic Bulletin, May, 1978, pp. 17-26.

* * *

GOLDBERG, Leonard S. 1936-

PERSONAL: Born March 19, 1936, in Charleston, SC. *Education:* Attended the Citadel, 1953-54, and College of Charleston, 1954-56; Medical College of South Carolina, M.D., 1959.

ADDRESSES: Home—Los Angeles, CA. *Agent*—Jane Jordan Browne, Multimedia Product Development, Inc., 410 South Michigan Ave., Suite 724, Chicago, IL 60605.

CAREER: St. Louis City Hospital, St. Louis, MO, intern and resident in medicine, 1960-61; Medical College of Virginia, Richmond, resident in medicine, 1963-64; Jackson Memorial Hospital, Miami, FL, resident in medicine, 1964-65; University of California, Los Angeles, fellow in hematology, 1965-66, research fellow in immunology, 1966-67; University of California, San Francisco, research fellow in immunology, 1967-68; University of California, Los Angeles, assistant professor, 1968-71, associate professor, 1971-75, professor, 1975-79, clinical professor of medicine, 1979—, clinical investigator of the Veterans Administration, 1968-71; Wadsworth Veterans Hospital, consultant in rheumatology, 1971—. American Board of Internal Medicine, diplomat in internal medicine, hematology, and rheumatology. *Military service:* U.S. Air Force, physician, 1961-63; served in Japan; became captain.

MEMBER: International Society of Hematology, American Association of Immunologists, American Federation for Clinical Research, American Rheumatism Association, American Society of Hematology, American College of Physicians (fellow), British Society for Immunology, Western Society for Clinical Research.

WRITINGS:

MEDICAL SUSPENSE NOVELS

Transplant, Signet (New York), 1980.
Deadly Medicine, Signet, 1992.
A Deadly Practice, Signet, 1994.
Deadly Care, Dutton (Bergenfield, NJ), 1996.

OTHER

Contributor of reviews to medical journals, including *Journal of Clinical Investigation, Clinical Immunology and Immunopathology, Journal of Laboratory and Clinical Medicine,* and *Annals of Internal Medicine.* Member of editorial advisory board, *Journal of the Life Sciences.*

* * *

GOMEZ DE LA SERNA, Ramon 1888-1963 (Tristan)

PERSONAL: Born on July 3 (one source says July 6), 1888, in Madrid, Spain; died on January 12, 1963, in Buenos Aires, Argentina; buried in Madrid's Panteon de Hombres Ilustres; son of Javier Gomez de la Serna y Laguna (an author and magazine editor) and Josefa Puig Coronado. *Education:* University of Madrid Law School, graduated, 1908.

CAREER: Writer. Held political post in Paris, France, 1909-11. Host of series of radio programs, Madrid, beginning 1930.

AWARDS, HONORS: Juan Paloma Award for literature, 1960; "Special" March Award, official March Award, awards from the Spanish provinces of Galicia and Catalonia, and lifetime monthly pension from Argentine Parliament in recognition of literary achievements, all 1962.

WRITINGS:

IN ENGLISH TRANSLATION

Cinelandia, Sempere (Valencia), 1923, reprinted, Nostromo, 1974, translation by Angel Flores published as *Movieland,* Macauley (New York), 1930.
Some greguerias (selections from *Greguerias* and *Flor de greguerias*), translation by Helen

Granville-Barker, W. E. Rudge's Sons (New York), 1944.
Dali, Espasa-Calpe, 1977, translation by Nicholas Fry and Elizabeth Evans published under same title, Morrow, 1979.

Contributor of stories and *greguerias* in English translation to journals, including *Broom,* May, 1922, *Criterion,* January, 1923, *Bookman,* June, 1928, *Alhambra,* June, 1929. Also contributor in English translation to anthologies, including *The Best Continental Short Stories of 1927,* edited by R. Eaton, *Great Spanish Short Stories,* edited by J. G. Gorkin, and *The European Caravan,* edited by S. Putnam.

IN SPANISH

Entrando en el fuego (title means "Entering the Fray"), Imprenta del Diario de Avisos (Segovia), 1905.
Morbideces, El Trabajo (Madrid), 1908.
Cuento de Calleja (play), Sociedad de Autores Espanoles (Madrid), 1909.
Ex-votos: Dramas (play collection), Aurora (Madrid), 1910.
La bailarina (title means "The Ballerina"), Aurora—Sociedad de Autores Espanoles, 1911.
El doctor inverosimil (title means "The Unlikely Doctor"; novel), La Novela de Bolsillo (Madrid), 1914, reprinted, Destino, 1981.
El Rastro (novel), Prometeo, 1915, reprinted, La Nave, 1931.
La viuda blanca y negra (title means "The Black and White Widow"; novel), Biblioteca Nueva, 1917, reprinted, Poseidon, 1943.
El circo (title means "The Circus"), Latina (Madrid), 1917, reprinted, Plaza & Janes, 1987.
Senos (title means "Bosoms"), Latina, 1917, AHR (Barcelona), 1968.
Greguerias, Prometeo (Valencia), 1917, enlarged edition published as *Greguerias, 1940-1945,* Espasa-Calpe (Buenos Aires), 1945, enlarged edition published as *Greguerias, seleccion 1910-1960,* Espasa-Calpe (Madrid), 1960.
(Editor, contributor, and author of epilogue) Silverio Lanza, *Paginas escogidas e ineditas de Silverio Lanza,* Biblioteca Nueva, 1918.
Pombo, Meson de Panos (Madrid), 1918, published as *Pombo: Biografia del celebre cafe y de otros cafes famosos,* Juventud (Buenos Aires), 1941, abridged edition, Juventud (Barcelona), 1960.
Muestrarios (title means "Samplings"), Biblioteca Nueva, 1918.
El alba y las cosas (title means "The Dawn and Things"), Saturnino Calleja (Madrid), 1918.

Toda la historia de la Puerta del Sol (title means "The Complete History of the Puerta del Sol"), La Tribuna, 1920.

Variaciones (title means "Variations"), La Tribuna, 1920.

Virguerias (title means "Virginal Glimpses"), self-published (Madrid), 1920.

El libro nuevo (title means "The New Book"), Meson de Panos, 1920.

Edgar Poe, Biblioteca Nueva (Madrid), 1920, revised edition published as *Edgar Poe, genio de America,* Losada, 1953.

Disparates (title means "Absurdities"), Calpe (Madrid), 1921.

Oscar Wilde, Biblioteca Nueva, 1921, reprinted, Poseidon, 1944.

El secreto del acueducto (title means "The Secret of the Aqueduct"), Biblioteca Nueva, 1922, EDHASA (Barcelona), 1962.

El incongruente: Novela grande, Calpe, 1922, reprinted, Picazo (Barcelona), 1972.

Leopoldo y Teresa, La Novela Corta (Madrid), 1922.

El gran hotel (title means "Grand Hotel"), America (Madrid), 1922.

Ramonismo (title means "Ramonism"), self-illustrated, Calpe, 1923.

El chalet de las rosas, Sempere (Valencia), 1923, reprinted, Centro (Madrid), 1975.

La quinta de Palmyra (title means "Palmyra's Country Villa"), Biblioteca Nueva, 1923, reprinted, Espasa-Calpe (Madrid), 1982.

El novelista (novela grande), Sempere, 1923, reprinted, Espasa-Calpe, 1973.

Azorin (biography), La Nave (Madrid), 1923, reprinted, Losada, 1957.

La sagrada cripta del Pombo (title means "Pombo, The Sacred Crypt"), Meson de Panos, 1924.

La malicia de las acacias: Novelas (novel collection), Sempere, 1924.

Cuentos para ninos (title means "Stories for Children"), Calpe, 1924.

Caprichos (title means "Caprices"; short sketches), La Lectura (Madrid), 1925, reprinted, Espasa-Calpe (Madrid), 1962.

El Prado, Libreria (Madrid), 1925.

El drama del palacio deshabitado: Dramas (contains title play and "La utopia", "Beatriz," "La corona de hierro", and "El lunatico"), America (Madrid), 1926.

Gollerias (title means "Tidbits"), self-illustrated, Sempere, 1926, expanded edition (also includes *Ramonismo* and *Variaciones*), Losada, 1946.

El torero Caracho (novel), Agencia Mundial de Libreria (Madrid), 1926, reprinted, Espasa-Calpe (Madrid), 1969.

La mujer de ambar (title means "The Amber Woman"), Biblioteca Nueva, 1927, reprinted, Espasa-Calpe (Madrid), 1968.

Seis falsas novelas (title means "Six False Novels"), Mundial (Paris), 1927, reprinted, Mondadori (Madrid), 1989.

El caballero del hongo gris: Novela humoristica (title means "The Gentleman in the Grey Top Hat"; novel), Agencia Mundial de Libreria, 1928, reprinted, Salvat (Madrid), 1970.

El dueno del atomo: Novelas (title means "The Master of the Atom: Novels"; collection), Historia Nueva (Madrid), 1928, reprinted, Losada, 1945.

Goya (biography), La Nave, 1928, reprinted, Consejo Nacional de Cultura (Havana), 1963.

Efigies, (biographical sketches), Oriente (Madrid), 1929, reprinted, Aguilar, 1944.

Los medios seres (title means "The Half-Beings"; play; first produced in Madrid, 1929), Prensa Moderna (Madrid), 1929.

Novisimas greguerias, 1929, E. Gimenez (Madrid), 1929.

La nardo (novela grande), Ulises (Madrid), 1930, reprinted, Bruguera, 1981.

Ismos (criticism), Biblioteca Nueva (Madrid), 1931, enlarged edition, Poseidon, 1943, reprinted, Brujula (Buenos Aires), 1968.

Elucidario de Madrid, Renacimiento, 1931, 2nd edition, Artes Graficas Municipales (Madrid), 1957.

Policefalo y senora (title means "Polycephalous and Wife"; novel), Espasa-Calpe (Madrid), 1932.

Chao: Novela, [Barcelona], 1933.

La hiperestetica (El regalo del doctor, La roja, El vegetariano): Novelas, Ulises, 1934.

Flor de greguerias, Espasa-Calpe (Madrid), 1935, expanded edition published as *Flor de greguerias, 1910-1958,* Losada, 1958.

El Greco: El visionario de la pintura, Nuestra Raza (Madrid), 1935, reprinted, Losada, 1950.

Las escaleras, Cruz y Raya (Madrid), 1935.

Los muertos y las muertas, y otras fantasmagorias (title means "Dead Men and Dead Women, and Other Phantasmagories"), Arbol (Madrid), 1935, corrected and enlarged edition, Espasa-Calpe (Madrid), 1961.

El colera azul, Sur (Buenos Aires), 1937.

Rebeca!: Novela inedita, Ercilla (Santiago de Chile), 1937, reprinted, Espasa-Calpe (Madrid), 1974.

Retratos contemporaneos (title means "Contemporary Portraits"), Sudamericana, 1941.

Don Francisco de Goya y Lucientes (biography), Poseidon, 1942.

Mi tia Carolina Coronado, Emece (Buenos Aires), 1942.

Lo cursi, y otros ensayos, Sudamericana, 1943.

El turco de los nardos, La Novela Actual (Madrid), 1943.

Don Diego de Velazquez, Poseidon (Buenos Aires), 1943.

Jose Gutierrez Solana, Poseidon, 1944, reprinted, Picazo, 1972.

Don Ramon Maria de Valle-Inclan (biography), Espasa-Calpe (Buenos Aires), 1944, reprinted, Espasa-Calpe (Madrid), 1969.

Dona Juana la loca y otras (seis novelas superhistoricas), Clydoc (Buenos Aires), 1944.

Lope de Vega, La Universidad (Buenos Aires), 1945, published as *Lope viviente* (title means "Living Lope"), Espasa-Calpe (Buenos Aires), 1954.

Nuevos retratos contemporaneos (title means "New Contemporary Portraits"), Sudamericana, 1945.

Norah Borges (monograph), Losada (Buenos Aires), 1945.

El hombre perdido (title means "The Lost Man"), Poseidon, 1947, reprinted, Espasa-Calpe (Madrid), 1962.

Trampantojos (title means "Tricks of Whimsy"), La Cuerda Floja (Buenos Aires), 1947.

Cuentos del fin del ano (title means "Stories for the End of the Year"), Clan (Madrid), 1947.

Greguerias completas, Lauro (Barcelona), 1947, published as *Total de greguerias,* self-illustrated, Aguilar, 1955.

Obras selectas, ten volumes, Plenitud (Madrid), 1947, published in one volume, with prologue by Pablo Neruda, AHR, 1971.

Explicacion de Buenos Aires, Prologo (Madrid), 1948.

Automoribundia, 1888-1948 (autobiography), Sudamericana, 1948, reprinted, Guadarrama (Madrid), 1974.

Cartas a las golondrinas (title means "Letters to the Swallows"), Juventud, 1949.

Las tres gracias (novela madrilena de invierno), Perseo (Madrid), 1949.

Interpretacion del tango, Ultreya, 1949, reprinted, Albino y Asociados (Buenos Aires), 1979.

Quevedo (biography), Espasa-Calpe (Buenos Aires), 1953.

Antologia: Cincuenta anos de literatura, edited by Guillermo de Torre, Losada, 1955.

Cartas a mi mismo (title means "Letters to Myself"), AHR, 1956.

Nostalgias de Madrid (title means "Nostalgias of Madrid"), El Grifon de Plata (Madrid), 1956.

Obras completas (title means "Complete Works"), two volumes, AHR, 1956-57.

Mis mejores paginas literarias (title means "My Best Pages of Literature"), Gredos, 1957.

Nuevas paginas de mi vida: Lo que no dije en mi Automoribundia (autobiography), Marfil, 1957, reprinted, Alianza, 1970.

Biografias completas (title means "Complete Biographies"; collection), Aguilar, 1959.

Piso bajo: Novela (title means "Ground Floor: Novel"), Espasa-Calpe (Madrid), 1961.

Retratos completos (title means "Complete Portraits"; collection), Aguilar, 1961.

Guia del Rastro (title means "Guide to the Rastro"), with photographs by Carlos Suara, Taurus (Madrid), 1961.

Cartas a las golondrinas. Cartas a mi mismo, Espasa-Calpe, 1962.

Ensayo sobre lo cursi. Escaleras: Drama en tres actos, Cruz del Sur (Santiago de Chile), 1963.

Greguerias: Seleccion, introduction and selection by Gaspar Gomez de la Serna, Anaya (Salamanca), 1963.

Ramon Gomez de la Serna (selections), edited by Luisa Sofovich, [Buenos Aires], 1963.

(Editor) Ramon de Mesonero y Romanos, *Escenas matritenses* (title means "Scenes of Madrid"), Espasa-Calpe (Madrid), 1964.

Retratos contemporaneos escogidos, Sudamericana, 1968.

Caprichos postumos, La Esquina, 1969.

Diario postumo, Plaza y Janes, 1972.

Descubrimiento de Madrid, Catedra (Madrid), 1974.

Also author of *El miedo al mar,* 1921; *La hija del verano,* 1922; *La gangosa,* 1922; *Por los tejados,* 1924; *En el bazar mas suntuoso del mundo,* 1924; *Aquella novela,* 1924; *La funebre falsa,* 1925; *Hay que matar el Morse,* 1925; *El hijo del millionario,* 1927; *Siluetas y sombras,* 1934; *Ruskin, el apasionado,* 1943; and *Ventura Garcia Calderon,* 1946. Also author of prologue to Carmen de Burgos's Spanish translation of John Ruskin's *Stones of Venice.* Columnist, *El Liberal* (Madrid newspaper), 1918-23, *El Sol,* 1923-1933, and *La Nacion* (Buenos Aires newspaper), beginning 1928. Contributor, occasionally under pseudonym Tristan, to periodicals, including *La Tribuna* (Madrid daily), *Revista de Occidente* (literary journal) and *Arriba* (newspaper). Editor, *Prometeo,* beginning 1912.

SIDELIGHTS: Spanish humorist, short story writer, playwright and novelist Ramon Gomez de la Serna's literary career began while he was still in his teens. The elder Gomez de la Serna financed the publication of young Ramon's first book, *Entrando en el fuego* ("Entering the Fray"; published when he was just sixteen), used his influence to obtain a political post

in Paris for his son so he could live in the city where authors such as Guillaume Apollinaire, Marcel Proust, Colette and others were writing, and later founded the literary magazine, *Prometeo,* and appointed Ramon its editor. Before the boy turned twenty, he had been honored at a literary banquet in his honor and had established himself as an innovative thinker. To many critics his subsequent work—spanning a period of nearly six decades—proved his early reputation to be justified and constituted a major contribution to Spanish letters.

One of the highlights of Gomez de la Serna's career was his invention of the *gregueria* in 1911. A chance glance out of his balcony window in Madrid recalled to the writer a similar view out of a balcony on the Arno River in Florence, Italy. As he longingly tried to recreate the scene in his mind, the idea struck him that maybe the river wished it could be in another location too or that the far bank of the river might want to exchange places with the near bank. Enchanted by the humor of his thoughts, Gomez de la Serna decided to name the concept *gregueria,* a Spanish word meaning a "confused hubbub of voices." In *The Literature of the Spanish People: From Roman Times to the Present* Gerald Brenan offered several examples of *greguerias* in English translation, including: "Stale bread is like a newly formed fossil" and "The seagulls were born from the handkerchiefs that wave goodbye in ports." Included in Rita Mazzetti Gardiol's *Ramon Gomez de la Serna* is the equation the writer used as his own definition of the term: "Humor + metaphor = *gregueria.*" These semi-aphoristic pieces, which often convey brilliant poetic images, have been seen by critics as precursors to several of the vanguardist schools of thought popular in Europe during the early years of the twentieth century.

The absurd humor of some of the *greguerias,* for example, brings to mind the writing of the surrealists who reveled in anything that would shock traditionalists. Gomez de la Serna attempted to do the same in his work nearly a decade before French writer Andre Breton's first surrealist manifesto. According to *Modern Fiction Studies* contributor Richard L. Jackson: "The power to startle consistently with surprising analogies is one of the major artistic achievements of the *gregueria.* The expression of this surprise, shock, and astonishment is one of the main objectives of this literary 'invention.'" Brenan wrote of the *greguerias:* "The best of them reveal the secret correspondences of things, employing for this a peculiar sort of poetic intuition. This kind of writing is of course surrealism, born long before that term was invented."

Other works that demonstrated Gomez de la Serna's surrealistic tendencies include the two early volumes, *Senos* ("Bosoms") and *El circo* ("The Circus"), published in 1917, the same year in which his first collection of *greguerias* was published. Both *Senos* and *El circo* can be considered collections, too, for they each contain long lists of images associated with the theme referred to in the book's title. In the former, Gomez de la Serna describes bosoms in chapters titled, for instance, "Bosoms in Art" and "Andalusian Bosoms." *El circo* focuses on the exciting and colorful world of the circus. This work was to provide its author with several opportunities to live out his surrealistic tendencies: once, when honored in Madrid for the book by a traveling circus, Gomez de la Serna chose to deliver a responding lecture entitled "The Complex Beauty of the Circus" from a circus trapeze. On the occasion of a similar tribute at the Cirque d'Hiver in Paris, he spoke about elephants while perched on the back of one.

In his listing of things or sensations associated with the circus, his listing of bosoms, and his listings of images in his *gregueria* collections, Gomez de la Serna revealed his love of looking for the logic behind what might at first glance appear to be a seemingly unconnected series of ideas or things. He gathered what appeared to be a confused jumble of thoughts and hoped, on completion of his work, to produce an understandable whole. Gardiol considered this characteristic of Gomez de la Serna's work an echo of a similar inclination towards enumeration in the writings of Spanish essayist Jose Martinez Ruiz (known by his pseudonym Azorin). But while Azorin merely offered detailed descriptions of things, Gomez de la Serna granted human qualities to the objects. In *El Rastro* (which included a dedication to Azorin) Gomez de la Serna describes the sights of Madrid's lively outdoor flea market of the same name where second-hand odds and ends spread out on blankets or stretch for miles in booths. In Gomez de la Serna's hands the sea of discards takes on a life of its own, each item has a story to tell. His love of things, which might typically be construed as a characteristic of the writing of a realist, was used by the author in a vanguardist manner. "Never is Ramon more Ramon—and less a realist—then when he seems to enjoy, to take delight in things," commented Spanish philosopher and essayist Julian Marias in an *Insula* article quoted in English translation by Gardiol.

Marias greatly admired Gomez de la Serna's work and, according to Jackson, "maintained that in Ramon's generation only three men reached the stature of genius: Ortega [y Gasset] in philosophy, Picasso in art, and Ramon in literature." All three men excelled in looking at their world in ways that upset traditional modes of thought. Gomez de la Serna, in fact, was influenced by Ortega y Gasset's views, including his theory advocating the dehumanization of art (the title of his most famous work) and his emphasis on the microstructure—those seemingly unimportant events—of life. Gomez de la Serna dedicated his novel *El secreto del acueducto* ("The Secret of the Aqueduct") to Ortega y Gasset and the work's structure reveals his indebtedness to the philosopher's thinking: Human characters diminish in importance, as in most of Gomez de la Serna's novels, while things, in this case the great Roman aqueduct of Segovia, gain in significance. The aqueduct becomes the focus of the author's attention and, at times, he even stops his narrative to admire its beauty. Other Gomez de la Serna works, such as *Ramonismo* ("Ramonism"), *Caprichos* ("Caprices"), and *Gollerias* ("Tidbits"), celebrate Ortega y Gasset's idea of the microstructure by emphasizing minute details.

Ramonismo, the word the author used to describe his attitude toward art and life, serves as the title to a collection of random thoughts on a variety of topics, including polka dot blouses, parrots, and awnings. In *The Generation of 1898 and After* Beatrice Patt and Martin Nozick described *ramonismo* as "an outrageously unconventional and purely arbitrary vision of facts and things." The *gregueria* is perhaps the best expression of *ramonismo* and Gomez de la Serna's most enduring contribution to Spanish literature. "He proved that literary language could be richer if it used images," wrote Spanish critic Arturo Barea in *Books Abroad,* "with the same freedom as did the symbol-studded talk of the Andalusian peasants and gypsies." The "symbol-studded" speech of Andalusian country folk was what was to similarly inspire the innovative use of metaphors found in the work of Garcia Lorca (whose first book of poetry was published a decade after Gomez de la Serna's creation of the *gregueria*) and other writers of his generation and after. As Gardiol noted, "Because [Gomez de la Serna's] creative innovations succeeded in expanding the expressive powers of the image, he has been recognized as a major influence on the Spanish poets of the Generation of '25 and one of the precursors of the 'new' Spanish literature."

The Town Hall of the City of Madrid houses a museum of Ramon Gomez de la Serna memorabilia.

BIOGRAPHICAL/CRITICAL SOURCES:

BOOKS

Brenan, Gerald, *The Literature of the Spanish People: From Roman Times to the Present,* World Publishing, 1957.
Contemporary Literary Criticism, Volume 9, Gale, 1978.
Gardiol, Rita Mazzetti, *Ramon Gomez de la Serna,* Twayne, 1974.
Patt, Beatrice, and Martin Nozick, editors, *The Generation of 1898 and After,* Harper, 1960.

PERIODICALS

Books Abroad, spring, 1953.
Insula, February 15, 1957.
Modern Fiction Studies, summer, 1976.*
—Sketch by Marian Gonsior

* * *

GOMEZ ROSA, Alexis 1950-

PERSONAL: Born September 2, 1950, in Santo Domingo, Dominican Republic; son of Juan Francisco Gomez (a certified public accountant) and Altagracia de la Rosa de Gomez; married Barbara Garcia Jimenez (in psychology), February 12, 1976; children: Berenice, Yelida, Adrian. *Education:* Attended Universidad Autonoma de Santo Domingo, 1970-74, and University of Massachusetts—Boston, 1983-85; State University of New York, Empire State College, B.A., 1988.

ADDRESSES: Home—514 West 176th St., New York, NY 10033. *Office*—Spanish Dept., New York University, 19 University Place, 4th floor, New York, NY 10003.

CAREER: Colegio Onesimo Jimenez (high school), Dominican Republic, teacher, 1972-74; copywriter for Young & Rubicam advertising agency, 1974; copywriter for RETHO advertising agency, 1975; teacher at Padre Billini High School, 1975-77; Dominican Export Promotion Center, publicist, 1978-83; Noticias del Mundo, publicist, 1983-90; poetry instructor in the public schools of Boston and

Dorchester, MA, 1984-85; Northern Manhattan Coalition for Immigrants Rights, New York City, community liaison, 1987-88; New York University, Spanish instructor. Journalist. Social worker with organizations and clubs of Washington Heights.

AWARDS, HONORS: First Prize for Poetry, Casa de Teatro, 1990; National Prize for Poetry, Salome Urena de Henriquez, 1991.

WRITINGS:

POETRY

Oficio de post-muerte, Williamsburg Print Shop, 1973.
(Contributor) *Los paraguas amarillos,* Ediciones del Norte, 1983.
High Quality, Ltd., Luna Cabeza Caliente (Santo Domingo, Dominican Republic), 1985.
(Contributor) *La poesia bisona,* Associated University Presses, 1986.
(Contributor) *Poesia dominicana de post-guerra,* Associated University Presses, 1986.
(Contributor) *Anthology of Contemporary Latin American Literature,* Associated University Presses, 1986.
(Contributor) *Antologia de la poesia hispanoamericana actual,* Siglo Veintiuno (Mexico), 1987.
Tiza & Tinta, Lluvia Editores (Lima, Peru), 1990.

Also author of *Pluroscopo* (Santo Domingo).

* * *

GONZALEZ, Cesar A.
　See GONZALEZ T(RUJILLO), Cesar A.

* * *

GONZALEZ T(RUJILLO), Cesar A. 1931-
　(Cesar A. Gonzalez)

PERSONAL: Born January 17, 1931, in Los Angeles, CA; son of Jose A. (a chef) and Camerina (a seamstress; maiden name, Trujillo) Gonzalez; married Bette Beattie (a teacher), August 30, 1969. *Education:* Gonzaga University, B.A., 1953, M.A., Ph.L., 1954; University of Santa Clara, M.S.T., S.T.L.,

1961; graduate study at University of California, Los Angeles, 1962-65; graduate study at University of New Mexico, 1986. *Politics:* "Registered Democrat." *Religion:* "Practicing Catholic."

ADDRESSES: Home—7252 Caminito Carlotta, San Diego, CA 92120. *Office*—Chicano Studies Department, San Diego Mesa College, 7250 Mesa College Dr., San Diego, CA 92111.

CAREER: Instituto Regional, Chihuahua, Mexico, teacher, 1954-57; Centro Laboral Mexico, Mexico City, worked at community development projects, 1965-68; Head Start, Los Angeles, CA, supervisor working for civil rights and Chicano educational reform, 1968-69; Operation SER, San Diego, CA, employment counselor, 1969-70; San Diego Mesa College, San Diego, founding chair and professor in Chicano studies department, 1970—.

MEMBER: National Association of Chicano Studies, American Federation of Teachers, La Raza Faculty Association, Chicano Federation of San Diego County, Centro Cultural de la Raza, Poets and Writers.

AWARDS, HONORS: Fulbright-Hays fellow in Peru, 1982; community service award from Chicano Federation of San Diego, 1982; member of first Chicano National Endowment for the Humanities fellowship group, 1984; outstanding instructor award from San Diego Mesa College, 1985, 1995; Editor's Choice Award, *Poet* magazine, 1993; Cesar Chavez Social Justice Award, 1994; Latina Latino Indigenous People Coalition Award, 1995; special congressional recognition, 1995.

WRITINGS:

(Editor, with others, under name Cesar A. Gonzalez) *What You Want to Know about English Grammar But Are Afraid to Ask: English Grammar for College Students,* San Diego Community College District, 1978.
(Editor and contributor, with others, under name Cesar A. Gonzalez) *Real Writing: English Composition for College Students,* San Diego Community College District, 1979.
Unwinding the Silence (poetry; includes "Sol Invernal," "Ancient Youth," "Damned," "In the Long Run," and "Quetzalcoatl and Christ"), introduction by Luis Leal, Lalo, 1987.
(Editor with Luis Alberto Urrea) *Fragmentos de Barro: The First Seven Years,* Tolteca, 1987.

(Editor and contributor) *Rudolfo A. Anaya: Focus on Criticism,* Massachusetts Bay, 1989.

Work represented in anthologies, including *First Chicano Literary Prize,* edited by Juan Villegas and others, Department of Spanish and Portuguese, University of California, Irvine, 1975; and *Southwest Tales: A Contemporary Collection,* edited by Alurista and Xelina Rojas-Urista, Maize, 1986. Contributor to periodicals, including *De Colores, Maize, Paperback Edition, Caracol, Citybender, Mesa Press,* and *Imagine.* Editor, with others, of literary contest publication *Fragmentos de Barro: Pieces of Clay,* 1976-81 and 1983.

SIDELIGHTS: Cesar A. Gonzalez T., who has spent much of his career teaching Chicano studies, philosophy, and English, is best known as a poet. A child during the Depression, he was deeply affected by the suffering and turmoil he witnessed, developing a strong sense of compassion for his fellow human beings and an awareness of the transitory nature of the world. Such feelings surface in his poetry, which is marked by its philosophical slant. In Gonzalez T.'s first collection of verse, *Unwinding the Silence,* the poet explores the opposition of good and evil and shows how love and companionship can transcend the impermanence of the world. *Dictionary of Literary Biography* contributor Ernesto Chavez Padilla observed, "His are songs of innocence and experience that probe life with the logical mind of the philosopher; and yet, in the end, Gonzalez abandons the rigor of philosophy for the mystical precept that man can sustain contraries in his approach to the perfection of love."

Gonzalez T. writes: "The Chicano movement, Chicano publications, and writing contests moved me to commit myself to writing in a dedicated and sustained way. I wanted to be part of a movement expanding the base of American literature, with its implicit redefinition of American reality.

"A great deal of what I write is done while I am on the move, sometimes at night, on a pad in the dark, by the side of the bed, writing something only when it must be written. I write in English or Spanish, at times using both languages in what Tino Villanueva has aptly called bisensitive writing. Both are public languages in the United States, with all of the attendant problems of publication. When I published my first collection, *Unwinding the Silence* with Lalo Press, I also made a linguistic statement.

"In my reading, reflection, and expression, I am fascinated by change and by the analogy of being. Hence, for all of its elusiveness, I read reality as a kaleidoscope of prisms, wherein everything is in everything. So whether we look outwards in our naming or inward from our necessarily limited apprehension of the totality of physical/psycho-moral space, we see the world which we continue to try to express through the particularity of our word.

"The poem 'Maldito / Damned' in *Unwinding the Silence* may be read as an expression of this fascination with anagogy, expressing the frustration of intuiting the whole, yet being unable to take in, comprehend, much less 'name the world,' or reality. I believe that aspirations for transcendence are not a chance hoax of nature, destined for frustration. Ending 'Maldito por no ser Dios! / Damned, I'm not God!' there is implicit an intuition of the existence of God.

"My faith and a certain privacy are very important to me. A friend remarked recently that in my writing I often seem to slip in traces of scholasticism. I learned this in my many years of studying and working with the Jesuits. Gerard Manly Hopkins, S.J., and Pierre Teilhard de Chardin, S.J., have been great influences. Thomas Aquinas and Jacques Maritain were also important in my formative years.

"An example of deliberate philosophical intent is found in the epilogue-poem of *Unwinding the Silence,* 'A la larga / In the Long Run.' While expressing affirmative expectations for the future of Chicano literature, it asserts that in the long run 'we will be / re-membered,' as a community once scattered in moral disjunction, creating personhood. We will be 're-newed' and 're-read for / what / we with art fully make, / with prudence truly do, with wisdom thought-full speculate and / say we do ourselves freely decide' our own ideals as a community in unity. I remember Aquinas speaking of wisdom as a virtue of the speculative intellect seeking truth for its own sake, as in metaphysics or pure science. Art, he goes on to say, is the virtue proper to the intellect being used for the practical purpose of making something; prudence guides the practical intellect in doing, that is in moving the will toward deliberate, responsible choice—which is the realm of ethics. The intellect acting for the practical purpose of guiding choice is more popularly known as conscience.

"My reading includes an extensive reading of Chicano literature, with a special interest in the writ-

ings of women. There are many excellent writers. The *Quinto Sol* prize winners (Tomas Rivera, Rudolfo A. Anaya, Rolando Hinojosa-Smith, and Estela Portillo Trambley) are notable. I share Anaya's interest in archetype and myth. When he speaks of myth as 'the truth in the heart,' I read this as intuitive, dimensional human nature, common to all across time and space, and also the foundation of natural law and *ius gentium*. The Aztecs—the inheritors of millenia of indigenous wisdom—spoke of this as an innate sense of 'what is fitting, what is right.'"

BIOGRAPHICAL/CRITICAL SOURCES:

BOOKS

Dictionary of Literary Biography, Volume 82: *Chicano Writers,* First Series, Gale, 1989.

* * *

GOODWIN, R(ichard) M(urphey) 1913-1996

OBITUARY NOTICE—See index for *CA* sketch: Born February 24, 1913, in New Castle, IN; immigrated to England, c. 1951; died resulting from heart problems, August 6, 1996, in Siena, Italy. Economist, educator, painter, and author. Goodwin was an economist of considerable merit who developed various economic models and inspired his students in the field. During his forty-year teaching career, Goodwin spent time painting; many of his works of art adorn the universities where he taught. Goodwin worked as an instructor at Harvard University beginning in 1942, becoming an assistant professor in 1945. In the 1930s, he had joined the Communist party along with many others in that era, but had resigned his membership during World War II. He was later investigated, however, by Senator Joseph McCarthy and the U.S. House of Representatives' subcommittee on un-American activities. In the early 1950s, Goodwin relocated to England and began more than twenty-five years at Cambridge University as part of the school's economic faculty. In 1979, he began teaching at the University of Siena in Italy as a professor, retiring in 1984. He spent many summers painting in India. His paintings were exhibited in the United States and England. He wrote and edited books, including *Elementary Economics from the Higher Standpoint, Essays in Linear Economic Structures, The Dynamics of a Capitalist Economy, Essays in Nonlinear Economic Dynamics,* and *Chaotic Economic Dynamics.*

OBITUARIES AND OTHER SOURCES:

PERIODICALS

New York Times, August 13, 1996, p. B6.
Times (London), August 15, 1996, p. 19.

* * *

GOODWIN, Ruby Berkley 1903-1961

PERSONAL: Born October 17, 1903, in DuQuoin, IL; died May 31, 1961; daughter of a coal miner; married; children: five. *Education:* San Gabriel College (San Diego State), A.B., 1949.

CAREER: Syndicated columnist of "Hollywood in Bronze," 1936-52; secretary and publicist for actor Hattie McDaniel, 1936-52; actor appearing in the films *The View from Pompey's Head,* 1955, *Strange Intruder,* 1956, *The Alligator People,* 1959, and *Wild in the Country,* 1961.

MEMBER: Los Angeles Urban League, Chaparral Poetry Society, Screen Actors Guild, Negro Actors Guild, Fullerton Council of Churchwomen, Fullerton Young Women's Christian Association (YWCA), Actors' Equity Association.

AWARDS, HONORS: Gold Medal, Commonwealth Award for best nonfiction by a California writer, 1953, for *It's Good to Be Black.*

WRITINGS:

From My Kitchen Window (poems), Wendell Malliet and Co., 1942.
A Gold Star Mother Speaks (poems), Orange County Printing Co., 1944.
It's Good to Be Black (autobiography), Doubleday, 1953.

Contributor to books, including *Twelve Negro Spirituals* (stories), Handy Brothers Music Co., 1937; *Negro Voices,* 1938; and *Ebony Rhythm,* 1938.

SIDELIGHTS: Although she started her college education late in life, Ruby Berkley Goodwin had pursued her writing career with vigor prior to beginning her undergraduate career. A wife and mother to five children, she maintained a dual career as a syndicated

columnist on black Hollywood and as the publicist and secretary to the screen actor Hattie McDaniel. It was during this time that her work "Stories of Negro Life" was published in *Twelve Negro Spirituals*.

Goodwin found success with the publication of her poetry collection *From My Kitchen Window*. In her introduction, she denounced the inherent injustice in racism, but expressed hope: "love instead of hate; helpfulness and encouragement instead of arrogance and disdain." Her poetry records daily and cumulative injuries and wrongs and shows how solace can be found in God. She also affirms the integrity and pride of black Americans.

In relating her childhood as the daughter of a coal miner at the turn of the twentieth century, Goodwin provided a portrait of a strong family in *It's Good to Be Black*. A critic in *Kirkus Reviews* described the autobiography as "a personal narrative which substitutes dignity for sensationalism, a quiet strength for the more embittered and embattled attack against discrimination."

BIOGRAPHICAL/CRITICAL SOURCES:

BOOKS

Goodwin, Ruby Berkley, *From My Kitchen Window,* Wendell Malliet and Co., 1942.

PERIODICALS

Kirkus Reviews, October, 1953.*

* * *

GRAY, Muriel

PERSONAL: Born in Scotland; married; children: one son.

ADDRESSES: Home—Glasgow, Scotland. *Office*—c/o Doubleday, 1540 Broadway, New York, NY 10036.

CAREER: Journalist and television personality in Scotland; appeared on *The Media Show;* host of talk show *Walkie Talkie,* beginning in 1989; owner, producer, and director of a television network in Glasgow, Scotland. Edinburgh University, rector, beginning 1988.

WRITINGS:

The Trickster (novel), Doubleday (New York), 1995.

WORK IN PROGRESS: A horror story.

SIDELIGHTS: The Trickster is the first novel of Muriel Gray, a Scottish television personality and network owner whom publisher Doubleday touts as "a female Stephen King." Commenting on Doubleday's claim, critic Dean Johnson, in a *Chicago Tribune* review, remarked: "I'm not so sure that what the world needs now is 'a female Stephen King' . . . but Muriel Gray's book will undoubtedly give even Mr. King a few shivers."

The Trickster is set in the Canadian Rockies in the town of Silver, where a string of grizzly murders has residents terrified. Gray's protagonist is Sam Hunt, a Kinchuinick Sioux, who anglicized his name from Hunting Wolf in protest after renouncing his tribe and the childhood of abuse he suffered on the reservation. Now married to a white woman and the father of two children, Sam has been experiencing blackouts, leaving him unable to account for his actions during prolonged periods of time. His rejection of his tribal heritage has made him vulnerable to an ancient demon known as "The Trickster" who is attempting to use Sam's seething anger to destroy the town. Because of his blackouts, Sam begins wondering if he, himself, is the murderer, but he eventually discovers that he is the town's salvation, for one of his ancestors had succeeded in defeating The Trickster. Therefore, because of his heritage, Sam is the one to rise to the occasion and confront the evil spirit.

The Trickster is rife with Native American folklore and superstition, and the novel explores in depth the relationship between Native Americans and whites. *Chicago Tribune* critic Johnson applauded Gray's treatment of her subject, observing: "She has obviously done her research; the Native American characters are certainly the most compelling." Kim Newman, writing in *New Statesman and Society,* noted that "Gray doesn't spare the nasty business" in her descriptions. Newman judged, "There's entertainment enough . . . but neither the author nor the reader are exactly stretched." A *Publishers Weekly* reviewer issued praise, characterizing the book as a

"tersely plotted" novel that is "an auspicious fiction debut."

BIOGRAPHICAL/CRITICAL SOURCES:

PERIODICALS

Chicago Tribune, August 22, 1995, section 5, p. 3.
Kirkus Reviews, July 1, 1995, pp. 880-81.
New Statesman and Society, December 1, 1989, p. 46; November 4, 1994, p. 37.
Publishers Weekly, January 23, 1995, pp. 44, 46; July 17, 1995, p. 222.*

* * *

GREENLAW, Lavinia (Elaine) 1962-

PERSONAL: Born July 30, 1962, in London, England; children: one daughter. *Education:* Kingston Polytechnic, B.A. (English; with honors), 1983; London College of Printing, diploma in publishing/production 1985.

ADDRESSES: Agent—Derek Johns, A. P. Watt, 20 John St., London WC1N 2DR, England.

CAREER: Imperial College of Science and Technology, London, England, publications editor, 1985-86; Allison and Busby, London, desk editor, 1986-87; Earthscan, London, managing editor, 1988-90; Southbank Centre, London, assistant literature officer, 1990-91; London Arts Board, principal literature officer, 1991-94; freelance writer and reviewer, 1994—. Writer-in-residence, Science Museum in London, 1994-95; British Council Fellow in Writing, Amherst College, fall, 1995.

AWARDS, HONORS: Eric Gregory award, 1990; Arts Council of England Writers' award, 1995.

WRITINGS:

POETRY

The Cost of Getting Lost in Space, Turret Books (London), 1991.
Love from a Foreign City, Slowdancer Press (London), 1992.
Night Photograph, Faber (London), 1993.

GREENWALD, Jeff 1954-

PERSONAL: Born March 6, 1954, in Bronx, NY; son of Robert Greenwald (in sales) and Roslyn Greenwald-Miller (an educator; maiden name, Yapalater). *Education:* Attended University of California at Santa Cruz. *Politics:* "Democratic socialist cynic." *Religion:* "Another Buddhist Jew." *Avocational interests:* Scuba diving, science fiction, tennis, Thai cooking.

ADDRESSES: Office—P.O. Box 5883, Berkeley, CA 94705. *E-mail*—73541.3207@compuserve.com. *Agent*—Jane Dystel, 1 Union Square, New York, NY 10013.

CAREER: World traveler, writer, photographer, videographer, and artist. *Santa Barbara News & Review,* Santa Barbara, CA, cultural and features editor, 1980-83; *Wired* magazine, San Francisco, CA, contributing writer, 1993—; Global Network, Navigator, CA, contributing travel editor, 1993—; Songline Studios, Sebastopol, CA, project director, 1995—. *Art/Life,* editor; designed urban playgrounds for UNICEF and Nepal Children's Organization; prepared exhibits, lectures and educational programs for Exploratorium (San Francisco), University of California, Body Shop International, and Asian Art Museum of San Francisco. Also engineer on the site of Khao-I-Dang, a Cambodian refugee camp.

MEMBER: PEN.

AWARDS, HONORS: Journalism Fellowship, Rotary International Foundation, 1983.

WRITINGS:

Mr. Raja's Neighborhood: Letters from Nepal, John Daniel, 1986.
Shopping for Buddhas, Harper (San Francisco), 1990.
(Editor) Alan Clements, *Burma: The Next Killing Fields?,* Odonian, 1992.
The Size of the World: Once Around without Leaving the Ground, Globe Pequot Press, 1995

Regular contributor to *Wired, HotWired, San Francisco Examiner, Los Angeles Times, Washington Post, Details, Conde-Nast Traveler,* and *Escape* as well as *Hotwired*'s "World Beat" on the Internet. Work represented in several anthologies, including the *Travelers' Tales* series. Also published art portfolio *eye.*

WORK IN PROGRESS: Snake Lake; Kanthaka; The 36 Unknown; research on Tibetan Buddhism, space travel, and the new seven wonders of the world.

SIDELIGHTS: Jeff Greenwald is the author of several travelogues. In his *The Size of the World: Once Around without Leaving the Ground,* he describes the worldwide trek he undertook shortly before his fortieth birthday. On his journey, Greenwald toured the globe using ground and water transportation, avoiding the skyways. A *Publishers Weekly* reviewer described the volume as "a travel book like no other," while a *Booklist* contributor noted that "Greenwald's skillful writing is always engrossing, blending insightful depictions of remote settings with introspective anecdotes."

In *Shopping for Buddhas,* Greenwald writes about Nepal, which he first visited in 1979. Containing his thoughts about the land and its people, the work also delineates his search for the perfect statue of the religious figure Buddha. "He recounts his sojourns," wrote Donna Seaman in *Booklist,* "with startling inventive descriptions." Melinda Stivers in *Library Journal* observed that "[Greenwald] takes us on a drug-induced, out-of-body experience reminiscent of . . . Timothy Leary." And a *School Library Journal* critic remarked that the volume includes "some strange, appalling, and extremely uplifting experiences."

Greenwald told *CA:* "My writing interests are mainly travel and science. All of my work is participatory; book contracts and magazine assignments provide no more than an excuse to meet amazing people, engage myself in extraordinary projects, or depart on harebrained expeditions.

"All of my books in print are travelogue. The clearest thing I ever said about my approach to the genre appeared in the *San Francisco Examiner* when the editor asked how I *felt* traveling through the twenty-six countries I visited while writing *The Size of the World.* The following was my reply:

"'It's a good question, because it addresses a contemporary phenomenon that must mark a watershed in human behavior. Never before have so many men and women traveled so lightly, so broadly, so *spontaneously.* It's a great freedom, but it poses an interesting dilemma for the individual traveler. On the one hand, you want to merge as seamlessly as possible with the culture you're visiting; you want to be a fly on the wall. On the other hand you can't help being a sort

of curiosity, an 'alien' just by virtue of the clothes you wear, the books you carry, the color of your skin.

"'There was an era in travel—by no means gone—when people clung to or even flaunted their separation, socially and economically, from the cultures they visited. Today, though, individual travelers compose a distinct culture of their own. Part of belonging to this culture involves the ability—executed with wildly varying degrees of success—of simply being yourself wherever you go. You don't isolate yourself from strange customs and situations, but you don't necessarily protect them from you either.

"'There are limits, of course. You don't wear shorts into a mosque, point your feet at a Thai monk, or bring Spam to a potluck in Israel. But if you begin with an assumption of mutual respect, cultivate a good heart, and allow yourself to be yourself wherever you go, you can feel at home, and in place, almost anywhere in the world.'

"The way I write both books and articles is straightforward: a detailed outline, and two three-hour shifts a day. I never take a break when I'm stuck; only in mid-thought or sentence. That way I know I can come back, sit down, and pick up writing again without delay."

BIOGRAPHICAL/CRITICAL SOURCES:

PERIODICALS

Booklist, June 15, 1990; October 1, 1995, p. 247.
Library Journal, July, 1990, p. 116.
Publishers Weekly, July 6, 1990, p. 63; August 28, 1995, p. 98.
School Library Journal, March, 1991, p. 234.

* * *

GROULX, Lionel (Adolphe) 1878-1967
(Alonie de Lestres, Lionel Montal)

PERSONAL: Born January 13, 1878, in Vaudreuil, Quebec; died May 23, 1967; son of Leon and Philomene Salomee (Pilon) Groulx. *Education:* Attended Seminaire de Ste.-Therese-de-Blainville (now renamed for Groulx), 1884-99; attended the Grand Seminaire de Montreal; studied in Rome, Paris, and Fribourg, 1906-1909. *Religion:* Roman Catholic.

CAREER: Ordained as a Roman Catholic priest, 1903; Seminaire de Valleyfield, teacher, 1901-1915; associated with Universite Laval de Montreal (now Universite de Montreal), 1915-49; free-lance writer, 1906-67. Editor of *L'Action francaise* (now *L'Action nationale*), 1921-28; founder of the Institut d'Histoire de l'Amerique Francaise and its *Revue,* 1946; visiting lecturer throughout Quebec, and on radio and television.

MEMBER: Ligue des Droits du Francais.

AWARDS, HONORS: Tyrrel Medal of the Royal Society of Canada; special recognition from the Canadian Historical Association; numerous awards from nationalist, historical, and literary groups in Quebec and France; honorary degrees from universities, including Universite de Montreal, Universite d'Ottawa, and Memorial University.

WRITINGS:

L'Education de la volonte en vue du devoir social, A.C.J.C. (Montreal), 1906.

Une Croisade d'adolescents, L'Action Sociale (Quebec City), 1912.

Les Rapaillages (vieilles choses, vieilles gens) (short stories), Le Devoir (Montreal), 1916.

La Confederation canadienne, Le Devoir, 1918.

La Naissance d'une race, Bibliotheque de l'Action Francaise (Montreal), 1919.

Chez nos ancetres, Bibliotheque de l'Action Francaise, 1920.

Lendemains de conquete, Bibliotheque de l'Action Francaise, 1920.

Vers l'emancipation, Bibliotheque de l'Action Francaise, 1921.

Notre maitre, le passe, first series, Bibliotheque de l'Action Francaise, 1924, second and third series, Granger (Montreal), 1936, 1944.

Dix ans d'Action francaise, Bibliotheque de l'Action Francaise, 1926.

L'Enseignement francais au Canada (two volumes), Volume 1, Albert Levesque (Montreal), 1931, Volume 2, Granger, 1933.

Le Francais au Canada, Libraire Delagrave (Paris), 1932.

Orientations, Editions du Zodiaque (Montreal), 1935.

Directives, Editions du Zodiaque, 1937.

Histoire du Canada francais depuis la decouverte (four volumes), L'Action Nationale (Montreal), 1950-52.

Pour batir, L'Action Nationale, 1953.

Rencontres avec Dieu, Fides (Montreal), 1956.

Une Femme de genie au Canada: La Bienheureuse Mere d'Youville, Comite des Fondateurs de l'Eglise Canadienne (Montreal), 1957.

Notre Grande Aventure: L'Empire francais en Amerique du Nord (1535-1760), Fides, 1958.

Dollard est-il un mythe?, Fides, 1960.

Le Canada francais missionaire, Fides, 1962.

Chemins de l'avenir, Fides, 1964.

La Decouverte du Canada: Jacques Cartier, Fides, 1966.

Constantes de vie, Fides, 1967.

Roland-Michel Barrin de La Galissoniere, 1693-1756, Presses de l'Universite Laval (Quebec City), 1970; translated by John Flinn, University of Toronto Press (Toronto), 1970.

Mes Memoires (four volumes; autobiography), Fides, 1970-74.

Abbe Groulx: Variations on a Nationalist Theme, translations by Joanne L'Heureux and Susan Mann Trofimenkoff, edited by Trofimenkoff, Copp Clark (Vancouver), 1973.

Lionel Groulx, Journal 1895-1911, Presses de l'Universite de Montreal (Montreal), 1984.

NOVELS; UNDER PSEUDONYM ALONIE DE LESTRES

L'Appel de la race, Bibliotheque de l'Action Francaise, 1922; translated by J. S. Wood as *The Iron Wedge,* Carleton Library (Ottawa), 1986.

Au Cap Blomidon, Le Devoir, 1932.

OTHER

Contributor of poems to periodicals, including *Le Semeur,* under the pseudonym Lionel Montal.

SIDELIGHTS: A Catholic priest and strong advocate of Quebec nationalism, Lionel Groulx was the author of many historical and political works. He primarily worked in the genres of nonfiction, but his volume of short stories, *Les Rapaillages (vieilles choses, vieilles gens),* proved very popular in his home province. He also authored two novels with French-Canadian nationalist themes, the first of which was translated into English as *The Iron Wedge.* Though Groulx is little known to English-speaking Canadians, Phyllis M. Senese reported in the *Dictionary of Literary Biography* that "[anyone] who attempts to understand Quebec and the Quebecois in the years before 1967 must come to terms with Groulx and the body of his writing."

Groulx was born in Quebec in 1878. A month after his birth, his father died of smallpox, and two of his

three siblings died during an outbreak of diphtheria. Following these tragedies, his mother remarried. His new family was apparently a happy one, and from childhood Groulx showed evidence of a strong religious faith. While studying for the priesthood, he began writing poetry. Some of this verse was eventually published in periodicals under the pseudonym Lionel Montal, but Groulx seems to have abandoned poetry later in his literary career. Ordained in 1903, Groulx continued his studies in Paris, Rome, and Fribourg. He taught at the seminary of Valleyfield and in 1915 started his long tenure at the University of Montreal.

Groulx's first book was published in 1906. Throughout his career he wrote in support of French Canadian nationalism, and some of the best known of these include *La Naissance d'une race, Notre maitre, le passe,* and *Chemins de l'avenir.* In these and other works, including a four-volume history of French-speaking Canada, Groulx advocated a deep commitment to Catholicism as a key element in preserving Quebec's cultural independence and in winning its political freedom. Senese explained that according to Groulx, "Catholicism was the paramount national characteristic. In a truly French Quebec, Catholic social values, not secular materialism, would inspire a society that was economically and politically modern and progressive." Groulx saw increasing secularization as a threat to Quebec's independence. But, in Senese's analysis, "Groulx never understood, or admitted, the extent to which nationalism exhibited a tendency to become a religion in its own right, destroying in its wake the spiritual values Groulx so keenly professed." Though Groulx's importance in and inspiration to the movement for Quebec's independence cannot be overestimated, and though, in Senese's words, "he had made separatism, as a political option, respectable," he was not entirely pleased by the direction that movement took. According to Senese "Groulx was distressed by much of what occurred. The impressive gains in nationalist terms were offset by the steady decline of Catholicism as the system of values guiding society."

Groulx also expressed his sentiments about French Canadian nationalism in novel form. Published in 1922 under the pen name Alonie de Lestres, his first novel, *The Iron Wedge,* concerns Jules de Lantagnac, a French Canadian who sacrifices his heritage to achieve financial and social success. He marries an Anglican woman, who, though she converts to Catholicism, is intensely proud of her English heritage. When Jules, at mid-life, suffers a crisis of faith and attempts to return to his French-speaking roots, his wife separates from him. Jules also risks his position in parliament by fighting against the elimination of French education in Ontario. Thus Groulx demonstrates both the cultural and the political odds against French-speaking Canadians, and, according to Senese, symbolically portrays "the disastrous 'mixed marriage' of French and English in the Canadian Confederation."

Groulx's other novel, *Au Cap Blomidon,* relates the story of Jean Berube, a young man of Acadian descent, whose ancestors had fled Nova Scotia for Quebec during the Acadian deportations of 1755. To fulfill a condition of his inheritance, Jean travels to Nova Scotia to reclaim the family homestead. Senese called *Au Cap Blomidon* "a platform on which Groulx could display his concerns about national survival, pride, and integrity. It also allowed him to expound at length on the virtue of struggle to achieve national strength and self-reliance."

In addition to his many writings, Groulx supported the Quebec nationalist movement in many other ways. He joined the Ligue des Droits du Francais, the political group which founded the magazine *L'Action francaise.* Groulx himself founded the Institut d'Histoire de l'Amerique Francaise in 1946, and edited its periodical, the *Revue.* He also lectured on French Canadian nationalism at universities and on radio and television. Groulx remained active until his death in 1967 at the age of eighty-nine; after his death he was honored by Quebec with a state funeral and an official day of mourning. Many streets, the seminary school at which he studied, and a subway station in Montreal now bear his name.

BIOGRAPHICAL/CRITICAL SOURCES:

BOOKS

Dictionary of Literary Biography, Volume 68: *Canadian Writers, 1920-1959, First Series,* Gale, 1988.
Giguere, Georges-Emile, *Lionel Groulx: Biographie,* Bellarmin, 1978.
Groulx, Lionel, *Mes Memoires* (four volumes), Fides, 1970-74.

PERIODICALS

L'Action Nationale, June, 1968.
Revue d'Histoire de l'Amerique Francaise, December, 1978.*

—Sketch by Elizabeth Wenning

GUIDO, Beatriz 1924-1988

PERSONAL: Born December 13, 1924, in Rosaria, Argentina; died March 4, 1988, in Madrid, Spain; daughter of Angel and Berta (Eirin) Guido; married Leopoldo Torres Nilsson (a film director), June 29, 1959. *Education:* Attended University of Buenos Aires and La Sorbonne, Paris, France.

CAREER: Writer. Argentine cultural attache in Spain.

AWARDS, HONORS: Premio Emece, 1954, for *La casa del angel.*

WRITINGS:

Regreso a los hilos, El Ateneo, 1947.
Estar en el mundo, El Ateneo, 1950.
La casa del angel (novel), Emece, 1954, translation by Joan Coyne MacLean published as *The House of the Angel,* McGraw, 1957.
La caida (novel), Losada, 1956, reprinted, 1981.
Fin de fiesta (novel), Losada, 1958.
La mano en la trampa (short stories), Losada, 1961.
El incendio y las visperas (novel), Losada, 1964, translation by A. D. Towers published as *End of a Day,* Scribner, 1966.
(Contributor) *Memorias de infancia,* selected by Piri Lugones, J. Alvarez, 1968.
Escandalos y soledades (novel), Losada, 1970.
El ojo unico de la ballena (short stories and plays), Merlin, 1971.
Los insomnes (short stories and interviews), Corregidor, 1973.
Une madre, Emece, 1973.
(With Luis Pico Estrada and husband, Leopoldo Torre Nilsson) *El Pibe Cabeza* (drama), Schapire, 1975.
Piedra libre, Galerna, 1976.
Quien le teme a mis temas?, Fraterna, 1977.
Todos los cuentos, Planeta Argentina, 1979.
La invitacion, Losada, 1979.
Apasionados, Losada, 1982.
Soledad y el incendiario, Abril, 1982.
12 mujeres cuentan, La Campana, 1983.

ADAPTATIONS: Guido collaborated with her husband, director Leopoldo Torres Nilsson, on film adaptations of several of her works, including *La casa del angel, La caida, Fin de fiesta,* and *La mano en la trampa.*

SIDELIGHTS: Beatriz Guido was a prominent Argentine writer known for her vivid depictions of the political and social conflicts in her native country. Among her most enduring works are *La casa del angel* (*The House of the Angel*), which offers commentary on corruption within Argentine society by focusing on a wealthy young girl's painful right of passage, and *El incendio y las visperas* (*End of a Day*), about an aristocratic family at the close of Juan Domingo Peron's regime.

BIOGRAPHICAL/CRITICAL SOURCES:

PERIODICALS

New York Times Book Review, June 5, 1966.

* * *

GUZMAN (FRANCO), Martin Luis 1887-1976

PERSONAL: Born October 6, 1887, in Chihuahua, Mexico; died in 1976; son of Martin L. Guzman and Carmen Franco Terrazas; married Anita West Villalobos, 1909; children: three sons. *Education:* Attended University of Mexico.

CAREER: Journalist and politician. Member of editorial staff, *El imparcial,* 1908; took part in Mexican Revolution, 1913; co-founder, *El honor nacional,* 1913; counselor to minister of war, 1914; in exile, 1914-20; editor in chief, *El heraldo de Mexico,* 1920; founder, *El mundo,* 1922; member, Chamber of Deputies, 1922-24; resided in Spain, 1924-30; founder, *Tiempo* (Mexico), 1942; ambassador to United Nations, 1951; president, Comision Nacional de los Libros de Texto Gratuiros, 1964.

WRITINGS:

La querella de Mexico, Imprenta Clasica Espanola, 1915.
A orillas del Hudson, Libreria Editorial Andres Boras e Hijo, 1920.
El aguila y la serpiente, Compania Ibero-americana de Publicaciones (Madrid), 1928, 16th edition, Compania General de Ediciones, 1974, published as *El aguila y la serpiente: Memorias de la revolucion mexicana,* edited by Ernest Richard Moore, Norton, 1943, translation by Harriet de Onis published as *The Eagle and the Serpent,* Knopf, 1930.
La sombra del caudillo (sequel to *El aguila y la serpiente*), Espasa-Calpe, 1929, 25th edition, Compania General de Ediciones, 1974.

Mina el mozo, heroe de Navarra, Espasa-Calpe, 1932.

Memorias de Pancho Villa: Segun el texto establecido y ordenado, Ediciones Botas, 1938, 23rd edition, Compania General de Ediciones, 1971, translation by Virginia H. Taylor published as *Memoirs of Pancho Villa,* University of Texas Press, 1965.

Javier Mina: Heroe de Espana y de Mexico, Compania General de Ediciones, 1955, 4th revised edition, 1972.

Muertes historicas, Compania General de Ediciones, 1958.

La querella de Mexico, A orillas del Hudson, Otras paginas, Compania General de Ediciones, 1958.

Academia: Tradicion, independencia, libertad, Compania General de Ediciones, 1959.

Islas Marias: Novela y drama; Guion para una pelicula, Compania General de Ediciones, 1959.

Filadelfia, paraiso de conspiradores y otras historias noveladas, Compania General de Ediciones, 1960.

Obras completas, two volumes, Compania General de Ediciones, 1961-63.

Febrero de 1913, Empresas Editoriales, 1963.

(With Alfonso Reyes and Federico de Onis) *Frente a la pantalla,* Direccion General de Difusion Cultural, UNAM, 1963.

Necesidad de cumplir las Leyes de Reforma, Empresas Editoriales, 1963.

Cronicas de mi destierro, Empresas Editoriales, 1964.

Antologia de Martin Luis Guzman, selected by Ermilo Abreu Gomez, Ediciones Oasis, 1970.

Martin Luis Guzman, selected by Andres de Luna, Senado de la Republica, 1987.

Martin Luis Guzman: Iconografia, selected by Hector Perea, Fondo de Cultura Economica, 1987.

Also author of *Aventuras democraticas,* 1929, *El hombre y sus armas,* 1938, *Campos de batalla,* 1939, *Panoramas politicos y la causa del pobre,* 1940, *Axkana Gonzalez en las elleciones,* 1960, and *Maestros rurales y piratas y corsarios,* 1960.

SIDELIGHTS: Much of Martin Luis Guzman's work focuses on the Mexican Revolution of 1913, in which Guzman himself took an active role. His novel *El aguila y la serpiente* reflects his revolutionary experiences, while his portrait of revolutionary leadership in *Memorias de Pancho Villa* has gained widespread critical acclaim. Guzman returned to politics late in life, when he became Mexico's ambassador to the United Nations in 1951.*

H

HANDLER, Evan 1961-

PERSONAL: Born January 10, 1961, in Queens, NY; son of Murry Raymond (an advertising designer) and Enid Irene (a mental health administrator; maiden name, Ostrov) Handler. *Education:* Attended Julliard School, 1979-81.

ADDRESSES: Agent—David Black Literary Agency, 156 5th Ave., #608, New York, NY.

CAREER: Actor, director, writer. Worked at Chelsea Theater Center in New York City as an intern. Actor in stage productions, including *Biography: A Game,* 1978; *Strider,* 1979; *Derelict,* 1982; *Solomon's Child* (Broadway debut), 1982; *Weapons of Happiness,* 1983; *Early Warnings,* 1983; and the following Broadway productions: *Brighton Beach Memoirs,* 1983; *Master Harold . . . and the Boys,* 1983-84; *Biloxi Blues,* 1985; *Broadway Bound,* 1987; *Six Degrees of Separation,* 1990-91; and *I Hate Hamlet,* 1991. Director of stage plays, including *Freeze Tag,* 1989. Actor in films, including *The Chosen,* 1980; *Taps,* 1981; *Dear Mr. Wonderful,* 1982; *The Children's War,* 1983, *Sweet Lorraine,* 1985, *Natural Born Killers,* 1994, and *Ransom,* 1996.

MEMBER: Actors' Equity Association, Screen Actors Guild, AFTRA.

WRITINGS:

Time on Fire (one-person show), produced at Second Stage, New York, 1993, published as an expanded, full-length book of memoirs under the title *Time on Fire: My Comedy of Terrors,* Little, Brown (Boston), 1996.

Time on Fire: My Comedy of Terrors was also published in England by London's Souvenir Press, 1996.

SIDELIGHTS: When Evan Handler was a successful young actor of twenty-four with a resume that included seven leading roles on Broadway, many more off-Broadway and others in television and film, he was struck with an often fatal form of leukemia. Over the next five years he struggled with the disease, and with the inhuman treatment he received at the hands of some members of the medical profession. He credits his almost miraculous recovery to the support of his family and former girlfriend, playwright Jackie Reingold, and to the bone-marrow transplant he received at the Johns Hopkins Medical Center in Baltimore. His story is the subject of his monologue, *Time on Fire,* which he later expanded into a book titled *Time on Fire: My Comedy of Terrors.* Handler's piercing observations of the behavior of those around him, and of his own inner life during this extended ordeal, make for a story that is "entertaining, harrowing and ennobling," according to a reviewer for *Publishers Weekly.* Handler explained to Patti Hartigan, a reporter for the *Boston Globe:* "People are desperate to confront the issue of death, but they're so used to having it presented in a sappy sentimental fashion." He added: "I'm trying to let them confront something terrifying in a way that makes them laugh, and through the laughter, through the joyous, aching pain, their fears are disarmed."

Many of the horrors discussed in Handler's *Time on Fire* occur in Manhattan's Memorial Sloan-Kettering Cancer Center, where he was first treated for acute myelogenous leukemia. There "Handler would be plunged into an emotional twilight zone, which he observes with a writer's sensitive but distant eye,"

wrote Laurie Winer in the *Los Angeles Times*. The author describes insensitive doctors, humiliating procedures, and a burning desire to live. Handler told the *Boston Globe*'s Hartigan: "The only way to survive was to disobey and to break the rules." He added that he "became kind of ruthless." Doctors from the hospital have seen the play and have recommended that it be performed for staff to help them understand more about the care of patients.

More than one critic remarked that Handler portrays himself in less-than-flattering light at times. During his bout with leukemia, he often combined the self-centeredness of the patient with the natural solipsism of the actor, which made him something of a tyrant to not only hospital staff but hapless family and friends. Nonetheless, it is that type of honesty, according to Lisa Jennifer Selzman of the *New York Times Book Review*, "combined with his ability to walk an edge between humor and despair, [that] makes *Time on Fire* moving and admirable." Jill Bernstein in the *San Francisco Review of Books* compared the emotional impact of Handler's narrative to Joseph Heller's slapstick indictment of war in the novel *Catch-22*. "[Handler] creates a wildly humorous, keenly observed journey from the aggressive self-absorption of youth to the complex, poignantly layered landscape of adulthood."

Both a widely well-received stage production (in venues such as Boston, Baltimore, Los Angeles, and Carnegie Hall) and a book, *Time on Fire* recounts actor Handler's struggle with his life-threatening illness and with the staff of the medical facilities where he was being treated. It serves as an indictment of the insensitivity of the medical establishment to its patients, an exploration of how the quality of life changes when the end of life seems to be in sight, and a humorous send-up of the human condition itself. *Time on Fire* wrung passionate responses from critics, whose reaction to his narrative combined horror and empathy, anger and admiration, through the power of laughter. Handler himself quipped in the *San Francisco Review of Books*, of the enormous success of his tale: "It's the concept of being alive I was writing about. And that's a subject a lot of living people can relate to." He told Hartigan: "Everyone who wishes they could snap back at a doctor will feel terribly vindicated" after seeing the production. Noting that the work is "not an exercise in self-pity," he added: "Yes, it's about death, but it's done from a gleefully defiant point of view."

BIOGRAPHICAL/CRITICAL SOURCES:

PERIODICALS

Boston Globe, September 5, 1993, p. A1.
Library Journal, November 1, 1995, p. 100.
Los Angeles Times, April 13, 1995, p. F1.
New York Times, May 12, 1993, p. C13; May 14, 1993, p. C3.
New York Times Book Review, February 18, 1996, p. 16.
Publishers Weekly, October 30, 1995, p. 50.
San Francisco Review of Books, January/February, 1996, p. 11.

* * *

HARRY, J. S. 1939-

PERSONAL: Born in 1939, in Adelaide, South Australia.

ADDRESSES: Home and office—P.O. Box 184, Randwick, New South Wales 2031, Australia.

CAREER: Writer. Australian National University, Canberra, writer-in-residence, 1989.

AWARDS, HONORS: Harri Jones memorial prize, 1971; P.E.N. International Lynne Phillips prize, 1987.

WRITINGS:

POETRY

The Deer under the Skin, University of Queensland Press (St. Lucia), 1970.
Hold, for a Little While, and Turn Gently, Island Press (Sydney), 1979.
A Dandelion for Van Gogh, Island Press, 1985.

* * *

HASKINS, Scott (M.) 1953-

PERSONAL: Born March 13, 1953, in Whittier, CA; son of Arch and Joan Haskins; children: Virginia, Francesca, James, Andrew. *Ethnicity:* "Caucasian."

Education: Ente Nazionale ACLI Istruzione Professionale, Lombardy Regional Conservation Center, Botticino, Italy, degree in art conservation (with honors), 1978. *Religion:* Church of Jesus Christ of Latter-day Saints (Mormons).

ADDRESSES: Home—4079-A Foothill Rd., Santa Barbara, CA 93110. *Office*—Fine Art Conservation Laboratories, P.O. Box 23557, Santa Barbara, CA 93121; fax 805-568-1178. *E-mail*—artdoc@earthlink .net. *Agent*—Cori Beutler, Publishers Distribution Center, Salt Lake City, UT.

CAREER: Private practice as a conservator of fine arts, 1976-77; Ex Monastero della Trinita Museum, intern, 1977-78; Brigham Young University, Provo, UT, director of conservation, 1978-84; Fine Art Conservation Laboratories, Santa Barbara, CA, chief conservator, 1984—, director, 1986—. Shroud of Turin Research Project, participant and consultant.

MEMBER: International Institute for Conservation (associate member), American Institute for Conservation (professional associate member; vice-chairperson of Conservators in Private Practice, 1990-93), Western Association for Art Conservation (vice-president, 1982-83; president, 1983-84; member of board of directors, 1984-85).

WRITINGS:

The Emergency Care Book for Your Possessions, Conservation Materials, 1994.
How to Save Your Stuff from a Disaster, Preservation Help Publications (Santa Barbara, CA), 1996.

WORK IN PROGRESS: How to Care for Your Things at Home, completion expected in 2000.

* * *

HASSELSTROM, Linda (Michele) 1943-

PERSONAL: Born July 14, 1943, in Houston, TX; daughter of John Hasselstrom (a rancher) and Florence Mildred Baker (a secretary); married Daniel G. Lusk, April 9, 1966 (divorced, June 27, 1973); married George R. Snell, March 10, 1979 (died, September 7, 1988). *Education:* University of South Dakota, Vermillion, B.A. (English and journalism), 1965; University of Missouri—Columbia, M.A. (American literature), 1969. *Avocational interests:* Camping, travel, black powder rifles, horses, Scottish pre-history, Western history, and the environment of the West.

ADDRESSES: Home—Cheyenne, WY. *Office*—P.O. Box 169, Hermosa, SD 57744.

CAREER: Writer, rancher, and educator. Cattle rancher, SD, 1953—; *Sioux City Journal,* IA, reporter, night staff, 1965-66; Christian College (now Columbia College), Columbia, MO, teacher of Journalism, and Director of Student Publications, 1966-69; University of Missouri—Columbia, instructor in English, 1969-71; Lame Johnny Press, Hermosa, SD, owner and publisher, 1971-85; *Sunday Clothes: A Magazine of the Fine Arts,* editor, 1971-82; National College, Rapid City, SD, instructor in English, 1987-88; Black Hills State College, Ellsworth AFB branch, Spearfish, SD, instructor in English, 1987-88; Oglala Lakota College, Rapid City, SD, teacher, 1989; South Dakota School of Mines, Rapid City, professor of English, 1989-90. Has taught dozens of writing workshops and conferences, including Wildwood Writers' Conference, Harrisburg Area Community College, 1995, Big Wind Confluence, Central Wyoming College, Riverton, 1993, and Jackson Hole Writers' Conference, 1992. Lectures and has given readings of her work at schools and colleges. Black Hills Energy Coalition, president; Technical Information Service, chair, 1985-94.

MEMBER: Poets & Writers, Authors Guild, Gallatin Institute, Western Writers of America, South Dakota State Historical Society, Coalition for Western Women's History, Women Writing the West, Custer Area Arts Council, Mari Sandoz Heritage Society.

AWARDS, HONORS: South Dakota Press Woman of Achievement Award, 1979; fellowships from the National Endowment for the Arts, 1984, and South Dakota Arts Council, 1989; named Author of the Year, South Dakota Hall of Fame, 1989; Governor's Award in Arts for Distinction in Creative Achievement, South Dakota, 1989; Western American Writer Award (first woman recipient), Center for Western Studies, Sioux Falls, SD, 1990; Elkhorn Poetry Prize, *Nebraska Territory,* 1991; *Land Circle* named one of four best books by Mountains and Plains Booksellers, 1992; Hasselstrom named one of ten West River Notables by *Rapid City Journal,* 1992; "Buffalo Winter" cited as one of 100 best essays of 1995 in *Best American Essays 1995;* Distinguished Achievement Award, South Dakota Newspaper Association, 1996.

WRITINGS:

EDITOR

Next-Year Country: One Woman's View, Lame Johnny Press, 1978.
A Bird Begins to Sing: Northwest Poetry and Prose, Lame Johnny Press, 1979.
Journal of a Mountain Man: James Clyman, Mountain Press, 1984.
(With Nancy Curtis and Gaydell Collier, and author of introduction) *Leaning into the Wind* (anthology), Houghton Mifflin, 1997.

NONFICTION AND POETRY

The Book Book: A Publishing Handbook (nonfiction), Lame Johnny Press, 1979.
Caught by One Wing (poetry), Holcomb, 1984, reprinted, Spoon River Poetry Press, 1990.
Roadkill (poetry), Spoon River Poetry Press, 1987.
Windbreak: A Woman Rancher on the Northern Plains (nonfiction), Barn Owl Books, 1987.
Going over East: Reflections of a Woman Rancher (nonfiction), Fulcrum, 1987.
Land Circle: Writings Collected from the Land (essays and poetry), Fulcrum, 1991.
Dakota Bones: The Collected Poems of Linda Hasselstrom, Spoon River Poetry Press, 1992.
A Roadside History of South Dakota (nonfiction), Mountain Press, 1994.

Author of introduction, *The Christmas of the Phonograph Records,* Mari Sandoz, reprinted by the University of Nebraska Press, 1996. Contributor to books, including *Graining the Mare: The Poetry of Ranch Women,* Gibbs-Smith, and *American Nature Writing 1994,* Sierra Club Books, both 1994; *Home Territory,* Yale University Press, and *Writers on the Range,* University Press of Colorado, both 1995. Contributor of poetry, fiction, and nonfiction to periodicals, including *American Poetry Review, Christian Science Monitor, Dakota Arts Quarterly, Elkhorn Review, Mother Earth News, Northern Lights, Reader's Digest,* and *South Dakota Review.*

WORK IN PROGRESS: "Untitled manuscript about loss and survival, has not yet been accepted by a publisher."

SIDELIGHTS: A poet, essayist, and former rancher, Linda Hasselstrom is known for work that celebrates life on the plains of South Dakota, despite the isolation and hardship that it often involves. Her poems and essays explore the personal, emotional, and political landscape as well as the physical one; she has written about the details of everyday life on the ranch, her grief over her husband's early death, her community of neighbors, in favor of sustainable agriculture, and on a variety of other environmental and social issues. According to *Western American Literature* contributor William Kittredge, Hasselstrom's "is one of those voices folks who grew up in the outback country of the American West were likely to hear every so often—a decent, experienced woman announcing her thoughts in a direct, passionate way, speaking straight from the trials of her life."

Hasselstrom explained to *CA* that much of her writing is inspired by a "sense of place": "Sense of place is the center of all good art, and William Faulkner is only one of the writers who have proved it in America's literary history. Intensely regional writing carries a conviction that makes it intensely universal.

"John Milton stated my belief well in the introduction to *Horizons: The South Dakota Writers' Anthology,* which I co-edited and published: 'For literature to be effective, meaningful, and honest, it must be written by intimates of not only the subject but the place and people as well.' Merely traveling through a region does not create intimacy, as midwesterners have seen eastern writers prove often in our history. To write truly, to speak with authority of this place, one must put down roots, become involved, be battered and tested by the terrain, the weather, and the people. Much of what I despise in contemporary writing comes from writers who have no sense of place, or even a sense that they need a place, but wander without convictions or connections over the scenery, seeing everything as if it were behind a television screen or car window. They are observers, not participators."

Hasselstrom's work is well-respected; she has received several awards and a fellowship from the National Endowment for the Arts. Her 1987 poetry volume *Roadkill* was so successful that Spoon River Poetry Press reprinted her first book of poems, *Caught by One Wing,* in 1990. She has also received favorable critical attention for *Windbreak: A Woman Rancher on the Northern Plains,* which chronicles a year of her life on her South Dakota ranch. From Hasselstrom's perspective, wrote Nancy Mairs in the *New York Times Book Review,* readers gain new insights and learn "to cherish with her all the fine small beauties of her strenuous life." According to *Publishers Weekly,* even the most ardent of urbanites will

come to admire Hasselstrom's "abiding loyalty to her difficult but satisfying way of life."

"Since I have always read voraciously," Hasselstrom told *CA,* "I soon noticed (at the age of five, reading *Black Beauty* books) that much of what was written about my neighborhood of western South Dakota, my parents' occupation as ranchers, and my interests of riding horseback and raising cows, was controlled by myth. Many people had written about all these topics, but usually from the perspective of outsiders, immersed in various untrue versions of western life: novels, movies, fantasy stereotypes.

"After *Windbreak* was published and I toured to promote it, I discovered that in spite of my efforts to be truthful in what was essentially my diary, people *still* mingled the realities of my work with their own preconceived myths from a century of romanticism. They'd say, 'I thought you'd be bigger,' or 'I thought you'd have a bigger dog.'"

Hasselstrom also garnered praise with an essay and poetry collection, *Land Circle: Writings Collected from the Land,* which was published in 1991. Each of the essays in *Land Circle* is accompanied by a poem, "a counterpoint that works well to bring out the ironies and unexpected subtleties of her material," notes Dianne Ganz Scheper in *Belles Lettres.* The pieces in *Land Circle* address subjects such as the importance of community, the complex moral issues involved in slaughtering cows for beef, the backbreaking work of the ranch, and her methods of coping with her husband's death. *Publishers Weekly* reports that in *Land Circle,* Hasselstrom employs "vivid images" and "speaks eloquently" on issues of the environment. And in his review of the book, Kittredge noted that the author's "greatest wisdom lies in her utter emotional honesty."

Hasselstrom revealed to *CA* that "I keep writing to understand my own life, and express the truth as I see it around me: the problems, strengths, and shortcomings of the people who really live in the West. I've been forced to leave the ranch for now and live in a city—an educational experience at fifty!—but I hope to stay in the region, because I think not only research, learning facts, but drinking the water, eating the beef, smelling the sage, and bending against the wind are necessary for writing about a region well."

Hasselstrom is also author of 1994's *A Roadside History of South Dakota* and has begun "studying and writing about rural and ecological problems from my own experiences in the Great Plains." She told *CA,* "As my knowledge expanded, I encouraged ranchers and farmers in better practices to help keep more rural people employed in agriculture. I wanted to help inform the American public about the ruinous costs to all of us of the kind of development we've seen in agriculture over the last fifty years.

"This writing, I believe, is closely connected to more 'artistic' writing—fiction and poetry—on environmental problems, giving me an opportunity to educate others about important problems. I see the plains as the final frontier, and in danger of utter destruction if it serves more populous areas only as an energy reservoir, source of labor, and waste repository.

"I believe one's work should complement the rest of one's life, and blend smoothly into a whole that keeps the physical body healthy while also working the mind. I worked to bring my life into a circle: writing things I can respect, publishing work I respect, laboring at riding, branding, gardening, taking care of the land, and doing it all with an awareness of how those things fit together. More and more, as I grow older, I feel that it is important to keep my roots in this arid soil, to learn from it all I can, in order to continue to grow as a writer and as a human being."

BIOGRAPHICAL/CRITICAL SOURCES:

PERIODICALS

Belles Lettres, spring, 1995, pp. 32-34.
Bloomsbury Review, July/August, 1992.
Life, July, 1989.
New York Times Book Review, August 9, 1987, p. 21.
Prairie Winds, fall, 1995, pp. 2-4.
Publishers Weekly, July 3, 1987; October 4, 1991.
Roundup, February, 1996, p. 39.
Small Press Review, February, 1980, p. 9; April, 1995, p. 6.
South Dakota Magazine, September/October, 1992.
South Dakota Review, autumn, 1992, pp. 130-55.
Western American Literature, February, 1995.
Writing!, September, 1988.

* * *

HAUPTMANN, Gerhart (Johann Robert) 1862-1946

PERSONAL: Born November 15, 1862, in Obersalzbrunn, Silesia, Germany; son of Robert (a

hotel owner) and Marie (maiden name, Straehler) Hauptmann; died of pneumonia, June 8, 1946, in Agneterdorf, Silesia, Poland; married Marie Thienemann, May 5, 1885. *Education:* Elementary schooling in Ober-Salzbrunn and Breslau, ended in 1878 due to family's financial difficulties; Royal Art and Trade School in Breslau, 1880 (expelled); private instruction under sculptor Robert Haertel; University of Jena (one year); Dresden Academy of Arts, 1884 (six weeks); University of Berlin, 1884-85 (two semesters).

CAREER: Student, through 1883, 1884-85; sculptor in Rome, 1883-84; writer, 1885-1946.

MEMBER: "Durch" ("Through"), 1887.

AWARDS, HONORS: Nobel Prize for Literature, 1912.

WRITINGS:

PLAYS

Vor Sonnenaufgang (produced in Berlin at the Lessingtheatre, 1889), S. Fischer (Berlin), 1889, translation by Leonard Bloomfield published as *Before Dawn,* R. G. Badger (Boston), 1909.

Das Friedenfest, S. Fischer, 1890, translation by Janet Achurch and C. E. Wheeler published as *The Coming of Peace,* C. H. Sergel (Chicago), 1900.

Einsame Menschen (produced in Berlin, 1890), S. Fischer, 1891, translation by Mary Morison published as *Lonely Lives,* De Witt (New York), 1898.

Kollege Crampton (produced in Berlin, 1892), S. Fischer, 1894.

Der Biberpelz (produced in Berlin at the Deutsches Theater, 1893), S. Fischer, 1893, translation published as *The Beaver Coat,* 1912.

Die Weber (produced in Berlin at the Deutsches Theater, 1893), S. Fischer, 1893, translation by Mary Morison published as *The Weavers,* W. Heinemann (London), 1899.

Hanneles Himmelfahrt (produced in Paris and London, 1894), S. Fischer (Berlin), 1894, translation by William Archer published as *Hannele,* W. Heinemann (London), 1894, translation by G. S. Bryan published as *The Assumption of Hannele* in *Poet Lore,* vol. XX, no. 3, 1909.

Florian Geyer (produced in Berlin, 1896), S. Fischer, 1896, translation published as *Florian Geyer,* 1929.

Die versunkene Glocke (produced in Berlin, 1896), S. Fischer, 1897, translation by Charles Henry Meltzer published as *The Sunken Bell,* Doubleday and McClure, 1899.

Fuhrmann Henschel (produced in Berlin, 1896), S. Fischer, 1899, translation by Marion A. Redlich published as *Fuhrman Henschel,* Dramatic Publishing Co. (Chicago), 1909.

Schluck und Jau (produced in Berlin, 1899), S. Fischer, 1900.

Michael Kramer (produced in Berlin, 1900), S. Fischer, 1900.

Die rote Hahn (produced in Berlin, 1901), S. Fischer, 1901.

Rose Bernd (produced in Berlin, 1903), S. Fischer, 1903.

Und Pippa tanzt! (produced in Berlin, 1905), S. Fischer, 1906, translation by Mary Harned published as *And Pippa Dances* in *Poet Lore,* vol. XVIII, no. 3, 1907.

Die Ratten (produced in Berlin, 1911), S. Fischer, 1911.

Die Winterballade (produced in Berlin, 1917), S. Fischer, 1917.

Indipohdi (produced in Berlin, 1920), S. Fischer, 1920.

Der Weisse Heiland (produced in Berlin, 1920), S. Fischer, 1920.

Vor Sonnenuntergang (produced 1932), S. Fischer, 1932.

Die goldene harfe (produced in Berlin, 1933), S. Fischer, 1933.

Iphigenie in Delphi (produced 1941), Haarlem (Berlin), 1944.

Magnus Garbe (produced 1942), S. Fischer, 1942.

Iphigenie in Aulis (produced 1943), Suhrkamp (Berlin), 1944.

Agamemnons Tod (produced 1947), published with *Elektra,* Suhrkamp, 1948.

Elektra (produced 1947), published with *Agamemnons Tod,* Suhrkamp, 1948.

POETRY

Promethidenlos, W. Issleib (Berlin), 1885.

Die blaue Blume, S. Fischer, 1924.

Des grossen kampffliegers, landfahrers, gauklers und magiers Till Eulenspiegel abenteuer, streiche, gaukeleien, gesichte und traume (poetry) S. Fischer, 1928; also published as *Till Eulenspiegel,* C. Bertelsman, 1955.

Der grosse Traum (poetry), Insel-Verlag (Leipzig), 1942.

PROSE FICTION

Der Apostel [and] Bahnwarter Thiel, S. Fischer, 1892, translation of *Bahnwarter Thiel* published as *Lineman Thiel* in *Lineman Thiel and Other Tales,* 1989.

Der Narr in Christo Emanuel Quint, S. Fischer, 1910, translation by Thomas Seltzer published as as *The Fool in Christ: Emanuel Quint,* B. W. Huebsch (New York), 1911.

Atlantis, S. Fischer, 1912, translation by Adele and Thomas Seltzer published as *Atlantis,* B. W. Huebsch, 1912.

Lohengrin, Ullstein (Berlin), 1913.

Parsival, Ullstein, 1914; translation by Oakley Williams published as *Parsival,* Macmillan (New York), 1915.

Der Ketzer von Soana, S. Fischer, 1918, translation by Bayard Quincy Morgan published as *The Heretic of Soana,* B. W. Huebsch, 1923.

Phantom, S. Fischer, 1922, translation by Bayard Quincy Morgan published as *Phantom,* B. W. Huebsch, 1922.

Die Insel der Grossen Mutter, S. Fischer, 1924, translation by Willa and Edwin Muir published as *The Island of the Great Mother; or, The Miracle of the Ile des Dames,* Viking, 1925.

Fasching, S. Fischer, 1925.

Der Damon, S. Fischer, 1927, also published as *Wanda,* S. Fischer, 1928.

Die Hochzeit auf Buchenhorst, S. Fischer, 1932.

Im Wirbel der Berufung, S. Fischer, 1936.

OTHER

Griechischer Fruhling (travel diary), S. Fischer, 1908.

Buch der Leidenschaft (fictional diary), S. Fischer, 1930; also published as *Neue Leidenschaft,* 1966.

Das Meerwunder (allegory), S. Fischer, 1934.

Das Abenteuer meiner Jugend (memoir), S. Fischer, 1937.

SIDELIGHTS: Gerhart Hauptmann's naturalistic plays of the late nineteenth century established him as a major artist in modern drama. Though he produced a vast assortment of works in various genres throughout his long career, it is these early dramas on which his literary standing was founded and endures. Hauptmann is recognized primarily for initiating the naturalist movement in German theater with his first drama, *Vor Sonnenaufgang (Before Dawn).* Influenced by the work of Ibsen and Zola, Hauptmann became his country's most prominent exponent of dramatic techniques that sought to portray the harsh realities of human existence, particularly focusing on the social problems of the lower classes. He did not, however, limit himself to this single artistic approach, and his work ranges over a variety of styles from naturalism to romanticism to symbolist fantasy. In 1912 Hauptmann was awarded the Nobel Prize in literature.

Hauptmann was born in Silesia, and he later used the dialect of this region in his dramas, along with local folklore and legends. After an unsuccessful academic career, during which he studied agriculture, sculpture, and history, he settled in Berlin. There he entered Berlin literary society and began producing his first works.

Before Dawn was an immediate success. Although recognized as a powerful vision of life, this and the later naturalistic plays have received criticism for depicting existence in an undramatic and fragmentary manner. Some critics also claim that Hauptmann's dramas convey no clear ideology; others contend that, like Shakespeare, Hauptmann reflects life in its true state of diversity and contradiction, not confining himself to a single world view.

In his most famous play, *Die Weber (The Weavers),* Hauptmann made use of a collective hero, a device that would be much exploited by collectivist writers. This work once again portrays the harsher aspects of human reality for which Hauptmann's naturalism is frequently noted. *Der Biberpelz (The Beaver Coat)* presents similar naturalistic themes in the genre of comedy, as does *Florian Geyer* in that of the historical drama. In *Hanneles Himmelfahrt (Hannele)* Hauptmann combines the methods of naturalism with those of symbolic fantasy. He follows a thoroughly symbolic style in the dream play *Die versunkene Glocke (The Sunken Bell).* In these later dramas Hauptmann focuses on characters as individuals rather than as representatives of a social body.

In 1907 Hauptmann visited Greece, afterwards recounting the experience in *Griechischer Fruhling.* Hauptmann's encounter with the birthplace of Western classical mythology proved a rich source of inspiration for his later works. The influence of pagan myth is visible in such novels as *Der Narr in Christo Emanuel Quint (The Fool in Christ, Emanuel Quint)* and *Der Ketzer von Soana (The Heretic of Soana),* these works being informed by a conflict between Christian compassion for humankind and pagan delight in physical gratification.

Between the wars Hauptmann produced what he regarded as his greatest work, *Till Eulenspiegel,* an epic poem that is a summation of the author's lifelong thought and learning set against the turmoil of Weimar Germany. During the Second World War Hauptmann did not follow the example of many German artists who left the country, and he consequently incurred much personal criticism for his wartime inactivity. The literary result of this period is *Die Atriden Tetralogie,* a reinterpretation of the myths surrounding the curse of Atreus, which was both an indictment of Naziism and a lament for the increasingly barbaric behavior of the German people.

Though highly praised during his lifetime as an innovative force in German literature, Hauptmann is no longer widely read. Ultimately his reputation seems to have suffered because of his versatility. Some critics contend that his concern for experimentation and innovation in drama, poetry, and prose kept him from attaining mastery in any single genre. Though his diversity has frustrated critical attempts to define his most essential concerns, one quality is often cited as a unifying element in Hauptmann's works—his humanism. A sincere compassion for humankind is fundamental to his entire literary output.

BIOGRAPHICAL/CRITICAL SOURCES:

BOOKS

Dussere, C.T., *The Image of the Primitive Giant in the Work of Gerhart Hauptmann,* Heinz, 1979.

Garten, Hugo F., *Gerhart Hauptmann,* Bowes & Bowes, 1954.

Holl, Karl, *Gerhart Hauptmann: His Life and His Work 1862-1912,* Gay & Hancock, 1913.

Knight, K. G., and F. Norman, eds., *Hauptmann Centenary Lectures,* University of London Institute of Germanic Studies, 1964.

Marshall, Alan, *The German Naturalists and Gerhart Hauptmann,* Lang, 1982.

Maurer, Warren R., *Gerhart Hauptmann,* Twayne, 1982.

McInnes, Edward, *German Social Drama 1840-1900: From Hebbel to Hauptmann,* Heinz, 1976.

Mellen, Philip, *Gerhart Hauptmann and Utopia,* Heinz, 1976.

Mellen, Philip, *Gerhart Hauptmann: Religious Syncretism and Eastern Religions,* Lang, 1984.

Osborne, John, *The Naturalist Drama in Germany,* Manchester University Press, 1971.

Perkins, Jill, *Joyce and Hauptmann: Before Sunrise,* Huntington Library, 1978.

Shaw, Leroy R., *Witness of Deceit: Gerhart Hauptmann as Critic of Society,* University of California Press, 1958.

Styan, J. L., *Modern Drama in Theory and Practice,* volume 1: *Realism and Naturalism,* Cambridge University Press, 1981.

Twentieth-Century Literary Criticism, Volume 4, Gale, 1981.

PERIODICALS

Comparative Literature Studies, summer, 1985.

German Life and Letters, vol. 3, 1949, pp. 32-41; October, 1977, pp. 13-22.

Germanic Review, October, 1958, pp. 176-180.

Maske und Kothurn, vol. 8, 1962, pp. 223-32.

Monatshefte, vol. 44, 1952, pp. 333-39.

Mosaic, spring, 1976, pp. 97-116.

* * *

HAYNES, David 1955-

PERSONAL: Born August 30, 1955, in St. Louis, MO. *Education:* Macalester College, B.A., 1977; Hamline University, M.A., 1989.

ADDRESSES: Home—St. Paul, MN. *Agent*—c/o Milkweed Editions, 430 1st Ave., N., Suite 400, Minneapolis, MN 5540-1743.

CAREER: C. V. Mosby Publishing Co., St. Louis, MO, associate editor, 1978-81; schoolteacher in St. Paul, MN, 1981-93; writer, 1993—. Morehead State University, visiting scholar, 1994; Mankato State University, visiting writer, 1994; teacher at Writer's Center, Bethesda, MD, 1994-95, and Hamline University, 1995—; Warren Wilson College, faculty of M.F.A. program for writers, Spring 1997 and 1997. National Board for Professional Teaching Standards, member of adolescent generalist standards committee, 1990—, teacher in residence, 1994—; Minnesota Humanities Commission, member of advisory committee, Teacher Institute, 1993-94. The Loft, member of board of directors, Regional Writing Center, 1985-89; New Rivers Press, member of board of directors, 1993—.

AWARDS, HONORS: Fiction prize from *City Pages,* 1984, for the story "Taking Miss Kezee to the Polls"; winner of Loft Mentor Series, 1985-86; fellowships from Cummington Community of the Arts, 1986-89, Ragdale Foundation, 1988-94, and Minnesota State

Arts Board, 1995; The Loft, residency prize, 1989, career initiative grant, 1996; winner of Regional Writers Contest, Lake Superior Contemporary Writers, 1989; awards from Virginia Center for the Creative Arts, 1989-95; *Right By My Side* was named "one of the best books for young adults" by American Library Association, 1994; fellow, Minnesota State Arts Board, 1995; *Somebody Else's Mama* was selected as one of the best of the young American novelists, *Granta,* 1996.

WRITINGS:

Right By My Side (novel), New Rivers Press (St. Paul, MN), 1993.
Somebody Else's Mama (novel), Milkweed Editions (Minneapolis, MN), 1995.
Live at Five (novel), Milkweed Editions, 1996.
Heathens (novel), New Rivers Press, 1996.
The Gumma Wars (juvenile), Milkweed Editions, 1997.
Business As Usual (juvenile), Milkweed Editions, 1997.
All American Dream Dolls (novel), Milkweed Editions, in press.

Work represented in anthologies, including *Imagining Home,* University of Minnesota Press (Minneapolis, MN), 1995. Contributor to periodicals, including *Other Voices, Glimmer Train,* and *Colors.*

* * *

HEANEY, Marie 1940-

PERSONAL: Born September 14, 1940, in Northern Ireland; daughter of Thomas F. (in business) and Eileen (a teacher; maiden name, O'Hare) Devlin; married Seamus Heaney (a poet), August 5, 1965; children: Michael, Christopher, Catherine.

ADDRESSES: Home—Dublin, Ireland.

CAREER: Teacher and journalist. Appeared on television in BBC Northern Ireland program, *Now and Then.* Has given readings of work in Ireland, Britain, and the United States.

WRITINGS:

Over Nine Waves (myths and legends), Faber (Winchester, MA), 1994.

Contributor of reviews to periodicals. Has written scripts for television and radio programs.

* * *

HEATH, Lorraine 1954-

PERSONAL: Born January 14, 1954, in Watford, Herfordshire, England; daughter of Curtis Rayburn and Lily Elizabeth (Gurney) Heath. *Ethnicity:* "Caucasian." *Education:* University of Texas at Austin, B.A., 1976.

ADDRESSES: Home—P.O. Box 941673, Plano, TX 75094-1673. *E-mail*—LorraineHe@aol.com; http://www.paintedrock.com/authors/heath.htm.

CAREER: Romance novelist, 1993—.

MEMBER: Romance Writers of America, Dallas Area Romance Authors, Fort Worth Area Romance Authors, Published Authors Special Interest Chapter.

AWARDS, HONORS: Booklovers Award for Best-Selling Americana, 1994; Reviewers Choice Award and Knight in Shining Silver Award, both from *Romantic Times;* ROMY Award for Best Americana Historical; Favorite First Book Award from Puget Sound Romance Readers.

WRITINGS:

HISTORICAL ROMANCE NOVELS

Sweet Lullaby, Diamond Books (New York), 1994.
Parting Gifts, Diamond Books, 1994.
The Ladies' Man, Jove (New York), 1995.
Always to Remember, Jove, 1996.
Texas Destiny, Topaz, in press.

WORK IN PROGRESS: Texas Glory, publication by Topaz expected in 1998; *Texas Splendor,* Topaz, 1999.

SIDELIGHTS: Lorraine Heath told *CA:* "I have always been fascinated with history, in particular the small events that involved ordinary people in extraordinary circumstances. I am very much interested in the common people, the people who did not make their way into the history books, and yet without them and their stories, we would have no history.

"Very often, the stories I discover while reading journals and personal accounts do not have happy endings. As a writer, I have the luxury of changing fact into fiction, and I often weave my stories around incidents or people who I have met through my research. The prologue to *Always to Remember* was based on a personal account of a man who was tortured during the Civil War because he refused to carry a rifle. He was to be executed and, as he stood before the firing squad, he said a prayer similar to the one that my character Clay said in *Always to Remember*. The soldiers lowered their rifles and refused to carry out their orders. The man was returned to his cell. Unfortunately, he had been tortured so severely beforehand that he died of his wounds. The man's story fascinated me and, although I knew nothing else about him, I saw him as a man of courage, a man of conviction—a man I wanted to portray in a story that would have a happier ending.

"Writing happy endings is one of the joys of being a romance writer. No matter what rough roads I force my characters to travel, I always know that the journey will lead them toward happiness and, of course, love: the strongest of human emotions and the most rewarding."

* * *

HEJINIAN, Lyn

PERSONAL: Born in San Francisco, CA; married Larry Ochs (a composer and musician); children: one child.

ADDRESSES: Home—Berkeley, CA. *Office*—Tuumba Press, Berkeley, CA.

CAREER: Tuumba Press, editor, and *Poetics Journal,* editor, both Berkeley, CA.

WRITINGS:

POETRY

A Thought Is the Bride of What Thinking, Tuumba Press (Willits, CA), 1976.
A Mask of Motion, Burning Deck (Providence, RI), 1977.
Writing Is an Aid to Memory, The Figures (Berkeley, CA), 1978.
Gesualdo, Tuumba Press, 1978.

Redo, Salt-Works Press (Grenada, MS), 1984.
The Guard, Tuumba Press, 1984.
(With Kit Robinson) *Individuals,* Tucson, Arizona, Chax Press, 1988.
The Cell, Sun and Moon Press (Los Angeles), 1990.
The Hunt, Zasterle Press (La Laguna, Islas Canarias), 1991.
The Cold of Poetry, Sun and Moon Press, 1994.

NOVELS

My Life, Burning Deck, 1980; revised edition published by Sun and Moon Press, 1987.
Oxota: A Short Russian Novel, The Figures (Great Barrington, MA), 1991.

OTHER

(Translator) *Description,* by Arkadii Dragomoshchenko, Sun and Moon Press, 1990.
(Translator, with Elena Balashova) *Xenia,* by Arkadi Dragomoschenko, Sun and Moon Press, 1993.

* * *

HEMPHILL, Essex 1956(?)-

PERSONAL: Born in c. 1956.

CAREER: Editor, poet, and essayist.

WRITINGS:

(Editor) *Brother to Brother* (anthology), Alyson Publications, 1991.
Ceremonies: Prose and Poetry, New American Library, 1992.

Also author of two self-published chapbooks of poetry, *Earth Life* and *Conditions,* both 1985; contributed to the films *Looking for Langston,* by Isaac Julien, and *Tongues Untied,* by Marlon Riggs.

SIDELIGHTS: Since the beginning of the modern gay liberation movement in the 1970s, a steadily growing body of literature by gay and lesbian writers has explored issues of gay identity, the gay community, and the place of gay men and lesbians in mainstream society. As an editor, poet, and essayist, Essex Hemphill has been a key figure in the emergence of a distinctive African American perspective in the field of gay literature.

Hemphill grew up in a working-class neighborhood in Washington, D.C., gradually becoming aware of the racism that proliferated around him. And as he entered adolescence and became increasingly aware of his own homosexuality, he had to contend with yet another kind of oppression. As Hemphill writes in his book *Ceremonies,* "My sexual curiosity would have blossomed in any context, but in Southeast Washington, where I grew up, I had to carefully allow my petals to unfold. If I had revealed them too soon they would have been snatched away, brutalized, and scattered down alleys. I was already alert enough to know what happened to the flamboyant boys at the school who were called 'sissies' and 'faggots.' I could not have endured then the violence and indignities they often suffered."

In his twenties, Hemphill was attracted to the ideas embodied in the black nationalist movement that flourished in the 1960s and 1970s. But as he got older, he began to question the rhetoric that had previously inspired him. "I moved away from black nationalism," Hemphill writes in *Ceremonies,* "as being too narrow a politic for the interests that reside in me." But he also found that a narrowly defined lesbian and gay political ideology could not adequately accommodate his personal vision, and went on to develop his own political and literary ideas.

Hemphill's literary voice had to accommodate the numerous conflicts that he faced, both as an African American male in a predominantly white society afflicted by racism and as a gay man in a predominantly heterosexual society afflicted by homophobia. And as many black gay writers, including Hemphill, have expressed repeatedly in recent years, being both black and gay carries a special burden. Throughout American history, the culture of slavery and racism often encouraged white men to bolster their own sense of masculinity by asserting their dominance over black men. In response to this violent and abusive history, the black community placed a high premium on strong male images. Homosexuality, understood only through stereotypes of effeminacy and submissiveness, was particularly repugnant in this context. Thus, where many white Americans were reluctant to tolerate homosexuals, many blacks were reluctant even to acknowledge that homosexuals existed in their community. Moreover, the racism that prevailed in mainstream American society could also be found in the newly emerging and predominantly white gay community, an especially frustrating and disheartening fact for the many black gay men and

lesbians seeking to participate in the newfound gay liberation of the past 25 years.

Given these multiple layers of oppression and rejection, black gay and lesbian writers were truly courageous in staking out a new literary terrain for themselves. The writings of 35 such black gay men were gathered by Hemphill in *Brother to Brother,* an anthology of poetry and prose. The pieces in this collection are primarily autobiographical, and lend a personal immediacy to discussions of racism, religious intolerance, homophobia, and life in the age of AIDS. Given the sensitivity of these topics, *Brother to Brother* could not help but be controversial. The book is divided into four sections, each with a distinct theme. The first section, called "When I Think of Home," focuses on varying notions of home and family, from those we grow up in to those we choose and create for ourselves as adults. The second section, called "Baby, I'm for Real," explores the false identities that black gay men create for themselves and hide behind, identities that often represent what they wish they could truly be or could truly have, including white skin or heterosexuality. The third section, called "Hold Tight, Gently," considers life in the age of AIDS, and includes personal accounts of dealing with the epidemic. The final section, "The Absence of Fear," contrasts the way black men are represented in mainstream culture with the way black men represent themselves. It includes discussions of homoerotic images of black men by the gay white photographer Robert Mapplethorpe, as well as recent films by and about black gay men, like Isaac Julien's *Looking for Langston* and Marlon Riggs's *Tongues Untied.* Hemphill himself contributes poetry which, according to Donald Suggs in his *Village Voice* review of the book, "effectively brackets and enlarges many of the conflicts in the anthology."

Ceremonies, an anthology of Hemphill's poetry and prose, spans the author's entire writing career, and includes pieces from his self-published 1985 chapbooks *Earth Life* and *Conditions* as well as previously unpublished work. As did the writings by Hemphill and others in *Brother to Brother,* the poems and essays in *Ceremonies* continue to explore the double burden of being a minority within a minority. "One of Hemphill's most persistent themes [is] the outsider confronting the dominant culture," wrote David Trinidad in his *Village Voice Literary Supplement* review of the book. Hemphill "has forged—with few role models to emulate, and with little or no support from the white gay literary establishment—an identity and a style characterized by anger and point-blank

honesty," according to Trinidad. In addition to overtly political pieces, Hemphill includes love poems, celebrations of sexuality, and affirmations of gay identity, along with heartfelt and moving accounts of the fears and dangers of growing up black and gay. "He makes passionate common sense," wrote Thomas Tavis in his *Library Journal* review, concluding that "this is urgent, fiercely telling work." According to Craig Allen Seymour II, writing in the *Advocate,* Hemphill "is poised to become the most widely known black gay writer since James Baldwin."

BIOGRAPHICAL/CRITICAL SOURCES:

PERIODICALS

Advocate, June 2, 1992, p. 38.
Library Journal, October 1, 1992, p. 88.
Los Angeles Times Book Review, September 8, 1991, p. 18.
The Village Voice, October 1, 1991, p. 74.
Village Voice Literary Supplement, June 1992, pp. 7-8.

* * *

HENDERSON, Hamish 1919-

PERSONAL: Born November 11, 1919, in Blairgowrie, Perthshire, Scotland; married; children: two daughters. *Education:* Attended Dulwich College; Downing College, Cambridge, M.A.

ADDRESSES: Office—University of Edinburgh, School of Scottish Studies, 27 George Sq., Edinburgh EH8 9LD, Scotland.

CAREER: School of Scottish Studies, University of Edinburgh, senior lecturer and research fellow, 1951-87, honorary fellow, 1987—. *Military service:* Highland Division during World War II.

AWARDS, HONORS: Somerset Maugham award, 1949. LL.D.: University of Dundee. Honorary Degrees: University of Dundee, Open University, University of Edinburgh.

WRITINGS:

POETRY

Elegies for the Dead in Cyrenaica, Lehmann (London), 1948.

Freedom Come-All-Ye published in *Chapbook* special issue (Aberdeen), volume 3, number 6, 1967.

OTHER

Alias MacAlias, Polygon (Edinburgh), 1990.
(Editor and contributor) *Ballads of World War II, Collected by Seumas Mor Maceanruig,* Caledonian Press (Glasgow), 1947.

* * *

HERBERT, Stephen 1951-

PERSONAL: Born December 20, 1951, in London, England; son of Albert Herbert and Betty (Hinton) Corne; married, 1976 (divorced, 1995); companion of Mo Heard; children: Claire. *Ethnicity:* "Caucasian." *Education:* South Thames College, Audio-Visual Technical Qualification, 1980.

ADDRESSES: Home and office—66 Culverden Rd., London SW12 9LS, England; fax 01-81-675-7622. *E-mail*—s_herbert@easynet.co.uk.

CAREER: University of London, Goldsmiths' College, London, England, film and video production technician, 1979-89; British Film Institute, London, deputy head of technical services for National Film Theatre, Museum of the Moving Image, and London Film Festival, 1989-91, head of technical services, 1991-96; freelance visual technology consultant, 1996—. Projection Box Publishers (optical toy designers), partner, 1993—.

MEMBER: National Stereoscopic Association, Projected Picture Trust, Magic Lantern Society (research officer).

WRITINGS:

(Editor with Dennis Crompton and David Henry) *Magic Images,* Magic Lantern Society, 1990.
(Editor with Luke McKernan) *Who's Who of Victorian Cinema,* BFI Publishing (London, England), 1996.

Contributor to periodicals, including *Movie Maker, Making Better Movies,* and *New Magic Lantern Journal.* Past newsletter editor, Projected Picture Trust.

WORK IN PROGRESS: An account of the work of inventor Theodore Brown.

SIDELIGHTS: Stephen Herbert told *CA:* "A lifelong interest in film and projected images led to research in the fields of pre-cinema and early (pre-1914) film. I have reconstructed early motion picture shows, and for the past five years have been the research officer for the Magic Lantern Society. In 1993 I formed a publication company with my partner Mo Heard. We are currently publishing monographs on pre-cinema, early film, and optical recreations, both facsimiles and new research."

BIOGRAPHICAL/CRITICAL SOURCES:

BOOKS

Williams, C., editor, *Cinema: The Beginnings and the Future,* University of Westminster, 1996.

* * *

HERMLIN, Stephan 1915-

PERSONAL: Born April 13, 1915, in Chemnitz, Germany. *Politics:* Communist.

ADDRESSES: Home—Kurt Fischerstrasse 39, III Berlin, Germany.

CAREER: Radio Frankfurt, editor, 1945-47; freelance writer since 1947. Exiled from Germany 1936-45. *Wartime Service:* participated in Spanish Civil War; fought with the French Resistance during World War II.

MEMBER: International PEN (vice president since 1975); Berlin Academy of Arts, Societe Europeenne de Culture, Venice.

AWARDS, HONORS: Heine Prize, 1948 and 1972; National Prize, 1950, 1954, 1975; Fatherland's Merit Order in Gold, 1980.

WRITINGS:

(With Hans Mayer) *Ansichten uber einige Bucher und Schriftsteller* (title means "Opinions on Some Books and Writers"), Volk und Welt (Berlin), 1947.
Die Strassen der Furcht, Oberbadischer Verlag, 1947.
Zweiundzwanzig Balladen (title means "Twenty-Two Ballads"), Volk und Welt (Berlin), 1947.

Russische Eindrucke (title means "Russian Impressions") Kultur und Fortschritt (Berlin), 1948.
Die Zeit der Gemeinsamkeit (title means "The Time of Loneliness"), Volk und Welt (Berlin), 1951.
Der Kapf um eine deutsche Nationalliteratur, Schriftseller-Verlag (Berlin), 1952.
Die Sache des Friedens (title means "The Matter of Peace"), Volk und Welt (Berlin), 1953.
Ferne Nahe (title means "Distant Closeness"), Aufbau-Verlag (Berlin), 1954.
Der Leutnant Yorck von Wartenburg (title means "The Lieutenant Yorck of Wartenburg") Oberbadische Druckerei und Verlagstanstalt, 1954.
Begegnungen (title means "Encounters"), Aufbau-Verlag (Berlin), 1954-60.
Dichtungen, Aufbau-Verlag (Berlin), 1956.
Nachdichtungen, Aufbau-Verlag (Berlin), 1957.
Die Stadte (title means "The Cities"), Bechtle (Munich), 1966.
Scardanelli, Wagenbach (Berlin), 1971.
Lekture, Suhrkamp (Frankfurt), 1974.
Stadte-Balladen (title means "City Ballads"), Reclam (Leipzig), 1975.
Gesammelte Gedichte (collected poems), Hanser (Munich), 1979.
Abendlicht, Wagenbach (Berlin), 1979, translation by Paul F. Dvorak published as *Evening Light,* Fjord Press (San Francisco), 1983.
Aufsatze—Reportagen—Reden—Interviews, edited by Ulla Hahn (collected writings), Hanser (Munich), 1980.
Lebensfrist (short stories; title means "Time to Live"), Wagenbach (Berlin), 1980.
Ausserungen 1944-1982 (title means "Utterings"), Aufbau-Verlag (Berlin), 1983.
Bestimmungsorte: Funf Erzahlungen (short stories), Wagenbach (Berlin), 1985.

Also published *Zwolf Balladen von den grossen Stadten,* 1945; *Zwei Erzahlungen* (Two Stories), 1947; with Hans Mayer, *Mansfelder Oratorium* (Mansfield Oratorio), 1951; *Der Flug der Taube* (The Flight of the Dove), 1952; *Mein Friede,* 1985; *Traum der Gemeinsamkeit,* 1987. Also author of radio plays and contributor to magazines.

SIDELIGHTS: Once a pillar of the artistic community in East Germany, Stephan Hermlin is considered to be one of the foremost lyric poets of his generation. Dedicated to Communism and the humanitarian principles that it promised to promote, Hermlin has struggled to reconcile his upbringing, his own artistic talents, and his political beliefs.

Born into a wealthy, cultured Jewish family in Germany, Hermlin was the son of a sophisticated Englishwoman and an industrialist who collected art. Growing up in Germany during the 1920s and 1930s, Hermlin witnessed great artistic and political upheavals. At age 16 he joined the Communist party; two years later, despot Adolf Hitler came to power in Germany, his popularity based in part on his promise to protect Germany from the threat of spreading Communism (not to mention the dictator's vow to eradicate the Jewish race), and the young man was forced underground. Hermlin passed several years of exile in the Near East, England, Spain, and France, fighting on the side of the republicans in the Spanish Civil War and later joining the French Resistance. During World War II, his father was sent to a Nazi concentration camp.

Hermlin returned home after the war to support the new socialist regime in East Germany. He began publishing poetry written during the war, ballads about exile, war, and death. Some of his new poetry served to glorify the Communists, but he also continued to write mournful poems. However, his lyric poetry—which has inspired tremendous international acclaim—soon proved to be problematic in the German Democratic Republic. Diether H. Haenicke described the situation in *World Literature Today:* "In the fifties Hermlin was severely admonished by Marxist critics to abjure his 'estheticist' leanings, which he himself considered weaknesses because they ran counter to a party esthetic which espouses its own socialist realism." Sacrificing his poetic aspirations for Party interests, Hermlin effectively stopped writing poetry and turned instead to stories, translations, and essays. However, he continued to focus in his fiction on the anguish of life in the violent years of the mid-twentieth century. In a *World Literature Today* review of a collection of Hermlin's short stories, *Lebensfrist,* Perter Firchow wrote, "It seems almost as if Hermlin can only see life through suffering eyes. . . .The only real truth is the truth of suffering, the only real life that which ends in brutal, self-sacrificial death."

Hermlin's 1979 memoir *Abendlicht* (translated as *Evening Light* in 1983), reflected on the author's poetic and political leanings and became the first of his works to be published in English. *Publishers Weekly* commented that it "somehow captures the strange, lyric quality of memory. . . .[it is a] graceful, oneric memoir." Joel Agee explained in the *New York Times Book Review,* that "after finishing it one has the impression of having read several different kinds of books . . . a serene and dignified summing up of a life dedicated to the difficult marriage of poetry and class struggle, of a militant secular faith and a religious temperament, that is evinced by virtually every sentence in this beautiful memoir."

By the time he produced his memoir, Hermlin had become a vocal critic of the East German government's treatment of artists. In 1976 he denounced the exile of poet Wolf Biermann and, later, he spoke out against the threatened expulsion of others. While less prominent authors suffered for expressing such opinions, Hermlin's stature was such that he was relatively safe. By the time the Berlin Wall fell in 1989 and Germany was reunified, the author had lost some status within the Communist Party, yet when Hermlin was seen in *November Days,* a film by Marcel Ophuls that documented the views of East and West Germans during the days surrounding the fall of the Berlin Wall, he still presented an image that at least one critic perceived as loyal to the Communist Party. Stanley Kauffmann commented in the *New Republic* that "the Communist poet and short-story writer Stephan Hermlin purrs over his pipe with an equanimity that presumably Party fidelity bought for him and that is unshaken."

BIOGRAPHICAL/CRITICAL SOURCES:

PERIODICALS

New Republic, June 1, 1992, pp. 36-37.
New York Times Book Review, September 18, 1983, p. 7.
Publishers Weekly, April 29, 1983, p. 50.
World Literature Today, winter 1981, p. 95; winter 1982, p. 111; spring 1982, p. 331, 467.*

* * *

HERRINGTON, Terri
See BLACKSTOCK, Terri

* * *

HERRNSTEIN, Richard J(ulius) 1930-1994

PERSONAL: Born May 20, 1930, in New York, NY; died of lung cancer, September 13, 1994, in Belmont, MA; son of Rezso and Flora Irene (Friedman)

Herrnstein; married Barbara Brodo, May 28, 1951 (divorced February, 1961); married Susan Chalk Gouinlock, November 11, 1961; children: (first marriage) Julia Manganaro; (second marriage) Max Gouinlock, James Rezso. *Education:* City College of New York, B.A., 1952; Harvard University, Ph.D., 1955.

CAREER: Walter Reed Army Medical Center, Washington, DC, research psychologist, 1956-58; University of Maryland, lecturer, 1957-58; Harvard University, Cambridge, MA, 1958-94, began as instructor, became Edgar Pierce Professor of Psychology, director of psychology labs, 1965-67, chair of psychology department, 1967-71. *Military service:* U.S. Army, 1956-58; became first lieutenant.

MEMBER: American Academy of Arts and Sciences, Phi Beta Kappa, Sigma Xi.

AWARDS, HONORS: Guggenheim Foundation fellowship, 1977-78; Sloan Foundation fellowship, 1982-83.

WRITINGS:

(Editor with Edwin G. Boring) *A Source Book in the History of Psychology,* Harvard University Press (Cambridge, MA), 1965.

(With Joseph C. Stevens and George S. Reynolds) *Laboratory Experiments in Psychology,* Holt (New York City), 1965.

I.Q. in the Meritocracy, Little, Brown (Boston), 1973.

(With Roger Brown) *Psychology,* Little, Brown, 1975.

(Editor with Michael L. Commons and Howard Rachlin) *Matching and Maximizing Accounts,* Ballinger (Cambridge, MA), 1982.

(Editor with Commons and Allan R. Wagner) *Discrimination Processes,* Ballinger, 1983.

(With James Q. Wilson) *Crime and Human Nature,* Simon & Schuster (New York City), 1985.

(With Charles Murray) *The Bell Curve: Intelligence and Class Structure in American Life,* Free Press (New York City), 1994.

Editor of *Psychological Bulletin,* 1975-81; contributor of articles to psychological journals and periodicals, including the *Atlantic Monthly.*

SIDELIGHTS: Psychologist Richard J. Herrnstein's views on the inheritance of intelligence, social standing, and criminal tendencies made him a controversial figure. In the ongoing nature versus nurture debate,

Herrnstein had joined those who countered the mainstream focus on environmental influences to human behavior. In articles and books, he had argued that because heredity was behind much of human nature, much of the public policy designed to overcome social ills was misguided. His views had prompted some to label him racist and classist; others had hailed him for his straight talk about important social issues that political correctness had tried to silence.

Yet, the controversy surrounding Herrnstein did not end with his death on September, 13, 1994. Just weeks after he died of lung cancer, his last book, *The Bell Curve: Intelligence and Class Structure in American Life,* was published. This book, coauthored with Charles Murray, ignited a firestorm of debate among scholars, politicians, and commentators. Magazines such as the *National Review* and the *New Republic* devoted their pages to reactions to *The Bell Curve.* Publishers scrambled to print collections of responses to the book. The debate attracted the media and the general public in large numbers. Even though the book was over 800 pages made heavy by statistical analyses, charts, graphs, appendices, and notes, it sold over 400,000 copies in its first two months.

Herrnstein began his career as a psychologist at Harvard University. During the late 1950s and early 1960s, he studied under and then worked with B. F. Skinner, the founder of behaviorism. "In research on laboratory animals," wrote Daniel Goleman in a *New York Times* obituary, "Dr. Herrnstein mapped with mathematical precision the link between behavior and rewards and formulated what is known as 'matching law,' which shows that animals learn to repeat an action in direct proportion to the degree the action is reinforced by a reward like food." In the 1970s, Herrnstein turned his attention to intelligence, especially as it was measured by tests of I.Q. or "intelligence quotient."

Herrnstein first moved into the spotlight of controversy when his 1971 article "I.Q." was published in the *Atlantic Monthly.* In this article, the psychologist offered an overview of the history of intelligence testing. He also argued that mental abilities were inherited, and that these abilities contributed to financial success, and thereby social standing. Herrnstein's vision of the "meritocracy" stated that the rich and powerful were so because they were smart; and, because intelligence was passed on to children, so was wealth and power. To the extent that I.Q. tests measured mental abilities, Herrnstein felt, they would also measure social success.

Herrnstein's findings led him to some other conclusions. One was that as arbitrary environmental (social, political, and cultural) differences among people were eliminated, innate differences would become more pronounced. "Greater wealth, health, freedom, fairness, and educational opportunity [in our society]," wrote Herrnstein in the *Atlantic Monthly,* "are *not* going to give us the egalitarian society of our philosophical heritage. It will instead give us a society sharply graduated, with ever greater separation between the top and the bottom, and ever more uniformity within families as far as inherited abilities are concerned." Herrnstein further developed these ideas in his 1973 book *I.Q. in the Meritocracy.* Both the article and the book attracted a great deal of attention. Some found Herrnstein's conclusions racist and classist; as a result, he became the object of student protests at Harvard.

In the 1990s, Herrnstein teamed with Charles Murray, a conservative political scientist and fellow at the American Enterprise Institute, to write *The Bell Curve.* In this book, Herrnstein and Murray presented discussion, documentation, statistical analyses, charts, graphs, scholarly references, and appendices to make their case on how intelligence affects class structure. They then used their conclusions to explain recent history and current events and to make projections about the future. Finally, they offered policy recommendations based on their findings.

Specifically, Herrnstein and Murray argued that, increasingly, inherited intelligence (not social status or other factors) is necessary for success in modern societies. As these societies are becoming more and more effective at selecting for intelligence, they are creating a "cognitive elite" at the top and a stagnant underclass at the bottom. The gap between these two groups is widening because the intelligent are getting richer, they are segregating themselves physically from others, and because they are intermarrying. Herrnstein and Murray also argued that intelligence affects social behavior. The social problems that we now face in the United States, the authors contended, are related to low intelligence. They presented evidence to support the idea that low intelligence causes poverty, unemployment, welfare dependence, school failure, family ills, and poor parenting. Their third thesis was that different ethnic groups differ in intelligence and that these differences can account for inequalities among groups.

According to Herrnstein and Murray, these phenomena explain why past and current public policy fail to make positive social change. The phenomena also suggest, in the authors' views, that the underclass will continue to grow because those with low intelligence have more children and because immigration policy allows those with low intelligence to enter. This will lead to increasing class strife. Instead of allowing these trends to continue, we should, in the opinion of Herrnstein and Murray, take cognitive ability into account and make changes. Chester E. Finn, Jr., paraphrased their recommendations in *Commentary:* "First, they say, we should restate the principle of equality in terms that require everyone to be accorded equal liberty, not vouchsafed equal outcomes. . . . Everyone, smart or slow, should be encouraged to find his own 'valued place' in society. And third, simplify the overcomplicated rules that permeate our lives."

The Bell Curve may be the most talked about and written about book of the last several years. "I cannot recall a serious book provoking such a gusher of commentary," observed Finn. Responses to it have filled talk radio, television news programs, magazines, book reviews, newspaper editorials, and letters to the editor. It has spawned books about the book. It has involved scholars, politicians, commentators, and the public. Whether positive or negative, the responses have focused on the book's presentation, its scientific foundation, its social and public policy implications, and its recommendations.

"The Bell Curve is a very sober, very thorough, and very honest book," wrote Thomas Sowell in *The Bell Curve Wars: Race, Intelligence, and the Future of America,* "on a subject where sobriety, thoroughness, and honesty are only likely to provoke cries of outrage." On the subject of intelligence testing and its social implications, added Sowell, the book "is an education . . . including the evidence pro and con on a wide variety of controversial issues. . . . In such candor, as well as the clarity with which technical issues are discussed without needless jargon, this book is a model that others might well emulate." In his review in *Commentary,* Finn pointed out that the authors maintained a balanced approach even while taking on the established view. "Though written with care (and often erring on the side of caution)," he commented, "[*The Bell Curve*] thumbs its nose at the taboos. It overturns innumerable applecarts. It challenges all manner of assumptions, social programs, and institutional arrangements. And it contains a trove of useful information, insight, and analysis."

Howard Gardner admitted in *The Bell Curve Wars* that the book "is well argued and admirably clear in

its exposition. The authors are, for the most part, fair and thorough in laying out alternative arguments and interpretations." Yet, Gardner also found that *The Bell Curve*'s authors used what he called "scholarly brinkmanship. Whether concerning an issue of science, policy, or rhetoric, the authors come dangerously close to embracing the most extreme positions, yet in the end shy away from doing so." This approach, concluded Gardner, "encourages the reader to draw the strongest conclusions, while allowing the authors to disavow this intention." In the *New York Times Book Review,* Malcolm W. Browne faulted Herrnstein and Murray for not clearly targeting their audience. "[The] authors seem unsure whether they are addressing ordinary (but scientifically literate) readers or professional scholars. In their indecision, they offer either too little or too much information."

The science of *The Bell Curve* has come under close scrutiny and elicited its own body of responses. In the opinion of Christopher Caldwell of the *American Spectator,* "*The Bell Curve* is a comprehensive, responsible treatment of its subject, never mean-spirited or gloating. It gives fair hearing to those who dissent scientifically from its propositions—in fact, it bends over backward to be fair." Caldwell added, "Its crucial data are supplied in appendices for the reader's independent examination. Its science is never fuzzy or self-contradictory." Browne cited a number of reasons to accept the book's central premise. He wrote, "Taken as a whole, the statistics are impressive; its seems hard to challenge the notion that I.Q. plays a statistically important role in the shaping of society." As Caldwell pointed out, these statistics included information "made available by the National Longitudinal Survey of Youth, a federally funded study of 12,686 students who were age 14 to 22 in 1979, and have been followed ever since." In addition to such long-term studies, noted Browne, "One of the strengths of *The Bell Curve* is that it devotes an entire section to the relationships between I.Q. and behavior among whites alone, thereby eliminating the complications arising from interracial comparisons."

Yet, *The Bell Curve* has also been criticized for its science. Some have contended that it is not fair and thorough. As Richard Lacayo pointed out in a *Time* magazine feature, "Specialists in the intelligence field complain that Herrnstein and Murray all but ignore what is known about brain development." Others have argued that the author's scientific method was flawed. Leon J. Kamin commented in *Scientific American* that "the caliber of the data in *The Bell Curve* is, at many critical points, pathetic." Kamin

went on to examine studies used by Herrnstein and Murray, such as those by Richard Lynn. He characterized Lynn's work as "distortions and misrepresentations of the data" and added that "it is a matter of shame and disgrace that two eminent social scientists . . . take Lynn as their scientific tutor and uncritically accept his surveys of research."

Thomas Sowell raised another issue. "Perhaps the most troubling aspect of *The Bell Curve* from an intellectual standpoint is its authors' uncritical approach to statistical correlations. One of the first things taught in introductory statistics is that correlation is not causation." The result, according to Kamin, was that the authors "draw many inappropriate conclusions." Stephen Jay Gould, writing in *The Bell Curve Wars,* questioned even the relationships offered by Herrnstein and Murray as evidence for their conclusions. Gould commented that the authors' "correlation coefficients are generally low enough by themselves to inspire lack of confidence."

By far the most volatile responses to *The Bell Curve* have concerned its social and public policy implications and its recommendations. Using their conclusions that intelligence is innate and unchangeable and that it is related to social success and failure, Herrnstein and Murray offered support to many items on the conservative political agenda. They argued that government intervention to improve education has had some affect on the below-average student, but it has "neglected the gifted minority who will greatly affect how well America does in the twenty-first century." They argued that affirmative action has worsened the relationship between the majority and minorities by favoring unprepared and unqualified minorities in education and employment. They also offered a case for "ending welfare to discourage births among low-IQ poor women," observed Lacayo, and "changing immigration laws to favor the capable."

In Stephen Jay Gould's view, "*The Bell Curve* is scarcely an academic treatise in social theory and population genetics. It is a manifesto of conservative ideology; the book's inadequate and biased treatment of data displays its primary purpose—advocacy. The text evokes the dreary and scary drumbeat of claims associated with conservative think tanks." Chester E. Finn, Jr., suggested, however, that the severe critics of Herrnstein and Murray were influenced by political correctness and a desire to silence the debate. He wrote, "Their main project has been to hurl enough brickbats to drive both book and authors out of the public square." Caldwell viewed the outrage to the

book as a sign of liberal insecurity. He commented, "November's electoral blowout [of 1994] and a bevy of polling data show that Americans have finally lost patience with the largely black urban underclass and with the government social programs that many blame for its existence. Anger and defensiveness are sure to greet a book that sees such impatience as well-founded, or further undermines the rationale for those programs. And this book does both."

Whatever the outcome of the debate over *The Bell Curve*, it added fuel to the mid-1990s political fire over the direction of the country and the fate of government social programs. There was no agreement on whether its effect would be positive or negative. "To give credence to such ideas," observed *Time*'s Lacayo, "is to resume some of the most poisonous battles of the late 1960s and '70s." Although he accepted their arguments, Richard John Neuhaus worried in a *National Review* article that Herrnstein and Murray would actually do harm to their cause. "The authors give us no compelling reason for having such a public discussion, and there are compelling reasons for not having it," he commented. "There are many other matters on which public debate should be generated, matters about which we can do something." Thomas Sowell concluded his response to *The Bell Curve*: "In one sense, the issues are too important to ignore. In another sense the differences between what Herrnstein and Murray said and what others believe is much smaller than the latter seem to think. . . . *The Bell Curve* deserves critical attention, not public smearing and uncritical private acceptance."

BIOGRAPHICAL/CRITICAL SOURCES:

BOOKS

Fraser, Steven, editor, *The Bell Curve Wars: Race, Intelligence, and the Future of America,* Basic Books (New York City), 1995.

Glauberman, Naomi, and Russell Jacoby, editors, *The Bell Curve Debate: History, Documents, Opinions,* Times Books/Random House (New York City), 1995.

Herrnstein, Richard J., and Charles Murray, *The Bell Curve: Intelligence and Class Structure in American Life,* Free Press (New York City), 1994.

PERIODICALS

American Spectator, January, 1995, pp. 62-67.
Atlantic Monthly, September, 1971, p. 43.

Commentary, January, 1995, pp. 76-80.
Nation, November 28, 1994, pp. 654-57, 659-62.
National Review, December 5, 1994, pp. 40-42.
New Republic, October 31, 1994, pp. 27-37.
New York Review of Books, November 17, 1994, pp. 7-13.
New York Times Book Review, September 8, 1985; October 16, 1994, p. 3.
Scientific American, February 1995, pp. 99-103.
Time, October 24, 1994.
Washington Post Book World, September 22, 1985.

OBITUARIES:

PERIODICALS

New York Times, September 16, 1994, p. B8.
Time, September 26, 1994, p. 17.*

—*Sketch by Bryan Ryan*

* * *

HILL, Anita Faye 1956-

PERSONAL: Born July 30, 1956, in Morris, OK; daughter of Albert (a farmer) and Irma Hill. *Education:* Oklahoma State University, B.S. (psychology), 1977; Yale University School of Law, LL.D., 1980.

ADDRESSES: Office—University of Oklahoma School of Law, 300 Timberland Rd., Norman, OK 73019.

CAREER: Attorney, educator, and activist. Ward, Harkrader, & Ross, Washington, DC, attorney, 1980-81; U.S. Department of Education, Washington, DC, personal assistant to the head of the Office of Civil Rights (Clarence Thomas), from 1981; Equal Employment Opportunity Commission, Washington, DC, personal assistant to the chair (Clarence Thomas), through 1983; Oral Roberts University School of Law, Tulsa, OK, civil rights professor, 1983-86; University of Oklahoma School of Law, Norman, professor of law, 1986—.

MEMBER: Oklahoma Bar Association.

AWARDS, HONORS: Ida B. Wells Award, National Coalition of 100 Black Women, 1991; named one of *Glamour* magazine's ten Women of the Year, 1991.

WRITINGS:

(Editor, with Emma Coleman Jordan, and contributor) *Race, Gender, and Power in America: The Legacy of the Hill-Thomas Hearings* (essays), Oxford University Press, 1995.

WORK IN PROGRESS: An autobiography and a book about sexual harassment.

SIDELIGHTS: Law professor Anita Faye Hill, an African American woman, became a household name and galvanized the women's movement in 1991 when she charged Clarence Thomas, an African American man and then a nominee for United States Supreme Court justice, with sexual harassment. The Senate Judiciary Committee hearings on the allegations, which captured the attention and divided the sympathies of the American public, became a melodrama infused with race and gender issues. Hill's motivation for coming forward and her credibility were repeatedly attacked, with some suggesting that she was part of an eleventh-hour plot to scuttle Thomas's nomination. Others supported her and accused the all-male, all-white Judiciary Committee of minimizing her complaint. Although Hill's charges were dismissed and Thomas's nomination was approved, Hill's composed and articulate hearing appearances helped focus attention on sexual harassment in the workplace. The hearings also made clear that women and people of color are underrepresented in the U.S. legislature and inspired a record number of women to campaign for office in 1992.

With Emma Coleman Jordan, Hill has edited and contributed to a book of essays, *Race, Gender, and Power in America: The Legacy of the Hill-Thomas Hearings,* which grew out of a conference at Georgetown University Law Center. The essays, by a number of legal and political scholars, address sexual harassment, the intersection of race and gender, relations between black men and women, the legacy of slavery, the treatment of black women, and the differing perspectives of black and white women on the hearings, among other topics. Hill writes about the dual impact of racism and sexism in "Marriage and Patronage in the Empowerment and Disempowerment of African-American Women": "Because of my race and because of my gender I was then [during the hearings] and continue to be on the fringe of both the African-American community and the community of women."

Race, Gender, and Power in America garnered mostly favorable reviews, although some critics commented that the quality of the essays was uneven. Writing in *Booklist,* Lillian Lewis noted that, as a complete work, the book is "quite intriguing." A *New York Times Book Review* contributor found an essay on the history of the treatment of black women written by former federal appellate judge A. Leon Higginbotham, Jr., to be "masterly." *Boston Globe* writer Sandy Coleman termed Hill's essay "one of the most well-written and intriguing in the book." Coleman concluded that *Race, Gender, and Power in America* "is an important book" filled with "provocative" essays.

BIOGRAPHICAL/CRITICAL SOURCES:

BOOKS

Contemporary Black Biography, Volume 5, Gale, 1994, pp. 117-20.
Hill, Anita Faye, and Emma Coleman Jordan, editors, *Race, Gender, and Power in America: The Legacy of the Hill-Thomas Hearings,* Oxford University Press, 1995.

PERIODICALS

Booklist, October 1, 1995.
Boston Globe, October 26, 1995, p. 63.
New Yorker, May 24, 1993, p. 90-96.
New York Times Book Review, November 5, 1995, p. 22.
Publishers Weekly, October 2, 1995.
Washington Post Book World, November 26, 1995, p. 8.*

* * *

HILLIARD, Asa G(rant) III 1933-

PERSONAL: Born August 22, 1933, in Galveston, TX; married; wife's name, Patsy Jo; children: Asa IV, Robi Nsenga Bailey, Patricia Nefertari, Hakim Sequenenre. *Education:* University of Denver, B.A., 1955, M.A., 1961, Ed.D., 1963.

ADDRESSES: Office—Georgia State University, P.O. Box 243, Atlanta, GA 30303.

CAREER: Denver Public Schools, Denver, CO, teacher, 1955-60; University of Denver, teaching fel-

low, 1960-63; San Francisco State University, San Francisco, CA, professor and dean of education, 1963-83; Georgia State University, Atlanta, distinguished professor of education, 1980—. Automated Services Inc., director of research, 1970-72; National Black Child Development Institute, member of board of directors, 1973-75; American Psychology Association, member of Board of Ethnic and Minority Affairs, 1982-84.

MEMBER: National Association for the Education of Young Children.

AWARDS, HONORS: Fellow, National Defense Education Act (University of Denver), 1960-63; Knight Commander of the Human Order of African Redemption, 1972; Distinguished Leadership Award, Association of Teacher Educators, 1983; award for outstanding scholarship, Association of Black Psychologists, 1984.

WRITINGS:

An Exploratory Study of Relationships between Student Teachers' Personality, Ability, Lower Division Grades, and the Student Teachers' Evaluation of Pupils, University Microfilms, 1963.
(Editor with Larry Williams and Nia Damali) *The Teachings of Ptahhotep: The Oldest Book in the World,* illustrated by Babatunde K. S. Abdullah, Blackwood Press, 1987.
The Maroon within Us: Selected Essays on African American Community Socialization, Black Classic Press (Baltimore, MD), 1995.

Also author of *Strengths: African American Children and Families,* 1982; and, with Betty M. Caldwell, *What Is Quality Child Care?,* 1985.*

* * *

HINDESS, Barry 1939-

PERSONAL: Born July 11, 1939, in Hitchin, England; son of Henry Gordon (an electrical engineer) and Mary Ann (Macbeth) Hindess. *Education:* Oxford University, B.A., 1961; University of Liverpool, Ph.D., 1975.

ADDRESSES: Office—Research School of Social Sciences, Australian National University, Canberra

0200, Australia; fax 06-249-3051. *E-mail*—b.hindess @coombs.anu.edu.au.

CAREER: University of Liverpool, Liverpool, England, began as lecturer, became professor of sociology, 1968-87; Australian National University, Canberra, professor of political science, 1987—.

MEMBER: International Political Science Association, International Sociological Association, Australian Political Science Association, Australian Sociological Association.

WRITINGS:

The Decline of Working Class Politics, MacGibbon & Kee (London, England), 1971.
The Use of Official Statistics in Sociology: A Critique of Positivism and Ethnomethodology, Humanities (Atlantic Highlands, NJ), 1973.
(With Paul Hirst) *Pre-Capitalist Modes of Production,* Routledge & Kegan Paul (Boston, MA), 1975.
(Editor and contributor) *Sociological Theories of the Economy,* Holmes & Meier (New York City), 1977.
Philosophy and Methodology in the Social Sciences, Humanities, 1977.
(With Hirst) *Mode of Production and Social Formation,* Macmillan (London), 1977.
(With Hirst, Tony Cutler, and Athar Hussain) *Marx's Capital and Capitalism Today,* Routledge & Kegan Paul, Volume I, 1977, Volume II, 1978.
Parliamentary Democracy and Socialist Politics, Routledge & Kegan Paul, 1983.
Freedom, Equality, and the Market: Arguments in Social Policy, Tavistock (London), 1986.
Politics and Class Analysis, Basil Blackwell (Oxford, England), 1987.
Choice, Rationality, and Social Theory, Unwin-Hyman (London), 1988.
Political Choice and Social Structure, Edward Elgar (London), 1989.
(Editor and contributor) *Reactions to the Right,* Routledge (New York City), 1990.
Democracy, Routledge, in press.
(Editor) *Individualism,* Routledge, in press.
(Editor with Mitchell Dean) *Governing Australia,* Cambridge University Press, in press.

Also author of *Discourses of Power: From Hobbes to Foucault,* Blackwell Scientific (Oxford, England).

HOAGLAND, Anthony Dey 1953-
(Tony Hoagland)

PERSONAL: Born November 19, 1953, Fort Bragg, NC; married Betty Sasaki, 1995. *Education:* Attended Williams College, 1971-73; University of Iowa, Iowa City, B.G.S., 1977; University of Arizona, M.F.A., 1983.

ADDRESSES: Home and office—47 Redington St., Waterville, ME 04901.

CAREER: Arizona Western College, Yuma, instructor, 1986; College of the Holy Names, Oakland, CA, instructor, 1989-90; St. Mary's College, Moraga, CA, instructor, 1990-91; University of Maine, Farmington, instructor, 1992. Writer-in-residence, Kalamazoo College, Kalamazoo, MI, summer, 1991. Warren Wilson College, Asheville, NC, faculty member, writing program, 1993—; Colby College, Waterville, ME, instructor, 1993—.

AWARDS, HONORS: National Endowment for the Arts fellowship, 1987, 1994; Pushcart prize in poetry, 1991, 1993; Brittingham prize, University of Wisconsin Press, 1992; John C. Zacharis prize, Emerson College, 1994. Fine Arts Work Center in Provincetown fellow, 1986. Member: Academy of American Poets.

WRITINGS:

POETRY, AS TONY HOAGLAND

A Change in Plans (chapbook), San Pedro Press (Sierra Vista, AZ), 1985.
Talking to Stay Warm (chapbook), Coffee Cup Press (Minneapolis, MN), 1986.
History of Desire (chapbook), Moon Pony Press (Tucson, AZ), 1990.
Sweet Ruin, University of Wisconsin Press, 1992.

* * *

HOAGLAND, Tony
See HOAGLAND, Anthony Dey

* * *

HOBBS, Mary 1923-

PERSONAL: Born September 7, 1923, in Sunderland, England; daughter of Louis (a lecturer) and Elizabeth Mary (Milburn) Ruderman; married Keith Hobbs (an archdeacon), May 8, 1950; children: Robin Michael. *Education:* University of London, B.A. (with honors), 1945, Ph.D., 1973. *Religion:* Church of England. *Avocational interests:* Drama, music, foreign travel, reading.

ADDRESSES: Home—10 St. Martin's Sq., Chichester, West Sussex PO19 1NR, England. *Office*—Cathedral Office, Cloisters, Chichester Cathedral, Chichester, West Sussex PO19 1PX, England.

CAREER: High school English teacher in Cambridgeshire, England, 1946-49, and Clifton, England, 1949-51; West London Institute of Higher Education, London, England, lecturer in English literature, 1971-78; Chichester Cathedral, Chichester, England, librarian, 1978—. Cathedrals Advisory Commission, member, 1987-91; Council for the Care of Churches, vice-chairperson, 1987-91.

MEMBER: Cathedral Librarians and Archivists Association, Society of Antiquaries (fellow).

WRITINGS:

The Young Milton (novel), Macdonald and Co., 1968.
(Editor) *The Stoughton Manuscript,* Scolar Press, 1990.
The Sermons of Bishop Henry King of Chichester, 1892-1969, Scolar Press, 1992.
(Editor) *Early Seventeenth-Century Verse Miscellany Manuscripts,* Scolar Press, 1992.
(Editor) *Chichester Cathedral: An Historical Survey,* Phillimore and Co. (Chichester, England), 1994.

Contributor to journals, including *Review of English Studies, Notes and Queries, Library, Book Collector,* and *Sussex Archaeology.*

WORK IN PROGRESS: Research on Henry King as poet and "middle-way theologian."

* * *

HODGINS, (Ian) Philip 1959-

PERSONAL: Born January 28, 1959, in Shepparton, Victoria, Australia; married Janet Shaw, 1989; children: two daughters. *Education:* Attended University of Melbourne, 1986-87.

ADDRESSES: Home—Rural Mail Box 2138, Maryborough, Victoria 3465, Australia.

CAREER: Macmillan Publishers, Melbourne, Australia, sales representative, 1978-85.

AWARDS, HONORS: New South Wales Premier's Literary award; Wesley Michel Wright Poetry prize, Australian Bicentennial Poetry Book award, Grace Leven Poetry prize.

WRITINGS:

POETRY

Blood and Bone, HarperCollins (Sydney), 1986.
Down the Lake with Half a Chook, Australian Broadcasting Commission (Sydney), 1988.
Animal Warmth, HarperCollins, 1990.
Il Linguaggio della Memoria, Supernova (Venice, Italy), 1990.
The End of the Season, Brindabella Press (Canberra), 1993.
Up on All Fours, HarperCollins, 1993.
Dispossessed, HarperCollins, 1994.

* * *

HOFMANNSTHAL, Hugo von 1874-1929

PERSONAL: Born February 1, 1874, in Vienna, Austria; died of a heart attack, July 15, 1929, in Rodaun, Austria; buried in Kalksburg Cemetery, Vienna; son of Hugo August (a bank director) and Anna Maria; married Gertrud Schlesinger, 1901; children: Christiane, Raimund, Franz. *Education:* Akademisches Gymnasium, 1892, University of Vienna, Ph.D., 1899.

CAREER: Dramatist, poet, novelist, and essayist. *Military service:* Austrian army, 1894-95.

WRITINGS:

Gestern: Studie in einem Akt, in Reimen, Verlag der Modernen Rundschau, 1891.
Die Frau im Fenster (performed under the title *Madonna Dianora,* 1898); *Die Hochzeit der Sobeide; Der Abenteurer und die Sangerin: Theater in Versen,* Fischer, 1899, *Die Hochzeit der Sobeide*

translated as *The Marriage of Sobeide* in *German Classics of the Nineteenth and Twentieth Centuries,* German Publishing Society, 1914.
Der Kaiser und die Hexe, Insel, 1900.
Der Thor und der Tod, Insel, 1900, translated as *Death and the Fool,* Badger, 1913.
Der Tod des Tizian: Ein dramatisches Fragment, Insel, 1901, translated as *The Death of Titian,* Four Seas, 1914.
(Author of introduction) Arthur Schnitzler, *Anatol,* Fischer, 1901, introduction translated in *Playing with Love,* Gay & Hancock, 1914.
Studie uber die Entwicklung des Dichters Victor Hugo, Verlag von Dr. Hugo von Hofmannsthal, 1901, republished as *Victor Hugo,* Schuster & Loeffler, 1904, republished as *Versuch uber Victor Hugo,* Bremer Presse, 1925.
Ausgewahlte Gedichte, Verlag der Blatter fur die Kunst, 1903.
Des kleine Welttheater oder Die Glucklichen, Insel, 1903, translated as *The Little Theater of the World,* Victor & Jacob Hammer, 1945.
Elektra: Tragodie in einem Aufzug frei nach Sophocles, Fischer, 1904, translated as *Electra: A Tragedy in One Act,* Brentanos, 1908.
Unterhaltungen uber literarische Gegenstande, Bard, Marquardt, 1904.
Das gerettete Venedig: Trauerspiel in funf Aufzugen, Fischer, 1905, translated as *Venice Preserved: A Tragedy in Five Acts,* Badger, 1915.
Das Marchen der 672. Nacht und andere Erzahlungen (comprises "Das Marchen der 672. Nacht," translated as "Tale of the Merchant's Son and His Servants," 1969, "Reitergeschichte," "Erlebnis des Marschalls von Bassompierre," "Ein Brief," translated as "The Letter," 1942) Wiener Verlag, 1905.
Oedipus und die Sphinx: Tragodie in funf Aufzugen, Fischer, 1906, translated as *Oedipus and the Sphinx,* Odyssey, 1968.
Kleine Dramen (2 volumes, contains *Gestern: Studie in einem Akt, in Reimen, Der Thor und der Tod, Der weisse Facher: Ein Zwischenspiel, Das Bergwerk zu Falun, Der Kaiser und die Hexe, Des kleine Welttheater oder Die Glucklichen*), Insel, 1906-07.
Die gesammelten Gedichte, Insel, 1907, translated as *The Lyrical Poems of Hugo von Hofmannsthal,* Yale University Press, 1918.
Die prosaischen Schriften gesammelt (5 volumes), Fischer, 1907.
Vorspiele, Insel, 1908.
Hersperus: Ein Jahrbuch, Insel, 1909.
(Translator) *Konig Odipus,* Fischer, 1910.

Cristinas Heimreise: Komodie, Fisher, 1910, translated as *Cristinas Journey Home: A Comedy in Three Acts,* Badger, 1917, revised as *Florindo,* Avalun, 1923.

Jedermann: Das Spiel vom Sterben des reichen Mannes erneuert, Fisher, 1911, translated as *The Salzburg Everyman: The Play of the Rich Man's Death,* Mora, 1911.

Grete Wiesenthal in Amor und Psyche und Das fremde Madchen: Szenen, Fischer, 1911.

Alkestis: Ein Trauerspiel nach Euripides, Insel, 1911.

Der Rosenkavalier: Komo die fur Musik, Fischer, 1911, translsated as *The Rose-Bearer,* Furstner, 1912.

Die Gedichte und kleinen Dramen, Insel, 1911.

(Editor) *Deutsche Erzahler* (4 volumes), Insel, 1912.

Ariadne auf Naxos: Oper in einem Aufzuge nebst einem Vorspiel, Furstner, 1912, translated as *Ariadne on Naxos: Opera in One Act, with a Prelude,* Boosey & Hawkes, 1924.

Die Wege und die Begegnungen, Bremer Presse, 1913.

Josephslegende, Furstner, 1914, translated as *The Legend of Joseph,* Furstner, 1914.

Der Burger als Edelmann: Komodie mit Tanzen von Moliere. Freie Buhnenarbeitung in drei Aufzugen, Furstner, 1914.

Prinz Eugen der edle Ritter: Sein Leben in Bildern, Seidel, 1915.

(Editor) *Osterreichischer Almanach auf das Jahr 1916,* Insel, 1915.

(Editor) Franz Grillparzer, *Grillparzers politisches Verma chtnis,* Insel, 1915.

Rodaunder Nachtrage (3 volumes), Amalthea, 1918.

Lucidor: Figuren zu einer ungeschriebenen Komodie, Reiss, 1919.

Die Frau ohne Schatten: Oper in drei Akten, Furstner, 1919, Boosey & Hawkes, 1964, translated as *The Woman without a Shadow,* Decca Records, 1957.

Die Frau ohne Schatten: Erzahlung, Fischer, 1919.

(Translator) Pedro Calderon de la Barca, *Dame Kobold: Lustspiel in drei Aufzugen,* Fischer, 1920.

(Author of introduction) *Die Erzahlungen aus den Tausendundeinen Nachten* (6 volumes), Insel, 1921-1928.

Der Schwierige: Lustpiel in drei Akten, Fischer, 1921.

Reden und Aufsatze, Insel, 1921.

Gedichte, Insel, 1922.

Das Salzburger grosse Welttheater, Insel, 1922.

Buch der Freunde, Insel, 1922, enlarged as *Buch der Freunde: Tagebuch-Aufzeichnungen,* Insel, 1929.

(Author of introduction) *Griechenland: Baukunst, Landschaft, Volksleben,* Wasmuth, 1922, translated as *Picturesque Greece: Architecture, Landscape, Life of the People,* Architectural Book Publishing Co., 1922.

(Editor) *Deutsches Lesebuch* (2 volumes), Bremer Presse, 1922-23.

(Editor) *Deutsche Epigramme,* Bremer Presse, 1923.

Der Unbestechliche: Lustspiel in funf Akten, produced 16 March 1923.

Die grune Flote: Ballettpantomime, Universal-Edition, 1923.

Augenblicke in Griechenland, Habbel & Naumann, 1924.

Der Turm: Ein Trauerspiel in funf Aufzugen, Bremer Presse, 1925, revised edition, Fischer, 1927, translated as *The Tower,* 1966.

Die Ruinen von Athen: Ein Festspiel mit Tanzen und Choren, Furstner, 1925.

(Author of afterword) Adalbert Stifter, *Der Nachsommer: Eine Erzahlung,* List, 1925.

(Editor) Johann Christoph Friedrich von Schiller, *Schillers Selbstcharakteristik aus seinen Schriften,* Bremer Presse, 1926.

Fruuheste Prosastucke, Gesellschaft der Freunde der Deutschen Bu cherei, 1926.

Szenischer Prolog zur Neueroffnung des Josefstadtertheaters, Johannes-Presse, 1927.

Das Schrifttum als geistiger Raum der Nation, Bremer Presse, 1927.

Drei Erzahlungen, Insel, 1927.

(Editor) *Wert und Ehre deutscher Sprache in Zeugnissen,* Bremer Presse, 1927.

Die agyptische Helena: Oper in zwei Aufzugen, Furstner, 1928, translated as *Helen in Egypt,* Furstner, Ricordi, 1928.

Loris: Die Prosa des jungen Hugo von Hofmannsthal, Fischer, 1930.

Die Beruhrung der Spharen, Fischer, 1931.

Wege und Begegnungen, Reclam, 1931.

Fragment eines Romans, privately printed, 1931, enlarged as *Andreas oder Die Vereinigten: Fragmente eines Romanes,* Fischer, 1932, translated as *Andreas: or, The United: Being Fragments of a Novel,* Dent, 1936.

Arabella: Lyrische Komodie, Furstner, 1933, translated as *Arabella: A Lyrical Comedy in Three Acts,* Boosey & Hawkes, 1955, 1965.

Semiramis; Die beiden Gotter, Rupprechtpresse, 1933.

Prolog zur Feier von Goethes 50. Geburtstag am Burgtheater zu Wien, Officina Vindobonensis, 1934.

Nachlese der Gedichte, Fischer, 1934.

Dramatische Entwurfe aus dem Nachlass, Johannes-Presse, 1936.

Beethoven: Rede gehalten an der Beethoven feier des Lesezirkels Hottingen in Zurich am 10. Dez. 1920, Reichner, 1938.

Festspiele in Salzburg, Bermann-Fischer, 1938.

Gesammelte Werke in Einzelausgaben (15 volumes), Fischer, 1945-59, reedited as *Gesammelte Werke in zehn Einzelbanden* (10 volumes), Fischer, 1979.

Das Theater des Neuen: Eine Ankundigung, Edition Komodie in Bindenschildverlag, 1947.

Dem Gedachtnis des Dichters Theodor Storm, in der Handschrift des Dichters, Hempe, 1951.

Aud dem Jugendwerk Hugo von Hofmannsthal (Loris), Editrice viscontia, 1951.

Danae oder Die Vernunftheirat: Szenarium und Notizen, Fischer, 1952.

Selected Writings: Selected Prose, Routledge & Kegan Paul, 1952.

Selected Essays, Blackwell, 1955.

Osterreichische Aufsa tze und Reden, Bergland, 1956.

Natur und Erkenntnis: Essays, Deutsche Buch-Gemeinschaft, 1957.

Ausgewahlte Werke (2 volumes), Fischer, 1957.

Komodie, Stiasny, 1960.

Selected Writings: Poems and Verse Plays: Bilingual Edition, Routledge & Kegan Paul, 1961, Pantheon, 1961.

Selected Writings: Selected Plays and Libretti, Pantheon, 1963, Routledge & Kegan, 1964.

Three Plays (comprises *Death and the Fool, Electra, The Tower*), Wayne State University Press, 1966.

Four Stories, Oxford University Press, 1968.

Das erzahlerische Werk, Insel, 1975.

Samtliche Werke: Kritische Ausgabe (28 volumes), Fischer, 1975-.

Also contributed to the journal *Insel.* Hugo von Hofmannsthal's papers are at the Bibliothek des Freien Deutschen Hochstifts (Library of the Free German Academy), Frankfurt am Main; at the Houghton Library at Harvard University; and in private collections.

SIDELIGHTS: Hugo von Hofmannsthal is considered the preeminent Symbolist writer of German literature. Although he is often identified with the German "art for art's sake" movement of the late nineteenth century, his work is distinguished by a rare combination of aestheticism and moral committment. Hofmannsthal's international reputation rests on his libretti for several of Richard Strauss's operas and on his role as one of the originators of the Salzburg

Festival, where his symbolic dramas, most notably *Jedermann (The Play of Everyman)* and *Das Salzburger grosse Welttheater (The Salzburg Great Theatre of the World),* are still performed.

Born and raised in Vienna, Hofmannsthal was the only child of a prominent family who encouraged his studies in the arts. While still in school, he wrote lyric poetry, critical essays on contemporary authors, and, at seventeen, published his first lyric drama, *Gestern.* Hofmannsthal's precocious literary activity brought him to the attention of such prominent German and Austrian men of letters as Stefan George and Arthur Schnitzler, who were astounded by the display of mature thought and form in the young Austrian's work. For a short time Hofmannsthal contributed literary works to *Die Blatter fur die Kunst,* the journal through which George promoted his idea of a new German spirit based on a glorification of youth and leadership. Hofmannsthal eventually grew uncomfortable with George's elitist view of art, and though he maintained a friendship with the German poet, he ended the master/disciple relationship George had tried to nurture. Along with other writers of his own generation, including Hermann Bahr and Richard Beer-Hofmann, Hofmannsthal formed the *Jung Wien* (Young Vienna), a coterie of writers who rejected the trend of naturalism in literature and who artistically allied themselves to the French Symbolist tradition. In 1899 Hofmannsthal graduated from the University of Vienna with a doctorate in philology but chose to continue his writing career rather than to teach at a university. Thereafter, with the exception of travelling to Italy and France and serving as a translator and courier during World War I, Hofmannsthal remained in his homeland, living a quiet, genteel life until his death in 1929.

Critics of Hofmannsthal's works usually divide his literary development into three overlapping phases. The early phase began when he was sixteen and lasted through the turn of the century. The poetry and lyric dramas of this period, such as *Gestern, Der Tod des Tizian (The Death of Titian),* and *Der Tor und der Tod (Death and the Fool,),* brought him attention as an aesthete associated with the "art for art's sake" movement. These works, which are usually set in the baroque era, are commonly concerned with cultivated men who reject society for a life devoted to art, arriving at a social consciousness only when they are confronted with death. Characterized by an egocentric aestheticism, the works in this early phase convey a dreamlike detachment from life—a mystical state Hofmannsthal later called "pre-existence." According

to Hofmannsthal, in this contemplative condition the writer is in harmony with the universe and intuitively understands life with a wisdom that exceeds his experiences. He attributed to "pre-existence" his ability to compose works seemingly beyond the artistic and spiritual range of his seventeen years.

The middle phase of Hofmannsthal's career began around 1900 and lasted to World War I. It was a transitional period in which he focused more on human concerns and less on the artistic preoccupation of his earlier stage. He now emphasized the need to accept the responsibilities of life. During this time Hofmannsthal despaired over the insufficiency of language to express a world view. This crisis is artfully expressed in his *Ein Brief* (*The Letter*), a fictional letter written by an Elizabethan gentleman to Francis Bacon, the sixteenth-century essayist and philosopher. *The Letter* is important not only as a description of Hofmannsthal's personal doubts about his creative abilities, but also as an indication of his belief that art should not supplant life; therefore, *The Letter* warned his contemporaries of the dangers of aestheticism. Hofmannsthal's aesthetic crisis precipitated his abandonment of lyric poetry and lyric drama for the more straightforward expression of prose drama. In 1903, he staged a successful adaptation of the Greek tragedy, *Elektra* (*Electra*). Throughout the drama, Hofmannsthal maintained morbid imagery which helped transform the title character from her traditional role as a woman who methodically seeks justice into a vengeful psychotic. His association with the composer Strauss began shortly after this production of *Electra*. Strauss regarded Hofmannsthal as a "born librettist" and together they created several classic operas. *Der Rosenkavalier* (*The Rose-Bearer*, also known as *The Cavalier of the Rose*) endures as the most popular of their creations. As a librettist, Hofmannsthal found that operatic expression often transcended the inadequacy of language through its music and grand theatrical staging. In 1911 he wrote an adaptation of the English morality play *Everyman*. The drama represents the apex of Hofmannsthal's middle phase and indicates the dominant concern of his later period—suppression of "self" and cultivation of a Christian spirit.

Hofmannsthal's last period produced several social comedies and the morality plays written for the Salzburg Festival. *Der Schwierige* (*The Difficult Man*), which is often praised for its subtle craftsmanship, is his best comedy in this post-war period. The protagonist of the drama, Hans Karl Buhl, is one of Hofmannsthal's most interesting characters, an aristocrat with a social conscience. Unlike the characters in Hofmannsthal's earlier works, Hans Karl is given the opportunity to develop fully his awareness of the world around him, realizing both the benefits and responsibilities of social relationships. With the establishment of the Salzburg Festival, Hofmannsthal hoped to restore Austrian culture, which had been devastated by war and the loss of an empire. This contemporary theater advocated a Christian ethic and appealed to the common audience through its use of simple peasant speech. Hofmannsthal's *Everyman* was the first festival production, followed by *The Salzburg Great Theatre of the World,* a spiritual drama based on the seventeenth-century Spanish play *The Great Theatre of the World* by Calderon. In this religious allegory, Hofmannsthal successfully rendered the metaphor of "the world as a stage" and created a timeless universal plane on which the play is acted. His third drama written for the festival theater, *Der Turm* (*The Tower*), is also an adaptation of a Calderon play, *Life Is a Dream.* As one of his most symbolic works, *The Tower* expresses the hopeless fate of human existence ravaged by the brutal forces of a modern world devoid of a Christian mission.

Though Hofmannsthal's works are usually discussed as if they formed discrete phases of his career, most critics agree that they possess consistent themes which demand that they be considered as a unified body of work. According to Lowell Bangerter, the dominant concern of Hofmannsthal's canon is "that of synthesis, of bringing all things harmoniously together—people, nations, art forms, traditions, ideas, past, present, future." His works insist upon social consciousness and moral commitment to life, qualities which can be awakened by art. Thus, while the expressed purpose of his contemporaries was "art for art's sake," Hofmannsthal's literary doctrine was "art for life's sake."

BIOGRAPHICAL/CRITICAL SOURCES:

BOOKS

Coghlan, Brian, *Hofmannsthal's Festival Dramas: "Jedermann, Das Salzburger Grosse Welttheater, Der Turm,"* Cambridge University Press, 1964.

Daviau, Donald G., and Buelow, Georg J., *The "Ariadne auaf Naxos" of Hugo von Hofmannsthal and Richard Strauss,* University of North Carolina Press, 1975.

Erken, Gunther, "Hofmannsthal-Chronik: Beitrag zu einer Biographie," *Literaturwissenschaftliches Jahrbuch,* new series 3, 1962, pp. 239- 313.

Kovach, Thomas A., *Hofmannsthal and Symbolism: Art and Life in the Work of a Modern Poet,* Lang, 1985.

Norman, F., ed. *Hofmannsthal: Studies in Commemoration,* University of London, 1963.

Schwarz, Alfred, "The Purgation of the Will: Tragic Theater in the Christian Tradition." In *From Buchner to Beckett: Dramatic Theory and the Modes of Tragic Drama,* Ohio University Press, 1978, pp. 223-59.

Sondrup, Steven P., *Hofmannsthal and the French Symbolist Tradition,* Lang, 1976.

Twentieth-Century Literary Criticism, Volume 11, Gale, 1983.

Volke, Werner, *Hugo von Hofmannsthal in Selbstzeugnissen und Bilddokumenten,* Rowohlt, 1967.

Yuill, W. E., and Patricia Howe, editors, *Hugo von Hofmannsthal (1874- 1929): Commemorative Essays,* Institute of Germanic Studies, 1981.

PERIODICALS

Comparative Literature, winter, 1961, pp. 1-15.
Conoisseur, November, 1989, p. 64.
The Germanic Review, December, 1945, pp. 261-86.
German Life and Letters, October, 1948, pp. 1-12; 1951-52, pp. 255-68.
Life and Letters, October, 1964, pp. 15-24.
Modern Austrian Literature, 1972, pp. 14-29.
Modern Drama, May, 1959, pp. 17-28.
The Modern Language Review, April, 1979, pp. 341-48.
New Yorker, December 11, 1989, p. 134; July 8, 1991, p. 68.
Opera News, February 14, 1987, p. 14; March 12, 1988, p. 8; December 24, 1988, p. 38; December 9, 1989, p. 38; February 19, 1994, p. 38.
PMLA, March, 1940, pp. 253-65 *Wisconsin Studies in Contemporary Literature* 8, No. 4, 1967, pp. 484-504.*

* * *

HORAK, Jan-Christopher 1951-

PERSONAL: Born May 1, 1951, in Germany; son of Jaromir V. (a chemical engineer) and Giselle (a teacher; maiden name, Offermanns) Horak; married Marth F. Schirn (a writer), 1988; children: Gianna Mei Li. *Ethnicity:* "European." *Education:* University of Delaware, B.A.; Boston University, M.S., 1975; University of Muenster, Ph.D., 1984. *Avocational interests:* Skiing, swimming, travel.

ADDRESSES: Home—Wittelsbacherstrasse 14, D-80469 Munich, Germany. *Office*—St. Jakobsplatz 1, D-80331 Munich, Germany; fax 011-49-89-233-239-31. *E-mail*—101657.3365@compuserve.com.

CAREER: George Eastman House, Rochester, NY, senior curator, 1984-94; Munich Film Museum, Munich, Germany, director, 1994—. University of Rochester, professor of English, 1985-94; Hochschule Fernsehen/Film, lecturer in film, 1995—; consultant to International Design Center, Edgar Reitz Films, and U.S. Information Agency.

MEMBER: International Association for Audio-Visual Media and History, Gesellschaft fuer Filmwissenschaft, Society of Cinema Studies, American Association of Moving Image Archivists (president), NYSCA.

WRITINGS:

IN ENGLISH

(Translator from German) Ute Eskildsen, *Helmar Lerski: Metamorphosis Through Light,* Laterna Verlag (Freren, Germany), 1983.

The Dream Merchants: Making and Selling Films in Hollywood's Golden Age, George Eastman House (Rochester, NY), 1989.

Lovers of Cinema: The First American Film Avant-Garde, 1919-1945, University of Wisconsin Press (Madison, WI), 1995.

Making Images Move: Photographers and Avant-Garde Cinema, Smithsonian Institution Press (Washington, DC), 1996.

Editor (with Hans-Juergen Wulff and Karl-Dietmar Moeller) of the bilingual work, *Bibliography of Film Bibliographies/Bibliographie der Filmbibliographien,* published in New York City, 1987. Contributor of articles and reviews to magazines.

OTHER

(Editor with Eskildsen) *Film und Foto der zwanziger Jahre,* Verlag Gerd Hatje (Stuttgart, Germany), 1979.

(With Eskildsen) *Helmar Lerski: Lichtbildner, Fotographien und Filme, 1910-1947,* Museum Folkwang (Essen, Germany), 1982.

Fluchtpunkt Hollywood: Eine Dokumentation zur Filmemigration nach 1933, MAkS-Verlag (Muenster, Germany), 1984, revised edition, 1986.

Anti Nazi Filme der deutschsprachigen Emigration von Hollywood, MAkS-Verlag, 1984.

Contributor of more than a hundred articles and reviews to periodicals published in French, German, Italian, and Hebrew.

WORK IN PROGRESS: Research on German exile cinema in France and the United States.

SIDELIGHTS: Jan-Christopher Horak told *CA:* "I have been a film historian for over twenty years now. Initially I planned to become a film reviewer, then I slipped into film archive work while continuing to conduct research and to write. My motivation for writing is that I enjoy the process of conducting historical research. It is a giant detective game, which can end happily or sometimes without success. The writing of history, then, becomes an integral part of that process, because it is only in the act of formulating a text (that is, of creating a historical narrative or a critical dialogue) that the 'holes' become visible.

"Writing has changed drastically. When I first started out, I was still writing by hand, then typing, making manual corrections, and retyping various drafts until I got it right. I used notecards, and often spent hours copying information from books. Today, I type directly into the computer. I do print out a hard copy, because I've found that mistakes are harder to find in a computer. I still use hand-written notes, though, because, I lose any sense of the material, when it is only available to me on disk.

"I have so many influences that I find it hard to list them all. Some, like the late George Pratt or George Bluestone, were my teachers and mentors. Others, like Andrew Sarris, have been people I read and admired."

* * *

HORAN, Richard (Vincent, Jr.) 1957-

PERSONAL: Born August 21, 1957, in Stamford, CT; son of Richard Vincent (a government consultant) and Yolanda Anne (Vitti) Horan; married Mary Sue Buckley (a singer), July 5, 1986; children: Katherine Nicole, Evelyn Frances. *Ethnicity:* "Irish/Italian." *Education:* Attended Denison University, 1976-78; Boston University, B.A., 1981; University of Pittsburgh, M.A.T., 1988. *Politics:* "Environmentalist." *Religion:* "Teaching of Krishnamurti." *Avocational interests:* Jazz trumpet, running, fishing, birding.

ADDRESSES: Home—1704 Oak St., South Milwaukee, WI 53172. *Office*—St. John's Northwestern Military Academy, Delafield, WI 53018-1498.

CAREER: Professional boxer, Brockton, MA, 1978-81; Wall Street Institute, Parma, Italy, teacher of English as a second language, 1984-86; New England College, Henniker, NH, adjunct teacher of journalism and composition, 1989-92; New Hampshire College, Manchester, teacher of English as a second language, 1992; U.S. Department of Defense, Washington, DC, English teacher at dependents' schools in Belgium, 1992-94, and South Korea, 1994-96; St. John's Northwestern Military Academy, Delafield, WI, English teacher, 1996—. High school teacher in Newport, NH, 1988-89, and Merrimack, NH, 1992; also worked as assistant college baseball coach.

MEMBER: Phi Delta Kappa.

WRITINGS:

Life in the Rainbow (novel), Steerforth Press (South Royalton, VT), 1996.

Columnist for *Korea Times.* Contributor to magazines and newspapers.

SIDELIGHTS: Richard Horan told *CA:* "My primary motivation for writing is a desire to share with the world my ecstasy and passion—to inspire joy and fun. The greatest influences on my writing, in order of importance, include Henry Miller, J. Krishnamurti, Henry David Thoreau, Jack Kerouac, Nikolai Gogol, Fyodor Dostoyevsky, W. E. Hudson, *The Bowery Boys* (Leo Gorcey and Huntz Hall), and *The Honeymooners* (Jackie Gleason, Art Carney, Audrey Meadows).

"I let a story ferment in my head for years, then finally I write it. *Life in the Rainbow* was inspired by actual experience. My next work will be inspired by my very own ideal of a life well lived."

HOWARD, Philip K. 1948-

PERSONAL: Born October 24, 1948, in Atlanta, GA; son of John R (a Presbyterian minister) and Charlotte Stewart Howard; married Alexandra Cushing (an architectural historian), November 23, 1972; children: Olivia, Charlotte, Lily and Alexander (twins). *Education:* Yale University, B.A., 1970; University of Virginia Law School, J.D., 1974. *Religion:* Protestant.

ADDRESSES: Home—Manhattan, NY. *Office*—Howard, Darby, and Levin, 1330 Ave. of Americas, New York, NY 10019.

CAREER: Writer and attorney. Howard, Darby, and Levin (law firm), cofounding partner, 1983—; special adviser to SEC Task Force of Simplification, 1996; consultant to other government officials and agencies.

MEMBER: New York Bar Association, American Academy in Rome (trustee), Municipal Art Society of New York.

AWARDS, HONORS: Howard named to the *Village Voice* Honor Roll of New York's Heroes and Heroines, 1988; *The Death of Common Sense* ranked among the best books of 1995 by the *New York Times, Washington Post,* and *Washington Monthly.*

WRITINGS:

The Death of Common Sense: How Law Is Suffocating America, Random House (New York), 1994.

Author of introduction to *Common Sense Government,* by Al Gore. Contributor to periodicals, including the *New York Times* and the *Wall Street Journal.*

WORK IN PROGRESS: Two essays, one on "how public employment kills the spirit of trust within it," and the other on "the responsibility of judges to make value judgements in the courtroom."

SIDELIGHTS: Philip K. Howard is the author of *The Death of Common Sense: How Law Is Suffocating America,* a book that examines how overgrown regulatory laws result in bureaucratic lethargy, stifled growth, and loss of individual accountability. The author focuses on three problematic legal areas: specificity, which deals with codes for such things as safety and health; process, which involves the time-consuming systems set up for such actions as civic employee dismissals and various review boards; and

finally, rights, which defines the extent to which a person may go to secure their personal freedom and privileges—the wellspring from which myriad lawsuits flow. As Howard explains, each of these areas began bureaucratic life as a noble concept; somewhere along the way, however, the original intent was lost amid inept management and unnecessary emendation. Howard cites the example in which Nobel Peace Prize-winner Mother Teresa and her Missionaries of Charity order sought to establish a homeless shelter in the South Bronx of New York. After going through more than two years of excessive paperwork and renovations to meet various safety and health codes, the nuns were told that, because the building was four stories high, city regulations called for the installation of an elevator at the additional cost of $100,000. Already having spent more time and money than they anticipated, the order walked away from the project, deeming the cost of the elevator above and beyond their means. As Howard points out, in following an inflexible regulatory system to the letter, the city lost out on a worthwhile and beneficial institution. Explaining to *People*'s Lisa Kay Greissinger why such action occurs, Howard stated: "It's because we have a system in which rules dictate results that don't make sense and bureaucrats don't take responsibility for decisions. No one is allowed to think on the spot."

Critical reaction to *The Death of Common Sense* was generally positive, with most reviewers, if not wholeheartedly supporting Howard's methods, agreeing with his concern for regulatory overgrowth. Stating that the alternative to too many rules would be much worse, *New York Times Book Review* contributor Cass R. Sunstein averred that "Philip Howard points in most of the right directions—toward much less governmental focus on how people do things, much more attention on real-world results." Sunstein concluded: "When we think about 'reinventing government,' [Howard's ideas are] a good place to start." Praising the author's ability to clearly relate his agenda, Mary Ann Glendon wrote in *Commonweal:* "It is no mean achievement to portray a society suffocating in the toils of regulatory law without suffocating the non-specialist reader. Howard solves that problem nicely with abundant examples that will have most readers nodding their heads in agreement as they recall their own run-ins with the administrative state and its legal apparatus." Not all reviews favored the extent to which Howard goes to make his point and offer solutions, however. *New Yorker* contributor Calin Romano stated that Howard's calls for less law and regulation does not get to the root of the prob-

lem: "Less law has rarely led to better bureaucrats, and Howard's 'common sense' recommendation merely invites a state ruled by bureaucrat-despots. 'Thinking in extremes might be our national disease,' he says. *The Death of Common Sense* offers us a case in point." Agreeing that the book has its flaws, *Time*'s Richard Lacayo ultimately found praise for the volume, stating that "not just anybody can make a best seller out of the bone-dry topic of regulatory law."

BIOGRAPHICAL/CRITICAL SOURCES:

PERIODICALS

Commonweal, March 24, 1995, pp. 20-22.
New Yorker, March 13, 1995, pp. 103-5.
New York Times, January 19, 1995, p. C22.
New York Times Book Review, February 12, 1995, p. 12.
People, May 1, 1995, pp. 87-89.
Time, April 10, 1995, pp. 40-41.
Wall Street Journal, May 30, 1995.
Washington Monthly, January/February, 1995.

* * *

HOWARD, Vanessa 1955-

PERSONAL: Born in 1955, in Brooklyn, NY.

CAREER: Poet and fiction writer. Participant in the Fort Greene Writing Workshop.

WRITINGS:

A Screaming Whisper (poetry), photographs by J. Pinderhughes, Holt, 1972.

Work represented in anthologies, including *Soulscript, Voice of the Children,* and *Tales and Stories.*

SIDELIGHTS: Vanessa Howard was still a teenager when *A Screaming Whisper,* a book of forty-four poems, was published. Among the works collected in the volume is "Observations of a Subway Train," in which Howard perceives both the projected images and the true personalities of other passengers on the train. Despite Howard's youth, Margaret A. Dorsey, a critic for the *Library Journal,* commended the author for her "maturity of understanding." In the En-

glish *Journal* John W. Conner found that Howard's "observations are poignant and real. She is restless and impatient with the age-old restlessness and impatience of youth."

BIOGRAPHICAL/CRITICAL SOURCES:

PERIODICALS

English Journal, May, 1973, p. 829.
Library Journal, December 15, 1972, p. 4078.*

* * *

HOWARTH, Lesley 1952-

PERSONAL: Born December 29, 1952, in Bournemouth, England. *Education:* Attended art college.

ADDRESSES: Office—c/o Candlewick Press, 2067 Massachusetts Ave., Cambridge, MA 02140. *Agent*—The Agency, 24 Pottery Lane, Holland Park, London W11 4LZ, England.

CAREER: Writer. Worked at market gardens, a pottery, and a home for the elderly.

MEMBER: Writers Guild of Great Britain.

AWARDS, HONORS: Shortlisted for Whitbread Children's Book Award, 1993, and *Guardian* Children's Fiction Award, 1994, both for *The Flower King;* shortlisted for Writers' Guild Award, 1994; *Guardian* Children's Fiction Award, shortlisted for W. H. Smith Mind Boggling Books Award and *Young Telegraph* Book Award, all 1995, all for *MapHead;* Smarties Book Prize, 9-11 category, 1995, for *Weather Eye.*

WRITINGS:

CHILDREN'S BOOKS

The Flower King, Walker Books (London, England), 1993.
MapHead, Walker Books, 1994.
Weather Eye, Walker Books, 1995. *The Pits,* Walker Books, 1996.
Fort Biscuit, Walker Books, 1996.

WORK IN PROGRESS: MapHead 2.

SIDELIGHTS: Lesley Howarth told *CA:* "My primary motivation for writing is to have fun! Loads of people have influenced me, but my big heroes are Robert Louis Stevenson, Raymond Carver, Alan Bennett, Paul Jennings, and the authors of all the classic books I read as a child, the 'Penguin Modern Poets,' et cetera.

"My writing process is simple. I get excited about an idea, read a lot (but not too much) around it, then sit down in front of my word processor and begin. I set up the most exciting situation and the most believable, if quirky, characters that I can, then I let 'em roll and see what happens. Then I have to keep control over the 'shape' of the story as it unfolds. I am never entirely sure it will all work out until I am almost through, but that's the excitement of it!

"What inspires me to write? It is the sheer excitement of reaching out to touch someone else with what I am excited about."

* * *

HUESTON, Frederick M. 1953-

PERSONAL: Born February 18, 1953, in Dover, NJ; married; wife's name, Christine E., April 21, 1974. *Education:* University of Central Florida, B.S., 1981.

ADDRESSES: Home—1053 Portsmouth Ln., Winter Park, FL 32792. *Office*—National Training Center for Stone and Masonry Trades, 941 Long Dale Ave., Longwood, FL 32750; fax 407-898-0370. *E-mail*—fhueston@aol.com.

CAREER: National Training Center for Stone and Masonry Trades, Longwood, FL, director, 1986—.

MEMBER: Marble Institute of America, Association for Preservation Technology.

WRITINGS:

Stain Removal Guide for Stone, BNP Publishing, 1995.
Marble and Tile: The Selection and Care of Stone and Tile Surfaces, NTC Publishing (Orlando, FL), 1996.

Contributor to magazines.

WORK IN PROGRESS: Marketing for the Service Business.

SIDELIGHTS: Frederick M. Hueston told *CA:* "I enjoy writing and producing information that will help people learn. The marble and tile business has little educational material to offer. I thought it was time to provide this information, and I am an expert in the field, so I began writing."

* * *

HUGHES, Tracy
See BLACKSTOCK, Terri

* * *

HUNCKE, Herbert E(dwin) 1915-1996

OBITUARY NOTICE—See index for *CA* sketch: Name rhymes with "junkie"; born January 9, 1915, in Greenfield, MA; died of congestive heart failure, August 8, 1996, in New York, NY. Hustler and writer. Friend to writers of the Beat Generation during the 1950s, Huncke helped coin the movement's name and was later featured in books by Jack Kerouac, Allen Ginsberg, William S. Burroughs, and others. Huncke had left home as a teenager and claimed that he began experimenting with drugs at the age of twelve. Within four years, he had begun hustling. Throughout his life, he was involved in a variety of thefts and spent more than a decade in prison. Despite his pursuits, he was befriended by those in what was to become the Beat literary movement, and he became a writer himself. Some critics praised his work for its sheer honesty and its conversational style. Some of his work was written in the men's room of the New York subway. Huncke penned several books, including *Huncke's Journal, Elsie John and Joey Martinez, The Evening Sun Turned Crimson, A Day in the Life: Tales from the Lower East: An Anthology of Writings and Art from the Lower East Side,* and *Guilty of Everything.* Huncke engaged in a lecture tour and taught at Ginsberg's poetry school, Naropa Institute, although he received much of his financial support from friends.

OBITUARIES AND OTHER SOURCES:

BOOKS

Writers Directory, St. James Press, 1995.

PERIODICALS

New York Times, August 9, 1996, p. B7.
Washington Post, August 10, 1996, p. B4.

* * *

HYDE, Douglas (Arnold) 1911-1996

OBITUARY NOTICE—See index for *CA* sketch: Born
April 8, 1911, in Worthing, Sussex, England; died
September 19, 1996. British political activist, editor
and author. Whether he was editing the Communist
Daily Worker, or professing his newfound Roman
Catholic faith, Hyde never ended his fight for social
justice. His books include 1950's *I Believed,* the 1966
novel, *God's Bandit: The Story of Don Orione, "Fa-
ther of the Poor,"* and 1972's *Communism Today.*
Hyde joined the Communist Party before he was 18
and was a reporter and news editor for the *Daily
Worker* in London. But the Stalinist crackdowns in
Europe after World War II soured Hyde on the Com-
munist Party and he resigned. He started practicing as
a Roman Catholic soon after and wrote for the *Catho-
lic Herald.* He split with the church in his later years,
but continued his activism, marching in demonstra-
tions against nuclear weapons.

OBITUARIES AND OTHER SOURCES:

PERIODICALS

Times (London), October 3, 1996, p. 23.

I-J

IGNATIEV, Noel 1940-

PERSONAL: Born December 27, 1940, in Philadelphia, PA; son of Irv (a newspaper carrier) and Carrier (a homemaker; maiden name, Glass) Ignatiev; children: Rachel, John Henry. *Education:* Attended Penn State University; received Ph.D. from Harvard. *Politics:* Radical. *Religion:* "None."

ADDRESSES: Office—Race Traitor, Box 603, Cambridge, MA 02140.

CAREER: Laborer, machinist, maintenance worker, and college instructor. Writer.

WRITINGS:

How the Irish Became White, Routledge (New York), 1995.
(With John Garvey) *Race Traitor,* Routledge, 1996.

Also author of numerous articles and pamphlets.

WORK IN PROGRESS: Manifesto of the New Abolitionism with John Garvey.

SIDELIGHTS: Noel Ignatiev's first book, *How the Irish Became White,* is a study of the change in status of Irish immigrants to the United States in the early 1800s. While the Irish were initially discriminated against, Ignatiev asserts that they became "white" themselves in order to improve their position in a competitive society. The Irish gained political power through voting solidarity and ousted blacks, sometimes using violence, out of shared neighborhoods and from widely held lower-class jobs. "Ignatiev writes perceptive capsule biographies of several Irish-American public figures, editors and/or officeholders, who gradually rejected the idea that their ethnic group and blacks had anything in common," remarked Michael Kazin of the *Washington Post Book World.* "Unfortunately, Ignatiev is far better at describing the political history of Irish Americans in the antebellum United States than at providing explicit answers to such questions" as how poor Irish immigrants quickly adopted the "whiteness" of the native-born Americans and why supporters of an independent Ireland could support the slavery of blacks in the United States. Historian Nell Irvin Painter, also writing in the *Washington Post Book World,* called *How the Irish Became White* "probably the most interesting history book of 1995."

As co-editor of the abolitionist magazine *Race Traitor,* activist Ignatiev maintains that the only race is the human race and that race as we know it is social concept that traps people in roles and stereotypes based on their skin color. "It is our contention that there are a lot of people out there who are nominally white and not quite satisfied with that definition of themselves and what it means and are looking for various kinds of alternatives," Ignatiev told Clarence Page of the *Chicago Tribune.* "The irony is that the future of each race is so tied to the other, that the feuding and bitterness that erupts between blacks and whites is of a type that can only erupt in a family quarrel," he added. Thus Ignatiev asserts that whites should become traitors to their race, which in an *Utne Reader* reprint he defined as "someone who is anominally classified as white, but who defies the rules of whiteness so flagrantly as to jeopardize his or her ability to draw upon the privileges of the white

skin." According to Ignatiev, through race treason a new, liberated humanity can emerge.

BIOGRAPHICAL/CRITICAL SOURCES:

PERIODICALS

Chicago Tribune, March 26, 1995, p. 3.
Library Journal, September 1, 1995, p. 189.
Publishers Weekly, August 14, 1995, p. 67.
Utne Reader, November-December, 1994, pp. 82-86.
Washington Post Book World, September 24, 1995, pp. 3, 6.

* * *

IMLAH, Mick 1956-

PERSONAL: Born in 1956. *Education:* Attended Magdalen College, Oxford University.

ADDRESSES: Agent—Chatto and Windus, 20 Vauxhall Bridge Rd., London SW1V 2SA, England.

CAREER: Oxford Poetry, founding editor, 1983; *Poetry Review,* editor, 1983-86; Chatto and Windus, poetry editor, 1989-93.

WRITINGS:

POETRY

The Zoologist's Bath and Other Adventures, Sycamore Press (Oxford, England), 1982.
Birthmarks, Chatto and Windus (London, England), 1988.

* * *

INCLAN, Ramon (Maria) del Valle
 See VALLE-INCLAN, Ramon (Maria) del

* * *

ISHIKAWA, Hakuhin
 See ISHIKAWA, Takuboku

ISHIKAWA, Takuboku 1886(?)-1912
(Hakuhin Ishikawa)

PERSONAL: Born Hajime Ishikawa, February 20, 1886 (some sources say 1885), in Hinoto Village, Iwate Prefecture, Japan; died of tuberculosis, April 13, 1912, in Tokyo, Japan; son of a Zen Buddhist priest; married, 1905.

CAREER: Worked as an assistant teacher and reporter; held a variety of jobs with print shops and newspapers; poet and essayist.

WRITINGS:

Akagore (poetry; title means "Aspiration"), [Japan], 1905.
Choei (novel; title means "Shadow of a Bird"), [Japan], 1908.
Romaji nikki (diary), 1909, published in English as *The Romaji Diary,* translation by Sanford Goldstein and Seishi Shinoda published with *Sad Toys,* Tuttle, 1985.
Ichiaku no suna (poetry), 1910, translation by Shio Sakanishi published as *A Handful of Sand,* Marshall Jones, 1934.
Kanashiki gangu (poetry), 1912, published in English as *Sad Toys,* translation by Sanford Goldstein and Seishi Shinoda published as *Sad Toys,* Purdue University Press, 1977, published with *The Romaji Diary,* Tuttle, 1985.
Yosuko to fue (poetry), [Japan], 1912.
Yobiko to kuchibue (poetry; title means "Piping and Whistling"), [Japan], 1913.
Takuboku nikki (diary; title means "Takuboku's Diary"), [Japan], 1948-49.
The Poetry of Ishikawa Takuboku, translation by H. H. Honda, Hokuseido Press, 1959.
From Yumi-cho: Poems to Eat, translation by Carl Sesar, woodcut illustrations by M. Kuwata, Kodansha International, 1966, translation by Sesar also published as *Poems to Eat,* Begos and Rosenberg, 1991.
Takuboku zenshu, 8 vols. (poetry, novels, short stories, criticism, and essays), [Japan], 1967-68.

Early poetry published in the poetry magazine *Myojo.* Some writings have appeared under the pseudonym Hakuhin Ishikawa.

SIDELIGHTS: Ishikawa Takuboku is acknowledged to be one of the most significant poets in modern Japanese literature. His most famous works fuse tanka form, a classic Japanese verse structure consisting of

thirty-one syllables, with intellectual and autobiographical subject matter that was not previously considered acceptable for such a traditional poetic form. For this innovation, Takuboku is credited with revitalizing Japanese poetry and strongly influencing the work of many twentieth-century Japanese poets.

Takuboku was born in rural northern Japan, the only son of a Zen priest who broke his vows and secretly married. Although his parents were quite poor, they were committed to providing Takuboku with the finest education they could afford. As a young student, Takuboku showed intellectual and literary ability. His aspirations to become a poet grew particularly strong in his adolescence. As an apprentice poet, Takuboku greatly admired the works of Tekkan Yosano and the romantic school to which Yosano belonged. He persistently submitted poems to Yosano's literary journal, *Myojo,* but met with no success until 1902, when *Myojo* finally accepted one of Takuboku's poems for publication. With renewed confidence and conviction in his future as a poet, Takuboku quit school and moved to Tokyo where he could study under Yosano. In 1905 he published his first volume of poetry, *Akagore,* which was primarily composed of longer lyrical poems written in the "shintai-shi" ("new style"), a form derived from the well-established Western models of poetry found in an 1882 anthology that had considerable impact on Japanese writers of the day. Unimpressed with Takuboku's tanka, Yosano had encouraged him to write poetry in the shintai-shi form, because it was in this mode that he thought Takuboku's poetic gifts would be best displayed. *Akagore* received warm, enthusiastic praise, but it contained little of the fierce individual voice Takuboku would develop a few years later. After the publication of *Akagore,* Takuboku married a woman he had known since childhood. These few months in 1905 marked the happiest and most fulfilling time in his life.

In 1906, Takuboku's father disappeared after being dismissed from the Hotoko Temple for misuse of temple funds, and upon his son devolved the responsibility of supporting the family. Takuboku left Tokyo and accepted a teaching position in a small village, but his meager income could not adequately provide for a family of five, which included his wife and child, his mother, and an ailing older sister. They all lived close to starvation and steadily declined in health. Unable to cope with these pressures, Takuboku left his teaching post after one year and traveled around Japan, during which time he worked at a variety of jobs, mostly with newspapers and print

shops, and continued to send money back to his family. At this time, he suffered from strong internal conflicts regarding his previous romantic perceptions of poetry and an emerging inclination toward naturalism, a movement which then exerted a strong influence on Japanese fiction writers. Takuboku recorded his perceptions of his gravitation toward naturalism, as well as many painful discoveries regarding his own character, in a notebook which is known as *Romaji nikki (The Romaji Diary)* because it was written in a westernized system of transliteration. Some critics consider *The Romaji Diary* an autobiographical Naturalistic novel, in which Takuboku depicts himself heroically struggling with ambition, self-doubt, and the stifling responsibilities life has thrust upon him. For the next five years, Takuboku attempted to write fiction, at which he was largely unsuccessful, and experimented with a new type of poetry which he believed more earnest and vital than the shintai-shi verse he had previously written. In this new poetry he used the verbally spare and precise tanka form to describe the everyday events and impressions that he now believed were essential subjects for poetry. This new verse was published in a volume entitled *Ichiaku no suna (A Handful of Sand).* During the last two years of his life, Takuboku continued to work when circumstances and his health permitted. Over a span of approximately eighteen months his newborn child died, his wife contracted tuberculosis, and he was operated on for a severe case of peritonitis. Takuboku's aged and ailing mother nursed the family until she too collapsed and died of tuberculosis. Close to death, Takuboku entrusted his last collection of poems, *Kanashiki gangu (Sad Toys),* to his friend Toki Zemmaro, a poet and scholar who promised to find a publisher for it. A publisher accepted the manuscript and gave Zemmaro a small advance. Takuboku died one week later of tuberculosis and was cremated in a pauper's funeral.

Although Takuboku's poetic career lasted only nine years, it developed rapidly and passed through three distinctive phases: romanticism, naturalism, and a period in which he produced politically conscious poetry. His first volume of poems, *Akagore,* contains the best examples of Takuboku's writing during his romantic period. The poems in *Akagore,* which have a restrained but musical language and a romantic belief in heightened individualism and spiritual awareness, were highly praised by the Tokyo literati. As his life became increasingly filled with poverty and hardship, Takuboku came to believe that poetry, if it was to have lasting meaning and truth, must confront and include these less sublime facts of life.

This marks the beginning of the naturalistic phase of his career, the period in which he would introduce new thematic possibilities of form and content to Japanese poetry. During this time, Takuboku gained confidence in his use of the tanka form, which became the exclusive mode of his second volume, *A Handful of Sand,* a highly original work that combines the formal simplicity of classic Japanese poetry with the pathos of life in the modern world. As Shio Sakanishi remarked of Takuboku in his introduction to this work: "Lifting it from anarchy and stiltedness, [he] again restored poetry to the human heart, extended its scope, and made language his willing servant." The following tanka, one of the most famous in *A Handful of Sand,* may serve to illustrate the unconventional nature of poetic expression achieved by Takuboku in this volume: "My sister pitied / my eyes that burned / with insatiable / craving for knowledge / she thought I must be in love." The ironic and intellectual nature of such verse revolutionized tanka, which had been largely devoted to pastoral subject matter. *Sad Toys,* Takuboku's last volume, exhibits his growing social and political awareness. In 1909 he had written a serialized essay, entitled "Poems to Eat," which summarized his emerging conceptions of the highest intentions of poetry. In Takuboku's own words true poetry means "poems written without putting any distance from actual life. They are not delicacies or dainty dishes, but food indispensible for us in our daily meals." The tanka in *Sad Toys* mix colloquial language with classical form, and it is in this volume that most critics feel that Takuboku achieves the artistic and socialistic goals he had sought to attain: the removal of Japanese poetry from its elitist pedestal and its distribution to the masses.

Although Takuboku wrote fiction and produced highly regarded and influential criticism, it is through his poetry that his literary reputation was established and endures. Considered one of the first modern voices in Japanese poetry, he brought to it unprecedented personalism and passion that has had a lasting impact on the poets who have succeeded him. His direct vision and spare but evocative language has also made his work extremely appealing to Western readers.

BIOGRAPHICAL/CRITICAL SOURCES:

BOOKS

Biographical Dictionary of Japanese Literature, International Society for Educational Information, 1976.

Cassell's Encyclopedia of World Literature, revised edition, Morrow, 1973.

Hijiya, Yukihito, *Ishikawa Takuboku,* Twayne, 1979.

Sakanishi, Shio, introduction to *A Handful of Sand,* Marshall Jones, 1934.

Takamine, Hiroshi, *A Sad Toy: A Unique and Popular Japanese Poet, Takuboku's Life and His Poems,* Tokyo News Service, 1962.*

* * *

IVERSON, Eric
 See TURTLEDOVE, Harry (Norman)

* * *

JABAVU, Davidson Don Tengo 1885-1959

PERSONAL: Born October 20, 1885, in Healdtown, South Africa; died of cancer, 1959; buried in Middlerift, Cape Province, South Africa; son of John Tengo and Elda (Sakuba) Jabavu; married Florence Nolwandle Tandiswa, September 2, 1916 (died 1951); children: Helen Nontan-o, Alexandra Nothemba, Tengo Max. *Education:* University of London, B.A. (with honors), 1912; Birmingham University (England), teacher's degree, 1916. *Religion:* Wesleyan Methodist. *Advocational interests:* Playing the piano and violin, singing.

CAREER: Native College at Fort Hare (now Fort Hare University College), South Africa, lecturer, 1916-42, professor of Bantu languages, Latin, English, and history, 1942-46, secretary of College Senate. *Imvo zabantsundu* ("Opinion of the Blacks," a newspaper founded by his father), co-editor and co-publisher, beginning in 1921. Organized the Cape African Teachers' Association, South African Federation of Native Teachers, Native Farmers' Association, and Cape Native Voters' Association; member of the Native Conferences sponsored by the Government, 1920-30; called the first All-African Convention, 1935, president, 1935-48; worked with Joint Councils of Europeans and Natives. South African Institute of Race Relations, vice-president, 1932-59. Established All-African Insurance Company, 1959.

AWARDS, HONORS: Honorary Ph.D., Rhodes University, 1946; medal created in his honor, Royal African Society, 1946; Freedom of New Brighton

award, May, 1954; a memorial stone was placed on Jabavu's grave, 1961.

WRITINGS:

POETRY

Izithuko (title means "Abuses"), Lovedale Press, 1954.

Izidungulwana (title means "Twigs"), Maskew Miller, c. 1960.

NONFICTION

The Black Problem, Lovedale Press, 1920, second edition, 1921.

Bantu Literature, Lovedale Press, 1921.

The Life of John Tengo Jabavu, Lovedale Press, 1922.

What Methodism Has Done for the Natives, Lovedale Press, 1923.

Incwadi Yaba Limi (title means "On Agriculture"), Lovedale Press, 1923.

The Segregation Fallacy, Lovedale Press, 1928.

E-Jerusalem (title means "To Jerusalem"), Lovedale Press, 1928.

(Editor) Richard Tainton Kawa, *I-bali lama Mfengu* (title means "The Story of the Mfengu People"), Lovedale Press, 1929.

(Editor) Chief Shadrach Fuba Zibi, *U'Kayakhulu,* Lovedale Press, 1930.

"Native Disabilities" in South Africa, Lovedale Press, 1932.

E-Amerika (title means "To America"), Lovedale Press, 1932.

The Influence of English on Bantu Literature, Lovedale Press, 1943.

E-Indiya nase-East Africa (title means "To India and East Africa"), Lovedale Press, 1951.

OTHER

Contributor to *International Review of Missions* (London).

BIOGRAPHICAL/CRITICAL SOURCES:

BOOKS

Herdeck, Donald E., *African Authors: A Companion to Black African Writing,* Volume 1: *1300-1973,* Black Orpheus Press, 1973.

Higgs, Catherine, *The Ghost of Equality: the Public Lives of D. D. T. Jabavu of South Africa, 1885-1959,* University Press (Athens, OH), 1996.*

* * *

JAMES, Luther 1928-

PERSONAL: Born August 8, 1928, in New York, NY; son of Joseph and Alice James; married Thelma (divorced); married Marguerite Brisby; children: (first marriage) Robin, Julian. *Education:* Attended Dramatic Workshop of the New School for Social Research, 1951.

ADDRESSES: Home—1308 South New Hampshire, Los Angeles, CA 90006. *Office*—Department of Theatre, University of California, San Diego, 9500 Gilman Rd., La Jolla, CA 92093.

CAREER: Affiliated with Comet Productions, 1950s; Luther James Theatre Workshop, New York City, teacher, 1958-68; Arena Productions, Metro-Goldwyn-Mayer (MGM), Culver City, CA, assistant to supervising producer, 1965-66; CBS-TV, Los Angeles, CA, executive producer, 1966-68; Negro Ensemble Company, New York City, instructor, 1968-69; WGBH-TV, Boston, MA, producer of *On Being Black,* 1968-70; TV writer and director, 1970-75. Teacher of drama, Portland State University, California State University, Los Angeles, and California State University, Northridge, 1971-73; University of California San Diego Department of Theatre, associate professor, 1975—. Director of plays, Oregon Shakespeare Festival, 1980—; theater editor, *Crisis* magazine, 1986—.

MEMBER: Directors Guild of America, Writers Guild of America.

AWARDS, HONORS: Recipient of John Hay Whitney fellowship, 1959-60; Ford Foundation fellowship, 1962.

WRITINGS:

Liberty (one-act play; telecast early 1970s), published in *Interactions,* Altshuler, 1972.

JAMES, Rebecca
 See ELWARD, James (Joseph)

* * *

JAMISON, Bill 1942-

PERSONAL: Born March 7, 1942, in Oklahoma; son of Braxton and Lois (Cleveland) Jamison; married Cheryl Alters (a writer), 1985; children: Heather Jamison Neale. *Education:* University of North Texas, B.A., 1964; doctoral study at University of Kansas, 1967.

ADDRESSES: Office—P.O. Box 1804, Santa Fe, NM 87504. *E-mail*—B_C_Jamison@MSN.com. *Agent*—Doe Coover, Doe Coover Agency, 58 Sagamore Ave., Medford, MA 02155.

CAREER: Writer.

AWARDS, HONORS: James Beard Awards, 1994, for *Smoke and Spice,* and 1995, for *The Border Cookbook: Authentic Home Cooking from the American Southwest and Northern Mexico.*

WRITINGS:

WITH WIFE, CHERYL ALTERS JAMISON

The Rancho de Chimayo Cookbook: The Traditional Cooking of New Mexico, Harvard Common (Boston, MA), 1991.
Texas Home Cooking, Harvard Common, 1993.
Smoke and Spice, Harvard Common, 1994.
The Border Cookbook: Authentic Home Cooking from the American Southwest and Northern Mexico, Harvard Common, 1995.
Best Places to Stay in Mexico, 3rd edition, Houghton (Boston), 1995.
Best Places to Stay in Hawaii, 3rd edition, Houghton, 1995.
Sublime Smoke: Bold New Flavors Inspired by the Old Art of Barbecue, Harvard Common, 1996.
The Insider's Guide to Santa Fe, Taos, and Albuquerque, 4th edition, Harvard Common, 1996.
Best Places to Stay in the Caribbean, 4th edition, Houghton, 1996.

WORK IN PROGRESS: A Good Times Guide to American Grilling, with Cheryl Alters Jamison, publication by Harvard Common expected in 1998.

* * *

JAMISON, Cheryl Alters 1953-

PERSONAL: Born June 17, 1953, in Illinois; daughter of Marcellus M. and Betty E. Alters; married Bill Jamison (a writer), 1985; children: Heather Jamison Neale (stepdaughter). *Education:* Illinois State University, B.S., 1975; University of Illinois at Springfield, M.A., 1977.

ADDRESSES: Office—P.O. Box 1804, Santa Fe, NM 87504. *E-mail*—B_C_Jamison@MSN.com. *Agent*—Doe Coover, Doe Coover Agency, 58 Sagamore Ave., Medford, MA 02155.

CAREER: Writer.

AWARDS, HONORS: James Beard Awards, 1994, for *Smoke and Spice,* and 1995, for *The Border Cookbook: Authentic Home Cooking from the American Southwest and Northern Mexico.*

WRITINGS:

WITH HUSBAND, BILL JAMISON

The Rancho de Chimayo Cookbook: The Traditional Cooking of New Mexico, Harvard Common (Boston, MA), 1991.
Texas Home Cooking, Harvard Common, 1993.
Smoke and Spice, Harvard Common, 1994.
The Border Cookbook: Authentic Home Cooking from the American Southwest and Northern Mexico, Harvard Common, 1995.
Best Places to Stay in Mexico, 3rd ed., Houghton (Boston), 1995.
Best Places to Stay in Hawaii, 3rd ed., Houghton, 1995.
Sublime Smoke: Bold New Flavors Inspired by the Old Art of Barbecue, Harvard Common, 1996.
The Insider's Guide to Santa Fe, Taos, and Albuquerque, 4th edition, Harvard Common, 1996.
Best Places to Stay in the Caribbean, 4th edition, Houghton, 1996.

WORK IN PROGRESS: A Good Times Guide to American Grilling, with Bill Jamison, publication by Harvard Common expected in 1998.

JAMISON, Kay Redfield

PERSONAL: Daughter of a meteorologist and a teacher; married second husband, Richard Wyatt (a medical researcher). *Education:* University of California, Los Angeles, Ph.D.

ADDRESSES: Home—Washington, DC. *Office*—School of Psychiatry and Behavioral Sciences, 4-181 Meyer Hospital, Johns Hopkins University, Baltimore, MD 21218. *Agent*—c/o Alfred A. Knopf, 201 E. 50th St., New York, NY 10022.

CAREER: Worked at University of California, Los Angeles; Johns Hopkins University, Baltimore, MD, associate professor of psychiatry; writer.

WRITINGS:

(With Bruce L. Baker and Michael J. Goldstein) *Abnormal Psychology: Experiences, Origins, and Interventions,* Little, Brown (Boston, MA), 1980.
(With Frederick K. Goodwin) *Manic-Depressive Illness,* Oxford University Press (New York), 1990.
Touched with Fire: Manic-Depressive Illness and the Creative Temperament, Free Press (New York), 1993.
An Unquiet Mind (memoir), Knopf (New York), 1995.

SIDELIGHTS: Kay Redfield Jamison is a psychologist and educator who is considered an authority on manic-depressive illness. Her 1990 volume *Manic-Depressive Illness,* compiled with Frederick K. Goodwin, is regarded as a key contribution to the study of manic-depressive illness, a biochemical disorder which results in periods of mania alternating with bouts of depression. *Manic-Depressive Illness* encompasses a range of issues and subjects, including diagnosis, clinical studies, psychological ramifications, and pathophysiological elements. Larry S. Goldman, reviewing *Manic-Depressive Illness* in the *New England Journal of Medicine,* acknowledged Jamison and Goodwin as "two highly regarded senior clinicians and researchers" and proclaimed their book "thorough and most readable." Goldman concluded, "It is hard to imagine a clinician working with patients with the illness . . . or a researcher in any part of the field of mood disorders who should not have this tour de force available."

In 1993 Jamison followed *Manic-Depressive Illness* with *Touched with Fire: Manic-Depressive Illness and the Creative Temperament,* a detailed account of the ties between artistic sensibilities and manic-depressive illness. While conceding that not all artists are manic-depressive, and that not all manic-depressives are artists, Jamison argues that a significant association exists between the artistic and manic-depressive temperaments. There is, for example, a high rate of suicide among both types. In her analysis, Jamison incorporates scientific-medical data, including diagnostic methods and genetic information, and she applies this data to a host of creative individuals, including the composer Robert Schumann, the painter Vincent Van Gogh, and such American writers as Ernest Hemingway, John Berryman, and Hart Crane. Jamison notes that many of the creative individuals considered in *Touched with Fire* had little recourse to any suitable psycho-medical care.

Since its appearance in 1993, *Touched with Fire* has been praised as a detailed and compelling study. "This book," reported Myrna M. Weissman in *Contemporary Psychology,* "provides information about the experience of manic depressive illness from unique and creative individuals, factual information about our current scientific understanding, and a forum for some 'very careful thought.'" She called Jamison "a scientifically knowledgeable and remarkable author." Another reviewer, Hugh Freeman, wrote in *Nature* that *Touched with Fire* constituted "an important work that should provoke some serious rethinking in several corners of academe," while Larry S. Goldman, in his *New England Journal of Medicine* appraisal, deemed Jamison's book "clear and enjoyable."

In 1995, Jamison's *An Unquiet Mind,* a memoir of her own experiences with manic depression, was published. In this volume Jamison recounts her extreme moodiness as a child and relates her first, exhilarating experience of mania when she was in her mid-teens. She notes that mania and depression sometimes exist simultaneously. It is during these periods, when the depths of despair are coupled with the impulsiveness characteristic of mania, that sufferers, according to Jamison, are more likely to consider suicide. Jamison discloses in *An Unquiet Mind* that she attempted to take her own life, and she credits psychotherapy with helping her realize greater acceptance and stability. *Time* reviewer Anastasia Toufexis hailed *An Unquiet Mind* as "a rare and insightful view of mental illness from inside the mind of a trained specialist." Sharon O'Brien, writing in the *New York Times Book Review,* also responded favorably, lauding Jamison's book as "an invaluable memoir of

manic depression, at once medically knowledgeable, deeply human and beautifully written."

BIOGRAPHICAL/CRITICAL SOURCES:

PERIODICALS

Atlantic Monthly, April, 1993, p. 133.
Contemporary Psychology, May, 1994, pp. 469-70.
Los Angeles Times Book Review, August 1, 1993, p. 6.
Nature, April 15, 1993, pp. 666-67.
New England Journal of Medicine, March 14, 1991, pp. 778-79; October 7, 1993, pp. 1133-34.
New York Times Book Review, October 1, 1995, pp. 16-18.
Time, September 11, 1995, p. 83.
Washington Post, May 6, 1993, p. D2.*

* * *

JARRY, Alfred 1873-1907

PERSONAL: Born September 8, 1873, in Laval, France; died from complications due to alcoholism and use of ether, November 1, 1907, in Paris, France; son of Anselme (a traveling merchant) and Caroline (Quernest) Jarry. *Education:* Lycee in Rennes, 1888-91; Lycee Henri IV, Paris, 1891-93.

CAREER: Co-founder, with Remy de Goncourt, and co-director of journal *L'Ymagier,* 1894-95; founder and publisher, *Perhinderion,* 1896; Theatre de l'Oeuvre, assistant to director, 1896; columnist, *La Revue Blanche,* 1900-03.

WRITINGS:

Les minutes de sable memorial, suivies de Cesar-Antechrist (prose and poetry), [France], 1894, Fasquelle editeurs (Paris), 1932.
Cesar-Antechrist (drama), [France], 1895; published as *Caesar Antichrist,* 1971.
Ubu roi (drama; first produced at the Theatre de l'Oeuvre in Paris, 1896), [France], 1896; published in England as *Ubu Roi; Drama in Five Acts,* translated by Barbara Wright, Gaberbocchus Press (London) 1951; published in the United States as *King Turd,* translated by Beverley Keaith and G. Legman, Boar's Head

Books (New York), 1953; translated by David Copelin, Pulp Press (Vancouver, British Columbia, Canada), 1977.
Messaline (novel), [France], 1900; published as *The Garden of Priapus,* translated by Louis Colman, illustrated by Arthur Zaidenberg, Blackhawk Press, 1936; as *Messalina: A Novel of Imperial Rome,* Atlas (London), 1985.
Ubu enchaine (drama), [France], 1900, reissued as *Ubu enchaine; suivi de Ubu sur la butte, des Paralipomenes, et d'Essais sur le theatre,* Fasquelle editeurs, 1938; published in England as *Ubu Enchained*), 1968.
Le surmale, roman moderne (novel), [France], 1902; translated from the French by Barbara Wright as *The Supermale: A Modern Novel,* Cape (London), 1968, translated by Wright and Ralph Gladstone, New Directions (New York), 1977.
Gestes et opinions du Docteur Faustroll, pataphysicien (novel), [France], 1911; published as *Exploits and Opinions of Doctor Faustroll, Pataphysician,* 1965.
L'amour absolu, avec des souvenirs du docteur Saltas et des notes de Charlotte Jarry, Les Marges, M. Seheur (Paris), 1932.
La dragonne, Gallimard (Paris), 1943.
Ubu cocu (drama), [France], 1944; published as *Turd Cuckolded,* 1953; published in England as *Ubu Cuckolded,* 1968.
Oeuvres poetiques complete, Gallimard, 1945.
Choix de textes, Guilde du livre (Lausanne), 1946.
L'Autre Alceste: Drame en cinq recits, [Paris], 1947.
Oeuvres completes, Editions du Livre (Monte Carlo), 1948, Schoenhof's Foreign Books, 1987.
La revanche de la nuit; poemes retrouves, Mercure de France (Paris), 1949.
L'objet aime, pastorale en un acte, Arcanes (Paris), 1953.
L'ouverture de la peche, College de pataphysique, 1953.
Le futur malgre lui, College de pataphysique (Paris), 1954.
Les jours et les nuits, Mercure de France, 1964; Schoenhof's Foreign Books, 1981; translated as *Days and Nights: Novel of a Deserter* (includes "The Other Alcestis"), Atlas (London), 1989.
Saint-Brieuc des Choux, Mercure de France, 1964.
Selected Works, edited by Roger Shattuck and Simon Watson Taylor, Methuen (London), 1965, Grove Press (New York), 1965.
The Ubu Plays (includes *Ubu Roi, Ubu Cuckolded,* and *Ubu Enchained,* edited and introduced by Simon Watson Taylor, Methuen, 1968, Grove Press (New York), 1988.

La Chandelle verte, Le Livre de poche (Paris), 1969.

Siloques, superloques, soliloques et interloques de pataphysique, Le Castor Astral, 1992.

Also author of the essay "De l'inutilite du theatre au theatre," (title means "Of the Futility of the 'Theatrical' in the Theater"), published in journal *Mercure de France,* and also in *Selected Works, 1965.*

SIDELIGHTS: Alfred Jarry's plays are forerunners of the theater of the absurd of Beckett, Artaud, and Ionesco and influenced the dadaists and surrealists as well. *Ubu roi* (which has been translated as *King Turd*) is Jarry's most famous and influential work. Regarded by some critics as combining elements from *Hamlet, Macbeth,* and *King Lear, Ubu roi* essentially eliminates all dramatic action and uses scatological humor and farcical situations to comment on art, literature, politics, and current events.

A brilliant student, Jarry won prizes in foreign languages and science as a youth. Even at this early age, however, the rebelliousness and caustic wit that would mark his life and career were already apparent. With his schoolmates, Jarry staged bawdy lampoons of Felix Hebert, his physics teacher, who he regarded as incompetent and physically repulsive. Jarry remained obsessed with the figure of Hebert for the rest of his life, using him as the model for the title character of *Ubu roi.* During his later years, which were marked by bizarre behavior, drug and alcohol abuse, and ill health, Jarry even began to affect the mannerisms of Ubu, speaking in a droning monotone and walking in a jerky, robot-like fashion.

Jarry did not have to wait long for critical recognition. On the night of *Ubu roi*'s first performance, riots broke out in the theater. Among those sitting in the audience for the opening night were Arthur Symons, William Butler Yeats, and Stephan Mallarme. Martin Esslin wrote, "Yeats rightly sensed that the scandalous performance marked the end of an era in art." While Yeats wrote of being stunned and saddened by the play, Mallarme was enthusiastic: "You have put before us, with a rare and enduring glaze at your finger-tips, a prodigious personage and his crew, and this is a sober and sure dramatic sculptor. He enters into a repertoire of high taste and haunts me."

Ubu roi is little different from the rest of Jarry's oeuvre. *Ubu enchaine* and *Ubu cocu* offer further variations on the same crude protagonist. In such essays as "De l'inutilite de theatre au theatre" and

"Questions de theatre," Jarry attempted to explain the theoretical framework and rationale for the farcical tone and techniques of his plays. Similarly, *Gestes et opinions du Docteur Faustroll, pataphysicien (Exploits and Opinions of Doctor Faustroll, Pataphysician)* is a work of fiction that presents the tenets of pataphysics—the science of absurd creations. Although Jarry's plays have had the greatest impact, his prose has also been praised. Roger Shattuck commented, "Jarry writes in a highly compressed, poetic, often mock-heroic prose that requires careful reading. Yet the sentences move at headlong speed and draw the reader unexpectedly into the action."

BIOGRAPHICAL/CRITICAL SOURCES:

BOOKS

Beaumont, Keith S., *Alfred Jarry: A Critical and Biographical Study,* St. Martins (New York), 1984.

Beaumont, Keith S., *Jarry, Ubu Roi,* Grant and Cutler (London), 1987.

Cooper, Judith, *Ubu roi: An Analytical Study,* Tulane University (New Orleans, LA), 1974.

LaBelle, Maurice Marc, *Alfred Jarry: Nihilism and the Theater of the Absurd,* New York University Press, 1980.

Lennon, Nigey, *Alfred Jarry: The Man with the Axe,* illustrated by Bill Griffith, Panjandrum Books (Los Angeles), 1984.

Shattuck, Roger, *The Banquet Years: The Origins of the Avant-Garde in France, 1885 to World War I,* Books for Libraries Press (Freeport, NY), 1968.

Stillman, Linda Klieger, *Alfred Jarry,* Twayne (Boston), 1983.

Twentieth-Century Literary Criticism, Volume 2, Gale, 1980.

* * *

JOE, Rita 1932-

PERSONAL: Born March 15, 1932, in Whycocomagh, Cape Breton, Nova Scotia, Canada; married Frank Joe, 1954 (died 1989); children: ten. *Education:* Attended Shubenacadie Indian Residential School, 1944-48.

Agent—c/o Ragweed Press, Box 2023, Charlottetown, Prince Edward Island, C1A 7N7, Canada.

CAREER: Writer.

MEMBER: Order of Canada.

AWARDS, HONORS: Nova Scotia Writers' Federation Competition, 1974.

WRITINGS:

POETRY

Poems of Rita Joe, Abanaki Press (Halifax, Nova Scotia, Canada), 1978.
Song of Eskasoni: More Poems of Rita Joe, Ragweed Press (Charlottetown, Prince Edward Island, Canada), 1988.
Lnu and Indians We're Called, Ragweed Press, 1991.

* * *

JOHNSON, Judith (Emlyn) 1936-

PERSONAL: Born October 3, 1936, in New York, NY; married James T. Sherwin, 1955 (divorced); children: three. *Education:* Attended the Dalton Schools, 1954; attended Radcliffe College, 1954-55; Barnard College, B.A. (cum laude), 1958; attended Columbia University, 1958-59.

ADDRESSES: Office—Department of English, State University of New York, Albany, NY 12222.

CAREER: Writer. Arrow Press, New York, promotion manager, 1961; Poetry Center, New York, instructor 1976, 1978, 1981; Wake Forest University, Winston-Salem, NC, poet-in-residence, 1980; State University of New York, Albany, poet-in-residence, 1980-81, assistant professor of English, 1981-87, associate professor, 1988-91, professor of English and women's studies, 1992—, chair of department of Women's Studies, 1995-96; Poetry Society of America, president, 1975-78, chair of Executive Committee, 1979-80; Associated Writing Programs, member of Board of Directors, 1994-97, president, 1995-96.

AWARDS, HONORS: Academy of American Poets prize, 1958; Yaddo fellowship, 1964; Poetry Society of America fellowship, 1964; Aspen Writers Workshop Rose fellowship, 1967; Yale Series of Younger Poets award, 1968; *St. Andrews Review* prize, 1975; *Playboy* award for fiction, 1977; National Endowment for the Arts fellowship, 1981; Poetry Society of America Alice Fay Di Castagnola award, 1992; D. Litt. Honoris Causa, St. Andrew's College, 1992.

WRITINGS:

POETRY

Uranium Poems, Yale University Press (New Haven, CT), 1969.
Impossible Buildings, Doubleday (New York), 1973.
Waste: The Town Scold, Transparencies, Dead's Good Company, Countryman Press (Taftsville, VT), 3 vols., 1977-79.
How the Dead Count, Norton (New York), 1978.
The Ice Lizard, Sheep Meadow Press (New York), 1992.

PLAYS

Belisa's Love, produced in New York, 1959.
En Avant, Coco, produced in New York, 1961.
Waste (multimedia), produced in London, 1972.

SHORT STORIES

The Life of Riot, Atheneum (New York), 1970.

OTHER

Hungry for Light: The Journal of Ethel Schwabacher, edited by Judith E. Johnson and Brenda S. Webster, Indiana University Press, 1993.

* * *

JOHNSON, Linton Kwesi 1952-

PERSONAL: Born in 1952, in Chapeltown, Jamaica; immigrated to England in 1963. *Education:* Goldsmith's College, University of London, B.A. (sociology), 1973.

ADDRESSES: Office—c/o Island Records Ltd., 22 St. Peters Sq., London W6 9NW, England.

CAREER: Race Today Collective, London, founding member; *Race Today* magazine, arts editor; Keskidee Arts Centre, library resource and education officer; London Borough of Lambeth, writer-in-residence. University of Warwick, Coventry, fellow. Producer of a ten-part program about Jamaican music, BBC

Television. Has made several recordings, including *Poet and the Roots,* Virgin, 1977; *Dread, Beat, and Blood,* Virgin, 1978; *Forces of Victory,* Island, 1979; *Bass Culture,* Island, 1980; *Making History,* Island, 1984; *In Concert with the Dub Band,* Rough Trade, 1985; *Dread Beat an' Blood,* Heartbeat, 1989.

AWARDS, HONORS: C. Day Lewis fellowship, 1977.

WRITINGS:

POETRY

Voices of the Living and the Dead (includes play), Towards Racial Justice (London), 1974.
Dread, Beat, and Blood, Bogle L'Ouverture (London), 1975.
Inglan Is a Bitch, Race Today (London), 1980.
Tings an Times: Selected Poems, Bloodaxe (Newcastle upon Tyne), 1991.

OTHER

Voices of the Living and the Dead (produced in London, 1973), included in *Voices of the Living and the Dead* (also contains poetry), Towards Racial Justice, 1974.

* * *

JONES, Brian 1938-

PERSONAL: Born in 1938, in London, England; married; children: two.

ADDRESSES: Office—c/o Carcanet Press, 208-212 Corn Exchange Buildings, Manchester M4 3BQ, England.

CAREER: Writer. English teacher at British grammar and secondary schools.

AWARDS, HONORS: Cholmondeley award, 1967; Eric Gregory award, 1968.

WRITINGS:

POETRY

Poems, Alan Ross (London), 1966.
A Family Album, Alan Ross, 1968.
Interior, Alan Ross, 1969.

The Mantis Hand and Other Poems, Arc (Gillingham, Kent), 1970.
For Mad Mary, London Magazine Editions (London), 1974.
The Spitfire on the Northern Line (for children), Chatto and Windus (London), 1975.
The Island Normal, Carcanet (Manchester), 1980.
The Children of Separation, Carcanet, 1985.
Freedom John, Carcanet, 1990.

OTHER

Author of a radio play, *The Lady with a Little Dog,* based on a story by Anton Chekhov, 1962.

* * *

JORDAN, Emma Coleman 1946-

PERSONAL: Born November 29, 1946, in Berkeley, CA; daughter of Earl and Myrtle Coleman; married Don Jordan; children: Kristen Elena, Allison Elizabeth. *Education:* California State University, B.A., 1969; Howard University, J.D., 1973.

ADDRESSES: Office—School of Law, Georgetown University, 600 New Jersey Ave., Washington, DC 20001-2075.

CAREER: Stanford Law School, teaching fellow, 1973-74; University of Santa Clara, assistant professor, 1974-75; Georgetown University Law Center, professor; University of California School of Law, acting professor, 1975-80, professor, 1980—. Special assistant to the Attorney General of the United States, 1981.

MEMBER: National Conference of Black Lawyers, National Bar Association, American Society of International Law, California State Board of Dental and Examiners, American Association of Law Schools (sections on Commercial Law and Contracts, Minority Groups), Charles Houston Bar Association, California Association of Black Lawyers (board of directors), Society of American Law Teachers (president, 1986-88), California State Bar Financial Institution Committee (chair), American Agricultural Law Association (AALA), Financial Institute and Consumer Financial Service Section (chair), Consumer Action (board member), National Consumer Union of Northern California (advisory committee), American Law Institute, Association of American Law Schools (ex-

ecutive committee, 1988-91, president-elect, 1991-92, president, 1992-93).

AWARDS, HONORS: Outstanding academic achievement award, Phi Alpha Delta, 1973; graduated first in class, Howard Law School, 1973.

WRITINGS:

(Editor, with Anita Faye Hill) *Race, Gender, and Power in America: The Legacy of the Hill-Thomas Hearing,* Oxford University Press (New York), 1995.

Has published several articles in state law reviews, including *Nebraska Law Review.*

SIDELIGHTS: Emma Coleman Jordan is a law school professor whose legal writings pertain predominantly to the area of affirmative action, the branch of the law that seeks to redress the historic inequality of opportunity for non-whites in the United States. Jordan is also the co-editor, with Anita Faye Hill, of the 1995 volume *Race, Gender, and Power in America: The Legacy of the Hill-Thomas Hearing.* An anthology of essays written by legal scholars and lawyers, *Race, Gender, and Power in America* grew out of a conference sponsored by the Georgetown University Law Center in 1992, one year after the controversial nomination hearings of Clarence Thomas to the United States Supreme Court. During those hearings, one of Thomas's former employees, Anita Hill, testified that the nominee had sexually harassed her, inciting intense public debate and nearly derailing Thomas's nomination. Jordan and Hill jointly edit this collection of essays, which seeks to assess the ramifications of the hearings.

The contributors to *Race, Gender, and Power in America* examine why the American public, as represented by the members of the Senate Judicial Committee, were unable to either believe or to take seriously the charge of sexual harassment made by a single, black, professional woman against a married, black, male professional. The reasons offered include society's historically suspicious treatment of a black woman lacking patronage or marriage; a belief among some African Americans that because she is African American Hill should have supported Thomas—also African American—and not disclosed her claims of sexual harassment; and one contributor traces the treatment of both Thomas and Hill as a consequence of the historical relationship between blacks and whites in the United States, dating back to the age of slavery.

Race, Gender, and Power in America was generally well-received as an important contribution to the ongoing debates on race and gender in America. Reviewers noted that the essays were of varying quality, from thoughtful, scholarly analyses to essays of less merit. "Ms. Hill's own essay . . . is required reading for those interested in this historic confrontation," maintained Neil A. Lewis in *New York Times Book Review.* Although *Boston Globe* reporter Sandy Coleman maintained that the volume "makes no attempt to be balanced," calling it "an all-out rally around Hill," she concluded: "*Race, Gender, and Power in America* is an important book that conjures up the haunting realities of the past and shows readers the ghosts that will continue to stalk the present if not faced and dealt with head on."

BIOGRAPHICAL/CRITICAL SOURCES:

PERIODICALS

Booklist, October 1, 1995.
Boston Globe, October 26, 1995, p. 63.
New York Times Book Review, November 5, 1995, p. 22.
Publishers Weekly, October 2, 1995, p. 60.
Washington Post Book World, November 26, 1995, p. 8.*

* * *

JOSEPH, Henry 1948-

PERSONAL: Born February 4, 1948, in Calhoun, GA; son of Frank Ernest (a civil servant) and Mary Frances (a civil servant) Joseph. *Education:* University of Georgia, B.A., 1970; West Georgia College, M.A., 1977. *Politics:* None. *Religion:* "Oneself dwells in all."

ADDRESSES: Home—P.O. Box 734, Bowdon, GA 30108. *Agent*—John Hawkins and Associates, 71 West 23rd St., Suite 1600, New York, NY 10010; fax (212) 807-9555.

CAREER: "Professional wanderer," 1970-90; writer.

WRITINGS:

Bloodwork: The New Rugged Cross (novel), Peregrine Smith/Gibbs M. Smith (Layton, UT), 1994.
Dinosaur Heaven, Gallimard (Paris, France), 1997.

A French translation of *Bloodwork* was published by Gallimard, and an omnibus edition of *Bloodwork* and *Dinosaur Heaven* is in press.

WORK IN PROGRESS: The Well Spent Death of Eightball Barnett, completed in 1995; *Outlaw Custom,* a sequel to *Bloodwork* and *Dinosaur Heaven,* has recently been completed.

SIDELIGHTS: Henry Joseph's debut novel, 1994's *Bloodwork: The New Rugged Cross,* is a thriller that follows the adventures of Jack Lee, a former marijuana smuggler who decides to come out of retirement temporarily to help an old friend with a drug deal. The deal goes bad, and Lee finds himself involved in a murder investigation after the mutilated bodies of his friend and two others are discovered in his friend's marijuana field, which also has been ravaged. The murder turns out to be the work of members of a religious cult with ties to a white supremacist group, and Jack decides to seek revenge. Frank Wilson, in his *New York Times Book Review* assessment of *Bloodwork,* praised the "brisk pace of the narrative" and concluded that while Joseph uses a "standard" plot and stock characters, the novel "succeeds on sheer storytelling brio." Although a *Library Journal* critic provided a negative assessment of *Bloodwork, Booklist*'s Elliott Swanson responded favorably, calling the novel "A solid effort."

Joseph told *CA:* "My favorite living author, Jorge Amado, once said that the writing of a novel is a 'solitary pleasure.' In this I concur. I write to please myself. Hang both criticism and praise! Advice to aspiring authors: Tell your story in your own way—in your own voice. Then fight like hell for your material."

BIOGRAPHICAL/CRITICAL SOURCES:

PERIODICALS

Booklist, May 1, 1994, p. 1586.
Library Journal, May 1, 1994, p. 142.

New York Times Book Review, October 2, 1994, p. 32.

* * *

JUSSAWALLA, Adil (Jehangir) 1940-

PERSONAL: Born April 8, 1940, in Bombay, India; married Veronik Jussawalla, 1971; children: one stepdaughter. *Education:* Attended Cathedral School, 1947-56; attended Architectural Association School of Architecture, London, 1957-58; attended Felsham House, 1958-60; University College, Oxford University, M.A., 1964.

ADDRESSES: Home—Palm Springs, Flat R2, Cuffe Parade, Bombay 400 005, India.

CAREER: Greater London Council, supply teacher, 1965; International Language Centre, London, language teacher, 1965-69; language teacher at various colleges in Bombay, 1970-72; St. Xavier's College, Bombay, lecturer in English language and literature, 1972-75; International Writing Program, University of Iowa, Iowa City, member, 1976; *Indian Express,* Bombay, book reviews editor, 1980-81; *Express Magazine,* Bombay, literary editor, 1980-82; *Science Age,* Bombay, literary editor, 1983-87; *Debonair,* Bombay, literary editor, 1987-89, editor, 1989—.

WRITINGS:

POETRY

Land's End, Writers Workshop (Calcutta), 1962.
Missing Person, Clearing House (Bombay), 1976.

OTHER

(Editor) *New Writing in India,* Penguin (London), 1974.
(Editor with Eunice de Souza) *Statements: An Anthology of Indian Prose in English,* Orient Longman (Bombay), 1976.

Author of television scripts, including *Train to Calcutta,* 1970; *War,* 1989.

K

KABAT-ZINN, Jon

PERSONAL: Education: Received Ph.D. from Massachusetts Institute of Technology.

ADDRESSES: Office—Stress Reduction Clinic, University of Massachusetts Medical Center.

CAREER: Worked as science teacher; University of Massachusetts Medical Center, MA, researcher, ending in 1979, founder, 1979, and director of Stress Reduction Clinic, 1979—; writer.

WRITINGS:

Full Catastrophe Living: Using the Wisdom of Your Body and Mind to Face Stress, Pain, and Illness, Delacorte (New York), 1990.
Wherever You Go, There You Are: Mindfulness Meditation in Everyday Life, Hyperion (New York), 1994.

Columnist for *Health* magazine. Contributor to periodicals.

SIDELIGHTS: Jon Kabat-Zinn is a biologist who has gained attention as director of the University of Massachusetts Medical Center's Stress Reduction Clinic. Kabat-Zinn began his career as a science teacher and then turned to researching molecular biology. He eventually became interested in mind activation as a means of maintaining health and realizing greater personal stability. In 1979 he founded the Stress Reduction Clinic, which provides instruction in meditation and yoga to people suffering a broad range of afflictions.

The Stress Reduction Clinic has been acclaimed for its achievements in helping individuals manage stress. James S. Gordon, for instance, wrote in the *Atlantic Monthly,* "The results that [Kabat-Zinn] and his colleagues have obtained, with people afflicted by disorders ranging from hypertension to cancer, anxiety to AIDS, are striking." And Dr. Keith Berndtson, a professor of preventive medicine, told the *Chicago Tribune* that Kabat-Zinn's Stress Reduction Clinic "is probably one of the best examples of what a meditation program can do." Kabat-Zinn attributes the success of the clinic to principles derived from long-lived religions and practices that remain relevant today. He related to the *Chicago Tribune* that "the principles were articulated in the most sophisticated and deepest way in Buddhism, Taoism, and yoga, but they really are universal and have to do with what it means to be fully human."

In 1990 Kabat-Zinn published *Full Catastrophe Living: Using the Wisdom of Your Body and Mind to Face Stress, Pain, and Illness,* and he followed that volume in 1994 with *Wherever You Go, There You Are: Mindfulness Meditation in Everyday Life.*

BIOGRAPHICAL/CRITICAL SOURCES:

PERIODICALS

Atlantic Monthly, May, 1991, pp. 115-22.
Chicago Tribune, January 23, 1994, Section 5, pp. 1, 3.
Psychology Today, July-August, 1993.*

KAGAN, Norman 1931-

PERSONAL: Born in 1931. *Education:* Attended New York University.

ADDRESSES: Agent—c/o Continuum Publishing Group, 370 Lexington Ave., Suite 1700, New York, NY 10017-6503.

CAREER: Film critic and short story writer.

WRITINGS:

The Cinema of Stanley Kubrick, Holt, Rinehart, and Winston (Orlando, FL), 1972.
The War Film, Pyramid (New York), 1974.
The Cinema of Oliver Stone, Continuum (New York), 1995.

Also published occasional science fiction short stories, including "The Mathenauts," published in *If,* 1964.

SIDELIGHTS: Norman Kagan writes about American films and filmmakers in a way that critics have often characterized as both engaging and informative. In his first book, 1972's *The Cinema of Stanley Kubrick,* Kagan surveys the career of a director whose films typify the *auteurist* theory of filmmaking in that they are the unique product of one person's vision. In 1974 Kagan contributed *The War Film* to the Pyramid Illustrated History of the Movies series, a series otherwise devoted to biographies of film stars. In Kagan's monograph, the author surveys more than fifty American films for their varying fictional portrayals of war. In his 1995 volume *The Cinema of Oliver Stone,* Kagan takes as his subject a filmmaker whose works have inspired heated debates over subject matter and treatment. Although some critics faulted Kagan's discussions as overly schematic and organized around invented categories into which he forces works that do not necessarily fit, Kagan is credited with presenting entertaining overviews of important films and filmmakers.

In *The Cinema of Stanley Kubrick* Kagan covers the first twenty years of the career of the filmmaker responsible for such divergent and controversial works as *2001: A Space Odyssey, Doctor Strangelove, Lolita,* and *A Clockwork Orange. Publishers*

Weekly dubbed Kubrick "one of this country's most provocative film directors," and praised Kagan's "acute analyses" of his subject's body of work. Some critics focused on Kagan's organization of Kubrick's films into five themes, including "imaginary worlds," "futility of intelligence," "journey to freedom," "triumph of obsessional hero," and "suicide-homicides"—all of which are found in some form, according to the author, in each of Kubrick's films. But "the effort to systematize Kubrick has led Kagan down the paths of glibness," maintained a *Kirkus Reviews* contributor. Nevertheless, Kagan's informal writing style and fascinating subject guarantee the success of his book, according to a reviewer for the *English Journal,* who wrote: "I predict that *The Cinema of Stanley Kubrick* will be popular reading for local film buffs!"

Kagan's *The War Film* is a chronological survey of fictional American war movies, described as a "useful for a quick review," by a critic for the *Journal of Popular Film and Television.* "The author finds the war movie a surprisingly ready source of Western spiritual and social history," observed a *New York Times Book Review* critic. Although *Library Journal* reviewer Jerry Cao asserted that Kagan's presentation of his material—arranged chronologically, with additional categories thrown in to cover certain themes—was "less successful" than that employed by others covering the same topic, he concluded that "Kagan's modest work is a good buy, particularly when read as American nostalgia."

In his next publication, *The Cinema of Oliver Stone,* Kagan discusses the film career of Oliver Stone, a director whose works include *Platoon, Born on the Fourth of July, The Doors, JFK,* and *Natural Born Killers,* each controversial in its own right. "Here's a book with a refreshing oddness to it," began Dennis Drabelle in the *Washington Post Book World,* who remarked upon Kagan's less-than-adulatory tone in his *The Cinema of Oliver Stone.* The author quotes from the filmmaker's critics as liberally as he does from his fans, and adds his own caveats into the mix, according to Drabelle. "The overall impression [Kagan] leaves is of a parade of films that are visually sumptuous but confused and shallow," Drabelle continued. Although Stephen Rees of *Library Journal* maintained that Kagan "gets bogged down in frequent plot summaries" and quotations from other critics, in the end failing to be as strong a personality as his own subject, he also assessed *The Cinema of Oliver Stone* as "well written, up-to-date, and sometimes informative."

BIOGRAPHICAL/CRITICAL SOURCES:

PERIODICALS

English Journal, May, 1973, p. 826.
Journal of Popular Film and Television, summer, 1990, p. 75.
Kirkus Reviews, July 15, 1972, pp. 839-40.
Library Journal, January 1, 1975, pp. 62-63; May 15, 1995, pp. 73-74.
New York Times Book Review, December 8, 1974, p. 37.
Publishers Weekly, July 10, 1972, p. 42.
Washington Post Book World, November 12, 1972, p. 8; August 13, 1995, p. 11.*

* * *

KAHLO, Frida 1907-1954

PERSONAL: Full name, Magdalena Carmen Frida Kahlo y Calderon; born in 1907, in Coyoacan, Mexico; died, 1954; daughter of a photographer; married Diego Rivera (an artist), 1929 (marriage ended; later remarried Rivera). *Ethnicity:* "Hispanic."

CAREER: Artist.

WRITINGS:

The Diary of Frida Kahlo: An Intimate Self-Portrait, with an introduction by Carlos Fuentes and essay and commentaries by Sarah M. Lowe, Abrams (New York), 1995.
The Letters of Frida Kahlo: Cartas Apasionadas, selected and edited by Martha Zamora, Chronicle Books (San Francisco), 1995.

SIDELIGHTS: Four decades after her death in 1954, the art of Mexican painter Frida Kahlo experienced a resurgence in critical and commercial popularity. Kahlo, who was married to the artist Diego Rivera, is best known for her unusual paintings—many of them self-portraits—that blend European influences such as surrealism with distinctly Latin American iconography. Despite the success she achieved as an artist, and her acquaintance with many notable figures of her day—including Leon Trotsky—Kahlo suffered immense psychological and physical pain for much of her life. The artist, who was stricken with polio at the age of six, also experienced continual back pain

and underwent several operations as a result of injuries sustained in a bus accident when she was a teenager. Often, she was forced to paint while lying on her back.

By the 1990s numerous books had been published on Kahlo as a result of the renewed interest in her work, and gallery and museum exhibitions brought her art to a wider audience while prices of her auctioned works rose. A film biography was even planned. In 1995 two more books were published in conjunction with this rediscovery of Kahlo. The first was her long-secreted diary, which had been stored in a bank vault in Mexico City for several years. Administrators of the Rivera estate had previously allowed only a select few, such as Kahlo's biographers, limited access to her writings. In 1994, however, the estate put the diary up for auction, and the art-book publisher Abrams was the highest bidder for these pages that Kahlo wrote during the last ten years of her life. The diary was reproduced in the 1995 book *The Diary of Frida Kahlo: An Intimate Self-Portrait.* Kahlo's sketches, often accompanied by captions and her written musings on a variety of introspective topics, form the book's core; it also contains an introductory chapter by Mexican critic and poet Carlos Fuentes, and an essay and commentaries by Kahlo biographer Sarah M. Lowe. Deborah Solomon, reviewing *The Diary of Frida Kahlo* for the *New York Times Book Review,* noted that it "is less pure diary than a hybrid creature mixing drawings and watercolors with casual prose-poems," and remarked that Kahlo's art seems to yield more clues to the artist herself than does the journal. Donna Seaman in *Booklist,* however, had a more favorable reaction to the diary, calling it "a remarkable and precious book."

Seaman and Solomon also reviewed *The Letters of Frida Kahlo: Cartas Apasionadas,* also published in 1995. The eighty letters chosen by Martha Zamora, one of Kahlo's biographers, include letters that the artist wrote as a teenager to her first boyfriend, as well as later missives that she sent to family, friends, and even her doctors. The documents provide a portrait of a woman who was perhaps not as dark and brooding as her paintings may have suggested; critics note that in many of them Kahlo writes profusely and affectionately of Rivera. Still, Solomon found something lacking. "All in all, Kahlo's letters and diaries are most revealing in their very lack of revelation," she observed in her *New York Times Book Review* piece. "They have the odd effect of dulling the edge of her originality, allowing her to command center stage while providing no hint of how or why she got

there." Seaman in *Booklist,* however, found that Kahlo's "frank, affectionate and energetic letters play in revealing counterpoint to her wrenching mythic paintings."

BIOGRAPHICAL/CRITICAL SOURCES:

BOOKS

Modern Arts Criticism, Volume 4, Gale, 1994.

PERIODICALS

Booklist, October 1, 1995, p. 244.
Library Journal, May 15, 1994, p. 72.
New York Times, August 10, 1994, p. C9.
New York Times Book Review, November 19, 1995, p. 12.
Publishers Weekly, October 9, 1995, p. 72.*

* * *

KANE, Paul
 See SIMON, Paul

* * *

KAPLAN, Alice Y.
 See KAPLAN, Alice Yaeger

* * *

KAPLAN, Alice Yaeger 1954-
 (Alice Y. Kaplan)

PERSONAL: Born June 22, 1954, in Minneapolis, MN; daughter of Sidney J. (an attorney) and Leonore (a social worker; maiden name, Yaeger) Kaplan. *Education:* University of California, Berkeley, B.A., 1975; Yale University, Ph.D., 1981.

ADDRESSES: Office—Program in Literature, 101-A Art Museum, Duke University, Durham, NC 27708.

CAREER: Duke University, Durham, NC, began as associate professor, became professor of Romance studies and literature, 1986—, and director of undergraduate studies for Program in Literature.

MEMBER: Modern Language Association of America, Association pour l'autobiographie et le patrimoine autobiographique, Societe des etudes celiniennes.

AWARDS, HONORS: Grant from National Humanities Center, 1989-90; *French Lessons* was named by the *New York Times* as a "notable book of 1993"; grant from Stanford Humanities Center, 1994-95; Guggenheim fellow, 1995-96.

WRITINGS:

Reproductions of Banality: Fascism, Literature, and French Intellectual Life, University of Minnesota Press (Minneapolis, MN), 1986.
Sources et citations dans "Bagatelles pour un massacre," Editions du Lerot, 1988.
French Lessons: A Memoir, University of Chicago Press (Chicago, IL), 1993.

Contributor of articles and reviews to periodicals, including *Yale French Studies* and *South Atlantic Quarterly.* Member of editorial board, *South Atlantic Quarterly.* Some writings appear under the name Alice Y. Kaplan.

WORK IN PROGRESS: A book on Paris in 1945 and the purge of collaborators, focusing on the treason trial of writer Robert Brasillach.

* * *

KATZ, Marshall P. 1939-

PERSONAL: Born September 17, 1939, in the United States; son of Joseph M. (a business executive) and Agnes R. Katz; married Wallis Fisk, June 13, 1965; children: Lauren S. *Ethnicity:* "Caucasian." *Education:* Cornell University, B.A., 1961. *Politics:* Republican. *Religion:* Jewish. *Avocational interests:* Contemporary art, fine wines, ceramics.

ADDRESSES: Home—4875 Ellsworth Ave., Pittsburgh, PA 15213. *Office*—Cavendish Holdings, Gateway Towers, Suite 24-A, Pittsburgh, PA 15222; fax 412-471-0250. *E-mail*—palissy@usaor.net.

CAREER: Papercraft Corp., Pittsburgh, PA, chairperson and chief executive officer of a consumer household products company, 1962-91. Member of board of directors, Carnegie Institute, Andy Warhol

Museum, Pittsburgh Symphony, Pittsburgh Opera, Pittsburgh Cultural Trust, and Joseph M. Katz Graduate School of Business, University of Pittsburgh. *Military service:* U.S. Coast Guard, 1961-62.

WRITINGS:

Nineteenth-Century French Followers of Palissy, privately printed, 1994.
(With Robert Lehr) *Palissy Ware: Nineteenth-Century French Ceramists from Avisseau to Renoleau,* Athlone Press (London, England), 1996.

Contributor to magazines, including *Antiques* and *Ceramics Monthly.*

WORK IN PROGRESS: Research on late nineteenth-century Portuguese ceramics.

* * *

KAUFFMAN, Stuart Alan 1939-

PERSONAL: Born September 28, 1939, in Sacramento, CA; married, 1967; children: one. *Education:* Dartmouth College, B.A., 1961; Oxford University, B.A., 1963; University of California, San Francisco, M.D., 1968.

ADDRESSES: Office—Department of Biochemistry and Physiology, University of Pennsylvania College of Medicine, Philadelphia, PA 19104.

CAREER: University of Chicago, Chicago, IL, assistant professor of theoretical biology, 1969-73, became assistant professor of medicine, 1970-73; Laboratory of Theoretical Biology, National Cancer Institute, research associate, 1973-75; University of Pennsylvania College of Medicine, associate professor of biochemistry-biology, 1975-81, became associate professor of biochemistry and biophysics, 1981—; associated with the Santa Fe Institute.

MEMBER: Philosophy of Science Association.

AWARDS, HONORS: Genetics fellowship, University of Cincinnati, 1968-69; Norbert Wiener Gold Medal, American Cybernet Society, 1970; MacArthur Fellow, 1987.

WRITINGS:

The Origins of Order: Self-Organization and Selection in Evolution, Oxford University Press (New York), 1993.
At Home in the Universe: The Search for Laws of Self-Organization and Complexity, Oxford University Press, 1995.

Contributor to *Molecular Evolution on Rugged Landscapes: Proteins, RNA, and the Immune System,* Addison-Wesley (Redwood City, CA), 1991.

SIDELIGHTS: Biologist Stuart Alan Kauffman is in the vanguard of a new science known as complexity theory, which he describes in *The Origins of Order: Self-Organization and Selection in Evolution* and *At Home in the Universe: The Search for Laws of Self-Organization and Complexity.* In *The Origins of Order,* Kauffman expounds on the question "What are the sources of the overwhelming and beautiful order which graces the living world?" Maintaining that the precepts of natural selection propounded by Darwin do not adequately explain nature's order, Kauffman proposes that natural selection coupled with an innate order of complex systems are the forces that create biological and social structures. He and other complexity theorists propose that self-organized systems exist in three possible states: rigid order, chaos, and a balance between rigid order and chaos, otherwise known as "the edge of chaos" or "complexity." Using simple mathematical formulas and computer simulations, Kauffman tries to outline the limits of natural selection within systems poised on the edge of chaos, proposes that the origin of life may have been a simple, predictable event, and discusses the development of embryos. Calling the search for the laws of complexity "a provocative quest," *Business Week* correspondent John Carey described the work of complexity theorists: "Much of this work is on the cutting edge of computer science. Some of the results are tantalizing."

Kauffman's books and the theories they propose have drawn both positive and negative responses from commentators. "Many biologists will react against the central message of *The Origins of Order,* as it threatens to replace the current world-view with one that encompasses emergence and self-organisation, concepts that are antithetical to modern biological thinking," predicted Roger Lewin, another complexity theorist, in a review for *New Scientist.* "And some biologists will label complexity theory and its implications as a fad," he continued. "But if its tenets

prove to be valid, *The Origins of Order* will be seen as a major work in the progression of biological theory. At the very least, Kauffman has made a persuasive case to have his bold hypothesis heard."

Several commentators found *The Origins of Order* difficult to penetrate. "The style is heady, sententious and dangerously seductive, with an audible breathlessness throughout," remarked Gabriel A. Dover in *Nature*. According to Matt Ridley, writing for the *Times Literary Supplement,* "The general effect is like throwing a smoke bomb into a fog. It is hard to distinguish his hypothesis among the slightly Malapropian verbiage, and, when one does, its implications prove elusive." He continued, "The lack of clarity in presentation is less forgivable than the immodesty. Kauffman's theories and the evidence he brings to support them are hidden in a jungle of jargon and the kind of scientific writing where it is obvious what it means once you know already what it means."

Gunter P. Wagner in *Science* also expressed reservations about complexity theory: "Successful science depends as much on an adequate style of thinking as it does on adequate experimental methods," he stated. "As attractive as Kauffman's thinking style is to the reviewer, a rational decision about its heuristic value will only be reached in retrospect. . . . I hope that Kauffman's book will be a strong stimulus for many scientists to search actively for the principles that govern the organization of living states of matter." About *At Home in the Universe,* a condensed version of *The Origins of Order,* a contributor to the *Economist* declared that Kauffman "lays out [the] rudiments" of complexity theory "in an accessible way with this challenging and audacious book. . . . Few real-life biologists will choose to abandon their wellies or microscopes in favour of Mr. Kauffman's networks, bytes and buzzwords. It would pay, however, to take him seriously."

BIOGRAPHICAL/CRITICAL SOURCES:

PERIODICALS

Business Week, November 6, 1995, pp. 21, 24.
Economist, October 21, 1995, p. 91.
Nature, October 21, 1993, pp. 704-706.
New Scientist, June 5, 1993, p. 46.
New York Times Book Review, October 1, 1995, pp. 30-31.

Science, June 4, 1993, pp. 1531-1533.
Times Literary Supplement, March 11, 1994, p. 31.*

* * *

KAUMEYER, Mary Leta Dorothy
See LAMOUR, Dorothy

* * *

KAY, Jackie
See KAY, Jacqueline Margaret

* * *

KAY, Jacqueline Margaret 1961-
(Jackie Kay)

PERSONAL: Born November 9, 1961, in Edinburgh, Scotland; children: one son. *Education:* University of Stirling, B.A. (honors; English), 1983.

ADDRESSES: Agent—Pat Kavanagh, Peters Fraser & Dunlop, 503/4 The Chambers, Chelsea Harbour, London SW10 0XF, England.

CAREER: Writer. Writer-in-residence, Hammersmith, London, 1989-91.

AWARDS, HONORS: Eric Gregory award, 1991; Scottish Arts Council Book award, 1991, for *The Adoption Papers;* Saltire First Book of the Year award, 1991, for *The Adoption Papers;* Forward prize, 1992, for *The Adoption Papers;* Signal Poetry award, 1993, for *Two's Company;* Somerset Maugham award for *Other Lovers.*

WRITINGS:

POETRY, AS JACKIE KAY

The Adoption Papers, Bloodaxe (Newcastle upon Tyne, England), 1991.
That Distance Apart (chapbook), Turret (London), 1991.
Two's Company (for children), Puffin (London), 1992.
Other Lovers, Bloodaxe, 1993.

Three Has Gone (for children), Blackie Children's (London), 1994.

* * *

KEFALA, Antigone 1935-

PERSONAL: Born May 28, 1935, in Braila, Romania; married Robert Kerr, 1959 (divorced 1963); married Usher Weinrauch, 1964 (divorced 1976). *Education:* Victoria University, B.A., 1958, M.A., 1960.

ADDRESSES: *Home*—12 Rose St., Annandale, New South Wales 2038, Australia.

CAREER: Writer. New South Wales Department of Education, Sydney, teacher of English, 1961-68; University of New South Wales, administrative assistant, 1968-69; Australia Council for the Arts, Sydney, arts administrator, 1971-87.

WRITINGS:

POETRY

The Alien, Makar Press (Brisbane), 1973.
Thirsty Weather, Outback Press (Melbourne), 1978.
European Notebook, Hale and Iremonger (Sydney), 1988.
Absence: New and Selected Poems, Hale and Iremonger, 1992.

NOVELS

The First Journey, Wild and Woolley (Sydney), 1975.
The Island, Hale and Iremonger, 1984.

OTHER

Alexia: A Tale of Two Cultures, illustrated by Warwick Hatton (for children), John Ferguson (Sydney), 1984.

* * *

KEMPER, R. Crosby (III) 1951-

PERSONAL: Born January 7, 1951, in Kansas City, MO; son of R. Crosby, Jr. (a banker) and Cynthia (Warrick) Kemper; married Kate Gill, August 14, 1974 (divorced, 1992); married Hilary Noonan, June 13, 1992; children: (first marriage) Tara, Susan; (second marriage) James Lawson. *Ethnicity:* "English, Scots, Irish, French, German, Cherokee, etc." *Education:* Yale University, 1974. *Politics:* Republican. *Religion:* Episcopalian. *Avocational interests:* Reading, theater, politics, movies, canoeing.

ADDRESSES: *Home*—4647 Pershing, St. Louis, MO 63108. *Office*—6 South Broadway, St. Louis, MO 63102; fax 314-632-8223.

CAREER: UMB Bank of St. Louis, St. Louis, MO, president, 1993—. UMB Financial Corp., vice-chairperson of board of directors. Heart of America Shakespeare Festival, co-founder, 1992, president, 1992-93; St. Louis Repertory Theater, vice-president and member of board of directors; Westminster College, member of board of trustees; Webster College, member of board of directors of Truman Library.

AWARDS, HONORS: Honorary doctorate from Park College.

WRITINGS:

(Editor) *Winston Churchill: Resolution, Defiance, Magnanimity, Good Will,* University of Missouri Press (Columbia, MO), 1995.

WORK IN PROGRESS: Essays on literary history.

* * *

KIBERA, Leonard 1940(?)-

PERSONAL: Born c. 1940, in Kenya.

CAREER: Writer.

AWARDS, HONORS: Third prize, British Broadcasting Corporation African drama contest, 1967, for play, *Potent Ash.*

WRITINGS:

Potent Ash (play; produced in London on the British Broadcasting Corporation's African Service, June, 1967), published in *New African Literature and the Arts,* Volume 2, edited by Joseph Okpaku, Thomas Y. Crowell, 1968.

(With Samuel Kahiga) *Potent Ash* (short stories), East African Publishing House, 1968.

Voices in the Dark (novel), East African Publishing House, 1970.

Also author of short story, "The Spider Web," published in *Presence Africaine,* second trimester, 1970.

* * *

KIMMEL, Michael S(cott) 1951-

PERSONAL: Born February 26, 1951, in New York, NY; son of Edwin H. and Barbara Diamond (Michtom) Kimmel. *Education:* Vassar College, B.A., 1972; Brown University, M.A., 1974; University of California, Berkeley, Ph.D., 1981.

ADDRESSES: Office—Department of Sociology, State University of New York at Stony Brook, Stony Brook, NY 11794.

CAREER: Bryant College, Smithfield, RI, instructor in sociology, 1973; State University of New York College at Oneonta, instructor in sociology, 1973-74; University of California at Berkeley, instructor in sociology, 1974-76; University of California at Santa Cruz, visiting lecturer, 1977-81; Rutgers University, New Brunswick, NJ, assistant professor of sociology, 1982-86; State University of New York at Stony Brook, professor of sociology, 1987—; editor and writer.

MEMBER: American Sociology Association; California Anti-sexist Men's Political Caucus; Institute for International Studies (fellow); Chancellor's Patent Fund (fellow); William A. Clark Memorial Library (fellow).

AWARDS, HONORS: Recipient of grants from the Spencer Foundation; fellowship from University of California at Berkeley, 1978-79.

WRITINGS:

Absolutism and Its Discontent: State and Society in Seventeenth-Century France and England, Transaction Books (New Brunswick, NJ), 1988.

(Author of introduction) *Mundus Foppensis* [and] *The Levellers,* William A. Clark Memorial Library (University of California at Los Angeles), 1988.

Revolution: A Sociological Interpretation, Temple University Press (Philadelphia), 1990.

Manhood in America: A Cultural History, Free Press (New York), 1996.

Contributor of articles and reviews to periodicals, including *New York Times Book Review, Los Angeles Times, Washington Post,* and *Harvard Business Review.*

EDITOR

Changing Men: New Directions in Research on Men and Masculinity, Sage (Newbury Park, CA), 1987.

(With Michael A. Messner) *Men's Lives,* Macmillan (New York), 1989.

Love Letters between a Certain Late Nobleman and the Famous Mr. Wilson, Haworth (New York), 1990.

Men Confront Pornography, Crown (New York), 1990.

(With Thomas E. Mosmiller) *Against the Tide: "Pro-Feminist" Men in the United States, 1776-1990, a Documentary History,* Beacon (Boston), 1992.

The Politics of Manhood: Profeminist Men Respond to the Mythopoetic Men's Movement (and Mythopoetic Leaders Answer), Temple University Press (Philadelphia), 1995.

Contributing editor of *San Francisco Review of Books,* 1977-85; corresponding editor of *Theory and Society,* 1979-84; book review editor of *Society,* 1981; book editor of *Changing Men,* 1983—.

SIDELIGHTS: Michael S. Kimmel is a sociologist who has published various volumes on male culture. Notable among his writings is *Manhood in America: A Cultural History,* which explores the ways that notions of masculinity have influenced, and have been influenced by, American culture. In this volume Kimmel argues that men have long been motivated by the desire or need to prove their masculinity. He traces the ways in which the American concept of masculinity, influenced by social and economic changes and pressure, has evolved. He also speculates on the ways in which notions—and representations—of masculinity might further change in the near future. "Kimmel has culled every testosterone tract of the last two centuries in order to find out not what men did, but what they were advised to do," Sam Fussell noted in his *Washington Post Book Review* critique of *Manhood in America.*

Kimmel has also edited various works on masculinity. Among these volumes are *Changing Men: New Directions in Research on Men and Masculinity; Men Confront Pornography; Against the Tide: "Pro-Feminist" Men in the United States, 1776-1990, a Documentary History,* on which he collaborated with Thomas E. Mosmiller; and *The Politics of Manhood: Profeminist Men Respond to the Mythopoetic Men's Movement (and Mythopoetic Leaders Answer).*

Although Kimmel is probably best known for his publications on masculinity, he has also written such works as *Absolutism and Its Discontent: State and Society in Seventeenth-Century France and England,* and *Revolution: A Sociological Interpretation.* In addition, he supplied the introduction to the 1992 volume *Mundus Foppensis* [and] *The Levellers.*

BIOGRAPHICAL/CRITICAL SOURCES:

PERIODICALS

Dissent, Fall 1992, pp. 539-41.
Voice Literary Supplement, April 1990, pp. 16-17.
Washington Post Book World, November 5, 1995, pp. 1, 14.

* * *

KNELLER, Marianna 1942-

PERSONAL: Born July 7, 1942, in Wimborne, Dorset, England.

ADDRESSES: Home—Exbury, England. *Office*—c/o Timber Press, 133 Southwest 2nd Ave., Suite 450, Portland, OR 97204.

CAREER: Writer.

AWARDS, HONORS: Medal from Royal Horticultural Society.

WRITINGS:

The Book of Rhododendrons, Timber Press (Portland, OR), 1995.

KOLATKAR, Arun (Balkrishna) 1932-

PERSONAL: Born November 1, 1932, in Kolhapur, Bombay.

ADDRESSES: Agent—c/o The Clearing House, Palm Springs, Cusse Parade, Bombay 400 005, India.

CAREER: Writer. Works as a graphic artist in an advertising agency, Bombay.

AWARDS, HONORS: Commonwealth Poetry prize, 1977.

WRITINGS:

POETRY

Jejuri, Bombay, Clearing House, 1976.

* * *

KORDER, Howard 1958(?)-

PERSONAL: Born c. 1958, in New York, NY.

ADDRESSES: Agent—c/o Dramatists Play Service, 440 Park Ave. South, New York, NY 10016.

CAREER: Playwright. Worked as a story editor on the television series *Kate and Allie* for CBS.

AWARDS, HONORS: Winner of a $50,000 production grant from "AT&T: Onstage," c. 1989, for *Search and Destroy;* Obie Award for playwriting, *Village Voice,* 1994, for *The Lights.*

WRITINGS:

PLAYS

Middle Kingdom (one act), first produced at the Intar Theater, New York City, 1985.
Episode 26 (two acts), Samuel French, 1985.
Lip Service, first produced at Manhattan Punchline, New York City, 1985; adapted by Korder for Home Box Office (HBO) cable television network, 1988.
Fun (one act; produced at the Judith Anderson Theater, New York City, 1987), published as *Fun; and Nobody: Two Short Plays,* Dramatists Play Service, 1988.

Nobody (one act; produced at the Judith Anderson Theater, 1987), published as *Fun; and Nobody: Two Short Plays,* Dramatists Play Service, 1988.

Boys' Life (produced at the Mitzi E. Newhouse Theater at Lincoln Center, New York City, 1988), Dramatists Play Service, 1988.

Wonderful Party! (one act), produced at the Judith Anderson Theater, 1989.

Search and Destroy (produced by South Coast Repertory, Costa Mesa, CA, 1989), Dramatists Play Service, 1992.

The Pope's Nose: Short Plays and Sketches, Dramatists Play Service, 1991.

The Lights, first produced at the Mitzi E. Newhouse Theater, 1993.

Night Maneuver, produced at Theatre 6470 at the Complex, Hollywood, CA, 1995.

ADAPTATIONS: Search and Destroy was adapted as a motion picture directed by David Salle and starring Griffin Dunne, Christopher Walken, John Turturro, and Illeana Douglas. *Lip Service* was adapted by Korder for Home Box Office (HBO) cable television network, 1988.

SIDELIGHTS: Howard Korder's success as a playwright may be measured by the fact that nearly a dozen of his plays were produced on Broadway or off-Broadway before he was thirty-five. Frequently compared to David Mamet (*Sexual Perversity in Chicago, Speed the Plow*), a playwright known for his blackly comic take on social issues and hard-hitting, realistic dialogue, Korder also credited Harold Pinter and Samuel Beckett as important influences on his choice of subject matter and method in an interview with *Los Angeles Times* critic Jan Herman. Critics often focus on the humor Korder manages to wring from the dingy or desperate circumstances in which he places his fumbling, often incompetent characters. And though Korder endures comparisons to Mamet and Pinter, he is also credited with showing more sympathy and respect for his female characters than either of his mentors.

Korder's early, one-act plays include *Middle Kingdom,* which centers on a couple's late night financial discussion in their kitchen, and *Wonderful Party!,* in which the hostess of a large gathering knows none of her own guests. Two related one-acts, *Fun* and *Nobody,* are often performed together and are published together as the volume *Fun; and Nobody: Two Short Plays.* In the first, two aimless teenagers spend a night in search of a diversion from their redundant existence in small-town America; in the second, the

father of one of the boys from *Fun* is, like Willy Loman in Arthur Miller's *Death of a Salesman,* a failure whom nobody understands. Although Walter Goodman in the *New York Times* noted that in these two plays Korder "lets the social critic take over the work of the dramatist," Kevin Kelly enthused that "both [plays] have the crackling energy of real talent," in his review for the *Boston Globe. Night Maneuver,* another play, centers on two brothers' various schemes to escape the dreary underclass. "*Night Maneuver* is bleak and fairly unformed," wrote Laurie Winer in a review in the *Los Angeles Times,* "with shots of humor and seeds of the full-bodied desperate dreamers and ruthless liars who populate the . . . plays *Boys' Life* and *Search and Destroy.*"

Boys' Life, one of Korder's first widely successful full-length plays, centers on a year in the life of three young men fresh out of college. In the absence of any more meaningful activity, the three spend the majority of their time in pursuit of women. "The stylized comic writing—staccato, pithy, unerringly attuned to the vernacular—is Mametesque," observed Frank Rich in the *New York Times.* Though several critics saw *Boys' Life* as little more than a 1980s reworking of Mamet's *Sexual Perversity in Chicago* (1975), "Korder's play can stand on its own," asserted Richard Christiansen, the entertainment editor for the *Chicago Tribune.* Like others, Christiansen remarked that the characters in *Boys' Life* engage the audience's sympathy even when they are the object of the playwright's social commentary or the butt of his jokes. "Korder may be relatively new to the theater, but his play-writing voice is already sure and distinct," David Richards wrote in the *Washington Post.*

Korder's play *Lip Service,* which concerns the devolution of an informative morning news show to a light-hearted program that blurs the line between entertainment and news, was adapted by the author for the Home Box Office (HBO) cable network following its successful stage run. The play centers on the show's two hosts, one a dignified newscaster whose somber manner and non-sensational delivery insures his demise, and the other an ambitious younger man whose affability and knack for mindless "infotainment" features propels him to success. "It's just brilliantly written and incredibly bitchy," admired David Mamet, who produced the television adaptation, to Neal Gabler of the *New York Times.* "It's vastly beyond acerbic." Although *New York Times* television critic John J. O'Connor felt that the adaptation lacked the taut energy of the stage produc-

tion, he nonetheless concluded: "Like his mentor Mr. Mamet, Mr. Korder has a talent for creating harrowingly vivid characters. . . . He and Mr. Korder and company should definitely poke around further in television land. They do make a welcome difference."

Martin Mirkheim, the protagonist of Korder's play *Search and Destroy,* is a man pursuing the American dream. "He is," Korder told *Los Angeles Times* correspondent Jan Herman, "a man with an idea. This is his delusion. But he is no more delusional than Henry Ford." A failed broker of circus acts, Mirkheim is in debt to the Internal Revenue Service; he therefore abandons his life in Florida to try to break into the movie business. Unfazed by his lack of resources or contacts in the business, Mirkheim travels throughout the country attempting to convince people, through means that are both questionably legal and less so, to help him make a film based on a story written by a New Age self-help guru. "This play deals with the myth of America as a land of infinite possibility," Korder told Herman. "Mirkheim believes the myth. He is a man whose head has been filled with the junk of our culture. He has grown up like a weed and flourished like a weed. His yearnings are universal."

Search and Destroy received mixed reviews in its theatrical run. (In 1995, the play was made into a film produced by Martin Scorsese, directed by David Salle, and starring Griffin Dunne as Mirkheim and Christopher Walken as a shady investor in the movie deal.) Critics noted the eerily empty character of Mirkheim, who, armed with the convenient philosophy of a cult leader, is unstoppably optimistic about his own future prospects, regardless of the reality of his limited abilities. While this is a frightening prospect, "What makes Mr. Korder's vision scarier still is his ability to portray his protagonist's emptiness as symptomatic of a larger, national condition," wrote Frank Rich in the *New York Times*. The American predilection for erasing the past has robbed the country of its moral legacy as well, according to Rich.

In *The Lights,* for which Korder won an Obie Award in 1994, the author leaves aside his signature comedic slant on social issues for what Robert Brustein called in the *New Republic* an "unfashionably grim study of the metaphysical perils of living in the modern city." Featuring two shopgirls among a large cast of faceless, menacing urban dwellers, *The Lights* confronted critics with a vision of life in the city as "deeply alien and repellent," according to Brustein. Although the play failed to capture a uniformly positive response,

William A. Henry III, *Time* magazine's theater critic, called *The Lights* "spellbinding."

Korder is an award-winning playwright whose works are often perceived as black comedies, combining fine-tuned social commentary and humor. Korder's signature style often marks him as a descendent of David Mamet: "We are, in short, in David Mamet Village, which is a hop and a skip from Harold Pinter City," quipped the *New York Times*'s O'Connor of Korder's characteristic dialogue in *Lip Service.* Korder has also garnered comparisons to Arthur Miller for his occasionally fierce rendition of life among the underclass. Although at times he has been faulted for allowing his social commentary to overshadow his artistry, Korder is generally considered an important young writer on the off-Broadway theater scene.

BIOGRAPHICAL/CRITICAL SOURCES:

PERIODICALS

Boston Globe, April 18, 1989.
Chicago Tribune, September 13, 1989.
Los Angeles Times, January 9, 1990, pp. F1, F6; February 2, 1995.
New Republic, November 29, 1993, pp. 29-30.
New York, November 15, 1993, p. 95.
New York Times, November 19, 1987; March 1, 1988, p. C13; March 24, 1988; October 16, 1988, sec. 2, p. 20; October 17, 1988; December 14, 1990, p. C3; February 27, 1992, p. C18.
Time, November 15, 1993, p. 101.
Washington Post, March 21, 1988.*

—Sketch by Mary Gillis

* * *

KRAKAUER, Jon

PERSONAL: Avocational interests: Mountain climbing.

ADDRESSES: Home—Seattle, WA. *Office*—c/o Villard Publishers, 201 East 50th St., New York, NY 10022.

CAREER: Journalist. Contributing editor to *Outside* magazine.

AWARDS, HONORS: Nominee, National Magazine Award, for an article that formed the basis of *Into the Wild.*

WRITINGS:

Eiger Dreams: Ventures among Men and Mountains (essay collection), Lyons and Burford (New York), 1990.
(Photographer) David Roberts, *Iceland: Land of the Sagas* (travelogue), Abrams (New York), 1990.
Into the Wild (nonfiction), Villard (New York), 1996.

Has published numerous articles in *Smithsonian, Outside,* and *Playboy* magazines.

SIDELIGHTS: Jon Krakauer is a journalist whose highly praised writings on mountain climbing and other sports combine the knowledge of the insider with the writer's sense of dramatic and well-timed storytelling. Critics recommended the author's first book-length publication, *Eiger Dreams: Ventures among Men and Mountains,* a collection of essays on mountain climbing, for armchair adventurers, novices, and experienced climbers alike, praising its thrilling subject matter and Krakauer's unpretentious prose style. Krakauer's second book, *Into the Wild,* reconstructs the last days of a young man who gave away all his possessions and traveled to the Alaskan wilderness only to die of starvation in an abandoned bus. Drawing on numerous interviews, Krakauer paints a touching picture of the troubled young man. Krakauer has also contributed photographs to *Iceland: Land of the Sagas.*

Eiger Dreams is a collection of twelve essays, several featuring famous eccentrics of the mountain-climbing set—including John Gill, who climbs boulders, and the Burgess twins, who without an income manage to travel the world climbing its most challenging peaks—while others center on the mountains themselves. The Eiger of the title is a fiercely difficult mountain in Switzerland that the author attempted and failed to climb, providing one of the occasional moments of humor in these adventure-filled pages. "Krakauer conveys well the formidable, even terrifying aspects of the sport," emphasized a reviewer for *Kirkus Reviews.* Tim Cahill, critic for the *New York Times Book Review,* singled out the author's avoidance of the cliches of "conquering" mountain peaks, and the trite epiphanies that occur there: "There is a beauty in his mountains beyond that expressed in conventional sermons. His reverence is earned, and it's entirely genuine."

Krakauer's next book, *Into the Wild,* is the nonfiction account of the life and death of a young man named Christopher McCandless. A brilliant young man from a loving and prosperous family, McCandless abandoned his upper-middle-class existence to live the simple unencumbered life of a wanderer, influenced by the example of writers such as Henry David Thoreau and Jack London. In April of 1992 he hitchhiked to Alaska, carrying with him only bag of rice, a .22-gauge shotgun, and some books. A few months later the boy's dead body was discovered alongside a desperate note in which he begged to be saved. Although McCandless's death was commonly greeted with derision or apathy by Alaskans, who pointed to the arrogance inherent in his ill-equipped and untutored attempt to live off the land, Krakauer manages to make his subject sympathetic, according to several reviewers. "The more we learn about him, the more mysterious McCandless becomes, and the more intriguing," wrote Thomas McNamee in the *New York Times Book Review.* Christopher Lehmann-Haupt similarly remarked in his review of *Into the Wild* in the *New York Times* that Krakauer mitigates the reader's desire to condemn McCandless by presenting him through the eyes of those who encountered him. The people Krakauer interviewed emphasize "how particularly intelligent, unusual and just plain likable this young man was," Lehmann-Haupt wrote. Lehmann-Haupt commented favorably on Krakauer's apt placing of McCandless's quest in the context of other spiritual daredevils and sons of dominating, successful fathers. In this latter context, Krakauer reveals his own survival of an adolescent trek up Devils Thumb, a treacherous mountain on the Alaska-British Columbia border. Although McNamee complained that the author too readily dismisses the possibility that McCandless's actions were at least partly the result of mental instability, he concluded: "Christopher McCandless's life and his death may have been meaningless, absurd, even reprehensible, but by the end of *Into the Wild,* you care for him deeply." Similarly, Lehmann-Haupt ended: "Mr. Krakauer has taken the tale of a kook who went into the woods, and made of it a heart-rending drama of human yearning."

BIOGRAPHICAL/CRITICAL SOURCES:

PERIODICALS

Kirkus Reviews, February 1, 1990, p. 159.
Los Angeles Times Book Review, September 3, 1995, p. 9.
New York Times, January 4, 1996, p. C17.

New York Times Book Review, June 10, 1990, p. 48; March 3, 1996, p. 29.
People, February 12, 1996, p. 35.
Publishers Weekly, February 2, 1990, p. 73; October 19, 1990, p. 44; November 6, 1995, p. 76.

* * *

KRAMER, Lotte (Karoline) 1923-

PERSONAL: Born Lotte Karoline Wertheimer, October 22, 1923, in Mainz, Germany; married Frederic Kramer, 1943; children: one son.

ADDRESSES: Home and office—4 Apsley Way, Longthorpe, Peterborough, Cambridgeshire PE3 9NE, England.

CAREER: Laundry hand, Berkhamsted, Hertfordshire, 1939-40, and Hampton, Middlesex, 1943-47; lady's companion, Oxford, 1940-43; dress shop assistant, Richmond, Surrey, 1953-57. Peterborough Museum, voluntary worker, 1977—. Also a painter: several individual exhibitions.

WRITINGS:

POETRY

Scrolls, Keepsake Press (Richmond, Surrey, England), 1979.
Ice-Break, Annakinn (Peterborough, Cambridgeshire, England), 1980.
Family Arrivals, Poet and Printer (Hatch End, Middlesex, England), 1981.
A Lifelong House, Hippopotamus Press (Frome, Somerset, England), 1983.
The Shoemaker's Wife and Other Poems, Hippopotamus Press, 1987.
The Desecration of Trees, Hippopotamus Press, 1994.
Earthquake and Other Poems, Rockingham Press (Ware, Hertfordshire, England), 1994.

* * *

KUBLY, Herbert (Oswald Nicholas) 1915-1996

OBITUARY NOTICE—See index for *CA* sketch: Born April 26, 1915, in New Glarus, WI; died August 7, 1996, in New Glarus, WI. Journalist, critic, educa-

tor, and author. Kubly is remembered for his first book, the National Book Award-winning *American in Italy,* which describes his recollections of the people and sites he encountered while in Italy on a Fulbright scholarship. Kubly spent his early career as a journalist and critic, working for newspapers and magazines such as the *Pittsburgh Sun-Telegraph, New York Herald Tribune,* and *Time.* In 1947 he began two years as national secretary for the Dramatist Guild of America. Then he initiated a thirty-five-year stint as an educator, first at the University of Illinois at Urbana-Champaign as an associate professor of speech.

Following positions at Columbia University, New School for Social Research, and San Francisco State College, he joined the faculty of the University of Wisconsin-Parkside as a professor of English and writer-in-residence. He became professor emeritus in 1984. In addition to his National Book Award, he was also named a MacDowell Colony fellow. Among his other books are *Easter in Sicily, The Whistling Zone, Gods and Heroes,* and *Native's Return.* Also a playwright, Kubly wrote dramas such as *Men to the Sea, Inherit the Wind,* and *Perpetual Care.* He also contributed to magazines such as *Holiday, Life, Town and Country,* and *Atlantic Monthly.*

OBITUARIES AND OTHER SOURCES:

BOOKS

Who's Who in America, 51st edition, Marquis, 1996.

PERIODICALS

New York Times, August 13, 1996, p. B6.
Washington Post, August 13, 1996, p. C6.

* * *

KUPPNER, Frank 1951-

PERSONAL: Born in 1951, in Glasgow, Scotland. *Education:* Attended University of Glasgow, became qualified electronics engineer.

ADDRESSES: Agent—c/o Polygon, 22 George Sq., Edinburgh EH8 9LF, Scotland.

CAREER: Engineer and writer.

WRITINGS:

POETRY

A Bad Day for the Sung Dynasty, Carcanet (Manchester), 1984.
The Intelligent Observation of Naked Women, Carcanet, 1987.

Everything Is Strange, Carcanet, 1994.

NOVEL

Ridiculous! Absurd! Disgusting!, Carcanet, 1989.
A Very Quiet Street, Polygon (Edinburgh), 1989.
A Concussed History of Scotland, Polygon, 1990.
Something Very Like Murder, Polygon, 1994.

L

LAMOUR, Dorothy 1914-1996

OBITUARY NOTICE—See index for *CA* sketch: Original name, Mary Leta Dorothy Kaumeyer; born December 10, 1914, in New Orleans, LA; died September 22, 1996, in Los Angeles, CA. Actor, singer, and comedian. Dubbed by the press as the "bond bombshell" during World War II for her work on war bond drives, Lamour was born to a poor family in Louisiana and went on to become one of the biggest screen stars of the 1930s and 1940s. She continued working on stage productions well into her sixties and made her final film appearance with a bit part in 1987's *Creepshow 2*. But it was Lamour's work playing the "straight" role to Bob Hope and Bing Crosby's wisecracking in the series of *Road* movies (*The Road to Singapore, The Road to Morocco,* etc.) that made her famous.

Her first movie was the hit *The Jungle Princess* and the sarong she wore in the film made her an instant star. (The sarong would later be retired to the Smithsonian Institution.) Lamour's beginnings were more humble, as she had to quit high school and find work to help the family. But after winning a beauty contest in 1931 and doing a stint on the New York nightclub circuit in the mid-1930s, Lamour found her niche in films. She became a "pinup" girl for thousands of American G.I.s during World War II and constantly worked war bond drives and danced with soldiers. She continued to star in popular movies like *Here Comes the Groom* and the aforementioned *Road* series after the war. Lamour retired from the film industry in the 1960s but returned to the stage in 1968 with the national tour of *Hello Dolly!* She also went back to the New York cabaret circuit in the early 1980s. In 1980, Lamour wrote the autobiography, *My Side of the Road,* and later in the decade made appearances on television specials.

OBITUARIES AND OTHER SOURCES:

BOOKS

A Biographical Dictionary of Film, Knopf, 1994.
Contemporary Theatre, Film, and Television, Volume 11, Gale, 1994.

PERIODICALS

Chicago Tribune, September 23, 1996, section 1, p. 13.
Los Angeles Times, September 23, 1996, p. A16.
New York Times, September 24, 1996, p. B9.
Times (London), September 24, 1996, p. 23

* * *

LANDAU, Paul Stuart 1962-
(Bucky Shaynoux)

PERSONAL: Born October 7, 1962, in New York, NY; son of Sidney I. (an editor in chief of a university press) and Sarah B. (a professor of art history) Landau. *Ethnicity:* "White." *Education:* Wesleyan University, Middletown, CT, B.A., 1984; University of Wisconsin—Madison, M.A., 1986, Ph.D., 1992. *Politics:* "Lefty." *Religion:* "None but a general sense of the spirit." *Avocational interests:* Artist, screenwriter.

ADDRESSES: Home—New Haven, CT. *Office*—Department of History, Yale University, P.O. Box 208324, New Haven, CT 06520. *E-mail*—plandau@ minerva.cis.yale.edu.

CAREER: University of New Hampshire, Durham, assistant professor of African history, 1992-95; Yale University, New Haven, CT, assistant professor of African history, 1995—.

MEMBER: American Historical Association, African Studies Association.

AWARDS, HONORS: Fulbright fellowship.

WRITINGS:

The Realm of the Word: Language, Gender, and Christianity in a Southern African Kingdom, Heinemann (Portsmouth, NH), 1995.

WORK IN PROGRESS: Editing *Images and Empires in Africa,* publication by Berkeley Press expected in 1998; *Other Worlds: Self-Narrative and the Spirit in Southern Africa,* completion expected in 1999; writing under the pseudonym Bucky Shaynoux.

SIDELIGHTS: Paul Stuart Landau told *CA:* "It is possible to understand faith and social history as aspects of each other without doing violence to either, and without reducing the discussion to 'missionaries and converts.' I tried to write a social history of Christian belief and practice without compelling the reader to patronize Africans' choices."

* * *

LANDIS, Jerry
See SIMON, Paul

* * *

LAURIE, Clayton D. 1954-

PERSONAL: Born October 23, 1954, in Cedar Falls, IA; son of George O. (an engineer) and Donna Rae (in retail sales; maiden name, Clayton) Laurie; married Sandra K. Hocking (a secondary schoolteacher), May 23, 1981; children: Ian A., Tyler J. *Ethnicity:* "White." *Education:* University of Northern Iowa,

B.A., 1977; University of Nebraska, Omaha, M.A., 1982; American University, Ph.D., 1990. *Politics:* Independent. *Religion:* Presbyterian. *Avocational interests:* Reading, camping, traveling, sailing.

ADDRESSES: Home—18302 Redbridge Ct., Olney, MD 20832-3022. *Office*—Conventional War Studies Branch, Histories Division, U.S. Army Center of Military History, 1099 14th St. N.W., Washington, DC 20005-3402; fax 202-761-5387.

CAREER: Public high school teacher in Council Bluffs, IA, 1977-84; U.S. Army Center of Military History, Washington, DC, military historian, 1986—. American University, adjunct lecturer, 1984-90; University of Maryland, Baltimore County, lecturer in history, 1991—.

MEMBER: American Historical Association, Society for Military History, Society of Historians of American Foreign Relations, Phi Alpha Theta.

AWARDS, HONORS: U.S. Department of the Army, Merit Commendations, 1990, 1992, 1993, fellowship, 1995-96; Throne/Aldrich Award from Iowa State Historical Society, 1995, for the article "Goebbels's Iowan: Frederick W. Kaltenbach and Nazi Propaganda Broadcasts to the United States, 1940-45."

WRITINGS:

The Propaganda Warriors: America's Crusade Against Nazi Germany, University Press of Kansas (Lawrence, KS), 1996.
The Role of Federal Military Forces in Domestic Disorders, 1877-1945, U.S. Army Center of Military History (Washington, DC), 1996.
The United States Army and Psychological Warfare Operations, 1918-1945, U.S. Army Center of Military History, in press.
(Editor) John H. Ohly, *The Emergency Operation of Industrial Facilities by the War Department During World War II, 1940-1945,* U.S. Army Center of Military History, in press.

Contributor of more than twenty articles to journals, including *Civil War Times Illustrated, Philippine Studies, Montana: Magazine of Western History, West Virginia History, War and Society,* and *Gate Heritage.*

WORK IN PROGRESS: Missions Other Than War: The United States Army and Humanitarian, Disaster, and Medical Relief, 1792-2001, for U.S. Army Cen-

ter of Military History; *The Organization and Operations of the Military Intelligence Division, War Department General Staff, 1941-1945;* and *MacArthur's OSS: The Allied Intelligence Bureau in the Southwest Pacific, 1942-1945.*

* * *

LAWRENCE, Paul Frederic 1912-

PERSONAL: Born March 20, 1912, in Paterson, NJ; son of Joshua and Louise Lawrence; married Vivian Ann Hall; children: Katherine Louise, Robin Ann. *Education:* Newark State Teachers College, B.S., 1935; Stanford University, M.A., 1946, Ed.D., 1947.

ADDRESSES: Home—4837 Crestwood Way, Sacramento, CA 95822.

CAREER: Princeton, NJ, schools, classroom teacher and art supervisor, 1935-41; Howard University, associate director of counseling, 1948-56; Willowbrook School District, superintendent of schools, 1956-60; California State College, associate dean of counseling, 1960-63; California State Department of Education, associate state superintendent, 1963-67; U.S. Office of Education, regional commissioner of education, 1967-73, deputy assistant commissioner at regional office, 1973-79, director, postsecondary liaison, 1979-82; Consultants in Educational Policy and Administration, chief executive officer, 1985—. Fair Play Council, Palo Alto, CA, board member, 1946-48; Southern Field Project National Scholarship Service Foundation, director, 1949-54; National Conference of Christians and Jews, Los Angeles region, board member, 1956-60; *Scholastic Magazine* Advisory Board member, 1964-68; College Placement Bureau, board member, 1966-70; National Academy of Sciences Engineering Council, pre-college council, chair, 1975-80; Stanford University Alumni Association, board member, 1984—. Settlement team member and federal court monitor in case of National Association for the Advancement of Colored People vs. San Francisco School District and California State Department of Education. Private consultant. *Military service:* U.S. Air Force, 22 years; became lieutenant colonel.

MEMBER: Phi Delta Kappa.

AWARDS, HONORS: Numerous military decorations; honorary doctorate, New Jersey State University, 1965; Kean College, D.H.L., 1965; Keys to City, Riverside, CA, 1966-70; two citations, California State Legislature (Senate and Assembly), 1967-68; service award, U.S. Office of Education, 1970; Distinguished Educator, National Alliance of Black School Educators, 1974.

WRITINGS:

College Primer for Negro Students, Pepsi-Cola Scholarship Board (Palo Alto, CA), 1948.

Also author of *College Primer for Negro Youth,* 1946, and *Primer for Compliance Monitoring,* 1989; co-author of *Negro American Heritage* (textbook), 1964.*

* * *

LAWRENCE, Vera Brodsky 1909-1996
 (Vera Brodsky)

OBITUARY NOTICE—See index for *CA* sketch: Born July 1, 1909, in Norfolk, VA; died September 18, 1996, in Manhattan, NY. American musician, music historian, educator, and author. Music history was a second career for Lawrence but one she pursued until her death. She left unfinished the third volume of her most recent project, *Strong on Music,* a look at music in nineteenth-century New York. The first volume, *Resonances,* was published in 1991, and the second, *Reverberations,* was published in 1995. Lawrence began her musical career at New York's Juilliard School and was a concert pianist for forty years. She retired from concerts in 1965 and devoted herself to music history. She played a large role in the ragtime revival of the mid-1970s after she compiled, edited and produced *The Collected Works of Scott Joplin,* one of her best-known works. In 1976, Lawrence also won the Deems Taylor Award from the American Society of Composers for her book *Music for Patriots, Politicians, and Presidents: Harmonies and Discords of the First Hundred Years.*

OBITUARIES AND OTHER SOURCES:

BOOKS

Baker's Biographical Dictionary of Musicians, 7th edition, Schirmer, 1984.

PERIODICALS

New York Times, September 22, 1996, p. 48.

* * *

LEBSOCK, Suzanne (Dee) 1949-

PERSONAL: Born December 1, 1949, in Williston, ND. *Education:* Carleton College, B.A., 1971; University of Virginia, M.A., 1973, Ph.D., 1977.

ADDRESSES: Office—Department of History, Rutgers University, P.O. Box 2101, New Brunswick, NJ, 08903.

CAREER: Rutgers University, New Brunswick, NJ, assistant professor of history, 1977—. Writer.

MEMBER: American Historical Association, Organization of American Historians.

AWARDS, HONORS: Grant from American Council of Learned Societies, 1978; Bancroft Prize from Columbia University, 1985, for *The Free Women of Petersburg: Status and Culture in a Southern Town, 1784-1860.*

WRITINGS:

"A Share of Honour": Virginia Women, 1600-1945 (essays), Project, 1984.
The Free Women of Petersburg: Status and Culture in a Southern Town, 1784-1860, Norton, 1984.
(Editor with Nancy A. Hewitt) *Visible Women: New Essays on American Activism,* University of Illinois Press (Urbabna, IL), 1993.

Contributor to periodicals, including *Journal of Southern History.*

SIDELIGHTS: Suzanne Lebsock is a historian known for her expertise on the history of southern American women. Among her writing is *The Free Women of Petersburg: Status and Culture in a Southern Town, 1784-1860,* which documents the lives of women in a slaveholding town during the period between the American Revolution and the Civil War. Wendy

Kaminer, writing in the *New York Times Book Review,* called Lebsock's book "a lively and illuminating review," showing that "the women of Petersburg . . . enjoyed increasing personal autonomy and economic independence" during what was in many ways an era of "strident domesticity."

BIOGRAPHICAL/CRITICAL SOURCES:

PERIODICALS

New York Times, April 5, 1985.
New York Times Book Review, February 26, 1984, p. 23; September 29, 1985, p. 54.
Publishers Weekly, April 26, 1985.*

* * *

LEE, Li-Young 1957-

PERSONAL: Born August 19, 1957, in Jakarta, Indonesia; became American citizen; married Donna L., 1978; children: two sons. *Education:* University of Pittsburgh, B.A., 1979; attended University of Arizona, 1979-80; attended State University of New York, 1980-81.

ADDRESSES: Agent—c/o Simon and Schuster, Simon and Schuster Bldg., 1230 Avenue of the Americas, New York, NY 10020.

CAREER: Writer.

AWARDS, HONORS: National Endowment fellowship, 1986, 1995; Delmore Schwartz award, 1986, for *Rose;* I. B. Lavan award, 1986; Guggenheim fellowship, 1987; Lamont award, 1990, for *The City in Which I Love You;* American Book award, Before Columbus Foundation, 1995, for *The Winged Seed.*

WRITINGS:

POETRY

Rose, BOA Editions (Brockport, NY), 1986.
The City in Which I Love You, BOA Editions, 1990.

OTHER

The Winged Seed, Simon and Schuster (New York), 1995.

LEHNINGER, Albert L(ester) 1917-1986

PERSONAL: Born February 17, 1917, in Bridgeport, CT; died of a respiratory ailment, March 4, 1986, in Baltimore, MD; buried in St. Thomas Episcopal Church cemetery, Owings Mills, MD; son of Albert O. and Wally Selma (Heymer) Lehninger; married Janet Wilson, March 12, 1942; children: James L., Erika L. Whitmore. *Education:* Wesleyan University, B.A., 1939; University of Wisconsin, Madison, M.S., 1940, Ph.D., 1942. *Avocational interests:* Sailing, golf.

CAREER: University of Wisconsin, Madison, Department of Physiological Chemistry, instructor, 1942-45; University of Chicago, Department of Biochemistry, Chicago, IL, assistant professor, 1945-49, associate professor, 1949-52; Johns Hopkins School of Medicine, Baltimore, MD, Department of Physiological Chemistry, DeLamar Professor and director, 1952-78, University Professor of Medical Sciences, beginning in 1978. Visiting professor, University of Frankfort, West Germany, 1951; visiting professor, Guy's Hospital, London, England, 1963. Fifth Jubilee lecturer, Biochemical Society, 1970. Member of President's panel on Biomedical Research, 1975-76; member of council on biological sciences, Pritzker School of Medicine, beginning in 1977.

MEMBER: American Association for the Advancement of Science, National Academy of Sciences (councilor, from 1976), American Academy of Sciences Institute of Medicine (councilor, from 1976), American Philosophical Society, American Society of Biological Chemists (president, 1972-73), Biochemical Society (London), Deutsche Akademie der Naturforscher Leopoldina, Phi Beta Kappa, Sigma Xi, Phi Nu Theta.

AWARDS, HONORS: Paul Lewis Award in enzyme chemistry, American Chemical Society, 1948; Guggenheim fellowship, 1951-52, 1964; distinguished service award, University of Chicago, 1965; Remsen Award, American Chemical Society, 1969; La Madonnina Award, City of Milan, Italy. Honorary degrees include D.Sc from Wesleyan University, 1954, University of Notre Dame, 1968, Acadia University, 1972, Memorial University of Newfoundland, 1973, Universite de Paris, 1977, and Universite de Louvain, 1978; honorary M.D. from University of Padua, Italy, 1966.

WRITINGS:

The Mitochondrion: Molecular Basis of Structure and Function, W. A. Benjamin, 1964.
Bioenergetics: The Molecular Basis of Biological Energy Transformations, W. A. Benjamin, 1965, 2nd edition, 1971.
Biochemistry: The Molecular Bases of Cell Structure and Function, Worth Publishers (New York City), 1970, 2nd edition, 1975.
A Short Course in Biochemistry, Worth Publishers, 1973.
Principles of Biochemistry, Worth Publishers, 1982, 2nd edition (with David L. Nelson and Michael M. Cox), 1993.

Also author of over 300 papers on biochemistry of energy transformation in mitochondrion and in cells in general. Editor, *Journal of Biological Chemistry.*

SIDELIGHTS: The late Albert L. Lehninger was one of the first biochemists to discover one of the major processes that cells use to make energy from nutrients. In 1948, while working with fellow biochemist Eugene P. Kennedy, Lehninger determined that the enzymes used by cells to respirate—to convert raw material into energy—are located in the walls and interior of the mitochondria: tiny globe- or rod-shaped particles common to almost all cells. Lehninger's findings enabled him to predict that mitochondria would prove to have a complex internal structure, a prediction that was confirmed several years later by means of electron microscopes.

The study of the process of cell respiration, which Lehninger pioneered, became known as bioenergetics after his book, *Bioenergetics: The Molecular Basis of Biological Energy Transformations,* published in 1965. Perhaps more influential than *Bioenergetics,* however, was his classic textbook *Biochemistry: The Molecular Bases of Cell Structure and Function.* That book, according to a *Boston Globe* obituary writer, "won him international recognition and was acclaimed by colleagues as 'the most influential and successful textbook of biochemistry ever written by a single author.'" It was adopted as a standard text by many medical schools and reportedly sold over 600,000 copies in its various editions. "With a clarity and a simplicity that often awed those who knew him," wrote Martin Evans in a Baltimore *News-American* obituary, "the wiry, sandy-haired man described to a generation how living things could be composed of lifeless molecules."

BIOGRAPHICAL/CRITICAL SOURCES:

PERIODICALS

Choice, June, 1966, p. 329; November, 1973, p. 1412.
Nature, March 10, 1983, p. 176.
Science, December 24, 1965, p. 1704.

OBITUARIES:

PERIODICALS

Boston Globe, March 7, 1986, p. 13.
Chicago Tribune, March 7, 1986, p. 6.
News-American (Baltimore), March 6, 1986.
New York Times, March 6, 1986.
Pittsburgh Press, March 6, 1986.*

* * *

LEHR, Robert 1919-

PERSONAL: Born December 5, 1919, in France; son of Simon (a manufacturer) and Fanny (Britch) Lehr; married December 8, 1966; wife's name, Sophie (an antiques dealer); children: Anne-Blanche. *Education:* Received Sc.D., 1953. *Religion:* Jewish.

ADDRESSES: Home—2 rue de l'Amirel de Coligny, 75001 Paris, France. *Office—Magnane,* 1369 ave. Michard Pelissier, 06410 Biot, France.

CAREER: Writer and pharmacologist.

WRITINGS:

(With Marilyn G. Karmason and Joan B. Stacke) *Majolica,* Abrams (New York), 1989.
(With Marshall P. Katz) *Palissy Ware: Nineteenth-Century French Ceramists from Avisseau to Renoleau,* Athlone Press (London, England), 1996.

Contributor to French art journals, including *L'Objet d'Art* and *Connaissance des arts.*

WORK IN PROGRESS: Research on nineteenth-century European ceramics.

LEISER, Gary 1946-

PERSONAL: Born April 9, 1946, in Chicago, IL; son of La Viere C. (a youth counselor) and Anne (a waitress, delicatessen chef, and real estate investor; maiden name, Just) Leiser; married Patricia Tarbell (a specialist in Islamic art), June 20, 1970; children: Evan, Todd. *Education:* British Middle East Centre for Arabic Studies, Shemlan, Lebanon, Certificate in Arabic, 1967; Portland State University, B.A. and Certificate in Middle Eastern Studies, both 1969; University of Pennsylvania, Ph.D., 1976.

ADDRESSES: Home—101 San Jose Ct., Vacaville, CA 95688. *Office*—400 Brennan Circle, Travis Air Force Base, CA 94535. *E-mail*—gleiser@amw60. travis.af.mil.

CAREER: Cabrini College, Radnor, PA, visiting lecturer in Middle Eastern history, 1976; University of Utah, Salt Lake City, visiting instructor in Middle Eastern history, 1976-77; Food Development Corp., Pasco, WA, Middle East consultant, 1978; U.S. Department of Defense, staff interpreter and Middle East specialist at technical liaison office, Ankara, Turkey, 1980-83, Arabic linguist and analyst for Lebanon at Fort Meade, MD, 1983-84; U.S. Air Force in Turkey, civilian historian, 1984-89; Travis Air Force Base, Travis Air Force Base, CA, civilian historian, 1989-96, curator of Travis Air Museum, 1996—. University of Maryland, European Branch, instructor, 1981; Air University, instructor, 1995; lecturer at educational institutions, including Boston University; consultant to Brightstar, Inc.

MEMBER: American Oriental Society.

AWARDS, HONORS: Sustained Superior Performance Awards, Department of the Air Force, 1986, 1987, 1988.

WRITINGS:

(Co-editor) *Papers and Discussions: Turkiye Is Bankasi International Symposium on Ataturk,* [Ankara, Turkey] 1984.
(Editor, translator from Turkish, and author of introduction) *A History of the Seljuks: Ibrahim Kafesoglu's Interpretation and the Resulting Controversy,* Southern Illinois University Press (Carbondale, IL), 1988.
(Editor and translator from Turkish) M. Fuad Koprulu, *Origins of the Ottoman Empire,* State

University of New York Press (Albany, NY), 1992.

(Editor and translator from Turkish) Koprulu, *Seljuks of Anatolia,* University of Utah Press (Salt Lake City, UT), 1992.

(Editor, translator from Turkish, and author of introduction) Koprulu, *Islam in Anatolia After the Turkish Invasion (Prolegomena),* University of Utah Press, 1993.

(Editor and translator from Turkish) *Vetluga Memoir: A Turkish Prisoner of War in Russia, 1916-18,* University Press of Florida (Gainesville, FL), 1995.

(Editor, translator from Turkish, and author of introduction) Koprulu, *Some Observations on the Influence of Byzantine Institutions on Ottoman Institutions,* Turkish Historical Society Press (Ankara, Turkey), 1996.

Contributor to books, including *Berlitz Travellers' Guide to Turkey.* Contributor to periodicals, including *Pennsylvania Gazette, Studia Islamica, Maghreb Review, Textile Museum Journal, Middle Eastern Studies,* and *Aerospace Historian.* Author of several classified publications for the U.S. Air Force.

WORK IN PROGRESS: Translating Koprulu's *Early Mystics in Turkish Literature,* with Robert Dankoff and John Woods; translating and editing a twelfth-century Arabic medical examination, with Noury Al-Khaledy; a brief history of Ankara, from ancient times to the present, with Toni Cross.

SIDELIGHTS: Gary Leiser told *CA:* "By training, I am a specialist in the history of the medieval Middle East, with the emphasis on Egypt and Syria in the twelfth and thirteenth centuries. As a result of the collapse of the academic job market in the mid-seventies, when I completed graduate school, I went to work for the U.S. Department of Defense on the strength of my linguistic skills. I subsequently spent eight years in Turkey, working in a liaison office with the Turkish General Staff and as a historian for the U.S. Air Force.

"While working in Turkey, I maintained my academic interests, but shifted their focus to twelfth- and thirteenth-century Anatolia (Turkey). In this respect, I became fascinated by the works of M. Fuad Koprulu, the most dynamic Turkish intellectual and scholar of the twentieth century. His prolific writings on Turkish literature and history (in the broadest sense) had a profound influence on the development of these disciplines in Turkey and earned him an international reputation. Yet, because Koprulu wrote primarily in Turkish, most of his important works have been inaccessible outside his native land. With this in mind, I have undertaken the translation and publication of selected works by Koprulu that are essential for understanding the early literature and history of the Turks.

"I am currently translating Koprulu's masterpiece, *Early Mystics in Turkish Literature.* This was one of the most important books written by a Middle Eastern scholar in his own language on any aspect of Middle Eastern culture and history in the century. *Early Mystics* laid the foundation for the modern study of early Turkish literary, religious, and social history in the region between Central Asia and Anatolia. In this work, Koprulu investigated the origin and early development of Turkish mystic/Sufi folk literature, which was at the heart of Turkish literature until the late Ottoman period. Moreover, this literature was what maintained Turkish linguistic identity until modern times. Koprulu's study was meant, in fact, to help establish a modern Turkish cultural and national identity. Furthermore, the sources that Koprulu presented were a feast for specialists in Persian and Arabic literature, the evolution of Islam and Sufism in general, as well as for those interested in Turkish cultural history.

"I have worked, traveled, and done extensive research in the Middle East, including Lebanon and Egypt: I lived with a family of Palestinians in Lebanon and was evacuated during the Six-Day War; I lived in Egypt following the October War; I witnessed the troubles on Cyprus in 1974 and was evacuated after the Turkish intervention. I also lived in Ankara during the military coup of 1980.

"With the exception of Iraq and the Arabian peninsula, I have traveled throughout the Middle East, North Africa, Uzbekistan, Mongolia, the northern Pacific (Guam, the Philippines, Korea, and Japan), and New Zealand. I visited Antarctica with Operation Deep Freeze."

* * *

LENFESTEY, (William Frederick) Thompson 1925-

PERSONAL: Born June 24, 1925, in Tampa, FL; son of George S. (president of a supply business) and Lena P. (a homemaker) Lenfestey; married Harriet

Biery (a museum curator and writer), December 19, 1949; children: Harriet, Tom, Hudson. *Ethnicity:* "WASP." *Education:* Tulane University, B.S., 1946, postgraduate study, 1947; attended University of Wisconsin; attended Cincinnati Conservatory of Music; attended the University of Tampa; attended University of Cincinnati. *Politics:* Republican. *Religion:* Presbyterian. *Avocational interests:* Sailing, historical research, maritime research.

ADDRESSES: Home—902 S. Dakota Ave., No. 3A, Tampa, FL 33606. *Office*—Erny-Lenfestey Supply Co., 5008 Linebaugh Ave., Tampa, FL 33624. *E-mail*—gunkholer@aol.com.

CAREER: Erny-Lenfestey Supply Co., Tampa, FL, president, 1953-73, sales executive, 1973—. *Military service*—U.S. Navy, served as an officer in both World War II and the Korean war.

MEMBER: Bay Area Professional Writers Guild, Tampa Rotary Club, Tampa Yacht Club.

WRITINGS:

NONFICTION

A Gunkholer's Cruising Guide to Florida's West Coast, 10th edition, Great Outdoors Publishing (St. Petersburg, FL), 1981.
(With son, Tom Lenfestey, Jr.) *Facts on File Dictionary of Nautical Terms,* Facts on File (New York, NY), 1994.

Also contributor of travel articles to periodicals, including *Sailing Magazine, Yachting Magazine, Sailors Gazette, Florida Waterways Pleasure Boating, Changing Homes, Cruising World, Florida Living,* and *Guest Informant.*

WORK IN PROGRESS: A guide to historical sites of Florida, to be published by Great Outdoors Publishing.

SIDELIGHTS: When Thompson Lenfestey took up writing, he turned to his experience in the U.S. Navy during World War II and the Korean war, his long-time enjoyment of sailing, and his knowledge of the waters surrounding his home state for inspiration. Lenfestey's first book, *A Gunkholer's Cruising Guide to Florida's West Coast,* was published in 1981. He has also penned several hundred articles for magazines, and collaborated with his son, Tom, on 1994's *Facts on File Dictionary of Nautical Terms.*

A Gunkholer's Cruising Guide tells readers both what perils to avoid and what natural and man-made wonders to look for when boating along the west coast of Florida including keys, lagoons, islands, beaches, and parks. Lenfestey also provides information on the area's history, and discusses the dockside restaurants where he has dined and which he considers worthy of a boater's attention. Critics in several boating-related periodicals praised Lenfestey's experienced, common sense approach to his subject matter. Chris Caswell in *Yachting* concluded that "this book should be aboard any yacht passing along Florida's Gulf Coast." *The Gunkholer's Cruising Guide* has since seen its tenth edition.

The Facts on File Dictionary of Nautical Terms not only provides definitions of over 8,500 words having to do with seafaring, but discusses them in differing contexts. For instance, a nautical term may have various shades of meaning in the Coast Guard, the Navy, or the Merchant Marine. The Lenfesteys have collected words that range in time from the days of the Roman Empire to the most modern technical terms for sophisticated radio equipment. A listing of the phonetic alphabet used in nautical radio transmissions is also included. In *Library Journal,* Robert E. Greenfield declared *The Facts on File Dictionary of Nautical Terms* to be "highly recommended for any library." A *Booklist* critic offered high praise for the book as well, citing the elder Lenfestey's "years of experience as a naval officer and a yachtsman" and noting that the text is aimed at "the serious sailor."

Lenfestey told *CA:* "My motive for writing is not very high-minded. If the royalties stopped coming, my motivation would take a serious nose dive. Since I write outdoor books and articles, the research is as much fun, however, as the actual writing process. As with actors, it is also the smell of the greasepaint and the roar of the crowd that keeps me writing. Along with the research, I do respond to my readers' comments in person and in writing. When my readers tell me how they followed my cruising guide and found new places they would not have otherwise found, or read something in the dictionary they did not know about, my writing soul is turned on.

"I usually write early in the morning when all is quiet, often beginning at three or soon after. By the time we have breakfast, I have several ideas I want my wife to think about with me. It may be an idea, a phrase, or a paragraph I wonder about; she is not reluctant to tell me if what I have said does not make sense—or worse, makes sense and is crazy. She is

also quick to tell me when something is just right and to quit tinkering with it.

"I like to find a niche market and fill it. There was no cruising guide for the west coast of Florida that did the job of telling people where to anchor, where to eat, and where to go aground, even though it is the most cruised piece of real estate in the world. So, I decided to write it myself. I then found that there was no comprehensive nautical dictionary in print at this time, so I wrote one that remains the most comprehensive, serious dictionary on marine subjects in print."

BIOGRAPHICAL/CRITICAL SOURCES:

PERIODICALS

Booklist, March 15, 1994, pp. 1389-90.
Library Journal, January, 1994, p. 108.
Lloyd's List, July, 1994.
Yachting, August, 1982, p. 34.

* * *

LESHOAI, Benjamin Letholoa 1920-

PERSONAL: Born July 1, 1920, in Bloemfontein, Orange Free State, South Africa. *Education:* Healdtown Missionary Institution, Teacher's Certificate, 1944; Fort Hare, B.A., 1947; University of Illinois, M.A., 1964.

ADDRESSES: Office—University College, Department of Theatre Arts, Dar es Salaam, Tanzania.

CAREER: High school in Pretoria, South Africa, English teacher, 1947-57, headmaster, 1957-60; Union Artists (Bantu players), Johannesburg, South Africa, assistant manager; English teacher, Ndola (while in exile in Zambia in 1963); Mufulira Teachers' College, Zambia, English teacher, 1965-68; University College, Department of Theatre Arts, Dar es Salaam, Tanzania, teacher, 1968—.

WRITINGS:

Masilo's Adventures and Other Stories, Longmans, 1968.

Also author of play, *The Wake,* published in *New Writing from Zambia,* number 2, Lusaka, 1968.

BIOGRAPHICAL/CRITICAL SOURCES:

BOOKS

Gerard, Albert S., *Four African Literatures,* University of California Press, 1971.*

* * *

LESTRES, Alonie de
 See GROULX, Lionel (Adolphe)

* * *

LEWES, Darby 1946-

PERSONAL: Surname is pronounced like "Lewis;" born October 6, 1946, in New York, NY; married Bobby Stiklus; children: Jennifer Stiklus Gray, Kimberley. *Education:* Saint Xavier College (now University), B.A. (with honors), 1984; Northwestern University, M.A., 1985; University of Chicago, Ph.D., 1991.

ADDRESSES: Home—R.D.2, Box 319, Pennsdale, PA 17756. *Office*—Department of English, Lycoming College, Williamsport, PA 17701-5192. *E-mail*—lewes@lycoming.edu.

CAREER: Saint Xavier University, Chicago, IL, lecturer in English, 1986-90; University of Chicago, Chicago, instructor in literature, 1991-93; Lycoming College, Williamsport, PA, assistant professor of English, 1993—. Loyola University of Chicago, lecturer, 1991-92, visiting assistant professor, 1992-93.

MEMBER: Modern Language Association of America, Society for Utopian Studies, Popular Culture Association, Midwest Victorian Studies Association, Southeastern Nineteenth-Century Studies Association, Northeastern Modern Language Association.

AWARDS, HONORS: Fellow of English-Speaking Union, Oxford University, 1985; Arthur O. Lewis Award, Society for Utopian Studies, 1992, 1994; honorary doctorate, Wilson College, 1997.

WRITINGS:

Dream Revisionaries: Genre and Gender in Women's Utopian Fiction, 1870-1920, University of Alabama Press (Tuscaloosa, AL), 1995.

Contributor to periodicals, including *Utopian Studies* and *Legacy*.

WORK IN PROGRESS: *Nudes from Nowhere: Utopian Sexual Landscapes,* completion expected in 1998.

* * *

LEWIS, Padmore
 See LEWIS, Susan Padmore

* * *

LEWIS, Sandra Padmore 1957-
 (Padmore Lewis)

PERSONAL: Born October 16, 1957, in Barbados; daughter of Desmond (a carpenter) and Etheline (a homemaker; maiden name, Padmore) Spooner; married David A. Lewis (an automotive body repairer), June 16, 1990. *Ethnicity:* "Black." *Education:* Pace University, B.B.A., 1986; Long Island University, M.B.A., 1991. *Avocational interests:* Walking, reading, "making a difference in another person's life."

ADDRESSES: *Home*—315 East 23rd St., Brooklyn, NY 11226. *Office*—Port Authority of New York and New Jersey, 1 World Trade Center, 69W, New York, NY 10048.

CAREER: Port Authority of New York and New Jersey, New York City, accountant, 1994—. Community volunteer.

MEMBER: Institute of Management Accounting (associate director, 1994—).

WRITINGS:

Some Things I Have Noticed, American Literary Press (Baltimore, MD), 1996.

Some writings appear under the name Padmore Lewis.

WORK IN PROGRESS: Two novels, *For the Love of Friends* and *Time and Years Have Changed Us.*

SIDELIGHTS: Sandra Padmore Lewis told *CA:* "I am an honest and sincere person who always wants to be of some comfort to another person. I want others to know that, no matter what they are going through, somebody else has walked that road before. My work is influenced by the experiences of others. I listen very carefully; then, in the form of poetry, I tell others what I hear them saying or what they should be saying. Then I look within my spirituality to find the most appropriate phrase to suit the occasion. My subjects are issues of an everyday nature: jealousy, loneliness, sickness, dying."

* * *

LILLICH, Richard B(onnot) 1933-1996

OBITUARY NOTICE—See index for *CA* sketch: Born January 22, 1933, in Amherst, OH; died of a heart attack, August 3, 1996, in Charlottesville, VA. Lawyer, educator, author. A champion of international human rights issues, Lillich began his career as an attorney in private practice in New York City in 1957. He turned to education in 1960, first at Indiana University-Bloomington and at Syracuse University from 1960 to 1969, followed by the remainder of his career at the University of Virginia. He was still teaching at Virginia at the time of his death. Lillich was involved in various human rights organizations. He was a cofounder of the International Human Rights Law Group in 1978. An editor of the *American Journal of International Law,* he also was an adviser to the Urban Morgan Institute of Human Rights, and he was a founder and one-time president of the Procedural Aspects of International Law Institute. The author and editor of numerous books, he penned works such as *International Claims: Their Adjudication by National Commissions, International Claims: Post War British Practice, International Human Rights Instruments, Human Rights Documents,* and *International Human Rights: Problems of Law, Policy, and Practice.* Among his edited works are *Humanitarian Intervention and the United Nations* and *U.S. Ratification of the Human Rights Treaties: With or Without Reservations.*

OBITUARIES AND OTHER SOURCES:

BOOKS

Who's Who in American Law, 7th edition, Marquis, 1991.

PERIODICALS

New York Times, August 16, 1996, p. A30.

* * *

LIMON, Jerzy 1950-

PERSONAL: Born May 24, 1950, in Malbork, Poland; son of Zenon (a physician) and Wanda (a nurse; maiden name, Gierasimowicz) Limon; married Justyna Marcinkiewicz (an English teacher), April 8, 1985; children: Tomasz (son). *Education:* Adam Mickiewicz University, Poznan, Poland, M.A., 1975; Ph.D., 1979. *Religion:* Roman Catholic.

ADDRESSES: Home—ul. 23 Marca 91/87, Sopot, 81-820 Poland. *Office*—Department of English, University of Gdansk, ul. Wita Stwosza 55., Gdansk-Oliwa, Poland. *Agent*—Stowarzyszenie Autorow "ZAiKS," ul. Hipoteczna 2, 00-092 Warsaw, Poland.

CAREER: Adam Mickiewicz University, Poznan, Poland, Department of English, instructor, 1975-79, lecturer, 1979-80; University of Gdansk, Gdansk, Poland, Department of English, assistant professor, 1980-85, associate professor, 1985—.

MEMBER: Stowarzyszenie Autorow "ZAiKS."

WRITINGS:

Munchhauseniada (novel), Wydawnictwo Poznanskie, 1980.
Gentlemen of a Company: English Players in Central and Eastern Europe, 1590-1660 (nonfiction), Cambridge University Press (Cambridge, England), 1986.
Dangerous Matter: English Drama and Politics in 1623-24 (nonfiction), Cambridge University Press, 1986.
The Masque of Stuart Culture (nonfiction), University of Delaware Press (Newark), 1990.
(Editor with Jay L. Halio) *Shakespeare and His Contemporaries: Eastern and Central European Studies* (nonfiction), University of Delaware Press, 1993.

SIDELIGHTS: Scholar Jerzy Limon has done much research into the English theatrical players who performed during the sixteenth and seventeenth centuries. In *Gentlemen of a Company* he recounts how in the early 1590s English troupes of theatrical players toured Europe, where they often became resident companies at different courts. The English players, finding ready accommodations in the Germanic areas, developed a highly physical form of acting, which they refined as they learned the German language. When the Thirty Years War made traveling in Europe hazardous and the theaters reopened in London under the Restoration, English players returned to England.

Scholars found much to praise about *Gentlemen of a Company.* According to Julie Hankey of the *Times Literary Supplement,* one of Limon's achievements is to have brought together the findings of various continental scholars for the English-speaking world. She suggests that because the book is made up of papers that have appeared elsewhere, "there is a sense of different audiences being addressed." She asserts that "the long introduction is kind on the general reader," yet the central section is geared chiefly for the specialist. Harold B. Segel in *Renaissance Quarterly* declared, "Although much has been written about the English players on the Continent from 1590 to 1660 in both English and German, Jerzy Limon's small book is a welcome addition." Segel added, "In his carefully researched account of the travels of the English players in Eastern Europe the author supplements the existing Western literature, thereby permitting the English-language reader a much more complete view of the subject that was previously possible."

Limon's *Dangerous Matter* is a very specialized study of the 1623-1624 London theatrical season and how the works staged during this time may have been part of a propaganda campaign designed and initiated by Prince Charles and the Duke of Buckingham to promote anti-Spanish policy in the wake of a failed attempt to arrange a marriage with the Spanish princess. In a review for *Choice,* H. L. Ford called *Dangerous Matter* "authoritative" and "generally well written and readable," adding that the notes, bibliography, and index are extensive and "valuable."

Limon told *CA:* "In accordance with a Chinese curse—'I wish you lived in interesting times'—I was lucky to be born into yet another interesting phase in Poland's history (this is why from time to time we all long for a 'normal' life). The permanent economic crisis notwithstanding, a writer in today's Poland faces a peculiar situation. He/she has the option of cooperating with at least three types of presses: the state-run big publishing houses (in which editors are often more captious than the censors), Catholic

presses (these are also censored), and underground presses. The presses reflect, in fact, the spheres of our cultural life: the 'official,' the 'tolerated,' and the 'illegal.' The existence of censorship has, of course, numerous consequences and one of the most difficult tasks for a writer is to avoid becoming his/her own censor (which is not that easy!). The other danger is that of becoming too topical, which makes the created texts incomprehensible to all foreign readers."

BIOGRAPHICAL/CRITICAL SOURCES:

PERIODICALS

Choice, February, 1987, p. 882; May, 1991, p. 1487.
English Historical Review, April, 1989, pp. 490-91.
Literature and History, spring, 1988, p. 119.
Renaissance Quarterly, volume 41, issue 1, spring, 1988, pp. 153-55; volume 41, issue 2, spring, 1988, pp. 252-56.
Times Literary Supplement, March 7, 1986, p. 250; February 20, 1987, p. 188.

* * *

LIPSON, Leon Samuel 1921-1996

OBITUARY NOTICE—See index for *CA* sketch: Born August 4, 1921, in Chelsea, MA; died of heart problems, September 20, 1996, in New Haven, CT. Educator, lawyer, writer. Lipson gained prominence in the field of international law. He began a thirty-five-year teaching career in 1957 at Yale University's Law School. Lipson was well-versed in Soviet law, as well as space law. In addition to his teaching career, Lipson also served as an adviser to the United Nations and as a member of the board of Social Science Research Council.

In 1961 he authored a project for NASA with Nicholas de Belleville Katzenbach, entitled *Report to the National Aeronautics and Space Administration on the Law of Outer Space.* He also contributed to *Soviet and Chinese Communism: Similarities and Differences* (Donald W. Treadgold, editor), *Prospects for Soviet Society* (A. H. Kassof, editor), and translated August Stern's *The U.S.S.R. Versus Dr. Mikhail Stern: Soviet Justice Versus Human Rights* (with Marco Carynnyk).

OBITUARIES AND OTHER SOURCES:

BOOKS

Who's Who in American Law, Marquis, 1991.

PERIODICALS

New York Times, September 26, 1996, p. D23.

* * *

LISLE, Janet Taylor 1947-

PERSONAL: Born February 13, 1947, in Englewood, NJ; daughter of Alden (in insurance) and Janet (an architect) Taylor; married Richard Lisle (a financial consultant), 1976; children: Elizabeth. *Education:* Smith College, B.A., 1969; attended Georgia State. *Avocational interests:* Choral singing, gardening.

ADDRESSES: Home—Rhode Island. *Agent*—c/o Gina Maccoby, c/o Orchard Books, 95 Madison Ave., New York, NY 10016.

CAREER: Writer. Has worked as a journalist in Georgia and New York; VISTA (Volunteers in Service to America), volunteer, Atlanta, GA, c. 1970.

AWARDS, HONORS: Honor Book designation, Society of Children's Book Writers, 1988, for *The Great Dimpole Oak;* Newberry Honor, 1990, for *Afternoon of the Elves.*

WRITINGS:

FOR CHILDREN

The Dancing Cats of Applesap, Bradbury Press (Scarsdale, NY), 1984.
Sirens and Spies, Bradbury Press, 1985.
The Great Dimpole Oak, Orchard (New York), 1987.
Afternoon of the Elves, Orchard, 1989.
The Light behind the Door, Orchard, 1989.
The Lampfish of Twill, Orchard, 1991.
Forest, Orchard, 1993.
The Gold Dust Letters, Orchard, 1994.
Looking for Juliette, Orchard, 1994.
A Message from the Match Girl, Orchard, 1995.
Angela's Aliens, Orchard, 1996.

SIDELIGHTS: The imaginative stories of author Janet Taylor Lisle draw young readers into a world where the everyday is peppered with magic: where cats

dance, miniature elves hide in the backyard lawn, and worlds exist below the sea. Praising the author's ability to both fascinate and challenge her audiences, Kay E. Vandergrift noted in *Twentieth-Century Children's Writers* that Lisle "is an elegant writer whose stories are carefully woven with just enough space left for readers to continue to wonder and to imagine new possibilities at the book's close."

After working as a journalist for several years, Lisle found her interest in writing fiction growing; she wrote her first children's book, *The Dancing Cats of Applesap,* in 1984 after being inspired by a writing workshop she attended in 1980. Based on Lisle's memories of growing up in a small Connecticut town, *The Dancing Cats* features a shy ten-year-old girl who helps a local soda fountain escape financial ruin by promoting the escapades of the store's resident felines. Balancing subtle humor with character development in what would become characteristic Lisle fashion, the book was followed a year later by *Sirens and Spies.* In this novel, two sisters become intrigued by their reclusive, foreign-born violin teacher's mysterious past. The younger sister discovers that Miss Fitch was actually condemned as a Nazi sympathizer as a result of a love affair with a German soldier stationed in France during World War II; she refuses to listen to any explanation for this "wrong" while the older sister exhibits greater tolerance and compassion and tries to understand her teacher's actions. Critically praised for its strong character development and ability to deal with developing moral character, *Sirens and Spies* was cited by Ilene Cooper in *Booklist* as "prov[ing] once again that fiction for children can be just as powerful and complex as that written for adults."

Lisle's other novels, such as *The Great Dimpole Oak, Afternoon of the Elves,* and *The Lampfish of Twill,* are also set in the Northeast United States, but each novel's setting reflects a different part of that area's character: small, rural towns, remote seaside communities, or the granite-strewn, wooded terrain of the yet-undeveloped New England countryside. In *The Lampfish of Twill,* a young boy begins to reevaluate his own preconceptions after he is led to an underwater world where the physical realities of the surface are radically altered: time has stopped and creatures are left "stuck," without the ability to move. The treetop haven that is home to a group of grey squirrels is invaded after a young girl runs away from home and takes to the woods in *Forest,* a novel which *New York Times Book Review* contributor Brock Cole characterized as dark in meaning: A "feeling of un-

certainty and weakness, of not being sure that one can cope with the irrational and violent impulses that threaten always to break out, lends an edge to her work that her way with words and her sense of humor can't always cloak," he noted of Lisle's 1993 novel.

Lisle told *CA:* "I believe in the unknown. There is a great deal we don't know about our world, like how big the universe is or what makes our brains work. Perhaps the human brain isn't smart enough or sensitive enough yet to detect certain secrets. I think of magic as being that which is still waiting to be discovered. I put it in my books so that readers (myself included) won't forget to keep a sharp eye out. The unknown is all around us. As the old fishcatcher in *The Lampfish of Twill* warns Eric, 'there are larger schemes in motion!'"

BIOGRAPHICAL/CRITICAL SOURCES:

BOOKS

Twentieth-Century Children's Writers, fourth edition, St. James (Detroit), 1995, pp. 586-87.

PERIODICALS

Booklist, July, 1984, p. 1550; May 15, 1985, p. 1333.
Boston Globe, February 21, 1988, p. 48.
Horn Book, September/October, 1989, p. 622.
New York Times Book Review, December 13, 1987, p. 36; November 12, 1989, p. 28; November 10, 1991, p. 31; November 14, 1993, p. 47.
Publishers Weekly, January 17, 1986, p. 69; October 9, 1987, p. 88; September 13, 1991, p. 80; May 31, 1991, p. 77; January 10, 1994, p. 62; August 1994, p. 158.
School Library Journal, November, 1993, p. 109.

* * *

LITTMAN, Jonathan (Russell) 1958-

PERSONAL: Born April 18, 1958, in San Francisco, CA; son of Allan Norman and Caroline (Russell) Littman. *Education:* University of California, Berkeley, B.A., 1982.

ADDRESSES: Office—c/o Little, Brown and Co., Inc., 1271 Avenue of the Americas, New York, NY 10020.

CAREER: PC World (magazine), San Francisco, CA, contributing editor, 1983-84; *PC Week* (magazine), Belmont, CA, staff reporter, 1984-86; *Mac World* (magazine), San Francisco, contributing editor, 1987—. Speaker at colleges and universities and on national television, 1985—.

WRITINGS:

Once upon a Time in ComputerLand: The Amazing, Billion-Dollar Tale of Bill Millard, Knight-Ridder (Tucson, AZ), 1987.
The Fugitive Game: Online with Kevin Mitnick, Little, Brown (New York), 1996.

Also contributor of articles and reviews to *PC/Computing, Personal Computing, Forbes, Los Angeles Times, Working Woman,* and *California.*

SIDELIGHTS: Jonathan Littman's first book, *Once upon a Time in ComputerLand: The Amazing, Billion-Dollar Tale of Bill Millard,* "provides an interesting insight" into the history and development of this particular company which "did not follow established business practices," comments Michael D. Kathman in *Library Journal.* The book, which chronicles the rise and demise of Millard's business career, addresses many of Millard's personal quirks and unusual behaviors. A *Booklist* reviewer notes that Littman "tells the tale with authority and verve," adding that the "details of various courtroom battles are particularly fascinating." A *Kirkus Reviews* critic describes the book as a "deft and devastating portrait of William Millard." The *Kirkus Reviews* critic further labels the book "a painstakingly documented account that rings true," concluding that the book contains "altogether splendid reportage."

In *The Fugitive Game: Online with Kevin Mitnick,* Littman "offers a convincing perspective on Kevin Mitnick's alleged computer crimes, developed from interviews, research and talks with the then-fugitive suspect," according to a *Publishers Weekly* reviewer. Published at the same time as two other books about the infamous computer hacker, *The Fugitive Game* treats the material from the perspective of Mitnick himself, unlike another of the books—*Takedown: The Pursuit and Capture of Kevin Mitnick, America's Most Wanted Computer Outlaw, by the Man Who Did It.* That work, by Tsutomu Shimomura with *New York Times* reporter John Markoff, examines the story from Shimomura's position as the highly respected cyber-security expert whose personal computer was hacked into by Mitnick himself. Joe

Accardi observes in the *Library Journal* that Littman questions the motives of Shimomura and Markoff. Littman observes that the book and film rights and public appearance fees surrounding their involvement in the case may have caused the authors to step over the line of journalistic ethics. In a similar vein, James Fallows remarks in the *New York Times Book Review* that, rather than focusing on Mitnick as the villain, Littman "seems to locate the menace in John Markoff and his accomplice, Tsutomu Shimomura." Dana Kennedy writes in *Entertainment Weekly* that while Littman has the benefit of Mitnick as a primary source for information and detail, he "pretty much squanders" that advantage in "clearly a bitter rivalry with Markoff" regarding the latter's media deals and profit motives.

BIOGRAPHICAL/CRITICAL SOURCES:

PERIODICALS

Booklist, October 15, 1987, p. 350.
Entertainment Weekly, February 2, 1996, pp. 50-51.
Globe and Mail (Toronto), January 30, 1988.
Kirkus Reviews, September 15, 1987, pp. 1372-73.
Library Journal, December, 1987, p. 107; January, 1996, pp. 130, 132.
New York Times Book Review, February 4, 1996, pp. 14-15.
Publishers Weekly, November 27, 1995, p. 59.*

* * *

LIVINGSTON, Myra Cohn 1926-1996

OBITUARY NOTICE—See index for *CA* sketch: Born August 17, 1926, in Omaha, NE; died of cancer, August 23, 1996, in Los Angeles, CA. Musician, critic, educator, poet, anthologist, and author. Livingston was one of the foremost American children's authors of the latter twentieth-century. She wrote scores of books and compiled about forty anthologies. Trained as a French horn player, she opted to write book reviews in 1948 for newspapers such as the *Los Angeles Daily News* and the *Los Angeles Mirror.* In 1950 she began working as a personal secretary for entertainer Dinah Shore; she also held a similar post with musician Jascha Heifetz, and was working on a biography of the violinist before her death. In 1958 she began a series of jobs as an instructor at such institutions as the Dallas Public Library and Dallas Public School System and the Uni-

versity of California-Los Angeles. From 1966 until 1984, she was poet-in-residence at the Beverly Hills United School District. Beginning in 1975, she was a poetry consultant to various publishers. She also taught classes for the International Reading Association, the National Council of Teachers of English, and other organizations.

A prolific poet for children, she wrote volumes such as *Whispers and Other Poems, A Lollygag of Limericks,* and *My Head Is Red and Other Riddle Rhymes.* Her most recent books include *Light and Shadow, Let Freedom Ring: A Ballad of Martin Luther King, Jr., Flights and Fancy and Other Poems,* and *Abraham Lincoln: A Man for All People.* Among her honors are the Kerlan Award from the University of Minnesota, the National Council of Teachers of English award for poetry, and a translation award from the International Board on Books for Young People for *Platero Y Yo/Platero and I.*

OBITUARIES AND OTHER SOURCES:

BOOKS

Who's Who in America, 51st edition, Marquis, 1996.

PERIODICALS

Los Angeles Times, August 27, 1996, p. A19.
New York Times, August 27, 1996, p. B8.
Washington Post, August 26, 1996, p. B5.

* * *

LLEWELLYN, Kate 1940-

PERSONAL: Born Katherine Jill Sky Brinkwath, in 1940, in Tumby Bay, South Australia; married Richard Dutton Llewellyn, 1960 (divorced 1975); one son, one daughter. *Education:* University of Adelaide, B.A., 1978.

ADDRESSES: Agent—Tim Curnow, Curtis Brown Literary Agents, 7 Union St., Paddington 2021, New South Wales, Australia.

CAREER: Royal Adelaide Hospital, South Australia, trainee nurse, 1954-58; registered nurse, Adelaide, 1958-60; Llewellyn Galleries, Dulwich, co-owner and director, 1968-75.

WRITINGS:

POETRY

Trader Kate and the Elephants, Friendly Street Poets (Adelaide), 1983.
Luxury, Redress Press (Sydney), 1985.
Honey, Hawthorn (Hudson), 1988.
Figs, Hawthorn, 1989.
Selected Poems, Hawthorn, 1992.

Also author of *Crosshatched,* 1994.

OTHER

The Waterlily, Hawthorn, 1986.
Dear You, Hawthorn, 1987.
The Mountain, Hawthorn, 1990.
Angels and Dark Madonnas—Travels in Italy and India, Hawthorn, 1991.
Lilies Feathers and Frangipani, HarperCollins (Sydney), 1993.
The Floral Mother and Other Essays, HarperCollins, 1995.
Gorillas Tea & Coffee (Travels in East Africa), HarperCollins, 1995.
(Editor) *The Penguin Book of Australian Women Poets,* Penguin (Melbourne), 1986.

* * *

LLORENS, Washington 1900-

PERSONAL: Born November 28, 1900, in Ponce, Puerto Rico.

CAREER: Pharmacist and writer; director of San Juan District Laboratory of the Alcohol Tax Unit, United States Internal Revenue Service, 1943—. Chairperson of the Commonwealth's Board of Pharmacy Examiners, 1941; lecturer at the Interamerican University of Puerto Rico.

MEMBER: Puerto Rico Academy of Arts and Sciences (president), Puerto Rico Society of Journalists and Writers (vice-president), Puerto Rico Academy of the Spanish Language, Royal Spanish Academy of Language (corresponding member), Puerto Rico Institute of Hispanic Culture (president), Pharmaceutical Association of Puerto Rico (secretary-treasurer).

AWARDS, HONORS: Journalism prizes from Institute of Puerto Rican Literature, 1956 and 1964; honorary degree from Temple University for outstanding contributions to pharmacy.

WRITINGS:

El espanol de Puerto Rico y la decimoctava edicion del Diccionario de la Real Academia Espanola, Club (San Juan Bautista, Puerto Rico), 1957.

Un intruso en la jardin de academo, Club, 1957.

Catorce pecados de humor y una vida descabellada, Club, 1959.

El humorismo, el epigrama y la satira en la literatura puertorriquena, Instituto de Cultura (San Juan, Puerto Rico), 1960.

El habla popular de Puerto Rico, Academia de Artes y Ciencias de Puerto Rico, 1968, revised edition, with introduction by Cesareo Rosa-Nieves, Edil (Rio Piedras), 1981.

Diez pecados de humor, Instituto de Cultura, 1977.

Humor, Epigram, and Satire in Puerto Rican Literature, Gordon Press, 1979.

La magia de la palabra, University of Puerto Rico, 1980.

Cazador de imposibles, Biblioteca de Autores Puertorriquenos (San Juan), 1981.

Editor of the literary publications *Alma Latina* and *Prensa Literaria;* editor of *Journal* of the Puerto Rico College of Pharmacy, and of *Revista Farmaceutica de Puerto Rico,* 1930-32.*

* * *

LOCKETT, Reginald (Franklin) 1947-

PERSONAL: Born November 5, 1947, in Berkeley, CA; son of Jewell and Alyce Irene (Matthis) Lockett; married Faye Arvis West, January 23, 1983 (divorced September 1, 1987); children: Maya Lomasi Lauren Aimee. *Education:* San Francisco State University, B.A., 1971, M.A., 1972.

ADDRESSES: Home—3717 Market St., Oakland, CA 94608. *Office*—Department of Language Arts, San Jose City College, 2100 Moorpark Ave., San Jose, CA 95128-2723.

CAREER: North Peralta Community College, Oakland, CA, instructor in English, 1973-75; Laney College, Oakland, instructor in English, 1975-76; San

Francisco State University, San Francisco, CA, lecturer in creative writing, 1976-78; City College of San Francisco, San Francisco, reading lab instructor, beginning in 1982; San Jose City College, San Jose, CA, member of department of language arts.

WRITINGS:

Good Times and No Bread (poetry), Jukebox Press, 1978.

Contributor of numerous poems to literary magazines and anthologies; editor, *Folio,* 1977.*

* * *

LOPEZ, Diana 1948-
(Isabella Rios)

PERSONAL: Born March 16, 1948, in Los Angeles, CA; daughter of Louis H. (a contracting business owner) and Valentine (a homemaker; maiden name, Ballesteros) Lopez; children: Jason Ho. *Education:* San Francisco State University, B.A., 1967, M.A., 1969; Nova University, Ed.D., 1979.

ADDRESSES: Home—1066 Via Arroyo, Ventura, CA 93003. *Office*—Department of Language Arts, Moorpark College, 7075 Campus Rd., Moorpark, CA 93021.

CAREER: Moorpark College, Moorpark, CA, English instructor, 1970—, assisted in establishing and taught in Bilingual Center and tutorial program for minority students; writer.

MEMBER: Ventura Writers' Club.

WRITINGS:

(Under pseudonym Isabella Rios) *Victuum,* Diana-Etna (Ventura, CA), 1976.

Contributor of poems and short stories to periodicals.

WORK IN PROGRESS: A revision of *Victuum,* and a sequel; a book of poetry.

SIDELIGHTS: Diana Lopez, who writes under the pseudonym Isabella Rios, will be remembered in Hispanic literature as the author of the first Chicana bildungsroman, *Victuum.* The story of a Hispanic

woman's coming of age and discovery of her psychic ability, *Victuum* also offers insight into the social and cultural changes Californian Chicano society underwent from the turn of the twentieth century to the present day. The book is based on the life and experiences of one of Rios's female relatives, whom Rios interviewed extensively for two years; woven into her story are bits of Lopez family history and Hispanic folklore.

Victuum begins with protagonist Valentina Ballesternos still in the womb, lamenting that once she is born she will not remember any of what she has learned in her past lives. As Rios follows her through birth and adolescence to marriage and motherhood she writes of the Chicano experience during the Prohibition era, the Depression, and World War II as Valentina lived it. Valentina's psychic powers manifest themselves as she matures, and when describing her later years *Victuum* becomes her spiritual biography. Eventually the narrative becomes dominated by Valentina's psychic experiences—visions and dreams peopled by such diverse figures as poet William Wordsworth, the prophet Isaiah, and Pope Eusebius. Thus Rios recreates the mystical landscape of Valentina's mind, raising questions about the very nature of reality.

BIOGRAPHICAL/CRITICAL SOURCES:

BOOKS

Dictionary of Literary Biography, Volume 82: *Chicano Writers, First Series,* Gale, 1989.

PERIODICALS

Minority Voices, spring, 1980.

* * *

LOUGHLIN, James 1948-

PERSONAL: Born October 24, 1948, in Portadown, Northern Ireland; married Jacinta Haddock, July 26, 1975; children: Caroline, Carmen. *Education:* Northern Ireland Polytechnic, B.A. (with first class honors), 1977; Trinity College, Dublin, Ph.D., 1983.

ADDRESSES: Home—40 Cashelmore Park, Londonderry BT48 0RU, Northern Ireland. *Office*—School of History, Philosophy, and Politics, Magee College, University of Ulster, Londonderry BT48 7JL, Northern Ireland.

CAREER: Substitute teacher in local secondary schools, 1982-83; University of Ulster, Londonderry, Northern Ireland, lecturer in modern European and British history, 1984-86; Queen's University of Belfast, Belfast, Northern Ireland, junior research fellow at Institute of Irish Studies, 1985, research associate, 1986-87, senior research fellow, 1987-88, lecturer in modern history and politics, 1985-86; University of Ulster, lecturer in history, 1988—.

MEMBER: Royal Historical Society (fellow).

WRITINGS:

Gladstone, Home Rule, and the Ulster Question, 1882-93, Gill & Macmillan (Dublin, Ireland), 1986, Humanities (Atlantic Highlands, NJ), 1987.
Ulster Unionism and British National Identity Since 1885, Cassell (London, England), 1995.

Contributor to books, including *Parnell in Perspective,* edited by D. G. Boyce and A. O'Day, Routledge & Kegan Paul (New York City), 1991. Contributor to periodicals, including *Retrospect, Irish Historical Studies, Eire-Ireland,* and *History.*

WORK IN PROGRESS: British Monarchy, National Identity, and Ireland, 1870-1921.

SIDELIGHTS: James Loughlin told *CA:* "The major research areas that interest me are Anglo-Irish relations in the nineteenth and twentieth centuries and the problems that have complicated them, especially problems of national identity. In this regard, a particular focus of my work has been the Ulster question since its inception as a specifically political problem in the mid-1880s. Aspects of the Ulster question have been covered in most of my published works. As it is the last significant issue in Anglo-Irish relations still to be resolved, I have been concerned especially to explore its complexity and the difficulties hampering its resolution. My most recent monograph examined a relatively neglected dimension of the question; that is, Ulster unionist conceptions of their national identity and their relationship with Britain.

"I shall continue to publish on Ulster, though the issue of national identity in the context of Anglo-Irish relations will be considered more widely in my next book."

LOW, Kathleen

PERSONAL: Born in California. *Education:* University of California, Davis, B.A., 1977; San Jose State University, M.L.S., 1979.

ADDRESSES: Office—California State Library, P.O. Box 942837, Sacramento, CA 94237-0001. *E-mail*—klow@library.ca.gov.

CAREER: University of California, Davis, cataloger, 1980-83; CLASS, San Jose, CA, online coordinator, 1983-84; California State Library, Sacramento, online reference librarian, 1984-88, database specialist, 1988-89, outreach manager, 1989-92, principal librarian, 1992—.

MEMBER: American Library Association, California Writers Club, Northern California Technical Processes Group.

WRITINGS:

Legislative Reference Services and Sources, Haworth Press (Binghamton, NY), 1995.
(Editor and contributor) *The Roles and Responsibilities of Reference Librarians,* Haworth Press, 1996.

Contributor to magazines, including *American Libraries, Link-Up, Online Access,* and *Reference Librarian.*

WORK IN PROGRESS: A book on recruitment, for Neal-Schuman (New York City).

* * *

LOWE, Sarah M. 1956-

PERSONAL: Born September 1, 1956, in Buffalo, NY; daughter of Charles U. (a physician) and Eileen (a musician) Lowe. *Education:* Vassar College, B.A., 1979; Graduate School and University Center of the City University of New York, M.Phil., 1989, Ph.D., 1996. *Politics:* Democrat. *Religion:* Jewish. *Avocational interests:* Gardening.

ADDRESSES: Home—Brooklyn, New York. *E-mail*—smlarthist@aol.com.

CAREER: Art historian; curator of exhibits at Hartwick College, 1987, and Brooklyn Museum, 1993; curator of traveling exhibits for Center for Photography at Woodstock, 1993, and Philadelphia Museum of Art, 1995. Lecturer at educational institutions, including Adelphi University, 1986, 1990, Kean College of New Jersey, 1987, and Montclair State College and State University of New York College at Purchase, both 1988. Lower East Side Printshop, New York City, member of board of directors, 1995-97.

MEMBER: Latin American Art Association, College Art Association of America, ArtTable, Inc., Women Writing Women's Lives Seminar.

WRITINGS:

Frida Kahlo, Universe Books (New York), 1991.
(Co-author) *Consuelo Kanaga: An American Photographer,* University of Washington Press (Seattle, WA), 1992.
Tina Modotti: Photographs, Abrams (New York), 1995.
(Author of essay and commentaries) *The Diary of Frida Kahlo: An Intimate Self-Portrait,* Abrams, 1995.

Contributor to periodicals, including *History of Photography* and *Women in the Arts.*

WORK IN PROGRESS: Research on women artists on the "Grand Tour," "focusing on photographer Louise Dahl-Wolfe's trip to Europe in 1927 and the diary she kept and illustrated with her own photographs."

* * *

LOWTHER, Pat(ricia Louise) 1935-1975

PERSONAL: Born July 29, 1935, in Vancouver, British Columbia, Canada; murdered, September 1975, near Squamish, British Columbia, Canada; daughter of Arthur (a caretaker) and Virginia (a dancer) Tinmuth; married Bill Domphousse, 1953 (divorced, c. 1957); married Roy Armstrong Lowther (a teacher and activist), 1963; children: (first marriage) Alan, Catherine, (second marriage) two daughters. *Education:* Took creative writing classes during the 1950s and early 1960s. *Politics:* Socialist.

CAREER: Worked in many clerical positions in Vancouver, British Columbia, during the 1950s and 1960s; secretary for one year for the New Democratic Party's Little Mountain Constituency, Vancouver, British Columbia, c. 1972; University of British Columbia, Vancouver, creative writing instructor, 1975.

MEMBER: League of Canadian Poets (co-chair, 1975).

AWARDS, HONORS: Two Canadian Council Grants; a memorial prize is given in her name annually.

WRITINGS:

This Difficult Flowering, illustrated by S. Slutsky, Very Stone House (Vancouver, British Columbia), 1968.

(Contributor) *Forty Women Poets of Canada,* edited by Dorothy Livesay, Ingluvin (Montreal, Quebec), 1971.

The Age of the Bird (limited edition unbound portfolio), Blackfish Press, 1972.

Milk Stone (includes "In the Continent Behind My Eyes" and "Moonwalk Summer"), Borealis (Ottawa, Ontario), 1974.

A Stone Diary, Oxford University Press (Toronto, Ontario), 1977.

Final Instructions: Early Uncollected Poems, edited by Dona Sturmanis and Fred Candelaria, *West Coast Review*/Orca Sound Publications (Vancouver, British Columbia), 1980.

Also contributor of poems to periodicals.

SIDELIGHTS: Poet Pat Lowther only lived for forty years, and her literary output was somewhat slender, but "her place in Canadian literature is assured," according to Hilda L. Thomas in the *Dictionary of Literary Biography.* Her first collection, *This Difficult Flowering,* saw print in 1968, and the most widely read and reviewed of her works, *A Stone Diary,* was published posthumously in 1977. Much of her poetry is concerned with the related topics of political repression—particularly as exemplified in South American history—and the concerns of modern feminism.

Lowther was born Patricia Louise Tinmuth in Vancouver in 1935. Her parents were of the working class, and, though she was bright and demonstrated a love of writing at an early age, Lowther left school at the age of sixteen to take a clerical job. She married her first husband, Bill Domphousse, when she

was only eighteen. Lowther had a son and daughter with Domphousse; when they divorced in 1957, she got custody of their daughter while he kept their son.

Following her divorce, Lowther began taking creative writing classes, which she continued to do through the early 1960s. There she made contacts with Canadian West Coast poets such as Dorothy Livesay and Pat Lane. By 1963 she had married her second husband, Roy Armstrong Lowther, a public school teacher who shared her socialist-leaning political views. Lowther's views, in fact, were so radical that eventually he was fired from his teaching position. After that, the couple periodically lived on welfare. Lowther had two more daughters with her second husband.

Lowther's friend Lane and another acquaintance, Seymour Mayne, owned a small press called the Very Stone House. They encouraged Lowther in her efforts to write poetry, and they eventually published her first volume of poetry, *This Difficult Flowering.* In *This Difficult Flowering,* Thomas judged, "already . . . there is the mark of an original voice, and evidence of Lowther's ability to develop and sustain a complex theme." The critic went on to explain that "the poems seek through a minute and particular observation of the natural world to achieve a dialectical understanding of the tensions and contradictions in human experience."

Lowther's next published collection was a limited edition unbound portfolio entitled *The Age of the Bird.* The poems in *The Age of the Bird* speak of revolution in South American countries; one of them is a eulogy for Chilean poet Pablo Neruda, whose work greatly influenced Lowther. Only one hundred and fifty copies of *The Age of the Bird* were printed.

More well-known is Lowther's third collection, *Milk Stone,* published in 1974. This volume includes the long poem "In the Continent Behind My Eyes," which, according to Thomas, "creates a mythic, prehistoric world . . . as a vision of evolving human consciousness." The other poems in *Milk Stone* concern themselves primarily with the experiences of women.

In the year following the publication of *Milk Stone,* Lowther had another volume of poetry accepted by Oxford University Press. She began teaching creative writing classes at the University of British Columbia, and had become a force within the League of Canadian Poets. Lowther's literary career was on the

brink of a major expansion, but she disappeared in September of 1975. Her body was found three weeks later in a creek near Squamish, British Columbia; nearly two years later, her second husband was convicted of Lowther's murder.

Lowther's last volume, *A Stone Diary,* was published by Oxford University Press in 1977. As she had in *The Age of the Bird,* the poet discusses upheaval in the country of Chile, and offers tribute once more to Neruda in a set of five letter-poems. There are many evocations of violence and pain in *A Stone Diary,* and a number of reviewers found in them ironic foreshadowings of the poet's death. In 1980, some unpublished and uncollected poems of Lowther's were gathered and edited by Dona Sturmanis and Fred Candelaria under the title *Final Instructions: Early Uncollected Poems.* Since Lowther's murder, a memorial prize has been established in her name.

BIOGRAPHICAL/CRITICAL SOURCES:

BOOKS

Dictionary of Literary Biography, Volume 53: *Canadian Writers Since 1960, First Series,* Gale, 1986.

PERIODICALS

Canadian, June 5, 1976, pp. 13-19.
Canadian Literature, autumn, 1977, pp. 21-29.*

—Sketch by Elizabeth Wenning

* * *

LUCKMANN, William H. 1926-

PERSONAL: Born January 15, 1926, in Cape Girardeau, MO; son of William A. and Leonora (Ochs) Luckmann; married June Kepner, November 26, 1949; children: Charles W., Nancy Luckmann Glass, Jill Luckmann Musselman, Carol Luckmann Parrish, John. *Education:* University of Missouri—Columbia, B.S., 1949; University of Illinois at Urbana-Champaign, M.S., 1951, Ph.D., 1956. *Politics:* Independent. *Religion:* Lutheran. *Avocational interests:* Fishing, woodworking, reading, gardening.

ADDRESSES: Agent—c/o Wiley Interscience, 605 Third Ave., New York, NY 10158.

CAREER: Author.

WRITINGS:

(Editor with Robert L. Metcalf) *Introduction to Insect Pest Management,* 3rd edition, Wiley (New York City), 1994.

* * *

LUENING, Otto (Clarence) 1900-1996

OBITUARY NOTICE—See index for *CA* sketch: Born June 15, 1900, in Milwaukee, WI; died September 2, 1996, in Manhattan, NY. Composer, educator, conductor, author. Luening is remembered as one of the forefathers of contemporary, electronic music. The son of a conductor, Luening and his family moved to Munich, Germany when he was twelve years old. At the age of sixteen, he began a career as a flutist. During World War I, the family relocated to Zurich, Switzerland; Luening joined the Tonhalle Orchestra and studied under Richard Strauss and Ferruccio Busoni. In 1920, he returned to the United States as the conductor of the American Grand Opera Company in Chicago. From 1925 to 1928, Luening served as the executive director of the opera department at the Eastman School of Music in Rochester, New York.

It was in 1940 that he cofounded the American Music Center in New York City. Luening began a thirty-four-year stint at Columbia University in 1944, and in 1948 he produced *Evangeline,* an opera based on Henry Wadsworth Longfellow's poem. In all, Luening composed more than three hundred works, including *Synthesis, Moonflight,* and *Fantasy in Space.* In the 1950s, Luening began experimenting with electronic music. With colleague Vladimir Ussachevsky, he founded the Columbia-Princeton Electronic Music Center in New York City. He contributed articles to music journals and penned *The Odyssey of an American Composer: The Autobiography of Otto Luening.*

OBITUARIES AND OTHER SOURCES:

BOOKS

Dictionary of Twentieth-Century Culture, Volume 1: American Culture After World War II, Gale, 1994.

PERIODICALS

Chicago Tribune, September 6, 1996, Section 3, p. 10.
New York Times, September 5, 1996, p. D21.

* * *

LUTHULI, Albert John 1898(?)-1967

PERSONAL: Born c. 1898, in Groutville, Natal, South Africa; died of injuries from being hit by a train, July 21, 1967, in Groutville; son of John and Mtonya Gumede Luthuli, and grandson of Zulu chief; married Nokukhanya Bhengu in 1927; children: two sons, five daughters. *Education:* Attended Groutville Mission School; Adams College; Methodist Institute, teacher training. *Politics:* African National Congress. *Religion:* Congregationalist.

CAREER: Adam's Mission Station College, South Africa, teacher, 1921-36; Abasemakholweni Tribe, South Africa, Chief, 1936-53; African National Congress, Natal Provincial Division, President-General, 1953-67. International Missionary Council, India, delegate, 1938; Christian Council of South Africa, representative and executive member; Congregational Churches of America, chairperson of the board; Natal Mission Conference, president.

AWARDS, HONORS: Nobel Prize for Peace, 1960; United National Human Rights Prize, 1968.

WRITINGS:

Fifty Years of Union (political review), South African Institute of Race Relations, 1960.
Freedom Is the Apex (speech), South African Congress of Democrats, 1960.
Let My People Go (autobiography), McGraw-Hill, 1962.
The Road to Oslo, and Beyond!, (contains Luthuli's Nobel lecture), [London], 1962.
(With others) *Africa's Freedom,* Allen & Unwin, 1964, Barnes & Noble, 1964.

Also contributor to *Ebony.*

BIOGRAPHICAL/CRITICAL SOURCES:

BOOKS

Benson, Mary, *Chief Albert Luthuli of South Africa,* Oxford University Press, 1963.
Luthuli, Albert John, *Let My People Go* (autobiography), McGraw-Hill, 1962.

PERIODICALS

New York Times, October 24, 1961, p. 22; July 22, 1967.

* * *

LUZMA
See UMPIERRE (HERRERA), Luz Maria

M

MACHADO de ASSIS, Joaquim Maria 1839-1908

PERSONAL: Born June 21, 1839, in Rio de Janeiro, Brazil; died September 29, 1908, in Rio de Janeiro, Brazil; son of a house painter; married, 1869; wife's name, Carolina.

CAREER: Worked as a printer, typesetter and proofreader before joining Brazilian civil service.

MEMBER: Brazilian Academy of Letters (named president for life, 1897).

WRITINGS:

NOVELS

Resurreicao, 1872, W. M. Jackson, 1937.

A mao e a luva, 1874, Garnier, 1922, translation by Albert I. Bagby, Jr., published as *The Hand and the Glove,* University Press of Kentucky (Lexington), 1970.

Helena, 1876, Garnier, 1929, translation by Helen Caldwell published under same title, University of California Press, 1984.

Yaya Garcia, 1878, Garnier, 1899, translation by R. L. Scott-Buccleuch published under same title, P. Owen (London), 1976.

Memorias posthumas de Braz Cubas, 1881, Garnier, 1914, translation by William L. Grossman published as *Epitaph of a Small Winner,* Noonday Press, 1952, translation by E. Percy Ellis published as *Posthumous Reminiscences of Braz Cubas,* Instituto Nacional do Livro, 1955.

Quincas Borba, 1891, 3rd edition, Garnier, 1899, translation by Clotilde Wilson published as *Philosopher or Dog?,* Noonday Press, 1954, same translation also published as *The Heritage of Quincas Borba,* W. H. Allen (London), 1954.

Dom Casmurro, 1899, Garnier, 1924, translation by Helen Caldwell published under same title, University of California Press (Berkeley), 1953, translation by R. L. Scott-Buccleuch published as *Dom Casmurro: Lord Taciturn,* P. Owen, 1992.

Esau e Jacob, 1904, Garnier, 1924, translation by Helen Caldwell published as *Esau and Jacob,* University of California Press, 1965.

Memorial de Ayres (also published as *Memorial de Aires*), 1908, Garnier, 1923, translation by Helen Caldwell published as *Counselor Ayres' Memorial,* University of California Press, 1972, translation by R. L. Scott-Buccleuch published as *The Wager: Aires' Journal,* P. Owen, 1990.

SHORT STORIES

Contos fluminenses, 1870, Garnier, 1924.

Historias de meia-noite, 1873, Garnier, 1923.

Historias sem data, 1884, revised edition, Garnier, 1924.

Papeis avulos, 1884, W. M. Jackson, 1937.

Varias historias, 1895, Garnier, 1924.

Paginas recolhidas, 1899, W. M. Jackson, 1937.

Reliquas de casa velha, 1906, Garnier, 1921.

The Psychiatrist, and Other Stories, translation by William L. Grossman and Helen Caldwell, University of California Press, 1963.

What Went on at the Baroness': A Tale with a Point, translation by Helen Caldwell, Magpie Press (Santa Monica, CA), 1963.

The Devil's Church, and Other Stories, translation by Jack Schmitt and Lorie Ishimatsu, University of Texas Press (Austin, TX), 1977.

PLAYS

Desencantos, produced in Rio de Janeiro, 1861.

Quase ministro, produced in Rio de Janeiro, 1864.

Os deuses de casaca, produced in Rio de Janeiro, 1866.

Tu, so tu, puro amor, Impresso por Lombaerts, 1881, translation published as *You, Love, and Love Alone,* 1972.

POETRY

Crisalidas, [Rio de Janeiro], 1864.

Phalenas, [Rio de Janeiro], 1869.

Americanas, Garnier, 1875.

Poesias completas, Garnier, 1901.

Also author of *Occidentais,* 1901.

OTHER

Teatro (essays), 1863, W. M. Jackson, 1937.

Novas reliquias, Editora Guanabara, Waissman, Koogan, 1932.

Conceitos e pensamentos, compilacao de Julio Cesar da Silva, Companhia editors nacional, 1934.

Chronicas (1859-1888), W. M. Jackson, 1937.

Correspondencia; colligida e annotada por Fernando Nery, W. M. Jackson, 1937.

Historias romanticas, W. M. Jackson, 1937.

O alienista e outras historias, Saraiva, 1957.

SIDELIGHTS: Joaquim Maria Machado de Assis is considered "the greatest and most complete man of letters in Brazil," according to Afranio Coutinho. He is particularly noted for the novels *Memorias posthumas de Braz Cubas* (1881; *Epitaph of a Small Winner,* 1952) and *Dom Casmurro* (1899; *Dom Casmurro,* 1953). His fiction has been called bitterly pessimistic and sardonic. Machado often used satire to illuminate trivial human vanities and selfishness, particularly among the white Brazilian upper middle class; he rarely addressed his own mulatto culture. Although his works have not found a large audience, Machado was, according to David T. Haberly, "the most original novelist to appear in the Western Hemisphere in the nineteenth century."

Machado was born in Rio de Janeiro, the son of a black house painter and Portuguese mother. After the early death of his mother, he was raised by his mulatto stepmother, Maria Ines, who is credited with introducing him to literature. At seventeen Machado was apprenticed to a printer and became a proof-reader and typesetter. In the course of his work he met many important literary figures, some of whom later helped him get his first works published. After his printing apprenticeship he joined the civil service and spent most of his life as a middle-level bureaucrat. Popular with readers and critics alike—he was already acclaimed in his native country by the time he was twenty-five—Machado was made president for life of the newly founded Brazilian Academy of Letters in 1897. He continued to write until his death in 1908.

Machado began his literary career by writing dramas and poetry. Most of these works went unpublished or unproduced, but his poetry collection *Occidentais,* which appeared in 1901, was well received. Critics have noted that while these poems are often stylistically mundane, they nevertheless faithfully reflect Machado's belief that life is essentially meaningless. They also convey the author's characteristic attitude of ironic resignation. These beliefs and attitudes are displayed more extensively and with greater artistic success in Machado's early novels. His first four—*Ressurreicao* (1872), *A mao e a luva* (1874; *The Hand and the Glove,* 1970), *Helena* (1876; *Helena,* 1984), and *Yaya Garcia* (1878; *Yaya Garcia,* 1976)—are products of the Romantic movement in Brazilian literature and are considered inferior to his later fiction. Like other works of this movement, Machado's novels, which center on thwarted love or ambition, are often criticized for their unrealistic situations and lack of character motivation. In these works Machado presented detailed portraits of female characters, meticulously examining the moral and social implications of the marriage of convenience. In his later works he abandoned both female protagonists and his concern with the delineation of class and social distinctions.

Epitaph of a Small Winner is the autobiography of a dead writer—"I am a deceased writer not in the sense of one who has written and is now deceased," writes the narrator, Braz Cubas, "but in the sense of one who has died and is now writing." This often humorous novel features an unreliable narrator and has been likened to Laurence Sterne's *The Life and Opinions of Tristram Shandy.* In *Epitaph of a Small Winner* Machado explored the effects of egotism, the absurdity of life, and the inevitability of death. Machado viewed human nature as fundamentally irrational and found self-love to be the only consistent motivating force in human behavior. While characterizing this worldview as pessimistic, critics have also noted that Machado's fiction conveys amusement rather than

bitterness toward the folly of selfish, passion-driven humanity. Throughout his novels, and particularly in *Epitaph of a Small Winner,* Machado mockingly challenged the accepted beliefs of society. Richard J. Callan noted that "at the heart of [Machado's] criticism of mankind lies the hope that he can move his readers to a reform of manners." Similarly, William L. Grossman argued that *Epitaph of a Small Winner* affirms important human values by destroying many false gods and illusions.

Like *Epitaph of a Small Winner, Dom Casmurro* is told by an unreliable narrator. This novel, which is considered Machado's masterpiece, is full of deception and ambiguity. The narrator's self-destructive conviction that his wife and best friend had an affair, and that his son is in fact theirs, was long accepted as a central fact of the novel. But critics have recently questioned whether the narrator's conclusion was perhaps based merely on suspicion, circumstantial evidence, and unfounded jealousy—all prevalent themes in Machado's novels. Recent commentators posit that the narrator seems to be pleading his case before a jury of readers in an attempt to let them decide for themselves if his cruelty toward those closest to him may be justified.

Machado's last two novels, *Esau e Jaco* (1904; *Esau and Jacob,* 1965) and *Memorial de Ayres* (1908; *Counselor Ayres' Memorial,* 1972), are considered extended allegorical interpretations of turn-of-the-century Brazilian social conflicts. The warring twins of *Esau and Jacob,* for example, have been interpreted as symbols of the emancipation period in Rio de Janeiro; they represent conflicts between liberal and conservative factions, between tradition and modern values, and between colonial life and the birth of an independent Brazil. In *Counselor Ayres' Memorial,* Machado again metaphorically evoked Brazil, but this time he expressed hope for his country, provided Brazilians learn to be guided by selfless love—the force that rejuvenates the jaded ambassador Ayres in the novel. Machado's affirmations of life and love in *Counselor Ayres' Memorial* are regarded as foils for the total pessimism he expressed in his earlier works.

Machado is also considered a master of the short story. Although he dealt with many of the same issues he treated in his novels—hidden or unconscious motives as well as human egotism and inadequacy—his range as a short story writer was much broader. This is especially evident in Machado's experimental use of styles and forms and the diversity of his subjects and techniques.

Critics have found Machado's racial heritage problematic in analyzing his works. Raymond S. Sayers commented: "One of the strange paradoxes of literature is that the greatest Brazilian novelist, [Machado], . . . was a mulatto who wrote very little about his fellow Negroes and their lives but instead drew most of his material for his novels from the lives of the upper classes of Carioca society, which were predominantly white." Because people of color rarely have more than minor roles in Machado's works, some critics have accused the author of denying his heritage and condemned him for not decrying slavery in Brazil. Yet he encountered discrimination in his life. David T. Haberly noted that of the "catalogue of social and physical handicaps that late nineteenth-century Brazilians would have defined as *taras,* or hereditary defects," Machado had not only weak health and epilepsy but he "was not white." Haberly argued that Machado consequently tried to hide his race. The process of becoming "white" is therefore a major facet of Machado's works, which, he added, "can be seen as a highly evasive and ambiguous journal of his passage from nonwhiteness to whiteness." Sayers, however, has maintained that Machado was interested in satirizing Brazilian society, not in rejecting his race. Thus blacks and mulattoes could not reasonably be targets for Machado. Sayers explained: "The Negro could not serve as a subject for the irony of Machado, for the Negro could never determine his own conduct or fix his own position in society; he was not a free agent, and therefore he could not be made a subject for satire."

Reviewers call Machado one of the greatest, if critically neglected, Latin American writers. "I am astonished," wrote Susan Sontag, "that a writer of such greatness does not yet occupy the place he deserves." Machado's reputation as a writer has grown in recent years, but his works remain ambiguous to critics. Waldo Frank noted: "Within the quiet courses a complex fugue: innocence cruelly punished and revealed as guilt; pleasure pleasurably crushed; the 'good' and the 'beautiful' on the wrack and dissolving into their contraries. The blood, indeed the core, of the fictive world of Machado de Assis is ambiguity—ambiguity raised to a principle and a substance."

BIOGRAPHICAL/CRITICAL SOURCES:

BOOKS

Caldwell, Helen, *The Brazilian Othello of Machado de Assis: A Study of 'Dom Casmurro,'* University of California Press, 1960.

Caldwell, *Machado de Assis: The Brazilian Master and His Novels,* University of California Press, 1970.

Haberly, David T., *Three Sad Races: Racial Identity and National Consciousness in Brazilian Literature,* Cambridge University Press, 1983.

Lisboa, Maria Manuel, *Machado de Assis and Feminism,* E. Mellen Press, 1996.

Machado de Assis, Joaquim Maria, *Epitaph of a Small Winner,* Noonday Press, 1952.

Maia Neto, Jose Raimundo, *Machado de Assis: The Brazilian Pyrrhonian,* Purdue University Press, 1994.

PERIODICALS

Hispania, March, 1966, pp. 81-7; May, 1966, pp. 211-17; December, 1966, pp. 778-86; September, 1967, pp. 430-41; May, 1970, pp. 198-206.
Luso-Brazilian Review, December, 1972, pp. 47-57.

* * *

MACKEY, Nathaniel (Ernest) 1947-

PERSONAL: Born October 25, 1947, in Miami, FL; married Pascale Gaitet, 1990; children: one daughter, one stepson. *Education:* Princeton University, A.B., 1969; Stanford University, Ph.D., 1975.

ADDRESSES: Agent—c/o Moving Parts Press, 70 Cathedral Dr., Santa Cruz, CA 95060.

CAREER: University of Wisconsin, Madison, professor, 1974-76; University of Southern California, Los Angeles, professor, 1976-79; University of California, Santa Cruz, professor, 1979—. Editor, *Hambone.* Has also made a recording, entitled *Strick: Song of the Andoumboulou 16-25,* Spoken Engine, 1995.

AWARDS, HONORS: Woodrow Wilson fellowship, 1969; National Poetry Series selection, 1985, for *Eroding Witness;* Whiting Writer's award, 1993.

WRITINGS:

POETRY

Four for Trane, Golemics (Los Angeles), 1978.
Septet for the End of Time, Boneset Press (Santa Cruz, CA), 1983.

Eroding Witness, University of Illinois Press (Urbana), 1985.
Outlantish, Chax Press (Tucson, AZ), 1992.
School of Udhra, City Lights Books (San Francisco, CA), 1993.
Song of the Andoumboulou: 18-20, Moving Parts Press (Santa Cruz, CA), 1994.

NOVELS

Bedouin Hornbook, Callaloo Fiction Series (Lexington, KY), 1986.
Djbot Baghostus's Run, Sun and Moon Press (Los Angeles, CA), 1993.

OTHER

Discrepant Engagement: Dissonance, Cross-Culturality and Experimental Writing, Cambridge University Press (New York), 1993.
(Editor with Art Lange) *Moment's Notice: Jazz in Poetry and Prose,* Coffee House Press (Minneapolis, MN), 1993.

* * *

MAFFI, Mario 1947-

PERSONAL: Born May 23, 1947, in Milan, Italy; son of Bruno (a translator) and Anna (a homemaker; maiden name, Pirini) Maffi; married Maria Matilde Merli (a headmistress), May 7, 1973; children: Alice. *Education:* University of Milan, received degree (summa cum laude), 1971. *Avocational interests:* Theater, travel.

ADDRESSES: Home—Milan, Italy. *Office*—Istituto di Anglistica, Piazza S. Alessandro 1, 20123 Milan, Italy. *E-mail*—maffluni@imiucca.csi.unimi.it. *Agent*—Grandi e Associati, Via Caradosso 12, 20123 Milan, Italy.

CAREER: State University of Milan, Milan, Italy, assistant professor of American studies, 1975—, and member of scientific board, Centro di Studi Stati Uniti. Member of Museum of Chinese in the Americas and Tenement Museum, both New York City.

MEMBER: European Association for American Studies, Italian Association for American Studies, American Studies Association, Society for the Study of the

Multi-Ethnic Literature of the United States (MELUS).

AWARDS, HONORS: Libro Giovane Award, from Unione Italiana per il Progresso della Cultura, 1975, for *La cultura underground.*

WRITINGS:

La cultura underground, Laterza (Bari, Italy), 1972, 3rd edition, 1980.
Le origini della sinistra extraparlamentare, Mondadori (Milan, Italy), 1976.
La giungla e il grattacielo: Gli scrittori e il "sogno americano," 1965-1920, Laterza, 1981.
(With Guido Fink, Franco Minganti, and Bianca Tarozzi) *Storia della letteratura americana,* Sansoni (Florence, Italy), 1991.
Nel mosaico della citta: Differenze etniche e nuove culture in un quartiere di New York, Feltrinelli (Milan), 1992, translation by the author published as *Gateway to the Promised Land: Ethnic Cultures in New York's Lower East Side,* Rodopi (Amsterdam, Netherlands), 1994, New York University Press (New York City), 1995.
New York: L'isola delle colline, Il Saggiatore (Milan), 1995.
(Editor) *Voci dal silenzio,* Feltrinelli, 1996.

Translator from English to Italian. Contributor to scholarly journals. Editor, *Acoma.*

WORK IN PROGRESS: Editing and translating a collection of Hispanic American writing; research on Mark Twain and the Mississippi culture.

SIDELIGHTS: Mario Maffi told *CA:* "As a scholar, writer, and teacher in the field of American studies, my primary interest is the study of the dialectics between culture and society: the way in which culture(s) speaks of society and society speaks through culture(s).

"My first book *La cultura underground* came out of my university dissertation. It dealt with the American youth counter-culture in the sixties, with chapters on literature, politics, music, theater, and the movies. As the first Italian attempt at a general (and critical) overview of that contradictory experience, the book has remained somewhat of a classic.

"In some ways, my second book continued that analysis, but projected itself back into the past by going over the great debates between Marx and Bakunin,

Lenin and the 'economicists,' Bordiga and Gramsci, the Third International, and 'council communism.' The book traced the non-Marxist origins of many youth movements born in the late sixties and early seventies.

"Then came *La giungla e il grattacielo: Gli scrittori e il "sogno americano," 1965-1920,* which explored the difficult, often ambiguous, but always exceptionally creative relationship between writers and society in the United States from the Civil War to World War I. The first part dealt with general themes (such as the city, the machine, the popular press, the dime novels, the utopian novel, the political novel), the second part with specific authors.

"During the eighties, I edited and translated the work of many American and British authors, including Abraham Cahan, Tom Kromer, Jack London, Upton Sinclair, James F. Cooper, Arthur Morrison, and George Orwell, as well as an anthology of new American dramatists and, more recently, the work of Robert L. Stevenson and Mark Twain. In addition, with three university colleagues I worked at the first history of American literature to be published in Italy in some thirty years, *Storia della letteratura americana.*

"My major activity during those years, however, was a long and complex study of New York's Lower East Side, mainly (but not only) centered on the 1880-1920 'golden' period of this multi-ethnic immigrant neighborhood. The book that came out of this extremely involved experience was written directly in English and then translated (by me) into Italian. Based upon a great wealth of data and sources, and ten years of first-hand experience with the life of the neighborhood, the book tells of its physical and material aspects, its history and economy, its multi-ethnic realities, the social struggles that developed there, its art, fiction, and theater, the way in which it always functioned as a magnet for social and cultural exploration and experimentation, and its present critical, but still quite creative, stimulating situation. At the core of the book are the ideas of such neighborhoods as veritable socio-cultural laboratories and of Americanization as an alchemic process through which immigrant cultures (then and now) confront America and negotiate with it, transforming America while transforming themselves.

"The impact of the Lower East Side and my personal involvement with the social and cultural realities there was great. It was only inevitable that I should

go back to it again. In fact, *New York: L'isola delle colline* is both a piece of travel writing, telling the story of my discovery of the city and of this multiethnic neighborhood, and an attempt at *writing a city* through my senses and through the words of its inhabitants, through the perception of its places and streets and through its memory and its micro- as well as macro-history. I have always been more interested in *telling,* in *narrating* American culture than in exploring this or that supposedly new theoretical trend. My approach to American culture and literature is a wide, comparative, and almost anthropological one, based on an interpretation of culture and literature in their dialectical relationship with classes and modes of production."

"I feel that the book *New York* represents a kind of turning point for me: toward a more personal and narrative style, even in the scholarly field. I don't know if this is a prelude to fiction, but I know that both my teaching and my writing have been taking a more involved and engaged (involving and engaging) aspect. When I think of the projects I have in mind (a book on islands, a book on Mark Twain and the Mississippi culture, perhaps another work on the Lower East Side and New York City), I surely think of them in this same form."

"Much of my recent writing and teaching still deals with related subjects and aspects—urban and ethnic cultures. I just edited the first anthology of Asian-American writing to come out in Italy, and I am presently working on another anthology of Chicano and Puerto Rican writing. Meanwhile I also translated *Porgy and Bess* for the Teatro alla Scala."

* * *

MAJOR-BALL, Terry 1932-

PERSONAL: Born July 2, 1932, in Old Malden, Surrey, England; son of Abraham Thomas (an acrobat, trapeze performer, baton swinger, actor, comedian, songwriter, and later a manufacturer of garden ornaments) and Gwendoline Minnie (a dancer and performer; maiden name, Coates) Major-Ball; married Shirley Mildred Wilson, September 3, 1960; children: Fiona, Mark. *Religion:* Church of England. *Politics:* Conservative (Tory).

ADDRESSES: Home and office—Surrey, England. *Agent*—Gillon Aitkin, Aitkin and Stone Ltd., 29 Fernshaw Rd., London, SW10 OTG, England.

CAREER: "Left school aged fifteen and entered the family business—Major's Garden Ornaments in July 1947, took over as manager in June 1952 due to father's ill heath, later becoming the owner after Father retired about 1954. Spent a couple of years working for F. W. Woolworth & Co. Ltd., where I met my wife, Shirley, who was employed in the invoice office. Spent a year in the plastics industry, eleven working for SEEB (South Eastern Electricity Board) followed by fifteen years with Philips Service (the service division of Philips Electronics). Retired in November 1989 and took up research into my father's stage career and the family history, which led to my writing *Major Major.* Have also made appearances on television chat and game shows, also making a short film for television called *Postcards to My Brother,* transmitted on BBC2." *Military service:* "National Service in the Royal Army Medical Corps from 18th January 1951, until 17th June 1952, having been given a compassionate early discharge due to my father's ill health."

WRITINGS:

Major Major: Memories of an Older Brother, Duckworth, 1994.

Contributor of articles to newspapers and various magazines; columnist for the *Daily Mail.*

SIDELIGHTS: Terry Major-Ball, the brother of British Prime Minister John Major M.P., tells his and his family's life history in his autobiography *Major Major: Memories of an Older Brother.* Eleven years older than his brother, Major-Ball recalls sitting with his sister as their father told them stories about his past experiences—tales which ranged from his boyhood in America, his experiences as an acrobat, actor, gambler, and temporary conscript in the Uruguayan Army, and as a member of the Walsall Swimming Club. He also describes his mother and her act, during which she became his father's second wife (following the death of Kitty, his father's first wife, in 1909). After describing his own childhood, Major-Ball focuses on the highs and lows of his business career. The more personal relationship with his wife, Shirley, is also explored, as are the joys Major-Ball experiences from his annual holiday and his garden.

John Wells in the *Evening Standard* said of *Major Major:* "Unquestionably this is one of the great comic books of the year, and yet it contains moments of such touching human grief I defy strong men not to weep." John Gaskell in the *Sunday Telegraph* called the book "a nineties cult classic." And London *Times* reviewer Keith Waterhouse, writing of Major-Ball's overwhelming niceness and goodness as portrayed in *Major Major,* concludes: "There is a faintly self-conscious air about his unworldliness, the same air one encounters in pub characters who are very aware that they have a reputation for being pub characters."

Major-Ball told *CA:* "The book is the truth told with a touch of humour and all the dates are accurate. The paperback version has two extra chapters, one of which describes my trip to the First International Gnome Festival in Christchurch, New Zealand. The book was great fun to write and the spin offs have been just as enjoyable. My one regret regarding my visit to New York was not seeing the inside of the Statue of Liberty, although I had a flight around it in a helicopter."

BIOGRAPHICAL/CRITICAL SOURCES:

PERIODICALS

Daily Express, July 29, 1994.
Daily Telegraph, August 13, 1994.
Evening Standard, August 15, 1994.
Guardian, August 12, 1994.
London Review of Books, October 20, 1994, p. 10.
Observer, August 14, 1994; August 21, 1994.
Private Eye, August 9, 1994.
Spectator, August 13, 1994.
Sunday Telegraph, August 14, 1994.
Times (London), July 29, 1994; August 15, 1994; August 21, 1994, p. 5.

* * *

MALLEA, Eduardo 1903-1982(?)

PERSONAL: Born August 14, 1903, in Bahia Blanca, Argentina; died of leukemia c. 1982, in Buenos Aires, Argentina; son of Narciso Segundo (a physician and writer) and Manuela (Aztiria) Mallea; married Helena Munoz Larreta, March 15, 1944. *Education:* Attended Colegio Nacional and Faculty of Law, Buenos Aires, beginning in 1920.

CAREER: Practiced law until 1927; *La Nacion,* Argentina, correspondent, 1927-31, literary editor, 1931-55; UNESCO, Paris, France, ambassador-at-large for Argentina, 1955-58; writer, 1958-82. Lecturer in Italy, 1934. Former member of board of directors of *Sur* and *Realidad.*

MEMBER: Argentine Society of Writers (president, beginning in 1940).

AWARDS, HONORS: Primer Premio Nacional de Letras, 1945; Gran Premio de Honor from Argentine Society of Writers, 1946; Premio Casavalle, 1955, for *La sala de espera;* Forti Glori prize, 1968; honorary doctorate from University of Michigan, 1968; Gran Premio in literature from Fondo Nacional de las Artes, 1970.

WRITINGS:

NOVELS AND NOVELLAS

Fiesta en noviembre, Club del Libro, 1938, translation by Alis de Sola published as *Fiesta in November,* Calder & Boyars, 1969.
La bahia de silencio, Sudamericana, 1940, translation by Stuart Edgar Grummon published as *The Bay of Silence,* Knopf, 1944.
Todo verdor perecera, Espasa-Calpe, 1941, translation by John B. Hughes and others published as *All Green Shall Perish, and Other Novellas and Stories,* edited and introduced by Hughes, Knopf, 1966.
Las aguilas (title means "The Eagles"), Sudamericana, 1943.
El vinculo, Los Rembrandts, [and] *La rosa de Cernobbio,* Emece, 1946.
Los enemigos del alma (title means "The Enemies of the Soul"), Sudamericana, 1950.
La torre (title means "The Tower"), Sudamericana, 1951.
Chaves, Losada, 1953, translation by Maria Mercedes Aspiazu and others published as *Chaves, and Other Stories,* Calder & Boyars, 1970.
La sala de espera (title means "The Waiting Room"), Sudamericana, 1953.
Simbad (title means "Sinbad"), Sudamericana, 1957.
El resentimiento: Los ensimismados, El resentimiento, [and] *La falacia,* Sudamericana, 1966.
La penultima puerta (title means "The Penultimate Door"), Sudamericana, 1969.
Gabriel Andaral, Sudamericana, 1971.

Triste piel del universo (title means "Sad Skin of the Universe"), Sudamericana, 1971.

En la creciente oscuridad, Sudamericana, 1973.

SHORT STORY COLLECTIONS

Cuentos para una inglesa desesperada (title means "Stories for a Desperate English Woman"), Gleizer, 1926, reprinted, Espasa-Calpe, 1969.

La ciudad junto al rio inmovil (title means "The City on the Motionless River"; includes "Sumersion," "Conversacion," and "La causa de Jacobo Uber, perdida"), Sur, 1936.

Posesion (title means "Possession"), Sudamericana, 1958.

La barca de hielo (title means "The Ice Ship"), Sudamericana, 1967.

La red (title means "The Net"), Sudamericana, 1968.

Also author of *La mancha en el marmol.*

OTHER

Conocimiento y expresion de la Argentina (title means "Knowledge and Expression of Argentina"), Sur, 1935.

Nocturno europeo (title means "European Nocturne"), Sur, 1935.

Historia de una pasion argentina (title means "History of an Argentine Passion"), Sur, 1937, expanded edition, prologue by Francisco Romero, Espasa-Calpe, 1940.

Meditacion en la costa (title means "Meditation at the Sea Shore"; essay collection), Imprenta Mercatali, 1939.

El sayal y la purpura (essay collection), Losada, 1941.

Rodeada esta de sueno (title means "Surrounded by Dreams"), two volumes, Espasa-Calpe, 1944.

El retorno (title means "The Return"), Espasa-Calpe, 1946.

Notas de un novelista (essay collection), Emece, 1954.

El gajo de enebro: Tragedia en tres actos, Emece, 1957.

La razon humana, Losada, 1959.

La vida blanca (title means "The Sterile Life"), Sur, 1960.

Las travesias (title means "The Crossings"), Sudamericana, Volume 1, 1961, Volume 2, 1962.

Obras completas, Emece, Volume 1 (contains *Cuentos para una inglesa desesperada, Conocimiento y expresion de la Argentina,*

Nocturno europeo, La ciudad junto al rio inmovil, Historia de una pasion argentina, Fiesta en noviembre, Meditacion en la costa, La bahia de silencio, Todo verdor perecera, and *El sayal y la purpura*), 1961, Volume 2 (contains *Las aguilas, Rodeada esta de sueno, El retorno, El vinculo, Los enemigos del alma,* and *La torre*), 1965.

La representacion de los aficionados: Un juego, Sudamericana, 1962.

La guerra interior (title means "The Inner War"), Sur, 1963.

Poderio de la novela (title means "The Power of the Novel"), Aguilar, 1965.

Los papeles privados, Sudamericana, 1974.

Co-founder of the magazine *Revista de America,* 1923. Contributor to periodicals, including *Revista de Occidente* and *Sur.*

SIDELIGHTS: During the 1930s and 1940s Eduardo Mallea was one of South America's leading writers. An essayist, short story writer, and novelist, Mallea was chiefly concerned with the absence of spirituality in the modern world, especially in his native Argentina. His fiction has been called existential because it often focuses on solitary figures who struggle to find meaning in life, usually without success. In addition to writing dozens of fiction and nonfiction works, Mallea earned distinction between 1931 and 1955 as *La Nacion*'s literary editor, a post that gave him considerable authority and influence in Argentine literary circles.

His popularity, however, began to wane as early as 1943 when Colonel Juan Domingo Peron came to power in Argentina, bringing with him a populist autocracy that disdained the elite class of which Mallea was a member. Gradually social writers like David Vinas and Gabriel Garcia Marquez began to dominate the South American literary scene, leaving philosophical writers like Mallea out of vogue.

Born into a prominent Argentine family descended from Spanish nobility, Mallea grew up under the shadow of his affectionate but authoritarian father, who was both a physician and a man of letters. His father's extensive library provided Mallea with an early exposure to such European writers as Charles Dickens, Leo Tolstoy, Friedrich Nietzsche, and Soeren Kierkegaard. The influence of European literature and culture played a prominent role not only in Mallea's early education but in his professional writings as well.

Beginning in 1914 Mallea lived and studied in Buenos Aires, a city that introduced him to many of his life-long literary compatriots and served as the subject of some of his more important writings. It was during his years as a law student in the 1920s that Mallea first became associated with the "Florida" group of writers. Named after a street in the affluent section of Buenos Aires, the Florida group consisted of elitist writers whose cosmopolitan outlook stood in direct contrast to the socialist, proletarian writings of the so-called "Boedo" group. H. Ernest Lewald observed in his book *Eduardo Mallea* that "the mainstream of Argentine literature has been traveling in either one of these two channels since the original division took place [in the 1920s]."

Against this backdrop Mallea began his own literary career by helping found the magazine *Revista de America* in 1923 and by publishing his first book, *Cuentos para una inglesa desesperada,* in 1926. The appearance of this collection of stories was considered important for two reasons: it encouraged Mallea to abandon his law career to pursue writing, and it gave him the requisite literary credentials to work as a correspondent for *La Nacion,* the major Argentine newspaper for which he became literary editor.

After taking a hiatus from book writing between 1927 and 1934—during which time he made two trips to Europe—Mallea began publishing essays concerning the national character of Argentina. In 1935 he wrote *Conocimiento y expresion de la Argentina.* This collection of essays foreshadowed the author's ongoing interest in reconciling spiritual values of the Old World with the emerging materialistic values of South America. Through an expository blend of personal and Argentine history, Mallea's volume concludes that large, modern cities like Buenos Aires alienate rather than unify people. Mallea further developed this thesis in his 1937 essay collection, *Historia de una pasion argentina.* The collection, which includes autobiographical essays, posits a visible and invisible Argentina: the former refers to the majority of the population whose empty lives, according to Mallea, reflect the emptiness of modern city life; the latter refers to the few enlightened individuals in whom the hope for a better Argentina resides. Mallea believed that the invisible Argentina would one day bring about a new, rejuvenated Argentina. Critics generally agreed that the ideas laid out in these essay collections, though central to Mallea's thinking, were better expressed through his fiction, beginning with *La ciudad junto al rio inmovil.*

Published in 1936, *La ciudad junto al rio inmovil* is a collection of stories featuring individuals who grapple with the materialism and loneliness of modern life. The story "Sumersion" tells how Avesquin, a European, comes to Buenos Aires seeking a new life only to return home disappointed; "Conversacion" is about an upper-middle-class couple's meaningless life of boredom and indecision; and "La causa de Jacobo Uber, perdida" recounts how a quiet desk clerk tries unsuccessfully to establish fulfilling relationships. Lewald felt "Sumersion" was especially reminiscent of the writings of Franz Kafka, citing in particular the story's "confrontation between the individual and an impersonal, all-pervasive entity that claims the mass-man and creates a deep feeling of anguish in those who, like Avesquin, are bearers of sensitivity and intelligence." Mallea's concern about the conflict between individual and state carried over into his novels as well.

La bahia de silencio, a novel later translated as *The Bay of Silence,* has been called autobiographical in that it details a Buenos Aires law student's quest to become a novelist. The story, told through the diary of Martin Tregau, is about the hero's journey toward self-knowledge and his interest in promoting the general welfare of his native Argentina. Some critics complained that the strictly sequential, first-person narrative grew wearisome after five hundred pages. Other reviewers, like William S. Lynch, whose *Saturday Review* article is quoted in *Modern Latin American Literature,* defended the novel's structure. While admitting the book was "talkative and disjointed" with "characters [who] are wooden," Lynch argued that the characters' dialogues are "pertinent to the intellectual biography of the man whose mental direction we follow. [The characters] are relevant, too, in their revelation of the winds of doctrine and opinion that blow with balm or blast not only across Argentina but wherever there are human beings assembled in what we call modern society."

Mallea's pessimistic view of modern civilization was most pronounced in his 1941 novel, *Todo verdor perecera,* later published in English as *All Green Shall Perish.* Heroine Agate Cruz is surrounded by sterility: her husband is a farmer who cannot produce a crop, and the couple's conjugal relations fail to produce any children. Cruz makes one last attempt at happiness after the death of her husband by moving to the city and having an affair with a lawyer, but this too ends in disappointment and later madness. Once again Mallea's familiar themes of alienation and desperation are present. Critical opinion ranged from

those who found the book too cold and lifeless to those who praised it as an important contribution to modern literature. Saying the narrative was told with "consummate skill," John A. Crow wrote in the *Saturday Review* that through Cruz "we see the tragedy of modern man, rootless and sterile, making the wrong crucial decisions, already beyond the point of intelligent communication, doggedly plodding toward what seems an inevitable destruction." Moreover, Piers Brendon averred in *Books and Bookmen* that the "book is a classic, a jewel among the dross [of other foreign works], shining luminously even through the additional murk of translation."

Along with *The Bay of Silence* and *All Green Shall Perish, Chaves* is generally cited as one of Mallea's best novels. This 1953 work marked a transition for the Argentine author in that it is shorter and less overtly philosophical than previous books. The story is about a quiet, unambitious man whose modest way of life as a sawmill worker changes when he decides to marry and start a family. After taking a job as a salesman Chaves becomes interested in the power of words over people. The rest of the novel depicts Chaves's struggle to find meaning and eloquence in words when his business fails and his wife and child die. Dejected by his attempts to find purpose through words, Chaves retreats into silence and returns to the humbling work at the sawmill. Reviewers found *Chaves* more appealing than many of Mallea's earlier writings, and Lewald explained why: "Gone are the endless discussions on art, literature, history, or philosophy; gone also the repetitious descriptions of bourgeois behavior and milieu; and gone are the morose soliloquies by protagonists whose main occupation consists of eating, drinking, walking, and talking."

Mallea continued his literary output through the 1970s, though he never fully regained the popularity he lost during the Peron administration. After Peron was ousted in 1955, however, Mallea enjoyed renewed influence and prestige when he became an Argentina representative at UNESCO in Paris. But his public approval declined again after 1958, when the Argentine author began writing full time only to discover that his country had become more interested in social rather than philosophical issues. Mallea remains nonetheless an important voice for a generation of Argentines who were concerned with the deterioration of values and loss of spirituality in the New World.

BIOGRAPHICAL/CRITICAL SOURCES:

BOOKS

Foster, David William and Virginia Ramos Foster, editors, *Modern Latin American Literature,* Ungar, 1975.
Lewald, H. Ernest, *Eduardo Mallea,* Twayne, 1977.
Ocampo, Victoria, *Dialogo con Mallea,* Sur, 1969.
Polt, John H. R., *The Writings of Eduardo Mallea,* University of California Press, 1959.

PERIODICALS

Books Abroad, autumn, 1970; winter, 1970; spring, 1971.
Books and Bookmen, February, 1968.
Hispania, May, 1983.
Times Literary Supplement, December 28, 1967; March 13, 1969; September 18, 1970.

* * *

MALLICK, Ross

PERSONAL: Education: York University, B.A. (with honors), 1976, M.A., 1978; Oxford University, M.Litt., 1984; Cambridge University, Ph.D., 1988.

ADDRESSES: Home and office—3 Banchory Cres., Kanata, Ontario, Canada K2K 2V4.

CAREER: Development consultant and writer.

WRITINGS:

Development Policy of a Communist Government: West Bengal Since 1977, Cambridge University Press (Cambridge, England), 1993.
Indian Communism: Opposition, Collaboration, and Institutionalization, Oxford University Press (New York City), 1994.

WORK IN PROGRESS: Development, Ethnicity, and Human Rights in South Asia; International Aboriginal Representation; Affirmative Action in North America and South Asia.

MANDINO, Augustine A.
See MANDINO, Og

* * *

MANDINO, Og 1923-1996

OBITUARY NOTICE—See index for *CA* sketch: Full name is Augustine A. Mandino; born December 12, 1923, in Boston, MA; died resulting from an aneurysm, September 3, 1996, in Antrim, NH. Insurance salesperson, author. Mandino gained prominence as the insurance salesperson turned motivational writer and speaker whose book *The Greatest Salesman in the World* met with huge success. After serving in the U.S. Army Air Corps during World War II, and receiving the Distinguished Flying Cross for his missions as a navigator, Mandino returned to a series of odd jobs before landing a position in 1948 with the Metropolitan Life Insurance Company in Boston. In 1960, he left Met Life for Combined Insurance Company in Chicago, and in 1965 he became the executive editor of *Success Unlimited,* a motivational and inspirational magazine. In 1968, *The Greatest Salesman in the World* was published. The book was based on a short story he wrote for *Success Unlimited,* about a young boy who gives his blanket to the baby Jesus. His other works include *A Better Way to Live, The Greatest Miracle in the World, The Christ Commission, Secrets for Success and Happiness,* and *Og Mandino's University of Success.*

OBITUARIES AND OTHER SOURCES:

BOOKS

Who's Who in Writers, Editors, and Poets, December Press, 1995.

PERIODICALS

New York Times, September 7, 1996, p. 13.
Washington Post, September 11, 1996, p. C5.

* * *

MARCUS, Frank 1928-1996

OBITUARY NOTICE—See index for *CA* sketch: Born June 30, 1928, in Breslau, Germany; immigrated to England in 1939; became British citizen; died of a pulmonary embolism, August 5, 1996, in London, England. Drama critic, playwright, translator, and screenwriter. Marcus is best remembered for his play *The Killing of Sister George,* a work that dealt with lesbianism. Although he was born in Germany, Marcus left his homeland for England when the Nazis gained power. He pursued an interest in drama, finding success with his first play, *The Formation Dancers,* in London in 1964. A year later his *The Killing of Sister George* was produced in London, followed by a Broadway run the next year. The work received the *Evening Standard's* Best Play of the Year Award, as well as similar honors from *London Critics' Variety* and *Plays and Players.* In addition to his plays, Marcus also worked as a drama critic for London's *The Sunday Telegraph.* During his career he also wrote for *Plays and Players* and Dramatists' Guild *Quarterly,* and he acted, directed, and designed sets at London's Unity Theatre. He also founded the International Theatre Group. Marcus continued to see some success with his plays, such as *Mrs. Mouse, Are You Within?, Notes on a Love Affair, Blind Date, Minuet for Stuffed Birds,* and *Studies of the Nude.* He also translated and adapted works and wrote for film and television. Among the stories he adapted are *Anatol* and *La Ronde.* His screen credits include *Blank Pages, The Snow Tiger,* and *A Temporary Typist.*

OBITUARIES AND OTHER SOURCES:

BOOKS

Writers Directory, St. James Press, 1995.

PERIODICALS

Chicago Tribune, August 11, 1996, Section 4, p. 4.
New York Times, August 9, 1996, p. B7.
Washington Post, August 12, 1996, p. B6.

* * *

MARCUS, K(aren) Melissa 1956-

PERSONAL: Born February 28, 1956, in Vancouver, British Columbia, Canada; daughter of Marvin (a professor of mathematics) and Arlen (an administrative assistant; maiden name, Sahlman; present surname, Bishop) Marcus; married Jorge Mezei, 1984 (divorced, 1987). *Ethnicity:* "Caucasian." *Education:*

Attended University of Pau, 1975, and University of Grenoble, 1975-76; University of California, Santa Barbara, B.A. 1978, M.A., 1981; attended University of Geneva, 1979-80; Stanford University, M.A., 1984, Ph.D., 1990; attended Ecole Normale Superieure de Jeunes Filles, Paris, 1984-85. *Politics:* Democrat. *Religion:* Jewish. *Avocational interests:* Yoga, walking, photography, travel, movies, reading.

ADDRESSES: Home—5303 East Cortland Blvd., No. B-4, Flagstaff, AZ 86004. *Office*—Department of Modern Languages, Northern Arizona University, P.O. Box 6004, Flagstaff, AZ 86011-6004; fax 520-523-0963. *E-mail*—Melissa.Marcus@nau.edu.

CAREER: U.S. Department of State, Washington, DC, intern in Office of Western European Affairs, 1979; freelance translator and French tutor, 1987; Stanford University, Stanford, CA, lecturer in French, 1989-90; Northern Arizona University, Flagstaff, assistant professor, 1990-96, associate professor of French, 1996—, co-founder of Literary Translators Consortium, 1996.

MEMBER: Coordination Internationale des Chercheurs Sur Les Litteratures Maghrebines, Modern Language Association of America, American Association of Teachers of French, American Council on the Teaching of Foreign Languages, American Literary Translators Association, Women in French, American Association of University Professors, American Association of University Women, Phi Beta Kappa, Alpha Lambda Delta, Phi Sigma Iota, Pi Delta Phi.

AWARDS, HONORS: Travel grants for France, Northern Arizona University, 1991-96.

WRITINGS:

(Translator) Nina Bouraoui, *Forbidden Vision* (novel), Station Hill Press (Barrytown, NY), 1995.
The Representation of Mesmerism in Honore de Balzac's "La Comedie Humaine," Peter Lang (New York), 1995.
(Translator) Malika Mokeddem, *L'Interdite,* University of Nebraska Press (Lincoln, NE), in press.

Contributor of articles and reviews to periodicals, including *Constructions.*

WORK IN PROGRESS: Research on North Africa, women and Islam, and feminism in Algeria.

MARECHAL, Leopoldo 1900-1970

PERSONAL: Born June 11, 1900, in Buenos Aires, Argentina; died June 26, 1970, in Buenos Aires, Argentina; son of Alberto (a mechanic) and Lorenza (Beloqui) Marechal; married Maria Zoraida Barreiro (deceased); married Elbia Rosbaco, 1950; children: Maria de los Angeles, Maria Magdalena. *Education:* Graduated from Escuela Normal de Professores "Mariano Austa" (Buenos Aires), 1922. *Politics:* Began as socialist; became a Peronist. *Religion:* Roman Catholic.

CAREER: Teacher and writer. President of general education board in Santa Fe province, Argentina, 1944; technical inspector general of schools in Buenos Aires, Argentina, 1944-46; section chief of ministry of justice and public education, beginning in 1944; president of national folklore commission, beginning in 1947; cultural director of ministry of education, c. 1950.

MEMBER: Sociedad Argentina de Escritores (vice president), Cursos de Cultura Catolica.

AWARDS, HONORS: Municipal Poetry Prize from City of Buenos Aires, c. 1929, for *Odas para el hombre y la mujer;* National Poetry Prize from Argentina, 1941, for *Cinco poemas australes, El centauro,* and *Sonetos a Sophia;* Forti Glori Prize, 1966, for *El banquete de severo Arcangelo.*

WRITINGS:

POETRY

Los aguiluchos (title means "The Eaglets"), Gleizer (Buenos Aires), 1922.
Dias como flechas (title means "Days Like Arrows"), Gleizer, 1926.
Odas para el hombre y la mujer (title means "Odes for Man and Woman"), Libra (Buenos Aires), 1929.
Laberinto de amor (title means "Labyrinth of Love"), Sur (Buenos Aires), 1936.
Cinco poemas australes (title means "Five Southern Poems"), Cursos de Cultura Catolica (Buenos Aires), 1937.
El centauro (title means "The Centaur"), Sol y Luna (Buenos Aires), 1940.
Sonetos a Sophia, y otros poemas (title means "Sonnets to Sophia, and Other Poems"), Sol y Luna, 1940.

El viaje de la primavera, Emece (Buenos Aires), 1945.

La poetica (canto of *Heptameron* [also see below]), Hombre Nuevo (Buenos Aires), 1959.

La patria, [Buenos Aires], 1960.

La alegropeya: Primer dia, Hombre Nuevo, 1962.

Heptameron, Sudamericana (Buenos Aires), 1966.

El poema de robot, Americalee (Buenos Aires), 1966.

Poemas de Marechal (anthology), Universitaria de Buenos Aires, 1966.

Antologia poetica (anthology), edited by Oscar Grandov, Kapelusz (Buenos Aires), 1969.

Antologia poetica (anthology), edited by Alfredo Andres, De La Flor (Buenos Aires), 1969.

Canto de San Martin, Castaneda (Buenos Aires), 1979.

Poemas de la creacion, Castaneda, 1979.

(With Jorge Luis Borges and others) *La generacion poetica de 1922* (anthology), edited by Maria Raquel Llagostera, America Latina (Buenos Aires), 1980.

Poesia (1924-1950) (anthology), edited by Pedro Luis Barcia, Del 80, 1984.

Translations of poetry published in *Anthology of Contemporary Latin American Poetry,* 1942, and *Tri-Quarterly Anthology of Contemporary Latin American Literature,* 1969.

NOVELS

Adan Buenosayres (title means "Adam Buenosayres"), Sudamericana, 1948, revised, 1982.

El banquete de severo arcangelo (novel; title means "The Banquet of Severo Arcangelo"), Sudamericana, 1965.

Megafon; o, La guerra (title means "Megafon; or, The War"), Sudamericana, 1970.

PLAYS

Antigona Velez, Citerea (Buenos Aires), 1965, recent edition, Colihue (Buenos Aires), 1981.

Las tres caras de Venus, Citerea, 1966.

La batalla de Jose Luna (title means "The Battle of Jose Luna"), Universitaria (Santiago, Chile), 1970.

Don Juan (three-act), Castaneda, 1978.

OTHER

Historia de la calle Corrientes, Municipalidad (Buenos Aires), 1937, recent edition, Paidos (Buenos Aires), 1967.

Descenso y ascenso del alma por la belleza (aesthetic commentary), Sol y Luna, 1939, recent edition, Salido (Buenos Aires), 1982.

El nino Dios (for children), Sudamericana, 1939.

Vida de santa Rosa de Lima (biography; title means "Life of St. Rose of Lima"), Emece, 1943, recent edition, Castaneda, 1977.

Alejandro Bustillo, Peuser (Buenos Aires), 1944.

(Editor with wife, Elbia R. de Marechal) *Antologia didactica de la prosa argentina* (anthology of Argentine literature), Kapelusz, 1954.

Autopsia de Creso, El Barrilete (Buenos Aires), 1965.

(With Julio Cortazar, Adolfo Prieto, and Graciela de Sola) *Las claves de "Adan Buenosayres"* (commentary on his novel *Adan Buenosayres;* includes one article by each author), Azor (Mendoza, Argentina), 1966, 2nd edition published as *Interpretaciones y claves de "Adan Buenosayres,"* Acali (Montevideo, Uruguay), 1977.

Cuaderno de navigacion, Sudamericana, 1966.

Palabras con Leopoldo Marechal (critical anthology), edited by Alfredo Andres, C. Perez (Buenos Aires), 1968.

El espia y otros relatos, Kiek (Buenos Aires), 1975.

"El beatle final" y otras paginas no recogidas en libro (previously uncollected writings), America Latina, 1981.

Contributor and editor for the periodicals *Martin Fierro* and *Proa,* during the 1920s.

SIDELIGHTS: Little known in the English-speaking world and underappreciated in his native Argentina for many years, Leopoldo Marechal has increasingly been seen as an important forerunner of the renaissance in Latin American fiction that began in the 1960s. In *Spanish American Writing Since 1941,* George R. McMurray ranked Marechal's achievement as a literary innovator beside that of his revered countryman Jorge Luis Borges.

Along with Borges, Marechal began his writing career as one of the iconoclastic young poets who flourished in Buenos Aires during the 1920s. He shared with his peers an enthusiasm for the linguistically innovative writing that was appearing in Europe at the time, and he helped to write and edit two influential new periodicals, *Martin Fierro* and *Proa,* that featured the work of such experimental writers as James Joyce and Federico Garcia Lorca. As a fledgling poet Marechal derived from Borges an interest in ultraism, a Spanish movement which proclaimed that poetry should consist primarily of new and startling meta-

phors. The author's first major work, the 1926 poetry collection *Dias como flechas* ("Days Like Arrows"), strongly reflects ultraist trends. Reviewer Francisco Luis Bernardez, writing in the periodical *Sur* and quoted in *Modern Latin American Literature,* called the work "a masterpiece of sensory rejoicing."

Thereafter Marechal began to evolve a more idiosyncratic literary style, based on his personal religious concerns. As a visitor to Europe in the mid-1920s he had relished the antiestablishment lifestyle of its artists, but by 1929 he had returned to Argentina and become filled with religious turmoil, spurred by the grave illness of a friend. He turned to the writings of classical philosophers and Christian theologians, rejoining the Catholic church. The author's poetry reflected his newfound interest in traditional values. The 1936 collection *Laberinto de amor* ("Labyrinth of Love"), for instance, describes the differences between love as a human emotion and as a spiritual need, and was written in rhymed couplets. Bernardez said the book "represents the clearest synthesis of today's aesthetic of torture and the prodigious serenity of yesterday and eternity." Marechal continued to write traditional poetry about broad philosophical themes for the rest of his life. *Cinco poemas australes* ("Five Southern Poems"), perhaps his best work of this variety, helped him to win Argentina's National Poetry Prize in 1941.

Meanwhile, in 1930 Marechal began a lengthy work of fiction that further elaborated on his religious interests. A mixture of philosophical discussion and sharp urban realism, expressed in visionary and poetic prose, the seven-hundred-page novel appeared in 1948 as *Adan Buenosayres* ("Adam Buenosayres"). Though the work is highly indebted to Joyce's 1921 novel *Ulysses,* it represents a bold departure from traditional Latin American fiction, which generally surveyed social problems in a straightforward, journalistic style. The first five of the seven parts of *Adan Buenosayres* bear the strongest resemblance to *Ulysses.* Here Marechal introduces the title character of Adan, a writer much like Marechal himself, and evokes the texture of urban life by showing Adan's excursions through Buenos Aires on two days in the 1920s. As if to underscore Adan's status as an outsider, the writer's best friend is an alienated Jewish philosopher named Tesler who rails at the teeming metropolis while enduring the jibes of anti-Semites. While Joyce's novel seems willing to accept life as it is—a mixture of comedy and pathos—Marechal's book conveys a growing sense of moral revulsion. Tesler and Adan both experience bouts of nausea,

symbolizing, according to Ambrose Gordon in *Comparative Literature Studies,* their basic disgust with the city.

In the last two sections of *Adan Buenosayres,* Marechal departs from the model of *Ulysses* to depict Adan's search for human love and spiritual insight. Section six is a diary of Adan's love for a cold-hearted northern European woman, a futile affair that he resolves by imagining her death and funeral in great detail. Section seven is apparently Adan's dream, in which he plunges beneath Buenos Aires for a journey that resembles the poet Dante's voyage through hell in *The Inferno.* Here Adan views "sinners" who resemble the inhabitants of the city above, except that their moral failings have met with grotesque punishment. At his journey's end Adan is shown an ultimate monstrosity which is simple, formless chaos. Marechal does not say whether Adan finds redemption because of his unsettling vision. When *Adan Buenosayres* was first published, according to *Modern Latin American Literature,* the respected Argentine fiction writer Julio Cortazar called it "an extraordinary event in Argentine literature."

The work went largely unpublicized, however, because of its author's increasingly conservative politics. By the time *Adan Buenosayres* appeared Marechal was identified with the administration of president Juan Peron, an Army officer whose authoritarianism made him an anathema to most of Argentina's intellectuals. Marechal's prominence in such posts as cultural director of Peron's ministry of education prompted fellow writers to shun him for years, and he retreated into obscurity after the president was deposed in 1955.

In 1965 Marechal released a second novel, *El banquete de severo arcangelo* ("The Banquet of Severo Arcangelo"), which discussed the emptiness of modern society by using the biblical imagery of Christ's Last Supper. Less intricate and sprawling than *Adan Buenosayres,* the book sold well and became an occasion for the Latin American literary world to come to terms with Marechal's life and work. "I am not . . . about to defend the political and religious ideology of Leopoldo Marechal," wrote Manuel Pedro Gonzalez in 1967 in *Cuadernos americanos,* quoted in *Modern Latin American Literature.* "One can, and even should, censure the . . . Peronist proclivity of the author and at the same time recognize the value of his writings." In particular Gonzalez praised *Adan Buenosayres,* which over the next few years went through several new printings—

including one by Casa de las Americas, the official publishing house of Marxist Cuba. Cortazar collaborated with Marechal and other writers on the book *Las claves de "Adan Buenosayres,"* a mixture of commentary and praise about the novel. The rediscovery of Marechal extended to Ernesto Sabato, an Argentine novelist who is often ranked beside Cortazar in prestige. Sabato, according to Gonzalez, called Marechal "one of our most notable writers, unjustly and perversely forgotten by the official literature."

BIOGRAPHICAL/CRITICAL SOURCES:

BOOKS

Foster, David William, and Virginia Ramos Foster, editors, *Modern Latin American Literature,* F. Ungar, 1975.
McMurray, George R., *Spanish American Writing Since 1941,* Ungar, 1987.

PERIODICALS

Comparative Literature Studies, Volume 19, 1982.
Hispania, March, 1972.
Latin American Theatre Review, Volume 9, number 1, 1975.*

—*Sketch by Thomas Kozikowski*

* * *

MARIN, Luis Munoz
 See MUNOZ MARIN, (Jose) Luis (Alberto)

* * *

MARKS, Kathy (L.) 1953-

PERSONAL: Born August 11, 1953, in Sutton, WV; daughter of Amos and Crystabel Johnston; married William Marks, June 2, 1983; children: Mary Beth Marks Baxter, Jennifer Marks Thompson, Jon, Jason. *Ethnicity:* "White." *Education:* Attended West Virginia University, 1971-73; Glenville State College, B.S.W., 1980; Southern Illinois University, M.S., 1994. *Politics:* Democrat.

ADDRESSES: Home—P.O. Box 305, Marion, IL 62959. *E-mail*—kmarks@midwest.com.

CAREER: West Virginia Department of Welfare, Sutton, child abuse investigator, 1973-80; Franklin-Williamson Human Services, community worker, 1984-86; Jackson County Probation Office, adult probation officer, 1988-90; Illinois Department of Children and Family Services, child protective investigator, 1990—. Mobile Unit 15, police training instructor.

MEMBER: Elk Ladies Association, Williamson County Democrat Organization.

WRITINGS:

Faces of Right Wing Extremism, Branden Publishing (Brookline Village, MA), 1996.

WORK IN PROGRESS: Research on current terrorist activities in the United States.

SIDELIGHTS: Kathy Marks told *CA:* "I have always been interested in current events and their investigatory aspects. The desire to inform the public of matters I believe to be of vital interest to all of us has particularly inspired me.

"When I began work on my master's degree and started researching the activities of the extreme edge of the right wing, I learned that there was little organized material available. This became a challenge to me to learn more. The more I researched and even contacted groups directly for more information, the more intrigued I became.

"My writing to this point has been nonfiction, and organization is my best characteristic. Deciding the point of the work to be written, what needs to be covered, and how to organize the information is very important."

* * *

MARS, Jean Price
 See PRICE-MARS, Jean

MARUYAMA, Masao 1914-1996

OBITUARY NOTICE—See index for *CA* sketch: Born March 22, 1914, in Osaka, Japan; died of liver cancer, August 15, 1996. Political scientist, educator, and author. Maruyama was a noted Japanese political scientist who wrote influential books about post-World War II politics. His works were considered to be anti-establishment and were important to Japan as the country began efforts to modernize. Maruyama had a lengthy career in education at schools such as the University of Tokyo, Harvard University, St. Antony's College at Oxford University, and the Institute for Advanced Study at Princeton. His memberships included the American Academy of Arts and Sciences, the Japan Academy, and the British Academy. In 1993 he received the Association for Asian Studies Award for Distinguished Contribution to Asian Studies. His books include *The Logic and Psychology of Ultranationalism, Thought and Behaviour in Modern Japanese Politics,* and *Studies in the Intellectual History of Tokugawa Japan.*

OBITUARIES AND OTHER SOURCES:

BOOKS

International Who's Who, 60th edition, Europa, 1996.

PERIODICALS

Chicago Tribune, August 21, 1996, Section 3, p. 11.

* * *

MASTER OF LIFE, THE
See OLISAH, Sunday Okenwa

* * *

MASTERSON, Peter 1934-

PERSONAL: Born June 1, 1934, in Houston, TX; son of Carlos Bee (a lawyer) and Josephine Yeager (Smith) Masterson; married Carlin Glynn (an actor), December 29, 1960; children: Carlin Alexandra, Mary Stuart, Peter Carlos. *Education:* Rice University, B.A. (history), 1957; attended Stella Adler Theatre School. *Religion:* Episcopalian.

ADDRESSES: Home—1165 Fifth Ave., New York, NY 10029.

CAREER: Actor and director; playwright. Stage acting credits include *The Trial of Lee Harvey Oswald,* 1967, *The Great White Hope,* 1968, and *The Poison Tree,* 1975; film acting credits include *Ambush Bay,* 1965, *In the Heat of the Night,* 1967, and *The Stepford Wives,* 1974. Stage directorial credits include *The Cover of Life,* 1994, and *The Young Man from Atlanta,* 1995; films directed include *The Best Little Whorehouse in Texas,* 1980, *The Trip to Bountiful,* 1985, *Night Game,* 1988, and *Convicts,* 1991.

MEMBER: Actors Equity Association, Screen Actors Guild, Society of Stage Directors and Choreographers, American Federation of Television and Radio Actors, Writers Guild, Actors Studio, Directors Guild.

AWARDS, HONORS: Drama Desk award for best director, 1978, and Antoinette Perry ("Tony") Award nomination for best director and best writer, 1979, both for *The Best Little Whorehouse in Texas.*

WRITINGS:

PLAYS

(With Larry L. King, and director) *The Best Little Whorehouse in Texas* (music and lyrics by Carol Hall), Samuel French (New York), 1978, adapted as a screenplay (with King and Colin Higgins), 1980.

Author, with King, and co-director, with Tommy Tune, *The Best Little Whorehouse Goes Public,* 1994. Author and producer of television play *City in Fear.*

SIDELIGHTS: Known primarily as a film director, Peter Masterson is the co-author, with Larry L. King and lyricist Carol Hall, of the popular musical *The Best Little Whorehouse in Texas.* First performed on Broadway in 1978 under Masterson's direction, the Tony-nominated play was adapted by Masterson and King into a motion-picture screenplay in 1980. The film version, which starred Dolly Parton and Burt Reynolds in the leading roles, received mixed reviews from critics; Gene Siskel noted in the *Chicago Tribune* that "there is much to enjoy in the movie, which moves along in fits and starts." The musical's plot revolves around the Chicken Ranch, a brothel that does a brisk business in rural Texas—the madame being a close personal friend of the town's sheriff—

until a defender of the public good agitates to have the establishment closed down. *The Best Little Whorehouse Goes Public,* which Masterson, King, and Hall wrote and produced as a Broadway musical in 1994, was less enthusiastically received.

Masterson has also directed several screenplay adaptations of plays written by his cousin, Horton Foote, including 1985's *The Trip to Bountiful* and 1991's *Convicts.* Masterson began his career as an actor in a number of stage productions and films, including the title role in the play *The Trial of Lee Harvey Oswald,* 1967, and a role in the 1974 motion picture thriller *The Stepford Wives.*

BIOGRAPHICAL/CRITICAL SOURCES:

PERIODICALS

Chicago Tribune, July 26, 1982.
New York Times, July 24, 1982; December 3, 1989, section 2, p. 15.

* * *

MATLOCK, Jack F., Jr. 1929-

PERSONAL: Born October 1, 1929, in Greensboro, NC; son of Jack Foust (a teacher and school administrator) and Nellie (a teacher) Matlock; married Rebecca Burrum (a teacher and art consultant), September 2, 1949; children: James G., Hugh B., Nell, David M., Joseph F. *Education:* Duke University, A.B. (summa cum laude), 1950; Columbia University, M.A., 1952; Russian Institute, certificate, 1952. *Politics:* Independent. *Religion:* Methodist. *Avocational interests:* Photography, bookbinding, hiking, bird watching.

ADDRESSES: Home—2913 P St. NW, Washington, DC 20007-3069; 63 Battle Rd., Princeton, NJ 08540. *Office*—c/o Institute for Advanced Study, Olden Lane, Princeton, NJ 08540.

CAREER: Dartmouth College, Hanover, NH, instructor of Russian literature and culture, 1953-56; American Foreign Service officer, 1956-91, three tours as member of Moscow staff (before touring as ambassador), beginning 1961, other posts include Czechoslovakia, Tanzania, Ghana, and Austria, ambassador to U.S.S.R., 1987-91; Vanderbilt University, Nashville, TN, visiting professor of political science, 1978-79;

National Security Council, Washington, DC, special assistant to the President, senior director of European and Soviet affairs, 1983-87; Columbia University, New York City, senior research fellow, 1991-93, Kathryn and Shelby Cullom Davis Professor in the Practice of International Diplomacy, 1993-96; Institute for Advanced Study, School of Historical Studies, Princeton, NJ, George F. Kennan Professor, 1996—. Associated with the American Program Bureau and Capitol Speakers, speaker in the fields of national and global affairs, Russia and the former Soviet Union, political leadership, and bureaucratic management.

MEMBER: American Academy of Diplomacy, Academy of Political Science, Washington Institute of Foreign Affairs, American Association for the Advancement of Slavic Studies, Council on Foreign Relations, Century Association of New York.

AWARDS, HONORS: Has received numerous awards for service, including the Masaryk Award, 1983; Baltic Freedom Award, 1986; Wilbur J. Carr Award, 1991; Statesman of the Year Award from the George Washington University School of Law, 1991; Award for Excellence from the Graduate Faculties, Columbia University, 1992; McIver Award for Distinguished Public Service, University of North Carolina at Greensboro, 1994. Honorary L.L.D.s: Greensboro College, 1989, Albright College, 1992, Connecticut College, 1993.

WRITINGS:

(With Fred C. Holling) *An Index to the Collected Works of J. V. Stalin,* United States Department of State External Research Paper, 1955, reissued by Johnson Reprint (New York), 1971.
Autopsy on an Empire: The American Ambassador's Account of the Collapse of the Soviet Union, Random House (New York), 1995.

Contributor of articles on United States-Soviet relations, United States and Russian foreign policy, literature, and culture, and the Soviet government to periodicals, including *American Slavic and East European Review, Russian Review, Saturday Review, New Republic, Survey, Political Science Reviewer, Studia Diplomatica* (Brussels), *Voprosy literatury, The World & I,* and the *New York Review of Books.* Also contributor to the *Wall Street Journal* and the *New York Times.*

WORK IN PROGRESS: Reagan and the Russians: Ending the Cold War; Understanding Russia; The Practice of Diplomacy.

SIDELIGHTS: In *Autopsy on an Empire: The American Ambassador's Account of the Collapse of the Soviet Union,* former U.S. ambassador to Moscow Jack F. Matlock, Jr. drew on first-hand knowledge to describe the political events that took place in the faltering Soviet Union between 1987 and 1991. He analyzed the strengths and weaknesses of the various political players in the drama, chiefly Mikhail Gorbachev and Boris Yeltsin, whose conflict provides the work's unifying thread. Matlock concluded the work with an epilogue in which he described the aftermath of the Soviet Union's collapse. In addition, he professed his belief that the Soviet Union was destined to fail and that it will not be recreated regardless of any nostalgic efforts to do so.

The book garnered praise from critics. *Autopsy on an Empire* is one of the most scrupulously sober, intelligent and fair-minded analyses of the Soviet collapse yet to appear," proclaimed Anatol Lieven in the *New York Times Book Review.* "And coming from a man who from 1987 to 1991 was closer than any other Westerner to the heart of the events he describes, it also has enduring value as a historical document." Likewise, George F. Kennan, writing for the *New York Review of Books,* called *Autopsy on an Empire* "a serious and in many respects masterful work, well-written, interesting throughout, unique in both concept and execution, and of high historical importance."

A specialist with impressive credentials in Soviet politics and history, Matlock was appointed ambassador by President Ronald Reagan and remained in this post when George Bush was elected. Matlock could have put himself in the middle of his narrative, but did not, as Kennan noted: "It must be said, to the author's credit, that he firmly resisted the temptation to be carried off into autobiography, and brought his own experiences into the picture only when they were indeed relevant to the inquiry at hand." Instead, Matlock analyzed the political leaders involved. He faulted George Bush for excessive caution in dealing with the Soviets and empathized with Gorbachev's precarious position. "His portrait of the last Soviet leader is psychologically acute, even moving, but Mr. Matlock is also well aware of Mr. Gorbachev's shortcomings," described Lieven. "It will be a long time before [*Autopsy on an Empire*] is overtaken by the more detached and specifically historical scholarly

studies that must eventually follow," commented Kennan. "For the present the book may stand . . . for what it is: a running and very useful account of the events of the decisive four-year period (1987-1991), as seen and commented upon by one who was not only uniquely prepared but also uniquely positioned for the task of understanding and judging them."

BIOGRAPHICAL/CRITICAL SOURCES:

BOOKS

Mayers, David, *The Ambassadors and America's Soviet Policy,* Oxford University Press (New York), 1995, pp. 245-52.

PERIODICALS

Business Week, December 11, 1995, p. 15.
New York Review of Books, November 16, 1995, pp. 7-10.
New York Times Book Review, November 26, 1995, p. 6.
Publishers Weekly, October 2, 1995, p. 62.
Reader's Digest, April, 1991, pp. 129-33.
Washington Monthly, December, 1995, p. 57.

* * *

MAUGHAN, Jackie Johnson 1948-

PERSONAL: Surname is pronounced "mawn"; born January 4, 1948, in Pueblo, CO; daughter of H. W. W. (an outfitter and guide) and Helen (a social worker; maiden name, Gittings) Johnson; married Ralph B. Maughan (a college professor), 1977; children: (stepchildren) Erika Maughan Briggs, Alison Maughan Wood. *Ethnicity:* "WASP (German, Swedish, English)." *Education:* University of Idaho, B.A. (journalism), 1974; Idaho State University, M.A. (English), 1987. *Politics:* Democrat. *Avocational interests:* Environmental politics, women's issues.

ADDRESSES: Home—P.O. Box 8264, Pocatello, ID 83209. *Office*—Department of English, Idaho State University, Pocatello, ID 83209. *E-mail*—maugjacq @isu.edu.

CAREER: San Francisco Newsreel (documentary film company), member, 1969-72; *Lewiston Morning Tribune,* Lewiston, ID, stringer, 1973-74; *Greater Renton News,* Renton, WA, managing editor, 1975;

Idaho State University, Pocatello, Office of University Relations, public relations, 1976-85, Admission Counseling Slideshow, producer and scriptwriter, 1982, 1984, 1985, 1987, instructor of English, 1986—; *Morning News,* Blackfoot, ID, stringer, 1977; U.S. Forest Service fire lookout: Selway District, Nez Perce National Forest, Idaho, summer, 1992; Burnt-Powder Fire Zone, Wallowa-Whitman National Forest, Oregon, summer, 1993 and summer, 1994; Williams Ranger District, Kaibab National Forest, Arizona, summer, 1996; writer and editor. Kelly Pearce for U.S. Congress Committee, member, 1976; Dwight Jensen for U.S. Senate Committee, Pocatello coordinator, 1978; Idaho Democratic Convention, delegate, 1976 and 1982; Beverly Bistine for Idaho House campaign, writer and media consultant, 1980; Bannock County Democratic Central Committee, precinct committeewoman, 1982-86; Dwight Horsch for Idaho Senate campaign, writer and media consultant, 1984.

MEMBER: Sierra Club (Eastern Idaho Group political chair), United Transportation Union (shop steward, 1971-72), Idaho Conservation League (board of directors, 1980-82), Outdoorsmen for Church (steering committee, 1980), Idaho Environmental Council (board of directors, 1978-82; newsletter editor, 1981-82), Citizens for Responsible Government (Pocatello Chapter, founder and treasurer, 1978).

AWARDS, HONORS: Honorable Mention, Best Documentary (group award), Cannes Film Festival, 1970, for *The Women's Film;* award, Poetic Brevity, from the *Bridge: Poetry Quarterly,* 1972, for "Spartacus"; Sweepstakes Award, multiple categories, from Idaho Press Women, 1978; Honorable Mention, Press Release, from the National Federation of Press Women, 1978; Second Place, Critic's Review, National Federation of Press Women, 1978; Second Place, Interview, National Federation of Press Women, 1978; Outstanding Young Women of America, 1978-81; First Place, Research Article (with Ralph B. Maughan), National Federation of Press Women, 1980; First Place, Publicity and Promotion, National Federation of Press Women Communications Contest, 1980; Zonta, international executive and professional women's service honorary, 1984-86; Outstanding Young Democrat, Idaho, 1986.

WRITINGS:

(With Ann Puddicombe) *Hiking the Backcountry: A Do-It-Yourself Guide for the Adventurous Woman,* Stackpole Books (Mechanicsburg), 1981.

(With Cathryn Collins) *The Outdoor Woman's Guide to Sports, Fitness, and Nutrition,* Stackpole Books, 1983.
(With husband, Ralph B. Maughan) *The Hiker's Guide to Idaho,* Falcon Press (Missoula, MT), 1985, 3rd edition, 1994.
(Editor and contributor) *Go Tell It on the Mountain: Writings by Fire Lookouts,* Stackpole Books, 1996.

Also author of the novel *A Pirate Looks at Forty,* an agented manuscript; author of documentary films, including *The Women's Film;* contributor to *Idaho Fiction at the Centennial,* Idaho State University Press, 1992. Contributor to periodicals, including *Women's Sports and Fitness, Family Camping, Backpacker, Timberline: A Literary Magazine,* and *Redneck Review of Literature.*

WORK IN PROGRESS: A novel, *Go Tell the Great Bear.*

SIDELIGHTS: Go Tell It on the Mountain: Writings by Fire Lookouts, a 1996 collection of stories and essays edited by Jackie Johnson Maughan, contains accounts written by nineteen fire lookouts—employees of the U.S. Forest Service who sit in remote stations to monitor wooded areas for signs of fire—that detail their experiences on the job. Maughan is an experienced writer who has coauthored three books on outdoor sports and writes regularly for periodicals dealing with outdoor sports. She also works as a fire lookout and has contributed her own account to the collection. *Go Tell It on the Mountain* includes narratives that describe the isolation faced by the lookouts and how they cope with it, as well as the constant, intense alertness required of them. The lookouts also provide commentary on the hazards they face while working, including lightning (a primary cause of forest fires), grizzly bears, rattlesnakes, and other wild animals. Herbert Kupterberg of *Parade* magazine called *Go Tell It on the Mountain* "a thoughtful collection," and a *Publishers Weekly* contributor asserted that it contains "several fascinating accounts."

Maughan told *CA:* "I've made my living as a professional writer (documentary films, advertising, news, public relations), but in recent years I've turned to fiction and creative nonfiction. This type of work is (for me) much more difficult both to create and to sell and as a consequence I've had to support myself by teaching college writing as a part-time, temporary employee.

"I believe that those of us who live in the West and write about it *do* help define it. The Old West has been canonized and mythologized, but what about the New West? What defines it? What makes Boise or Pocatello different from, say, Beverly Hills, or Memphis, or the Mekong Delta?

"While I'm not particularly concerned about how we're perceived outside of the region, I am deeply concerned about telling the truth about our lives here. That's what I hope my work accomplishes."

BIOGRAPHICAL/CRITICAL SOURCES:

BOOKS

Maughan, Jackie Johnson, editor and contributor, *Go Tell It on the Mountain: Writings by Fire Lookouts,* Stackpole Books, 1996.

PERIODICALS

Parade, July 7, 1996, p. 10.
Publishers Weekly, January 15, 1996, p. 456.

* * *

McBRIDE, James C. 1957-

PERSONAL: Born in 1957; son of Andrew McBride (a minister; deceased in 1957) and Ruth McBride Jordan (a homemaker; born, Rachel Shilsky).

ADDRESSES: Office—c/o Riverhead Books, 200 Madison Ave., New York, NY 10016-3903.

CAREER: Worked variously as a jazz saxophonist, composer, and producer; *Washington Post,* journalist; *Boston Globe,* journalist; freelance writer.

WRITINGS:

The Color of Water: A Black Man's Tribute to His White Mother (memoir), Riverhead Books (New York), 1996.

WORK IN PROGRESS: A novel.

SIDELIGHTS: For Mother's Day in 1981 journalist James C. McBride penned an essay about his mother for the *Boston Globe.* Readers, moved by the piece, wrote to McBride and encouraged him to write a book. More than a decade after McBride first approached his mother about writing her story Ruth Jordan finally acquiesced. In 1996 *The Color of Water: A Black Man's Tribute to His White Mother* rolled off the presses. The title of the book reflects Jordan's answer to her son's childhood inquiry about the color of God's skin.

The Color of Water is told in chapters that alternate between the mother's recollections and her son's commentary. Jordan explains how she was born in Poland, the daughter of an Orthodox Jewish rabbi-turned-grocer who emigrated to the American South. To escape sexual abuse by her father, Jordan says she fled the South, ending up in New York City. There she met and married minister Andrew McBride, helped him establish an all-black Baptist church, and gave birth to eight children. James was the youngest and never met his father, who died shortly before his birth. McBride described how Jordan remarried, had four more children, and raised him and his siblings in lower-income neighborhoods in Brooklyn and Queens. To protect her children from stigma, Ruth led her children to believe that she was a light-skinned black, and until late in his childhood, McBride did not question her. When McBride did ask his mother whether he was white or black, her response was: "You're a human being. Educate yourself or you'll be a nobody." The author explains that during his adolescence, he rebelled against his mother and stepfather's authority and was involved in petty crime. Yet he and his siblings overcame many obstacles, earning college degrees and self-respect. McBride gives much credit for the success of their family to his mother's Orthodox background combined with his father's Christianity.

Some reviewers have compared *The Color of Water* with *Divided to the Vein,* by Scott Minerbrook, another African American journalist whose mother was white and father was black. Writing in *Booklist,* Alice Joyce called *The Color of Water* and *Divided to the Vein* "remarkably candid," adding "these memoirs reflect earnestly on issues of self stemming from the interracial marriages of their parents." In the *Chicago Tribune,* John Blades wrote: "Though McBride's disillusionment was not so severe as Minerbrook's, his memoir just as forcefully points out how 'divided to the vein' America remains, not just between black and white but also between black and black." He added: "Similar but very different, the two books are both eye- and mind-opening about the eternal convolutions and paradoxes of race in America, as seen from up-close and microcosmic perspectives."

As he delved into his past, McBride came to take pride in his Jewish heritage and became more empathetic to people of all kinds. "The lingering effects of slavery and color consciousness continue to push us in directions we shouldn't go," according to McBride, as reported by Blades. "What I'd like people to come away with is that we have a lot more in common than we think," he told Norman Oder in *Publishers Weekly.* Blades quoted McBride: "I think America is integrating itself kicking and screaming. But it's absolutely essential that we do. We can't survive any other way." According to a reviewer in *Publishers Weekly:* "This moving and unforgettable memoir needs to be read by people of all colors and faiths."

BIOGRAPHICAL/CRITICAL SOURCES:

BOOKS

McBride, James C., *The Color of Water: A Black Man's Tribute to His White Mother,* Riverhead Books, 1996.

PERIODICALS

Booklist, January 1 and 15, 1996, p. 782.
Chicago Tribune, TEMPO section, February 26, 1996, p. 1.
Library Journal, January, 1996, p. 110.
Publishers Weekly, October 30, 1995, pp. 24-25; January 15, 1996, p. 454.
USA Today, January 29, 1996, p. D4.
Wall Street Journal, February 9, 1996, pp. A10, A12.
Washington Post, January 14, 1996, p. 4.*

*　　*　　*

McCOY, Max 1958-
(Rheuben Buckner, a pseudonym)

PERSONAL: Born October 30, 1958, in Baxter Springs, KS; son of Carl J. (in sales) and Mary (Carter) McCoy. *Education:* Pittsburg (KS) State University, B.A. (communication), 1988; Emporia State University, M.A. (English), 1994. *Politics:* "Democrat by nature." *Religion:* "I consider myself a spiritual, not a religious person." *Avocational interests:* Scuba diving, black powder weapons, classic Mustangs.

ADDRESSES: Home—P.O. Box 1607, Pittsburg, KS 66762. *Agent*—Robin Rue, Anita Diamant Agency, 310 Madison Ave., New York, NY 10017.

CAREER: Pittsburg Morning Sun, Pittsburg, KS, reporter, 1980-83, reporter and photographer, 1983-89; *Joplin Globe,* Joplin, KS, reporter and photographer, 1982-83; Pittsburg State University, part-time instructor, 1989-90; *Parsons Sun,* Parsons, KS, county government reporter, 1992; Emporia State University, instructor in creative and professional writing, 1994.

MEMBER: Western Writers of America, Mensa, Ozark Writers League, Midwest Diving Council, Jayhawk Divers.

AWARDS, HONORS: H. G. Roberts First Amendment Freedom Award, 1983; Hibakusha Travel grant, 1986; second place award, Inland Daily Press/University of Wisconsin Investigative Reporting Contest, 1986, for "An Uncertain Legacy"; Medicine Pipe Bearer's Award, Western Writers of America, 1992, for *The Sixth Rider;* Oxbow Award for Short Western Fiction, Ozark Writers League, 1983, for "Spoils of War"; finalist for best western novel award, Western Writers of America, 1994, for *Sons of Fire.*

WRITINGS:

NOVELS

The Sixth Rider, Doubleday (Garden City, NY), 1991.
Sons of Fire, Doubleday, 1995.
The Wild Rider (sequel to *The Sixth Rider*), Bantam (New York City), 1995.
Home to Texas (sequel to *Sons of Fire*), Bantam, 1995.

FOR CHILDREN

Indiana Jones and the Philosopher's Stone, Bantam, 1995.
Indiana Jones and the Dinosaur Eggs, Bantam, 1996.

OTHER

Contributor to *Ozark Writers on Writing,* edited by L. Pate, Seven Oaks Publishing (Conway, AR), 1995. Contributor of nonfiction to periodicals, sometimes under the pseudonym Rheuben Buckner.

SIDELIGHTS: Kansas-based writer and journalist Max McCoy found his niche penning westerns and adventure novels known for their enticing storylines and historical authenticity. His first novel, *The Sixth Rider,* about a group of nineteenth-century western outlaws known as the Dalton Gang, won the Medicine Pipe Bearer's Award (a prize for best first novels) from the Western Writers of America in 1992. McCoy has also written several installments in the *Indiana Jones* adventure series for younger readers, each based on the characters from the popular motion picture trilogy.

Growing up in southeast Kansas, McCoy found his school years to be a test of endurance—for both him and his teachers. He was a troublemaker and was often bored with classes. "I was what they now call an *at risk* student," he told *CA.* "But I always knew I was going to be a writer, even when my high school guidance counselor advised me to 'give up these pipe dreams' and do the sensible thing by joining the military. A very few teachers, however, encouraged my writing, and to them I will be eternally grateful."

McCoy worked as a reporter and photographer at various newspapers for nearly ten years before publishing his first novel. "Although I started writing when I was in my early teens, making up long, novel-length stories to entertain my friends, it wasn't until I became a full-time newspaper reporter at the age of twenty that I began to develop an appreciation for local history—and began to cast about in search of a voice for the outlaw spirit," he recalled. After several years of research, he wrote *The Sixth Rider*—in a mere six weeks. "When my subconscious is ready, things tend to go quickly and almost effortlessly," he explained in an article in *Ozark Writers on Writing.* "The story tumbles out. I go into a kind of trance, a kind of waking dream, in which I vividly imagine characters and events."

"My first book was inspired not by history, but by the *experience* of growing up in southeast Kansas," McCoy explained to *CA*—"it was, for me, a special kind of agony, filled with alienation and conflict, and made worse by the hypocrisy of small-town life. I had heard the stories of the outlaw Daltons, the Youngers, and the James Gang when I was a kid, but they didn't seem to make much of an impression at the time. Like most people who grow up in small towns, I had the feeling that 'nothing ever happened here.' I know first-hand that it is not the glorification of crime that makes an outlaw, but the isolation one feels from the rest of society."

Although McCoy's books have been marketed as western novels, he doesn't consider himself to be a "western" writer. "In fact, I didn't read westerns when I was growing up," he admits, "with the exception of two terrific books from the sixties which many people don't consider westerns: *True Grit* by Charles Portis and *Little Big Man* by Thomas Berger. Other early influences were Mark Twain, Jules Verne, and H. G. Wells. Add lots of comic books, *Mad Magazine,* some *Playboy* interviews and science fiction into the mix. Later came Hemingway and Fitzgerald, and more recently, Joseph Campbell."

BIOGRAPHICAL/CRITICAL SOURCES:

BOOKS

Pate, L., editor, *Ozark Writers on Writing,* Seven Oaks Publishing (Conway, AR), 1995, pp. 123-44.

* * *

McCRORIE, Edward (P.) 1936-

PERSONAL: Born November 19, 1936, in Central Falls, RI; son of Charles and Helen (Pollitt) Mc-Crorie; married Beatrice Beebe (a psychologist), May 12, 1995; children: Jeanne, Julia, Joyce, Cynthia. *Education:* Assumption College, B.A., 1962; Villanova University, M.A., 1964; Brown University, Ph.D., 1970. *Politics:* Independent. *Religion:* "Christian Taoist." *Avocational interests:* The environment, travel, all the arts, "physical challenge."

ADDRESSES: Home—84 Prospect St., Pawtucket, RI 02860. *Office*—Department of English, Providence College, Providence, RI 02918.

CAREER: Providence College, Providence, RI, professor of English, 1964—.

WRITINGS:

After a Cremation (poems), Thorp Springs (Berkeley, CA), 1975.
(Translator) *The Aeneid of Virgil,* University of Michigan Press (Ann Arbor, MI), 1995.

WORK IN PROGRESS: Love Life, poems; translating *The Odyssey of Homer;* research on "a model of love for the twenty-first century."

SIDELIGHTS: Edward McCrorie told *CA:* "I am moved to write from within. It is a desire or need to make something beautiful and socially acceptable out of confused, painful turmoil inside. Making a poem is good therapy; it should also be good art, and a good comment on our common lives and labors at the end of this century.

"Life influences my work first: a great sycamore, a frozen river, swifts over Rome, mosquitoes at Mount Monadnoc; people around me who are in pain, especially those to whom I am close; and other writers, not only poets, but especially Sappho, Thoreau, Derek Walcott, Maxine Kumin. If I could be sure who 'inspires' me, I'd tell the world!"

* * *

McDOUGALL, Colin (Malcolm) 1917-1984

PERSONAL: Born July 13, 1917, in Montreal, Quebec, Canada; died June 3, 1984; son of Errol (a judge) and Mary Wynifred (Rankin) McDougall; married Diana Ekers, January 4, 1941; children: one son, three daughters. *Education:* Attended Lower Canada College, 1929-36; McGill University, B.A., 1940. *Religion:* Anglican.

CAREER: McGill University, Montreal, Quebec, student counsellor, 1946-47, director of placement service, 1947-57, registrar, 1957-73, secretary general, 1973-84. First president of the Service for Admission to Colleges and Universities, 1966-68; member of the College Entrance Exam Board and the Committee on International Education. *Military service:* Served in Italy in World War II as part of Princess Patricia's Canadian Light Infantry; attained rank of major.

AWARDS, HONORS: First prize in *Maclean's* fiction contest, and President's Medal from the University of Western Ontario for best Canadian short story, both c. 1953, both for "The Firing Squad"; Governor General's Award, and Quebec Literary Prize, both 1959, both for *Execution.*

WRITINGS:

Execution (novel), St. Martin's (New York), 1958.

Contributor of short stories, including "Cardboard Soldiers," "The Firing Squad," and "Love Is for the Birds," to *Maclean's* during the early 1950s.

SIDELIGHTS: Canadian author Colin McDougall spent most of his career in education, holding various positions throughout nearly four decades of service at Montreal's McGill University. He published only one novel and a few short stories, but the critical acclaim and literary prizes awarded his works have guaranteed him a place in Canadian literature. *Execution,* McDougall's 1958 novel set in World War II, has drawn comparisons to the works of American novelists Ernest Hemingway, Stephen Crane, Norman Mailer, and Joseph Heller. It garnered the prestigious Governor General's Award in 1959, as well as the Quebec Literary Prize the same year.

McDougall was born in Montreal, Quebec, in 1917. His father was a noted Canadian judge. McDougall began his secondary education at Lower Canada College, completing his bachelor's degree at McGill in 1940. He served in World War II after his graduation, reaching the rank of major within Princess Patricia's Canadian Light Infantry. McDougall became a company commander while he and his unit were stationed in Italy; it is this experience that inspired the bulk of his fiction.

Following the war, McDougall began his long career at McGill, where he worked in student counselling and placement services, followed by seventeen years as registrar and more than a decade as secretary general, a post he held at the time of his death. As Hallvard Dahlie observed in the *Dictionary of Literary Biography,* "it is possible to see [the author's] writing career merely as one of many activities he pursued throughout a balanced, orderly, and fruitful life." He began submitting short stories to *Maclean's* in the early 1950s; the first to see print in that periodical was "Cardboard Soldiers." Much better known, however, was the later "Firing Squad." This tale won both the *Maclean's* fiction contest and a President's Medal from the University of Western Ontario for best Canadian short story.

"The Firing Squad" also became the basis for the novel *Execution,* ostensibly a war story whose "fundamental substance," according to Dahlie, "is philosophical and moral rather than military." The novel is, at one level, about two executions: the first of some Italian deserters whom Dahlie described as "harmless"; the second of "innocent" young Rifleman Jones, whose death is demanded by both Canadian and American officials. In Dahlie's analysis, McDougall uses the literal examples of the two executions to frame an examination of the moral, ethical, and "metaphysical implications" of the relation-

ships between and among those responsible for ordering and carrying out the executions and those sentenced to the punishment. Wrote Dahlie, the characters of "Bazin, Adam, and Jones are all personally implicated in the initial execution Throughout the subsequent action Bazin and Adam attempt to exorcise their own personal guilt and to rationalize the guilt of mass man, as represented by their company." Jones, a simpler man who feels no guilt, continues as usual until his accidental involvement in the death of an American soldier requires his execution. Among the characters in *Execution* is a soldier named Krasnick, originally from Manitoba, who has no trouble killing German soldiers, but refuses to shoot horses. Dahlie concluded that "McDougall's novel avoids sentimentality and didacticism, and in its blend of objective realism and carefully controlled symbolism it allows for both a credibility and an expansible interpretation that have confirmed its continuing relevance and significance."

BIOGRAPHICAL/CRITICAL SOURCES:

BOOKS

Dictionary of Literary Biography, Volume 68: *Canadian Writers, 1920-1959, First Series,* Gale, 1988.

PERIODICALS

Canadian Literature, winter, 1966, pp. 20-31.*

* * *

McGEE, Spike
See MOODY, Fred

* * *

McGIRT, James E(phraim) 1874-1930

PERSONAL: Born September, 1874; died June 13, 1930; son of Madison (a farmer) and Ellen Townsend McGirt. *Education:* private and public schools; Bennett College, North Carolina, B.A., 1895.

CAREER: Poet, songwriter, and publisher of *McGirt's Magazine.* Founder of the Constitutional Brotherhood of America.

WRITINGS:

Avenging the Maine, A Drunken A.B., and Other Poems, Edwards & Broughton, 1899, revised and enlarged edition, 1900, second revised edition, Lasher, 1901.
Some Simple Songs and a Few More Ambitious Attempts, Lasher, 1901.
For Your Sweet Sake: Poems, Winston, 1906, enlarged edition, 1909.
The Triumphs of Ephraim, McGirt, 1907.

SIDELIGHTS: James E. McGirt made a notable contribution to African American literature through his publication of *McGirt's Magazine,* which reprinted and disseminated the work of major black writers, gave voice to the political aims of the African American community, and encouraged blacks to gain autonomy through voting and education.

Immediately following his college career, McGirt made a modest but comfortable career in business, working as a launderer and drayman. His first collection of poems, *Avenging the Maine, A Drunken A.B., and Other Poems,* was published by Edwards and Broughton in 1899. The work received generally unfavorable reviews, which McGirt was not to better even with two expanded editions of the same book in 1900 and 1901. His poetry follows the folk dialect style popularized by Paul Laurence Dunbar and James D. Corrothers. But according to Walter C. Daniel in the *Dictionary of Literary Biography,* in at least one poem, "Memory of Lincoln and the Yankees," McGirt "fails to achieve the unity in structure or the high level of poetic skill that characterize Dunbar's work."

McGirt sought a mentor from among the prominent poets and scholars of his day, both black and white. Lacking a patron, he featured his own work in *McGirt's Magazine,* which was published first in Greensboro, North Carolina, then from Philadelphia, where he moved in 1903. He also printed the work of Dunbar, W. E. B. Du Bois, Benjamin T. Tanner, Frances E. W. Harper, and other prominent black writers. Although McGirt never found sustaining support from among the literary circle of his day, he was encouraged by Du Bois, whose political orientation was in alignment with his own.

McGirt's Magazine served as the official voice of the Constitutional Brotherhood of America, which McGirt founded in an effort to increase the power of blacks within the Republican Party. Through his pe-

riodical, he also supported the National Afro-American Council and the Niagara Movement, the latter cause being led by Du Bois.

In 1906, while McGirt was in Philadelphia, his second collection of poems was published. Some poems were written in the sentimental style which reached its zenith in the mid-nineteenth century; others were in dialect form. Again, McGirt's work was deemed uneven by critics. In 1909 his publishing company failed, and he returned to his home in Greensboro the following year. Upon returning home, McGirt turned around a fledgling family cosmetics business, building it into one of the preeminent black-owned businesses in North Carolina. He also met with success as a realtor. Even with his business obligations, he continued to be a prolific writer, shifting from poetry to short stories perhaps hoping to receive more favorable reviews. In 1907, he self-published *The Triumphs of Ephraim,* a collection of his prose pieces. However, McGirt never achieved recognition for his poetry or fiction, and his strident, committed editorship of *McGirt's* remains his chief legacy. Selected copies of the magazine can be found at Howard University in Washington, D.C.

BIOGRAPHICAL/CRITICAL SOURCES:

BOOKS

Dictionary of Literary Biography, Volume 50, *Afro-American Writers before the Harlem Renaissance,* Gale, 1987, pp. 212-17.

PERIODICALS

Crisis, May, 1953, pp. 287-89.
Negro History Bulletin, March, 1953, pp. 123-26.

* * *

McNEILL, Christine 1953-

PERSONAL: Born April 4, 1953, in Vienna, Austria; daughter of Hans and Hermine (Illner) Rabensteiner; married Ralph McNeill, May 24, 1975 (divorced, October 21, 1992). *Education:* International House, London, Teachers' Training Certificate in Teaching English as a Foreign Language (TEFL), 1975; Linguaphone Institute, London, Business German, 1976. *Politics:* Socialist. *Religion:* "Follow personal beliefs."

ADDRESSES: Home and office—31 Burnt Hills, Cromer, Norfolk NR27 9LW, England.

CAREER: Linguaphone Institute, London, tutor of German and TEFL, 1976-78; Inner London Education Authority, English as a Second Language (ESL) tutor, 1976-81; North Norfolk District Council, tutor of German, 1989—.

AWARDS, HONORS: Richard Ellmann Award, joint winner for poetry.

WRITINGS:

Kissing the Night (poetry), Bloodaxe Books (Newcastle upon Tyne, England), 1993.

Contributor of poetry to periodicals, including *London Magazine, Verse, Observer, New Statesman and Society, Critical Quarterly,* and *Writing Women.*

WORK IN PROGRESS: Contrasting Bodies, a poetry collection.

SIDELIGHTS: Christine McNeill told *CA:* "I left Vienna in 1970 because I felt the need to adopt another language (English) and culture in order to analyse and integrate my personal background and my country's history. My writing reflects my post-war Viennese upbringing, and explores psychological states in relation to physical and historical alienation. I examine repressed sexuality, loss, the ironies of history, art in relation to daily life, failure in communication between individuals, and unexpressed love in relationships.

"Many of my poems in *Kissing the Night* are shadowed by the guilt of my parents' generation as I act out their painful stories and uneasy reminiscences of life during the War. . . . I am interested in the kinship of past and present, ideas and emotions, and in my work try to weave disparate elements together in order to find and show links."

Just such disparate images and ideas are described by McNeill in the poetry collection *Kissing the Night.* The author's background as a language teacher, as well as the fact that English is her second language, bring interesting characteristics to the poems as well, resulting in combinations of uniquely constructed phrases. "McNeill unsettles expectations by dwelling on the meeting-point of jarring value systems, and her own style mingles influences from both German and Anglo-American literary culture," observed Ian

Gregson in the *Times Literary Supplement*. In the poem "Foreign Language," for example, McNeill portrays a language teacher working in the Far East to emphasize that cultures, like languages, are not always easily translated. Gregson also praised McNeill's expression of her ideas on the effects of a native language through the use of various aspects of narration. Many of the events narrated deal with both Austrian and German experiences during and after World War II. Because of the cultural and language differences between the two countries, these events must be continuously re-examined from numerous perspectives. "The unstable hybrid that results can be seen as a version, at the level of literary style, of what happens when cultures meet, and as such demonstrates how a mother tongue can be too single-minded," explained Gregson.

BIOGRAPHICAL/CRITICAL SOURCES:

PERIODICALS

Times Literary Supplement, September 23, 1994.

* * *

MEDINA, Robert C. 1924-

PERSONAL: One source lists first name as Roberto; born February 11, 1924, in Las Cruces, NM; son of Jesus (a painter) and Petra (Cisneros) Medina; married Mary Louise Medina, January 5, 1948; children: Carol M. Maze, Agatha Rodriguez, Cathy Garcia, Mark, Pete, Rose S. Galgay. *Education:* Attended New Mexico State University. *Politics:* Democratic. *Religion:* Catholic.

ADDRESSES: Home—121 Ridgecrest Dr., Las Cruces, NM 88005. *Office*—Bilingue Publications, P.O. Drawer H, Las Cruces, NM 88004.

CAREER: Federal Government Civil Service, White Sands Missile Range, NM, worked for over thirty years as a photo-optical equipment operator; Bilingue Publications, Las Cruces, NM, owner, 1974—.

MEMBER: Knights of Columbus.

WRITINGS:

(Also editor) *Two Ranges* (novel), introduction by Patricio Quintana, Bilingue Publications, 1974.

(Also editor) *Fabian no se muere: novela de amor* (novel; also see below), Bilingue Publications, 1978.

(Also editor) *Fabian Doesn't Die* (condensed drama of *Fabian no se muere* in English; produced 1990), Bilingue Publications, 1981.

(Editor, with Virginia Lark, of daughter Carol's book) Carol M. Maze, *Mexican Microwave Cookery,* Bilingue Publications, 1984.

SIDELIGHTS: Robert C. Medina's second novel, *Fabian no se muere: novela de amor,* is the story of a young Chicano man (Fabian) who, after moving from the country to pursue a new life in the city, returns to operate his family's farm. A contributor to *Chicano Literature: A Reference Guide* notes Medina "establishes endearing images of Chicano culture" that "deal with the various levels of familial ties and cultural means by which they are preserved: religion, language, and the work ethic." The contributor also describes Medina's use of *calo,* a mixture of Spanish, English, and Nahuatl (an Indian language), as Fabian's "way of identifying with big-city folk" that "establishes both an era and a locale—the 1940s in southern New Mexico and west Texas." Moreover, the contributor continues, "Medina's novels are telling examples of the view that *calo* is a vehicle of communication that must be recognized in fiction as an inescapable social datum. In this sense, . . . Medina's novels are in the tradition of promoting the Southwest as a pluralistic society that both affects and is affected by Chicanos in their efforts to find their unique place within it."

BIOGRAPHICAL/CRITICAL SOURCES:

BOOKS

Lomeli, Francisco A., and Donaldo W. Urioste, *Chicano Perspectives in Literature: A Critical and Annotated Bibliography,* Pajarito Publications, 1976.

Martinez, Julio A., and Francisco A. Lomeli, editors, *Chicano Literature: A Reference Guide,* Greenwood Press, 1985.

* * *

MENENDEZ PIDAL, Ramon 1869-1968

PERSONAL: Born March 13, 1869, in La Coruna, Spain; died November 14, 1968, in Madrid, Spain;

married Maria Goyri, 1900; children: Jimena, Rodrigo. *Education:* Ph.D., 1893; studied at Universities of Madrid and Toulouse.

CAREER: Ateneo, School for Higher Studies, Madrid, Spain, reader, 1896-99; University of Madrid, Madrid, professor of Romance philology, 1899-1939. Founder of Center for Historical Studies, Madrid, 1907, and director, beginning 1910; president of Royal Spanish Academy, 1925-39 and 1947-68. Minister in Spanish cabinet, 1912 and 1918. Visiting professor, University of Buenos Aires, 1914, and Columbia University, 1937-38. *Comisario regio* in settlement of border dispute between Ecuador and Peru, 1904-08.

AWARDS, HONORS: Special citations from Spanish History Academy, 1893, for *Cantar del Mio Cid: Texto, gramatica y vocabulario,* and 1896, for *La leyenda de los Infantes de Lara;* honorary degrees from numerous universities, including the Universities of Toulouse, Oxford, Tuebingen, Paris, Louvain, and Brussels.

WRITINGS:

IN ENGLISH TRANSLATION

(Editor) *Poema del Cid,* annotated edition, [Madrid], 1900, abridged edition published with modern Spanish prose version by Alfonso Reyes as *Poema del Cid,* 1938, reprinted, 1967, abridged Spanish edition with translation by W. S. Merwin published as *Poema del Cid/Poem of the Cid* (bilingual edition), Las Americas (New York), 1960.

La Espana del Cid, two volumes, Plutarca (Madrid), 1929, revised edition, Espasa-Calpe, 1956, translation by Harold Sunderland of original Spanish edition published in one volume as *The Cid and His Spain,* J. Murray, 1934, reprinted, F. Cass, 1971.

(Editor and author of preface) *Historia de Espana,* seven volumes, [Madrid], 1947, translation by Walter Starkie of preface published as *The Spaniards in Their History: An Analysis of Spain's National Characteristics,* Norton, 1950.

IN SPANISH

(Editor) *La leyenda de los Infantes de Lara,* [Madrid], 1896, 2nd edition, [Madrid], 1934, revised edition, Espasa-Calpe, 1971.

(Editor) *Cronicas generales de Espana: Catalogo de la Real Biblioteca,* Sucesores de Rivadeneyra (Madrid), 1898, 3rd edition corrected and enlarged, [Madrid], 1918.

Notas para el Romancero del Conde Fernan Gonzalez, [Madrid], 1899.

(Editor) *Antologia de prosistas castellanos,* [Madrid], 1899, 2nd edition, Clasica Espanol (Madrid), 1917, 5th edition published as *Antologia de prosistas espanoles,* Hernando (Madrid), 1928, reprinted, Espasa-Calpe, 1964.

(Editor) *"El condenado por desconfiado," por Tirso de Molina,* [Madrid], 1902.

La leyenda del Abad Don Juan de Montemayor, [Dresden], 1903.

Manual elemental de gramatica historica espanola, [Madrid], 1904, 3rd edition, V. Suarez, 1914, published as *Manual de gramatica historica espanola,* 1918, reprinted, Espasa-Calpe, 1977.

(Editor) Alfonso X, *Primera cronica general de Espana que mando componer Alfonso el Sabio y se continuaba bajo Sancho IV en 1289,* [Madrid], 1906, 2nd edition, 1916, reprinted, Gredos, 1977.

(Editor) *Cantar del Mio Cid: Texto, gramatica y vocabulario,* three volumes, [Madrid], 1908-11, 3rd edition with corrections, Espasa-Calpe (Madrid), 1954-56.

El romancero espanol: Conferencias dadas en la Columbia University de New York los dias 5 y 7 de abril de 1909, bajo los auspicios de the Hispanic Society of America, Hispanic Society of America (New York), 1910.

(Editor and author of introduction and notes) *Poema del Mio Cid,* La Lectura (Madrid), 1913.

(Editor with wife, Maria Goyri) *La serrana de la vera, de Luis Velez de Guevara,* [Madrid], 1916.

Documentos linguisticos de Espana, Volume I: *Renio de Castilla,* Centro de Estudios Historicos, 1919, reprinted, Revista de Filologia Espanola, 1966.

Estudios literarios, Ateneo (Madrid), 1920, reprinted, Espasa-Calpe, 1968.

Un aspecto en la elaboracion del "Quijote," Ateneo, 1920.

(Contributor) *Cursos de metodologia y alta cultura: Curso de linguistica,* [Barcelona], 1921.

El Cid y la historia, Jimenez y Molina (Madrid), 1921.

Poesia popular y poesia tradicional en la literatura espanola, Oxford University Press, 1922.

El rey Rodrigo en la literatura, Bulletin of the Royal Spanish Academy, 1924.

Poesia juglaresca y juglares: Aspectos de la historia literaria y cultural de Espana, Revista de

Archivos (Madrid), 1924, 4th edition, corrected and enlarged, Instituto de Estudios Politicos (Madrid), 1957.

(Editor) *Rodrigo: El ultimo godo,* Volume I: *La edad media,* La Lectura, 1925, reprinted, Espasa-Calpe, 1958.

Origenes del espanol: Estudio linguistico de la peninsula iberica hasta el siglo XI (also see below), Hernando, 1926, 4th edition, corrected and greatly enlarged, Espasa-Calpe, 1956.

El idioma espanol en sus primeros tiempos (previously published as part of *Origenes del espanol: Estudio linguistico de la peninsula iberica hasta el siglo XI*), Voluntad (Madrid), 1927, reprinted, Espasa-Calpe, 1968.

(Editor) *Flor nueva de romances viejos que recogio de la tradicion antigua y moderna R. Menendez Pidal,* Revista de Archivos, Bibliotecas y Museos, 1928, expanded edition, 1943, reprinted, Espasa-Calpe, 1968, original edition published as *Flor nueva de romances viejos,* Espasa-Calpe (Buenos Aires), 1939, reprinted, 1967.

El romancero: Teorias e investigaciones, Paez (Madrid), 1928.

Historia y epopeya (also see below), Hernando, 1934.

(Editor) *Epopeya y romancero: Pliegos impresos hasta julio de 1936 bajo los auspicios de la Hispanic Society of America* (also see below), Hernando, 1936.

Los romances de America y otros estudios, Espasa-Calpe (Buenos Aires), 1939, reprinted, Espasa-Calpe (Madrid), 1958.

De Cervantes y Lope de Vega, Espasa-Calpe, 1940, reprinted, 1973.

Idea imperial de Carlos V, La condesa traidora, El romanz del infant Garcia, Adefonsus, imperator toletanus (includes three essays previously published in *Historia y epopeya*), Espasa-Calpe (Buenos Aires), 1941, reprinted, Espasa-Calpe (Madrid), 1963.

Poesia arabe y poesia europea, con otros estudios de literatura medieval, Espasa-Calpe (Buenos Aires), 1941, reprinted, Espasa-Calpe (Madrid), 1963.

La lengua de Cristobal Colon, El estilo de Santa Teresa, y otros estudios sobre el siglo XVI, Espasa-Calpe, 1942.

Mio Cid: El de Valencia, Universidad Literaria de Valencia, Facultad de Filosofia y Letras, 1943.

Castilla: La tradicion, el idioma, Espasa-Calpe (Buenos Aires), 1945.

La epopeya castellana a traves de la literatura espanola, Espasa-Calpe, 1945, (originally published in French translation by Henry Merimee from the original Spanish manuscript as *L'Epopee castillane a travers la litterature espagnole,* with preface by Ernest Merimee, [Paris], 1910), 2nd edition, Espasa-Calpe (Madrid), 1969.

(Author of introduction) *Cancionero de romances impreso en Amberes sin ano,* facsimile edition, Consejo Superior de Investigaciones Cientificas (Madrid), 1945.

Como vivio y como vive el romancero, E. Lopez Mezquida (Valencia), 1947.

(Author of introduction) Guillermo Diaz Plaja, editor, *Historia general de las literaturas hispanicas,* five volumes, Barna (Barcelona), 1949-58.

El imperio hispanico y los cinco reinos: Dos epocas en la estructura politica de Espana, Instituto de Estudios Politicos (Madrid), 1950.

De primitiva lirica espanola y antigua epica, Espasa-Calpe (Buenos Aires), 1951, reprinted, Espasa-Calpe (Madrid), 1977.

Los espanoles en la historia y en la literatura: Dos ensayos (also see below), Espasa-Calpe (Buenos Aires), 1951.

Los origenes de las literaturas romanicas a la luz de un descubrimiento reciente, Publicaciones de la Universidad Internacional Menendez Pelayo (Santander), 1951.

(Editor) *Reliquias de la poesia epica espanola* (also see below), Espasa-Calpe (Madrid), 1951.

Miscelanea historica-literaria, Espasa-Calpe (Buenos Aires), 1952.

Los Reyes Catolicos segun Maquiavelo y Castiglione, with a biographical sketch by Damaso Alonso, [Madrid], 1952.

Romancero hispanico (hispano-portugues, americano y sefardi): Teoria e historia, two volumes, Espasa-Calpe (Madrid), 1952.

(Contributor) Gonzalo Menendez Pidal and Elisa Bernis, editors, *Antologia de cuentos de la literatura universal,* Labor, 1953.

(Contributor) *Como vive un romance: Dos ensayos sobre tradicionalidad,* Revista de Filologia Espanola (Madrid), 1954.

Espana: Eslabon entre la Cristianidad y el Islam, Espasa-Calpe (Madrid), 1956.

Los godos y la epopeya espanola, "chansons de geste" y baladas nordicas, Espasa-Calpe, 1956.

(Editor with Goyri) *Romancero tradicional de las lenguas hispanicas (espanol, portugues, catalan, sefardi),* Gredos, 1957.

Mis paginas preferidas: Estudios linguisticos e historicos, Gredos (Madrid), 1957.

Mis paginas preferidas: Temas literarios, Gredos, 1957.

Espana y su historia, two volumes, Minotauro (Madrid), 1957.

El padre las Casas y Victoria, con otros temas del siglo XVI y XVII, Espasa-Calpe, 1958.

Tres poetas primitivos: Elena y Maria, "Roncesvalles," Historia troyana polimetrica, Espasa-Calpe (Buenos Aires), 1958.

La epica francesa y el tradicionalismo, University of Barcelona, Facultad de Filosofia y Letras, 1958.

La Chanson de Roland y el neotradicionalismo (origenes de la epica romanica), Espasa-Calpe (Madrid), 1959.

(Author of prologue) *Pliegos poeticos espanoles en la Universidad de Praga,* [Madrid], 1960.

Los espanoles en la literatura, Espasa-Calpe (Buenos Aires), 1960.

(Contributor) *Seis temas peruanos,* Espasa-Calpe (Madrid), 1960.

Estudios de linguistica: Las leyes foneticas, Menendez, el diccionario ideal y otros, Espasa-Calpe, 1961.

(Contributor) Francisco Javier Sanchez Canton, *La casa de Lope de Vega,* Real Academia Espanola (Madrid), 1962.

En torno a la lengua vasca, Espasa-Calpe (Buenos Aires), 1962.

El dialecto leones, Instituto de Estudios Asturianos (Oviedo), 1962.

Los Reyes Catolicos y otros estudios, Espasa-Calpe, 1962.

El padre las Casas: Su doble personalidad, Espasa-Calpe (Madrid), 1963.

En torno al poema del Cid, EDHASA (Barcelona), 1963, reprinted, 1983.

(Editor) *Crestomatia del espanol medieval* (manuscript completed and revised by Rafael Lapesa y Maria Soledad de Andres), Gredos, 1965.

Toponimia prerromanica hispana, Gredos, 1968.

Textos medievales espanoles: Ediciones criticas y estudios, Espasa-Calpe, 1977.

(Editor) *Reliquias de la poesia epica espanola; acompanadas de Epopeya y romancero* (Arabic, Latin, and Spanish text), Gredos, 1980.

Also editor of *Floresta de leyendas heroicas espanolas.* Founder and editor of *Revista de Filologia Espanola,* beginning 1914.

SIDELIGHTS: Called "the most profound and well informed scholar of the Spanish epic tradition" by Guillermo Diaz Plaja in his *History of Spanish Literature,* Spanish literary historian and philologist Ramon Menendez Pidal was the first scholar elected to the presidency of the prestigious Royal Spanish Academy who was not a member of the nobility or a politician. His election came after he had become well-known for his historical grammar of the Spanish language, *Manual de gramatica historica espanola,* and his most important work, an exhaustive study of Spain's twelfth-century epic poem, the *Cantar del Mio Cid.*

His work on the *Cantar* spawned a renewed interest in Spain's rich medieval heritage which literary historians had previously neglected. A student of the great Spanish critic and historian Marcelino Menendez y Pelayo, Menendez Pidal in turn left a legacy for scholars who would make substantial contributions to Spanish literary studies, including essayist Alfonso Reyes, historian Americo Castro, and critic Damaso Alonso.

Menendez Pidal's scholarly approach to ancient texts opened new avenues of research to Castilian philologists and provided fresh insights into the methodology of historical study. He became so enamored of the Cid legend that he named his children after characters from the story, naming his son Rodrigo after the Cid (whose real name was Rodrigo Diaz de Vivar) and his daughter Jimena after the Cid's wife. "His whole life [was] devoted to the Spanish Middle Ages," Walter Starkie commented in his biographical essay on the historian published as a preface to *The Spaniards in Their History,* "but so profound [was] his knowledge of the obscure workings of the human race in those centuries that he [became] universal, and his researches [were] no less significant to the Hispanists of England, France, Holland or Italy than they [were] to those of North and South America. For this reason his prestige . . . united the scholars of both hemispheres."

BIOGRAPHICAL/CRITICAL SOURCES:

BOOKS

Diaz Plaja, Guillermo, *A History of Spanish Literature,* New York University Press, 1971.

OBITUARIES:

PERIODICALS

New York Times, November 16, 1968.

MEREDITH, George 1828-1909

PERSONAL: Born February 12, 1828, in Portsmouth, Hampshire, England; died May 18, 1909, in Dorking, Surrey, England; son of Augustus and Jane Eliza (Macnamara) Meredith; married Mary Ellen Peacock Nicolls, August 9, 1849 (separated after she eloped to Italy with Henry Wallis, 1858; died in 1861); married Marie Vulliamy, September 20, 1864 (died in 1885); children: (first marriage) Arthur Gryffydh; (second marriage) William Maxse, Marie Eveleen. *Education:* Attended two boarding schools in England and Moravian School, Neuwied, Germany, 1843-44.

CAREER: Author and journalist. Apprenticed as law clerk to Richard Charnock in London, 1846; founder, with Charnock and others, of *Monthly Observer,* late 1840s; literary critic for *Westminster Review;* journalist for *Ipswich Journal,* a Tory newspaper, around 1858-68, and contributor to other Conservative papers, including the *Morning Post* and *Pall Mall Gazette;* manuscript reader and literary adviser for Chapman and Hall, 1860-95, and reader for Saunders & Otley; war correspondent for *Morning Post,* covering Italy's battle for independence from Austria during the summer of 1866; contributor to *Fortnightly Review,* beginning 1867, served as editor, 1867-68; moved to Flint Cottage, near Dorking, England, 1868; became active in politics, canvassing for Frederick Maxse's unsuccessful campaign for a seat in Parliament, 1868; published series of dialogues in *Graphic,* December, 1872, to January, 1873; lectured on comedy at London Institute, 1877; London Library, vice president, 1902; continued to write for periodicals until shortly before his death.

MEMBER: Society of Authors (president, 1892).

AWARDS, HONORS: Order of Merit, 1905; Gold Medal of the Royal Society of Literature, 1905; D.C.L., Oxford University.

WRITINGS:

Poems, Parker, 1851, Scribner, 1898.
The Shaving of Shagpat: An Arabian Entertainment, Chapman & Hall, 1856, Roberts Brothers, 1887.
Farina: A Legend of Cologne, Smith, Elder, 1857.
The Ordeal of Richard Feverel: A History of Father and Son, 3 volumes, Chapman & Hall, 1859, 1 volume, Roberts Brothers, 1887.
Evan Harrington; or, He Would Be a Gentleman, Harper, 1860, 3 volumes, Bradbury & Evans, 1861.

"Modern Love" and Poems of the English Roadside, with Poems and Ballads, Chapman & Hall, 1862, edited by E. Cavazza, Mosher, 1891.
Emilia in England, 3 volumes, Chapman & Hall, 1864, published as *Sandra Belloni,* Chapman & Hall, 1886, Roberts Brothers, 1887.
(Editor and author of introduction and concluding chapters) *The Cruise of the Alabama and the Sumter: From the Private Journals and Other Papers of Commander R. Semmes,* Saunders & Otley, 1864, Carleton, 1864.
Rhoda Fleming: A Story, 3 volumes, Tinsley, 1865, 1 volume, Roberts Brothers, 1886.
Vittoria, 3 volumes, Chapman & Hall, 1866, Roberts Brothers, 1888.
The Adventures of Harry Richmond, 3 volumes, Smith, Elder, 1871, 1 volume, Roberts Brothers, 1887.
Beauchamp's Career, 3 volumes, Chapman & Hall, 1876, 1 volume, Roberts Brothers, 1887.
The House on the Beach: A Realistic Tale, Harper, 1877.
The Egoist: A Comedy in Narrative, 3 volumes, Kegan Paul, 1879, Harper, 1879.
The Tragic Comedians: A Study in a Well-Known Story, 2 volumes, Chapman & Hall, 1880, 1 volume, Munro, 1881.
Poems and Lyrics of the Joy of Earth, Macmillan, 1883, Roberts Brothers, 1883.
Diana of the Crossways, 3 volumes, Chapman & Hall, 1885, 1 volume, Munro, 1885.
Ballads and Poems of Tragic Life, Macmillan, 1887, Roberts Brothers, 1887.
A Reading of Earth, Macmillan, 1888, Roberts Brothers, 1888.
Jump-to-Glory Jane, privately printed, 1889, Sonnenschein, 1892.
The Case of General Ople and Lady Camper, Lovell, 1890.
The Tale of Chloe: An Episode in the History of Beau Beamish, Lovell, 1890.
One of Our Conquerors, 3 volumes, Chapman & Hall, 1891, 1 volume, Roberts Brothers, 1891.
Poems: The Empty Purse, with Odes to the Comic Spirit, to Youth in Memory and Verses, Macmillan, 1892, Roberts Brothers, 1892.
The Tale of Chloe; The House on the Beach; The Case of General Ople and Lady Camper, Ward, Lock & Bowdon, 1894.
Lord Ormont and His Aminta: A Novel, 3 volumes, Chapman & Hall, 1894, 1 volume, Scribner, 1894.
The Amazing Marriage, 2 volumes, Constable, 1897, Scribner, 1897.

An Essay on Comedy and the Uses of the Comic Spirit (first published in *New Quarterly,* 1877), Constable, 1897, Scribner, 1897.

Selected Poems, Constable, 1897, Scribner, 1897.

The Nature Poems, Constable, 1898.

Odes in Contribution to the Song of French History, Constable, 1898, Scribner, 1898.

The Story of Bhanavar the Beautiful, Constable, 1900.

A Reading of Life, with Other Poems, Constable, 1901, Scribner, 1901.

Last Poems, Constable, 1909, Scribner, 1909.

Chillianwallah, Marion Press, 1909.

Love in the Valley, and Two Songs: Spring and Autumn, Seymour, 1909.

Poems Written in Early Youth, Poems from "Modern Love," and Scattered Poems, Constable, 1909, Scribner, 1909.

Celt and Saxon, Constable, 1910, Scribner, 1910.

Up to Midnight: A Series of Dialogues Contributed to the "Graphic," Luce, 1913.

The Works of George Meredith, De Luxe Edition, 39 volumes, Constable, 1896-1912, Library Edition, 18 volumes, Constable, 1897-1910, Boxhill Edition, 17 volumes, Scribner, 1897-1919, Memorial Edition, 27 volumes, Constable, 1909-11, Scribner, 1909-11.

The Poetical Works of George Meredith, edited by G. M. Trevelyan, Constable, 1912.

The Letters of George Meredith, edited by C. L. Cline, 3 volumes, Clarendon Press, 1970.

The Poems of George Meredith, edited by Phyllis B. Bartlett, 2 volumes, Yale University Press, 1978.

Also author of *Short Stories,* 1898; *The Sentimentalists* (play), produced 1910; *The Contributions to the Monthly Observer,* edited by H. Buxton Forman, 1928; *The Notebooks,* edited by Gillian Beer and Margaret Harris, 1983; and *Selected Poems,* edited by Keith Hanley, 1983.

Meredith's papers are in the Altschul Collection at the Beinecke Rare Book and Manuscript Library, Yale University; the Berg Collection at the New York Public Library; and the Henry E. Huntington Library, San Marino, CA.

SIDELIGHTS: George Meredith was a major Victorian novelist whose career developed in conjunction with an era of great change in English literature during the second half of the nineteenth century. While his early novels largely conformed to Victorian literary conventions, his later novels demonstrated a concern with character psychology, modern social problems, and the development of the novel form that has led to his being considered an important precursor of English Modernist novels. In particular, Meredith is noted as one of the earliest English psychological novelists and as an important experimenter with narrative told from a variety of shifting, unreliable perspectives, reflecting a modern perception of the uncertain nature of both personal motivation and of social or historical events.

Meredith was born in Portsmouth, England. His father inherited a seemingly prosperous Portsmouth naval outfitters and tailor shop from Meredith's grandfather but soon discovered that one reason for the shop's popularity with customers was that delinquent bills were rarely pursued. The Merediths ran the failing business at a loss for several years while living extravagantly on the dowry that Meredith's mother had brought into the marriage. Considering themselves superior to ordinary tradespeople, the Merediths unsuccessfully attempted to establish themselves as the social equals of the elegant patrons of the tailor shop. Meredith was sent to private schools and quickly learned to say nothing of his family's position, instead encouraging the assumption that he was of the gentry. Meredith remained secretive about his origins all his life, and much is unknown about his childhood because of his unwillingness to disclose details of this period.

When Meredith was five his mother died, leaving her money in a trust for her son's education. Lacking access to these funds for his business, Meredith's father was forced into bankruptcy. The boy was sent to boarding schools and had very little contact with his father thereafter. At fourteen Meredith was sent to school in Neuwied, Germany, where he remained for two years, leaving with a love of German culture, especially music, that lasted the rest of his life. Upon Meredith's return to England, his father wanted to apprentice him to a bookseller and publisher, but Meredith, disinclined to follow the advice of a man he considered "a muddler and a fool," found a post for himself assisting an attorney, for whom he worked for five years.

As he entered his early twenties, Meredith began writing poetry, influenced in particular by John Keats and Lord Tennyson. He became acquainted with Edward Gryffydh Peacock and Mary Nicolls, the son and widowed daughter of the satirist Thomas Love Peacock, a man he admired. With the younger Peacock he collaborated on the publication of a privately circulated literary magazine, the *Monthly Observer,*

to which he submitted his own poetry and critical essays. A tempestuous relationship with Nicolls culminated in their marriage in 1849, but the marriage was neither a happy nor a lasting one, in part due to Meredith's precarious financial situation. Although his father-in-law offered to secure him an office position, Meredith preferred to try to make his living by his pen. However, his first book, *Poems,* a volume published at his own expense, attracted little notice and never recouped printing costs. During the first years of their marriage Nicolls suffered several miscarriages and stillbirths, while Meredith developed nervous and digestive disorders that led him to demand a highly specialized diet. Nicolls turned this to financial advantage by writing and publishing, with her father's help, a successful cookbook. In 1853, with Nicolls again pregnant, the couple's financial difficulties forced them to move in with Thomas Love Peacock. Peacock could not adjust to the disruption of his household, which was exacerbated by the birth of the Merediths' son Arthur later that year, and he eventually quit his own house to take rooms elsewhere.

By 1856 Meredith and his wife were living apart, and in 1858 she left for Italy with another man, leaving Meredith alone with five-year-old Arthur. When she returned to England years later, alone and seriously ill, Meredith refused to let her see their son until shortly before her death. Meredith's lifetime of reticence about his early years carried over into a stolid refusal to discuss his first marriage, though critics maintain that the sonnet cycle *Modern Love,* which painstakingly details the dissolution of a marriage, actually chronicles that event. Meredith's subsequent relationships with women proved for some time unsatisfactory. He fell in love with a much younger woman whose socially prominent parents cultivated the rising novelist as a valuable social asset, but refused to consider him a suitable match for their daughter. Meredith lived alone or with male friends for years, traveling extensively in Switzerland, France, and Italy. In London he shared a house briefly with Dante Gabriel Rossetti and Algernon Charles Swinburne, but, unprepared for their unconventional way of life, soon took single lodgings. Upon his second marriage in 1864, Meredith settled at Box Hill, Surrey, where he lived the rest of his life.

During the 1850s Meredith began to receive an income from magazine writing and was thus encouraged to attempt a longer prose work. His first work of fiction, *The Shaving of Shagpat: An Arabian Enter-*

tainment, is a lighthearted fantasy that contains a number of themes that recur throughout Meredith's career, including ridicule of social conventions and disdain for social climbers, and features as a central character a young man whose growth to maturity is aided by a woman. The favorable reception of *Shagpat* inspired Meredith to write a serious novel, *The Ordeal of Richard Feverel: A History of Father and Son.* In this partially autobiographical work, a man is abandoned with an infant son by his wife and brings up the child according to a strict scientific system designed to insure that the boy will accept his father's social, political, and ideological beliefs, and will ultimately select an ideal mate who will prove faithful. However, the son eventually rebels against the debilitating and stifling environment created by his father and marries a woman of the lower classes. The novel contained a great deal of irony at the expense of both the characters and the conventions of Victorian society and created a stir due to its sarcastic tone and freethinking atheism. Moreover, many reviewers misread the work as an attack on science or scientific systems in general, despite Meredith's claim that "the moral is that no System of any sort succeeds with human nature, unless the originator has conceived it purely independent of personal passion." The novel also lost many readers when Mudie's lending library refused to circulate it because it depicted extramarital sex. Thus, after promising early sales, the novel fell both in critical and public regard.

Following the failure of *The Ordeal of Richard Feverel,* Meredith entered into a complex relationship with his readers, attempting, according to Ioan Williams, "to reconcile his artistic purpose with the demands of the reading public." Most critics agree that during the period from 1860 to 1875, Meredith was very responsive to the desires of the book-buying public. Several critics have theorized that Meredith tried in each new novel to correct the faults that had been criticized in the last, and to incorporate elements that would appeal to Victorian readers. As a part-time reader for Chapman and Hall publishers, Meredith was able to observe literary trends and to employ them in his early novels. In *Emilia in England* and its sequel *Vittoria,* for example, Meredith was inspired by the current interest in local-color fiction to give the heroine a vividly realized Italian background and to introduce historical figures and events into the story. Despite the introduction of fictional devices and elements that had proved successful for many other writers of the time, Meredith was unable to attract either readers or favorable critical notice. Some critics contend that Meredith's attempts

to craft his books to the public taste by utilizing literary conventions was a calculated attempt on his part to couch his radical ideas concerning the impermanent nature of human values and the inconstancy of human nature in a form that would be acceptable to his readers. It is now commonly accepted by critics that Meredith possessed what Judith Wilt has called a "sensitive and aggressive awareness of the presence, at the heart of his creative art, of the reader." This assumption contradicts the widely held belief that he wrote in lofty disregard of his readers out of a single-minded dedication to his own artistic values. This estimation was reached by some commentators when Meredith, after years of courting a broad readership, professed his contempt for readers in angry statements that his books were ignored by an unworthy and hypocritical public. Once he despaired of reaching a large audience, Meredith began to write primarily to please himself and the small circle of admirers who had defended and praised his works from the first. It was then that he found his works more popular than at any other time in his career.

Meredith's early novels share a number of characteristics of plot and style. Walter F. Wright has written that "without being autobiography, Meredith's creative work manifests the qualities revealed in his own life," and this is most noticeable in the novels written before 1876. The novels often open with a single father, abandoned by his wife or widowed, raising a son alone. The son's growth to young manhood and experiences with first love—often ending in tragedy—occupy many of the early novels. Many of them portray the marriage of an upper-class man with a woman of the lower classes, and the antagonisms resulting from differences between the classes is a recurring subject. These early novels contain Meredith's nascent attempts at psychological portraiture, and are typically concerned with demonstrating the instability of human nature as they satirically attack egoism, pretense, snobbery, and false values.

Meredith's most critically acclaimed work is the 1877 lecture *An Essay on Comedy and the Uses of the Comic Spirit,* printed in the *New Quarterly Magazine* and published separately twenty years later. In this essay, which Arthur Symons called "his most brilliant piece of sustained writing," Meredith did not discuss comedy in general terms, but rather expounded on the comic approach that characterized his own fiction. Meredith contended that great comedy rectifies the excesses of human behavior by permitting audiences to laugh at their own foibles, depicting, according to Joseph Warren Beach, "the discrepancy between the real and the supposed motive" for human actions. True comedy thus has a beneficial social effect. For that reason Meredith asserted that true comedy is both "impersonal" and "thoughtful" and can only appear in a civilized nation. The novel *The Egoist,* written immediately after the essay on comedy, is the most successful example of his comic method and remains his most critically praised novel. In this comedy of manners, Meredith attacked a widely embraced element in the thought of John Stuart Mill, who held that individuals could think and do as they wished provided that they did no harm to others. Meredith demonstrated through the character of Sir Willoughby Patterne that such a belief was both alienating and harmful in that it ultimately denied the legitimacy of other opinions through the domination of egoistic individuals. Critical consensus is that with this work Meredith most successfully combined his theory of comedy, writing style, and thematic concerns. With *The Egoist,* Meredith finally achieved popular success and his popularity grew with subsequent novels.

Following *The Egoist,* Meredith was most concerned with writing psychological novels that portrayed the tangled motivations of individuals and explored the disparity between the public and private aspects of self. These later novels demonstrate a heightened social awareness, a more tolerant view of human folly, and a corresponding softening of the satiric and ironic portraits of individuals. In these works there is no clear explanation of individual behavior, but rather an examination of the various ways that individuals and their actions are perceived. Often it is unclear what actually happens in the novels, and the reader is forced to extract the truth from the gossip, half-truths, and misdirection arising from the different characters' perceptions; in many cases Meredith gave several versions of the same event through the eyes of several characters. Critics contend that in Meredith's experiments with the novel form and with complex characterizations can be seen the germ of the modern psychological novel. Throughout these works Meredith sought to demonstrate that most human motivations are concealed and that, while much in life is relative, including morality, actions are not: once something has happened, it is unchangable and often irredeemable.

The most popular and artistically successful of Meredith's later works was *Diana of the Crossways,* a novel inspired by a scandal involving an adulterous woman accused of selling a state secret. It has been theorized that readers were attracted by the belief that

in this novel Meredith was revealing some inside information about this widely discussed affair; in fact, so many readers assumed that the novel reflected the facts of the scandal that later editions contained disclaimers disallowing any connection between Meredith's creation and the affair. The character of Diana, who leaves her husband to pursue a writing career, became a favorite with feminists and the prototype of many subsequent novel heroines who, misunderstood and unappreciated, strike out boldly on their own. Throughout his career Meredith had explored the circumscribed role of women in society, a topic known in his day as "the woman question," and had long contended that civilization can only flourish when men and women are equal. It was in *Diana* that his didactic intentions, novelistic devices, and analysis of character achieved their greatest unity.

Critics have been united in comparing Meredith with Thomas Hardy as a "poet-novelist" who considered poetry his true literary vocation but turned to writing novels for financial reasons. Meredith's poetry has received increasing attention in recent years and critics have noted that it follows the same course of development as his novels, moving from early examinations of the self in society to a later concern with broader social issues and defiance of the conventions of the form. In particular, Meredith explored new meters and stanzaic forms and experimented dramatically with syntax and grammar. Critics characterize his poetry as verbally dense, allusive, and metaphorical, and in many ways reflective of the late nineteenth-century inclination toward aesthetic artifice. Although *"Modern Love"* is considered his most important poetic achievement, several of his late poems provide important perspectives on his fiction, particularly a series of odes on the purpose of literature and the nature of the historical process. In these works, as well as in his novels, Meredith demonstrated his desire to challenge and overcome what he perceived as narrow and constrictive world views.

At the time of his death Meredith was considered one of England's premier men of letters. In the years since, his critical reputation has undergone several reassessments, although he has never enjoyed the resurgence in general popularity enjoyed by such Victorian novelists as Charles Dickens and Anthony Trollope. Several reasons have been cited for this. Meredith's novels feature very little action, relying instead on dialogue, or what Meredith called "action of the mind," to advance the story. This resulted in a popular perception of his novels as static and

"talky." However, Meredith's prose is most often identified as the barrier that makes his works inaccessible to readers. Meredith's narrative style, making extensive use of metaphor, allusion, and aphorism, has been described by his admirers and detractors alike as so difficult that close rereadings of passages are frequently necessary to extract the meaning. Some critics contend that Meredith became so enamored of his mannered style that style itself became the end of his work and not the means to tell a story. His supporters, however, praise the poetic quality of Meredith's prose, maintaining that each line of Meredith's work is written in the allusive, rich language usually reserved for poetry. Although Meredith's career has undergone several reappraisals as new generations of critics rediscover his works, the difficulties presented by his narrative style have been cited as the factor that has discouraged a resurgence of widespread interest. However, as has been true throughout the history of commentary on Meredith, there remains a dedicated group of admirers who contend, with J. B. Priestley, that Meredith's difficult style, requiring as it does the full and undivided attention of the reader, paved the way for the public acceptance of much subsequent serious fiction, helping to shape "the modern attitude towards fiction and the modern novel itself."

BIOGRAPHICAL/CRITICAL SOURCES:

BOOKS

Auchincloss, Louis, *Reflections of a Jacobite,* Houghton, 1961, pp. 85-94.

Bailey, Elmer James, *The Novels of George Meredith: A Study,* Scribner, 1907.

Beach, Joseph Warren, *The Comic Spirit in George Meredith,* Longman, 1911.

Beer, Gillian, *Meredith: A Change of Masks; A Study of the Novels,* Athlone Press, 1970.

Bernstein, Carol L., *Precarious Enchantment: A Reading of Meredith's Poetry,* Catholic University of America Press, 1979.

Booth, Thornton Y., *Mastering the Event: Commitment to Fact in George Meredith's Fiction,* Utah State University Press, 1967.

Concise Dictionary of British Literary Biography, Volume 4: *Victorian Writers, 1832-1890,* Gale, 1991.

Crees, J. H. E., *George Meredith,* B. H. Blackwell, 1918.

Curle, Richard H. P., *Aspects of George Meredith,* Dutton, 1908.

Dictionary of Literary Biography, Gale, Volume 18: *Victorian Novelists after 1885,* Gale, 1983, Volume 35: *Victorian Poets after 1850,* 1985, Volume 57: *Victorian Prose Writers after 1867,* 1987.

Ellis, S. M., *George Meredith: His Life and Friends in Relation to His Work,* Dodd, Mead, 1920.

Fletcher, Ian, editor, *Meredith Now: Some Critical Essays,* Routledge & Kegan Paul, 1971.

Gindin, James, *Harvest of a Quiet Eye: The Novel of Compassion,* Indiana University Press, 1971, pp. 57-77.

Gretton, Mary Sturge, *The Writings and Life of George Meredith: A Centenary Study,* Harvard University Press, 1926.

Kelvin, Norman, *A Troubled Eden: Nature and Society in the Works of George Meredith,* Stanford University Press, 1961.

Lindsay, Jack, *George Meredith: His Life and Work,* Bodley Head, 1956.

Moses, Joseph, *The Novelist as Comedian,* Schocken Books, 1983, pp. 164-183.

Muendel, Renate, *George Meredith,* Twayne, 1986.

Priestley, J. B., *George Meredith,* Macmillan, 1926.

Pritchett, V. S., *George Meredith and the English Comedy,* Chatto & Windus, 1970.

Reference Guide to English Literature, second edition, St. James Press, 1991.

Sassoon, Siegfried, *Meredith,* Viking, 1948.

Shaheen, Mohammad, *George Meredith: A Reappraisal of the Novels,* Macmillan (London), 1981.

Stevenson, Lionel, *The Ordeal of George Meredith: A Biography,* Scribner, 1953.

Williams, David, *George Meredith: His Life and Lost Love,* Hamish Hamilton, 1977.

Williams, Ioan, editor, *Meredith: The Critical Heritage,* Routledge & Kegan Paul, 1971.

Wilt, Judith, *The Readable People of George Meredith,* Princeton University Press, 1975.

Wright, Walter F., *Art and Substance in George Meredith: A Study in Narrative,* University of Nebraska Press, 1953.

* * *

MERRY, Robert William 1946-

PERSONAL: Born March 5, 1946, in Tacoma, WA; son of Robert Ellsworth (a newspaper editor) and Carol Beatrice (a hospital executive; maiden name, Rasmussen) Merry; married Susan Diane Pennington (an association executive), September 20, 1969; children: Robert Ellsworth II, Johanna Lynn, Stephanie Ann. *Education:* University of Washington, B.A., 1968; Columbia University, M.S., 1972. *Politics:* Independent. *Religion:* Protestant. *Avocational interests:* Jogging, biking, hiking, biography, movies.

ADDRESSES: Home—1313 Merrie Ridge Road, McLean, VA 22101. *Office*—Congressional Quarterly Inc., 1414 22nd St. N.W., Washington, DC 20037-1003.

CAREER: Denver Post, reporter and copy editor, 1972-74; *National Observer* (Dow Jones Inc.), reporter, 1974-77; *Wall Street Journal,* reporter, 1977-86; *Roll Call* (newspaper of Capitol Hill), editor, 1986-87; *Congressional Quarterly,* managing editor, 1987-89, became executive editor, 1990—. *Military service:* U.S Army, 1968-71.

MEMBER: National Press Club, Cosmos Club.

WRITINGS:

Taking on the World: Joseph and Stewart Alsop—Guardians of the American Century (biography), Viking (New York), 1996.

Contributor to *First Among Equals: Outstanding Senate Leaders of the Twentieth Century,* CQ Press (Hicksville, NY), 1991.

SIDELIGHTS: Career journalist and executive editor of the *Congressional Quarterly,* Robert Merry focused on the lives of two prominent figures in the history of twentieth-century journalism in *Taking on the World: Joseph and Stewart Alsop—Guardians of the American Century.* From the 1930s to the 1970s, Joseph and Stewart Alsop covered the political scene for the *New York Herald,* the *Saturday Evening Post,* and *Newsweek* magazine. Merry recounts how the brothers had been born into the East Coast establishment and received Ivy League educations. As well-known journalists they cultivated personal ties with an elite that included presidents. After they both served in World War II, the Alsop brothers jointly penned a political column for more than a dozen years and wrote widely on Washington politics for other national publications. During the Vietnam war the brothers took opposing positions, with Joseph supporting the war and Stewart admitting that it was a lost cause. Stewart died fifteen years before Joseph, after battling leukemia for three years. In his later years, Joseph retired from the political scene to write about history and art.

Taking on the World elicited largely favorable reviews. Writing for the *Wall Street Journal,* Richard J. Tofel lauded the biography as "a very readable—and painstakingly researched—account of the Alsop saga" and a "masterful portrayal of journalists easily seduced by proximity to power." *Washington Post Book World* reviewer James Fallows described the book as "absorbing," though he faulted Merry for occasional overwriting and "needless portentousness." Fallows added, nevertheless, "If the layer of sociology is ignored and *Taking on the World* is considered solely as a re-creation of two lives, it becomes rich and rewarding, with plenty of incidental insights on topics ranging from the history of journalism to the twists of sibling rivalry." Fallows continued, "Merry does a good job of recreating the controversies of the 1950s and showing how the Alsops placed themselves in the middle of these fights." In the *New York Times Book Review,* David M. Kennedy called *Taking on the World* a "rich and fascinating book," commending it "as a sensitive portrait, executed with respect and affection but also with critical acumen, of two American lives and an American era that are well worth the remembering."

BIOGRAPHICAL/CRITICAL SOURCES:

PERIODICALS

Boston Globe, January 23, 1996, p. 57.
New York Times Book Review, February 25, 1996, section 7, p. 11.
Wall Street Journal, February 15, 1996, p. A12.
Washington Post Book World, February 18, 1996, pp. 1, 14.

* * *

MILLARD, Charles W(arren III) 1932-

PERSONAL: Born December 20, 1932, in Elizabeth, NJ; son of Charles Warren, Jr. and Constance Emily (Keppler) Millard. *Education:* Princeton University, A.B. (magna cum laude), 1954; Harvard University, M.A., 1963, Ph.D., 1971.

ADDRESSES: Home—P.O. Box 811, Chapel Hill, NC 27514.

CAREER: William Hayes Fogg Art Museum, Harvard University, assistant to the director, 1963-64; Dumbarton Oaks, Washington, DC, assistant to the director, 1965-66; Washington Gallery of Modern Art, director, 1966-67; Los Angeles County Museum of Art, curator of nineteenth-century European art, 1971-74; Hirshhorn Museum, Washington, DC, chief curator, 1974-86; Ackland Art Museum, University of North Carolina, Chapel Hill, director, 1986-93. Art editor, *Hudson Review,* 1972-87; writer. Adjunct professor of art history, Johns Hopkins University, 1983-86, University of North Carolina, 1986-93. Chair, visiting committee to the art history department, Boston University, 1977-80. *Military service:* U.S. Navy, 1956-59.

MEMBER: International Association of Art Critics.

WRITINGS:

The Sculpture of Edgar Degas, Princeton University Press (Princeton, NJ), 1976.
Miro: Selected Paintings (exhibition catalog), Smithsonian Institution Press (Washington, DC), 1980.
Friedel Dzubas (exhibition catalog), Smithsonian Institution Press, 1983.

Author of numerous exhibition catalogs and articles in journals.

SIDELIGHTS: Noted for his work in the field of nineteenth-century European fine art, former museum director Charles W. Millard has authored several works that have been heralded by critics within the art community. In his 1976 volume *The Sculpture of Edgar Degas,* an adaptation of his doctoral dissertation at Harvard University, Millard "provides valuable new material on the chronology of the sculptures, their relation to the artist's oeuvre, and his sources and inspiration," according to a *Choice* reviewer. Critic John Russell asserted in *Times Literary Supplement* that "Degas in his art—as in his life, and in his sonnets too—just didn't know how to be dull, and Charles Millard has unriddled many of the secrets with which he surrounded his activity in sculpture." Praised as well for both its thorough bibliography and engaging prose style, Millard's examination of the noted French painter's work in plaster (from which bronze casts were made after Degas's death in 1917) has been followed by several exhibition catalogues for the Hirshhorn Museum and Sculpture Garden. The year 1977 saw the publication of *Miro: Selected Paintings* and in 1983 Millard completed *Friedel Dzubas;* both works were published by the Smithsonian Institution. In addition, Millard served as art editor for the *Hudson Review* from 1972

to 1987 and has contributed to several journals on his area of expertise.

BIOGRAPHICAL/CRITICAL SOURCES:

PERIODICALS

Choice, June, 1977, p. 522.
Nation, December 17, 1977, p. 661.
New York Times Book Review, February 27, 1977, p. 6.
Times Literary Supplement, March 18, 1977, p. 315.

* * *

MILLER, Blair 1955-

PERSONAL: Born October 28, 1955, in Columbus, OH; son of John L. (a doctor) and Carol (a nurse) Farrell. *Ethnicity:* "Caucasian." *Education:* Nazareth College of Rochester, B.S., 1987. *Politics:* Republican. *Religion:* United Methodist. *Avocational interests:* Going to the movies, self-improvement, bicycling, weight-lifting, current events, local history, visiting museums.

ADDRESSES: Home—1 Pannel Cir., Apt. 1, Fairport, NY 14450. *Office*—Citibank Student Loan Corp., 99 Garnsey Rd., Pittsford, NY 14534.

CAREER: Citibank Student Loan Corporation, Pittsford, NY, promissory note clerk, 1991—.

MEMBER: International Laurel and Hardy Society; Utopia Tent of the Sons of the Desert.

WRITINGS:

American Silent Film Comedies: An Illustrated Encyclopedia of Persons, Studios, and Terminology (nonfiction), McFarland & Company, 1995.

WORK IN PROGRESS: Researching a book which will detail silent comedy filmmaking in Jacksonville, Florida.

SIDELIGHTS: Blair Miller is the author of 1995's *American Silent Film Comedies: An Illustrated Encyclopedia of Persons, Studios, and Terminology.* As the title implies, many aspects of silent film comedy are covered in the volume. Entries—of which there are over four hundred—range from those on actors in the genre such as Charlie Chaplin and Fatty Arbuckle, to those on subjects such as "blacks in silent film comedies." People important to the technical aspects of the early films are discussed as well, including American inventor Thomas Edison. Entries on the various studios involved in making silent comedies include filmographies.

W. P. Hogan in *Choice* reviewed *American Silent Film Comedies,* noting that "Miller's lucid explanations of the business aspects of the early film industry are exceptionally valuable." A *Booklist* reviewer complimented Miller's effort as well, observing that it "provides ample *see* and *see also* references," and concluding that "public libraries, academic libraries, and film libraries may want to consider purchase."

In addition to his writing work, Miller has a position with a bank specializing in student loans. He plans another project about the silent film industry, this time concentrating on the filmmaking that took place in Jacksonville, Florida. He told *CA:* "My writing process involves writing and rewriting, until a polished presentation results. Usually I'll write, and then come back to it a few days later to revise. Using a Macintosh computer also helps, both in organizing material and ease of making revisions and adding new information to each entry as additional facts are discovered.

"This is the book I wish I'd had, when I first got interested in silent film comedies."

BIOGRAPHICAL/CRITICAL SOURCES:

PERIODICALS

Booklist, October 1, 1995, p. 344.
Choice, January, 1996, pp. 754, 756.

* * *

MINEHAHA, Cornelius
 See WEDEKIND, (Benjamin) Frank(lin)

* * *

MINNELLI, Vincente 1913(?)-1986

PERSONAL: Born February 28, 1913 (some sources say 1903 or 1910), in Chicago, IL; died of heart

failure, July 25, 1986, in Los Angeles, CA; son of May Le Beau (an actor); married Judy Garland (an actor), June 15, 1945 (divorced, 1952); married Georgette Magnani, February, 1954 (divorced, 1958); married Denise Gigante, December 31, 1960 (divorced, August, 1971); married (Margaret) Lee Anderson, 1980; children: (first marriage) Liza Minnelli, (second marriage) Christiana Miro. *Education:* Studied painting at the Art Institute of Chicago.

CAREER: Film and stage director, art and set designer. Performed with Minnelli Brothers Dramatic Tent Show as a child; Balaban & Katz (vaudeville chain), then Paramount Theatre, New York City, costume director and stage assistant; Radio City Music Hall, art director, 1933-35; producer of Broadway shows, including *At Home Abroad,* 1935, *Ziegfeld Follies,* 1936, and others; Paramount Pictures, Hollywood, producer-director, 1936-37; Metro-Goldwyn-Mayer, Hollywood, production assistant, then director, beginning 1940. Directorial credits include *Cabin in the Sky,* 1942; *Meet Me in St. Louis,* 1944; *Father of the Bride,* 1950; *An American in Paris,* 1951; *Lust for Life,* 1956; *Gigi,* 1958; *On a Clear Day You Can See Forever,* 1970; and *A Matter of Time,* 1976.

AWARDS, HONORS: Academy Award for best director, 1958, for *Gigi;* Commander Nationale Legion d'honneur (France), 1986.

WRITINGS:

(With Hector Arce) *I Remember It Well* (autobiography), Doubleday (Garden City, NY), 1974.

Illustrator, *Casanova's Memoirs,* 1931.

SIDELIGHTS: Heralded as one of the most influential directors of Hollywood film musicals, Vincente Minnelli worked with some of the best-known actors of the twentieth century during a career in film that spanned more than four decades and included over thirty-five films. Fred Astaire, Leslie Caron, Kirk Douglas, Judy Garland—to whom Minnelli was married for four years—Gene Kelly, Dean Martin, and Spencer Tracy are but a few of the talents that graced his films, which included the classics *An American in Paris, Lust for Life, Gigi* (which garnered him an Academy Award for best director), and *Meet Me in St. Louis.*

The noted director chronicled his life in the autobiography *I Remember It Well,* published in 1974. Begin-

ning his career as a performer with his family's vaudeville troupe, young Minnelli quickly realized that his talents lay elsewhere; he graduated from a job as a department store window dresser through the ranks of the Broadway theatre world to arrive at Hollywood's Metro-Goldwyn-Mayer studio in 1940. Minnelli's first directorial credit was 1942's *Cabin in the Sky,* a groundbreaking film because of its all-black cast, which included actor Lena Horne.

Minnelli went on to refine the style that would characterize much of his work throughout the forties and fifties, particularly the dance sequences known as "dream ballets." "What makes Minnelli's dream ballets distinctive is the incredible palette he brings to them," film curator and Minnelli biographer Stephen Harvey told Howard Reich in the *Chicago Tribune.* "He was quite well versed in 19th- and 20th-century painting, and he brings the look of canvases by Dali, Toulouse-Lautrec and so on right onto the screen."

In addition to musicals, Minnelli directed several dramatic films, including *Lust for Life,* the biography of Vincent Van Gogh that starred Kirk Douglas, and the comedy *Father of the Bride,* starring Spencer Tracy and a young Elizabeth Taylor. (The movie was later remade with Steve Martin in the starring role.) Since his death in 1986 many film retrospectives have reintroduced Minnelli's work to younger audiences. With all of his successes, one of the personal triumphs in Minnelli's career came when he directed his daughter, Liza Minnelli, in the film *A Matter of Time* in 1976.

BIOGRAPHICAL/CRITICAL SOURCES:

BOOKS

Casper, Joseph, *Vincente Minnelli and the Film Musical,* A. S. Barnes (South Brunswick, NJ), 1976.
Film Encyclopedia, Crowell (New York), 1979.
Harvey, Stephen, *Directed by Vincente Minnelli,* Museum of Modern Art (New York), 1989.
Lang, Robert, *American Film Melodrama: Griffith, Vidor, Minnelli,* Princeton University Press (Princeton, NJ), 1989.
Minnelli, Vincente, with Hector Arce, *I Remember It Well,* Doubleday (Garden City, NY), 1974.
Naremore, James, *The Films of Vincente Minnelli,* Cambridge University Press (Cambridge), 1993.
Schickel, Richard, *Men Who Made the Movies,* Atheneum (New York), 1975.

PERIODICALS

Booklist, November 15, 1974, p. 314.
Chicago Tribune, July 27, 1986; December 10, 1989, p. 10.
Publishers Weekly, June 30, 1975, p. 61.
New York Times, July 27, 1986.
Times (London), July 28, 1986.
Washington Post, July 27, 1986; July 28, 1986.*

* * *

MOFOLO, Thomas (Mokopu) 1875(?)-1948

PERSONAL: Born August 2, 1875 (some sources say 1876), in Khojane, Basutoland (now Lesotho); died in September, 1948, in Teyateyaneng, Lesotho. *Education:* Educated at a Bible School.

CAREER: Novelist.

WRITINGS:

NOVELS

Moeti oa bochabela [Morija, Lesotho], 1907; translation by H. Ashton published as *The Traveller of the East,* S.P.C.K., 1934.
Pitseng [Morija, Lesotho], 1910.
Chaka [Morija, Lesotho], 1925; translation by F. H. Dutton published as *Chaka: An Historical Romance,* International Institute for African Languages and Culture, 1931.

SIDELIGHTS: Mofolo is considered the first great author of modern African literature. Written in the Sesotho language, his three novels are concerned with the radical effect of Christian teachings on traditional African society. *Chaka,* Mofolo's most highly regarded work, is often interpreted as a depiction of the negative moral consequences of paganism unchecked by Christian ethics; a respect for traditional African customs and beliefs pervades the work, however, especially in the heroic portrayal of the Zulu king Chaka. This respect, in part, caused missionary publishers to suppress Mofolo's manuscript until thirteen years after its completion. Today the novel is considered an epic tragedy of literary and historical significance and has served as the model for numerous subsequent works about Chaka, one of the most celebrated legendary figures in African literature.

Mofolo was born in Kojane, Basutoland (now Lesotho), a small country surrounded by the Republic of South Africa. The third son of Christian parents, he was educated at local religious schools and then sent to Morija to work as a houseboy for the Reverend Alfred Casalis, who headed the bible school, printing press, and book depot there. In 1894 Casalis enrolled Mofolo in the bible school, and two years later Mofolo entered the teacher training college, earning a teaching certificate in 1899. He then began work as an interpreter at the printing press, but the operation was suspended during the South African War (also known as the Boer War or Anglo-Boer War), which began in October 1899 and continued until 1902. Mofolo studied carpentry for two years and taught at various schools until 1904, when he returned to Morija as secretary to Casalis and proofreader for the press.

Exposed to a variety of books at the Morija Book Depot, Mofolo read religious works, African and European histories, and novels by such writers as H. Rider Haggard and Marie Corelli. Several missionaries encouraged him to write works of his own, and his Christian allegory *Moeti oa bochabela (The Traveller to the East),* published in 1907, became the first novel written in Sesotho. His next novel, *Pitseng,* the story of two exemplary youths inspired by an African Christian teacher, was published in 1910. During this period Mofolo also began research for a novel based on the life of the Zulu warrior-king Chaka. Travelling to Pietermaritzburg, the former Zulu capital Mgungundluvu, Mofolo visited Chaka's gravesite and collected historical data, recollections, and legends which had been passed on through oral literature. The manuscript of *Chaka* was submitted to the Morija printers around 1912. Despite acknowledgement of the novel's extraordinary qualities, the missionaries were deeply divided over whether to publish the work, with those who opposed it citing their fear that the novel's depiction of traditional Africa would entice the indigenous reader to return to a non-Christian way of life. After a campaign by supporters and the excision of some material, *Chaka* was published in 1925. Mofolo, however, had left the Morija press after the novel was rejected. Disillusioned and feeling betrayed, he gave up writing.

Mofolo afterward held various jobs, including recruiter and labor agent for diamond mines, sugar plantations, and large farms, manager of a postal route, and trade store proprietor. In 1933 Mofolo returned to his home district, where he purchased a large farm from a white landowner; the farm was

confiscated by the government, however, under provisions of the Land Act of 1914 because one end of the property touched that of another African landowner. Mofolo spent several years and much money in an unsuccessful court fight to regain his land. In 1940, impoverished and ill, he retired to live on a pension until his death in 1948.

Chaka has been called by many critics a masterpiece of world literature. Regarded by contemporary reviewers as an "Africanized" Christian tract, the novel has more recently been assessed as a sophisticated fusion of Christian philosophy, African praise-poetry and myth, and Western literature. Although it is a fictionalized historical biography, *Chaka* retains much that is factual. The story depicts the rise and decline of the early-nineteenth-century Zulu monarch Chaka, who systematically conquered Natal and by 1824 ruled over 50,000 subjects. The illegitimate son of chief Senzangakona and Nandi, a woman from a neighboring tribe, Chaka is ostracized by his father, maligned and physically brutalized by his peers, and, in retaliation, resolves to lead a life of vengeful aggression. He becomes an innovative chief and then a warrior-king whose egoism and bloodlust give rise to a reign of terror that ends when he is murdered by his half-brothers.

There are many Christian readings of *Chaka* as an illustration of the battle between good and evil. In such interpretations, Chaka's death at the hands of his brothers is considered just punishment for his sinful paganism. Many critics, however, note that much of the so-called Christian morality in the novel is in fact based on African traditions in which nature, the tribal community, and the gods are indivisible. Chaka's illegitimacy, for example, is fateful according to this tradition because it opposes tribal law, a law established before the introduction of Christianity to Africa. Similarly, Chaka ensures his destruction when he murders his mother, which breaks the ultimate taboo against shedding the blood of kin. Ben Obumselu contends that a critical reading of the work as Christian morality cannot sufficiently account for the novel's complexity, which is most apparent in the portrayal of Chaka's psychological development. While this careful attention to the events of Chaka's early childhood and his reaction to them does not excuse his behavior, it provides an explanation for his actions which goes beyond that of a simplistic pagan symbolism promoted by those who read the novel as a Christian allegory. Several critics have also commented on the sympathetic nature of Mofolo's eulogy for Chaka and the Mazulus at the end of the novel.

Daniel P. Kunene, for instance, believes that the passage reveals Mofolo's conscious or unconscious loyalty to Sesotho culture and its traditions of heroism and virility. Albert S. Gerard similarly considers the eulogy a passage wherein Mofolo sets aside religion to reflect on the Mazulu empire, pondering the "past greatness of his race and its present subjugation."

Mofolo employed several diverse stylistic elements in *Chaka,* including the rhythm and narrative devices of African praise poems, which were performed to honor Bantu monarchs; the didactic elements of African oral narratives, which traditionally served as vehicles for moral instruction; and Biblical terminology, which reflected his missionary schooling. Because the novel form is not intrinsically African, Mofolo also utilized some of the conventions of the Western novel. He combined these various stylistic forms throughout *Chaka,* shifting from one to another when appropriate for dramatic or thematic emphasis. Mofolo's use of witch doctors in the novel demonstrates the extent to which these various traditions are skillfully synthesized. Essential to the portrayal of Chaka's drive for power, the role of the witch doctor has been interpreted as a literal commentary on good and bad witch doctors in the tribal community; a symbolic revelation of Chaka's personality traits and true desires reminiscent of the witches in MacBeth; and an allegorical rendering of a Mephistophelean devil with whom the Faustian Chaka makes a pact.

Chaka demonstrates Mofolo's respect for Chaka and traditional African ways of life, unlike the negative depictions of these subjects by white historians. For this reason, Mofolo has profoundly influenced such African authors as Leopold Sedar Senghor, Abdou Anta Ka, and Djibril Tamsir Niane, whose works go beyond his novel in celebrating Chaka's military and political genius. Translated into English, French, German, and several African languages, *Chaka* remains one of the great works of African literature.

BIOGRAPHICAL/CRITICAL SOURCES:

BOOKS

Burness, Donald, "Shaka, King of the Zulus," in *African Literature,* Three Continents Press, 1976, pp. 1-24.

Heywood, Christopher, editor, *Aspects of South African Literature,* African Publishing Company, 1976, pp. 54-65.

Interdisciplinary Dimensions of African Literature, Three Continents Press, 1985, pp. 113-27.

PERIODICALS

English in Africa, May, 1986.
The French Review, April, 1984.
The Literary Criterion, No. 2, 1985.
The Nation, January 27, 1932.
Research in African Literatures, Spring, 1987.
South African Journal of African Languages, No. 1, 1988; November, 1989.
Spectator, August 15, 1931.

* * *

MOLNAR, Ferenc 1878-1952

PERSONAL: Original name, Ferenc Neumann; born January 12, 1878, in Budapest, Hungary; immigrated to the United States in January, 1940; U.S. citizen, 1947; died of stomach cancer, April 1, 1952, in New York, NY; buried in Linden Hill Cemetery, New York, NY; son of Mor (a physician) and Jozepha (Wallfisch) Neumann; married Margit Veszi, 1906 (divorced, 1910); married Sari Fedak (an actor), 1922 (divorced, 1924); married Lili Darvan, 1926 (separated, c. 1932); longtime domestic partnership with Wanda Bartha ended with her suicide in 1947; children: (first marriage) one daughter. *Education:* Studied law at University of Budapest, beginning 1895; completed legal studies at the Swiss University in Geneva.

CAREER: Novelist and playwright; worked as a journalist in Budapest, beginning 1896; war correspondent for the Budapest daily *Az Est,* beginning 1914.

MEMBER: Petofi Society, Kisfaludy Society.

AWARDS, HONORS: Order of Franz Josef, 1916; French Cross of the Legion of Honor, 1927.

WRITINGS:

FICTION

"Magdolna" es egyeb elbeszelesek (title means "'Magdalena' and Other Stories"; novella and short stories), [Budapest], 1898.
"A csokok ejszakaja" es egyeb elbeszelesek (title means "'The Kiss at Night' and Other Stories"), [Budapest], 1899.
Az ehes varos (title means "The Hungry City"; novel), [Budapest], 1901.

Egy gazdatlan csonak torteenete (novel), [Budapest], 1901, translation by Emil Lengyel published as *Eva and the Derelict Boat,* Bobs-Merrill (Indianapolis), 1926.
Eva (novel), [Budapest], 1903, translation by Emil Lengyel published as *Eva and the Derelict Boat,* Bobs-Merrill, 1926.
Egy pesti leany tortenete (title means "A Budapest Girl's Story"), [Budapest], 1905.
A Pal utczai fiuk (novel), [Budapest], 1907, Lampel (Budapest), 1923, translation by Louis Rittenberg published as *The Paul Street Boys,* Macy-Masius (New York City), 1927.
Muzsika (title means "Music"; short stories), [Budapest], 1908.
"Baro Marczius" es egyeb elbeszekesek (title means "'Marczius Baro' and Other Stories"), [Budapest], 1913.
Kis harmaskonyv (title means "Three in One"; short stories), [Budapest], 1914.
"Az orias" es egyeb elbeszelesek (title means "'The Giant' and Other Stories"), [Budapest], 1917.
Szentolvajok, [Budapest], 1918.
Andor (title means "Andor"), [Budapest], 1918.
A gozoszlop (title means "The Steam Chimney"; novel), Franklin-tarsulat (Budapest), 1926.
A zenelo angyal (novel), 1935, translation published as *Angel Making Music,* H. Smith and R. Haas (New York City), 1935.
A zold huszar (title means "The Green Hussar"), Athenaeum (Budapest), 1937.
Oszi utazas (title means "Autumn Journey"; novel), Athenaeum, 1939.
A kekszemu (stories), 1940, translation published as *The Blued Eyed Lady,* Viking (New York City), 1942.
Isten veled szivem (novel), 1947, translation published as *Farewell My Heart,* Simon and Schuster (New York City), 1945.
Companion in Exile (autobiography), Gaer Associates (New York City), 1950.
Stories for Two (short stories), Horizon Press (New York City), 1950.

STAGE WORKS

A Doktor ur (produced in Vigszinhaz, Budapest, 1902), [Budapest], 1902, translation published as *The Lawyer,* in *Plays of Molnar,* Jarrolds (London), 1927.
Jozsi (produced in Vigszinhaz, 1904), [Budapest], 1902.
Az ordog (produced Vigszinhaz, 1907), [Budapest], 1907, translation by Oliver Herford published as

The Devil, M. Kennerley (New York), 1908, and in *Plays of Molnar,* Jarrolds, 1927.

Liliom (produced in Vigzinhaz, 1909), [Budapest], 1909, translation by Benjamin Glazer published as *Liliom,* Boni and Liveright, 1921; several subsequent translations under same title, 1909.

A vacsora (produced in Vigszinhas, 1915), [Budapest], 1909, translation published as *Dinner,* in *Smart Set,* number 67, 1922; as *The Host,* in *One-Act Plays for Stage and Study,* 1925; as *As Anniversary Dinner,* in *Romantic Comedies,* Crown (New York City), 1952.

A testor (produced in Vigszinhaz, 1910), [Budapest], 1910, translation published as *The Guardsman,* 1910, translation by Frank Marcus published as *The Guardsman: A Comedy in Three Acts,* Eyre Methuen (London), 1978.

A farkas (produced in Magyar Szinhaz, Budapest, 1912), Franklin-tarsulat, 1912, translation published as *The Tale of the Wolf,* in *Plays of Molnar,* Jarrolds, 1927; translation by Henric Hirsch and Frank Hauser published as *The Wolf: A Play,* Samuel French (London), 1975.

A fehler felho (produced in Nemzeti Szinhaz, 1916), [Budapest], 1916, translation published as *The White Cloud,* in *Plays of Molnar,* Jarrolds, 1927.

Farsang (produced in Vigszinhaz, 1916), Franklin-tarsulat, 1917, translation published as *Carnival,* in *Plays of Molnar,* Jarrolds, 1927.

Uri divat (produced in Nemzeti Szinhaz, Budapest, 1917), Franklin-tarsulat, 1917, translation by Benjamin Glazer published as *Fashions for Men,* with *The Swan,* Boni and Liveright, 1922; and in *Plays of Molnar,* Jarrolds, 1927.

A hattyu (produced in Vigszinhaz, 1920), [Budapest], 1921, translation by Benjamin Glazer published as *The Swan,* with *Fashions for Men,* Boni and Liveright, 1922; and in *Plays of Molnar,* Jarrolds, 1927.

Szinhaz: Elojatek Lear Kiralyhoz, Marshall, and *The Violet* (one act plays; produced in Magyar Szinhyaz, 1921), [Budapest], 1929; individual titles: *Elojhatek Lear Kiralyhoz,* translation published as *Prologue to "King Lear,"* in *Plays of Molnar,* Jarrolds, 1927; *Marsall,* translation published as *Marshal,* in *Plays of Molnar,* Jarrolds, 1927; *Az ibolya,* translation published as *The Violet,* in *Plays of Molnar,* Jarrolds, 1927.

Egi es foldi szerelem (produced in Magyar Szinhaz, 1923), Pantheon (Budapest) 1922, translation published as *Heavenly and Earthly Love,* in *Plays of Molnar,* Jarrolds, 1927.

A voros malom (produced in Magyar Szinhaz, 1922), Franklin-tarsulat, 1923, translation published as *Mima,* in *Plays of Molnar,* Jarrolds, 1927.

Husbands and Lovers (nineteen dialogues), translation by Benjamin Glazer, Boni and Liveright, 1924.

Az uvegcipo (produced in Vigszinhaz, 1924), Franklin-tarsulat, 1924, translation published as *The Glass Slipper,* in *Plays of Molnar,* Jarrolds, 1927.

Riviera (produced at Theater in der Josefstadt, Vienna, 1925), [Budapest], 1926, translation published as *Riviera,* in *Plays of Molnar,* Jarrolds, 1927.

Csendelt (produced in Vigszinhaz, 1925), translation published as *Still Life,* in *Plays of Molnar,* Jarrolds, 1927.

Jatek a kastelyban (produced in Magyar Szinhaz, 1926), 1926, translation by P. G. Wodehouse published as *The Play's the Thing,* Brentano's, 1927, and in *Plays of Molnar,* Jarrolds, 1927; adapted by Tom Stoppard as *Rough Crossing,* Faber and Faber (London), 1985.

A boszorkany (produced in Andrassy-uti Szinhaz, Budapest, 1927), translation published as *The Witch,* in *Plays in Molnar,* Jarrolds, 1927.

Olympia (produced in Magyar Szinhaz, 1928), Franklin-tarsulat, 1928, translation by Sidney Howard published as *Olympia,* Brentano's, 1928, and in *Plays of Molnar,* Jarrolds, 1927.

Egy, ketto, harom (produced in Vigszinhaz, 1929), [Budapest], 1929, translation published as *President,* in *Romantic Comedies,* Crown, 1952.

A jo tunder (produced in Vigszinhaz, 1930), [Budapest], 1930, translation by Jane Hinton published as *The Good Fairy,* R. Long and R. R. Smith (New York City), 1932, and in *Romantic Comedies,* Crown, 1952.

Valaki (produced in Velvarosi Szinhaz, Budapest, 1932), Franklin-tarsulat, 1932, translation published as *Arthur,* in *Romantic Comedies,* Crown, 1952.

Harmonia (produced in Mazyar Szinhaz, 1932), Athenaeum, 1932.

Menyegzo (produced in Andrassy-uti Szinhaz, 1935), 1933.

Csoda a hegyek kozt (produced in Vigszinhaz, 1936), Athenaeum, 1933.

Az ismeretlen lany (produced in Vigszinhaz, 1934), Athenaeum, 1934.

A cukraszne (produced in Andrassy-uti Szinhaz, 1935), [Budapest], 1934, translation by Gilbert Miller published as *Delicate Story,* Samuel French, 1941.

Nagy szerelem (produced in Vigszinhaz, 1935), Athenaeum, 1935.

Delila (produced in Pesti Szinhaz, Budapest, 1937), Athenaeum, 1937, translation published as *Blue Danube,* in *Romantic Comedies,* Crown, 1952.

The King's Maid, produced at Bass Rocks Theater, Gloucester, Massachusetts, 1941.

Panoptikum (produced in Akademietheater, Vienna, 1948), [Budapest], 1941, translation published as *Waxworks,* in *Romantic Comedies,* Crown, 1952.

A csaszar, produced in Vigszinhaz, 1946.

Pit-a-Pat (produced as *Das Spiel des Herzen,* Theater in der Josefstadt, 1971), translation published as *Game o Hearts,* in *Romantic Comedies,* Crown, 1952.

COLLECTIONS

Plays (includes *Liliom; Husbands and Lovers; Fashions for Men;* and *The Swan*), translation by Benjamin F. Glazer, [New York], 1927.

Molnar Ferenc muvei (collected works in 20 volumes), [New York], 1928.

Plays of Molnar (includes *The Lawyer; The Devil; Liliom; The Guardsman; The Tale of the Wolf; The White Cloud; Carnival; Fashions for Men; The Swan; A Prologue to "King Lear"; Marshal; The Violet; Heavenly and Earthly Love; Mima; The Glass Slipper; Riviera; Still Life; The Play's the Thing; The Witch;* and *Olympia*), translated and introduced by Benjamin F. Glazer, edited by Louis Rittenberg, Jarrolds, 1927; published as *All the Plays of Molnar,* Garden City Publishing (Garden City, NY), 1937.

Romantic Comedies (includes *Actor from Vienna; President; Waxworks; Arthur; Blue Danube; The Good Fairy; Anniversary Dinner;* and *Game of Hearts*), Crown, 1952.

Szinhaz (selected works), Szepirodalmi Konyvkiado (Budapest), 1961.

OTHER

Gyerekek (for children), [Budapest], 1905.

Ketten beszelnek (sketches), [Budapest], 1909, translation published as *Stories for Two,* Horizon Press, 1950.

Pesti erkolscok (title means "Metropolitan Morals"), [Budapest], 1909.

Hetagup sip (title means "Pipes of Pan"), [Budapest], 1911.

Ma, tegnap, tegnapelott (title means "Today, Yesterday, Tomorrow"; journalism), [Budapest], 1912.

Egy haditudosito emlekei (title means "A War Correspondent's Diary"), [Budapest], 1916.

Ismerosok (title means "Acquaintances"), [Budapest], 1917.

Toll (title means "Pen"), [Budapest], 1928.

Szulofalum, Pest (miscellany), [Budapest], 1962.

ADAPTATIONS: Liliom was adapted for the American stage by Richard Rogers and Oscar Hammerstein, and produced as *Carousel.*

SIDELIGHTS: The author of light comedies praised for their charm and technical excellence, Ferenc Molnar was the first Hungarian dramatist to achieve international acclaim. His plays often depict relationships between men and women, generally portraying men as victims of their scheming but irresistible partners. His most successful play, *Liliom,* gained fame through its adaptation by Richard Rodgers and Oscar Hammerstein as the musical *Carousel.*

Molnar was the second son of a successful Budapest physician, Mor Neumann, and his wife, Jozepha Wallfisch. As was usual among the Hungarian upper class, he was educated by private tutors until the age of nine. He then entered a Calvinist secondary school, where he printed his own periodicals and staged his first play at the age of fourteen. Upon completion of secondary school in 1895, Molnar studied law at the University of Budapest and at the Swiss University in Geneva. During this period he published articles in Hungarian newspapers and wrote his first novellas and short stories. In 1896 Molnar returned to Budapest, abandoning his law studies to become a full-time journalist. His essays and sketches for leading newspapers were praised for their originality and stylistic excellence, and Molnar was quickly accepted into Budapest's most prominent literary circles, where he earned a reputation as a brilliant conversationalist. In 1901 he published his first novel, *Az ehes varos* ("The Hungry City"). Generally disparaged by critics, the novel was immediately popular with readers and became a Hungarian bestseller.

Molnar eventually turned to drama, the genre for which he became famous, and his first professionally produced play, *A Doktor ur* (*The Lawyer*), was staged in 1902. This and subsequent productions of Molnar's plays were overwhelmingly successful with audiences. While gaining renown as a dramatist, he continued to be extremely prolific in other genres. According to S. N. Behrman, Molnar's self-imposed literary program for the twenty years preceding World War I required the completion of "a feuilleton or a short dialogue for the papers every day, a short story every week, and a play and a novel every year." He became a celebrity as the result of both the popularity of his works and the scandalous nature of his numerous love affairs, several of which resulted in highly publicized marriages. Molnar's personal relationships were often dramatized in his works;

according to Clara Gyorgyey in *Ferenc Molnar,* "the gossip-hungry Budapest populace stormed the theaters to watch the new developments in the playwright's private life."

At the outbreak of World War I, Molnar was sent by the Budapest daily *Az Est* to accompany Austro-Hungarian troops into battle. His resulting reports, which were also published in the *London Morning Post* and the *New York Times,* were praised for their realistic portrayal of the horrors of war. After 1920 Molnar lived a life of luxury and celebrity, residing in the finest hotels of Budapest, Vienna, Karlsbad, Venice, and Nice. Acclaimed throughout the world, he was decorated with the French Cross of the Legion of Honor and was received by President Calvin Coolidge. By 1937, however, the growing threat of war began to affect Molnar's enthusiasm for life. He became subject to bouts of anxiety and depression and abandoned society life for semi-seclusion. He immigrated to the United States in 1940, a move which biographers note had a temporary rejuvenating effect on the author, who rapidly completed a series of plays and short stories. In 1943, however, a massive heart attack and news about the atrocities of the war combined to destroy Molnar's emotional equilibrium. According to Gyorgyey, "he became apathetic, morose, a misanthrope." In 1947 his despondency was compounded by the suicide of Wanda Bartha, his longtime secretary and companion. Molnar immersed himself in his writing, maintaining that "there is only one consolation on earth, and that is work." His plays and novels from this period, which critics find uncharacteristically melancholy and didactic, are not as highly regarded as his earlier works. After a period of failing health, Molnar died of stomach cancer in 1952.

Molnar's plays reflect his central preoccupations, frequently depicting theater life, the aristocracy, and, most often, relationships between the sexes. Many contain fantastic or supernatural elements, such as *Az ordog* (*The Devil*), which was the first of his dramas to achieve acclaim outside of Hungary. *The Devil* portrays the efforts of the title character to encourage a young woman to leave her husband for the man she loves. Like many of his works, the play dramatizes a conflict from Molnar's personal life. According to acquaintances, it was written as a challenge to his mistress and precipitated a duel with her jealous husband that led to a jail sentence for Molnar. Critics note that the play demonstrates Molnar's interest in psychology; most agree with Behrman's assessment that the character of "the devil is merely the materi-

alized subconscious of the troubled and vacillating characters." In *A testor* (*The Guardsman*), *Jatek a kastelyban* (*The Play's the Thing*), and three one-act plays published together as *Szinhaz: Elojatek Lear Kiralyhoz, Marshall, and The Violet,* Molnar again portrayed domestic triangles while addressing another of his favorite themes: the relationship between illusion and reality and their intermingling in the world of the theater. In *The Guardsman,* perhaps the best known of the group, an actor masquerades as a Russian guardsman to test his wife's fidelity. Despite an ostensible reconciliation between the characters, an ambiguous resolution leaves the audience uncertain of the wife's loyalty, and the play concludes on a note of cynicism. The characters are typical of Molnar's comedies: the woman is beautiful, fickle, and cunning, while the man is jealous, somewhat befuddled, and ultimately defeated by the woman. As Joseph Remenyi and others have noted, in Molnar's plays "man generally suffers because of a woman and the woman almost never suffers because of a man." *Elojatek Lear Kiralyhoz* (*Prologue to "King Lear"*), the most successful of the *Szinhaz* plays, is based on a situation similar to that in *The Guardsman:* a husband discovers his wife's infidelity and attempts to confront her lover, an actor who is costumed as King Lear. The actor takes advantage of the dignity of his role and the husband finds it impossible to chastise him, lamenting, "My wife's seducer hides from me behind the mask and stands in the guise of a majestic figure, an unhappy mythical king and father whose fate has often stirred me . . . I'm paralyzed." Gyorgyey observes that "Molnar adorns the Shakespearean characters with so much authority that the play's actual characters are compelled to admit their own lack of substance and, after being deflated, they scramble off into their dim, makeshift reality." In such works as *A hattyu* (*The Swan*) and *Olympia,* Molnar treated the theme of jealousy in a different setting, satirizing the snobbishness of the aristocracy in their romantic liaisons. *The Swan,* one of Molnar's most popular plays, has often been praised for its sparkling dialogue and subtle characterization.

In *Liliom,* widely acknowledged to be his finest play, Molnar once again combined the theme of love with elements of the supernatural. The plot concerns a carnival barker whose rough exterior conceals a gentle heart, yet who is nevertheless unable to refrain from inflicting pain on his loved ones. After his death and fifteen years in purgatory, Liliom is allowed to return to earth to visit his family and redeem himself by doing one good deed. He fails, slapping his daughter in exasperation when she refuses a gift; however,

the blow does not hurt the child, whose mother explains: "It has happened to me too . . . it is possible, dear, that someone may beat you and beat you and beat you—and not hurt you at all." Critics identify the play's protagonist with the author, who demonstrated similar qualities of cruelty and remorse, and view *Liliom* as Molnar's public apology to his first wife and tribute to her endurance. The play has been variously interpreted as commentary on the fate of the outcast unable to conform to society, on the futility of the struggle for salvation of a man predestined to damnation, and on the nature of love, which penetrates beyond externals and endures all abuse. Critics attribute Molnar's artistic success in *Liliom* to his rejection of facile entertainment in favor of sincere exploration of eternal truths. According to John Gassner, writing in *Masters of the Drama,* "*Liliom* is a play of rare beauty, one of the most gratifying romantic plays of the twentieth century."

Molnar wrote fourteen novels, the majority of which are even more overtly autobiographical than his plays. According to Gyorgyey he used the genre as therapy for his personal traumas, writing a novel "each time he suffered a deep wound—genuine or imagined—in the forever-raging combats with the 'weaker sex.'" His novels are therefore dominated by troubled sexual relationships and often end in tragedy. At the time of their publication, Molnar's novels were almost invariably popular with readers but attacked by critics, who considered them superficial and lacking in artistic merit. The single exception was *A Pal utczai fiuk* (*The Paul Street Boys*), which was acclaimed by both critics and readers as a classic of juvenile literature. *The Paul Street Boys,* which is also unique among Molnar's novels for its nonsexual subject matter, successfully combines naturalistic descriptions with a sentimental theme to depict the heroic sacrifice of a schoolboy, and is praised for its insight into the psychology of children. Molnar was also the author of numerous short stories, which are notable primarily for their skillful use of dramatic dialogue.

Although Molnar's plays continue to be popular with audiences all over the world, critical opinion is divided as to their literary value. While some critics praise his works for their brilliant dialogue and technical craftsmanship, others dismiss them as insignificant and superficial, maintaining that Molnar sacrificed artistry to commercial ends. Some commentators, however, contend that Molnar aspired to be an entertainer, not an artist. He readily achieved this

goal in twenty-four plays of wit, charm, and sophistication, becoming the most popular Hungarian dramatist of the first half of the twentieth century.

BIOGRAPHICAL/CRITICAL SOURCES:

BOOKS

Gassner, John, *Masters of the Drama,* Dover Publications, 1940, pp. 467-94.

Gergely, Emro Joseph, *Hungarian Drama in New York: American Adaptations, 1908-1940,* University of Pennsylvania Press, 1947.

Gyorgyey, Clara, *Ferenc Molnar,* Twayne Publishers, 1980.

Middleton, George, *These Things Are Mine: The Autobiography of a Journeyman Playwright,* Macmillan, 1947, pp. 363-73.

Nathan, George Jean, *Theatre Book of the Year: 1946-1947,* Alfred A. Knopf, 1947, pp. 373-76.

Theatre Book of the Year: 1947-1948, Alfred A. Knopf, 1948, pp. 358-60.

PERIODICALS

Nation, May 11, 1921; November 5, 1924; August 11, 1945.

New Republic, May 4, 1921.

New York Herald Tribune Books, June 6, 1926; December 4, 1927.

Psychoanalytic Review, January, 1922.

Spectator, October 5, 1934.*

* * *

MONTAL, Lionel
See GROULX, Lionel (Adolphe)

* * *

MONTERROSO, Augusto 1921-

PERSONAL: Born in 1921, in Guatamala; immigrated to Mexico.

CAREER: Writer.

AWARDS, HONORS: El Aguila Azteca, 1989.

WRITINGS:

Monterroso (lectures and essays), compiled by Jorge Ruffinelli, Centro de Investigaciones Linguistico-Literarias, Universidad Veracruzana, 1976.

La oveja negra y demas fabulas, Seix Barral, 1981.

Movimiento perpetuo, Seix Barral, 1981.

Obras completas (y otros cuentos) (short stories), Seix Barral, 1981.

Mr. Taylor and Co., Ciudad de la Habana, 1982.

Lo demas es silencio: la vida y la obra de Eduardo Torres, Seix Barral, 1982.

Viaje al centro de la fabula, M. Casillas, 1982.

La palabra magica, Era, 1983.

Las ilusiones perdidas, Fondo de Cultura Economica, 1985.

Der Frosch, der ein richtiger Frosch ein Wollte, Reclam, 1986.

La letra e, Era, 1987.

Sinfonia concluida y otros cuentos, Monte Avila Editores Latinamericana, 1994.

Complete Works and Other Stories, translated by Edith Grossman, University of Texas Press, 1995.

Also author of *Estado religioso y la santidad,* 1967—.*

* * *

MOODY, Fred 1949-
(Spike McGee)

PERSONAL: Born March 14, 1949, in Missoula, MT; son of Fred R. (a court reporter) and Anna (a probation officer; maiden name, McGee) Moody; married Anne Moehring (an adoption counselor), April 1, 1974; children: Erin, Caitlin, Jocelyn. *Education:* Fairhaven College, B.A., 1972; University of Michigan, A.M.L.S., 1975. *Religion:* "Pataphysics." *Avocational interests:* Bicycling.

ADDRESSES: Agent—Nat Sobel, Sobel-Weber Associates, 146 E. 19th St., New York, NY 10003-2404.

CAREER: Ardis Publishers, Ann Arbor, MI, editor, 1974-80; Melmoth Typesetting, Seattle, WA, owner, 1980-86; *Seattle Weekly,* Seattle, staff writer, 1983—; freelance writer. Secretary of Bainbridge Foundation, 1988-90.

WRITINGS:

Ten Russian Bibliographies of Twentieth-Century Literature (reference), Ardis (Ann Arbor, MI), 1977.

Fighting Chance: An NFL Season with the Seattle Seahawks (nonfiction), Sasquatch (Seattle, WA), 1989.

I Sing the Body Electronic: A Year with Microsoft on the Multimedia Frontier (nonfiction), Viking (New York), 1995.

Also the author of writings under the pseudonym Spike McGee.

WORK IN PROGRESS: Research on the industry of virtual reality.

SIDELIGHTS: Fred Moody, a writer for the *Seattle Weekly* newspaper, is the author of two books that reveal the inner workings of two large organizations, the Seattle Seahawks of the National Football League, and the Microsoft Corporation, the fastest-growing producer of computer products.

In the first of these volumes, *Fighting Chance: An NFL Season with the Seattle Seahawks,* Moody covers virtually every aspect of the Seahawks' 1988 season, from contract negotiations and new ownership, to injuries, poor refereeing, and odd occurrences on the field. He also shares highlights of conversations he had with the coaches, the managers, the players, and their wives, as well as anecdotes about activity in the locker room and the superstitious practices of some team members. Commenting on Moody's comprehensive coverage of the Seattle franchise, a *Publishers Weekly* reviewer predicted: "Hardcore football fans will enjoy this game-by-game, play-by-play commentary on the Seattle Seahawks' first division-winning season."

Moody's next effort, *I Sing the Body Electronic: A Year with Microsoft on the Multimedia Frontier,* took him to the Redmond, Washington, headquarters of the Microsoft Corporation, where he observed a team of software designers for one year. Involved in the development of "Sendak," a multimedia encyclopedia for children, the team encountered numerous hurdles during the program's production, especially conflicts between the artistic designers and the practical programmers. Moody reports, however, that the most nerve-wracking process in the program's development was the design team's presentation to Microsoft founder and chair Bill Gates. Eventually, Gates ap-

proved the project, released in 1994 as "Explorapedia."

I Sing the Body Electronic was applauded by critics who enjoyed Moody's behind-the-scenes reportage at Microsoft, which focuses as much on the average programmer as on the more publicly visible Gates. Technology reporter Steve Lohr, for example, wrote in his *New York Times Book Review* assessment of *I Sing the Body Electronic* that "Mr. Moody has not written a Gates book, but Mr. Gates is an animating presence throughout. . . . It is pretty much the world according to Microsoft. Still, Mr. Moody explains that his intent was 'to capture as accurately as possible the working conditions and emotional state of the Microsoft worker.' By that standard, he has succeeded admirably." Lohr also found Moody "has done a remarkable reporting job and written a first-rate work of narrative description, rendering the look and feel of life inside Microsoft—its youth, its management ethos and its corporate culture. He offers his portrait with scant judgment or analysis."

Moody told *CA:* "I do my most concentrated writing from 4:30 a.m. to 7:30 a.m., and work sporadically from then on, throughout the day. I took to writing in early middle age because I finally discovered that I had neither the skill, the aptitude, the interest, nor the attention span to do anything else for a living. I was unable to begin writing at an earlier age because of a crippling awe of the following writers: Vladimir Nabokov, Raymond Queneau, Brian Moore, Steven Millhauser, and the great memoirist and moralist Nadezhda Mandelstam.

"I write nonfiction rather than fiction for two reasons: I lack the imagination to be a great or even a decent novelist; and I like to augment reality by employing the techniques of fiction in the telling of nonfictional stories. I believe that it is at least as important for the writer to entertain as to inform. I have the heart and soul of a novelist, but the mind and imagination, alas, of a journalist.

"I like writing because it is the only pastime I have ever tried that requires concentration sufficient to distract me from my depressing problems, most of which are financial. I also like writing because it allows the writer to improve on reality. The favorite part of my job is the crafting of sentences and the savoring of their sound; the second-favorite part of my job is getting people to tell me things that are none of my business."

BIOGRAPHICAL/CRITICAL SOURCES:

PERIODICALS

Library Journal, July 1995, p. 110; September 1, 1989, p. 197.
New York Times Book Review, September 3, 1995, p. 8.
Publishers Weekly, August 4, 1989, p. 85; August 7, 1995, p. 454.

* * *

MOORE, Alison 1951-

PERSONAL: Born November 6, 1951, in Pittsfield, MA; daughter of Herbert (a publisher) and Audley (an editor; maiden name, Thomas); *Ethnicity:* "White." *Education:* Warren Wilson College, M.F.A., 1990. *Avocational interests:* Photography.

ADDRESSES: Home— 3560 West Goret Rd., Tucson, AZ 85745. *Office*—University of Arizona, College of Humanities, Department of English, Tucson, AZ 85721. *Agent*— Ellen Levine, 15 East 26th St., Suite 1801, New York, NY 10010.

CAREER: University of Arizona, Tucson, AZ, professor of creative writing, 1995—; ArtsReach (nonprofit organization for the instruction of creative writing to Native American children), Tucson, AZ, publications director, 1991.

MEMBER: PEN Center West.

AWARDS, HONORS: Notable Book of the Year, American Library Association, 1993, for *Small Spaces between Emergencies: Stories;* creative writing fellowship from the National Endowment for the Arts, 1993.

WRITINGS:

Small Spaces between Emergencies: Stories, Mercury (San Francisco), 1992.
Synonym for Love (novel), Mercury, 1995.

WORK IN PROGRESS: A novel, *Almost Egypt.*

SIDELIGHTS: Alison Moore's fiction often portrays loneliness and the wary quest for human connection. "Moore is a perceptive observer of the distances

between individuals and of the cautious efforts to bridge the divide," Yvonne Fraticelli commented in *Belles Lettres.* Often featuring characters who feel compelled to move frequently, Moore's writings are noted for the strong sense of place they impart through evocative, metaphor-rich language. "Every object of situation seems to be a character in and of itself, every sentence a beautiful composition," Sharon Lennon observed in *Ms.* Reviewers noted that despite the author's dark view of the human condition, her works often end on a note of hope.

Small Spaces between Emergencies: Stories, Moore's first book-length publication, features stories about people compulsively running away, unable or unwilling to connect with those around them. In "Leaving by the Window," one of the collection's most accomplished stories according to some critics, a teen-age girl and her newly-widowed father travel together until the girl, inspired by her father's stories of his youth, runs away to New York, where she is raped. In "News from Another World," an elderly woman escapes from a nursing home and kidnaps a baby for the afternoon so that she can sit in the park and pretend to be part of a family. According to Linda Barrett Osborne in the *New York Times Book Review,* the stories contained in *Small Spaces between Emergencies* focus on "the capacity of the human spirit to create the fragile but necessary conditions we need to survive."

Some reviewers singled out Moore's understated, poetic style for praise. A critic for the *Los Angeles Times Book Review* wrote of *Small Spaces,* "In these stories, Moore shows originality, an acute, if slightly skewed, view of relationships and a style that, beneath a quiet surface, hums with metaphor." At times, wrote a contributor to the *Kirkus Reviews,* "such metaphors dazzle and often transcend the bleakness here." While some critics found certain pieces in *Small Spaces* more original and moving than others, the book as a whole was widely considered a memorably promising debut.

Moore's second book, *Synonym for Love,* a novel, follows Matty Grover as she travels from place to place, finally settling for a season in the Sonoran Desert where she meets Della, with whom she forms a tentative friendship and to whom she reminisces about her youth. Matty is on a quest to unearth the secrets of her troubled family and of her own identity. According to Starr E. Smith in *Library Journal,* the character's progression is portrayed "movingly."

In the predominantly positive reviews of *Synonym for Love,* critics singled out, as with Moore's short story collection, the author's poetic prose style, which some credited as the major strength of the novel. Although the structure of Moore's novel, which requires the main action of the story to occur in flashbacks during the narrator's reminiscences, was called "ungainly" by a reviewer for *Publisher's Weekly,* that same critic also remarked that this flaw is compensated by "striking imagery" and "dense, passionate writing." Critics praised the novel's strong evocations of what Abby Frucht in the *New York Times Book Review* called "both inner and outer landscapes." Additionally, *Synonym for Love* was found to be a moving testament to the sometimes unknown strengths of the human heart. Kathleen Hughes of *Booklist* stated that *Synonym for Love* "clearly reveals what we are to each other and applauds the strength and capacity for renewal of the human spirit."

BIOGRAPHICAL/CRITICAL SOURCES:

PERIODICALS

Belles Lettres, winter, 1992-93, pp. 59-60.
Booklist, June 1-15, 1995, p. 1731.
Kirkus Reviews, April 15, 1992, p. 6.
Library Journal, June 1, 1995, p. 164.
Los Angeles Times Book Review, July 12, 1992, p. 6.
Ms., July/August, 1995, pp. 76-77.
New York Times Book Review, September 6, 1992, p. 15; September 17, 1995, p. 25.
Publishers Weekly, April 20, 1992, p. 36; May 8, 1995, p. 287.

* * *

MORALES, Edmundo 1943-

PERSONAL: Born November 9, 1943, in Peru; naturalized U.S. citizen; son of Lucas (a farmer) and Felicitas (Bayona) Morales; married, wife's name Norma (a registered nurse), November 25, 1978; children: Angel, Edmundo, Jr. *Education:* Richmond College, B.A., 1977; New York University, M.A., 1980; Graduate School of the City University of New York, Ph.D., 1983. *Politics:* Democrat. *Religion:* Roman Catholic. *Avocational interests:* Photography.

ADDRESSES: Home—101 North Five Points Rd., Apt. H-11, West Chester, PA 19380. *Office*—West

Chester University, West Chester, PA 19383; fax 610-436-2525. *E-mail*—emorales@wcupa.edu.

CAREER: West Chester University, West Chester, PA, associate professor of sociology, 1988—.

AWARDS, HONORS: Fulbright scholar, 1992, 1996.

WRITINGS:

Cocaine: White Gold Rush in Peru, University of Arizona Press (Tucson, AZ), 1989.
The Guinea Pig: Healing, Food, and Ritual in the Andes, University of Arizona Press, 1995.

* * *

MORALES, Jorge Luis 1930(?)-

PERSONAL: Born October 27, 1930 (one source says 1932), in Ciales, Puerto Rico; son of Rafael Morales Rubero (a writer) and Julia Gonzalez Gonzalez (a writer); married Maria Socorro Villalobos (an executive secretary), September 17, 1954; children: Jorge Luis, Ruben Shelley, Alga Solange. *Education:* University of Puerto Rico, B.A. (cum laude), 1951, M.A., 1963; University of Madrid, Ph.D., 1965.

ADDRESSES: Office—Department of Spanish Language and Literature, University of Puerto Rico, Rio Piedras, Puerto Rico.

CAREER: Writer. Secondary school teacher, radio host, and school administrator in Puerto Rico, 1951-57; University of Puerto Rico, Rio Piedras, professor of Spanish language and literature, 1957-88, distinguished poet-in-residence, 1988—. Editor for Editorial Universitaria, 1959—; founder and president of Editorial ASOL. Founder and director of Instituto Nacional de Bellas Letras in Puerto Rico, beginning in 1981.

AWARDS, HONORS: First National Literature Awards from Puerto Rican Institute of Literature, 1960, for *La ventana y yo,* 1975, for *Nueva antologia poetica,* 1980, for *Alfonso Reyes y la literatura espanola,* and 1983, for *Salvado Margen;* Gold Medal from Mexico's Cultural Olympiads, 1968, for "Los rios redimidos"; Puerto Rican Award and Honor Medal, both from Arts and Sciences Academy of Puerto Rico; Manuel Alonso Award, 1980; has received numerous honorary degrees.

WRITINGS:

Metal y piedra: Poemas, 1949-1951 (poetry), Imprenta Soltero, 1952.
Mirada en el olvido, Orfeo, 1953.
Inspiracion del viaje, Ediciones de Repertorio Americano, 1953.
Decir del propio ser (poetry), Las Americas, 1954.
La ventana y yo, Editorial Universitaria, Universidad de Puerto Rico, 1960, translation by Juan Duque published as *The Window and I,* Editorial ASOL, 1981.
Acto poetico, Facultad de Estudios Generales, Universidad de Puerto Rico, 1961.
Journada precisa, Ediciones Rumbos, 1962, 2nd edition, Ediciones Juan Ponce de Leon, 1963.
Discurso a los pajaros, Coleccion Morivivi, 1965, translation by Pedro Juan Duque published as *Address to the Birds,* Editorial ASOL, 1981.
Antologia poetica, Editorial Universidad de Puerto Rico, 1968, 2nd edition published as *Nuevo antologia poetica,* 1975.
Los rios redimidos, Editorial Universitaria, Universidad de Puerto Rico, 1969.
(Editor) *Las cien mejores poesias liricas de Puerto Rico,* Editorial Edil, 1973.
Espana en Alfonso Reyes, Editorial Universitaria, Universidad de Puerto Rico, 1976.
(Editor) *Poesia afroantillana y negrista,* Editorial Universitaria, Universidad de Puerto Rico, 1976, revised edition, 1981.
Buho entre ruinas, Editorial ASOL, 1976.
Libertad por la poesia, Colegio Regional de Cayey, 1976.
Albores del pensamiento religioso en grecia, Universidad de Puerto Rico, Revista La Torre, c. late 1970s.
Alfonso Reyes y la literatura espanola, Editorial Universitaria, Universidad de Puerto Rico, 1980.
Tiempo y fabula, Editorial ASOL, 1980.
Alto en ventana, Editorial ASOL, 1981.
Pura nieve, Editorial ASOL, 1981.
Estacion del canto, Editorial ASOL, 1981.
Frente a las cosas, Editorial ASOL, 1981.
De la tormenta y el rayo, Editorial ASOL, 1981.
Sea de todos, Editorial ASOL, 1981.
La Poesia salva y lecciones de teoria poetica, Editorial ASOL, 1983.
Salvado Margen, Editorial ASOL, 1983.
Estas en mi, Editorial ASOL, 1983.
Poetria: Sagrada biblia poetica, Instituto Nacional de Bellas Artes, 1995.

Also author of *Constancia lirica de la mujer puertorriquena,* Editorial Universitaria, Universidad de Puerto Rico, *Poetas extranjeros en la Universidad de Puerto Rico,* Editorial Universitaria, Universidad de Puerto Rico, *Teoria del poema,* Editorial ASOL, *Medida libertad,* Editorial ASOL, *Del sentir morivivi,* Editorial ASOL, *Historia de mis libros,* Editorial ASOL, and *Marian arzola,* Editorial ASOL, all published in 1980s.

Author of columns, including "Alfabeto y abaco," 1970, and "Desde mi biblioteca," in *El Vocero,* 1979. Contributor to periodicals, including *Revista del Instituto de Cultura Puertorriquena, Asomante,* and *El Mundo.* Editor for periodicals, including *La Torre* and *PLERUS.*

WORK IN PROGRESS: Manuel joglar cacho, for Editorial ASOL; *Jorge Luis Morales: Una jornada precisa; El rio y los mares* (title means "The River and the Seas"), an eight-hundred-page poem; *Sartoria labor,* a one-thousand-page history of humankind; *Obelisco,* a poetry collection; *Ontiatria* (title means "Medicine of the Self Itself"), a treatise on medicine; two novels; a short story collection; various other volumes.

SIDELIGHTS: Jorge Luis Morales is widely regarded as Puerto Rico's greatest poet in the years since World War II, and his poetry, though frequently specific in its concerns with Puerto Rican life, is considered generally accessible in its depictions of modern life.*

* * *

MORGAN, Dareion
 See WALZ, Marjorie A.

* * *

MORI, Kyoko 1957(?)-

PERSONAL: Born in Japan; immigrated to U.S. in 1977; naturalized U.S. citizen.

ADDRESSES: Office—St. Norbert's College, Green Bay, WI. *Agent*—c/o Henry Holt, New York, NY.

CAREER: St. Norbert's College, Green Bay, WI, teacher of creative writing; writer.

WRITINGS:

Shizuko's Daughter (young-adult novel), Holt (New York, NY), 1993.
The Dream of Water (memoir), Holt, 1995.
One Bird (young-adult novel), Holt, 1995.

SIDELIGHTS: Kyoko Mori is a Japanese-born American writer who has distinguished herself with a memoir and two volumes of young-adult fiction. She began her literary career in 1993 with *Shizuko's Daughter,* the autobiographical story—written for young-adult readers—about a young girl, Yuki, whose mother commits suicide, whereupon the girl's aloof father installs his long-time mistress in the home. Yuki soon falls victim to her step-mother's maliciousness. But a warm relationship with her aging grandparents, together with a prospering appreciation for nature and the arts, provides Yuki with a measure of reassurance and contentment. Liz Rosenberg, writing in the *New York Times Book Review,* described *Shizuko's Daughter* as "a work of art" and that it is "a jewel of a book, one of those rarities that shine out only a few times in a generation."

Mori followed *Shizuko's Daughter* with *The Dream of Water,* a memoir that relates, among other things, her own harrowing experiences as a child in Japan. The memoir begins with Mori leaving the United States and returning to her hometown of Kobe in Japan. Like Yuki, the heroine of *Shizuko's Daughter,* Mori too experienced the loss of her mother from suicide. Mori's own father, however, was more cruel, both emotionally and physically, than Yuki's surviving parent. Mori's father emotionally tormented her, beat her, and even threatened to kill her. Mori's step-mother is likewise more monstrous than the character depicted in *Shizuko's Daughter.* Not surprisingly, Mori prefers to board with strangers—friends of friends—rather than ingratiate herself with surviving relatives. Eventually, though, she reunites with her father and step-mother. That reunion, as John Burnham Schwartz noted in the *New York Times Book Review,* is "a painful, bitter meeting." Schwartz described *The Dream of Water* as an "affecting . . . memoir," and Richard Eder, writing in the *Los Angeles Times Book Review,* proclaimed Mori's book "chilly and fragile, and honest."

One Bird, Mori's third work, is a young-adult novel about Megumi, a Japanese teenager forced to fend for

herself after her mother leaves home and her father devotes himself increasingly to his mistress in another city.

Consequently, Megumi fears becoming a social outcast at her school. Her Christianity fails to bring any solace. Indeed, the death of a friend causes Megumi to reconsider the validity of a religion that perceives pain and anguish as positive spiritual experiences. However, a friendship with a veterinarian helps Megumi maintain her self esteem and achieve a greater understanding of the seemingly inscrutable world. Francine Prose wrote in the *New York Times Book Review* that *One Bird* is "gracefully written" and "full of small radiant scenes and glints of observation."

BIOGRAPHICAL/CRITICAL SOURCES:

PERIODICALS

Los Angeles Times Book Review, June 20, 1993, p. 3; January 5, 1995, p. 7.
New York Times Book Review, August 22, 1993, p. 19; February 5, 1995, pp. 13-14; November 12, 1995, p. 50.
Washington Post Book World, February 19, 1995, p. 8.*

* * *

MORRIS, (Margaret) Jean 1924-
(Kenneth O'Hara)

PERSONAL: Born January 15, 1924, in Sevenoaks, Kent, England; children: one daughter. *Education:* University of London, B.A. (with honors).

ADDRESSES: Home—Flat 1, 56 Pevensey Road, Eastbourne, East Sussex BN21 3HT, England.

CAREER: Writer.

MEMBER: PEN.

AWARDS, HONORS: Arts Council of Great Britain bursary award, 1955, for drama; *The Donkey's Crusade* was a runner-up for Great Britain's prestigious Whitbread writer's award in 1983.

WRITINGS:

NOVELS

Man and Two Gods, Cassell (London), 1953, Viking (New York), 1954.
Half of a Story, Cassell, 1957.
The Adversary, Cassell, 1959.
The Blackamoor's Urn, Cassell, 1962.
A Dream of Fair Children, Cassell, 1966.

NOVELS; AS KENNETH O'HARA

A View to a Death, Cassell, 1958.
Sleeping Dogs Lying, Cassell, 1960, Macmillan (New York), 1962.
Underhandover, Cassell, 1961, Macmillan, 1963.
Double Cross Purposes, Cassell, 1962.
Unknown Man, Seen in Profile, Gollancz (London), 1967.
The Birdcage, Gollancz, 1968, Random House (New York), 1969.
The Company of St. George, Gollancz, 1972.
The Delta Knife, Gollancz, 1976.
The Ghost of Thomas Penry, Gollancz, 1977.
The Searchers of the Dead, Gollancz, 1979.
Nightmares' Nest, Gollancz, 1982, Doubleday (Garden City, NY), 1983.
Death of a Moffy, Doubleday, 1987.

FOR CHILDREN

The Path of the Dragons, Hutchinson (London), 1980.
Twist of Eight (short stories), Chatto & Windus (London), 1981.
The Donkey's Crusade, Bodley Head (London), 1983.
The Song under the Water, Bodley Head, 1985.
The Troy Game, Bodley Head, 1987.
The Paper Canoe, Bodley Head, 1988.
A New Magic, Bodley Head, 1990.
A New Calling, Bodley Head, 1992.

PLAYS

The Spongees, published in *Eight Plays 1,* edited by Malcolm Stuart Fellows, Cassell, 1965.
Anne of Cleves, televised 1970, published in *The Six Wives of Henry VIII,* edited by J. C. Trewin, Elek (London), 1972.

Author of stage play *Island of Gulls,* 1956; author of numerous radio plays for the British Broadcasting Corp. (BBC), including *Safety of the City,* 1961, *The*

Heretic, 1962, *The Mislaid Cause,* 1964, and *Travelling in Winter,* 1971.

OTHER

(Translator, with Radost Pridham) *The Peach Thief and Other Bulgarian Stories,* Cassell, 1968.

The Monarchs of England, Charterhouse (New York), 1975.

ADAPTATIONS: The television play *Anne of Cleves* was adapted for the stage by Herbert E. Martin, Dramatic Publishing (Chicago), 1973.

SIDELIGHTS: Author of novels for both adults and young people, writer Jean Morris has received critical acclaim for her historical fantasy fiction for teen readers, which includes *The Path of the Dragons,* 1980, *Twist of Eight,* 1981, *The Donkey's Crusade,* 1983, and 1992's *A New Calling.* Critics' most favorable response concerns Morris's knowledgeable and sophisticated perspective on the historical epochs she brings to life in her fiction for young people, as well as her insistence that young readers engage themselves intellectually and come away from her work with a strengthened vocabulary. "Morris is always an entertaining writer, witty and quotable," Naomi Lewis noted in *Twentieth-Century Children's Writers,* adding that the writer's books "are a young (or older) connoisseur's discovery, and they gain more and more with each rereading. This can be said of very few works of junior fiction today."

In the short story collection *Twist of Eight,* Morris reworks several classic children's stories, throwing a new light on an old tale, and showing the action as it unfolds from a secondary character's point of view. In "The Waking Beauty," for example, the princess changes places with a young housemaid just prior to the arrival of the evil witch and her curse; bored with royal life, she elopes with the stable boy while her naive replacement must deal with the pricked finger that eventually nets her a handsome prince. *The Donkey's Crusade,* a 1983 runner-up for Great Britain's prestigious Whitbread writer's award, revolves around a novice monk's quest for a religious man who can aid in the capture of the holy city of Jerusalem during the Crusades of the thirteenth century. "The ever-changing scenery is vivid, the characters pulsate with personality," remarked author Geoffrey Trease in his review for the *Times Educational Supplement.* Declaring that Morris's style is

"like listening to some strange melody played on a wind instrument with effortless command," Trease concluded that *The Donkey's Crusade* "is a richly textured book, subtle in humour and humanity."

Morris's fiction for young people is characteristic in its integration of a subtle magic; in *A New Calling,* as well as its prequel, *A New Magic,* the world of magic takes center stage as an evil witch named Miss Maldrew joins forces with twentieth-century technology in an attempt to enslave the residents of Great Britain, and then the world—including the four children who try to thwart her. Spells, charms, anagrams, extrasensory perception (ESP), shifts of the time continuum, and shape changing—several of the children turn into foxes or cats during the course of the novel—keep the action moving as protagonists Aspasia, Gareth, Sophie, and Leo attempt to save the world from the clutches of the maleficent Maldrew.

Under the pseudonym Kenneth O'Hara, Morris has also built a reputation for well-crafted adult suspense novels replete with mystery, horror, and the supernatural, including *Unknown Man, Seen in Profile, The Birdcage,* and *Nightmares' Nest.* In a review of *Unknown Man, Seen in Profile,* a *Times Literary Supplement* contributor declared: "The telling is sophisticated and urbane, sometimes almost to the point of classy copywriting." Allen J. Hubin contended in the *New York Times Book Review* that *The Birdcage,* which he dubbed "a novel cinematic in expression" in its depiction of a doctor hunted by a psychotic former patient, "plumbs the crevices of a psychosis with delicate skill."

In addition to her work in the fiction genre, Morris has also written *The Monarchs of England,* an illustrated collection of biographies of kings and queens from Alfred the Great to Elizabeth II that, in the words of a *Publishers Weekly* reviewer, "transforms the history of the monarchy in to something extraordinary by taking the *long view.* . . . [Morris's] insistent questioning sweeps away cobwebs." She has also written the 1970 television play *Anne of Cleves,* as well as several scripts for BBC-Radio broadcast.

BIOGRAPHICAL/CRITICAL SOURCES:

BOOKS

Lewis, Naomi, "Jean Morris," in *Twentieth-Century Children's Writers,* St. James Press (Detroit), 1995.

PERIODICALS

New York Times Book Review, November 2, 1969, p. 20.

Observer, November 29, 1981, p. 27; December 11, 1983, p. 35; August 6, 1989, p. 40.

Publishers Weekly, June 2, 1975, p. 52.

School Librarian, September 1981, p. 238; May 1993, p. 73.

School Library Journal, August 1982, p. 103; March 1986, p. 178.

Times Educational Supplement, January 13, 1984, p. 42; June 5, 1987, p. 64; March 10, 1990, p. B14; January 11, 1991, p. 31; February 19, 1993, p. R6.

Times Literary Supplement, May 4, 1967; April 7, 1978, p. 368; December 31, 1982, p. 1448; November 29, 1985, p. 1357; April 3, 1987, p. 355.*

* * *

MORROW, Lance 1939-

PERSONAL: Born September, 1939, in Philadelphia, PA; son of Hugh (a journalist, speechwriter, and political advisor) and Elise (a journalist; maiden name, Vickers) Morrow; married first wife, Brooke (divorced); married second wife, Susan; children: (first marriage) James, Justin. *Education:* Harvard University, graduate (with honors), 1963.

ADDRESSES: Office—Time Magazine, Time & Life Bldg., Rockefeller Center, New York, NY 10020.

CAREER: As a teenager, worked summers as a Senate page in Washington, DC, and as a reporter-photographer with the *Danville News,* Danville, PA; *Washington Star,* Washington, DC, copyboy, 1958-59, reporter, 1963-65; *Time* Magazine, New York, NY, 1965—, currently senior writer and essayist.

AWARDS, HONORS: National Magazine Award, 1981, for essays appearing in *Time* Magazine.

WRITINGS:

The Chief: A Memoir of Fathers and Sons (autobiography), Random House (New York), 1984.
America: A Rediscovery, Holt (New York), 1987.
Fishing in the Tiber (essays), Holt (New York), 1988.

Safari: Experiencing the Wild (essays), photographs and notes by Neil Leifer, Reader's Digest Association (New York), 1992.
Heart: A Memoir, Warner Books (New York), 1995.

SIDELIGHTS: "A heart attack, like the prospect of the noose in the morning—or, more closely, like the rope itself that morning, tightening up hard and starting to cut the neck—concentrates the mind." Thus observes veteran *Time* magazine essayist Lance Morrow in his 1995 book *Heart: A Memoir,* a reflection on what forces in his life might have caused him to suffer not one, but two, severe heart attacks by the age of fifty-three.

The first attack occurred in 1976 while Morrow was in Kansas City, Missouri, covering the Republican National Convention for his employer. It was followed soon after by coronary bypass surgery. He was only thirty-six, but as he readily admits in his book, "I managed to pack a great deal of aging into a small container of birthdays. . . . I had the bad habits of two or three grown-ups: a journalist . . . with the trade's behaviors, smoking and drinking; like a chimney and like a fish."

Yet even then, in the midst of his fright and anger over being betrayed by his own body, Morrow sensed there was something more behind what had happened to him. He slowly began to regard his heart attack not as a natural consequence of his smoking and drinking or his genes (there was no history of early-onset heart disease in either side of his family) but as some sort of warning or punishment.

This feeling grew stronger in 1992 after Morrow suffered his second heart attack and again was forced to undergo coronary bypass surgery—despite the fact that he had given up his bad habits for the most part following his first attack. The experience triggered a period of intense self-examination, during which time his thoughts turned to the past, specifically to his family.

Morrow's father, Hugh, was a well-known journalist who served for more than twenty years as a speechwriter, political advisor, and confidant to Nelson Rockefeller, the former governor of New York and vice president during the administration of President Gerald Ford. His mother, Elise, was also a noted journalist. Theirs was a troubled marriage in which alcohol abuse, money problems, ambition, "revenge, recrimination, blind rage, [and] apocalyptic follies" figured prominently, recalls their son. Ab-

sorbed in themselves and their careers and often neglectful of their responsibilities as parents, they maintained a certain distance from their children that early on forced Lance and his brothers and sisters to function as "little adults."

It was Elise Morrow in particular, however, who emerged as the focus of her son's search for answers. A brilliant and passionate woman, she was subject to especially savage bouts of fury. All her life, she struggled to cope with her hatred of an overbearing father. (He had rejected both her and her mother and ordered them out of the house, and he eventually had his wife committed to a mental hospital.) In addition, she fiercely resented her second-class status in a society that refused to consider her an equal to men.

As Lance Morrow contemplated these bittersweet memories during his recovery, he came to realize that he, too, had been consumed with "blood-clotting" anger throughout his life. It was a rage that ran so deep he thought it might have been inherited from his mother and perhaps from his maternal grandfather as well. At any rate, he notes in his memoir, he began to think of the sensation in his chest as he was having a heart attack as "a glowing toxin of some kind. . . . Ever since the second heart attack, I have felt that I brought it on by harboring, inside myself, an accumulation of palpable rage that finally, after years, arose against the saner regime and tried to stop the heart, and killed the muscle, taking it as a kind of tribute, a sacrifice of myself to the rage god."

This image serves as the premise of *Heart:* that "the past (traumas, golden ages, irretrievable horrors and treasures) may become so transfixing that it ends by ruining and thwarting the present—occludes the present moment, which is alive, as a clot blocks the heart, and makes the muscle (the life) die." Morrow then takes an imaginative leap and applies the same metaphor to various situations he has observed around the world as a journalist. In places like Bosnia or the Middle East, he theorizes, it is a similar kind of obsessive rage and "clogging, enduring hatred" that have fueled decades (and sometimes centuries) of conflict between people who cannot set aside ancient grievances.

Writing in the *New York Times Book Review,* Richard Selzer described Morrow's memoir as "gripping" with its juxtaposition of the "rich experience of external life and the unseen wound within." As the reviewer concluded, "One closes [the book] giving thanks that the gifted, charismatic, humane and ut-terly likable Lance Morrow lived to write it." John Stone also admired the author's skill with words, declaring in the *Atlanta Journal-Constitution* that his prose "is sometimes so good it almost hurts." Commenting on *Heart* and its "searing" recollections in the *Chicago Tribune,* Chris Petrakos remarked that the memoir has "a wild courage . . . that is difficult to forget."

While *New York Times* critic Christopher Lehmann-Haupt praised Morrow's "beguiling fluency" in discussing his heart attacks and his family history, he felt that trying to draw parallels between one man's inner rage and subsequent health problems with events in the outside world is a bit of a stretch. "You begin to get the feeling that he is filling up space," noted Lehmann-Haupt. Steve Oney, whose assessment of *Heart* appeared in the *Los Angeles Times Book Review,* made a similar observation. He found Morrow's theory "interesting," but he questioned whether it truly stands up under closer scrutiny. "This is the sort of thinking a writer can take only so far, and sadly, Morrow doesn't know when to stop," declared Oney. All in all, though, he characterized the memoir as "by any measure a triumph, a transfusion of rich images and insights."

Sherwin B. Nuland, a surgeon and author of *How We Die: Reflections on Life's Final Chapter* (winner of the 1994 National Book Award), offered up his views on *Heart* in an article published in *Time.* Like the others, he found it "evocative" and "almost poetic" in its style and language, with the power to "draw the reader in from the start." By the end, said Nuland, "Morrow's luminous study of self . . . strikes an unexpectedly universal chord. . . . So the author deals not only with the inner torment of Lance Morrow but also with that of all of us."

BIOGRAPHICAL/CRITICAL SOURCES:

BOOKS

Morrow, Lance, *The Chief: A Memoir of Fathers and Sons,* Random House (New York), 1984.
Morrow, *Heart: A Memoir,* Warner Books (New York), 1995.

PERIODICALS

Atlanta Journal-Constitution, September 17, 1995, p. L8.
Chicago Tribune, September 22, 1995.

Los Angeles Times Book Review, September 17, 1995.

Newsweek, February 18, 1985, p. B81.

New York Times, September 18, 1995, p. C16.

New York Times Book Review, January 27, 1985, p. 3; October 8, 1995, p. 37.

Time, February 11, 1985, pp. 89-91; October 16, 1995.

—*Sketch by Deborah Gillan Straub*

* * *

MOTT, N(evill) F(rancis) 1905-1996
(Sir Nevill Mott)

OBITUARY NOTICE—See index for *CA* sketch: Born September 30, 1905, in Leeds, England; died following a brief illness, August 8, 1996, in Milton Keynes, England. Physicist, educator, and author. Mott was knighted for his contributions to the field of physics, which led to significant developments with computer memory, and such work also earned him the Nobel Prize at the age of seventy-two. Mott began more than forty years as an educator at Cambridge University's Gonville and Caius College in 1930. In 1933 he became a physics professor at the University of Bristol, taking on the directorship of the school's Henry Herbert Wills Physical Laboratories in 1948. During World War II, he served as a scientific adviser to the Anti-Aircraft Command in England. He conducted influential work with radio waves and explosives. He returned to Cambridge in 1954 as the Cavendish Professor of Physics at the Cavendish Laboratory; earlier he had studied under Lord Rutherford, who headed Cavendish at that time. In 1959 he became master of Gonville and Caius College. He became professor emeritus in 1971 and began working on his research pursuits with renewed enthusiasm. He shared the Nobel Prize for Physics in 1977 and was named Chevalier of the French National Order of Merit the same year. During his career, he also was chairperson and later president of Taylor and Francis publishers, chaired the education committee for the Royal Society, was president of the International Union of Physics, and was an educational adviser to Israel, Greece, and several African countries. In 1995 he was appointed to Companion of Honour. His writings included *An Outline of Wave Mechanics, The Beginnings of Solid State Physics, A Life in Science* (as Sir Nevill Mott), *Can Scientists Believe?,* and *Polaron Theory of High Temperature Superconductors.*

OBITUARIES AND OTHER SOURCES:

BOOKS

Who's Who in the World, 13th edition, Marquis, 1996.

PERIODICALS

New York Times, August 10, 1996, p. 30.

Times (London), August 12, 1996, p. 19.

* * *

MOTT, Sir Nevill
See MOTT, N(evill) F(rancis)

* * *

MQHAYI, S(amuel) E(dward) K(rune Loliwe) 1875-1945

PERSONAL: Born December 1, 1875, in Gqumahashe, Chumie Valley, Cape Province, South Africa; died July 29, 1945; son of Ziwani Mqhayi; married twice; second wife's name, Amy Cukudu. *Education:* Attended school in Evergreen, and later Lovedale, both in South Africa; took a teacher's training course.

CAREER: West Bank Location, East London, South Africa, teacher, beginning in 1897; *Izwi labantu* ("The Voice of the Bandu"), sub-editor, 1897-1900, 1905-09; taught in Centane, South Africa, 1900-06; Lovedale Press, proofreader, beginning in 1922.

WRITINGS:

Ityala lamawele (novella and short stories), Lovedale Press (South Africa), 1914, eighth edition, 1930, enlarged edition published as *Ityala lamawele* (novella, short stories, and poetry), 1931, English translation by August Collingwood, published as *The Case of the Twins,* 1966; also known as *The Lawsuit of the Twins.*

Ama gora e Mendi (poetry; title means "The Heroes of the Mendi"), Lovedale Press, c. 1920.

U-Sogqumahashe: Ishikhumbuzo sika Ntsikana (biography), Lovedale Press, 1921.

(Translator into Xhosa) William G. Dowsley, *Farming for Schools,* Nasionale Pers (South Africa), 1922.

U-bomi bom-fundisi John Knox Bokwe (biography; title means "The Life of the Reverend J. K. Bokwe"), Lovedale Press, 1925.

(With others) *Imihobe nemibongo yokufundwa ezikolweni* (poetry; title means "Lullabies to Be Studied in School"), Sheldon Press (London), 1927.

U-Don Jadu (novel), Lovedale Press, 1929.

(Translator into Xhosa) E. S. Smith, *Aggrey of Africa,* Sheldon Press, 1935.

U-Mhlekazi u-Hintsa: um-bongo ewasiya izibongo zamadoda ngomnyaka we (poetry), Lovedale Press, 1937; also known as *Hintsa the Great.*

U-Mqhayi wase-Ntab'ozuko (autobiography; title means "Mqhayi from the Mountain of Glory"), Lovedale Press, 1939.

I-Nzuzo (poetry; title means "Reward"), Witwatersrand University Press, 1943; also known as *Gain.*

(Translator into Xhosa) G. C. Hobson and S. B. Hobson, *Mees van die Kalahari,* Lovedale Press, 1945.

Mqhayi in Translation (abridged autobiography and translation), edited by Patricia E. Scott, Rhodes University, 1976.

Also author of *U-Samson* (novel), 1907; *I-Bandla laBantu* (poetry; title means "The Church of the People"), 1923; *Isikumbuzo zomPolofiti u-Ntsikana* (biography), 1926. Work represented in anthologies, including *Imibengo* (title means "Tidbits"), edited by William Govan Bennie, Lovedale Press, 1939; *Zemk' inkomo magwale ndini* (title means "Away Go the Cattle, You Cowards"), edited by Walter B. Rubusana, Butler and Tanner (London), 1906.

OTHER

Editor of John Tengo Jabavu's *Imvo zabantsundu.* Also author of lyric titled "Nkosi sikelel' Afrika" (African National Anthem). Contributor to periodicals. Editor of *Iim Vo zaba Ntsundu,* 1920-22.

Mqhayi's works have been translated into German.

SIDELIGHTS: S. E. K. Mqhayi is recognized as a leading Xhosa-language poet and prose writer. He is remembered primarily for his *izibongo,* traditional African lyric poems that gained him the title *imbongi yesizwe,* equivalent to poet laureate of his people. Hailed by Albert S. Gerard in *Four African Literatures* as "perhaps the last of the great tribal bards" for his contributions to Xhosa poetry, Mqhayi is also credited with introducing the Western genre of prose fiction into Xhosa literature in the early twentieth century. According to R. H. W. Shepherd: "His contributions to Xhosa literature . . . were outstanding in quality, and by them and in other ways he helped in no small measure to stabilize and purify the Xhosa language."

Mqhayi was born in Gqumahashe (or Gqamahashe) in the Victoria East District of Cape Province. He attended school in Evergreen from 1882 to 1885, when his family moved to Centane in the Transkei, where Mqhayi's great-uncle Ngonzana (or Nzazana) was a local chieftain. Mqhayi took great interest in the official activities he witnessed at his uncle's judicial court, the "Great Place," and later wrote: "I thank my father for taking me to Centane, for it was the means of my getting an insight into the national life of my people." After completing a teaching course, Mqhayi worked as an educator and journalist for several years. During that time he contributed to influential Xhosa newspapers and periodicals, including *Izwi labantu* and *Iim Vo zaba Ntsundu,* which he edited from 1920 to 1922. He retired from education in 1922 to assist in programs designed to standardize Xhosa grammar and syntax and the Xhosa-language Bible. In 1925 Mqhayi settled near King William's Town in a hilltop retreat named Ntab'ozuko, or "Mount of Glory." From there he traveled widely among the Xhosa-speaking peoples, who acknowledged him as the "poet of the race." He died in 1945.

One of Mqhayi's earliest prose works, the novel *U-Samson* (1907), presents an adaptation of the biblical story of Samson, imaginatively rendered to critique South African society in the era following the Anglo-Boer War. However, another biblically inspired work, the novella *Ityala lamawele,* has received considerably more critical attention. Published in 1914, though written several years earlier, *Ityala lamawele* is based on the biblical story of Tamar's sons in Genesis 38:27-29 as well as on Mqhayi's memories of Ngonzana's law court at the "Great Place" in Centane. The novella relates the tale of twins whose dispute over their birth order—and thus, inheritance rights—is decided through the native justice system. According to Gerard in *Four African Literatures,* "it was Mqhayi's aim [in *Ityala lamawele*] to vindicate traditional native justice threatened by the colonial

administration." Another major prose work is the utopian novel *U-Don Jadu* (1929), which describes a culturally and racially integrated Christian society in twentieth-century South Africa that combines the best of European and African cultures.

While Mqhayi's prose works are highly regarded by critics, it is as a poet that he is chiefly remembered. Working in the oral tradition of tribal court bards, he composed many *izibongo,* traditional praise poems that proclaim the accomplishments of chiefs and other public figures, celebrate cultural holidays, or comment on current events. These poems are not purely laudatory; A. C. Jordan has explained that tribal bards "had not only to praise the chief but also to criticize him." Mqhayi has been noted for treating modern themes in this ancient traditional form: some of his *izibongo* discuss British colonialism in Africa, and several are addressed to British royalty and administrators, albeit often ironically. Late in his career, Mqhayi experimented with European forms unfamiliar in Xhosa poetry, such as the sonnet and the heroic couplet, but most critics have expressed disappointment with these attempts to force Xhosa into foreign forms, especially noting the flatness of his rhymes. Most critics concur with Wandile Kuse that "Mqhayi was at his best when he wrote or recited poetry in the oral tradition."

While a lack of translations has hampered Mqhayi's international reputation, his work is beloved and renowned among Xhosa-speaking peoples and has received high praise from other South African writers. Jordan attested to Mqhayi's literary achievement when, in an obituary tribute, he wrote: "Mqhayi takes the highest place in Xhosa literature. He has done more than any other writer to enrich Xhosa. In his hands it receives a fresh impress, and he has revealed all its possibilities as a powerful medium of expression of human emotion."

BIOGRAPHICAL/CRITICAL SOURCES:

BOOKS

Gerard, Albert S., *Four African Literatures,* University of California Press, 1971.
Westermann, Diedrich, *Afrikaner erzahler ihr Leben,* Essen, 1938.

PERIODICALS

South African Outlook, Volume 75, 1945.*

MUIR, Kenneth (Arthur) 1907-1996

OBITUARY NOTICE—See index for *CA* sketch: Born May 5, 1907, in London, England; died September 30, 1996, in Birkenhead, England. Scholar, critic, and author. Muir was a Shakespearean scholar and was recognized as a leading authority on the subject. He gained fame in academic circles in the early 1950s when he edited new editions of *Macbeth* and *King Lear,* both of which were published in the United States. Muir was also a critic and author, with his favorite subject being Shakespeare's imagery. In 1937, he co-authored *The Voyage to Illyria* with Sean O'Loughlin, and the book became an early bench mark for the study of Shakespeare's imagery. Muir was educated at Epsom College and Oxford University's St. Edmund Hall and went on to teach at St. John's College in York and Leeds University. His later works include translations with A. L. Mackenzie of Calderon's *La Cisma de Inglaterra* (1990) and *Jealousy the Worst Monster* (1993).

OBITUARIES AND OTHER SOURCES:

BOOKS

Who's Who, 146th edition, St. Martin's, 1994.

PERIODICALS

New York Times, October 7, 1996, p. B13.

* * *

MUNOZ MARIN, (Jose) Luis (Alberto) 1898-1980

PERSONAL: Born February 18, 1898, in San Juan, Puerto Rico; died of a heart attack, April 30, 1980, in San Juan, Puerto Rico; son of Luis Munoz Rivera and Amalia Marin; married Muna Lee (divorced); married Ines Maria Mendoza de Palacios; children: (first marriage) Luis, Muna (deceased); (second marriage) Victoria, Viviana. *Education:* Attended Georgetown University and Georgetown Law School.

CAREER: Journalist, orator, essayist, poet, and politician. Secretary to resident commissioner of Puerto Rico in Washington, DC, 1916-18; active in Pan American Labor movement; served in secretariat of Pan American Union during Havana Conference, 1929; elected to Puerto Rico Senate as a Liberal, 1932, and as the founder of the Popular Democratic

Party, 1940 and 1944; president of Senate, 1941; economic commissioner of Puerto Rico in United States; chairperson of commission on political status of Puerto Rico, 1946; elected first governor of Puerto Rico, 1949-65.

WRITINGS:

(Contributor) Felix Ojeda Reyes, editor, *Yo soy aquel que ayer no mas decia; retrato de un colonizado,* Ediciones Puerto Rico (Rio Piedras, Puerto Rico), 1972.

Luis Munoz Marin: Pensamiento politico, economico, social y cultural, segun exprasado en los discursos oficiales, Corporacion de Servicios Bibliotecarios (Rio Piedras), 1973.

Mensajes al Pueblo Puertorriqueno: Pronunciados ante las Cameras Legislativas, 1949-1964, Inter American University Press, 1980.

Memorias: Autobiografia publica, 1898-1940, Universidad Interamericana de Puerto Rico, 1982.

Historia del Partido Popular Democratico, El Batey (San Juan, Puerto Rico), 1984.

Celebracion del 88vo. aniversario del natalicio de Don Luis Munoz Marin, Departamento de Instruccion Publica, Estado Libra Asociado de Puerto Rico, 1986.

Also author of *Borrones* and *Madre Haraposa,* 1917. Contributor to *American Mercury, Nation, New Republic, New York Herald Tribune,* and the *Baltimore Sun.* Editor and publisher of *La Democracia,* 1926-27. Editor of *El Imparcial, El Batey,* 1946, and *Revista de Indias,* a journal about Pan American culture.

SIDELIGHTS: Government official, translator, and author, Luis Munoz Marin was the first elected governor of Puerto Rico. Architect of the "Operation Bootstrap" program that encouraged the establishment of U.S. corporations in Puerto Rico, Munoz Marin witnessed improved economic conditions in his country. Munoz Marin's father, Luis Munoz Rivera, had also been active in politics and had worked for the country's autonomy from Spain; after the Spanish-American War of 1898 granting Puerto Rico to the United States, he held a non-voting seat in the U.S. House of Representatives. Munoz Marin accompanied his father to Washington, D.C., and studied briefly at Georgetown University and Law School. Upon his father's death in 1916, Munoz Marin left school and began a literary career. During the 1920s, he lived in New York City and contributed articles to several periodicals. According to Manuel Suarez in a *New York Times'* obituary: "He had the mind of a politician and the soul of a poet. . . . He would write essays on United States foreign policy one day and articles on the Broadway theatre the next." When he returned to Puerto Rico, he favored socialism and Puerto Rican independence. As founder of the Popular Democratic Party, he assisted Puerto Rico in becoming a commonwealth in 1952 but campaigned against statehood during the 1970s. As Suarez observed, Munoz Marin "firmly believed that only commonwealth status safeguarded the island's Hispanic culture while simultaneously giving it the security and economic base it required."

BIOGRAPHICAL/CRITICAL SOURCES:

BOOKS

Aitken, Thomas, *Poet in the Fortress: The Story of Luis Munoz Marin,* New American Library, 1964.

Alexander, Robert J., editor, *Biographical Dictionary of Latin American and Caribbean Political Leaders,* Greenwood Press, 1988.

Bernier-Grand, Carmen T., *Poet and Politician of Puerto Rico: Don Luis Munoz Marin,* Orchard Books, 1995.

Rosario Natal, Carmelo, *Luis Munoz Marin y la independencia de Puerto Rico, 1907-1946,* Producciones Historicas, 1994.

PERIODICALS

Chicago Tribune, May 1, 1980.
Newsweek, May 12, 1980.
New York Times, May 1, 1980.
Time, May 12, 1980.
Times (London), May 2, 1980.
Washington Post, May 1, 1980.*

N-O

NATANSON, Maurice (Alexander) 1924-1996

OBITUARY NOTICE—See index for *CA* sketch: Born November 26, 1924, in New York, NY; died of prostate cancer, August 16, 1996, in Santa Cruz, CA. Philosopher, educator, and author. Schooled in philosophy and social science, Natanson worked to familiarize American students with the renown philosophers Edmund Husserl and Jean-Paul Sartre. He accomplished this work by writing definitive books, such as the National Book Award-winning *Edmund Husserl: Philosopher of Infinite Tasks,* and by teaching at universities throughout the United States. Natanson's early teaching posts took him to the University of Nebraska, New School for Social Research, University of Houston, University of North Carolina at Chapel Hill, and the University of California at Santa Cruz. In 1976, he began nearly twenty years at Yale University as a professor of philosophy. He retired in 1995. During his career, he also was a guest professor of sociology at the University of Konstanz in West Germany. He was a prolific author penning works such as *Literature, Philosophy, and the Social Sciences, The Journeying Self: A Study of Philosophy and Social Role,* and *Anonymity: A Study in the Philosophy of Alfred Schutz.* He was the editor of works, including *Phenomenology and Social Reality,* and was a member of the editorial advisory board of *Phenomenology and Human Sciences.* Princeton University Press will publish his final work, *The Erotic Bird: Phenomenology in Literature.*

OBITUARIES AND OTHER SOURCES:

BOOKS

Who's Who in America, 51st edition, Marquis, 1996.

PERIODICALS

New York Times, August 20, 1996, p. B6.

* * *

NESBITT, John D. 1948-

PERSONAL: Born December 14, 1948, in Lompoc, CA; son of A. D. (a farmer, rancher, and hired hand) and Elizabeth Margaret (an artist and writer; maiden name, Schneider) Nesbitt; married Laura Stokes, September 17, 1977 (marriage ended, February 14, 1983); married Liesa Jensen, January 4, 1988 (marriage ended, August 3, 1990); married Rocio Perez, July 21, 1995. *Ethnicity:* "Caucasian." *Education:* University of California, Los Angeles, B.A. (magna cum laude), 1971; University of California, Davis, M.A., 1974, Ph.D., 1980; attended University of Wyoming, 1988; Instituto de Filologia Hispanica, Saltillo, Mexico, Diploma in Spanish Philology, 1994. *Avocational interests:* Hunting, camping, gardening.

ADDRESSES: Home—P.O. Box 973, Torrington, WY 82240. *Office*—Eastern Wyoming College, 3200 West C St., Torrington, WY 82240.

CAREER: Eastern Wyoming College, Torrington, instructor in English and Spanish, 1981—.

MEMBER: Western Writers of America, Western Literature Association, Wyoming Writers, Phi Beta Kappa.

AWARDS, HONORS: Fellow of Wyoming Council for the Humanities and Wyoming Council on the Arts, both 1988; best short story award from *West Wind Review,* 1989; first place fiction awards from Wyoming Writers competitions, 1994 and 1995.

WRITINGS:

Adventures of the Ramrod Rider (stories), privately printed, 1991.

One-Eyed Cowboy Wild (novel), Walker and Co. (New York City), 1994.

Twin Rivers (novel), Walker and Co., 1995.

One Foot in the Stirrup: Western Stories, privately printed, 1995.

(Editor) *Wyoming Journeys* (poetry chapbook), WyoPoets, 1995.

I'll Tell You What: Fiction with Voice (stories), privately printed, 1996.

Wild Rose of Ruby Canyon (novel), Walker and Co., in press.

Black Diamond Rendezvous (novel), Leisure Books (New York City), in press.

Work represented in anthologies, including *Critical Essays on the Western American Novel,* G. K. Hall (Boston, MA), 1980; *VeriTales: Note of Hope,* Fall Creek Press (Fall Creek, OR), 1993; and *New Trails,* edited by John Jakes and Martin H. Greenberg, Doubleday (New York City), 1994. Contributor of dozens of stories, poems, articles, and reviews to periodicals, including *Lines in the Sand, New Trails, American Literary Review, Western American Literature, South Dakota Review,* and *Wyoming Horizons.* Editor, *Westering,* 1986-92.

WORK IN PROGRESS: Contemporary and Old West fiction; research on western American fiction.

SIDELIGHTS: John D. Nesbitt told *CA:* "I grew up in a rural setting, in northern California, and I spent a large portion of my first thirty-three years working outdoors—at farm and ranch work, construction, landscaping, and gardening. I also developed a strong interest in camping and hunting. Since coming to Wyoming in 1981, I have continued my interests in hunting, camping, hiking, and working outdoors. I live in the plains country of Wyoming, where I do a variety of work on my own country place. I have a few animals of my own, and I have daily opportunities for observing wild plant and animal life.

"I write with the hope that other people will be interested in life as I see it. I write about human na-

ture, human relationships, the Western outdoors, and the interplay between people and the environment. Most of my work is about people in the places where they live. Place is important in the lives of my characters, no doubt because it is important to me. I hope to communicate the importance of understanding the natural world and of not losing touch with it.

"I have done academic writing, and I expect to do more. I do not think that academic training or academic employment must be a detriment to one's creativity, but there are certainly competing demands on one's time and energy. I have heard many writers make snide remarks about academics, and I think that's too bad. It doesn't hurt to have had disciplined training and to have learned something in a field. I did have a professor in graduate school who told me that I would never get anywhere by studying Western American literature. I suppose he would have even less generous things to say about my having become a writer of traditional westerns, but I don't judge academic endeavor on the basis of people like him. Formal education, as a whole, is much greater than some of its parts.

"As a generalist in British and American literature, I have read widely. I like just about all the major fiction writers from Fielding onward, and it would be difficult to cite major influences. If pressed, I would say I feel the strongest affinities with Charles Dickens, A. B. Guthrie, Jr., and Alice Munro. I also feel some sort of artistic affinity with such songwriters and singers as Woody Guthrie, Merle Haggard, and Ian Tyson. Merely by mentioning these half-dozen, I feel I am slighting the hundreds of other writers and singers whose work has inspired me along the way."

* * *

NEWTON, Candelas 1948-

PERSONAL: Born November 13, 1948, in Santander, Spain; naturalized U.S. citizen; daughter of Jose (in business) and Isabel (a homemaker; maiden name, Gala) Sanchez; married Richard L. Newton, July, 1974; children: Isabel Gala, Ryan Antonia. *Education:* Official School of Languages of Madrid, Certificate in French, 1968; Conservatorio Vizcaino de Musica Juan Crisostomo de Arriaga, Piano Teaching Credential, 1968; University of Salamanca, B.A.,

1972; University of Pittsburgh, M.A., 1978, Ph.D., 1980. *Politics:* Democrat. *Religion:* Roman Catholic. *Avocational interests:* Playing the piano, opera, physical fitness, Mahler, cross-stitch, dogs and cats.

ADDRESSES: Home—470 Heritage Dr., Lewisville, NC 27023. *Office*—Department of Romance Languages, Wake Forest University, 7566 Reynolda Station, Winston-Salem, NC 27109; fax 910-759-4432. *E-mail*—newtonc@wfu.edu.

CAREER: Teacher at a grammar school in London, England, 1972-73; Carlow College, Pittsburgh, PA, lecturer, 1973-74; Wake Forest University, Winston-Salem, NC, instructor, 1978-81, visiting assistant professor, 1981-82, assistant professor, 1982-85, associate professor, 1985-91, professor of Spanish, 1991—, chairperson, Department of Romance Languages, 1996—, director of Salamanca Semester Abroad Program, 1980, 1991, director of Wake Forest-Universidad de Los Andes exchange scholarship, 1981—, member of university judicial council, 1990-95; chairperson, Subcommittee on Technology and the Teaching of Foreign Languages, 1996—. Volunteer translator, Winston-Salem Police Department and Baptist Hospital.

MEMBER: Asociacion Internacional de Hispanistas, Modern Language Association of America, American Association of Teachers of Spanish and Portuguese, American Association of University Professors, Asociacion de Letras femeninas, Asociacion de Licenciados y Doctores Espanoles en los Estados Unidos, Philological Association of the Carolinas (member of executive committee; president, 1988-89), South Atlantic Modern Language Association, Northeast Modern Language Association, Midwest Modern Language Association, Wake Forest Humanities Club (vice president, 1990-91; president, 1991-92).

AWARDS, HONORS: Exchange scholar, University of Colorado, Boulder, 1972; grant from National Endowment for the Humanities, 1983; travel grants for Spain, Archie Fund, 1987, 1989.

WRITINGS:

Lorca: Libro de poemas o las aventuras de una busqueda, Ediciones Universidad de Salamanca (Salamanca, Spain), 1986.

Lorca: Una escritura en trance; Libro de poemas y Divan del Tamarit (monograph), John Benjamins (Philadelphia, PA), 1992.

Understanding Federico Garcia Lorca, University of South Carolina Press (Columbia, SC), 1995.

Translator of English-language education books into Spanish. Contributor of articles and reviews to academic journals, including *Garcia Lorca Review, Foreign Language Journal, Revista Hispanica Moderna, Revista de estudios hispanicos, Hispanic Journal,* and *Letras peninsulares.* Member of editorial board, *Critica Hispanica,* 1991.

WORK IN PROGRESS: A book on twentieth-century women poets from Spain.

* * *

NISBET, Robert A(lexander) 1913-1996

OBITUARY NOTICE—See index for *CA* sketch: Born September 30, 1913, in Los Angeles, CA; died of prostate cancer, September 9, 1996, in Washington, DC. Sociologist, educator, historian, and author. A noted sociologist, Nisbet was a conservative thinker whose ideas appeared in more than a dozen books and received much debate and acceptance. Nisbet studied at the University of California at Berkeley before service in the U.S. Army during World War II. He began his teaching career at Berkeley in 1939, followed by stints at the University of California at Riverside as professor of sociology and dean of the College of Letters and Science, and at the University of Arizona. In 1974, Nisbet became the Albert Schweitzer Professor of Humanities until achieving emeritus status in 1978. He served as resident scholar at the American Enterprise Institute from 1978 until 1980, turning to adjunct scholar status from 1980 until 1986. He also worked in visiting capacities at schools such as University of Bologna in Italy and the University of Pennsylvania, and for organizations such as the American Psychiatric Association. Nisbet often lectured on and wrote about the history of ideas. His books include *The Quest for Community, Roosevelt and Stalin, History of the Idea of Progress, Prejudices: A Philosophical Dictionary, The Present Age, Conservatism: Dream and Reality, The Making of Modern Society,* and *Teachers and Scholars.*

OBITUARIES AND OTHER SOURCES:

PERIODICALS

Chicago Tribune, September 13, 1996, section 3, p. 11.

Los Angeles Times, September 13, 1996, p. A30.
New York Times, September 12, 1996, p. D19.
Washington Post, September 11, 1996, p. C5.

OTHER

Complete Marquis Who's Who on CD-ROM, Marquis Who's Who/Reed Reference Electronic Publishing, 1996.

* * *

NJOROGE, J(ames) K(ingangi) 1933-

PERSONAL: Born May 18, 1933, in Kangemi, Kenya; son of John Kingagi and Phylis (Wanjiru) Thiongo; married Lizzie Nyambura, January 3, 1959; children: John, Jane, Mary, Patrick. *Education:* Makerere University College, B.A., 1958; Royal College, Nairobi, diploma in education, 1962, and public administration.

ADDRESSES: Home—P.O. Box 48525, Nairobi, Kenya.

CAREER: Fiction writer and poet, 1966—. Associated with Njiris High School, 1958-61; Kenyan Government, assistant secretary, 1961, member of the ministry of state for constitutional affairs and administration, 1962, under secretary, ministry of commerce and industry, 1962, permanent secretary, ministries of commerce and industry, education, information, and defense, 1963-70; East African Rys. Corporation, Nairobi, resident director; Industrial Development Corporation, vice chair, 1963-64. Member of finance and general purpose committees, University of Dar-es-Salaam, 1965-70; member of the board of directors, Pan-Foods Co., Kenya.

MEMBER: Kenya National Union of Teachers (treasurer and general secretary, 1958-61), Table Tennis and Gardening Club.

WRITINGS:

FICTION

Tit for Tat and Other Stories, East African Publishing House, 1966.
The Proud Ostrich and Other Stories, East African Publishing House, 1967.

Pestle and Mortar, East African Publishing House, 1969.

POETRY

Spectrum: A Book of Poems, Equatorial Publishers, 1970.*

* * *

NORMAN, Charles 1904-1996

OBITUARY NOTICE—See index for *CA* sketch: Born May 9, 1904, in Russia; immigrated to the U.S., 1910; naturalized U.S. citizen, 1924; died September 10, 1996, in Newport, RI. Journalist, biographer, poet, and author. Norman gained recognition as a biographer and prolific author of children's books; most notably, the *Mr. Upstairs and Mr. Downstairs* series, chronicling the exploits of the Jonquil family. Born in Russia, Norman and his family moved to the United States when he was a young boy. In 1924 Norman's first compilation of poetry was published; *The Far Harbor: A Sea Narrative* was based on his experiences aboard a freighter bound for South America. During the 1920s, he became a reporter for the *Paris Times* and later worked for the North American Newspaper Alliance, United Press International, Associated Press, and newspaper *P.M.* During World War II he produced two books of poetry, *A Soldier's Diary* and *The Savage Century,* both based on his wartime experiences in the U.S. Army. Norman also wrote many biographies including *The Magic Maker: E. E. Cummings, So Worthy a Friend: William Shakespeare,* and *Ezra Pound. A Study in Mauve, To a Different Drum: The Story of Henry David Thoreau,* and *The Hornbeam Tree and Other Poems* are among his other works.

OBITUARIES AND OTHER SOURCES:

BOOKS

Dictionary of Literary Biography, Volume 111: *American Literary Biographers,* Gale, 1991.

PERIODICALS

New York Times, September 14, 1996, p. 10.
Washington Post, September 17, 1996, p. D5.

NOUWEN, Henri J(osef Machiel) 1932-1996

OBITUARY NOTICE—See index for *CA* sketch: Born January 24, 1932, in Nijerk, Netherlands; came to the United States in 1964; died of a heart attack, September 21, 1996, in the Netherlands. Theologian, educator, psychologist, and author. Nouwen was a Dutch priest, ordained in 1957, who served at Roman Catholic churches in the Netherlands and the United States. In 1966 he turned his attention to education at the University of Notre Dame as a visiting professor of psychology. Posts at the University of Utrecht and Catholic Theological Institute followed. He joined Yale in 1971 as an associate professor, becoming professor of pastoral theology from 1977 until 1981. In 1983 he worked with the Harvard Divinity School as Lenz lecturer, and until 1985 he also served as professor of theology. In 1986, he began to serve as priest-in-residence for the L'Arche Daybreak Community, a residence for the mentally impaired in Toronto, Ontario, Canada. Nouwen authored a number of books, including *Out of Solitude: Three Meditations on the Christian Life, The Living Reminder: Service and Prayer in Memory of Jesus Christ, Clowning in Rome: Reflection on Solitude, Celibacy, and Contemplation, Cry for Mercy, Lifesigns,* and *Seeds of Hope.*

OBITUARIES AND OTHER SOURCES:

BOOKS

Writers Directory, St. James Press, 1994.

PERIODICALS

Los Angeles Times, September 26, 1996, p. A20.
New York Times, September 23, 1996, p. B7.

* * *

NUYTTEN, Bruno 1945-

PERSONAL: Born August 28, 1945, in Paris, France; son of a physician and a pharmacist; children: (with Isabelle Adjani) Barnabe Nuytten. *Education:* Attended Institut des Hautes Etudes Cinematographiques, Paris, France, and Institut des Arts du Spectacle, Brussels, Belgium.

ADDRESSES: Office—c/o French Film Office, 745 Fifth Ave., New York, NY 10151.

CAREER: Cinematographer, director, and screenwriter. Cinematographer for films, including *Les Valseuses* (also known as *The Waltzers* and *Going Places*), Societe Nouvelle Productions/Almi Cinema V/Interama, 1973; *L'Asassin musicien* (also known as *The Musician Killer*), Sunchild Productions, 1975; *India Song,* Artificial Eye, 1975; *La Meilleure Facon de marcher* (also known as *The Best Way to Walk*), AMLF/Oppidan, 1975; *Souvenirs d'en France* (also known as *French Provincial* and *Inside Memories of France*), AMLF, 1975; *Barocco,* Films la Boetie, 1976; *Le Camion* (also known as *The Truck*), Cinema 9/Films Moliere, 1977; *L'Exercice du pouvoir,* Camera One, 1977; *Mon Coeur est rouge* (also known as *My Heart Is Red*), Films Moliere, 1977; *Les Soeurs Bronte* (also known as *The Bronte Sisters*), Gaumont International/Roissy, 1978; *French Postcards,* Paramount, 1979; *Zoo-Zero,* Panoceanic Films, 1979; *The Best Way,* Filmoblic, 1980; *Brubaker,* Twentieth Century-Fox, 1980; *La Tortue sur le dos* (also known as *Like a Turtle on Its Back*), World Marketing Films/New Line Cinema, 1981; *Garde a vue* (also known as *The Inquisitor*), Gala Film Distributors, 1981; *Possession,* New Realm Distributors/Limelight International, 1981; *Hotel des Ameriques* (also known as *Hotel of the Americans*), Parafrance, 1982; *Tchao Pantin* (also known as *So Long, Stooge*), Roissy/AMLF/European Classics, 1983; *La Vie est un roman* (also known as *Life Is a Bed of Roses*), Spectrafilm, 1983; *Les Enfants* (also known as *The Children*), Productions Berthemont, 1984; *Fort Saganne,* Roissy/AAA, 1984; *La Pirate* (also known as *The Pirate*), AMLF/Films du Scorpion, 1984; *Detective,* Spectrafilm/Union Generale Cinematographique, 1985; *Jean de Florette,* AMLF/Orion Classics, 1986; *Manon des sources* (also known as *Manon of the Spring*), Orion Classics/Cannon Releasing/AMLF/Roissy, 1986; and *Double Messieurs* (also known as *Double Gentlemen*), Mallia Films/Saltzgeber/Mutual Reception, 1986; also cinematographer for *Invitation au voyage,* c. 1982. Director of films, including *Camille Claudel,* Pathe Releasing/Gaumont/Orion Classics/Roissy, 1988; and *Albert Souffre* (also known as *Albert Suffers*), AMLF, 1992. Camera operator, first assistant, *Nathalie Granger,* French Consulate/Moullet et Compagnie, 1972.

AWARDS, HONORS: Prize for artistic contribution, Cannes Film Festival, 1982, for *Invitation au voyage;* Academy Award nomination for best foreign-language film, 1989, for *Camille Claudel;* awards for best cinematography, British Academy of Film and Television Arts, for *Jean de Florette* and *Manon des sources;* Cesar awards, for *Tchao Pantin, La*

Meilleure Facon de marcher, and *Barocco;* Cesar Award nominations, for *Les Soeurs Bronte, Possession, La Vie est un roman, Fort Saganne, Jean de Florette,* and *Manon des sources.*

WRITINGS:

SCREENPLAYS

(With Jean-Francois Stevenin and Jackie Berroyer) *Double Messieurs* (also known as *Double Gentlemen*), Mallia Films/Saltzgeber/Mutual Reception, 1986.

(With Marilyn Goldin) *Camille Claudel* (adaptation of the book *Camille Claudel, 1864-1943,* by Reine-Marie Paris, 1984), Pathe Releasing/Gaumont/Orion Classics/Roissy, 1988.

Albert Souffre (also known as *Albert Suffers*), AMLF, 1992.

WORK IN PROGRESS: A novel.

SIDELIGHTS: A highly acclaimed cinematographer, Bruno Nuytten has been praised for his use of compelling images and a style that captures visual contrasts, shadows, and movement of light. Nuytten has served as director of photography on more than thirty feature films, including the critically acclaimed and internationally popular *Jean de Florette* and its sequel *Manon of the Spring.* His work as a cinematographer is reflected in his screenplay for *Camille Claudel,* co-written with Marilyn Goldin, which relies heavily on images to convey the narrative. Nuytten also made his directorial debut with *Camille Claudel,* which was nominated for an Oscar in the best foreign-language film category.

Camille Claudel tells the true story of the French sculptress who struggled in the shadow of her renowned and volatile lover, Auguste Rodin, and ultimately went mad. The film documents Claudel's passion for art and her struggle to assert herself as an artist against prevailing prejudices and the active opposition of the men in her life: Rodin, her father, and her brother, the poet Paul Claudel. Hal Hinson, in a laudatory review in the *Washington Post,* praised the film's "tempestuous spirit," and continued: This is a movie of miraculous moments; even when you're uncertain about the thematic point of [a] scene, you can feel the pulses of the actors. . . The truly rare and great accomplishment of the film . . . is that it manages to express the impulses that drive artists in their work." Kevin Thomas, writing in the *Los Angeles Times,* described *Camille Claudel* as "a romantic tragedy in the grand manner, accompanied by a stormy score and unfolding amid settings that are period perfect." *Chicago Tribune* reviewer Dave Kehr, however, found the film overly melodramatic, and commented of Nuytten's visual style: "The movie takes on a painterly, studied look that contradicts its subject—extreme emotions, creative agony—at the most fundamental level, that of form."

BIOGRAPHICAL/CRITICAL SOURCES:

PERIODICALS

Chicago Tribune, March 9, 1990, p. B32.
Los Angeles Times, December 21, 1989, pp. F11, 13.
Maclean's, February 5, 1990, p. 61.
Newsweek, March 12, 1990, pp. 86-87.
Washington Post, December 21, 1989, pp. D1, 16.*

*　　*　　*

ODEKU, Emmanuel Latunde 1927-

PERSONAL: Born June 29, 1927, in Awe, Nigeria; son of Daniel Lapido and Regina Eyinade Folowiyo (Adensina) Odeku; married Katherine Jille Adcock, 1971; children: Lenora Folawiyo, Peter Glenn, Alan John Lapapo. *Education:* Howard University, B.S. (summa cum laude), 1950, M.D., 1954; University of Michigan, proficiency certificate neurosurgery, 1960.

ADDRESSES: Home—University of Ibadan Campus, Ibadan, Nigeria.

CAREER: Howard University College of Medicine, Washington, DC, instructor in neuroanatomy and neurosurgery, 1961-62; University of Ibadan, Ibadan, Nigeria, member of faculty, 1962—, professor of neurosurgery and dean of the Faculty of Medicine, 1968-70, head of surgery department, 1969-71. University College Hospital, Ibadan, member of board of management, 1968-70. Western State, Nigeria, member of medical advisory board, 1970—.

MEMBER: Kappa Pi.

AWARDS, HONORS: Fellow A.C.S., Association of Surgeons of West Africa, International College of Surgeons, Medical Council in Surgery, Nigeria.

WRITINGS:

POETRY

Twilight: Out of the Night, Abiodun Printing Works (Idaban, Nigeria), 1964.

Also author of *Whispers from the Night,* 1969.*

* * *

OGALI, Ogali A(gu) 1931-

PERSONAL: Born in 1931, in Umuafia, Iboland, Nigeria.

CAREER: Playwright and fiction writer, 1956—. Worked at United Africa Company, Ltd., and Nigerian Railway Corporation.

WRITINGS:

PLAYS

Veronica, My Daughter, Zik Enterprises (Enugu, Nigeria), 1956.
Adelabu, [Nigeria], 1958.
Mr. Rabbit Is Dead, Zik Enterprises, 1958.
Patrice Lumumba, 4th edition, distributed by Tabansi Bookshops (Onitsha), 1961.
The Ghost of Lumumba, [Nigeria], 1961.
Veronica, My Daughter and Other Onitsha Market Plays and Stories, Three Continents Press (Washington, DC), 1980.

FICTION

Long, Long Ago, Omaliko and Sons, 1957.
Smile Awhile, Zik Enterprises, 1957.
Okeke the Magician, [Nigeria], 1958.
Eddy, the Coal-city Boy, [Alayi], 1959.
Caroline the One Guinea Girl, 1960, Goodwill Press and Bookshop, 1965.
Coal City, Fourth Dimension Publishers (Enugu, Nigeria), 1977.
The Juju Priest: A Novel, Fourth Dimension Publishers, 1978.

Also author of *Fireside: African Folklore,* University Publishing Company.

BIOGRAPHICAL/CRITICAL SOURCES:

PERIODICALS

World Literature Today, winter, 1981, p. 166.*

* * *

OGUNYEMI, Wale 1939(?)-

PERSONAL: Born in 1939 (some sources say 1932), in Yoruba country, Western Nigeria.

CAREER: Playwright and scholar. Institute of African Studies, University of Ibadan, senior assistant artist/ writer.

AWARDS, HONORS: Top prize for new work, *African Arts,* 1971, for the screenplay *The Vow.*

WRITINGS:

PLAYS

Ijaye War, A Historic Drama, Orison Acting Editions (Ibadan, Nigeria), 1970.
Eshu Elegbara (based on the Yoruba creation myth "The coming to the world of the gods and goddesses"), Orison Acting Editions, 1970.
Kiriji (historic drama based on Ekita Parapo War in the nineteenth century), African Universities Press (Lagos), 1976.
The Divorce, Onibonoje Press (Ibadan, Nigeria), 1977.
The Vow, Macmillan (London), 1985.
Eniyan: A Morality Play, Ibadan University Press (Ibadan, Nigeria), 1987.

Also author of "Be Mighty, Be Mine," *Nigeria Magazine,* 1968; and "Aare Akogun" (adaptation of *Macbeth*), *Nigeria Magazine,* 1969.

OTHER

Partners in Business, University Press (Ibadan, Nigeria), 1991.

Contributor to *Three Nigerian Plays,* with introduction and notes by Ulli Beier, Longmans, 1967.*

O'HARA, Kenneth
 See MORRIS, Jean

* * *

OLISAH, Sunday Okenwa 1936-1964
 (The Strong Man of the Pen, The Master of Life)

PERSONAL: Born in 1936, in Ibo country, eastern Nigeria; died in 1964.

CAREER: Fiction writer, playwright, biographer, and pamphleteer. Principal of Lisabi Grammar School in Aeokuta, Western Nigeria.

WRITINGS:

Drunkards Believe Bar as Heaven, Chinyelu Printing Press (Onitsha, Nigeria), c. 1955.
(Under pseudonym The Strong Man of the Pen) *How to Live Bachelor's Life and Girl's Life without Much Mistakes,* New Era Printers (Onitsha, Nigeria), c. 1955.
How to Live Better Life and Help Yourself, Okenwa Publications (Onitsha, Nigeria), c. 1955.
The Life Story and the Death of Mr. Lumumba (play), [Onitsha, Nigeria], 1964.
(Under pseudonym The Master of Life) *No Condition Is Permanent,* N. Njoku (Onitsha, Nigeria), c. 1964.
The Ibo Native Law and Custom, New Era Press (Onitsha, Nigeria), c. 1965.
Money Hard to Get But Easy to Spend, J.O. Nnadozie (Onitsha, Nigeria), c. 1965.

Author of numerous novelettes or "chapbooks" and pamphlets published in and around Onitsha, Nigeria, in the 1950s and 1960s, including *The World Is Hard,* 1957; *Money Palaver,* 1960; *The Story about Mammy-Water, Dangerous Man Vagabond versus Princess,* 1960; *Half-Educated Messenger,* 1960; *Elizabeth My Lover,* early 1960s, reprinted by Kraus Reprint; *Life Turns Man Up and Down, Money and Girls Turn Man Up and Down,* c. 1963; *The Life of the Prison Yard,* 1966.

Also author of a play, *My Seven Daughters Are after Young Boys,* and biographies, and *Mr. Lumumba and President Kasavubu in Congo Politics.*

BIOGRAPHICAL/CRITICAL SOURCES:

BOOKS

Herdeck, Donald E., *African Authors: A Companion to Black African Writing,* Volume 1: *1300-1973,* Black Orpheus Press, 1973.*

* * *

OLIVELLA, Manuel Zapata
 See ZAPATA OLIVELLA, Manuel

* * *

O.L.S.
 See RUSSELL, George William

* * *

O'NEAL, Charles E. 1904-1996

OBITUARY NOTICE—See index for *CA* sketch: Born January 6, 1904, in Raeford, NC; died August 29, 1996, in Los Angeles (one source says Beverly Hills), CA. Actor, journalist, and writer. O'Neal is best remembered as the author of *The Three Wishes of Jamie McRuin,* the story of an Irishman who gets three wishes and asks for travel, a wife, and a son. The work won him the Christopher Book Award in 1949. He later worked with several others to adapt the story into a musical, produced on Broadway. O'Neal, nicknamed "Blackie," pursued a career as an actor following several years at college. He worked a series of odd jobs, including bank clerk and horse groom, and found work as an actor in theatrical productions in Illinois, California, and New York. (His son, Ryan, and granddaughter, Tatum, would later follow in his footsteps and find success as actors.) O'Neal joined San Diego's Old Globe Shakespearean Repertory. In the 1940s he began writing screenplays such as *The Missing Juror, I Have a Mystery, The Seventh Victim,* and *Return of the Badmen.* The decade also brought him fame with *The Three Wishes of Jamie McRuin.* He continued to write, penning *The Thirty-second Day* with Victor Trivas, as well as the play *Praise Hoyes,* and the screenplays *Montana* and *Golden Girl.* He also wrote for television series, in-

cluding *The Untouchables* and *Lassie.* Furthermore, O'Neal wrote a column that was issued by the Copley newspaper group.

OBITUARIES AND OTHER SOURCES:

PERIODICALS

Los Angeles Times, September 4, 1996, p. A14.
New York Times, September 5, 1996, p. D21.

* * *

O'NEILL, Brian Juan 1950-

PERSONAL: Born January 29, 1950, in New York, NY; son of George Caracena (a professor of anthropology) and (Betty) Nena (an anthropologist and writer; maiden name, Dross) O'Neill; married Isabel Maria Monteiro Rua Pinto (a social worker), September 27, 1986; children: Barbara Carlota. *Education:* Columbia College, B.A. (cum laude), 1972; University of Essex, M.A. (with distinction), 1974; London School of Economics, Ph.D., 1982. *Politics:* Democrat. *Religion:* Catholic.

ADDRESSES: Home—Lisboa, Portugal. *Office*—Department of Social Anthropology, ISCTE (Instituto Superior de Ciencias do Trabalho e da Empresa), Av. das Forcas Armadas, 1600 Lisboa, Portugal.

CAREER: Gulbenkian Institute of Science, Oeiras, Portugal, research fellow in historical sociology, 1982-85; Centro de Estudos de Antropologia Social, Instituto Superior de Ciencias do Trabalho e da Empresa (ISCTE), Lisbon, Portugal, research fellow and vice president, 1986-87, then president, 1988-89; ISCTE, assistant professor, 1986-94, associate professor of social anthropology, 1995—, department president, 1996—. Visiting professor at Universities of Parix X Nanterre, 1989, Tarragona, 1990, and Santiago de Composela, 1992.

MEMBER: Royal Anthropological Institute (London), American Anthropological Association, American Ethnological Society, European Association for Southeast Asian Studies.

AWARDS, HONORS: Calouste Gulbenkian Foundation research grants, 1976-77, 1981; Raymond Firth Prize, London School of Economics, 1979; Radcliffe-Brown Memorial grant, Royal Anthropological Insti-

tute, 1981; International Prize in Ethno-Anthropological Studies (Italy), 1985, for *Proprietarios, Lavradores e Jornaleiras: Desigualdade Social numa Aldeia Transmontana 1870-1978;* senior research scholar, CNRS (Paris), 1989; Orient Foundation Research Scholarship (Lisbon), 1993-96.

WRITINGS:

Proprietarios, Lavradores e Jornaleiras: Desigualdade Social numa Aldeia Transmontana 1870-1978, Dom Quixote (Lisbon), 1984, translated as *Social Inequality in a Portuguese Hamlet: Land, Late Marriage, and Bastardy, 1870-1978,* Cambridge University Press (Cambridge), 1987.

Author of articles in anthologies and international journals, including *Analise Social, Cahiers de Literature Orale, Critique of Anthropology, Etudes Rurales,* and *Peasant Studies.*

WORK IN PROGRESS: Editorship of various books on Portuguese society and, currently, on the Portuguese Eurasian Creole community in Malacca, Western Malaysia.

SIDELIGHTS: Educator Brian Juan O'Neill's family background has contributed significantly to his choice of vocation: the specialization in the study of European peasant societies. Both his parents were closely involved in archaeology and anthropology; numerous childhood trips accompanying them to pre-Columbian excavations and monuments in Mexico formed the impetus for his later study of Iberian cultural themes within a sociological/anthropological context. O'Neill's parents wrote the 1972 bestselling book on modern American conjugal life, *Open Marriage: A New Life Style for Couples.* This work along with his own paternal Andalusian genealogical roots in Seville would also interweave as well as contrast with one of the major topics of his doctoral research at the London School of Economics. That work was the examination of late marriage, non-marriage, celibacy, concubinage, and bastardy in Fontelas, a remote northeastern Portuguese village. This research would be published in translation in 1987 as *Social Inequality in a Portuguese Hamlet: Land, Late Marriage, and Bastardy, 1870-1978.*

O'Neill's study of "alternative" European kinship practices has been valuable in helping to document social practices in an as yet relatively uncharted corner of Europe. Countering images of harmonious,

egalitarian rural communities promoted by other Iberian anthropologists by drawing on parish records that illuminate the lot of poorer peasant families, O'Neill's work has been praised for its thorough documentation and readable style. Calling *Social Inequality* "an honest and thorough book, needing ideally a bit of compression perhaps, but with a clear argument and some lively discussion," Juliet du Boulay notes in the *Times Literary Supplement* that O'Neill's oeuvre "will be a useful resource for anthropologists and historians interested in household structure, property, and inheritance."

BIOGRAPHICAL/CRITICAL SOURCES:

PERIODICALS

American Anthrologist, September, 1988, pp. 721-22.
American Historical Review, April, 1990, pp. 523-24.
Annales E.S.C., March-April, 1989, pp. 433-36.
Anthropos, Volume 85, 1990, pp. 258-60.
Choice, May, 1988, p. 1438.
L'Homme, number XXIX, 1989.
Man (The Journal of the Royal Anthropological Institute), June, 1989.
Times Literary Supplement, February 26, 1988, p. 226.

* * *

O'NEILL, Timothy J. 1949-

PERSONAL: Born February 7, 1949, in Bethesda, MD; son of Donald J. and Mary Jean (Kelly) O'Neill; married Lynn Norman, August 24, 1974; children: William, James. *Education:* Claremont McKenna College, B.A., 1971; University of California, Berkeley, M.A., 1974, Ph.D., 1981.

ADDRESSES: Office—Department of Political Science, Wellesley College, Wellesley, MA 02181.

CAREER: Brookings Institution, Washington, DC, research fellow, 1978-79; Tulane University, New Orleans, LA, assistant professor of political science, 1979-82; Wellesley College, Wellesley, MA, assistant professor of political science, 1982—. Liberal arts fellow in law and politics, Harvard Law School, Harvard University, Cambridge, MA, 1985-86. *Military service:* U.S. Army, 1971-73.

MEMBER: American Political Science Association, Society for Public Administration, Committee on the Constitutional System, Natural Law Society.

AWARDS, HONORS: Edward S. Corwin Prize, American Political Science Association, 1982, for best dissertation in public law; National Science Foundation graduate fellow, 1973-76.

WRITINGS:

Bakke and the Politics of Equality: Friends and Foes in the Classroom of Litigation, Wesleyan University Press (Middletown, CT), 1985.

Contributor to journals, including *American Political Science Review, Annals of the American Academy of Political and Social Science,* and *Law and Policy.*

WORK IN PROGRESS: Law as Metaphor, a book manuscript exploring the metaphorical basis of legal reasoning; "Is the American Constitution Unconstitutional?," a study of the conflict between the principles of the American founders and those of liberal constitutionism.

SIDELIGHTS: An educator in the area of political science, Timothy J. O'Neill is the author of 1985's *Bakke and the Politics of Equality: Friends and Foes in the Classroom of Litigation.* Based on a 1978 U.S. Supreme Court case that challenged Title VII of the Civil Rights Act of 1964, O'Neill's book examines the case of Allan Paul Bakke, a former U.S. Marine who was rejected by the Board of Admissions of the University of California Medical School in favor of "less qualified" applicants due to that institution's need to fulfill minority enrollment requirements.

O'Neill focuses on the role of the U.S. Supreme Court in providing both a legally sound and responsibly precedent-setting decision. In a close study of over one hundred *amicus curiae* briefs submitted before the court by such organizations as the National Association for the Advancement of Colored People, the American Civil Liberties Union, and the American Federation of Teachers, O'Neill shows how the case led to an increased understanding of the "affirmative action" policies of Title VII and cites the process as a model of democracy in action. Calling the work "an ambitious book," reviewer Kenneth Minogue notes in the *Times Literary Supplement* that in *Bakke and the Politics of Equality* O'Neill "is fair minded. He has written a notable contribution to the

view that democracy requires the discussive participation of all citizens."

BIOGRAPHICAL/CRITICAL SOURCES:

PERIODICALS

Choice, July, 1985, p. 1697.
Times Literary Supplement, August 16, 1985, p. 899.

* * *

OTERO, Miguel Antonio (II) 1859-1944

PERSONAL: Born October 17, 1859, in St. Louis, MO; died August 7, 1944, in Santa Fe, NM; son of Miguel Antonio (a banker, business person, and lawyer) and Mary Josephine (Blackwood) Otero; married Caroline Virginia Emmett, December 19, 1888; married Maud Paine Frost, October 1, 1913; children: (first marriage) Miguel A. III (died in infancy), Miguel A. IV, Elizabeth Emmett. *Education:* Attended St. Louis University and University of Notre Dame. *Politics:* Democrat.

CAREER: Bookkeeper for Otero, Sellar, & Co., late 1870s; San Miguel National Bank, Las Vegas, NM, cashier, 1880-85; City of Las Vegas, NM, treasurer, 1883-84; San Miguel County, NM, probate clerk, 1886-90; U.S. District Court, Fourth Judicial District (NM), clerk, 1890-93; Territory of New Mexico, governor, 1897-06, treasurer, 1910-11; New Mexico Board of Penitentiary Commissioners and Parole Board, president, 1913-17; Panama Canal Zone, Isthmus of Panama, U.S. marshall, 1917-21. President of board of regents, New Mexico Normal University, 1923-25, 1933-34; chair of state advisory board, Federal Emergency Administration of Public Works, 1933. Officer or director of several business enterprises. Republican Party national delegate, 1892, 1900, 1904, 1908; Progressive Party national delegate, 1912, 1916; member of Democratic National Committee, and national delegate, 1920, 1924.

MEMBER: Masons, Elks, Santa Fe Club.

WRITINGS:

(Editor with Paul A. F. Walter and Frank W. Clancy, and contributor) *Colonel Jose Francisco Chaves, 1833-1924,* Historical Society of New Mexico, 1926.

My Life on the Frontier, Volume 1: *1864-1882,* Press of the Pioneers, 1935, reprinted, University of New Mexico Press, 1987, Volume 2: *1882-1897,* University of New Mexico Press, 1939.
The Real Billy the Kid: With New Light on the Lincoln County War, R. F. Wilson, 1936.
My Nine Years as Governor of the Territory of New Mexico, 1897-1906, edited and with a foreword by Marion Dargan, University of New Mexico Press, 1940.
Otero: An Autobiographical Trilogy (contains *My Life on the Frontier,* Volumes 1-2, and *My Nine Years as Governor of the Territory of New Mexico, 1897-1906*), Arno Press, 1974.

Also author of *Conquistadores of Spain and Buccaneers of England, France and Holland,* 1925. The University of New Mexico has compiled papers and photographs of Otero in the Miguel A. Otero Collection.

SIDELIGHTS: "Miguel Antonio Otero's three-volume autobiography is one of the best documentations of life on the American frontier during the last half of the nineteenth century," Luis Leal asserted in a *Dictionary of Literary Biography* essay. The son of a prominent businessman and former congressional delegate, Otero grew up in the frontier Midwest and Southwest, and there he met such legendary figures as "Wild Bill" Hickok, "Buffalo Bill" Cody, and William H. Bonney, who became infamous as "Billy the Kid." The first volume of *My Life on the Frontier* contains tales of these men, as well as stories of the Old West that Otero learned from his mother. In making "observations about life on the frontier as seen first through the eyes of a boy and then of a young man," Leal reported, the author "made use of his early impressions to elaborate the early part of his memoirs." The result, the critic continued, is that "the reader . . . is impressed with the vividness of the narration and receives the impression that it was written shortly after the mentioned events took place," even though Otero did not begin to write until after his retirement.

The second volume of Otero's autobiography relates his growing involvement in the development of the Southwest; making "greater use of quotations from newspapers and even books . . . to document his studies," summarized Leal, Otero gave "less emphasis to personal experiences and more to territorial matters." But Otero's work in local government and with the Republican Party was leading to a position in which he would directly affect political concerns; in 1897, President William McKinley appointed his

friend to the governorship of New Mexico, making Otero the first Hispanic governor of a southwestern territory. Despite his disregard for the existing political machinery, Otero forged a strong alliance with the Legislature and led his territory to a stronger economy and eventually, application for statehood.

This period of Otero's life is recalled in *My Nine Years as Governor of the Territory of New Mexico, 1897-1906,* and includes the governor's stormy relationship with President Theodore Roosevelt. Although the two men collaborated on the creation of the Rough Riders regiment, their disagreement over the conditions for New Mexico's statehood led Roosevelt to replace Otero as governor in 1906. Otero remained politically active well into his seventies, however, and eventually switched his allegiance to the Democratic Party. "Not an intellectual but rather a politician and a man of action, Otero was able to leave an autobiography that is vigorous, warm, and full of life," observed Leal. "His writings reflect his personality, which was that of a man of strong convictions who did not hesitate to fight those who opposed him, nor to help his friends." The trilogy consisting of *My Life on the Frontier*'s two volumes and *My Nine Years as Governor* "remains one of the most important sources of information about life in the Southwest during a critical period," the critic concluded. "Otero's autobiography is one of the most important and worthy antecedents of a genre that has been a favorite among contemporary Chicano writers."

BIOGRAPHICAL/CRITICAL SOURCES:

BOOKS

Crocchiola, F. L. Stanley, *The Otero, New Mexico, Story* (Pantex, TX), 1962.
Dictionary of Literary Biography, Volume 82: *Chicano Authors, First Series,* Gale, 1989.
Otero, Miguel Antonio, *My Life on the Frontier,* Volume 1: *1864-1882,* Press of the Pioneers, 1935, reprinted, University of New Mexico Press, 1987, Volume 2: *1882-1897,* University of New Mexico Press, 1939.
Otero, Miguel Antonio, *My Nine Years as Governor of the Territory of New Mexico, 1897-1906,* edited and with a foreword by Marion Dargan, University of New Mexico Press, 1940.

OBITUARIES:

PERIODICALS

New York Times, August 8, 1944.*

OTTLEY, Roi (Vincent) 1906-1960

PERSONAL: Born August 2, 1906, in New York, NY; died October 1, 1960; buried in Burr Oak Cemetery, Chicago, IL; son of Jerome P. and Beatrice (Brisbane) Ottley; married Gladys Tarr, April 27, 1941 (marriage ended); married Alice L. Dungey, February 14, 1951; children: Lynne. *Education:* Attended St. Bonaventure College, 1926-27, University of Michigan, two years, Columbia University, 1934-35, New York University, 1935-36, and St. John's University School of Law. *Religion:* Roman Catholic.

CAREER: Amsterdam Star News, New York City, reporter, beginning 1930, columnist, 1932-37, became an editor, c. 1935, columnist and theatrical and sports editor, 1937-38; editor with New York City Writers Project, 1937; free-lance writer, 1937-41; National C.I.O. War Relief Committee, director of public relations, 1943; war correspondent for *Liberty* and *P.M.,* 1944, and *Pittsburgh Courier* and Overseas News Agency, 1945; *Chicago Tribune,* columnist, 1945-60. Social worker, 1932-37; director, Drexel National Bank, Chicago, and Victory Mutual Life Insurance Company.

MEMBER: National Geographic Society, War Correspondents' Association, P.E.N., Chicago Press Club.

AWARDS, HONORS: Houghton Life in America Award and Rosenwald fellowship, both 1944, for *New World A-Coming;* Ainsworth Award, 1944; Peabody Award, 1945; *New World A-Coming* radio series won Schomburg Award, 1945; Brotherhood Award from Chicago Conference for Brotherhood, Inc.

WRITINGS:

"New World A-Coming": Inside Black America, Houghton, 1943.
Black Odyssey: The Story of the Negro in America, Scribner, 1948.
No Green Pastures, Scribner, 1951.
The Lonely Warrior: The Life and Times of Robert S. Abbott, Regnery, 1955.
White Marble Lady (novel), Farrar, Straus, 1965.
(Editor with William J. Weatherby) *The Negro in New York: An Informal Social History,* New York Public Library, 1967, published as *The Negro in New York: An Informal Social History, 1626-1940,* Praeger, 1969.

Also coauthor of scripts for radio series *New World A-Coming,* WMCA (New York), 1944-46. Work rep-

resented in anthologies, including *Radio Drama in Action*, 1945. Contributor to periodicals, including *Pittsburgh Courier*, *Baltimore Afro-American*, *Herald-Tribune*, and *New York Times*.

BIOGRAPHICAL/CRITICAL SOURCES:

PERIODICALS

New York Times, October 2, 1960.
Publishers Weekly, October 17, 1960.

OBITUARIES:

BOOKS

Current Biography, December, 1960.

PERIODICALS

New York Times, October 2, 1960.
Publishers Weekly, October 17, 1960.*

* * *

OVERMEYER, Eric 1952(?)-

PERSONAL: Born c. 1952. *Education:* Attended Reed College, Oregon, and Asolo Conservatory, Sarasota.

ADDRESSES: Office—American Conservatory Theater, 30 Grant Ave., San Francisco, CA 94108-5800.

CAREER: Playwright. Playwrights Horizons, New York, NY, literary manager, 1979-84; Yale University School of Drama, New Haven, CT, professor, 1991-92.

WRITINGS:

PLAYS

Native Speech (produced at Center Stage, Baltimore, 1984), published in *Collected Plays*, Smith and Kraus, 1993.
In a Pig's Valise (produced at Center Stage, c. 1984), published in *Collected Plays*, Smith and Kraus, 1993.
On the Verge, or The Geography of Yearning (produced at Center Stage, 1985), published in *Collected Plays*, Smith and Kraus, 1993.

In Perpetuity throughout the Universe, produced at the Hudson Guild, New York City, 1988.
Dark Rapture, produced at Empty Space Theatre, Seattle, 1992.
(Author of book and lyrics) *The Heliotrope Bouquet by Scott Joplin & Louis Chauvin* (produced at Playwrights Horizons, New York City, 1993), published in *Collected Plays*, Smith and Kraus, 1993.
The Dalai Lama Goes Three for Four, Magic Theater Southside, San Francisco, 1995

Writer of scripts for television series, including *St. Elsewhere*, *The Days and Nights of Molly Dodd*, and *The Cosby Mysteries*.

SIDELIGHTS: In an era when the visual in art predominates, playwright Eric Overmeyer has taken the opposite approach. A connoisseur of words, Overmeyer has astonished and at times befuddled audiences with his virtuosic use of language in a handful of plays: *Native Speech*, about a talk show host, *On the Verge, or The Geography of Yearning*, about Victorian women explorers, *In Perpetuity throughout the Universe*, about a right-wing conspiracy, *In a Pig's Valise*, a hard-boiled detective musical, *The Heliotrope Bouquet by Scott Joplin & Louis Chauvin*, about the genesis of ragtime, and *Dark Rapture*, a crime story. To quote Jessica Werner of the American Conservatory Theatre Board, Overmeyer is "one of this country's most imaginative playwrights."

Overmeyer credits many writers as influences. "I've been very influenced by novelists with mandarin styles like Don DeLillo, John Barth and Ishmael Reed," Overmeyer told Stephen Holden of the *New York Times*. "Beckett, Pinter and Chekhov, the playwrights who have influenced me the most, all used poetic language and imagery." Indeed, Overmeyer's creative use of language has become a hallmark of his work. Because he presents complex themes through dialogue, theater commentators have compared him to Harold Pinter, Tom Stoppard, and Mac Wellman. Calling Overmeyer a "deviously comic playwright," Mel Gussow of the *New York Times* elaborated: "Both [Overmeyer and Wellman] are extraordinarily funny writers who make one laugh even when the reason for the laughter remains obscure." Critics have likened Overmeyer's work to that of other American writers as well, particularly that of such late-twentieth-century "heightened language" dramatists as Jeffrey Jones, Suzan-Lori Parks, Erik Ehn, and Len Jenkins. "Eric manages to strike a nice bal-

ance between verbal imagery and the visual worlds he creates," notes Goodman Theater director David Petrarca. "The beauty of Eric's language is that it is both a joy to be heard in and of itself, as well as a great, open system which allows for many points of view."

While reading a book about explorers, Overmeyer learned about women explorers of the Victorian age and became interested enough in them to write *On the Verge,* a one-act surrealist comedy about a trio of Victorian women explorers from 1888 who travel through time to America in the 1950s, where they encounter such foreign objects as ice cream bars, an eggbeater, Burma Shave, a motorcycle, and a Jacuzzi. They puzzle over the vast changes that have taken place in the world and solve some of the mysteries. The play itself underwent a metamorphosis: over a three year period *On the Verge* grew into a full-length work and was mounted in more than a dozen regional theaters before being staged in New York City, where it was Overmeyer's first work to appear before New York audiences. "I think of the play as a long poem," Overmeyer told Holden. "I hope the play works in the way that a poem does by resonating with meanings rather than by being explicit."

On the Verge garnered compliments from reviewers. Holden praised the work highly: "*On the Verge* is a delight to the ear because its language is a funny, musically conceived torrent of Victorian language and modern slang, overflowing with amusing puns and delicious alliteration." "I love Eric's writing," director Garland Wright was quoted as saying in a *New York Times* review by Leslie Bennetts. "He's a writer of language, and he writes about the imagination, and he writes specifically for the theater. But also I'm attracted to the play because it's a play with hope, and one rarely in these times runs across plays like that," he continued. "It treasures the individual's imagination and the imagination's ability to transcend realities that can be crushing, or can be looked at negatively. It celebrates the act of exploring and discovering, which is what I hope theater is," enthused Wright. Holden concluded, "The language of the play is so charged and the characters so sympathetic and brave, that *On the Verge* leaves audiences in a good mood."

Inspired by the detective novels of Raymond Chandler, Overmeyer wrote his own hard-boiled detective story—*In a Pig's Valise*—over an eight-year period. "To me the detective story is one aspect of American

mythology," Overmeyer explained to Holden. "It's our version of Greek legends. We live with a gold mine of American mythology that's all stuck together." Overmeyer wrote some twenty drafts, and worked with six different composers before collaborating with pop band leader August Darnell of Kid Creole fame. (Overmeyer had been a fan of Darnell's work since 1981 but at the time thought there would be little chance of getting the artist to collaborate.) According to Holden, who called the play "a bold experiment in language," "the story swirls together American legends ranging all the way from [Walt] Disney to John Dillinger, from Philip Marlow to Huey Newton, with a giddy, insouciant playfulness and in a mix of musical genres that include calypso, funk, pop, cool jazz country, reggae, hard rock and rap." More specifically, the plot involves a detective hired to find a missing girl in an underworld fraught with sleaze and danger. "I was drawn to the detective form because it is so American," Overmeyer told Holden. "The piece is really about American vernacular, both linguistic and musical."

Like *In a Pig's Valise, Dark Rapture* is a rendition of a modern American crime novel for the stage. In what Werner described as "a wild ride through contemporary American culture," the action revolves around a screenwriter who, presumed to have died in a fire, decides to adopt a new identity and tries to escape a past full of dangerous underworld figures. "There is a very American mythology that is central to *Dark Rapture*. This incredible, yet uninformed, optimism at the core of who we are enables us to throw off our pasts without realizing the possible dangers in doing so," Petrarca explained.

Directors producing Overmeyer's plays have found casting to be a difficult matter. Actors and actress must be especially well trained in order to perform Overmeyer's verbal gymnastics with aplomb. Because his style is often terse, performers often feel inclined to paraphrase or add words that seem to be missing from the dialogue—often compromising the rhythmic effect in the process. So whenever he can, Overmeyer is at the scene himself to aid the director. Overmeyer's plays have been successfully mounted in a number of regional theaters across the country, and *On the Verge* and *In a Pig's Valise* were performed Off-Broadway. About the New York experience Overmeyer commented to *New York Times* reviewer Michael Bloom, "Being produced in New York is a brutal experience. It's not about the work. It's about the critical and commercial consequences."

BIOGRAPHICAL/CRITICAL SOURCES:

PERIODICALS

Choice, March, 1994, p. 1130.
New York, February 27, 1989, p. 138.
New Yorker, February 27, 1989, pp. 66-67; March 15, 1993, p. 122.
New York Times, February 22, 1987, section 2, p. 5; March 27, 1987, p. 19C; October 29, 1988; February 12, 1989, pp. 5, 28; February 11, 1990.
Publishers Weekly, September 6, 1993, p. 88.
Variety, July 24-30, 1995, pp. 78-79.

OTHER

American Conservatory Theater Board Internet homepage, August 15, 1996: www.act-sfbay .com/darkessay.html#second.*

P

PARIS, Barry

PERSONAL: Education: Institute for the Study of the USSR, certificate, 1968; Columbia University, B.A., 1969; University of Pittsburgh, graduate studies, 1976-78. *Avocational interests:* Fluent in Russian, Spanish, French, German, Czech/Slovak, and Ukrainian.

ADDRESSES: Office—c/o WQED, 4802 Fifth Ave., Pittsburgh, PA 15213.

CAREER: Journalist, biographer, film, dance, and theater critic, teacher, and translator. *Wichita Eagle,* film and theater critic and reporter, 1969-72; *Prairie Journal,* Wichita, KS, editor and publisher, 1972-74; KAKE-TV, Wichita, performing arts critic, 1972-76; *Wichita Sun,* feature editor and film critic, 1974-76; *Pittsburgh Post-Gazette,* editorial writer and editor, 1976-79, film and music critic and reporter, 1980-86; *Miami Herald,* feature editor, 1979-80; "Sunday Arts Magazine," WQED-FM, Pittsburgh, PA, host and critic-at-large, 1982—. Presidential biography researcher, American Political Items Collectors, 1965—; Columbia University Tutorial Service, instructor, 1965-69; Manhattan Commercial Corp., New York City, translator, 1967; Catholic Diocesan Schools, Wichita, KS, instructor, 1969-70; Wichita State University, instructor, 1970-76; editing for R. Buckminster Fuller, University of Southern Illinois, 1971.

AWARDS, HONORS: Named Best Weekly Newspaper, Kansas Press Association, 1974, for *Prairie Journal;* Golden Quill, Pittsburgh Press Club, 1978, for Best Editorial Writing; Matrix Award, Women in Communications, 1980, 1981, for Best News Series; Golden Quill, Pittsburgh Press Club, 1982, for Best Cultural Reporting; named Best Local Newspaper Reporter, *Pittsburgh Magazine,* 1982; Pennsylvania Association of Broadcasters award, 1987, for Best Editorial; Golden Quill, Pittsburgh Press Club, 1989, for Best Political Commentary; Film Biography of the Year award, ABC-TV, 1990, for *Louise Brooks.*

WRITINGS:

Louise Brooks, Knopf (New York), 1989.
(With Tony Curtis) *Tony Curtis: The Autobiography,* Morrow (New York), 1993.
Garbo: A Biography, Knopf, 1995.
Audrey Hepburn, Putnam (New York), 1996.

Also author of a screenplay, *Pierce in Oblivion: The Life of Franklin Pierce.* Contributor to periodicals, including *New Yorker, Vanity Fair, Art & Antiques, Interview, Washington Post, Cosmopolitan* (UK), and *American Film.*

WORK IN PROGRESS: The edited dramatic lectures of Stella Adler for Knopf.

SIDELIGHTS: An award-winning journalist and arts critic, Barry Paris is noted for his extensive research and sympathetic approach toward the subjects of Hollywood film star biographies. Paris's insights into his subjects' emotional and psychological composition have been deemed intriguing and even fascinating by critics.

Paris's first celebrity biography, *Louise Brooks,* describes the rise and fall of a woman who, at the height of her fame in the 1920s, "was being touted as the quintessential flapper—a hedonistic good-time gal

whose photographs graced magazines everywhere," according to *New York Times Book Review* critic Neal Gabler. A dancer by training and vocation, Brooks grew up in Kansas, and left home at the age of fifteen to join the Denishawn dance school in New York City. She was forced to leave the school two years later due to her licentious behavior, but later joined the Ziegfeld Follies and was discovered by Hollywood film representatives.

Though her film career was shortlived, Brooks "made an indelible mark" on Hollywood, according to *Washington Post Book World* critic John Simon. Hardly successful in her own day, having quit Hollywood at the age of thirty-two to teach dance briefly, work as a salesperson, and even as a prostitute, film historians tend to perceive Brooks as intentionally self-destructive. "The fascinating details of this systematic self-destruction, as chronicled in Barry Paris's biography, suggest something larger than laziness, sloppiness and carelessness (although those too). There was a conscious or unconscious wish to fail," remarked Simon.

Although *Louise Brooks* was reviewed widely, Paris's writing style was the subject of some negative commentary. "As a love object Brooks inspired frenzy, and she seems to have had the same effect on her biographer," Gabler observed. The result is "a fat, richly documented, doting and exhaustive book that treats Brooks's life as seriously as if she had been Winston Churchill." Seemingly echoing Gabler, Simon called Paris's *Louise Brooks* "for both better and worse, a labor of ardent love," but concluded: "Paris's writing is fluent except for some faulty grammar and occasional purple patches. The story he tells is fascinating not only for what it says about Brooks, but also for its generous sidelights on the whole jazz-and-flapper age."

For his next publication, Paris collaborated with actor Tony Curtis to produce the star's autobiography. In *Tony Curtis: The Autobiography,* the authors unabashedly discuss Curtis's good looks, his many love affairs both while married and single, and other movie stars, according to several reviewers. *New York Times Book Review* contributor Janet Maslin cautiously praised *Tony Curtis:* "Mr. Paris, whose own impressions of Mr. Curtis's films are interspersed throughout the book, daringly describes his subject as 'one of the most dynamic, complex and enduring popcultural figures of our time. . . .' This is not a memoir to justify that claim, but it is a candid, very readable portrait of a man who has no trouble saying

what's on his mind." *Newsweek*'s Peter Plagens was more enthusiastic: "*Tony Curtis: The Autobiography* is a highly readable, candid reminiscence of a guy who never stopped thinking it was still 1948 and he was the hot new hunk on the Universal lot."

As with his biography of Louise Brooks, critics again spotlighted Paris's prodigious research in reviews of his next project, entitled *Garbo: A Biography.* A mysterious figure renowned for her love of solitude and secrecy, Greta Garbo has been the subject of numerous biographies. Paris's book is based on these earlier works as well as on newly available material, including Garbo's fifty-year correspondence with Salka Viertel and a hundred hours of taped telephone conversations between the subject and Sam Green, an art dealer who became her friend late in the actress's life. "As a result," remarked Kenneth Turan in *Los Angeles Times Book Review,* "if there is any fact to be discovered about Greta Garbo it can be found here."

Reviewers noted, with mixed reactions, Paris's faithful rendering of the minutiae of his reclusive subject's life. "Paris's book . . . does a solid job of tracing the actress's story through its by-now familiar paces, enthusiastically correcting misinformation whenever necessary," observed Turan. But *New York Times Book Review* critic Patrick McGilligan complained that despite Paris's attention to every detail, "[t]he encyclopedic footnotes cover Berlin hookers, fringe lawsuits, Garbo's look-alike stand-in, Scandinavian folk tales, [and] Alsatian dogs, Garbo . . . strolls through the pages a riddle unto herself, making cryptic, usually terse statements." Turan and McGilligan both state, however, that Garbo is a particularly difficult subject, and Turan asserts that of all the books dedicated to the actress's life, Paris's *Garbo: A Biography* is "in many ways the most successful."

BIOGRAPHICAL/CRITICAL SOURCES:

PERIODICALS

London Review of Books, March 8, 1990, pp. 11-12.
Los Angeles Times Book Review, March 12, 1995, p. 4.
Newsweek, November 1, 1993, pp. 70-71.
New York Times Book Review, October 22, 1989, p. 11; December 19, 1993, p. 12; April 2, 1995, p. 3.
Publishers Weekly, December 5, 1994, p. 60.
Times (London), March 10, 1990.
Washington Post Book World, November 26, 1989.

PARKERSON, Michelle (Denise) 1953-

PERSONAL: Born January 11, 1953, in Washington, DC. *Education:* Temple University, B.A., 1974.

ADDRESSES: Home—1716 Florida Ave. N.W., No. 2, Washington, DC 20009.

CAREER: WRC-TV, Washington, DC, television engineer, 1975; WTTG-TV Metromedia Inc., Washington, DC, television engineer, 1976-83; Eye of the Storm Productions Inc., Washington, DC, director and producer, 1982—. Director and producer of films, including *Sojourn,* 1973, and *But Then, She's Betty Carter,* 1980; producer of video *Gotta Make This Journey,* 1983; affiliated with Robert Flaherty Film Seminar, Cornell University, 1984. University of Delaware, visiting instructor, 1985; Temple University, assistant professor, 1986; lecturer.

MEMBER: American Film Institute, Association of Independent Video and Filmmakers.

AWARDS, HONORS: Sojourn won the Judges Prize, American Women in Radio and Television, 1975; grand prize, New York Black Film Festival, 1976; National Endowment for the Arts fellow, 1980; grants from District of Columbia Commission on Arts and Humanities, 1980-81 and 1984-85, Corporation for Public Broadcasting, 1983, and Gay Education Fund, 1983; Edith Blum Lecture Performance Series Award, Washington Women's Arts Center, 1983; ENIK Arts Society Award, 1984; Community Recognition Award, University of the District of Columbia, 1984; Jerry Heil Memorial Award, Gertrude Stein Democratic Club, 1985; *Gotta Make This Journey* won the Leigh Whipper Award, Philadelphia International Film Festival, 1985.

WRITINGS:

Waiting Rooms (poetry), illustrated by Jean Vallon, Common Ground Press, 1983.

Contributor of essays, reviews, poetry, and fiction to periodicals.*

* * *

PARKIN, Sara (Lamb) 1946-

PERSONAL: Born April 9, 1946, in Aberdeen, Scotland; daughter of George Lamb and Marie Munro (Rankin) McEwan; married Donald Maxwell Parkin, 1969; children: two sons. *Education:* Edinburgh Royal Infirmary, R.G.N., 1970. *Avocational interests:* Reading, films, gardening, walking, camping, opera, plays.

ADDRESSES: Office—c/o Pandora Publishing, 77-85 Fulham Palace Road, Hammersmith, London W6 8JB, England.

CAREER: University of Edinburgh, Edinburgh, Scotland, research assistant, 1973-74; Edinburgh Brook Advisory Center, council member, 1974-76; Leeds Area Health Authority, Leeds, England, family planning nurse, 1976-80; Green Party, international liaison secretary, 1983-90, speaker, 1989-92, executive chairperson, 1992; Forum for the Future, director, 1992—. Co-secretary of European Green Coordination, 1985-90.

MEMBER: New Economics Foundation (trustee), Friends of the Earth Trust, Population Concern.

AWARDS, HONORS: Hon. D.Sc. from Ball State University, 1993, Institution of Civil Engineers, 1996.

WRITINGS:

Green Parties: An International Guide, Heretic Books (London), 1989.
Green Futures: Agenda for the Twenty-First Century, Fount (London), 1991.
(Editor) *Green Light on Europe,* Heretic Books, 1991.
The Life and Death of Petra Kelly, Pandora (London), 1994.

Contributor to periodicals, including *New Scientist* and *New Statesman and Society.* Contributor to newspapers and books.

SIDELIGHTS: Sara Parkin is a former nurse who is probably best known for her work with the United Kingdom's Green Party from the mid-1970s to the early 1990s, and for establishing the European Green Party coordination during the 1980s. After a career in nursing, Parkin joined the Green Party in 1977. She held the post of international liaison secretary until 1990, then serving as a speaker, mainly on international issues. In 1992 she became the Green Party's executive chairperson. In that capacity, as was noted

in *New Statesman and Society,* Parkin displayed "undoubted skills as an outstanding advocate of green politics" and proved herself "a good strategic planner and manager."

But after Parkin's substantial role in the party's record fifteen percent showing in the 1989 elections to the European Parliament, the Green Party proved itself unable to build on that success, and subsided into internal conflicts. Parkin resigned, at odds with the direction of the party's strategy and policy, in 1992. A *New Statesman and Society* writer reported that "the sheer grind of endless mid-slinging . . . explains why people like Sara Parkin feel unable to continue" within the Green Party.

During her fifteen years with the Green Party, Parkin produced various party-related publications, including *Green Parties: An International Guide,* a 1989 volume delineating the issues and ethics pertinent to Green causes. She followed this work with *Green Futures: Agenda for the Twenty-First Century,* which appeared in 1991. That same year, she also was commissioned as editor of *Green Light on Europe.*

In 1994 Parkin published *The Life and Death of Petra Kelly,* an account of the German Green Party figure whose life ended violently in 1992. Kelly rose to prominence within the Green Party in the 1980s, and as a Green candidate she eventually won election to the West German parliament. But as the German Green Party declined due to internal strife, Kelly's prominence within the party faded. In October, 1992, she was found dead from a gunshot wound. Also found dead was Gert Bastian, a retired Army general who was one of Kelly's lovers. Although the deaths of Kelly and Bastian were initially seen as suicides, evidence indicates that Kelly may have been murdered by Bastian. In *The Life and Death of Petra Kelly,* Parkin suggests that Bastian's fears of publicity linking him to East Germany's secret police may have led him to kill Kelly and himself. London *Times* reviewer Peter Millar observed, "As a study of a remarkable woman . . . Parkin's work is authoritative and detailed in its reference to original sources."

BIOGRAPHICAL/CRITICAL SOURCES:

PERIODICALS

New Statesman and Society, September 4, 1992, p. 26.
Times (London), September 25, 1994.
Times Literary Supplement, October 20, 1989.

PARSON, Ann B(olton) 1950-

PERSONAL: Born August 25, 1950, in Blue Hill, ME; daughter of George A. Parson and Katharine (Bolton) Rodgers. *Education:* Boston University, B.A., 1972. *Avocational interests:* Science journalism.

ADDRESSES: Home and office—65 Forest St., Brookline, MA 02167. *E-mail*—aparson@acs.bu.edu. *Agent*—Doe Coover Agency, 58 Sagamore Ave., Medford, MA 02155.

CAREER: Boston University, Boston, MA, adjunct professor of science journalism, 1990—.

MEMBER: National Association of Science Writers, New England Science Writers.

WRITINGS:

(With Isaac Schiff) *Menopause: The Massachusetts General Hospital Guide,* Times Books (New York City), 1996.

Contributor to periodicals, including *McCall's* and *Golf for Women.*

WORK IN PROGRESS: A book on medical genetics, for a general audience.

* * *

PARSON-NESBITT, Julie 1957-

PERSONAL: Born March 12, 1957, in Chicago, IL. *Education:* University of Wisconsin-Madison, B.A., 1980; University of Pittsburgh, M.F.A., 1994. *Religion:* Jewish.

ADDRESSES: Office—Writer's Voice, Duncan Young Men's Christian Association, 1001 West Roosevelt Rd., Chicago, IL 60608.

CAREER: Duncan Young Men's Christian Association, Chicago, IL, director of Writer's Voice, 1996—. Poet, literary arts organizer, and fundraiser.

AWARDS, HONORS: Significant Illinois Poet Award from Gwendolyn Books, 1989.

WRITINGS:

(Editor with Lilliam Anguiano, Paula Berg, and others) *Naming the Daytime Moon: Stories and Poems by Chicago Women,* Another Chicago Press (Chicago, IL), 1989.

Finders (poems), West End Press (Albuquerque, NM), 1996.

WORK IN PROGRESS: A collection of poems.

* * *

PEKKANEN, John 1939-

PERSONAL: Born February 11, 1939, in New Haven, CT; son of Robert Rudolph and Lucille (Podvin) Pekkanen; married Lynn Kopke (an investigator), September 29, 1961; children: Robert, Sarah, Benjamin. *Education:* Attended St. Johns College, 1957-61; attended Harvard University, 1970-71.

ADDRESSES: Home and office—5101 Newport Ave., Bethesda, MD 20816. *Agent*—John Boswell, 123 East 54th St., New York, NY 10022.

CAREER: Life (magazine), New York City and Chicago, IL, bureau chief, 1967-71; freelance writer, 1972-87; *Washingtonian* (magazine), Washington, DC, senior writer, 1982-87; *Reader's Digest* (magazine), Pleasantville, NY, roving editor, 1987—.

AWARDS, HONORS: Penney-Missouri Award, 1982, for best medical science article; National Headliner Award, 1982; National Magazine Award, American Society of Magazine Editors, 1982 and 1985; National Press Club Award, 1985.

WRITINGS:

The American Connection: Profiteering and Politicking in the "Ethical" Drug Industry, Follett (Chicago, IL), 1973.

Victims: An Account of a Rape, Dial Press (New York, NY), 1976.

The Best Doctors in the U.S.: A Guide to the Finest Specialists, Hospitals, and Health Centers, Seaview (New York, NY), 1979, revised edition, 1981.

(With Elmo Zumwalt, Jr. and Elmo Zumwalt III) *My Father, My Son,* Macmillan (New York, NY), 1986.

Donor: How One Girl's Death Gave Life to Others, Little, Brown (Boston, MA), 1986.

M.D.: Doctors Talk about Themselves, Delacorte (New York, MA), 1988.

Contributor of articles to periodicals.

SIDELIGHTS: John Pekkanen has worked and written for many periodicals, including *Life, Washingtonian,* and *Reader's Digest.* He has also written several books, including one on rape and another on the effects of the defoliant Agent Orange used during the Vietnam War. But, as with his articles, most of his books pertain to medical matters. Pekkanen explained to *CA* that his "interest is to explain, and humanize the subject of medicine for lay readers."

Pekkanen's 1973 book, *The American Connection: Profiteering and Politicking in the "Ethical" Drug Industry,* caused much debate when it was published. Critics hailed it; Joseph A. Page in *Commonweal,* for instance, called it "a persuasive indictment of the drug industry's responsibility for the misuse of its products." Rosalie H. Lipsett in *Library Journal* called *The American Connection* "a fascinating and frightening book." In *The American Connection* Pekkanen argued that the legitimate corporations that manufacture legal, prescription drugs are to blame for many more cases of drug addiction than illegal pushers of drugs like heroin and marijuana. The drug companies, Pekkanen proposes, have accomplished this by producing much more of their products than are medically needed, promoting over-prescription through advertisements in medical journals, and selling drugs to Mexican markets cheaply, so they may be easily smuggled back to the United States and sold on the black market. According to Pekkanen, the drug companies are also a powerful lobbying force, preventing Congress from passing any truly effective laws to prevent their unethical practices.

Another of Pekkanen's important works is the reference guide, *The Best Doctors in the U.S.: A Guide to the Finest Specialists, Hospitals, and Health Centers,* which he first issued in 1979 and updated in 1981. To obtain his information, Pekkanen polled more than five hundred physicians, asking them which of their colleagues they would turn to if they or their family members needed treatment in various medical fields. The result was a list of two thousand five hundred doctors "in every major medical and surgical specialty," as Jacalyn Coghlin-Strom explained in the *Library Journal.* Pekkanen also included general guidelines for choosing a doctor and information on

how to be sure a particular physician is competent. A *Saturday Review* critic, comparing *The Best Doctors in the U.S.* to an issue of *Consumer Reports,* concluded that Pekkanen had made it "almost as easy to shop for doctors as for stereos, throw rugs, or eggplants."

Pekkanen has also collaborated with Admiral Elmo Zumwalt, Jr. and Lieutenant Elmo Zumwalt III on *My Father, My Son,* the story of how one military family was affected by the use of the defoliant Agent Orange during the Vietnam War. Zumwalt, Jr. ordered the defoliant used "along the river banks and naval outposts in Vietnam to help prevent ambushes against the light naval craft patrolling these waterways," noted Martin M. Goldstein in the *Los Angeles Times Book Review.* Zumwalt, Jr.'s son served as the commander of the boats that patrolled the areas that were sprayed with Agent Orange, and after the war came down with two different, rare forms of cancer, in addition to fathering a child with severe birth defects. Their story, according to Alden Whitman in *Tribune Books,* "has an enormous emotional impact on the reader."

In addition, Pekkenan wrote *Donor: How One Girl's Death Gave Life to Others,* published in 1986, the same year as *My Father, My Son.* In it he tells the personal stories of the different people involved in one case of organ transplantation: from the family of a seventeen-year old accident victim, to the head of the Organ Procurement Center in Baltimore, Maryland, to the people who receive the dead girl's corneas and kidneys, including a four-year-old boy who has had other, failed kidney transplants previously. William A. Nolen in the *Washington Post* judged that *Donor* was "well worth reading," and declared that "each of these stories is poignant and dramatic; each contains moments of happiness and despair."

M.D.: Doctors Talk about Themselves is Pekkanen's 1988 effort. In it, he interviews more than seventy anonymous doctors in many different medical specialties to uncover how they feel about their jobs. They discuss mistakes they have made, their feelings of inadequacy, and, as Paul Galloway reported in the *Chicago Tribune,* "they decry the type of training they receive in medical school, citing the exhausting regimen and an overemphasis on diagnosis; they denounce the difficulties in getting rid of bad doctors; they condemn their peers who are more interested in money than healing." Mike Oppenheim in the *New York Times Books Review* labeled *M.D.* "relentlessly entertaining," and added that other books of this nature do not reveal "such honesty and feeling."

BIOGRAPHICAL/CRITICAL SOURCES:

PERIODICALS

Chicago Tribune, November 6, 1988.
Commonweal, March 8, 1974, pp. 19-20.
Library Journal, November 1, 1973, p. 3248-49; July, 1976, p. 1546; January, 1986, p. 94; October 1, 1979, p. 2084.
Los Angeles Times Book Review, October 12, 1986, pp. 3, 7.
New York Times Book Review, July 7, 1974, p. 14; October 30, 1988, p. 27.
Saturday Review, August, 1979, p. 47.
Tribune Books, October 12, 1986, p. 7.
Washington Post, February 21, 1986; September 23, 1986.

—*Sketch by Elizabeth Wenning*

* * *

PELENSKI, Jaroslaw 1929-

PERSONAL: Born April 12, 1929, in Warsaw, Poland; naturalized U.S. citizen. *Education:* University of Munich, Ph.D., 1957; Columbia University, certificate, 1964, Ph.D., 1968.

ADDRESSES: Office—Department of History, University of Iowa, Iowa City, IA 52242.

CAREER: King's College, PA, instructor, then assistant professor of German language and literature, 1958-61; American University, Washington, DC, assistant professor of history, 1964-67; University of Iowa, Iowa City, associate professor, 1967-71, research professor, 1971, professor of history, 1971—.

MEMBER: American Historical Association, American Association for the Advancement of Slavic Studies, American Association of University Professors.

AWARDS, HONORS: Fulbright fellowship, 1970-71; American Council of Learned Societies grant, 1971-72.

WRITINGS:

Russia and Kazan: Conquest and Imperial Ideology (1438-1560s), Mouton (The Hague, Netherlands), 1974.

(Editor) *The American and European Revolutions, 1776-1848: Sociopolitical and Ideological Aspects,* University of Iowa Press (Iowa City), 1980.

(Editor) *The Political and Social Ideas of Vjaceslav Lypyns'kyj,* Harvard University Press (Cambridge, MA), 1987.

(Editor, with Peter P. Potichnyj, Marc Raeff, and Gleb N. Zekulin) *Ukraine and Russia in Their Historical Encounter,* Canadian Institute of Ukrainian Studies Press (Hamilton, Ontario), 1995.

Contributor to journals, including *Slavic Review.*

SIDELIGHTS: A historian, educator, and author, Jaroslaw Pelenski began teaching Russian and East Central European history at the University of Iowa in 1967; he became full professor of history in 1971. In addition to his commitment as an educator, Polish-born Pelenski has channelled his expertise on Muscovite Russia and Eastern European history into several books, including *Russia and Kazan: Conquest and Imperial Ideology (1438-1560s),* published in 1974.

In addition to *Russia and Kazan,* Pelenski served as editor of 1980's *The American and European Revolutions, 1776-1848: Sociopolitical and Ideological Aspects,* and of 1987's *The Political and Social Ideas of Vjaceslav Lypyns'kyj,* which David Saunders describes in the *English Historical Review* as "placing [radical Ukrainian political theorist Lypyns'kyj's] ideas in context and according them a respect they have rarely received." The 1995 historiographic study *Ukraine and Russia in Their Historical Encounter,* which Pelenski co-edited, was based on papers read at a Canadian conference held in 1981. While, as Mark Sandle notes in *History Today,* "the only regrettable feature of an otherwise impressive volume is the failure to update the papers (except in a couple of cases, and then only cursorily) in the light of the momentous changes in historical interpretation which have occurred since 1985," *Ukraine and Russia* includes an interview between Pelenski and former Soviet dissident Aleksandr Solzhenitsyn, in which the two men assess Russian-Ukrainian relations in light of the demise of post-*glastnost* Stalinist orthodoxy. A contributor of articles to academic journals, Pelenski was honored with a Fulbright fellowship in 1970 and as a fellow of the American Council of Learned Societies from 1971 to 1972.

BIOGRAPHICAL/CRITICAL SOURCES:

PERIODICALS

American Historical Review, February, 1976, p. 183; February, 1990, pp. 204-205.
English Historical Review, April, 1991, pp. 517-518.
History Today, July, 1995, p. 53.
New York Review of Books, September 19, 1983, pp. 18-27.*

* * *

PELLICER, Carlos 1899-1977

PERSONAL: Born November 4, 1899, in Villahermosa, Tabasco, Mexico; died February 15, 1977, in Mexico City, Mexico; son of Carlos (an army colonel) and Deifilia Camara de Pellicer. *Education:* Escuela Nacional Preparatoria, graduate.

CAREER: Served in Mexican diplomatic corps in Columbia and other countries; university professor of modern poetry; director of the Ministry of Fine Arts; founding curator, Museo-Parque de la Venta, Villahermosa, Mexico; director, Palacio de Bellas Artes.

MEMBER: Congress of Latin American Writers (president, 1965).

AWARDS, HONORS: National Literature Prize, Mexico, 1964.

WRITINGS:

Colores en el mar y otros poemas, Libreria Cultura, 1921.
Piedra de sacrificios, Poema iberoamericano, Editorial Nayarit S.A., 1924.
6, 7 poemas, Aztlan-Editores, 1924.
Bolivar, Secretaria de Educacion Publica, 1925.
Hora y Veinte, Editorial Paris-America (Paris), 1927.
Camino, Talleres de Tipografia Solsona (Paris), 1929.
Esquemas para una oda tropical, Secretaria de Relaciones Exteriores, 1933.
Estrofas del mar marino, Imprenta Mundial, 1934.
Hora de junio, Ediciones Hipocampo, 1937, reprinted, Fondo de Cultura Economica, 1979.

Recinto y otras imagenes, Edicion Tezontle, 1941, reprinted, Fondo de Cultura Economica, 1979.

Exagonos, Nueva Voz, 1941.

(Contributor) *Three Spanish American Poets: Pellicer, Neruda, and Andrade,* Swallow & Critchlow (Albuquerque), 1942.

Subordinaciones: Poemas, Editorial Jus, 1949.

Sonetos, [Mexico], 1950.

(With Salvador Toscano) *Julio Castellanos, 1905-1947,* Editorial Netzahualcoyotl, 1953.

Practica de vuela, Edicion Tezontle, 1956.

Museo de Tabasco: Guia Oficial, Instituto Nacional de Antropologia e Historia, 1961.

Material poetico, 1918-1961, Universidad Nacional Autonoma de Mexico, 1962.

Con palabras y fuego, Fondo de Cultura Economica, 1962.

Teotihuacan, y 13 de agosto: ruina de Tenochtitlan, Ediciones Ecuador, 1964.

Simon Bolivar, Secretaria de Educacion Publica, Subsecretaria de Asuntos Culturales, 1965.

(With Jose Vasconcelos and Manuel R. Mora) *Geopolitica de Tabasco,* Editorial Politica Nueva, 1965.

(With Ruth Rivera and Dolores Olmedo de Olvera) *Anahuacalli: Museo Diego Rivera,* Artes de Mexico, 1965.

Leonardo Nierman, Artes de Mexico, 1967.

(Author of text with Max Mittler) *Mexiko,* Atlantis Verlag (Zurich), 1968.

(Editor with others) *Primera antologia poetica: Poemas liricos, heroicos, en el paisaje y religiosos,* Fondo de Cultura Economica, 1969.

(Author of prologue and three poems) *Jose Maria Velasco: Pintures, dibujos, acuarelas,* Fondo Editorial de la Plastica Mexicana, 1970.

Noticias sobre Nezahualcoyotl y algunos sentimientos, Gobierno del Estado de Mexico, 1972.

(With Justino Fernandez and Gonzalo Obregon) *Los manos del mexicano,* Grupo Financiero Comermex, 1975.

Esquemas para una oda tropical, Fondo de Cultura Economica, 1976.

Reincidencias, Fondo de Cultura Economica, 1978.

Cosillas para el nacimiento, Editorial Latitudes, 1978.

Practica de vuela, Fondo de Cultura Economica, 1979.

Cuaderno de viaje, Ediciones del Equilibrista, 1987.

Also author, with Negrete Martinez, of *Es un pais lejano,* Impreso por Foto-Ilustradores.

SIDELIGHTS: Carlos Pellicer was a Mexican poet known for a "dazzling and sensuous tropicalism,"

according to Edward J. Mullen in his book-length study *Carlos Pellicer.* The poet's place in contemporary Mexican literature is secure. As Mullen stated, "Pellicer's celebration of the physical and cosmic splendors of the New World, his constant identification with the immediate world of the senses, and pervasive concern for social justice, clearly place him in the mainstream of twentieth-century Spanish-American literature."

BIOGRAPHICAL/CRITICAL SOURCES:

BOOKS

Mullen, Edward J., *Carlos Pellicer,* Twayne, 1977.

OBITUARIES:

PERIODICALS

New York Times, February 18, 1977.*

* * *

**PENA, Ramon Jose Simon del Valle y
 See VALLE-INCLAN, Ramon (Maria) del**

* * *

PEREZ GALDOS, Benito 1843-1920

PERSONAL: Born May 10, 1843, in Las Palmas, Grand Canary Island, Canary Islands, Spain; died January 4, 1920, in Madrid, Spain; buried in Madrid's Almudena Cemetery; son of Sebastian Perez (a lieutenant colonel in the army) and Maria de los Dolores Galdos; children: (with Lorenza Cobian) Maria. *Education:* Studied law at University of Madrid, Spain, 1862-65.

CAREER: Writer. Partner, with Miguel Honorio de Camara y Cruz, in publishing business, 1874-96; founder of publishing company, 1898. Elected to Spanish parliament as Liberal Party representative for the Guayama district of Puerto Rico, 1886, as Republican Party representative for Madrid, 1907, and as Republican Party representative for Las Palmas, 1914.

WRITINGS:

NOVELS; "NOVELAS ESPANOLAS CONTEMPORANEAS" SE-
RIES

La desheredada, [Madrid], 1881, reprinted, La
Guirnalda, 1890, translation by Guy E. Smith
published as *The Disinherited Lady: A Novel,*
Exposition Press (New York), 1957, translation
by Lester Clark published as *The Disinherited,*
Folio Society (London), 1976.

El amigo Manso (title means "Friend Manso"),
[Madrid], 1882, reprinted, Losada (Buenos
Aires), 1939, edited with an introductory note by
Federico Carlos Sainz de Robles, Aguilar, 1969,
translation by Robert Russell published as *Our
Friend Manso,* Columbia University Press, 1987.

El Doctor Centeno, two volumes, [Madrid], 1883,
published in one volume, La Guirnalda, 1896.

Tormento, [Madrid], 1884, translation by J. M.
Cohen published as *Torment,* Weidenfield &
Nicolson, 1952, Farrar, Straus, 1953.

La de Bringas, La Guirnalda, 1884, translation by
Gamel Woolsey published as *The Spendthrifts,*
introduction by Gerald Brenan, Farrar, Straus,
1952, reprinted, Arden Library, 1978.

Lo prohibido (title means "The Prohibited"), two
volumes, La Guirnalda, 1884-85, edited with in-
troduction and notes by Jose F. Montesinos,
Castalia, 1971.

Fortunata y Jacinta (dos historias de casadas), four
volumes, [Madrid], 1886-87, reprinted, Her-
nando, 1979, translation by Clark of original
Spanish edition published as *Fortunata and
Jacinta: Two Stories of Married Women,* Pen-
guin, 1973, translation by Agnes Moncy Gullon
published under same title, University of Georgia
Press, 1986.

Miau (title means "Meow"), La Guirnalda, 1888,
edited with introduction by Ricardo Gullon,
Ediciones de la Universidad de Puerto Rico,
1957, translation by J. M. Cohen published under
same title, Methuen, 1963, Dufour, 1965.

La incognita, La Guirnalda, 1889, edited by R.
Gullon, Taurus, 1976.

Torquemada en la hoguera, [Madrid], 1889, re-
printed, Tello (Madrid), 1898, edited with intro-
duction and notes by Angel del Rio, Instituto de
las Espanas en los Estados Unidos (New York),
1932, edited with an introduction by J. L.
Brooks, Pergamon, 1973, translation by N.
Round of original Spanish edition published as
Torquemada in the Fire, University of Glasgow,
Department of English Literature, 1985.

Realidad: Novela en cinco jornadas, La Guirnalda,
1890, edited by R. Gullon, Taurus, 1977.

Angel Guerra, three volumes, La Guirnalda, 1890-91,
reprinted, Hernando, 1970.

Tristana, La Guirnalda, 1892, translation by R.
Selden Rose published under same title, R. R.
Smith (Peterborough, NH), 1961.

La loca de la casa (title means "The Mad Woman of
the House"), [Madrid], 1892, reprinted, Revista
Literaria—Novelas y Cuentos (Madrid), 1963,
translation published as *The Theatre of Galdos,*
Edwin Mellen Press (Lewiston, NY), 1995.

Torquemada en la Cruz (title means "Torquemada on
the Cross"), La Guirnalda, 1893.

Torquemada en el purgatorio (title means
"Torquemada in Purgatory"), La Guirnalda,
1894.

Torquemada y San Pedro (title means "Torquemada
and Saint Peter"), La Guirnalda, 1895.

Nazarin, La Guirnalda, 1895, reprinted, Hernando,
1969.

Halma, La Guirnalda, 1895.

Misericordia, [Madrid], 1897, published with a spe-
cial preface by the author, Nelson, 1913, edited
with notes by Jose Padin and prologue by
Federico de Onis, Heath, 1928, college edition
edited with introduction, notes, vocabulary, and
questions by Angel del Rio and McKendree
Petty, Dryden Press (New York), 1946, transla-
tion by Tony Talbot of original Spanish edition
published as *Compassion: A Novel,* Ungar, 1962,
translation by Joan MacLean of original Spanish
edition published as *Compassion,* American R.
D. M. Corp., 1966.

El abuelo (novela en cinco jornadas) (title means
"The Grandfather [Five-Act Novel]"), Tello,
1897, reprinted, Hernando, 1956.

Casandra (novela en cinco jornadas) (title means
"Casandra [Five-Act Novel]"), [Madrid], 1905,
with prologue by Sainz de Robles, Aguilar, 1961.

El caballero encantado (cuento real . . . inverosimil),
Perlado, Paez, 1909, edited by Julio Rodriguez-
Puertolas, Catedra, 1977.

*La razon de la sinrazon: Fabula teatral absolutamente
inverosimil,* [Madrid], 1915.

Torquemada (translation by Frances M. Lopez-
Morillas of *Torquemada en la hoguera,
Torquemada en la Cruz, Torquemada en el
purgatorio, Torquemada y San Pedro*), Colombia
University Press, 1986.

NOVELS; EPISODIOS NACIONALES: FIRST SERIES

Trafalgar, [Madrid], 1873, corrected edition, Tello,
1901, reprinted, Losada, 1939, translation by

Clara Bell of original Spanish edition published as *Trafalgar: A Tale,* W. S. Gottsberger (New York), 1884, abridged edition adapted and edited by Ramon Espinosa and Alden R. Hefler, Oxford University Press (New York), 1941.

La corte de Carlos IV, [Madrid], 1873, corrected edition, Tello, 1900, translation by Bell of original Spanish edition published as *The Court of Charles IV: A Romance of the Escorial,* W. S. Gottsberger, 1888, corrected Spanish edition reprinted, Hernando, 1970.

El 19 de marzo y el 2 de mayo (title means "March Nineteenth and May Second"), [Madrid], 1873, reprinted, Obras de Perez Galdos (Madrid), 1898.

Bailen, [Madrid], 1873, corrected edition, Obras de Perez Galdos, 1900, reprinted, Alianza Hernando, 1976.

Napoleon en Chamartin (title means "Napoleon in Chamartin"), [Madrid], 1874, corrected edition, Tello, 1899, reprinted, Alianza, 1976.

Zaragoza, [Madrid], 1874, corrected edition, Tello, 1901, edited with introduction, notes, and vocabulary by John Van Horne, Ginn, 1926, translation of original Spanish edition by Minna Caroline Smith published as *Saragossa: A Story of Spanish Valor,* Little, Brown, 1899.

Gerona, [Madrid], 1874, corrected edition, Obras de Perez Galdos, c. 1897, reprinted, Alianza, 1976.

Cadiz, [Madrid], 1874, corrected edition, Obras de Perez Galdos, 1901.

Juan Martin, el Empecinado, [Madrid], 1874, corrected edition, Obras de Perez Galdos, 1898, edited with introduction, notes, and vocabulary by Paul Patrick Rogers, Stanford University Press, 1929, corrected Spanish edition reprinted, Alianza, 1976.

La batalla de los Arapiles, [Madrid], 1875, corrected edition, Obras de Perez Galdos, c. 1898, abridged edition, edited by Juan B. Rael, Odyssey Press (New York), 1941.

Trafalgar; La corte de Carlos IV, Critica (Barcelona), 1995.

NOVELS; EPISODIOS NACIONALES: SECOND SERIES

El equipaje del rey Jose, [Madrid], 1875, corrected edition, Obras de Perez Galdos, 1899, reprinted, Alianza/Hernando, 1976.

Memorias de un cortesano de 1815 (title means "Memoirs of a Cortesan of 1815"), [Madrid], 1875, corrected edition, Obras de Perez Galdos, 1897.

La segunda casaca, [Madrid], 1876, corrected edition, Obras de Perez Galdos, 1899, reprinted, Alianza, 1976.

El Grande Oriente, [Madrid], 1876, corrected edition, Obras de Perez Galdos, 1898, reprinted, Alianza, 1976.

7 de julio (title means "July Seventh"), [Madrid], 1876, corrected edition, Obras de Perez Galdos, 1899, reprinted, Alianza, 1976.

Los cien mil hijos de San Luis, [Madrid], 1877, corrected edition, Obras de Perez Galdos, 1899, reprinted, Alianza, 1976.

El terror de 1824 (title means "The Terror of 1824"), [Madrid], 1877, corrected edition, Obras de Perez Galdos, 1899, reprinted, Alianza, 1976.

Un voluntario realista, [Madrid], 1878, corrected edition, Obras de Perez Galdos, 1900, reprinted, Alianza, 1976.

Los apostolicos, [Madrid], 1879, corrected edition, Obras de Perez Galdos, 1899, reprinted, Hernando, 1932.

Un faccioso mas y algunos frailes menos, [Madrid], 1879, corrected edition, Tello, 1898.

NOVELS; EPISODIOS NACIONALES: THIRD SERIES

Zumalacarregui, [Madrid], 1898, reprinted, Perlado, Paez, 1906.

Mendizabal, [Madrid], 1898, Obras de Perez Galdos, 1900.

De Onate a la Granja, [Madrid], 1898, reprinted, Hernando, 1930, reprinted, Alianza, 1977.

Luchana, [Madrid], 1899, reprinted, Perlado, Paez, 1906, reprinted, Alianza/Hernando, 1976.

La campana del Maestrazgo, Obras de Perez Galdos, 1899, reprinted, Hernando, 1953.

La estafeta romantica, [Madrid], 1899, reprinted, Obras de Perez Galdos, 1900, reprinted, Alianza, 1978.

Vergara, [Madrid], 1899, reprinted, Perlado, Paez, 1906, reprinted, Alianza, 1978.

Montes de Oca, [Madrid], 1900, reprinted, Hernando, 1930, reprinted, Alianza, 1978.

Los Ayacuchos, [Madrid], 1900, reprinted, Alianza/Hernando, 1978.

Bodas reales (title means "Royal Wedding"), [Madrid], 1900, corrected edition, Obras de Perez Galdos, 1903, reprinted, Alianza, 1978.

NOVELS; EPISODIOS NACIONALES: FOURTH SERIES

Las tormentas del 48 (title means "The Storms of '48"), Tello, 1902, reprinted, Alianza/Hernando, 1978.

Narvaez, Obras de Perez Galdos, 1902, reprinted, Alianza, 1979.

Los duendes de la camarilla, Obras de Perez Galdos, 1903.

La revolucion de julio, Obras de Perez Galdos, 1903, reprinted, Historia 16 (Madrid), 1995.

O'Donnell, Obras de Perez Galdos, 1904, reprinted, Alianza, 1979.

Aita Tettauen, Obras de Perez Galdos, 1905, reprinted, Alianza, 1979.

Carlos VI en la Rapita, Obras de Perez Galdos, 1905, reprinted, Alianza/Hernando, 1979.

La vuelta al mundo en la Numancia, Perlado, Paez, 1906, reprinted, Alianza/Hernando, 1980.

Prim, Perlado, Paez, 1906, reprinted, Alianza, 1980.

La de los tristes destinos, Perlado, Paez, 1907, reprinted, Alianza/Hernando, 1980.

NOVELS; EPISODIOS NACIONALES: FINAL SERIES

Espana sin rey (title means "Spain without a King"), Perlado, Paez, 1908.

Espana tragica (title means "Tragic Spain"), Perlado, Paez, 1909.

Amadeo I, Perlado, Paez, 1910.

La primera Republica (title means "The First Republic"), Perlado, Paez, 1911, reprinted, Alianza, 1980.

De Cartago a Sagunto, Perlado, Paez, 1911, reprinted, Alianza, 1980.

Canovas, Perlado, Paez, 1912, reprinted, Alianza, 1980.

PLAYS

Realidad: Drama en cinco actos (title means "Reality: Five-Act Drama"; adapted from his novel; first produced in Madrid at Teatro de la Comedia, March 15, 1892), [Madrid], 1892.

La loca de la casa: Comedia en cuatro actos (four-act; adapted from his novel; first produced in Madrid at Teatro de la Comedia, January 16, 1893), La Guirnalda, 1893, edited with introduction, notes, exercises, and vocabulary by J. Warshaw, Holt, 1924.

Gerona (four-act drama; adapted from his novel), first produced in Madrid, February 3, 1893.

La de San Quintin: Comedia en tres actos (three-act; first produced in Madrid at Teatro de la Comedia, January 27, 1894), La Guirnalda, 1894, translation by Philip M. Hayden published as "The Duchess of San Quintin—La de San Quintin," in *Masterpieces of Modern Spanish Drama,* [New York], 1917.

Los condenados (three-act drama with prologue), first produced in Madrid at Teatro de la Comedia, December 11, 1894.

Voluntad: Comedia en tres actos (title means "Will Power: Three-Act Play"; first produced in Madrid at Teatro Espanol, December 20, 1895), [Madrid], 1907.

Dona Perfecta: Drama en cuatro actos (four-act drama; based on his novel; first produced in Madrid at Teatro de la Comedia, January 28, 1896), [Madrid], 1896.

La fiera (three-act drama), first produced in Madrid at Teatro de la Comedia, December 23, 1896.

Electra: Drama en cinco actos (first produced in Madrid at Teatro Espanol on January 30, 1901), Obras de Perez Galdos, 1901, published in English translation by C. A. Turrell under same title in *Contemporary Spanish Dramatists,* [Boston], 1919.

Alma y vida: Drama en cuatro actos precedido de un prologo (title means "Soul and Life: Four-Act Drama Preceded by a Prologue"; first produced in Madrid at Teatro Espanol, April 9, 1902), Obras de Perez Galdos, 1902.

Mariucha: Comedia en cinco actos (five-act comedy; first produced in Barcelona at Teatro Eldorado, July 16, 1903), [Madrid], 1903, edited with an introduction, notes, and vocabulary by S. Griswold Morley, Heath, 1921.

El abuelo: Drama en cinco actos (adapted from his novel; first produced in Madrid at Teatro Espanol, February 14, 1904), [Madrid], 1904, edited by H. Chonon Berkowitz, Century, 1929, translation by Elizabeth Wallace published as *The Grandfather (Drama in Five Acts),* R. G. Badger, 1910.

Barbara: Tragicomedia en cuatro actos (four-act tragicomedy), first produced in Madrid at Teatro Espanol, March 28, 1905.

Amor y ciencia: Comedia en cuatro actos (four-act tragicomedy; first produced in Madrid at Teatro de la Comedia, November 17, 1905), [Madrid], 1905.

Pedro Minio (two-act comedy), first produced in Madrid at Teatro de Lara, December 15, 1908.

Casandra (four-act drama; adapted from his novel), first produced in Madrid at Teatro Espanol, February 28, 1910.

Celia en los infiernos: Comedia en cuatro actos (four-act comedy; first produced in Madrid at Teatro Espanol, December 9, 1913), [Madrid], 1913.

Alceste: Tragicomedia en tres actos (three-act tragicomedy; first produced in Madrid at Teatro de la Princesa, April 21, 1914), [Madrid], 1914.

Sor Simona: Drama en tres actos y cuatro cuadros (title means "Sister Simone: Drama in Three Acts and Four Scenes"; first produced in Madrid at Teatro de la Infanta Isabel, December 1, 1915), [Madrid], 1916.

El tacano Salomon: Comedia en dos actos (two-act comedy; first produced in Madrid at Teatro de Lara, February 2, 1916), [Madrid], 1916.

Santa Juana de Castilla: Tragicomedia en tres actos (three-act tragicomedy; first produced in Madrid at Teatro de la Princesa, May 8, 1918), [Madrid], 1918.

Anton Caballero: Comedia en tres actos (three-act; posthumous work adapted by Serafin y Joaquin Alvarez Quintero; first produced in Madrid at Teatro del Centro on December 16, 1921), Hernando, 1922.

Teatro selecto (collection), Escelicer (Madrid), 1972.

Also author of "Un joven de provecho" (four-act comedy; written c. 1867), published in *PMLA,* 1935, and "Quien mal hace, bien no espere" (one-act dramatic experiment; written 1861), 1974.

OTHER

La fontana de oro: Novela historica (title means "The Golden Fountain: Historical Novel"), privately printed (Madrid), 1870, reprinted, Brockhaus, 1883, special commemorative edition celebrating the centenary of the author's birth, Losada, 1943.

La sombra, [Madrid], 1871, reprinted, La Guirnalda, 1890, Spanish text edited with English introduction by Rodolfo Cardona, Norton, 1964, translation of original Spanish edition by Karen O. Austin, published as *The Shadow,* Ohio University Press, 1980.

El audaz: Historia de un radical de antano (novel), [Madrid], 1871, reprinted, La Guirnalda, 1891, edited with a prologue by Elias Lynch Rivers, Geminis (Montevideo), 1975.

Dona Perfecta (novel), [Madrid], 1876, reprinted, Hernando, 1969, translation by D. P. W. published as *Dona Perfecta: A Tale of Modern Spain,* Tinsley (London), 1880, translation by Mary Wharton published as *Lady Perfecta,* Independent Novel Series, 1894, translation by Mary Jane Serrano published as *Dona Perfecta,* Harper, 1896, Serrano's translation reprinted, Arden Library, 1979, translation by Harriet de Onis with her introduction published under same title, Barron's, 1960.

Gloria, two volumes, [Madrid], 1876-77, translation by N. Wetherell published under same title, two

volumes, [London], 1879, translation by Bell published under same title, two volumes, W. S. Gottsberger, 1882, Bell's translation reprinted, Fertig, 1974, corrected Spanish edition, Obras de Perez Galdos, 1900-01, published as *Gloria: Novela de costumbres,* edited with notes, exercises and vocabulary by Alexander H. Krappe and Lawrence M. Levin, Century (New York), 1927.

Marianela (novel), [Madrid], 1878, corrected edition, Obras de Perez Galdos, 1899, translation by Bell published under same title, W. S. Gottsberger, 1883, translation by Helen W. Lester published as *Marianela: A Story of Spanish Love,* A. C. McClurg and Co. (Chicago, IL), 1892, Lester's translation reprinted, Arden Library, 1979, translation by Wharton published as *Marianela,* Digby & Long (London), 1893, corrected Spanish edition edited by Nicholson B. Adams, reprinted, Ginn, 1951.

La familia de Leon Roch (title mean "The Family of Leon Roch"; novel), three volumes, [Madrid], 1878-79, reprinted with prologue by Sainz de Robles, Aguilar, 1960, translation by Bell of original Spanish edition published as *Leon Roch: A Romance,* W. S. Gottsberger, 1888, reprinted, Fertig, 1974.

Guerra de la independencia: Extractada para uso de los ninos (title means "War of Independence: Extracts for Use by Children"; abridged juvenile edition of novels of "Episodios nacionales: First Series"), Hernando, c. 1906.

Memoranda, Perlado, Paez, 1906.

Casa de Shakespeare. Portugal. De vuelta de Italia., A. Lopez (Barcelona), c. 1920.

Obras ineditas (title means "Unpublished Works"), Volume 1: *Fisonomias sociales,* Renacimiento, 1923, Volume 2: *Arte y critica* (title means "Art and Criticism"), Renacimiento, 1923, Volumes 3 and 4: *Politica espanola* (title means "Spanish Politics"), Renacimiento, 1923, Volume 5: *Nuestro teatro,* Renacimiento, 1923, Volumes 6 and 7: *Cronicon,* Renacimiento, 1924, Volume 8: *Toledo (su historia y su leyenda)* (title means "Toledo [Her History and Her Legend]"), Renacimiento, 1924, Volume 9: *Viajes y fantasias* (title means "Travels and Fantasies"), Compania Ibero-Americana de Publicaciones (Madrid), 1928, Volume 10: *Memorias,* Renacimiento, 1930, Volume 11: *Cronica de Madrid (1865-1866),* Castro (Madrid), 1933.

La novela en el tranvia: Obra inedita, Ercilla, 1936.

Obras completas, edited by Sainz de Robles, six volumes, Aguilar, 1941-42.

Cartas de Perez Galdos a Mesonero Romanos (correspondence), Seccion de Cultura e Informacion (Madrid), 1943.

Cronica de la quincena, edited with a preliminary study by William H. Shoemaker, Princeton University Press, 1948.

Episodios nacionales: Narrados a los ninos (title means "National Episodes: Told to Children"), school edition edited by daughter, Maria Perez Galdos, Hernando, 1948.

Antologia (title means "Anthology"), edited by Amando de Miguel, Doncel (Madrid), 1960.

Benito Perez Galdos y la Revista del Movimiento Intelectual de Europa, Madrid, 1865-1867 (collection of journalistic pieces), compiled by Leo J. Hoar, Jr., Insula, 1968.

Los articulos de Galdos en "La Nacion," 1865-1866, 1868, edited with a preliminary study by Shoemaker, Insula, 1972.

Las cartas desconocidas de Galdos en "La Prensa" de Buenos Aires (title means "The Undiscovered Letters of Galdos in 'La Prensa' of Buenos Aires"), edited by Shoemaker, Cultura Hispanica, 1973.

Rosalia, Catedra, 1984.

Author of numerous prologues. Translator of Charles Dickens's *Pickwick Papers,* 1868. Contributor of "The Battle of Salamanca: A Tale of the Napoleonic War," translated by Rollo Ogden, to *Lippincott's Monthly Magazine,* 1895. Contributor to periodicals, including *La Nacion* (newspaper), *El Debate* (newspaper), *La Guiralda* (magazine), *El Oceano* (magazine), and *La Prensa* (Buenos Aires newspaper). Contributor to and editor of *Revista de Espana* (magazine), 1872-73.

ADAPTATIONS: Marianela was adapted by Serafin and Joaquin Quintero for a play of the same title, 1916; *El audaz: Historia de un radical de antano* was adapted by Jacinto Benavente for a play of the same title, 1919; *Tristana* was adapted for a film of the same title by Luis Bunuel, 1970.

SIDELIGHTS: Benito Perez Galdos (usually referred to by his maternal surname) is regarded as the most important Spanish novelist since Cervantes. Many critics, such as noted Spanish scholar Salvador de Madariaga, assign him a position among the giants of nineteenth-century European letters. In *The Genius of Spain and Other Essays on Spanish Contemporary Literature,* Madariaga noted, "In European literature Galdos undoubtedly deserves to rank with the great novelists of the century, in line with Dickens, Balzac,

and Dostoievsky." Although Galdos's works are intimately linked with nineteenth-century Spain, his ability to appeal to audiences outside his own time and culture appeared to be confirmed when several of his most important novels were released in English translation in the 1980s to general critical approval.

Galdos showed his inclination toward the writing profession at an early age when he began contributing articles to local papers while still a secondary-school student living in his native Canary Islands, an archipelago under Spanish jurisdiction off the coast of Africa. While he had considered continuing his education with university studies in architecture, his mother was insistent that her youngest child become a lawyer. Duly enrolled at the University of Madrid's Law School, Galdos soon found his interests lay elsewhere and rarely attended classes after the first year. He preferred to study the city which was to become the backdrop for most of his novels on innumerable walks through its picturesque lower-class neighborhoods. He established himself as a regular at several of the capital's popular cafes where he could spend hours observing its colorful types and colloquial language. He also tried to learn as much as he could about Madrilenian customs by reading the works of authors such as Ramon de la Cruz, who produced many short plays depicting the customs of eighteenth-century Madrid.

During Galdos's first decade in the Spanish capital he concentrated on his journalistic endeavors, including contributing to a variety of periodicals and working as an editor. Eventually, finding himself drawn to the theater, he wrote several plays for which he was unable to find a producer or publisher. A trip to Paris in May, 1867—which strengthened his recently awakened interest in the French novelist Honore de Balzac—seemed to be the catalyst the young writer needed to finally attempt to write in the genre which would become his life's work: the novel. The following summer he wrote *La fontana de oro: Novela historica,* his first published novel, while once again in France, and in 1871 two of his novels, *La sombra* and *El audaz: Historia de un radical de antano,* were published in serial form by two of Madrid's leading periodicals. Two years later, encouraged by the success of these early writings, Galdos abandoned most of his journalistic activities and began to write a series of novels he called "Episodios nacionales" ("National Episodes"), which established his reputation as Spain's foremost novelist.

The novels were written at an incomparable speed; the first series of ten were completed by 1875. At

that time, Galdos immediately began a new series which he finished writing before the end of the decade. The first series was an account of Spanish history beginning at the Battle of Trafalgar in 1805, concluding with the end of the Napoleonic invasion of Spain at the Battle of Los Arapiles in 1812. The second series dealt with the struggle of the Spanish people to gain independence from the oppressive reign of King Ferdinand VII and ended with the monarch's death in 1934. Eventually, the series included forty-six volumes in five separate series spanning the first three quarters of the nineteenth century.

The interconnectedness between volumes in each series, through repetition of characters and related events, led to a comparison with the similarly constructed *Comedie humaine* of Balzac and the "Rougon-Macquart" novels of Emile Zola. Despite these foreign influences, Galdos's focus in the "Episodes" was fixed on his native country. "The aim of the novels was nothing less," wrote Lester Clark in his introduction to his English translation of Galdos's *Fortunata y Jacinta (dos historias de casadas),* "than the regeneration of Spain through the awakening of a new national conscience." Using newspaper accounts and eyewitness testimonies, weaving historical fact with vibrant fiction, Galdos was able to paint a grand portrait of Spain's history. In *Hispania* Hayward Keniston called the series "the great national epic of the first half of the past century."

Although some critics find the novels of the later series less appealing than those of the first two, together the "Episodes" are considered to form an unequalled literary achievement. "In these stories," observed Clyde Chew Glascock in the *Texas Review,* "historical personages live again whose names were indistinctly engraven on the memory of Spaniards. [Galdos] gave them precision and personality, a body and a soul. These books are indeed a faithful reproduction of the national incidents and characters of the epoch, of the inner and outer life of Spaniards during the nineteenth century." Madariaga similarly commented: "In these forty-six volumes, many of which are admirable, and none of which can be passed over, Galdos gave us the history of Spain as seen from the drawing-room of contemporaries, not from the study of the historian. It is . . . a vivid and dramatic interpretation of the life of the people through the events of the century, their hopes, feelings, thoughts, and disappointments." In L. B. Walton's *Perez Galdos and the Spanish Novel of the Nineteenth Century,* the critic proclaimed, "The ['Episodes'] are not

. . . historical romances, in the orthodox sense of the term; but, inasmuch as they are an endeavor to interpret history in terms of the human spirit, they belong to the historical genre—of which, in modern Spanish literature, Galdos is, indisputably, the creator."

While the "Episodes" were extremely popular, Galdos felt confined by their historical outline. While he was writing the ten volumes of the second series he also composed four non-series novels: *Dona Perfecta, Gloria, La familia de Leon Roch,* and *Marianela.* Galdos used the first three works to express his vehement anti-clericalism. While not anti-Catholic, he felt that the heavy influence of the Roman Catholic church in Spain was a hindering block to Spain's intellectual and cultural growth. Of the three volumes, *Dona Perfecta* was, by far, the most popular and through several translations introduced Galdos to an enthusiastic international audience. The work was first published in 1876 in serial form in the prestigious Spanish magazine, *Revista de Espana,* for which Galdos had served as editor a few years earlier.

The novel takes place in the fictional provincial Spanish town of Orbajosa which W. D. Howells referred to in *Criticism and Fiction and Other Essays* as "the microcosm of bigoted and reactionary Spain." The story revolves around the monstrous figure of Dona Perfecta who permits her nephew, Pepe Rey, a liberal intellectual from Madrid, to be murdered rather than have her daughter marry him. Although the novel could be read as the struggle between an aunt and her nephew, critics noted that the characters are essentially symbols for the conflict Galdos saw in Spanish society at large. "The confrontation of Perfecta and Pepe," wrote John Devlin in *Spanish Anticlericalism: A Study in Modern Alienation,* "has all the tell-tale signs of the larger confrontation of clericalism and sincere liberalism that was taking place in Spain, and that was to culminate eventually in the murder and bloodshed of the Civil War." While some critics, such as Sherman H. Eoff, fault the novel for Galdos obvious manipulation of the story line to further his didactic purpose, they find in his portrait of Dona Perfecta the novel's redeeming quality. In *The Novels of Perez Galdos: The Concept of Life as Dynamic Process,* Eoff wrote: "The characterization of Dona Perfecta, nevertheless, more than counterbalances the novel's technical flaws. The portrait of her personality overshadows all else in the story and bears strong testimony to the assertion that Galdos' fundamental strength as a novelist is psychological."

Rodolfo Cardona praised Galdos's skill as a novelist in the introduction to his edition of *Dona Perfecta,* noting that only an author of Galdos's stature could keep the emotionally-charged atmosphere of the novel from becoming excessively melodramatic. In particular, he pointed out how Galdos used name symbolism (a technique found in other Galdosian works as well) to highlight at every opportunity the issue that Cardona saw as the novel's theme: hypocrisy. As Pepe Rey travels toward Orbajosa he notices that the names of some of the ugliest areas through which he must pass carry the most poetic names and he gives the examples of Valleameno ("Pleasant Valley") and Valdeflores ("Valley of the Flowers"). The litany of characters and places with fraudulent names continues throughout the novel: Dona Perfecta is not perfect, the town's conniving cleric, Don Inocencio, is not innocent, and Orbajosa, which Orbajosans fancy an "Urbs Augusta", is revealed as an "Orbajosa" or dunghill. "It is . . . ," Cardosa commented, "the contact of these two perspectives [inherent in the duality of each of the names] that causes the violent collision of the characters, which, in the context of the entire novel, is also seen as the collision between Orbajosa—the Spanish province—and Madrid—the metropolis—and what these places represent."

According to Cardosa, Galdos's ability to raise this story of familial strife to the height of a classical confrontation between good and evil endows the work with an universal appeal. Glascock also observed the timeless quality of the tale, noting: "The backwardness of country people in conforming to new conditions produced by the advance of education is found in every land. . . . The ill-feeling aroused in a little Spanish town because of difference in religious opinion due to differences of education and rearing might have been intense in almost any place if brought about by similar circumstances." And for this reason *Dona Perfecta* excited universal interest. Cardosa concluded, "The reason that Galdos's successful thesis novels, like *Dona Perfecta,* can continue to be read today is that they embody not doctrines but specific insights."

Although his "National Episodes" and his novels like *Dona Perfecta* were very popular, in 1879 Galdos announced that he would never write another historical novel (a promise he was later to break for financial reasons) and began work on a series of novels which he called his "Novelas contemporaneas espanolas" ("Contemporary Spanish Novels"). Although this series did not sell as well as his previously published works, it represents his most critically acclaimed writing. These "Contemporary Spanish Novels" show Galdos as a keen observer of daily life and a master of character delineation. Comparing these newer novels to Galdos's earlier production, Gerald Brenan wrote in *The Literature of the Spanish People: From Roman Times to the Present:* "There is a change of accent from the earlier works. In them the principal characters personified ideas, now he draws individuals." Glascock offered his comparison of the new series of novels to the old with the observation: "After passing through a didactic, anticlerical stage . . . Galdos began a series of more realistic novels in which he aimed to present truth as he saw it and let the reader draw conclusions. The purpose does not obtrude, or is supposed not to do so, and interfere with art."

General critical consensus names *Fortunata y Jacinta (dos historias de casadas)* (*Fortunata and Jacinta: Two Stories of Married Women*) one of the "Contemporary Spanish Novels" and the longest the novelist ever wrote, as Galdos's masterpiece. Eoff called the novel, "one of the richest and most elaborate examples of nineteenth-century realism." Amongst its pages are found the characteristics of Galdos's work that align him with the great novelists of his day. "Sharing the determination of Balzac, Dickens, and Zola to present a faithful record of bourgeois society," wrote *Village Voice* contributor William Grimes, "he takes the reader down unfamiliar streets and peers behind the city's anonymous facades. He is a prolific creator of characters and types. Like Dostoyevski and Tolstoy, he regards his creations as spiritual beings, wrestling with questions that will determine the fate of their immortal souls." Critics also noted in this and in *La desheredada* and *Lo prohibido,* two other novels from the series, Galdos's growing affinity for the naturalism of Zola, with its emphasis on the debased side of human life.

Although influenced by Zola's ideas, Galdos never completely adopted the naturalist's tendencies, even though many of the twenty-four volumes of the "Contemporary Spanish Novels," including *Fortunata and Jacinta,* depict Madrid's lower classes in great detail. Galdos believed that in order to engender change in his society, the novelist had to depict every part of that society without exception. His descriptions of Madrid in *Fortunata and Jacinta,* in particular, are so accurate that one can trace the footsteps of the novel's characters on a map of modern day Madrid without difficulty. Galdos offers a social panorama of

Madrid as well as a geographical one: By choosing one of his title characters, Jacinta, from Madrid's middle class, and the other, Fortunata, from Madrid's slum area, he was able to present a complete cross-section of Madrid's society in the 1870s. The novel explores the interactions of the childless Jacinta with her husband, Juanito, and his mistress, Fortunata, who bears him a child. The highlight of the work is found in Galdos's psychological portrait of the two women mentioned in the title. Commenting on this aspect of the novel, Brenan maintained: "His two women—Jacinta especially—are drawn with marvelous skill and delicacy. No writer, except perhaps Tolstoy, has shown such a deep and intimate understanding of women's characters and feelings."

Because the "Contemporary Spanish Novels" did not draw as many readers as his historical novels, Galdos found himself facing mounting debts and in 1898 returned to writing his "National Episodes." During this last period of his life, he also wrote nearly two dozen plays, including several adapted from his novels, and attempted to enact the reforms indicated in his fiction by re-entering politics as a member of the Spanish parliament (he had served one term in parliament nearly twenty years earlier). In 1905, he suffered a stroke that left him partially paralyzed, and in 1912 became blind. That same year, the Spanish Royal Academy answered those who had been attempting to gain the Noble prize for the aging author by refusing to sponsor his candidacy for the award, largely due to his liberal, anticlerical philosophy. By October, 1919, he was confined to his bed after an attack of uremia. The novelist died three months later, on January 4, 1920, and, the following day, was laid in state in Madrid's City Hall where tens of thousands of Madrilenos thronged to pay their last respects.

According to many critics Galdos was the father of the modern Spanish novel, for the genre was nearly nonexistent in Spain when he began his literary career. His sweeping portrait of Spanish history, his fierce criticism of Spanish society, and his skill at drawing memorable individuals has led commentators to universally acknowledge Galdos as the premier novelist of nineteenth-century Spain. "Superior to all others in Spain in writing historical novels, in characterizing contemporary Spaniards of the middle class, in fertility of invention and in versatility of production," Glascock concluded, "his fame appears secure, not merely for our day, but as well for time to come."

BIOGRAPHICAL/CRITICAL SOURCES:

BOOKS

Bell, Aubrey F. G., *Contemporary Spanish Literature,* Knopf, 1925.

Brenan, Gerald, *The Literature of the Spanish People: From Roman Times to the Present,* 2nd edition, Cambridge University Press, 1953, reprinted, 1976.

Devlin, John, *Spanish Anticlericalism: A Study in Modern Alienation,* Las Americas, 1966.

Eoff, Sherman H., *The Novels of Perez Galdos: The Concept of Life as Dynamic Process,* Washington University Studies, 1954.

Eoff, Sherman H., *The Modern Spanish Novel: Comparative Essays Examining the Philosophical Impact of Science on Fiction,* New York University Press, 1961.

Ford, J. D. M., *Main Currents of Spanish Literature,* Holt, 1919.

Kirk, Clara Marburg, and Rudolf Kirk, editors, *Criticism and Fiction and Other Essays,* New York University Press, 1959.

Madariaga, Salvador de, *The Genius of Spain and Other Essays on Spanish Contemporary Literature,* Oxford at the Clarendon Press, 1923.

Pattison, Walter T., *Benito Perez Galdos,* Twayne, 1975.

Perez Galdos, Benito, *Dona Perfecta,* edited with notes and introduction by Rodolfo Cardona, Anaya, 1974.

Perez Galdos, Benito, *Fortunata and Jacinta: Two Stories of Married Women,* translated by Lester Clark, Penguin, 1973.

Walton, L. B., *Perez Galdos and the Spanish Novel of the Nineteenth Century,* Dent, 1927.

PERIODICALS

Hispania, October, 1920.
Los Angeles Times Book Review, July 13, 1986.
New York Times Book Review, February 22, 1987.
Texas Review, January, 1923.
Times Literary Supplement, October 12, 1973; August 28, 1987.
Village Voice, November 4, 1986.*

—*Sketch by Marian Gonsior*

* * *

PEREZ-MARCHAND, Monelisa L(ina) 1918-

PERSONAL: Born January 7, 1918, in Ponce, Puerto Rico.

CAREER: Professor at University of Puerto Rico, Rio Piedras; chair, Puerto Rican Commission to study the history of ideas.

WRITINGS:

Dos etapas ideologicas del siglo XVIII en Mexico a traves de los papeles de la Inquisicion, El Colegio de Mexico, 1945.
Historia de las ideas in Puerto Rico, Instituto de Cultura Puertorriquena, 1960, translation published as *History of Ideas in Puerto Rico,* Gordon Press, 1979.

Also author of monographs and essays. Assistant editor, *Asomante* (literary review).*

* * *

PERRY, Brighton
 See SHERWOOD, Robert E.

* * *

PETERSON, Louis (Stamford, Jr.) 1922-

PERSONAL: Born June 17, 1922, in Hartford, CT; son of Louis Peterson, Sr. (a bank employee) and Ruth Peterson (a bank employee; maiden name, Conover); married Margaret Mary Feury, July 21, 1952 (divorced, 1961). *Education:* Morehouse College, B.A., 1944; attended Yale University, 1944-45; New York University, M.A., 1947.

CAREER: Playwright and screenwriter for film and television. Actor in stage plays, including productions of Edwin Bronner's *A Young American,* 1946, Theodore Ward's *Our Lan',* 1947, and Carson McCullers's *The Member of the Wedding,* 1951; worked as a technician at an insurance company, c. 1960s; affiliated with State University of New York at Stony Brook, Department of Theatre Arts, beginning 1972.

AWARDS, HONORS: Benjamin Brawley Award for Excellence in English, 1944; *Take a Giant Step* was named as one of the best plays of 1953-54 by *Burns Mantle Yearbook.*

WRITINGS:

STAGE PLAYS

Take a Giant Step (produced in New York, 1954), Samuel French, 1954.
Entertain a Ghost, produced in New York, 1962.
Crazy Horse, produced in New York, 1979.
Another Show, produced at Stony Brook, New York, 1983.

FILM SCREENPLAYS

(With Alberto Lattuada) *The Tempest,* Cinecitta, 1957.
(With Julius Epstein) *Take a Giant Step* (adapted from Peterson's play), United Artists, 1958.

TELEVISION PLAYS

"Padlocks," *Danger,* CBS, 1954.
"Class of '58," *Goodyear Theatre,* NBC, 1954.
"Joey," *Goodyear Theatre,* NBC, 1956.
"Emily Rossiter Story," *Wagon Train,* NBC, 1957.
"Hit and Run," *Dr. Kildare,* NBC, 1961.

SIDELIGHTS: Louis Peterson established himself with his first play, *Take a Giant Step,* a coming-of-age story featuring a young black man, Spencer, who grows up in a predominantly white, middle-class area and faces the insidious racism meted out by his teachers and schoolmates. The play owes much to Peterson's own experience. He grew up in a largely white section of Hartford, Connecticut, and his parents, like Spencer's, worked in a bank. In a *New York Times* interview with Charles Peck, Peterson described his childhood surroundings as "very pleasant" though he also noted that "there were frictions" among the various ethnic groups in the area.

Beginning when Peterson was very young, his parents stressed that a college education was crucial to his success. Peterson's initial pursuit was music, having played the piano since youth. He shifted his major to English, however, and graduated from Morehouse College in Atlanta in 1944. Another interest was the theatre, and Peterson acted in several plays at Morehouse and later pursued graduate studies in drama at Yale and New York universities.

After obtaining his master's degree, Peterson won a minor role in a Broadway play in 1947. He continued to study acting with Stanford Meisner at New York's Neighborhood Playhouse School of the Theatre, but

maintained his desire to write. While studying acting with Lee Strasberg at the Actors Studio, he also took instruction in play writing from Clifford Odets. Odets mentored Peterson, sometimes working with him through the night.

In 1951, while touring as an actor in Carson McCullers's *The Member of the Wedding,* Peterson began to write *Take a Giant Step,* and he completed the play in 1952. Louis Gossett, Jr., then a high school senior, won the role of Spencer in the Broadway production of Peterson's debut play. Though it closed after just 76 performances, the play received a warm critical reception, and it was named as one of the best plays of 1953-54 by the *Burns Mantle Yearbook.*

Speaking about the play in Peck's *New York Times* interview, Peterson said that he felt "almost defensive" that the play did not address the more blatant forms of racism that were especially prevalent in the Southern United States. But as Steven R. Carter noted in *Dictionary of Literary Biography, Take a Giant Step* addressed "quieter, subtler forms" of racism, including "the racist version of Afro-American history in the 1950s, the overwhelming isolation of blacks living away from other blacks, and the fear that made many black parents seek to hobble proud, gifted children lest their strength provoke white fury."

These issues are played out as Spencer faces challenges and insults from his classmates and his teacher. In response to the instructor's assertion that black slaves were too stupid to gain their own freedom, Spencer calls the teacher ignorant and is subsequently suspended from school. His parents, although they fostered his pride in himself, do not support Spencer fully in his conflict and encourage him to avoid confrontations with whites. In a climactic speech, Spencer's mother tells him: "You think it's easy for me to tell my son to crawl when I know he can walk and walk well? I'm sorry I ever had children." In Carter's opinion, this passage prompts Spencer to modify his behavior; he apologizes to his mother for his actions and later distances himself from his white friends, minimizing the chances of further conflicts.

A later play, *Crazy Horse,* written in the late 1970s, was also semi-autobiographical and also employed the same realistic approach as *Take a Giant Step. Crazy Horse* is the account of a marriage between a black journalist and a white woman which crumbles under the opposition of both spouses' families. Peterson's 1983 work, *Another Show,* depicts a college student's suicide and the fallout experienced by those who knew him. Though several of Peterson's plays have been staged since *Take a Giant Step,* critics have suggested that the playwright's debut has had the most lasting impact of all his writing. "For the public and the critics," Carter wrote in *Dictionary of Literary Biography,* "his most significant work is indisputably his stirring, insightful and sensitive portrayal of a black adolescent modeled on himself in *Take a Giant Step."*

BIOGRAPHICAL/CRITICAL SOURCES:

BOOKS

Carter, Steven R., in *Dictionary of Literary Biography,* Volume 76: *Afro-American Writers, 1940-1955,* Gale, 1988, pp. 134-39.
Peterson, Louis, *Take a Giant Step,* Samuel French, 1954.

PERIODICALS

New York Times, September 20, 1953, section 2, p. 1; April 10, 1962, section 1, p. 48; November 12, 1979, section 3, p. 13; February 20, 1983.*

* * *

PETROPOULOS, Jonathan G. 1961-

PERSONAL: Born January 10, 1961, in Los Angeles, CA; son of George (an aerospace engineer) and Maureen (a dressage teacher) Petropoulos; married, May, 1994; wife's name, Kimberly (a university administrator). *Ethnicity:* "Caucasian." *Education:* Attended University of London, 1981-82; University of California, Los Angeles, B.A. (with honors), 1983; Harvard University, Ph.D., 1990, A.M., 1994. *Avocational interests:* Tennis, basketball.

ADDRESSES: Office—Department of History, Loyola College, 4501 North Charles St., Baltimore, MD 21210; fax 410-617-2832. *E-mail*—petropoulos@ loyola.edu.

CAREER: Harvard University, Cambridge, MA, lecturer in history, 1990-93; Loyola College, Baltimore, MD, assistant professor of history, 1993—. Consult-

ant to Kuenstlerhaus, Vienna, Austria, and Los Angeles County Museum of Art.

MEMBER: American Council on Germany, German Studies Association, Phi Beta Kappa.

WRITINGS:

Art as Politics in the Third Reich, University of North Carolina Press (Chapel Hill, NC), 1996.

Contributor of articles and reviews to periodicals.

WORK IN PROGRESS: Research on the art world during the Third Reich.

* * *

PFISTER, Patrick 1949-

PERSONAL: Born October 14, 1949, in Detroit, MI.

ADDRESSES: *Home*—Lauria 81, 3, 1a, 08009 Barcelona, Spain.

CAREER: Writer.

WRITINGS:

Pilgrimage (travel book), Academy Chicago Publishers (Chicago, IL), 1995.

WORK IN PROGRESS: A novel, *North Beach Hotel.*

* * *

PHILLIPS, John 1914-1996

OBITUARY NOTICE—See index for *CA* sketch: Born November 13, 1914, in Bouira, Algeria; immigrated to the U.S.; naturalized U.S. citizen; died August 22, 1996, in Manhattan, NY. Photojournalist, photographer, educator, and author. Phillips made a name for himself as a photojournalist for *Life* magazine, receiving acclaim for his wartime work. His stint with *Life* began in 1936 and ended in 1959. His photography was featured in exhibitions and his works are contained in permanent collections at several muse-

ums worldwide. He also taught at Manhattan's International Center of Photography. In addition to his photojournalism, Phillips wrote a number of books, including *Odd World: A Photo-Reporter's Story, The Italians: Face of a Nation, The Yugoslav Story,* and *It Happened in Our Lifetime: A Memoir in Words and Pictures.* He left behind an autobiography, which was near completion.

OBITUARIES AND OTHER SOURCES:

PERIODICALS

New York Times, August 26, 1996, p. B9.

* * *

PICKARD, Nancy 1945-

PERSONAL: Born in 1945.

ADDRESSES: *Home*—5740 Windsor Dr., Fairway, KS 66205.

CAREER: *The Squire,* Overland Park, KS, reporter and editor, 1967-69; Western Auto, Kansas City, MO, writer and supervisor, 1969-72; writer, 1973—.

MEMBER: Mystery Writers of America, Sisters in Crime (president, 1988-89).

AWARDS, HONORS: Anthony Award, 1985; Macavity Award for novel, 1987, for short story, 1989; Shamus Award, 1991, for short story "Dust Devils."

WRITINGS:

"JENNY CAIN" MYSTERIES

Generous Death, Avon (New York), 1984.
Say No to Murder, Avon, 1985.
No Body, Scribner (New York), 1986.
Marriage Is Murder, Scribner, 1987.
Dead Crazy, Scribner, 1989.
Bum Steer, Pocket Books (New York), 1990.
I.O.U., Pocket Books, 1991.
But I Wouldn't Want to Die There, Pocket Books, 1993.
Confession, Pocket Books, 1994.

OTHER

The 27 Ingredient Chili Con Carne Murders (based on characters and a story created by Virginia Rich), Delacorte (New York), 1993.

Also author of numerous short stories.

SIDELIGHTS: The first eight of Nancy Pickard's lighthearted mysteries feature the investigative exploits of the lovely and chirpy Jennifer Cain. As the director of the Port Frederick Civic Foundation in a small Massachusetts seaside town, Cain encounters a variety of foul play, including arson, suicide, and murder. In Cain's first case, *Generous Death,* she uses her brains, sense of humor, home computer, and handsome police officer boyfriend to crack a case involving a series of wealthy patrons who die under mysterious circumstances. In *Say No to Murder* a small-town waterfront mall project provides the backdrop as Jenny Cain tells her story in "a somewhat stumbling, over-explanatory first-person narrative," to quote reviewer Douglas Hill in Toronto *Globe and Mail.* But, Hill continued, the novel "does well with the local color and characters."

After 1986's *No Body,* "a wickedly funny expose of funeral-business scams," according to Jean M. White in *Washington Post Book World,* Pickard turned to a grim topic, battered wives who may or may not be killing their husbands, with her subsequent book, *Marriage Is Murder.* This uncharacteristically serious subject, wrote White, "casts a shadow over Pickard's witty and bright style," but the author does provide some amusing touches along the way. *Dead Crazy,* the fifth Jenny Cain mystery, drew mixed reviews. When Cain tries to buy an abandoned church to make over into a recreation center, she encounters community opposition, not to mention two brutal murders. Reviewer Marilyn Stasio in the *New York Times Book Review* found numerous unrealistic details, while conceding that perky heroines who effortlessly solve murders come with the genre.

Pickard's next mystery, *Bum Steer,* is a case involving a strange bequest to Jenny Cain's foundation, one that takes her to the Crossbones ranch in Kansas and other places far from her coastal Massachusetts home. Next, in *I.O.U.,* the detective probes into Cain family matters in a first-person tale that offers insight into the heroine's character. After *But I Wouldn't Want to Die There,* the eighth Jenny Cain mystery, Pickard was chosen to complete an unfinished story, Virginia Rich's *The 27 Ingredient Chili Con Carne*

Murders. Rich, who died in 1984, had written three popular and much-imitated culinary mysteries and was working on a fourth. The elderly heroine, Eugenia Potter, a widow, serves one of her renowned meals—after which three of the diners drop dead. Mrs. Potter takes off on the trail of the villain who poisoned her entree. She gets the guilty guest, of course, and Stasio in the *New York Times Book Review* applauded Pickard for imbibing Rich's protagonist with renewed vigor.

BIOGRAPHICAL/CRITICAL SOURCES:

PERIODICALS

Globe and Mail (Toronto), September 3, 1985, p. 8.
New York Times Book Review, December 11, 1988, p. 34; March 4, 1990, p. 35; May 5, 1991, p. 24; January 3, 1993, p. 15.
Publishers Weekly, July 29, 1988, p. 223.
Washington Post Book World, October 18, 1987, p. 8.*

* * *

**PIDAL, Ramon Menendez
 See MENENDEZ PIDAL, Ramon**

* * *

PIERCE, F(ranklin) David 1947-

PERSONAL: Born October 24, 1947, in Denver, CO; married Gayle Foulks, June 14, 1968. *Education:* University of Utah, B.S., 1970, M.S.P.H., 1984.

ADDRESSES: Home and office—Strategic Solutions, Inc., 1505 Waters Lane, Sandy, UT 84093; fax 801-576-0361.

CAREER: Westinghouse Electric Corp., Ogden, UT, manager of safety, environment, and security, 1984—. Strategic Solutions, Inc., director, 1994—.

MEMBER: American Society of Safety Engineers (president of Utah chapter, 1993-95).

WRITINGS:

Total Quality for Safety and Health Professionals, Government Institutes (Rockville, MD), 1995.

Shifting Safety and Health Paradigms, Government Institutes, 1996.

Mastering Change: A Safety and Health Professional's Guide to Future Success, Government Institutes, in press.

Contributor to magazines.

SIDELIGHTS: F. David Pierce told *CA:* "I have been teaching and lecturing on safety and health management for many years. Frustrated by the small number of people and the short amount of time I could impact using a classroom or conference setting, I began writing. Good management techniques and concepts are just not taught to safety and health professionals, and they are urgently needed if worker safety and health is to improve in America. My first book was based on a total quality management course I teach. In turn, it spawned many articles in professional magazines and journals. In my second book, I broadened my approach and focused on an evaluation of the entire management system for worker safety and health in America. Written less as a how-to text and more as a thought-provoking expose, *Shifting Safety and Health Paradigms* explores the nooks and crannies of the management system that is supposed to make workers safer and healthier in our workplaces.

"I have been greatly influenced by those outside the practice of safety and health. These influences include an extensive knowledge of Japanese management methods and thought and non-mainstream management authors such as Joel Barker, Chuck Coonradt, Meg Wheatley, and others. I continue to go to the 'edge' of current management thought for new information or new challenges to traditional paradigms. I use a lot of examples from real life and analogies to 'teach' what I am writing. This allows the reader to become part of the book through similar experiences and the ability to 'see' what I am writing.

"Not being formally taught how to write books, I come at each new subject by building a skeleton for the manuscript. From the skeleton, I add meat in what resembles an expanded, sentence-type, outline format. After dividing the outline into logical parts that become chapters, I start writing a chapter to which I feel particularly close at that point in time. I may finish the entire chapter following the outline, modify the outline entirely, or stop and start somewhere else in the manuscript. In a piecemeal fashion, I pick through the book, writing as inspired until the total picture becomes crystal clear and the writing effort moves to auto-pilot. Once a manuscript is com-

pleted, my editor Alex Padro steps in and molds the final product."

* * *

PIERPOINT, Katherine 1961-

PERSONAL: Born August 16, 1961, in Northampton, England. *Ethnicity:* "British." *Education:* University of Exeter, B.A. (with honors), 1984.

ADDRESSES: Home—c/o Left Bank, 17 North St., Mears Ashby, Northampton NN6 0DW, England.

CAREER: Dorling Kindersley Lt. (publishers), London, rights assistant, 1985-86; Channel 4 Television, London, publishing and producer's assistant, 1986-88; Eastern Arts Association, Cambridge, England, arts administrator, 1988; Acorn Computers Ltd., Cambridge, communications co-ordinator, 1988-90; freelance writer, editor, researcher, and translator, 1990—. Has given poetry readings at locations throughout the United Kingdom; has appeared on radio programs in the United Kingdom.

MEMBER: Society of Authors, Poetry Society.

AWARDS, HONORS: Hawthornden International Creative Writing Fellowship, 1993; John Downes-Oppenheim Award, 1994; *Truffle Beds* received a Poetry Book Society Recommendation, and was shortlisted for the T. S. Eliot Prize, both 1995.

WRITINGS:

Truffle Beds (poetry), Faber & Faber (London), 1995.

(Contributor) *Earth Ascending* (poetry anthology; includes "Open Headland"), edited by Jay Ramsay, Stride Publications (London), 1997.

Also contributor of poems to periodicals, including *Columbia, Independent, Sunday Times, Rialto,* and *New Yorker.*

WORK IN PROGRESS: A second poetry collection.

SIDELIGHTS: Katherine Pierpoint's book of poetry, *Truffle Beds,* was received warmly by the British press. Sarah Maguire, writing in the *Times Literary Supplement,* cited the collection's "supple, observant use of language." Pierpont was hailed as "a spirited,

resourceful, eerily inventive talent" by Alan Brownjohn, reviewing the volume in the London *Times.* "She makes our spirits float," concluded Kate Kellaway of Pierpoint in the *Observer.*

BIOGRAPHICAL/CRITICAL SOURCES:

PERIODICALS

Observer, June 11, 1995, p. 16.
Times (London), February 26, 1995, p. 11.
Times Literary Supplement, July 7, 1995, p. 14.

* * *

PIKE, Douglas Eugene 1924-

PERSONAL: Born July 27, 1924, in Cass Lake, MN; son of Clarence E. (a contractor) and Ester (a school teacher; maiden name, Jensen) Pike; married Myrna Johnson (a freelance editor), September 15, 1953; children: Andrew Jefferson, Victoria Louise, Ethan Edward. *Education:* University of California, Berkeley, A.B., 1953; American University, M.A., 1957; postgraduate work at Massachusetts Institute of Technology, 1963-64. *Politics:* Independent. *Religion:* Methodist.

ADDRESSES: Home—2265 Alva Ave., El Cerrito, CA 96540. *Office*—Indochina Archive, University of California, 6701 San Pablo Ave., Berkeley, CA 94720.

CAREER: Writer for the United Nations in Korea, 1950-52; U.S. Government State Department, foreign service officer in Washington, DC, Saigon, Hong Kong, Tokyo, and Taipei, Taiwan, 1958-82; University of California, Berkeley, director of Indochina Archive and Indochina studies program, 1982—. Frequent consultant to U.S. Senate foreign affairs committee, House of Representatives, and various other congressional foreign relations committees. *Military service:* U.S. Army, combat correspondent in the South Pacific and Japan, 1944-46.

MEMBER: Authors Guild, Authors League of America, Army-Navy Club, Foreign Service Club, University of California Faculty Club.

AWARDS, HONORS: Massachusetts Institute of Technology Center for International Studies fellow,

1964-65; Superior Honor Award, U.S. Department of State, 1969; Secretary of Defense Medal, 1982.

WRITINGS:

Vietcong: The Organization and Techniques of the National Liberation Front of South Vietnam, M.I.T. Press (Cambridge, MA), 1966.
War, Peace, and the Viet Cong: A Study of Current Communist Strategy in Vietnam, M.I.T. Press, 1969.
The Viet-Cong Strategy of Terror, M.I.T. Press, 1970.
History of Vietnamese Communism: 1925-1976, Hoover Institution Press (Stanford, CA), 1978.
PAVN: People's Army of Vietnam, Presidio Press (Novato, CA), 1986.
Vietnam and the Soviet Union: Anatomy of an Alliance, Westview Press (Boulder, CO), 1987.
(Editor) *The Bunker Papers: Reports to the President from Vietnam, 1967-1973,* Asian Foundation (San Francisco), 1990.

Also author of *Politics of the Viet Cong* (Saigon), 1968. Contributor of articles and reviews to periodicals, including *American Annals of Political and Social Science, Current History,* and *Los Angeles Times.*

WORK IN PROGRESS: Vietnam Leadership: Past, Present, Future; editing *Who's Who in Vietnam, Cambodia and Laos.*

SIDELIGHTS: The director of Indochina studies and the Indochina Archive at the University of California at Berkeley, Douglas Eugene Pike is considered one of the foremost U.S. experts on Vietnamese affairs. Drawing on two decades of experience gained as a foreign service officer stationed in Vietnam, Pike has published numerous papers and is the author of seven books containing his analysis of Vietnamese politics and culture. His knowledge of that area of Southeast Asia has been tapped by various U.S. government agencies in the process of formulating policies involving that war-ravaged country. As journalist Henry Raymont commented in the *New York Times:* "Mr. Pike has a reputation for scholarly and objective analysis of North Vietnamese and Vietcong policies and planning." As Pike himself told *CA:* "I write because I have a passion for getting people told."

Among Pike's earliest publications on Vietnam are 1966's *Vietcong: The Organization and Techniques of the National Liberation Front of South Vietnam,* and

War, Peace, and the Viet Cong: A Study of Current Communist Strategy in Vietnam. Both volumes are published by the Massachusetts Institute of Technology's Center for International Studies, where the author was a fellow in 1964 and 1965. Pike's first book-length work, *Vietcong,* was deemed "a long needed assessment of the little-known men of the NLF [National Liberation Front]" by reviewer Gavin Young, writing in *New Statesman.* Calling Pike's book "essential," Young continued by praising the book as "the best guide on the Vietcong there is—outside Hanoi." *War, Peace, and the Viet Cong,* published in 1969, was similarly praised as an authoritative look at North Vietnamese Communists—known as the Viet Cong—and their role in the conflict against South Vietnam. A *New York Times Book Review* critic described Pike as "a heavyweight analyst," and declared that Pike "has written what remains the only comprehensive work on the political organization and strategy of the Vietcong."

Pike's 1986 publication, *PAVN: People's Army of Vietnam,* traces the development of one of the world's largest armies. Pike follows PAVN from its inception at the end of World War II, when thirty-four men and women espousing Communist ideals first joined together as the Armed Propaganda Team, to its rise to military prominence in the mid-1980s, when the force boasted more than one million comrades. In his book, Pike analyzes the power of this military force, depicting the PAVN's influence on Vietnamese economics and culture as well as its threat to the rest of the world during the late twentieth century. Again, critics applauded Pike's book, among them *Washington Post Book World* contributor Harry G. Summers, Jr., who declared: "Although certainly one of America's foremost experts on Vietnam, Pike himself acknowledges that he is not a military strategist. . . . But there is much more to *PAVN: People's Army of Vietnam* than Pike's assessment of North Vietnamese strategy. It is without question the best work available on what is now the world's third largest military force."

Pike's subsequent book, *Vietnam and the Soviet Union: Anatomy of an Alliance,* delves deeply into the effects that the Communist ideology has had on Vietnam by studying the then-Soviet Union's influence on Vietnamese politics. He distinguishes between the manner in which Communism manifested itself in each nation: Although both Vietnam and the former U.S.S.R. embraced Marxism and Leninism, Pike explains in *Vietnam and the Soviet Union* that Vietnam remains a fiercely independent country resistant to many aspects of Russian economic policy and rule. Considered by *Journal of Asian Studies* contributor William S. Turley as Pike's best book, *Vietnam and the Soviet Union* has been hailed as an important contribution to the literature on Vietnam. *Russian Review* contributor Surendra K. Gupta, for example, deemed it "an important work that adds a great deal to our understanding of the dynamics of Soviet and Vietnamese foreign policies," while Donald W. Treadgold, writing in *American Historical Review,* concurred: "Douglas Pike has produced a valuable work, unemotional to the point of flatness, using Vietnamese materials extensively, sources in Russian much less, but sources on the Soviet Union and the People's Republic of China amply, much of it all drawn from Berkeley's Indochina Archive." Of the few remaining experts on Vietnam, Treadgold concluded, "Pike is among the foremost."

BIOGRAPHICAL/CRITICAL SOURCES:

PERIODICALS

American Historical Review, April, 1989, p. 506.
Journal of Asian Studies, November, 1988, pp. 947-48.
Los Angeles Times Book Review, August 9, 1987, p. 4.
Nation, October 20, 1969, pp. 414, 416.
New Statesman, February 10, 1967, p. 190.
New York Times, May 4, 1969.
New York Times Book Review, July 20, 1969.
Perspective, winter, 1988, p. 39.
Publishers Weekly, January 17, 1986, p. 58.
Russian Review, July, 1989, pp. 344-45.
Washington Post Book World, June 1, 1986, pp. 3, 5.

* * *

PILLING, John 1946-

PERSONAL: Born October 5, 1946, in Salisbury, Wilshire, England; son of Kenneth Newton (a clerk) and Pamela (a homemaker; maiden name, Rowell) Pilling. *Education:* University College, London, B.A., Ph.D., 1965-71.

ADDRESSES: Office—Department of English, University of Reading, P.O. Box 218, Reading, Berkshire RG6 2AA, England.

CAREER: University of Reading, Reading, Berkshire, England, lecturer in English, 1971-85, reader in En-

glish, 1985-93, professor of English and European literature, 1993—. Visiting professor of English, University of California-Santa Barbara, 1984-85.

WRITINGS:

Samuel Beckett, Routledge and Kegan Paul (London), 1976.

(With James Knowlson) *Frescoes of the Skull: The Later Prose and Drama of Samuel Beckett,* John Calder, 1979, Grove Press, 1980.

Autobiography and Imagination: Studies in Self-Scrutiny, Routledge, 1981.

An Introduction to Fifty Modern European Poets, Pan/Heinemann, 1982, published as *A Reader's Guide to Fifty Modern European Poets,* Barnes and Noble (New York), 1983.

(Editor, with Mary Bryden) *The Ideal Core of the Onion: Reading Beckett Archives,* Beckett International Foundation, 1992.

(Editor) *The Cambridge Companion to Beckett,* Cambridge University Press, 1994.

Beckett before Godot: The Formative Years, 1929-46, Cambridge University Press, in press.

Journal of Beckett Studies, editor, 1978-85; The White Knights Press, Reading, England, deputy editor, 1983—. Contributing editor to *Poetry Nation Review.*

SIDELIGHTS: John Pilling's scholarly works on modern writers have garnered praise for the author's exhaustive research into the lives and works of his subjects as well as for the clarity and accessibility of his critical arguments. Pilling's first publication, *Samuel Beckett* (1976), which focuses on one of the twentieth century's premier dramatists, was warmly received by critics. In the volume the author discusses Beckett's life, characteristic style, and influences. Derek Mahon commented in the *New Statesman:* "Pilling's book . . . is an extremely illuminating general guide. It is also mercifully free of the exhibitionism and mytho-mania that bedevil so much Beckett criticism." *Library Journal* contributor Shernaz Mehta Mollinger noted, along with several other reviewers, that the significance of Pilling's work lies in his ability to gather and clearly discuss the massive amount of scholarship that already exists on his subject. While George H. Szanto of *Western Humanities Review* remarked that while Pilling chose not to explore why or how Beckett was able to capture the zeitgeist of the modern era, the critic nonetheless enthusiastically recommended *Samuel Beckett,* remarking: "Altogether the study . . . is very

learned, yet casual in style; very thorough, yet controllable by the reader; very helpful to the student, yet sophisticatedly discursive in its presentation. In short, if one looks for a book simply about Beckett the writer, I know of no single better volume."

Pilling's next publication, *Frescoes of the Skull: The Later Prose and Drama of Samuel Beckett,* written with James Knowlson, focuses on Beckett's later fiction and drama, emphasizing the evolution of the dramatic pieces and offering detailed textual readings of the prose. Pilling turned to the personal writings of several famous authors with his *Autobiography and Imagination: Studies in Self-Scrutiny.* In this work Pilling relies on psychoanalytic concepts to analyze the autobiographical writings of such figures as Henry Adams, Henry James, W. B. Yeats, Boris Pasternak, Michel Leiris, Jean-Paul Sartre, and Vladimir Nabokov. Some critics judged that Pilling's arguments lacked the clarity and focus of his earlier works. Pilling has also written *A Reader's Guide to Fifty Modern European Poets,* which a reviewer in *Choice* recommended as "an important, though necessarily limited" introduction to those poets widely considered the most important in the "modern" canon.

BIOGRAPHICAL/CRITICAL SOURCES:

PERIODICALS

Choice, April, 1983, p. 1130.
Library Journal, July, 1976, p. 32.
New Statesman, April 23, 1976, p. 545.
Times Literary Supplement, November 7, 1980, p. 1271; November 27, 1981, p. 1402.
Western Humanities Review, winter, 1977, pp. 83-85.
World Literature Today, spring, 1982, p. 411.

* * *

PINERO, Arthur Wing 1855-1934

PERSONAL: Surname is pronounced "Pee-*nair*-o"; born May 24, 1855, in London, England; died following emergency surgery, November 23, 1934, in London, England; son of John Daniel (a solicitor) and Lucy (Daines) Pinero; married Myra Moore (an actress; stage name, Myra Holme), April 19, 1883 (died 1919). *Education:* Studied elocution at Birbeck Literary and Scientific Institution, 1870-74.

CAREER: Writer and actor. Worked in father's law office from the age of ten. Left home at nineteen to join the Theatre Royal Company in Edinburgh, and appeared in a series of non-speaking acting roles. Held utility actor position at Royal Alexandra Theatre, Liverpool, 1875-76; appeared in the dramatization of Wilkie Collins' Armadale in 1876, a role which led to permanent position with the Lyceum Theatre, 1876-81; moved to the Haymarket Theatre, 1881-85. First one-act play, Two Hundred a Year, produced October 6, 1877. First full-length comedy, The Squire, produced 1881, after which he was able to retire from acting. Secretary and provident, Benevolent Fund for Actors, beginning 1881—; chairperson of the Royal General Theatrical Fund, 1893. Chairperson of executive committee, Ellen Terry Jubilee Celebrations, 1906. Chairperson, First Battalion, United Arts Rifles, Central London Regiment (Volunteers), during World War I. Honorary examiner in elocution, Birbeck College, 1893-1904. Vice president, Birbeck College Council, 1891-1921. Member, Council of the Royal Academy of Dramatic Arts, 1906-26.

MEMBER: Garrick Club, Athenaeum Club.

AWARDS, HONORS: Knighted, 1909; Royal Society of Literature (fellow).

WRITINGS:

PLAYS

Two Hundred a Year, produced in London at Globe Theatre, 1877.

La Comete; or, Two Hearts, produced in Croydon at Theatre Royal, 1878.

Two Can Play at That Game, produced in London at Lyceum Theatre, 1878.

Daisy's Escape, produced at Lyceum Theatre, 1879.

Hester's Mystery (produced in London at Folly Theatre, 1880), Lacy's Acting Edition of Plays, 1893.

Bygones, produced at Lyceum Theatre, 1880.

The Money Spinner (produced in Manchester at Prince's Theatre, 1880), Samuel French, 1900.

Imprudence, produced at Folly Theatre, 1881.

The Squire (produced in London at St. James's Theatre, 1881), J. Miles, 1881, Samuel French, 1905.

Girls and Boys: A Nursery Tale, produced in London at Toole's Theatre, 1882.

The Rector: The Story of Four Friends, produced in London at Court Theatre, 1883.

Lords and Commons, produced in London at Theatre Royal, Haymarket, 1883.

The Rocket (produced in Liverpool at Prince of Wales's Theatre, 1883), Samuel French, 1905.

Low Water, produced at Globe Theatre, 1884.

(From Georges Ohnet) The Iron-Master, produced at St. James's Theatre, 1884.

In Chancery (produced in Edinburgh at Lyceum Theatre, 1884), Samuel French, 1905.

Mayfair (from a play by Sardou), produced at St. James's Theatre, 1885.

The Magistrate (produced at Court Theatre, 1885), United States Book Company, 1892.

The Schoolmistress (produced at Court Theatre, 1886), W. H. Baker, 1894.

The Hobby-Horse (produced at St. James's Theatre, 1886), United States Book Company, 1892.

Dandy Dick (produced at Court Theatre, 1887), United States Book Company, 1893.

Sweet Lavender (produced in London at Terry's Theatre, 1888), W. H. Baker, 1893.

The Weaker Sex (produced in Manchester at Theatre Royal, 1888; revised version produced in 1889), W. H. Baker, 1894.

The Profligate (produced in London at Garrick Theatre, 1889), United Stated Book Company, 1891.

The Cabinet Minister (produced at Court Theatre, 1890), J. W. Lovell, 1891, Oberon, 1988.

Lady Bountiful: A Story of Years (produced at Garrick Theatre, 1891), United States Book Company, 1892.

The Times (produced at Terry' Theatre, 1891), United States Book Company, 1891.

The Amazons (three acts; produced at Court Theatre, 1893), W. H. Baker, 1895.

The Second Mrs. Tanqueray (produced at St. James's Theatre, 1893), W. H. Baker, 1894.

The Notorious Mrs. Ebbsmith (produced at Garrick Theatre, 1895), W. H. Baker, 1895; edited by C. M. Selle, in The New Drama, 1963.

The Benefit of the Doubt (produced in London at Comedy Theatre, 1895), Mershon, 1895.

The Princess and the Butterfly; or, The Fantastics (produced at St. James's Theatre, 1897), Chiswick Press, 1896, Samuel French, 1897.

Trelawny of the "Wells" (produced at Court Theatre, 1898), Chiswick, 1897, De Witt, 1898.

(With J. Comyns Carr) The Beauty Stone, music by Arthur Sullivan (produced in London at Savoy Theatre, 1898), Chappell, 1898.

The Gay Lord Quex (produced at Globe Theatre, 1899), R. H. Russell, 1900.

Iris (produced at Garrick Theatre, 1901), R. H. Russell, 1902.

Letty (produced in London at Duke of York's Theatre, 1903), W. H. Baker, 1905.

A Wife without a Smile: A Comedy in Disguise (produced in London at Wyndham's Theatre, 1904), Chiswick Press, 1904, W. H. Baker, 1905.

His House in Order (produced at St. James's Theatre, 1906), Heinemann, 1906, W. H. Baker, 1907.

The Thunderbolt; An Episode in the History of a Provincial Family (produced at St. James's Theatre, 1908), W. H. Baker, 1909.

Mid-Channel (produced at St. James's Theatre, 1909), W. H. Baker, 1910; edited by Gerald Weales, in *Edwardian Plays,* 1962.

Preserving Mr. Panmure (produced at Comedy Theatre, 1911), Chiswick Press, 1912.

The "Mind the Paint" Girl (produced at Duke of York's Theatre, 1912), Chiswick Press, 1912.

The Widow of Wasdale Head: A Fantasy (produced at Duke of York's Theatre, 1912), Chiswick Press, 1912, published in *Representative Plays,* edited by Barrett H. Clark, 1921.

Playgoers (produced at St. James's Theatre, 1913), Samuel French, 1913.

The Big Drum (produced at St. James's Theatre, 1915), W. H. Baker, 1915.

Mr. Livermore's Dream (produced in London at Coliseum, 1917), Chiswick Press, 1916.

The Freaks: An Idyll of Suburbia (produced in London at New Theatre, 1918), Chiswick Press, 1917.

Monica's Blue Boy (music by Frederic Cowen), produced at New Theatre, 1918.

Quick Work; A Story of a War Marriage (produced in Springfield, MA, 1919), Chiswick Press, 1918.

The Enchanted Cottage (produced at Duke of York's Theatre, 1922), Chiswick Press, 1921.

A Seat in the Park (produced in London at Winter Garden Theatre, 1922), Chiswick Press, 1922.

Dr. Hamer's Holidays (produced in Washington, DC, at Shubert Theatre, 1931), Chiswick Press, 1924.

A Private Room (produced in London at Little Theatre, 1928), Chiswick Press, 1926, Samuel French, 1928.

Childman, Chiswick Press, 1928.

Dr. Harmer's Holidays, produced in London, 1931.

A Cold June (produced in New York at Duchess Theatre, 1932), [London], 1932.

Also author of *The Bulkeley Peerage,* 1914.

OTHER

Robert Louis Stevenson: The Dramatist, The Critic Company, 1903, published as *Robert Louis*
Stevenson as a Dramatist, with an introduction by Clayton Hamilton, Dramatic Museum of Columbia University, 1914, reprinted, Folcroft Library Editions, 1976.

COLLECTIONS

The Plays of A. W. Pinero, Heinemann, 1891.

The Pinero Birthday Book, selected and arranged by Myra Hamilton, Heinemann, 1898.

The Pinero Calendar; A Quotation from the Works of Sir Arthur Pinero for Every Day in the Year, selected by Myra Hamilton, F. Palmer (London), 1912.

The Social Plays of Arthur Wing Pinero, edited by Clayton Hamilton, four volumes, Dutton, 1917-22, reprinted, AMS Press, 1967.

Two Plays by Arthur Pinero (includes *Dr. Harmer's Holidays* and *Childman*), Heinemann, 1930.

The Collected Letters of Sir Arthur Pinero, edited by J. P. Wearing, University of Minnesota Press, 1974.

Three Plays (includes *The Magistrate, The Second Mrs. Tanqueray, Trelawny of the "Wells"*), edited by Stephen Wyatt, Methuen, 1985.

Plays (includes *The Schoolmistress, The Second Mrs. Tanqueray, Trelawny of the "Wells," The Thunderbolt; An Episode in the History of a Provincial Family*), edited with an introduction and notes by George Rowell, Cambridge University Press, 1986.

Trelawny of the "Wells" and Other Plays (includes *The Magistrate; The Schoolmistress; The Second Mrs. Tanqueray;* and *Trelawny of the "Wells"*), edited with an introduction by J. S. Bratton, Clarendon Press, 1995.

SIDELIGHTS: Arthur Wing Pinero was the most popular and prolific English dramatist of his time, dominating the London stage throughout the late nineteenth and early twentieth centuries. His early works display the artificial plots and tight structure of the French *piece bien faite,* or well-made play, while his later works additionally exhibit the realism and social awareness promulgated by the dramas of Norwegian playwright Henrik Ibsen. Because his works reflected continental techniques and trends during an especially stagnant period in the history of the English stage, Pinero has frequently been credited with the revitalization of the English drama. His works are also regarded as significant in marking the transition in England from traditional theater to modern theater.

Pinero was born in suburban London to a wealthy family of Portuguese descent. His father and grand-

father were solicitors, and it was assumed that Pinero would also practice law; toward that end, he was obliged to work in his father's office from the age of ten. However, Pinero found the law unendurably dull and aspired to an acting career, leaving home at the age of nineteen to join a theater company in Edinburgh. Although his involvement in the Edinburgh company was limited to a series of non-speaking parts, he soon graduated to more substantial roles on the London stage, including an appearance in the 1876 dramatization of Wilkie Collins's popular novel, *Armadale*. Pinero's performance in *Armadale* attracted the attention of Henry Irving, the most influential of London's many actor-managers, and Irving subsequently offered the young actor a permanent position at the renowned Lyceum Theater.

During his acting apprenticeship, Pinero began to write one-act plays, known as "curtain-raisers," and the first of these, *Two Hundred a Year,* was produced on October 6, 1877, by one of Pinero's former employers, R. C. Carton. Irving, impressed with this work, agreed to produce Pinero's play, *Daisy's Escape.* Over the next four years Irving accepted several more of Pinero's curtain-raisers, often casting Pinero in the central roles. In 1881, the young playwright achieved popular success with his first full-length comedy, *The Squire,* and one year later he retired from acting in order to devote his full attention to writing. During the remainder of the 1880s, Pinero wrote a series of increasingly well-received farces and sentimental comedies, most notably *The Magistrate, The Schoolmistress, Dandy Dick,* and *Sweet Lavender.*

Having achieved popularity and wealth with his comedies, Pinero turned to serious drama in 1889, hoping, in his own words, "to write great plays, regardless of the predilections of the public." His first attempt at tragedy, *The Profligate,* which portrayed the downfall and demise of an immoral man, was neither a popular nor a critical success. However, his second attempt resulted in one of his most highly regarded dramas, *The Second Mrs. Tanqueray.* Described by Denzil England as "nothing less than the most important serious play in the English language for two hundred years," *The Second Mrs. Tanqueray* was a huge success, running for 225 performances and bringing fame to Mrs. Patrick Campbell, the actress who first played the eponymous heroine. Pinero continued to write serious dramas for the next twenty years, and he frequently directed performances of his plays. In 1909, at the peak of his popularity, he was

honored with a knighthood for his accomplishments in the theater.

During the latter portion of his career, Pinero experimented with various dramatic styles, producing a propaganda play for the English government during World War I, a fantasy entitled *The Enchanted Cottage,* a pantomime, and several social satires. However, these plays were artistically and commercially unsuccessful, and Wilbur Dunkel has suggested that, despite Pinero's attempts to modernize his art after 1910, he "failed utterly to live in the new social order brought on by the World War." Nevertheless, continuing productions of his earlier plays maintained Pinero's popularity throughout this period, and, ignoring repeated failures, he continued to write new plays until shortly before his death in 1934.

Critics frequently cite Pinero's skillful exploitation of the major theatrical trends and techniques of his time as his greatest achievement. The most important and enduring influence on his work was the French well-made play, a genre characterized by intricate, carefully developed plots and most commonly used as a vehicle for comedy. However, critics contend that in creating his early works, which were predominantly comedies of the well-made type, Pinero improved significantly upon the conventions of the genre as practiced by mid-nineteenth-century French dramatists by substituting believable, well-defined individuals for such stock characters as the jealous husband, the miser, and the buffoon. This focus on characterization reflects one of Pinero's primary artistic aims, which was to portray the action of his plays not as a series of episodes contrived to advance a comic plot, but as the natural result of the personal qualities of his characters. In *Dandy Dick,* for example, the events of the play are initiated by the naivete of a highly respected cleric, who allows himself to be drawn into the morally ambiguous world of horse racing and thus triggers a series of calamities that threaten his reputation. Pinero used this formula consistently throughout his comedies, leading Walter Lazenby, writing in *Arthur Wing Pinero,* to describe the characters in these works as "possible people doing improbable things."

In his later works, Pinero ·continued to utilize the form of the well-made play, while transferring its conventions from the realm of comedy to that of tragedy. Beginning with *The Profligate,* Pinero's works also reflect the influence of the dramatic realism that had been introduced to a limited extent into English drama during the latter half of the nineteenth century

and had been exploited on the European continent with some success by Gerhart Hauptmann, Maurice Maeterlinck, and Ibsen. Pinero denied the influence of Ibsen, but he freely acknowledged his debt to the mid-nineteenth-century English playwright Tom Robertson, who had called for the use of more realistic sets and had rejected conventions such as the soliloquy and the aside. Pinero added to Robertson's innovations by having characters speak in a colloquial manner and by creating an even greater sense of realism in his staging effects. Despite Pinero's assertions to the contrary, critics find the influence of Ibsen in the subject matter of his tragedies, which were often called "problem plays" or "social dramas" because they consistently dealt with social concerns of the day. The problem most commonly addressed in Pinero's tragedies is that of the moral double standard implicit in Victorian society, which demanded sexual propriety from women but not from men; this topic is central to *The Second Mrs. Tanqueray, The Notorious Mrs. Ebbsmith, Iris, Letty,* and *His House in Order,* all of which feature female protagonists whose moral conduct was considered scandalous by Victorian audiences. Yet, while Pinero's audiences found his frank treatment of such concerns daring and controversial, some critics, most notably Bernard Shaw and Max Beerbohm, argued that Pinero failed to exonerate his heroines from blame, thereby implicitly subscribing to the very standards he ostensibly condemned.

Although critics were nearly unanimous in their praise for Pinero's comedies, his attempts at serious drama drew a mixed response. With the enormous success of *The Second Mrs. Tanqueray,* a number of commentators hailed Pinero as the greatest English dramatist since the Restoration period of the seventeenth century. Recent commentators, acknowledging that Pinero was clearly a skilled dramaturgist, argue that his serious plays lack intellectual depth and generally agree with John Russell Taylor's suggestion that Pinero had "no 'philosophy of life,' no message that he was burning to deliver to the public, no deep-rooted personal obsessions." Nevertheless, Pinero's social dramas are considered significant in advancing the trend toward dramatic realism, and several critics have noted that, while Pinero clearly lacked the iconoclastic vigor of Ibsen and Bernard Shaw, he did display great intellectual courage in his sympathetic portrayals of female characters whose behavior departed radically from Victorian standards. Moreover, Pinero remains celebrated as the creator of well-crafted, highly entertaining comedies, several of which remain an integral part of the modern repertoire.

BIOGRAPHICAL/CRITICAL SOURCES:

BOOKS

Armstrong, Cecil Ferard, *Shakespeare to Shaw,* Books for Libraries, 1968, pp. 206-45.
Boas, Frederick, *From Richardson to Pinero,* Columbia University Press, 1937, pp. 250-80.
Dawick, John, *Pinero: A Theatrical Life,* University Press of Colorado, 1993.
Dunkel, Wilbur Dwight, *Sir Arthur Pinero; A Critical Biography with Letters,* Kennikat Press, 1967.
Lazenby, Walter, *Arthur Wing Pinero,* Twayne, 1972.
Nicoll, Allardyce, *History of Late Nineteenth Century Drama, 1850-1900,* Volume 1, Cambridge University Press, 1946, pp. 178-82.
Smith, Leslie, *Modern British Farce: A Selective Study of British Farce from Pinero to the Present Day,* Barnes and Noble, 1989.

PERIODICALS

Contemporary Review, May, 1955, pp. 313-18.
Quarterly Review, April, 1930, pp. 292-310.*

* * *

PINSON, Hermine (Dolorez) 1953-

PERSONAL: Born July 20, 1953, in Beaumont, TX; daughter of Robert B. (a surgeon) and Enid D. (a school teacher) Harris; married Donald Pinson (a pre-trial officer), September 10, 1976; children: Leah Courtney. *Education:* Fisk University, B.A., 1975; Southern Methodist University, M.A., 1979; Rice University, Ph.D., 1991.

ADDRESSES: Home—24 Bromley Drive, Williamsburg, VA 23185. *Office*—Department of English, College of William and Mary, Williamsburg, VA 23185.

CAREER: College of William and Mary, Williamsburg, VA, professor.

MEMBER: Modern Language Association, South Central Modern Language Association, Southern Conference on Afro-American Studies, Lambda Iota Tau Literary Honor Society.

AWARDS, HONORS: Certificate for Outstanding Teacher, National Geographic Society, Texas Southern University, 1990.

WRITINGS:

Ashe (poetry), Wings Press, 1992.

Contributor to books, including *Loss of Ground Note: Women Writing about the Death of Their Mothers,* Clothespin Fever Press, 1992; and *Common Bonds: Stories by and about Modern Texas Women,* Southern Methodist University Press, 1990. "Journal Entries," *Life Notes,* edited by Patricia Bell-Scott, Norton, forthcoming. Contributor to journals, including *Sage.*

WORK IN PROGRESS: Girlchild.

SIDELIGHTS: Hermine Pinson, author of a doctoral dissertation on the poet Melvin B. Tolson, shows his influence in her verse, not only in allusions to his epics *Libretto for the Republic of Liberia* and *Harlem Gallery* but in the richness of her resourceful and redolent language and in her wide range of reference. Pinson's poems range from the deceptively simple "Sugar's Blues," with its echo of traditional blues lyrics mingled with the onomatopoeic scatting of trains and bebop saxophone solos, to poems like "From Beaumont to Benin" that show the influence of Marianne Moore's refined and distancing imagism: "yes, it can devour the body/like ashes eat a cigarette/by the millimeter."

Pinson's themes run from portraits of strong black women to montage-like renditions of the spectrum of current social problems: urban decay, racial rioting, and the invasion of drugs. Critics note that pulsing through her poems is a jazzy vitality and a rhythmic sense of verbal improvisation that propels each poem into a new dimension of feeling, even when the subject of the poem promises to be what is expected. The poetry also is filled with the rhetorics of popular music, the black church, street talk, and the cacophony of media overload, giving her verse a contemporary sound that some reviewers suggest is delightful to read aloud. Like contemporary poets such as Jane Cortez and Nikki Giovanni, Pinson is moving into bringing her poetry to a wider audience through recordings with musical accompaniment.

BIOGRAPHICAL/CRITICAL SOURCES:

BOOKS

Pinson, Hermine, *Ashe,* Wings Press, 1992.*

PIRANDELLO, Luigi 1867-1936

PERSONAL: Born June 28, 1867, in Agirgenti, Sicily, Italy; died December 10, 1936, in Rome, Italy; son of a sulfur merchant; married Antonietta Portulano, 1894; children: two sons, one daughter. *Education:* Attended University of Palermino, Rome, 1886-87, and University of Rome, 1887-89; University of Bonn, doctorate in Romance philology. *Politics:* Joined Fascist Party, 1924.

CAREER: Playwright, novelist, short story writer, essayist, and poet. Teacher, Regio Istituto Superiore di Magistero Femminile, 1897-22; co-editor, *Ariel,* 1898. Director, Teatro Mediterraneo Troupe, Rome, 1919; co-founder, Teatro d'Arte di Roma, 1925-28.

AWARDS, HONORS: Nobel Prize in literature, 1934; named Commander of the Crown by Italian government; inducted into Legion of Honor by French government; named High Commander of St. Maurice.

WRITINGS:

FICTION

Mal giocondo (poetry), [Italy], 1889.
Amori senza amore (short stories), [Italy], 1894.
Beffe della morte e della vita (short stories; two volumes), F. Lumachi, 1902.
Quand'ero matto. . . , [Italy], 1902.
Il turno, [Italy], 1902, A. Mondadori, 1980.
Bianche e nere (short stories), [Italy], 1904.
Il fu Mattia Pascal (novel), [Italy], 1904, revised edition, R. Bemporad, 1921, translation published as *The Late Mattia Pascal,* Hippocrene Books (New York), 1923, translation by William Weaver published under same title, Eridanos Press (Hygiene, CO), 1987.
Erma bifronte (short stories), Fratelli Treves, 1906.
L'esclusa (novel), [Italy], 1908, translation by Leo Ongley published as *The Outcast,* Dutton (New York), 1925.
L'umorismo (essay), [Italy], 1908, L. Battistelli, 1920, translation by Antonio Illiano and Daniel P. Testa published as *On Humor,* University of North Carolina Press, 1974.
La vita nuda, [Italy], 1910, translation by Arthur and Henrie Mayne published as *The Naked Truth,* John Lane, 1934.
Suo marito, [Italy], 1911.
Terzetti, [Italy], 1912.
I vecchi e i giovani (novel; two volumes), [Italy], 1913, translation by C. K. Scott-Moncrieff published as *The Old and the Young,* Dutton, 1928.

Le due maschere, [Italy], 1914, translation published as *Tu Ridi,* 1920.

La trappola, [Italy], 1915.

Erba del nostro orton, [Italy], 1915.

Si gira (novel), [Italy], 1916, translation by C. K. Scott-Moncrieff published as *Shoot! The Notebooks of Serafino Gubbio, Cinematograph Operator,* Dutton, 1926, published as *The Notebooks of Serafino Gubbio, or Shoot!,* Hippocrene Books (New York), 1990.

Un cavallo nella luna, [Italy], 1918, translation by Samuel Putnam published as *The Horse in the Moon,* Dutton, 1932.

Berecche e la guerra, [Italy], 1919.

Il carnevale dei morti (short stories), [Italy], 1919.

In Silenzio, R. Bemporad, 1923.

Uno, nessuno e centomila (novel), [Italy], 1926, translation published as *One, None, and a Hundred Thousand,* Eridanos Press, 1933.

Candelora, R. Bemporad, 1928.

Horse in the Moon (short stories), [New York], 1931.

Novelle per un anno (short stories; 15 volumes; includes *Horse in the Moon, Better Think Twice about It, The Naked Truth,* and *The Medals*), A. Mondadori, 1932-37, translation by Giovanni R. Bussino published as *Tales of Madness: A Selection from Luigi Pirandello's Short Stories for a Year,* Dante University of America Press, 1984, and as *Tales of Suicide: A Selection from Luigi Pirandello's Short Stories for a Year,* Dante University of America Press, 1988.

Better Think Twice about It (short stories), Ayer (New York), 1934.

The Naked Truth, and Eleven Other Stories (short stories), [New York], 1934.

A Character in Distress, Duckworth, 1938.

Medals and Other Stories (short stories), Dutton, 1939.

Four Tales, 1939, translation published as *"Limes from Sicily" and Other Stories,* PAJ (Chicago), 1942.

Better Think Twice about It, and Twelve Other Plays, translation by Arthur and Henrie Mayne, Books for Libraries Press, 1976.

The Oil Jar and Other Short Stories, translation by Stanley Appelbaum, Dover (New York), 1995.

Lettere a Marta Abba, A. Mondadori, 1995, translation by Benito Ortolani published as *Pirandello's Love Letters to Marta Abba,* Princeton University Press, 1994.

Also author of *Short Stories,* edited by Frederick May, 1965, and *Tales of Suicide,* translated by Giovanni R. Bussino, 1988.

POETRY

Mal giocondo, [Italy], 1889.

Pasqua di Gea, [Italy], 1891.

Pier Gudro, [Italy], 1894.

Elegie renane, [Italy], 1895.

Zampogna, [Italy], 1901.

Fuori de chiave, [Italy], 1912.

PLAYS

Liola (drama), produced in Italy, 1916, 3rd edition, A. Mondadori, 1957.

Cosi e (se vi pare) (drama), produced in Italy, 1917, D.C. Heath, 1930, translation published as *Right You Are! (If You Think So),* 1922.

Il piacere dell'onesta (drama), produced in Italy, 1917, translation published as *The Pleasure of Honesty,* 1923.

L'uomo, la bestia e la virtu (drama), produced in Italy, 1919.

Maschere nude (dramas; includes *Cosi e (se vi pare),* *Sei personaggi in cerca d'autore,* and *Enrico IV*), Fratelli Treves, 1919-22, translation by Eric Bentley published as *Naked Masks: Five Plays,* Dutton (New York), 1952.

Sei personaggi in cerca d'autore (drama), produced in Italy, 1921, translation by Frederick May published as *Six Characters in Search of an Author,* W. Heinemann, 1958, Penguin, 1995; produced in Rome, 1922.

Enrico IV (drama), produced in Italy, 1922, 4th edition, R. Bemporad, 1926, translation published as *Henry IV,* 1922.

Three Plays (dramas; contains *Right You Are! (If You Think So),* *Six Characters in Search of an Author,* and *Henry IV*), Dutton, 1922.

Vestire gli ignudi (drama), produced in Italy, 1922, translation published as *Naked,* 1923.

Each in His Own Way, and Two Other Plays (contains *The Pleasure of Honesty, Naked,* and *Each in His Own Way*), Dutton, 1923.

Ciascuno a suo modo (drama), produced in Italy, 1924, translation by Arthur Livingston published as *Each in His Own Way,* Dutton, 1923.

The One-Act Plays (includes *The Vise; Sicilian Limes; The Doctor's Duty; The Jar; By Judgement of the Court; Chee-Chee; The Imbecile; At the Gate; The House with the Column; The Man with the Flower in His Mouth;* and *Our Lord of the Ship*), translation by Elisabeth Abbott, Arthur Livingston, and Blanche Valentine Mitchell, Dutton, 1928.

Come tu mi vuoi (drama), produced in Italy, 1930, A. Mondadori, 1934, translation by Samuel Putnam published as *As You Desire Me,* Dutton, 1931.

Questa sera si recita a soggetto (drama), produced in Italy, 1930, translation by Samuel Putnam published as *Tonight We Improvise,* Dutton, 1932.

I giganti della montagna (drama), 1937, produced in Italy, translation by Marta Abba published in *"The Mountain Giants" and Other Plays* (includes *The New Colony* and *When Someone Is Somebody*), Hart Stenographic Bureau, 1956.

Three Plays (includes *Right You Are (If You Think You Are), The Rules of the Game,* and *Henry IV*), translated by F. May and R. Rietty, [New York], 1969.

Collected Plays, edited by Robert Rietty, J. Calder, 1988-92.

OTHER

Also author of *Laute und Lautentwicklung der Mundart von Girgenti,* 1891, and *Arte e Scienza,* 1908. Translator of *La filologia romanza,* 1893, and *Elegie romane,* 1896.

Author of screenplays, *Pantera nera,* 1920, *Acciaio,* 1933, and *Pensaci Giacomino!,* 1935, A. Mondadori, 1949.

SIDELIGHTS: One of the most important dramatists of the twentieth century, Luigi Pirandello prompted a reevaluation of traditional stagecraft through his innovative use of philosophical themes and experimentation with dramatic structure. Obsessed by the relationships of reality to appearances and of sanity to madness, he often portrayed characters who adopt multiple identities, or "masks," in an effort to reconcile social demands with personal needs. He was closely associated with the Theater of the Grotesque, a dramatic school that stressed the paradoxes and contradictions of life, and was also deeply concerned with making literature a more truthful and effective means for conveying human experience. Toward this end he developed the aesthetic theory of "humorism," which he defined as a mingling of comedy and tragedy to produce simultaneous emotional awareness of both of these aspects of the human condition.

Pirandello was born in Sicily to a prosperous sulphur merchant. Although his father initially sent him to study commerce at the local technical institute, Pirandello lacked interest in the subject and transferred to an academic secondary school, where he excelled in oratory and literature. He began writing at

a young age, and by the time he was twelve had produced his first play, *Barbaro,* with siblings and friends. He also wrote poetry and fiction, publishing his first poem in 1883 and his first story a year later. After graduation, Pirandello attended universities in Palermo, Rome, and finally Bonn, where he earned a doctorate in Romance philology. He then returned to Rome, living on a remittance from his father while trying to establish himself as a writer. After his father arranged Pirandello's marriage to Antonietta Portulano, the daughter of a business partner, the couple settled together in Rome and had three children. To support his family, Pirandello was forced to increase his literary output and to take a position as professor at a women's school. In 1904 he realized his first critical success with the novel *Il fu Mattia Pascal* (later translated as *The Late Mattia Pascal*), but this was overshadowed when his father's sulphur mines, in which Pirandello was heavily invested, were destroyed in a flood. All of Pirandello's wealth, including his wife's dowry, was wiped out. Upon hearing the news, Antonietta suffered an emotional collapse; she subsequently became obsessively jealous and delusional. Although subjected to relentless accusations and abuse, Pirandello refused to have his wife committed; instead, he took refuge in his study, where he lost himself in writing short stories, novels, and essays. He also wrote several plays, but was unable to get them produced.

Pirandello's early works were strongly influenced by verism, an Italian naturalist movement led by Giovanni Verga. Writing in his native Sicilian dialect, Pirandello skillfully described the landscape and inhabitants of Sicily. While his first successful novel, *The Late Mattia Pascal,* displays a naturalistic style, it also suggests the philosophical themes of his later work. Portraying a man who assumes a false identity in order to escape the circumstances of his life, *The Late Mattia Pascal* deals with the relationship of personal identity to the social definition of an individual. Pirandello's 1926 novel, *Uno, nessuno e centomila* (later translated as *One, None, and a Hundred Thousand*), expands upon this theme by examining Vitangelo Moscarda's efforts to free himself from the restrictions of his social identity. Unlike Mattia Pascal, who after abandoning his social identity painfully realizes that it is impossible to establish a new one, Moscarda seeks to rid himself permanently of those characteristics by which others have identified him. Pirandello's techniques of characterization parallel the struggles of his protagonists to deconstruct their superficial identities: instead of constructing a coherent character through a cumulative revelation of

detail, Pirandello first described a character in superficial terms and then later contradicted what he had written.

In his essay *L'umorismo* (later translated as *On Humor*), which he dedicated "To the Memory of Mattia Pascal, Librarian," Pirandello articulated the major aesthetic principle that guided his work. Pirandello's theory of humorism is based upon his vision of the conflict between surface appearances and deeper realities. According to Pirandello, when an opposition exists between a character's situation and an audience's expectations, the audience gains an "awareness" of this opposition, and the situation appears comic. When the audience additionally recognizes a character's suffering beneath the comic appearance, the audience gains a "sentiment" or "feeling" of this opposition. Catharsis occurs when, through a combination of opposing reactions, the audience achieves both a compassionate understanding of the character's situation in the fictional world and a deeper insight into the real world. Pirandello was thus more interested in the audience's direct emotional experience of the theater than in the purely abstract and philosophical aspects of his plays.

Pirandello described his dramatic works as a "theater of mirrors" in which the audience sees what passes on stage as a reflection of their own lives: when his characters doubt their own perceptions of themselves, the audience experiences a simultaneous crisis of self-perception. In questioning the distinction between sanity and madness, Pirandello attacked abstract models of objective reality and theories of a static human personality. For these reasons, many critics have labelled him a pessimist and a relativist; others, noting the strong sense of compassion that Pirandello conveys for his characters, contend that Pirandello is not preaching a definable ideology, but is simply expressing his acute consciousness of the absurdities and paradoxes of human life. As Pirandello once explained: "My works are born from live images which are the perennial source of art, but these images pass through a veil of concepts which have taken hold of me. My works of art are never concepts trying to express themselves through images. On the contrary. They *are* images, often very vivid images of life, which, fostered by the labors of my mind, assume universal significance quite on their own, through the formal unity of art."

In his most famous play, *Six Characters in Search of an Author,* Pirandello described the plight of six characters who interrupt the rehearsal of another Pirandello play to demand that their stories be acted out. His acknowledgement of the stage as the location of a theatrical performance—a place where life is only simulated—startled audiences and critics alike and heralded the self-conscious use of the theater that is a hallmark of modernist drama. Summarizing the effect of Pirandello's play, Antonio Illiano has written that the "sudden and unexpected appearance of live characters, who claimed to belong to the stage and could actually be seen and heard, was like a bombshell that blew out the last and weary residues of the old realistic drama." At the first performance of the play in Rome, the audience was so infuriated that a riot broke out. The play was next performed several months later in Milan, but after the notoriety of the play's earlier performance, as well as the intervening publication of the text, the audience knew what to expect and the performance was a triumphant success. Pirandello's new technique created an ironic parallel between the relationship of the six characters to the stage manager and actors on the one hand, and the relationship of the performance of *Six Characters* to the actual audience on the other. When the characters argue that they are more real than the stage manager because their lives are fixed and unchanging in the roles that they eternally relive, they are actually challenging the audience's belief in the stable reality of their own personalities. Pirandello followed the success of *Six Characters* with *Henry IV,* which many critics consider his greatest work. Written four years after he had his wife committed, *Henry IV* is the last and most eloquent expression of the theme of madness that had been prevalent in Pirandello's personal life and in his art. It uses none of the modernistic dramatic techniques of *Six Characters* and instead draws upon and enriches classical dramatic patterns; the influence of *Hamlet* is especially evident. The play depicts a man who, as the result of an injury suffered at the hands of a rival, believes he is Henry IV. Eventually, he regains his sanity but in a fit of rage kills his rival, so that he must feign continued madness if he wants to avoid the consequences of his deed. Considered an apology for madness, *Henry IV* examines the practical reasons that make insanity and the construction of illusions the only logical response to a reality that is too painful to bear.

Pirandello is today viewed with a more sophisticated appreciation for his philosophical themes and with near universal esteem for all his works, including his later dramas. What was previously scorned as overly intellectual and incoherent is now respected for its provocative treatment of relativism and

antirationalism. Pirandello foresaw the abatement of the critical controversy that he inspired during his lifetime, and looked to that time when his works would be judged according to the artistic terms in which they were created: "The commotion aroused almost everywhere [by my work] is not the ideal environment for it. For me it is no more than a pledge for the future. Before it is attacked, as every human creation inevitably is, the meaningless clamor around it must be silenced; and there will be a moment when, in the first lull it will come to life . . . clear as it once was in my mind when I contemplated it in its finished form and, for an instant, thought it perfect."

BIOGRAPHICAL/CRITICAL SOURCES:

BOOKS

Bentley, Eric, *The Playwright As Thinker: A Study of Drama in Modern Times,* Reynal & Hitchcock, 1946, pp. 159-190.
Brustein, Robert, *The Theatre of Revolt: An Approach to the Modern Drama,* Atlantic-Little, Brown, 1964, pp. 281-317.
Budel, Oscar, *Pirandello,* Bowes & Bowes, 1966.
MacClintock, Lander, *The Age of Pirandello,* Indiana University Press, 1951.
Vittorini, Domenico, *The Drama of Luigi Pirandello,* University of Pennsylvania Press, 1935.

PERIODICALS

Nation, November 22, 1922, p. 556; February 18, 1931, pp. 198-199.
New Republic, November 22, 1922, pp. 335-36; September 28, 1959, pp. 21-24.
New York Times, June 25, 1967.*

* * *

PITCHER, Oliver 1923(?)-

PERSONAL: Born in 1923 (some sources say 1924), in Massachusetts. *Education:* Attended Bard College; studied at the Dramatic Workshop of the New School and the American Negro Theatre.

ADDRESSES: Agent—c/o Eaton, 945 Old Trade Road, Palo Alto, CA 94306.

CAREER: Poet, playwright, actor, and drama teacher. Vassar College, Poughkeepsie, NY, teacher

of black drama, 1970s; Atlanta University Center, Atlanta, GA, poet-in-residence. Has acted professionally and in college and small theater productions.

WRITINGS:

POETRY

Dust of Silence, Troubador, 1960.

Also author of *Prose Poems.* Contributor to anthologies, including *Beyond the Blues,* edited by Pool, 1962; *American Negro Poetry,* edited by Arna Bontemps, 1963; *New Negro Poets: USA,* edited by Hughes, 1964; *Kaleidoscope,* edited by Hayden, 1965; *3000 Years of Black Poetry,* edited by Lomax and Abdul, 1970; and *The Poetry of Black America,* edited by Adoff, 1972. Contributor of poetry to periodicals, including *Negro Digest, Presence Africaine, The Tiger's Eye, Totem, Points of Light,* and *Umbra.* Editor of *Atlanta University Center Sampler.*

PLAYS

Spring Beginning (poetic drama; full-length), produced in Harlem at 115th St. People's Theatre, in 1940s.
Snake! Snake!, produced in New York at the Poet's Theatre, c. 1961.
The Bite (one-act), published in the *Atlanta University Sampler,* 1970.
The One (monologue; one-act; produced as a work in progress in New York by Negro Ensemble Company, 1971), published in *Black Drama Anthology,* King & Milner, 1972.
Shampoo, published in *Atlanta University Sampler,* number 3, 1972.

Also author of *So How're You Wearing Your Strait-jacket?* (one-act play), 1963; *The Daisy* (avant-garde drama; two acts), pre-1975; and *The Meaning of Strings* (one-act drama), pre-1975.

BIOGRAPHICAL/CRITICAL SOURCES:

BOOKS

Page, James A., *Selected Black American Authors: An Illustrated Bio-Bibliography,* G. K. Hall, 1977, p. 218.
Peterson, Bernard L., *Contemporary Black American Playwrights and Their Plays: A Biographical Directory and Dramatic Index,* Greenwood, 1988, p. 383-384.

Rush, Theressa Gunnels, Carol Fairbanks Myers, and Esther Spring Arata, *Black American Writers Past and Present,* Scarecrow Press, 1975, p. 595.*

* * *

POIRIER-BURES, Simone 1944-

PERSONAL: Name is pronounced "See-*mun* Pwar-yea-*Bursh*"; born October 5, 1944, in Halifax, Nova Scotia, Canada; daughter of Arthur L. (a wholesaler of penny candy) and Leonie (a teacher and writer; maiden name, Comeau) Poirier; married John N. Deely, September 1, 1966 (divorced, 1978); married Allen L. Bures (a professor), March 11, 1979; children: (first marriage) Matthew. *Ethnicity:* "French Acadian." *Education:* Newton College, B.A., 1965; University of New Brunswick, M.A., 1970; Hollins College, M.A., 1990. *Avocational interests:* Travel, cooking.

ADDRESSES: Home—7547 Cedar Grove Lane, Radford, VA 24141-8981. *Office*—Department of English, Virginia Polytechnic Institute and State University, 304 Williams Highway, Blacksburg, VA 24061; fax 540-231-5692. *E-mail*—poirier@vt.edu.

CAREER: Worked variously as an English teacher in Crete, an actor with the Organic Theater, an elementary schoolteacher, and a property manager; Virginia Polytechnic Institute and State University, Blacksburg, English teacher, 1982—. University of Dubuque, Dubuque, IA, director of continuing education; Bures and Associate, Inc., workshop presenter and consultant.

AWARDS, HONORS: Three fellowships at Virginia Center for the Creative Arts; winner of Sherwood Anderson Contest; four prizes from Irene Leache Contest, for short stories and an essay; *Candyman* was listed among the top books of 1995, *Halifax Chronicle Herald.*

WRITINGS:

Candyman (novel), Oberon Press (Ottawa, Ontario), 1994.
That Shining Place (memoir), Oberon Press, 1995.

Work represented in anthologies, including *VeriTales: Beyond the Norm,* Fall Creek Press (Fall Creek, OR), 1994; *Bless Me, Father: Stories of Catholic Childhood,* Penguin (New York City), 1994; and *Mother of the Groom,* Distinctive Publishing (Salt Lake City, UT), 1995. Contributor of essays and stories to periodicals, including *Virginia Quarterly Review, Belles Lettres, Dalhousie Review,* and *Short Story.*

WORK IN PROGRESS: A novel.

SIDELIGHTS: Simone Poirier-Bures told *CA:* "I write, I think, out of a need to understand and share my experience. When I began writing what eventually became *Candyman,* I set out to write a memoir. It was November, near the anniversary of my father's death. I tended to remember my father as he had been in his later years—old, ill, and defeated. My father was fifty-four when I was born so, in many ways, he seemed more like a grandfather; he died when I was twenty. That November I got to remembering what it was like when I was a child and he would take us out in his old truck for rollicking Sunday drives. What a wonderful thing it was to be a candyman's daughter, to have a basement full of candy, to be the envy of all the neighborhood children! So I began writing things down—whatever I remembered. It seemed a way of celebrating my father, celebrating my family's survival through some very difficult times. Eventually I realized that my random recollections didn't add up to much of a story. There were so many blanks! I put my imagination to work, inventing the life that I imagined my parents must have experienced. I lied, in a way, to tell the truth. In the process I discovered the man who was my father.

"*That Shining Place,* ironically, started as a novel and became a memoir. That too sprang from a need to understand and explain my experience. When I was twenty-one, I hitchhiked through Europe and spent time teaching on the Greek island of Crete. I lived in a five-hundred-year-old house with no indoor plumbing and very few comforts. It was my life's great experiment. I wanted to live in a non-materialistic, joyful way and thought I would learn how to do this from the Greeks. What began as an idyll turned ugly, and I had to leave. Twenty-five years later I went back to Crete, to try to find the woman who had befriended me back then, and to come to terms with my younger, more idealistic self. I tried writing all this as a novel, but it didn't work. It needed the ring of truth as well as the play and power of memory. It became a memoir. I have learned that you can't always impose your will on material; it finds its own form.

POPPERWELL, Ronald G(eorge) (?)-1983

PERSONAL: Born in Loughton, Essex, England; died December 22, 1983, in Cambridge, England. *Education:* King's College, Cambridge, Ph.D., 1951.

CAREER: Educator, translator, and author. Worked in an insurance office after leaving school at the age of 16, until 1940; volunteered for the Intelligence Corps, 1940, spending four years in Shetland; Cambridge University, lecturer in Norwegian, beginning 1953, Fellow of Clare Hall, beginning 1965, chair of the Faculty Board, 1968-72, 1974, director of the Literary and Linguistic Computer Centre, beginning 1971, head of the Department of Scandinavian Studies, beginning 1979. University College London, W. P. Ker Lecturer, 1951-52, Special Lecturer in Norwegian, 1977-81; visiting professor at University of Wisconsin, 1965-66; chair of inter-university committee of enquiry into Scandinavian studies, 1976-78.

MEMBER: International Association of Scandinavian Studies (founder member; British secretary, beginning 1962), Modern Humanities Research Association.

AWARDS, HONORS: Appointed Knight First Class of the Royal Norwegian Order of St. Olav, 1975.

WRITINGS:

(With Elias Bredsdorff and Brita Mortensen) *An Introduction to Scandinavian Literature from the Earliest Time to Our Day,* Cambridge University Press, 1951, Greenwood Press, 1970.
The Pronunciation of Norwegian, Cambridge University Press, 1963.
(Translator) Johan Falkberget, *Fourth Night Watch,* University of Wisconsin Press, 1968.
The Year's Work in Modern Language Studies, Modern Humanities Research Association, Volume 31, 1969, Volume 32, 1970.
Norway, Benn, 1972.
(Editor) *Expression, Communication and Experience in Literature and Language: Proceedings of the XII Congress of the International Federation for Modern Languages and Literatures held at Cambridge University 20 to 26 August 1972,* Modern Humanities Research Association, 1973.
(With Torbjorn Stoverud) *Norsk litteraturantologi: tekster, opptak, kommentarer,* Modern Humanities Research Association, 1976.

Also translator of *Floodtide of Fate,* by O.J. Dunn, 1960.

SIDELIGHTS: A noted expert in Scandinavian studies, Ronald G. Popperwell presents a panorama of one country in *Norway.* Published in 1972, this introduction to Norway discusses various aspects of Norway's heritage, including history, material culture, and its rich artistic tradition. Popperwell even covers the debate concerning the two Norwegian languages, an issue most foreigners have trouble comprehending, and he does this with full understanding of Norway's linguistic situation.

Popperwell covers Norway's economy and modern life, but critics have faulted him for paying insufficient attention to everyday matters. For example, a *Times Literary Supplement* reviewer pointed out that the author fails to describe the life of an average modern-day Norwegian citizen. This reviewer, however, praised Popperwell's "truly encyclopedic knowledge of the Norwegian arts," adding that the author's presentation of Norwegian history is concise, balanced, and accurate. Despite *Norway*'s incomplete coverage of certain aspects of Norwegian life, "as a cultural and historical guide to Norway it is a remarkable achievement," asserted the *Times Literary Supplement* contributor. Terje I. Leiren, writing in the *Wilson Quarterly,* similarly concluded that *Norway* is "the best book on Norway's past and present."

BIOGRAPHICAL/CRITICAL SOURCES:

PERIODICALS

Choice, May, 1973, p. 520.
London Times, December 24, 1983.
Times Literary Supplement, November 14, 1972, p. 1423.
Wilson Quarterly, spring, 1984, pp. 140-41.*

* * *

PREM, Hanns J(uergen) 1941-

PERSONAL: Born January 18, 1941, in Vienna, Austria; son of Karl Julius (a jeweler) and Vlasta (Drazsky) Prem; married Ursula Dyckerhoff (an ethnohistorian), April 4, 1978. *Education:* Attended Freie Universitaet Berlin, 1959-61; University of Hamburg, D.Phil., 1966; University of Munich, D.Phil., 1978.

ADDRESSES: Home—Schlegelweg 10, D-3400 Goettingen, Germany. *Office*—Institut fuer Voelkerkunde, Theaterplatz 15, D-3400 Goettingen, Germany.

CAREER: University of Munich, Munich, Germany, professor of anthropology, 1980-84; University of Goettingen, Goettingen, Germany, professor of anthropology, 1984—.

WRITINGS:

Matricula de Huexotzinco, Akademische Druck und Verlagsanstalt, 1974.
Milpa y Hacienda, tenencia de la tierra indigena y espanola en la cuenca del Alto Atoyac, Puebla, Mexico, Steiner Verlag, 1978.
(Editor with H. R. Harvey) *Explorations in Ethnohistory: Indians of Central Mexico in the Sixteenth Century,* University of New Mexico Press (Albuquerque, NM), 1984.
Geschichte Altamerikas, R. Oldenbourg (Munich, Germany), 1989.

Also author of television report series, "Das Mexico-Projekt der Deutschen Forschungsgemeinschaft," 1975. Editor of journal, *Mexicon,* 1981—.

WORK IN PROGRESS: Ethnonyme und Toponyme im Klassischen Aztekischen; co-editing, with Ursula Dyckerhoff, *Das Alte Mexico;* researching Aztec history of the fifteenth century, chronological problems.

* * *

PRICE-MARS, Jean 1875-1969

PERSONAL: Born October 15, 1875, in Grande-Riviere du Nord, Haiti; died March 2, 1969, in Port-au-Prince, Haiti; married Clara Perez, 1930; children: one daughter, two sons. *Education:* Attended University of Dakar, French West Africa.

CAREER: Diplomat, educator, and author. Professor and rector of the University of Haiti; member of Haitian Senate; served in Haitian diplomatic service in Germany, the U.S., France, the Dominican Republic, and at the United Nations, and as minister of foreign affairs, beginning in 1900. Founder of Institute of Ethnology, Haiti; president of African Society of Culture.

MEMBER: Academie des Sciences d'Outre Mer (Paris, France).

AWARDS, HONORS: LL.D. from University of Dakar, French West Africa.

WRITINGS:

Silhouettes de negres et de negrophiles, Presence Africaine (Paris, France), 1960.
Antenor Firmin, [Haiti], 1964.
(With Robert Cornevin) *Ainsi parla l'oncle,* [Montreal, Quebec], 1973, translated by Magdaline W. Shannon as *So Spoke the Uncle,* Three Continents Press, 1983.

Also author of *Le Sentiment de la valeur personnelle chez Henry Christophe,* 1933, *Formation ethnique: Folklore et culture du peuple haitien,* and *Une Etape de l'evolution haitienne.* Contributor to *Tomorrow,* 1954.

BIOGRAPHICAL/CRITICAL SOURCES:

BOOKS

Shannon, Magdaline W., *Jean Price-Mars: The Haitian Elite and the American Occupation, 1915-1935,* St. Martin's (New York), 1996.

PERIODICALS

Ebony, July, 1966, p. 98.

OBITUARIES:

BOOKS

Biographical Dictionary of Parapsychology, with Directory and Glossary: 1964-1966, Garret Publications, 1964.
Encyclopedia of Occultism and Parapsychology, 2nd edition with revisions, Gale, 1979.
Dictionary of Afro-Latin American Civilization, Greenwood Press, 1980.
Obituaries on File, Facts on File, 1979.*

* * *

PRIMACK, Richard B. 1950-

PERSONAL: Born January 15, 1950, in Boston, MA; son of Saul (a roofer) and Shirley (a bookkeeper;

maiden name, Lechten) Primack; married Margaret Huong, 1983; children: Daniel, William. *Education:* Harvard University, B.A., 1972; Duke University, Ph.D., 1976. *Avocational interests:* Jogging, basketball, hiking, creative writing.

ADDRESSES: Office—Department of Biology, Boston University, 5 Cummington St., Boston, MA 02215; fax 617-353-6340. *E-mail*—primack@bio.bu.edu.

CAREER: Boston University, Boston, MA, professor of plant ecology, 1978—. Member of board of directors, Tropical Forest Foundation, Tropical Ecosystems Directorate, and U.S. Man and the Biosphere Program.

MEMBER: Society for Conservation Biology (book editor).

WRITINGS:

Essentials of Conservation Biology, Sinauer Associates (Sunderland, MA), 1993.
A Primer of Conservation Biology, Sinauer Associates, 1995.
(Editor) *Ecology, Conservation, and Management of Southeast Asian Forests,* Yale University Press (New Haven, CT), 1995.
Conservation and Community Development in the Maya Forest of Belize, Guatemala, and Mexico, Island Press, in press.

WORK IN PROGRESS: Research on the natural history of Borneo.

SIDELIGHTS: Richard B. Primack told *CA:* "My primary motivation to write is a desire to share information with other people. There was a great need to have a good textbook in conservation biology, as there was no book covering this new and rapidly growing field. Conservation biology is an important subject; it documents the loss of biological diversity and the need and strategies for protecting species and biological communities. Many people had written on this subject from a popular or technical perspective, but I decided to produce a synthesis for university students, government officials, and researchers. My first effort was a long textbook, followed by a shorter version. I am now working with scientists from Germany, Japan, China, India, Indonesia, and Thailand to produce translations of my books that include local examples and materials."

PROUDFOOT, Lindsay 1950-

PERSONAL: Born November 22, 1950, in St. Helier, Jersey, United Kingdom; son of Lindsay and Catherine Leitch (Crawford) Proudfoot; married Jennifer Crawford (a teacher), August 8, 1975; children: Gillian, Robin (son). *Ethnicity:* "Scottish." *Education:* Queen's University, B.A. (with honors), 1973, additional study, 1989; University of Birmingham, M.A., 1974, Ph.D., 1976. *Politics:* Conservative. *Religion:* Protestant. *Avocational interests:* Painting, music, running, travel.

ADDRESSES: Home—2 Carlston Ave., Whinney Hill, Holywood, County Down BT18 0NF, Northern Ireland. *Office*—Department of Geosciences, Queen's University, Belfast BT7 1NN, Northern Ireland.

CAREER: Queen's University, Belfast, Northern Ireland, lecturer, 1977-96, reader in geography, 1994—.

MEMBER: Economic History Society of Ireland, Historical Geography Research Group, Association of University Teachers.

WRITINGS:

(Editor with B. J. Graham, and contributor) *An Historical Geography of Ireland,* Academic Press (London, England), 1993.
(With Graham) *Urban Improvement in Provincial Ireland, 1700-1840,* Irish Settlement Studies (Dublin, Ireland), 1994.
Urban Patronage and Social Authority: The Management of the Duke of Devonshire's Towns in Ireland, 1760-1890, Catholic University of America Press (Washington, DC), 1995.
(Editor and contributor) *County Down: History and Society; Interdisciplinary Essays on the History of an Irish County,* Geography Publications (Dublin), 1996.
(Editor with Russell King and B. J. Smith, and contributor) *The Mediterranean: Environment and Society,* Edward Arnold, 1996.

Contributor to books, including *Urban Historical Geography: Recent Progress in Britain and Germany,* edited by D. Denecke and G. Shaw, [Cambridge, England], 1988; *Waterford: History and Society; Interdisciplinary Essays on the History of an Irish County,* edited by W. Nolan and T. P. Power, Geography Publications, 1992; and *The Oxford Companion to Irish History,* edited by S. J. Connolly, Oxford

University Press (Oxford, England), in press. Contributor of articles and reviews to academic journals, including *Historical Geography, Irish Economic and Social History, Journal of Urban History, Planning Perspectives,* and *Geography Forum.*

WORK IN PROGRESS: Research on place and identity in nineteenth-century Ireland; research on "painting Irish history."

SIDELIGHTS: Lindsay Proudfoot told *CA:* "I am interested in exploring the diverse cultural identities that constitute contemporary society in Ireland, together with their historical provenance. I am inspired by a fascination with the historical laboratory that is Ireland, past and present. I have determined that, in a divided and polarized society such as that in Ireland, where conflicting identities are historically constructed, contemporary protagonists should be challenged at every level over their ready, oversimple use of potentially destructive ethnic, social, cultural, and political stereotypes.

"My writing process is best described as evolutionary. It involves copious cups of coffee and follows extensive archival and field work, wide reading and thought, usually while jogging. Writing is essentially a time-consuming, cost-ineffective, solitary, self-indulgent, and lonely process."

Q-R

QUINONES, Ricardo J(oseph) 1935-

PERSONAL: Born July 9, 1935, in Allentown, PA. *Education:* Northwestern University, B.A., 1957; Harvard University, Ph.D. (comparative literature), 1963.

ADDRESSES: Home—605 Purdue Dr., Claremont, CA 91711-3417. *Office*—Department of Comparative Literature, Claremont McKenna College, 890 Columbia Ave., Claremont, CA 91711.

CAREER: Claremont McKenna College, Claremont, CA, assistant professor, became associate professor beginning in 1963, served as associate professor ending in 1975, professor of English and comparative literature, 1975—, chairperson of literature department, 1977-80. National Endowment for the Arts younger fellow, 1968-69; visiting professor at City University of New York graduate center, 1970-71; visiting fellow at Villaci Tatti, Florence, Italy, 1981.

MEMBER: Renaissance Society of America, Dante Society of America, Modern Language Association.

WRITINGS:

The Renaissance Discovery of Time, Harvard University Press (Cambridge, MA), 1972.
Dante Alighieri, Twayne (Boston), 1979.
Mapping Literary Modernism: Time and Development, Princeton University Press (Princeton, NJ), 1985.
(Editor, with Monique Chefdor and Albert Wachtel) *Modernism: Challenges and Perspectives,* University of Illinois Press (Urbana), 1986.
The Changes of Cain: Violence and the Lost Brother in Cain and Abel Literature, Princeton University Press, 1991.
Foundation Sacrifice in Dante's Commedia, Pennsylvania State University Press (University Park), 1994.

SIDELIGHTS: Ricardo J. Quinones has been on the English and comparative literature faculty at Claremont McKenna College since 1963. He is the author of several books in his field, the first being *The Renaissance Discovery of Time.* In the volume he explains how the Renaissance awareness of time as an expendable resource emerged, thus changing the way people viewed history and progress, and allowing them to adapt to industrialization and innovation. In a subsequent book, *Mapping Literary Modernism: Time and Development,* Quinones further studies the theme of time as it is handled in the literature of the Modernists, among them James Joyce, T. S. Eliot, D. H. Lawrence, and Virginia Woolf. These authors, Quinones writes, longed to return to pre-Renaissance ideals, which were relatively free of the constraints on time.

Quinones discusses four periods of Modernism in *Mapping Literary Modernism,* beginning with a discourse on *Women in Love, The Rainbow,* and *Buddenbrooks,* three novels Quinones suggests reflect the Modernist move away from Renaissance views of time. According to Margaret Dickie in a review for the *Journal of English and Germanic Philology,* "this phase, discussed more fully than any other, interests Quinones because it dramatizes most clearly what he calls the 'paradox of time,' 'the theory that accounts for this strange reversal whereby the temporally most sophisticated come to resemble the most primitive.'

The strongest efforts to control time came in the end only to the barrenness of repetition." The three remaining phases of Modernism, according to Quinones, as quoted by Dickie, move from a "complex central consciousness," to the discovery of self as illustrated in *Finnegan's Wake* and *Joseph and His Brothers,* to the Modernists' finding that order, conventionality, and history are, after all, essential elements of human experience.

Mapping Literary Modernism was generally well-received. Richard Brown, in his *Times Literary Supplement* assessment of the book, remarked that, "Quinones is remarkable for the justice of his generalizations but also for the freshness and sincerity of some of his remarks." Dickie, too, expressed appreciation for Quinones' effort, opining: "What Quinones contributes to this discussion is the perspective he brings from his studies in the Renaissance. . . . The Modernism he presents is neither an extension of Romanticism nor a persistently adversarial or avant-garde movement, but rather a lengthy period of creative activity that had a cohesive and purposeful development. Because the idea of Modernism itself seemed to deny history, the history of the movement has been neglected. The value of Quinones' book is its willingness to open that discussion."

Several critics, however, took exception to Quinones' comparisons of Modernism with Romanticism. Jeffery M. Perl, for instance, wrote in *Clio* that "Quinones' belief in the originality of these modernist solutions induces him to devalue the originality of romanticism. . . . Yet, while unflattering things might be said of the romantics' revival and the tactics of its proponents. . . , the same things could be said of Stravinsky's and Eliot's attempts to quash romanticism. Re-engaging this controversy can come to no good." Nevertheless, Perl concluded: "Much that is good can be said of it. *Mapping Literary Modernism* is an intelligent book, which attempts, with considerable success, to do for this century what Walter Houghton's *The Victorian Frame of Mind* did for the last." Similarly, *Los Angeles Time Book Review* critic Merle Rubin judged Quinones "is strongest when elucidating the Modernist world view, because he does full justice to the subtlety and complexity of their thought. He is weakest when he strains to prove the superiority of the Moderns to the Romantics."

Another of Quinones' widely-reviewed books is *The Changes of Cain: Violence and the Lost Brother in Cain and Abel Literature,* a comprehensive look at the Cain and Abel theme in literature, from the classics to the present.

Quinones discusses the various ways authors have incorporated and interpreted the Biblical theme of Cain's greed, jealousy, and eventual murder of his brother, Abel. Cain and Abel, Quinones suggests, can be found in various forms in the literature of Philo, Augustine, Dante, Shakespeare, Melville, Conrad, and Hesse, just to name a few. And Byron, Quinones asserts, was one of the first to portray Cain as a hero, who killed Abel because Abel's bourgeois inferiority infuriated him. "Quinones is helpful on every such aspect and variant reading of the story," Denis Donoghue remarked in the *New York Review of Books.* "He carries his learning gracefully. Over a remarkably wide range of literatures, he is informative on the unregenerate Cain, envious Cain, Cain the sacred executioner, and in the nineteenth century the transformed Cain, Byron's hero, the Cain we are supposed to recognize as our contemporary."

The Changes of Cain also elicited positive remarks from James Finn Cotter in his *Hudson Review* critique. "Quinones writes with true eloquence and conviction," Cotter wrote, although noting some errors overlooked by Quinones' copy editor. "These are trivial pursuits, however, that should not obscure the major quest this study undertakes: to make readers aware of a (or *the*) central theme in literature and how it permeates our culture. Quinones leaves up to his readers to make connections with current plays and films in order to discover for themselves how Cain and Abel still act out their ancient ritual of life and death, violence and self-identity, rebellion and regeneration. One learns a lot from reading Quinones, and not the least is to want to read more of his many sources." *World Literature Today*'s reviewer Gerald Gillespie wrote of *The Changes of Cain:* "In the sweep and verve of his new exploration, Ricardo Quinones more than lives up to the high expectations of readers familiar with his generously proportioned studies of epochal consciousness in *The Renaissance Discovery of Time* . . . and *Mapping Literature Modernism: Time and Development* . . . and in his monograph on an axial poet, *Dante Alighieri.*" Gillespie continued, "Because his findings are so apposite, he whets our appetite for various extensions of his arguments. . . . By offering deep substance, Quinones promotes real dialogue among the direct inheritors in Europe and the Americas, and therefore readers on other continents touched by modernism will certainly be eager to consult him, too."

BIOGRAPHICAL/CRITICAL SOURCES:

PERIODICALS

Clio, spring, 1985, pp. 344-46.
Hudson Review, summer, 1992, p. 345-50.
Journal of English and Germanic Philology, July, 1986, pp. 468-70.
Journal of the History of Ideas, April, 1992, p. 348.
Los Angeles Times Book Review, September 15, 1985.
New York Review of Books, December 18, 1986, pp. 66-74; November 5, 1992, p. 46.
Times Literary Supplement, September 27, 1985, p. 1075.
World Literature Today, winter, 1993, pp. 245-46.*

* * *

QUINTERO, Jose (Benjamin) 1924-

PERSONAL: Born October 15, 1924, in Panama City, Panama; son of Carlos Rivira and Consuelo (Palmorala) Quintero. *Education:* University of Southern California, B.A., 1948; attended Goodman Theatre Dramatic School, c. 1948-49.

ADDRESSES: Office—The Lantz Office, 888 7th Ave., Suite 2500, New York, NY 10106.

CAREER: Theater director, producer, and actor. Circle in the Square (theater), New York, NY, director and producer of plays, c. 1951-63; Brandeis University, Waltham, MA, artistic director of Spingold Theater, beginning in 1983; affiliated with Chaplin-O'Neill Theater, Los Angeles, CA. Director of numerous plays, including *The Glass Menagerie* and *Riders to the Sea,* 1949, *Dark of the Moon,* 1950, *Bonds of Interest, The Enchanted, Yerma,* and *Burning Bright,* 1951, *Summer and Smoke,* 1952, *In the Summer House, The Grass Harp,* and *American Gothic,* 1953, *The Girl on the Via Flaminia* and *Portrait of a Lady,* 1954, *La Ronde* and *Cradle Song,* 1955, *The Innkeepers, Long Day's Journey into Night,* and *The Iceman Cometh,* 1956, *Lost in the Stars, Children of Darkness,* and *The Quare Fellow,* 1958, *The Triumph of St. Joan, Macbeth,* and *Our Town,* 1959, *Camino Real, Laurette,* and *The Balcony,* 1960, *Look, We've Come Through* and *Under Milkwood,* 1961, *Great Day in the Morning, Pullman Car Hiawatha,* and *Plays for Bleecker Street,* 1962, *Strange Interlude* and *Desire Under the Elms,* 1963,

Marco Millions and *Hughie,* 1964, *Diamond Orchid* and *Matty and the Moron and the Madonna,* 1965, *More Stately Mansions,* 1967, *The Seven Descents of Myrtle,* 1968, *Gandhi,* 1970, *Johnny Johnson* and *The Big Coca-Cola Swamp in the Sky,* 1971, *A Moon for the Misbegotten,* 1973, *Gabrielle,* 1974, *The Skin of Our Teeth,* 1975, *Knock Knock,* 1976, *Anna Christie* and *A Touch of the Poet,* 1977, *The Human Voice,* 1978, *Faith Healer,* 1979, *Clothes for a Summer Hotel, Welded,* and *Ah! Wilderness,* 1980, and *Cat on a Hot Tin Roof,* 1982. Director of the television productions *Medea* and *Our Town,* 1959, and the film *The Roman Spring of Mrs. Stone,* 1961. Producer or co-producer of plays, including *Long Day's Journey into Night,* c. 1956.

MEMBER: Directors Guild of America, Society of Stage Directors and Choreographers.

AWARDS, HONORS: Obie Award for best director from *Village Voice,* 1956, for *The Iceman Cometh;* Antoinette Perry (Tony) awards from League of American Theatres and Producers, 1957, as co-producer of *Long Day's Journey into Night,* and 1974, as director of *A Moon for the Misbegotten;* Drama League Unique Contributions to the Theatre Award, 1987, for directing plays by Eugene O'Neill; Caballero de la Order de Vasco Nunez de Balboa; special citation from Asamblea Nacional de Panama.

WRITINGS:

If You Don't Dance They Beat You (memoir), Little, Brown, 1974.
Gabrielle (play), produced in Buffalo, NY, at Studio Arena, 1974.

Contributor to periodicals, including *New York Times.*

SIDELIGHTS: Panamanian-born Jose Quintero is an acclaimed director of plays by Eugene O'Neill, a Nobel Prize-winning American author whose work is renowned for its pessimism and dramatic power. "Other directors have staged O'Neill," wrote Barbara Gelb in the *New York Times,* "but—even during the dramatist's lifetime—none with anything like Quintero's mastery." After growing up in Panama, Quintero came to the United States in the 1940s and studied acting. By 1949 he had joined a group of young actors in founding a short-lived theater in Woodstock, New York, where he realized that he preferred directing plays to performing in them. He accompanied his friends to New York City, where they turned a cramped and disused nightclub into

Circle in the Square, one of most acclaimed small theaters of the 1950s. Here Quintero directed a variety of up-and-coming young actors, including Geraldine Page and, most notably for Quintero's career, Jason Robards. Quintero and Robards joined forces to restore the sagging reputation of O'Neill, beginning with their Obie Award-winning revival of *The Iceman Cometh* in 1956. The production so impressed O'Neill's widow Carlotta that she chose the young director to stage the American premiere of O'Neill's autobiographical masterpiece, *Long Day's Journey into Night*. The success of the ensuing production secured Quintero's status as a major director. Though Quintero left Circle in the Square in the early 1960s due to artistic differences, he has continued to direct well-received productions of O'Neill plays in succeeding years, often working with Robards.

In 1974 Quintero released a memoir of his years in the theater, *If You Don't Dance They Beat You*. The book focuses on the people Quintero has encountered during his career, including the Circle in the Square troupe, O'Neill's widow and children, and many others, such as an unhappy child dancer whose "stage mother" beat her to make her perform. In the *New York Times Book Review* drama critic Brooks Atkinson praised the work, saying it contains "the essence of theater." "The reader soon understands why Mr. Quintero is so able," Atkinson observed. "He is a free spirit and he draws his knowledge of directing out of his knowledge of people."

BIOGRAPHICAL/CRITICAL SOURCES:

BOOKS

Martinez, Al, *Rising Voices*, New American Library, 1974.
Quintero, Jose, *If You Don't Dance They Beat You*, Little, Brown, 1974.
Van Italie, J. C., *Behind the Scenes*, Holt, 1971.

PERIODICALS

Americas, September, 1955; November, 1958.
Cue, January 23, 1954.
Horizon, January, 1978.
New York Times, January 28, 1974; November 18, 1974; December 11, 1977; February 18, 1983; June 16, 1988.
New York Times Book Review, November 24, 1974.
Theatre Arts, May, 1960.*

RAYMOND, Ellsworth (Lester) 1912-1996

OBITUARY NOTICE—See index for *CA* sketch: Born May 8, 1912, in Fort Ann, NY; died of a pulmonary embolism, August 20, 1996. Foreign service adviser, educator, and author. Raymond was a noted Kremlinologist who used his knowledge of the Soviet Union as teacher and author. Working as a researcher on Soviet politics and economics at the U.S. Embassy in Moscow beginning in 1938, Raymond later served with the U.S. Army's military intelligence service during World War II. He also assisted the U.S. War Department during the war as section chief and researcher on Soviet economics. Raymond switched to a teaching career in 1949, joining the faculty at New York University. While at the University, he also headed the Russian area studies. He became professor emeritus of politics in 1978. Raymond, who contributed to encyclopedias such as Colliers and Americana, translated the book *Industrial Management in the U.S.S.R.* He also authored books such as *Soviet Economic Progress*, *The Soviet State*, *Soviet Power and Policy*, *Karl Marx*, and *The Russian Revolution*.

OBITUARIES AND OTHER SOURCES:

BOOKS

Writers Directory, St. James Press, 1995.

PERIODICALS

New York Times, August 23, 1996, p. A25.

* * *

REDD, Louise 1967-

PERSONAL: Born October 9, 1967, in Memphis, TN; daughter of True (a photographer) and Lady Margaret (Fyfe) Redd. *Education:* Johns Hopkins University, B.A., 1989; University of Houston, M.A., 1992. *Avocational interests:* Gardening.

ADDRESSES: Home—Austin, TX. *E-mail*—louise @io.com; http://www.io.com/~louise/Louise.html.

CAREER: Writer.

WRITINGS:

Playing the Bones (novel), Little, Brown (Boston, MA), 1996.

Contributor to periodicals.

WORK IN PROGRESS: A novel.

SIDELIGHTS: Louise Redd told *CA:* "I have been writing fiction for as long as I can remember. Until I started getting paid to do so, I supported myself by teaching school (sixth, eighth, ninth, and eleventh grade English), cleaning houses, answering phones, and taking dictation from arrogant lawyers. Now I write fiction and book reviews.

"In many ways, the act of moving through other women's houses and caring for other women's things took on a fictional quality. It allowed me to move with ease through the minds of the characters I created. The anger I sometimes felt toward the big-haired women who left on their copper countertops long lists addressed to 'Cleaning Girl' fueled the anger that Lacy Springs, the red-headed star of *Playing the Bones,* began to feel about her past, and it fed her sense of humor as well. So my influences are less literary and more vocational.

"In particular, the women whose houses I cleaned strengthened my determination to write. They were all wealthy and could have done whatever they wanted with their time. I couldn't understand why they didn't all spend their days reading and writing. I spent my own days delirious on the fumes of cleaning products and my nights writing about Lacy and the blues luminary Black Jesus. I think I was having a lot more fun than any of my employers were. I wouldn't have traded places with them for anything."

* * *

REINHOLD, Robert 1941-1996

OBITUARY NOTICE—See index for *CA* sketch: Born December 18, 1941, in New York, NY; died of complications from a brain tumor, August 28, 1996, in Los Angeles, CA. Journalist. Reinhold established himself as a successful reporter, first with the *New York Times* and later with the *Los Angeles Times.* He began work at the New York paper as a copyboy after studies in science at Johns Hopkins University. The job began while he was pursuing his master's degree at Columbia University in 1964. Reinhold would remain at the *New York Times* for some thirty years, working on stories ranging from science, travel, and urban affairs, and serving as bureau chief in Los Angeles and Houston. In 1994, Reinhold joined the staff of the *Los Angeles Times* and contributed edito-

rials. During his prolific journalism career, he camped out with geologists at work in Antarctica to gain a better perspective for his story, and he also covered the San Francisco earthquake of 1989, the rebuilding of damaged structures after the Los Angeles riots, and demographics and urban affairs in Washington.

OBITUARIES AND OTHER SOURCES:

PERIODICALS

New York Times, August 30, 1996, p. B7.

* * *

REISER, Paul 1957-

PERSONAL: Born March 30, 1957, in New York, NY; married; wife's name, Paula; children: Ezra. *Education:* State University of New York—Binghamton, B.F.A. (music), 1977.

ADDRESSES: Office—c/o *Mad About You,* NBC, 3000 West Alameda Ave., Burbank, CA 91523. *Agent*—Cynthia Shelton, United Talent, 9560 Wilshire Blvd., Suite 500, Beverly Hills, CA 90211.

CAREER: Comedian, actor, writer, and producer. Stand-up comedy performer in numerous clubs, including Catch a Rising Star, The Comic Strip, and The Improv, New York City, 1979—. Actor in motion pictures, including *Diner,* Metro-Goldwyn-Mayer/United Artists, 1982; *Beverly Hills Cop,* Paramount, 1984; *Odd Jobs,* 1986; *Aliens* (also known as *Alien II*), Twentieth Century-Fox, 1986; *Beverly Hills Cop II,* Paramount, 1987; *Cross My Heart,* Universal, 1987; *Crazy People,* Paramount, 1990; *The Marrying Man,* Buena Vista, 1991; *Family Prayers,* Arrow Releasing, 1993; *Mr. Write,* SGE/RS Entertainment, 1994; and *Bye Bye, Love,* Twentieth Century-Fox, 1995. Actor in television pilots, including *Diner,* CBS, 1983, and *Just Married,* ABC, 1985. Actor in television series, including *My Two Dads* (also known as *Who's Dad*), NBC, 1987-1990; and *Mad About You* (also known as *Loved By You*), NBC, 1992—. Actor in made-for-television movies, including *Sunset Limousine,* 1983, and *The Tower,* Fox, 1993.

Has appeared in television specials, including *Paul Reiser: Out on a Whim* (also known as *On Location*),

HBO, 1987; *Comic Relief II,* HBO, 1987; "Just for Laughs," *Showtime Comedy Spotlight,* Showtime, 1987; (host) *US Magazine—Live at the Emmys!,* Fox, 1989; (host and commentator) *18th Annual Sunkist Fiesta Bowl Parade,* NBC, 1989; *Comic Relief III,* HBO, 1989; (host) *11th Annual ACE Awards* (also known as *The Golden ACE Awards*), syndicated, 1990; (host) *42nd Annual Primetime Emmy Awards* (creative arts presentation; New York and Los Angeles only), FBC, 1990; *Paul Reiser: 3 1/2 Blocks from Home,* Showtime, 1991; (host) *Hard Rock Cafe New Year's Eve Special,* CBS, 1991; (presenter) *The 44th Annual Primetime Emmy Awards,* Fox, 1992; (host) *Bob Hope: The First Ninety Years,* NBC, 1993; (host) *The Ninth Annual Soap Opera Awards,* NBC, 1993; (presenter) *The 14th Annual CableACE Awards,* Lifetime, 1993; (presenter) *The 45th Annual Primetime Emmy Awards,* ABC, 1993; *NBC Super Special All-Star Comedy Hour,* NBC, 1993; *Together for Our Children: M.U.S.I.C.,* syndicated, 1993. Actor in episodic television productions, including "You Ruined My Life," *Disney Sunday Movie,* ABC, 1987, and *Alan King: Inside the Comedy Mind,* Comedy Central, 1991. Has appeared on numerous television talk shows, including *Late Night with David Letterman,* NBC, *Late Show with David Letterman,* CBS, and *The Tonight Show,* NBC. Executive producer, *Paul Reiser: 3 1/2 Blocks from Home,* Showtime, 1991; creator and producer, *Mad About You* (also known as *Loved By You*), NBC, 1992—.

MEMBER: Screen Actors Guild.

AWARDS, HONORS: Emmy Award nomination, best lead actor in a comedy series, 1994, for *Mad About You.*

WRITINGS:

TELEVISION SPECIALS

Paul Reiser: Out on a Whim (also known as *On Location*), HBO, 1987.
Paul Reiser: 3 1/2 Blocks from Home, Showtime, 1991.

TELEVISION PILOTS AND THEMES

Mad About You (also known as *Loved By You*), NBC, 1992.

OTHER

Couplehood, Bantam (New York), 1994.

SIDELIGHTS: Raised in Manhattan, Paul Reiser studied music at the State University of New York—Binghamton before launching his career in show business as a stand-up comic in some of New York's most popular comedy clubs. His break from the club routine came in 1982 when Barry Levinson cast him in the role of "Modell" in the motion picture *Diner.* Reiser was featured subsequently in a string of films, including *Beverly Hills Cop* and its sequel, as well as *Aliens, Crazy People,* and *Bye Bye, Love.*

Reiser's work in television consisted of stand-up comedy appearances on late-night talk shows and an occasional role in a television pilot or film until 1987, when he landed the role of Michael Taylor in the NBC situation comedy *My Two Dads.* That same year he starred in *Paul Reiser: Out on a Whim,* an HBO production that he also wrote. *My Two Dads* was canceled in 1990, but Reiser was, nevertheless, gaining in popularity and recognition. He wrote and starred in another special, Showtime's *Paul Reiser: 3 1/2 Blocks from Home* in 1991, then was approached by NBC to do another series, which became Reiser's creation *Mad About You.* The continuing saga of married life in the '90s as told through characters played by Reiser and actress Helen Hunt, *Mad About You* debuted in 1992 and earned Reiser a 1994 Emmy Award nomination for lead actor in a comedy series.

In 1994, Reiser added "published author" to his list of accomplishments with his first book, *Couplehood.* Like *Mad About You, Couplehood* explores the throes of marriage and showcases Reiser's humorous outlook on relationships. The book opens on page 145, rather than page one, with an anecdote about his somewhat clumsy proposal to his own wife, Paula. A *Time* review by Richard Zoglin quoted Reiser on his unconventional page numbering: "This way," [Reiser] goes, "you can read the book for two minutes, and if anybody asks you how far along you are you can say, 'I'm on 151—and it's really flying.'"

Although his book enjoyed several months on the Top 10 bestsellers' list, Reiser admits he is not an expert on couples. "I don't claim to know anything about relationships," he told Nancy Mills in an interview for the *Chicago Tribune.* "The last thing I wanted to write was an instruction manual. Both the show [*Mad About You*] and the book come out of things that amuse and interest me. We all notice them, but comedians carry a pencil. . . . The things that are the most private are also the most universal. Everybody goes to the bathroom. Everybody has been naked with somebody else at some point. If I put something out

there and people respond and laugh, I feel better. 'Oh good, I'm not alone.'"

Reiser joins comedians Jerry Seinfeld, Ellen DeGeneres, and Tim Allen in becoming a published author, but some reviewers, among them Zoglin, have deemed these books by comedians "not really books. They're comedy routines on paper," Zoglin declared, adding: "They have the rhythms of stand-up monologues. Lots of conversational asides, jokey hyperbole and the sort of slangy sentence structure you don't usually see in print." Alex Tresmowski, however, reviewing the books written by Reiser and Allen for *People Weekly,* found *Couplehood* "allows Reiser to exploit his *Mad About You* persona—sensitive, sometimes cranky but lovable—and enhance his bid to be the '90s ideal husband. . . . It should be enough for fans of these performers that their first books capture much of their unique comic voices."

BIOGRAPHICAL/CRITICAL SOURCES:

BOOKS

Contemporary Theatre, Film, and Television, Volume 12, Gale (Detroit), 1994.

PERIODICALS

Chicago Tribune, September 14, 1994, Tempo section, p. 3.
People Weekly, October 3, 1994, pp. 34-35.
Time, November 7, 1994.*

* * *

REJALI, Darius M. 1959-

PERSONAL: Name is pronounced "Da-*ri*-us Re-*ja*-li"; born November 1, 1959, in Tehran, Iran; son of Davood (a professor and college dean) and Sallie Ann (a professor; maiden name, Yarborough) Rejali. *Education:* Swarthmore College, B.A., 1981; McGill University, M.A., 1983, Ph.D. (with honors), 1987. *Politics:* "Yes, every day." *Avocational interests:* Travel, friends, music, yoga.

ADDRESSES: Office—Department of Political Science, Reed College, Portland, OR 97202-8199.

CAREER: McGill University, Montreal, Canada, lecturer, 1988; Reed College, Portland, OR, assistant professor, 1989-94, associate professor of political science, 1994—, chair of political science department, 1993-97, chair of division of history and social science, 1996—. Visiting assistant professor at Union College, 1988-89. Has delivered papers at conferences in locations including Coventry, England; Bielefeld, Germany; Toronto, Ontario, Canada; Madrid, Spain; Vancouver, British Columbia, Canada; Williamstown, MA; Calgary, Alberta, Canada; and Portland, OR; board member of the International Gay and Lesbian Human Rights Commission, 1995-97; volunteer with the Cascade AIDS Project, 1989-95.

MEMBER: International Sociological Association, American Political Science Association, Western Political Science Association, Oregon Academy of Sciences.

AWARDS, HONORS: Max Bell open fellowship, 1983-84; Binz fellowship, 1984-85; Friends of McGill fellowship, 1985-87; Reed College summer research grant, 1990; travel grant, American Council of Learned Societies, 1990; research grants from the Oregon Council for the Humanities, and from the Hewlett Program in Comparative and International Policy, both 1994.

WRITINGS:

NONFICTION

(Contributor) *Vigilantism and the State in Modern Latin America: Essays in Extralegal Violence,* edited by Martha K. Huggins, Praeger (New York), 1991.
Torture and Modernity: Self, Society, and State in Modern Iran, Westview Press (Boulder, CO), 1994.

Also contributor to periodicals, including *Peace Review, PS: Political Science and Politics,* and *Social Science Forum.*

WORK IN PROGRESS: Articles, including "HIV Testing in Comparative Perspective" and "The Fox and the Lion: Machiavelli's Metaphor of Freedom."

SIDELIGHTS: Academician and author Darius M. Rejali was born in Tehran, Iran and his birthplace figures prominently in his 1994 book, *Torture and Modernity: Self, Society, and State in Modern Iran.* The volume began as his doctoral thesis, and was published by Westview Press.

One of Rejali's major arguments in *Torture and Modernity* is that the Islamic fundamentalist Iranian Revolution of the 1970s has failed in its goal of ridding Iran of the corrupting Western influences brought in by the country's previous rulers, the Pahlavi shahs—at least in terms of its employment of torture as a state tool. Rather than reverting to the ritualized, though brutal methods used under ancient Islamic rule, the Revolutionary government of Iran (led by an Ayatollah) has continued many of the same practices they fought against under the last shah. "Even in the few cases when it has amputated according to Islamic law," reported Daniel Chirot, reviewing *Torture and Modernity* in *Contemporary Sociology*, "since the mid-1980s the Ayatollahs' judicial police has used an electric machine that 'severs the hand in a tenth of a second.'" More importantly, according to Rejali, torture in Islamic Iran still has a modernist aim—as Margaret Lynd phrased it in *Middle East Journal*, "torture is intended to reform and normalize, to transform real, potential, or wholly imagined dissidents into docile and obedient subjects by invading the minds and bodies of its victims."

Rejali also asserts in *Torture and Modernity* that torture is made more likely by the nature of the modern state, and, as Lynd put it, even when modern states "do not actively participate in torture, [they] almost certainly have in place the disciplinary structures that allow them to slip easily into the aggressive use of torture to contain potentially subversive subjects." Rejali agrees in many ways with French deconstructionist philosopher Michel Foucault's writings on torture, but differs from Foucault in placing major emphasis on diversity between cultures as an important factor in the questions of if and how torture is used.

Torture and Modernity has been well received by critics. Lynd noted that "this book probably will not receive much attention outside the world of Middle East scholarship and that is a likelihood much to be regretted." Chirot called the volume "an excellent introduction to postmodernism. . . . [L]earned, often fascinating, and in many places elegantly witty—no mean feat when dealing with this subject." An English translation of Payman Vahhabzadeh's review of *Torture and Modernity* in the Iranian exile publication *Iran Nameh* noted that it "is without a doubt a book not only for those interested in Iranian problems but also a valuable book for everyone who studies and struggles against methods of control, repression, and discipline in politics in our age." Similarly, a *Times Literary Supplement* critic found *Torture and Moder-*

nity to be "of immense importance to anyone wanting to understand how rationality has failed to banish the wilful infliction of pain by the state."

Rejali told *CA:* "I write the way I speak and teach. I didn't always do this. As a student, I wrote heavy, ponderous prose imitating the articles that I was often assigned. I was lucky to find a friend, Brian Walker, who took writing as a craft extremely seriously, and who taught me a great deal of what I now practice. I was also fortunate enough to find several writers of philosophy who seemed to me to be exemplary writers: Charles Taylor, Alasdair MacIntyre, and Hilary Putnam. These writers took the most abstract, jargonized philosophy and rendered it comprehensible in plain prose. In this way, I started writing seriously, particularly after I left graduate school. I am still, I suspect, a better teacher than writer, but I'm working at it.

"I did not think much about my working habits as a whole until 1988 when visiting Anthony Parel, the great Machiavelli scholar, in Calgary. My legs fell asleep while we were talking and so awkwardly delayed my departure. This prompted Parel to remark: 'As St. Thomas would say, you need to care for your *habitus*. The constellation of habits you develop in your first years of your professional career are the ones you keep for life. After that it is much harder to change.' That is how I came by the habits I now have.

"I write or type standing. Brian Walker made my desk in the model of nineteenth-century standing desks you can see in pictures of Rainer Maria Rilke. For better posture, I have a footrest to shift my weight while keeping my spine straight. I avoid haphazard writing materials: I habitually prefer certain types of pens, paper, research notebooks (Clairefontaines only), lighting (halogens mainly), computers, and computer programs. When walking, I always have my pocket notebook. I keep my notebook as strictly as authorities these days keep track of registered aliens; no thought passes unquestioned into the night.

"I always write as much as I can before I turn to books. Since childhood I have always had books as companions, I find their company distracting when I write. All my books are shelved in a large walk-in closet; the door is usually shut. All this is out of my great respect for the power of books. If I want to speak to other authors, I go to the room where they dwell.

"I wrote *Torture and Modernity* as my dissertation, so it was in the first instance a disciplinary exercise. I found it extremely difficult to write about torture. *Torture and Modernity* took ten years to write (1983-1993) and went through many revisions. Although I first turned to the topic out of intellectual interest in Foucault, I found the material would not permit a dispassionate approach and eventually I had to make the topic my own. Finding a rhetorical manner of writing which was at once factual, personal and moral was one of the greatest challenges of writing this book.

"*Torture and Modernity* proposes to discuss torturers and the world they live in, and that meant trying to see things through the eyes of a torturer. This exercise forces one to look very closely at the darkest sides of the ideals one holds. You inquire how you came by them, who taught them to you, and what their history is. In my case, I investigated closely the ideals of both my American-Protestant heritage and my Persian aristocratic ancestors. There can be no thoughtful criticism of such evils as torture that is not born out of self-criticism. The benefit of this exercise appears to be that others hear the main theses of the book, and its relevance to their lives quite clearly. This is very gratifying.

"Ralph Waldo Emerson urges in *The American Scholar* that a scholar's first task is to read the book of the world, *liber mundi,* and that, more than anything else, is a test of real literacy. Unfortunately, the kind of training I received as a student, with the exception of a few extraordinary teachers, taught me to value books over the book of the world. What is more, the book of the world cannot be read as one would read a book, that is, by concentration. Rather, it seems to require quite the opposite psychological skills, the ability to open oneself, shut up, and attend to what's going on. I cannot say I excel at this, but I have tried as well as I can to attend to the ordinary.

"Attentiveness does not imply passivity. In fact, attentiveness is possible mainly through acting, not talking and thinking. I have always served public causes because one is forced to deal not only with the world but also with the fears that get in the way of such attentiveness. That is why for some years I have volunteered with AIDS service organizations and worked for the right of sexual minorities. Without confronting one's own fears, writing will always fall short of the world and seem unconnected with anything important. Whenever possible, I try to write about something I am doing rather than what I am thinking.

"At any rate, whenever I find this kind of attentiveness to the world in a book, I am drawn to it. So I turn often to the philosophy of the late Ludwig Wittgenstein, the poetry of Paul Celan, the writings of Michel Proust, Frantz Fanon, Hannah Arendt, Memmi, Sa'adi, Machiavelli, Aristotle, Pascal, Jorge Luis Borges, Francis Yates, George Steiner, James Thurber, and Paul Monnette as well as to a host of others. None of these are substitutes for the book of the world. I learned long ago that what I love to read is not necessarily what I should try to write."

BIOGRAPHICAL/CRITICAL SOURCES:

PERIODICALS

Contemporary Sociology, September, 1994, pp. 678-80.
The Historian, spring, 1995, pp. 587-88.
Iran Nameh, winter and spring, 1995.
Middle East Journal, winter, 1995, pp. 145-47.
Times Literary Supplement, April 22, 1994, p. 28.

* * *

RETTIE, Dwight F. 1930-

PERSONAL: Born March 27, 1930, in New Haven, CT; son of James C. (an economist) and Lois (a teacher; maiden name, Morris) Rettie; married Karen Ross (a consultant), August 3, 1984; children: Stuart, Cathy Rettie Melton, Thomas. *Ethnicity:* "Scottish." *Education:* Yale University, B.A. (with honors), 1952; University of California, Berkeley, M.A., 1955. *Politics:* Democrat. *Religion:* Unitarian-Universalist. *Avocational interests:* Sailing his forty-two-foot boat, especially in the Caribbean.

ADDRESSES: Home and office—607 Mandy Ct., Morehead City, NC 28557; fax 919-240-2386. *E-mail*—farwathie@coastalnet.com.

CAREER: U.S. Forest Service, Washington, DC, worked as a forest fire dispatcher, smoke chaser, and lookout in western Montana, summers, 1948-52; U.S. Treasury Department, Washington, DC, junior management assistant in Bureau of the Public Debt, 1955-57; U.S. Department of the Interior, Washington, DC, director of information for Bureau of Land Management, 1957-62; U.S. Fish and Wildlife Service, Washington, DC, director of public affairs for Office of the Commissioner, 1962-63; U.S. Depart-

ment of the Interior, staff assistant to the under-secretary, 1964-66; U.S. Department of Housing and Urban Development, Washington, DC, director of Open Space and Urban Beautification Division, 1966-71, representative on Advisory Council on Historic Preservation, 1967-71; National Recreation and Park Association, Arlington, VA, executive director, 1971-75; National Park Service, Washington, DC, special assistant to the deputy director, 1975-78, deputy chief of park planning and development, 1978-81, chief of Office of Policy Development, 1981-86; retired, 1986. East Carolina University, instructor in political science, 1995—; Carteret Community College, instructor, 1995—; consultant to National Parks and Conservation Association. Boy Scouts of America, member of national council, 1958-62; Arlington County Public Utilities Commission, chairperson, 1967-73; Arlington TeleCommunications, Inc., member of board of directors, 1973-79; Northern Virginia Regional Park Authority, member of governing board, 1973-81; U.S. Board on Geographic Names, deputy member, 1981-86. *Military service:* U.S. Army, 1952-54; became staff sergeant.

WRITINGS:

Our National Park System: Caring for America's Greatest Natural and Historic Treasures, University of Illinois Press (Champaign, IL), 1995.

WORK IN PROGRESS: The Fortunes of War, a Civil War novel; research on "the emerging economic royalty in the United States."

SIDELIGHTS: Dwight F. Rettie told *CA:* "I wrote the equivalent of several books during my professional life, almost none of it bearing my name. Now that I am retired, I have published one important book and have another in the early stages. The substance and shape of my book was formulated over nearly a decade while I was still working for the National Park Service. I retired, and my wife and I moved aboard our sailboat to do several years of world cruising. During much of that seven years, I often remarked about starting the book I was then 'carrying around in my head.' The trouble was that, as long as we were cruising, serious writing was just not possible.

"So, in 1991, we temporary stopped our cruising. We were in Fort Lauderdale, Florida, at the time. It turned out that the Broward County Library is something like the seventh largest public library in the United States, and it has excellent facilities and ser-

vices. The manuscript was finished after about thirteen months.

"Writing is hard work for me. I was inspired to write the book because I knew that no one else could do it. I was the chief of policy for the National Park Service. The book contains information and analysis available nowhere else. I believe it will make an important long-term contribution to the literature about our national park system.

"My next major project is a novel about an incident that happened during the Civil War. My wife and I are doing the research now. The plot and principal characters are all in hand; what I need is the historical details to flesh out the narrative.

"I am also looking into a serious study of the emerging economic royalty in the United States, a royalty that was created a century or more ago as a modern version of hereditary royalty in Europe. Such royalty here in the United States is also hereditary, holds enormous political, economic, and social power, and is largely unaccountable to the people and institutions whose lives and social structures are influenced and controlled by its members. Most Americans shrug off the very notion that any real royalty is being created here, but it is happening in ways that undermine democratic institutions and concentrate political and economic power in elites responsible only to themselves."

　　　　　　　*　　*　　*

REYLES, Carlos　1868-1938

PERSONAL: Born in 1868, in Uruguay; died in 1938.

CAREER: Wealthy landowner and writer.

WRITINGS:

El embrujo de Sevilla (novel), first published in 1922, translation by Jacques Le Clercq published as *Castanets,* [New York], 1929, recent edition, Gordon Press, 1977.
Cuentos completos, Arca, 1968.
Diario, Arca, 1970.

Also author of *Por la vida,* 1888; and the novels *Beba,* 1894, *La raza de Cain,* 1900, *El terruno,* 1916, and *El gaucho Florido,* 1932.

SIDELIGHTS: A regional writer influenced by French naturalists such as Emile Zola, Carlos Reyles is best known for his novel *La raza de Cain,* in which he offers a psychological and sociological analysis of characters from the ranches and cities of Uruguay.

BIOGRAPHICAL/CRITICAL SOURCES:

BOOKS

Torres Rioseco, Arturo, *Grandes novelistas de la America Hispana,* University of California Press, 1947.

PERIODICALS

Hispania, May, 1968.*

* * *

RHEIMS, Maurice 1910-

PERSONAL: Born January 4, 1910, in Versailles, France; son of Leon (a general) and Jeanne (Levy) Rheims; married Lili Krahmer, 1951 (divorced); children: Bettina, Louis, Nathalie. *Education:* L'Ecole du Louvre, received diploma; Sorbonne, University of Paris, received diploma. *Religion:* Jewish.

ADDRESSES: Office—25 Rue de Faubourg-Saint-Honore, 75008 Paris, France.

CAREER: Auctioneer, art critic, and novelist. Worked as an appraiser and auctioneer (*commissaire-priseur*) at Paris auction houses, including the Hotel-Drouot, 1935-1972. Vice president, administrative council of Bibliotheque Nationale, Paris, 1983—; president, Fonds de developpement culturel de la Fondation de France. *Military service:* Active in French Resistance, 1939-1945; received Croix de Guerre and Medaille de la Resistance.

MEMBER: Academie Francaise.

AWARDS, HONORS: Literary prize for *Le cheval d'argent;* Prix Broquette-Gonin, l'Academie Francaise, 1970, for *La vie d'artiste;* named commandeur, Legion d'Honneur, 1979; grand prize for black humor, 1983, for *Le Saint-Office.*

WRITINGS:

NONFICTION

La vie etrange des objets: Histoire de la curiosite, Plon (Paris), 1959, translated by David Pryce-Jones as *The Strange Life of Objects: Thirty-Five Centuries of Art Collecting and Collectors,* Atheneum (New York), 1961.
L'objet 1900 (exhibition catalogue), Arts & Metiers Graphiques (Paris), 1964, expanded as *L'Art 1900; ou, Le style Jules Vernes,* 1965, translated by Patrick Evans as *The Flowering of Art Nouveau,* Abrams (New York), 1966, as *The Age of Art Nouveau,* Thames & Hudson (London), 1966.
Dictionnaire des mots sauvages (title means "Dictionary of Savage Words"), Larousse (Paris), 1969.
La vie d'artist, Grasset (Paris), 1970.
La sculpture au XIXe siecle, Arts & Metiers Graphiques, 1972, translated by Robert Wolf as *Nineteenth-Century Sculpture,* Abrams, 1977.
(With others) *Musees de France,* Realites (Paris), 1973.
Haute curiosite (memoir), Laffont (Paris), 1975, translated by Patrick Evans as *The Glorious Obsession,* St. Martin's (New York), 1980.
(Author of introduction) Yves Devaux, *L'univers des bronzes et des fontes ornementales: Chefs-d'oeuvre et curiosites, 1850-1920,* Pygmalion (Paris), 1978.
L'enfer de la curiosite: De Marat au bain au petit pan de mur jaune (literary and art criticism), A. Michel (Paris), 1979.
Dix-Neuvieme siecle, Hachette (Paris), 1979.
Les collectionneurs: De la curiosite, de la beaute, du gout, de la mode, et de la speculation, Ramsay (Paris), 1981.
Bernard Buffet, graveur, 1948-1980 (exhibition catalogue), Editions d'Art de Francony (Nice), 1983.
Por l'amour de l'art, Gallimard (Paris), 1984.
Hector Guimard, Bibliotheque des arts (Paris), 1985, translated, Abrams, 1988.
Les fortunes d'Apollon: L'art, l'argent, les curieux de Cresus aux Medicis, Seuil (Paris), 1990.
Apollon a Wall Street, Seuil, 1992.

Also author of *Les chefs d'oeuvre des musees de Province,* 1974, *Haarlem . . . noir,* 1986, *En tous mes Etats: Entretien avec Francois Duret-Robert,* 1993; *La vie de Gauguin,* and (with others) *La vie de Tolouse-Lautrec.*

FICTION; NOVELS, EXCEPT WHERE NOTED

Le cheval d'argent (short stories), Julliard (Paris), 1961.

Un Carpaccio en Dordogne (short stories), Julliard, 1963.

Le luthier de Mantoue, Flammarion (Paris), 1972.

Le main, Laffont, 1977, translated by Simon Watson Taylor as *The Hands*, Weidenfeld & Nicolson, 1963.

Le Saint-Office, Gallimard, 1983.

Attila, laisse donc ta petite soeur tranquille, Flammarion, 1985.

Les greniers de Sienne, Gallimard, 1989.

Les forets d'argent, Gallimard, 1995.

Author of screenplays *Martin Soldat*, 1966, *L'homme presse*, 1977, *L'enfer de la curiosite*, 1979, and *L'amour de l'art*, 1984.

SIDELIGHTS: One of France's most well-known auctioneers, Maurice Rheims has supplemented his long career as a *commissaire-priseur*—since the end of World War II he has been involved in selling art objects gleaned from such places as the Sphinx and the palaces of Egypt's King Farouk to some of the world's most wealthy collectors—by using his writing skills to cultivate readers' appreciation for the art of the late nineteenth century. The period between 1880 and 1910 holds a special fascination for Rheims, who has written a number of books on both the artists and works of that era.

The Flowering of Art Nouveau, a translation of Rheims's 1964 work entitled *L'objet 1900* that includes approximately six hundred black-and-white illustrations and a dozen color plates, goes beyond the artistic mode of its title; as a critic noted in the *Times Literary Supplement*, the common thread in the volume "is not so much any particular repertoire of stylistic motifs, let alone any deeper shared aesthetic, but a certain strain of the bizarre. . . . as might be expected of an old enthusiast for surrealism." Echoing Rheims's appreciation of the artistic eccentricity of that era is *Hector Guimard*. This equally well-illustrated 1988 volume profiles the career of the world-renowned architect who created the Paris Metro Stations that remain among that city's most recognizable landmarks. Praising the volume in the *Chicago Tribune*, Paul Gapp asserted that "Rheims' . . . text is authoritative, concise, and free of academic babble."

Rheims's abilities as a stylist are reflected in his fictional works; he is the author of several novels and short stories in addition to his critical writings. Among his fiction, literary honors have been bestowed upon *Le cheval d'argent* (1961) and *Le Saint-Office* (1983); in addition, Rheims's nonfiction work *La vie d'artist* was the recipient of the 1970 Prix Broquette-Gonin awarded by the French Academy. In another reflection of his literary capabilities, Rheims has compiled the *Dictionnaire des mots sauvages* (or "Dictionary of Savage Words"). Divided into sections such as "Military," "Religious," "Gastronomic," "Criminal," and "Political," this collection of historic literary expressions was praised by a reviewer in the *Times Literary Supplement*: "These are words that have not made it officially, that have not been admitted into the inner sanctum. . . . There is a lot of dross, a lot more silliness; but [Rheims]'s haul includes a number of artificial pearls that are well worth rescuing and that are often more expressive than those that they imitate."

BIOGRAPHICAL/CRITICAL SOURCES:

PERIODICALS

Chicago Tribune, May 11, 1989, p. 8.

Connoisseur, January, 1985, pp. 96-73.

National Review, December 13, 1966, p. 1282.

New York Times Book Review, June 29, 1967, p. 10; December 4, 1977, p. 81.

Times Literary Supplement, December 15, 1966, p. 1169; October 16, 1970, p. 1197.

* * *

RHODES, Colin 1963-

PERSONAL: Born December 17, 1963, in Yorkshire, England; married Nicky Mayo, July 7, 1990; children: Tom, Anna, Tess. *Education:* Goldsmith's College, London, B.A. (with honors), 1986; University of Essex, M.A., 1987, Ph.D., 1993.

ADDRESSES: Home—7 High St., Silverstone, Towcester, Northants NN12 8US, England. *Office*—Loughborough College of Art and Design, Epinal Way, Loughborough, Leicestershire LE11 3GE, England; fax 01509 265515. *E-mail*—C.Rhodes@lcad.ac.uk.

CAREER: Loughborough College of Art and Design, Loughborough, Leicestershire, England, lecturer, 1991-93, head of department of contextual studies, 1993—. Has served as a tutor for Headington School in Oxford, England, 1988-91, and the Open University, 1991-93; external examiner for Winchester School of Art, 1992-95, Courtauld Institute of Art, 1993—, and Liverpool John Moores University, 1993—. Guest lecturer or conference participant at institutions and events including Keele University; Trinity College, Dublin; University of Essex; Manchester International Festival of Expressionism; Courtauld Institute; Association of Art Historians Annual Conference, Birmingham and Newcastle; Manchester Zurich Dada Conference; Oxford Brookes University; Whitechapel Art Gallery; and Hayward Gallery.

MEMBER: College Art Association, Association of Art Historians.

AWARDS, HONORS: British Academy Grant, for master's and doctoral study, 1986-90.

WRITINGS:

NONFICTION

Primitivism and Modern Art, Thames and Hudson (London), 1994.
(With M. Minichiello) *Festival of Illustration* (exhibition catalogue), Southwold, England, 1995.

Contributor to books, including *Expressionism Reassessed,* edited by Behr, Fanning, and Jarman, Manchester University Press (Manchester, England), 1993; *Zurich Dada,* edited by Michael Howard, Manchester University Press, in press; *The Dictionary of Art;* and *Art,* De Agostini Editions (London), in press. Contributor to periodicals, including *Art History* and the *Burlington Magazine.*

WORK IN PROGRESS: A monograph on artist E. L. Kirchner and a general work for Thames and Hudson entitled *Outsider Art,* completion expected in 1997.

SIDELIGHTS: British author and academician Colin Rhodes obtained his doctorate in the history and theory of art from the University of Essex in 1993. Since then, he has been head of the department of contextual studies at Loughborough College of Art and Design, an institution where he lectured while still completing his studies. He has also taught art

history in several other capacities, including teaching part-time to sixth form students at Headington School in Oxford, England, and serving as a tutor for the Open University. Rhodes has contributed articles on primitivism and expressionism, as well as German art of the nineteenth and twentieth centuries, to volumes such as *The Dictionary of Art, Expressionism Reassessed,* and *Zurich Dada.* His work, and his reviews of the work of his colleagues, have appeared in the periodicals *Art History* and the *Burlington Magazine.* His first full-length book, 1994's *Primitivism and Modern Art,* brought him respectful reviews from critics.

In *Primitivism and Modern Art,* Rhodes declares that his purpose is "to give an overview of, and to highlight and clarify the often confused major issues and values at stake in the Primitivist world view through a discussion that focuses on the modern artists most closely associated with it." He primarily selects artists from Russia, France, and Germany to achieve this goal, beginning with French painter Paul Gaugin and continuing through to coverage of the Surrealist and Abstract Expressionist movements. For the most part, as Lynne Cooke reported in the *Times Literary Supplement,* Rhodes organizes the volume by topic, rather than by the chronological fashion common to most works of Western art criticism. According to Allen Wardwell in *Art Book* magazine, Rhodes also gives the reader background information about the ways in which primitivist artists viewed the primitive cultures to which they paid tribute with their art, and how the views of the artist meshed with the views of society as a whole.

Cooke praised Rhodes for succeeding in his aim in *Primitivism and Modern Art,* proclaiming that "in many ways, this book supersedes the currently available standard general works on the subject, most notable of which is Robert Goldwater's *Primitivism in Modern Art.*" Wardwell also compared Rhodes' effort to that of Goldwater, observing that "he follows the lead established" by the other art expert in taking "a very broad view of the nature and sources of primitivism" because he includes children's and folk art along with the more tribal cultures traditionally associated with primitive art. Speaking of the historic arguments among scholars of primitivism, Wardwell judged that "for coming to grips with this confusion and controversy, Mr. Rhodes is to be admired and congratulated." He lauded the author's "well organised and cogent manner" of tackling his subject, and concluded that "in these politically correct times, he is willing to ask hard questions and does not duck

the issues that are raised today at the mere mention of the words primitive and primitivism."

BIOGRAPHICAL/CRITICAL SOURCES:

BOOKS

Rhodes, Colin, *Primitivism and Modern Art,* Thames and Hudson (London), 1994.

PERIODICALS

African Arts, winter, 1996, pp. 18, 20, 21.
Art Book, Volume 2, number 1, p. 30.
Times Literary Supplement, November 24, 1995, p. 19.

* * *

RHODES, Zandra (Lindsey) 1940-

PERSONAL: Born September 19, 1940, in Chatham, Kent, England; daughter of Albert James (a truck driver) and Beatrice Ellen (a fitter and educator; maiden name, Twigg) Rhodes. *Education:* Medway College of Art, diploma, 1961; Royal College of Art School of Textile Design, DesRCA (with first-class honors), 1964. *Avocational interests:* Touring museums, drawing and painting, traveling.

ADDRESSES: Office—87 Richford St., Hammersmith, London W6 7HJ, England.

CAREER: Fashion, costume, and textile designer. Established own studio, beginning in 1965; produced dresses using own fabric in partnership with Sylvia Ayton, 1966; Fulham Clothes Shop, London, co-founder, 1967, designer, 1967-68; freelance fashion designer, 1968-75; Zandra Rhodes Co., London, managing director, 1975—. Part-time teacher, Birmingham College of Art, Ravensbourne College of Art, and Royal College of Art, 1964-66. Painter, with exhibits at the Dyansen Gallery, Boston. Fashions in collections and exhibited at galleries, including the Victoria and Albert Museum, London, 1971; Parsons School of Design, New York City, 1982; Royal Ontario Museum, Toronto, and Metropolitan Museum, New York City. Has created costumes for television productions, including *Romeo & Juliet on Ice.*

MEMBER: Society of Industrial Artists and Designers (fellow).

AWARDS, HONORS: Designer of the Year award, British Clothing Institute, 1972; Royal Designer for Industry award, 1977; citation from City of Philadelphia, 1978; award from Moore College of Art, 1978; fellow, Society of Industrial Artists and Designers, 1982; Emmy Award for costume design, 1984, for *Romeo & Juliet on Ice;* honorary D.F.A., International Fine Arts College, 1986; Dr. honoris causa, Royal College of Art, 1991; received National Diploma of Design from British government.

WRITINGS:

(With Anne Knight) *The Art of Zandra Rhodes,* J. Cape (London), 1984, Houghton (Boston, MA), 1985.

SIDELIGHTS: Patterned, gossamer chiffons, hand silk-screened prints on silk, intricate traceries of beading, and vibrant colors are characteristic of the clothing creations of London designer Zandra Rhodes. Grouped with such designers as Karl Lagerfeld, Giorgio Armani, and Perry Ellis as one of the world's top fashion designers, Rhodes has made a name for herself as one of the most eclectic talents in the world of high fashion. Riding the fashion tide from the "Mod" influences of the 1960s through the punk wave that crashed through the 1970s, her work has been groundbreaking in introducing new trends. *The Art of Zandra Rhodes,* which the designer co-authored with Anne Knight in 1984, provides a detailed look at the theory and inspiration behind her work.

Beginning her career as a textile designer in 1965, the determined and hard-working Rhodes taught her craft at local colleges several days a week in order to fund her own company. Ten years later she had become an established designer with a London shop under her own name (Zandra Rhodes Co.); international fame was quick to follow. "I feel that one of the major contributions to the world of fashion I have been able to make is my originality of textile print design," she notes in the introduction to *The Art of Zandra Rhodes,* "and the way I have allowed the textiles to influence the garment shapes."

Rhodes finds inspiration during her many trips abroad, not only to such exotic locales as India and China, but also to the U.S. Southwest, where the

native cactus so caught her fancy that it appeared as a textile motif for years afterward. But travel is not the only thing that can inspire a new creation, a new direction: the film *Star Wars* acted as a spark in inspiring an entire collection of space-aged evening wear, and Rhodes's own work designing the costumes for a production of the ice ballet "Romeo and Juliet" carried over into a line of ready-to-wear fashions that bore her name. While Rhodes's designs of the 1980s reflected her desire to create what she considers timeless and feminine styles, she achieved fame earlier in her career for unconventional finishes that flaunted couturier conventions; the chains, safety pins, holes, and rips that appeared in her clothing in the mid-1970s—as well as her personal predilection for spiky, dyed hair—even prefigured the punk rock styles of the era. Rhodes has constantly worked to keep ahead of current trends and the pendulum of public taste that continues to sway, like politics, between extremes.

The Art of Zandra Rhodes provides intimate details of the authors' design process, and includes copies of many of the sketches Rhodes has made in moments of inspiration. Such sketches have been translated into textile designs, or into patterns for beading, sequined ornament, or applique, handcrafted elements that Rhodes considers the foundation of her art. "My book has become a cult book in the Middle West of your country," Rhodes explained to Julie Hatfield of the *Boston Globe,* "where there is some very exciting craft work coming out of places such as Minneapolis and St. Paul, Minnesota, and Columbus, Ohio. The world is going back to crafts, and 'art' clothes are part of the crafts."

BIOGRAPHICAL/CRITICAL SOURCES:

BOOKS

Contemporary Newsmakers, Gale (Detroit), 1986, pp. 322-34.
Rhodes, Zandra, and Anne Knight, *The Art of Zandra Rhodes,* J. Cape (London), 1984, Houghton (Boston, MA), 1985, p. 9.

PERIODICALS

Boston Globe, June 20, 1989, p. 57.
London Review of Books, February 21, 1985, pp. 11-12.

RICHARDS, Beah
(Beulah Richardson)

PERSONAL: Born in Vicksburg, MS; married Hugh Harrell. *Education:* Attended Dillard University, New Orleans, Louisiana, and San Diego Community Theater.

ADDRESSES: Agent—c/o Gores/Fields Talent Agency, 10100 Santa Monica Blvd., Ste. 700, Los Angeles, CA 90067.

CAREER: Stage and film actor; playwright. Appeared in numerous Off-Broadway and other stage productions, including *Take a Giant Step,* 1956, *A Raisin in the Sun,* and *The Miracle Worker,* 1959, *Purlie Victorious,* 1961, *The Amen Corner* and *Arturo Ui,* 1963, *The Little Foxes,* 1967, *One Is a Crowd,* 1970, *A Black Woman Speaks,* 1975, *Iago—An Evening with Beah Richards,* 1979. Appeared in films, including *Take A Giant Step,* 1959, *The Miracle Worker,* 1962, *Gone Are the Days,* 1963, *Guess Who's Coming to Dinner,* 1967, *Hurry Sundown,* 1967, *In the Heat of the Night,* 1967, *The Great White Hope,* 1970, *The Biscuit Eater,* 1972, *Mahogany,* 1975, *Inside Out,* 1986, *Big Shots,* 1987. Appeared in television programs, including *Hawaii Five-O,* 1969, *The Bill Cosby Show,* 1970-71, *Just an Old Sweet Song,* 1976, *Roots: The Next Generations,* 1979, *The Sophisticated Gents,* 1981, *As Summers Die,* 1986, and *Frank's Place,* c. 1988.

MEMBER: Actors' Equity Association, Screen Actors Guild, Congress of Racial Equality, National Association for the Advancement of Colored People.

AWARDS, HONORS: Best Plays citation and *Theater World* Award, both 1964, for *The Amen Corner;* nominated for Antoinette Perry (Tony) Award for best dramatic actress, American Theatre Wing, 1965, for *The Amen Corner;* Academy Award nomination for best supporting actress, Academy of Motion Picture Arts and Sciences, 1967, for *Guess Who's Coming for Dinner;* All-American Press Association Award, 1968; inducted into Black Filmmakers Hall of Fame, 1974; Emmy Award for outstanding guest performer in a comedy or drama series, Academy of Television Arts and Sciences, 1988, for *Frank's Place.*

WRITINGS:

A Black Woman Speaks and Other Poems (includes *A Black Woman Speaks,* one-act dramatic mono-

logue, first produced in Chicago, 1950; published in *Freedomways* under name Beulah Richardson, 1964), Inner City Press, 1974.

One Is a Crowd, first produced in Los Angeles, CA, 1970.

Work represented in anthologies, including *Nine Plays by Black Women,* 1986.*

* * *

RICHARDSON, Beulah
See RICHARDS, Beah

* * *

RIDDLE, Jean
See WEIHS, Jean

* * *

RINGKAMP, Jonathan 1929-1986

PERSONAL: Religious name is Brother Jonathan; born March 6, 1929, in Brooklyn, NY; died of pneumonia, September 19, 1986, in New York, NY; buried in Holy Cross Cemetery, New York, NY; son of Francis Bernard and Margaret Louise (Mercier) Ringkamp. *Education:* Pratt Institute, B.F.A., 1961, M.F.A., 1967; studied as a Fulbright Scholar at Accademmia di Belli Arti, Venice, Italy, 1961-62.

ADDRESSES: Agent—Flora Roberts, 65 East 55th St., New York, NY 10022.

CAREER: Franciscan monk, educator, and playwright. Joined Order of St. Francis, Roman Catholic Church, 1955; first vows, 1956; final vows, 1961. Taught at New York University, Boston University, Brooklyn College, St. Francis College, Kingsborough Community College, and several Catholic elementary and secondary schools. Established, with Geraldine Fitzgerald, the Everyman Theatre of Brooklyn, 1967, artistic director, 1968-78; member of Ensemble Studio Theatre, New York City, beginning 1972; play-

wright, directors unit, Actors Studio, New York City, beginning 1982.

MEMBER: Writers Guild, New York City Cultural Council.

AWARDS, HONORS: Fulbright Scholarship, 1961-62; runner-up, CAPS and Sergel Prize.

WRITINGS:

PLAYS

Bella Figura, produced at Ensemble Studio Theatre, New York City, 1982.
Poisoner of the Wells, produced at Ensemble Studio Theatre, 1983.

Also author of several other plays, including (with Geraldine Fitzgerald) *Everyman and Roach* (rock opera), produced as street theater, and at La Mama, New York City; (with Fitzgerald) *Mister Estevan,* produced as street theater, and at Lincoln Center (outside), New York City; *Elena,* produced as street theater, and at Brooklyn Academy of Music, New York City; *The Dog Ran Away,* produced at Ensemble Studio Theatre and later, Milwaukee Repertory Theatre, WI; *You Didn't Have to Tell Me,* produced at Ensemble Studio Theatre; *Jack Swift American Myth,* produced as street theater; *Play Dead,* produced at Ensemble Studio Theatre and Actors Studio, New York City; *Veteran,* produced at Ensemble Studio Theatre and Everyman Theatre, New York City; (with Harry Chapin) *The Zinger* (musical), 1976; *The Arbor,* produced at Manhattan Theatre Club, New York City; *Change of Mind,* produced at Ensemble Studio Theatre; *Ground Lies Fallow,* produced at Actors Studio; *Shakespeare on Shakespeare,* produced at Strasberg Institute, New York City; and *MidEast Crisis,* 1982.

SCREENPLAYS

Author of screenplays for films, including *Clairvoyant,* 1981; *Rappallo and Sons,* 1983; and *The Killing Hour.* Also author of television screenplays for *Visions,* 1975.

OTHER

Author of the manuscripts *If God Wouldn't Eat with a German, The Wall at Higgs Memorial Beach,* and *Gregorius the Great.*

SIDELIGHTS: Well-respected and known in both Off-Broadway and other theater circles in New York City and London, playwright Jonathan Ringkamp began his early career as a member of the Franciscan Order. Joining in 1955, Ringkamp took his final vows in 1961; around the same time he studied painting at Pratt Institute and was awarded a Fulbright Scholarship to attend the Accademmia di Belli Arti in Venice, Italy. The year 1967, however, saw his career change dramatically when he founded a street theater company, the Everyman Theatre of Brooklyn, with Geraldine Fitzgerald. This venture led to many successes; Ringkamp's plays were subsequently produced at top Off-Broadway theaters as well as at venues in London and Milwaukee.

Drawing on his personal knowledge of Franciscan spirituality, Ringkamp filled his emotionally charged plays with characters often in crisis. Among these characters are fellow Franciscans trying to overcome the difficulties of living in the modern world. Ringkamp's most important works are three such plays, The Dog Ran Away, The Arbor, and Bella Figura, which together comprise a trilogy about the Franciscan way of life. "Brother Jonathan's work is psychological realism," described Willem O'Reilly in the Biographical Dictionary of Contemporary Catholic American Writing. "His essential theme is the relationship of the alienated yet passionate individual to his community, to tradition, and ultimately, to God."

BIOGRAPHICAL/CRITICAL SOURCES:

BOOKS

Tynan, Daniel J., editor, Biographical Dictionary of Contemporary Catholic American Writing, Greenwood Press, 1989.

OBITUARIES:

PERIODICALS

New York Times, September 20, 1986.*

* * *

RIOS, Isabella
 See Lopez, Diana

ROBERTS, Leigh
 See SMITH, Lora R(oberts)

* * *

ROBERTS, Lora
 See SMITH, Lora R(oberts)

* * *

ROCHA, Rina Garcia
 See GARCIA ROCHA, Rina

* * *

RODHAM CLINTON, Hillary
 See CLINTON, Hillary Rodham

* * *

ROESKE, Paulette 1945-

PERSONAL: Surname is pronounced "Res-key"; born September 30, 1945, in Bloomington, IL; daughter of Paul Henry Rudolph (a pharmacist and store manager) and Helen Virginia (Reise) Roeske; married John Terrence Becker, June 17, 1967 (divorced, 1978); children: Adrienne Lee. Education: University of Iowa, B.A., 1967; Northwestern University, M.A., 1968; Warren Wilson College, M.F.A., 1982. Avocational interests: Taekwon-do (first-degree black belt), travel (especially in Asia).

ADDRESSES: Home—1200 Harvard Terrace, Evanston, IL 60202. Office—Department of English, College of Lake County, 19351 West Washington St., Greyslake, IL 60030; fax 847-548-3383. E-mail—com 426@clc.cc.il.us.

CAREER: Harper High School, Chicago, IL, English teacher, 1968-69; College of Lake County, Greyslake, IL, professor of English, 1969—. Christ Church College (Canterbury, England), teacher, 1995. School of the Art Institute of Chicago, member of board of directors of Poetry Center of Chicago, 1987—, vice president, 1987-92; Ragdale Foundation,

member of selection committee, 1989—; judge of poetry competitions; workshop leader; gives readings from her works.

MEMBER: Academy of American Poets, Associated Writing Programs, Modern Poetry Association, Poetry Society of America, Poets and Writers, PEN Midwest Associates, Illinois Writers, Inc.

AWARDS, HONORS: Poets and Patrons Award for Free Verse, 1978; Jo-Anne Hirschfield Memorial Poetry Award, Evanston Library, 1979, for "Dream of Trains;" Illinois Arts Council, Literary Awards, 1981, 1989, 1990, fellowship, 1989; winner of Chicago Cultural Center Poetry Competitions, 1983, for "Shortcut through the Park" and "Waiting for This," and 1989, for "Sestina: Her Life with Chopin;" New Poetry Broadsides Award, 1983, for "Waiting for This;" Pushcart Prize nominations, 1986, for poems in *Indiana Review,* and 1988; award from *South Coast Poetry Journal,* 1988; Goodman Award, Thorntree Press, 1989; resident, Ragdale Foundation, 1990, 1991, 1992, 1995; first place award, Chester H. Jones Foundation National Poetry Competition, 1990; Teaching Excellence Award, National Institute for Staff and Organizational Development, 1991; first place award, poetry chapbook competition, Illinois Writers, Inc., 1992, for *The Body Can Ascend No Higher;* fellow of National Endowment for the Humanities at Chinese Culture and Civilization Institute, 1993; Fulbright fellow, 1994; Japan Foundation fellow, 1995; *Divine Attention* was awarded the 1996 Carl Sandburg Award.

WRITINGS:

Breathing Under Water (poems), Stormline Press (Urbana, IL), 1988.
The Body Can Ascend No Nigher (poetry chapbook), Illinois Writers (Normal, IL), 1992.
Divine Attention (poems), Louisiana State University Press (Baton Rouge, LA), 1995.

Work represented in anthologies, including *The Anthology of Magazine Verse and Yearbook of Contemporary American Poetry,* edited by Alan F. Pater, Monitor Book (Beverly Hills, CA), 1983; *Woman Poet: The Midwest,* edited by Elaine Dallman, Women-in-Literature, Inc. (Reno, NV), 1985; and *Benchmark: Anthology of Contemporary Poetry in Illinois,* edited by James McGowan and Lynn DeVore, University of Illinois Press (Urbana), 1988. Contributor of dozens of poems and stories to periodicals, including *Whetstone, Poetry Northwest, As-*

cent, Short Fiction Review, Other Voices, and *Cottonwood Review.* Editor, *Willow Review,* 1983—.

WORK IN PROGRESS: The Ecstasy of Magda Brummer: A Novella and Stories; an untitled collection of poems, completion expected in 1998.

SIDELIGHTS: Paulette Roeske told *CA:* "I settled on the notion of writing poems in 1978, at age thirty-three, when it occurred to me, as the divorced mother of a five-year-old daughter, that I could improve my lot by completing graduate work that would permit advancement on the salary scale at the College of Lake County, where I had been teaching freshman composition to dazed Vietnam veterans. My less than 'anything-for-art's-sake' motive catapulted me from column A to column E, disproving Robert Frost's maxim, 'Never write a poem to pay a bill, because you won't.'

"The following year, 'Dream of Trains,' one of my first poems, was selected by Lisel Mueller to tie for first place in the Evanston Library's first annual Jo-Anne Hirschfield Memorial Poetry Competition. Lisel would later become my first teacher and a lifelong friend, who would continue to offer her sure hand, her cool wisdom and clarity in all matters, both on and off the page. These many years later, she is the one I imagine looking over my shoulder as I write.

"Frost, of course, was right, but by the time I learned that, I was already being paid in spiritual currency, and it was too late to turn back.

"I came to writing through reading, a habit cultivated in childhood as an escape from the noise of the family. The only closed door ever respected was the bathroom door, so it was there my life as a reader began. After childhood's typical fare, I turned to autobiography—these even before Nancy Drew and Cherry Ames, those stalwart young women who never learned the extent of their limitations, and long before *Gone with the Wind,* which I read at an age young enough to believe it was pornographic, although that was not a word I knew.

"On the bottom shelf in the grade school library, the autobiographies, arranged alphabetically, occupied several running feet. The books were all the same length, about a hundred pages, I should imagine, with large, uniform print that gave the impression of reading one multi-volume story with a large cast of characters. I began with Clara Barton and, even before I reached Benjamin Franklin, the end of the shelf

reared up like a spooked horse, and beyond it, what? The end.

"Always an unhappy child, I had finally found something I liked. The tight fist of panic clenched in my stomach at the thought of reading the last word in the last book at the end of that shelf. Looking back, I think this fear that the story would end was my childhood apprehension of mortality.

"My fascination with stories directed me through undergraduate and graduate school, as an English major whose blissful task it was to read a book a week for each of five literature courses that comprised my schedule by the time I was a junior. I loved everything I read, but preferred the Russian novels—for their length, still hoping, I suppose, to stave off the end.

"When I began to write, my poems, in contrast, were short lyrics with no story at all. Only at Goddard College in my work with Stephen Dobyns did I come to study his poems and realize the narrative potential in my own subjects. This was the first development in my writing. The result was the long narratives in *Divine Attention,* which Li-Young Lee referred to as 'an autobiographical novel.'"

BIOGRAPHICAL/CRITICAL SOURCES:

PERIODICALS

Chicago Tribune, May 15, 1995.

* * *

ROGERS, Joel Augustus 1880(?)-1966

PERSONAL: Born September, 1880 (some sources say 1883), in Jamaica, West Indies; immigrated to the United States, 1906; naturalized citizen, 1917; died January, 1966, in New York, NY; son of Samuel and Emily Rogers. *Education:* Self-educated.

CAREER: Historian, journalist, newspaper columnist, and writer. Correspondent and columnist for *Pittsburgh Courier,* Pittsburgh, PA; free-lance journalist. *Military service:* Served in British army for four years.

MEMBER: American Geographical Society, American Academy of Political Science, Societe d'Anthropologie (Paris, France).

WRITINGS:

From Superman to Man, M. A. Donohue, 1917.

As Nature Leads: An Informal Discussion of the Reason Why Negro and Caucasian Are Mixing in Spite of Opposition, M. A. Donohue, 1919.

The Approaching Storm and How It May Be Averted: An Open Letter to Congress and the 48 Legislatures of the United States of America, self-published, 1920.

The Maroons of the West Indies and South America, self-published, 1921.

The Ku Klux Klan Spirit: A Brief Outline of the History of the Ku Klan Past and Present, Messenger, 1923.

World's Greatest Men of African Descent, self-published, c. 1931.

100 Amazing Facts about the Negro, with Complete Proof: A Short Cut to the World History of the Negro, F. Hubner, 1934, revised and enlarged edition, 1957, revised edition, Sportshelf, 1963.

Real Facts about Ethiopia, self-published, c. 1935.

World's Greatest Men and Women of African Descent, self-published, 1935.

Sex and Race: Negro-Caucasian Mixing in All Ages and All Lands, three volumes, self-published, 1940-44.

World's Great Men of Color, two volumes, self-published, 1946-47, edited and introduced by John Henrik Clarke, Macmillan, 1972.

Nature Knows No Color Line: Research into the Negro Ancestry in the White Race, Helga M. Rogers, 1952.

Africa's Gift to America: The Afro-American in the Making and Saving of the United States, self-published, 1959, published with new supplement, *Africa and Its Potentialities,* Sportshelf, 1961.

Facts about the Negro, Lincoln Park Studios, 1960.

She Walks in Beauty (novel), Western, 1963.

Selected Writings of Joel Augustus Rogers, edited by Kinya Kiorgozi, Pyramid, 1989.

Also author of novels *Blood Money,* 1923, and *The Golden Door,* 1927. Contributor to periodicals, including *Freedomways, American Mercury, Survey Graphic,* and *Journal of Negro History.* Author of special feature, "Your History from the Beginning of Time to the Present," *Pittsburgh Courier,* 1940.

SIDELIGHTS: Joel Augustus Rogers was, for more than fifty years, a prominent black journalist and historian. Rogers became a journalist for the *Pittsburgh Courier* and was assigned to cover the coronation of the Emperor of Ethiopia in 1930. He was

subsequently assigned to cover the Italo-Ethiopian War in 1935, and became the first Black war correspondent in the history of the United States. In the 1950s he went on to publish numerous books on African American history. According to a *Negro Almanac* reviewer, Rogers's researches were extraordinary "at a time when Negro historians were virtually non-existent in the U.S."

BIOGRAPHICAL/CRITICAL SOURCES:

BOOKS

Negro Almanac, Bellwether, 1971.

PERIODICALS

Library Journal, November 1, 1992, pp. 47, 49.*

* * *

ROJAS, A. R.
 See ROJAS, Arnold R.

* * *

ROJAS, Arnold R. 1896(?)-1988
 (A. R. Rojas)

PERSONAL: Born September 25, 1896 (one source says 1899), in Pasadena, CA; died September 8, 1988. *Education:* Attended elementary school.

CAREER: Vaquero at V7 Ranch, San Luis Obispo, CA, San Emideo Ranch, and Rancho Tejon until 1935; Bar-O Stable, Bakersfield, CA, owner, 1935-50; equine dentist and horse trainer, beginning 1950; writer. Rodeo chairman in Bakersfield, c. late 1940s.

WRITINGS:

California Vaquero, Academy Library Guild, 1953.
Lore of the California Vaquero, Academy Library Guild, 1958.
Last of the Vaqueros, Academy Library Guild, 1960.
The Vaquero, illustrations by Nicholas S. Firfires, McNally & Loftin, 1964.
(Under name A. R. Rojas) *Bits, Bitting and Spanish Horses: The Chief Rojas Fact Book about Successful Horse Training and the Proper Use of Equipment,* Kimberly Press, 1970.

These Were the Vaqueros: Collected Works of Arnold R. Rojas, illustrations by Rich Rudish, privately printed, 1974.
Vaqueros and Buckeroos, privately printed, 1979.

Contributor to *Bakersfield Californian.*

SIDELIGHTS: Grounded in personal experience, Arnold R. Rojas's books about the life of California's vaqueros—Mexican cowboys—are regarded as regional classics. A vaquero himself, he heard many anecdotes and legends around campfires and in bunkhouses and set them down, along with his own observations of cowboys, horses, Indians, and cattle, in "brief tales that hover on the line between fiction and history," according to Gerald Haslam in *Dictionary of Literary Biography.* Rojas, whose formal schooling ended at third grade, learned to write through the tradition of oral story-telling and the example of authors such as Alexandre Dumas, Miguel de Cervantes, Rudyard Kipling, Robert Louis Stevenson, Emile Zola, and Jack London. His first writings were thumbnail sketches of several vaqueros written for the *Bakersfield Californian* as publicity for a rodeo Rojas was organizing. These led to regular contributions to the paper and the Academy Library Guild's offer to publish his work in book form. Observed Haslam: "It is the unexpected and magical that readers find in Rojas's work. He captured in print a time and a culture whose human qualities would otherwise have been forgotten."

BIOGRAPHICAL/CRITICAL SOURCES:

BOOKS

Dictionary of Literary Biography, Volume 82: *Chicano Writers, First Series,* Gale, 1989.*

* * *

ROJAS, Guillermo 1938-

PERSONAL: Born January 18, 1938, in Victoria, TX. *Education:* North Texas State University, B.A., 1963, M.A., 1965; University of Illinois at Urbana-Champaign, Ph.D., 1970.

ADDRESSES: Office—Department of Mexican-American Studies, University of California, Davis, CA 95616.

CAREER: Southern University, Baton Rouge, LA, assistant professor of Spanish and German, 1966-67; University of California, Davis, assistant professor of Spanish, 1970—.

MEMBER: American Association of Teachers of Spanish and Portuguese, Modern Language Association.

AWARDS, HONORS: National Endowment for the Humanities fellowship, 1972-73.

WRITINGS:

Characterization of Pancho Villa and Other Historical Figures in the Major Works of Martin Luis Gazman, University of Illinois at Urbana-Champaign, 1971.

Camino abierto, Ediciones ECLCA, 1986.

(Editor) *Chicano Studies: Nuevos Horizontes,* Prisma Books, 1988.

Contributor to numerous periodicals. Associate editor of *Anuario de Letras Chicanas,* 1977—.*

* * *

ROJAS (SEPULVEDA), Manuel 1896-1973

PERSONAL: Born January 8, 1896, in Buenos Aires, Argentina; died in 1973.

CAREER: Writer.

AWARDS, HONORS: Premio Nacional de Literature, 1957.

WRITINGS:

Hombres del sur (short stories), prologue by Raul Silva Castro, Nascimento, 1927.

Tonada del transeunte (poems), Nascimento, 1927.

El delincuente (short stories), Sociedad Chilena de Ediciones, 1929, reprinted, Zig-Zag, 1963.

Lanchas en la bahia (novel), Empresa Letras, 1932, reprinted, Zig-Zag, 1959.

Travesia (short stories), Nascimento, 1934, reprinted, Editorial Nascimento, 1973.

La ciudad de las cesares (novel), Ediciones Ercilla, 1936, reprinted, Zig-Zag, 1972.

De la poesia a la revolucion, Ediciones Ercilla, 1938.

El bonete maulino, Cruz del Sur, 1943.

Hijo de ladron (novel), Nascimento, 1951, translation by Frank Gaynor published as *Born Guilty,* Library Publishers, 1955.

Deshecha rosa (poems), 2nd edition, Babel, 1954.

(Editor) *Chile: 5 navegantes y 1 astronomo,* Zig-Zag, 1956.

Imagenes de infancia y adolescencia, Babel, c. 1956, reprinted, Zig-Zag, 1983.

Antologia de cuentos, prologue by Enrique Espinoza, Zig-Zag, 1957.

(With Mary Canizzo) *Los costumbristas chilenos,* Zig-Zag, 1957.

Mejor que el vino (novel), Zig-Zag, 1958.

El vasa de leche y sus mejores cuentos, Nascimento, 1959.

Punta de rieles, Zig-Zag, 1960.

(Editor) Alberto Blest Gana, *Blest Gana: Sus mejores paginas,* Ercilla, 1960.

El arbol siempre verde, Zig-Zag, 1960.

Obras completas, Zig-Zag, 1961.

Apuntes sobre la expresion escrita, [Caracas], c. 1961.

Antologia autobiografica, Ercilla, 1962.

Cuentos del sur y diario de Mexico, Ediciones Era, 1963.

(Editor) *Esencias del pais chileno: Poesias,* Universidad Nacional Autonoma de Mexico, 1963.

El Hombre de la rosa, Editorial Losada, 1963.

Sombras contra el muro (novel), Zig-Zag, 1963.

Pase por Mexico un dia, Zig-Zag, 1964.

Manual de literatura chilena, Direccion de Cursos Temporales, 1964.

Historia breve de la literatura chilena, Zig-Zag, 1965.

A pie por Chile, Editora Santiago, 1967.

El bonete maulino, y otros cuentos, Editorial Universitaria, 1968.

Viaje al pais de los profetas, Ediciones Zlotopioro, 1969.

Cuentos, Editorial Sudamericana, 1970.

La oscura vida radiante, Editorial Sudamericana, 1971.

Obras, prologue by Jorge Campos, Aguilar, 1973.

Mares libres, edited by Norman Cortes L., Ediciones Universitarias de Valparaiso, Universidad Catolica de Valparaiso, 1975.

El colocolo y otros cuentos, Ediciones Huracan, Editorial Arte y Literatura, 1977.

BIOGRAPHICAL/CRITICAL SOURCES:

BOOKS

Yates, Donald A., editor, *Tres cuentistas hispanoamericanos,* Macmillan, 1969.

PERIODICALS

World Literature Today, spring, 1965; winter, 1965.*

* * *

ROMANO, Octavio I. 1932-

PERSONAL: Born in 1932. *Education:* Received B.A. and M.A. from University of New Mexico; University of California, Berkeley, Ph.D., 1964.

ADDRESSES: Office—Tonatiuh/Quinto Sol International, Inc., P.O. Box 9275, Berkeley, CA 94709; and Department of Public Health, University of California, Berkeley, Berkeley, CA 94720.

CAREER: Associate professor of behavioral science at University of California, Berkeley; president of Tonatiuh-Quinto Sol International, Inc., Berkeley. Member of California State Advisory Commission on Compensatory Education, 1967-68; former chair of Spanish Speaking People's Institute for Education.

WRITINGS:

(Editor) *El Espejo—The Mirror: Selected Mexican-American Literature,* Tonatiuh/Quinto Sol International, 1969.
(Editor) *The Grito del Sol Collection: Anthology, Winter, 1984,* Tonatiuh/Quinto Sol International, 1985.
Geriatric Fu, Tonatiuh/Quinto Sol International, 1989.

Contributor of articles and short stories to periodicals, including *El Grito* and *Grito del Sol.* Editor of *Grito del Sol: A Chicano Quarterly.* *

* * *

ROSA, Alexis Gomez
See GOMEZ ROSA, Alexis

* * *

ROSENFELD, Samuel
See TZARA, Tristan

ROSENSTOCK, Sami
See TZARA, Tristan

* * *

ROSENSTOCK, Samuel
See TZARA, Tristan

* * *

ROSS, Becki L. 1959-

PERSONAL: Born March 16, 1959, in Sudbury, Ontario, Canada; daughter of Chuck and Carol (Van Horne) Ross; companion of Ingrid E. Stitt. *Ethnicity:* "Scottish/Dutch." *Education:* University of Western Ontario, B.A., 1982; Queen's University, Kingston, Ontario, M.A., 1984; University of Toronto, Ph.D., 1992. *Politics:* "Socialist, feminist, anti-racist." *Avocational interests:* Golfing, curling, swimming, going to films.

ADDRESSES: Home—402-2875 Osoyoos Cres., Vancouver, British Columbia V6T 2G3, Canada. *Office*—Department of Anthropology and Sociology, University of British Columbia, 6303 Northwest Marine Dr., Vancouver, British Columbia V6T 1Z1, Canada. *E-mail*—becki@unixg.ubc.ca.

CAREER: Toronto Centre for Lesbian, Gay, Bisexual, and Transgender Studies, Toronto, Ontario, co-chairperson, 1992-94; University of British Columbia, Vancouver, assistant professor of anthropology, sociology, and women's studies, 1995—.

MEMBER: Canadian Sociology and Anthropology Association, Canadian Women's Studies Association, Canadian Historical Association, Canadian Socialist Studies Association, Canadian Lesbian and Gay Studies Association.

WRITINGS:

The House That Jill Built: A Lesbian Nation in Formation, University of Toronto Press (Toronto, Ontario), 1995.
(With Brenda Cossman, Shannon Bell, and Lise Gotell) *Bad Attitude/s: Feminism, Pornography, and the Butler Decision,* University of Toronto Press, 1996.

Contributor to periodicals, including *Journal of the History of Sexuality.*

WORK IN PROGRESS: A socio-cultural analysis of *Better Homes and Gardens* magazine in the 1960s and on Canadian lesbians in the 1950s; research on pornography and censorship.

SIDELIGHTS: Becki L. Ross told *CA:* "My primary motivation for writing is a desire to communicate research and analysis I've completed on complex aspects of women's experiences. I am most intrigued by the intersections of gender, sexuality, race/ethnicity, and class as they structure the lives of lesbians, or women engaged in homoerotic relations, in the Canadian context from the nineteenth century to the present. To date, this has meant examining the movement of lesbian feminists in the 1970s to specify a critique of compulsory heterosexuality, and to enact new modes of collective living, decision-making, and political protest. I have also looked at the complicated relations forged by the Staff at Street Haven hostel and the 'homeless, wayward girls' they served in the 1960s and in Toronto's 'tenderloin' district. In doing this combined archival and interview-based research, I am indebted to Joan Nestle, Esther Newton, George Chauncey, Allan Berube, Jonathon Ned Katz, Liz Lapovsky Kennedy, Madeline Davis, Gary Kinsman, and Donna Penn, who, among others, have opened up and popularized the field of 'queer history.' I write whenever I have time, outside the rigors of full-time teaching, graduate supervision, and committee work at the University of British Columbia. My own hunger for knowledge of a queer past and my commitment to transmitting this knowledge to younger generations of queer youth comprise the engine that drives my research practice and my belief in the value of publishing finished work. I consider all my work to be embedded in, and informed by, personal and political interests in enabling justice and social change in increasingly conservative and moral regulatory times."

* * *

ROUTIER, Simone 1901-1987
(Marie de Villiers)

PERSONAL: Born March 4, 1901, in Quebec, Canada; died November 6, 1987; daughter of Alfred-Charles (a jeweler) and Zelia (La Force) Routier; married J.-Fortunat Drouin, April 8, 1958. *Educa-tion:* Attended Convent des Ursulines, Quebec, Universite Laval, and Sorbonne (Universite de Paris). *Religion:* Catholic.

CAREER: Lecturer and poet. Canadian Archives, Paris, France, draftsman, 1930-40; Canadian Archives, Ottawa, Ontario, assistant archivist, 1940-50; Canadian Embassy, Brussels, Belgium, press attache, 1950-54; Canadian consulate, Boston, MA, vice consul, 1954-58.

MEMBER: Academie Canadienne-Francaise, Societe des Poetes (Paris), Societe des Ecrivains Canadiens-Francais, Societe des Poetes de Quebec.

AWARDS, HONORS: Prix David, 1928, for *L'Immortel Adolescent;* Diplome aux Jeux Florauz du Languedoc, France, 1931; Medaille Carrel, 1931; Lieutenant Governor's Medal, 1934, for *Ceux qui seront aimes.*

WRITINGS:

L'Immortel Adolescent, Le Soleil (Quebec), 1928, revised and enlarged edition, 1929.
Ceux qui seront aimes, Pierre Roger (Paris), 1931.
Paris-Amour-Deauville, Pierre Roger (Paris), 1932.
Les Tentations, La Caravelle (Paris), 1934.
Adieu, Paris! Journal d'une evacuee canadienne, 10 mai-17 juin 1940, Le Droit (Ottawa), 1940, revised and enlarged edition, Beauchemin (Montreal), 1944.
(Under pseudonym Marie de Villiers) *Reponse a "Desespoir de vielle fille,"* Beauchemin (Montreal), 1943.
Les Psaumes du jardin clos, La Lyre et La Croix/ Editions du Levrier (Paris/Montreal), 1947.
Je te fiancerai, La Lyre et La Croix (Paris), 1947, published as *Le Long Voyage,* La Lyre et La Croix (Paris), 1947.
(With Soeur Paul-Emile) *Notre Dame du bel amour,* Le Droit (Ottawa), 1947.
Le Choix de Simone Routier dans l'oeuvre de Simone Routier, Presses Laurentiennes (Notre-Dames-des-Laurentides, Quebec), 1981.

Contributor of poetry to several anthologies, including *The Oxford Book of Canadian Verse,* edited by A. J. M. Smith, Oxford, 1960; *Un siecle de litterature canadienne,* edited by G. Sylvestre, HMH, 1967. Also contributor to *Canadian Poetry, Ecrits du Canada francais,* and *Poesie.* Routier's manuscripts, letters, and other documents are held in the Bibliotheque Nationale du Quebec.

SIDELIGHTS: "Simone Routier's name," writes Louise H. Forsyth in her *Dictionary of Literary Biography* essay, "is usually cited among those of the significant poets of the first half of the twentieth century." Her early work provides a unique perspective on the life and loves of a young French Canadian woman. Her first book, *L'Immortel Adolescent,* may have been based in part on Routier's relationship with her fellow Quebecois poet Alain Grandbois. "A close relationship seems to have developed between the two young poets, which lasted for two years (1920-1922) and then dissolved with some measure of bitterness and misunderstanding," Forsyth explains. A later relationship, with an English-speaking Protestant boy, also ended, because Routier's family disapproved of the match. *L'Immortel Adolescent* traces the transformation of Routier's emotions from those of a disappointed young woman to those of a poet.

L'Immortel Adolescent helped to forge Routier's reputation. On the basis of it, she was admitted to the Societe des Poetes Canadiens-Francais and awarded the Prix David. "By the time she published *Les Tentations*" in 1934, Forsyth declares, "Routier had achieved mastery of her craft." However, her personal romantic life was in turmoil. "The early years of World War II were for her a period of tragedy," the critic explains. "Her fiance, Louis Courty, was killed by an exploding shell two days before their wedding. A short time later she had to leave France, abandoning all her belongings, including her manuscripts, the work of ten years." Routier spent another ten years in her homeland, and her work during this period—among the last of her work published during her lifetime—introduces an interest in a serene life and in religion. "While this represents a new departure in her writing," Forsyth asserts, "Routier's sensitivity remains unchanged: spiritual fulfillment can come only through full acceptance of experience in the material world."

BIOGRAPHICAL/CRITICAL SOURCES:

BOOKS

Blais, Jacques, *De l'ordre et de l'aventure,* Presses de l'Universite Laval (Quebec), 1975.
Dantin, Louis, *Poetes de l'Amerique francaise,* 2nd series, Albert Levesque (Montreal), 1934.
DesRochers, Alfred, *Paragraphes,* Action Canadienne-Francaise, 1931.
Dictionary of Literary Biography, Volume 88: *Canadian Writers, 1920-1959, Second Series,* Gale, 1989.

Hebert, Maurice, . . . *Et d'un livre a l'autre,* Albert Levesque (Montreal), 1932.
Marcotte, Gilles, *Une litterature qui se fait,* HMH (Montreal), 1962.
Pageau, Rene, *Rencontres avec Simone Routier, suivies des lettres d'Alain Grandbois,* Parabole (Joliette, Quebec), 1978.

PERIODICALS

Ecrits du Canada francais, Volumes 44/45, 1982, pp. 227-74.
Liaison, May, 1947, pp. 268-72.*

* * *

ROY, Jacqueline 1954-

PERSONAL: Born January 2, 1954, in London, England; daughter of Namba (a painter, sculptor, and novelist) and Yvonne (an actress and teacher; maiden name, Shelly) Roy. *Education:* University of North London, B.A., 1989; University of Leeds, M.A., 1990. *Politics:* Labour.

ADDRESSES: Home—49 Salford Rd., London SW2 4BL, England. *Office*—Manchester Metropolitan University, Lower Ormond St., Manchester M15, England. *Agent*—Rosemary Sandberg, 44 Bowerdean St., London SW6 3TW, England.

CAREER: Manchester Metropolitan University, Manchester, England, lecturer, 1992—; writer.

MEMBER: Society of Authors.

WRITINGS:

(Editor) Namba Roy, *No Black Sparrows: A Vivid Portrait of Jamaica in the 1930s,* Heinemann, 1989.
Soul Daddy, HarperCollins, 1990.
King Sugar, HarperCollins, 1993.

Also author of the short stories "A Family Likeness" and "Joshua's Friend."

WORK IN PROGRESS: Fat Chance, a novel; research in black British women's writing.

SIDELIGHTS: Jacqueline Roy commented: "I was born in London of an English mother and a Jamaican

father, and this inevitably raises questions of cultural identity, which I try to explore in my fiction. My late father, Namba Roy, was also a writer. He was a Maroon, a people originally composed of escaped slaves who fled to the mountains in Jamaica and established a community there, which tried to hold on to African traditions. In Africa, the oral tradition is of great importance, and histories, both personal and public, were usually passed on by word of mouth. For this reason, the storyteller has always been a valued member of the community, and the role was passed down through the generations. My father was the storyteller for the Maroons, and although he had settled in England, when he died it was hoped that at least one of his children would succeed him. Therefore, writing is particularly important in my family; my brother and sister are writers too. In addition to producing my own fiction, I edited my father's novel, *No Black Sparrows*. This increased my sense that writing was a family tradition.

"At school, I was very aware of the lack of interest in Afro-Caribbean history and culture, and partly for this reason, I left without taking A-levels; like many young people, I was not sure what an all-white curriculum could say to me and much of the teaching seemed irrelevant. I worked in various places. At one point I cut cheese in a local supermarket—a job I really wasn't too good at. Customers asking for a quarter pound usually ended up with at least twice that! Working in a bookshop was a lot more interesting than this, but my real ambition was still to write, and I spent my spare time writing stories for all age groups from small children to adults.

"Eventually, bored with shop work, I decided to take a degree in English at the Polytechnic of North London (now the University of North London). The course included studies of African, West Indian, and Indian literature, and I found it exciting and stimulating. On graduating, I went on to do an M.A. in Commonwealth Literature at Leeds University. While at the poly, I wrote *Soul Daddy,* which explored identity on two levels: firstly, the need for a racial and/ or cultural identity, and secondly, the wish to create an identity within the family. Twinship featured strongly and was a device for looking at the way in which we see ourselves and how this often changes and develops as other people come into our lives. I wanted to show that the family structure is not stable or fixed but fluctuates, just as the social structure does.

"*King Sugar,* my second book for teenagers, concerns Alex, a young actress who gets a part in a West End production. She plays Poll, a young slave, and as she gets into the role, Poll seems to appear to her. Poll says that the way she is presented in the play is inaccurate, and she wants to tell her story. As Alex listens, she is forced to question versions of history and to ask herself whose story the play is telling—that of the masters, or that of the slaves? Just as sugar is central to the life of a Caribbean slave, it is also central to Alex's life—she has diabetes and is not sure if Poll is a ghost or a symptom of her illness. Alex has a friend called Denise, who becomes the target of the right wing extremists who operate in the area in which the girls live. Denise's victimization, as well as her resilience, show Alex that life is still a struggle for Afro-Caribbeans, but that courage and the will to survive are part of her inheritance.

"*Fat Chance* is for a slightly younger age group (ten to thirteen). It is about the friendship between two misfits, Jasper and Tessa, who are despised and disliked at school and who offer hope to each other. Tessa is overweight and believes slimness is the key to popularity. As she diets and gets thinner, her friendship with Jasper suffers, but he stands by her and helps to prevent her from slipping into anorexia nervosa.

"My books are mainly about young women and the expectations they believe they must meet, whether these are social or personal or relating to the family. For black youngsters, the problems are particularly intense because expectations of them are either very low and negative, or very high, by way of compensation.

"My particular interests are Caribbean and Afro-American women's fiction and the role of women in society in general. Toni Morrison is my favorite writer for adults, and for young people's authors I like Rosa Guy and Marlene Phillip. I also like music—everything from soul and reggae to jazz and classical. Aretha Franklin and Laura Nyro are my favorite singers. I enjoy walking and wish I had a dog, as they're so much fun to take out, but that's difficult in British cities—there aren't enough places for them to run. I also love street markets; the bustle, the color, and the variety make them exciting places to be. I have a large collection of teddy bears, which have virtually taken over the house, and more books than I've got space for. My favorite foods are chocolate and ice cream, though I'm trying to cut back on the chocolate!

"I have just begun to teach in higher education. I had such a good experience of degree work as a mature student that I'd like to be able to pass on some of the skills and interests I developed. Education is an invaluable tool in voicing social and political concerns, and it is something which is often denied to the black and/or underprivileged communities. It is therefore vital to ensure that it does not remain in the hands of the privileged few."

* * *

RUSSELL, George William 1867-1935
(A.E., Y.O., O.L.S., Gab)

PERSONAL: Born April 10, 1867, in Lurgan, County Armagh, Ireland; died July 17, 1935, in Bournemouth, England; son of Thomas and Marianne Russell; married Violet North, June 11, 1897 (died February, 1932). *Education:* Attended Rathmines School and the Metropolitan School of Art. *Religion:* Theosophist. *Avocational interests:* Painting.

CAREER: Writer, published his works under the pseudonyms A.E., Y.O., O.L.S., and Gab; worked as a cashier, 1890; accepted full-time position with Horace Plunkett's Irish Agricultural Organization Society, 1897; edited *Irish Homestead,* 1905-23; edited *Irish Statesman,* 1923-30.

MEMBER: Theosophical Society, Irish National Theatre Society.

WRITINGS:

POETRY

Homeward: Songs by the Way, Whaley, 1894.
The Earth Breath, and Other Poems, John Lane/Bodley Head, 1897.
The Divine Vision, and Other Poems, Macmillan, 1904.
Collected Poems, Macmillan, 1913.
Voices of the Stones, Macmillan, 1925.
Vale and Other Poems, Macmillan, 1931.
The House of the Titans and Other Poems, Macmillan, 1934.
Selected Poems, Macmillan, 1935.

Also author of *Gods of War,* 1915.

ESSAYS

Co-operation and Nationality: A Guide for Rural Reformers from This to the Next Generation, Maunsel, 1912.
Imaginations and Reveries, Maunsel, 1915.
The National Being: Some Thoughts on an Irish Polity, Maunsel, 1916.
Song and Its Fountains (essays), Macmillan, 1932.
The Living Torch, edited by Monk Gibbon, Macmillan, 1937.
Selections from the Contributions to the Irish Homestead, edited by Henry Summerfield, Colin Smythe, 1978.
The Descent of the Gods, Comprising the Mystical Writings of G.W. Russell, "A.E.," edited by Baghavan Iyer and Nandini Iyer, Colin Smythe, 1988.

OTHER

Deirdre (play), performed at the Irish National Theatre, in 1902.
The Candle of Vision (autobiography), Macmillan, 1918.
The Interpreters (novel), Macmillan, 1922.
The Avatars: A Futurist Fantasy (novel), Macmillan, 1933.
AE's Letters to Minanlabain, Macmillan, 1937.
Letters from AE, edited by Alan Denson, Abelard-Schuman, 1961.

SIDELIGHTS: A key figure in the Irish Literary Revival, George William Russell contributed more to the movement through his personality than through his artistry. He was a gifted conversationalist, a popular lecturer, and a generous man who brought many of the members of the Revival together. Although Russell's interests were varied, he earned a modest literary reputation based on his mystical poems and his drama, *Deirdre.* He was central to the rise of the Irish National Theatre, and, with W. B. Yeats, J. M. Synge, and Lady Gregory, was one of the founders of the Abbey Theatre. Through his work and his charismatic personality, Russell was an important influence on the writers of the Irish Revival, a generation which sought to reduce the influence of English culture and create an Irish national literature.

Russell had a pious upbringing and from his youth was inclined toward mysticism. While studying painting at the Dublin Metropolitan School of Art, Russell

met Yeats, who became his lifelong friend. Through Yeats, Russell became involved in the theosophical movement, in which he found a channel for his mystical interests. These interests were a mixture of belief in Buddhism, theosophy, magic, reincarnation, pantheism, and elements of Irish mythology that served as the inspiration for his early poems, collected in *Homeward: Songs by the Way, The Earth Breath, and Other Poems,* and *The Divine Vision, and Other Poems.* The poems of these early volumes are characterized by their colorful imagery, archaic language, and exaltation of the Earth as a life-sustaining mother, which is a recurring motif throughout Russell's work. It was during this period that Russell's unusual pseudonym, A.E., was acquired. A typesetter was unable to decipher the scribbled pen name Aeon, with which Russell had signed an article, and so printed only the first two letters. Russell was delighted with the result and used the pseudonym throughout his life.

By 1905, Russell had become a guiding force behind the Agricultural Cooperative Movement and was appointed editor of its chief organ, the *Irish Homestead,* which later became the *Irish Statesman.* The political essays he published in the magazine and in his book *The National Being: Some Thoughts on an Irish Polity* propose plans for the development of a more practical Irish government. Russell promoted Irish Home Rule, but unlike many of his fellow nationalists, he stressed the importance of political moderation and reconciliation with Great Britain. One of Russell's most widely read books of political essays, *The National Being,* definitively states the author's economic policies, calling for a cooperative commonwealth for the new Republic of Ireland. In addition to his political activities, Russell was very involved in the cultural life of Ireland at this time. His only play, *Deirdre,* treats the ancient legend of the Red Branch, and was, with Yeats's *Cathleen ni Houlihan,* one of the earliest productions of the modern Irish theater. Together, the two dramas contributed to the period now known as the Celtic Twilight, a late nineteenth-century period when Irish artists attempted to give Irish art and culture a distinct national and spiritual identity based on ancient Celtic legend. Always interested in encouraging and promoting other Irish authors, Russell hosted a weekly gathering at his home, attracting such artists as Yeats, George Moore, Padraic Colum, and James Stephens. As editor of the *Irish Statesman,* he also provided a forum for these writers. In his last years, broken by the death of his wife and saddened by the increasing factional hatred and violence in Ireland, Russell retired to England, where he died.

Russell was devoted to the work of Ralph Waldo Emerson, and shared with him an interest in pantheism and transcendentalism as well as a desire to wed spiritual beliefs with social action. Russell also recognized his own vision in the life-affirming poetry of William Blake. In *The Candle of Vision,* a work often referred to as his spiritual autobiography, Russell expressed a thorough and thoughtful elucidation of his development from childhood to adulthood. His discussion of visions and intuition led Leslie Shepard to claim that *The Candle of Vision* "is an essential key, not only to Russell, but also to the mystic life itself, which is the inheritance of everyone." The book won Russell recognition and respect as a mystic both in Ireland and North America. The essay collection *Song and Its Fountains* is Russell's explanation for the creation of poetry. Stating that poetry originates from the divine inner being rather than from experience, Russell relates his mystical revelations in an autobiographical style similar to that of *The Candle of Vision.*

Although his poetry is generally characterized by monotonous repetitions of themes and images, critics praise the sincerity of Russell's thought and inspiration. Some critics, such as Ernest Boyd, suggest that the repetitiveness of his verse results "because words as fresh as the emotion prompting them are not always to be found." Yeats, whose poetry overshadows Russell's, referred to him as "the most subtle and spiritual poet of his generation." But other critics question the legitimacy of Russell's spiritual inclinations, and believe that his mystical ideals often outweigh his artistry, and that his poetry is highly derivative and facile. The critical consensus is that he survives not as a painter, poet, or politician, but as the embodiment of the beliefs and principles of the Irish Revival.

BIOGRAPHICAL/CRITICAL SOURCES:

BOOKS

Bose, Abinash Chandra, *Three Mystic Poets: W. B. Yeats, A.E., and Rabindranath Tagore,* Folcroft Press, 1970.

Boyd, Ernest, *Ireland's Literary Renaissance,* Barnes & Noble, 1968.

Canby, Henry Seidel, *American Estimates,* Kennikat, 1968.

Davis, Robert Bernard, *George William Russell ("AE"),* Twayne, 1977.

Denson, Alan, *Printed Writings by George W. Russell (AE): A Bibliography,* Northwestern University Press, 1961.

Eglinton, John, *A Memoir of AE: George William Russell,* Macmillan, 1937.

Figgis, Darrell, *AE (George W. Russell): A Study of a Man and a Nation,* Maunsel, 1916.

Howarth, Herbert, *The Irish Writers 1880-1940,* Rockliff, 1958.

Kain, Richard M., and James H. O'Brien, *George Russell (A.E.),* Bucknell University Press, 1976.

Loftus, Richard J., *Nationalism in Modern Anglo-Irish Poetry,* University of Wisconsin Press, 1964.

Moore, George, *Hail and Farewell: Ave, Salve, Vale,* Macmillan, 1976.

Phelps, William Lyon, *Autobiography with Letters,* Oxford University Press, 1939.

Skelton, Robin, and Ann Saddlemyer, editors, *The World of W. B. Yeats,* University of Washington Press, 1965.

Summerfield, Henry, *That Myriad-Minded Man: A Biography of George William Russell ("A.E."), 1867-1935,* Rowan and Littlefield, 1975.

Thompson, William Irwin, *The Imagination of an Insurrection, Dublin, Easter, 1916: A Study of an Ideological Movement,* Oxford University Press, 1967.

PERIODICALS

Ariel, Vol. 11, number 3, July, 1980, pp. 69-82.

Atlantic Monthly, February, 1943, pp. 51-57.

Colby Library Quarterly, Vol. IV, number 2, May, 1955.

Eire-Ireland, Vol. VI, number 4, winter, 1971, pp. 38-48; Vol. VIII, number 3, autumn, 1973.

Ireland-American Review, number 1, September, 1938, pp. 36-49.

Kenyon Review, number 2, spring, 1965, pp. 336-43.

Nation, Vol. CXVI, number 3016, April 25, 1923, p. 499.

New Republic, Vol. 87, number 1119, May 13, 1936, pp. 23-24.

North American Review, Vol. 202, number 717, August, 1915, pp. 251-61.

Poet Lore, Vol. XVI, number IV, winter, 1905, pp. 82-86; Vol. XLVII, number 3, autumn, 1941, pp. 240-49.

Sewanee Review, Vol. XV, number 2, spring, 1907, pp. 148-65.

Times Literary Supplement, number 1864, October 23, 1937, pp. 765-66.

Virginia Quarterly Review, Vol. 15, number 1, winter, 1939, pp. 41-57.

Yale Review, Vol. XXIX, number 1, September, 1939, pp. 60-88.*

RUSTOW, Dankwart A(lexander) 1924-1996

OBITUARY NOTICE—See index for *CA* sketch: Born December 21, 1924, in Berlin, Germany; immigrated to the U.S.; naturalized U.S. citizen; died of non-Hodgkins lymphoma, August 3, 1996, in Manhattan, NY. Political scientist, educator, and author. Rustow specialized in Middle Eastern studies, teaching for some forty-five years at schools in the United States and abroad. His early career saw work at Oglethorpe University from 1950 to 1952 followed by seven years at Princeton University, which included field research in Turkey. Next, Rustow joined the Columbia University faculty for eleven years, ultimately serving as professor of international social forces. He rounded out his career at City University of New York from 1970 until 1995. He also found time for visiting lecturer or professor stints at schools such as Hunter College, Yale University, University of Heidelberg, and London School of Economics and Political Science. During his career, Rustow was on the governing board of the Middle East Institute and was a vice president of the Middle East Studies Association. He authored and edited numerous books, including *The Politics of Compromise: A Study of Parties and Cabinet Government in Sweden, Politics and Westernization in the Near East, Succession in the Twentieth Century, A World of Nations: Problems of Political Modernization,* and *Middle Eastern Political Systems.*

OBITUARIES AND OTHER SOURCES:

PERIODICALS

New York Times, August 5, 1996, p. A14.

*　　*　　*

RYAN, Craig 1953-

PERSONAL: Born December 14, 1953, in Shawnee, OK; son of Eugene S. (a geologist) and Joyce A. (Salmon) Ryan; married Kathy L. Narramore, January 9, 1973; children: Jessy R., Caitlin S. *Education:* Attended Webster College, 1972-74; Reed College, B.A., 1977; Brown University, M.A., 1982.

ADDRESSES: Home—4303 S.W. Jerald Way, Portland, OR 97221. *Agent*—Albert Zuckerman, Writers House, 21 West 26 St., New York, NY 10010.

CAREER: Nonfiction writer, technical writer and editor. Software engineering manager, Sequent Computer Systems.

AWARDS, HONORS: Transatlantic Review Award, Henfield Foundation, 1982, for fiction; award of achievement, International Society for Technical Communication, 1990, for "Technical Writer's Guide."

WRITINGS:

The Pre-Astronauts: Manned Ballooning on the Threshold of Space (history), Naval Institute Press (Annapolis, MD), 1995.

Also author of text for travel-photo books, *Beautiful New Mexico* and *Beautiful New York.*

SIDELIGHTS: In *The Pre-Astronauts: Manned Ballooning on the Threshold of Space,* Craig Ryan brings to light the foundation of the American space program in the experiments of high-altitude balloonists in the 1950s and 1960s. Ryan tells the story of daredevils such as Joe Kittinger and John Paul Stapp of the U.S. Air Force who convinced their reluctant superiors that manned balloon flights could provide valuable information on the earth's stratosphere and the effect on equipment and the human body of atmospheric pressure at high altitudes. The pre-astronauts, as Ryan calls them, invented what became the prototypes for the space suits and capsules that went into outer space with the first actual American astronauts. "*The Pre-Astronauts* is a eulogy for the brave and brilliant individuals who took mankind to the threshold of outer space," wrote James Reinbold in *Brown Alumni Monthly.* "Their achievements and the lessons they imparted have been largely forgotten," Reinbold continued, "[but] Craig Ryan has assured their place in history."

Critics singled out Ryan's riveting accounts of the dangerous early balloon flights, in particular Kittinger's ascent to over one hundred thousand feet in an open gondola and subsequent free-fall at near the speed of sound before opening his parachute to land safely on the earth. *The Pre-Astronauts* was likened to Tom Wolfe's best-selling *The Right Stuff,* about the early days of NASA. "Ryan adroitly braids the many strands of balloon-borne research and documents how it was surpassed by the space program," wrote Carl Posey in *Air & Space/Smithsonian.* Others compared Ryan's effective translation of the inherent

excitement of his subject in a nonfiction format to the art of fiction. *The Pre-Astronauts* "is a thorough chronicle of a little-heralded achievement in American space development," remarked Charles P. Thobae in the *Houston Chronicle.* "Yet some of it reads like a Tom Clancy thriller," Thobae continued, "as Ryan superbly narrates harrowing moments experienced by the balloonists."

Ryan told *CA:* "I studied fiction at Reed College and wrote a novel (unpublished) under the tutelage of detective novelist James Crumley. The summer after graduating I wrote the text for a couple of travel-photo books, *Beautiful New Mexico* and *Beautiful New York,* published by an Oregon publisher. At the Brown Writer's Workshop I wrote lots of stories (several of which comprised my master's thesis) and wrote another novel, this time under the guidance of the great fiction writer R. V. Cassill. I never published the novel, but the first chapter did win a Henfield Foundation Grant (The Transatlantic Review Award, 1982). While at Brown, I also taught fiction writing to undergraduates for a semester.

"Out of college with a family to support, I returned to Portland and took a job in the high-tech industry as a technical writer and published a few articles in computer trade journals, later taking a job as a technical editor. Today I manage software engineering projects for Sequent Computer Systems and do my writing at night and on weekends.

"Part of my motivation for writing *The Pre-Astronauts* was to fill in what I perceived to be a gap in American aviation and astronautical history. We knew about the development of rockets and the genesis of Project Mercury following the Russians' success with Sputnik, but we didn't know much about the stratospheric ballooning and high-altitude biomedical research that had been done by the U.S. Air Force and U.S. Navy in the 1950s. I argue that the high-altitude balloonists were in fact the pioneers of American space exploration. The balloon programs contributed much that was later adopted—often without acknowledgment—by NASA. (I'm happy to say that Space Center Houston, a museum at NASA, hosted an exhibition in the summer of 1996 celebrating the link between stratospheric ballooning and the space program—an exhibition based entirely on my book.)

"Another part of my motivation was to bring to life the myriad dramas I discovered in the course of my research and interviews for the book. I believe my background in fiction and my work with technical

topics gave me the perfect background to tackle this subject.

"It may be true that we live in the 'golden age of nonfiction,' and I particularly admire the work of Robert Caro, Alvin Josephy, Shelby Foote, and Peter Guralnick. My taste in fiction includes Chekhov, Faulkner, Wallace Stegner, and Cormac McCarthy."

BIOGRAPHICAL/CRITICAL SOURCES:

PERIODICALS

Air & Space/Smithsonian, October/November, 1995.
Brown Alumni Monthly, September, 1995, p. 19.
Houston Chronicle, September 3, 1995, pp. 21, 24.

S

SAAVEDRA, Luis Spota
 See **SPOTA (SAAVEDRA), Luis**

* * *

SABINES, Jaime 1925(?)-

PERSONAL: Born in 1925 (one source says 1926) in Tuxtla Gutierrez, Chiapas, Mexico. *Education:* Attended school in Mexico City, Mexico.

CAREER: Writer.

WRITINGS:

Horal, Departamento de Prensa y Turismo (Tuxtla Gutierrez, Mexico), 1950.
Tarumba, Coleccion Metafora, 1956, translation by Philip Levine and Ernesto Trejo published as *Tarumba: The Selected Poems of Jaime Sabines* (bilingual edition), Twin Peaks Press, 1979.
Poesia de la sinceridad (anthology), [Tlaxcala, Mexico], 1959.
Diario semanario y poemas en prosa, Universidad Veracruzana (Xalapa, Mexico), 1961.
Recuento de poemas (includes poems previously published in other volumes), Universidad Nacional Autonoma de Mexico, 1962.
Yuria, J. Mortiz, 1967.
Maltiempo, J. Mortiz, 1972.
Algo sobre la muerte del mayor Sabines, J. Mortiz, 1973.
Nuevo recuento de poemas (includes *Horal, Tarumba, Diario semanario y poemas en prosa, Yuria, Algo sobre la muerte del mayor Sabines,* and *Maltiempo*), J. Mortiz, 1977.

Poemas sueltos, Papeles Privados, 1981.
Poesia, Casa de las Americas, 1987.

Also author of *La senal,* 1951, and *Dona Luz,* 1969. Contributor to literary reviews, including *Pajaro Cascabel.*

BIOGRAPHICAL/CRITICAL SOURCES:

BOOKS

Hernandez Palacios, Esther, editor, *La poesia de Jaime Sabines: Analisis poetico estrutural de "Algo sobre la muerte del mayor Sabines,"* Centro de Investigaciones Linguistico-Literarias, Instituto de Investigaciones Humanisticas, Universidad Veracruzana, 1984.
Rodriguez Monegal, Emir, editor, *The Borzoi Anthology of Latin American Literature,* Volume II: *The Twentieth Century—From Borges and Paz to Guimaraes Rosa and Donoso,* Knopf, 1986.

PERIODICALS

Times Literary Supplement, May 18, 1973.*

* * *

SALAMON, Lynda B(rown) 1942-

PERSONAL: Born August 3, 1942, in Potsdam, NY; daughter of George K. (a college administrator) and Edna (a medical technician; maiden name, Dougherty) Brown; married Lester M. Salamon (a college professor), 1965; children: Noah Benjamin,

Matthew William. *Education:* Carnegie-Mellon University, B.A., 1965; Boston University, M.A., 1966; University of Maryland at College Park, Ph.D., 1989.

ADDRESSES: Home—Arnold, MD. *Office*—Department of English, Essex Community College, Baltimore, MD 21237; fax 410-974-4792.

CAREER: Essex Community College, Baltimore, MD, associate professor of English, 1989—.

MEMBER: Modern Language Association of America, American Literature Association, Two-Year College Association.

WRITINGS:

(Editor with C. Ralph Stephens) *The Craft of Peter Taylor,* University of Alabama Press (Tuscaloosa, AL), 1995.

WORK IN PROGRESS: James Fenimore Cooper; research on captivity narratives and on women's autobiographical writings.

* * *

SALVERSON, Laura Goodman 1890-1970

PERSONAL: Born December 9, 1890, in Winnipeg, Manitoba, Canada; died July 13, 1970; daughter of Laurus and Ingiborg (Gudsmundotte) Goodman; married George Salverson (a railway dispatcher), 1913; children: one son. *Education:* Attended public school in Duluth, MN.

CAREER: Novelist and poet.

AWARDS, HONORS: Governor General's Award for fiction, 1937, for *The Dark Weaver;* Gold Medal for literary merit, Paris Institute of Arts and Letters, 1938; Governor General's Award for nonfiction, 1939, for *Confessions of an Immigrant's Daughter;* Ryerson Fiction Award, 1954, for *Immortal Rock.*

WRITINGS:

The Viking Heart, McClelland & Stewart (Toronto), 1923.
Wayside Gleams (poetry), McClelland & Stewart (Toronto), 1925.
When Sparrows Fall, T. Allen (Toronto), 1925.

Lord of the Silver Dragon: A Romance of Lief the Lucky, McClelland & Stewart (Toronto), 1927.
The Dove, Ryerson (Toronto), 1933.
The Dark Weaver, Ryerson (Toronto), 1937.
Black Lace, Ryerson (Toronto), 1938.
Confessions of an Immigrant's Daughter (autobiography), Ryerson (Toronto), 1939.
Immortal Rock: The Saga of the Kensington Stone, Ryerson (Toronto), 1954.

SIDELIGHTS: Laura Goodman Salverson "was one of the pioneers of Canadian prairie fiction, perhaps Canada's first native prairie novelist," declared Paul Hjartarson in his *Dictionary of Literary Biography* essay. Born in Winnipeg, Manitoba—then the edge of the frontier—to desperately poor Icelandic immigrant parents, Salverson and her family moved often in attempts to escape their poverty. At various points during her youth, Salverson lived in North Dakota, Minnesota, and Mississippi. Partly because of this, and partly because she was sickly as a child, Salverson started school and learned English late. Her education was frequently interrupted by her family's poverty; she worked in a tailor's shop and in a hospital to earn a living. "As a result of her childhood experiences," Hjartarson explained, "[Salverson] developed a sympathy for the poor and an awareness of the plight of women that inform her writing."

Salverson's Icelandic heritage influenced almost all her work, from her first and most famous novel, *The Viking Heart,* to her autobiography, *Confessions of an Immigrant's Daughter.* However, while *The Viking Heart, The Dark Weaver,* and *When Sparrows Fall* are all about immigrants and the ways they adapt to their new land, the rest of her prose draws on history for its inspiration. *Black Lace* is set in the France of the Sun King, Louis XIV, while *Lord of the Silver Dragon, The Dove,* and *The Immortal Rock* are all based on Icelandic or Norse history and legend. *Lord of the Silver Dragon* recounts Leif Ericson's voyages to Greenland and the Atlantic coast of North America. *The Immortal Rock* is a fiction based on the Kensington Stone, a slab of rock discovered in Minnesota in 1898, which supposedly recounts the tale of a fourteenth-century Norse expedition to the Midwest. Salverson's story depicts the last twenty-four hours of the survivors. *The Dove,* on the other hand, tells of the fate of an Icelandic woman carried off to slavery in Algiers. "In her books," Hjartarson declared, Salverson "attempts to reconcile the narrative form of the Icelandic saga with that of the popular romance in order to interpret Icelandic life for English-speaking readers."

BIOGRAPHICAL/CRITICAL SOURCES:

BOOKS

Dictionary of Literary Biography, Volume 92: *Canadian Writers, 1890-1920,* Gale, 1990.
Eggleston, Wilfrid, *The Frontier and Canadian Letters,* Ryerson (Toronto), 1957.
Harrison, Dick, *Unnamed Country: The Struggle for a Canadian Prairie Fiction,* University of Alberta Press (Edmonton), 1977.
Ricou, Laurence, *Vertical Man/Horizontal World,* University of British Columbia Press (Vancouver), 1973.
Twentieth Century Romance and Historical Writers, 3rd edition, St. James, 1990.

* * *

SANCHEZ, Florencio 1875-1910

PERSONAL: Born in 1875, in Uruguay; died in 1910.

CAREER: Journalist, political activist, playwright, and writer.

WRITINGS:

PLAYS

La gringa (four-act comedy), [Uruguay], 1904, reprinted, introduction and notes by Jay Thomas Lister and Ruth Richardson, Knopf, 1927, reprinted, Huemul (Buenos Aires), 1970, translation by A. Coester published as "The Foreign Girl" in *Plays of the Southern Americas,* Books for Libraries Press (Freeport, N.Y.), 1971.
Barranca abajo (three-act drama), [Uruguay], 1905, reprinted, Prometeo, 1981.

POSTHUMOUS PUBLICATIONS

Los muertos (three-act drama), Argentores (Buenos Aires), 1935, reprinted, La Pampa (Buenos Aires), 1961.
M'hijo el dotor (three-act drama), prologue by Fermin Estrella Gutierrez, Kapelusz (Buenos Aires), 1953, reprinted, Juventud (La Paz, Argentina), 1981.
En familia (three-act comedy), La Pampa, 1961, reprinted, Colihue, 1981.

Also author of articles, letters, and short prose works; other plays include *Canillita, Nuestros hijos, El caudillaje criminal en Sud America, Los curdas, Mano santa, Los derochos de la salud, Un buen negrocio,La pobre gentle, El pasado, El desalojo, La tigre, Moneda falsa, Marta Gruni* (farce), and *Cartas de un flojo.*

COLLECTIONS

El teatro del uruguayo Florencio Sanchez, Cervantes (Barcelona), 1926.
Teatro de Florencio Sanchez, Sopena Argentina, 1939.
Teatro completo de Florencio Sanchez, compiled by Dardo Cuneo, Claridad (Buenos Aires), 1941.
Teatro completo, prologue by Vicente Martinez Cuitino,"El Ateneo," 1951.
Representative Plays of Florencio Sanchez, translated by Willis Knapp Jones, Pan American Union (Washington), 1961.
Obras completas, compiled with introduction by Jorge Lafforgue, Schapire (Buenos Aires), 1968.

Works also published in multititle volumes and in other collections; works represented in anthologies, including *Teatro uruguayo contemporaneo,* Aguilar (Madrid), 1960.

BIOGRAPHICAL/CRITICAL SOURCES:

BOOKS

Rela, Walter, *Florencio Sanchez, persona y teatro,* Ciencias, 1981.

* * *

SANCHEZ (y SANCHEZ), George I(sidore) 1906-1972

PERSONAL: Given names sometimes spelled Jorge Isidoro; born October 4, 1906, in Albuquerque (one source says Barela), NM; died April 5, 1972, in Austin, TX; son of Telesfor and Juliana (Sanchez) Sanchez; married Virginia Romero, June 15, 1925 (divorced, 1947); married Luisa G. Guerroro, August 30, 1947; children: George Eugene, Juliana Consuelo. *Education:* University of New Mexico, A.B., 1930; University of Texas, M.S., 1931; University of California, Ed.D., 1934.

CAREER: Teacher, principal, and supervisor in schools of rural New Mexico, 1923-30; New Mexico State Department of Education, Santa Fe, director of division of information and statistics, 1930-35; Julius Rosenwald Fund, Chicago, IL, research associate, 1935-37; Government of Venezuela, Caracas, asesor tecnico general for Ministerio de Educacion and director of Instituto Pedagogico Nacional, 1937-38; University of New Mexico, Albuquerque, research associate and associate professor of education, 1938-40; University of Texas, Austin, professor of Latin American education, 1940-72, chairman of department of history and philosophy of education, 1951-59, director of Center for International Education, beginning 1963. Visiting lecturer at University of Southern California, Colorado State College of Education, and University of Mexico. Conducted education surveys of Navajo for U.S. Office of Indian Affairs, 1946, in Venezuela for U.S. Office of Education, 1961, and in Peru for U.S. Agency for International Development, 1962; member of Citizens Committee on a New Frontier Policy in the Americas, 1960, and of advisory council of Peace Corps, 1961; consultant to numerous government agencies. Member of board of Travis Junior College.

MEMBER: League of United Latin American Citizens (president, 1941-42), National Education Association, Progressive Education Association, Southwest Council on the Education of Spanish-Speaking People (president, 1945-72), New Mexico Education Association (president), Sociedad Mexicana de Geografia y Estadistica, Sociedad Nacional Argentina de Estudios Historicos, Phi Delta Kappa, Phi Kappa Phi, Sigma Delta Pi.

AWARDS, HONORS: Grant from Carnegie Corporation for study of the people of rural New Mexico, 1938-39; grant from Carnegie Endowment for study of education in Mexico, 1941-42.

WRITINGS:

Mexico: A Revolution by Education, foreword by Rafael Ramirez, Viking, 1936, reprinted, Greenwood Press, 1971.

The Equalization of Educational Opportunity: Some Issues and Problems, University of New Mexico Press, 1939.

Forgotten People: A Study of New Mexicans, University of New Mexico Press, 1940, reprinted, Calvin Horn, 1967.

The Development of Higher Education in Mexico, King's Crown Press (New York), 1944, reprinted, Greenwood Press, 1970.

The People: A Study of the Navajos, foreword by William Zimmerman, Jr., U.S. Indian Service, 1948.

(With Howard Putnam) *Materials Relating to the Education of Spanish-Speaking People in the United States: An Annotated Bibliography,* Institute of Latin American Studies, University of Texas, 1959.

Arithmetic in Maya, [Austin, Tex.], 1961.

The Development of Education in Venezuela, U.S. Department of Health, Education, and Welfare, Office of Education, 1963.

Mexico, Ginn, 1966.

Editor of *Inter-American Education: Occasional Papers,* for University of Texas Press, beginning 1946. Contributor to periodicals, including *Curriculum Journal, Journal of Applied Psychology,* and *Journal of Social Psychology.* Editorial consultant to *The Nation's Schools,* beginning 1944.

SIDELIGHTS: George I. Sanchez was a lifelong advocate for Hispanic Americans of the southwestern United States. After using a Carnegie grant to study the inhabitants of rural New Mexico during the late 1930s, Sanchez was inspired to write his 1940 book, *Forgotten People.* The book focuses on the descendants of New Mexico's early Spanish-speaking settlers, depicting their struggles to earn a living and to preserve their culture after the area was annexed by the United States during the mid-nineteenth century. Reviewing a reprint of the work for the *Nation* in 1968, Philip Darraugh Ortego wrote: "*Forgotten People* is as relevant today as it was in 1940. It is one of the great books in the literature of the Southwest." Sanchez spent the last years of his life campaigning to make bilingual education available to Hispanics in Texas.

BIOGRAPHICAL/CRITICAL SOURCES:

BOOKS

Humanidad: Essays in Honor of George I. Sanchez, Chicano Studies Center Publications, University of California, Los Angeles, 1977.

PERIODICALS

Nation, April 8, 1968.*

SARAMAGO, Jose 1922-

PERSONAL: Born November 16, 1922, in Azinhaga, Portugal; married Pilar del Rio; children: one.

ADDRESSES: Office—R. Dos Ferreiros a Estrela 32-1, Lisbon 1200, Portugal. *Agent*—Ray-Guede Mertin, 1 Friedrichstrasse, 6380 Hamburg 1, Germany.

CAREER: Writer.

AWARDS, HONORS: Winner of Grinzane Cavour Prize, Mondello Prize, and Flaliano Prize; honorary doctorates from the University of Turin (Italy) and the University of Sevilla (Spain), both 1991.

WRITINGS:

NOVELS IN ENGLISH TRANSLATION

Memorial do convento (title means "Memoirs of the Convent"), Caminho (Lisbon, Portugal), 1982, translation by Giovanni Pontiero published as *Baltasar and Blimunda,* Harcourt (San Diego, CA), 1987.

O ano da morte de Ricardo Reis, Caminho, 1984, translation by Pontiero published as *The Year of the Death of Ricardo Reis,* Harcourt, 1991.

A jangada de pedra, Caminho, 1986, translation by Pontiero published as *The Stone Raft,* Harcourt, 1994.

O Evangelho Segundo Jesus Cristo, Caminho, 1991, translation by Pontiero published as *The Gospel According to Jesus Christ,* Harvil (London, England), 1993, Harcourt, 1994.

OTHER NOVELS

Manual de pintura e caligrafia (title means "Manual of Painting and Calligraphy"), Moraes (Sao Paulo, Brazil), 1976.

Levantado do chao (title means "Raised from the Ground"), Caminho, 1980.

Historia do Cerco de Lisboa (title means "The History of the Siege of Lisbon"), Caminho, 1989.

POETRY

Os poemas possiveis, Portugalia, 1966.

Provavelmente Alegria, Horizonte (Lisbon), 1970, revised edition, Caminho, 1985.

O an de 1993, Futura (Lisbon), 1975.

PLAYS

A noite, Caminho, 1979.

Que farei com este livro?, Caminho, 1980.

A Segunda vida de Francissco de Assis, Caminho, 1987.

In nomine Dei, Caminho, 1993.

OTHER

Deste mundo e do outro, Arcadia, 1971.

A bagagem do viajante, Futura, 1973.

O embargo, Estudios Cor, 1973.

Os opinioes que o D. L. teve, Seara Nova, 1974.

Os apontamentos, Seara Nova, 1976.

Objecto quase, Moraes, 1978.

Viagem a Portugal, Circulo de Leitores, 1981.

Entre a historia e aa ficcao, uma saga de Portugueses, Dom Quixote (Lisbon, Portugal), 1989.

Also author of *Blimunda* (opera libretto for Azio Corghi's musical score; adapted from Saramago's novel *Baltasar and Blimunda;* also see above), 1990. Editor of *O poeta perguntador,* 1979.

SIDELIGHTS: Jose Saramago is an accomplished Portuguese writer who has distinguished himself as an author of fiction, poetry, plays, and essays. Saramago is best known, both in his native Portugal and among English-language readers, for his novels. He was already in his early fifties when he published his first novel, *Manual de pintura e caligrafica* (which means "Manual of Painting and Calligraphy"), in 1976. This work concerns the maintaining of ideals in a world of materialism and superficial values, and is narrated by an unnamed, mediocre painter who adheres to his own sense of dignity and artistic purpose while fulfilling a commission from a rich patron. A conflict eventually develops between painter and patron, and the painting commission ends abruptly. The narrator thereupon rejects payment, choosing to retain the incomplete painting instead of compromising himself.

Saramago followed *Manual de pintura e caligrafica* with *Levantado do chao* (which means "Raised from the Ground") in 1980, a grim tale of repression set during the dictator Salazar's reign in Portugal from the mid-1930s to the late 1950s. Gerald M. Moser, reviewing *Levantado do chao* in *World Literature Today,* praised Saramago as "a born storyteller." Neither *Manual de pintura e caligrafica* nor *Levantado do chao* has been translated into English.

In 1982 Saramago published *Memorial do convento* (which means "Memoirs of the Convent" but which has been translated into English, by Giovanni Pontiero, as *Baltasar and Blimunda*), a novel that is often ranked foremost among his artistic triumphs. *Baltasar and Blimunda* is set in eighteenth-century Portugal during the Inquisition, and concerns the efforts of two young people, handicapped war veteran Baltasar and visionary Blimunda, to transport themselves into the heavens. The vehicle for this unlikely journey is a flying machine created by a priest similarly eager to leave behind the Inquisition. The existence of this flying machine, built by Baltasar and powered, fantastically enough, by human wills that have been captured by the hypersensory Blimunda, ultimately brings the main characters into opposition with the Inquisition's repressive church leaders. Running parallel to the tale of the flying machine in *Baltasar and Blimunda* is a narrative concerning the construction of the Mafra Convent, by seemingly all available Portuguese men, prior to a date foretold as that of King John V's death. In recounting this storyline Saramago provides compelling depictions of the construction process and detailed descriptions of life in the Portuguese royal court.

Baltasar and Blimunda has been hailed as a masterful blend of the fantastic and the historical, the romantic and the realistic. *New York Times* reviewer Walter Goodman described the novel as "a romance and an adventure, a rumination on royalty and religion in 18th-century Portugal and a bitterly ironic comment on the uses of power." Irving Howe, writing in the *New York Times Book Review,* called *Baltasar and Blimunda* a "full-bodied novel" and noted that it is "organized as a series of contrasts between rulers and ruled, those who luxuriate and those who labor." And Richard Eder, in his critique for the *Los Angeles Times Book Review,* deemed Saramago's novel "elaborate" and added that it concerns "the melancholy of magnificence." John Gledson, meanwhile, wrote in the *Times Literary Supplement* that *Baltasar and Blimunda* is "a strange but exciting novel."

The Year of the Death of Ricardo Reis, Saramago's 1991 novel, is a rich tale set in Portugal during the early years of Salazar's dictatorship. Ricardo Reis, the novel's protagonist, is a middle-aged poet-physician who has recently arrived in Lisbon after a stay in Rio de Janeiro. Once back in Lisbon, Reis finds himself romantically drawn to Marcenda, a young woman with a deformed arm. Reis commences a physical relationship, however, with Lydia, a thirty-year-old maid, and the relationship develops as Reis

begins to appreciate Lydia as more than a mere physical entity. Also prominent in this tale is the ghost of Fernando Pessoa, the great Portuguese poet who died in 1935. It is Pessoa's ghost who proves to be Reis's fitting companion as the hero lives his final hours.

Upon translation by Pontiero into English in 1991, *The Year of the Death of Ricardo Reis* gained approval as further indication of Saramago's impressive, imposing talent. *New York Times* reviewer Herbert Mitgang called the book "a rare, old-fashioned novel—at once lyrical, symbolic and meditative" and characterized it as being "written in a classical style, formal and cerebral, with a surreal story that lingers in the imagination." Likewise, Shaun Whiteside wrote in *New Statesman and Society* that *The Year of the Death of Ricardo Reis* constituted "very much a novel of ideas, subtly textured and rich in symbolism, written in a style redolent of the age of high modernism." And Gabriel Josipovici, writing in the *Times Literary Supplement,* concluded that Saramago's novel "is the work of a fine and interesting writer."

O Evangelho Segundo Jesus Cristo, which Saramago originally published in 1991, was translated by Pontiero and published in English in 1994 as *The Gospel According to Jesus Christ.* This controversial novel provides what John Butt, writing in the *Times Literary Supplement,* described as "an idiosyncratic, satirical, bitter and frequently comical account of Jesus' life." In Saramago's tale, the immaculate conception is a questionable explanation of Christ's origin. Similarly, Christ's rather unworldly holiness is itself portrayed as rather dubious in Saramago's rendering. In the book Christ is, in essence, the wandering son of a carpenter. Inevitably human, he even enters into sexual relations with Mary Magdalene. God serves as the villain of Saramago's tale. Butt noted that Saramago portrays God as a "cynical bureaucrat, cheerfully disposed to extend his influence by founding on the blood of an innocent a religion that will bring pain, death and intolerance to mankind." God's exploitation of Christ, as delineated in the novel, results in a concluding crucifixion that is undeniably moving, if blasphemous by some readers' standards.

With *The Gospel According to Jesus Christ,* Saramago drew further recognition as an important writer. *Nation* reviewer Ilan Stavans noted that in *The Gospel According to Jesus Christ* "Saramago works wonders with the Passion story." Stavans added that the novel "is enough to assure [Saramago] a place in

the universal library and in human memory." Richard A. Preto-Rodas, writing in *World Literature Today*, noted the novel's controversial, provocative nature, and he concluded, "It is obvious that [*The Gospel According to Jesus Christ*] will hardly validate traditional beliefs, but it will definitely provide much food for thought."

The Stone Raft, another of Saramago's novels translated by Pontiero in 1994, concerns events that ensue after the Iberian peninsula breaks free from the European mainland and begins drifting through the Atlantic Ocean. This unlikely incident sparks considerable bureaucratic chaos even as the drifting Iberians struggle to cope with their extraordinary predicament. Prominent among these people are five individuals who undergo some typically incredible experiences, and eventually come together to realize a greater understanding of the entire Iberian phenomenon. Richard Eder, writing in the *Los Angeles Times Book Review*, speculated that *The Stone Raft* "may be Saramago's finest work," while Amanda Hopkinson, in her review for *New Statesman and Society*, hailed Saramago's novel as "the best new book I have read [in 1994]."

BIOGRAPHICAL/CRITICAL SOURCES:

PERIODICALS

Chicago Tribune Book World, January 27, 1991, p. 7; March 6, 1994, p. 7.
London Review of Books, March 23, 1995, p. 26.
Los Angeles Times Book Review, December 13, 1987, p. 3; May 28, 1995, pp. 3, 11.
Nation, May 16, 1994, pp. 675-76.
New Statesman and Society, August 28, 1992, pp. 34-35; August 27, 1993, p. 40; November 18, 1994, pp. 54-55.
New York Review of Books, October 5, 1995, pp. 35-36.
New York Times, November 15, 1987; December 5, 1987; April 30, 1991, p. C17.
New York Times Book Review, November 1, 1987, pp. 7, 9.
Observer, March 6, 1988, p. 42.
Times Literary Supplement, March 18-24, 1988, p. 301; September 11, 1992, p. 24; October 22, 1993, p. 22.
World Literature Today, winter, 1984, p. 78; spring, 1986, p. 297; winter, 1987, pp. 27-31; winter, 1988, p. 88; winter, 1990, p. 84; autumn, 1992, p. 697.*

SAUNDERS, James Robert 1953-

PERSONAL: Born April 4, 1953, in Richmond, VA; son of James Robert (a military officer) and Marjorie (a teacher; maiden name, Wilson) Saunders; married Renae Shackelford (a college instructor), July 6, 1982; children: Monica. *Ethnicity:* "African-American." *Education:* University of Virginia, B.A. (cum laude), 1975, M.A., 1981; Harvard University, J.D., 1978; University of Michigan, D.A., 1986. *Religion:* Southern Baptist. *Avocational interests:* Reading, biking, jogging, attending plays.

ADDRESSES: Home—3530 Daleview Dr., Ann Arbor, MI 48105. *Office*—Department of English, University of Toledo, Toledo, OH 43606.

CAREER: University of Virginia, Charlottesville, resident advisor, 1973-74, instructor, 1973, 1974, 1982, 1980-82, student coordinator of the Afro-American and African studies program, 1980-81; Human Relations Commission, Richmond, intern, summer, 1975; State of Virginia, appeals examiner, summer, 1977; Central National Bank, Richmond, VA, management trainee, 1978; Department of Welfare, Richmond, VA, research analyst, 1979; Mary Washington College, Fredericksburg, VA, lecturer, 1981-82; University of Michigan, Ann Arbor, academic advisor, 1984-85, writing skills specialist, summer, 1985; Washtenaw County Community College, Ann Arbor, MI, instructor, 1984; University of Toledo, Toledo, OH, instructor, 1985-86, assistant professor, 1986-90, associate professor, 1990-96, professor of English, 1996—. Has lectured or presented papers in various locations, including Auburn, AL; Washington, DC; Chicago, IL; Akron, OH; Columbus, OH; Toledo, OH; West Chester, PA; and Charlottesville, VA.

AWARDS, HONORS: Z Society Recognition Award for Scholarly Achievement and Academic Service, University of Virginia, 1972; Graduate and Professional Opportunity Program Fellowship, University of Virginia, 1979-82; Horace H. Rackham Fellowship, University of Michigan, 1982-86; faculty research fellowships, University of Toledo, 1988, 1990, and 1995; Certificate of Excellence, Options, Inc. (affiliated with Toledo Public Schools), 1996; Black Student Union Recognition Award for outstanding work with black students at the University of Toledo and surrounding community, 1996.

WRITINGS:

The Wayward Preacher in the Literature of African American Women (literary criticism), McFarland & Company (Jefferson, NC), 1995.

Contributor to books, including *Gloria Naylor: Critical Perspectives Past and Present,* edited by Henry Louis Gates, Amistad Press (New York, NY), 1993. Contributor of articles to periodicals, including *Hollins Critic, Southern Literary Journal, Journal of the Short Story in English, Langston Hughes Review, Journal of the Society for the Study of the Multi-Ethnic Literature of the United States (MELUS)* and *College Literature.*

WORK IN PROGRESS: Tightrope Walk: Identity, Survival and the Corporate World in African American Literature, forthcoming from McFarland and Company; research with wife, Renae Shackelford, on a book-length project entitled "Vinegar Hill: An Oral History of Urban Renewal in a Southern Black Community."

SIDELIGHTS: James Robert Saunders earned a law degree from Harvard University, but quickly decided to return to his first love, English literature. Saunders specializes in African-American literature—especially that by women authors—and teaches classes in the literature of Africa and the Caribbean. His 1995 book, *The Wayward Preacher in the Literature of African American Women,* discusses stories and novels by Gloria Naylor, Zora Neale Hurston, Nella Larsen, Paule Marshall, and Terry McMillan. As Vicki L. Kroll, interviewing Saunders for the *UTimes* of the University of Toledo, put it: "Each writer, in her own way, has shaken societal and discriminatory shackles to depict a more realistic image of men of the cloth." Saunders told Kroll that "[f]or so long, certain topics have been taboo in terms of what African-American women have and have not been able to discuss openly. Criticizing black men was especially taboo, and criticisms of male preachers were even more thoroughly forbidden." Saunders also noted, however, that despite African-American solidarity concerning their preachers, "one imagines that there comes a time when an oppressed group of people must look inward to determine whether or not a source of oppression is one of their own."

Saunders told *CA:* "My earliest memories include having always been a voracious reader. A crucial point in my life was when, at my all-black elementary school in Richmond, Virginia, I was informed that I could check out as many as ten books a week, return that ten, and then check out another ten books ad infinitum. It was the beginning of a habit that I have had now for several decades. It would seem to be in the natural order of things that I myself would one day wish to be involved in the process of serious writing.

"Much of my thought about what to write has been woman-based due, I think, to the fact that I was reared primarily by my mother. So as much as I have tried to write about men (and I have written several essays about male writers), I am constantly being pulled back (emotionally) to the concerns of women. I was at the point of finishing up a book-length manuscript on John Edgar Wideman when I was brought to the realization that I first had to write a book about women authors. The need to write about women first was so strong that I tore up the Wideman manuscript as a prerequisite to being able to begin the first pages of *The Wayward Preacher in the Literature of African American Women,* a book that while ostensibly about preachers is actually more a book about the ordeals that women have had to endure in their quests for fulfillment and dignity.

"Now I am free to pursue other literary matters. Harvard Law School, needless to say, had a profound impact on my life. Though I finished law school, I did not enjoy the study of law. Yet I was, for many years, virtually obsessed, trying to figure out how to include the subject of law in my writing. The result is *Tightrope Walk: Identity, Survival and the Corporate World in African American Literature.* In this book, I use novels such as Ralph Ellison's *Invisible Man,* Brent Wade's *Company Man,* and Bebe Moore Campbell's *Brothers and Sisters* (among others) to convey the difficulties that can occur when a person is the only black (or one of but a few blacks) in a particular work place. All of my writing is therapeutic, and in writing *Tightrope Walk* I was able to cast out many of the demons that had been haunting me since my days during the 1970s at Harvard Law School. In the introduction to this book, I explain the sense of alienation that I felt at law school and argue that a similar alienation can occur as corporate America rewards homogeneity among its employees and sacrifices individuality."

BIOGRAPHICAL/CRITICAL SOURCES:

PERIODICALS

UTimes (Toledo, OH), March 6, 1995, p. 2.

SAYER, Karen (Anne) 1967-

PERSONAL: Born January 20, 1967, in Great Yarmouth, England; daughter of Peter Edward (a certified driving instructor) and Iris Margaret (in business) Sayer; companion of Matthew Charles Hoskins (an electronic publisher). *Ethnicity:* "White." *Education:* Portsmouth Polytechnic, B.A. (with first class honors), 1988; University of Sussex, D.Phil., 1992. *Politics:* "Green, feminist, generally left-wing." *Religion:* "None." *Avocational interests:* Gardening.

ADDRESSES: Home—Bedford, England. *Office*—Faculty of Humanities, University of Luton, 75 Castle Dr., Luton, Bedfordshire LU1 3AJ, England; fax 01-58-248-9014. *E-mail*—karen.sayer@luton.ac.uk.

CAREER: University of Sussex, Brighton, England, lecturer, 1988-91; University of Luton, Luton, England, lecturer in literary studies, 1992—. Portsmouth Polytechnic, lecturer, 1988-91.

MEMBER: Fawcett Society (member of executive committee, 1992-98; vice-chairperson, 1995-97), Women's Studies Network Association (member of executive committee, 1994-97), Women's History Network (member of national steering committee, 1996), University Association for Continuing Education.

WRITINGS:

Women of the Fields: Representations of Rural Women in the Nineteenth Century, Manchester University Press (New York City), 1995.

Contributor of articles and reviews to periodicals, including *Modern History Review, Gender Studies, Women's Studies International Forum, Women's History Review,* and *Bulletin of the Society for the Study of Labour History.* Member of editorial board, *Imprimatur: A Journal of Criticism and Theory.*

WORK IN PROGRESS: A Cottage in the Country, a social and cultural history of the English country cottage, publication by Manchester University Press expected in 1998; research on "envisioning alternatives, pastoral utopias in literary science fiction."

SIDELIGHTS: Karen Sayer told *CA:* "I write about working-class rural women in England primarily because I came from a working-class background and grew up in the countryside. I looked for my own history when I began to write, but I found mostly urban studies. This prompted me to explore the place and people that I came from. Originally I wanted to write an empirical history of rural women, but then I found that the available sources obscured, rather than revealed, their lives, so I began looking at representations of these women instead. This involved studying the wider cultural context in which the representations were formed, so that *Women of the Fields* turned out to be a very interdisciplinary text. In it I argued that there was a traffic between the images of the women and the women's concrete/lived experiences. Legislation enacted in the nineteenth century, which restricted women's access to agricultural work, was passed on the basis of the dominant representation of the rural woman as a kind of ideal happy homemaker, which, when explored by government officials, was found to be untrue.

"The book began as an undergraduate essay, moved on to become a dissertation and then a doctoral project. Writing it therefore involved a kind of 'organic' or evolutionary process, while the project as a whole was very close to my heart. This raises interesting issues around the question of academic objectivity, and I have recently been reflecting on this.

"My best friend, Gail, has been very influential in my work and, in fact, sparked my current interest in the English country cottage. Two very dilapidated workers' cottages near the house she rents were sold off recently for quite a large sum. They have no electricity or gas, no water supply or sewage disposal, no telephone. They even had to be taken apart brick by brick and rebuilt to one side of their original site. This prompted Gail and me to wonder what made the country cottage so desirable.

"Continuing to think about representations of the countryside and its people, pursuing this interdisciplinary study, and teaching in a similar way at my university has also caused me to move gradually into a new 'home' discipline. I now work within literary studies and have begun work on the ideas of the pastoral in radical, utopian science fiction. Bringing my long-standing love of science fiction into my research has enabled me to look at those radical alternative visions of the future which focus on the rural, and incorporate green and anarchist politics."

SCHIFF, Isaac 1944-

PERSONAL: Born January 8, 1944, in Montreal, Quebec, Canada; naturalized U.S. citizen; son of Max and May (Levine) Schiff; married Jan Kirsch, June 15, 1969; children: Julie, Daniel. *Education:* McGill University, B.S., 1964, M.D.C.M., 1968.

ADDRESSES: Home—12 Abbott Rd., Wellesley, MA 02181. *Office*—Department of Obstetrics and Gynecology, Massachusetts General Hospital, VBK113, Boston, MA 02114; fax 617-726-7548. *E-mail*—schiffi@a1.mgh.harvard.edu.

CAREER: Montreal General Hospital, Montreal, Quebec, rotating intern, 1968-69, resident in medicine, 1969-71; Boston Hospital for Women, Boston, MA, resident in obstetrics and gynecology, 1971-73; New England Medical Center, Boston, resident in surgery, 1974; Boston Hospital for Women, fellow in reproductive endocrinology, 1974-76, assistant obstetrician and gynecologist, 1974-76, instructor in obstetrics and gynecology, 1974-78, founder of Menopause Clinic, 1976; Harvard University, Harvard Medical School, Boston, assistant professor, 1978-81, associate professor, 1981-88, Joe Vincent Meigs Professor of Gynecology, 1988—, senior fellow for pathophysiology, Cannon Society, 1990—, chairperson of departmental executive committee, 1996. Brigham and Women's Hospital, associate director of reproductive endocrinology, 1980-86, director, 1986-88, obstetrician and gynecologist, 1976—; Massachusetts General Hospital, chief of Vincent Memorial Gynecology Service, 1988-93, and Vincent Memorial Obstetrics and Gynecology Service, 1993—, chairperson of Laser Safety Committee, 1990—, and Surgical Day Care Committee, 1990-92, vice-chairperson of general executive committee, 1993-95, co-chairperson of Domestic Violence Task Force, 1995—; Mount Auburn Hospital, member of consulting staff, 1990—; American Board of Obstetrics and Gynecology, diplomate; consultant to Dana-Farber Cancer Institute, National Institute on Aging, and American Medical Association. Speaker at colleges and universities, including University of Kentucky, George Washington University, University of Montreal, Brown University, Columbia University, Yale University, State University of New York Downstate Medical Center, University of Vermont, and Yeshiva University.

MEMBER: North American Menopause Society (president, 1992), American College of Obstetricians and Gynecologists, Society of Andrology, American Fertility Society, Endocrine Society, Society for Gynecologic Investigation, Society of Reproductive Surgeons, Association of Gynecology and Obstetrics, Royal College of Surgeons (fellow), Suffolk District Medical Society (member of council, 1992—), Obstetrical Society of Boston (fellow; vice-president, 1994-96; president, 1996—).

AWARDS, HONORS: Prize Paper Awards from American College of Obstetricians and Gynecologists, 1977, for "Vaginal Absorption of Estrone and 17B-Estradiol," and 1979, for "Effects of Estrogens on Sleep and Psychological State of Hypogonadal Women;" A.M. from Harvard University, 1988; Women's Health Achievement Award, clinical science category, from Society for the Advancement of Women's Health Research, 1995; grants from National Institutes on Health.

WRITINGS:

(Editor with Robert L. Barbieri, and contributor) *Reproductive Endocrine Therapeutics,* Alan Liss (New York City), 1988.

(Editor with C. B. Hammond and F. P. Haseltine, and contributor) *Menopause: Evaluation, Treatment, and Health Concerns,* Alan Liss, 1989.

(Editor with Samuel Smith, and contributor) *Modern Management of Premenstrual Syndrome,* Norton (New York City), 1993.

(Editor with K. J. Carlson, S. A. Eisenstat, and F. D. Frigoletto, Jr., and contributor) *Primary Care of Women,* Mosby (St. Louis, MO), 1995.

(With Ann B. Parson) *The Massachusetts General Hospital Guide to Menopause: What It Is, How to Treat It, How to Cope With It,* Times Books (New York City), 1996.

Contributor to books, including *Kistner's Gynecology: Principles and Practice,* edited by Barbieri, K. J. Ryan, and R. Berkowitz, Yearbook Medical Publishers (Chicago, IL), 1990; *Addictive States,* edited by C. P. O'Brien and J. H. Jaffe, Raven Press (New York City), 1992; and *Textbook of Reproductive Medicine,* edited by B. R. Carr and R. E. Blackwell, Appleton & Lange (Norwalk, CT), 1993. Editor of the series "Clinical Perspectives in Obstetrics and Gynecology," Springer-Verlag (New York City), 1991. Contributor of more than a hundred-fifty articles to medical journals. Editor in chief, *Menopause,* 1994—; member of editorial board, *Journal of Women's Health,* 1992—; member of editorial advisory board, *Obstetrics and Gynecology Forum,* 1992—, and *Menopause Management,* 1996—.

SCHROEDER, Joan V(annorsdall) 1951-

PERSONAL: Born November 20, 1951, in New Haven, CT; daughter of John W. Vannorsdall (a theologian) and Patricia (an artist; maiden name, Ellis) Vannorsdall; married Mark D. Schroeder (a physician), April 27, 1974; children: Matthew, Olivia, Jordan. *Education:* St. Olaf College, B.A., 1973; University of Minnesota, M.A., 1976.

ADDRESSES: Home—2344 Jones Rd., Winchester, VA 22602. *Agent*—Ronald Goldfarb, 918 Sixteenth St. NW, Washington, DC 20006.

CAREER: Novelist, essayist, book reviewer, and author of short stories.

WRITINGS:

Solitary Places (novel), Putnam (New York), 1994.

Contributor of numerous essays, short stories and book reviews to periodicals, including *New York Times, Washington Post, Yankee,* and *Journal of Small Business Management.*

SIDELIGHTS: Joan V. Schroeder told *CA:* "Although I've been writing essays and magazine articles for years, I'm a relative newcomer to fiction, having had my first short story published in late 1987. Fiction always seemed very risky to me, a far cry from the relative safety of the facts and mappable construction of a magazine piece, or the justifiable indignation of an op-ed submission. Now, though I still write some nonfiction when some idea strikes my fancy, and am a dedicated book reviewer, I consider myself primarily a novelist.

"The scope of the novel intrigues me: the ability to tell a story that reverberates, that leaves its reader a different person than she was when she opened the book's covers. I'm fascinated by community, dangerous love, cause and effect, the inescapability of one's past, and passionate commitment. The writing of *Solitary Places* took nearly three years, working three or four hours a day five days a week; the editing went on nearly a full year, a process which taught me more about my writing than any writing course or textbook.

"Anyone who sits down to write a novel had better be in love with the story: feel very strongly about its importance and be obsessively intrigued by its possibilities. One must be prepared to kill off boring, peripheral characters and to hear voices late at night. Most of all, one must be scrupulously honest and always tell the truth, removing any words/pages/chapters that aren't straight-sighted. What is left after all the unnecessary words are taken away will matter."

Schroeder's first novel, *Solitary Places,* tells the story of the fight to save the Virginia mountain community of Collier from the serious health hazards caused by a nearby landfill. Basing her story on a real-life experience protesting a similar noxious landfill, Schroeder creates four characters who in turn describe the environmental battle with their own unique insights on the proceedings. First to notice the possibly toxic garbage is nursing home aide Reba Walker whom Joanne Wilkinson in *Booklist* called, "an almost perfect portrait of an activist." Abandoned by her husband and with her son in jail, Walker nevertheless relies on what Wilkinson referred to as "tunnel vision and raw candor" to organize the town against the landfill's owners.

Reba Walker is just one of three women whose narrations carry the plot forward. Also contributing to the story are Lucy McComb, the former schoolteacher who used to own the land on which the dump is located, and Sara Rose McComb, the wife of Lucy's nephew and Reba's former classmate. In his *Washington Post* review of the novel, Frank Levering pointed out that although Lucy is long-dead she acts as "an omniscient narrator who knows the hearts and minds of the community." Much the opposite of Reba, Sara Rose is hesitant to join her neighbors in any overt acts of protest, but she soon finds that there is no other way to save the life she has always known. Rounding out the list of Schroeder's narrators is young Jesse Paxton, the twelve-year-old son of a landfill worker. Referring to the book as an "auspicious debut," Levering compared Schroeder to Charles Dickens, noting among other traits, her ability to "paint scenes and themes in broadly obvious strokes, with sharp contrasts" like the great British novelist. The critic found her characterization of the three women narrators "extraordinarily well-realized."

Generally favorable reviews greeted the publication of *Solitary Places. New York Times Book Review* contributor David Masello called it an "accomplished first novel."

BIOGRAPHICAL/CRITICAL SOURCES:

PERIODICALS

Booklist, October 1, 1994, p. 240.
Library Journal, September 15, 1994, p. 92.
New York Times Book Review, January 29, 1995, p. 16.
Publishers Weekly, September 5, 1994, pp. 88-89.
Washington Post, January 3, 1995.

* * *

SCOTT, Duncan Campbell 1862-1947

PERSONAL: Born on August 2, 1862, in Ottawa, Ontario, Canada; died on December 19, 1947, in Ottawa, Ontario, Canada; son of William Scott (a Methodist minister) and Janet Campbell MacCallum; married Belle Warner Botsford (a concert violinist) in 1894 (died, 1929); married Desiree Elise Aylen in 1931; children: (first marriage) Elizabeth Duncan (died at age 12). *Education:* Wesleyan College, Stanstead, Quebec, 1877-79.

CAREER: Indian Branch (later Department of Indian Affairs), Ottawa, Canada: clerk third class, 1879-93, chief clerk, 1893-96, secretary of the department, 1896-1909, superintendent of Indian education, 1909-23, deputy superintendent general, 1923-32. Toronto *Globe,* columnist, 1892-93.

MEMBER: Ottawa Drama League (president), Canadian Authors Association (president, 1931-33).

AWARDS, HONORS: D. Litt., University of Toronto, 1922; Lorne Pierce Medal, 1927; LL.D., Queens University, 1939; fellow, 1899, honorary secretary, 1911-21, president, 1921-22, Royal Society of Canada; fellow, Royal Society of Literature (United Kingdom); C.M.G. (Companion, Order of St. Michael and St. George), 1934.

WRITINGS:

POETRY

The Magic House, and Other Poems, Durie, 1893.
Labor and the Angel, Copeland & Day, 1898.
New World Lyrics and Ballads, Morang, 1905.
Via Borealis, Tyrrell, 1906.
Lundy's Lane and Other Poems, McClelland, Goodchild & Stewart, 1916.

Beauty and Life, McClelland & Stewart, 1921.
The Poems of Duncan Campbell Scott, McClelland & Stewart, 1926.
The Green Cloister: Later Poems, McClelland & Stewart, 1935.
Selected Poems, edited by E. K. Brown, Ryerson, 1951.
Powassan's Drum: Selected Poems of Duncan Campbell Scott, edited by Raymond Souster and Douglas Lochhead, Tecumseh, 1985.

Also wrote *To the Canadian Mothers and Three Other Poems,* 1916 and *The Poems,* 1926. Poetry also collected in *Powassan's Drum: Poems,* edited by Raymond Souster and Douglas Lochhead, 1985.

FICTION

In the Village of Viger, Copeland & Day, 1896.
The Witching of Elspie: A Book of Stories, McClelland & Stewart, 1923.
Selected Stories of Duncan Campbell Scott, edited by Glenn Clever, University of Ottawa Press, 1972.
Untitled Novel, ca. 1905, University of Toronto Press, 1979.

OTHER

(Editor with Pelham Edgar and W. D. LeSeur) *The Makers of Canada,* 22 volumes, Morang, 1903-08, 1916; revised edition, 12 volumes, edited by W. L. Grant, Oxford University Press, 1926.
John Graves Simcoe (biography), Morang, 1905.
(Contributor) *Canada and Its Provinces,* edited by Adam Shortt and Arthur Doughty, Glasgow, Brook, 1914.
Poetry and Progress (criticism), Royal Society of Canada, 1922.
(Author of foreword) Elise Aylen *Roses of Shadow,* Macmillan, 1930.
The Administration of Indian Affairs in Canada, Canadian Institute of International Affairs, 1931.
(Author of foreword and editor with E. K. Brown) Archibald Lampman *At the Long Sault and Other New Poems,* Ryerson, 1943.
The Circle of Affection, and Other Pieces in Prose and Verse, McClelland & Stewart, 1947.
(Editor and contributor) Archibald Lampman *Selected Poems,* Ryerson, 1947.
Some Letters of Duncan Campbell Scott, Archibald Lampman, & Others, edited by Arthur S. Bourinot, published by the editor in Ottawa, 1959.

More Letters of Duncan Campbell Scott, edited by Bourinot, published by the editor in Ottawa, 1960.

(With William Wilfred Campbell and Archibald Lampman) *At the Mermaid Inn,* University of Toronto Press, 1979.

The Poet and the Critic: A Literary Correspondence Between D. C. Scott and E. K. Brown, edited by Robert L. McDougall, Carleton University Press, 1983.

Also wrote the following plays: *Pierre,* produced 1921, published in *Canadian Plays from Hart House Theatre I,* edited by Vincent Massey, 1926; *Prologue,* produced 1923, published in *The Poems,* 1926; and *Joy! Joy! Joy!,* produced 1927.

SIDELIGHTS: Duncan Campbell Scott is best remembered as one of the leading poets of the "Confederation group." Writing in an era following the formation of the Dominion of Canada, Scott, along with poets Bliss Carman, Archibald Lampman, and Charles G. D. Roberts, helped create and cultivate a sense of national identity. Early cast as a regional writer of the northern wilderness, especially its Indian life, Scott is being reappraised in our time as a writer of great diversity with a complex, though unified, vision and a distinctly Canadian spirit.

Scott's lifelong interest in Native Americans began in his childhood when, with his missionary father, his family spent several years among the Indians. He later entered the civil service in Ottawa's Department of Indian Affairs, spending fifty-two years in a successful administrative career which culminated with his position as Deputy Superintendent General. On his frequent trips in this service, Scott became acquainted with the Canadian wilds and visited many Indian tribes, gaining insight into their customs and life. From these experiences came the material for his narrative poems of Indian life such as "At Gull Lake, 1810" and "The Forsaken." Scott's first poetry writing, however, was prompted by his close friendship with an associate in the civil service, the young poet Archibald Lampman. Together they collaborated with Wilfrid Campbell on a weekly literary column, "At the Mermaid Inn," which appeared in the *Toronto Globe* from 1892-93 and served as a guide to prevailing tastes. A collection of the columns was published as *At the Mermaid Inn* in 1979.

Scott has been praised as a lyric and as a dramatic poet. His best lyric poems are found in the collections *The Magic House, and Other Poems, Beauty and Life,* and *The Green Cloister: Later Poems.* Nature, its moods and seasons, are often the subject of these lyrics, and critics are unfailing in noting Scott's mastery at painting vivid, colorful descriptions and creating a mysterious and compelling atmosphere. Scott's dramatic poems are also highly regarded, especially the narrative pieces on Indian life. Violence emerges as an important theme in many of these narrative studies as well as in Scott's lyric poems. The dialectic of tension and resolution is, in fact, central to Scott's vision—from these conflicts, in nature and between people, issue beauty and peace. An outstanding example of such a dialectic is "The Piper of Arll," called by some Scott's masterpiece, which portrays the role of the artist and the nature of artistic experience. Filled with the tensions of contrasts (secluded bay and wild ocean, rustic shepherd and traveled sailors) and paradoxes (life in death, fulfillment in self-sacrifice), the poem culminates in a transcendent peace.

In the past decade Scott's stories, long neglected by critics, have begun to receive recognition. His two volumes of short stories, *In the Village of Viger* and *The Witching of Elspie: A Book of Stories,* are often contrasted with each other: the first, a prose counterpart to *The Magic House,* is light and pleasurable; the second, wild and bloody stories of the lonely fur-trade areas, is stark and harsh. Recent publication of Scott's only novel, *Untitled Novel, ca. 1905,* sheds new light on his prose, proving Scott an early innovator in the portrayal of the modern antihero. Some critics now conjecture that Scott may be remembered for his prose rather than his poetry.

Despite a long career as a civil servant, Scott received many awards in his lifetime that were a tribute to his literary artistry, including the Lorne Pierce Medal, which honors Canadians for significant achievements in imaginative or critical literature. He was elected a Fellow of the Royal Society of Canada in 1899 and became its President in 1921. Scott is recognized as a commanding poet of distinct Canadian sensibility.

BIOGRAPHICAL/CRITICAL SOURCES:

BOOKS

Brown, E. K., *On Canadian Poetry,* Ryerson, 1944, pp. 118-43.

Dragland, S. L., *Duncan Campbell Scott: A Book of Criticism,* Tecumseh, 1974.

ECW's Biographical Guide to Canadian Poets, ECW Press, 1993, pp. 65-69.

Monkman, Leslie, *A Native Heritage,* University of Toronto Press, 1981.

New, W. H., *Dreams of Speech and Violence,* University of Toronto Press, 1987.

Such, K. P., editor, *The Duncan Campbell Scott Symposium,* University of Ottawa Press, 1979.

Titley, Brian, *A Narrow Vision: Duncan Campbell Scott and the Administration of Indian Affairs in Canada,* University of British Columbia Press, 1986.

Twentieth-Century Literary Criticism, Gale, Volume 6, 1982.

PERIODICALS

Antigonish, fall-winter, 1991-92, pp. 138-45.

Books in Canada, December, 1979, p. 10.

Canadian Literature, summer, 1959, pp. 13-25; autumn, 1962, pp. 43-52; summer, 1968, pp. 15-27; summer, 1979, pp. 142-43; winter, 1986, pp. 10-25, 27-40; autumn, 1990, pp. 176-79; summer, 1994, pp. 86-106.

Canadian Poetry, spring, 1988, pp. 49-67.

Dalhousie Review, April, 1927, pp. 38-46.

Essays on Canadian Writing, fall-winter, 1979-80, pp. 70-77.

Journal of Canadian Fiction, number 16, 1976, pp. 138-43.

* * *

SEGRIFF, Larry 1960-

PERSONAL: Born July 14, 1960, in Cedar Rapids, IA; son of Raymond Eugene (in insurance) and Lorna Clarice (a secretary; maiden name, Bell) Segriff; married Marlys Ann Brunsting, September 9, 1982; children: Megan Elizabeth, Caitlin Erin. *Ethnicity:* "Caucasian." *Education:* Attended University of Iowa. *Avocational interests:* Fencing (former competitor), volunteer soccer coach.

ADDRESSES: Home—P.O. Box 9576, Green Bay, WI 54308. *Office*—Tekno-Books, P.O. Box 8196, Green Bay, WI 54308; fax 414-437-6721. *E-mail*—lsegriff@netnet.net. *Agent*—Susan Gleason, 325 Riverside Dr., New York, NY 10025.

CAREER: Editorial assistant to author Ed Gorman, Cedar Rapids, IA, 1992-94; Tekno-Books (book packaging and editing firm), Green Bay, WI, vice-president, 1994—. Free-lance computer programmer and consultant.

MEMBER: Science Fiction and Fantasy Writers of America, Mystery Writers of America, Horror Writers of America.

WRITINGS:

Spacer Dreams (science fiction), Baen Books (Riverdale, NY), 1995.

(With William R. Forstchen) *The Four Magics* (fantasy), Baen Books, 1996.

(Editor with Martin H. Greenberg) *Future Net* (science fiction), DAW Books (New York), 1996.

Work represented in anthologies, including *Science Fiction, Fantasy, Mystery,* and *Horror.*

WORK IN PROGRESS: Alien Dreams, a sequel to *Spacer Dreams;* research on virtual reality, quantum mechanics, dream states, and chaos theory.

SIDELIGHTS: Larry Segriff told *CA:* "I think that, to make a broad and sweeping generalization, there are two main types of writers: storytellers and stylists. Storytellers are motivated mostly by the sense of the story, by the desire to create some wonderful place, people it with interesting characters, and then share that place with others. Stylists, on the other hand, are in love with the beauty of language, motivated by the desire to work with words. I am primarily a storyteller and, while I find great beauty in words, my primary motivation is the desire to tell a story.

"I suspect that many writers come to our craft after many years of reading for pleasure. Certainly that was the route I took. As a result, my voice, my style, my entire approach to storytelling has been shaped by the authors I've read. In addition, I studied many different authors in an attempt to learn how they handled scene construction and character development, or how they structured and paced a novel, as opposed to a short story. Of them all, Roger Zelazny has been my greatest influence. He combined style with storytelling in a way that I doubt will ever be duplicated, and every story I write is touched by the memories of his work.

"There are two halves to the writing process: the external, or physical, element and the internal, philosophical part. I write in the morning, before

heading out to my day job. I used to be more of a spurt writer: writing in great bursts, but sporadically. That has changed. With maturity has come discipline. Now, when I am on deadline, I try to write a minimum of a thousand words per day. These must be new words, not a rewriting of a previous day's output.

"My internal approach has changed as well, evolving as I have grown and developed. Writing is still, and will always be, a calling, but it is more than that, too. It is a business, and writing requires the same degree of professionalism as any other occupation. I think that is one of the reasons it takes so long for most writers to break in. It is not enough to learn to write well; it is also important to learn to write commercially—to understand and recognize market trends and to learn the concept of audience and how to write for one. Like many authors, I started out an *artiste* and became a craftsman.

"What inspires me to write on the subjects I choose? That's a tough question. I work in many areas and genres—science fiction, fantasy, mystery, and horror—each of which is vastly different from the others, and each of which brings its own combination of inspiration and desire. In all honesty, though, I consider myself a fantasist first and a science fiction/mystery/horror writer second. I have always been drawn to the concept of empowerment: my teenage dreams were all about the ninety-eight-pound weakling suddenly developing psychic or magical powers and saving the beautiful girl. It is this concept—not the teenage fantasies—that underlies much of my work, and that inspires me to find the stories I write."

* * *

SEN, Zekai 1947-

PERSONAL: Born October 25, 1947, in Kastamonu, Turkey; son of Zekeriya (a worker) and Hatice (a homemaker) Sen; married Fatma Ozturk, September 12, 1971; children: Zekeriya, Tevhide, M. Fatih. *Education:* Istanbul Technical University, B.Sc., 1971; Imperial College of Science and Technology, London, M.Sc. and D.I.C., 1972; University of London, Ph.D., 1974. *Religion:* Islamic.

ADDRESSES: Home—Hatbogu Cikmazi, Topbas, Sitesi Blok B, Daire 15, Erenboy, Istanbul, Turkey. *Office*—Faculty of Aeronautics and Astronautics, Istanbul Technical University, Maslak, 80626 Istanbul, Turkey; fax 212-285-3139.

CAREER: Istanbul Technical University, Istanbul, Turkey, member of hydraulics faculty, 1975-82; King Abdulaziz University, member of hydrogeology faculty, 1982-92; Istanbul Technical University, professor of meteorology, 1992—. City of Istanbul, chief consultant for water resources management. *Military service:* Served in 1975.

MEMBER: American Institute of Hydrology, Bernoulli Society (France).

AWARDS, HONORS: Turkish Science Prize, 1993.

WRITINGS:

Applied Hydrogeology for Scientists and Engineers, Lewis Publishers (New York), 1995.

WORK IN PROGRESS: Research on fuzzy logic, atmospheric sciences, chaos theory, water sciences, and the philosophy and history of science.

SIDELIGHTS: Zekai Sen told *CA:* "Science is a common property of humanity, and scientific activities should have beneficial targets in the sense of serving humanity. It is not necessary that each individual should be involved in science but, for a society to prosper, there must be a sufficient number of individuals who are responsible for scientific tasks.

"I write in order to share my views with others in distant parts of the world, to receive constructive criticisms that pave the road for better works in the future. I also write to disseminate useful information that might be of some help to other individuals that I cannot meet personally. Writing provides a fertile soil for even minor ideas to flourish and give fruit. For a scientist, the production of new ideas is not so difficult, but to make them understandable to others through one's writings is harder."

* * *

SERNA, Ramon Gomez de la
See GOMEZ DE LA SERNA, Ramon

SHAYNOUX, Bucky
 See LANDAU, Paul Stuart

* * *

SHERRED, T(homas) L. 1915-1985

PERSONAL: Born August 27, 1915, in Grand Rapids, MI; died April 16, 1985, in Detroit, MI; married; wife's name, M. L. *Education:* Attended Wayne State University. *Avocational interests:* History, particularly the Roman Empire and American Civil War.

CAREER: Worked in the auto industry, advancing from tool rooms to technical writing and public relations.

WRITINGS:

Alien Island (novel), Ballantine (New York), 1970.
First Person, Peculiar (short stories; includes "E for Effort," "Cue for Quiet," "Eye for Iniquity," and "Cure Guaranteed"), Ballantine (New York), 1972.
(With Lloyd Biggle, Jr.) *Alien Main* (novel), Doubleday (Garden City, NY), 1985.

Work represented in anthologies, including *Again, Dangerous Visions,* edited by Harlan Ellison, 1972.

SIDELIGHTS: T. L. Sherred was the author of a slim body of science fiction, consisting of a collection of stories, a novel, and the beginning of a novel that was completed by another author after Sherred's death in 1985. Dubbed by at least one critic as "blue-collar SF," Sherred's stories were often set in Detroit and featured the down-to-earth laborers with which the author was acquainted through his career in the automotive field.

Sherred saw publication of his first novel, *Alien Island,* in 1970. A darkly humorous tale, *Alien Island* revolves around the devastating events that occur when aliens covertly inhabit Earth. Also marked by humor and melancholy are the four stories collected in Sherred's subsequent publication, *First Person, Peculiar.* The lead story of the four, "E for Effort," also exhibits Sherred's love of the Roman Empire and American Civil War history, as the story deals with the invention of a time machine, through which one can view the past.

At his death in 1985, Sherred left an unfinished sequel to *Alien Island,* which author Lloyd Biggle, Jr., completed and published as *Alien Main.* Set on Earth some two hundred years after aliens nearly destroyed life on the planet, the novel finds descendants of the aliens returning to atone for the atrocities committed by their ancestors. They find that the inhabitants of Earth are now living in tribes, with no connections except for a common belief in a goddess, whose return they await. While a *New York Times Book Review* critic deemed *Alien Main* "not very ambitious," the reviewer nevertheless found the work offers a "pleasant blend of surprise and predictability." The reviewer concluded: "Books such as this are the nourishing bread and butter of science fiction."

BIOGRAPHICAL/CRITICAL SOURCES:

PERIODICALS

New York Times Book Review, September 8, 1985, p. 28.

OBITUARIES:

PERIODICALS

Analog, December, 1985.
Locus, June/July, 1985.*

* * *

SHERWOOD, Robert E(mmet) 1896-1955

PERSONAL: Born April 4, 1896, in New Rochelle, New York; died November 14, 1955, in New York, New York; son of Arthur Murray and Rosina Emmet Sherwood; married Mary Brandon, 1922 (divorced 1934); married Madeline Hurlock Connelly, 1935; children: one daughter. *Education:* Harvard University, B.A., 1918.

CAREER: Playwright and screenwriter. Drama critic, *Vanity Fair,* 1919-1920; *Life,* movie critic, 1920-28, editor, 1924-28; *Scribner,* literary editor, 1928; served as speechwriter and adviser to President Franklin Roosevelt, as special assistant to the Secretary of War and the Secretary of the Navy, and as director of the Overseas Branch of the Office of War Information during World War II. Co-founder, Playwrights' Producing Company, 1938, and of the Com-

mittee to Defend America by Aiding the Allies. *Military service:* Served in Canadian Black Watch Regiment, 1918-19; wounded in action.

MEMBER: Dramatists Guild (president).

AWARDS, HONORS: Megrue Prize for comedy, 1932, for play *Reunion in Vienna;* Drama Study Club award, 1936, for *Idiot's Delight;* Pulitzer Prize for drama, 1936, for *Idiot's Delight,* 1939, for *Abe Lincoln in Illinois,* and 1940, for *There Shall Be No Night;* Academy Award, 1946, for *The Best Years of Our Lives;* Pulitzer Prize for nonfiction, 1948, for *Roosevelt and Hopkins.*

WRITINGS:

SCREENPLAYS

(Author of scenario with James T. Donohue) *The Lucky Lady,* Famous Players—Lasky/Paramount, 1926.

(Author of screen story with Bertram Bloch) *Oh, What a Nurse,* Warner Bros., 1926.

(Author of commentary) *Around the World in 80 Minutes with Douglas Fairbanks,* United Artists, 1931.

(With Charles Lederer) *Cock of the Air,* United Artists, 1932.

(Author of screen story with George S. Kaufman) *Roman Scandals,* United Artists, 1933.

(With Arthur Wimperis) *The Scarlet Pimpernel,* United Artists, 1935.

The Ghost Goes West, United Artists, 1936.

(With Aben Kandel and Akos Tolnay) *Thunder in the City,* Columbia, 1937.

The Adventures of Marco Polo, United Artists, 1938.

(With Lajos Biro) *The Divorce of Lady X,* United Artists, 1938.

Idiot's Delight, Metro-Goldwyn-Mayer, 1939.

Abe Lincoln in Illinois, RKO, 1940.

(With Joan Harrison) *Rebecca,* United Artists, 1940.

The Best Years of Our Lives (based on the novel *Glory for Me* by MacKinlay Kantor), RKO, 1946.

(With Leonardo Bercovici) *The Bishop's Wife,* RKO, 1947.

Man on a Tightrope, Twentieth Century-Fox, 1953.

(Author of screen story) *Main Street to Broadway,* MGM, 1953.

PLAYS

Barnum Was Right, produced by the Hasty Pudding Club, Harvard University, 1917.

The Road to Rome (produced in New York City, 1927), Scribner (New York City), 1927.

The Love Nest (based on a story by Ring Lardner), produced in New York City, 1927.

The Queen's Husband (produced in New York City, 1928), Scribner, 1928.

Waterloo Bridge (produced in New York City, 1930), Scribner, 1930.

This Is New York (produced in New York City, 1930), Scribner, 1931.

Reunion in Vienna (produced in New York City, 1931), Scribner, 1932.

Acropolis, produced in London, 1933.

The Petrified Forest (produced in New York City, 1935), Scribner, 1935.

Idiot's Delight (produced in New York City, 1936), Scribner, 1936.

Tovarich (based on novel of same title by Jacques Deval; produced in New York City, 1936), Random House (New York City), 1937.

Abe Lincoln in Illinois (produced in New York City, 1938), Scribner, 1939.

There Shall Be No Night (produced in New York City, 1940), Scribner, 1940.

The Rugged Path, produced in New York City, 1945.

Miss Liberty, produced in New York City, 1949.

Small War on Murray Hill (produced in New York City, 1957), Dramatists Play Service (New York City), 1957.

OTHER

Roosevelt and Hopkins, Harper (New York City), 1940, published as *The White House Papers of Harry L. Hopkins,* 2 volumes, Eyre & Spottiswoode (London), 1949.

Robert E. Sherwood: Film Critic, Revisionist Press (New York City), 1973.

Also editor of *The Best Moving Pictures* (annual), 1922-23, and of *Who's Who in the Movies and the Yearbook of the American Screen,* 1923. Also author of novel *The Virtuous Knight,* 1931 (published as *Unending Crusade,* 1932). Also author of television scripts in the early 1950s. Contributor to *New York Times Magazine, New York Herald* and other publications. Editor, *Harvard Lampoon,* 1917.

SIDELIGHTS: Robert E. Sherwood was a popular playwright whose work was informed by his opposition to the tyranny of power and ideas. Critics, however, find that his desire to entertain his audience often obscured the serious themes of his plays. His thematic intentions, as stated in the prefaces to his

works, are often left undeveloped in the midst of slick showmanship.

The evolution of Sherwood's thought is typical of the changing attitude of the generation that came of age with the First World War. Like so many other writers of his generation, Sherwood served in the war and was thoroughly disillusioned by the senselessness and horror of his experience. War is a constant presence in his work and his attitude toward it evolved in three stages: an early group of plays that ridiculed traditional concepts of honor and glory, as in *The Road to Rome;* a group of plays as typified by *The Petrified Forest,* peopled with frustrated idealists who passively sacrifice themselves for others; and his ultimate position, exemplified in *The Rugged Path,* that fighting, however personally abhorrent, is sometimes necessary to insure basic freedoms. All of his work reflects his concern with the power of the individual to shape or alter events.

Sherwood received Pulitzer Prizes for three of his plays: *Idiot's Delight, Abe Lincoln in Illinois,* and *There Shall Be No Night.* In 1940 he became a speechwriter and advisor to President Franklin D. Roosevelt and this experience led to his historical work, *Roosevelt and Hopkins,* for which he received his fourth Pulitzer Prize.

Although Sherwood's dramatic works are infrequently staged today, they are valuable as a mirror of his generation's changing attitudes toward war. His most lasting contribution was in the area of cinema: the film version of *The Petrified Forest,* with acclaimed performances by Humphrey Bogart, Leslie Howard and Bette Davis, remains a revered classic, and *The Best Years of Our Lives,* for which Sherwood wrote an Academy Award-winning screenplay, is widely considered one the best American films dealing with World War II and its aftermath. Sherwood was also a pioneer in his early work as a movie reviewer, as one of the first commentators to treat film as a serious art form.

BIOGRAPHICAL/CRITICAL SOURCES:

BOOKS

Brown, John Mason, *The Worlds of Robert E. Sherwood: Mirror to His Times, 1896-1939,* New York, Harper, 1962.
Gessner, Robert, *The Moving Image: A Guide to Cinematic Literacy,* New York, Dutton, 1968.

Gould, Jean, *Modern American Playwrights,* Dodd, 1966.
Meserve, Walter J., *Robert E. Sherwood: Reluctant Moralist,* New York, Pegasus, 1970.
Shuman, R. Baird, *Robert E. Sherwood,* New York, Twayne, 1964.

PERIODICALS

Journal of Popular Film, spring, 1972, pp. 81-104.
New York Times Book Review, October 24, 1948.
Saturday Review of Literature, August 6, 1949.
Theatre Arts Monthly, February, 1956.

* * *

SHOGAN, Robert 1930-

PERSONAL: Born September 12, 1930, in New York, NY; son of Albert and Millie (Jacobs) Shogan; married Ellen Shrewsbury, May 26, 1959; children: Cynthia, Amelia. *Education:* Syracuse University, B.A., 1951; attended Institute of Public Administration, University of Michigan, 1951-52, and Columbia University, 1952.

ADDRESSES: Home—3513 Raymond St., Chevy Chase, MD 20815. *Office—Los Angeles Times,* 1875 I St. NW, Suite 1100, Washington, DC 20006-5409. *Agent*—Carl Brandt, 1501 Broadway, New York, NY 10036.

CAREER: Journalist and author. *Detroit Free Press,* Detroit, MI, reporter, 1956-59; *Miami News,* Miami, FL, telegraph editor, 1959-61; *Wall Street Journal,* New York City, assistant editor, 1961-65; Peace Corps, Washington, DC, evaluation officer, 1965-66; *Newsweek* magazine, Washington DC, correspondent, 1966-73; *Los Angeles Times,* Los Angeles, national political correspondent from Washington, DC, 1973—. Professional-in-residence, Annenberg School of Communication, University of Pennsylvania, 1993. *Military service:* U.S. Army, 1952-54.

MEMBER: Phi Beta Kappa.

AWARDS, HONORS: First prize for feature writing, Michigan Associated Press, 1959; Public Affairs award for distinguished reporting, American Political Science Association, 1969; Scribes Award, 1973, for *A Question of Judgement;* McCormick fellow, Hoover Presidential Library, 1993.

WRITINGS:

(With Tom Craig) *The Detroit Race Riot: A Study in Violence,* Chilton (Philadelphia), 1964.

A Question of Judgement: The Fortas Case and the Struggle of the Supreme Court, Bobbs-Merrill (Indianapolis), 1972.

Promises to Keep: Carter's First Hundred Days, Crowell (New York), 1977.

None of the Above: Why Presidents Fail—And What Can Be Done about It, New American Library (New York), 1982.

The Riddle of Power: Presidential Leadership from Truman to Bush, Dutton (New York), 1991.

Hard Bargain: How F.D.R. Twisted Churchill's Arm, Evaded the Law, and Changed the Role of the American Presidency, Dutton, 1995.

The New Political Order, Turner, in press.

Also contributor to periodicals, including *American Heritage, Public Opinion,* and *New Republic.*

SIDELIGHTS: Robert Shogan has distinguished himself as a political journalist and historian throughout his career, which began in 1961. Washington, DC, correspondent for the *Los Angeles Times* and the author of several books on U.S. politics, Shogan has also been a staff member at both the *Wall Street Journal* and *Newsweek* magazine. In such works as 1983's *None of the Above: Why Presidents Fail—and What Can Be Done about It* and *The Riddle of Power: Presidential Leadership from Truman to Bush,* published in 1991, Shogan provides in-depth analyses of twentieth-century American politics. "I have a broad and continuing interest in contemporary public affairs," Shogan explained to *CA,* "with particular emphasis on politics, government, and the law."

Several of Shogan's early books grew out of his own interest in stories he covered as a print journalist. 1964's *The Detroit Race Riot: A Study in Violence* drew on the first-hand knowledge of how circumstances present in the economically depressed areas served to spark Detroit's racially charged atmosphere that Shogan gained through his work as a *Detroit Free Press* reporter during the late 1950s. *A Question of Judgement: The Fortas Case and the Struggle for the Supreme Court,* in which Shogan investigates the efforts of the Nixon White House to oust one of the Supreme Court's more liberal justices in favor of a conservative appointee to the U.S. high court, was an extension of Shogan's work as a Washington, DC, correspondent for *Newsweek* magazine. Although Shogan's investigation alarmed his subject to the

point at which former justice Abe Fortas reportedly contemplated taking legal action against Shogan, *New York Times Book Review* contributor Geoffrey Cowan asserted: "The book is fair, even sympathetic to Fortas, perhaps because the man did so much good, fell so low and was, finally, more humane and decent than his enemies."

Broader in scope than its predecessor, Shogan's *None of the Above,* an examination of U.S. presidential leadership throughout the decades of the 1960s and 1970s, makes a distinction between promise-laden politicking and the actual legislative track record of elected officials. Citing a problematic electoral process and the entrenched relationship between Congress and the executive branch of government, Shogan suggests proposals for reforms and changes in the federal government. Although he praised the work as an "elegant history of presidential politics," *Washington Post Book World* reviewer Godfrey Hodgson contended that "Shogan is far better at describing what has gone wrong than at suggesting what might be done about it."

More concerned with individual ideology, values, and moral character, *The Riddle of Power* profiles each of the nine men who assumed the office of the president in the shadow of Franklin D. Roosevelt. Herbert Mitgang called the work "a lively and straightforward primer on leadership," in his review for the *New York Times,* and *Boston Globe* critic Charles E. Claffey hailed the work as "a valuable book on the changing American presidency, as well as a useful tool to voters trying to assess the qualities of our future leaders."

Considered by many Americans to be the most effective and respected president of the twentieth-century, Franklin Delano Roosevelt is subject to Shogan's scrutiny in 1995's *Hard Bargain: How F.D.R. Twisted Churchill's Arm, Evaded the Law, and Changed the Role of the American Presidency.* In the late spring and summer of 1940, Roosevelt and recently elected British Prime Minister Winston Churchill negotiated the so-called "destroyers for bases" deal that would help in the defense of England against Nazi Germany by allowing Churchill the use of fifty U.S. destroyers, in return for which the United States would gain leaseholds—and thereby a defensible interest—in British-owned bases in the Atlantic. F.D.R.'s machinations in implementing this agreement, which ultimately propelled the United States into the war against fascism, are cited by Shogan as examples of politically unprincipled

policymaking that have since collectively served as a precedent for the excessive exercise of presidential power under the guise of "national security." Characterized as "a marvelous and compelling tale of intrigue, deception, vision, rank politics and grand strategy" by Thomas Oliphant in the *Boston Globe, Hard Bargain* "sustains a fine narrative pace and includes a wide range of well-drawn biographical sketches," according to a reviewer for *Foreign Affairs.*

BIOGRAPHICAL/CRITICAL SOURCES:

PERIODICALS

American Spectator, June, 1991, p. 37.
Boston Globe, April 1, 1991, p. 45; June 6, 1995, p. 15.
Chicago Tribune Book World, August 28, 1983, p. 31.
Foreign Affairs, May/June, 1995, pp. 175-76.
Los Angeles Times, February 6, 1983, p. 6; June 7, 1995, p. E5.
Nation, May 8, 1972, pp. 601-02.
New York Review of Books, June 29, 1972, p. 14.
New York Times, March 9, 1991, p. A16.
New York Times Book Review, May 28, 1972, p. 1; September 25, 1977, p. 16; April 30, 1995, p. 11.
Publishers Weekly, January 25, 1991, p. 43; February 20, 1995.
Washington Post Book World, October 31, 1982, p. 9; April 28, 1991, p. 11; April 9, 1995, p. 4.

* * *

SHRADER, Charles R. 1943-

PERSONAL: Born July 3, 1943, in Nashville, TN; son of Reginald W. (a noncommissioned air force officer) and Freda O. (a secretary; maiden name, Presley) Shrader; married Carole A. Analore (a secretary), August 18, 1963; children: Peter R., Sheila L. Shrader Bixby. *Ethnicity:* "Caucasian." *Education:* Vanderbilt University, B.A. (cum laude), 1964; Columbia University, Ph.D., 1976. *Politics:* Republican. *Religion:* Roman Catholic.

ADDRESSES: Home and office—910 Forbes Rd., Carlisle, PA 17013; fax 717-249-5625. *E-mail*—heriger@aol.com.

CAREER: U.S. Army, career officer, 1964-87, retiring as lieutenant colonel; independent historian and consultant, 1987—. U.S. Army War College, General of the Army George C. Marshall Professor of Military Studies, 1983-84. U.S. Commission on Military History, member, 1986—; Carlisle Municipal Authority, member.

MEMBER: American Historical Association, Mediaeval Academy of America, Society for Military History (executive director, 1992—), Oral History Association, American Association for State and Local History, Society of Historians of American Foreign Relations, Oral History in the Mid-Atlantic Region, Inter-University Seminar on the Armed Forces and Society, Phi Beta Kappa.

AWARDS, HONORS: Military: Legion of Merit; Bronze Star with oak leaf cluster; Meritorious Service Medal with oak leaf cluster; Joint Service Commendation Medal; Army Commendation Medal. *Other:* Grant from American Philosophical Society, 1980; Faculty Writing Prize from Army War College Foundation, 1982, for the article "The Influence of Vegetius's 'De Re Militari'"; grants from U.S. Army Military History Institute, 1987-88, and National Endowment for the Humanities, 1989.

WRITINGS:

(Editor) *Selected Readings in Military History: The Evolution of U.S. Army Logistics,* U.S. Army Command and General Staff College (Fort Leavenworth, KS), 1978.
(General editor) *Reference Guide to United States Military History,* five volumes, Facts on File (New York City), 1991-94.
U.S. Military Logistics, 1607-1990: A Research Guide, Greenwood Press (Westport, CT), 1992.
Communist Logistics in the Korean War, Greenwood Press, 1995.
(With Theodore J. Crackel) *A Guide to the Papers of the Commanding Generals and Chiefs of Staff, United States Army, 1775-1987,* Greenwood Press, in press.

Contributor to books, including *The U.S. Army War College Guide to the Battle of Antietam,* edited by Jay Luvaas and Harold W. Nelson, South Mountain Press (Carlisle, PA), 1987; and *The Great War, 1914-1918: Essays on the Military, Political, and Social History of the First World War,* edited by R. J. Q. Adams, Texas A & M University Press (College Station, TX), 1990. Contributor of articles and reviews to

history and military studies journals, including *Mediaeval Studies, Army Logistician, Military Review, Army Historian,* and *Military Affairs.*

WORK IN PROGRESS: An Historical Anthology of Army Logistics, 1775-1991, for U.S. Army Center of Military History (Washington, DC); *The First Helicopter War: Logistics and Mobility in Algeria, 1954-1962; Logistics in the First Indochina War, 1946-1954,* two volumes; *Logistical Support of the Communist Insurgency in Greece, 1946-1949;* research on the medieval manuscripts of Vegetius's *De re militari.*

SIDELIGHTS: Charles R. Shrader told *CA:* "In general, my continuing research interests include American military biography and the institutional and intellectual history of the United States Army, 1865-1915; the history of military logistics; medieval manuscript studies (including paleography and codicology); and the ecclesiastical, intellectual, and military history of the Middle Ages.

"My research and writing efforts are currently focused on a study of the logistical aspects of the revolution in Indonesia in the late 1960s and on the compilation of a comprehensive handbook of statistical and reference data for American military historians. I also have research in progress for a number of article-length studies, including a descriptive handlist of the known, extant manuscripts of the Eucharistic writings of Heriger of Lobbes; a study of the influence of American business management methods on the United States Army, 1900-1980; a military analysis of the battle of Tagliacozzo in 1268; and a biographical study of Colonel Arthur L. Conger, a United States Army intelligence operative and later world leader of the Theosophical Society.

"I continue to work actively on a long-term project designed to produce a multi-volume, comprehensive, descriptive catalog of the three-hundred-twenty-four known, extant codices containing the *De re militari* of Flavius Vegetius Renatus. I have assembled microfilm copies of more than fifty pre-1300 manuscripts that will be described in the first volume.

"For some time I have also been working on a biography of Eugene O. Fechet, who served in both the United States Army and the army of the Khedive Ismail of Egypt in the late nineteenth and early twentieth centuries. The project involves the use of official records, private letters and diaries (including Fechet's own Egyptian exploration journals) and in-

terviews with surviving acquaintances and relatives of Fechet. I hope to produce a biography that will elucidate Civil War and post-Civil War military life and the involvement of the United States government and American military officers in the development of the Egyptian khedival army in the late 1870s.

"My other long-range research and writing projects include a full-scale biography of Adolphus W. Greely, Arctic explorer and Chief Signal Officer of the United States Army; a comprehensive study of medieval tactical doctrine, illustrated by systematic analysis of the data available on selected medieval battles; and an essay on military thought as a reflection of the trends in general philosophy dominant in various eras of history."

*　　*　　*

SICKELS, Noelle 1945-

PERSONAL: Born December 24, 1945, in Teaneck, NJ; married Victor Parra (a psychotherapist); children: Jude Parra-Sickels. *Education:* University of Delaware, B.A., 1968; University of Pennsylvania, M.A., 1971; Glassboro State College, M.A., 1973. *Avocational interests:* Camping, making artists' books.

ADDRESSES: Home—Los Angeles, CA. *Agent*—Tom Epley, Potomac Literary Agency, 19062 Mills Choice Rd., Suite 5, Gaithersburg, MD 20879.

CAREER: North Caroline High School, Denton, MD, and Caroline County Migrant School, Preston, MD, teacher of life skills, 1971-72; Philadelphia Child Guidance Clinic, Philadelphia, PA, psycho-education specialist, 1974-77; Behavioral Health Services, Gardena, CA, coordinator of medicine education program, 1977-79; childbirth educator in Rosemont, PA, and Los Angeles, CA, 1980-89; Neighborhood Nursery School, Los Angeles, CA, teacher, 1984-93, teacher-director, 1995—; Sequoyah School, Pasadena, CA, assistant to the director, 1993-95. Served on the board of the December Rose Association for Creative Seniors, 1991-94, and also served as coordinator of that group's annual writing competition; interviewed on *Connie Martinson Talks Books,* on various cable television channels, 1995. Has given readings in locations such as Los Angeles, CA, Pasadena, CA, Torrance, CA, Mission Viejo, CA, Marlton, NJ, Paramus, NJ, Philadelphia, PA, Bryn

Mawr, PA, Wilmington, DE, Rockville, MD, Santa Barbara, CA, La Jolla, CA, Glendale, CA, and Claremont, CA.

MEMBER: PEN Center, USA West, The Women's Building (writing committee).

AWARDS, HONORS: Grant from the Cultural Affairs Department of Los Angeles to conduct writing workshops for senior citizens and adolescents, 1993-94; awarded writer's residency at Dorland Mountain Arts Colony in Temecula, CA, 1994.

WRITINGS:

(Editor) *Time Was* (reminiscences collection), Cultural Affairs Department (Los Angeles), 1992.
Walking West (novel), St. Martin's Press (New York), 1995.

Contributor to short story anthologies, including *Snakeskin,* edited by Bayle Winters, Anaconda Press (Chicago, IL), 1991; *American Fiction 3,* edited by Michael White, Birch Lane Press (New York), 1991; *Each in Her Own Way,* edited by Elizabeth Claman, Queen of Swords Press (Eugene, OR), 1994. Contributor to poetry anthologies, including *Lovers and Liars,* edited by Cynthia Walker, Saturday Afternoon Press (Los Angeles, CA), 1992; *A Sense of Place,* edited by Rob Morris, Saturday Afternoon Press, 1993; *True Confessions,* edited by Elvin Whitesides, Saturday Afternoon Press, 1995; *Women's Words,* edited by Marilyn Sewell, Beacon Press (Boston), 1996. Essay contributor to *The Book Group Book,* edited by Ellen Slezak, Chicago Review Press (Chicago), 1995; *An Intricate Weave,* edited by Marlene Miller, Iris Editions, Laguna Beach, CA, 1997.

Collaborated on the scripts for two television documentaries, *History Told on Walls: The Bas Reliefs of Abomey* and *Columbus 92: The Crossing of the Atlantic.* Also contributor of stories, poems, and articles to periodicals, including *Fathoms, Ignis Fatuus Review, Wordplay, Mediphors, Poems That Thump in the Dark, American Baby, L.A. Weekly, New Directions for Women, Childbirth Educator, Expecting, Growing Parent, Living With Children, Scouting, Wet Set Gazette, Beyond Doggerel,* and *Raconteur.*

WORK IN PROGRESS: Two novels, one to be titled *Relics,* the other to be named *The Shopkeeper's Wife.*

SIDELIGHTS: Author, poet, and educator Noelle Sickels began her career teaching life skills to mi-

grant workers. She has taught creative writing to both adolescents and senior citizens, and spent several years giving childbirth preparation classes to expectant parents. She has developed courses on the proper medications to be given senior citizens in various states of health, and served as the assistant director of a private elementary school. Sickels has also taught at and served as director of a nursery school. She has performed her educational duties in locations ranging from Los Angeles, California, to Philadelphia, Pennsylvania. Sickels' writing, however, has not been restricted to articles on education and parenting. She has contributed poetry to such anthologies as *Lovers and Liars* and *Women's Words,* and her short stories have been featured in volumes such as *American Fiction 3* and *Each in Her Own Way.* In 1995, Sickels saw the publication of her first novel, *Walking West.*

Walking West has been acclaimed by reviewers and readers for telling the story of western settlement in the United States from a woman's point of view. The novel's heroine is Alice Muller, who in 1852 travels with her husband, in-laws, and several other people in a wagon train west, despite being pregnant during the journey. Another important character is Bailey Jeffers, an unmarried female artist, who joins the wagon train searching for a better life. The party loses approximately half of its members to illness, drowning, or exhaustion en route. As *Ocala Star-Banner* contributor Rima L. Firrone put it, these characters die "without encountering nasty opposition . . . simply because they were unprepared for the mundane." Alice survives, and when she reaches her destination, she decides—because of the inspiration she has received from Bailey—to continue the writing she had begun merely as a means to chronicle the trip westward.

Critics expressed respect and affection for Sickels' achievement in *Walking West.* Dick Roraback of the *Los Angeles Times Book Review* asserted that the author "has garbed her first novel in such authenticity that she may as well have been there herself," and labeled it "homespun, with patches of poetry." Susan Saxton D'Aoust in the *River Journal* singled out for praise a descriptive passage in which Alice is pushed to the limits of her physical strength helping to steady one of the wagons as it moves downhill. Firrone concluded that *Walking West* is a "gentle and compassionate tale."

Sickels told *CA:* "I am interested in how men and women perceive the world differently and in what people decide to reveal about themselves and what they choose to keep secret."

BIOGRAPHICAL/CRITICAL SOURCES:

PERIODICALS

Los Angeles Times Book Review, October 1, 1995.
Ocala Star-Banner, July 16, 1995.
River Journal, October 30, 1995.

* * *

SIMON, Paul (Frederick) 1941-
(Paul Kane, Jerry Landis)

PERSONAL: Born October 13, 1941, in Newark, NJ; son of Louis (a musician and teacher) and Belle (a teacher) Simon; married Peggy Harper (divorced, 1975); married Carrie Fisher (an actress and writer), 1983 (divorced); married Edie Brickell (a musician), 1992; children: (with Harper) Harper; (with Brickell) Adrian Edward. *Education:* Queens College, B.A.; attended Brooklyn Law School.

ADDRESSES: Office—Paul Simon Music, 1619 Broadway, Suite 500, New York, NY 10019.

CAREER: Musician, producer, and songwriter. Performed (as Jerry Landis) with Art Garfunkel in the high school duo Tom and Jerry, 1957-1958; performed with Garfunkel in the duo Simon and Garfunkel, 1964-71, reunited briefly with Garfunkel, 1982 and 1993; recorded as a solo artist, 1972—. Actor in films, including *Monterrey Pop,* 1968, *Annie Hall,* 1977, *All You Need Is Cash,* 1978, *One Trick Pony,* 1980, and *Steve Martin Live,* 1985. Has made appearances in television shows, including *Paul Simon Special,* 1978, *Paul Simon's Graceland: The African Concert,* 1987, *Live: The Hard Rock Cafe,* 1988, *Paul Simon: Born at the Right Time,* 1992.

AWARDS, HONORS: Grammy Awards, National Academy of Recording Arts and Sciences: two in 1968 (with Simon and Garfunkel) for the soundtrack recording from the film *The Graduate,* six in 1970 (with Simon and Garfunkel) for the record album *Bridge over Troubled Water,* two in 1975 for the record album *Still Crazy after All These Years,* in 1986 and 1987 for the record album *Graceland;* Emmy Award, 1977, for the television show *Paul Simon Special;* inducted with Garfunkel into Rock and Roll Hall of Fame, 1990.

WRITINGS:

RECORDINGS, PERFORMED WITH ART GARFUNKEL

Wednesday Morning, 3 A.M., Columbia, 1964.
The Sounds of Silence, Columbia, 1966.
Parsley, Sage, Rosemary and Thyme, Columbia, 1966.
Simon and Garfunkel, Allegro, 1967.
The Graduate (soundtrack), Columbia, 1968.
Bookends, Columbia, 1968.
Bridge over Troubled Water, Columbia, 1970.
Simon and Garfunkel's Greatest Hits, Columbia, 1972.
The Simon and Garfunkel Collection (boxed set), CBS, 1981.
The Concert in Central Park, Warner Bros., 1982.

RECORDINGS, PERFORMED AS A SOLO ARTIST

The Paul Simon Song Book, CBS, 1965.
Paul Simon, Columbia, 1972.
There Goes Rhymin' Simon, Columbia, 1973.
Live Rhymin': Paul Simon in Concert, Columbia, 1974.
Still Crazy after All These Years, Columbia, 1975.
Greatest Hits, etc., Columbia, 1977.
One Trick Pony, Warner Bros., 1980.
Hearts and Bones, Warner Bros., 1983.
Graceland, Warner Bros., 1986.
Negotiations and Love Songs, 1971-1986, Warner Bros., 1988.
The Rhythm of the Saints, Warner Bros., 1990.
Paul Simon's Concert in the Park, Warner Bros., 1991.
Paul Simon, 1964-1993 (boxed set), Warner Bros., 1993.

BOOKS

The Songs of Paul Simon, Knopf (New York), 1972.
New Songs, Knopf, 1975.
One-Trick Pony (screenplay), Knopf, 1980.
At the Zoo (for children), illustrated by Valerie Michaut, Doubleday, 1991.

Some writings have appeared under the name Paul Kane.

WORK IN PROGRESS: A musical, *Capeman.*

SIDELIGHTS: Paul Simon's career has spanned nearly five decades of American popular music. He

learned his craft in the late 1950s, achieved considerable success as half of Simon and Garfunkel in the 1960s, made his mark as a soloist in the 1970s, and has remained an innovative and popular artist through the 1980s and 1990s. He has been noted as an intelligent and artful lyricist, a tasteful musician, and a dedicated explorer of new musical territory.

Simon's musical career began in 1957, while he was still in high school. He and his friend Art Garfunkel renamed themselves Tom and Jerry and, singing a catchy brand of doo-wop music, had a Top 40 hit with the song "Hey! Schoolgirl." But success was fleeting; no more hits followed, and the boys went back to high school.

Simon spent the next several years at Queens College, where he majored in literature. Influenced by the books he was reading and the earnest, exciting folk music scene prevalent in New York's Greenwich Village, Simon began writing songs that were more sophisticated than anything Tom and Jerry had attempted. He and Garfunkel revived their partnership under their own names, and landed a contract with Columbia Records. Their debut album, *Wednesday Morning, 3 A.M.,* was released in 1964. The record did not gain immediate attention. Its introspective lyrics and folky sound were overshadowed by the big-beat exuberance of the Beatles, who dominated the airwaves in those days. Simon left the U.S. to spend the summer in England. His first solo album, *The Paul Simon Songbook,* was released in England in 1965, and contained several songs that would appear in the next Simon and Garfunkel collaboration, *The Sounds of Silence* (1966).

While Simon was in England, his career took a decisive turn. One track from Simon and Garfunkel's album was receiving repeated requests over the radio. Tom Wilson of Columbia Records decided to cash in on this spark of interest. He overdubbed electric guitar, bass and drums onto the original recording, which simply featured vocals and acoustic guitar. With its new folk-rock sound, "The Sound of Silence" shot to No. 1 on the U.S. charts. Simon returned home to find that he and Garfunkel were stars.

Enormous success followed. Album by album, Simon and Garfunkel solidified their reputation for intelligent, poetic songs that captured the spirit of the times. Simon did all the songwriting, and was quickly tagged as a poet of alienation. Some critics dismissed his work as pretentious and moody. But many more hailed him as a voice of the times, turning his generation's yearnings and confusions into serious and carefully crafted songs.

Simon and Garfunkel recorded eight albums together, and every one earned a Gold Record. Their partnership culminated in 1970 with *Bridge over Troubled Water,* which won an unprecedented six Grammy Awards. In the wake of this triumph, the duo broke up, Garfunkel to pursue an acting career, Simon to record his songs on his own terms. "I'm really happy to be by myself now and not have to share decisions," Simon explained to a reviewer in *New York Times* in 1972. "Now I do things almost entirely to my taste." The two revived their partnership briefly on several separate occasions. In 1975, they recorded the single "My Little Town," which also appeared on Simon's *Still Crazy after All These Years* and Garfunkel's *Breakaway.* In 1978, along with James Taylor, they recorded another single, the Sam Cooke classic "Wonderful World" for Garfunkel's *Watermark* album. Then in 1982, the duo reunited in front of a half-million people in a free concert in New York City's Central Park. But they soon split up again, the freedom of solo work outweighing the benefits of collaboration.

His "taste" has served him well time and again. His solo album, *Still Crazy after All These Years,* won a Grammy Award in 1975, and his 1986 album *Graceland* won two. Simon has continued to hone his skill as a songwriter. The songs on *Graceland* have been described as complex and ambitious, more mature and more worldly than even the best of his earlier work. But the artistry of his words is not the only constant in Simon's music. He has consistently opened himself up to challenging musical influences. In the early 1970s, he had used Caribbean and South American musical textures on his recordings at a time when those types of music were virtually unknown in the United States. With *Graceland,* he took the same concept to a new level. The record is a collaboration between Simon and musicians from South Africa, where it was recorded. The fusion of Simon's urbane style and this strongly rhythmic, colorful music led many to characterize *Graceland* as a milestone in American pop. Simon's exploring did not end in Africa. His next recording, 1990's *The Rhythm of the Saints,* is steeped in the music of Brazil.

Paul Simon has also worked in film. He began with a small role in Woody Allen's 1977 film *Annie Hall.* 1980 saw the release of *One-Trick Pony,* a semi-autobiographical film about life in the music business. Simon wrote the screenplay and the musical score,

and plays the lead role. He also appeared in the concert film, *Monterrey Pop* (1968), and in *All You Need Is Cash* (1978) and *Steve Martin Live* (1985). But it is as a songwriter and musician that Paul Simon has made his mark, crafting mature, poetic pop songs and widening the boundaries of the genre.

BIOGRAPHICAL/CRITICAL SOURCES:

BOOKS

Bonds, Ray, ed., *The Harmony Illustrated Encyclopedia of Rock,* Harmony Books (New York), 1982, pp. 209-11.

Contemporary Literary Criticism, Volume 17, Gale, 1981.

Dalton, David, and Lenny Kaye, *Rock 100,* Grossett & Dunlap, 1977.

Humphries, Patrick, *Paul Simon: Still Crazy after All These Years,* Doubleday, 1988.

Jahn, Mike, *Rock: From Elvis Presley to the Rolling Stones,* Quandrangle/New York Times (New York), 1973.

Kingston, Victoria, *Simon and Garfunkel: The Definitive Biography,* Sidgwick and Jackson, 1996.

Leigh, Spencer, *Paul Simon: Now and Then,* Raven Books, 1973.

Miller, Jim, ed., *The Rolling Stone Illustrated History of Rock & Roll,* Random House, 1976.

Simon, George T., *Best of the Music Makers,* Doubleday, 1979.

PERIODICALS

Harper's, April, 1976, pp. 103-4.

Los Angeles Times, June 26, 1989.

Newsweek, December 15, 1975, p. 98; March 15, 1976, p. 48.

New Yorker, September 2, 1967, pp. 24-7; May 4, 1968, pp. 179-80; April 29, 1972, p. 32; October 5, 1981, pp. 9-11.

New York Times, October 13, 1968, Magazine, p. 48; February 27, 1972, section II, p. 15; September 7, 1979, p. C6; October 3, 1980, p. C14; February 28, 1982.

Observer (London), June 10, 1973.

Rolling Stone, May 14, 1970, pp. 56, 58; May 28, 1970, p. 36; March 2, 1972, p. 56; August 3, 1972, pp. 38, 40; June 21, 1973, p. 62; December 4, 1975, pp. 57-8; January 25, 1979, p. 18; October 16, 1980, pp. 54-5; October 30, 1980, pp. 42-5; October 15, 1981, p. 51; March 18, 1982, pp. 26-8.

Saturday Review, February 28, 1970, pp. 91, 98; June 12, 1976, pp. 43, 44, 59.

Time, April 19, 1968, p. 46; January 31, 1972, p. 36.

Village Voice, September 3, 1980, p. 53.

Washington Post, September 17, 1988.*

* * *

SIMPSON, Jeffrey (Carl) 1949-

PERSONAL: Born February 17, 1949, in New York, NY; son of Robert Lawrence and Eve Cloud (Matheson) Simpson; immigrated to Canada, 1959; married Wendy Elizabeth Bryans, June 15, 1974; children: Tait, Danielle, Brook. *Education:* Attended University of Toronto Schools, 1967; Queen's University, B.A., 1971; London School of Economics, M.Sc. (International Relations), 1972. *Religion:* Anglican. *Avocational interests:* Skiing, tennis, music, reading.

ADDRESSES: Office—165 Sparks Street, 3rd Floor, Ottawa, Ontario K1P 5B9, Canada. *Home*—413 Third Ave., Ottawa, Ontario, Canada K1S 2K6. *Agent*—David Lavin Agency, 24 Duncan St., Toronto, Ontario, Canada M5V 2B8.

CAREER: Globe and Mail, Toronto, Ontario, Canada, reporter, 1973-79, Ottawa bureau chief, 1979-81, European correspondent, 1981-83, London correspondent, 1981-84, columnist, 1984—.

AWARDS, HONORS: Governor General's Award in nonfiction, Canada Council, 1980, for *Discipline of Power: The Conservative Interlude and the Liberal Restoration;* John S. Knight Fellow, Stanford University, 1993. Distinguished Visitor, University of Alberta; John V. Clyne Fellow, University of British Columbia; Skelton-Clark Fellow, Queen's University; Hymon Solomon Award for Public Policy Journalism.

WRITINGS:

Discipline of Power: The Conservative Interlude and the Liberal Restoration, Personal Library (Toronto), 1981.

(With Ged Martin) *The Canadian Guide to Britain,* Macmillan (New York City), 1985.

Spoils of Power: The Politics of Patronage, Collins (New York City), 1988.

(With Martin) *Canada's Heritage in Scotland,* Dundurn Press (Toronto), 1989.

Faultlines, HarperCollins (Scranton, PA), 1993.

The Anxious Years, Lester Publishing (Toronto, Ontario), 1996.

Contributor to periodicals, including *Saturday Night.*

SIDELIGHTS: "Widely read in political history, and no mean historian in his own right, [Jeffrey Simpson] is one of the most scholarly of Canadian journalists," declared Michael Bliss in *Saturday Night.* Simpson is not a native Canadian, however, having been born in the United States. He immigrated to Canada at the age of ten. Educated in University of Toronto schools, Simpson later received his bachelor's degree from Queen's University in 1971. Further graduate study took him to England where he received a masters degree from the London School of Economics in 1972. Returning to Canada, Simpson has had a long career as a journalist with the Toronto *Globe and Mail.* His duties have ranged from reporter to bureau chief, foreign correspondent, and columnist. He has also written six books examining the state of Canadian politics. His first volume, *Discipline of Power: The Conservative Interlude and the Liberal Restoration,* received the Canadian Governor General's Award in nonfiction in 1980.

Discipline of Power is a descriptive analysis of the limitations and cultural context in which the modern politician must confront the realities of running for office and governing. In his in-depth study of the 1979 election of Conservative Joe Clark as Canadian Prime Minister, Simpson examines Clark as a candidate, the role of television, the manipulation of political images, the sudden collapse of the Clark government after only 259 days, and the return of Liberal government under Pierre Trudeau.

Simpson viewed the 1979 election as a watershed in the history of Canadian elective politics that signaled the increased use of negative campaigning, and marked "the triumph of partisan politics over government," as noted in *Discipline of Power.* Essentially, Simpson concludes, the Conservatives were elected in 1979 because voters had basically grown weary of the incumbent Trudeau administration. Furthermore, upon taking office the Conservatives could not wield the type of political power needed to sustain themselves nor provide a clear direction for Canada's future. They lacked the discipline necessary to be effective agents of change. Sixteen years as the opposition party, according to Simpson, made the Conservatives reactive and unaccustomed to ruling. In particular, Simpson cites the Conservative Party's mistakes concerning a "no confidence" budget vote that

began the downward spiral of the Clark government and signaled the rise of Trudeau's comeback in 1980.

A critic in *Publisher's Weekly* praised *Discipline of Power* as "deeply analytical" and "well-written." Writing in *Saturday Night,* Ramsay Cook cited Simpson's "talent for lucid explanations" and called *Disciple of Power,* "the work of an intelligent and informed political reporter who is anxious to understand what has been going on in [Canadian] politics." In writing the volume, Simpson draws on inside information from meetings of the cabinet and party managers, Conservative Party documents, and interviews. "The result," judged Cook, "is an informative work which advances a clear and convincing argument."

Turning from political topics to travel, Simpson's next book written with coauthor Ged Martin, *The Canadian Guide to Britain,* is a tour of places in England with a special connection to Canada. In the introduction to the guide, the authors welcome the readers with a simple entreaty: "Leave all the 'how to' and 'where to' questions for others. This book is about Canada in Britain, the intermingling of two histories, a guide and perhaps an inspiration for the thousands of Canadians who visit Britain every year to look about them and discover part of their country's own history." The guide includes all sorts of hotels, monuments, statues, and places, such as the location of the Canadian Red Cross Hospital. Built on the grounds of Lady Astor's estate, the staff of this hospital treated thousands of Canadian soldiers during World War I and World War II. At England's largest military cemetery, Brookwood Cemetery in Surrey, the traveler can view the graves of approximately 2000 Canadian World War II service personnel. Unusual places are also listed, like the boyhood home of the famous Canadian Indian named Grey Owl. Writing in the Toronto *Globe and Mail,* Alan Pearson observed: "*The Canadian Guide to Britain* is a compendium of well researched and interesting information, much of it surprisingly new."

Following along the lines of his descriptive analysis of *Discipline of Power,* Simpson set his aim on the method politicians use to reward supporters—patronage. His effort, *Spoils of Power: The Politics of Patronage,* is a "wonderfully rich account of the role played by patronage in Canadian political history," according to Joseph Wearing, writing in the Toronto *Globe and Mail.* Broadly, the book focuses on the historical development of patronage (the practice of rewarding supporters with advantageous posts, con-

tracts, and other perks) at the federal level and in the ten Canadian provinces, and offers historical references, such as how nineteenth-century politicians wielded appointments and used the perks of office to help build a cohesive party system. Tracing patronage in politics as far back as the 1840s, Simpson shows in the *Spoils of Power* how it has been used skillfully and abusively throughout the nation's history. He contends that reforms have had some impact, albeit mostly limited. "Meticulously researched and fluidly written, *Spoils of Power* is a serious book about a controversial subject," stated Pamela Young in *Maclean's*. Michael Bliss, writing in *Saturday Night*, concluded: "*Spoils of Power* is a richly detailed study of a major aspect of Canada's old political system."

BIOGRAPHICAL/CRITICAL SOURCES:

BOOKS

Simpson, Jeffrey, *Discipline of Power: The Conservative Interlude and the Liberal Restoration,* Personal Library, 1981.
Simpson, Jeffrey, and Ged Martin, *The Canadian Guide to Britain,* Macmillan, 1985.

PERIODICALS

Globe and Mail (Toronto), May 25, 1985; September 24, 1988.
Maclean's, October 10, 1988, pp. 61-62; November 28, 1988, p. 42.
Publishers Weekly, July 24, 1981, p. 141.
Saturday Night, November, 1980, pp. 73-75; November, 1988, pp. 63-65.*

* * *

SINOR, John 1930-1996

OBITUARY NOTICE—See index for *CA* sketch: Surname is pronounced "*Sigh*-ner"; born December 24, 1930, in Elk City, OK; died of heart and kidney failure, August 28, 1996, in San Diego, CA. Journalist, educator, and author. Sinor was a noted newspaper columnist whose work was syndicated in some six hundred newspapers and won him the National Headliners Award. Sinor got his start as a copy runner at the *Sacramento Bee*. Beginning in 1948, he worked as a freelance journalist. He saw service in the U.S. Air Force during the Korean War. He wrote the weekly "John Sinor Column" for Copley News Service and prepared a daily commentary for the *San Diego Tribune* (later the *San Diego Union-Tribune*). According to a contributor in the *Los Angeles Times,* Sinor's columns concerned "everyday problems of everyday people." He retired in 1992. In addition to his journalism, Sinor wrote books including *Eleven Albatrosses in My Bluebird Tree, Ghosts of Cabrillo Lighthouse, Finsterhall of San Pasqual, Finsterhall Goes over the Wall, Best of San Diego,* and *Some Ladies in My Life. Finsterhall of San Pasqual* was adapted for the screen and filmed by Disney Studios.

OBITUARIES AND OTHER SOURCES:

BOOKS

Science Fiction and Fantasy Literature, 1975-1991, Gale, 1992.

PERIODICALS

Los Angeles Times, September 6, 1996, p. A18.

* * *

SLOAN, John 1948-

PERSONAL: Born November 11, 1948, in Scotland. *Education:* Oxford University, M.A., D.Phil.

ADDRESSES: Home—Oxford, England. *Office*—Harris Manchester College, Oxford University, Oxford OX1 3TD, England.

CAREER: Oxford University, Oxford, England, lecturer in English at Balliol College, 1985-96, fellow, tutor, and lecturer in English at Harris Manchester College, 1996—.

WRITINGS:

George Gissing: The Cultural Challenge, Macmillan, 1989.
John Davidson: First of the Moderns, Oxford University Press (Oxford, England), 1995.
(Editor) *Selected Poems and Prose of John Davidson,* Clarendon Press (New York City), 1995.

WORK IN PROGRESS: Research on the literature of the 1890s and on the English novel.

SIDELIGHTS: John Sloan told *CA:* "My primary motivation for writing is a desire to promote the enjoyment of literature. I am very old-fashioned and write my first drafts in longhand with a pencil before even thinking of going to the word processor. As for inspiration, it is my experience that a writer does not so much choose his subject—especially for a biography—but that the subject chooses him."

* * *

SMITH, Hallett (Darius) 1907-1996

OBITUARY NOTICE—See index for *CA* sketch: Born August 15, 1907, in Chattanooga, TN; died August 15, 1996, in Duarte, CA. Educator, researcher, and author. Smith established a reputation for his work in Shakespearean and Elizabethan studies. He began his career as an educator at Williams College in 1931, rising to professor of English at the school in 1946. Three years later, he joined the California Institute of Technology faculty as a professor, and he also chaired its Division of Humanities and Social Sciences. In 1970, he began some twenty years as a senior research associate at Huntington Library. During his career, he was a visiting professor at Columbia University and the University of British Columbia. In the early 1950s, he received the Poetry Chap-Book prize from the Poetry Society of America. He was a fellow in the American Academy of Arts and Sciences. Smith wrote and edited numerous books, including *The Critical Reader, Elizabethan Poetry: A Study in Conventions, Meaning and Expression, The Norton Anthology of English Literature, Twentieth Century Interpretations of "The Tempest,"* and *Shakespeare's Romances: A Study of Some Ways of the Imagination.*

OBITUARIES AND OTHER SOURCES:

BOOKS

Who's Who in America, 51st edition, Marquis, 1996.

PERIODICALS

Los Angeles Times, August 24, 1996, p. A22.

SMITH, Lora R(oberts) 1949-
(Lora Roberts; Leigh Roberts, a pseudonym)

PERSONAL: Born December 29, 1949, in Marshall, MO; daughter of Howard Ridgeway (a teacher) and Evelyn (a teacher) Roberts; married Jerry Smith (an engineer), March 28, 1970; children: Matthew R., Jeremy R. *Ethnicity:* "White." *Education:* University of Missouri—Rolla, B.A., 1971. *Politics:* "Mine." *Religion:* "Also mine." *Avocational interests:* Gardening, sewing, reading.

ADDRESSES: Home—Palo Alto, CA. *Office*—P.O. Box 957, Palo Alto, CA 94303; fax 415-328-0378. *E-mail*—myslora@hooked.net. *Agent*—Ruth Cohen, Inc., P.O. Box 7626, Menlo Park, CA 94025.

CAREER: Writer.

MEMBER: Mystery Writers of America (member of board of directors), Sisters in Crime (member of board of directors).

WRITINGS:

Revolting Development, Perseverance Press (Menlo Park, CA), 1989.

UNDER NAME LORA ROBERTS

Murder in a Nice Neighborhood, Fawcett (New York), 1994.
Murder in the Marketplace, Fawcett, 1995.
Murder Mile-High, Fawcett, 1996.
Murder Bone by Bone, Fawcett, in press.

ROMANCE NOVELS, UNDER PSEUDONYM LEIGH ROBERTS

Moonlight Splendor, Harlequin (New York), 1983.
Love Circuits, Harlequin, 1984.
Siren Song, Harlequin, 1985.
Birds of a Feather, Harlequin, 1986.
Head Over Heels, Harlequin, 1987.
The Wishing Pool, Harlequin, 1988.
A Piece of Cake, Harlequin, 1990.
Built to Last, Harlequin, 1992.

WORK IN PROGRESS: Mr. Sigerson's Case, a mystery featuring Sherlock Holmes; *Murder with Bells On,* a Liz Sullivan mystery; research on Edwardian England.

SIDELIGHTS: Lora R. Smith told *CA:* "I didn't apply myself to more lucrative disciplines in school, con-

vinced that I would be a writer. When it was time to go to work, I discovered that English majors had few choices—clerical work, public relations work, or actually attempting to write for a living. I did all those things, and I am still writing, although I have a sideline in editing that puts a little cornbread on the table.

"Like many another author, I began writing romances. It was a good way to be paid for learning to write novels, but my true love has always been the mystery genre. I grew up in a house full of siblings, arguments, and books; more than half of those books were mysteries. My mother was hard-boiled (Mickey Spillane, Brett Holiday), my dad was more moderate in his gore requirements (Erle Stanley Gardener, Agatha Christie). I read all of these, horrifying my mother by asking, when I was eleven, 'What is this cognac they drink all the time?' My tastes ran with my dad's, however. I liked the novel of detection, the amateur sleuth, the comfortable confines where violence can be hidden, the placid surfaces with raging currents beneath them.

"Those who love crime fiction divide it into many sub-genres—espionage, private investigator, police procedural, cozy. Mine, I like to think, are semi-cozy. There is violence, but it is not dwelt on in loving detail. There is humor, but that is not the focus. The characters, as in all good fiction, carry the story, but the story makes definite progress toward a satisfying resolution.

"Ah, that resolution! That is one of the reasons why I love reading and writing mysteries. One reviewer once damned a book of mine because the ending was too tidy. Well, I like that tidy ending. As a child, I loved the books in which the characters, though tossed by turbulent action, ended up tucked into bed, snug and safe for the night. I want my characters to enjoy that same feeling at the end of the book, after I have put them through harsh and uncomfortable action, made them confront their weaknesses and exploit strengths they didn't know they had. It is not, perhaps, literarily fashionable, but it sure is great to read. Since I write for entertainment, I am not going to worry my pretty little head over whether the novel is literary or not. I just want my readers to be glued to the pages, unable to sleep until the end, when they shut the book with a sigh of satisfaction and tuck themselves away in their burrows—er, beds.

"I have written four Liz Sullivan books and plan to write at least two more. I am also exploring other possible series, including one with Sherlock Holmes

in it. Writing for a living is the most deeply satisfying job I've ever had, and in my time I've had plenty of jobs. I just hope I can continue doing this one."

* * *

SOGOLOW, Rosalie (K.) 1939-

PERSONAL: Born August 25, 1939, in Chicago, IL; daughter of Jack and Edith (Tarantur) Krulan; married Sidney R. Sogolow (an obstetrician and gynecologist), March 20, 1960; children: Wendi Sogolow Fast, Lawrence William. *Ethnicity:* "Jewish/Russian." *Education:* Attended University of Illinois, 1957-59; National College of Education, B.A., 1960; attended San Jose State University, 1992. *Religion:* Jewish. *Avocational interests:* Travel, photography.

ADDRESSES: Home—19695 Versailles Way, Saratoga, CA 95070.

CAREER: Chicago Public Schools, Chicago, IL, teacher, 1960-63; Rosalie's Accents, Saratoga, CA, interior designer, 1979-94; Jewish Family Service of Santa Clara Valley, Los Gatos, CA, teacher of English as a second language (ESL), principal of senior ESL program, 1987—. Board member and editor of San Jose *Hadassah Lifeline;* member and study group leader of Brandeis National Women's Committee; member of Hospice of the Valley Service League.

MEMBER: American Association of University Women.

AWARDS, HONORS: Dr. Cal Lubrin Memorial Award from Jewish Family Service, for community service, 1990; Chai Award from the Jewish Federation, 1995; J.C. Penney Golden Rule Award, 1995.

WRITINGS:

(Editor) *Memories from a Russian Kitchen: From Shtetl to Golden Land* (nonfiction), Fithian Press (Santa Barbara, CA), 1996.

WORK IN PROGRESS: Two Soups from One Chicken (and Other Bubbe Stories): Home Remedies and Amusing Anecdotes, completion expected in 1998; research on home remedies, superstitions, and folk tales.

SIDELIGHTS: Rosalie Sogolow has had a varied career. She obtained her bachelor's degree in educa-

tion, and went to work as a teacher in the Chicago public school system. Then, after her family moved to California, she tried her hand at interior design. Later, Sogolow became involved in the Jewish Family Service's English as a Second Language program; she focused especially on more elderly immigrants from the former Soviet Union. Her work with these people inspired her to edit a collection of both their remembrances and their recipes, 1996's *Memories from a Russian Kitchen: From Shtetl to Golden Land.* Sogolow has also served as an editor for the Jewish-American women's publication, *Hadassah Lifeline.*

Memories from a Russian Kitchen includes recollections from many eras of Russian-Jewish history, including the Communist Revolution in 1917 and the siege of Leningrad (now St. Petersburg) during World War II. Pogroms against the Jewish people, as well as times of celebration are recounted. A reviewer in *Publishers Weekly* hailed the volume as "a treat . . . warm and engaging." A critic in *Moment* summed it up as "a tasty mix of ethnic recipes with family accounts and anecdotes," but *Library Journal* emphasized that *Memories from a Russian Kitchen* is "much more than a cookbook, this is an oral history."

Sogolow intends to continue her research into Russian-Jewish culture. She told *CA*: "As a teacher, principal, and organizer of Jewish Family Service's senior ESL program, I have been privileged to work with hundreds of elderly (primarily Russian) emigres—wonderful, fascinating people, who have shared their lives with me and allowed me to become one of their 'family.' They have also given me a priceless gift: a better understanding of their history and culture.

"As eyewitnesses of an amazing century of Russian/Jewish life they have a treasure of experience to share. Helping them unlock these memories and preserve them for posterity has been a great joy to me and a motivational force in my writing."

BIOGRAPHICAL/CRITICAL SOURCES:

PERIODICALS

Library Journal, March 15, 1996.
Moment, April, 1996.
Publishers Weekly, January 8, 1996.

SOLORZANO, Carlos 1922-

PERSONAL: Born May 1, 1922, in San Marcos, Guatemala; married Beatrice Caso, September 3, 1946; children: one son, two daughters. *Education:* National University of Mexico, B.A., 1939, M.A., 1944, Ph.D., 1946.

ADDRESSES: Home—Condor 199, Col. Alpes Tlacopac, Mexico 01010 DF, Mexico.

CAREER: Playwright, novelist, and essayist. National University of Mexico, artistic director of the university theatre, 1952-62, professor, 1960-85, professor emeritus, 1985—. Director of National Theatre, 1977-82. Visiting lecturer at numerous universities in Mexico and abroad.

MEMBER: International P.E.N., Hispanic Society of America (corresponding member), Playwrights and Composers Society, Spanish Royal Academy of Language (corresponding member), Latin American Community of Writers Society.

WRITINGS:

Del sentimiento de lo plastico en la obra de Unamuno, [Mexico], 1944.
Dona Beatriz, la sin ventura (produced 1952), published in *Cuadernos americanos,* no. 59, 1951, published in book form, 1954.
El hechicero: tragedia en tres actos (produced 1952), Ediciones Cuadernos Americanos, 1955.
Las manos de Dios (produced in Mexico City, 1956), B. Costa-Amic, 1957, reprinted, Center for Curriculum Development, 1971, translation by W. Keith Leonard and Marlo T. Soria published as *The Hands of God,* Hiram College, 1968.
Mea Culpa (produced 1956), published in *Teatro Breve,* 1977.
El crucificado (produced 1958), published in *Tres actos,* 1959, translated as *The Crucifixion* in *The Orgy: Modern One-Act Plays from Latin America,* edited by Gerardo Luzuriaga and Robert S. Rudder, University of California Press, 1974.
Los fantoches (produced 1958), published in *Tres Actos,* 1959.
Cruce de vias (produced 1959), published in *Tres actos,* 1959, translation published as *Crossroads* in *Selected Latin American One-Act Plays,* edited by Francesca Colecchia and Julio Matas, University of Pittsburgh Press, 1973.
Tres actos, El Unicornio, 1959.

El sueno del angel (produced 1960), published in *Teatro,* 1972.

Teatro latinoamericano del siglo XX, Nueva Vision, 1961.

(Editor) *Teatro guatemalteco contemporaneo,* Aguilar, 1964.

(Editor) *El teatro hispanoamericano contemporaneo,* Fondo de Cultura Economica, 1964, reprinted, 1981.

El zapato (produced 1966), published in *Cosmos 2,* 1966, in *Teatro breve,* 1977.

El visitante (produced 1966).

(Editor) *Teatro breve hispano-americano contemporaneo,* Aguilar, 1970.

Las celdas, J. Mortiz, 1971.

Teatro, Editorial Universitaria Centroamericana, 1972.

(Editor and author of introduction) *El teatro actual latinoamericano,* De Andrea, 1972.

Testimonios teatrales de Mexico, Universidad Nacional Autonoma de Mexico, 1973.

Los falsos demonios, J. Mortiz, 1973.

Teatro breve, J. Mortiz, 1977.

Work has been included in numerous anthologies including *Uno, dos, tres: tres dramas mexicanos en un acto,* edited by Jeanine Gaucher-Shultz and Alfredo O. Morales, Odyssey Press, 1971, and *Teatro centroamericano contemporaneo,* del Pulgarcito, 1977. Contributor to journals and magazines.

SIDELIGHTS: Carlos Solorzano's works have been translated into English, French, Russian, Italian, Hungarian, Polish, and German.*

* * *

SOMMERS, Christina Hoff

PERSONAL: Daughter of Dolores; married Fred Sommers; children: Tamler (stepson), David.

ADDRESSES: Office—Department of Philosophy, Clark University, 950 Main St., Worcester, MA 01610.

CAREER: Clark University, Worcester, MA, associate professor of philosophy. Appointed to U.S. advisory panel on cultural diversity requirements in the college-accrediting process, 1991.

AWARDS, HONORS: Mellon Faculty Development Grant, Higgins Research Grant, both from Clark University.

WRITINGS:

(Compiler) *Vice and Virtue in Everyday Life: Introductory Readings in Ethics,* edited by Robert J. Fogelin, Harcourt Brace Jovanovich (San Diego, CA), 1985.

(Compiler) *Right and Wrong: Basic Readings in Ethics,* edited by Fogelin, Harcourt Brace Jovanovich, 1986.

Who Stole Feminism?: How Women Have Betrayed Women, Simon & Schuster (New York), 1994.

Contributor of articles to journals and periodicals, including *Chicago Tribune, New England Journal of Medicine, New Republic,* and *Wall Street Journal.*

SIDELIGHTS: Christina Hoff Sommers attracted wide attention for her controversial 1994 book, *Who Stole Feminism?: How Women Have Betrayed Women,* an indictment of the contemporary feminist movement. A teacher of ethics, history, and feminist theory, Sommers has also compiled two volumes of readings on ethics and was appointed by U.S. Education Secretary Lamar Alexander to a government advisory committee on cultural diversity requirements in the college accrediting process in 1991.

In *Who Stole Feminism?,* Sommers argues that feminism has turned from its beginnings in what the author calls "equity feminism"—an attempt at gaining equal opportunity and protection under the law—to what she labels "gender feminism"—proclaiming women's inherent difference from men and trying to change the legal, economic, educational, and political systems to favor this view of women. To illustrate her theories, Sommers offers accounts of proceedings at women's studies conferences she has attended and provides descriptions of how statistics have been misquoted to reinforce the picture of women as victims of society. For instance, according to Jean Bethke Elshtain in the *New Republic,* Sommers challenges a citation from feminist Gloria Steinem that "'in this country alone . . . about 150,000 females die of anorexia each year,'" and "discovers from the president of the American Anorexia and Bulimia Association that. . . . The organization's newsletter had written of 150,000 to 200,000 estimated *sufferers* from eating disorders." Elshtain further quotes Sommers as saying "[t]he National Center for Health

Statistics reported 101 deaths from anorexia in 1983 and sixty-seven deaths in 1988."

Opinions of *Who Stole Feminism?* range from Nina Auerbach's judgment in *New York Times Book Review* that the book "is so overwrought and underargued that it is unlikely to amuse or persuade," to *National Review* contributor Mary Lefkowitz's assertion that Sommers's work is an "excellent new book, which everyone interested in the subject ought to read, even if he is prepared to dislike it." Elshtain observed that "Sommers's analytical achievements here are owed to her journalistic stubbornness, to her energy in tracking down and exposing 'factoids' that have gained the status of 'fact'." Gertrude Himmelfarb, reviewing *Who Stole Feminism?* in *Times Literary Supplement,* hailed it as a "riveting account of the 'gender war'" taking place in the United States.

BIOGRAPHICAL/CRITICAL SOURCES:

PERIODICALS

Boston Globe, November 14, 1991, p. 24.
National Review, July 11, 1994, pp. 55-57.
New Republic, July 11, 1994, pp. 32-36.
New York Times Book Review, June 12, 1994, p. 13.
Times Literary Supplement, November 11, 1994, p. 20.*

* * *

SPASH, Clive L(aurence) 1962-

PERSONAL: Born March 10, 1962, in Reading, England; son of David (an engineer) and Patricia (a needlework teacher; maiden name, Fitzgerald) Spash. *Education:* University of Stirling, B.A. (with honors), 1984; University of British Columbia, M.Sc., 1987; University of Wyoming, Ph.D., 1993. *Politics:* Green.

ADDRESSES: Home—19 Silver Street, Cambridge, England, CB39EP. *Office*—Cambridge Research for the Environment, Department of Land Economy, University of Cambridge, England. *E-mail*—cls27@cam.ac.uk.

CAREER: University of Stirling, Stirling, Scotland, lecturer in environmental economics, 1990-95, assistant director of Environmental Economics Research Group, 1992-95, University of Cambridge, Lecturer, Department of Land Economy, 1996—, Director, Cambridge Research for the Environment; writer. Visiting lecturer at Lincoln University, New Zealand, 1993-94, Visiting Professor, Universite de Versailles, France 1996.

MEMBER: International Society for Ecological Economics, International Society for Environmental Ethics, Worldwide Fund for Nature, National Wildlife Federation, American Economics Association, Association of Environmental and Resource Economists, Cousteau Society, Green Action Movement, European Association of Environmental and Resource Economists, Royal Economic Society, Scottish Economic Association, Sea Shepherd Conservation Society, European Society of Ecologicial Economics (vice president, 1996—).

AWARDS, HONORS: Post-graduate scholarship from University of British Columbia, 1985-87; doctoral fellowship from University of Wyoming, 1987-90; award for outstanding dissertation in social sciences from University of Wyoming, 1993.

WRITINGS:

(With Nick Hanley) *Cost-Benefit Analysis and the Environment,* Edward Elgar (Cheltenham, UK), 1993.
Greenhouse Economics: Value and Ethics, Routledge, in press.

Contributor to books, including *Ecological Economics: The Science and Management of Sustainability,* edited by Robert Constanza, Columbia University Press (New York), 1991; *The New Global Oil Market: Understanding Energy Issues in the World Economy,* edited by Siamack Shojai, Praeger (Westport, CT), 1995; *Sustainable Development: Science, Ethics, and Law,* edited by John Lemons and Donald A. Brown, Kluwer Academic Publishers (Dordrecht, Netherlands), 1995; *Environmental Economics,* edited by John Foster, Routledge (London), 1996. *Natural Resource Economics: A Book of Readings,* edited by C. Gopalakrishnan, University of California Press (Berkeley, CA), in press.

Contributor to periodicals, including *Ecological Economics, Environmental Ethics,* and *Review of Political Economy.* Editor of *Green Values: Scottish Environmental Economics Discussion Group Newsletter,* 1990-93; co-editor of *European Association of Environmental and Research Economists News,* 1994—.

WORK IN PROGRESS: With Nick Hanley, *The Economics of Resource Use and Environmental Quality*, publication by Edward Elgar expected in 1998; research in biodiversity, environmental valuation, enhanced greenhouse effect, and ecological economics.

SIDELIGHTS: Clive L. Spash is an educator and author known for his expertise in environmental economics. From 1990 to 1995, he lectured on this subject at the University of Stirling in Scotland. At Stirling he also served as assistant director of the school's Environmental Economics Research Group from 1992 to 1995. In 1996, Spash joined the University of Cambridge as a lecturer in the Department of Land Economy and Director of Cambridge Research for the Environment.

Among Spash's writings is *Cost-Benefit Analysis and the Environment,* on which he collaborated with Nick Hanley. This book contains considerable analysis of relevant economic issues—including non-market valuations—and explores the ethics of environmental economics at a time when cost effectiveness sometimes takes precedent over environmentally responsible action. Reviewer Ross Cullen, writing in *Economic Journal,* declared that *Cost-Benefit Analysis and the Environment* "provide[s] an accessible and useful survey of the techniques employed on environment and resource issues." Cullen added that the volume "is valuable because it provides clear . . . treatments of topics," and he noted that it includes "excellent comprehensive references" and "useful appendices."

Spash is also the author of *Greenhouse Economics: Value and Ethics,* which is expected to appear in 1997.

Spash told *CA:* "My motivation has been a deep concern for the environment and the way in which humans impact upon ecosystems. There have been numerous people trying to get the environmental message across to policy makers, but few were on the inside of the institutional structures. This has slowly been changing, and I hope my work encourages that kind of change while adding to the voice of external lobby groups.

"In *Cost-Benefit Analysis and the Environment,* Nick Hanley and I were trying to take the reader from the theoretical to the practical and provide criticism along the way. This book will be followed by *The Economics of Resource Use and Environmental Quality,* a book critically explaining the use of environmental and resource economics in analyzing policy problems.

These two books will give a critical appraisal of the current economic approach to the environment.

"For me, writing is one part of expressing a concern for environmental responsibility and must be accompanied by often difficult changes in lifestyle. The environmental economists who forget the environment when they shut the office door at the end of the day are symptomatic of the society I am trying to change."

BIOGRAPHICAL/CRITICAL SOURCES:

PERIODICALS

Economic Journal, November, 1994, pp. 1488-1490.

* * *

SPLICHAL, Joachim 1954-

PERSONAL: Born July 22, 1954, in Spaichingen, Germany; son of Helmut and Berta Renk; came to United States in 1981; married, July 7, 1984; wife's name, Christine; children: two. *Education:* Attended Hotel Management School, Montreux, Switzerland.

ADDRESSES: *Office*—Patina/Pinot Corporate Offices, 5955 Melrose Ave., Los Angeles, CA 90038.

CAREER: Regency Club, Los Angeles, CA, chef, beginning 1981; Seventh Avenue Bistro, Los Angeles, co-developer and chef, c. 1982; Max Au Triangle, Los Angeles, owner and chef, beginning 1984; Patina Restaurant, Los Angeles, owner and chef, 1989—; also owner of restaurants: Patinette at MOCA, Pinot Bistro, Cafe Pinot, and Pinot Hollywood, and of Patina Catering; teacher of cooking classes. Worked in various restaurants throughout Europe; worked in France as chef saucier at La Bonne Auberge in Antibes, and L'Oasis in La Napoule, and as sous chef for four years at Chantecler Restaurant in the Hotel Negresco, Nice. Former consultant to Highlands Inn, Carmel, CA, Ventana Inn, Big Sur, CA, and Canyon Ranch resorts in Tucson, AZ, and Lenox, MA; consultant to Windstar Cruises.

AWARDS, HONORS: "Youngest and Most Creative Chef" award, Cercle Epicurien Society, Germany;

named "Best California Chef," 1991, and "Best Chef of the Year," 1991 and 1994, both from James Beard Foundation.

WRITINGS:

(With Charles Perry) *Patina Cookbook: Spuds, Truffles, and Wild Gnocchi,* Collins (San Francisco, CA), 1995.

SIDELIGHTS: Joachim Splichal, writes *Gourmet* contributor Caroline Bates, "dazzled diners in the early days of the late Seventh Street Bistro with his potato artistry and an all-vegetable *prix-fixe* menu—a revolutionary idea in the Los Angeles of 1985." Born in Germany, trained in Switzerland and France, Splichal played an important part in the renaissance of California cuisine in the 1980s with a series of restaurants, beginning with the Seventh Street Bistro mentioned by Bates. In 1989, he opened Patina, a Melrose Avenue eating establishment, followed by four other eateries in the Los Angeles area. Restaurant critic John Mariani, writing in *Esquire,* praised Patina as "L. A.'s finest haute-cuisine restaurant."

In Splichal's first cookbook, *Patina Cookbook: Spuds, Truffles and Wild Gnocchi,* the chef includes more than sixty recipes, including "Potato Oyster Ravioli" and the making of a gourmet club sandwich. These two dishes, along with others in the book, uphold Splichal's reputation for what the *Publisher Weekly* reviewer called "tweaking traditional recipes." As an example, in these two instances, the potatoes replace the pasta in the first recipe; while in the second, sweetbreads, spinach, and duck liver are used instead of more typical sandwich ingredients. Observing that the complex recipes in the book are not intended for those interested in quick and easy cooking, the reviewer noted that "Splichal's spirit, devotion and talent shine through" them all. Attesting to Splichal's reputation, the *Patina Cookbook* is the first in a "Great Chefs/Great Restaurants" series planned by Collins.

BIOGRAPHICAL/CRITICAL SOURCES:

PERIODICALS

Esquire, November, 1993, pp. 53-54.
Gourmet, October, 1995, pp. 38, 40; May, 1996, p. 66.
Publishers Weekly, April 3, 1995, p. 59.

SPOTA, Luis
See SPOTA (SAAVEDRA), Luis

* * *

SPOTA (SAAVEDRA), Luis 1925-1985

PERSONAL: Born July 13, 1925, in Mexico City, Mexico; died of pancreatic cancer, January 20, 1985, in Mexico City, Mexico.

CAREER: Journalist and writer. Television news commentator.

AWARDS, HONORS: City of Mexico prizes for *Mas cornadas da el hambre,* 1950, *Las grandes aguas,* 1951, and *Vagabunda;* National Literature Prize for the play *El area de los Sometidos.*

WRITINGS:

De la noche al dia (stories), Tollocan, c. 1945.
El coronel fue echado al mar (novel; title means "The Colonel Was Tossed to the Sea"), [Mexico], 1947.
Mas cornadas da el hambre (novel), [Mexico], c. 1948, 2nd edition, D. F. Porrua, 1959, translation by Barnaby Conrad published as *The Wounds of Hunger,* Houghton, Mifflin, 1957.
Murieron a mitad del rio (novel; title means "They Died in the Middle of the River"), [Mexico], 1948, 4th edition, Costa-Amic, 1973.
Vagabunda (novel), [Mexico], 1950, 2nd edition, D. F. Porrua, 1959.
La estrella vacia (novel; title means "The Empty Star"), Libreria de M. Porrua, 1950.
Casi el paraiso (novel), Fondo de Cultura Economica, 1956, revised edition, Diana, 1970, translation by Ray Morrison and Renate Morrison published as *Almost Paradise,* Doubleday, 1963.
Las horas violentas (novel; title means "The Violent Hours"), 1958, 2nd edition, Libro Mex, 1959, reprinted, Costa-Amic, 1981.
La sangre enemiga (novel), Fondo de Cultura Economica, 1959, revised edition, Grijalbo (Mexico), 1981, translation by Robert Molloy published as *The Enemy Blood,* Doubleday, 1961.
El tiempo de la ira (novel), Fondo de Cultura Economica, 1960, reprinted, Grijalbo (Mexico), 1981, translation by Robert Molloy published as *The Time of Wrath,* Doubleday, 1962.

El area de los sometidos (play; title means "The Area of the Vanquished"), Costa-Amic, 1962.

La pequena edad (novel; title means "The Tender Age"), Fondo de Cultura Economica, 1964.

La carcajada del gato (novel; title means "The Cat's Laugh"), Mortiz, 1964, reprinted, Grijalbo (Barcelona), 1977.

Los suenos del insomnio (novel; title means "The Dreams of Insomnia"), Mortiz, 1966, reprinted, Grijalbo (Barcelona), 1977.

Lo de antes (novel; title means "What Went Before"), Diana, 1968, reprinted, Grijalbo (Mexico), 1981.

Las cajas (novel), Mortiz, 1973.

El viaje, Mortiz, 1973.

Palabras mayores (novel), Grijalbo (Barcelona), 1975, revised, 1981.

Retrato hablado (novel), Grijalbo (Barcelona), 1975.

El rostro del sueno, Grijalbo (Mexico), 1979.

Mitad oscura, Grijalbo (Mexico), 1982.

Paraiso 25, Grijalbo (Mexico), 1983.

Also author of *Las grandes aguas, La plaza, Sobra la marcha,* and *El primer dia,* all novels. Author of essays, plays, and biographies. Contributor to *Hoy, Excelsior, Novedades, Politica,* and *Espejo.*

SIDELIGHTS: Luis Spota was one of Mexico's most popular and prolific novelists. Though his works sometimes met with mixed reviews, he three times won the City of Mexico Prize, one of the country's highest literary honors, and his novels are widely read in his country.

Spota was born into wealth, but his family lost its fortune in 1934, and Spota left school to support himself with a variety of jobs, including brief stints as a bullfighter, seaman, waiter, and encyclopedia salesman. He eventually obtained work as an office boy at a weekly magazine in Mexico and thus began his journalism career. Spota worked for several Mexican newspapers, developing the brash, sometimes sensational journalistic style that would also characterize his novels.

Many of Spota's early novels are autobiographical, incorporating knowledge gained from his various occupations. The 1947 *El coronel fue echado al mar* ("The Colonel Was Tossed to the Sea") drew on his experiences aboard a steamer. In the novel an American ship is carrying wounded soldiers, but hiding this fact from the enemy. Several patients die, but no "burials" occur. After each death a great abundance of meat is served and the crew begins to suspect they are eating the dead. A nurse clears up the mystery, explaining that the bodies require storage in the refrigerators for preservation until autopsies can be performed. The grotesque humor of the story became a trademark of later novels. Though Walter M. Langford, writing in *Mexican Novel Comes of Age,* did not consider *El coronel fue echado al mar* one of Spota's best novels, he asserted that "two characteristics that are to become basic to his style are readily visible in this work: a true capacity for creating dialogue that is natural to the characters and the circumstances, and an equal talent for narration that holds the reader's attention from start to finish."

Spota's familiarity with the bullring served him in the novel *Mas cornadas da el hambre,* later translated as *The Wounds of Hunger.* The story tells of man driven to become a bullfighter because, as the bullfighters say, "the wounds of hunger wound worse" than gorings by the bulls. Praised for its unromantic, brutal depiction not only of bullfighting but of poverty, the novel received the City of Mexico Prize in 1950. Spota, who described himself as a political leftist, continued to focus on social concerns in other novels. His 1948 novel, *Murieron a mitad del rio* ("They Died in the Middle of the River"), for instance, describes the lives of Mexicans who illegally immigrate to the United States and suffer exploitation as laborers, while the 1958 *Las horas violentas* ("The Violent Hours") focuses on the control over Mexican labor unions, depicting twelve hours of a strike in a canning factory.

Spota's highly acclaimed and popular 1956 novel, *Casi el paraiso,* translated as *Almost Paradise,* satirizes Mexico's upper class, "lay[ing] bare the sham, hypocrisy, and false values of many among the highest echelon of Mexican society," wrote Langford. The protagonist—a self-styled Italian playboy/prince—almost achieves paradise by marrying into a wealthy Mexican family, but his plans fail when his true origins come to light.

With the publication in 1960 of *El tiempo de la ira,* translated as *The Time of Wrath,* Spota turned to the subject of dictatorship, a familiar theme in Latin-American literature. Beginning with Cesar Dario's plans to overthrow the government, the novel traces the fictional leader's rise to power until his assassination by an aide. Langford named *El tiempo de la ira* among the most outstanding novels on the topic, praising the detailed characterization of Dario as a leader concerned about his country's welfare, but ruthless in protecting his own power.

La carcajada del gato, published in 1964, also met with critical approval. Recalling *Casi el paraiso* with its dark, pessimistic tone, *La carcajada del gato* concerns a demented father who imprisons his family at home, forbidding any contact with the outside world in an effort to fashion a new version of humanity. This results in such sordid developments as incest—and eventually—the family's plot to murder the father.

While some reviewers have objected to the violence and cynicism that pervades much of Spota's writings, they have praised his reforming satiric voice evident in other works. Spota's direct, bold prose, together with fast-paced narratives and imaginative plots, makes for arresting and suspenseful fiction.

BIOGRAPHICAL/CRITICAL SOURCES:

BOOKS

Langford, Walter M., *The Mexican Novel Comes of Age,* University of Notre Dame Press, 1971.
Spota, Luis, *The Wounds of Hunger,* Houghton, Mifflin, 1957.

OBITUARIES:

PERIODICALS

Chicago Tribune, January 23, 1985.
Washington Post, January 23, 1985.

* * *

SRIVASTAVA, C(handrika) P(rasad) 1920-

PERSONAL: Born July 8, 1920, in Unnao, India; son of B. B. Srivastava; married Nirmala Salve, April 7, 1947; children: Kalpana (daughter), Saphana Srivastava Varma. *Education:* Lucknow University, B.A. (with first class honors), 1940, B.A. (with honors), 1941, M.A. (with first class honors), 1942, LL.B. (with first class honors), 1944. *Politics:* "One world, one human family." *Religion:* "Vishwa Nirmala Dharma (universal pure religion)." *Avocational interests:* Music, tennis, reading.

ADDRESSES: Home—Pratishthan, P.B.2, N.D.A. Rd., Poona, India. *Office*—International Maritime Organization, 4 Albert Embankment, London SE1 7SR, England and Palazzo Doria, 15060 Cahella Ligure, Alessandria, Italy; fax 0039-143-99384.

CAREER: Indian Ministry of Commerce, under-secretary, 1948-49; City of Lucknow, India, city magistrate, 1950; District of Meerut, India, district magistrate, 1951-52; Directorate General of Shipping, officer on special duty, 1953, deputy director general, 1954-57; Ministry of Transport, deputy secretary, 1958; Directorate General of Shipping, senior director general, 1959-60; Shipping Corp. of India Ltd., Bombay, managing director, 1961-64; Office of the Prime Minister of India, joint secretary, 1964-66; Shipping Corp. of India Ltd., managing director and chairperson of board of directors, 1966-73; International Maritime Organization, London, England, secretary general, 1974-89, secretary general emeritus, 1989—. Indian Institute of Foreign Trade, member of governing body, 1970; Indian Institute of Management, Ahmedabad, member of governing body, 1972-73; Institute of Marine Technologists of India, president, 1972-89; Seatrade Academy, member of advisory board, 1978-89; Plymouth Polytechnic, honorary fellow, 1979; World Maritime University, founding chancellor, 1983-91, chancellor emeritus, 1991—. Central Inland Water Transport Corp., director, 1967; Mogul Line Ltd., chairperson of board of directors, 1967-73; Indian National Shipowners Association, president, 1971-73; Reserve Bank of India, director of Central Board, 1972-73; Bombay Chamber of Commerce and Industry, member of general committee, 1971; International Chamber of Commerce, member of board of International Maritime Bureau, 1981-89, member of board of directors of Centre for Maritime Cooperation, 1985-89; Lloyd's Register, specially elected member of General Committee, 1989. United Nations Plenipotentiary Conference on the Code of Conduct for Liner Conferences, president, 1973-74; chairperson of Seatrade Annual Award for Achievement, 1988, and Indian Register of Shipping, 1991; vice-president of Sea Cadet Council, 1970-73, Welsh Centre for International Affairs of the United Kingdom, 1989, and Advisory Committee on Pollution of the Sea, 1989; member of National Shipping Board of India, 1959-73, Merchant Navy Training Board of India, 1959-73, National Welfare Board for Seafarers of India, 1966-73, American Bureau of Shipping, 1969, and National Harbour Board of India, 1970-73.

MEMBER: International Federation of Shipmasters Associations (honorary member), International Maritime Pilots Association (honorary member), Institution of Marine Technologists of India (honorary

member), Royal Society of Arts (England; fellow), Marine Society of the United Kingdom (life member of governing board), Royal Institute of Navigation (England; honorary member), Nautical Institute (England; fellow), Warsash Association (England; honorary member), Anglo-Belgian Club (London), Willingdon Sports Club (Bombay), Poona Club.

AWARDS, HONORS: Padma Bhushan, 1972; Colombian Admiral Padilla Award and Gran Amigo del Mar Award, both 1978; Commandeur du Merite, French Maritime Award and Commander, Norwegian Order of St. Olav, both 1982; Italian Grande Ufficiale dell'Ordine al Merito, Portuguese Order of Prince Henry the Navigator, Polish Gold Order of the Distinguished Seafarer, and Greek Nautical Medal, first class, all 1983; Gold Mercury International Award, Ad Personam and Orden Cruz Peruana al Marito Naval, both 1984; LL.D., Bhopal University, 1984; Panamanian Orden de Manual Amador Guerrero, 1985; Brazilian Orden do Merito Naval and Commander's Cross, Polish Order of Merit, both 1986; LL.D, University of Wales, 1987; Silver Medal of Honor, City of Malmo, Sweden, 1988; LL.D., University of Malta, 1988; Knight Great Band from Liberian Humane Order of African Redemption, Seatrade Award for Achievement from Seatrade Organization, BIMCO Appreciation Award from Baltic and International Maritime Council, Commander's Cross of the Order of Merit of the Federal Republic of Germany, and Commander Grand Cross, of Sweden's Royal Order of the Polar Star, all 1989; Knight Commander, British Order of St. Michael and St. George, 1990; Order of Merit, first grade, from Arab Republic of Egypt, 1990; International Maritime Prize from United Nations International Maritime Organization, 1992; Encomienda de Numero, Spanish Orden de Isabel la Catolica, 1994.

WRITINGS:

'*Lal Bahadur Shastri, Prime Minister of India, 1964-1966: A Life of Truth in Politics,* Oxford University Press (Oxford, England), 1995.

Contributor to shipping journals and newspapers.

WORK IN PROGRESS: Research on secularism in India.

SIDELIGHTS: C. P. Srivastava told *CA:* "I am motivated by love of my country, a firm belief in the concept of one human family, one God, and a hu-mane society. My work has been influenced by Aristotle, Abraham Lincoln, and Gandhi. I am inspired by the integrity, moral purity, complete dedication to right conduct, humility, and wisdom of Mr. Lal Bahadur Shastri."

* * *

STACKPOLE, Michael A(ustin) 1957-

PERSONAL: Born November 27, 1957, in Wausau, WI; son of James Ward (a physician) and Janet (an educator and community volunteer; maiden name, Kerin) Stackpole; companion of Elizabeth Turner Danforth (an artist). *Ethnicity:* "Caucasian/Irish-American." *Education:* University of Vermont, B.A., 1979. *Politics:* Democrat. *Religion:* Roman Catholic. *Avocational interests:* Indoor soccer, arena football, gaming, shooting.

ADDRESSES: Home—Scottsdale, AZ. *Office*—P.O. Box 60333, Phoenix, AZ 85082-0333. *Agent*—Ricia Mainhardt, 612 Argyle, No. 5-L, Brooklyn, NY 11230.

CAREER: Flying Buffalo, Inc., Scottsdale, AZ, game designer, 1979-87; writer, 1987—.

MEMBER: Game Manufacturers Association (chairperson of Industry Watch Committee), Science Fiction and Fantasy Writers of America, Academy of Gaming Arts and Design, Phoenix Skeptics (executive director, 1988—).

AWARDS, HONORS: H. G. Wells Awards, best role playing adventure, 1983, for *Citybook I,* and 1984, for *Stormhaven;* Best Adventure Game, Computer Gaming World, 1988, for *Wasteland,* and 1989, for *Neuromancer; Wasteland* was inducted into the Computer Gaming World's Hall of Fame, 1993; Meritorious Service Award, Game Manufacturers Association, 1993; inducted into Academy of Gaming Arts and Design Hall of Fame, 1994.

WRITINGS:

NOVELS

Natural Selection, FASA Corp. (Chicago, IL), 1992.
Assumption of Risk, FASA Corp., 1993.
Bred for War, FASA Corp., 1994.
Once a Hero, Bantam (New York), 1994.

Mutant Chronicles: Dementia, FASA Corp., 1994.
Malicious Intent, FASA Corp., 1996.
Talion: Revenant (fantasy), Bantam, in press.
A Hero Born (fantasy), Harper, in press.
Grave Covenant (science fiction), FASA Corp., in press.

"WARRIOR" SERIES

Warrior: En Garde, FASA Corp., 1988.
Warrior: Riposte, FASA Corp., 1988.
Warrior: Coupe, FASA Corp., 1989.

"BLOOD OF KERENSKY" SERIES

Lethal Heritage, FASA Corp., 1990.
Blood Legacy, FASA Corp., 1990.
Lost Destiny, FASA Corp., 1991.

"DARK CONSPIRACY" SERIES

A Gathering Evil, Game Designers Workshop (Bloomington, IL), 1991.
Evil Ascending, Game Designers Workshop, 1991.
Evil Triumphant, Game Designers Workshop, 1992.

"STAR WARS X-WING" SERIES

Rogue Squadron, Bantam, 1996.
Wedge's Gamble, Bantam, 1996.
The Krytos Trap, Bantam, 1996.
The Bacta War, Bantam, in press.

GAMES

Citybook I, Flying Buffalo (Scottsdale, AZ), 1983.
Stormhaven, Flying Buffalo, 1984.
Wasteland, Electronic Arts/Interplay Productions, 1988.
Neuromancer, Interplay Productions, 1989.

OTHER

(Editor with Liz Danforth) *Mages Blood and Old Bones,* Flying Buffalo, 1992.

Author of nonfiction books on gaming. Work represented in anthologies, including *Shrapnel,* FASA Corp., 1988; *Into the Shadows,* FASA Corp., 1990; *An Armory of Swords,* edited by Fred Saberhagen, Tor Books (New York), 1995; *Warriors of Blood and Dreams,* Avon (New York), 1995; *Superheroes,* Ace (New York), 1995; and *Insufficient Evidence: Distant Planes,* Harper, 1996. Contributor of short stories to magazines, including *Amazing Stories, Challenge, Star Wars Adventure Journal, Kage, Autoduel Quarterly,* and *Space Gamer.*

WORK IN PROGRESS: Eyes of Silver, a fantasy novel, publication by Bantam expected in 1998; research on World War I, serial killers, folklore, and mythology.

SIDELIGHTS: Michael A. Stackpole told *CA:* "My writing process is pretty basic. I tend to work in three-hour blocks, morning and afternoon, usually turning out a chapter per session. I work very fast by comparison with many of my peers. It is often suggested that a writer who works fast cannot do good work, but I think that's utterly fallacious. People in all manner of professions work at different speeds and, in almost all of them, efficiency and speed is considered a good thing. Whether I write well when writing fast is a matter for each reader to decide.

"I believe that writers and readers are involved in an elaborate game of 'Name That Tune.' A reader's job is to say to himself, 'Okay, it's page ninety-seven, and I know how this story will end.' The writer's job is to keep laying the story out in a manner that precludes the reader from being right. When it is done correctly, the reader can look back and find all the clues laid out there. While I seldom reread novels myself, I know my readers do, so I like to toss in little details that emerge only on a second or third read.

"My motivations for writing are simple. I want to write the kind of story I like to read. I want to create stories that entertain the readers. I want to make readers feel for characters and care about what happens to them because, by involving a reader on an emotional level, a book can allow the reader to experience things that are outside the purview of a normal life. I also write for money, because bills have to be paid.

"Much of my work is set in brand-name universes, areas where other writers refuse to work because they think they will be too restricted. I don't feel restricted, because I do my research and learn very quickly what is out of bounds and what areas I am free to explore. I also make a corner of that universe my own, so I am at home there and can tell the kind of story I like to tell. Readers bring to these books a set of assumptions about the kind of story that will be told, and that allows me to thwart them, distract them, and ultimately surprise them. No one really

wants to read a story in which they know what will happen, so I constantly work at exploding preconceptions while providing an entertaining story.

"A number of writers have influenced me. From Edgar Rice Burroughs I learned how to structure a plot, and I got a refresher course in that from Fredrick Forsyth. Walter Gibson, Lester Dent, and Rex Stout all showed me how to make fascinating characters from individuals who are largely unknowable. J. R. R. Tolkien showed how a contemporary author can tap into the elements of myth, Dennis L. McKiernan and Stephan Donaldson showed how it could be done differently and better, and Roger Zelazny showed how the use of detail can suggest whole universes.

"Much of my work is military in nature. I find warfare fascinating and decidedly terrifying. Except for a natural disaster, war is the most catastrophic thing that can happen to a human being. Despite its horrors, war is a crucible that creates heroes, and it is their stories that I like to tell. My books don't praise war, but they praise the triumph of individuals over war.

"I also include politics in my books, because I find the games people play to obtain and preserve power are very interesting. Political maneuvering often resembles a game of chess, with gambits set up, exchanges offered, and traps set. The fun part about stories is that, every so often, a pawn can stand up and refuse to be used. Politics is not an exact science, and that makes it tricky to deal with and fun to write about (and vilifying politicians is so cathartic!)."

* * *

STAPLES, Brent 1951-

PERSONAL: Born in 1951, in Chester, PA; son of Melvin (a truck driver) and Geneva (a homemaker; maiden name, Patterson) Staples. *Education:* Widener University, B.A. (cum laude), 1973; University of Chicago, Ph.D., 1977.

ADDRESSES: Office—*New York Times,* 229 W. 43rd St., New York, NY 10036.

CAREER: Adjunct professor of psychology at colleges in Pennsylvania and Illinois, 1977-81; *Chicago Sun-Times,* Chicago, IL, reporter, 1982-83; *New York Times,* New York, editorial writer, 1983—.

AWARDS, HONORS: Danforth Fellowship for graduate study.

WRITINGS:

Parallel Time: Growing Up in Black and White (autobiography), Random House (New York), 1994.

Contributor of articles to periodicals, including *New York Woman.*

SIDELIGHTS: New York Times editorial writer Brent Staples is the author of *Parallel Time: Growing Up in Black and White,* an autobiography that details his rise from an underprivileged childhood to his acquisition of a prestigious post at the *Times.* Although Staples is an African-American, his book is not about what has been called the "black experience;" in fact, Staples is quoted by Paul Galloway, writing in the *Chicago Tribune,* as saying: "I despise the expression ['black experience']. . . . Black people's lives in this country are too varied to be reduced to a single term. . . . I'm writing about universal themes—family and leaving home and developing your own identity—which all Americans can enjoy and understand. . . . Being black enriches my experience; it doesn't define me." Staples, therefore, objected to his book's release during Black History Month, which he says "ghettoizes literature." But reviewers of *Parallel Time* appeared to recognize the autonomous stance Staples assumes in his book. *New York Times* contributor Michael Eric Dyson, for example, wrote: "Staples has surpassed the need for imitation, revealing a resolutely distinct voice as he negotiates the treacherous shoals of racial identity in American culture. . . . [Staples's book] reminds us that the best personal writing is born of the courage to confront oneself." Abigail Thernstrom, in a *Times Literary Supplement* review, concurred: "Staples is speaking for himself; he has written a deeply personal, moving memoir that contains no overt 'message for our time.'"

The oldest son of nine children, Staples was born and raised in Chester, Pennsylvania, then a prosperous shipbuilding center, where his father worked as a truck driver. Although he can recall a time when the family's needs were met, Staples writes that his father's increasingly heavy drinking caused the family's decline and loss of security. In the 1960s the family was further devastated by the poverty that came to Chester as some 40,000 people were suddenly jobless as a result of plant closings. Staples and his family moved seven times before he finished jun-

ior high school, running from landlords before they were evicted, and eluding creditors. "The chaos of these moves swallowed things that would never be seen again," Staples wrote in an excerpt of *Parallel Time* published in the *New York Times*. "Family portraits. Volumes from the set of encyclopedias. Legal documents of every sort, including birth certificates, leaving some of us uncertain of when we were born. Each new house was a change of skin."

Despite the interruptions in his life caused by frequent moves, Staples managed to graduate from high school, but with little thought of going to college. A chance meeting with a college professor, however, resulted in his acceptance into Project Prepare, a program that recruited 23 black students for attendance at PMC Colleges (Pennsylvania Military College and Penn Morton College), later to become Widener University. There, Staples thrived; he was president of his freshman class, he was regularly on the dean's list, he graduated cum laude, and he earned a Danforth Fellowship to assist him in pursuing graduate studies.

Staples studied for his doctorate in behavioral sciences at the University of Chicago. He was at once enthralled with the gray turrets and towers of the university, and enjoyed taking long walks along Lake Michigan at night. His peaceful solitude was disrupted one night, however, by the realization that his presence made others uneasy, especially whites, as they passed by this tall, broad-shouldered black man in the dark. "I'd been a fool," Staples writes in *Parallel Time*. "I'd been grinning at people who were frightened to death of me. I did violence to them by just being. . . . I became expert in the language of fear. Couples locked arms or reached for each other's hand when they saw me. . . . I tried to be innocuous but didn't know how." At first when he realized others were afraid of him, Staples went out of his way, literally, to ease their fears, taking a different path or changing his pace so that others would know he was not following them. Or he would begin whistling; his melodic renditions of Beatles tunes or Vivaldi compositions seemed to render him harmless in the minds of passersby.

One day, however, Staples tired of accommodating the unwarranted fears of others. As a white couple approached him, he saw them draw close to one another, and heard their conversation abruptly halt, as though their attention turned from conversing to avoiding harm. Normally Staples would have begun whistling and moving out of their way. For some

reason, on this night he deviated, heading towards them so they had to separate for him to pass through. The fear in their eyes caused Staples to break out in laughter, and from then on he found great amusement in playing "Scatter the Pigeons," as he dubbed his game. Commenting on Staples's pastime, Jack E. White wrote in his *Time* magazine review of *Parallel Time:* "There are few better examples in literature of the contained fury toward whites that grips even the most outwardly docile black man."

Staples earned his Ph.D. in 1977 with his thesis on the mathematics of decision-making and went on to hold several teaching positions before accepting a reporter's position at the *Chicago Sun-Times*. He later joined the staff of the *New York Times,* where he serves on the editorial board, writing editorials on politics and culture. His first full-length publication, *Parallel Time,* is Staples's autobiography detailing his rise to success. But it is also the grim story of his younger brother Blake, a drug dealer who was killed by a drug customer. Staples had tried to help Blake escape from his life as a drug-dealer, even offering to buy him a plane ticket to a new start in life, but Blake never managed to change his situation. Blake's death came as no shock to Staples, who had prepared himself over and over again, imagining Blake's death and rehearsing his funeral, as he became resigned to the increasing likelihood that Blake was never going to escape his bleak existence and would die young. Reviewer Verlyn Klinkenborg, writing in the *New York Times Book Review,* found that an "important parallel in *Parallel Time*" is "the one between black and black. Brent Staples has a shadow in this book: his younger brother Blake. . . . Because he died, Blake Staples is quintessentially the young man who did not escape Chester, who barely escaped adolescence. Had he lived, he might have been able to grow into something less quintessential." Nevertheless, Klinkenborg observed: "*Parallel Time* is not a tract or apologia, nor is it intended to be a chronicle of injustice. It is a complex portrait of a worldly education, written at times with affection, at times with a sting." Klinkenborg added: "a memoir is not a door through which others can flee the past. No one gets out but the author."

BIOGRAPHICAL/CRITICAL SOURCES:

BOOKS

Contemporary Black Biography, Volume 8, Gale (Detroit), 1995.
Staples, Brent, *Parallel Time: Growing Up in Black and White,* Random House (New York), 1994.

PERIODICALS

Chicago Tribune, March 7, 1994.
Nation, April 25, 1994, pp. 562-565.
New York Review of Books, April 6, 1995, pp. 41-46.
New York Times, February 6, 1994; March 21, 1994, pp. C1, C5.
New York Times Book Review, February 20, 1994, p. 1.
Time, March 7, 1994, p. 68.
Times Literary Supplement, June 10, 1994, pp. 14-15.*

* * *

STARBUCK, George (Edwin) 1931-1996

OBITUARY NOTICE—See index for *CA* sketch: Born June 15, 1931, in Columbus, OH; died of Parkinson's disease, August 15, 1996, in Tuscaloosa, AL. Editor, educator, and poet. Starbuck was the author of comic verse that addressed issues of importance to its creator, such as anti-Vietnam war sentiments. According to a contributor in the *New York Times* he was "once called the thinking man's Ogden Nash." Starbuck got his start in the publishing business in 1958 at Houghton Mifflin Co. as an editor in its trade department. After two years in Italy as an American Academy fellow, he joined the faculty at the State University of New York. From 1964 to 1967, he was an associate professor at the Writers Workshop at the University of Iowa, which was followed by three years as director of the program. In 1971, he began work at Boston University as a professor of creative writing and as director of its graduate programs. He left Boston University nearly two decades later. Starbuck received recognition for his poetry in 1960 as the winner of the Yale Series of Younger Poets Award. He later received an American Academy and Institute of Arts and Letters award. His volumes of poetry include *Bone Thoughts, White Paper, Elegy in a Country Church Yard, Desperate Measures, Talkin' B.A. Blues: The Life and a Couple of Deaths of Ed Teashack, or How I Discovered B.U., Met God, and Became an International Figure,* and *The Argot Merchant Disaster: Poems, New and Selected.*

OBITUARIES AND OTHER SOURCES:

BOOKS

Writers Directory, St. James Press, 1995.

PERIODICALS

New York Times, August 17, 1996, p. 26.

* * *

STEINBERG, Clarence B. 1929-

PERSONAL: Born June 3, 1929, in Brooklyn, NY; son of Israel J. (a farmer) and Bella (a farmer) Steinberg; married August, 1960; wife's name, Judith S. (died, 1992); children: Claude M., Mark E. *Ethnicity:* "White." *Education:* City College of New York (now City College of the City University of New York), A.B., 1952; University of Connecticut, M.A., 1957; attended Yale University, 1957-58; University of Pennsylvania, Ph.D., 1969. *Politics:* Democrat. *Religion:* Jewish. *Avocational interests:* Archaeology, classical music, theater, literature, travel.

ADDRESSES: Home—9503 Wire Ave., Silver Spring, MD 20901. *Office*—United States Department of Agriculture, Agricultural Marketing Service, Fourteenth and Independence Ave., Washington, DC 20250.

CAREER: Delaware Valley College, Doylestown, PA, assistant professor of English, 1960-68; University of Maryland, College Park, MD, assistant professor of language and literature, 1968-75; Board of Veterans Appeals, Washington, DC, management analyst, 1980-86; U.S. Department of Agriculture, Washington, public affairs specialist, 1986—. Served as community association vice president; and as co-president of his local Parent Teacher Association, 1978-83.

MEMBER: Modern Language Society of Helsinki, Office of Professional Employees of U.S. Department of Agriculture.

WRITINGS:

(With Abraham D. Lavender) *Jewish Farmers of the Catskills: A Century of Survival,* University Press of Florida (Gainsville, FL), 1995.

WORK IN PROGRESS: Research in Mayan history and on Eastern European partisans during World War II.

SIDELIGHTS: Clarence B. Steinberg was able to draw on a great deal of personal data for his 1995 volume, *Jewish Farmers of the Catskills: A Century of Survival,* while his coauthor, Abraham D. Lavender, was responsible for some of the interviews which help fill out the history of the Jewish farming communities of the Catskill mountain range. The book begins with an overview of the role of farming in Jewish history, and moves into early Zionist projects to promote farming among Jews. The authors also discuss the greater freedom available to U.S. Jews to farm: often these people emigrated from European countries in which they were not allowed to own land because of their religion and ethnicity. The effects of the Great Depression and World War II upon Jewish farms are enumerated and explained, as are the adjustments made by farming families to economic times not as hospitable to farmers. For instance, in some homes, the father worked in New York City except for the summers, when he devoted his efforts to farming, while the mother and children took care of the farm all year round. Other families turned their farms into the popular Jewish resorts of the Catskills, where Jewish comedians often got their start in show business. The role of religion in the Jewish farmers' lives, as well as their integration as a community with non-Jews, is also explicated in *Jewish Farmers of the Catskills.* In addition, the book recounts the Jewish farmers of the Catskills pioneering development of farming cooperatives.

Many reviewers had kind words for *Jewish Farmers of the Catskills.* M. F. Jacobson, holding forth in *Social and Behavioral Sciences,* called the volume "carefully executed social history, nicely vivified by oral history and other firsthand accounts." Jerome E. Fischer, critiquing the book in *Contemporary Jewry,* praised it as "carefully researched" and "richly documented," further declaring that "the scholar will delight in the detailed documentation and the layperson will find pleasure in browsing. It is a valuable contribution to the history of Jews in America." Sylvia Jorrin, discussing *Jewish Farmers of the Catskills* in the *Delaware County Times,* concluded it to be "an important one to read for anyone interested in the past or future of farming in America today," because "the examples given are of hard times, punctuated with stick-to-itiveness and courage that typifies the voluntary American immigrant. The underlying thread of a combination of self and mutual help is an inspiration." She went on to emphasize: "This is a book worth reading."

Steinberg told *CA:* "I suppose I write for the same reasons that most people do, to tell significant truths. Some are known but denied, some unknown but embraceable if teased from hiding. I like to tease them out of hiding, whether explicating a Chaucerian or a Beowulfian passage, or tracing Tudor themes in Shakespeare's dark comedies, or describing lives of the Catskill Jewish farmers. Shaped when plain people read history and literature, I think automatically in history's two dimensions—events, and causes and effects of events. Then, depending on circumstance, I elaborate to literature's third—description and characterization. I've not written fiction, but am toying with some themes from antiquity.

"I wrote *Jewish Farmers* in three-hour evening spurts as a Federal worker, doing library research weekends and interviewing the book's people over several years. Then I sent a draft to my co-author, who added sections from interviews he took, and which, in turn, I attempted to render into a consistent style.

"Ideally, I'd craft a rough text quickly after getting my background straight, and fill in the blanks later. I do revise both for style and substance, especially for substance, when the materials I call on provoke new insights. That happens about a third of the way through a project, generally with good result.

"I began writing *Jewish Farmers* as simple history. Interviews and photos moved it almost to characterization and description. I suppose Clifford Geertz's 'thick brush' for historical writing comes closest to the style of the book's penultimate manuscript, which, rightly trimmed for its genre, was published.

"I hope *Jewish Farmers* fingers the intersects of men and their institutions, providing a mode for understanding other groups' lives. I hope its intersects also shed worthwhile light on Jewish life in this century. For scholars of the period, our apparatus, much of which is Abe Lavender's, surely does that."

BIOGRAPHICAL/CRITICAL SOURCES:

PERIODICALS

Contemporary Jewry, volume 16, 1995.
Delaware County Times (Delhi, NY), August 11, 1995, pp. 14-15.
Social and Behavioral Sciences, November, 1995.

STEINBERG, Mark D(avid) 1953-

PERSONAL: Born June 8, 1953, in San Francisco, CA; son of Norman E. (a shopkeeper) and Dina (a shopkeeper; maiden name, Gilbert) Steinberg; married Jane T. Hedges (a manuscript editor and translator), August 10, 1980; children: Alexander Hedges. *Education:* University of California, Santa Cruz, B.A., 1978; University of California, Berkeley, M.A., 1982, Ph.D., 1987.

ADDRESSES: Office—Department of History, 309 Gregory Hall, University of Illinois at Urbana-Champaign, 810 South Wright St., Urbana, IL 61801.

CAREER: Worked as taxicab driver, New York City, 1975, and printer's apprentice and messenger, New York City, 1978-79; University of Oregon, Eugene, visiting instructor in Russian history, 1987; Harvard University, Cambridge, MA, assistant professor of Russian history, 1987-89; Yale University, New Haven, CT, assistant professor, 1989-94, associate professor of Russian history, 1994-96, Morse junior faculty fellow in humanities, 1991-92, Fox faculty fellow in Moscow, Yale Center for International and Area Studies, 1993; University of Illinois at Urbana-Champaign, professor of Russian history, 1996—. Consultant to National Geographic Television.

MEMBER: American Historical Association, American Association for the Advancement of Slavic Studies.

AWARDS, HONORS: Research scholar, Kennan Institute for Advanced Russian Studies, Woodrow Wilson Center for International Scholars, Smithsonian Institution, 1989; fellow of Social Science Research Council, 1990-92; grant for the Soviet Union, International Research and Exchanges Board, 1991-92; fellow, National Endowment for the Humanities, 1995.

WRITINGS:

Moral Communities: The Culture of Class Relations in the Russian Printing Industry, 1867-1907, University of California Press (Los Angeles, CA), 1992.

(Editor with Stephen Frank, and contributor) *Cultures in Flux: Lower Class Values, Practices, and Resistance in Late Imperial Russia,* Princeton University Press (Princeton, NJ), 1994.

(With Vladimir Khrustalev) *The Fall of the Romanovs: Political Dreams and Personal Struggles in a Time of Revolution,* Yale University Press (New Haven, CT), 1995.

(Author of introduction, chronology, and index) Maxim Gorky, *Untimely Thoughts: Essays on Revolution, Culture, and the Bolsheviks, 1917-1918,* Yale University Press, 1995.

Contributor to books, including *Making Workers Soviet: Power, Class, and Identity,* edited by Lewis H. Siegelbaum and Ronald Grigor Suny, Cornell University Press (Ithaca, NY), 1994; and *Trauma in Eastern European Therapists and Their Patients.* Contributor of articles and reviews to periodicals, including *Russian Review, Alternatives Newsletter, Journal of Social History,* and *Russian History.*

WORK IN PROGRESS: Editing *The Russian Revolution,* with Daniel Orlovsky and Genrikh Ioffe, for Yale University Press; *Proletarian Imagination: The Quest for the Cultural Self in Russia, 1910-1925.*

SIDELIGHTS: Mark D. Steinberg told *CA:* "My book *The Russian Revolution* is a collection of translated letters from peasants, soldiers, and workers in Russia during the year 1917, selected from many hundreds I examined in Russian archives, often from previously closed collections. The collection is introduced by an analysis of the ways in which lower-class Russians understood and responded to the months of crisis and revolution.

"*Proletarian Imagination* is a study of poetry and fiction written by urban, lower-class Russians before and after the revolution, focusing on popular conceptions and uses of such key cultural ideas as the individual and the collective, the city and the machine, suffering and death, and religion.

"My aim in exploring Russian history, as both author and teacher, has been less to describe and explain past events (a sort of history-telling that, frankly, I have often found to be superficial and tedious) than to discover what the past meant for individuals who experienced and influenced the world around them. Thus, whether studying Nicholas II or workers and employers, to mention the subjects of two of my books, I ask similar questions: what were their values, how did they perceive and judge right and wrong, how did they make earthly life appear sensible and meaningful, and what caused them to act as they did?

"In trying to answer these sorts of questions, I have learned how much is revealed, not just in what people say, but also in how they say it—in their choices of vocabulary and images. Beyond looking for evidence of material interests and collective identities, I have also seen the centrality in human consciousness, ethics, religion, and emotion. Equally important, I try not to assume more coherence in the past (or more honesty and self-understanding in the texts I read) than likely ever existed. People in the past (and this is reflected in past events) often thought and acted on the basis of conflicting ideas and values, ambiguity, ambivalence, and even paradox. Making matters even more complex, their stories about themselves and their times contain plenty of silences and misrepresentations. In all of this complexity are the textures of real human life, but also obstacles to understanding. Thus, like many historians who share this essentially cultural and critical approach to the past, I have to admit the necessary tentativeness of any answers. It is better to ask hard questions and admit that certain answers remain elusive than boldly to flatten out human experience in order to construct a seamless narrative and interpretation of the past."

* * *

STEINMAN, David 1958-

PERSONAL: Born August 29, 1958, in Los Angeles, CA; son of Jesse (a sea captain and engineer) and Rose (a teacher) Steinman; married Terri Lynn Breen, May 17, 1993; children: Spenser Carl Max. *Ethnicity:* "American." *Education:* Columbia University, B.A.; University of Oregon, M.A. *Politics:* "Conservative (not Republican)." *Religion:* "Do right." *Avocational interests:* The outdoors.

ADDRESSES: Home—Topanla, CA. *Office*—*Journal of Longevity Research,* 330 Washington Blvd., 9th Floor, Marina del Rey, CA 90292. *Agent*—Madeleine March, 2M Communications, 121 West 27th St., No. 601, New York, NY 10001.

CAREER: Journal of Longevity Research, Marina del Rey, CA, editor, 1991—.

AWARDS, HONORS: Two Pulitzer Prize nominations; Best of the West Award; award from Sierra Club.

WRITINGS:

Diet for a Poisoned Planet: How to Choose Safe Foods for You and Your Family, Harmony, 1990.
Seafood Safety, National Academy Press (Washington, DC), 1991.
(Coauthor) *The Safe Shopper's Bible,* Macmillan (New York City), 1995.
Living Healthy in a Toxic World, Putnam (New York City), 1996.
The Breast Cancer Prevention Bible, Macmillan, in press.

WORK IN PROGRESS: Children's Bible, publication by Macmillan expected in 1998; *The Wetlands,* a work of fiction, completion expected in 1998; research on children's health and on class conflicts.

SIDELIGHTS: David Steinman told *CA:* "I write because it is liberating and because it creates visions of what can be. My work is influenced by my life, the people I meet, and the books I read. I am a hard worker and persistent. I select my subjects because I am America's Consumer Cop and because I have a vision and a message to bring to all people."

* * *

STEPHEN, Felix N. 1925-

PERSONAL: Born in 1925, in Eastern Nigeria.

CAREER: Fiction writer.

WRITINGS:

NOVELETTES

The Life Story of Boys and Girls, Chinyelu Printing Press, 1962.
How to Play Love, Njokuandsons, 1963.
The Trials and Death of Lumumba, M. Allan Ohaejesi, 1963.
The Temple of Love, B.C. Okara and Sons, 1964.
Pamphlet Literature from Onitsha, Kraus Reprint, 1965.
Lack of Money Is Not Lack of Sense, Chinyelu Printing Press, 1966.

OTHER

"The Sweetness of Love," in *The Work of Love* by Cyril Nwakuma Ariruguzo, Ariruguzo and Sons, 1963.

Also author of *How to Speak and Write to Girls for Friendship,* published by Njoko and Sons.*

* * *

STERN, Harold S. 1923(?)-1976

PERSONAL: Born c. 1923; died May 25, 1976.

CAREER: Drama critic, magazine editor, and fiction writer.

MEMBER: National Academy of Recording Arts and Sciences.

WRITINGS:

Blackland (novel), Doubleday, 1970.

Drama and nightclub critic for the *Brooklyn Eagle* and drama critic for WNEW-AM. Syndicated columnist for Woman's News Service, North American Newspaper Alliance, Inter-Press Feature Syndicate, and King Features. Contributing editor, *After Dark* magazine; editor, *Youth Beat, Applause,* and *Broadway Sign Post;* entertainment editor, Bell-McClure Syndicate.

BIOGRAPHICAL/CRITICAL SOURCES:

PERIODICALS

New York Times, May 30, 1976.

* * *

STEWART, Daniel Blair 1951-

PERSONAL: Born March 1, 1951, in Salt Lake City, UT; son of Robert Daniel (a chemist) and Elaine Naomie (a homemaker; maiden name, Rapp) Stewart; married Ayla Meadow, 1982 (marriage ended, 1989); children: River Nova. *Ethnicity:* "Caucasian."

Avocational interests: Unidentified flying objects and other phenomena, scuba diving.

ADDRESSES: Office—383 South Main St., No. 180, Willits, CA 95490.

CAREER: Self-employed writer and artist.

WRITINGS:

Akhunaton: The Extraterrestrial King, North Atlantic Books (Berkeley, CA), 1995.

WORK IN PROGRESS: A novel about Nikola Tesla; research for a novel about Rasputin.

SIDELIGHTS: Daniel Blair Stewart told *CA:* "I write to explore reality. Our world is filled with mysteries. Unanswered questions abound. Researching events, discoveries, and historical figures leads me to uncover ideas for historical fiction and science fiction. I have chosen to write about the mysteries of science and human history, because that strange and enigmatic side of reality is real and accessible to me. What influences my work is an adventurous lifestyle."

* * *

STILLMAN, (John) Whit(ney) 1952(?)-

PERSONAL: Born c. 1952, in New York, NY; son of John Sterling (in politics); married; wife's name, Irene; children: one daughter. *Education:* Harvard University, B.A.

ADDRESSES: Home—New York, NY. Agent—William Morris Agency, 151 El Camino Dr., Beverly Hills, CA 90212-2775.

CAREER: Screenwriter and director. Director and producer, *Metropolitan,* 1990; director, *Barcelona,* 1994. Worked at Doubleday publishers, New York City; distributor of Spanish films; Riley Illustration (a cartoonist's agency), New York City, owner and operator.

MEMBER: Directors Guild of America, Writers Guild of America.

AWARDS, HONORS: Academy Award nomination, best screenplay, 1991, for *Metropolitan.*

WRITINGS:

SCREENPLAYS

Metropolitan (also known as *Metropolitan: Doomed. Bourgeois. In Love.*), New Line Cinema, 1990, published in *Barcelona and Metropolitan: Tales of Two Cities,* Faber & Faber, 1995.

Barcelona, Castle Rock/Fine Line, 1994, published in *Barcelona and Metropolitan: Tales of Two Cities,* Faber & Faber, 1995.

OTHER

Contributor to periodicals, including *American Spectator.*

SIDELIGHTS: Whit Stillman is screenwriter and director of two critically acclaimed independent films, *Metropolitan* and *Barcelona. Metropolitan,* a romantic comedy of manners with roots in the works of F. Scott Fitzgerald, Jane Austen, and Philip Barry (the screenwriter of such 1940s class comedies as *Holiday* and *The Philadelphia Story*) is a semi-autobiographical look at New York City's upper crust (Urban Haute Bourgeoisie or UHB as Stillman has dubbed them). According to *New York* magazine contributor David Denby, Stillman stated that he was inspired to create *Metropolitan* because there is "an absence in American cinema of accurate portraits of the American upper class." The result, wrote London *Times* contributor John Marriot, is "a warmly critical essay on New York's debutante set. With a fresh, eager eye which lifts the urban movie beyond the grasp of usual tired imagery, [Stillman] homes in on the Upper East Side and . . . outlines the strengths, foibles and anxieties of a disappearing class."

Metropolitan, which is subtitled "Doomed. Bourgeois. In Love.," focuses on a group of debutantes and their male friends—escorts in class-speak—who call themselves the Sally Fowler Rat Pack. Told in short, episodic segments, the film follows the characters from balls to after parties filled with earnest discussions of philosophy, class burdens (one fatalistic character's is obsessed with falling from upper class grace), and politics. Tom Townsend, whose parent's divorce, socialist leanings, and reduced economic circumstances have made him a bit of an outsider, falls in with the group when an "escort shortage" makes him sought-after for the Christmas season's debutante balls. These details of Tom's circumstances parallel that of a young Stillman, who, according to *New York Times* reviewer Alessandra

Stanley, serves up *Metropolitan* with "an edge of gentle irony." As Stillman told *Washington Post* interviewer Martha Sherrill, "I like to like the people I'm approaching satirically. And a lot of the stuff in the film is really just my own attitudes of 15 or 20 years ago. And so it would be masochistic to be too brutal about it."

Stillman also directed and produced *Metropolitan,* which was made on a very low budget by Hollywood standards (under a million dollars, according to the director) and sported a cast of unknown, inexperienced actors. He wrote the script over four years, whenever he had time out from his work as an agent for cartoonists and illustrators, and admits that he was still reading "how-to-direct-a-movie" books when filming began.

Despite Stillman's lack of experience, the film generated considerable word-of-mouth at the prestigious Sundance and Cannes film festivals and received glowing reviews from a number of respected critics. According to *Los Angeles Times* reviewer Sheila Benson, "Stillman's gift for quiet, scrupulous observation grows on you. . . . [He] understands caste, class and deportment as perfectly as . . . Jane Austen and by the time he's through, so do we." Calling the work "immensely likable," *New York* reviewer David Denby also likened Stillman's class acuity to Austen and proclaimed that, despite an occasional weakness, "most of *Metropolitan* is funny and graceful. That such a film exists at all is almost a miracle." The *Nation*'s Stuart Klawans agreed, professing to have "thoroughly enjoyed" Stillman's film. Klawans stated that the writer/director's accomplishment with *Metropolitan* was "so satisfying that nothing more could be wanted." Some critics, however, saw Stillman's portrayal of the UHB world as too esoteric for mass consumption; *Washington Post* contributor Desson Howe remarked that "true appreciation for this movie may be restricted to those with firsthand experience in this kind of world, or a certain upper-haute stamina."

Stillman's second film, *Barcelona,* retains much of *Metropolitan*'s episodic nature, but the film uses these narrative flashes in the service of a larger, more distinct plot. As the screenwriter explained in an interview with *Film Comment* contributor Donald Lyons, he wrote *Metropolitan* with the idea that "life is essentially an eventless affair and to make a movie full of plot and incident would be a false and inauthentic repetition of genre movie cliches. In the interval between the two scripts I changed my mind: life does have melodramatic turns."

Barcelona, set in the Spanish title city, concerns Ted, a sales representative for an American company, and his cousin Fred, a U.S. Navy lieutenant who is the advance man for a visit by the U.S. Sixth Fleet. Ugly American Fred arrives in Barcelona unannounced and makes himself at home in his relative's apartment, upending Ted's precariously ordered life. Ted, who expresses a Puritan sensibility, reads motivational books, and studies the Bible while dancing to Glenn Miller music, offers a marked contrast to Fred's uncensored opinions, egotistical confidence, and deep patriotism. The men find a small patch of common ground in their appreciation for and romantic involvement with the Spanish women working at a trade fair. The cousins' odd-couple antics and romantic escapades take a serious turn when Fred's outspoken politics and aloof manner lead him to be mistaken as a CIA agent; Barcelona's anti-American fervor leads to an act of violence against the Naval officer. The event leads Ted to a reassessment of his feelings toward his cousin, his job, his ideals of womanhood, and ultimately his life. As James Bowman commented in the *American Spectator,* "all the way through, the expected things do not happen and unexpected ones do, prejudices are upended and firm opinions proven wrong, including the two cousins' opinions of each other."

Barcelona garnered some very enthusiastic reviews, although the overall response was mixed. *New Yorker* contributor Terrence Rafferty noted that although the film "begins promisingly, its charm peters out fast: it's all attitude, no story." *National Review* critic John Simon registered a similar complaint, remarking, "What Mr. Stillman has is a good situation, but no story." Bowman, however, praised *Barcelona*'s "freshness and wit." The critic stated further that it "takes someone like Whit Stillman, from outside the film culture, to make a film that is not burdened with that culture's simple-minded view of America." *New Republic* critic Stanley Kauffmann commented that "*Barcelona* makes *Metropolitan* look retrospectively like a warm-up. . . . [I]t is immediately apparent that [Stillman's] sheer cinematic fluency has taken a great leap forward." Lyons also compared *Barcelona* favorably to Stillman's first film: "The brilliant *Barcelona* shows, in its greater richness than that of *Metropolitan,* the kind of growth we always hope for in a major artist."

BIOGRAPHICAL/CRITICAL SOURCES:

PERIODICALS

American Spectator, October, 1994, pp. 67-68.

Film Comment, July-August, 1994, pp. 82-83, 85.
Los Angeles Times, August 10, 1990.
Nation, August 13-20, 1990, pp. 178-80.
National Review, September 12, 1994, pp. 87-88.
New Republic, August 15, 1994, pp. 30-31.
New York, August 13, 1990, pp. 64-65.
New Yorker, August 15, 1994, p. 77.
New York Times, July 29, 1990; January 20, 1991, p. 13, 18.
Times (London), November 22, 1990.
Washington Post, September 14, 1990, pp. C1, C9.*

* * *

ST. MARTIN, Hardie 1924-
(Jonathan Casart, Julian Casart)

PERSONAL: Born February 23, 1924, in Belize; U.S. citizen. *Ethnicity:* "White." *Education:* Regis College, B.A., 1944; Columbia University, graduate study, 1946-49. *Religion:* Roman Catholic.

ADDRESSES: Home—Sugranyes 39-41, Atic 2, 08028 Barcelona, Spain; fax 34-422-3077.

CAREER: Writer and translator.

AWARDS, HONORS: Guggenheim fellow, 1965-66; shared P.E.N. International Translation Award, 1974; Islands and Continents Award, 1977; fellow, Comite Conjunto Hispano-Norteamericano, 1980-81.

WRITINGS:

(Translator) *Twenty Poems of Blas de Otero,* Sixties Press (Madison, WI), 1964.
(Translator) *Gazapo,* by Gustavo Sainz, Farrar, Straus (New York), 1968.
(Editor with Timothy Baland, and translator) *Selected Poems: Miguel Hernandez and Blas de Otero,* Beacon Press (Boston, MA), 1971.
(Translator with Ronald Mades) *The Obscene Bird of Night,* by Jose Donoso, Knopf (New York), 1973, reprinted, David R. Godine (Lincoln, MA).
(Editor and contributor) *Roots and Wings,* Harper (New York), 1976.
(Translator) *Memoirs,* by Pablo Neruda, Farrar, Straus, 1976.
(Translator) *Play by Play,* by Isaac Goldemberg, Persea Books (New York), 1985.

(Translator) *The Ships,* by Robert Quesada, Four Walls Eight Windows Press (New York), 1991.

(Translator) *The Garden Next Door,* by Donoso, Grove Weidenfeld (New York), 1992.

(Editor and contributor) *Small Hours of the Night: Selected Poems of Roque Dalton,* Curbstone Press (Willimantic, CT), 1996.

Work represented in anthologies in the United States, Canada, and England. Some translations appear under the pseudonyms Jonathan Casart and Julian Casart.

WORK IN PROGRESS: Translating *Selected Poems of Juan Gelman,* for Curbstone Press.

* * *

STOETT, Peter J. 1963-

PERSONAL: Born July 16, 1963, in Tillsonburg, Ontario, Canada; son of F. A. and Irene Stoett; married Betty McKee (marriage ended); children: Alexandra. *Ethnicity:* "Canadian-Dutch." *Education:* University of Guelph, B.A. (with honors), 1988, M.A., 1989; Queen's University, Ph.D., 1994. *Avocational interests:* Athletics, music.

ADDRESSES: Office—Department of Political Studies, University of Guelph, Guelph, Ontario, Canada N1G 2W1; fax 519-824-4120, extension 3535. *E-mail*—pstoett@css.uoguelph.ca.

CAREER: Queen's University, Kingston, Ontario, lecturer in politics, 1992-94; University of British Columbia, Vancouver, visiting assistant professor of political science, 1994-95; University of Guelph, Guelph, Ontario, visiting assistant professor of political studies, 1995—. Frontier College, tutor with Prison Literacy Initiative, 1992; University of Waterloo, lecturer, 1993-94; Simon Fraser University, sessional lecturer, 1995; consultant to Feannex Foundation.

MEMBER: Canadian Political Science Association.

AWARDS, HONORS: Melvin Gelber Essay Prize, International Journal, 1995, for the article "This Age of Genocide: Conceptual and Institutional Implications."

WRITINGS:

Atoms, Whales, and Rivers: Global Environmental Security and International Organization, Nova Science Publishers (Commack, NY), 1995.

Cetapolitics: The International Relations of Whaling, University of British Columbia Press (Vancouver, British Columbia), 1996.

Contributor to books, including *Crisis and Transformation,* edited by P. Dutkiewicz and B. Berman, Centre for International Relations, Queen's University (Kingston, Ontario), 1993; *Environmental Policies in Developing Countries: A Comparative Analysis,* edited by O. P. Dwivedi and D. K. Vajpeyi, Greenwood Press (Westport, CT), 1995; and *Asia: Who Pays for Growth? Women, Environment, and Popular Movements,* edited by J. Lele and W. Tettey, Dartmouth (Aldershot, England), 1996. Contributor of articles and reviews to journals and newspapers, including *Sea Wind: Bulletin of Ocean Voice International, International Journal, Journal of Forecasting, Planning, and Policy, Environmental Politics, Global Governance: A Review of Multilateralism and International Organizations, Journal for the Northwest Environment,* and *Canadian Foreign Policy.*

WORK IN PROGRESS: International Relations: Convergence and Divergence, with Allen Sens, publication by Nelson Canada expected in the year 2000; a text on the effects of ecological concerns on international relations theory, with Eric Laferriere; *Coming to Terms: Genocide, Ecocide, Refugee, and Security.*

SIDELIGHTS: Peter J. Stoett told *CA:* "Most of my professional work relates to global environmental problems and their political implications. Inspiration is derived from my daughter Alexandra, whose children will face even greater challenges than we do."

* * *

STRAUSS, Anselm L(eonard) 1916-1996

OBITUARY NOTICE—See index for *CA* sketch: Born December 18, 1916, in New York, NY; died of a heart attack, September 5, 1996, in San Francisco, CA. Sociologist, psychologist, educator, author. Strauss is remembered for his work in the field of social science research, particularly his studies of chronic pain and patients who die while hospitalized.

Trained in sociology and psychology, Strauss taught at schools such as Wisconsin's Lawrence College, the University of Chicago, and Indiana University. In 1958 he became the director of the social science laboratory at Michael Reese Hospital. Two years later he joined the faculty at the University of California at San Francisco as a sociology professor. In 1987 he entered emeritus status. During his career, Strauss was instrumental in establishing the field of medical sociology, and he cofounded a research approach called grounded theory. He wrote a number of books, including *Mirrors and Masks: The Search for Identity, Awareness of Dying, Where Medicine Fails, Social Psychology,* and *Negotiations: Varieties, Contexts, Processes and Social Order.*

OBITUARIES AND OTHER SOURCES:

PERIODICALS

Los Angeles Times, September 17, 1996, p. A24.
New York Times, September 15, 1996, Section 1, p. 52.

* * *

STRONG MAN OF THE PEN, THE
See OLISAH, Sunday Okenwa

* * *

STRYJKOWSKI, Julian 1905-1996

OBITUARY NOTICE—See index for *CA* sketch: Born April 27, 1905, in Stryj, Poland; died August 8, 1996, in Warsaw, Poland. Journalist, short story writer, and novelist. Stryjkowski is best remembered for his books that described small town Jewish life during the first few decades of the twentieth century. After growing up in Poland, Stryjkowski followed a variety of political ideologies during his life, from Zionism, to Communism, to Solidarity. He survived Hitler's rise to power and the genocide against the Jews by relocating to Russia. When he heard of the Jewish insurrection in the Warsaw Ghetto, he was compelled to chronicle Jewish life in a trilogy entitled *Glosy w ciemnosci* (title means "Voices in the Dark"), which was written in the 1940s but not published until 1956. Also following the war, he wrote for the Polish PAP news agency covering Rome.

Stryjkowski also wrote short stories, collected in volumes such as *Bieg do Fragala* (title means "Course to Fragala"), *Czarna roza* (title means "The Black Rose"), and *Na Wierzbach nasze skrzypce* (title means "On Willows Our Fiddles"). He wrote a biblical trilogy, which included *Krol Dawid zyje* (title means "King David Is Alive"). After he revealed his homosexuality, he wrote a gay novel, *Milczenie* (title means "Silence"). In 1980 he was honored with the Alfred Jurzykowski Foundation Award.

OBITUARIES AND OTHER SOURCES:

PERIODICALS

New York Times, August 11, 1996, p. 37.
Washington Post, August 12, 1996, p. B6.

* * *

SUBOTNIK, Rena F. 1948-

PERSONAL: Born March 10, 1948, in New York, NY; daughter of Louis (a certified public accountant) and Emma (a homemaker and dress designer; maiden name, Bouskela) Subotnik. *Ethnicity:* "Jewish." *Education:* City College of the City University of New York, B.A., 1969; Columbia University, M.A., 1974; University of Washington, Seattle, Ph.D., 1984. *Politics:* Democrat. *Religion:* Jewish. *Avocational interests:* Reading, hiking, travel.

ADDRESSES: Home—New York City. *Office*—Educational Foundations, Hunter College of the City University of New York, 695 Park Ave., New York, NY 10021; fax 212-772-4722. *E-mail*—rsubotni@ shiva.hunter.cuny.edu.

CAREER: Gifted specialist at elementary and public schools in Seattle, WA, 1977-81; West Virginia University, Morgantown, assistant in special education, 1984-86; Hunter College of the City University of New York, New York City, assistant in educational foundations, 1986-91, associate, 1991—. Western Washington University, visiting professor, summers, 1986-88; Simon Fraser University, visiting professor, summer, 1995. Judge for National Alliance for Excellence, academic category, 1993—, and District Academic Olympics, 1995; Greenpeace International, curriculum evaluator, 1989-91; Rockefeller University, member of Science Outreach Group, 1994—; City-Wide Gifted and Talented Coordinators, mem-

ber, 1992—; consultant to National Research Center for the Gifted and Talented.

MEMBER: National Association for Gifted Children (chairperson of Research and Evaluation Division, 1992-94), American Educational Research Association, National Research Center for the Gifted and Talented, Advocacy for Gifted and Talented Education in New York State (member of board of directors, 1991—), Pi Lambda Theta.

AWARDS, HONORS: Shuster grants, 1987, 1989; grants from Pi Lambda Theta, 1988, 1995, National Science Foundation, 1988-90, Spencer Foundation, 1990, and U.S. Department of Education, 1990-93; Early Scholar Award, National Association for Gifted Children, 1990.

WRITINGS:

(With L. Kassan, E. Summers, and A. Wasser) *Genius Revisited: High IQ Children Grown Up,* Ablex Publishing (Norwood, NJ), 1993.
(Editor with K. D. Arnold, and contributor) *Beyond Terman: Contemporary Longitudinal Studies of Giftedness and Talent,* Ablex Publishing, 1994.
(Editor with Arnold and K. D. Noble, and contributor) *Remarkable Women: Perspectives on Female Talent Development,* Hampton (Cresskill, NJ), 1996.

Contributor to books, including *International Handbook of Research on Giftedness and Talent,* edited by K. A. Heller, F. J. Monks, and A. H. Passow, Pergamon (Oxford, England), 1993; *Problem Finding, Problem Solving, and Creativity,* edited by M. Runco, Ablex Publishing, 1994; and *Multicultural Education: Issues and Perspectives,* edited by J. A. Banks and C. McGee Banks, 3rd edition, Allyn & Bacon (Boston, MA), 1996. Author of the columns "Veritable Gifts," 1995, and "Educating Daughters," 1996. Contributor of articles and reviews to academic journals, including *International Journal of Educational Research, Journal for the Education of the Gifted, Educational Forum, International Journal of Science Education, Questioning Exchange: A Multidisciplinary Review,* and *Gifted Child Quarterly. Roeper Review,* editor of special issues, 1993, 1995, contributing editor, 1988-89, member of editorial board, 1989-91, 1994-96; co-editor, *Hunter Outreach Newsletter,* 1989—; member of editorial board, *Creativity Research Journal,* 1988-91, *American Educational Research Journal,* 1992—, *Journal for Secondary Gifted Education,* 1994—, and *Educational Horizons,* 1995—.

WORK IN PROGRESS: Continuing interviews with masters in the arts and sciences.

SIDELIGHTS: Rena F. Subotnik told *CA:* "I write to convey the excitement I feel about the work my colleagues and I are conducting and to provide insights into understanding and supporting talent and creativity in children and adults. I read voraciously and jot down ideas that seem to stick and that I want to savor. When I am asked to produce a manuscript and have some freedom to choose a topic, I go through my list of ideas and use one or two of them as jumping-off points for a new project or research study.

"Generating an outline of arguments to present is a pleasant pastime for me, but fleshing out the argument in writing is not. That step is too often left until an approaching deadline raises my anxiety to an unbearable level. Working collaboratively on a piece with someone who is less of a procrastinator is an effective strategy for me to get through this stage. I love the polishing process that takes place before I send off a manuscript. Finding just the right word or phrase is like completing a challenging crossword puzzle.

"I have been studying giftedness and talent in children and adults for more than twenty-five years. The more I dive into this topic, the more I find that needs to be said to educators and to the general public. Sometimes I wish I were champion of a less controversial cause than special services for gifted children. However, if there were easy answers to the dilemma of how to use limited resources (to support those with the most difficulties and challenges or those with the most potential for creative productivity) there wouldn't be much to write about. Containing my passionate feelings on the topic is a constant source of frustration, and publishing my ideas forces me to think through what I want to say in a logical and convincing manner."

* * *

SWINTON, Elizabeth de Sabato 1937-

PERSONAL: Born November 18, 1937, in Philadelphia, PA; daughter of Vincent and Barbara (a homemaker; maiden name, Coll; present surname, Attig) de Sabato; married Neil W. Swinton, Jr. (a physi-

cian), June 8, 1957; children: Neil W. III, Elizabeth Swinton Schoen, Barbara Swinton de Butts, Anne Swinton Ruggles. *Ethnicity:* "American of Western European ancestry." *Education:* Bryn Mawr College, A.B., 1958; Boston University, M.A., 1969; Harvard University, A.M., 1973, Ph.D., 1980. *Religion:* Episcopalian. *Avocational interests:* Gardening, cooking, American history.

ADDRESSES: Home—121 Suffolk Rd., Chestnut Hill, MA 02167. *Office*—Worcester Art Museum, 55 Salisbury St., Worcester, MA 01609; fax 508-798-5646.

CAREER: Worcester Art Museum, Worcester, MA, research curator for Asiatic art, 1978-81, consulting curator, 1981-84, curator of Asian art, 1985—, director of curatorial affairs, 1995—. Higgins Armor Museum, member of collections and exhibitions committees. Tufts University, assistant professor, 1977-84; Harvard University, research associate at Edwin O. Reischauer Institute of Japanese Studies, 1980—, lecturer, 1981; teacher of adult education courses.

MEMBER: Association of Asian Studies, College Art Association of America, American Association of Museums.

AWARDS, HONORS: Kinnicutt Foreign Travel Award for India, Worcester Art Museum, 1982; grant for China and Korea, Asian Cultural Council, 1987; grant for Japan, Northeast Asia Council, Association of Asian Studies, 1990.

WRITINGS:

The Graphic Art of Onchi Koshiro (1891-1955): Innovation and Tradition, Garland Publishing (New York), 1985.
The Women of the Pleasure Quarter: Painting and Prints of the Floating World, Hudson Hills Press (New York), 1996.

Author of exhibition catalogs. Contributor to books, including *The Locked Casket Whose Key Was Lost: New Russian and Japanese Encounters, 1868-1926,* edited by J. Thomas Rimer, Stanford University Press (Stanford, CA), 1994. Contributor to art history and Asian studies journals, including *Orientations, Asian Art,* and *Archives of Asian Art.*

SYKES, Charles J.

PERSONAL: Son of Jay G. Sykes (a professor). *Education:* Graduated from University of Wisconsin, Madison.

ADDRESSES: Home—Milwaukee, WI. *Agent*—c/o St. Martin's Press, 175 Fifth Ave., New York, NY 10010.

CAREER: Milwaukee Magazine, Milwaukee, WI, editor; *Milwaukee Journal,* Milwaukee, reporter; writer.

WRITINGS:

ProfScam: Professors and the Demise of Higher Education, Regnery (Washington), 1989.
The Hollow Men: Politics and Corruption in Higher Education, Regnery, 1990.
(Editor with Brad Miner) *The National Review College Guide: America's Top Liberal Arts Schools,* introduction by William F. Buckley, Wolgemuth & Hyatt, 1991, revised edition, Simon & Schuster (New York), 1992.
A Nation of Victims: The Decay of the American Character, St. Martin's (New York), 1992.
Dumbing Down Our Kids: Why America's Children Feel Good about Themselves But Can't Read, Write, or Add, St. Martin's, 1995.

SIDELIGHTS: Charles J. Sykes is a celebrated journalist who has won acclaim and courted controversy with his investigations of respected American institutions, notably higher education. His 1989 book, *ProfScam: Professors and the Demise of Higher Education,* depicts academia as a racket in which professors connive to further their reputations and careers at the expense of the very institution that they are presumably hired to honor and serve. As Roger Kimball noted in the *New York Times Book Review,* the contemporary university, at least as viewed by Sykes, is "like something of a scam." *ProfScam* presents an academic world rife with con artist professors who exploit the citation-counting system by conspiring to quote each other in essays and articles.

In *ProfScam,* the petty machinations and slightly dishonorable deeds of professors are seen to exact a dramatic toll on the system of higher education: Professors sacrifice teaching to concentrate on the research that will presumably lead to publications that will, in turn, enhance reputations and result in greater

job security (i.e., tenure) and an increase in what may be seen as already disproportionate wages. Sykes sees the salvation of higher education through the elimination of both tenure and the research-and-publish scheme. Teachers, Sykes argues, must teach.

ProfScam has been hailed as an important and provocative work. *National Review* writer Jeffrey Hart called *ProfScam* "an extraordinary book about higher education in America." Kimball expressed similar sentiments, writing in the *New York Times Book Review* that *ProfScam* is an "engaging and polemical overview" and adding that it is "an incisive and convincing document that deserves to be read by anyone concerned about the future of American higher education." Thomas Short explained, in a review of *Profscam* in *Commentary,* that Sykes "has shown that higher education is indeed a national disgrace."

Not all reactions to *ProfScam* were positive. The *Los Angeles Times* quoted one education professor, Claremont's Jack H. Schuster, as deeming Sykes's book "real garbage," and the same publication noted that Ernest Boyer, head of the Carnegie Foundation for the Advancement of Teaching, believed Sykes to be guilty of excessive generalization. In the *Los Angeles Times* piece, Boyer charged Sykes with producing "caricatures of the problem." Sykes maintained that it was not his intention to provide a balanced appraisal of academia; rather, he intended to concentrate on what he perceived as failings within the system of higher learning. He also disclosed that *ProfScam* derived from a paper published by his father, a journalism professor.

In 1990 Sykes followed *ProfScam* with *The Hollow Men: Politics and Corruption in Higher Education,* in which he presents further discussion of the weaknesses of academia. In *The Hollow Men,* Sykes focuses on Dartmouth College and reports on what he perceives as a general degeneration of quality education in recent decades. Colleges attempt to increase status by hiring high-profile specialists, reports Sykes. But such superficial improvements are sometimes made at the expense of education itself, because skilled but lesser-known professors, usually untenured, must be released to make way for the more celebrated specialists, who may or may not possess quality teaching skills. In addition, institutions have unnecessarily relinquished authority to the faculty, thus allowing teachers to determine what courses they teach and what works they assign. As a result, Sykes alleges, the curriculum of great books— those works that one has presumably studied if one is

to be considered educated—has been slighted. This, in turn, diminishes the quality of education realized by students today. Jeffrey Hart, writing in *National Review,* found *The Hollow Men* to be a timely and important work. He wrote that the book "is in the best tradition of investigative journalism" and contended that "it will have a national impact."

In 1991 Sykes collaborated with Brad Miner in editing *The National Review College Guide: America's Top Liberal Arts Schools.* This volume, which was revised in 1992, emphasizes the importance of a traditional curriculum and stresses the value of an intellectual environment comprised not only of teachers and students but administrators and even neighboring citizens. Jim Bencivenga, assessing *The National Review College Guide* in *Christian Science Monitor,* hailed the volume as a "keenly discriminating guide to liberal arts colleges" and concluded that "this book will temper utilitarian goals with the high ideals of a traditional liberal arts education." Less impressed was Jon Wiener, who contended in the *Nation* that the schools recommended by Sykes and Miner "are mostly little-known Christian colleges where almost everyone is white and majors in business."

In his 1992 volume *A Nation of Victims: The Decay of the American Character* Sykes continues to expose failure and folly in America, and decries the general lack of morality and honor in American society. Here Sykes stresses that there is a lack of self-accountability in individuals' behavior. He sees a distressing prevalence of what he terms "victimization," whereby individuals forsake personal responsibility and concentrate instead on ways in which they are compromised by the system or each other. Victimization occurs, Sykes states, in cases such as one in which a car thief perishes in an accident and surviving relatives sue the car owner for failing to safeguard the car, or in which a black official convicted of narcotics possession attributes his conviction to racial discrimination. For Sykes, the American public, which he sees as largely self-absorbed and irresponsible, needs a return to morality and a code of conduct stressing temperance and personal accountability.

A Nation of Victims has been acknowledged as a provocative examination of contemporary American values and behavior. In an *American Spectator* review, John R. Dunlop noted that *A Nation of Victims* "offers compelling reasons to suppose that American culture is in a bad way," and added that it "draws together an extremely useful compendium of insights

into the American character." *New York Times* contributor Michiko Kakutani characterized Sykes's suggestions as "flippantly delineated," and Charles R. Kessler, in his *National Review* assessment, found Sykes's appraisal adequately broad but lacking depth. Kessler added, however, that "Sykes has given us a timely warning of the consequences of Americans' turn from pride to pity as the principle of republican government."

In his 1995 book, *Dumbing Down Our Kids: Why America's Children Feel Good about Themselves But Can't Read, Write, or Add,* Sykes tackles the issue of school reform, which he sees as one in which the students' feelings are regarded with greater concern than are the students' actual thinking skills and ability to learn necessary information. Sykes decries the present climate in American schools as one in which the manner in which a subject is presented—politically correct and with sensitivity toward the students' own inclinations—too often overwhelms the actual substance of the subject.

In *Dumbing Down Our Kids,* Sykes blames much of the school systems' shortcomings to a sequence of progressive acts dating from the late 1910s. The introduction of the Cardinal Principles at that time, according to Sykes, began the shift in priority away from imparting knowledge. Furthermore, Sykes sees the present situation in education as one rife with jargon, political correctness, and bizarre priorities, all of which, he claims, undermine the actual process of education.

To remedy what he sees as deficiencies in American education, Sykes calls for greater diversity in the backgrounds and priorities of teachers, and he advocates—as he did in *ProfScam*—the elimination of the tenure system. *Wall Street Journal* reviewer Joseph Adelson reported that *Dumbing Down Our Kids* "shows us just how we have decreased our demands in teaching; who has undertaken a project of deliberately dumbing down the curriculum . . . and what the effects have been."

BIOGRAPHICAL/CRITICAL SOURCES:

PERIODICALS

American Spectator, May, 1989, p. 45; December, 1992, pp. 72-73.
Christian Science Monitor, February 11, 1991, p. 13.
Commentary, July, 1989, pp. 68-70.
Los Angeles Times, March 7, 1989.
Nation, February 24, 1992, pp. 236-39.
National Review, April 21, 1989, p. 39; October 15, 1990, pp. 72-74; January 18, 1993, pp. 48-49; September 20, 1993, pp. 74-75.
New York Review of Books, January 28, 1993, pp. 12-15.
New York Times, November 13, 1992, p. C28.
New York Times Book Review, February 19, 1989, p. 16; December 9, 1990, p. 28; November 12, 1995, pp. 14-16.
Wall Street Journal, October 20, 1995, p. A10.*

* * *

SZABO, Sandor 1954-

PERSONAL: Born April 16, 1954, in Hungary.

ADDRESSES: Office—Department of Mathematics, University of Bahrain, P.O. Box 32038, Bahrain.

CAREER: Author. Affiliated with department of mathematics at University of Bahrain.

WRITINGS:

(With Sherman Stein) *Algebra and Tiling,* Mathematical Association of America (Washington, DC), 1994.

T-U

TARNOPOLSKY, Yuri 1936-

PERSONAL: Born October 14, 1936, in Kharkov, U.S.S.R. (now the Ukraine); immigrated to the United States, 1987; naturalized citizen; son of Ilya (a manager) and Bella (an accountant; maiden name, Zelichenok) Tarnopolsky; married Olga Tupikina (a teacher), 1970; children: Irina. *Education:* Polytechnical Institute, Kharkov, M.S., 1960; Moscow Mendeleev Institute, Ph.D., 1964. *Religion:* Jewish. *Avocational interests:* Poetry, music, history.

ADDRESSES: Home—84 Pettaquamscutt Lake Rd., Narragansett, RI 02874. *Office*—Technic Inc., 1 Spectacle St., Cranston, RI 02910.

CAREER: Siberian Institute of Technology, Krasnoyarsk, U.S.S.R. (now Russia), professor of chemistry, 1964-77; SepTech, Inc., Wakefield, RI, senior scientist, 1988-91; Technic, Inc., Cranston, RI, senior scientist, 1994—.

MEMBER: American Chemical Society.

AWARDS, HONORS: Prix de la Liberte, French PEN Club, 1985; named honorary citizen of Chicago, 1987; Gimprich Award to a Distinguished Refugee Scientist, 1992.

WRITINGS:

La Clairiere dans la Pinede (poetry), Cahiers Bleu (Paris, France), 1985.
Memoirs of 1984 (nonfiction), foreword by Paul Simon, University Press of America (Lanham, MD), 1993.

Also contributor of articles to Russian and American chemical journals.

WORK IN PROGRESS: The New and the Different, a book on complexity.

SIDELIGHTS: Scientist, poet, and author Yuri Tarnopolsky was born in the former Soviet Union, but he fought for his right to emigrate from the Soviet Union, and was put into a Siberian labor camp for several years. His alleged crime was attempting "to steal state property from the Soviet Government"; the property in question was himself, and presumably his scientific knowledge. While he was serving his sentence, Tarnopolsky's first collection of poetry, *La Clairiere dans la Pinede,* was published in France. Eventually, he was released and allowed to immigrate to the United States, where he became a research chemist in Rhode Island. In 1993, his account of his experiences as a Soviet prisoner, *Memoirs of 1984,* was published.

Memoirs of 1984 takes its title from British author George Orwell's anti-utopian novel, *1984.* Tarnopolsky found it interesting that the actual year 1984 found him in a labor camp in a country where the novel had been forbidden. Among his assertions in *Memoirs* is that life in the camp in which he was interred differed only by the intensity of a person's discomfort from the life of the average Soviet citizen. At another point in the volume, he discusses his "trial" by fellow convicts who accused him of what Cathy Young, critiquing the work in the *New York Times Book Review,* described as "breaking the thieves' honor code." Tarnopolsky claims that this "trial" was much more fair than the one that actually landed him in the camp: "I had a chance to defend

414

myself . . . the outcome was not predetermined." In fact, he was found innocent by the other inmates, because they agreed with his defense: as a political prisoner he lived by another set of rules than their own.

Tarnopolsky offers up to readers of *Memoirs* his faith in what he calls "American materialism," though he tells of coming to respect the viewpoint of another political prisoner who supported the old rule of the Russian Czars. Tarnopolsky does not hold out much hope for change in Russia despite the fall of the Soviet Empire, feeling that there is something in the Russian people that is susceptible to totalitarianism. Though he compares his old country with his new one and finds many important differences between them, he warns that the kind of political and social oppression which took place under the former Soviet regime can surface in any nation, even the United States.

Young praised the author's command of the English language. However, she criticized the way in which Tarnopolsky adjusted the names of the people of his story for American readers. "The Tonys, Als and Mikes cropping up against a very Russian backdrop seem artificial and confusing." Nevertheless, she hailed *Memoirs* as a "vivid, eccentric, often gripping narrative." In his foreword to *Memoirs,* U.S. Senator Paul Simon lauded the volume as "a living testament to the power and force of freedom and a tribute to those, who by their very sacrifice and dedication to human values, perpetuate the ideals of freedom and democracy throughout the world."

Tarnopolsky told *CA:* "Since my childhood I wanted to be a writer because I had already been an ardent reader and I wished to reverse the enchanting process. I became a chemist, probably, because chemistry was also a kind of magic, next in the row after writing. Instead of building structures from words, I took up building structures from atoms. It was not enough, and I wrote poetry with no chance to publish it in Soviet Russia. A small part of it was published much later in France. Anyway, I felt comfortable in both rarely compatible habitats (sciences and humanities), like an amphibian.

"I came to America in 1987 after eight years of struggling for an exit visa as a *refusenik,* three of them spent in a Siberian labor camp as a political prisoner. I breathed the oxygen of freedom through both lungs and gills: I worked as a research chemist and wrote *Memoirs of 1984* in my spare time.

"I never intended to write prison memoirs. I was interested in the conflict between a person who was a planet of his own and a country that was consistent and solid enough to be regarded a person. I considered my experience in Russia as an experiment with history, conducted on myself. Fortunately, I was able to watch the decline and fall of the Soviet Empire—an event comparable with the fall of the Roman Empire. Most of all, however, I have been interested in America. I am concerned about the American sprouts of what I thought was indigenous Soviet vegetation—political correctness, for example.

"I am working on my next book, *The New and the Different*—a popular science treatise on the complexity of Everything. It will not be a compilation, but, hopefully, a new blend of mathematics and poetry, both of them discussed in the book as sister games of the mind. It will be about America, too.

"Writing in English—the language that is not my native—gives me the same sweet pain that only the self-imposed bondage of writing rhymed poetry can give."

BIOGRAPHICAL/CRITICAL SOURCES:

BOOKS

Tarnopolsky, Yuri, *Memoirs of 1984,* foreword by Paul Simon, University Press of America (Lanham, MD), 1993.

PERIODICALS

New York Times Book Review, February 6, 1994, p. 37.

* * *

TAVIANI, Paolo 1931-

PERSONAL: Born November 8, 1931, in San Miniato, Pisa, Italy. *Education:* Attended University of Pisa.

ADDRESSES: Home—Via dell'Ongaro 41, Rome, Italy, 06/5817231.

CAREER: Screenwriter and director of motion pictures. Co-founder, with brother Vittorio, of a film club.

AWARDS, HONORS: Golden Palm and International Critics Prize, Cannes Film Festival, 1977, for *Padre Padrone;* Special Jury Prize, Cannes Film Festival, 1982, and best director award, National Society of Film Critics, 1983, both for *Night of the Shooting Stars.*

WRITINGS:

PUBLISHED SCREENPLAYS WRITTEN AND DIRECTED WITH BROTHER, VITTORIO TAVIANI

San Michele aveva un gallo/Allonsafan (*San Michele aveva un gallo* released in 1971; *Allonsafan* released in 1974), introduction by Guido Aristarco, Cappelli, 1974.

Padre Padrone (title means "Father Master"; adapted from Gavino Ledda's book; Radio Italiano, 1977; released in the United States as *Padre Padrone,* New Yorker Films), introduction by Mino Argentieri, Cappelli, 1977.

(With Tonino Guerra) *Good Morning, Babylon* (released as *Good Morning Babilonia,* Filmtre/MK2/Pressman/RAI/Films A2, 1986; released in the United States as *Good Morning, Babylon,* Vestron, 1987), [London], 1987.

OTHER SCREENPLAYS WRITTEN AND DIRECTED WITH VITTORIO TAVIANI

(With Valentino Orsini) *Un uomo da bruciare* (title means "A Man for Burning"; title also translated as "A Man for the Killing"), 1962.

I fuorilegge del matrimonio, 1963.

I sovversivi (title means "The Subversives"), Ager, 1967.

Sotto il segno dello scorpione (title means "Under the Sign of the Scorpion"), 1969.

Il prato, 1979, released in the United States as *The Meadow,* New Yorker Films.

(With Tonino Guerra and Giuliani G. De Negri) *La notte di San Lorenzo* (title means "The Night of San Lorenzo"), RAI Radiotelevisione/Agner Cinematografica/Premier, 1982, released in the United States as *The Night of the Shooting Stars,* United Artists Classics, 1983.

(With Guerra) *Kaos* (adapted from Luigi Pirandello's short stories "The Other Son," "The Jar," "Requiem," and "Moon Sickness"), Metro-Goldwyn-Mayer/United Artists Classics, 1984.

(With Guerra) *Il sole anche di notte* (adapted from Leo Tolstoy's short story "Father Sergius"), Filmtre/Raiuno/Capoul/Inerpool/Sara Film/

Direkt Film, 1990, released in the United States as *Night Sun.*

(With Sandro Petraglia) *Fiorille,* Fine Line Features, 1993.

DOCUMENTARY SCREENPLAYS WRITTEN AND DIRECTED WITH VITTORIO TAVIANI

Also joint author of documentary screenplays, including *San Miniato, luglio '44,* 1954; *Voltera, commune medievale,* 1955; *Curtatone e Montanara,* 1955; *Carlo Pisacane; Ville della Brianza; Lavatori della pietra; Pittori in citta; I Pazzi della domenica; Moravia; Carbunara,* 1959; and contributor to *L'Italia non e un paesa povero.*

SIDELIGHTS: Brothers Paolo Taviani and Vittorio Taviani are an acclaimed filmmaking team who have written and directed some of Italian cinema's most significant works of recent decades. David Denby, writing in *New York,* declared that the Tavianis "seem possessed of a true folk imagination, both elemental and rigorous, harsh and responsive."

Both Tavianis were born in Pisa, and both eventually attended the university there. In 1950, together with Valentino Orsini, the Tavianis established a film club in Pisa. Next they teamed with Cesare Zavattini—writer of such films as director Vittorio De Sica's neorealist masterwork *The Bicycle Thief*—on a documentary project. By the mid-1950s, the Tavianis and Orsini had begun making their own documentary films.

By 1960 the Tavianis—sometimes in collaboration with Orsini—had written and directed ten documentaries. In 1962 the trio decided to attempt feature filmmaking. The result of their efforts was *Un uomo da bruciare* (referred to in English as "A Man for Burning" or "A Man for the Killing"). In this film a political activist returns to his native Sicily and promptly runs afoul of organized criminals who are exploiting local peasants. The Tavianis came to regard *Un uomo da bruciare* as a homage to Italy's neorealist classics.

The Tavianis next wrote and directed *I sovversivo* (which means "The Subversives"), a compelling drama depicting the effect of a communist leader's death on four individuals in Italy. In one storyline, a woman commences a lesbian tryst while her husband is attending the funeral; another narrative concerns a Venezuelan who is inspired to abandon his wealthy

lover and devote himself to sparking a revolution in his homeland. Peter Bondanella, in his study *Italian Cinema: From Neorealism to the Present,* deemed *I sovversivi* "an interesting study."

With their following achievement, *Allonsanfan,* the Tavianis continued to explore political themes. Here a Jacobean aristocrat in mid-eighteenth-century Italy is reluctantly drawn, by a former mistress, into a peasant rebellion in Sicily. His return to activism holds harrowing, even fatal, consequences. Although *I sovversivo* and *Allonsanfan* were both well received in Europe, they failed to make a significant impact on the United States.

More successful among American audiences was *Padre Padrone,* a disturbing, rather surreal portrait of a son's life under a crude, domineering father. The film traces the life of the son from childhood, spent as a shepherd under his cruel and abusive father in mountainous Italy, into young adulthood, when the son finally escapes from his grim circumstances by entering the military. *Padre Padrone,* which was based on actual events, won the Golden Palm and International Critics Prize at the 1977 Cannes Film Festival, and it received further praise after it was shown at the New York Film Festival later that year.

In 1982 the Tavianis scored further success with *Night of the Shooting Stars,* in which a woman recalls her childhood experiences in a small Italian town towards the close of World War II. Various figures unite and desert the village rather than risk the continued wrath of the occupying Nazis who are themselves preparing to elude invading Allied forces. During the sojourn, friendships and romances develop among the travellers, although their journey holds considerable danger. Like *Padre Padrone* before it, *Night of the Shooting Stars* received recognition as a magical, emotionally compelling examination of the human condition. The film was awarded the Special Jury Prize at the Cannes Film Festival.

Kaos, another Taviani feature, is derived from tales by Luigi Pirandello, the prolific Italian writer who is probably best known in the United States for his absurdist play *Six Characters in Search of an Author.* In *Kaos,* the Tavianis adapt four of Pirandello's unusual tales. Perhaps most notable in *Kaos* is "Moon Sickness," which concerns a newly married farmer who becomes convulsive during the full moon. *Time*'s Richard Corliss described this particular episode as "surrealism made simple."

With *Good Morning, Babylon* the Tavianis made their first English-language production. In this film two Italian brothers seek fame and fortune in the United States during the twentieth-century's second decade, a time when Hollywood established itself as the American film capitol. The brothers, Nicola and Andrea, eventually find love and happiness while working on director D. W. Griffith's epic *Intolerance.* That happiness, though, is shattered by America's involvement in World War I, whereupon the brothers are compelled to choose between their lives in America and their obligations to their Italian family and friends. *Newsweek*'s David Ansen acknowledged the "willfully naive vision" of *Good Morning, Babylon,* and while he conceded that the film's perspective is rather fragile, he concluded that it nonetheless constitutes "a lovely reverie."

Night Sun, which the Tavianis completed in 1990, marks a return to their more disturbing, yet characteristically inspirational fare, such as *Padre Padrone.* In *Night Sun,* which the brothers loosely fashioned from Leo Tolstoy's short story "Father Sergius," a dashing baron becomes a monk who realizes true salvation only after compromising his religious convictions. Janet Maslin, writing in the *New York Times,* acknowledged the "rapturous visual style" of *Night Sun,* and though she found that the opulent style ultimately overwhelmed the film's simple humanism, she nonetheless conceded that portions of the film "are rendered with particular beauty."

The Tavianis continued filmmaking in the 1990s with *Fiorile,* a multi-generation tale of ghosts and revenge. A family is afflicted by a curse when the thievery of a woman's brother brings about her lover's execution during the Napoleonic era. The woman, unaware that her brother's own treachery caused her lover's demise, invokes a curse on those responsible, and in the following years, even as her family amasses considerable wealth, they become victims of bad fortune. *New York Times* reviewer Stephen Holden called *Fiorile* a "sweeping and sensuous fable," and he added that the film "offers many pleasures."

For more information on Vittorio Taviani, please see his entry in this volume.

BIOGRAPHICAL/CRITICAL SOURCES:

BOOKS

Bondanella, Peter, *Italian Cinema: From Neorealism to the Present,* Ungar, 1983, pp. 175-78, 341-45.

PERIODICALS

American Film, June, 1987, pp. 26-31.
American Spectator, July, 1990, p. 36.
Nation, December 27, 1986, p. 748.
Newsweek, August 3, 1987, p. 68.
New York, July 27, 1987, pp. 59-60.
New York Times, September 28, 1990, p. C10; October 13, 1993, p. C21; October 14, 1993, p. B4.
Time, January 27, 1986, p. 64.*

* * *

TAVIANI, Vittorio 1929-

PERSONAL: Born September 20, 1929, in Miniato, Pisa, Italy. *Education:* Attended University of Pisa.

ADDRESSES: Home—Via Orti D'Alibert 4, Rome, Italy, 06/6541834.

CAREER: Director and screenwriter of motion pictures. Co-founder with brother Paolo of a film club.

AWARDS, HONORS: Golden Palm and International Critics Prize, Cannes Film Festival, 1977, for *Padre padrone;* Special Jury Prize, Cannes Film Festival, 1982, and best director award, National Society of Film Critics, 1983, both for *Night of the Shooting Stars.*

WRITINGS:

PUBLISHED SCREENPLAYS WRITTEN AND DIRECTED WITH BROTHER, PAOLO TAVIANI

San Michele aveva un gallo/Allonsafan (*San Michele aveva un gallo* released in 1971; *Allonsafan* released in 1974), introduction by Guido Aristarco, Cappelli, 1974.
Padre Padrone (title means "Father Master"; adapted from Gavino Ledda's book; Radio Italiano, 1977; released in the United States as *Padre Padrone,* New Yorker Films), introduction by Mino Argentieri, Cappelli, 1977.
(With Tonino Guerra) *Good Morning, Babylon* (released as *Good Morning Babilonia,* Filmtre/MK2/Pressman/RAI/Films A2, 1986; released in the United States as *Good Morning, Babylon,* Vestron, 1987), [London], 1987.

OTHER SCREENPLAYS WRITTEN AND DIRECTED WITH PAOLO TAVIANI

(With Valentino Orsini) *Un uomo da bruciare* (title means "A Man for Burning"; title also translated as "A Man for the Killing"), 1962.
I fuorilegge del matrimonio, 1963.
I sovversivi (title means "The Subversives"), Ager, 1967.
Sotto il segno dello scorpione (title means "Under the Sign of the Scorpion"), 1969.
Il prato, 1979, released in the United States as *The Meadow,* New Yorker Films.
(With Tonino Guerra and Giuliani G. De Negri) *La notte di San Lorenzo* (title means "The Night of San Lorenzo"), RAI Radiotelevisione/Agner Cinematografica/Premier, 1982, released in the United States as *The Night of the Shooting Stars,* United Artists Classics, 1983.
(With Guerra) *Kaos* (adapted from Luigi Pirandello's short stories "The Other Son," "The Jar," "Requiem," and "Moon Sickness"), Metro-Goldwyn-Mayer/United Artists Classics, 1984.
(With Guerra) *Il sole anche di notte* (adapted from Leo Tolstoy's short story "Father Sergius"), Filmtre/Raiuno/Capoul/Inerpool/Sara Film/Direkt Film, 1990, released in the United States as *Night Sun.*
(With Sandro Petraglia) *Fiorille,* Fine Line Features, 1993.

DOCUMENTARY SCREENPLAYS WRITTEN AND DIRECTED WITH PAOLO TAVIANI

Also joint author of documentary screenplays, including *San Miniato, luglio '44,* 1954; *Voltera, commune medievale,* 1955; *Curtatone e Montanara,* 1955; *Carlo Pisacane; Ville della Brianza; Lavatori della pietra; Pittori in citta; I Pazzi della domenica; Moravia; Carbunara,* 1959; and contributor to *L'Italia non e un paesa povero.*

SIDELIGHTS: For an essay describing the Tavianis brothers' work, please see the entry on Paolo Taviani in this volume.

BIOGRAPHICAL/CRITICAL SOURCES:

BOOKS

Bondanella, Peter, *Italian Cinema: From Neorealism to the Present,* Ungar, 1983, pp.175-78, 341-45.

PERIODICALS

American Film, June, 1987, pp. 26-31.
American Spectator, July, 1990, p. 36.
Nation, December 27, 1986, p. 748.
Newsweek, August 3, 1987, p. 68.
New York, July 27, 1987, pp. 59-60.
New York Times, September 28, 1990, p. C10; October 13, 1993, p. C21; October 14, 1993, p. B4.
Time, January 27, 1986, p. 64.*

* * *

TAYLOR, William N(athaniel, Jr.) 1952-

PERSONAL: Born September 26, 1952, in Miheola, NY; son of William Nathaniel (a chemical engineer) and Earline (a homemaker; maiden name, Merritt) Taylor; married Susan Presley (a registered nurse), June 25, 1982 (divorced); children: Three. *Education:* University of West Florida, B.S., 1975; University of Tennessee, M.S., 1976; University of Miami School of Medicine, M.D., 1981. *Religion:* Christian. *Avocational interests:* Body building, marathon running, golf, swimming, cycling, tennis, fishing.

ADDRESSES: Office—University of Central Florida, Department of Exceptional and Physical Education, 4000 Cental Blvd., Orlando, FL 32816. *E-mail*—wntaylor@pegasus.cc.ucf.edu.

CAREER: B. F. Goodrich Chemical Co., Avon Lake, OH, research scientist, 1976-77; Abtec Chemical Company, Louisville, KY, technical service engineer and research engineer, 1977; Medical Center Hospital, Punta Gorda, FL, director of emergency medicine, 1982-83; Sun Bay Hospital, St. Petersburg, FL, emergency medicine physician, beginning 1983; University of Central Florida, Orlando, associate professor of exceptional and physical education, c. 1995—. Physician crew chief for United States Olympic Committee Drug Education Program, 1984-88; assistant professor of sports medicine for United States Sports Academy, 1986; director of Lifefitness Clinic. Speaker at various medical symposia. Has served as medical advisor to American Running and Fitness Association. Appeared in several television segments on human growth hormone broadcast on Canadian and British television.

MEMBER: American Academy of Sports Physicians (board of governors, 1989, 1990), American College of Sports Medicine, American Institute of Chemical Engineers, American Chemical Society, American Medical Joggers' Association, Alpha Omega Alpha Medical Honor Society.

WRITINGS:

Anabolic Steroids and the Athlete, McFarland (Jefferson, NC), 1982.
Marathon Running: A Medical Science Handbook, McFarland, 1982.
Hormonal Manipulation: A New Era of Monstrous Athletes, McFarland, 1985.
Macho Medicine: A History of the Anabolic Steroid Epidemic, McFarland, 1991.
Osteoporosis: Medical Blunders and Treatment Strategies, McFarland, 1996.

Contributor to books, including *Sports Medicine: Fitness and Training Injuries,* 3rd edition, edited by Appenzeller and Atkinson, Urban & Schwaarzenberg Medical Publishers (Baltimore, MD), 1986; and *Winter Sports Medicine,* edited by J. C. Murray, Human Kinetics Publishers (Champaign, IL), 1988. Contributor to periodicals, including *Polymer Engineering and Science, Annals of Sports Medicine, Psychology Today,* and *J. Neurological and Orthopedic Medicine and Surgery.* Contributing editor to *Muscle Digest Magazine, Iron Man Magazine, Muscle and Fitness Magazine, Runner's World Magazine, Southern Bodybuilder,* and *Track and Field News.*

BIOGRAPHICAL/CRITICAL SOURCES:

PERIODICALS

Christian Science Monitor, January 3, 1986, p. B7.
Library Journal, January 15, 1983.

* * *

TEAHAN, Sheila 1961-

PERSONAL: Born January 3, 1961. *Education:* University of Toronto, B.A., 1982; Yale University, Ph.D., 1989.

ADDRESSES: Office—Department of English, Michigan State University, East Lansing, MI 48824.

CAREER: Michigan State University, East Lansing, assistant professor, 1989-95, associate professor of English, 1995—.

WRITINGS:

The Rhetorical Logic of Henry James, Louisiana State University Press (Baton Rouge, LA), 1995.

* * *

THOMAS, (Philip) Edward 1878-1917 (Edward Eastaway)

PERSONAL: Born March 3, 1878, in London, England; killed in action during World War I, April 9, 1917, at Battle of Arras in Arras, France; son of a railway clerk; married Helen Noble, c. 1895. *Education:* Attended St. Paul's School, London, and Lincoln College, Oxford.

CAREER: Freelance writer and reviewer for various publications. *Military service:* Served in British Army, infantry, 1915-1917.

WRITINGS:

POETRY

(Under pseudonym Edward Eastaway) *Six Poems,* Pear Tree Press, 1916.
Poems, Holt, 1917.
Last Poems, Selwyn & Blount, 1918.
Collected Poems, Selwyn & Blount, 1920, Seltzer, 1921, enlarged edition, Ingpen & Grant, 1928, reprinted, Faber & Faber, 1979.
Two Poems, Ingpen & Grant, 1927.
The Poems of Edward Thomas, edited by R. George Thomas, Oxford University Press, 1978.
Edward Thomas: A Mirror of England, edited by Elaine Wilson, Paul & Co., 1985.

CRITICISM

Richard Jefferies, His Life and Work, Little, Brown, 1909.
The Feminine Influence on the Poets, Secker, 1910, John Lane, 1911.
Maurice Maeterlinck, Dodd, Mead, 1911.
Algernon Charles Swinburne, A Critical Study, Kennerley, 1912.
George Borrow, The Man and His Books, Dutton, 1912.

Lafcadio Hearn, Houghton Mifflin, 1912.
Walter Pater, A Critical Study, Kennerley, 1913.
Keats, Dodge, c.1916.
A Literary Pilgrim in England, Dodd, Mead, 1917, Oxford University Press, 1980.

ESSAYS

Horae Solitariae, Dutton, 1902.
Beautiful Wales, Black, 1905.
The Heart of England, Dutton, 1906.
The South Country, Dutton, 1909, Tuttle, 1993.
Rest and Unrest, Dutton, 1910.
Light and Twilight, Duckworth, 1911.
The Last Sheaf, Cape, 1928.

PROSE

The Woodland Life (essays and diary), Blackwood, 1897.
Oxford, Black, 1903.
Rose Acre Papers, Brown, Langham, 1904.
Windsor Castle, Blackie, 1910.
The Tenth Muse, Secker, 1911.
Celtic Stories, Clarendon (Oxford), 1911, Clarendon (New York), 1913.
The Isle of Wight, Blackie, 1911.
Norse Tales, Clarendon, 1912.
The Happy-Go-Lucky Morgans (novel), Duckworth, 1913.
The Icknield Way, Dutton, 1913.
The Country, Batsford, 1913.
In Pursuit of Spring, Nelson, 1914.
The Life of the Duke of Marlborough (biography), Chapman & Hall, 1915.
Cloud Castle and Other Papers, Dutton, c.1923.
The Childhood of Edward Thomas (autobiography), Faber, 1938.
The Friend of the Blackbird, Pear Tree Press, 1938.
The Prose of Edward Thomas, edited by Roland Gant, Falcon Press, 1948.
A Pilgrim and Other Tales (short stories and essays), Tuttle, 1992.

OTHER

Four-and-Twenty Blackbirds (fairy tales), Duckworth, 1915.

SIDELIGHTS: Despite affinities with the Georgian movement of the early twentieth century, Edward Thomas's verse consistently defies classification. Like the work of his Georgian contemporaries, his

verse displays a profound love of natural beauty and, at times, an archaic use of diction. However, Thomas's personalized voice and intensity of vision give his poetry an artistic force which the Georgians never approached.

Thomas was born of Welsh parents in London. His father was a railway clerk who neglected his six sons in favor of politics and intellectual pursuits. Temperamentally, he was the opposite of his son, and the two disagreed on nearly all matters, including Thomas's desire for a literary career. Much later Thomas was to portray this adversarial relationship with his father in the poem *"P.H.T."* In 1894, while attending St. Paul's School, Thomas met the successful literary journalist James Ashcroft Noble, who encouraged Thomas in his literary ambitions and was instrumental in getting his first book, *The Woodland Life,* accepted for publication. Shortly thereafter, while still a student at Lincoln College in Oxford, Thomas married Noble's daughter, Helen. Faced with the necessity of supporting a growing family, Thomas began accepting assignments of all sorts from London publishers. Much of the work he received was uncongenial hackwork, but Thomas wrote steadily, sometimes producing as many as three books a year. His work included essays, natural history, criticism, biographies, reviews, fiction, introductions, and topographical descriptions. Thomas wrote his first poems in 1914 at the urging of the American poet Robert Frost. Two years later his first book of verse, *Six Poems,* was published. Due to Thomas's fear that it would be unfairly dismissed by the critics if it were published under his own name, this collection was published under the pseudonym of Edward Eastaway. These six were the only poems that Thomas lived to see in print: in 1915 he enlisted in the infantry and was killed two years later in the Battle of Arras, while the first edition of his *Poems* was being prepared for press.

Thomas's many reviews and critical studies—such as *Richard Jefferies, Walter Pater,* and *The Feminine Influence on the Poets*—represent the best of his prose work. Much of Thomas's prose was written according to the demands and deadlines of his publishers. Many critics believe that Thomas wasted his talents on hack work, and the author himself felt that his artistic potential was being destroyed under the strain of constant production. In spite of these circumstances, Thomas developed into a respected critic, and his reviews for various newspapers and journals were widely quoted. All of Thomas's criticism has been praised for its lucid style, precision of speech, and intelligent observations. Vernon Scannell has said that Thomas's "verse criticism shows not merely an intuitive awareness of what poetry should be about, but an intelligent familiarity with refinements of technique and a fine sense of the historical continuity of English literature."

While an accomplished prose writer, Thomas is of far more interest for the poetry which he began to write relatively late in his career. From his first poems, Thomas demonstrated, according to John Lehmann, an "intensity of vision" which set him apart from his contemporaries. His earliest poems bear the influence of Frost in their treatment of nature and in their simple style. However, Frost's influence was to decrease as Thomas discovered his own personal voice. Numerous critics, including Jeremy Hooker and J. P. Ward, have stressed the two principal themes in Thomas's verse: one, the presence of war and its effect on the individual; the other, the poet's profound sense of solitude. Though he wrote only one war poem per se— *"This Is No Case of Petty Right or Wrong"*—throughout his poetry Thomas subtly portrays the influence of war on the natural order. Thomas's sense of solitude has led Ward to consider him an early existentialist. Though this might be an isolated point of view, most critics agree that Thomas remains appealing to the modern reader—while many of his contemporaries have fallen out of favor—because his poetry expresses an awareness of individual alienation commonly associated with existentialism.

Such prominent critics and authors as Walter de la Mare and Aldous Huxley have called Thomas one of England's most important poets. In recent years much serious consideration has been given to Thomas's work. Most critics would agree with Andrew Motion, who states that Thomas occupies "a crucial place in the development of twentieth-century poetry" for introducing a modern sensibility, later found in the work of such poets as W. H. Auden and Ted Hughes, to the poetic subjects of Victorian and Georgian poetry.

BIOGRAPHICAL/CRITICAL SOURCES:

BOOKS

Leavis, F. R., *New Bearings in English Poetry,* Chatto & Windus, 1932.
Thomas, R. George, *Edward Thomas: A Portrait,* Oxford University Press, 1985.

THORNDIKE, John 1942-

PERSONAL: Born November 6, 1942, in New York, NY; son of Joseph J. (an editor) and Virginia (a doctor) Thorndike; married Clarisa Rubio Betancourt (divorced, 1974); children: Janir Daniel. *Education:* Harvard University, B.A., 1964; Columbia University, M.A., 1966.

ADDRESSES: Home—630 East Alameda, Santa Fe, NM 87501. *E-mail*—76745,110@compuserve.com. *Agent*—Kathy Anderson, Scovil, Chichek, Galen, 381 Park Ave. S., Suite 1020, New York, NY 10016.

CAREER: Writer.

WRITINGS:

Anna Delaney's Child (novel), Macmillan (New York), 1986.
The Potato Baron (novel), Villard (New York), 1989.
Another Way Home: A Single Father's Story, Crown (New York), 1996.

* * *

THORNTON, Yvonne S(hirley) 1947-

PERSONAL: Born November 21, 1947, in New York, NY; daughter of Donald E. (a laborer) and Itasker F. (a domestic worker; maiden name, Edmonds) Thornton; married Shearwood J. McClelland (an orthopedic surgeon), June 8, 1974; children: Shearwood III, Kimberly Itaska. *Education:* Monmouth College, B.S., 1969; Columbia University, M.D., 1973, M.P.H., 1996. *Politics:* Democrat. *Religion:* Baptist. *Avocational interests:* Competitive ballroom dancing, tennis, needlepoint, saxophonist, vocalist.

ADDRESSES: Home—Teaneck, NJ. *Office*—100 Madison Ave., Morristown, NJ 07962. *Agent*—The Richard Parks Agency, 138 East 16th St., New York, NY 10003. *E-mail*—yst1@columbia.edu.

CAREER: Roosevelt Hospital, New York City, resident in obstetrics and gynecology, 1973-77; Columbia-Presbyterian Medical Center, New York City, fellow in maternal-fetal medicine, 1977-79; Uniformed Services University of Health Sciences, Bethesda, MD, assistant professor of obstetrics and gynecology, 1979-82; Cornell University Medical College, New York City, assistant professor, 1982-89, associate professor of obstetrics and gynecology, 1989-92, assistant attending, 1982-89; New York Lying-in Hospital, New York City, assistant attending, 1982-89, associate attending of obstetrics and gynecology, 1989-92; New York Hospital-Cornell Medical Center, directory of clinical services department of obstetrics and gynecology, 1982-88, director of chorionic villus sampling program, 1984-92, Rockefeller University Hospital, New York City, visiting associate physician, 1986—; Columbia University College of Physicians and Surgeons, New York City, associate clinical professor, 1995—. Director of perinatal diagnostic testing center at Morristown Memorial Hospital, 1992-; saxophonist in Thornton Sisters ensemble, 1955-76. *Military service:* United State Navy, medical corps, 1979-82, became Lieutenant commander.

MEMBER: American Board of Obstetrics and Gynecology (diplomate), National Board of Medical Examiners, American College of Obstetricians and Gynecologists (fellow), American College of Surgeons, American Medical Association, American Society of Human Genetics, New York Academy of Medicine, Association of Women Surgeons, Society of Perinatal Obstetricians, American Federation of Musicians.

AWARDS, HONORS: Daniel Webster Oratorical Competition (Washington, DC), first place, 1996; the audiotape of *The Ditchdigger's Daughters* was named one of 1996's Best Audiobooks by *Publisher's Weekly; The Ditchdigger's Daughters* was named to the American Library Association's Best Books for Young Adults list, 1996.

WRITINGS:

(With Jo Coudert) *The Ditchdigger's Daughters: A Black Family's Astonishing Success Story* (autobiography), Birch Lane Press (New York), 1995.
Woman to Woman: Everything You Wanted to Know about Women's Health, Plume/Dutton, 1997.

ADAPTATIONS: The Ditchdigger's Daughters was adapted as a book on tape.

SIDELIGHTS: Yvonne S. Thornton, an accomplished physician, is the author of *The Ditchdigger's Daughters: A Black Family's Astonishing Success Story,* which she wrote with author Jo Coudert. Born before the Civil Rights movement, Thornton and her four sisters were raised by a hard-working, ditch-digging father and a house-cleaning mother, whose college

education was cut short by a lack of money. Both of Thornton's parents were determined that their own daughters would be educated and successful in life, despite the odds stacked against them because they were poor, black, and female in a society that oppressed such qualities. The personification of tough love, Thornton's father instilled in his daughters the belief that through hard-work and study, they could do anything they dreamed of; but without discipline and an education, Donald Thornton warned his girls, they would live a hard life of physical labor and little respect. In her book, Thornton recalls how her father would drive home his point: once, when one of her sisters brought home a "C" on a test, her parents showed little reaction. Early the next morning, however, her parents woke the girl and ordered her to scrub the kitchen floor, to show her what she would be doing for the rest of her life if she did not study harder. Thornton's father also continually reminded them of the importance of being smart; society would not accept their dark skin, he told them, but if they were smart, they would gain respect and honor. "The most valuable lesson he taught us," Thornton told *Detroit Free Press* writer Cassandra Spratling, "was that the only person who can stop you from reaching your goal is you. You set a goal, you aim your sights on that goal and that's it. . . . Whatever you do, you keep going till you reach your goal."

The Ditchdigger's Daughters is Thornton's account of how she and her sisters reached their goals and fulfilled their father's dreams for his daughters' success. Each is a professional: Yvonne and one of her sisters are medical doctors, while one is an oral surgeon, another is a lawyer, and the oldest sister is a court stenographer. They financed their educations by performing as the Thornton Sisters, a musical group, with Yvonne on saxophone. Popular on college campuses, the band also garnered spots on *Ted Mack's Amateur Hour* and *Amateur Night at the Apollo Theater.*

Reviewers have warmly received *The Ditchdigger's Daughters* as an inspiring story of the power of a family's love, with most observing that the Thornton family's accomplishments are tremendous for people of any color or social standing. *Wall Street Journal* contributor Joseph Perkins, for example, found Thornton's story "shows that a family that stays together, that holds fast to traditional values, can make a quantum leap up the social mobility scale in a single generation. This holds true no matter how poor a family may start out and no matter what the family's racial heritage." Reviewer Marilyn Sanders Mobley,

writing in the *Washington Post,* also appreciated the values dominating *The Ditchdigger's Daughters.* "At a moment in this nation's history when experts are lamenting the demise of the family and the loss of so-called family values," Mobley declared, "this book not only tells the story of a black family's success but also serves as a corrective to those who have underestimated the strength of the values that have historically enabled black families to survive and even thrive. . . . While the story of each daughter's life path is interesting, Yvonne's personal dream to become an obstetrician-gynecologist is remarkable."

BIOGRAPHICAL/CRITICAL SOURCES:

BOOKS

Thornton, Yvonne S. and Jo Coudert, *The Ditchdigger's Daughters: A Black Family's Astonishing Success Story,* Birch Lane Press (New York), 1995.

PERIODICALS

Booklist, May, 1995.
Detroit Free Press, April 12, 1995, pp. E 1, 3.
New York Daily News, April 16, 1995.
New York Times Book Review, October 1, 1995, p. 29.
Philadelphia Inquirer, June 18, 1995.
Plain Dealer (Cleveland), May 14, 1995.
Publishers Weekly, April 17, 1995, p. 47.
USA Today, May 18, 1995.
Wall Street Journal, September 6, 1995, p. A 16.
Washington Post, May 11, 1995, p. D 2.

* * *

TRAINOR, Bernard E. 1928-

PERSONAL: Born September 2, 1928, in New York, NY; married, June 13, 1959; wife's name, Peggy; children: Kathleen, Theresa, Eileen, Claire. *Ethnicity:* "Caucasian." *Education:* College of the Holy Cross, B.S., 1951; University of Colorado, M.A., 1962, and further graduate study; Air War College, Distinguished Graduate; attended Marine Corps Command and Staff College. *Politics:* Independent. *Religion:* Roman Catholic.

ADDRESSES: Home—80 Potter Pond, Lexington, MA 02173. *Office*—John F. Kennedy School of Gov-

ernment, Harvard University, 79 John F. Kennedy St., Cambridge, MA 02138; fax 212-223-0720. *Agent*—Robbins Office, 866 Second Ave., New York, NY 10017.

CAREER: U.S. Marine Corps, career officer, 1951-85, including service in Korea and Vietnam, as deputy chief of staff for plans, policies, and operations, and as deputy to the joint chiefs of staff, retiring as lieutenant general; *New York Times,* New York City, military correspondent, 1985-90; Harvard University, Cambridge, MA, director of National Security Program and adjunct lecturer in public policy, John F. Kennedy School of Government, 1990—. Presidential Commission for Roles and Missions, member; World Affairs Council, member of board of directors; Marine Toys for Tots Foundation, member of board of directors. Military analyst, American Broadcasting Co. and *NBC News.*

MEMBER: International Institute for Strategic Studies, Council on Foreign Relations.

WRITINGS:

Military Perspectives on Humanitarian Intervention and Military-Media Relations (Chester W. Nimitz Memorial Lectures in National Security), University of California Press, 1995.
(With Michael R. Gordon) *The Generals' War: The Inside Story of the Conflict in the Gulf,* Little, Brown (Boston, MA), 1995.

Contributor to books, including *Newsmen and National Defense,* 1991; *After the Storm,* 1992, and *Perspectives on Warfighting,* 1992. Weekly columnist, New York Times Syndicate.

WORK IN PROGRESS: Research on the military in the 1950s.

* * *

TREUER, David 1970-

PERSONAL: Born October 21, 1970, in Washington, DC; son of Rober (a writer) and Margaret (a lawyer) Treuer. *Ethnicity:* "Native American." *Education:* Princeton University, A.B., 1992; University of Michigan, M.A., 1996.

ADDRESSES: Home—1207 Farmstead Lane N.E., Bemidji, MN 56601.

CAREER: Writer.

WRITINGS:

Little (novel), Graywolf Press (St. Paul, MN), 1995.

* * *

TRISTAN
 See **GOMEZ DE LA SERNA, Ramon**

* * *

TURTLEDOVE, Harry (Norman) 1949-
 (Eric Iverson)

PERSONAL: Born in 1949. *Education:* Received a Ph.D. in Byzantine history.

ADDRESSES: Agent—Scott Meredith, 845 Third Ave., New York, NY 10022.

CAREER: Science fiction novelist and short story writer.

AWARDS, HONORS: Recipient of Hugo award for science fiction.

WRITINGS:

NOVELS

(As Eric Iverson) *Wereblood,* Belmont Tower (New York), 1979.
(As Iverson) *Werenight,* Belmont Tower, 1979.
A Different Flesh, Congdon & Weed (New York), 1988.
Noninterference, Ballantine (New York), 1988.
A World of Difference, Ballantine, 1990.
The Guns of the South: A Novel of the Civil War, Ballantine, 1992.
The Case of the Toxic Spell Dump, Ballantine, 1994.
Prince of the North, Baen (New York), 1994.
(With Richard Dreyfuss) *The Two Georges,* Tor (New York), 1996.

FANTASY NOVELS; "VIDESSOS CYCLE"

The Misplaced Legion, Ballantine, 1987.
An Emperor for the Legion, Ballantine, 1987.
The Legion of Videssos, Ballantine, 1987.
Swords of the Legion, Ballantine, 1987.
Krispos Rising, Ballantine, 1991.
Krispos of Videssos, Ballantine, 1991.
Krispos the Emperor, Ballantine, 1994.
The Stolen Throne, Ballantine, 1995.

SCIENCE-FICTION NOVELS; "WORLDWAR" SERIES

Worldwar: In the Balance, Ballantine, 1994.
Worldwar: Tilting the Balance, Ballantine, 1995.
Worldwar: Upsetting the Balance, Ballantine, 1996.

SHORT STORIES

Agent of Byzantium, Congdon & Weed, 1987 revised
 edition, 1994.
Kaleidoscope, Ballantine, 1990.
Earthgrip, Ballantine, 1991.
Departures, Ballantine, 1993.

Contributor of short stories to *The Magazine of Fantasy and Science Fiction* and *Analog.*

OTHER

(Translator) *The Chronicle of Theophanes: An English Translation of Anni Mundi 6095-9305 (A.D. 602-813),* University of Pennsylvania Press (Philadelphia, PA), 1982.

WORK IN PROGRESS: A fourth volume in the "Worldwar" series; another series on an alternative World War I.

SIDELIGHTS: In addition to writing novels and short stories in both the fantasy and science fiction genres, writer/historian Harry Turtledove has been credited by reviewers with creating yet another science fiction genre: "a combination of 'straight' SF and alternative history," in the words of M. Hammerton in *St. James Guide to Science Fiction Writers,* which the reviewer further defines as "the working out of the effect, over a fairly long period of time, of a particular act or a specified change of conditions."

In his popular multi-volume "Videssos Cycle," Turtledove has drawn on his vast knowledge of Byzantine history to recount the exploits of a Roman legion that finds itself transported to an alternate Roman Empire called Videssos. "The major appeal of the series remains Turtledove's competent handling of historical material," observed Roland Green in his *Booklist* review of *The Legion of Videssos.* Drawing once again upon his expertise, Turtledove wrote *Agent of Byzantium,* a collection of stories about Basil Argyros, a fourteenth-century secret agent of an alternate Byzantine Empire that never fell to crusaders, in a world where Mohammed converted to Christianity and became a saint. A *Kirkus Reviews* critic commented that "the backdrop is intriguing but Basil and his adventures are hard to believe in."

A more modern example of Turtledove's "alternate history SF" is his "Worldwar" series. The novels that comprise this series present an alternate-history saga of World War II in which Allied and Axis forces join together to combat technically superior alien invaders. *Library Journal* reviewer Jackie Cassada remarked in a review of *Worldwar: Tilting the Balance,* "Turtledove exhibits his genuine feel for crafting believable answers to historical 'what ifs'."

While the story collection *Kaleidoscope* and the novels *Noninterference* and *Earthgrip* can be classified as mainstream science fiction, much of Turtledove's work is "speculative fiction." In the seven stories comprising *A Different Flesh,* for example, the author envisions a world where *homo erectus* co-exists with *homo sapiens. Library Journal* reviewer James E. Cook noted that "Turtledove's gift for historical speculation is always provocative." Other worlds explored by Turtledove include an alternate Mars at war in the novel *A World of Difference,* a victorious Confederacy following the U.S. Civil War in *The Guns of the South,* and an alternate America that remains a colony of Great Britain in the novel *The Two Georges,* which was co-authored by actor Richard Dreyfuss. "Henry Turtledove is probably the best practitioner of the classic alternate-history since L. Sprague de Camp," summarized Russell Letson in *Locus,* "and his virtues are just those of the master: meticulous research and thorough knowledge of his period, an understated but firm way with storytelling, and a sense of the exotic appeal of the past combined with a recognition of the ordinariness of ordinary life."

BIOGRAPHICAL/CRITICAL SOURCES:

BOOKS

St. James Guide to Science Fiction Writers, edited by Jay P. Pederson, St. James Press (Detroit), 1995, pp. 939-40.

PERIODICALS

Booklist, February 15, 1987, p. 878; May 1, 1987, p. 1336; June 15, 1987, p. 1565; August 1987, p. 1722; October 1, 1987, p. 222; May 1, 1990, p. 1688; May 15, 1990, p. 1785; December 1, 1993, p. 678; January 1-15 1996, p. 799; February 1, 1996, p. 899.

Kirkus Reviews, May 1, 1987, p. 682; March 15, 1988, p. 417; August 1, 1992, p. 947.

Library Journal, April 15, 1988, p. 98; September 1, 1992, p. 217; November 15, 1993, p. 102; December 1995, p. 163.

Locus, June, 1990, p. 33; March, 1991, p. 60; October, 1991, pp. 31, 56; February, 1994, p. 75; April, 1994, pp. 23-24.

Publishers Weekly, January 23, 1987, p. 66; May 22, 1987, p. 69; March 18, 1988, p. 76; March 16, 1990, p. 66; January 11, 1991, p. 98; August 24, 1992, p. 63; December 6, 1993, p. 60; February 20, 1995, p. 200; January 22, 1996, p. 61; February 5, 1996, p. 80.

Science Fiction Chronicle, October, 1987, p. 41; January, 1988, p. 49; April, 1988, p. 52.

Voice of Youth Advocates, June, 1992, p. 116.

Washington Post Book World, June 27, 1993, p. 12.*

* * *

TUTHILL, John Wills 1910-1996

OBITUARY NOTICE—See index for *CA* sketch: Born November 10, 1910, in Montclair, NJ; died of cancer, September 9, 1996, in Washington, DC. Banker, educator, diplomat, author. Tuthill is best remembered for his years as ambassador to the European Economic Community and for his thirty years as a diplomat. At the beginning of his career, Tuthill held several banking positions, initially with the First National Bank in Paterson, New Jersey, then at Bankers Trust Company in New York City. From 1937 until 1940 he taught at Northeastern University. Then he began a lengthy term with the U.S. Department of State. His work with the State Department included stints as vice-consul in Windsor, Ontario, Canada, and Mazatlan, Mexico, secretary in the U.S. political adviser's office in Shaef, special assistant to the U.S. ambassador in London, England, and several directorships in the Office of Economic Affairs in Bonn, West Germany. In 1961 he became ambassador to the Organization for Economic Cooperation and Develop-

ment. He then served as ambassador to the European Economic Community and later to Brazil. He returned to teaching in 1969 as professor of international politics at Johns Hopkins University's Bologna Center in Italy. That same year he became director-general of the Atlantic Institute for International Affairs in Paris, France, until 1976; he continued his association with the Institute until 1986. From 1977 until 1985 he served as president of the Salzburg Seminar in American Studies in Cambridge, Massachusetts, and from 1978 until 1980 he was a visiting fellow at the Woodrow Wilson National Fellowship Foundation at Princeton. He rounded out his career as executive director and trustee of the American-Austrian Foundation from 1985 until 1988. Tuthill wrote *The Decisive Years Ahead* and a book of memoirs called *Some Things to Some Men: Serving in the Foreign Service.*

OBITUARIES AND OTHER SOURCES:

BOOKS

Who's Who in America, 49th edition, Marquis, 1994.

PERIODICALS

New York Times, September 22, 1996, p. 48.

* * *

TZARA, Tristan 1896-1963
(Samuel Rosenfeld, Samuel Rosenstock, Sami Rosenstock)

PERSONAL: Surname is pronounced "*tsa*-ra"; born Samuel Rosenfeld; name legally changed, 1925; born April 4, 1896 (some sources say April 16, 1896), in Moinesti, Bacu, Romania; immigrated to Switzerland, 1916; immigrated to France, 1919, naturalized citizen at the end of World War II; died December 24, 1963, in Paris France. *Education:* Bucharist University, 1914-15. *Politics:* Member of Communist Party, 1935-63. *Religion:* Jewish.

CAREER: Poet, dramatist, essayist, and critic. Founder, with Ion Vinea, of journal *Simbolul,* 1912; founder, with Ion Vinea, of journal *Chemarea,* 1915; founder, with Hugo Ball, Emmy Hennings, Marcel Janco, Richard Huelsenbeck, and Hans Arp, of Dadaist movement, Zurich, 1916. Member of Surre-

alist group of writers in Paris, 1929-34. Cultural ambassador to the Spanish Republic for the Writers' Association for the Defense of Culture; lecture tour through Central and Eastern Europe for French Ministry of Foreign Affairs, 1946. *Military service:* Served with Loyalists during the Spanish Civil War; directed the cultural broadcast of the French Resistance in the south of France, 1943-44, and wrote for Resistance magazines.

MEMBER: Writers' Association for the Defense of Culture.

AWARDS, HONORS: Taormina International Grand Prize for Poetry, 1961.

WRITINGS:

La premiere aventure celeste de Monsieur Antipyrine (poetry), [Paris], 1916.
Vingt-cinq poemes (poetry), Fontaine, 1918.
Anthologie Dada, Mouvement Dada, 1919.
Cinema calendrier du coeur abstrait maisons (poetry), [Paris], 1920.
La coeur a gaz (drama), [Paris], 1920, translation by Michael Benedikt published as *The Gas Heart,* 1964.
(With Hans Arp and Max Ernst) *Dada au grand air,* [Paris], 1921.
Faites vos jeux (unfinished autobiographical novel), [Paris], 1923.
De nos oiseaux (poetry), [Paris], 1923, translation by Lee Harwood published as *Cosmic Realities Vanilla Tobacco Dawnings,* Arc Publications, 1975.
Sept manifestes dada (essays), [Paris], 1924, translation by Barbara Wright published as *Seven Dada Manifestos and Lampisteries,* Calder, 1977.
Mouchoir de nuages (drama), Editions de la Galerie Simon, 1925.
Indicateur des chemins de coeur (poetry), [Paris], 1928.
L'arbre des voyageurs (poetry), [Paris], 1930.
Essai sur la situation de la poesie (essay), [Paris], 1931.
L'homme approximatif (poetry), Fourcade, 1931, translation by Mary Ann Caws published as *Approximate Man, and Other Writings,* Wayne State University Press, 1973.
Ou boivent les loups (poetry), [Paris], 1932.
L'antitete (prose poems), Editions des Cahiers libres, 1933.
Parler seul (poetry), Caracteres, 1933.
Abrege de la nuit (poetry and prose), [Paris], 1934.

Grains et issues (essay), Les Editions Denoel et Steele, 1935.
La main passe (poetry), [Paris], 1935.
Sur le champ, [Paris], 1937.
Vigies, [Paris], 1937, Alexandre Loewy, 1963.
La deuxieme aventure celeste de Monsieur Antipyrine (poetry), [Paris], 1938.
Midis gagnes (poetry), [Paris], 1939.
Ca va, [Paris], 1944.
Une route seul soleil, [Paris], 1944.
Entre-temps (poetry), [Paris], 1946.
Le signe de vie (poetry), Bordas, 1946.
Terre sur terre (poetry), Editions des Trois collines, 1946.
La fuite (drama), Gallimard, 1947.
Morceaux choisis, Bordas, 1947.
Le surrealisme et l'apres-guerre (essay), Nagel, 1947.
Picasso et les chemins de la connaissance, A. Skira, 1948.
Phases, P. Seghers, 1949.
Sans coup ferir (prose poem), [Paris], 1949.
De memoire d'homme (poetry), [Paris], 1950.
L'art oceanien, [Paris], 1951.
La premiere main, [Paris], 1952.
La face interieure (poetry), [Paris], 1953.
Picasso et la poesie (essay), [Paris], 1953.
L'Egypte face a face, Guilde du livre, 1954.
La bonne heure (poetry), [Paris], 1955.
A haute flamme (poetry), [Paris], 1955.
Le temps naissant, [Paris], 1955.
Le fruit permis (poetry), Caracteres, 1956.
(With Philippe Bonnet) *Peintures,* Berggruem and Cie, 1956.
(With Hans Arp and Richard Huelsenbeck) *Dada: Die Geburt des Dada,* Im Verlag der Arche, 1957.
Frere bois (poetry), PAB, 1957.
La rose et le chien (poetry), [Paris], 1958.
Juste present, [Paris], 1961.
De la coupe aux levres, Edizioni Rapporti europei, 1961.
Les premiers poemes (poetry), translation from Romanian into French by Claude Sernet (Mihail Cosma), Seghers, 1965, translation into English by Michael Impey and Brian Swann published as *Primele poeme/First Poems,* New Rivers Press, 1976.
Thirteen Poems (poetry), [Paris], 1969.
Destroyed Days, [Paris], 1971.
Oeuvres completes (poetry, dramas, essays, and criticism), 6 vols., edited by Henri Behar, Flammarion, 1975-91.
Selected Poems (poetry), translation by Lee Harwood, Trigram Press, 1975.

Selections of Tzara's works in English translation appear in *Axel's Castle,* by Edmund Wilson, 1932; *Surrealism,* by J. Levy, 1936; and *The Dada Painters and Poets,* by R. Motherwell, 1951.

SIDELIGHTS: Tristan Tzara is remembered as a proponent and theoretician for Dadaism, an intellectual movement of the World War I era whose adherents espoused intentional irrationality and urged individuals to repudiate traditional artistic, historical, and religious values. In response to the alienation and absurdity of World War I and the staid, unimaginative art forms predominant in Europe during that era, Tzara and other European artists sought to establish a new style in which random associations would serve to evoke a vitality free from the restraints of logic and grammar. Tzara articulated the aesthetic theories of Dadaism in his seminal collection of essays, *Sept manifestes dada* (1924; "Seven Dada Manifestos"). This volume, in which Tzara advocates "absolute faith in every god that is the immediate product of spontaneity," represents a chaotic assault on reason and convention. Although his work often defies standard classification and is regarded by most contemporary English-speaking scholars as little more than a literary curiosity, Tzara is esteemed in France for his large and diverse body of poetry, which is unified by his critique of and search for a universal language and cosmic wisdom.

Tzara's first published poetry appeared in a literary review in 1912. Many of these poems, written in Rumanian and influenced by French symbolist writers, appear in *Les premiers poemes* (1965; "Primele poemes: First Poems"). Tzara immigrated to Switzerland from Rumania in 1916. Together with Jean Arp, Hugo Ball, and others, Tzara founded Dadaism and staged Dadaist performances at the Cabaret Voltaire in Zurich. Tzara left Switzerland in 1919 and settled in Paris, where he engaged in Dadaist experiments with such literary figures as Andre Breton and Louis Aragon. Serious philosophical differences caused a split between Tzara and Breton in 1921; soon after, Breton founded Surrealism, and by 1922 the Dada movement had dissolved. Tzara's early Dadaist verse, written between 1916 and 1924, utilizes agglomerations of obscure images, nonsense syllables, outrageous juxtapositions, ellipses, and inscrutable maxims to perplex readers and to illustrate the limitations of language. Volumes such as *Vingt-cinq poemes* (1918) and *De nos oiseaux* (1923) display the propositions outlined in Tzara's manifestos and critical essays,

often blending criticism and poetry to create hybrid literary forms.

From 1929 to 1934, Tzara participated in the activities of the Surrealist group in Paris. In this environment, he created a more sustained and coherent poetry that places less emphasis on the ridiculous than his Dadaist verse. Tzara's works published during this period include *L'homme approximatif* (1931; "Approximate Man and Other Writings"), an epic poem that is widely considered a landmark of twentieth-century French literature. This work portrays an unfulfilled wayfarer's search for a universal knowledge and language. Roger Cardinal asserted: "[In] this apocalyptic explosion of language, Tzara finally approaches the primal seat of creativity, the point where the naked word reveals the naked truth about the world." This and Tzara's later Surrealist volumes—*L'arbre des voyageurs* (1930), *Ou boivent les loups* (1932), *L'antitete* (1933), and *Grains et issues* (1935)—reveal his obsession with language, his vision of humanity's destiny of tedium and alienation, and his concern with the struggle to achieve completeness and enlightenment.

In 1934, Tzara left the Surrealists to join France's communist party. As his commitment to left-wing politics increased, his poetry included greater political content and stressed revolutionary and humanistic values while maintaining his lifelong interest in free imagery and linguistic experiments. *Midis gagnes* (1939) focuses on Tzara's impressions of Spain during the country's Civil War, while *La fuite* (1947) depicts the frantic German evacuation of Nazi-occupied France during World War II. The prose poems *Sans coup ferir* (1949) and *A haute flamme* (1955) also address political topics related to the Second World War. Critics generally regard such later works as *Terre sur terre* (1946), *Parler seul* (1950), and *Le fruit permis* (1956) as less vigorous and inventive but more controlled than his earlier poetry.

Tzara's dramas have received less critical attention than his manifestos and poetry. Written during his Dadaist phase, Tzara's best-known plays, *La coeur a gaz* (1920; "The Gas Heart") and *Mouchoir de nuages* (1925), rely on absurdity and wordplay, parodying such literary forms as classical Greek and Shakespearean theater and French symbolist poetry. In *Essai sur la situation de la poesie* (1931), a collection of critical essays, Tzara celebrates poetry as a liberating force from conventional modes of expression.

BIOGRAPHICAL/CRITICAL SOURCES:

BOOKS

Ball, Hugo, *Flight Out of Time: A Dada Diary,* Viking Press, 1974.

Browning, Gordon Frederick, *Tristan Tzara: The Genesis of the Dada Poem or from Dada to Aa,* Akademischer Verlag Heinz, 1979.

Erickson, John D., *Dada: Performance, Poetry, and Art,* Twayne Publishers, 1984.

Harwood, Lee, *Tristan Tzara: A Bibliography,* Aloes Books, 1974.

Janco, Marcel, *Dada: Monograph of a Movement,* St. Martin's Press, 1975.

Ko, Won, *Buddhist Elements in Dada: A Comparison of Tristan Tzara, Takahashi Shinkichi, and Their Fellow Poets,* New York University Press, 1977.

Lewis, Helena, *The Politics of Surrealism,* Paragon House Publishers, 1988.

PERIODICALS

Architectural Digest, Volume 48, April, 1991, pp. 104-09.

Miorita: A Journal of Romanian Studies, Volume 9, numbers 1-2, 1985, pp. 1-18.*

* * *

UMPIERRE (HERRERA), Luz Maria 1947-

PERSONAL: Born October 15, 1947, in Santurce, Puerto Rico; daughter of Eduardo (an executive with the motor vehicle department of Puerto Rico) and Providencia (a telephone operator for Chase Manhattan Bank; maiden name, Herrera) Umpierre. *Education:* Universidad del Sagrado Corazon, B.A., 1970; Bryn Mawr College, M.A., 1976, Ph.D., 1978; postdoctoral studies at University of Kansas, 1981-82.

ADDRESSES: Office—Department of Foreign Languages and Literature, SUNY, Brockport Tower, Building 103A, Brockport, NY 14420.

CAREER: Academia Maria Reina, Rio Piedras, PR, instructor in Spanish and head of Spanish department, 1971-74; Haverford College, Haverford, PA, instructor in Spanish, 1975-76; Rutgers, the State University of New Jersey, New Brunswick, NJ, assistant professor, 1978-84, associate professor, department of Spanish and Portuguese, 1984-89; Western Kentucky University, Bowling Green, professor and chair, Modern Languages and Intercultural Studies, 1989—91; SUNY, Brockport, professor and chair, 1991—. Director of Spanish House, Bryn Mawr College, 1974-77. Visiting lecturer, Immaculata College, 1978—. Guest writer at several colleges and universities in the United States; lecturer and/or chair at numerous Latin American and women's literature conferences in the United States. Conducts poetry readings. Consultant to National Endowment for the Humanities. Secretary for New Jersey Voters for Civil Liberties. Speaker at March on Washington for Gay and Lesbian Rights; has made guest appearances on radio programs.

MEMBER: Modern Language Association (Ethnic Studies representative, Delegate Assembly, 1985-87), American Association of Teachers of Spanish and Portuguese, Feministas Unidas, National Organization of Women, Phi Sigma Iota.

AWARDS, HONORS: First prize for essay, Chase Manhattan Bank, 1976; first prize for poetry, International Publications, 1977; National Research Council/Ford Foundation fellowship, 1981-82; grants from Rutgers University, 1981, 1985, and 1986; Coalition of Lesbians/Gays in New Jersey Lifetime Achievement Award, 1990.

WRITINGS:

Una puertorriquena en Penna, Masters (San Juan), 1979.

En el pais de las maravillas, Third Woman Press (Indiana University), 1982.

Nuevas aproximaciones criticas a la literatura puertorriquena contemporanea, Cultural (Puerto Rico), 1983.

Ideologia y novela en Puerto Rico, Playor (Spain), 1983.

. . . Y otras desgracias / And Other Misfortunes . . . , Third Woman Press, 1985.

The Margarita Poems, Third Woman Press, 1987.

(Contributor) Elizabeth and Timothy Rogers, editors, *In Retrospect: Essays on Latin American Literature,* Spanish Literature Publications, 1987.

Poems represented in anthologies. Translator, with Nancy Gray Diaz, of Rosario Ferre's "Opprobium." Contributor to *Bibliographical Dictionary of Hispanic Literature in the United States* and *Encyclopedia of World Literature—20th Century.* Contributor of ar-

ticles and reviews to numerous journals and other periodicals in the United States and Latin America, including *Revista Chicano-Riquena, Gay Studies Newsletter, Plural, Latin American Theatre Review, Hispanic Journal, Revista de Estudios Hispanicos, Sojourner, Hispania, Third Woman,* and *Bilingual Review-Revista Bilingue;* contributor of poems to journals and newspapers, including *El Mundo.* Associate editor, Third Woman Press, 1982—; reader and consultant, *Latin American Theater Review,* 1983—, *Revista Chicano-Riquena,* 1984—, and *National Women Studies Association Journal,* 1987.

WORK IN PROGRESS: A book of essays on lesbian and gay writing; a book of poems on "women who have had an impact on me but who have died"; research on gay and lesbian literature.

SIDELIGHTS: Luz Maria Umpierre stated: "Most of my writings rise from my condition as a Lesbian and Puerto Rican woman in the United States. My poetry books deal with the alienation I have felt in the U.S.A. I also want the literature of my country, Puerto Rico, to be better known and to this effect I have devoted many of my research pieces to it. I am also interested in women writers and have made a serious commitment to myself since 1982 to write mostly on women."

BIOGRAPHICAL/CRITICAL SOURCES:

BOOKS

Marting, Diane, editor, *Women Writers of Spanish America,* Greenwood Press, 1987.

OTHER

"Puerto Rican Writers in the U.S.A." (film), produced by Zydnia Nazario, 1988.

* * *

UNGER, David 1950-

PERSONAL: Born November 6, 1950, in Guatemala City, Guatemala; immigrated to United States; son of Luis (a restaurant worker) and Fortuna (a secretary; maiden name, Yarhi) Unger; married Esti Dunow (an artist), May 15, 1977; children: Mia, Zoe. *Educa-*

tion: Attended Boston University, 1968-71; University of Massachusetts, B.A., 1973; Columbia University, M.F.A., 1975.

ADDRESSES: Home—209 West 86th St., No. 801, New York, NY 10024. *Office*—Division of Humanities, NAC 6293, City College of New York, New York, NY 10031. *Agent*—Susan Bergholz, 340 West 72nd St., New York, NY 10023.

CAREER: Columbia University, Translation Center, New York City, publicist for Latin American Writer Exchange Program, 1978-79; high school English teacher at Walden School, 1979-82; Teachers and Writers Collaborative, New York City, writer in residence at various schools, 1983-87; co-director, Latin American Book Fair, 1983—; Latin American Writers Institute, New York City, co-director, 1987—. Adjunct faculty, College of New Rochelle, School of New Resources, 1978-87; guest translator, Columbia University, 1979—; instructor in Spanish and Portuguese Department, University of Massachusetts, summers, 1984-85; teacher of graduate seminar, New York University, 1988; Guadalajara International Book Fair, U.S. representative, 1992—.

AWARDS, HONORS: Pushcart Prize Citation, 1978; translation grants from Translation Center, 1978, and New York State Council on the Arts, 1981 and 1983; Spanish Government Tourist Board Award for *Spain: An Insight Guide,* 1989.

WRITINGS:

(Translator with Jonathan Cohen and John Felstiner) Enrique Lihn, *The Dark Room and Other Poems,* New Directions, 1978.
(Contributor of translations) *A Longing for the Light,* Harper, 1979.
(Contributor) *Echad: An Anthology of Latin American Jewish Writers,* Micah Publications, 1980.
(Translator with Lewis Hyde) Vicente Aleixandre, *World Alone,* Penmaen Press, 1981.
(Translator with the author) Isaac Goldemberg, *Just Passing Through,* Point of Contact/Ediciones del Norte, 1981.
(Editor and co-translator) Nicanor Parra, *Antipoems: New and Selected,* New Directions, 1985.
(Contributor) *Anthology of Contemporary Latin American Literature,* Fairleigh Dickinson University Press, 1986.
Neither Caterpillar nor Butterfly (poetry), Es Que Somos Muy Pobres Press (New York), 1986.

(Contributor) *Spain: An Insight Guide,* APA Productions, 1987.

Contributor of poetry, articles, translations, and reviews to periodicals, including *New York Times Book Review.*

SIDELIGHTS: David Unger stated: "Critics have pointed out the dual nature of my writing: Latin American in subject matter/content, and North American in style and structure. The fact that I came to the United States at a young age and write in English may have much to do with this. Still, I would say that my literary preference runs toward Latin American poetry: the work of Peruvian Cesar Vallejo and Chileans Pablo Neruda and Nicanor Parra."

UZODINMA, E(dmund) C(hukuemeka) C(hieke) 1936-

PERSONAL: Born in 1936, in Eastern Nigeria. *Education:* Attended Ibadan University; received B.A. from University of London.

CAREER: Teacher at Our Lady's High School in Onitsha, Nigeria; principal of Aguata Community Grammar School, Nigeria; writer.

WRITINGS:

Brink of Dawn: Stories of Nigeria, Longman of Nigeria, 1966.
Our Dead Speak (novel), Longman, 1967.*

V

VALDER, Peter 1928-

PERSONAL: Born June 10, 1928, in Sydney, Australia; son of George Ernest (an orchardist) and Isa Wyatt (a homemaker; maiden name, Harrison; present surname Watson) Valder. *Ethnicity:* "Anglo-Saxon." *Education:* University of Sydney, B.Sc.Agr. (with first class honors), 1951; Cambridge University, Ph.D., 1956. *Politics:* "Variable." *Avocational interests:* Art, opera, music, visiting gardens in England, North America, France, Italy, Spain, China, Japan, and Korea.

ADDRESSES: Home and office—4C/55 Darling Point Rd., Darling Point, New South Wales 2027, Australia.

CAREER: Department of Agriculture, New South Wales, Australia, plant pathologist, 1951-62; University of Sydney, Sydney, Australia, mycologist and senior lecturer in botany, 1963-88; writer, 1988—. Lecturer at universities and botanic gardens in the United States and Canada, 1984. Friends of the Royal Botanic Gardens, Sydney, committee member, 1983—.

MEMBER: Horticultural, botanical, and scientific societies, including Australian Rhododendron Society (life member).

AWARDS, HONORS: Honorary Horticultural Associate, Royal Botanic Gardens, Sydney, 1995; Medal of Order of Australia, 1996.

WRITINGS:

Wisterias, Florilegium (Balmain, Australia), 1995.

Garden Plants of China: A Companion, Florilegium, in press.

Author and presenter of the film *A Curious and Diverse Flora,* 1981. Contributor to magazines.

WORK IN PROGRESS: Research for *A Chinese Garden Tour.*

SIDELIGHTS: Peter Valder told *CA:* "My motivation for writing is a desire to record some of the knowledge I have accumulated during my life, particularly with regard to botany, horticulture, and gardening, with much reference to historical and cultural matters. Having retired from the University of Sydney, I still find it hard to devote time to writing amongst my other activities, which include appearing on an Australian television series to talk about plants."

* * *

VALENCY, Maurice 1903-1996

OBITUARY NOTICE—See index for *CA* sketch: Born March 22, 1903, in New York, NY; died September 28, 1996, in Manhattan, NY. Educator, drama critic, playwright, author. Valency gained prominence as the winner of several New York Drama Critics Circle awards for adaptations of plays by Jean Giraudoux and Frederick Duerenmatt. While an associate professor at Columbia University, Valency adapted Giraudoux's *The Madwoman of Chaillot,* for which he received his first award in 1949. He followed this with adaptations of another of Giraudoux's plays, *Ondine,* and Duerenmatt's *The Visit,* among others.

He also wrote adaptations of librettos and television plays, including "Feathertop" and "The Man Without a Country" for CBS. He wrote several criticisms and novels, including *The End of the World: An Introduction to Contemporary Drama, The Cart and the Trumpet: The Plays of George Bernard Shaw, Julie,* and *Tragedy.*

OBITUARIES AND OTHER SOURCES:

BOOKS

International Authors and Writers Who's Who, Melrose, 1991.

PERIODICALS

New York Times, September 29, 1996, Section 1, p. 45.

* * *

VALLE-INCLAN, Ramon (Maria) del 1866-1936

PERSONAL: Name originally Ramon Jose Simon del Valle y Pena; also known as Don Ramon, Don Ramon Maria del Valle-Inclan, and Don Ramon Maria del Valle-Inclan y Montenegro; born October 28, 1866, in Villaneuva de Arosa, Galicia, Spain; died of bladder cancer, January 5, 1936, in Santiago de Compostela, Spain; buried in Santiago de Compostela, Spain (some sources say burial was in Boisaca); son of Ramon del Valle-Inclan Bermudez (a poet and journalist) and Dolores de la Pena y Montenegro del Valle-Inclan; married Josefina Angela Blanco (an actress), August 24, 1907 (divorced, 1932); six children (second son drowned). *Education:* Studied law at Instituto de Santiago de Compostela, 1887-89.

CAREER: Playwright, novelist, poet, short story writer, and essayist, who from 1895 to the 1930s wrote twenty-four plays, twelve novels, seven story collections, three volumes of poetry, and assorted other titles, as well as translating and adapting many works from the French, Italian, and Portuguese; wrote for Spanish newspapers *Globo* and *Diario de Pontevedra,* 1880s; wrote for Mexican newspapers *Correo Espanol* and *Universal,* early 1890s; served as correspondent on the Western Front during World War I for the Spanish paper *Imparcial;* named by

Spanish Republic as Director of the Spanish School of Fine Arts at Rome, Italy.

AWARDS, HONORS: Named by Spanish Republic as Curator of the Artistic Patrimony.

WRITINGS:

Femeninas: Seis historias amorosas (short stories; title means "Females"), Landin (Pontevedra), 1895.

Epitalamio: Historia de amores (novella; title means "Epithalamium"), Marzo (Madrid), 1897.

Cenizas (play; title means "Ashes"; first produced in Madrid, 1899), Rodriguez y Perma (Madrid), 1899.

(Translator) Jose Maria Eca de Queiros, *El crimen del padre Amaro,* Maucci (Barcelona), 1901.

(Translator) Paul Alexis, *Las chicas del amigo Lefevre,* Pueblo (Valencia), 1902.

(Translator) Eca de Queiros, *La reliquia,* Maucci, 1902.

(Author of prologue) Almagro San Martin, *Sombras de vida,* Marzo, 1902.

Sonata de otono: Memorias del marques de Bradomin (novel), Perez (Madrid), 1902, translation by May Heywood Broun and Thomas Walsh published in *The Pleasant Memoirs of the Marquis de Bradomin: Four Sonatas*, Harcourt (New York), 1924.

Corte de amor: Florilegio de honestas y nobles damas, Marzo, 1903.

Jardin umbrio (short stories; title means "Shady Garden"), Rodriguez Serra (Madrid), 1903.

Sonata de estio: Memorias del marques de Bradomin (novel), Marzo, 1903, translation by Heywood Broun and Walsh published in *The Pleasant Memoirs of the Marquis de Bradomin: Four Sonatas,* Harcourt, 1924.

Flor de santidad: Historia milenaria (novel; title means "Flower of Holiness"), Marzo, 1904.

(Translator) Eca de Queiros, *El primo Basilio,* Maucci, 1904.

Sonata de primavera: Memorias del marques de Bradomin (novel), Marzo, 1904, translation by Heywood Broun and Walsh published in *The Pleasant Memoirs of the Marquis de Bradomin: Four Sonatas,* Harcourt, 1924.

Sonata de invierno: Memorias del marques de Bradomin (novel), Archivos, Bibliotecas y Museos (Madrid), 1905, translation by Heywood Broun and Walsh published in *The Pleasant Memoirs of the Marquis de Bradomin: Four Sonatas,* Harcourt, 1924.

Jardin novelesco: Historias de santos, de almas en pena, de duendes y de ladrones, Archivos, Bibliotecas y Museos, 1905, enlarged edition, Maucci, 1908.

Aguila de blason: Comedia barbara dividida en cinco jornadas (play; title means "The Emblazoned Eagle"), Granada (Barcelona), 1907.

Aromas de leyenda: Versos en loor de un santo ermitano (poetry; title means "Aromas of Legend"; includes "Flor de la tarde" [title means "Afternoon Flower"] and "No digas de dolor" [title means "Do Not Talk about Pain"]), Villavicencio (Madrid), 1907.

El marques de Bradomin: Coloquios romanticos, Pueyo (Madrid), 1907.

Historias perversas, Maucci, 1907.

(Translator) Matilda Serao, *Flor de pasion,* Maucci, 1907.

Romance de lobos: Comedia barbara dividida en cinco jornadas (play; title means "Ballad of Wolves"), Pueyo, 1908.

El yermo de las almas: Episodios de la vida intima (title means "The Desert of Souls"), Balganon & Moreno (Madrid), 1908.

Los cruzados de la causa (novel), Balganon & Moreno, 1908.

El resplandor de la hoguera (novel), Pueyo, 1909.

Gerifaltes de antano (novel), Suarez (Madrid), 1909.

La guerra carlista (title means "The Carlist War"; includes *Los cruzados de la causa, El resplando de la hoguera,* and *Gerifaltes de antano,*), Suarez, 1909.

Cofre de sandalo, Suarez, 1909.

Una tertulia de antano, Cuento Semanal (Madrid), 1909.

Cuento de abril: Escenas rimadas en una manera extravagante, Pueyo, 1910.

Las mieles del rosal, Alemana (Madrid), 1911.

Voces de gesta: Tragedia pastoril (play), Alemana, 1912.

Obras completas, 19 volumes, edited by Perlado Paez, Renacimiento (Madrid), 1912-28.

La marquesa Rosalinda: Farsa sentimental y grotesca (play; title means "The Marchioness Rosalinda"), Alemana, 1913.

El embrujado: Tragedia de tierras de Salnes, Perlado & Paez (Madrid), 1913.

La cabeza del dragon (play), Perlado & Paez, 1913, translation by Heywood Broun published as *The Dragon's Head,* R. G. Badger (Boston), 1919; published as *Farsa infantil de la cabeza del dragon* in *Tablado de marionetas.*

La lampara maravillosa: Ejercicios espirituales (essays; title means "The Marvelous Lamp: Spiri-

tual Exercises"), Helenica (Madrid), 1916, translation by Robert Lima published as "The Lamp of Marvels: Spiritual Exercises," Lindisfarne Press, 1986.

Eulalia, Novela Corta (Madrid), 1917.

La media noche: Vision estelar de un momento de guerra (essays; title means "Midnight: Starry Vision of a Moment of War"), Clasica Espanola (Madrid), 1917.

Rosita, Novela Corta, 1917.

Mi hermana Antonia, Blass (Madrid), 1918.

Cuentos, estetica y poemas, edited by Guillermo Jimenez, Cultura (Mexico City), 1919, translation by Robert Lima published as *Autobiography, Aesthetics, Aphorisms,* 1966.

La pipa de kif (poetry; title means "The Hashish Pipe"; includes "Aleluya" [title means "Hallelujah"], "La tienda del herbolario" [title means "The Herbalist Shop"], "Rosa de sanatorio" [title means "The Sanatorium Rose"], "Fin de carnaval" [title means "The End of Carnival"], and "El crimen de Mendinica"), Sociedad General Espanola de Libreria (Madrid), 1919.

Divinas palabras (play; title means "Divine Words"), Yagues (Madrid), 1920, translation, Heinemann/ National Theatre (London), 1977.

Farsa de la enamorada del rey: Dividida en tres jornadas (title means "Farce of the King's Sweetheart"), Sociedad General Espanola de Libreria, 1920, published as *Farsa italiana de la enamorada del rey* in *Tablado de marionetas.*

El pasajero: Claves liricas (poetry; title means "The Passenger"; includes "Rosa del sol" [title means "Sun Rose"], "Rosa metrica" [title means "Metric Rose"], "Rosa hiperbole" [title means "Hyperbole Rose"], "Rosa matinal" [title means "Morning Rose"], "Rosa de caminante" [title means "The Traveler's Rose"], "Rosa de turbulos" [title means "Rose of Trouble"], "Alegoria" [title means "Allegory"], "Rosa vespertina" [title means "Evening Rose"], "Rosa de zoroastro" [title means "Zoroaster Rose"], "Rosa gnostica" [title means "Gnostic Rose"], "Rosa de Job" [title means "Job's Rose"], and "Karma"), Yagues, 1920.

Zacarias el cruzado, Artistica Saez Hermanos (Madrid), 1920.

Farsa y licencia de la reina castiza (play; title means "Farce and License of the Chaste Queen"), Artes de la Ilustracion (Madrid), 1922.

Cara de plata: Comedia barbara (play; title means "Silver Countenance"), Renacimiento, 1923.

The Pleasant Memoirs of the Marquis de Bradomin: Four Sonatas (novels; includes *Sonata de otono,*

Sonata de estio, Sonata de primavera, and *Sonata de invierno*), translation by May Heywood Broun and Thomas Walsh, Harcourt, 1924.

"La rosa de papel" y "La cabeza del Bautista": Novelas macabras (includes "La rosa de papel" [also known as "The Paper Rose Sacrilege"]), Prensa Grafica (Madrid), 1924.

(Author of prologue) Victoriano Garcia Marti, *De la felicidad (Eternas inquietudes),* Mundo Latino (Madrid), 1924.

Luces de Bohemia: Esperpento (play; title means "Lights of Bohemia"), Cervantina (Madrid), 1924, translation by Anthony N. Zahareas and Gerald Gillespie published as *Lights of Bohemia,* University of Pennsylvania Press (University Park), 1969.

Opera omnia, Rivadeneyra (Madrid), 1924-33.

Cartel de ferias: Cromos isabelinos, Prensa Grafica, 1925.

Los cuernos de don Friolera: Esperpento (play; title means "The Horns of Don Friolera"), Cervantina, 1925.

Ecos de Asmodeo, Novela Mundial (Madrid), 1926.

El terno del difunto, Novela Mundial, 1926.

Las galas del difunto (title means "The Corpse's Regalia"), Rivadeneyra, 1926.

Ligazon: Auto para siluetas, Novela Mundial, 1926.

Tablado de marionetas (plays; includes *Farsa italiana de la enamorada del rey, Farsa infantil de la cabeza del dragon,* and *Farsa y licencia de la reina castiza*), Rivadeneyra, 1926, published as *Tablado de marionetas para educacion de principes,* Espasa-Calpe (Madrid), 1961.

Tirano Banderas (novel), Rivadeneyra, 1926, published as *Tirano Banderas: Novela de Tierra caliente,* Espasa-Calpe (Buenos Aires), 1937; translation by Margarita Pavitt published as *The Tyrant (Tirano Banderas): A Novel of Warm Lands,* Holt (New York), 1929.

(Author of prologue) Ricardo Baroja, *El Pedogree,* Caro Ragio (Madrid), 1926.

La corte de los milagros: El ruedo iberico (novel), Rivadeneyra, 1927.

Estampas isabelinas: La rosa de oro, Novela Mundial, 1927.

La hija del capitan (play), Novela Mundial, 1927.

Retablo de la avaricia: La lujuria y la muerte, Rivadeneyra, 1927.

Fin de un revolucionario: Aleluyas de la Gloriosa, Moderna (Madrid), 1928.

Las reales antecameras, Atlantida (Madrid), 1928.

Teatrillo de enredo, Moderna, 1928.

Viva mi dueno: El ruedo iberico (novel), Rivadeneyra, 1928.

Otra castiza de Samaria, Novela de Hoy (Madrid), 1929.

(Author of prologue) S. J. Sender, *El problema religioso en Mexico,* Cenit (Madrid), 1929.

Claves liricas: "Aromas de leyenda," "El pasajero," "La pipa de Kif" (poetry), Rivadeneyra, 1930.

Martes de carnaval: Esperpentos (title means "Shrove Tuesday"; contains *Las galas del difunto, Los cuernos de don Friolera,* and *La hija del capitan*), Rivadeneyra, 1930.

Flores de almendro, Bergua, 1936.

Opera lirica (contains *Voces de gesta* and *Cuento de abril*), Rua Nueva (Madrid), 1943.

Obras completas de Don Ramon del Valle-Inclan, 2 volumes, Rivadeneyra, 1944.

Publicaciones periodisticas anteriores a 1895, edited by William L. Fichter, Colegio de Mexico (Mexico City), 1952.

Baza de espadas, AHR (Barcelona), 1958, published as *Baza de espadas: Fin de un revolucionario,* Elliot's Books, 1993.

Obras escogidas, prologue by Gaspar Gomez de la Serna, Aguilar (Madrid), 1958.

Teatro selecto, Escelicer (Madrid), 1969.

El trueno dorado, Nostromo (Madrid), 1975.

Articulos completos y otras paginas olvidadas, Istmo (Madrid), 1987.

Also author of *La cara de Dios* (novel), 1900.

SIDELIGHTS: An acknowledged master of prose style, Ramon del Valle-Inclan was one of the great modernizers of twentieth-century Spanish drama. He invented a new genre: the *esperpento,* in which all the elements of drama are satirically distorted to create Goyaesque images of horror and comedy. Conveying a sense of dehumanization and senseless struggle in an irrational world, the *esperpentos* are now seen as the forerunners of Absurdist works such as those of Samuel Beckett and Eugene Ionesco. Valle-Inclan's literary work is not, however, limited to his dramas. In addition to his *esperpentos,* he is also known for his novels, particularly the *Sonatas,* elegantly styled, fictive memoirs of the rakish Marquis de Bradomin.

Valle-Inclan was born to a family of disinherited aristocrats at Villaneuva de Arosa in the Spanish region of Galicia, and spent his youth in this rugged land of primitive Celtic customs. Educated in Pontevedra, he studied law briefly at the University of Santiago de Compostela, where he also began to write poetry and prose. Often described as restless and eager for adventure, he left for Mexico in 1890,

claiming that he went there because "it was the only country whose name is written with an X." He worked as a journalist in America for three years, then returned to Galicia. In the interim, he transformed his physical appearance: Valle-Inclan now wore long hair, a beard, and a cape, often carried a cane, and presented himself as an eccentric, bohemian writer. After publishing his first book, *Femeninas: Seis historias amorosas,* in 1895, he traveled to Madrid and began to participate in the capital's literary circles. By the turn of the century, Valle-Inclan had begun work on his *Sonatas,* the series of four novels that brought him fame in the early twentieth century. He recorded his impressions of World War I in *La media noche: Vision estelar de un momento de guerra* (1917), a collection of essays written while he served as a newspaper correspondent on the Western Front. Following the war, Valle-Inclan wrote his first *esperpento, Luces de bohemia* (1924; *Lights of Bohemia*), and also composed dramas and novels, wherein he incorporated the satirical and grotesque elements of the *esperpento* form. He began his *El ruedo iberico* cycle, a projected series of nine novels, in the late 1920s, but finished only two of the works—*La corte de los milagros: El ruedo iberico* (1927) and *Viva mi dueno: El ruedo iberico* (1928)— before his death in 1936.

Valle-Inclan's literary development is generally divided into two periods. The first, extending from 1895 until World War I, is characterized by fin-de-siecle decadence, reminiscent of Barbey d'Aurevilly and Gabriel D'Annunzio. In *Femeninas,* a collection of love stories, Valle-Inclan employed an exquisite, romantic style while treating erotic themes. Similarly, in the *Sonata de otono: Memorias del Marques de Bradomin* (1902) he projected an overtly romantic portrait of himself as the Marquis de Bradomin. Also in this period, Valle-Inclan wrote the novel *Flor de santidad* (1904) and the first two dramas known collectively as the *comedias barbaras, Aguila de blason* (1907) and *Romance de lobos* (1908), which draw on the traditions and folklore of his native Galicia. His *La guerra carlista* trilogy (1908-1909), historical novels of the Carlist Wars in Spain, mark a first departure from the eroticism of his earlier works.

Following the first World War, a drastic change took place in Valle-Inclan's writing. In 1916 he outlined his new aesthetic theory in *La lampara maravillosa: Ejercicios espirituales.* Discarding the Decadents' notion of the artist as one who finds pleasure in beauty, Valle-Inclan now expressed a disillusioned vision, which he hoped would achieve an objective view of reality and allow things to, in the words of Manuel Salas, "reveal their flaws and imperfections, their absurdities and dissonances." In *Lights of Bohemia* and the *esperpentos* that followed—*Los cuernos de don Friolera* (1925), *La hija del capitan* (1927), and *Las galas del difunto* (1930)—Valle-Inclan pursued this aesthetic, producing serio-comic distortions of reality. These later dramas focus on society and its conventions and deal with contemporary life, satirizing institutionalized vice, militarism, political corruption, and human frailty—all of which aligned Valle-Inclan more closely with the socially progressive Generation of 1898. His novels continue in the same spirit, as in *Tirano Banderas: Novela de Tierra caliente* (1926, *The Tyrant*), the story of a rebellion in the fictional Latin American state of Tierra Caliente wherein he analyzes the failures of Spanish society; or, the first novels of the *El reudo iberico* cycle which indict Isabella II's government.

Valle-Inclan's oeuvre has thus been discussed by critics largely in terms of temporal divisions. His early works, especially the *Sonatas,* won him popularity, though many critics disparaged their eroticism. Reaction to his later writing was likewise mixed. Some scholars objected to the grotesqueness of his *esperpentos* and the severity of the political satire in his later writings; however, his contemporaries, including the writer Jose Martinez Ruiz and the philosopher Jose Ortega y Gasset, admired Valle-Inclan for his adept, innovative style and unique use of language. Modern critics have followed these writers in appraising Valle-Inclan: Manuel Salas, for example, has called him "a musician with words, a sovereign artist, a master stylist."

BIOGRAPHICAL/CRITICAL SOURCES:

BOOKS

Bell, Aubrey F. G., *Contemporary Spanish Literature,* Knopf (New York), 1925, pp. 39-150.

Diaz-Plaja, Guillermo, *Las esteticas de Valle-Inclan,* Gredos (Madrid), 1965.

Dictionary of Literary Biography, Volume 134: *Twentieth-Century Spanish Poets, Second Series,* Gale (Detroit), 1994.

Edwards, Gwynne, *Dramatists in Perspetive: Spanish Theatre in the Twentieth Century,* St. Martin's (New York), 1985, pp. 36-74.

Guerrero, Obdulia, *Valle-Inclan y el novecientos,* Magisterio Espanol (Madrid), 1977.

Lima, Robert, *Ramon del Valle-Inclan,* Columbia University Press (New York), 1972.

Lyon, John, *The Theatre of Valle-Inclan,* Cambridge University Press (Cambridge), 1983.

Madariaga, Salvador de, *Genius of Spain and Other Essays on Spanish Contemporary Literature,* Oxford University Press (London), 1923, pp. 128-47.

Severa Bano, Jose, *Ramon del Valle-Inclan,* Jucar (Madrid), 1983.

Smith, Verity, *Valle-Inclan: Tirano Banderas,* Grant & Cutler, Ltd., 1971.

Smith, *Ramon del Valle-Inclan,* Twayne (New York), 1973.

Tolman, Rosco N., *Dominant Themes in the "Sonatas" of Valle-Inclan,* Coleccion Plaza Mayor Scholar (Madrid), 1973.

Twentieth-Century Literary Criticism, Volume 5, Gale, 1981.

Zahareas, Anthony N., editor, *Ramon del Valle-Inclan: His Life and Works,* Las Americas (New York), 1968.

PERIODICALS

Bulletin of Hispanic Studies, Volume 33, 1956, pp. 152-64; July, 1962, pp. 177-87; Volume 46, number 2, 1969, pp. 132-52.

Drama Critique, spring, 1966, pp. 69-78.

Drama Survey, spring-summer, 1967, pp. 3-23.

Educational Theatre Journal, December, 1967, pp. 455-66.

Hispania, May, 1961, pp. 266-68; September, 1974, p. 600.

Hispanic Review, January, 1961, pp. 120-33.

International P.E.N. Bulletin of Selected Books, Volume 21, number 1, 1970, pp. 108-112.

Modern Language Quarterly, September, 1964, pp. 330-37.

PMLA, March, 1967, pp. 128-35.

Revista de estudios hispanicos, January, 1972, pp. 33-93.

* * *

VALLEJO, Cesar (Abraham) 1892-1938

PERSONAL: Born March 16, 1892, in Santiago de Chuco, Peru; died April 15, 1938, of a chronic illness variously reported as tuberculosis, acute intestinal infection, and malaria; married Georgette Phillipart. *Education:* Trujillo University, B.A., 1915, and law degree, c. 1917; studied medicine at University of San Marcos in Lima, 1911.

CAREER: Poet and freelance writer. Worked in his father's notary office, in mine offices, as a tutor, and in an estate accounts office; teacher, Centro Escolar du Verones and Colegio Nacional de San Juan, 1913-17; lived in Lima, Peru, 1917-23; teacher, Colegio Barros, 1918-19, and another school, 1920; involved in political riot, Santiago de Chuco, Peru, and imprisoned, 1920-21; teacher, Colegio Guadalupe, 1921-23; lived in Europe after 1923; secretary, Iberoamerican press agency, 1925. Worked as journalist and helped publish *Nuestra Espana* in Spain during the Spanish Civil War, 1936-38.

AWARDS, HONORS: National short story contest winner, c. 1921.

WRITINGS:

POETRY

Los heraldos negros (title means "The Black Messengers"), includes "Canciones de hogar," [Lima], 1918, Peru Nuevo, 1959, published as *Los heraldos negros, 1918,* Losada (Buenos Aires), 1961, translation by Kathleen Ross and Richard Schaaf published as *The Black Heralds,* edited by Yvette E. Miller, introduction by Jean Franco, Latin American Literary Review Press, 1990.

Trilce, Talleres Tipografia de la Penitenciaria (Lima), 1922, second edition with introduction by Jose Bergamin, Cia Iberoamericana de Publicaciones (Madrid), 1931, published with essays by Antenor Orrego and Bergamin, Fondo de Cultura Popular, 1962, translation by David Smith, Grossman (New York), 1973.

Poemas humanos, Presses Modernes (Paris), 1939, Peru Nuevo, 1959, translation by Clayton Eshleman published as *Poemas Humanos: Human Poems,* Grove Press, 1969.

Espana, aparta de mi este caliz, with introductory essay "Profecia de America" (title means "Prophecy of America"), Seneca (Mexico), 1940, translation by Alvaro Cardona-Hine published as *Spain, Let This Cup Pass from Me,* Red Hill, 1972, translation by Eshleman and Jose Rubia Barcia published as *Spain, Take This Cup from Me,* Grove Press, 1974.

Antologia de Cesar Vallejo, compiled by Xavier Abril, Claridad, 1942.

Antologia, compiled by Edmundo Cornejo U., Hora del Hombre, 1948.

Poesias completas (1918-1938), compiled by Cesar Miro, Losada, 1949.

Los mejores versos de Cesar Vallejo, [Buenos Aires], c. 1956.

La vida, y quince poemas: antologia poetica, compiled by Jose Escobar and Eugenio Martinez Pastor, Baladre, 1958.

Poemas, compiled with notes by Ramiro de Casabellas, Perrot (Buenos Aires), 1958.

Poemas escogidos, compiled with prologue by Gustavo Valcarcel, Latinoamericana, 1958.

Poemas humanos (1923-1938) [and] Espana, aparta de mi este caliz (1937-1938), Losada, 1961.

Poesias completas, Volume 1: *Los heraldos ·negros,* Volume 2: *Trilce,* Volume 3: *Espana, aparta de mi este caliz,* Volume 4: *Poemas humanos,* Peru Nuevo, 1961.

Cesar Vallejo: Sus mejores obras, (includes *Los heraldos negros, Trilce,* and *Rusia en 1931: Reflexiones al pie del Kremlin*), Ediciones Peru, 1962.

Twenty Poems (bilingual edition), selection and translations by Robert Bly, James Wright, and John Knoepfle, with essay by Wright, Sixties Press, 1962.

Antologia poetica, with introduction by Valcarcel, Impresiones Nacional de Cuba, 1962.

Los heraldos negros y Trilce, Ediciones Peru, 1962.

Poesias completas, with prologue by Roberto Fernandez Retaman, Casa de las Americas (Havana), 1965.

Antologia, edited with notes by Julio Ortega, Universitaria, 1966.

Cesar Vallejo, edited by wife, Georgette de Vallejo, P. Seghers (Paris), 1967.

Seven Poems, translation by Eshleman, R. Morris, 1967.

Obra poetica completa, with manuscript facsimiles, edited by G. de Vallejo, (includes *Los heraldos negros* and *Poemas humanos*), F. Moncloa, 1968.

Obras completas (three volumes), Mosca Azul (Lima), Volume 1: *Contra el secreto profesional: A proposito de Pablo Abril de Vivero,* 1968, Volume 2: *El arte y la revolucion,* 1968, Volume 3: *Obra poetica completa,* with revised biographical essay by G. de Vallejo, 1974.

Cesar Vallejo: An Anthology of His Poetry, edited with an introduction and notes by James Higgins, Pergamon Press, 1970.

Un hombre pasa, translation by Michael Smith, New Writers' Press, 1970.

Ten Versions from Trilce, translations by Charles Tomlinson and Henry Gifford, San Marcos Press, 1970.

Neruda and Vallejo: Selected Poems, translation by Bly, Wright, and Knoepfle, edited by Bly, Beacon Press, 1971.

Poesias completas de Cesar Vallejo, J. Pablos (Mexico), 1971.

Selected Poems, edited by Gordon Brotherston and Ed Dorn, Penguin, 1976.

Cesar Vallejo: The Complete Posthumous Poetry, translation by Eshleman and Barcia, University of California Press, 1978.

Perfil de Cesar Vallejo: Vida y obra antologia poetica, edited by Juan Larrea and others, Grafica San Andres, 1978.

Poesia completa, Premia (Mexico), 1981.

Canciones de hogar: Songs of Home, translation by Richard Schaaf and Kathleen Ross, Ziesing Bros., 1981.

Selected Poems of Cesar Vallejo, translation by H. R. Hays, Sachem, 1981.

Obra poetica completa: Cesar Vallejo, with introduction by Americo Ferrari, Alianza, 1982.

Palms and Guitar, translation by J. C. R. Green, Aquila/Phaethon Press, 1982.

Asi es la vida, tal como es la vida, edited with introduction by Juan Antonio Massone, Nascimento, 1982.

Poemas humanos; Espana, aparta de mi este caliz, Laia (Barcelona), 1985.

Selected Poetry, edited by Higgins, F. Cairns, 1987.

Poemas en prosa; Poemas humanos, Espana, aparta de mi este caliz, Catedra, 1988.

Poesia completa, Ediciones Consejo de Integracion Cultura Latinoamericana, 1988.

Works also collected in *Poesia completa,* edited by Larrea, 1978. Contributor to literary magazines in Peru and Europe.

FICTION

Escalas melografiadas (short stories), Talleres Tipografia de la Penitenciaria (Lima), 1923.

Fabla salvaje (novella), [Lima], 1923, Editorial Labor, 1965.

El tungsteno: La novela proletaria, Editorial Cenit (Madrid), 1931, first Peruvian edition published as *Tungsteno,* Ediciones de Cuadernos Trimestrales de Poesia, 1958, translation by Robert Mezey with preface by Kevin O'Connor published as *Tungsten: A Novel,* Syracuse University Press, 1988.

Novelas: Tungsteno, Fabla salvaje, Escalas melografiadas, Hora del Hombre, 1948.

Tungsteno y Paco Yunque, J. Mejia Baca & P. L. Villanueva, 1957.

Novelas y cuentos completos, F. Moncloa (Lima), 1967, 2nd edition, Moncloa-Campodonico, 1970.

Paco Yunque, [Lima], 1969, first Honduran edition with illustrations by Pablo Picasso, Girandula (Honduras), 1981.

OTHER

Rusia en 1931: Reflexiones al pie del Kremlin, Ulises (Madrid), 1931, published in two volumes, Peru Nuevo, 1959.

El romanticismo en la poesia castellana, Juan Mejia Baca & P. L. Villanueva, 1954.

Articulos olvidados, compiled with prologue by Luis Alberto Sanchez, Asociacion Peruana por la Libertad de la Cultura, 1960.

Rusia ante el segundo plan quinquenal, Grafica Labor, 1965.

Literatura y arte, Ediciones del Mediodia (Buenos Aires), 1966.

Desde Europa, edited by Jorge Puccinelli, Instituto Raul Porras Barranchea (Lima), 1969, Ediciones Fuente de Cultura Peruana, 1987.

Cartas a Pablo Abril, Rodolfo Alonso (Buenos Aires), 1971.

Battles in Spain, translation by Eshleman and Barcia, Black Sparrow Press, 1978.

Teatro completo, two volumes, La Catolica, 1979.

Epistolario general (letters), Pre-Textos, 1982.

Autopsy on Surrealism, translation by Schaaf, edited by James Scully, Curbstone, 1982.

The Mayakovsky Case ("El caso Maiakovski," a critical essay), translation by Schaaf, edited by Scully, Curbstone, 1982.

Cronicas (prose works; in several volumes), Volume 1, Universidad Nacional Autonoma de Mexico, Direccion General de Publications, 1984.

La cultura Peruana: Cronicas (collected essays), selection by Aguirre, Mosca Azul, 1987.

Also author of "Lockout," a play. Translator of *L'Elevation,* by Henri Barbusse, 1931. Works represented in *Espadana,* published in Leon, Spain, 1944-51, and in *Aula Vallejo,* a serial publication of Instituto del Nuevo Mundo, Universidad Nacional de Cordoba, 1961—. Contributor of articles to *Mundial, El Comercio, Variedades,* and to newspapers in Spain and France. Cofounder and contributor, *Favorables-Paris-Poemas.*

SIDELIGHTS: Peruvian expatriate Cesar Vallejo was a major poet, known for the authenticity and originality of his work. Deeply rooted in his mixed European and Peruvian Indian heritage, his poetry expressed universal themes related to the human condition.

Sometimes called a surrealist poet, "Vallejo created a wrenching poetic language for Spanish that radically altered the shape of its imagery and the nature of its rhythms. No facile trend setter, Vallejo forged a new discourse in order to express his own visceral compassion for human suffering," Edith Grossman writes in *Los Angeles Times Book Review.* "A constant feature of his poetry is a compassionate awareness of and a guilt-ridden sense of responsibility for the suffering of others," observes James Higgins in *The Poet in Peru: Alienation and the Quest for a Super-Reality.* His compassion was informed by his own painful experience as an inmate in a Trujillo prison, as an expatriate political activist, and as a witness of the devastating Spanish Civil War. He also endured poverty and a chronic illness of which he died in 1938. Grossman relates, "He saw the world in piercing flashes of outrage and anguish, terror and pity. . . . A passionate, tragic poet, he mourned our loss of moral innocence and despaired of the injustice that moves the world."

Vallejo was born in Santiago de Chuco, a small village in the northern Andes mountains. Raised Catholic and encouraged to become a priest, he discovered that he could not adhere to the requirement of celibacy. His family relationships remained secure and close. For a time, he was a clerk in his father's notary office. His mother's friendship, in particular, was a sustaining force in his life until her death in 1923 (some sources say 1918). The comfort of his rural life set for Vallejo a standard against which all later experiences seemed arduous and painful.

Early poems in his first collection *Los heraldos negros* (*"The Black Messengers"*) relate Vallejo's bewilderment when struck with the harshness of city life in Trujillo and Lima, where he studied medicine, literature, and law. Introduced to the ideas of Marx, Darwin, and Rationalist philosophers, Vallejo felt that the faith in which he was raised was no longer viable. Together with other intellectuals, he became actively interested in his pre-Columbian heritage and was anguished to learn of the suffering of aboriginals in his country. When the parents of his lover broke off their relationship for reasons he did not understand, he attempted suicide. Higgins summarizes that Vallejo's "arrival in Lima therefore, marks his initiation into a seemingly absurd and senseless world whose meaning escapes him." Unable to replace the caring family he had lost, Vallejo felt alienated in the city. Alienation and the apparent senselessness of his suffering became his recurrent themes.

Poems in *Los heraldos negros,* like most Latin American poetry of that time, follow the conventions of the *modernista* movement. The *modernistas,* D. P. Gallagher explains in *Modern Latin American Literature,* highlighted the melodic quality of language; breaking a taboo, Vallejo added erotic lyrics to the descriptions of beautiful landscape common to this style. *Modernista* poets Leopoldo Lugones and Julio Herrara y Reissig influenced the young Vallejo significantly. "They were both masters of the violently surprising image, and their poetry is free of the jaded air of fatigued mimicry that many *modernista* poems had come to display," Gallagher comments. By the end of *Los heraldos negros* in the "Canciones de hogar" ("Songs of Home") section, Vallejo had given voice to concerns which would remain his major themes: he lamented his status as an orphan unprepared for the brutality of life in a world where God himself seemed powerless to intervene. In addition, the urgency of personal statement and original idiom in these poems show that Vallejo had outgrown his dependence on traditional literary models. Thus he presented a mature original voice having more social relevance and literary importance than his *modernista* mentors, Gallagher adds.

After a number of years in Trujillo and Lima, in 1920 Vallejo returned to his birthplace where he became involved in a political insurrection during which the town's general store burned down. He was accused of instigating the conflict and was jailed for three months. Added to the death of his mother, the isolation and savagery of jail conditions affected him deeply. "The subject of a number of poems, that experience reinforced his belief in the world's arbitrary cruelty and his sense of inadequacy in the face of it," Higgins writes in *A History of Peruvian Literature.* Accordingly, poems written in prison (collected in *Trilce*) are markedly different from the idyllic poems of *Los heraldos negros.*

Trilce is more difficult, more intense, and more original than Vallejo's first volume. Pared of all ornamental language, these poems convey the poet's personal urgency as he cries out against the apparent meaninglessness of his suffering. *Trilce* introduces the wrenched syntax that allows Vallejo to get beyond the constraints of received linguistic conventions to a language that is true to his experience. Writing in *A History of Peruvian Literature,* Higgins catalogues the elements of Vallejo's diction: "Vallejo confounds the reader's expectations by his daring exploitation of the line pause, which often leaves articles, conjunctions and even particles of words dangling at the end

of a line, by his frequent resort to harsh sounds to break the rhythm, by employing alliterations so awkward as to be tongue-twisters. He distorts syntactic structures, changes the grammatical function of words, plays with spelling. His poetic vocabulary is frequently unfamiliar and 'unliterary,' he creates new words of his own, he often conflates two words into one, he tampers with cliches to give them new meaning, he plays on the multiple meaning of words and on the similarity of sound between words. He repeatedly makes use of oxymoron and paradox and, above all, catachresis, defamiliarising objects by attributing to them qualities not normally associated with them."

Vallejo's wrenched syntax is not a mere literary performance; it is the means necessary "to discover the man that has been hitherto hidden behind its decorative facades. The discovery is not a pleasant one, and the noise in the poems make it consequently aggressive and not beautiful," Gallagher observes. Out of Vallejo's self-discovery comes an "unprecedented, raw language" that declares Vallejo's humanness despite his confinement to make a statement "about the human problems of which Vallejo is a microcosm," Gallagher adds. *New York Review of Books* contributor Michael Wood explains, "With Vallejo it is an instrument—the only possible instrument, it seems—for the confrontation of complexity, of the self caught up in the world and the world mirrored in the self. It is an answer, let us say, to the simultaneous need for a poetry that would put heart into an agonizing Spain and for a poetry that will not take wishes for truths." Gallagher suggests that Vallejo was "perhaps the first Latin American writer to have realized that it is precisely in the discovery of a language where literature must find itself in a continent where for centuries the written word was notorious more for what it concealed than for what it revealed, where 'beautiful' writing, sheer sonorous wordiness was a mere holding operation against the fact that you did not dare really say anything at all."

The facade separating Vallejo from the truth about himself—and all men—was one of many boundaries he strove to break through by means of writing. This is most evident in *Trilce* where the poet recognizes his imprisonment as a symbol of the human struggle against all limitations. For example, for Vallejo, the Spanish Civil War points to the existence of man's greater struggle, a predetermined conflict between an individual and his desires for transcendence, as he phrased it in *Poemas humanos.* "More than a political event," states Gallagher, to Vallejo the war was yet another facet of entropy, "that dismemberment of

unity which we have seen him observing even in his own body."

Vallejo saw that beyond the obvious constraints of government, society, and culture, man is incarcerated by time, space, and his biological limitations. Repeatedly the later poems complain of "the frustration of the poet's spiritual aspirations by the limitations of the flesh," relates Higgins in *The Poet in Peru*. The poet's hope of freedom seems to be precluded by an inescapable biological determinism, Jean Franco notes in *Cesar Vallejo: The Dialectics of Poetry and Silence*. "While his spirit holds up to him a vision of a higher life, his experience of hunger and illness brings home to him the extent to which his existence is lived on an elemental level, through that frail, decaying body of his which constantly demands satisfaction of its appetites and repeatedly breaks down under the effects of illness and age," Higgins elaborates. He adds, "Much more serious, the poet-doctor insinuates, is the malaise brought on by reasoning which, by destroying illusions and laying bare the vanity of things, insidiously undermines his spiritual health. Since man is unable to find any meaning to life, he has no real existence and lives only through the anguished sense of futility which is slowly destroying him and which has become contagious in an age when all human values seem to have failed." Though it becomes more subtle in later books, the theme of man versus his limits continues throughout Vallejo's work.

In 1923, Vallejo moved to Europe. Until 1930, when he was expelled from France for his unorthodox politics, he lived in Paris, where he wrote articles about the need to get beyond the superficiality of much contemporary poetry. Literary posturing sustained by simple mimicry of the style currently in vogue may disguise a poet's lack of talent but will not render a vital contribution to life or art, he maintained in *Literatura y arte*. The harshness of his standards is perhaps forgivable in that he applied them relentlessly to his own work, Gallagher comments. By achieving authenticity in innovative language, Vallejo influenced many younger poets to embrace nontraditional techniques.

In the 1920s and 1930s Vallejo became more engaged in politics. His three visits to the Soviet Union—the first in 1928—aided the formulation of his political views, and he subsequently produced political tracts including *Rusia en 1931* and *Reflexiones al pie del Kremlin,* first published in Spain and not printed in Peru until almost thirty years later. He also wrotes

the novel *El tungsteno* (*"Tungsten"*), which condemns an American company for exploiting its Peruvian workers to get the element it needed to make weapons. Political statements emerge in his other works as well, but they do not dominate. Vallejo was an ambivalent Marxist. Gallagher reports, "Vallejo regards Communism, in *Poemas humanos* and *'Espana, aparta de mi este caliz,'* as . . . just the vague sighting of a way out from a world that nevertheless remains as hermetically frontier-bound as that of *Trilce*." Higgins finds evidence in *Poemas humanos* that Vallejo sometimes admired the single-mindedness of those who could submit themselves to "the cause," but again found it impossible to subject himself without question to Marxist or communist ideals. He moved to Spain during its war years to work as a journalist and lend support to his friends in defense of the Spanish Republic. At the same time, Vallejo admired the brotherhood achieved among the activists who gave their lives to serve what they believed was the improvement of life for the poor.

After he died in 1938, his widow Georgette de Vallejo selected poems for publication in *Poemas humanos*. Gallagher maintains that the style of this volume is best described as "eccentric," in two senses of the word. *Poemas humanos* was written in a highly personal idiom. Vallejo expressed the suffering of people in general, for instance, in the terms of his own specific experience in a violently contorted language. Secondly, Vallejo's word choice was often "ex-centric" or off center to parallel the ambiguous nature of contemporary experience. In Vallejo's poems, things and events do not function as symbols; they signify no apparent cause, no meaning behind the objects and events of daily life. At the same time the poems are haunted by the dread that meaning does exist, but humanity cannot grasp it. If man's "a priori" contest is "beyond reckoning," as Vallejo wrote in *Poemas humanos,* it must also lay somewhat beyond words. Vallejo's unique diction is a natural extension of his personal crisis.

Though he won little critical acclaim before his death, Vallejo came "to be recognized as an artist of world stature, the greatest poet not only of Peru but of all Spanish America," Higgins sums up in *The History of Peruvian Literature*. Gallagher concludes, "There is no poet in Latin America like Vallejo, . . . who has bequeathed so consistently personal an idiom, and no poet so strictly rigorous with himself. It is a curiously subtle, menacing world that he has left us in his mature works." Vallejo will be remembered for discovering a unique poetic language that

expresses what he perceived as the frustration inherent in the human condition and the chaos of the world. Franco comments that for Vallejo, using that language was a vital exercise of freedom: "Vallejo knew that with every automatic word and gesture man contributes to his own damnation and imprisonment. His great achievement as a poet is to have interrupted that easy-flowing current of words which is both a solace and the mark of our despair, to have made each poem an act of consciousness which involves the recognition of difficulty and pain." Vallejo is seen as the progenitor of many innovations in poetic technique. *New York Times Book Review* contributor Alexander Coleman observes that Vallejo, "the standard for authenticity and intensity" in Hispanic literature, opened the way for future poets by leaving to them "a language swept clean, now bright and angular, ready for the man in the street."

BIOGRAPHICAL/CRITICAL SOURCES:

BOOKS

Abril, Xavier, *Cesar Vallejo a la teoria poetica,* Taurus (Madrid), 1962.

Abril, *Exegesis trilcica,* Labor, 1980.

Aguierre, Enrique Ballon, *Vallejo como paradigma: un caso especial de escritura,* Instituto de Cultura, 1974.

Asturrizaga, Juan Espejo, *Cesar Vallejo: Itinerario del hombre, 1892-1923,* Libreria-Editorial Juan Mejia Baca, 1965.

Chavez, Ivan Rodriguez, *La ortografia poetica de Vallejo,* Compania de Impresiones y Publicidad, 1974.

Coyne, Andre, *Cesar Vallejo y su obra poetica,* Letras Peruanas, 1957.

Daydi-Tolson, Santiago, *The Post-Civil War Spanish Social Poets,* Twayne, 1983.

de Vallejo, Georgette, in Vallejo, Cesar, *Obra poetica completa,* F. Moncloa, 1968.

de Vallejo, *Vallejo: alla ellos, alla ellos, alla ellos!,* Zalvac, 1980.

Escobar, Alberto, *Como leer a Vallejo,* P. L. Villanueva, 1973.

Ferrari, Americo, *El universo poetico de Cesar Vallejo,* Monte Avila (Caracas), 1972.

Flores, Angel, editor, *Aproximaciones a Vallejo,* two volumes, Las Americas (New York), 1971.

Flores, editor, *Cesar Vallejo, Sintesis biographica, bibliografia y indice de poemas,* Premia Editora, 1982.

Franco, Jean, *Cesar Vallejo: The Dialectics of Poetry and Silence,* Cambridge University Press, 1976.

Fuentes, Victor, *El cantico material y espiritual de Cesar Vallejo,* Anthropos Editorial del Hombre, 1981.

Gallagher, D. P., *Modern Latin American Literature,* Oxford University Press, 1973.

Garcia, Francisco Martinez, *Cesar Vallejo; acercamiento al hombre y al poeta,* Colegio Universitario de Leon, 1976.

Higgins, James, *Vision del hombre y de la vida en las ultimas obras poeticas de Cesar Vallejo,* Siglo Veintiuno, 1970.

Higgins, *The Poet in Peru: Alienation and the Quest for a Super-Reality,* F. Cairns, 1982.

Higgins, *A History of Peruvian Literature,* F. Cairns, 1987.

Hispanic Literature Criticism, Gale, 1994.

Larrea, Juan, *Cesar Vallejo; o, Hispanoamerica en la cruz de su razon,* Universidad de Cordoba, 1958.

Larrea, *Cesar Vallejo: Heroe y martir indo-hispano,* Biblioteca Nacional (Montevideo), 1973.

Larrea, *Cesar Vallejo y el surrealismo,* A. Corazon (Madrid), 1976.

Larrea, *Al amor de Vallejo,* Pre-Textos, 1980.

Larrea, and others, *Perfil de Cesar Vallejo,* Grafica San Andres, 1978.

Mariategui, Jose Carlos, in *Siete ensayos de la realidad peruana,* 9th edition, Biblioteca Amauta (Lima), 1964.

Merino, Antonio, and Julio Velez, editors, *Espana en Cesar Vallejo,* Editorial Fundamentos, 1984.

More, Ernesto, *Vallejo en la encrucijada del drama peruano,* Libreria y Distribuidores Bendezu (Lima), 1968.

Neale-Silva, Eduardo, *Cesar Vallejo en su fase trilcica,* University of Wisconsin Press, 1975.

Ortega, Julio, editor, *Cesar Vallejo,* Taurus (Madrid), 1974.

Ortega, *La teoria poetica de Cesar Vallejo,* DelSol Editores, 1986.

Osuna, Yolanda, *Vallejo, el poema, la idea,* Universidad Central de Venezuela, 1979.

Paoli, Roberto, *Poesie di Cesar Vallejo,* Lecrici, 1964.

Paoli, *Mapas anatomicos de Cesar Vallejo,* D'Anna, 1981.

Twentieth Century Literary Criticism, Gale, Volume 3, 1980, Volume 56, 1995.

Vallejo, Cesar, *Poemas humanos,* 1939, Nuevo Peru, 1959, translation by Clayton Eshleman published as *Poemas humanos: Human Poems,* Grove Press, 1969.

Vallejo, *Literatura y arte,* Ediciones del Mediodia (Buenos Aires), 1966.

Vega, Jose Luis, *Cesar Vallejo en "Trilce",* Universidad de Puerto Rico, 1983.

Yurkievich, Saul, in *Fundadores de la nueva poesia latinoamericana,* Barral (Barcelona), 1971.

Zilio, Giovanni Meo, *Stile e poesia in Cesar Vallejo,* Liviana (Padua, Italy), 1960.

PERIODICALS

Amaru, number 13, October, 1970.

Americas, November-December, 1968, pp. 46-48, 48-49.

Aula Vallejo, number 1, 1961; number 2/4, 1963; number 5/7, 1967; number 8/10, 1971; number 11/13, 1974.

Bulletin of Hispanic Studies, Volume 43, number 1, 1966, pp. 47-55.

Courier, June, 1988.

Cuadernos Americanos, January, 1957.

Fiction International, summer, 1986.

Hispamerica, April 6, 1974.

Hispania, September, 1987; March, 1989, pp. 42-48.

Hispanic Review, Volume 50, number 3, 1982.

Hudson Review, winter, 1979.

Kentucky Romance Quarterly, Volume 17, number 3, 1970, pp. 247-58.

Library Journal, June 15, 1992, p. 79; August, 1992, p. 106.

Los Angeles Times Book Review, January 1, 1989.

Nation, October 28, 1968.

New Republic, July 12, 1993, p. 34.

New York Review of Books, December 21, 1978.

New York Times Book Review, March 23, 1969; June 8, 1969; February 26, 1989; May 7, 1972.

Poetry, June, 1969; January, 1981.

Publishers Weekly, May 4, 1992, p. 52; July 13, 1992, p. 51.

Revista Hispanica Moderna, January-April, 1969, pp. 268-84.

Revista Iberoamericana, April, 1970 (special Vallejo issue).

Times Literary Supplement, September 25, 1969, p. 1098; August 5, 1977, p. 964; January 18, 1980; June 14, 1989.

Tri-Quarterly, fall, 1968.

Village Voice, March 21, 1989.

Virginia Quarterly Review, winter, 1980.

Vision del Peru, number 4, 1969.

Western Humanities Review, winter, 1969.

West Indian Review, July, 1939.*

* * *

VALLE Y PENA, Ramon Jose Simon del
See VALLE-INCLAN, Ramon (Maria) del

VAN CISE, Jerrold G(ordon) 1910-1996

OBITUARY NOTICE—See index for *CA* sketch: Born May 21, 1910, in Newark, NJ; died of pneumonia, July 21, 1996, in New London, NH. Attorney, educator, and author. Van Cise was an authority on antitrust law, serving on various national and state committees and writing books on the subject. Van Cise graduated with a J.S. from Yale University in 1935 and joined the firm of Cahill, Gordon and Reindel in New York that same year. After ten years, he was made a partner at the firm, and he remained there until his retirement in 1980. He also began a dual career as a writer in 1949. In addition, he taught at the Practicing Law Institute, chaired the antitrust section of the American Bar Association from 1960 to 1961 and the New York State Bar Association from 1961 to 1962, and worked to advance continuing legal education. Among his books are *How to Comply with the Antitrust Laws,* edited with C. W. Dunn, *Understanding the Antitrust Laws,* and *The Federal Antitrust Laws.* In 1985 he received Colby-Sawyer College's Susan Colgate Cleveland Award.

OBITUARIES AND OTHER SOURCES:

BOOKS

International Authors and Writer's Who's Who, 10th edition, International Biographical Centre, 1986.

PERIODICALS

New York Times, August 4, 1996, p. 41.

* * *

VAN DUZER, Chet A. 1966-

PERSONAL: Born March 10, 1966, in Stanford, CA; son of Victor E. (an engineer) and J. Noreen (a nurse; maiden name, Kelly) Van Duzer. *Education:* University of California, Berkeley, B.A., 1987.

ADDRESSES: Home—12177 Winton Way, Los Altos Hills, CA 94024.

CAREER: Freelance writer.

MEMBER: Phi Beta Kappa.

AWARDS, HONORS: National Writing Award and Nancy Hanks Memorial Award, *Scholastic,* both 1984, for the essay "The Aesthetics of Mathematics."

WRITINGS:

Duality and Structure in the Iliad and Odyssey, Peter Lang (New York), 1996.

WORK IN PROGRESS: The Palace of Mirrors: Reflexivity in Ancient Greek Vase Painting, a study of compositional patterns in the scenes portrayed on ancient Greek vases; research on the mythology of sacred centers and on medieval culture.

* * *

Van STAAVEREN, Jacob 1917-

PERSONAL: Born April 9, 1917, in Polk County, OR; son of Siet and Christina (Strickwerda) Van Staaveren; married Elizabeth Kelly (an economist, librarian, and genealogist), August 4, 1961. *Education:* Linfield College, B.A., 1939; University of Chicago, M.A., 1943, doctoral study, 1945-46, 1948-49. *Avocational interests:* History, genealogy, classical music.

ADDRESSES: Home and office—1008 Cascade Way, McMinnville, OR 97128-9512.

CAREER: Worked for National Labor Relations Board, Chicago, IL, 1942-43; Public Administration Clearing House, Chicago, worked for Council of State Governments and Municipal Finance Officers Association, 1944-46; Yananashi Military Government Team, Japan, civil information and education officer, 1946-48; Office of the Supreme Commander, Allied Powers, Tokyo, Japan, historian in Civil Historical Section, 1949-51; U.S. Air Force, historian in Korea, 1951-53; Far East Command, United Nations Command, Tokyo, historian at Military History Liaison Office, 1954-56; Strategic Air Command, historian, 1957-58; Office of Air Force History, Washington, DC, historian, 1958-81. Appeared in the documentary series *Nippon: Japan Since 1945,* televised by the British Broadcasting Corp. in England and by Arts and Entertainment in the United States; lecturer at colleges and universities; public speaker.

MEMBER: Association for Asian Studies, American Historical Society, National Association of Scholars.

AWARDS, HONORS: Superior Performance Awards and Outstanding Performance Awards for work as a government historian.

WRITINGS:

(Co-author) *The United States Air Force in Southeast Asia, 1961-1973,* U.S. Government Printing Office, 1977, revised edition, 1984.
Interdiction in Southern Laos, 1960-1968: A Military-Political History of the Air War along the Ho Chi Minh Trail in Southern Laos, U.S. Government Printing Office, 1994.
An American in Japan: A Civilian View of the Occupation, 1945-1946, University of Washington Press (Seattle, WA), 1994.
The Air War against North Vietnam, 1965-1966, U.S. Government Printing Office, in press.

* * *

VAZQUEZ AMARAL, Jose 1913-1987

PERSONAL: Born April 1, 1913, in Los Reyes, Jalisco, Mexico; died of a heart condition, February 24, 1987, in Summit, NJ; married Mary Helen Madiraca; children: Pedro, Lydia Watson, Marta Alicia Lopez, Maria Elena, Jacinta Rosa Amaral. *Education:* Escuela Nacional de Preparatoria, Ph.B. and B.Litt., 1935; Universidad Nacional Autonoma de Mexico, Licenciar en Derecho, 1941.

CAREER: National University of Mexico, Ciudad Universitaria, professor of English, 1935-42; visiting professor of Latin American literature at Tulane University, New Orleans, LA, 1942-43, and Swarthmore College, Swarthmore, PA, 1943-47; Rutgers, The State University, New Brunswick, NJ, began as associate professor and Latin America specialist, became professor of romance languages, 1947-87, head of Spanish and Portuguese department, 1947-82. Former lawyer, Hill-de la Sierra, Prado, Mexico Atlantic seaboard representative, Mexico Minister of Education.

MEMBER: International Institute of Iberoamerican Literature (secretary, 1943).

AWARDS, HONORS: Thornton Niven Wilder Prize from Translation Center of Columbia University, 1987; Distinguished Service Medal of the President

of Mexico; National Prize for Linguistics and Literature (Mexico).

WRITINGS:

Los Gringos, Costa Amic, 1969.
The Contemporary Latin American Narrative, Las Americas, 1970.
(Translator) *The Cantos of Ezra Pound,* Joaquin Mortiz, 1975.

Also translator of *Walt Whitman* and *Biography of Mexico.*

BIOGRAPHICAL/CRITICAL SOURCES:

PERIODICALS

New York Times, February 26, 1987.*

* * *

VERRIER, Suzanne 1942-
 (Suzy Verrier)

PERSONAL: Born June 15, 1942, in Portland, ME; daughter of Robert (a commercial contractor) and Valda Verrier; married Jack Henderson, 1969 (divorced, 1974); married Peter Rysman, 1976 (divorced, 1990); children: Stacy Verrier, Molly Rysman. *Ethnicity:* "French-American." *Education:* Attended Goucher College and Philadelphia Museum College of Art. *Politics:* Democrat. *Religion:* "None." *Avocational interests:* Plants, gardening, garden design, plant photography.

ADDRESSES: Home and office—36 Atlantic St., Portland, ME 04101; fax 207-871-1072.

CAREER: Illustrator of children's books, 1969-75; Forevergreen Farm, founder, owner, and operator, 1983-93; White Flower Farm, Litchfield, CT, consulting rosarian, 1994—.

AWARDS, HONORS: Award from Society of Illustrators, 1971, for *Titus Tidewater.*

WRITINGS:

Titus Tidewater (self-illustrated children's book), Doubleday (New York City), 1970.

Rosa Rugosa, Capability's Books (Deer Park, WI), 1991 *Rosa Gallica,* Capability's Books, 1996.
Rosa: Species, Capability's Books, in press.

Contributor of articles and photographs to magazines, including *Horticulture, Flower and Garden, Country Living, Gardener, American Rose Annual,* and *American Nurseryman.* Some writings appear under the name Suzy Verrier.

SIDELIGHTS: Suzanne Verrier told *CA:* "I was originally trained in art. Gardening became my art form, and my writing evolved simply to express my experience, enthusiasm, and ideas on this subject. My primary focus of interest in roses. I try to tackle areas not formerly clarified, or I attempt to set right misconceptions about my favorite subject.

"In my writing, I try to convey myself as a personality and communicate my zeal for the subject in a chatty, non-pontificating manner. I place great import on the correctness and validity of material in my writing. I am anti-computer and against the proliferation of errors generated by this medium. My books and articles are all handwritten."

* * *

VERRIER, Suzy
 See VERRIER, Suzanne

* * *

VILARINO, Idea 1920-

PERSONAL: Born August 18, 1920, in Montevideo, Uruguay; daughter of Leandro Vilarino (a poet) and Josefina Romani.

ADDRESSES: Home—Presidente Battle 2592, Apartado Postal 11600, Montevideo, Uruguay.

CAREER: Teacher of literature at a preparatory school, 1952-55; teacher at Instituto "Alfredo Vazquez Acevedo," 1955-73. Co-founder and co-director of literary review, *Numero,* 1949-55.

AWARDS, HONORS: "Rodo" literary prize from Intendencia Municipal de Montevideo, 1987.

WRITINGS:

POETRY

La suplicante (title means "The Supplicant"), self-published, [Montevideo], 1945.

Cielo, cielo (title means "Sky, Sky"), self-published, [Montevideo], 1947.

Paraiso perdido (1945-1948) (title means "Paradise Lost"), Numero (Montevideo), 1949.

Por aire sucio (title means "Through Dirty Air"), Numero, 1950.

Nocturnos (title means "Nocturnes"), Numero, 1955, reprinted, Schapire (Buenos Aires), 1976.

Poemas de amor (title means "Love Poems") [Montevideo], 1957, 2nd edition, Alfa (Montevideo), 1962.

Pobre mundo (title means "Poor World"), Banda Oriental (Montevideo), 1966.

Treinta poemas (title means "Thirty Poems"), Tauro, 1967.

Poesia, 1941-1967 (title means "Poetry . . ."), Arca (Montevideo), 1970.

Segunda antologia (title means "Second Anthology"), Calicanto (Montevideo), 1980.

No, Calicanto, 1980.

Poesia, Cal y Canto (Montevideo), 1994.

Contributor of poems in English translation to *The Borzoi Anthology of Latin American Literature,* Volume 2: *The Twentieth-Century—From Borges and Paz to Guimaraes Rosa and Donoso,* edited by Emir Rodriguez Monegal with the assistance of Thomas Colchie, Knopf, 1986.

OTHER

Julio Herrera y Reissig: Seis anos de poesia (title means "Julio Herrera y Reissig: Six Year of Poetry"; monograph), Numero, 1950, reprinted, Tecnica, c. 1974, published as *Julio Herrera y Reissig: Poemas comentados* (title means "Julio Herrera y Reissig: Annotated Poems"), 1978.

Grupos simetricos en poesia (title means "Symmetrical Groups in Poetry"), Universidad de la Republica (Montevideo), 1958.

Las letras de tango: La forma, temas y motivos (title means "Tango Lyrics: Form, Themes and Motifs"), Schapire, 1965.

(Editor) Juan Parra del Riego, *Nocturnos y otros poemas* (title means "Nocturnes and Other Poems"), Siete Poetas Hispanoamericanos (Montevideo), 1965.

(Compiler) *Antologia de la violencia* (title means "Anthology of Violence"), Schapire, 1972.

Los salmos (title means "The Psalms"), Casa de Estudiantes (Montevideo), 1974, 2nd edition, 1977.

La literatura biblica: El Antiguo Testamento (title means "Biblical Literature: The Old Testament"), Tecnica, 1976.

(Translator) W. H. Hudson, *La tierra purpura; Alla lejos y hace tiempo,* Ayacucho (Caracas), 1980.

Introduccion a literatura biblica, Tecnica (Montevideo), 1981.

(Editor) *Tangos: Antologia* (title means "Tangos: Anthology"), Centro Editor de America Latina (Buenos Aires), 1981.

El tango, CEDAL, 1981.

(Editor and author of prologue) *El tango cantado* (title means "The Sung Tango"), Calicanto, 1981.

Conocimiento de Dario (title means "Understanding Dario"), Arca, 1988.

La masa sonora del poema: Sus organizaciones vocalicas. Indagaciones en algunos poemas de Ruben Dario, Arca, 1989.

La sudicia luce del Giorno (anthology), Spanish and Italian texts, Urbino, 1989.

Also author of *Grupos simetricos en la poesia de Antonio Machado,* 1951, *Pius Servien y los ritmos,* 1952, and *La rima en Herrera y Reissig,* 1955. Also translator of works by William Shakespeare. Contributor to periodicals, including *Clinamen, Asir, Hiperion, Marcha,* and *Puente.*

SIDELIGHTS: In his *Spanish-American Literature: A History* Enrique Anderson-Imbert describes Uruguay's Idea Vilarino as the most representative poet of the generation that surfaced in that country immediately after World War II. Like the other members of the group, Vilarino focuses on death and hopelessness in her poetry. "The appearance of Idea's first book, *La suplicante,* in 1945," note Emir Rodriguez Monegal and Thomas Colchie in *The Borzoi Anthology of Latin American Literature,* "was an extraordinary event in Uruguayan poetry, not only because of the freshness in rhythm and language that her work represented . . . , but also because of the desolate, sincere, pathetic vision of the world that, in well-minted verses, the new and implacable voice transmitted." Rodriguez Monegal and Colchie also observe that Vilarino has written "some of the most devastating love poems written in Spanish today" and place her work in the tradition of erotic poetry developed in Latin America by Uruguayan poet Delmira

Agustini and the Nobel prize-winning Chilean poet Gabriela Mistral.

BIOGRAPHICAL/CRITICAL SOURCES:

BOOKS

Anderson-Imbert, Enrique, *Spanish-American Literature: A History,* Volume 2: *1910-1963,* 2nd edition revised and updated by Elaine Malley, Wayne State University Press, 1969.

Diccionario de literatura uruguaya, Arca-Credisol, 1987.

Rodriguez Monegal, Emir, with the assistance of Thomas Colchie, editors, *The Borzoi Anthology of Latin American Literature,* Volume 2: *The Twentieth Century—From Borges and Paz to Guimaraes Rosa and Donoso,* Knopf, 1986.

* * *

VILLIERS, Marie de
 See ROUTIER, Simone

* * *

VITALI, Julius 1952-

PERSONAL: Born July 1, 1952, in Queens, New York, NY; son of Victor (an electrical engineer) and Rose (in sales; maiden name, Tardio) Vitali; married Terry Niedzialek (an artist), August 25, 1985 (divorced). *Ethnicity:* "Italian-American." *Education:* State University of New York College at Fredonia, B.A., 1974; attended State University of New York at Buffalo, 1975. *Politics:* "Anarchist." *Religion:* "All religions." *Avocational interests:* Bicycling, ping pong, macrobiotic cooking.

ADDRESSES: Home and office—P.O. Box 75, Flicksville, PA 18050; fax 610-588-6423.

CAREER: Pennsylvania Press Service, Flicksville, photojournalist, 1987—. August House, Inc. (Easton, PA), director of development, 1992—; Open Space Gallery (Allentown, PA), vice-president. Artist, with work in public and private collections, including Bibliotheque Nationale, Paris, and Polaroid Corp. Pennsylvania Council on the Arts, member of Arts in Education Program; Hunger Through the Arts Foundation, member of board of directors. Guest on television programs, including *The Late Show with David Letterman.*

AWARDS, HONORS: Grants from National Endowment for the Arts, Pennsylvania Council on the Arts, Adolph and Esther Gottlieb Foundation, Kodak, and Polaroid.

WRITINGS:

The Fine Artist's Guide to Marketing and Self-Promotion: Innovative Techniques to Build Your Career as an Artist, Allworth Press (New York), 1996.

Contributor to periodicals, including *Petersen's Photographic, School Arts, Studio Photography, Domus,* and *Video-Actor.*

WORK IN PROGRESS: The Fine Artist's Guide to Practical Writing; research on "artists organized," a history of the shows and tips for current artists.

SIDELIGHTS: Julian Vitali told *CA:* "The information put forward in *The Fine Artist's Guide to Marketing and Self-Promotion: Innovative Techniques to Build Your Career as an Artist* was and continues to be lived. It was written by a professional practicing visual artist (with interdisciplinary leanings) over a two-and-a-half-year period, but it was lived for seventeen years. I lived by my wits, exhibiting, writing grants, doing illustrations for magazines. As I look toward the future, the book is my 'social security.' As a result of the nature of this book, I will be teaching survival skills for artists in workshops at art centers, colleges, and universities."

* * *

VOGEL, Frederick G. 1934-

PERSONAL: Born January 20, 1934; son of Frederick William and Marion (Lawlor) Vogel; married Mary Howitt (a transportation planner), August 30, 1970. *Education:* Received A.B. and A.M. from George Washington University. *Politics:* "New Deal Democrat." *Religion:* Episcopalian.

ADDRESSES: Home and office—47 Dunnell Rd., Maplewood, NJ 07040.

CAREER: Washington Post, Washington, DC, staff reporter, 1956-61; Crowell-Collier Publishing Co., Inc., New York City, book editor, 1961-67; Cowles Communications, Inc., New York City, magazine editor, 1968-80; freelance writer and editor, 1981— . *Military service:* U.S. Marine Corps, 1953-56.

WRITINGS:

(With Richard Fehr) *Lullabies of Hollywood: Movie Music and the Movie Musical, 1915-1992,* McFarland and Co. (Jefferson, NC), 1993.
World War I Songs, McFarland and Co., 1996.

WORK IN PROGRESS: A History of the Academy Awards; research on the history of popular songs, 1900-1920, and on the biographies of bandleaders of the 1930s.

SIDELIGHTS: Frederick G. Vogel told *CA:* "I have an abiding interest in American films (1929-1958) and in American popular music from the twenties through the forties. I enjoy researching and writing articles and books on these subjects, mostly I think to 'convert' fans of current popular music to my point of view. It is a most challenging avocation."

* * *

VOGT, Gregory L.

PERSONAL: Born in Milwaukee, WI; father's name: Kenneth W. Vogt; married Margaret Brunner; children: three daughters. *Education:* University of Wisconsin at Milwaukee, B.S., M.S.; Oklahoma State University, Ph.D.

CAREER: Writer and scientist. National Aeronautics and Space Administration (NASA), Educational Affairs Division, Johnson Space Center, Houston, TX, developer of educational videos for schools; has also worked with NASA's Teacher in Space program and as a writer and editor at NASA's Education Publications office in Washington, DC. Formerly at Oklahoma State University, adjunct assistant professor; Discovery World Museum of Science, Economics and Technology, Milwaukee, WI; executive director; Milwaukee Public School System, eighth-grade science teacher; planetarium lecturer; educational consultant to National Wildlife Federation.

WRITINGS:

FOR CHILDREN

Mars and the Inner Planets, Watts (New York), 1982.
Model Rockets, illustrated by Anne Canevari Green, Watts, 1982.
A Twenty-Fifth Anniversary Album of NASA, Watts, 1983.
The Space Shuttle: Projects for Young Scientists, Watts, 1983.
Electricity and Magnetism, Watts, 1985.
Generating Electricity, Watts, 1986.
Space Satellites, Watts, 1986.
An Album of Modern Spaceships, Watts, 1987.
Halley's Comet: What We've Learned, Watts, 1987.
Predicting Earthquakes, Watts, 1989.
Predicting Volcanic Eruptions, Watts, 1989.
Forests on Fire: The Fight to Save Our Trees, Watts, 1990.
Volcanoes, Watts, 1993.
The Search for the Killer Asteroid, Millbrook Press (Brookfield, CT), 1994.
The Solar System: Facts and Exploration, Twenty-First Century Books (New York), 1995.
Space Exploration: Projects for Young Scientists, Watts, 1995.

"SPACE LIBRARY" SERIES

Space Walking, Watts (New York), 1987.
Space Laboratories, Watts, 1989.
Spaceships, Watts, 1989.
Space Explorers, Watts, 1990.
Space Stations, Watts, 1990.

"MISSIONS IN SPACE" SERIES

Viking and the Mars Landing, Millbrook Press (Brookfield, CT), 1991.
Apollo and the Moon Landing, Millbrook Press, 1991.
Voyager, Millbrook Press, 1991.
Magellan and the Radar Mapping of Venus, Millbrook Press, 1992.
The Hubble Space Telescope, Millbrook Press, 1992.

"GATEWAY SOLAR SYSTEM" SERIES

Jupiter, Millbrook Press (Brookfield, CT), 1993.
Neptune, Millbrook Press, 1993.
Saturn, Millbrook Press, 1993.

Uranus, Millbrook Press, 1993.
Mercury, Millbrook Press, 1994.
Mars, Millbrook Press, 1994.
Pluto, Millbrook Press, 1994.
Venus, Millbrook Press, 1994.
Asteroids, Comets, and Meteors, Millbrook Press, 1996.
Earth, Millbrook Press, 1996.
The Sun, Millbrook Press, 1996.

SIDELIGHTS: Although some of Gregory L. Vogt's science books for young people, such as *Forests on Fire: The Fight to Save Our Trees* or *Electricity and Magnetism,* deal with the physical forces at work in the world around us, the majority of his titles explore the mysteries of outer space. Books in his "Space Library" series explain various aspects of space exploration, while his other two series, "Missions in Space" and "Gateway Solar System," provide detailed information about National Aeronautics and Space Administration (NASA) space programs and each of the planets in the solar system respectively.

Many of Vogt's books about space benefit from his inside knowledge of NASA gathered during years of work for the organization in various capacities including developer of educational videos and writer and editor of educational publications. Along with pertinent facts and accurate data, his ability to explain complex subjects to his young readers is the key to his efforts. His works combine a wealth of information and numerous photographs with an enjoyable writing style, according to reviewers. "He brings narrative skill and historical perspective to his task," a *Kirkus Reviews* critic writes of *Apollo and the Moon Landing.* In *Science Books and Films,* reviewer Sidney Rosen calls another volume in Vogt's "Missions in Space" series, *Magellan and the Radar Mapping of Venus,* "well-written" and finds it similar to "a Fodor's guide to the planets." Works in Vogt's "Gateway Solar System" series are equally appealing as Patsy Ann Giese notes in *Appraisal:* "These books contain an interesting blend of facts about planets, details from history and descriptions of astronomers' work. The vastness, complexity and beauty of the solar system are conveyed."

BIOGRAPHICAL/CRITICAL SOURCES:

PERIODICALS

Appraisal, spring, 1988, pp. 35-36; fall, 1994; spring/summer, 1995, pp. 55-56.

Booklist, April 15, 1986, p. 1228; May 15, 1990, p. 1808; July, 1990, p. 2096.
Kirkus Reviews, February 1, 1991, p. 178.
School Library Journal, December, 1983, p. 70, 71; May, 1986, p. 110; January 15, 1988, p. 871; December, 1990, p. 134, December, 1991, p. 131.
Science Books and Films, October, 1992, p. 207.
Voice of Youth Advocates, June, 1984, p. 111.

* * *

VOLBACH, Walther R(ichard) 1897-1996

OBITUARY NOTICE—See index for *CA* sketch: Born December 24, 1897, in Mainz, Germany; immigrated to the U.S., 1936; became naturalized U.S. citizen; died August 5, 1996. Theater director, educator, and author. Volbach devoted his career to the theater, first as a stage director in Berlin, Zurich, Kiel, Danzig, Stuttgart, and Vienna, and later as an educator in the subjects of drama and opera at universities in the United States. Volbach's stage career spanned sixteen years, before his immigration to the United States and a job at Marquette University from 1939 to 1941. He was the director of opera at the Cleveland Institute of Music for the next two years, followed by a twelve-year stint as a professor of drama and director of theater and opera at Texas Christian University. From 1958 until 1965, he led the school's department of theater arts. Beginning in 1965, he was a visiting professor at the University of Massachusetts. A translator of plays by writers such as Schiller and Montherlant, he wrote a biography of Appia called *Adolphe Appia: Prophet of the Modern Theater.* His other writings include *Problems of Opera Production* and *Memoirs of Max Reinhardt's Theatres, 1920-1922.*

OBITUARIES AND OTHER SOURCES:

PERIODICALS

New York Times, August 6, 1995, p. A15.

* * *

VON HOFMANNSTHAL, Hugo
See HOFMANNSTHAL, Hugo von

von KALNEIN, Wend 1914-

PERSONAL: Born May 24, 1914, in Ludwigslust, Germany; son of Erhard (an army officer) and Erna (maiden name, Reichel; later surname, von der Recke) von Kalnein; married Livia von Thielmann, 1959; children: Heinrich, Albrecht, Alexandra. *Education:* Attended University of Grenoble, 1932, and University of Heidelberg, 1933; University of Bonn, Phil.D., 1955. *Religion:* Protestant. *Avocational interests:* Languages, history, archaeology.

ADDRESSES: Home—Bayerham 70, A-5201 Seekirchen, Salzburg, Austria. *Office*—Residenzplatz 9 Kunsthist. Institut, Universitaet Salzburg, A-5020 Salzburg, Austria.

CAREER: University of Bonn, Bonn, Germany, assistant at Institute of the History of Art, 1953-54; Zaehringer Museum, Baden-Baden, Germany, director, 1954-61; National Museum of Fine Arts, Kassel, Germany, curator, 1961-64; Museum of Fine Arts, Duesseldorf, Germany, director, 1964-79; University of Salzburg, Salzburg, Austria, teacher and professor, 1979-95. International Committee of Glass, chairperson, 1971-79. *Military service:* 1936-38.

MEMBER: Art Historians Association of Austria.

WRITINGS:

Das kurfuerstl. Schloss Clemensruhe in Poppelsdorf, Schwann (Duesseldorf, Germany), 1956.

Meisterwerke der Markgr. BaDISCHEN Sammlungen im Neuen Schloss, Wesel (Baden-Baden, Germany), 1960.

(With Michael Levey) *Art and Architecture of the Eighteenth Century in France,* Pelican, 1972, revised edition, 1994.

Schloss Anif, Anton Pustet (Salzburg, Austria), 1988.

Contributor to periodicals. Editor, *Kataloge d. Kunstmuseums Duesseldorf,* 1964-79.

WORK IN PROGRESS: Research on Romantic architecture in Austria.

SIDELIGHTS: Wend von Kalnein is the author, with Michael Levey, of the respected work *Art and Architecture of the Eighteenth Century in France.*

Kalnein told *CA:* "Writing is part of the business of an art historian. When you are in a museum, you usually spend your time with publishing articles on almost everything: works of art, catalogs, exhibitions, conservation, education, and so on. When you are interested in architecture or special monuments, it is very much the same. You start with research and, having found out something essentially new about origin, author, historical background, or general connections, there is a special moment when you feel you have to write it down and publish it. It is hard work, however, before you are able to do so, and you can't write it down like a novel. Personally, I need a lot of scribble sheets before I get the definite form."

W

WALLIS, Hal B.
See WALLIS, Harold Brent

* * *

WALLIS, Harold Brent 1898(?)-1986
(Hal B. Wallis)

PERSONAL: Surname originally Walinsky; professionally known as Hal B. Wallis; born September 14, 1898 (some sources say 1899), in Chicago, IL; died of complications from diabetes, October 5, 1986, in Rancho Mirage, CA; buried in Forest Lawn Park, Glendale, CA; son of Jacob and Eva (Blum) Walinsky; married Louise Fazenda (an actress), November 24, 1927 (died, 1962); married Martha Hyer (an actress); children: (first marriage) Hal Brent.

ADDRESSES: Home—Rancho Mirage, CA.

CAREER: Film producer and writer. Worked as clerk in Chicago, IL, c. 1913-16; General Electric Co., Chicago, assistant sales and advertising manager, 1916-22; Garrick Theater, Los Angeles, CA, manager, 1922-23; Warner Brothers, Los Angeles, assistant publicity director, 1923-24, publicity director, 1924-28, studio manager and production executive, 1928-33, head of production, 1933-44; founded Hal Wallis Productions, 1944. Producer of motion pictures, including *I Am a Fugitive from a Chain Gang,* 1932; *The Adventures of Robin Hood,* 1938; *The Roaring Twenties,* 1939; *High Sierra,* 1941; *The Maltese Falcon,* 1941; *Now, Voyager,* 1942; *Yankee Doodle Dandy,* 1942; *Casablanca,* 1943; *My Friend*

Irma, 1949; *The Rainmaker,* 1956; *Blue Hawaii,* 1961; *True Grit,* 1969; *Mary, Queen of Scots,* 1972; and *Rooster Cogburn,* 1975.

AWARDS, HONORS: Academy of Motion Picture Arts and Sciences, Irving Thalberg Awards for lifetime achievement, 1938 and 1943, and Academy Award, 1943, for *Casablanca.*

WRITINGS:

(With Charles Higham) *Star Maker: The Autobiography of Hal Wallis,* foreword by Katharine Hepburn, Macmillan (New York), 1980.

SIDELIGHTS: Harold Brent Wallis was a prominent Hollywood film producer whose career extended from the early 1930s to the mid-1970s. Wallis came to Los Angeles, California in 1922 and soon found work managing a film theater. The following year he obtained a position as assistant to the head of publicity at Warner Brothers, a major film studio. In 1928 he became studio manager, and two years afterward he produced his first films, including Howard Hawks's war story *Dawn Patrol* and Mervyn LeRoy's gangster drama *Little Caesar,* both of which are considered classics.

In 1933 Wallis produced Michael Curtiz's *Mystery of the Wax Museum* and the musicals *Footlight Parade* and *Forty Second Street.* The successes of these films served as further indication of Wallis's impressive prowess in the production field. Two years later, by which time he had been named executive producer in charge of production, Wallis produced the swashbuckler *Captain Blood,* which helped establish actor Erroll Flynn as a major film actor, and *A Midsummer*

Night's Dream, the Shakespearean comedy co-directed by the innovative director Max Reinhardt.

By the end of the 1930s, Wallis was clearly established as one of Hollywood's most successful film producers. He was known for his particular expertise in assembling appropriate talent—actors, writers, directors—for specific projects. It was probably for his use of performers, though, that he was most respected, having launched the career of gangster-genre mainstay Edward G. Robinson in *Little Caesar* as well as Erroll Flynn. In addition, he enjoyed a highly successful series of collaborations with actress Bette Davis, whom he cast in both period dramas such as *Jezebel* and melodramas such as the acclaimed *Now, Voyager.*

Wallis continued his run of success in the early 1940s when he produced such prominent Warner Brothers productions as *High Sierra,* with Humphrey Bogart as a forlorn criminal; *The Maltese Falcon,* director John Huston's debut, with Bogart as Dashiell Hammett's sleuth Sam Spade; *Sergeant York,* with Gary Cooper as a World War I hero; *Yankee Doodle Dandy,* with versatile James Cagney in an impressive song-and-dance turn; and the classic love story *Casablanca,* another Bogart vehicle, with the actor as a sardonic nightclub operator caught up in international intrigue with a former love.

In the mid-1940s Wallis left Warner Brothers and formed Hal Wallis Productions. The next few years were hardly the most significant of Wallis's career, but in 1949 he produced the first of several films featuring the enormously popular comedy team of Dean Martin and Jerry Lewis. The duo made several films with Wallis, including their final and, perhaps, most innovative endeavors, *Artists and Models* and *Hollywood or Bust.*

In addition, Wallis continued to further the careers of promising performers. He cast Burt Lancaster in melodramas such as *Come Back, Little Sheba,* in which the versatile actor played a spouse abusing alcoholic, and paired him with Kirk Douglas in the compelling western *Gunfight at the O. K. Corral.* Perhaps Wallis's greater financial successes, though, came with a series of vehicles for pop singer Elvis Presley, including *Blue Hawaii* and *Girls! Girls! Girls!*

Wallis's career slowed slightly toward the end of the 1960s, and it ended altogether in the mid-1970s. In his final working years, however, he still managed to maintain a certain standard of quality; notable among his films from this period are the historical dramas *Anne of the Thousand Days* and *Mary, Queen of Scots.* His final film, *Rooster Cogburn,* teamed John Wayne with Katharine Hepburn in the sequel to Wayne's Oscar-winning performance in *True Grit.*

In 1980 Wallis wrote—with Charles Higham—*Star Maker: The Autobiography of Hal Wallis,* in which he recalls his triumphs with such films as *Casablanca* and his collaborations with such personalities as Martin and Lewis, Cagney, and Presley. Pat McGilligan, writing in the *Los Angeles Times Book Review,* acknowledged Wallis as "the last of the great veteran movie producers," and described *Star Maker* as "an unassuming reminiscence chock with . . . typical producer's turf."

Wallis died in 1986 at his home in Rancho Mirage, California. In various obituaries he was recalled as an especially successful film producer, and several obituaries noted that Wallis's four hundred films amassed more than one hundred Academy Award nominations and collected on thirty two of them.

BIOGRAPHICAL/CRITICAL SOURCES:

BOOKS

Contemporary Newsmakers 1987, Gale, 1987.
Wallace, Harold Brent, and Charles Higham, *Star Maker: The Autobiography of Hal Wallis,* foreword by Katharine Hepburn, Macmillan, 1980.

PERIODICALS

Film Comment, July-August, 1989, pp. 40-46.
Los Angeles Times Book Review, October 12, 1980, pp. 6-7.

OBITUARIES:

PERIODICALS

Chicago Tribune, October 9, 1986.
Los Angeles Times, October 8, 1986, p. D30; October 9, 1986, p. D27.
Newsweek, October 20, 1986, p. 63.
New York Times, October 8, 1986, October 9, 1986.
Time, October 20, 1986, p. 78.
Times (London), October 9, 1986.
Washington Post, October 8, 1986.*

WALZ, Marjorie A. 1939-
(Dareion Morgan)

PERSONAL: Born December 10, 1939, in Birmingham, AL; daughter of Alfred W. (a steelworker) and Grace (an elementary schoolteacher; maiden name, Rollins) Walz. *Ethnicity:* "White." *Education:* Washington University, A.B., 1960; University of Alabama, M.S., 1968; University of Mississippi, Ph.D., 1980. *Politics:* "Moderate." *Religion:* Methodist. *Avocational interests:* Astronomy, art, needlework, gardening.

ADDRESSES: Home—Birmingham, AL.

CAREER: St. Louis University, St. Louis, MO, postdoctoral fellow in pharmacology, 1982-87; writer.

MEMBER: American Association for the Advancement of Science, Arkansas Archeological Society, Sigma Xi, Rho Chi.

AWARDS, HONORS: National Research Service Award, National Institutes of Health, 1984.

WRITINGS:

(Under pseudonym Dareion Morgan) *Sophie's Legacy* (science fiction), Aegina Press (Huntington, WV), 1995.

Author of seventeen scientific articles.

WORK IN PROGRESS: Research on ancient Mediterranean (including biblical) history; research on the Latin language.

SIDELIGHTS: Marjorie A. Walz told *CA:* "My first love in life is human behavior—history, archaeology, psychology, even watching people on the street. I have a doctorate in biochemistry of the brain—underlying behavior and changes in biochemistry and behavior brought about by drugs. After early years as an introvert and due to an excellent speech teacher in college, I discovered I had a streak of the 'ham' in me, and I actually enjoyed public speaking. Recent part-time jobs have involved meeting the public and, much to my surprise, I have loved it.

"Among my earliest memories are making up stories and imagining that they were written in books and that people enjoyed reading them. Since early childhood I have read voraciously in history and science.

I was particularly fond of the historical novels of Joseph A. Altsheler, and I became enamored of science fiction later from watching *Star Trek.*

"During a very difficult career in scientific research, I wrote primarily to keep my head on straight. Now I have a pile of sixteen novels on computer disks. About half are science fiction, and the other half are historical fiction, ranging from the Trojan War to the American Civil War. There is one contemporary novel based on my research experiences. A few years ago, I gave up on the research and returned to my home town of Birmingham, Alabama, to concentrate on writing and marketing my work.

"There are four words (at least) in the English language meaning 'common, garden-variety': mean, vulgar, obscene, and ornery. It seems we common, garden-variety human beings are walking atrocities! I want people coming home from a day of mean, vulgar, obscene, ornery human behavior at the office, lab, or plant to be able to pick up one of my books and be reminded that—if only in human imagination—right can triumph and endings can be happy. If we lose the mental image of a world where good wins and justice reigns, we are damned!"

* * *

WASSON, R(obert) Gordon 1898-1986

PERSONAL: Born September 22, 1898, in Great Falls, MT; died December 23, 1986, in Binghamton, NY; son of Edmund Atwill (a minister) and Mary Matilda (DeVeny) Wasson; married Valentina Pavlovna Guercken (a pediatrician), 1926 (died, 1958); children: Peter, Mary Xenia. *Education:* Columbia University, B.Litt., 1920; attended the University of Lyons, France, and the London School of Economics.

CAREER: Columbia College, New York City, instructor in English, 1921-22; *New Haven Register,* New Haven, CT, editorial writer and political correspondent, 1922-24; associate editor of *Current Opinion,* 1924-25; financial reporter for *New York Herald Tribune,* 1925-28; associated with Guaranty Co., in New York City, 1928-34, and Morgan Guaranty Trust Co., in New York City, 1934-63, became vice president, 1943; writer. Honorary research fellow in ethnomycology at the Botanical Museum of Harvard University, beginning in 1957; honorary research

associate and honorary manager of the New York Botanical Garden, 1957-86. Correspondent for the National Museum of Natural History, Paris, France. *Military service:* Served in the U.S. Army (Signal Corps) during World War I.

MEMBER: Medieval Academy of America (member of executive committee), Sigma Xi, Century Association.

AWARDS, HONORS: Pulitzer Traveling Scholarship, 1920; Sarah Gildersleeve Fife Memorial Award from New York Botanical Gardens, 1958; Hon. D.Sc., from University of Bridgeport, 1974; Addison Emery Verrill Medal from Yale University's Peabody Museum of Natural History, 1983.

WRITINGS:

The Hall Carbine Affair: A Study in Contemporary Folklore, privately printed, 1941, third edition published as *The Hall Carbine Affair: An Essay in Historiography,* 1971.
(With wife, Valentina Pavlovna Wasson) *Mushrooms, Russia, and History* (two volumes), Pantheon (New York), 1957.
Soma: Divine Mushroom of Immortality, Mouton (The Hague), 1968, Harcourt (New York), 1971.
(Editor with others) *Maria Sabina and Her Mazatec Mushroom Velada* (text in Mazatec with English and Spanish translation), Harcourt, 1974.
(With Albert Hofmann and Carl A. P. Ruck) *The Road to Eleusis: Unveiling the Secret of the Mysteries,* Harcourt, 1978.
The Wondrous Mushroom: Mycolatry in Mesoamerica, McGraw (New York), 1980.
(With Stella Kramrisch, Jonathan Ott, and Ruck) *Persephone's Quest: Entheogens and the Origins of Religion,* Yale University Press (New Haven, CT), 1986.

Also author of leaflets published by the Botanical Museum of Harvard University, including *The Hallucinogenic Fungi of Mexico: An Inquiry into the Origins of the Religious Idea among Primitive Peoples,* 1961; *Soma and the Fly-Agaric; Mr. Wasson's Rejoinder to Professor Brough,* 1972; and *The Role of "Flowers" in Nahuatl Culture: A Suggested Interpretation,* 1973. Contributor to periodicals, including *Life.* Collaborator with wife, Valentina Pavlovna Wasson, on recording, *Mushroom Ceremony of the Mazatec Indians of Mexico,* Folkways, 1957. Wasson's works have been translated into French.

SIDELIGHTS: R. Gordon Wasson was a prominent banker and amateur botanist who is best known, at least to the general public, as the author of volumes espousing the various virtues—from the hallucinogenic to the merely aesthetic—of mushrooms. Wasson was born in 1898 in Great Falls, Montana. After studying journalism at Columbia University, he worked in the 1920s as a writer for various newspapers, including the *New Haven Register* and the *New York Herald Tribune,* and served as associate editor of *Current Opinion.* Towards the end of the 1920s Wasson left journalism and began his banking career by joining the Guaranty Company in New York City. In 1934 he left that company for the Morgan Guaranty Trust Company, of which he became vice president in 1943. Wasson stayed at Morgan's company until he retired from the banking profession in 1963.

In 1926, before Wasson turned to banking, he married Valentina Pavlovna Guercken, a Russian pediatrician. In the ensuing three decades, while Wasson maintained his banking career, he and his wife launched a new science they described as "ethnomycology," the study of mushrooms in various cultures throughout the world. With his wife, Wasson studied mushrooms in Russia and produced the two-volume *Mushrooms, Russia, and History.* This work, hailed by many as beautifully executed and lavishly illustrated, came to be prized by specialists, who considered it a classic of its kind.

In 1957, the same year that *Mushrooms, Russia, and History* was published, Wasson and his wife traveled to Mexico to study the Mazatec Indian rituals involving mushrooms. The couple recorded these rituals, which were released as *Mushroom Ceremony of the Mazatec Indians of Mexico,* the first recording of its kind. Also that year Wasson became an honorary research fellow in ethnomycology at the Botanical Museum of Harvard University.

After his wife died in 1958, Wasson continued his research into mycology. In 1969 he published *Soma: Divine Mushroom of Immortality,* which is probably his best-known book. In this volume Wasson recounts his four-year search to discover the legendary soma, a strength-inducing substance that was also worshipped as a god, noted in various ancient Sanskrit writings of India and Iran. In the work Wasson identifies soma as a poisonous, hallucinogenic mushroom commonly known as fly-agaric and speculates on its use in Vedic cult rituals. He asserts that the drug maintained its hallucinogenic properties even after it was expelled from the body. Thus, Wasson contends,

poor individuals availed themselves of soma's effects simply by drinking the urine of the priests who had recently consumed the mushroom.

Daniel H. H. Ingalls, writing in the *New York Times Book Review,* lauded Wasson's achievement in producing *Soma.* Ingalls described Wasson as "the first Westerner to have set out to find the soma plant not in his library but in the field," and he hailed *Soma* as "an important addition to cultural history." Ingalls's enthusiasm was not unequivocal, however. He disagreed with Wasson's contention of the way the poor consumed soma—Ingalls believed it was filtered through a trough, not through the priests—and in this regard he claimed that "Wasson's imagination carries him too far." But Ingalls nonetheless declared, "In Wasson's way lies discovery—occasional error perhaps, but a true widening of human knowledge." A *Times Literary Supplement* reviewer similarly appraised Wasson's literary achievement, deeming *Soma* "a joy to look at, a pleasure to read, and a mine of curious information not always relevant to the subject at hand."

Among Wasson's ensuing books are *Maria Sabina and Her Mazatec Mushroom Velada,* a 1974 volume on which he served as co-editor, *The Road to Eleusis: Unveiling the Secret of the Mysteries,* a 1978 work that he wrote with Albert Hofmann and Carl A. P. Ruck, and *The Wondrous Mushroom: Mycolatry in Mesoamerica,* a 1980 publication in which Wasson recounts his experiences as a participant decades earlier in mushroom rituals. In this volume he also traces the cult of mushroom worship in Mesoamerican cultures. Another volume that he co-edited, *Persephone's Quest: Entheogens and the Origins of Religion,* appeared in 1986.

BIOGRAPHICAL/CRITICAL SOURCES:

BOOKS

Riedlinger, Thomas J., editor, *The Sacred Mushroom Seeker: Essays for R. Gordon Wasson,* Dioscorides Press (Portland, OR), 1990.

PERIODICALS

New York Times, December 26, 1986, p. B19.
New York Times Book Review, September 5, 1971, p. 15; June 10, 1973, p. 34.
Times Literary Supplement, May 22, 1969, p. 562; December 17, 1971, p. 1586; December 23, 1988, p. 1412.*

WEDEKIND, (Benjamin) Frank(lin) 1864-1918
(Cornelius Minehaha)

PERSONAL: Born July 24, 1864, in Hanover, Germany; died March 9, 1918, in Munich, Germany.

CAREER: Playwright; sometimes published under the name Cornelius Minehaha. Also worked in the circus and in business, and as an actor and singer.

WRITINGS:

PLAYS

Der Schnellmaler oder Kunst und Mammon (performed in Munich, July 29, 1916), Schnabelitz, 1889.
Fruhlings Erwachen (performed in Berlin, November 22, 1906), Gross, 1891, translated by Francis J. Ziegler as *The Awakening of Spring,* Brown, 1909.
Der Erdgeist (performed in Leipzig, February 25, 1898), published as *Der Erdgeist: Eine Tragodie,* Langen, 1895, translated by Elio as *Erdgeist (Earth-Spirit): A Tragedy in Four Acts,* Boni, 1914.
Der Kammersanger (performed in Berlin, December 10, 1899), published as *Der Kammersanger: Drei Szenen,* Langen, 1899, translated by Alber Wilhelm Boesche as *The Court Singer,* German Publication Society, 1914.
Der Marquis von Keith (performed in Berlin, October 11, 1901), published as *Der Marquis von Keith (Munchner Scenen): Schauspiel in funf Aufzugen,* Langen, 1901, translation by Beatrice Gottlieb as *The Marquis of Keith,* University of Denver Press, 1952.
So ist das Leben (performed in Munich, February 22, 1902, revised as *Konig Nicolo oder So ist das Leben,* performed in Leipzig, January 15, 1919), published as *So ist das Leben: Schauspiel in funf Akten,* Langen, 1902, translated by Ziegler as *Such Is Life,* Brown, 1912.
Liebstrank, performed in Nuremberg, October 24, 1903.
Die Buchse der Pandora: Eine Tragodie in drei Aufzugen, performed in Nuremberg, February 1, 1904.
Die Buchse der Pandora: Eine Monstretragodie (performed in Hamburg, February 13, 1988), Cassirer, 1904, revised, Muller, 1911; translated by Carl Richard Mueller as *Pandora's Box,* in *The Lulu Plays.*

Karl Hetmann: Der Zwerg-Riese, performed in Munich, Febraury 18, 1905.

Lulu (performed in Nuremberg, April 18, 1905), published in *Lulu: Tragodie in funf Aufzugen mit einem Prolog,* Muller, 1913.

Totentanz (performed in Nuremberg, May 2, 1906, revised as *Tod und Teufel,* performed in Berlin, April 29, 1912), published as *Totentanz: Drei Szenen,* Langen, 1906, translated by Samuel Eliot as *Damnation!,* translated by Stephen Spender as *Death and Devil.*

Musik (performed in Nuremberg, January 11, 1908), published as *Musik: Sittengermalde in vier Bildern,* Langen, 1908.

Die junge Welt (performed in Munich, April 22, 1908).

Die Zensur (performed in Munich, July 27, 1909), published as *Die Zensur: Theodizee in einem Akt,* Cassirer, 1908.

Der Stein der Weisen, performed in Vienna, January 23, 1911.

Oaha: Die Satire der satire (performed in Munich, December 23, 1911, revised as *Till Eulenspiegel,* performed in Munich, December 1, 1916), published as *Oaha: Schauspiel in funf Aufzugen,* Cassirer, 1908, revised as *Der Stein der Weisen oder Laute, Armbrust und Peitsche: Eine Geisterbeschworung,* Muller, 1920.

Felix und Galathea (performed in Munich, July 25, 1914), Meyer, 1911.

Franziska (performed in Munich, November 30, 1912), Muller, 1912.

Simson oder Scham und Eifersucht (performed in Berlin, January 24, 1914), Muller, 1914.

Schloss Wetterstein (performed in Zurich, November 17, 1917), Muller, 1912, translated by Spender as *Castle Wetterstein,* in *Five Tragedies of Sex.*

Elins Erweckung (performed in Hamburg, March 16, 1919).

Herakles (performed in Munich, September 1, 1919), Muller, 1917.

Das Sonnenspektrum (performed in Berlin, September 23, 1922).

Bismarck (performed in Weimar, October 30, 1926), Muller, 1916.

BOOKS

Kinder und Narren: Lustspiel in vier Aufzugen, Warth, 1891, revised as *Die junge Welt: Komodie in drei Aufzugen und einem Vorspeil,* Langen, 1896.

Die Furstin Russalka, Langen, 1897, translated by Frederick Eisemann as *Princess Russalka,* Luce, 1919.

Der Liebestrank: Schwank in drei Aufzugen, Langen, 1899.

Mine-Haha oder Uber die korperliche erziehung der jungen Madchen: Aus Helene Engels schriftlichem Nachlass heraugegeben, Langen, 1903.

Hidalla oder Sein und Haben: Scauspiel in funf Akten, Larchlewski, 1904, revised as *Karl Hetmann, der Zwerg-Riese (Hidalla): Schauspiel in funf Akten* Muller, 1911.

Die vier Jahreszeiten: Gedichte, Langen, 1905.

Feuerwerk: Erzahlungen, Langen, 1906, translated by Francis Ziegler as *The Grisley Suitor,* Brown, 1911.

In allen Satteln gerecht: Komodie in einem Aufzug, Muller, 1910.

Schauspielkunst: Ein Glossarium, Muller, 1910, translated by Mueller as "The Art of Acting: A Glossary," in *The Modern Theatre,* Macmillan, 1964.

In allen Wassern gewaschen: Tragodie in einem Aufzug, Muller, 1910.

Mit allen Hunden gehetzt: Schauspiel in einem Aufzug, Muller, 1910.

Uberfurchtenichts, Muller, 1917.

Lautenlieder: 53 Lieder mit eigenen und fremden Melodien, edited by Artur Kutscher, Drei Masken, 1920.

Rabbi Esra, Muller, 1924.

Ein Genussmensch: Schauspiel in vier Aufzugen, Muller, 1924.

Das arme Madchen: Ein Chanson, Thorbecke, 1948.

Chansons, Desch, 1951.

Gedichte und Chansons, Bucherei, 1968.

Die Tagebucher: Ein erotisches Leben, edited by Gerhard Hay, Athenaum, 1986.

COLLECTIONS

Gesammelte Werke, 9 volumes, edited by Artur Kutcher and Joachim Friedenthal, Muller, 1912-21.

Ausgewahlte Werke, edited by Fritz Strich, Volksverband der Bucherfreunde, 1923.

Werke in drei Banden, 3 volumes, edited by Manfred Han, Aufbau, 1969.

EDITIONS IN ENGLISH

Rabbi Ezra; The Victim: Two Stories, translated by Francis J. Ziegler, Brown, 1911.

Tragedies of Sex, translated by Samuel A. Eliot Jr., Henderson, 1923.

Five Tragedies of Sex, translated by Frances Fawcett and Stephen Spender, Vision, 1952, Theatre

Arts, 1952, reprinted without *Spring's Awakening* as *The Lulu Plays and Other Sex Tragedies,* translated by Spender, Riverrun, 1977.

The Lulu Plays, translated by Carl Richard Mueller, Fawcett, 1967.

Spring Awakening, Heinemann, 1988.

The Diary of an Erotic Life, Blackwell, 1990.

The First Lulu, Applause Theatre Books, 1993.

SIDELIGHTS: Frank Wedekind's dramas were primarily concerned with attacking the hypocrisies of society, particularly the prohibitions against discussing sexuality. Though Wedekind avoided identification with any literary movement, his attacks on naturalism and his theatrical innovations made him a forerunner of both expressionism and the theater of the absurd. Wedekind's works introduced many of the techniques of modern dramaturgy to the German stage, including stylized, nonrealistic dialogue, an episodic format, grotesque characters, and bizarre plots.

The son of a physician and an actress, Wedekind was born in Hanover, Germany. In 1872 the Wedekinds moved to Switzerland to escape Germany's instability and social repression. As a young man Wedekind reluctantly obeyed his father's request to attend classes at the University of Zurich's law school, foregoing his literary interests, but his father's unexpected death freed Wedekind from his studies and his inheritance allowed him to enjoy life in Paris and London for some time. Whether abroad or back home in Germany, Wedekind chose the bohemian life, expressing contempt for what he considered the repressed, hypocritical middle class.

Wedekind's first produced play, *Fruhlings Erwachen (Spring's Awakening),* shocked its audience, for it dealt graphically with adolescent sexuality. Critics commended the work for shedding light on a taboo subject; enraged citizens, however, attacked Wedekind's portrayal of parents and teachers as repressive for keeping children ignorant of basic biological facts. The theme of sex and its power recurs in all of Wedekind's works. In the "Lulu" plays, *Erdgeist (Earth Spirit)* and *Die Buchse der Pandora (Pandora's Box),* Lulu, the sensual, predatory female, attracts and destroys men through their own passions until she meets a grisly death at the hands of Jack the Ripper. Though Lulu is sexually adept, she is portrayed by Wedekind as a primitive individual in constant conflict with a hypocritical society. Such characters are found throughout Wedekind's works. Because him aim was to force his audience to recognize how distorted conventional views of life were,

Wedekind's characters are not fully realized portraits but exaggerated caricatures that embody specific ideas. They speak not *to* each other, but *at* each other, suggesting the alienation of modern life. The plays themselves are often disjointed and loosely connected and invariably concern the confrontation between society and the social outcast. Because Wedekind considered antisocial behavior heroic, criminals and prostitutes are usually the most admirable characters in his dramas. For example, in *Der Marquis von Keith (The Marquis of Keith)* the protagonist is a clever con-man who almost succeeds in duping society by preying upon its weaknesses.

The audience of Wedekind's day regarded his plays as pornographic and his work was repeatedly banned by the German censor. In addition, he received a prison term in 1899 for writing a poem satirizing Kaiser Wilhelm. Although his professed aim was usually to shock, Wedekind did so with the hope of enlightening and reeducating the public; for this reason he became very outspoken in defense of his work. After the turn of the century his plays became more autobiographical, often portraying a misunderstood artist in revolt against society. He acted major roles in these plays, and often entertained in cabarets by performing his ballads. The public eventually grew used to him and his later dramas were met with a modest level of acclaim.

Wedekind's work exerted a strong influence on twentieth-century German drama, particularly on the plays and aesthetic theories of Bertolt Brecht, who called Wedekind "one of the great educators of the new Europe." His work forms a solid bridge between naturalistic realism and modern German drama. Though banned by the Nazis and neglected after World War II, his plays were frequently revived throughout the 1960s, when the shock value of his work had been dissipated and more serious attention could be paid to his ideas. According to Martin Esslin, Wedekind was "a pioneer of sexual freedom, for men as well as for women, and played in Germany in the first two decades of this century the part which D. H. Lawrence assumed in Britain."

BIOGRAPHICAL/CRITICAL SOURCES:

BOOKS

Allen, Ann Taylor, *Satire and Society in Wilhelmine Germany: "Kladderadatsch" and "Simplicissimus" 1890-1914,* University of Kentucky Press, 1984.

Bentley, Eric, *The Playwright as Thinker: A Study of Drama in Modern Times*, Reynal & Hitchcock, 1946, reprinted edition, Harcourt, 1967.

Best, Alan, *Frank Wedekind*, Wolff, 1975.

Boa, Elizabeth, *The Sexual Circus: Wedekind's Theatre of Subversion*, Blackwell, 1987.

Brecht, Bertolt, *Brecht on Theatre*, edited by John Willet, Methuen, 1964.

Carter, Angela, *Nothing Sacred: Selected Writings*, Virago, 1982.

Chick, Edson, *Dances of Death: Wedekind, Brecht, Durrenmatt, and the Satiric Tradition*, Camden House, 1984.

Diethe, Carol, *Aspects of Distorted Sexual Attitudes in German Expressionist Drama: Wedekind, Kokoschaka, Kaiser*, Lang, 1988.

Esslin, Martin, in *Modernism: 1890-1930*, edited by Malcolm Bradbury and James McFarlane, Penguin Books, 1974.

Finney, Gail, *Women in Modern Drama*, Cornell University Press, 1989.

Garten, H. F., *Modern German Drama*, Methuen & Co., 1964.

Harris, Edward, *The Turn of the Century: German Literature and Art 1890-1915*, edited by Gerald Chapple and H. H. Schulte, Bouvier, 1981.

Jelavich, Peter, *Munich and Theatrical Modernism: Politics, Playwriting, and Performance 1890-1914*, Harvard University Press, 1985.

Lenman, Robin, *Society and Politics in Wilhelmine Germany*, edited by Richard J. Evans, Croom Helm, 1978.

Osborne, John, *The German Theatre: A Symposium*, edited by Ronald Hayman, Oswald Wolff, 1975.

Seehaus, Gunter, *Frank Wedekind in Selbstzeugnissen und Bilddokumeneten*, Rowohlt, 1974.

Shaw, Leroy, *Alogical Modern Drama*, edited by Kenneth White, Rodopi, 1982.

Skrine, Peter, *Hauptmann, Wedekind and Schnitzler*, Macmillan, 1989.

Timms, Edward, *Karl Kraus: Apocalyptic Satirist*, Yale University Press, 1986.

Vincon, Hartmut, *Frank Wedekind*, Metzler, 1987.

Wedekind, Tilly, *Lulu: Die rolle meines Lebens*, Rutter & Loehning, 1969.

PERIODICALS

Boston University Journal, Volume XXIII, number 2, 1975, pp. 40-47.

Central European History, September, 1979, pp. 203-36.

Chicago, May, 1992, pp. 71-72.

Colloquia Germanica, Volume 19, 1986, pp. 47-67.

Germanic Review, Volume XLIII, 1968, pp. 163-87, summer, 1982, pp. 115-22.

German Life and Letters, April, 1985, pp. 205-32, January, 1989, pp. 113-28.

German Quarterly, March, 1966.

German Studies Review, February, 1984, pp. 27-38.

Modern Language Review, July, 1979, pp. 631-47, April, 1984, pp. 336-55, January, 1987, pp. 119-41.

Monatshefte, Volume 72, 1980, pp. 26-38.

New Literary History, winter, 1983, pp. 359-72.

New Statesman & Society, March 22, 1991, p. 37, November 6, 1992, p. 45.

New York, August 22, 1988, p. 141-42.

New York Times Book Review, November 18, 1990, p. 13.

Opera News, March 26, 1988, p. 28-32.

Oxford German Studies, Volume 9, February, 1978, pp. 105-18.

Performing Arts Journal, Volume 30, number 10, 1986-1987, pp. 102-17.

Publications of the English Goethe Society, Volume 56, 1987, pp. 56-73.

Seminar, spring, 1969, pp. 21-35; Volume 15, 1979, pp. 235-43, pp. 244-50.*

* * *

WEIDENFELD, (Arthur) George 1919-

PERSONAL: Born September 13, 1919, in Vienna, Austria; son of Max and Rosa Weidenfeld; married Jane Sieff, 1952 (divorced); married Barbara Connolly, 1956 (divorced, 1961); married Sandra Payson Meyer, 1966 (divorced); children: (first marriage) a daughter. *Education:* Attended University of Vienna and Konsular Akademie (Diplomatic College). *Avocational interests:* Travel, opera.

ADDRESSES: Office—c/o Orion House, 5 Upper St. Martin's Lane, London WC2H 9EA, England.

CAREER: Affiliated with British Broadcasting Corporation (BBC) Monitoring Service, 1939-42; BBC News, BBC Empire, and North American service, commentator on European affairs, 1942-46; founder of Contact Magazines and Books, 1945; cofounder and chairperson of Weidenfeld and Nicolson Ltd., England, 1948—; founder with Ann Getty of the Wheatland Corporation, New York, and Weidenfeld & Nicolson New York (publishing company), 1985 (merged with Grove Press to become Grove

Weidenfeld, 1989). Political adviser and chief of cabinet of President Weizmann of Israel. Chairperson of the University of Negev Foundation.

MEMBER: Reform Club.

AWARDS, HONORS: Knighted, 1969; awarded life peerage by Prime Minister Harold Wilson, 1976, for contributions to the cause of European unity.

WRITINGS:

Remembering My Good Friends: An Autobiography, HarperCollins (New York), 1994.

Also author of *The Goebbels Experiment,* 1943. Author of weekly foreign affairs column for the *News Chronicle,* 1943-44.

SIDELIGHTS: Born in Vienna, George Weidenfeld was just eighteen years old when he fled Austria for Britain during Germany's pre-World War II annexation of his homeland. The abrupt move proved profitable for Weidenfeld, as he eventually positioned himself in the center of London's social scene, a place of prominence he has enjoyed for more than fifty years.

In the early 1940s, Weidenfeld represented the British Broadcasting Corporation; affiliated first with its Monitoring Service, he subsequently became a commentator on European affairs and the author of a weekly newspaper column. In 1945 Weidenfeld commissioned his first book as a publisher, *New Deal for Coal,* a work by the future British prime minister Harold Wilson. In 1948, he founded the publishing house Weidenfeld and Nicolson, which issued works of nonfiction, especially history books and lavish, illustrated volumes. Weidenfeld also specialized in the publication of biographies, including the memoirs of Harold Wilson and Charles de Gaulle, as well as the British editions of books by Americans including Lyndon B. Johnson, Henry Kissinger, and Nancy Reagan.

In 1985, Weidenfeld brought his publishing skills to the United States to join with Ann Getty in the creation of the Wheatland Corporation and Weidenfeld and Nicolson New York, which later merged with Grove Press to become Grove Weidenfeld. According to industry observers, the publishing house suffered numerous blows from its competition and internal difficulties.

In *Remembering My Good Friends: An Autobiography,* Weidenfeld focuses little on the problems he encountered in business ventures and partnerships, preferring to speak kindly about those who have touched his life. Weidenfeld treats his three ex-wives with respect, causing *Sunday Times* reviewer Anthony Howard to write: "The trouble with George . . . is that he has always been the great networker—and that sort of exercise always involves never treading on anyone's toes. . . . For all the dash Weidenfeld has cut on London's social scene for half a century, the author of these memoirs has missed his vocation. . . . What a wonderful ornament for the diplomatic profession he would have made."

BIOGRAPHICAL/CRITICAL SOURCES:

BOOKS

Weidenfeld, George, *Remembering My Good Friends: An Autobiography,* HarperCollins, 1994.

PERIODICALS

New York Times, October 22, 1989, pp. 36-37, 47-48, 51.
Sunday Times, December 18, 1994, p. 5.*

* * *

WEIHS, Jean 1930-
(Jean Riddle, Jean Riddle Weihs)

PERSONAL: Born November 12, 1930, in Ottawa, Ontario, Canada; daughter of Walter Rowland and Greta (Miller) Northgrave; married John Douglas Riddle, September 25, 1954 (died August 15, 1964); married Harry Weihs (a consulting engineer), January 25, 1975; children: (first marriage) John Cameron; (second marriage) Frederick Harry and Ronald Carl (stepsons). *Ethnicity:* "British." *Education:* Queen's University, Kingston, Ontario, B.A., 1951; University of Toronto, B.L.S., 1953, Specialist in School Librarianship, 1965. *Avocational interests:* Skiing, reading, hiking, theater and other arts.

ADDRESSES: Home and office—Technical Services Group, 6 Edgar Ave., Toronto, Ontario M4W 2A9, Canada; fax 416-925-4704. *E-mail*—76265.2144@ compuserve.com.

CAREER: University of Toronto, Toronto, Ontario, bibliographer, 1953-59; North York Public Library, general reference librarian, 1960-64; school librarian at public schools in Scarborough, Ontario, 1965-66; head of technical services for public schools in East York, Ontario, 1967-69; Seneca College of Applied Arts and Technology, director of library techniques course, 1969-86; Technical Services Group, Toronto, principal, 1986—. Ontario Institute for Studies in Education, cataloger, 1966; Ontario Ministry of Education, instructor, 1968-69; University of California, Los Angeles, visiting professor, 1988; Simmons College, visiting professor, 1989. Joint Advisory Committee on Nonbook Materials, member, 1970-95; Canadian Committee on Cataloging, chairperson, 1981-86; Joint Steering Committee for Revision of Anglo-American Cataloging Rules, chairperson, 1984-89.

MEMBER: Canadian Library Association (co-chairperson of Task Force on the Roles of Librarians and Library Technicians, 1986-89), American Library Association, Online Audiovisual Catalogers, Ex Libris Association, Ontario Library Association (cochairperson of education committee, 1992-95).

AWARDS, HONORS: Ruby E. Wallace traveling fellow, Canadian Library Association, 1968; Canada Council grant, 1969; Queen's Jubilee Medal, Governor General of Canada, 1977; Margaret Mann Citation in Cataloging and Classification, American Library Association, 1986; award for outstanding contributions to research librarianship and library development, Ontario College and University Library Association, 1988; Blackwell's Award for Distinguished Academic Librarian, Canadian Association of College and University Libraries, 1990; John Comaromi Lecturer, American Library Association, 1994.

WRITINGS:

(Under name Jean Riddle; with Shirley Lewis and Janet Macdonald) *Nonbook Materials: The Organization of Integrated Collections,* preliminary edition, Canadian Library Association (Ottawa, Ontario), 1970, 3rd edition (under name Jean Weihs; with Lewis), 1989.

(Under name Jean Riddle Weihs) *Library Technician* (monograph), Guidance Centre, College of Education, University of Toronto (Toronto, Ontario), 1971, 4th edition, 1981.

Accessible Storage of Nonbook Materials, Oryx Press (Phoenix, AZ), 1984.

(With Lynne Howarth) *A Brief Guide to AACR2: 1988 Revision and Implications for Automated Systems,* Canadian Library Association, 1988.

(With Sheila S. Intner) *Standard Cataloging for School and Public Libraries,* Libraries Unlimited (Littleton, CO), 1990, 2nd edition, 1996.

The Integrated Library: Encouraging Access to Multimedia Materials, 2nd edition, Oryx Press, 1991.

Facts about Canada, Its Provinces and Territories, H. W. Wilson (Bronx, NY), 1995.

Special Library Cataloging, Libraries Unlimited, in press.

Contributor to books, including *Canadian Libraries in Their Changing Environment,* edited by Lorraine Spencer Garry and Carl Garry, Centre for Continuing Education, York University (Toronto), 1977; *The Nature and Future of the Catalog,* edited by Maurice J. Freedman and S. Michael Malinconico, Oryx Press, 1979; and *Bibliographic Control of Nonbook Materials,* edited by Intner and Richard P. Smiraglia, American Library Association (Chicago, IL), 1987. Contributor of more than a hundred articles and reviews to library journals. Editor, *OLA Newsletter,* 1972-73; member of editorial board, *Technicalities,* 1980-86.

BIOGRAPHICAL/CRITICAL SOURCES:

PERIODICALS

Library Resource and Technical Services, October/December, 1986, p. 423.

* * *

WEIHS, Jean Riddle
See WEIHS, Jean

* * *

WEIR, Charlene 1937-

PERSONAL: Born November 10, 1937, in Nortonville, KS; daughter of George Julius (a Lutheran minister) and Clara Ernestine (a homemaker; maiden name, Wissman) Kettner; married John M. Weir, 1958 (divorced, 1984); children: Jon Christopher, Leslie Alane. *Ethnicity:* "Caucasian."

Education: Attended Fort Scott School of Nursing, 1955-58, and University of Oklahoma, 1958-60.

ADDRESSES: Agent—Meg Ruley, Jane Rotrosen Agency, 318 East 51st St., New York, NY 10022.

CAREER: Author.

MEMBER: International Association of Crime Writers, Mystery Writers of America, Sisters in Crime, Crime Writers Association.

AWARDS, HONORS: Malice Domestic Award from St. Martin's, 1992, for *Winter Widow.*

WRITINGS:

MYSTERY NOVELS

Winter Widow, St. Martin's (New York), 1992.
Consider the Crows, St. Martin's, 1993.
Family Practice, St. Martin's, 1995.
Take Two, St. Martin's, 1997.

SIDELIGHTS: Charlene Weir told *CA:* "I came late to writing and got into it by accident. Authors seem to know from the day they're born that's who they are. Their first words are, 'Could I have a pencil and some paper?' Before they are famous, they get up at four in the morning and work on novels, then go off to jobs in lion taming or underwater search and rescue. This gives them interesting material to put under the photograph on the book jacket. I never wanted to be a writer, never thought about writing, never did any, and have never done anything interesting.

"I wanted to study nursing, but hadn't gotten very far when illness intervened. I was diagnosed with multiple sclerosis and told to curtail physical activities, avoid over-exertion, and avoid stress. That took care of nursing.

"I have always been a reader. Put printed words in front of me, and I will read them. I can't help it. Included in all this reading were mysteries: I read them all. Where else in this world we live in do all the questions get answered—does everything get explained? My life is filled with troubles and woes? Read about somebody who's worse off—like dead.

"Mysteries went through my hands in such quantity that one day I commented, 'I have read so many of these I should be able to write one of my own.' My husband looked at me and said, 'Well?' 'Don't be

ridiculous! It was one of those meaningless remarks one sometimes makes.'

"He pushed me into a life of crime. Not, I think because he thought I would be good at it, but simply to give me something to do while I was curtailing physical activities and avoiding stress. Writing may not involve much in the way of physical activities, unless you engage in rigorous research, maybe, but I am not sure how much stress it avoids. There is nothing scarier than blank paper.

"A recurring theme runs through my novels: life is what gets in the way of all your plans."

*　　*　　*

WEISSBOURD, Bernice (Targ)　1923-

PERSONAL: Born January 25, 1923, in Chicago, IL; daughter of Max and Fannie (Wexler) Targ; married Bernard BenZion Weissbourd, October 31, 1946; children: Burt, Ruth Weissbourd Grant, Robert, Rick. *Ethnicity:* "Caucasian." *Education:* Attended University of Chicago, 1940-43; American Conservatory of Music, B.Mus., 1943; attended Juilliard School, 1943-45; Columbia University, M.A., 1945; further graduate study at University of Chicago, 1961-62, and University of Illinois at Urbana-Champaign, 1973; doctoral study at Northwestern University; also attended Institute for Psychoanalysis. *Religion:* Jewish.

ADDRESSES: Home—2737 Sheridan Rd., Evanston, IL 60201. *Office*—Family Focus, Inc., 310 South Peoria St., Suite 510, Chicago, IL 60607-3534; fax 312-421-8185.

CAREER: Family Focus, Inc., Chicago, IL, president; University of Chicago, lecturer in social service administration; Family Resource Coalition, president. Zero to Three: National Center for Clinical Infant Programs, member of board of directors and co-chairperson of Heart Start Task Force; Voices for Illinois Children, member of board of directors and Work Group on Early Childhood. Member of board of directors, Child Care Action Campaign, Institute for Responsive Education, and Ounce of Prevention Fund; member of Advisory Committee on Services for Families with Infants and Toddlers, Administration for Children and Families; member of advisory board, Erikson Institute of Loyola University, Chi-

cago Children's Museum, Parenting Resources's Television Series for Parents of Young Children, Parent Television, and Institute for Family-Centered Care; member of leadership advisory group, Governor's Task Force on Human Services Reform; member of Governor's Task Force on Family Support and Family Preservation; honorary board member, Chicago Institute for Psychoanalysis; consultant to Journal Films and local public television channels.

MEMBER: American Orthopsychiatric Association (past president), National Association for the Education of Young Children (vice-president, 1982-86), Illinois Infant Mental Health Association (past member of board of directors), Chicago Association for the Education of Young Children (founder and past chairperson of Commission on Infants and Toddlers; past executive vice-president), Evanston Mental Health Society (past member of board of directors).

AWARDS, HONORS: Outstanding Leadership Award from Young Women's Christian Association, 1981; World of Children Award from UNICEF, 1983; awards from National Forum for Women, 1985, and American Orthopsychiatric Association, 1986; Patrick Zimmerman Award, 1987; Deborah Award for Outstanding Women from American Jewish Congress, 1989; honorary doctorate from Columbia College, 1989; Keepers of the Dream Award from Martin Luther King Center, 1991; award from Harvard Club of Chicago, 1992; Humanitarian Award from Institute for Clinical Social Work, 1994; honorary doctorate from Loyola University, 1994; For the Love of Children Award from Children's Home and Aid Society, 1996; 100 Big Hearts for Young Heroes Award from La Rabida Children's Hospital, 1996.

WRITINGS:

(Editor with L. B. Wallach) *Creating Drop-In Centers: The Family Focus Model,* Family Focus (Evanston, IL), 1979.
(Editor with J. Musick) *Infants: Their Social Environments,* National Association for the Education of Young Children (Washington, DC), 1981.
(Editor with S. L. Kagan, D. R. Powell, and E. F. Zigler) *America's Family Support Programs: Perspectives and Prospects,* Yale University Press (New Haven, CT), 1987.
(Editor with Kagan) *Putting Families First: America's Family Support Movement and the Challenge of Change,* Jossey-Bass (San Francisco, CA), 1994.

Contributor to books, including *Giving Children a Chance: The Case for More Effective National Policies,* edited by George Miller, Center for National Policy Press (Washington, DC), 1989; *Families as Nurturing Systems: Support Across the Life Span,* edited by Powell and D. G. Unger, Haworth Press (New York City), 1990; and *Visions of Entitlement: The Care and Education of America's Children,* edited by M. Jensen and S. Goffin, State University of New York Press (Albany, NY), 1993. Columnist, *Parents.* Contributor of articles and reviews to magazines, including *Young Children, Growing Times, Children Today, American Journal of Orthopsychiatry,* and *Infants and Young Children.*

SIDELIGHTS: Bernice Weissbourd told *CA:* "My writing is related to the principles and practices of family support, and to the policies that promote the wellbeing of children and families. It is a commitment to increase understanding of the link between the healthy development of children and strong families and communities, and of the responsibility of society to assure that families are supported in their child-rearing roles.

"As an early childhood educator in child care settings, I became keenly aware of the importance of the earliest years in a child's life, the years from birth to three, years previously ignored in education and social services. In my writing, I advocate programs for those years. Giving children and families support from birth is becoming increasingly important on the national agenda, and I keep trying to make it so."

* * *

WELCH, Lew(is Barrett, Jr.) 1926-1971(?)

PERSONAL: Born August 16, 1926, in Phoenix, AZ; died c. May 23, 1971; son of Lewis Barrett (a bank teller) and Dorothy (Brownfield) Welch; married Mary Garber, c. 1953; *Education:* Attended Stockton Junior College, 1946, Reed College, 1948-50, University of Chicago, c. 1951-55, and San Francisco State University, 1957.

CAREER: Writer. Worked in retail advertising for Montgomery Ward in Chicago, IL, 1953-57, and San Francisco, CA, c. 1957-58; taxi driver, c. 1959; rubber cutter for Bemis Bag Co., 1959; dock worker, 1963; teacher of poetry at University of California,

San Francisco, 1964; teacher of poetry and poet in residence at Colorado State University, Greeley, 1970. *Military service:* U.S. Air Force, 1945-46.

WRITINGS:

POETRY

Wobbly Rock, Auerhahn Press, 1960.
On Out, Oyez (Kensington, CA), 1965.
Hermit Poems, Four Seasons Foundation (San Francisco, CA), 1965.
At Times We're Almost Able to See, Don Carpenter, 1965.
The Basic Con, Unicorn Press (Monmouth Junction, NJ), 1967.
Courses: No Credit, No Blame, No Balm, Dave Haselwood, 1968.
The Song Mt. Tamalpais Sings, Maya (Concord, CA), 1969.
Redwood Haiku, and Other Poems, Crainium Press, 1972.
Ring of Bone: Collected Poems, 1950-1971, Grey Fox Press (San Francisco, CA), 1973.
(With Jack Kerouac and Albert Saijo) *Trip Trap: Haiku along the Road from San Francisco to New York, 1959,* Grey Fox Press, 1973.
Selected Poems, preface by Gary Snyder, edited by Donald Allen, Grey Fox Press, 1976.

Work represented in anthologies.

Contributor to periodicals, including *Contact* and *Poetry.*

OTHER

How I Work as a Poet, and Other Essays/Plays/Stories, Grey Fox Press (San Francisco, CA), 1977.
I, Leo (unfinished novel), Grey Fox Press, 1977.
I Remain: The Letters of Lew Welch with the Correspondence of His Friends (two volumes), edited by Donald Allen, Grey Fox Press, 1980.

SIDELIGHTS: Lew Welch is one of several of the writers and artists known collectively as the Beats. The Beat movement, which also included such notables as the poet Allen Ginsberg and the novelist Jack Kerouac, came to prominence in the 1950s, and exerted considerable influence on American culture into the ensuing decades.

Welch was born in 1926 in Phoenix, Arizona. His mother hailed from one of the city's wealthiest fami-lies. Consequently, she was accustomed to the social and economic benefits of upper-class life. Welch's father, however, was a man utterly lacking in financial means. Though Welch conceded that his parents' relationship, at least initially, was a loving one, he would also allow that it soon degenerated, especially after Welch was born.

After his parents separated in 1929, Welch traveled with his mother and sister to California. There they commenced fifteen years of random travel northward that inevitably left Welch an outsider in the numerous schools that he attended. At this time Welch immersed himself in reading, showing a preference for adventure tales and the work of such poets as Robert Service.

In 1945, after graduating from high school, Welch enlisted in the U.S. Air Force. When World War II ended, though, Welch returned to civilian life and enrolled in Stockton Junior College. There he again found himself—as a slightly older student and, furthermore, as a veteran—somewhat outside the school's social milieu. Nevertheless, he read extensively. One book, Gertrude Stein's *Three Lives* exerted considerable influence on Welch, and he later credited that work with inspiring him to pursue a literary career.

After two years at Stockton, Welch entered Reed College, a school known for its arts programs. At Reed, Welch befriended Gary Snyder and Philip Whalen, both of whom were aspiring poets. By this time Welsh was also writing poems. Soon Welch and his friends Snyder and Whalen became known about Reed for their poetic endeavors. And when the celebrated poet William Carlos Williams arrived at the school for a reading, Welch and cohorts were sent to fetch him from the airport. The students quickly established a rapport with the older poet, who expressed particular praise for Welch's thesis on Gertrude Stein.

Responding to an invitation from Williams, Welch eventually traveled east and visited the poet at his New Jersey home. At this time Welch determined to settle in New York City and devote himself to what he imagined would soon be a successful writing career. But events conspired against Welch: Williams suffered a stroke and was thus inaccessible to the younger poet, who had grown increasingly morose as a consequence of his failure to interest publishers in either his poems or the Stein thesis.

In 1951 Welch abruptly entered the University of Chicago with the intention of studying philosophy. He soon switched to English, but then plunged again into despair when he found his own interests incompatible with the English department's more conventional, critical approach. Welch thereupon succumbed to another bout of despair, and eventually experienced a mental breakdown.

Through the aid of a psychoanalyst, Welch was able to sufficiently recover his mental and emotional stability. In 1953 he found work in the advertising department of the Montgomery Ward merchandise company. During this period, perhaps the most conventional of Welch's life, he also married, though the marriage soon proved difficult. As Welsh lamented both his marital problems and his overall dissatisfaction with his life, he began drinking to excess.

For the next few years Welch remained in Chicago and continued both studying at the university there and working at Montgomery Ward. Then, in 1957, renewed correspondence with Snyder and Whalen spurred Welch to begin writing poetry again. Hoping to rejoin his friends, Welch obtained a transfer to Montgomery Ward's office in Oakland. He arrived in nearby San Francisco with his wife, whom he was already hoping to divorce, and soon found himself involved in the city's hectic literary scene. He was not ready to break entirely from convention, however, and he soon entered graduate school at San Francisco State University.

The ensuing few years proved a pivotal period for Welch. Under the increasing influence of the Beats, who expressed disdain for conventional dress and conduct, Welch soon came to show an increasing disregard for the wishes of his employers, who responded by firing him. For Welch, the dismissal was happy proof that he was assuming more of the Beat lifestyle.

A this time, Welch's poetry showed influences of both Snyder and Whalen. Like Snyder, he expressed respect for nature, and like Whalen he showed an inclination for humor. But though his poetry bore the influences of his friends, it also evidenced Welch's preference for prose-like simplicity and directness.

By the late 1950s, Welch had been fired from another job, as a rubber cutter, and had broken from his wife. He moved into a communal home and further engaged in his practice of heavy drinking. After a cross-country trek with novelist Jack Kerouac, Welch left his San Francisco home and headed to Reno, where he hoped to live with his mother and write a novel. That work, published posthumously as *I, Leo,* went unfinished, and was later appraised as unimpressive. Welch's poetry, however, was finally meeting with success. In 1960 a San Francisco printer produced Welch's *Wobbly Rock,* a long autobiographical poem written with the prose-like simplicity characteristic of Welsh's most successful verse.

Around the time of *Wobbly Rock*'s publication, Welch returned to San Francisco and once again immersed himself in the Beat lifestyle. He drank heavily, entered into an unhappy romance, and incurred another mental collapse. He eventually abandoned the city and, like other Beats, began living in the woods. During this time alcohol exerted considerable influence over Welch's life.

In the mid-1960s Welch managed to take advantage of the Beats' greater prominence, and he appeared at poetry readings and on radio broadcasts. His prior poems were collected as *On Out,* and his ensuing poems were published as the volumes *Hermit Poems* and *At Times We're Almost Able to See.* These works further established Welch, particularly in comparison to other Beats, as a relatively objective, if inevitably autobiographical, poet.

In 1970 Welch further capitalized on his newfound acclaim and contracted to produce a major volume of his collected poems. He also obtained a teaching position at Colorado State University. His drinking, though, had scarcely subsided, and he eventually resorted to Antabuse—a drug that induces sickness when combined with alcohol—in a futile effort to gain control of his drinking problem. But he would periodically cease the Antabuse and return to alcohol. His continued drinking—together with his periodic use of Antabuse, which has, as a side effect, the ability to produce extreme depression—perhaps contributed to his final phase of personal despair. In the spring of 1971, after appointing a literary executor and settling his financial affairs, Welch armed himself and wandered into a forest, never to be seen again.

Interest in Welch, and appreciation for his work, has grown in the years since his death. The volume *Selected Poems,* with a preface by Snyder, appeared in 1976 and probably contributed to interest in Welsh. In addition, a prose collection entitled *How I Work as a Poet, and Other Essays/Plays/Stories,* appeared in 1977, and the two-volume *I Remain: The Letters of*

Lew Welch with the Correspondence of His Friends followed in 1980.

Compared to such beats as Kerouac or Snyder, Welch was not particularly celebrated during his own lifetime. In the years since his death, however, he has won increasing recognition as a particularly talented and tragic poet. As Samuel Charters wrote in *Dictionary of Literary Biography,* Volume 16: *The Beats: Literary Bohemians in Postwar America,* Welch shared the Beat reverence for nature and the mysteries of life, and he "expressed all of this . . . with an intensity and bitter rage that left him hollowed out and too worn to live at age forty-four but that also left a group of poems that are among the purest and the most precise of all the Beat creations."

BIOGRAPHICAL/CRITICAL SOURCES:

BOOKS

Allen, Donald, editor, *On Bread and Poetry: A Panel Discussion with Gary Snyder, Lew Welch, and Philip Whalen,* Grey Fox Press, 1977.
Dictionary of Literary Biography, Volume 16: *The Beats: Literary Bohemians in Postwar America,* Gale, 1983.
Meltzer, David, editor, *The San Francisco Poets,* Ballantine, 1971.
Saroyan, Aram, *Genesis Angels: The Saga of Lew Welch and the Beat Generation,* Morrow, 1979.*

* * *

WESSELMAN, Hank (Henry Barnard) 1941-

PERSONAL: Born August 20, 1941, in New York, NY; son of Henry B. Wesselman (an attorney) and Alice Wade Sholes (a homemaker); married Jill Kuykendall (a physical therapist), September 9, 1979; children: Erica, Anna. *Education:* University of Colorado—Boulder, B.A., 1964, M.A., 1969; University of California—Berkeley, Ph.D., 1982. *Politics:* "Humanist/Pacifist." *Religion:* "Animist/Panpsychist/Buddhist." *Avocational interests:* Archeology, sculpture, painting, bonsai, suiseki.

ADDRESSES: Home—P.O. Box 549, Fairoaks, CA 95628. *Agent*—Candice Fuhrman, 201 Morningsun Ave., Mill Valley, CA 94941.

CAREER: Scientist, professor of anthropology. University of Colorado Museum, research assistant, 1963-64, curatorial assistant, 1968-69; Kiriji Memorial College, Igbajo, Nigeria, biology instructor, 1964-65; Adeola Odutola College, Ijebu-Ode, Nigeria, biology instructor; Department of Biology, University of Colorado—Boulder, teaching assistant, 1967-69; Department of Anthropology, University of California—Berkeley, teaching assistant, 1970-72, Omo Research Expedition, research assistant, 1971-82; Department of Anthropology, University of Hawaii at Hilo, West Hawaii Campus, Kealakekua, instructor, 1987-89; Department of Anthropology, University of California—San Diego, La Jolla, visiting lecturer, 1989-90. Department of Anthropology, Sierra College, Rocklin, CA, instructor, 1991—; Department of Anthropology, American River College, Sacramento, CA, instructor, 1991—; Department of Anthropology, California State University-Sacramento, instructor, 1993. *Military service:* U.S. Peace Corps volunteer, Nigeria, 1964-66.

Paleoanthropological consultant to the California Academy of Sciences, San Francisco, 1974-75; paleontological consultant to the Institute of Human Origins, Berkeley, CA, 1989.

MEMBER: American Anthropological Association, Society for the Anthropology of Consciousness, Foundation for Shamanic Studies.

AWARDS, HONORS: NDEA Title IV fellowship for graduate study, University of California—Berkeley, 1969-74; Excellence in Teaching Award, University of Hawaii at Hilo, 1989.

WRITINGS:

Spiritwalker: My Journeys through the Visionary Gateway, Bantam, 1995.

Contributor, with J. J. Jaeger, to books, including *Earliest Man and Environments in the Lake Rudolf Basin: Stratigraphy, Paleoecology and Evolutions,* edited by Y. Coppens, et al., University of Chicago Press, 1976; *The Omo Micromammals: Systematics and Paleoecology of Early Man Sites from Ethiopia,* edited by M. K. Hecht and F. S. Szalay, S. Karger (Basel, Switzerland), 1984; *The Longest Record, the Human Career in Africa,* 1986; and *Paleoclimate and Evolution with Emphasis on Human Origins,* edited by E. S. Vrba, et al., Yale University Press (New Haven, CT), 1995. Has published numerous scientific articles on human evolution.

WORK IN PROGRESS: Medicinemaker, expected completion 1996-97. Research on Paleoecology and microvertebrate analysis of the Aramis early hominid sites, Ethiopia.

SIDELIGHTS: Hank Wesselman told *CA:* "I have worked for more than twenty-five years with an international group of scientists, including Tim White, Don Johanson, and members of the well-known Leakey family, investigating the mystery of human origins out of East Africa's Great Rift Valley. In the early 1970s, while doing fieldwork with an expedition in the remote arid landscapes of southern Ethiopia, I began to experience spontaneous expanded states of awareness similar to those of traditional shamans. In an attempt to understand this, I went beyond scholarly research into direct, personal contact with the ancient, time-tested methods for achieving mystical states practiced by tribal peoples. Years later, this search would bring me face to face with a series of visionary encounters that form the core of *Spiritwalker,* a book based on some decidedly different fieldwork I did while living on my farm on the island of Hawaii in the late 1980s.

"I remain actively involved in paleoanthropology and am currently working with an expedition to the Middle Awash River area of the Ethiopian Rift headed by Professor Tim White of UC Berkeley. In the winter of 1994-95, the international team of scientists uncovered about 50 percent of a fossilized human skeleton that is 4.5 million years old and may well prove to be the missing link between humans and apes that Charles Darwin predicted would eventually be discovered. I am one of several specialists involved in trying to reconstruct the paleoenvironments of the site at the time it was laid down."

Hank Wesselman's book, *Spiritwalker: My Journeys through the Visionary Gateway,* is a record of the author's spiritual contact with a Hawaiian shaman named Nainoa five thousand years in the future. Through Nainoa's consciousness, Wesselman experiences a vastly altered American continent, devastated by the sudden melting of the polar ice caps brought on by the greenhouse effect. Human beings, living in sparse settlements scattered throughout the continent, live as hunters and gatherers, without the aid of metal tools, and trade stories of the Great Age of the Americans, before the Fall and the Great Flood. Critics compared *Spiritwalker* to Carlos Castaneda's detailed visionary fables, and recommended it to fans of New Age literature. *Kirkus Reviews* called Wesselman's book "a minatory vision that will im-press the credulous and lovers of superficial, eclectic mysticism."

BIOGRAPHICAL/CRITICAL SOURCES:

PERIODICALS

Kirkus Reviews, May 15, 1995, p. 700.
Publishers Weekly, June 5, 1995, p. 47.

* * *

WESTFALL, Richard S(amuel) 1924-1996

OBITUARY NOTICE—See index for *CA* sketch: Born April 22, 1924, in Fort Collins, CO; died of a heart attack, August 21, 1996, in Bloomington, IN. Educator and author. Westfall received critical recognition for his biography *Never at Rest: A Biography of Isaac Newton,* about scientist Isaac Newton, which was twenty years in the making. He also held a lengthy career as a history teacher, beginning in 1952 at the California Institute of Technology. Stints at the University of Iowa and Grinnell College followed. Westfall, who was often referred to by his nickname Sam, then began twenty-five years at Indiana University as professor of the history of science. He later served as a department chair and advanced to professor emeritus in 1989. He wrote a number of books in addition to his Pfizer Award-winning *Never at Rest.* They include *Science and Religion in Seventeenth Century England, Force in Newton's Physics, The Construction of Modern Science, Essays on the Trial of Galileo,* and *The Life of Isaac Newton.* He won another Pfizer Award in 1972 and a Sarton medal in 1985. He was a fellow in the American Academy of Arts and Sciences and served in the U.S. Navy during World War II.

OBITUARIES AND OTHER SOURCES:

BOOKS

Who's Who in America, 51st edition, Marquis, 1996.

PERIODICALS

Chicago Tribune, September 6, 1996, section 3, p. 10.
New York Times, September 1, 1996, section 1, p. 46.
Washington Post, September 5, 1996, p. B5.

WHELEHAN, Imelda 1960-

PERSONAL: Born May 16, 1960, in Exeter, England; daughter of Thomas (a district nurse) and Doris (a staff nurse; maiden name, Churchouse) Whelehan; married David Sadler (a university academic), August 19, 1995; children: one. *Ethnicity:* "White English-Irish." *Politics:* "Socialist/feminist." *Religion:* None. *Avocational interests:* Politics, history, walking.

ADDRESSES: Home—Leicester, England. *Office*—School of Humanities, DeMontfort University, The Gateway, Leicester LE1 9BH, England; fax 01-16-257-7199.

CAREER: DeMontfort University, Leicester, England, principal lecturer, 1989—.

WRITINGS:

Modern Feminist Thought: From the Second Wave to "Post-Feminism," Edinburgh University Press (Edinburgh, Scotland), 1995, New York University Press (New York), 1996.

Contributor to books, including *Gendering the Reader,* edited by Sara Mills, Harvester Press, 1994; *(Hetero)Sexual Politics,* edited by M. Maynard and J. Purvis, Taylor & Francis (London, England), 1995; and *War Culture,* edited by P. Kirkham and D. Thoms, Lawrence & Wishart (London), 1995.

WORK IN PROGRESS: This Book Changes Lives, for Edinburgh University Press; research on feminism in the 1990s.

* * *

WIGGINS, Melanie 1934-

PERSONAL: Born October 15, 1934, in Ft. Smith, AR; daughter of Ralph J. (in business) and Melanie (Holt) Speer; children: William Fiveash, Edward Fiveash. *Ethnicity:* "White." *Education:* Hollins College, B.A., 1956; attended Newcomb College. *Politics:* Republican. *Religion:* Episcopalian. *Avocational interests:* Photography, piano, choir.

ADDRESSES: Home and office—League City, TX.

CAREER: Manages 12,000 acres of family land on Texas's Bolivar Peninsula, beginning c. 1978.

MEMBER: Texas Gulf Historical Association, Galveston Historical Foundation (member of board of advisors), Galveston County Historical Commission.

WRITINGS:

NONFICTION

They Made Their Own Law: Stories of Bolivar Peninsula, Rice University Press (Houston, TX), 1990.
Torpedoes in the Gulf: Galveston and the U-Boats, 1942-43, Texas A & M University Press (College Station, TX), 1995.

WORK IN PROGRESS: A collection of factual U-boat stories from World War II, to be finished by the end of 1996; research on factual stories of Vietnamese people in the United States.

SIDELIGHTS: Melanie Wiggins is descended from Charles Taylor Cade, who owned large quantities of land in Texas's Bolivar Peninsula at the turn of the twentieth century. At present, Wiggins manages these lands for her family, and the peninsula, as well as other Texas locales on the Gulf of Mexico, have helped provide her with inspiration for her books, 1990's *They Made Their Own Law: Stories of Bolivar Peninsula* and 1995's *Torpedoes in the Gulf: Galveston and the U-Boats, 1942-43.*

In *They Made Their Own Law,* Wiggins tells the history of the Bolivar Peninsula, from the prehistoric Native Americans who were the first humans to dwell there to events of the 1980s. She focuses on the turn of the twentieth century, however, and includes interviews with elderly denizens who remember those times. The work's title comes at least in part from the fact that most of the peninsula lies in Chambers County, but that county's seat was extremely far away in pre-automotive days, and therefore so was official government.

As the title of *Torpedoes in the Gulf* implies, the book concerns a little-known but interesting facet of World War II history—that German submarines occasionally entered the Gulf of Mexico for surveillance purposes. Wiggins interviewed German U-boat personnel, including Admiral Otto Kretschmer, for her second full-length work.

Wiggins told *CA:* "I never intended to be a writer, but my job as family business manager necessitated letters and reports about various wild happenings on

our Bolivar Peninsula land. At the urging of my sister, I attempted to produce a book dealing with peninsula history, but the manuscript was rejected many times. One editor advised me to take some writing courses, and I followed his advice, rewrote the book, and *They Made Their Own Law: Stories of Bolivar Peninsula* was published. However, in rewording the manuscript I kept the individual oral histories intact, because I felt they were too charming and original to integrate into the text.

"About a year passed while I searched for ideas for a second book. One presented itself when a friend pointed out the old blimp base at Hitchcock, close to Galveston. When he said that blimps in World War II had patrolled the Gulf of Mexico looking for U-boats, I really didn't believe it. At the library I found that he was correct and that no one had written a complete book on the subject. Therefore, my second effort, *Torpedoes in the Gulf: Galveston and the U-boats, 1942-1943*. Because oral histories were such an important ingredient in my first book, I sought out as many German submarine veterans as possible, and especially any who had patrolled the Gulf. The few that I did find added immeasurably to the overall picture, giving the reader a chance to travel with commanders and crew members inside submarines and to understand their thinking.

"Project number three is a result of *Torpedoes,* in that my searches in Germany turned up many U-boat veterans of all ranks, who remembered their adventures in other seas and countries during and just after the war. Their old diaries, photographs, letters and reports are the basis for my present work, and I am hoping again to provide an intimate insight into a world seldom glimpsed.

"More than anything, I want to make reading history *fun.*"

* * *

WILLIAMS, Kimmika L(yvette Hawes) 1959-

PERSONAL: Born January 7, 1959, in Philadelphia, PA; daughter of Samuel S., Jr. and Lillian Yvonne (Curry) Hawes; children: Essence, Tenasha. *Education:* Howard University, B.A., 1980; Temple University MFA Candidate, 1996.

ADDRESSES: Office—Writer in Residence, Bushfire Theatre, 52nd and Locust Sts., Philadelphia, PA 19139.

CAREER: Philadelphia Tribune, Philadelphia, PA, reporter/columnist, 1984-86; Pennsylvania Prison Society, Philadelphia, instructor, 1985-89; Bob Lott Productions, Philadelphia, scriptwriter, 1986-89; WXPN-FM, Philadelphia, arts host and producer, 1989-90; Village Arts Center, Philadelphia, instructor, 1990—; Walnut Street Theatre, Philadelphia, outreach instructor and actress, 1990—. Writer in residence, Bushfire Theatre.

MEMBER: International Women's League for Peace and Freedom, National Black Authors Tour, National Black Storytellers, Theater Association of Pennsylvania, Philadelphia Dramatist Center.

AWARDS, HONORS: American Poetry Center Grant, Teacher's Fellowship, 1990; Playwright's Fellowship, Theatre Association of Pennsylvania, 1990-91; Artist Grant, Philadelphia Neighborhood Arts Project, 1990; Minneapolis Playwrights Center Exchange Grant, 1993; Writing Partnership Teachers Grant, 1995; Future Faculty Fellow, Temple University, 1996.

WRITINGS:

It Ain't Easy to Be Different, In the Tradition Publishing, 1986.
(Under name Kimmika Williams) *Negro Kinship to the Park,* Selrahc Publications, 1990.

Also author of *The Pack, Halley's Comet,* and *God Made Men Brown,* Selrahc Publications. Contributor to the poetry anthology *On the Move,* edited by Sharon Goodman, In the Tradition Publishing, 1985.*

* * *

WILLIAMS, Terry Tempest 1959(?)-

PERSONAL: Born c. 1959, in Nevada; daughter of Diane (Dixon) Williams. *Education:* Attended Teton Science School; University of Utah, B.A. (English), M.A. (environmental education).

ADDRESSES: Office—c/o Utah Museum of Natural History, Salt Lake City, UT.

CAREER: Writer. Worked as teacher at Navajo Reservation in Montezuma Creek, UT; naturalist in residence at Utah Museum of Natural History.

AWARDS, HONORS: Children's Science Book Award in younger category from New York Academy of Sciences, for *The Secret Language of Snow.*

WRITINGS:

(With Ted Major) *The Secret Language of Snow* (for children), illustrations by Jennifer Dewey, Sierra Club (San Francisco), 1984.

Pieces of White Shell: A Journey to Navajo Land, Scribner (New York), 1984.

Between Cattails (verse; for children), illustrations by Peter Parnall, Scribner, 1985.

Coyote's Canyon, Gibbs Smith, 1989.

Refuge: An Unnatural History of Family and Place, Random House (New York), 1992.

The Graywolf Annual Ten: Changing Community, Graywolf Press (St. Paul, MN), 1993.

Stone Time, Southern Utah: A Portrait and a Meditation, Clear Light (Weehawken, NJ), 1994.

Atomic Ghost: Poets Respond to the Nuclear Age, Coffee House Press (Minneapolis), 1995.

Desert Quartet: An Erotic Landscape, Pantheon (New York), 1995.

An Unspoken Hunger: Stories from the Field (essays), Random House, 1995.

Sacred Land of the Southwest, Monacelli Press, 1996.

Testimony: Writers in Defense of the Wilderness, Milkweed Editions (Minneapolis), 1996.

A Love that Is Wild, Random House, in press.

Work represented in anthologies, including *On Nature's Terms: Contemporary Voices,* edited by Rick Bass, Texas A & M University Press (College Station), 1992; and *The Owl in Monument Canyon, and Other Stories from Indian Country,* edited by H. Jackson Clark, University of Utah Press (Salt Lake City), 1993.

Contributor to periodicals, including *Northern Lights, Orion, Sierra,* and *Wilderness.*

SIDELIGHTS: Terry Tempest Williams is a prolific writer of nature books for children and for adults. In 1984 she began her career as a book writer with *The Secret Language of Snow,* a children's book—written with Ted Major—that explains snow's role in nature and explores its effects on both wildlife and plantlife. A reviewer for *Scientific American* noted that the creators of *The Secret Language of Snow* "know their

snow" and concluded, "Any good reader close enough to snow . . . will find this work a fine introduction."

In 1984 Williams also published *Pieces of White Shell: A Journey to Navajo Land,* an examination of Navajo culture. Here Williams emphasizes folklore in explicating various aspects of Navajo life. The next year she published *Between Cattails,* a free-verse children's book about marsh life, and she followed that volume with *Coyote's Canyon,* an account of the American southwest.

Williams gained significant attention as the author of *Refuge: An Unnatural History of Family and Place,* in which she writes of two seemingly disparate subjects: the rise of the Great Salt Lake and the death of her mother. Here she recounts how the rising of the lake threatens a bird sanctuary and the general stability of the area's rather fragile ecosystem. Interwoven among the environmental accounts are commentaries on her mother's experience with cancer, the same illness that had already claimed other members of the Williams family. Williams ties her mother's cancer to environmental changes by contending that the illness derives from nuclear tests conducted in the Nevada desert in the 1950s and 1960s. Williams notes the high rate of cancer among "downwinders," individuals so called because they lived downwind from the nuclear test sites and were, thus, at greater risk of exposure to dangerous radiation.

For Williams, a greater familiarity with nature leads to a greater understanding of death and, thus, a greater awareness of the life-death cycle. As she explained to a *Bloomsbury Review* interviewer, "That's the premise of *Refuge*—that an intimacy with the natural world initiates an intimacy with death, because life and death are engaged in an endless, inseparable dance."

Refuge has prompted positive reactions from reviewers. Marilyn R. Chandler, writing in *Women's Review of Books,* described *Refuge* as "a chronicle of sadness and rage," and she observed that the book serves as a testament "to the courage it takes to live through the sicknesses of our time." Meanwhile, Julie J. Nichols, in her *Belles Lettres* appraisal, deemed *Refuge* "remarkable" and added, "In it we are privileged to experience the vision of a woman of unusually enlightened consciousness."

Williams continued to write about nature, to a greater or lesser extent, in such works as *The Graywolf*

Annual Ten: Changing Community, Stone Time, Southern Utah: A Portrait and a Meditation, Atomic Ghost: Poets Respond to the Nuclear Age, and *Desert Quartet: An Erotic Landscape.*

In 1994 Williams published one of her more prominent works, *An Unspoken Hunger: Stories from the Field,* which is a collection of essays on subjects such as nuclear protesting and on places such as the African Serengeti Plain and Utah's Great Basin. John Hanson Mitchell, writing in the *New York Times Book Review,* noted an inevitably feminist perspective to *An Unspoken Hunger* when he wrote that "the idea of women as intermediary between earth and human conduct is interwoven throughout the book." Mitchell added that Williams "has a knack for integrating topical issues and detailed observations of nature into her narratives."

An Unspoken Hunger has been acknowledged as a rich and varied volume. *Newsweek*'s James N. Baker wrote, "This is not an exercise in didacticism: these are wide-ranging pieces as varied in tone as they are in subject matter." Similarly, Jan Zita Grover reported in *Women's Review of Books* that *An Unspoken Hunger* constituted "a various collection," though she noted that Williams's family inevitably plays a prominent role in the various proceedings. A particularly enthusiastic appraisal was expressed by Stephen Lyons, who wrote in *Bloomsbury Review* that the "writings in *An Unspoken Hunger* are well-crafted stories that prove the maxim that what is most personal is often most universal." He described Williams's language as "lean and intimate." And Suzanne Koehler concluded in *Workbook* that Williams's book provides "a year-round reminder of what being human on a fragile planet is all about."

Williams followed *An Unspoken Hunger* with such volumes as *Sacred Land of the Southwest, Testimony: Writers in Defense of the Wilderness,* and *A Love that Is Wild.*

BIOGRAPHICAL/CRITICAL SOURCES:

BOOKS

Pearlman, Mickey, *Listen to Their Voices: Twenty Interviews with Women Who Write,* Norton, 1993, pp. 121-33.

PERIODICALS

Belles Lettres, winter, 1991-92, pp. 60-61; spring, 1995, pp. 32-34.

Bloomsbury Review, December, 1991, pp. 8-9; November/December, 1994, p. 12.
Georgia Review, fall, 1994, pp. 601-09.
Newsweek, May 2, 1994, p. 58.
New York Times Book Review, September 4, 1996, p. 6.
Rocky Mountain Review of Books, Volume 49, number 1, 1995, pp. 106-12.
Scientific American, December, 1984, pp, 27-30.
Women's Review of Books, March, 1992, p. 10; June, 1995, pp. 17-18.
Workbook, winter, 1994-95, p. 176.*

* * *

WILLIAMSON, Margaret 1947-

PERSONAL: Born December 6, 1947, in Ilford, Essex, England; daughter of Jack Gifford (a college lecturer) and Winifred (a teacher) Williamson. *Ethnicity:* "White, Anglo-Saxon Protestant." *Education:* Cambridge University, B.A. (with honors), 1970; University of Toronto, M.A., 1972; University of London, Ph.D., 1990. *Religion:* "None."

ADDRESSES: Home—London, England. *Office*—St. Mary's University College, University of Surrey, Waldegrave Rd., Twickenham TW1 4SX, England; fax 01-81-240-4255. *E-mail*—mwilliamson@smnc.demon.co.uk. *Agent*—Frances Kelly, 111 Clifton Rd., Kingston upon Thames, Surrey KT2 6PL, England.

CAREER: University of Reading, Reading, England, lecturer in classics, 1979-82; University of Surrey, St. Mary's University College, Twickenham, England, senior lecturer in classical studies, 1989—. Oxford University, lecturer at Magdalen College, 1990-91.

WRITINGS:

Sappho's Immortal Daughters (monograph), Harvard University Press (Cambridge, MA), 1995.
(Editor with S. Blundell) *The Sacred and the Feminine in Ancient Greece,* Routledge & Kegan Paul (England), in press.

WORK IN PROGRESS: Research on gender in archaic lyric; research on gender, collectivity, and the chorus.

WOLFF, Egon 1926-

PERSONAL: Born in 1926, in Chile.

CAREER: Chemical engineer; author; playwright, 1958—.

WRITINGS:

Ninamadre (three-act play), Instituto Chileno-Norteamericano de Cultura (Santiago, Chile), 1966.

Los invasores (two-act play), Ercilla (Santiago, Chile), 1970.

Paper Flowers: A Play in Six Scenes, translated from the Spanish by Margaret Sayers Peden, University of Missouri Press, 1971.

El signo de cain (includes the play "Discipulos del miedo"), Ediciones Valores Literarios (Santiago, Chile), 1971.

(With Frieda Wolff) *Judeus no Brasil Imperial: Uma pesquisa nos documentos e no noticiario carioca da epocha* (nonfiction), Centro de Estudos Judaicos (Sao Paulo), 1975.

Sepulturas de israelitas, Universidade de Sao Paulo, 1976. <L>*Teatro,* Nascimento, 1978.

(With Frieda Wolff) *A odisseia dos judeus de Recife* (nonfiction), Centro de Estudos Judaicos, 1979.

Sepulturas de israelitas—II: Uma pesquisa em mais de trinta cemiterios nao israelitas, (nonfiction), Cemiterio Comunal Israelita (Rio de Janeiro), 1983.

Participacao e contribuicao de judeus ao desenvolvimento do Brasil (nonfiction), [Rio de Janeiro], 1985.

(With Frieda Wolff) *Campos: Ascensao e declinio de uma coletividade* [Rio de Janeiro], 1986.

Pareja de trapo: La balsa de la Medusa, Universitaria (Santiago, Chile), 1988.

Depoimentos, [Rio de Janeiro], 1988.

Invitacion a comer; Cicatrices, Univeristaria (Santiago), 1995.

Also author of the plays "Mansion de lechuzas," "Discipulos del miedo," and "Alamos en la azotea." Editor, with Frieda Wolff, of *Dicionario biografico,* 1986—. Work represented in anthologies, including *Tres obras de teatro,* Casa de las Americas, 1970; *Three Contemporary Latin-American Plays,* edited by Ruth S. Lamb, Xerox College Pub., 1971; and *Teatro chileno contemporaneo,* Bello, 1982.*

WOOD, Audrey 1905-1985

PERSONAL: Born February 28, 1905, in New York, NY; died after four years in a stroke-induced coma, December 27, 1985, in Fairfield, CT; daughter of William H. (a theater manager) and Ida M. (Gaubatz) Wood; married William Liebling (a talent representative), March 24, 1938 (died December 29, 1969). *Ethnicity:* "Caucasian." *Education:* Attended Hunter College, 1925. *Religion:* Lutheran.

CAREER: Century Play Co., New York City, play reader, c. 1927; Liebling-Wood, Inc. (a New York City-based artists' representatives agency), co-founder (with William Liebling), 1937, and co-owner (with Liebling), 1937-1954; MCA (Music Corporation of America), New York City, associate, 1954-62; Ashley Famous Agency (now International Creative Management), New York City, agent, 1962-81. Advisor, Eugene O'Neill Memorial Theater Foundation, 1965; taught a beginning playwrights' course, Wesleyan College, 1967; headed a playwrights' workshop sponsored by the University of Florida at the Asolo Theater of Sarasota, FL, 1968.

MEMBER: American National Theater and Academy (board member), American Theater Wing, New Dramatists' Committee, Society of Authors' Representatives.

AWARDS, HONORS: Received a D.H.L. from Florida State University, 1970; honored with the Richard L. Coe award at the Kennedy Center for the Performing Arts, 1981, for her contributions to the theater; a scholarship in Wood's name at the Yale School of Drama and Repertory Theatre was established in 1982 for young playwrights; a theater on 48th St. in New York City was renamed the Audrey Wood Theater in 1984.

WRITINGS:

(With Max Wilk) *Represented by Audrey Wood* (autobiography), Doubleday (Garden City, NY), 1981.

SIDELIGHTS: Literary agent Audrey Wood chronicled her long career bringing the works of talented writers to the American stage in her 1981 autobiography, *Represented by Audrey Wood.* Co-authored with Max Wilk, the book's final draft was handed over just a few days before Wood suffered a stroke that left her in a coma for four years; she died

in 1985. In these memoirs, Wood chronicles a life on Broadway spent behind the scenes, first as the daughter of a theater manager, and later as a script reader searching for a potential box-office hit. In 1937 she joined with casting agent William Liebling to form their own agency, Liebling-Wood, Inc. The partnership was a success from the start, as Wood writes. Their first stage project was a hit, and she and Liebling were married the following year, though at first they attempted to keep this a secret because of differing religious backgrounds.

As *Represented by Audrey Wood* details, the Liebling-Wood agency helped launch the careers of some of the most influential names in American theater. Wood is credited with bringing the works of William Inge and Tennessee Williams to the stage, and she spends many pages chronicling the tempestuous professional relationship she suffered at the hands of Williams, who eventually cast blame on her when his plays were unsuccessful. In 1954 Wood and Liebling sold their agency to entertainment conglomerate MCA, but continued in their roles handling literary and stage talent; Wood later headed the playwrights' department at International Creative Management. Her book makes mention of the numerous luminaries she befriended, and includes accounts of Charles Laughton reciting Bertolt Brecht and Bette Davis during rehearsals. Though her partner and husband passed away in 1969, Wood continued working until her 1981 stroke. Richard Gosswiller, writing in the *Chicago Tribune Book World,* faulted *Represented by Audrey Wood* for sections that "are little more than party reminiscences" and "an occasional banality," but assessed its content more favorably in light of Wood's significant contributions to the American theater in bringing such works as *Porgy and Bess* and *A Streetcar Named Desire* to the stage. Gosswiller pointed out that "it is not every day an author's agent writes a book—or has reason to. . . . Whatever the book's shortcomings, it is worthwhile having her recollections in print."

BIOGRAPHICAL/CRITICAL SOURCES:

BOOKS

Notable Names in the American Theater, James T. White (Clifton, NJ), 1976.
Robinson, Alice M., Vera Mowry Roberts, and Milly S. Barranger, eds., *Notable Women in American Theater: A Biographical Dictionary,* Greenwood Press (New York, NY), 1989.

PERIODICALS

Booklist, December 1, 1981, p. 477.
Chicago Tribune Book World, November 1, 1981.
Kirkus Reviews, September 15, 1981, p. 1225.
Library Journal, December 1, 1981, p. 2330.
Los Angeles Times, January 1, 1986, sec. II, p. 2.
Newsweek, January 13, 1986.
New York Times, December 29, 1985, p. 22; December 31, 1985; January 16, 1986.
Publishers Weekly, September 4, 1981, p. 52.
West Coast Review of Books, May, 1982, p. 30.*

* * *

WOOLF, S. J.
 See WOOLF, Stuart J(oseph)

* * *

WOOLF, Stuart J(oseph) 1936-
 (S. J. Woolf)

PERSONAL: Born January 23, 1936, in London, England; married Anna Debenedetti; children: one daughter. *Ethnicity:* "White." *Education:* Merton College, Oxford, B.A., 1956; Oxford University, M.A., D.Phil., 1960; Cambridge University, Ph.D. (by incorporation), 1961; Oxford University, D.Litt, 1991.

ADDRESSES: Office—Department of History, University of Essex, Wivenhoe Park, Colchester, Essex CO4 3SQ, England.

CAREER: Pembroke College, Cambridge, England, fellow and assistant director of studies in history, 1961-65; University of Reading, Reading, England, reader in Italian history and director of the Centre for the Advanced Study of Italian History, 1965-74; University of Essex, Colchester, England, professor of history, 1975—, research and history professor, 1992—. Affiliated with the European University Institute, Florence, Italy, 1983-92.

MEMBER: Royal Historical Society (fellow).

AWARDS, HONORS: John Florio Translation Prize, 1965.

WRITINGS:

(With M. V. Posner) *Italian Public Enterprise,* Harvard University Press (Cambridge), 1964.

A History of Italy, 1700-1860: The Social Constraints of Political Change, Methuen (London), 1979.

(With Jean-Claude Perrot) *State and Statistics in France, 1789-1815,* Harwood Academic Publishers (New York), 1984.

The Poor in Western Europe in the Eighteenth and Nineteenth Centuries, Routledge (London), 1984.

Napoleon's Integration of Europe, Routledge (London), 1990.

EDITOR

(And contributor) *European Fascism,* Random House (New York), 1968, revised edition published as *Fascism in Europe,* Routledge, 1981.

The Nature of Fascism, Random House, 1968.

(With E. L. Jones) *Agrarian Change and Economic Development: The Historical Problems,* Methuen, 1969.

The Rebirth of Italy, 1943-50, Humanities Press (New York), 1972.

(And author of introduction) F. Venturi, *Italy and the Enlightenment: Studies in a Cosmopolitan Century,* translated from the Italian by Susan Corsi, Longmans (London), 1972, New York University (New York), 1973.

Domestic Strategies: Work and Family in France and Italy, 1600-1800, Cambridge University Press (Cambridge), 1988.

Nationalism in Europe: A Reader, Routledge, 1995.

TRANSLATOR

Levi Primo, *If This Is a Man* (original title, *Se questo e un uomo*), New English Press (London), 1962.

Primo, *The Truce: A Survivor's Journey Home from Auschwitz* (original title, *Le Tregua*), Bodley Head (London), 1965.

(And adaptor) Marongiu, Antonio, *Medieval Parliaments: A Comparative Study* (original title, *Il Parlamento nel medio evo e nell'eta moderna*), Eyre & Spottiswoode (London), 1968.

OTHER

(Compiler) *The Italian Risorgimento,* Longmans, 1969.

Contributor to the periodicals, including the *Times Literary Supplement, English History Review,* and *Economic History Review.*

SIDELIGHTS: European history, and particularly the subjects of Italy and Fascist movements, is the specialty of British academic Stuart J. Woolf. A professor at the University of Essex for several years, he has also spent time in Italy for the purpose of research as well as through his affiliation with the European University Institute in Florence. Woolf has won acclaim as the translator of two works by the Italian writer Primo Levi, *If This Is a Man,* the 1962 translation of Levi's *Se questo e un uomo,* and 1965's *The Truce: A Survivor's Journey Home from Auschwitz.*

One of the first works under Woolf's name to attract attention was the 1968 collection of essays he edited, *European Fascism.* Much of the book's content had been taken from an academic seminar on the topic held at the University of Reading, where Woolf was at the time reader in Italian history and director of its Centre for the Advanced Study of Italian History. He contributed a piece on the Mussolini era to 1968's *European Fascism;* the other essays discuss right-wing nationalist movements in other European countries during the era between world wars. In a review of the 1968 edition for the *Observer,* Philip Toynbee termed it "a serious and thoughtful book," and declared "Dr. Woolf's introduction combines with Professor Trevor-Roper's excellent general article to form a finely definitive statement in a field where definition was greatly needed."

Aside from his editorship of numerous other titles, Woolf is also the author of academic works such as 1979's *A History of Italy, 1700-1860: The Social Constraints of Political Change* and *The Poor in Western Europe in the Eighteenth and Nineteenth Centuries,* published in 1986. For this latter volume, Woolf examined civil administration records from the era to determine who among the population were classified as poor during the era, and what kind of assistance they might have received from state or church agencies. Some of the work was originally published in Italian academic journals and specifically treats the Napoleonic era in Tuscany. As Woolf's research points out, more often than not the poor were children, the elderly, and female-headed households—and in some areas they may have numbered as much as three-quarters of the population. There is also a long introductory chapter providing an overview of social and political conditions in Europe leading up to the framework of the book. This first section, asserted J. N. Ball in the *Historian,* "is balanced and sympathetic in tone, and is clearly the mature reflections of a scholar who has worked for many years in his field."

In Woolf's 1991 work *Napoleon's Integration of Europe,* the academic examines a brief period of European history during which France assumed control over much of the continent. As his book explains, an army of bureaucrats inspired by the progressive ideals of the Enlightenment spread across counties such as Italy and helped usher in a new, more modern era. *Napoleon's Integration of Europe* also provides a glimpse as to why the famed conqueror's effort to model the rest of Europe after modernized France was doomed to fail. "Based on extensive reading in five languages, Stuart Woolf's book offers a unique picture of how Napoleonic Europe both worked and malfunctioned," noted the *Times Literary Supplement*'s William Doyle. The critic described it as "a genuinely original contribution to a field where recycling is too often the norm. Statesmen perplexed by the continuing problem of European integration should also study it."

BIOGRAPHICAL/CRITICAL SOURCES:

PERIODICALS

American Historical Review, October, 1992, p. 1206.
Choice, February, 1987, p. 929.
English Historical Review, November, 1994, pp. 1295-96.
Historian, May, 1989, pp. 486-88.
Journal of Economic History, December, 1993, pp. 930-31.
Journal of Interdisciplinary History, summer, 1993, pp. 138-40.
Journal of Modern History, March, 1994, pp. 124-26.
Observer, July 28, 1968.
Times Literary Supplement, April 24, 1992.
Washington Post Book World, August 10, 1969.

* * *

WYATT, Wilson (Watkins, Sr.) 1905-1996

PERSONAL: Born November 21, 1905, in Louisville, KY; died June 11, 1996; son of Richard H. and Mary (Watkins) Wyatt; married Anne Kinnaird Duncan, June 14, 1930; children: Mary Anne, Nancy Kinnaird, Wilson Watkins Jr. *Education:* University of Louisville, J.D., 1927. *Politics:* Democrat. *Religion:* Presbyterian.

ADDRESSES: Home—1400 Willow Ave. No. 1205, Louisville, KY 40204. *Office*—Citizens Plaza, 28th Fl., Louisville, KY 20202.

CAREER: Peter, Heyburn, Marshall, & Wyatt (law firm), Louisville, KY, founding partner, 1935-41; mayor, City of Louisville, 1941-45; National Housing Agency, housing expeditor, 1946; Wyatt, Grafton, & Sloss (law firm), senior partner, 1947-80; lieutenant governor, State of Kentucky, 1959-63. Delegate-at-large to Democratic conventions, 1944-68; Democratic National Committee representative for Kentucky, 1960-64. Chairperson, Louisville Community Foundation, 1984—, Leadership Kentucky, 1984-86, and Shakertown Roundtable, 1985—; vice-chairperson, Kentucky Economic Development Corporation, 1984—, and Kentucky Council on Science and Technology, 1987-90; and director, National Center for Family Literacy, 1989—. Member, Bingham Fund for Excellence in Teaching, Transylvania University, 1987—; and Gaines Center for Humanities, University of Kentucky, 1987-90.

MEMBER: American Bar Association, Kentucky Bar Association, American Law Institute, Forest Farmers Association, Rotary International, New York Century Club.

AWARDS, HONORS: U.S. Treasury Distinguished Service Award, 1955; Brotherhood Award, National Conference of Christians and Jews, 1974; Lawyer of the Year, Kentucky Bar Association, 1974, 1976, and 1981; Municipal Leadership Award, 1987; Alumnus of the Year, University of Kentucky, 1987; First Amendment Prize, Society of Professional Journalists, 1991; Community Service Award, 1991; Fleur-de-Lis Award, Louisville Forum, 1993; Hall of Fame, Junior Achievement Kentuckiana, 1994; various honorary degrees.

WRITINGS:

Whistle Stops: Adventures in Public Life (memoir), University Press of Kentucky (Louisville), 1985.

SIDELIGHTS: A former lieutenant governor of Kentucky, Wilson Wyatt had long and illustrious careers in both law and politics. In his 1985 memoir, *Whistle Stops: Adventures in Public Life,* he described his varied and intermittent career in municipal, state, and federal government that, together with his successful law practice, spanned half a century. The volume includes accounts of Wyatt's administration of Presi-

dent Harry S Truman's federal housing program after World War II; recollections of serving as special emissary to Indonesia to avert a crisis over oil expropriation during the Kennedy Administration; his role as delegate-at-large to seven Democratic National Conventions; and his work as campaign manager during former Illinois governor Adlai Stevenson's failed bids for the U.S. presidency in 1952 and 1956.

Whistle Stops garnered mixed reviews. Carl M. Brauer, writing for the *Journal of Foreign Affairs,* called the book a "gentle and modest memoir," though adding that, "To experts on this period, Wyatt has little new to offer in the way of insight or information." On the other hand, political and diplomatic reporter Chalmers M. Roberts remarked in the *Washington Post Book World:* "It is too bad that Wyatt . . . waited, for example, until the history of the postwar era of the Democratic Party up to and including Adlai E. Stevenson's two failed attempts to defeat Dwight D. Eisenhower for the presidency is all but set in verbal concrete. Twenty years ago, say, he might have added something to those histories; now this is just another addendum to the literature." While noting that "the most fascinating part to this book is Wyatt's description of the Stevenson campaigns and of the candidate himself," Roberts maintained that, "the more poignant parts concern the might-have-beens in Wyatt's own life."

Several commentators remarked on the section of *Whistle Stops* dealing with the feud between U.S. oil companies and the Indonesian government during the early 1960s. A reviewer for the *Journal of American History* called this episode "interesting," while Roberts deemed it "text book stuff for schools of diplomacy, especially in showing the uses of flattery and of a promise of a presidential visit." Brauer summed up *Whistle Stops* by asserting, "This is essentially a book that will be enjoyed by Wyatt's admirers and friends, and possibly by some young readers who are unfamiliar with the events and personalities he describes."

BIOGRAPHICAL/CRITICAL SOURCES:

PERIODICALS

Journal of American History, June, 1987, pp. 224-26.
Journal of Foreign Affairs, spring, 1986, p. 880.
Washington Post Book World, February 16, 1986, p. 4.

WYER, Robert S. (Jr.) 1935-

PERSONAL: Born April 18, 1935, in Delhi, NY; son of Robert S. (a photographer) and Wilhelmina (a teacher) Wyer; married first wife, Joan M., 1960 (divorced); married Darlene Goodhart (died, 1995); married Rashmi Adaval (a marketing researcher), May 19, 1995; children: Kathryn L., Natalie A. *Ethnicity:* "Caucasian." *Education:* Rensselaer Polytechnic Institute, B.E.E., 1957; New York University, M.S.E.E., 1959; University of Colorado, Ph.D., 1962. *Avocational interests:* Music, athletics.

ADDRESSES: Home—401 West Delaware St., Urbana, IL 61801. *Office*—Department of Psychology, University of Illinois at Urbana-Champaign, 613 East Daniel St., Champaign, IL 61820; fax 217-244-5876. *E-mail*—rwyer@s.psych.uiuc.edu.

CAREER: Bell Telephone Laboratories, Whippany, NJ, staff member, 1957-59; Hughes Aircraft Co., Culver City, CA, staff member, 1961-63; University of Iowa, Iowa City, assistant professor, 1963-65; University of Illinois at Urbana-Champaign, professor of psychology, 1965—.

MEMBER: Society of Experimental Social Psychology.

AWARDS, HONORS: Alexander von Humboldt Special Research Prize for Distinguished Scientists; grants from National Science Foundation and National Institute of Mental Health.

WRITINGS:

Cognitive Organization and Change, Lawrence Erlbaum (Mahwah, NJ), 1974.
(With Donal E. Carlston) *Social Cognition, Inference, and Attribution,* Lawrence Erlbaum, 1979.
(Editor with Thomas K. Srull) *Handbook of Social Cognition,* three volumes, Lawrence Erlbaum, 1984, 2nd edition, 1994.
(With Srull) *Memory and Cognition in Its Social Context,* Lawrence Erlbaum, 1989.
(Editor with Srull, and contributor) *Advances in Social Cognition,* Lawrence Erlbaum, Volume I: *A Dual Process Model of Impression Formation,* 1988, Volume II: *Social Intelligence and Cognitive Assessments of Personality,* 1989, Volume III: *Content and Process Specificity in the Effects of Prior Experiences,* 1990, Volume IV: *The Content, Structure, and Operation of Thought*

Systems, 1991, Volume V: *The Representation of Trait and Behavioral Knowledge about Self,* 1992, Volume VI: *Towards a General Theory of Anger and Emotion,* 1993, Volume VII: *Associated Systems Theory,* 1994.

Also editor of *Knowledge and Memory,* Lawrence Erlbaum. Contributor to books, including *Reconsidering the Democratic Public,* edited by C. E. Marcus and R. L. Hanson, Pennsylvania State University Press (University Park, PA), 1993; *The Cognitive Basis of Interpersonal Communication,* edited by D. E. Hewes, Lawrence Erlbaum, 1994; and *Social Cognition: Contributions to Classical Issues in Social Psychology,* edited by P. Devine, D. Hamilton, and T. Ostrom, Academic Press (San Diego, CA), 1994. Contributor of more than a hundred-fifty articles to scholarly journals, including *Social Cognition, Journal of Consumer Psychology, Journal of Personality and Social Psychology, Advances in Consumer Research, Psychological Review,* and *American Political Science Review.* Editor, *Journal of Experimental Social Psychology,* 1978-81.

SIDELIGHTS: Robert S. Wyer told *CA:* "I am a research psychologist whose interests (and, therefore, writing) surround the cognitive processes that underlie people's use of information to make judgments and behavioral decisions. The work I have done has touched on such diverse topics as person impression formation, the manner in which narratives are represented in memory, belief and attitude change, the determinants of humor elicitation, emotional communication in close relationships, and political information processing."

* * *

WYNTER, Sylvia 1928-

PERSONAL: Born May 11, 1928 (one source says 1932), in Holguin Oriente Province, Cuba; daughter of Percival and Lola Maude (Reed) Wynter; married, c. 1955 (divorced); husband's surname, Isachsen (a Norwegian pilot); married Jan Carew (a writer), c. 1960 (marriage ended, July, 1971); children: Annemarie, Christopher. *Education:* King's College, University of London, B.A. (with honors), 1949, M.A., 1953.

ADDRESSES: *Office*—Stanford University, Department of Spanish and Portuguese, Stanford, CA 94305.

CAREER: Worked variously as an actor, dancer, and writer in Europe, 1954-59; British Broadcasting Corporation (BBC), commentator, writer, and translator, 1958-62; University of the West Indies, Jamaica, lecturer in Hispanic literature, 1963-74; University of California, San Diego, lecturer in Hispanic literature, 1974-76, coordinator of the Literature and Society Program; Department of Spanish and Portuguese, Stanford University, professor of Spanish and chair of African and Afro-American Studies, 1977—.

WRITINGS:

The Hills of Hebron: A Jamaican Novel, Simon & Schuster, 1962.
Black Midas (juvenile; adaptation of Jan Carew's novel), illustrated by Aubrey Williams, Longmans, 1970.
Jamaica's National Heroes (nonfiction), National Commission (Kingston, Jamaica), 1971.
(With Annemarie Isachsen) *Rody and Rena, The Sea Star Readers,* Jamaica Publishing House, 1975.

PLAYS

(With Jan Carew) *The University of Hunger,* BBC, 1961, televised as *The Big Pride,* BBC, 1962.
Ssh . . . It's a Wedding (musical), produced in Jamaica, c. 1961.
(With J. Carew) *Miracle in Lime Lane,* produced in Spanish Town, Jamaica, at Folk Theatre, 1962.
Brother Man (adaptation of Roger Mais's novel), produced in Jamaica, 1965.
1865 Ballad for a Rebellion (epic story of Morant Bay Rebellion), produced in Jamaica, 1965.
(Translator) Francisco Cuevas, *Jamaica Is the Eye of Bolivar,* Vantage Press, 1979.
(With Alex Gradussov) *Rockstone Anancy* (Jamaican Pantomime), produced in Jamaica, 1970.

OTHER

Contributor to anthologies, including *Out of the Kumbla: Caribbean Women and Literature,* African World Press, 1990. Also contributor to journals, including *Jamaica Journal 2* and *Jamaica Journal 4, Savacou 5, Caribbean Studies,* and *New World Quarterly 5.*

SIDELIGHTS: West Indian author Sylvia Wynter is perhaps best known for her belief in the validity of folk culture. In his essay on Wynter in *Fifty Caribbean Writers,* Victor L. Chang notes that as early as the late 1960's the author publicly took to task such well-known male Caribbean literary critics as W. I.

Carr, Louis James, Wayne Brown, John Hearne, Cameron King, and Mervyn Morris for privileging European culture over West Indian folk culture in their critical writings. Chang further states that Wynter claims that for her the folk culture represents "the only living tradition in the Caribbean," and that any authentic national literature could come only from the life of the West Indian peasant.

The Hills of Hebron: A Jamaican Novel, published in 1962, was a literary milestone, for as Janice Lee Liddell points out in her essay published in the anthology *Out of the Kumbla: Caribbean Women and Literature,* Wynter was "the first Black woman novelist from the English-speaking Caribbean." The story, set in rural Jamaica, centers around a religious folk group, the New Believers, who follow their leader Moses Barton from the worldly village of Cockpit Center to the hills of Hebron in search of spiritual salvation and a better life. When Moses dies, a struggle for power ensues. Obadiah Brown, in the midst of a severe drought, takes over the leadership and vows celibacy for one year and a day in a covenant with God to protect the Hebronites. But Miss Gatha, Moses' widow, wants the leadership for her own son, Isaac, who is away at school. So when it becomes obvious that Rose, Obadiah's wife, is indeed pregnant, Obadiah is dismissed as a hypocrite, and Miss Gatha assumes temporary leadership as she awaits her son's return. Finally, it is revealed that not only has Isaac raped Rose and is thus responsible for her pregnancy, but has stolen the money that his mother was holding for the New Believers, and will never return to the community. The work ends on a symbolic note of hope when, as Miss Gatha holds her newborn grandson in her arms, the skies open and the rains come down, thus ending the drought.

Although she concedes that the primary thematic concern of this work is certainly not with women, Liddell approaches the work from the perspective of Miss Gatha and the other women whom she sees as living their lives and seeking their identity solely through their roles as wives and mothers. That these women living in what she calls a "patriarchal and patrilineal" society are able to achieve any semblance of autonomy she finds highly unusual and commendable. The primacy that this society places on these "female roles," she suggests, both victimizes and debilitates the Caribbean woman. On that same note, Chang states that although the main character is a man, the work could be called "a woman's novel." He sees the women as demonstrating the "strengths and enduring qualities of the folk culture" and providing "support and sustenance for their men."

The Hills of Hebron was met with mixed reviews. The most frequent criticism was that the author attempts to deal with too many issues at once. Kenneth Ramchand in *The West Indian Novel and Its Background* states that "*The Hills of Hebron* is an overloaded work by a West Indian intellectual anxious to touch on as many themes as possible." Chang, writing along similar lines, believes that "Wynter invests [the work] with so much of her concerns that the medium is too freighted with the message."

On the more positive side, Chang lists other areas in which he believes Wynter achieves "some fine effects" in this work. Citing the language used, Chang explains that while *The Hills of Hebron* is narrated in "Standard English," Wynter captures the "Creole patterns and rhythms" of the folk dialect in the speaking voices of her characters, as well as the "pervasive influence of the King James version of the Bible." He finds commendable the rich "Biblical echoes and allusions" in the place names, character names, and what he calls "near paraphrases [of Biblical events]." Chang also credits the author with being very successful in capturing and depicting rural Jamaica, which he thinks lends the novel "an air of authenticity." And a reviewer in *Library Journal* acknowledges that although "the book is marred by unevenness and a too diverse viewpoint, . . . the author's creativity and knowledge of people make it, on the whole, a distinctive and sensitive study of fanaticism."

BIOGRAPHICAL/CRITICAL SOURCES:

BOOKS

Dance, Daryl Cumber, editor, *Fifty Caribbean Writers: A Bio-Bibliographical Critical Sourcebook,* Greenwood Press, 1986.

Davies, Carole Boyce and Elaine Savory Fido, editors, *Out of the Kumbla: Caribbean Women and Literature,* African World Press, 1990.

Herdeck, Donald E. and others, editors, *A Bio-Bibliographical-Critical Encyclopedia,* Three Continents Press, 1979.

Ramchand, Kenneth, *The West Indian Novel and Its Background,* Faber & Faber, 1970.

PERIODICALS

Library Journal, July, 1962.
New York Times Book Review, July 15, 1962, p. 24.
Times Literary Supplement, September 28, 1962, p. 765.*

Y-Z

YAROSHINSKAYA, Alla 1953-

PERSONAL: Born February 14, 1953, in Zhitomir, U.S.S.R. (now the Ukraine); daughter of Alexander Yaroshinsky (in the military) and Lubov Yaroshinskaya (a lawyer; maiden name, Poddubnaya); married Alexander Kalko (in the military), August 18, 1982; children: Milan, Alexander. *Ethnicity:* "Ukrainian." *Education:* Kiev State University, Ph.D., 1976; attended the professional course of the Japan Newspapers and Editors Association, 1992; attended the U.S. Agency for International Development's Academy of Education, 1994. *Avocational interests:* "Politics, freedom of the press, nuclear ecology, and nuclear weapons."

ADDRESSES: *Home*—Rubliovskoe Shosse, 34-2-437, Moscow, Russia 121609. *Office*—Alla Yaroshinskaya Fund, Bersenevskaya Naberezkaya, 20\2, Moscow Russia 103790, GSP; fax 7095 230 1417; 415-53-79. *E-mail*—yaro@glas.apc.org.

CAREER: *Radyanska Zhitomirshina* (newspaper), journalist, 1976-89; U.S.S.R. Parliament, member of parliament serving on committees on glasnost, human rights, and the environment, and chief of the International Committee for the Defense of Journalists' Rights and Press Freedom, 1989-91; European Parliament, appointed member, 1990-91; Ministry of Press and Information of the Russian Federation, chief of mass media department, 1991-92; Federal Information Center of the President of the Russian Federation, chief of the International Liaison of Mass Media department, 1992-93; adviser to Russian President Boris N. Yeltsin, 1993—; president and founder of the Alla Yaroshinskaya Charity Fund to assist victims of nuclear disasters, 1993—. Has lectured in many countries, including France, Germany, the Netherlands, Sweden, Switzerland, Japan, and the United States.

MEMBER: International Network of Engineers and Scientists for Global Responsibility, Helsinki International Committee on Human Rights, Russian Branch of the International Green Cross Fund (headed by former Soviet leader Mikhail Gorbachev), Journalists Union of the Russian Federation (secretary).

AWARDS, HONORS: All-Union Golden Pen Award for outstanding journalism, city of Kiev, Ukraine, 1980; International Journalists' Prize, Soviet Union and Czechoslovakia, for best publication, 1985; co-recipient of the Right Livelihood Award, Right Livelihood Foundation, 1992, for her work in exposing and trying to ameliorate the effects of the nuclear disaster in Chernobyl.

WRITINGS:

(Coauthor) *Earth Is Alarmed* (nonfiction), Progress (Moscow, Russia), 1990.

Chernobyl Is with Us (nonfiction), Kniga (Moscow, Russia), 1991; French translation published as *Chernobyl: Verite Interdite,* L'Ob (Paris, France), 1993; English translation published as *Chernobyl: Prohibited Truth,* Jon Carpenter (Oxford, England), 1994, University of Nebraska Press (Lincoln, NE), 1995.

Chernobyl: Top Secret (nonfiction), Drugie Berega (Moscow, Russia), 1992; Japanese translation published under the same name by Heibonsha Limited (Tokyo, Japan), 1994; German translation published as *Prohibited Chernobyl,* BasicDruc (Berlin, Germany), 1994; English

translation, University of Nebraska Press (Lincoln, NE), 1995.

(Coauthor and editor-in-chief) *Nuclear Encyclopedia*, Yaroshinskaya Charity Fund Publishing House (Moscow, Russia), 1996.

Contributor of articles to periodicals.

WORK IN PROGRESS: Research on the non-proliferation and abolition of nuclear weapons.

SIDELIGHTS: Born in the Zhitomir region of the Ukraine, Russian journalist and activist Alla Yaroshinskaya has received awards for her reporting. She is especially known for her work about the accident at the Chernobyl nuclear power facility in 1986, an event that signalled a turning point in her own life. Some of her writings concerning the disaster were collected as *Chernobyl: Top Secret* in 1992.

Yaroshinskaya trained as a journalist at Kiev University. She worked more than a dozen years for her local newspaper as a correspondent. She told *CA:* "At university I had been a political dissident. During my work I consistently tried to expose party corruption and suffered administrative penalties. At the end of 1986 I began to feel uneasy about the supposed evacuation of areas which had been contaminated by radiation from the Chernobyl accident in April, and I began to investigate."

Yaroshinskaya requested permission to travel to the affected areas in order to prepare a story. When her supervisors denied this request, she used her days off to travel to the nearby areas of the Ukraine that had been exposed to the most radiation. "I discovered that people from highly contaminated villages were being resettled in hardly less contaminated villages nearby; that their health problems were serious but officially denied and ignored; that their new accommodation was grossly inadequate; and that people could not survive without eating the highly radioactive food being grown in the area." She learned that people affected by the accident, including many children, were experiencing radiation sickness; produce was grown in areas where the soil was radioactive. The Soviet government had tried to cover up these facts, issuing official reports and newspaper articles that downplayed the severity of the situation near Chernobyl.

Yaroshinskaya penned her news story; however, it was rejected not only by *Radyanska Zhitomirshina* but by the well-known Soviet papers *Pravda* and *Izvestia*

as well. Under the regime of Soviet leader Mikhail Gorbachev, more freedom was allowed in the press, and, ironically, while *Izvestia* did not print her reports on Chernobyl, they did print a story about the way Yaroshinskaya's work was being repressed. Undaunted, Yaroshinskaya illegally circulated her news stories about Chernobyl through the underground press known as *samizdat.*

Yaroshinskaya was pressured by Soviet government officials to end her actions, but she had gained great popularity among the people, who nominated her for election to the Soviet Parliament. She won her seat in 1989. As a politician, Yaroshinskaya continued her work on behalf of the victims of the Chernobyl accident. Her work has included gaining access to official government documents about Chernobyl. These revealed that a cover-up of the accident's severity, and the essentially flawed design of the nuclear reactor involved, had been perpetrated upon international authorities.

After the 1991 coup that transformed the Soviet Union into the Russian Federation, Yaroshinskaya was able to print an article about Chernobyl entitled "Forty Secret Protocols of the Kremlin Wise Men" in *Izvestia.* The article was picked up by papers worldwide. Even though official policy was more open than it had been under the Soviet regime, Yaroshinskaya still faced danger for her efforts. She told *CA* that after speaking about Chernobyl on Russian television in 1992, "strange happenings began to take place: once, narrowly missing my face, a brick dropped from the roof. The second time it was a piece of iron."

She added: "In the course of my campaigning for publicity and truth about Chernobyl, the false party press, especially that in Zhitomir, attacked me almost daily and even used insults. Three times I had to resort to the courts against three party newspapers to defend my honor and dignity during 1990 and 1991. They also tried to initiate a criminal case against me because of my exposure of the situation, but the office of public prosecutor, having studied the documents I presented in my case, refused to permit a criminal procedure."

In that same year, however, Yaroshinskaya received the Right Livelihood Award—known in many circles as the alternative Nobel Prize—for her work on the Chernobyl problem. She used the monetary prize to set up the Alla Yaroshinskaya Charity Fund, which gives assistance to the victims of nuclear disasters.

She continues to work in the Russian government as an adviser to President Boris N. Yeltsin, and offered this statement to *CA:* "The peoples of the world should be aware of the explosion at Chernobyl and about its global effects, those effects actually changing the ecology of the entire earth."

American critics have been receptive to *Chernobyl: Top Secret.* A reviewer in *Publishers Weekly* hailed it as "a convincing, absorbing, alarming and important book," while J. L. Lesso, in the *Library Journal,* praised it as "a shocking yet fascinating personal account."

Yaroshinskaya also told *CA:* "Throughout the campaigning on the Chernobyl issue, I was attacked by the authorities in Ukraine and Zhitomir with whom I was in any case unpopular because of my earlier attempts at exposing their misdeeds. After the failed putsch in August 1991, I learned that my name was at the top of the local list for internment had the putsch succeeded. The elections in Ukraine following the break-up of the Soviet Union returned practically the same politicians to power in Zhitomir whom I had consistently attacked. I also heard that I would be unlikely to get a job in Kiev. So, I stayed in Russia where I currently head the department for mass media at the Russian Press Ministry. My Right Livelihood Award will be used to expose the truth about the Chernobyl accident and to help some of its victims."

BIOGRAPHICAL/CRITICAL SOURCES:

BOOKS

Mazumoto, Kenzi, *Chernobyl: Five Years After,* Asahi (Tokyo, Japan), 1990.
Nuclear Encyclopedia, Yaroshinskaya Charity Fund Publishing House (Moscow, Russia), 1996.
Read, Piers Paul, *The Story of the Heroes and Victims of Chernobyl,* Random House (New York), 1993.

PERIODICALS

Allmant (Finland), December 12, 1992.
California Monthly, February, 1993.
Current Digest of the Soviet Press, Vol. 18, No. 17, 1991, p. 13.
Izvestia (USSR), June 6, 1987; December 31, 1987; January 29, 1989; April 10, 1989; November 15, 1990; November 22, 1991; (Russia) March 16, 1992; April 25, 1992; April 17, 1993; June 4, 1993; March 3, 1994.

Komsomolskaya Pravda (USSR), October 18, 1990; April 26, 1991; October 16, 1991; (Russia) April 21, 1992; October 4, 1995.
Kylat Toimivat (Finland), No. 4, 1992.
Library Journal, September 1, 1995, p. 204.
Literaturnaya Gazeta (USSR), February 15, 1989; March 22, 1989; April 12, 1989; (Russia) June 17, 1992; October 14, 1992; January 20, 1993.
Milio Framtid (Sweden), No. 8, 1992.
Molod Ukraini (USSR), May 4, 1989; February 18, 1990; (Ukraine) July 1, 1995.
Nedelaya (USSR), No. 40, 1989.
Neue Zeit (Germany), December 10, 1992.
Nezavisimost (Ukraine), July 17, 1992.
Oikumena (USSR), No. 2, 1991.
Pravda (USSR), August 9, 1988.
Publishers Weekly, July 3, 1995, p. 55.
Russkaya Mist (France), July 3, 1992; September 25, 1992; March 25-31, 1994.
Stoliza (USSR), No. 3, 1991; (Russia) No. 12, 1992; No. 26, 1992; No. 31, 1992; No. 49, 1992.
Trud (Russia), February 1, 1992; July 2, 1992.
Ukraine (USSR), March, 1990.
Uppsala Nya (Sweden), October 8, 1992.

* * *

Y.O.
See RUSSELL, George William

* * *

YOUNG, Robert A. 1950-

PERSONAL: Born November 16, 1950, in Toronto, Ontario, Canada; son of Gordon A. and Katharine Young. *Education:* McGill University, B.A., M.A.; Oxford University, D.Phil.

ADDRESSES: Office—Department of Political Science, University of Western Ontario, London, Ontario N6A 5C2, Canada; fax 519-661-3904.

CAREER: McGill University, Montreal, Quebec, assistant professor of political science, 1980-81; University of Western Ontario, London, assistant professor, 1981-85, associate professor, 1985-92, professor of political science, 1992—. University of Toronto, visiting associate professor, 1987-88; Queen's Uni-

versity, Kingston, Ontario, visiting research fellow at Institute of Intergovernmental Relations, 1991-92.

MEMBER: Canadian Political Science Association.

WRITINGS:

The Breakup of Czechoslovakia (monograph), Institute of Intergovernmental Relations, Queen's University (Kingston, Ontario), 1994.

The Secession of Quebec and the Future of Canada, Institute of Intergovernmental Relations, Queen's University, 1995.

WORK IN PROGRESS: Research on Canadian federalism, voting behavior, and interest groups.

* * *

ZAPATA OLIVELLA, Manuel 1920-

PERSONAL: Born March 17, 1920, in Lorica, Colombia; son of Anthonio and Edelmira (Olivella) Zapata; married Rosa Bosch, December 23, 1962; children: Harlem, Edelma. Education: University of Cartagena, Colombia, B.A., 1937, graduate study, 1938; National University, Bogota, Colombia, M.D., 1948.

ADDRESSES: Home—Calle 23A, No. 19-68, Bogota, Colombia.

CAREER: Physician, psychiatrist, and author. Intern at clinic of Dr. Alfonso Ortiz Tirado, Mexico City, Mexico, 1944, Hospital Floresta, Mexico, 1945, and Psychiatric Hospital for Women, Bogota, Colombia, 1948; general practitioner of medicine in El Cesar, Colombia, 1948-52, Cordoba, Colombia, 1953-55, Atlantico, Colombia, 1955, Bolivar, Colombia, 1959-60, and Bogota, 1960 and 1967-68; birth clinic of Dr. Lamaze, Paris, France, assistant in psycho-prophylaxis, 1958. Visiting professor at numerous universities, including Howard University, University of Kansas, and University of Toronto. Co-founder and artistic director of Colombian Folkloric Dances, 1958; chief of National Ministry of Education's division of popular culture, 1966; organizer of First Congress of Colombian Culture and of First Colombian Dramaturgists cycle of play reading, both 1966; founder, publisher, and director of literary periodical Letras nacionales. General secretary of Second Na-

tional Folklorists Congress, Ibague, Colombia, 1965; second general secretary of Latinoamerican Writers Congress, Mexico City, 1967; judge for First National University Folkloric Group Exhibition, Colombia, 1968; Director, producer, and script writer of Colombian radio and television programs.

AWARDS, HONORS: First National Play Theater Prize from Spiral; First National Novel Prize from Colombian Language Academy; Second National Novel Prize from Colombian Language Academy.

WRITINGS:

Hotel de vagabundos (play), Espiral (Bogota, Colombia), 1955.

Cuentos de muerte y libertad, [Bogota], 1961.

He visto la noche (travel book), Impr. Nacional de Cuba (San Rafael, Argentina), 1962, published as He visto la noche: Las raices de la furia negra, Bedout (Medellin, Colombia), 1969.

Corral de negros (novel), Casa de las Americas (Havana, Cuba), 1963, published as Chambacu: Corral de negros, Bedout, 1967.

Detras del rostro (novel), Aguilar (Madrid), c. 1963.

En Chima nace un santo, Seix Barral (Barcelona), c. 1963.

Tierra mojada (novel), Bullon (Madrid), 1964.

Quien dio el fusil a Oswald? y otros cuentos (short stories), Revista Colombiana (Bogota), 1967.

Tradicion oral y conducta en Cordoba: Estudio investigativo elaborado para la Division de Desarrollo Social Campesino del INCORA (essay collection), Publicacion de INCORA (Bogota), 1972.

Caronte liberado (play), published in Teatro, Instituto Colombiano de Cultura (Bogota), 1972.

El hombre colombiano: Con un resumen en ingles al final (essay collection), Canal Ramirez-Antares (Bogota), c. 1974.

El folclor en los puertos colombianos (essay collection), Puertos de Colombia (Bogota), 1977.

Chango: El gran putas, Oveja Negra (Bogota), c. 1983.

Etnografia colombiana (essay collection), ICFES (Bogota), 1984.

El fusilamiento del diablo, Plaza & Janes (Bogota), 1986.

Nuestra voz: Aportes del habla popular latinoamericana al idioma espanol (essay collection), Ecoe (Bogota), 1987.

Also author of Pasion vagabunda, 1948, China Six A.M., 1962, and La calle diez, 1962, and of the plays

Pasos del Indio, 1963, *Las tres Monedas de Oro,* 1966, and *El Retorno de Cain.*

SIDELIGHTS: Manuel Zapata Olivella is a well-known black Latin American author who has written short stories, plays, and novels along with essay collections on sociology, history, and music. A physician and psychiatrist involved in several Colombian cultural programs, Zapata Olivella writes works that seek to free blacks and other races from all forms of repression. One of his best-known novels, *Corral de negros,* reflects many of the author's persistent concerns and features an often-jailed political activist who is killed while trying to advance civil rights in his community.

BIOGRAPHICAL/CRITICAL SOURCES:

BOOKS

Jackson, Richard L., *The Black Image in Latin American Literature,* University of New Mexico Press, 1976.*

* * *

ZEDRIC, Lance Q. 1961-

PERSONAL: Born August 26, 1961, in Havana, IL; son of Leslie E. (a livestock buyer) and Peggy A. (an antiques buyer; maiden name, Culp) Zedric; married Deborah Susanne Healey, September 3, 1988 (divorced February 5, 1993). *Ethnicity:* "White." *Education:* Monmouth College, B.A., 1983; U.S. Army Intelligence School, graduated, 1988; Western Illinois University, M.A., 1993. *Politics:* Independent. *Religion:* Christian. *Avocational interests:* Foreign travel, weightlifting, cooking.

ADDRESSES: Home—232 West Chestnut, No. 18, Canton, IL 61520. *Office*—352 South Second Ave., Canton, IL 61520; fax 309-647-2439. *E-mail*—zee61@aol.com.

CAREER: Monmouth College, Monmouth, IL, director of public information, 1983-85; in private business, Hannibal, MO, 1985-88; Jackal Scrap Co., Canton, IL, yard manager, 1993—. *Military service:* U.S. Army, intelligence analyst, 1988-92; served in Southwest Asia and Kuwait; received Army Commendation Medal with oak leaf cluster, Southwest Asia Campaign Medal, and Liberation at Kuwait Medal.

MEMBER: American Legion, Veterans of Foreign Wars, Association of the U.S. Army.

WRITINGS:

Silent Warriors of World War II: The Alamo Scouts behind Japanese Lines, Pathfinder Publishing (Ventura, CA), 1995.
(With Michael F. Dilley) *Elite Warriors: 300 Years of America's Best Fighting Troops,* Pathfinder Publishing, 1996.
Losers, Users, and Parasites: A Host's Guide to Ridding Your Life of Unwanted People (humorous self-help), Pathfinder Publishing, 1996.

SIDELIGHTS: Lance Q. Zedric told *CA:* "I enjoy writing about the exploits of obscure or unknown military units. Being a veteran, I believe it is important that the men and women of these units receive historical recognition for their sacrifice and service. It is also easier to get a book published when the topic is new and fresh.

"In researching and writing about military units, I begin with a stop at my local library, where I search all available databases for extant works on the unit. If no work exists, such as was the case with the Alamo Scouts, the unit described in my first book, I consult histories of other units that operated in the same theater of operations at approximately the same time. A thorough search of the index and bibliography usually yields some valuable information. If not, I contact the chief of military history in Washington, DC, for assistance. Through that office, I obtain information on any veterans' organizations or associations that might provide a starting point for my research.

"Once I obtain a name and address of one veteran, the fun begins. I telephone the veteran and record the conversation and, of course, obtain the names of fellow soldiers who served in the unit. I ask for copies of any diaries, orders, awards, et cetera, that may verify the veteran's claims. Throughout the process, I continue doing broad research on the particular geographical area and general military situation in the unit's area of operations. When the interviews are completed, I formulate an outline based on the information I have thus far.

"The writing process is the most difficult. Generally, I try to write at least two pages per day. On those days that I don't feel like writing, I make follow-up calls or work on some other aspect of the book, such

as the bibliography or the proposal to a publisher. For me, the key to writing a book is persistence. Every day is valuable, and it is important to stick to a schedule. No one just sits down and writes a book. Writing is a long, hard process, but it can be done."

* * *

ZIGAL, Thomas 1948-

PERSONAL: Born October 20, 1948, in Galveston, TX. *Education:* University of Texas at Austin, B.A., 1970; Stanford University, M.A., 1974.

ADDRESSES: Agent—Esther Newberg, International Creative Management, 40 West 57th St., New York, NY 10019.

CAREER: Writer.

AWARDS, HONORS: Austin Book Award, 1982, for *Western Edge;* award, Texas Institute of Letters, best short story of 1983.

WRITINGS:

Western Edge (stories), Calliope Press (North Hollywood, CA), 1982.

Playland (mystery novel), Thorp Springs Press (Austin, TX), 1982.
Into Thin Air (mystery novel), Delacorte (New York City), 1995.
Hardrock Stiff (mystery novel), Delacorte (New York City), 1996.

* * *

ZISKIN, Harriet 1933-

PERSONAL: Born June 26, 1933, in New York, NY. *Ethnicity:* "Jewish."

ADDRESSES: Office—c/o Calyx Books, P.O. Box B, Corvallis, OR 97339.

CAREER: Writer.

WRITINGS:

The Blind Eagle (nonfiction), Early Stages Press, 1982.
The Adventures of Mona Pinsky (novel), Calyx Books (Corvallis, OR), 1995.

WORK IN PROGRESS: A novel.